BUTTERWORTHS SPANISH/ENGLISH LEGAL DICTIONARY

DICCIONARIO JURÍDICO ESPAÑOL/INGLÉS BUTTERWORTHS

GUILLERMO CABANELLAS de las CUEVAS
Abogado, Licenciado en Economía y Doctor en Ciencias Jurídicas. Profesor Titular
Universidad de Buenos Aires. Profesor Adjunto de la Universidad de Illinois.
L.L.B., Lic. in Economics and J.S.D. Professor, University of Buenos Aires.
Adjunct Professor, University of Illinois.

ELEANOR C. HOAGUE
Abogada. Miembro del Colegio de Abogados del Estado de Washington.
J.D. Member of the Washington Bar.

BUTTERWORTHS SPANISH/ENGLISH LEGAL DICTIONARY

2	SPANISH/ENGLISH ESPAÑOL/INGLÉS

DICCIONARIO JURÍDICO ESPAÑOL/INGLÉS BUTTERWORTHS

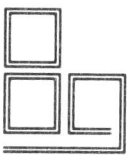

BUTTERWORTH LEGAL PUBLISHERS

ISBN   0-40925-668-4
ISBN   0-40925-669-2 *(2-vol. set)*

o de Compañías Butterworth

tados Unidos

tterworth Legal Publishers, Austin, Texas; Clearwater, Florida (D & S Publishers); ·ford, New Hampshire (Equity Publishing); St. Paul, Minnesota; y Salem, New Hamp- ire

ino Unido

tterworth & Co. (Publishers) Ltd., Londres y Edimburgo

·nadá

tterworths Canada Ltd., Toronto y Vancouver

·stralia

tterworths Pte Ltd., Sydney, Melbourne, Brisbane, Adelaida y Perth

·ueva Zelandia

tterworths (New Zealand) Ltd., Wellington y Auckland

·erto Rico

·uity de Puerto Rico, Inc., Hato Rey

·ngapore

·alayan Law Journal Pte Ltd., Singapore

PORTED BOOKS
P. O. Box 4414
las, Texas 75208
(214) 941-6497

Printed in U.S.A.

To my parents: it is easy to write a dictionary when your parents write dictionaries.

_____ Guillermo Cabanellas de las Cuevas

To my parents for their love and especially to my husband, Marc, for his support and encouragement.

Eleanor C. Hoague

PRÓLOGO

El permanente crecimiento de las comunicaciones, y el acercamiento en tre naciones que ello implica, ha conducido a que la interacción entre los distin tos sistemas jurídicos, sea cada vez más intensa. Ello ha dado origen a un volu men, hoy en día de enorme magnitud, de traducciones explícitas o implícitas, c uno a otro lenguaje jurídico. Explícitas, en la medida en que textos jurídicos d ben ser vertidos a otro idioma; implícitas, en cuanto se leen y utilizan textos ju rídicos correspondientes a idiomas que no son los del lector o usuario.

Esta relación entre lenguajes jurídicos es particularmente intensa y dif cultosa entre el inglés y el español. Intensa, desde múltiples perspectivas: por la relaciones comerciales entre países anglo e hispanoparlantes, por la existenc de amplios núcleos de población de habla hispana en los Estados Unidos, p la utilización de textos jurídicos en inglés -por distintos motivos- en los países c lengua española, por el hecho de que el Reino Unido y España sean miembr del Mercado Común Europeo, etc. Dificultosa, por cuanto no se trata aquí c trasladar un mismo concepto de uno a otro idioma, sino de encontrar en otr lenguaje jurídico conceptos que guarden semejanza o cumplan funciones equ valentes a los de otro lenguaje, ante la imposibilidad de dar con el mismo cor cepto en ambos idiomas.

En efecto, el sistema jurídico anglo-norteamericano, en relación con cual se ha formado la mayor parte de la terminología jurídica en lengua ingles difiere, prácticamente desde sus conceptos más fundamentales hasta los más l terales, del sistema de raíz romana que ha dado origen a la terminología jurídic en español. Sobre tal base, pretender encontrar en uno de estos idiomas el equ valente de los términos utilizados por el otro es un esfuerzo no sólo inútil sin que lleva consigo el grave peligro de dar no ya equivalentes de un término en otr idioma, sino crear un seudolenguaje que no es sino un símil sonoro en una len gua de las palabras que efectivamente se usan en la otra.

Para evitar estos peligros, se suministran equivalente de cada palabra e el otro idioma sólo cuando efectivamente los haya, en caso contrario, se explic el significado de la palabra carente de traducción exacta. También se da esa e plicación, de ser necesaria, en los casos en que existe traducción precisa.

Surge del enfoque aquí adoptado que este diccionario no puede suplir conocimiento, creatividad y criterio del traductor, éste debe optar entre distint acepciones, incluir, en un texto determinado, sobre la base del significado de l palabra a traducir, el término que en otro idioma mejor supla al traducido, aur que no lo haya exacto. Este diccionario es así un instrumento para una tarea qu hoy requiere la flexibilidad del talento humano. No es una suerte de maquinar impresa, que daría una apariencia de certeza y univocidad, donde no la hay.

PROLOGUE

The constant growth of communications and the resulting rapprochement between nations has brought about an increasingly intense interaction between different legal systems. Recently, this has given rise to an enormous volume of legal translations. These may be either explicit, as when legal writings must be translated from one language to another, or implicit as when legal writings which are read and used, are in a language which is not that of the writer or user.

This interaction becomes particularly intense and difficult when it concerns Spanish and English legal language. The intensity arises out of a variety of sources, including the commercial relationship between Spanish and English speaking countries, the existence of large populations of Spanish speakers in the United States, the use in Spanish speaking countries of legal texts written in English, the fact that Great Britain and Spain are both members of the Common Market, etc.. The main difficulty in English - Spanish legal translations is that one is not translating one identical concept from one language to another, but rather finding a legal concept in one language that is similar and fulfills equivalent functions of that in the other language.

The Anglo-North American legal system from which the largest part of legal terminology in the English language was developed and the Roman system which has been the source of Spanish legal terminology differ from their most fundamental concepts to those farthest afield. Bearing this in mind, it is useless to try to always find the equivalent in one language of a term used in the other; to do so also runs the risk of not providing the equivalent of the term in the other language, but of creating a pseudoterm which only sounds similar to the words actually used in the other language.

To avoid these dangers, we have provided the equivalent of each word only when one actually exists in the other language. When there is no precise equivalent, the meaning of the word has been explained. Even in cases in which a precise translation does exist, an explanation has also been provided where necessary.

It is obvious from these comments that this dictionary cannot supplant the knowledge, creativity and judgment of a translator. A careful translator must choose between different meanings, including a term or description which in the other language best provides the true interpretation of the term to be translated. This dictionary is thus a tool which must be used with the human flexibility and inventiveness. An accurate translation cannot be created by mechanically replacing words from one language with words from another: such work would merely give the appearance of certainty and equivalence where there is none.

INDICACIONES PARA LA CONSULTA Y EL MANEJO DE ESTA OBRA

1. *Las voces se encuentran ordenadas alfabéticamente, según el orde alfabético del idioma al que corresponden. Debe así recordarse, por ejemplo, qu en español la ll es una letra, que alfabéticamente va antes de la m y después c la l, similarmente, la ch es en español una letra, que alfabéticamente va ante de la d y después de la c.*

2. *Tratándose de voces compuestas, la alfabetización se basa en l primera de las palabras que la componen. Las voces compuestas cuya primer palabra es común son luego ordenadas en función de la alfabetización de la palabras que siguen a la primera.*

3. *Las siglas se consideran como si fueran una voz unitaria.*

4. *Las palabras y locuciones que se usan en uno de los idiomas, pero qu pertenecen a otros idiomas y no han sido incorporadas al idioma en relación co el cual se usan, se colocan entre comillas. Tal el caso, en particular, de las voce latinas que se utilizan en relación con el inglés y el español pero no han sido in corporadas a estos idiomas.*

5. *Respecto de las voces en español, se indica antes de las mismas si so sustantivos masculinos (m), sustantivos femeninos (f), verbos (v), adjetivo (adj) o adverbios (adv).*

6. *Cuando una voz tiene varios sentidos posibles, las traducciones cor respondientes a esos distintos sentidos se separan mediante barras.*

7. *En general, se incluyen los equivalentes en un idioma de las voces de otro, acompañándolos, cuando se lo considera necesario, por una explicació del sentido de la palabra que se traduce. Cuando no es posible dar tale equivalentes, se comienza directamente con la explicación de la voz de que s trate.*

8. *Tratándose de la traducción del inglés al español, en general se la de respecto de las voces según se las utiliza tanto en Estados Unidos como en Gran Bretaña. En la traducción del español al inglés se utiliza la ortografía empleadc normalmente en los Estados Unidos.*

SUGGESTIONS FOR THE USE OF THIS DICTIONARY

1. Terms are arranged alphabetically in each language.
Accordingly, one must remember, for example, that in Spanish "ll" is a
ter which come after "l" and before "m"; similarly, "ch" is a letter which come
ter "c" and before "d".
2. Phrases are alphabetized by their first words. Phrases that have a first
rd in common are alphabetized by the following word or words.
3. Abbreviations have been treated as if they were a single word.
4. Words foreign to both Spanish and English are placed in quotation
arks. In particular, this has been done with Latin terms that are not fully incor-
rated into the language in which they are being used.
5. Spanish terms are listed with a description of their grammatical function
d, as appropriate, their gender: verb (v), adjective (adj), adverb (adv), mas-
line (m), feminine (f).
6. When a given term has a variety of possible meanings, the various trans-
tions have been separated by two slanted lines.
7. In general, the precise equivalents of a term has been supplemented by
explanation only where it was deemed necessary for clarity. When no equiva-
nt exists, only an explanation is provided.
8. English terms have been translated according to their use and meaning
the United States as well as in Great Britain. Spanish terms have been trans-
ed using the U.S. spelling.

A BAJO PRECIO.
cheap, at a low price.

A BENEFICIO DE INVENTARIO.
Literally: for the benefit of the inventory. State of inheritance which allows the heir to determine if he or she will accept or reject the estate, usually on the basis of whether or not the estate assets exceed liabilities. Compare with ACEPTACION DE LA HERENCIA, REPUDIACION DE LA HERENCIA and PASIVIDAD.

A BORDO.
aboard; on board. Used in law of wills and nationality, and maritime and commercial law.

A BUEN PRECIO.
expensive; with effort or sacrifice; remunerated, paid.

A BUENA CUENTA.
on account.

A CARGO DE.
in charge of; payable by. In labor matters, refers to the relationship by which one receives the economic support of another person. In administrative law, designates the public office or position which a person holds. In tax law, refers to the party who is responsible for a taxable event. In commercial law, refers to person who is responsible for payment.

A CIEGAS.
completely without information.

A COMISIÓN.
on a commission basis.

A CONDICIÓN.
on condition that (words preliminary to the formulation of a requirement).

A CONTRARIO SENSU.
a contrario sensu; on the other hand.

A CORTO PLAZO.
short term.

A CRÉDITO.
on credit. Descriptive of contract by ˇ payment is postponed.

A CUALQUIER RIESGO.
at any risk.

A CUENTA.
against the account of; to the account of. cates partial payment of a debt.

A DESCUBIERTO.
unsecured (loan).

A DESTAJO.
by piece. Used in reference to piecework payment thereof.

A DÍA DETERMINADO.
See A DIA FIJO.

A DÍA FIJO.
on a fixed day; on a pre-determined date upon which contractual obligation mat Commonly used in commercial paper.

A DÍAS O MESES FECHA.
days or months from issuance. Expre used in commercial paper to indicate the upon which payment is due, by referen passage of days or months from the date issuance.

A DÍAS O MESES VISTA.
days or months from acceptance or pro Expression used in commercial paper to to date upon which payment is due, by r ence to passage of days or months from day after the date upon which it is accept drawee or maker, or protested by payee.

A DISTANCIA.
at a distance. Used to refer to measu

ysical boundary between neighboring
ns, plantations, and buildings.
)MICILIO.
home. In labor matters, used to refer to
rk site which is not the employer's. In com-
rce, used to designate place of delivery.
;CONDIDAS.
retly, clandestinely, undercover.
VOR DE.
avor of, for the benefit of ‖ with the aid of,
means of.
)RTIORI.
ortiori, with stronger reason.
,UAL TRABAJO,
JAL SALARIO.
r equal work, equal pay.
A FUERZA.
force, forcibly, violently; against one's will;
necessity.
A GRUESA.
rtaining to bottomry.
A LETRA.
the letter, exactly ‖ according to the literal
aning of the words.
A ORDEN.
your service ‖ up to date, current; to the or-
r of. Used to denote order paper (commer-
l instrument).
A PAR.
par ‖ at the same time, simultaneously.
A PRESENTACIÓN.
e A LA VISTA.
A PRIMERA PALABRA.
m the first moment.
A VISTA.
on presentment, at sight. Commercially,
ed to refer to sale in which payment is made
on delivery. In banking law, used in comercial instruments to denote that payment
st be made upon presentment.
IMINE".
mine ‖ from the beginning. Used to express
e dismissal of a complaint for failure to be
operly drafted.
ITE".
legal proceedings.
O LETRADO.
cording to the practices of lawyers or of the
rum.
ALA PARTE.
rversely, with bad intentions.

A MALAS.
with bad or evil intention.
A MANO.
by hand. Commercially, used to describe anything done or carried by hand.
A MANO AIRADA.
violently; angrily.
A MANO ARMADA.
armed. In criminal law, used to characterize
seriousness of offense.
A MANO REAL.
by executive means ‖ by official means.
"A MARITO".
of the husband, of a married man. Used in reference to power or responsibility within marriage.
A MEDIAS.
by halves ‖ between two parties ‖ partially.
Used to refer to incomplete statement which
may indicate culpability.
A MEDIDA.
to size, to proportion, to needs.
A MERCED.
without a fixed salary; at the mercy of.
A MI LEAL SABER
Y ENTENDER.
to the best of my knowledge and belief.
"A MINIMA".
lessened, minimized. Used in criminal law to
describe a lower court sentence thought to be
too light.
A MUERTE.
until death, until dead, to death.
A MUTUO.
on loan.
A NATIVITATE.
from birth. Used to describe physical defects
existing at birth.
"A NON DOMINO".
of the non-owner. Used to refer to the transfer
of property to non-owner.
A NOVO.
de novo, over again. Used to refer to submission of a case to a new court.
A OBSCURAS.
without knowledge ‖ in the dark.
A OJO.
by rough estimate, by calculated guess, in
one's judgment.
A PECHO DESCUBIERTO.
without protection ‖ sincerely.

A PEDIMENTO.
upon or on request.

"A PEREGRE".
from a foreign country, alien.

A PLAZO.
See A PLAZOS.

A PLAZOS.
in installments, on credit, on time.

A PLEITO.
subject to litigation ‖ conditioned upon a court decision.

A PLURALIDAD DE VOTOS.
by simple majority.

A PONENTE.
to be examined and preliminarily decided by a judge (who acts as PONENTE).

A POSTERIORI.
a posteriori, from what comes after.

A PREGÓN.
announced publicly.

A PREVENCIÓN.
just in case, as prevention. Used to refer to judge who, due to his preliminary hearing of a case, knows the case to the exclusion of other competent judges.

A PRIORI.
a priori, from what goes before.

A PRORRATA.
on a pro rata basis, proportionally.

A PRUEBA.
on approval, on a trial basis.

"A PUERO".
from infancy. Applies to habits and teachings learned at an early age.

A PUERTA CERRADA.
behind closed doors ‖ in camera. Used to refer to trial which is heard privately, due to possibility of scandal, to the nature of the crime, to the honesty or shyness of the damaged party or to avoid prejudice to state security.

A QUO.
a quo, a qua, from which. Used to refer to court from which case has been removed. Also used to designate time from which certain legal effects run.

A RAZÓN.
at the rate of.

A REGLAMENTO.
pursuant to regulation or rule. Used in reference to work slow-down.

A RUEGO.
upon friendly request.

A SABIENDAS.
with knowledge, consciously, deliberatel premeditation.

A SALVAMANO.
without risk of danger.

A SALVO.
out of danger, safe.

A SU TIEMPO.
opportunely, at the proper time; in due prior to expiration.

A SUELDO.
on salary, on the payroll.

A TÉRMINO.
upon maturity, at end of term ‖ future futures market).

A TÍTULO.
for a reason or purpose ‖ according tc principle.

A TÍTULO DE ANTICIPO.
as an advance.

A TÍTULO GRATUITO.
gratuitous, under gratuitous title; subj no obligation, without consideration. U reference to contracts and gifts.

A TÍTULO ONEROSO.
onerous, under onerous title ‖ subject tc gation, with consideration. Used in refe to contracts.

A TÍTULO PRECARIO.
under temporary use and enjoyment, for porary use and enjoyment. Used to de that which is given gratuitously subje unilateral revocation with no right of in nification.

A TÍTULO SINGULAR.
pursuant to specific title. Used to refer quisition or transfer of specific right on ticular thing. In wills, used to refer to con of heir to whom specified thing is given.

A TÍTULO UNIVERSAL.
pursuant to general title. Used to re transfer or acquisition of all or part of e In wills, used to describe passage of per age or all of estate.

A TORNAPEÓN.
subject to cooperative effort. Used in pa Spain, to refer to agreement to work on n boring farm in exchange for equal amou work on one's own farm.

RAICIÓN.
torously, with treachery. In criminal law,
d to characterize seriousness of the offen-

NA VOZ.
animously ‖ at the same time.

ERO DOMINO".
der true title, of the true owner, for the true
ner.

STA DE.
front of, in the presence of ‖ in considera-
n of, taking into consideration that ‖ in
nparison to, in contrast with or to.

VA FUERZA.
lently, combatively, by force.

)LUNTAD.
luntarily, freely ‖ with discretion ‖ capri-
usly.

)Z DE APELLIDO.
name call.

ACTIS".
actis, clerk of court ‖ public functionary in
irge of a public record.

INITIO".
initio, from the beginning or start.

NTESTATO.
intestato, ab intestate, from the intestate,
hout will ‖ see also ABINTESTATO.

IRATO.
irato, in anger, by one who is angry. In
minal law, used to describe state of emotion
accused, usually to minimize gravity.

ORIGINE".
m the beginning or start ‖ from the origins.

CERÍA.
etail food store, grocery.

CTOR.
abactor ‖ horse thief, cattle rustler.

JO FIRMADO.
dersigned.

NDERAMIENTO.
act of registering a ship under nation s flag.

NDERAR.
to register foreign ship (with flag of natio-
lity).

NDERARSE.
to obtain flag of nationality for foreign ship.

NDONADO.
, abandoned ‖ renounced.

NDONAR.
to abandon, leave (a person or place) ‖ to
fail to comply with, default, breach (an obligation) ‖ to abandon, waive, drop (a claim, appeal, etc.).

ABANDONARSE.
v, to breach or fail to fulfill an obligation ‖ to
give in, surrender (to desires or vices) ‖ to become slovenly or careless in one's appearance)
‖ to reveal confidences.

ABANDONO.
m, abandonment, act of abandonment ‖ resignation (of employment or a position) ‖ breach
of a duty; waiver, abandonment, dropping (of
a claim or appeal) ‖ evasion, flight ‖ desertion.

ABANDONO DE ACCIÓN.
abandonment or dropping of an action or lawsuit.

ABANDONO DE ANIMALES.
abandonment of animals. Occurs upon
owner's failure to go in search of animals after
their escape.

ABANDONO DE APELACIÓN.
abandonment or dropping of appeal.

ABANDONO DE BIENES.
abandonment of chattels or goods.

ABANDONO DE BUQUE.
desertion or junking of a ship or vessel.

ABANDONO DE CÓNYUGE.
abandonment of husband or wife.

ABANDONO DE COSAS.
See ABANDONO BE BIENES.

ABANDONO DE COSAS ASEGURADAS.
abandonment of insured property.

ABANDONO DE DERECHOS.
abandonment of rights.

ABANDONO DE DESTINO.
act of being away without leave or AWOL,
military crime of being away from station
without permission.

ABANDONO DE EMPLEO.
renunciation or resignation of employment ‖
leaving of employment without cause.

ABANDONO DE FAMILIA.
desertion of family.

ABANDONO DE FLETE.
abandonment of freight or cargo.

ABANDONO DE HIJOS.
abandonment of children. May occur by actual physical abandonment, or failure to provide proper physical or emotional care.

ABANDONO DE HOGAR.
abandonment of domicile.

ABANDONO DE HOGAR CONYUGAL.
abandonment of or leaving the family home.
ABANDONO DE INMUEBLE HIPOTECADO.
renunciation of rights to mortgaged real estate (normally by the mortgager).
ABANDONO DE INSTANCIA.
abandonment of action. May refer to PRETENSIÓN PROCESAL (abandonment of action alone), or PRETENSIÓN JURÍDICA (abandonment of the right to bring an action).
ABANDONO DE MENORES.
desertion of minors, abandonment of minors ‖ failure of father to provide for children.
ABANDONO DE MENORES INCAPACITADOS.
desertion of disabled minors.
ABANDONO DE MERCADERÍAS.
rejection of goods or merchandise.
ABANDONO DE MINAS.
abandonment of mining activities (by owner or licensee).
ABANDONO DE NIÑOS.
abandonment of children.
ABANDONO DE PERSONAS.
abandonment of persons, crime of intentionally endangering the physical safety of a person who cannot care for him or herself.
ABANDONO DE QUERELLA.
abandonment of prosecution, refusal to litigate criminal action ‖ injured party's abandonment of right to litigate a criminal action (whether or not the action has been filed).
See QUERELLA.
ABANDONO DE RECURSO.
See ABANDONO DE APELACIÓN.
ABANDONO DE RESIDENCIA.
See ABANDONO DE DESTINO.
ABANDONO DE SERVICIO.
dereliction of duties (of a professional) ‖ desertion of post or position.
ABANDONO DEL BUQUE Y DE LOS FLETES.
abandonment of ship and freight on board.
ABANDONO DEL DOMICILIO.
abandonment of domicile. Requires both physical abandonment and intent of the party to do so.
ABANDONO DEL HOGAR PATERNO.
abandonment of the parental home (by minor children).

ABANDONO DEL TRABAJO.
abandonment of work (whether temporary permanent).
ABARATAMIENTO.
m, act of reducing price.
ABARATAR.
v, to cheapen ‖ to reduce in price (to acc with governmentally fixed prices).
ABARCAR.
v, to embrace, cover, include, encompass ‖ undertake, carry out (a variety of different tivities) ‖ to monopolize or corner the mar‖ to comprise, contain.
ABARRAGANARSE.
v, to live in concubinage ‖ to cohabit (with being married).
ABARROTAR.
v, to stock (a shop) to the limit with goods ‖ overstock ‖ to monopolize, corner.
ABARROTARSE.
v, to lose wares due to overstocking.
ABASTECEDOR.
m, provider; supplier, purveyor.
ABASTECER.
v, to supply, furnish ‖ to provide (food a other necessities).
ABASTECIMIENTO.
m, supply ‖ supplying, provisioning.
ABASTECIMIENTOS.
m, provisions, supplies (e.g. food and otl necessities).
ABASTO.
m, provision, supply (of food and other nec sities).
ABDICACIÓN.
f, abdication ‖ voluntary renunciation of so reign powers by ruler of country, or of otl status or position by nobleman. May be par or total, express or implied, but never involu tary.
ABDICACIÓN DE LA PATRIA.
renunciation of nationality. Must be expr and voluntary.
ABDUCCIÓN.
f, abduction (of person), kidnapping. M occur due to fraud, violence or persuasion.
ABERCIDAR.
v, to deprive of a view ‖ to prohibit entry ‖ refuse a gift.
"ABERRATIO CAUSAE".
by mistake or error. Used in criminal law

er to criminal act carried out by means dif-
ent than those intended by perpetrator.
ERRATIO DELICTI".
mistake in the delict. Used in criminal law
characterize crime which perpetrator in-
ded to carry out against one thing or per-
, but due to mistaken identity of victim, is
ried out against another.
ERRATIO ICTUS".
mistake ‖ by mistaken act. Used in criminal
 to refer to crime which, due to inadver-
ce or lack of skill in criminal act, is carried
 against unintended victim.
URREA.
proprietary landmark, property boundary
st.
ERTO.
, open ‖ clear, evident ‖ frank.
GEAR.
o steal livestock or beasts.
GEATO.
theft of livestock.
GEO.
livestock thief.
GERO.
e ABIGEO.
NTESTATO.
type of intestate probate proceeding to
ermine heirs of intestate and distribute
estate's property.
e also AB INTESTATO.
URACIÓN.
abjuration, disavowal, recantation upon
th ‖ renunciation, repudiation ‖ rejection.
URAR.
to abjure, recant, disavow upon oath, re-
unce, repudiate ‖ to give new testimony
re or less contradictory to prior testimony.
LATIO".
, taken, removed. Used in criminal law to
er to phase of theft in which thing is taken
m its original location, but prior to its
noval from the owner's premises.
LOCARE".
to rent a house.
CAMIENTO.
 interview, conference, meeting (to put
gether a plan or deal with a matter) ‖ ap-
aching, nearing.
GABLE.
, pleadable.

ABOGACÍA.
f, formal course of study to be a lawyer ‖ legal
profession ‖ legal staff; activity of a lawyer.
ABOGADA.
f, woman attorney.
ABOGADEAR.
v, to involve oneself in legal matters and ad-
vocacy without proper title or training.
ABOGADERAS.
f, captious or tricky or fallacious arguments.
ABOGADESCO.
adj, pertaining to lawyers (derogatory).
ABOGADIL.
adj, pertaining to legal profession.
ABOGADILLO.
m, attorney of low standing.
ABOGADISMO.
m, excessive meddling by lawyers in public affairs, government or politics.
ABOGADO.
m, one who is authorized to practice law, who
may bring or defend legal actions in court, who
may give legal advice ‖ attorney (at law),
lawyer, legal adviser, legal counsel, counsellor,
advocate; (G.B.) barrister, solicitor. ABOGA-
DO refers to male or female attorney in some
countries and exclusively male in others. In
contrast to the British system, but similar to
that of the United States, in most civil law systems, an ABOGADO is admitted to practice
before the bar and is also permitted to give
legal advice extrajudicially.
ABOGADO ACUSADOR.
counsel for the plaintiff, plaintiff's counsel ‖
prosecuting attorney.
ABOGADO ADUANERO.
customs attorney.
ABOGADO ASOCIADO.
associate counsel.
ABOGADO AUXILIAR.
junior counsel ‖ attorney assisting lead counsel.
ABOGADO CIVILISTA.
attorney who specializes in matters regulated
in the civil code. See DERECHO CIVIL.
ABOGADO CONSULTOR.
consulting attorney ‖ legal consultant or advisor ‖ attorney who pronounces judgment, in
writing or orally, in a legal proceeding.
ABOGADO DE OFICIO.
appointed counsel, court-appointed counsel.

ABOGADO DE PATENTES.
patent attorney.
ABOGADO DE POBRES.
counsel for indigents.
ABOGADO DE SECANO.
pettifogger, shyster attorney (derogatory) ‖
attorney who neither practices law nor is capable of doing so ‖ person who attempts to practice law without being an attorney.
ABOGADO DE SOCIEDAD.
corporate attorney (either in-house or private counsel).
ABOGADO DEFENSOR.
defense counsel or attorney, counsel for the defense (both in criminal and non-criminal matters).
ABOGADO DEL DIABLO.
devil's advocate.
ABOGADO DEL ESTADO.
prosecuting attorney ‖ state attorney; attorney who represents government interests.
ABOGADO DESPRESTIGIADO.
attorney in poor professional repute.
ABOGADO EN EJERCICIO.
practicing attorney.
ABOGADO FIRMON.
attorney who signs documents without having drafted them.
ABOGADO FISCAL.
prosecuting or state's or government attorney.
ABOGADO LITIGANTE.
trial attorney.
ABOGADO NOTARIO.
attorney who is a special notary public. This usually entails further legal studies after having become an attorney. See NOTARIO PUBLICO and ESCRIBANO.
ABOGADO PENALISTA.
criminal attorney, attorney who specializes in criminal law.
ABOGADO PICAPLEITOS.
ambulance chaser ‖ attorney who is in poor professional repute.
ABOGADO PRINCIPAL.
lead counsel.
ABOGADO PRIVADO.
private attorney.
ABOGADO QUE CONSTA.
attorney of record.
ABOGADO SECUNDARIO.
junior counsel.

ABOGAR.
v, to advocate, plead, defend a case ‖ to ﹞
tice as an attorney ‖ to intercede.
ABOLENGO.
m, ancestors to whom one is related in asc
ing line (including and prior to grandpar‹
‖ property or inheritance coming from gr
parents or other removed relatives ‖ ance
lineage.
ABOLICIÓN.
f, abolition, revocation, abrogation ‖ repe
nullification (of a legal decree, use or cust
ABOLICIONISMO.
m, abolitionism.
ABOLIR.
v, to repeal, abrogate, abolish, revoke.
"ABOLITIO".
m, abolition.
ABOLORIO.
See ABOLENGO.
ABONADO.
m, subscriber ‖ the assured ‖ person for w
a guaranty is given ‖ adj, reliable, trustwc
‖ paid.
ABONADOR.
m, guarantor, bondsman, surety, person
vouches for another.
ABONAMIENTO.
m, surety, guaranty, bail ‖ security ‖ guara
ing, act of guarantying ‖ means by whi‹
nuncupative will is elevated to status
public document (see DOCUMENTO PUBLI
‖ subscription (e.g. to a club).
ABONAR.
v, to guarantee, be bondsman ‖ to credit ar
count ‖ to make a payment (on an accour
other contract) ‖ to pay.
ABONAR AL CONTADO.
to pay cash.
ABONAR DE MÁS.
to overcredit ‖ to overpay.
ABONAR EN CUENTA.
v, to pay into an account ‖ to credit an acco‹
ABONARÉ.
m, promissory note, I.O.U. ‖ due-bill.
ABONERO.
m, street vendor who sells on installments.
ABONO.
m, payment, installment ‖ credit entry ‖ sﹳ
ty, warranty, guaranty, bond ‖ voucher; yᵉ
of employment counted toward retirem

ough not necessarily worked) ‖ means by
h a roll-over of a loan is guaranteed ‖
ing ‖ allowance; subscription ‖ discount.

NO A CUENTA.
nent on account, partial payment.

NO DE INTERÉS.
ry interest payment (may refer to agree-
t by which interest is paid on the dowry,
n the time the agreement to marry is sig-
to the wedding; or, upon the dissolution of
marriage from the death of one of the
uses until the dowry property is properly
ributed) ‖ interest payment (incorrect
n of ABONO DE INTERESES).

NO DE INTERESES.
rest payment, payment of interest ‖ pay-
t of interest by financial institutions on
ey deposited.

NO DE PRISIÓN PREVENTIVA.
lit of pre-trial incarceration or detention
, calculation of time spent in prison by ac-
d prior to court decision to be counted
inst final court sentence.

NO DE TESTIGOS.
racter proof ‖ proof offered by third parto demonstrate the fit and truthful charac-
of witnesses who made sworn statements
out the other party being present or who
absent or dead.

NO DE TIEMPO DE PRISIÓN.
lit of (pre-conviction) time spent in jail.

NO FORTUITO.
ABONO CASUAL.

NO PARCIAL.
ial payment ‖ payment on account.

RDADO.
hip that has suffered a collision ‖ adj, boar-
, aboard.

RDAJE.
collision between or fouling of (two or mo-
hips) ‖ naval attack (of one warship against
ther, which may constitute piracy).

RDAJE CASUAL.
negligent or unavoidable collision be-
en ships.

RDAJE CULPABLE.
ligent or intentional fouling of ships.

RDAJE FORTUITO.
ABORDAJE CASUAL.

RDAJE RECÍPROCO.
ling of ships where both are at fault.

ABORDO.
m, attack ‖ collision.

ABORTAR.
v, to abort, provoke the expulsion of fetus
prior to its being viable ‖ to fail, be unsuccessful, abort.

ABORTICIDIO.
m, killing of a fetus by abortion.

ABORTISTA.
m, f, abortionist.

ABORTIVO.
m, aborted fetus ‖ abortion causing agent ‖
adj, abortive ‖ premature.

ABORTO.
m, abortion, artificially caused miscarriage
(may be crime) ‖ miscarriage ‖ failure.

ABORTO AGRAVADO.
abortion which results in the death of the
embryo and the mother.

ABORTO CULPOSO.
abortion caused by criminal negligence, want
of care or knowledge.

ABORTO ÉTICO.
abortion performed on a woman who has
been the victim of rape, incest, or defloration
as a minor.

ABORTO EUGENÉSICO.
abortion performed on a woman who has
serious mental or physical abnormalities, to
prevent the birth of a similarly deformed child.

ABORTO LETAL.
abortion which causes the death of the mother.

ABORTO PRETERINTENCIONAL.
abortion caused by aggression against the
mother, but without direct intent to provoke
the abortion.

ABORTO TENTADO.
abortion caused by lack of assistance to the
mother during delivery ‖ attemp to commit an
abortion.

ABRAZADO.
m, prisoner ‖ adj, in jail, in the clink (col) ‖ em-
braced.

ABREVAR.
v, to water an animal ‖ to use an easement for
watering animals.

ABREVIACIÓN.
n, abridgment ‖ abbreviation.

ABREVIADO.
adj, abbreviated, reduced ‖ summarized,
abridged ‖ condensed, succinct, concise.

ABRIR A LA MANO.
v, to accept bribes, be open to bribery.

ABRIR A PRUEBA.
v, to open testimony, begin taking testimony and other evidence.

ABRIR CRÉDITO.
v, to open up a loan or line of credit ‖ to give a credit or loan.

ABRIR EL JUICIO.
v, to open the case, begin trial.

ABRIR EL OJO.
to be on the aware's, be alert.

ABRIR EXPEDIENTE.
to initiate an investigation (which may end in a criminal proceeding).

ABRIR LA LICITACIÓN.
v, to open the bidding.

ABRIR LA MANO.
to be openhanded, liberal ‖ to accept gifts or tips; to loosen the grip ‖ to be lenient.

ABRIR LA SESIÓN.
to open the meeting or session, call the meeting or session to order.

ABRIR LOS LIBROS.
v, to open the accounting books.

ABRIR LOS OJOS.
to understand a situation ‖ to open one's eyes to something.

**ABRIR MANO
DE UNA PERSONA.**
to repudiate, turn away (a person).

ABRIR PRECIO.
to place an opening price on.

ABRIR PROPUESTAS.
v, to open bids.

ABRIR UNA CUENTA.
v, to open an account.

ABROGABLE.
adj, annullable, cancelable, repealable.

ABROGACIÓN.
f, abrogation, nullification, repeal, revocation, annulment (of law or regulation). May be TÁCITA (implied) or EXPRESA (express).

ABROGADO.
adj, abolished, without force or effect.

ABROGAR.
v, to repeal, annul, abolish, abrogate ‖ to set aside, revoke.

ABSENTISMO.
m, absenteeism, state of persons who live abroad and who receive income from property

in another country, or those who live far f their property.

ABSENTISMO LABORAL.
employee absenteeism ‖ failure to be pre at work without cause.

ABSENTISTA.
m, absentee, one who lives abroad ‖ adj, taining to absenteeism.

ABSOLUCIÓN.
f, acquittal, absolution ‖ dismissal of c plaint against defendant ‖ pardon. Ma used in either criminal or civil proceedings

ABSOLUCIÓN CON RESERVA.
dismissal without prejudice.

ABSOLUCIÓN CONDICIONADA.
conditional acquittal, acquittal without pr dice to continue the case at a later point in ti

ABSOLUCIÓN DE HECHO.
acquittal in fact.

ABSOLUCIÓN DE DERECHO.
acquittal in law.

ABSOLUCIÓN DE LA DEMANDA.
finding for the defendant, dismissal of c plaint (e. g. for failure to state a claim.)

ABSOLUCIÓN DE LA INSTANCIA.
acquittal, verdict of not guilty; dismissa criminal case (due to lack of evidence, leaving room for doubt as to guilt of accuse

ABSOLUCIÓN DE POSICIONES.
answer to interrogatories or requests for missions, sworn answer to questions in a l suit ‖ oral or written statements made by parties in judicial proceedings.

ABSOLUCIÓN DEL JUICIO.
dismissal of action.

ABSOLUCIÓN JUDICIAL.
acquittal (criminal) or dismissal (civil).

ABSOLUCIÓN LIBRE.
criminal acquittal, verdict of not guilty.

ABSOLUCIÓN PERENTORIA.
summary dismissal of criminal complaint.

"ABSOLUTIO".
m, absolution, freedom ‖ compliance ‖ recei

ABSOLUTISMO.
m, absolutism; despotism.

ABSOLUTISMO DEL DOMINIO.
absoluteness of ownership. Refers to the st of complete control of owner over property

ABSOLUTO.
adj, absolute, without limits, without restr tion; independent, unrestricted, unlimited.

SOLUTORIO.
ij, absolving, acquitting, pertaining to acquit-
l.

SOLUTUS CREDITOR".
, creditor who has been paid in full.

SOLVENTE.
, f, one who answers legal questions, usually
party.

SOLVER.
to absolve, acquit ‖ to release (from obliga-
ons) ‖ to answer interrogatories or requests
r admissions or oral or written questions.

SOLVER DE LA INSTANCIA.
acquit for lack of evidence.

SOLVER LAS POSICIONES.
answer interrogatories or requests for ad-
issions or oral or written questions.

SOLVER LAS PREGUNTAS.
answer questions or interrogatories.

**SOLVER LAS
ROPOSICIONES.**
ee ABSOLVER LAS POSICIONES.

SORBER LA PÉRDIDA.
absorb the (economic) loss.

SORCIÓN.
type of corporate merger in which one cor-
oration acquires all the assets of another cor-
oration which is subsequently dissolved ‖ ab-
orption, merger (of lesser crimes in principal
rime) ‖ transfer of funds (from one account
another).

SORCIÓN DE EMPRESAS.
orporate merger or acquisition ‖ take-over.
ee ABSORCIÓN.

SURDIDAD.
absurdity.

SURDO.
, absurdity ‖ adj, absurd.

BSQUE NULLA CONDITIONE".
ithout any conditions, unconditional (e.g.
bligation).

STENCIÓN.
abstention ‖ refusal to use a right ‖ neutra-
ty (in the face of armed conflict) ‖ lack of opi-
ion.

**STENCIÓN DE FUNCIONARIOS
UDICIALES.**
oluntary recusal or abstention of court of-
icers.

STENCIÓN DE JUECES.
oluntary recusal or abstention of judges.

ABSTENCIÓN DE PROCEDIMIENTOS.
refusal to prosecute, refusal to proceed with
the case. May be an obligation or a crime.

ABSTENCIÓN DE SENTENCIA.
refusal to sentence.

ABSTENCIÓN DE TESTIGOS.
refusal to testify.

ABSTENCIÓN DELICITIVA.
See DELITO DE OMISIÓN.

ABSTENCIONISMO ELECTORAL.
electoral non-participation, refusal to vote or
participate in an election. Where voting is
obligatory, may be a crime.

ABSTINENCIA MARITAL.
sexual abstinence (in marriage) ‖ mutual renunciation of marital obligations.

ABSTRACTO.
adj, abstract ‖ without cause, without reason.

ABSUELTO.
adj, absolved, acquitted ‖ released ‖ answered. See ABSOLVER.

ABUELASTRA.
f, step-grandmother ‖ second wife of a grandfather.

ABUELASTRO.
m, step-grandfather ‖ second husband of a
grandmother.

ABUELOS.
m, grandparents ‖ grandfathers.

ABUSAR.
v, to abuse, take advantage of, misuse ‖ to
rape ‖ to misuse, mistreat ‖ to sexually abuse
‖ to break into, break and enter ‖ to impose
upon ‖ to trick, fool.

ABUSIVAMENTE.
adv, abusively, improperly, illegally.

ABUSIVO.
m, abuser, person who abuses others ‖ adj,
abusive, with abuse ‖ misused, misapplied.

ABUSO.
m, abuse, misuse ‖ injustice, unfairness ‖ corruption ‖ offense ‖ imposition.

ABUSO CONTRA LA HONESTIDAD.
sexual abuse (excepting sexual intercourse).

ABUSO DE ARMAS.
assault with arms. In criminal law, describes
the firing of a weapon at a person which does
not result in injury.

ABUSO DE AUTORIDAD.
abuse of office ‖ abuse of authority, misuse by
public official of his or her authority.

ABUSO DE CARGO.
abuse or misuse of office or position.
ABUSO DE CONFIANZA.
breach of trust, betrayal or abuse of confidence.
ABUSO DE CRÉDITO.
abuse of credit, overborrowing, excessive use of credit. In bankruptcy proceedings, refers to act which qualifies bankrupt as fraudulent.
ABUSO DE DERECHO.
See ABUSO DEL DERECHO.
ABUSO DE DISCRECIÓN.
abuse of discretion.
ABUSO DE FIRMA EN BLANCO.
type of fraud, crime of completing an incomplete form or document which has been previously signed, and which acts to the detriment of the signer or a third party.
ABUSO DE FIRMA SOCIAL.
type of corporate or partnership fraud, use of corporate or partnership signature by one shareholder or partner to the prejudice of other shareholders or partners.
ABUSO DE INCAPACES.
abuse of incompetents, taking advantage of the inabilities and desires of an incompetent. May be a crime.
ABUSO DE MENORES.
child abuse ‖ abuse of minors, taking advantage of the inexperience and desires of a minor. May be a crime.
ABUSO DE PODER.
See ABUSO DE AUTORIDAD.
ABUSO DE PRIVILEGIO.
abuse of privilege.
ABUSO DE SUPERIORIDAD.
excessive self-defense.
ABUSO DEL DERECHO.
abuse of process ‖ abuse of right, legally protected act or omission to the detriment of a legal interest ‖ abuse of right, abnormal, excessive or antisocial use of a legal right. This is a concept commonly used in civil law countries for which there is no equivalent in Anglo-american law. In each case, constitutes a tort.
ABUSO DESHONESTO.
sexual abuse (excepting sexual intercourse).
"ABUSUS".
m, right of owners to abuse their property.
ACABILDAR.
v, to deal with a case jointly ‖ to unite opinions

or decisions (for a specific purpose) ‖ to together persons (to reach a common pla
ACADEMIA.
f, academy ‖ public school or college or ed tional institution of arts and sciences ‖ p where academics meet.
ACALONIAR.
v, to accuse (of a crime) ‖ to charge with a me in court.
ACALOÑAR.
See ACALONIAR.
ACALORADAMENTE.
adv, ab irato, angrily, heatedly.
ACANTONAMIENTO.
m, quartering (of troops) ‖ place where mi ry troops are located ‖ cantonment.
ACAPARADOR.
m, person who corners the market.
ACAPARAMIENTO.
m, cornering the market ‖ hoarding ‖ mon olizing, monopolization ‖ taking possessio
ACAPARAR.
v, to monopolize, corner (a market) ‖ to p chase goods to produce a scarcity in orde raise prices ‖ to hoard, buy up ‖ to take p session.
ACAPARRARSE.
v, to come to terms or to an agreement close a deal.
ACÁPITE.
m, paragraph, subheading.
ACARREAR.
v, to haul, transport, carry, convey ‖ to ca or produce damage or other negative cor quences.
ACARREO.
m, carriage, transportation, transport of go (by cart, wagon or truck) ‖ freight.
ACATAMIENTO.
m, respect for authority ‖ compliance with observance of laws, regulations and orders
ACATAR.
v, to comply with, observe ‖ to accept; to sh respect for, revere.
ACCEDENTE.
m, person who agrees or concedes (to agreement or pact) ‖ adj, acceding, concedi
ACCEDER.
v, to concede, consent (to a request) ‖ to ag ‖ to accede to (a position) ‖ to have access a place.

CEPTUS LIBERARE".
to close an account.
CEPTUM ROGARE".
to request the closure of an account.
CESIÓN.
accession ‖ property obtained by accession ‖
reement, acquiescence; increase, augmen-
tion, addition ‖ right of property owner to all
oduced thereby, added thereto, or incor-
rated therewith.
CESIÓN CONTINUA.
ght to accessions through ACCESIÓN NATU-
AL, ACCESIÓN INDUSTRIAL, or ACCESIÓN
IXTA.
CESIÓN DE ANIMALES.
ght to animals which wander onto and stay
n one's property.
CESIÓN DE POSESIONES.
cking, addition of ownership period of prior
wner to that of the present owner in order to
ain a longer uninterrupted period of owner-
ip.
CESIÓN DISCRETA.
atural accession, accession of offspring or
rm produce.
CESIÓN FÍSICA.
hysical addition of personal property to real
roperty.
CESIÓN INDUSTRIAL.
ccession to property resulting from human
ffort.
CESIÓN MIXTA.
ccession to property resulting from ACCE-
IÓN INDUSTRIAL and ACCESIÓN FÍSICA.
CESO.
a, access, entrance ‖ road, path.
CESO CARNAL.
exual intercourse by penetration of penis into
ody of another, regardless of sex.
CESO COACTIVO.
emporary right to enter property of another
ounded in necessity, with or without owner or
ser's permission.
CESO FORZOSO.
ape (of a woman) ‖ forcible entry ‖ right of
vay, easement of access.
CESO JUDICIAL.
ee INSPECCIÓN JUDICIAL.
CESO VIOLENTO.
ape, forcible sexual intercourse ‖ forcible en-
ry of a place.

ACCESORIAS DE LA CONDENA.
See PENA ACCESORIA.
ACCESORIAS LEGALES.
f, secondary claims ‖ legal claims complementary to primary claim (e.g. interests and costs.)
ACCESORIO.
m, accessory, additional thing ‖ fixture, attachment ‖ accession ‖ adj, accessory, secondary ‖
additional ‖ subordinate ‖ dependant.
"ACCESSIO PERSONAE".
third party accessories (to a contract). They
usually have no right to pursue legal remedies
or to excuse performance.
"ACCESSORIUM SEQUITUR PRINCIPALE".
An agent follows his principal ‖ the legal status
of the principal is transferred to the accessory.
ACCIDENTADO.
m, accident victim.
ACCIDENTAL.
adj, accidental ‖ causal ‖ unnecessary, non-essential ‖ incidental, secondary ‖ chance ‖ temporary, interim.
ACCIDENTALMENTE.
adv, accidentally, inadvertently.
"ACCIDENTALIA".
incidental parts.
"ACCIDENTALIA NEGOTII".
incidental clauses to a contract, clauses which
may be included in a contract without changing its essential purpose.
ACCIDENTE.
m, accident, mishap ‖ unexpected occurrence
‖ chance.
ACCIDENTE CORPORAL.
personal injury accident.
ACCIDENTE DE CIRCULACIÓN.
See ACCIDENTE DE TRANSITO.
ACCIDENTE DE TRABAJO.
occupational accident, industrial accident.
ACCIDENTE DE TRÁNSITO.
traffic accident.
ACCIDENTE EN EL TRAYECTO.
accident on the way to or from work.
ACCIDENTE INCULPABLE.
See ENFERMEDAD INCULPABLE.
ACCIDENTE INEVITABLE.
unavoidable accident, accident which is not
caused by negligence ‖ accident caused by for-
ce majeure.
ACCIDENTE "IN ITINERE".
See ACCIDENTE EN EL TRAYECTO.

ACCIDENTE MORTAL.
fatal accident.
ACCIDENTE OPERATIVO.
industrial accident.
ACCIDENTE PROFESIONAL.
occupational accident.
ACCIDENTES DEL MAR.
perils of the sea, marine risks ‖ accidents at sea.
ACCIÓN.
f, lawsuit, action, case, legal action, suit ‖ right of action ‖ stock, share, stock share, stock certificate ‖ act, action, activity ‖ plaintiff's legal complaint against another party.
ACCIÓN A QUE HUBIERE LUGAR.
action which may lie. See ACCIÓN.
ACCIÓN ACCESORIA.
subsidiary or collateral (legal) action. There are three types: PREPARATORIA (prior to instituting the principal action), PREVENTIVA (which protects the interests prior to instituting the principal action), and INCIDENTAL (during the course of the principal action). See ACCIÓN.
ACCIÓN "AD EXHIBENDUM".
(legal) action to produce or exhibit personal property ‖ preliminary proceeding to clarify it more precisely. See ACCIÓN.
ACCIÓN ADMINISTRATIVA.
administrative action or lawsuit ‖ administrative act or action or activity. See ACCIÓN.
ACCIÓN AMIGABLE.
friendly suit, amicable action. See ACCIÓN.
ACCIÓN CAMBIARIA.
collection action based on a negotiable instrument. See ACCIÓN.
ACCIÓN CAMBIARIA DE REGRESO.
collection action against secondary endorsers of a negotiable instrument.
See ACCIÓN.
ACCIÓN CAUCIONABLE.
bailable share. See ACCIÓN.
ACCIÓN CAUCIONAL.
placing or putting up bond.
ACCIÓN CAUTELAR.
(legal) action for a provisional remedy. (e.g. temporary restraining order, temporary injunction, etc.). See ACCIÓN.
ACCIÓN CIVIL.
civil action, (legal) action deriving from a private right. See DERECHO PRIVADO.
See ACCIÓN.

ACCIÓN COMERCIAL.
commercial law action, action for rece based on commercial law.
ACCIÓN COMPULSORIA.
nuisance action (regarding real property ACCIÓN.
ACCIÓN CON LUGAR.
action which lies. See ACCIÓN.
ACCIÓN CONFESORIA.
action for the recognition and enforceme a servitude or easement ‖ dispossess pro ings, ejectment action, unlawful detaine tion. See ACCIÓN.
ACCIÓN CONJUNTA.
joint action. See ACCIÓN.
ACCIÓN CONSTITUTIVA.
(legal) action which attempts to establish dify, or abolish a legal right.
See ACCIÓN.
ACCIÓN CONTRA LA COSA.
action in rem. See ACCIÓN.
ACCIÓN CONTRADICTORIA.
incompatible action; (legal) action which not be filed simultaneous with or after anc (legal) action. See ACCIÓN.
ACCIÓN CONTRADICTORIA DEL DOMINIO INSCRITO.
quiet title action, in rem proceeding chal ing the ownership of real property of a] who is registered as owner in the Real Prc ty Registry. See ACCIÓN.
ACCIÓN CONTRARIA.
(legal) action of debtor against creditc contractu to establish that all debtor ob tions have been fulfilled and to recover c damages or expenses incurred by the del See ACCIÓN.
ACCIÓN CRIMINAL.
criminal act, delinquent activity ‖ crimina tion, criminal prosecution. See ACCIÓN.
ACCIÓN CUASISERVIANA.
(legal) action to recover pledged goods. ACCIÓN.
ACCIÓN DE ABANDONO.
(legal) action to transfer title to insured g from insured party to insurer.
See ACCIÓN.
ACCIÓN DE AGRAVACIÓN.
(legal) action for reconsideration (of a la accident claim) based on worsened conditi See ACCIÓN DE REVISIÓN and ACCIÓN.

ÓN DE ALIMENTOS.
l) action for payment of support ‖ lawsuit
quire another party to provide basic sus-
nce. See ACCIÓN.
ÓN DE AMPARO.
UICIO DE AMPARO and AMPARO.
ÓN DE APREMIO.
n for monies owing ‖ summary process
ollection of taxes. See ACCIÓN.
ÓN DE COBRO DE DINERO.
n for moneis due and owing. See ACCIÓN.
ÓN DE COLACIÓN.
tion action, action to restore goods which
w must be given to certain relatives to dent's estate. See ACCIÓN and COLACIÓN
IENES.
ÓN DE COMPLEMENTO.
o enforce the right to property due a legal
See LEGADO FORZOSO.
ÓN DE CONDENA.
inal prosecution. See ACCIÓN.
ÓN DE CONDUCCIÓN.
nt's action to keep possession.
ACCIÓN.
ÓN DE DAÑOS Y PERJUICIOS.
l) action for damages, lawsuit to collect
conomic injury suffered, whether or not
ding in contract. See ACCIÓN.
ÓN DE DERECHO COMÚN.
loyee injury action, civil lawsuit to collect
ages suffered due to an occupational in-
. Opposed to labor law employee injury
n. See ACCIÓN.
ÓN DE DESAHUCIO.
tment action, unlawful detainer action,
ossess proceedings. See ACCIÓN.
ÓN DE DESALOJO.
ACCIÓN DE DESAHUCIO. See ACCIÓN.
ÓN DE DESCONOCIMIENTO DE LA
TERNIDAD.
rnity action (brought to negate or prove
ntage). See ACCIÓN.
ÓN DE DESCONOCIMIENTO DE LA
ERNIDAD.
rnity action (brought to negate or prove
ntage). See ACCIÓN.
ÓN DE DESLINDE.
n to settle real property boundaries. See
IÓN.
ÓN DE DESPOJO.
tment action (to recover physical posses-

sion of real property), unlawful detainer ac-
tion, dispossess proceedings. See ACCIÓN.
ACCIÓN DE DIFAMACIÓN.
defamation action, libel or slander lawsuit. See
ACCIÓN.
ACCIÓN DE DIVISIÓN DE COSA COMÚN.
(legal) action for partition. See ACCIÓN.
ACCIÓN DE DIVORCIO.
action for divorce. See ACCIÓN.
ACCIÓN DE DOLO MALO.
actio de dolo malo, action for fraud.
See ACCIÓN.
ACCIÓN DE DOMINIO.
action to recover property or to quiet title. See
ACCIÓN.
ACCIÓN DE DOMINIO REIVINDICATORIA.
See ACCIÓN DE DOMINIO and ACCIÓN.
ACCIÓN DE ENRIQUECIMIENTO
INDEBIDO.
(legal) action for unjust enrichment, (legal)
action to claim an overpayment or improper
delivery of a thing. See ACCIÓN.
ACCIÓN DE ESTADO.
(legal) action to determine or modify one's
marital status. See ACCIÓN.
ACCIÓN DE ESTADO CIVIL.
See ACCIÓN DE ESTADO.
ACCIÓN DE EVICCIÓN.
legal action of purchaser or other transferees
against seller or other transferors for money
owing, based on prior right of another to the
thing purchased or property acquired. See
ACCIÓN.
ACCIÓN DE "IN REM VERSO".
(legal) action for unjust enrichment.
See ACCIÓN.
ACCIÓN DE INDEMNIZACIÓN.
(legal) action for indemnification.
See ACCIÓN.
ACCIÓN DE INTERDICCIÓN DE BIENES.
(legal) action to prohibit husband from using
or managing dowry. See ACCIÓN.
ACCIÓN DE INVESTIGACIÓN DE LA
MATERNIDAD.
maternity action instigated by child to deter-
mine the identity of mother. See ACCIÓN.
ACCIÓN DE INVESTIGACIÓN DE LA
PATERNIDAD.
paternity action instigated by child to deter-
mine the identity of father.
See ACCIÓN.

ACCIÓN DE JACTANCIA.
See JACTANCIA, JUICIO DE JACTANCIA and ACCIÓN.

ACCIÓN DE LITISEXPENSAS.
(legal) action by wife against husband whom she is suing in another action to have him pay for the costs of the other action, when her funds are insufficient for that purpose. See ACCIÓN.

ACCIÓN DE LOCACIÓN.
(legal) action for rent, rent collection action ‖ (legal)action for tenant's breach of a rental contract. See ACCIÓN.

ACCIÓN DE MANDAMIENTO.
mandamus action. See ACCIÓN.

ACCIÓN DE MUTUO.
(legal) action on a loan, action by lender to require borrower to repay principal and interest owing. See ACCIÓN.

ACCIÓN DE NULIDAD.
(legal) action to declare a contract or transaction null and void. May be based on illegal or immoral purpose, contractual incapacity, lack of consent, etc. See ACCIÓN.

ACCIÓN DE NULIDAD DE TESTAMENTOS.
action to contest will, lawsuit brought by legal heir who should receive part of a decedent's estate, but who has been excluded therefrom. See ACCIÓN and LEGADO FORZOSO.

ACCIÓN DE NULIDAD DE MATRIMONIO.
annulment action, (legal) action to annul a marriage. See ACCIÓN.

ACCIÓN DE PARTICIÓN DE HERENCIA.
(legal) action to instigate probate proceedings. Action may not be brought if all the heirs have agreed temporarily not to divide the goods. See ACCIÓN.

ACCIÓN DE PETICIÓN DE DOTE.
(legal) action for dowry, lawsuit by husband against the family of the wife or any other party who agreed to donate to wife's dowry. See ACCIÓN.

ACCIÓN DE PETICIÓN DE HERENCIA.
type of probate proceeding, brought by legitimate or testamentary heir or certain relatives of the heirs to divide estate. See ACCIÓN.

ACCIÓN DE POSESIÓN.
possessory action. See ACCIÓN.

ACCIÓN DE QUERELLA DE INOFICIOSO TESTAMENTO.
(legal) action against faulty probate proceed-

ing (brought by heir who has not receive share of the estate, against heirs who received, for reintegration of property) ACCIÓN and LEGADO FORZOSO.

ACCIÓN DE REDUCCIÓN.
type of probate proceeding (brought by heir against another for receipt of share tate in excess of that permitted by law) ACCIÓN.

ACCIÓN DE REGRESO.
type of (legal) action for payment (broug holder or bearer of a bill of exchange ag the issuer, endorser, acceptor, or guara for failure to pay such bill in a timely fash See ACCIÓN.

ACCIÓN DE REIVINDICACIÓN.
See ACCIÓN REIVINDICATORIA.

ACCIÓN DE RENDICIÓN DE CUENTA
(legal) action for accounting, (legal) actio failure to properly account for funds he trust. See ACCIÓN.

ACCIÓN DE REPETICIÓN.
(legal) action for improper delivery, lav brought by creditor for return of goods ag party who fraudulently or mistakenly rece goods. See ACCIÓN.

ACCIÓN DE RESARCIMIENTO.
See ACCIÓN DE DAÑOS Y PERJUICIOS.

ACCIÓN DE RESCISIÓN.
See ACCIÓN RESCISORIA.

ACCIÓN DE RESPONSIBILIDAD.
(legal) action for damages arising out of e tort or contract.
See ACCIÓN.

ACCIÓN DE RESTITUCIÓN IN INTEGRUM.
restitution action or lawsuit by minors and tain institutions for return of things belon to them and taken from them by frau negligence. See ACCIÓN.

ACCIÓN DE REVISIÓN.
(legal) action for reconsideration (e.g. law by employee or party who indemni employee to revise the amount of mo awarded for an occupational or industrial cident in light of subsequent change employee's condition). See ACCIÓN.

ACCIÓN DE SANEAMIENTO.
(legal) action by buyer against seller to c the legal defects of the thing purchased (title, liens, etc.). See ACCIÓN.

ÓN DE SIMULACIÓN.
of declaratory judgment action to invali-
a private agreement which frau-dulently
ears to be a transaction with a third party.
ACCIÓN.

ÓN DE SUPLEMENTO.
of probate proceeding by legal heirs to
m less than that legally required has been
n, to receive their legal share. See ACCIÓN
LEGADO FORZOSO.

IÓN DECLARATIVA.
laratory judgment action, declaratory ac-
. See ACCIÓN.

IÓN DEL ENEMIGO.
of a public enemy ‖ hostile act or action.

IÓN DETERMINATIVA.
ACCIÓN CONSTITUTIVA.

IÓN DIRECTA.
on which arises from the words and spirit
he law ‖ creditor's action brought by pled-
creditor to recover costs and expenses ‖
emnity action brought by injured party to
over damages directly from insurer of the
ty responsible for the injury ‖ direct action.
ACCIÓN.

IÓN DISPOSITIVA.
ACCIÓN CONSTITUTIVA.

IÓN DIVISORIA.
tition action or lawsuit. See ACCIÓN.

IÓN EJECUTIVA.
ion of plaintiff to initiate a summary lawsuit
collect on a negotiable instrument. See
CIÓN.

IÓN EJERCITORIA.
ion against ship owner for services and sup-
es contract signed on his behalf by the cap-
n. See ACCIÓN.

IÓN EMPTI.
io empti.

IÓN EN COBRO DE DINERO.
lection action, action for monies due. See
CIÓN.

IÓN ENEMIGA.
e ACCIÓN DEL ENEMIGO.

IÓN ESPECIAL.
raordinary action, any lawsuit which is not
bject to ordinary legal procedure or trial.
e ACCIÓN.

IÓN ESTIMATORIA.
anti minoris ‖ action by buyer against seller
reduce the price because of defects in the

thing. Must be based on (1) transfer of the
good for valuable consideration and (2) the
existence of defect(s), hidden from the buyer
prior to the transfer. See ACCIÓN.

ACCIÓN EX EMPTO.
See ACCIÓN EMPTI.

ACCIÓN EX STIPULATU.
actio ex stipulatu, action to enforce a stipulation. See ACCIÓN.

ACCIÓN EXHIBITORIA.
See ACCIÓN "AD EXHIBENDUM".

ACCIÓN FAMILIAE ERCICUNDAE.
actio familiae ercicundae, action for division of
an inheritance. See ACCIÓN.

ACCIÓN FURTI.
actio furti, action for conversion.
See ACCIÓN.

ACCIÓN HIPOTECARIA.
foreclosure action or proceedings.
See ACCIÓN.

ACCIÓN IMPRESCRIPTIBLE.
action for which there is no statute of limitations. See ACCIÓN.

ACCIÓN INCIDENTAL.
accessory action. See ACCIÓN.

ACCIÓN IN REM.
action in rem. See ACCIÓN.

ACCIÓN IN SOLIDUM.
joint action. See ACCIÓN.

ACCIÓN INCIDENTAL.
accessory action or lawsuit. See ACCIÓN.

ACCIÓN INCOMPATIBLE.
See ACCIÓN CONTRADICTORIA.

ACCIÓN INDIRECTA.
See ACCIÓN OBLICUA.

ACCIÓN INMOBILIARIA.
(legal) action relating to real estate.
See ACCIÓN.

ACCIÓN INTERDICTAL.
motion for an injunction.

ACCIÓN INTERROGATORIA.
technical procedure to request clarification of
remedy requested.

ACCIÓN INTRANSMISIBLE.
non-assignable right of action, action which is
extinguished upon death of party in interest.
See ACCIÓN.

ACCIÓN JUDICIAL.
lawsuit, suit, case, legal action. See ACCIÓN.

ACCIÓN JURÍDICA.
legal activity or action. See ACCIÓN.

ACCIÓN LABORAL.
labor law action, action for recovery based on labor law. See ACCIÓN.

ACCIÓN LITIGIOSA.
See ACCIÓN JUDICIAL.

ACCIÓN MANCOMUNADA.
joint action, legal action brought by parties who together bring the action based on the same claim. See ACCIÓN.

ACCIÓN MIXTA.
quasi-in-rem action. See ACCIÓN.

ACCIÓN MOBILIARIA.
(legal) action relating to personal property. See ACCIÓN.

ACCIÓN NEGATORIA.
(legal) action to quiet title (regarding easement). See ACCIÓN.

ACCIÓN OBLICUA.
subrogation action, (legal) action which permits the creditor to exercise all his debtor's rights excepting those of inheritance, in partial or total satisfaction of the debtor's obligation. See ACCIÓN.

ACCIÓN ORDINARIA.
ordinary (legal) action. Opposed to ACCIÓN EJECUTIVA.

ACCIÓN PARA CUENTA Y RAZÓN.
action for accounting. See ACCIÓN.

ACCIÓN PARTICULAR.
personal action. See ACCIÓN.

ACCIÓN PAULIANA.
type of action whereby creditors move to void all acts by which a debtor defrauded or injured them. See ACCIÓN.

ACCIÓN PENAL.
criminal action or proceeding. See ACCIÓN.

ACCIÓN PERPETUA.
(legal) action which has a statute of limitations of 30 or 40 years.
See ACCIÓN INPRESCRIPTIBLE.

ACCIÓN PERSONAL.
personal action, (legal) action in personam. See ACCIÓN.

ACCIÓN PETITORIA.
petitory action, (legal) action to reclaim goods or real property. See ACCIÓN.

ACCIÓN PIGNORATICIA.
actio pignoraticia, (legal) action pertaining to contracts by which goods were pledged. May be DIRECTA (action by debtor to recover the thing pledged after satisfying the contractual

obligation) or CONTRARIA (action by credit for indemnity of the losses suffered). See ACCIÓN.

ACCIÓN PLENARIA.
plenary proceeding ‖ ordinary proceedi (versus summary proceeding). See ACCIÓN.

ACCIÓN POPULAR.
public interest action ‖ (legal) action broug by citizen(s) on behalf of the public intere See ACCIÓN.

ACCIÓN POR DAÑOS Y PERJUICIOS.
See ACCIÓN DE DAÑOS Y PERJUICIOS.

ACCIÓN POR INCUMPLIMIENTO DE CONTRATO.
action on the contract, contract action, actic ex contractu. See ACCIÓN.

ACCIÓN POR PROMESA MATRIMONIAI
(legal) action for broken marriage promise (aft the banns have been published in church). See ACCIÓN.

ACCIÓN POSESORIA.
possessory action, (legal) action to acquire recover what is not in plaintiff's possession to keep what is in his possession. See ACCIÓ

ACCIÓN PREJUDICIAL.
pre-trial proceeding or action ‖ incidental pr ceeding. See ACCIÓN.

ACCIÓN PRESCRIPTIBLE.
(legal) action which has a statute of limit; tions. See ACCIÓN.

ACCIÓN PRENDARIA.
See ACCIÓN PIGNORATICIA.

ACCIÓN PRESCRITA.
(legal) action barred by statute of limitation See ACCIÓN.

ACCIÓN PRESERVATIVA.
(legal) action for provisional remedy or fc remedy pendente lite (e.g. temporary restrair ing order, temporary injunction, etc.). See ACCIÓN.

ACCIÓN PREVENTIVA.
See ACCIÓN PRESERVATIVA.

ACCIÓN PRINCIPAL.
main action, lawsuit from which any subsidiar actions arise. See ACCIÓN.

ACCIÓN PRIVADA.
private action, (legal) action arising out of pri vate law (see DERECHO PRIVADO) ‖ crimina action prosecuted by private party with no in volvement of public prosecutor or other pu blic authority). See ACCIÓN.

CIÓN PROCEDENTE.
ion which lies. See ACCIÓN.
CIÓN PROCESAL.
ans of litigating ‖ suit by individual against
state; lawsuit, legal action.
ACCIÓN.
CIÓN PROHIBITORIA.
e ACCIÓN CONFESORIA.
CIÓN PÚBLICA.
minal (legal) action, except those set aside
private actions by statute (opposed to AC-
ÓN PRIVADA) ‖ public action, action arising
t of public law ‖ (legal) action which may
ought without regard to standing, on behalf
public interests. See ACCIÓN.
CIÓN PUBLICIANA.
tion to acquire property by prescription. See
CIÓN.
CIÓN QUOD METUS CAUSA.
tio quod metus causa. See ACCIÓN.
CIÓN REAL.
al action, (legal) action in rem. See ACCIÓN.
CIÓN REAL Y PERSONAL.
xed action. See ACCIÓN.
CIÓN REDHIBITORIA.
dhibitory action; (legal) action on a contract
r purchase of a thing which is later discove-
d to be defective.
e ACCIÓN.
CIÓN REGRESIVA.
e ACCIÓN CAMBIARIA.
CIÓN REIVINDICATORIA.
gal) action to quiet title or obtain title. See
CIÓN.
CIÓN REIPERSECUTORIA.
rect action by plaintiff against a prior posses-
r of property without regard to privity be-
veen the two parties. See ACCIÓN.
CIÓN RERUM AMOTARUM.
tio rerum amotarum. See ACCIÓN. ACCIÓN
ESCISORIA. (legal) action for rescission; (leal) action to rescind a contract which has
amaged minors or absentees and others de-
gnated by law. See ACCIÓN.
CIÓN RESOLUTORIA.
ction or suit for enforcement of a right to ter-
inate a contractual or other obligation.
CIÓN REVOCATORIA.
ee ACCIÓN PAULIANA.
CIÓN SIN LUGAR.
ction which does not lie. See ACCIÓN.

ACCIÓN SINDICAL.
(legal) action filed by labor union.
See ACCIÓN.
ACCIÓN SOLIDARIA.
action in solidum, joint and several action. See
ACCIÓN.
ACCIÓN SOSTENIBLE.
action which lies. See ACCIÓN.
ACCIÓN SUBROGATORIA.
See ACCIÓN OBLICUA.
ACCIÓN SUBSIDIARIA.
in court request or motion for a remedy sub-
sidiary to that set forth in the original com-
plaint. See ACCIÓN.
ACCIÓN SUMARIA.
summary proceeding. See ACCIÓN.
ACCIÓN SUMARÍSIMA.
expedited summary proceeding.
See ACCIÓN.
ACCIÓN TEMPORAL.
(legal) action with a statute of limitations, (legal) action with a time limit. See ACCIÓN.
ACCIÓN TEMPORALIS.
See ACCIÓN TEMPORAL.
ACCIÓN ÚTIL.
action brought on standards of fairness and
justice rather than on legal principles. See
ACCIÓN.
ACCIONADO.
m, defendant, accused ‖ one against whom a
legal action is brought ‖ adj, propelled, driven
‖ forced.
ACCIONANTE.
m, plaintiff, prosecutor ‖ one who brings a legal action.
ACCIONAR.
v, to litigate, bring suit, file an (legal) action,
bring a legal action ‖ to operate.
ACCIONARIADO.
m, entirety of shareholders ‖ system and rules
pertaining to a particular type of share.
ACCIONARIADO OBRERO.
employee's stock sharing plan ‖ system by
which employee receives stock, generally with
restricted rights, in the employer-company.
ACCIONARIO.
m, shareholder, stockholder; adj, share, pertaining to shares (in a corporation) ‖ of shares.
ACCIONES.
f, shares, stock, shares of stock, stock certificates ‖ plural of ACCIÓN.

ACCIONES AL PORTADOR.
non-registered stock, bearer stock. Opposed to ACCIONES NOMINATIVAS.

ACCIONES COMPATIBLES.
compatible actions, suits which may be carried at the same time.

ACCIONES COMUNES.
common stock.

ACCIONES CUBIERTAS.
paid-up stock.

ACCIONES DE BENEFICIO.
stock issued for services.

ACCIONES DE CAPITAL.
capital stock ‖ stock issued in exchange for valuable consideration.

ACCIONES DE COMPAÑÍAS.
corporate shares ‖ individual share of corporate capital.

ACCIONES DE CONOCIMIENTO.
processes that result in a judicial decision after a full presentation of the legal claims, proof and allegations. May be ACCIÓN CONSTITUTIVA, ACCIÓN DECLARATIVA, or ACCIÓN DE CONDENA.

ACCIONES DE DISFRUTE.
certificates giving certain limited rights to holders of retired stock.

ACCIONES DE FUNDACIÓN.
founders' shares, shares issued to the parties who initially incorporated company. May have special privileges or be issued free.

ACCIONES DE FUNDADOR.
See ACCIONES DE FUNDACIÓN.

ACCIONES DE GOCE.
See ACCIONES DE DISFRUTE.

ACCIONES DE INDUSTRIA.
stock issued for services rendered.

ACCIONES DE NO PAGO.
stock issued in exchange for services.

ACCIONES DE PAGO.
stock issued in exchange for valuable consideration.

ACCIONES DE PREFERENCIA ACUMULATIVA.
cumulative preferred stock.

ACCIONES DE PREFERENCIA NO ACUMULATIVA.
noncumulative preferred stock.

ACCIONES DE PRIMA.
type of stock issued by founders to those who have contributed in some way to the company.

ACCIONES DE TESORERÍA.
treasury stock.

ACCIONES DE TRABAJO.
stock issued to employees.

ACCIONES DESERTORAS.
See ACCIONES DESIERTAS.

ACCIONES DESIERTAS.
stock which has not been paid for and is default.

ACCIONES DIFERIDAS.
deferred stock, shares which receive dividen‹ only after the other stockholders have r ceived their share of the profits ‖ shares whi‹ receive a prorated portion of corporate pro. after the dividends have been paid to the or‹ nary, preferred, and privileged shares.

ACCIONES EN CAJA.
treasury stock.

ACCIONES EN ESPECIE.
stock issued in exchange for property.

ACCIONES EN TESORERÍA.
See ACCIONES EN CAJA.

ACCIONES ENDOSABLES.
endorsable or indorsable shares.

ACCIONES EXHIBIDAS.
fully paid shares.

ACCIONES HABILITANTES.
qualifying shares.

ACCIONES INDIVISIBLES.
types of legal actions which may be brougt only if all those parties having a right thereit are party thereto.

ACCIONES INDUSTRIALES.
See ACCIONES DE INDUSTRIA.

ACCIONES LABORALES.
See ACCIONES DE TRABAJO.

ACCIONES LIBERADAS.
shares issued in exchange for property or ser vices ‖ bonus shares ‖ fully paid-in stock.

ACCIONES NO LIBERADAS.
stock not fully paid-in.

ACCIONES NOMINALES.
See ACCIONES NOMINATIVAS.

ACCIONES NOMINATIVAS.
nominative or registered stock, shares issue‹ and registered in the name of the holder.

ACCIONES ORDINARIAS.
common stock.

ACCIONES PAGADAS.
fully paid shares.

CIONES PARTICIPANTES
EFERENTES.
rticipating preferred stock.
CIONES PREFERENTES.
eferred stock.
CIONES PREFERIDAS.
e ACCIONES PREFERENTES.
CIONES PRIVILEGIADAS.
eferred stock.
CIONES REDIMIBLES.
deemable stock.
CIONES SIN VALOR NOMINAL.
-par-value stock.
CIONES VOTANTES.
ting stock.
CIONISTA.
, shareholder, stockholder.
CIONISTA COMANDITARIO.
older of stock in a limited partnership.
CIONISTA PREFERIDO.
older of preferred stock.
CIONISTA REGISTRADO.
ockholder of record.
CIONISTAS CONSTITUYENTES.
unding stockholders.
CIONISTAS DE LA MINORÍA.
inority stockholders.
CIONISTAS DISIDENTES.
ssenting stockholders.
CIONISTAS MINORITARIOS.
inority stockholders.
COLA.
inhabitant, occupant, occupier (of an area) ‖
eighbor.
ECINAMIENTO.
, assassination.
ECHADOR.
, spy, observer, look-out.
ECHAR.
, to spy, observe, watch ‖ to lie in ambush.
EFALÍA.
lack of organizational leader or chief. Used
refer to the state of government when the
residential seat is vacant due to death or
esignation.
EFALISMO.
ee ACEFALÍA.
ÉFALO.
, country, society, association, party, tribunal
r community which lacks its governing or
uling leader.

ACENDRADO.
adj, pure, without fault or blemish whatsoever.
ACENSAR.
See ASENSUAR.
ACENSO.
m, real property rental.
ACENSUADO.
adj, real property which is subject to a special
charge called a CENSO.
ACENSUADOR.
m, one who is recipient of a type of yearly rent
on real estate.
ACENSUAR.
v, to charge a yearly rental on real property
pursuant to a CENSO.
ACEPCIÓN.
f, one of various possible meanings of words .
ACEPTACIÓN.
f, acceptance, agreement (of a contract) (may
be express or tacit) ‖ acceptance (of a bill of
exchange to show agreement to pay them
upon maturity) ‖ acceptance (see ACEPTA-
CIÓN DE LA HERENCIA).
ACEPTACIÓN A BENEFICIO DE
INVENTARIO.
limited acceptance of inheritance by heir. See
ACEPTACIÓN DE LA HERENCIA.
ACEPTACIÓN ABSOLUTA.
absolute acceptance.
ACEPTACIÓN BANCARIA.
banker's acceptance.
ACEPTACIÓN CAMBIARIA.
acceptance of a bill of exchange.
ACEPTACIÓN COMERCIAL.
trade acceptance.
ACEPTACIÓN CONTRACTUAL.
acceptance of a contract ‖ consent to contract.
ACEPTACIÓN DE CARGO.
acceptance of employment, position, or work.
ACEPTACIÓN DE DÁDIVAS.
acceptance of gratuities by a public official as
a gift or bribery. Usually constitutes a crime.
ACEPTACIÓN DE FAVOR.
accommodation acceptance.
ACEPTACIÓN DE LA DONACIÓN.
acceptance by donee of a gift. The necessity of
acceptance here is a matter of dispute, but as
a gift is deemed to be a contract, acceptance is
usually required.
ACEPTACIÓN DE LA HERENCIA.
acceptance of estate in full by heir. This act

usually requires the heir to answer for estate debts in order to obtain the right to the assets.

May be PURA (the heir's personal assets may be used to answer for the estate debts) or A BENEFICIO DE INVENTARIO (only the estate assets may be used to answer for estate debts).

ACEPTACIÓN DE LA LETRA DE CAMBIO.

acceptance of bill of exchange (which consists of writing the word "ACEPTO" or "ACEPTAMOS").

ACEPTACIÓN DE LOS LEGADOS.

acceptance of special bequests ‖ acceptance of a testamentary heir to receive by will. Unless refused, there is a presumption of acceptance.

ACEPTACIÓN DE PODER.

acceptance of power of attorney (to litigate) ‖ agreement to represent (a client in litigation).

ACEPTACIÓN DEL MANDATO.

acceptance of agent to represent a principal.

ACEPTACIÓN EN BLANCO.

blank acceptance.

ACEPTACIÓN EXPRESA.

express acceptance.

ACEPTACIÓN FORZOSA.

acceptance required or implied by law (not in fact).

ACEPTACIÓN IMPLÍCITA.

implied acceptance.

ACEPTACIÓN LEGAL.

legal acceptance, acceptance in accord with all legal requirements.

ACEPTACIÓN LIBRE.

general acceptance.

ACEPTACIÓN MERCANTIL.

trade acceptance.

ACEPTACIÓN POR ACOMODAMIENTO.

accommodation acceptance.

ACEPTACIÓN POR COMISIÓN.

type of commissioned bank acceptance ‖ acceptance which a bank agrees to perform for a client who wishes the bank to obtain the acceptance of bills of exchange which are not immediately payable.

ACEPTACIÓN POR INTERVENCIÓN.

acceptance by third party (of a bill of exchange which has been refused by acceptance party). To be accepted in this manner, it must be done under protest (see PROTESTO) before a special public notary.

ACEPTACIÓN PURA.

full acceptance of inheritance by heir.

ACEPTACIÓN DE LA HERENCIA.

ACEPTACIÓN PURA Y SIMPLE.

unconditional acceptance.

ACEPTACIÓN TÁCITA.

implied acceptance.

ACEPTADO.

adj, accepted ‖ admitted ‖ honored.

ACEPTADOR.

m, acceptor, party who accepts.

ACEPTADOR DE PERSONAS.

person who shows favoritism or grants fa⸱ for reasons of friendship or private interes⸱ public posts, it is a crime.

ACEPTANTE.

See ACEPTADOR.

ACEPTAR.

v, to accept, agree ‖ to admit.

ACEPTAR A BENEFICIO DE INVENTARIO.

to accept subject to an inventory of the heritance. See ACEPTACIÓN DE LA HEREN⸱

ACEPTAR CON RESERVA.

to accept conditionally or with reservation.

ACEPTAR POR CUENTA DE.

to accept on behalf of or for the account o⸱

ACEPTILACIÓN.

f, acceptilation ‖ payment of debts.

ACEPTO.

m, acceptance ‖ adj, accepted ‖ acceptab⸱ pleasing.

ACERCAMIENTO.

m, nearing, physical approximation ‖ rapp⸱ chement.

ACERROJAR.

v, to lock, bolt up tight; to watch over carefu⸱

ACERTAMIENTO INCIDENTAL.

m, ruling which forms basis for further actio⸱

ACERTAR.

v, to determine a question of law.

ACERVO.

m, undivided assets (of corporations, ⸱ heritances, bankruptcies, etc.).

ACERVO HEREDITARIO.

assets of an estate.

ACERVO SOCIAL.

corporate assets.

ACLAMACIÓN.

f, acclamation ‖ authorization by public acc⸱ mation to assume a position.

_ARACIÓN.
:larification, investigation, inquiry. Used in
ninal law to refer to criminal inquiry.

_ARACIÓN DE SENTENCIA.
rifying decision (written after an earlier de-
ion by the same judge or tribunal, to em-
asize a point, explain an ambiguity, or cor-
:t an omission).

)BARDAR.
o cause fear, frighten, intimidate, daunt. Its
: nullifies consent.

)CHINAR.
to kill brutally, (especially with reference to
)erson who cannot defend himself or flee).

)GER.
to receive, accept; to honor; to hide, conceal
o protect, shelter.

)GER UN GIRO.
honor a draft.

)GERSE.
to take refuge, hide oneself ‖ to make use

)GIDA.
acceptance.

OGIDA DE UNA LETRA.
)noring or acceptance of a draft.

OGIDO.
, refugee, asylee. Used especially to refer to
:destitute person who takes refuge in a poor-
)use.

OGIMIENTO.
, protection, shelter, concealment; system
ad agreement used in Spain by which one
mily who inherits an estate, accepts other
milies (related or not) into their own, form-
,g one communal family, for purposes of
·oduction, consumption , earnings, and to
)me degree, inheritance.

OGIMIENTO
. LA CASA.
ractice in Spain whereby the owners of a
ome recognize the right arising out of mar-
age or inheritance of a person to live in the
ome, be fed, clothed, cared for in sickness
nd health, with or without the corresponding
bligation to work in the home.

:OGIMIENTO FAMILAR.
ractice of sheltering a child in one's home as
ne's own child, without the benefit of adop-
on. It creates no on-going rights or obliga-
ons for either party.

ACOLLARARSE.
v, to cohabit (as husband and wife without
being married).

ACOMENDAR.
v, to entrust (something to the care of another).

ACOMETEDOR.
m, attacker, provocateur.

ACOMETER.
v, to assault, attack ‖ to attempt, try, undertake ‖ to overcome ‖ to incite, provoke.

ACOMETIMIENTO.
m, assault.

ACOMETIMIENTO Y AGRESIÓN GRAVE.
aggravated assault and battery.

ACOMETIMIENTO Y AGRESIÓN
SIMPLE.
assault and battery.

¡COMODADO.
adj, rich, wealthy ‖ accommodated ‖ convenient.

ACOMODO.
m, favoritism in the work place.

ACOMODO DE GANADOS.
pasturing rights ‖ right to rent common pasture.

ACOMODO DE PASTOS.
custom in parts of Spain of farmers to share
pasture land communally for their animals
during the summer months.

ACOMPAÑADO.
adj, accompanied.

ACOMPAÑAR.
v, to accompany ‖ to assist another in carrying
out their duties.

ACOMPAÑARSE.
v, to gather two or more experts in order to
come to agreement or exchange ideas on an
issue concerning their area of expertise which
will be offered at a trial or hearing.

ACONSEJADO.
m, advisee, person who has received advice;
adj, advised, prudent.

ACONSEJADOR.
m, advisor, counselor; adj, advising, counselling, advisory.

ACONSEJAR.
v, to advise. In criminal law, advice which is the
determinative cause of a criminal act; is a
crime in itself.

ACONSEJARSE.
v, to take advice.

ACOPIADOR.
m, hoarder.
ACOPIAR.
v, to hoard (usually for one's own use).
ACOQUINAR.
v, to intimidate.
ACORDADA.
v, court resolution, decision, order, ruling (by judges sitting en banc).
ACORDADO.
adj, agreed ‖ decided (by judges sitting en banc).
ACORDAR.
v, to dictate a judicial decision (to be sent to the parties in the suit) ‖ to decide, resolve ‖ to agree ‖ to remind ‖ to grant, allow.
ACORDAR UNA DILACIÓN.
to grant a delay.
ACORDAR UN DIVIDENDO.
to declare a dividend.
ACORDAR UNA PATENTE.
to grant or approve a patent.
ACORDARSE.
v, to remember ‖ to come to an agreement, come to terms.
ACORDE.
adj, agreed, harmonious.
ACORDEMENTE.
adv, in agreement ‖ by common agreement or consent.
ACORRALARSE.
v, to flee justice, be on the lam, be on the run.
ACORRERSE.
v, to be a refugee; to search for asylum or refuge.
ACORRIMIENTO.
m, help, assistance, asylum, refuge ‖ recourse, remedy.
ACORTARSE.
v, to use excessive respect, timidity in drafting a complaint.
ACOSAR.
v, to harass, pursue unswervingly, hound.
ACOSTUMBRADO.
adj, customary ‖ accustomed.
ACOTACIÓN.
f, marginal annotation or note (placed in a writing, a file, or a judicial ruling).
ACOTADO.
m, fugitive (for whom there is a reward) ‖ adj, with notes or footnotes placed in the margin.

ACOTAMIENTO.
m, boundary mark ‖ demarcation of proper limits by marker with secondary purpose limiting trespassers.
ACOTAR.
v, to stake out, mark boundaries ‖ to mak footnotes, annotate ‖ to be a character witne ‖ to cite texts or authorities in support of opinion or allegation.
ACRECENCIA.
f, augmentation, accretion. Used to refer right which heirs have to a proportional in crease in the inheritance if a portion of the in heritance is not claimed or is expressly rep diated.
ACRECENTAMIENTO.
See ACRECENCIA.
ACRECER.
See DERECHO DE ACRECER.
ACREDITACIÓN.
f, accreditation (of diplomatic acts ratifyir the authenticity of powers granted to a repre sentative in another nation) ‖ crediting, act crediting an account.
ACREDITADO.
adj, accredited, reputable ‖ accepted. Used refer to diplomatic act of one nation in accep ing a diplomat sent to represent another.
ACREDITAR.
v, to give credit to (a person's reputation) ‖ credit, authorize a deposit (to the account o ‖ to prove, evidence, show ‖ to prove that person possesses the attributes necessary t fulfill a certain diplomatic function or post.
ACREEDOR.
m, creditor, lender.
ACREEDOR ALIMENTARIO.
person to whom alimony is to be paid.
ACREEDOR ANTICRESISTA.
See ACREEDOR ANTICRÉTICO.
ACREEDOR ANTICRÉTICO.
holder of a right in rem to possess real proper ty and receive that produced by the proper in payment of interest on a loan or if in exces of interest, in payment of the capital of th loan. If the property is in the city, the holde may occupy or rent it. If the property is in th country, the holder may cultivate or rent i The holder may make claim against debtor account for betterments made ‖ request th sale of the property once the loan is due

return the land and request that payment be made by other means ‖ encumber the property with easements (with the owner's permission). The holder must repair damage that he has caused, put it to the same use as the legal owner, return it immediately upon payment of the debt, protect and care for it.

CREEDOR CENSUALISTA.
creditor of a debt guaranteed by a CENSO.

CREEDOR COMÚN.
general creditor. Opposed to secured creditor.

CREEDOR CON PRIVILEGIO ESPECIAL.
See ACREEDOR PRIVILEGIADO.

CREEDOR CON PRIVILEGIO GENERAL.
See ACREEDOR PRIVILEGIADO.

CREEDOR DE DOMINIO.
creditor who claims title to estate assets. Refers to: owners of goods which were deposited, loaned, rented to or administrated by debtor without transfer of ownership ‖ holders of non-endorsable bills of exchange and credit documents ‖ sellers of goods which have not yet been fully paid for ‖ inheritors and heirs ‖ the married female as to the goods brought from her family and the resulting fruits of such goods.

CREEDOR DE LA HERENCIA.
See ACREEDOR HEREDITARIO.

CREEDOR DE LA MASA.
special preferred creditor of a bankrupt, party who becomes a creditor of the bankrupt, due to his actions in the bankruptcy on behalf of the creditors after the declaration of bankruptcy ‖ creditor of an estate in receivership.

CREEDOR DE LA SUCESIÓN.
creditor of a decedent's estate.

CREEDOR DEL HEREDERO.
creditor of an heir.

CREEDOR DEL CONCURSO.
special preferred creditor who has a right which is enforceable against the estate of the bankrupt, due to his actions on behalf of the creditors after the declaration of bankruptcy.

CREEDOR DEL FALLIDO.
creditor of a bankrupt.

CREEDOR DEL QUEBRADO.
See ACREEDOR DEL FALLIDO.

CREEDOR DE REGRESO.
creditor who demands payment of a dis-

honored bill of exchange. From the issue or previous indorsers.

ACREEDOR EJECUTANTE.
execution creditor.

ACREEDOR EMBARGANTE.
attaching or garnishing creditor.

ACREEDOR ESCRITURARIO.
creditor whose loan was recorded before a special public notary.

ACREEDOR GARANTIZADO.
secured creditor.

ACREEDOR HEREDITARIO.
creditor of deceased person's estate. These creditors have an absolute preference over heirs or other inheritors.

ACREEDOR INFERIOR.
junior creditor.

ACREEDOR HIPOTECARIO.
mortgagee.

ACREEDOR MANCOMUNADO.
joint creditor ‖ creditor who with others is owed money by debtor and who can request only his or her portion, not the full debt.

ACREEDOR ORDINARIO.
general creditor.

ACREEDOR PERSONAL.
unsecured creditor with general rights.

ACREEDOR PETICIONARIO.
petitioning creditor.

ACREEDOR PIGNORATICIO.
secured creditor with a pledge, creditor in possession of mortgaged good.

ACREEDOR POR CONTRATO SELLADO.
speciality creditor.

ACREEDOR POR FALLO.
judgment creditor.

ACREEDOR POR JUICIO.
See ACREEDOR POR FALLO.

ACREEDOR POR SENTENCIA.
See ACREEDOR POR FALLO.

ACREEDOR PREFERENTE.
See ACREEDOR PRIVILEGIADO.

ACREEDOR PRENDARIO.
pledge or chattel mortgage creditor.

ACREEDOR PRIVILEGIADO.
preferred creditor ‖ creditor who has right to preferential payment. There are two types: 1) ACREEDORES SINGULARMENTE PRIVILEGIADOS or ACREEDORES CON PRIVILEGIO ESPECIAL (specially privileged creditors) ‖ and 2) ACREEDORES SIMPLEMENTE PRIVILE-

GIADOS or ACREEDORES CON PRIVILEGIO GE-NERAL (ordinarily privileged creditors). The first type is made up of a variety of secured creditors with rights in specific property; the second type is made up of unsecured creditors whose claims are paid out of the debtor's unsecured property as a whole.

ACREEDOR PROPIETARIO.
creditor who has a right of action in rem against debtor.

ACREEDOR QUIROGRAFARIO.
general creditor.

ACREEDOR REAL.
secured creditor (with in rem rights). See IN REM.

ACREEDOR RECURRENTE .
See ACREEDOR PETICIONARIO.

ACREEDOR REFACCIONARIO.
creditor who loans or advances money or materials to construct or repair a building. These are preferred creditors.

ACREEDOR SENCILLO.
general creditor.

ACREEDOR SIMPLE.
See ACREEDOR COMUN.

ACREEDOR SIN PRIVILEGIO.
See ACREEDOR COMUN.

ACREEDOR SOCIAL.
corporate creditor.

ACREEDOR SOLIDARIO.
joint and several creditor ‖ creditor who jointly with others is owed money by the debtor and who may receive the payment in full from the debtor on behalf of the other creditors.

ACREEDOR SUBSECUENTE.
subsequent creditor.

ACREEDOR SUPERIOR.
senior creditor.

ACREEDOR TESTAMENTARIO.
party who has a right emanating from a will against one or more heirs.

ACREEDOR VERBAL.
creditor whose right to payment springs from an oral contract.

ACREENCIA.
f, credit ‖ right of creditor to payment from debtor ‖ amount due, credit balance.

ACRIBILLADO.
adj, with many wounds or blows.

ACRIBILLAR.
v, to wound a person repeatedly with a gun.

ACRIMINACIÓN.
f, accusation (of a crime).

ACRIMINADO.
adj, accused of a crime.

ACRIMINADOR.
m, accuser ‖ adj, incriminatory.

ACRIMINAR.
v, to accuse of a crime, incriminate, char with an offense ‖ to exaggerate the gravity an offense.

ACRISOLAR.
v, to clarify (by testimony and proof).

ACRÓPOLIS.
f, acropolis ‖ asylum, refuge (of rulers or s diers).

ACTA.
f, written record ‖ minutes to a meeting document which certifies compliance with law or which outlines the breach thereof ‖ ce tification of an election ‖ act of the legislatur

ACTA AUTÉNTICA.
authentic act.

ACTA AUTORIZADA.
See ACTA AUTÉNTICA.

ACTA CONSTITUTIVA.
incorporation agreement ‖ incorporatic documents.

ACTA CONSULAR.
consular act ‖ formal action taken by a co sular officer abroad.

ACTA
DE ASAMBLEA.
minutes of a meeting (usually taken and swo to by the secretary). In most civil law countri these minutes must be kept in a permane minute book.

ACTA DE AUDIENCIA.
record of parties' and witnesses' testimon kept by judge's clerk.

ACTA DE AVENIMIENTO.
memorandum of agreement.

ACTA DE CESIÓN.
conveyance, transfer, assignment.

ACTA DE CONSTITUCIÓN.
See ACTA CONSTITUTIVA.

ACTA DE DEFUNCIÓN.
death certificate.

ACTA DE DEPÓSITO.
notarial certificate that certain things an documents have been deposited with notar public.

A DE DESLINDE.
cription of property line ‖ certificate defin-
dividing boundary line.

A DE MATRIMONIO.
ord of a marriage, marriage certificate.

A DE NACIMIENTO.
h certificate.

A DE NOTIFICACIÓN.
e of service of process, notarial certificate
ich notifies a party of legal proceeding, is-
:d at the request of an individual or govern-
nt uthority.

A DE ORGANIZACIÓN.
orporation papers.

A DE POSESIÓN.
tificate of office ‖ certificate of possession.

A DE PRESENCIA.
e of notarization, notarial certification is-
:d upon verifying the truth of the subject
tter contained in the document.

A DE PROTESTO.
arial certificate of failure to pay a bill of ex-
ange or other commercial document.

A DE PROTOCOLIZACIÓN.
arial certificate that certifies that a docu-
nt has been entered in the special public
ary book called a PROTOCOLO.

A DE RECEPCIÓN.
rmal act by which a finished work is deli-
red (especially with relation to public con-
cts).

A DE REFERENCIA.
tarial certificate that certain statements
ve been made in front of the notary.

A DE REGISTRO.
il registry ‖ registration of marital status.

A DE TESTAMENTO
RRADO.
tarial or public clerk's act (to certify that all
legal formalities of a proper will have been
mplied with).

A DE ÚLTIMA VOLUNTAD.
t will and testament, will, testament.

A DE UNA REUNIÓN.
e ACTA DE SESION.

A ELECTORAL.
ection certificate. Document which the
esident and participants of a meeting sign to
knowledge an election and the results.

A JUDICIAL.
cument issued by a judge's clerk to certify

facts or statements or agreements which have
occurred in the litigation.

ACTA LEGALIZADA.
See ACTA AUTÉNTICA.

ACTA NOTARIAL.
notarial certificate ‖ notarial acknowledgement.

ACTAS.
minutes of a meeting ‖ proceedings‖ docket,
file, papers.

ACTAS DE JUICIOS.
court records.

"ACTIO".
m, action ‖ right or cause of action. Refers not
only to the lawsuit but to the right which is in
contest.

ACTIO AD EXHIBENDUM.
See ACCIÓN "AD EXHIBENDUM".

ACTIO AESTIMATORIA.
See ACCIÓN ESTIMATORIA.

ACTIO CONFESSORIAE.
See ACCIÓN CONFESORIA.

ACTIO DE DOLO MALO.
See ACCIÓN DE DOLO MALO.

ACTIO DE IN REM VERSO.
action for unjust enrichment.

ACTIO EMPTI.
actio empti.

ACTIO EMPTU.
See ACTIO EMPTI.

ACTIO FAMILIAE ERCISCUNDAE.
See ACCIÓN FAMILIAE ERCISCUNDAE.

ACTIO FURTI.
See ACCIÓN FURTI.

ACTIO IN REM.
See ACCIÓN IN REM.

ACTIO PIGNORATICIA.
See ACCIÓN PIGNORATICIA.

ACTIO QUOD
METUS CAUSA.
See ACCIÓN QUOD METUS CAUSA.

ACTIO REDHIBITORIA.
See ACCIÓN REDHIBITORIA.

ACTIO RERUM AMOTARUM.
See ACCIÓN RERUM AMOTARUM.

ACTIO VENDITI.
See ACCIÓN VENDITI.

ACTITADERO.
adj, pending lawsuit.

ACTITAR.
v, to carry out ‖ to act as a special public notary

or country clerk in a legal proceeding ‖ to file a lawsuit.

ACTIVIDAD.
f, activity ‖ action ‖ promptness ‖ diligence, efficiency.

ACTIVIDAD LUCRATIVA.
lucrative activity.

ACTIVO.
m, personal or corporate property in toto ‖ assets ‖ adj, active. Used in criminal law to distinguish active versus passive participation.

ACTIVO A MANO.
cash assets.

ACTIVO APROBADO.
proven or admitted assets.

ACTIVO CIRCULANTE.
floating or working capital ‖ liquid assets ‖ current assets.

ACTIVO COMPUTABLE.
admitted assets.

ACTIVO CONFIRMADO.
See ACTIVO APROBADO.

ACTIVO CORRIENTE.
current assets ‖ liquid assets ‖ floating assets.

ACTIVO DE ORDEN.
See CUENTAS DE ORDEN.

ACTIVO DEMORADO.
deferred assets.

ACTIVO DISPONIBLE.
assets available, cash assets ‖ cash on hand in bank accounts, in checks, and merchandise which is easily convertible into money.

ACTIVO EFECTIVO.
cash assets.

ACTIVO EN CIRCULACIÓN.
See ACTIVO CIRCULANTE.

ACTIVO EVENTUAL.
contingent assets.

ACTIVO EXIGIBLE.
assets payable on demand.

ACTIVO FIJO.
fixed assets, capital assets.

ACTIVO INMOVILIZADO.
See ACTIVO FIJO.

ACTIVO NOMINAL.
goodwill ‖ intangible assets.

ACTIVO PERMANENTE.
See ACTIVO FIJO.

ACTIVO FLOTANTE.
current or circulating assets.

ACTIVO INTANGIBLE.
intangible assets ‖ passive assets.

ACTIVO INVISIBLE.
goodwill ‖ concealed assets.

ACTIVO LÍQUIDO.
net worth ‖ liquid assets.

ACTIVO NETO.
net worth.

ACTIVO OCULTO.
hidden assets.

ACTIVO REALIZABLE.
current assets ‖ liquid assets.

ACTIVO SOCIAL.
partnership or corporate assets.

ACTO.
m, action, act, manifestation of will ‖ fac‹ moment when action takes place ‖ ceremo‹ solemnity ‖ meeting ‖ time period in a trial hearing ‖ legal document.

ACTO A TÍTULO GRATUITO.
gift ‖ gratuitous transaction. See A TÍTU‹ GRATUITO.

ACTO A TÍTULO ONEROSO.
act of mutual obligations, act for which the is consideration paid. See A TÍTULO ONEROSO.

ACTO ATRIBUTIVO.
(legal) act of transferring a right to anoth‹ person.

ACTO AUTÉNTICO.
document which requires no supporting e‹ dence.

ACTO BÉLICO.
act of war.

ACTO CAUSADO.
act or legal transaction which sets forth t‹ basis upon which the obligation exists.

ACTO COMPLEJO.
joint action of parties with a common intere‹ or which joins different legal institutions; cor‹ plex transaction.

ACTO CONSERVATIVO.
See ACTO CONSERVATORIO.

ACTO CONSERVATORIO.
act which tends to preserve a right or thing the possession of a person.

ACTO CONCILIATORIO.
See ACTO DE CONCILIACIÓN.

ACTO CONSTITUYENTE.
constitutional act. See ACTO.

O CONTINUO.
tinuing act or action, act occurring imme-
tely after another event or act.
O DE ADMINISTRACIÓN.
ninistrative activities to preserve or impro-
property. Used in domestic relations, con-
ts, and wills.
O DE BUENA FE.
d faith act or action.
O DE COMERCIO.
nmercial transaction ‖ act regulated by
nmercial laws ‖ act carried out by a mer-
nt.
O DE COMISIÓN.
of commission.
O DE CONCILIACIÓN.
ciliatory action, act of conciliation ‖ settle-
nt or conciliation proceedings. If an agree-
nt is reached, the judge must enforce it as
dgment.
O DE DOCUMENTACIÓN.
rt records (of legal proceedings).
O DE EJECUCIÓN.
cution proceeding ‖ action to execute a
gment.
O DE GUERRA.
ACTO BÉLICO.
O DE IMPULSO
OCESAL.
which moves a legal proceeding forward.
O DE INSOLVENCIA.
of bankruptcy or insolvency.
O DE OMISIÓN.
t of omission.
O DE OTORGAMIENTO.
cution, carrying out.
O DE POSESIÓN.
ion by means of which possession is exer-
ed.
O DE PRESENCIA.
mal appearance.
O DE QUIEBRA.
of bankruptcy.
O DIPLOMÁTICO.
lomatic act, action carried out by diplo-
tic agent.
O DISIMULADO.
ion carried out to conceal the true action ‖
nulated or apparent action carried out to
oid performing an obligation or complying
h a law.

ACTO EJECUTIVO.
executive action, action of executive authority
in accord with laws and regulations of nation.
ACTO FACULTATIVO.
voluntary action ‖ act which is not obligatory
or required.
ACTO FORMAL.
See ACTO SOLEMNE.
ACTO INSCRIBIBLE.
act which is able to be registered in the Registry of Property or other government registries.
ACTO JUDICIAL.
judicial act ‖ action taken or decision made by
a judge or tribunal.
ACTO JURÍDICO.
juridical or legal act or activity ‖ act which has
legal effects. Refers to voluntary acts in accord
with the law the purpose of which is to establish, modify, transfer, preserve or extinguish
the legal relationship between the parties.
ACTO LEGAL.
legal act ‖ act which conforms with the law and
regulations. May be both morally wrong and
unjust, but it must be in accord with the law.
ACTO
MODIFICATIVO.
modifying action ‖ act which produces profit
or loss from the sale or purchase of corporate
assets.
ACTO NOTARIAL.
notarized document, document witnessed by a
notary public, in his capacity as such.
ACTO OMISIVO.
act of omission.
ACTO POSESORIO.
See ACTO DE POSESIÓN.
ACTO PROCESAL.
act which is done in the course of a legal
proceeding and which creates, modifies, or extinguishes procedural rights or relationships ‖
lawsuit, suit, legal action.
ACTO PÚBLICO.
act witnessed by notary public, court clerk, or
other public officer, in his or her capacity as
such ‖ public law action ‖ public ceremony.
ACTO-REGLA.
judicial act which imposes obligations on third
parties to action.
ACTO REGLAMENTARIO.
regulatory act, which administrative authority
carries out by virtue of the power delegated it

by the legislative branch, to complete the details of the law.

ACTO SOLEMNE.
action which must comply with certain formal requisites for it to be valid and binding.

ACTO TRASLATIVO.
act which transfers a thing or right to another party.

ACTOR.
m, plaintiff, claimant, complainant ‖ accuser.

ACTOR CIVIL.
plaintiff who requests civil remedy only.

ACTOR CRIMINAL.
prosecutor.

ACTOR EJECUTANTE.
party who requests the issuance of an order to seize and sell the goods of debtor in an attachment proceeding.

ACTORA.
f, female plaintiff.

ACTOS ABSTRACTOS.
legal acts in which the purpose or underlying transaction (CAUSA) is not designated. See ACTO.

ACTOS ACCESORIOS.
secondary or subordinate acts. Opposed to ACTOS PRINCIPALES. See ACTO.

ACTOS ADMINISTRATIVOS.
administrative acts carried out pursuant to public law. See ACTO.

ACTOS ANULABLES.
voidable acts or actions. See ACTO.

ACTOS BILATERALES.
bilateral acts or actions (i.e. those requiring consent of two parties). See ACTO.

ACTOS COLECTIVOS.
multilateral acts or actions (i.e. those requiring consent of two or more parties) ‖ acts carried out by a collective body (e.g. an assembly, a group of shareholders). See ACTO.

ACTOS CONSERVATORIOS.
acts to preserve rights.

ACTOS CONSTITUTIVOS.
acts or actions creating a right or obligation. See ACTO.

ACTOS DE AUTORIDAD.
administrative acts or actions which prohibit or authorize. See ACTO.

ACTOS DE DISPOSICIÓN.
acts or actions to dispose of property. Op-

posed to ACTO DE ADMINISTRACIÓN. See ACTO.

ACTOS DE GESTIÓN.
acts of agency ‖ activities which may be carrie out by an agent. See ACTO.

ACTOS DE GOBIERNO.
governmental acts or activities. See ACTO.

ACTOS DE SERVICIO.
acts or actions carried out by a public officia See ACTO.

ACTOS DE ÚLTIMA VOLUNTAD.
testamentary acts or actions (to be carried ou upon death). See ACTO.

ACTOS DECLARATIVOS.
declaratory acts or actions (to declare the pre existing state of affairs).

ACTOS EN FRAUDE DE ACREEDORES.
See ENAJENACIÓN EN FRAUDE DE ACREE DORES.

ACTOS ENTRE VIVOS.
inter vivos acts or actions.

ACTOS EXTINTIVOS.
acts or actions which extinguish (a right o obligation).

ACTOS GRATUITOS.
See ACTO A TÍTULO GRATUITO.

ACTOS ILÍCITOS.
illegal acts or actions.

ACTOS INAMISTOSOS.
unfriendly acts or actions.

ACTOS INDIVIDUALES.
individual acts or actions ‖ acts or action which only one person can carry out.

ACTOS INEXISTENTES.
void acts or actions (e.g. for failure to compl with legal requisites). These acts or actions de not meet the conditions to qualify as the act or actions they suppose to be.

ACTOS LIBIDINOSOS VIOLENTOS.
violent sexual acts.

ACTOS LÍCITOS.
legal acts or actions (i.e. those which do no violate the law).

ACTOS LUCRATIVOS.
lucrative acts or actions.

ACTOS NULOS.
void acts or actions.

ACTOS ONEROSOS.
See ACTO A TÍTULO ONEROSO.

ACTOS PRINCIPALES.
principal or primary acts or actions. Opposed to ACTOS ACCESORIOS.

ACTOS REGLADOS.
See FACULTADES REGLADAS.

ACTOS UNILATERALES.
unilateral acts or actions. Opposed to ACTOS BILATERALES and ACTOS COLECTIVOS.

ACTUABLE.
adj, actionable.

ACTUACIÓN.
f, performance, result of action ‖ record. See ACTUACIONES.

ACTUACIÓN JUDICIAL.
legal proceeding ‖ judicial action, all acts emanating from a trial and for which there is documentary evidence.

ACTUACIONES.
f, records (of the entirety of all legal acts that make up the file, proceedings, lawsuit, whether judicial or administrative).

ACTUACIONES SECRETAS.
in camera legal proceedings in which all attendance by the public or coverage by the press is prohibited (for a period of time, at least).

ACTUACIONES TRIBUNALICIAS.
court proceedings.

ACTUAL.
adj, present, current.

ACTUALIDAD.
f, actuality, reality ‖ present, present time, here and now ‖ event or person or doctrine which focuses attention on a present state of affairs.

ACTUALIDAD EN LA AGRESIÓN.
reality or actuality or present existence of aggression.

ACTUALIZACIÓN.
f, bringing current, updating (e.g. for inflation, changes in monetary value, etc.) ‖ overcoming a delay in a process or step.

ACTUAR.
v, to act, discharge a duty ‖ to write up court proceedings ‖ to bring an action, prosecute, litigate ‖ to perform judicial acts.

ACTUARIO.
m, actuary ‖ clerk of the court, county clerk ‖ person who is responsible for transcribing legal proceedings for judge and who swears on oath as to the truth of what he has transcribed. In some jurisdictions the ACTUARIO has additional functions within a legal proceeding.

ACTUARIO DE SEGUROS.
actuary, insurance actuary.

"ACTUS".
m, act or action ‖ position, office, employment.

ACUADRILLAR.
v, to form a group or a band. In criminal law this constitutes an aggravating circumstance.

ACUAGIO.
m, right to construct or exploit aqueducts; monopoly to distribute water.

ACUCHILLADO.
adj, knifed, hurt or killed by bladed weapon ‖ having experience gained from work or adversarial situation ‖ cautious due to experience.

ACUCHILLAR.
v, to knife, stab ‖ to gore.

ACUDIR.
v, to appear (in response to a summons) ‖ to present oneself, attend ‖ to object, oppose ‖ to go in help of another, aid.

ACUERDISTA.
m, person who defends an agreement or pact between two factions or parties.

ACUERDO.
m, agreement, accord, understanding, pact ‖ decision (made by tribunal, meeting, or corporation, etc.) ‖ meeting of magistrates to consider a matter ‖ sentence, verdict, judicial order, decree, resolution, order ‖ governmental decision ‖ cabinet meeting, meeting of ministers ‖ confirmation by Senate of executive nomination.

ACUERDO ADMINISTRATIVO.
administrative decision.

ACUERDO ARMÓNICO.
gentlemen's agreement.

ACUERDO CONCILIATORIO.
settlement ‖ agreement to resolve discrepancies. Enforceable as a contract.

ACUERDO CRIMINAL.
criminal conspiracy ‖ criminal pact or agreement.

ACUERDO DE CABALLEROS.
See ACUERDO ARMÓNICO.

ACUERDO DE LA MAYORÍA.
majority decision (taken at a meeting).

ACUERDO DE MINISTROS.
meeting of ministers ‖ cabinet meeting ‖ meeting without the head of state.

ACUERDO DE VOLUNTADES.
meeting of the minds.
ACUERDO DELICTIVO.
See ACUERDO CRIMINAL.
ACUERDO EXPRESO.
express agreement.
ACUERDO EXTRAJUDICIAL.
settlement out of court, out of court settlement.
ACUERDO INTERNACIONAL.
international treaty or pact or agreement.
ACUERDO NORMATIVO.
collective bargaining agreement.
ACUERDO NO SELLADO.
unstamped or unsealed agreement; oral agreement.
ACUERDO PLENARIO.
decision of all divisions of the appellate courts dealing with a specific area of the law to unify en banc previously conflicting case law. The decision is binding on the courts which adopted it and on lower courts, until it is overturned by another ACUERDO PLENARIO.
ACUERDO REGIONAL.
regional agreement; agreement reached between nations in a given region (usually economic).
ACUERDO SIMPLIFICADO.
simplified pact; treaty between two nations which takes immediate effect without subsequent ratification.
ACUERDO TRANSACCIONAL.
accord and satisfaction.
ACUERDO VERBAL.
oral agreement.
ACUERDO-LEY.
agreement with force of law.
ACUERDOS FISCALES INTERNACIONALES.
international tax agreements.
ACUMULABLE.
adj, cumulative.
ACUMULACIÓN.
f, accumulation; joinder; combination.
ACUMULACIÓN DE ACCIONES.
joinder of claims; plaintiff's combination of a variety of claims. They may not be contradictory, must all be within the jurisdiction of the same judge, and must emanate from the same legal matter. The joinder may be PASIVA (passive) if the variety of claims stems from the

variety of defendants; MIXTA (mixed) if th variety of claims stems from the variety c plaintiffs and defendants ‖ ACTIVA (active) i the variety of claims stems from the variety c plaintiffs. These three types may be SUBJETIV. (subjective) if they arise from the existence o different parties or OBJETIVA (objective) i they arise due to the existence of differen material bases of claims.
ACUMULACIÓN DE AUTOS.
technical joinder of legal actions or claims i process into one, in order that they be pre sented in one trial. The case is decided by on opinion and occurs upon request of the judg or parties, but must receive judicial approval.
ACUMULACIÓN DE BENEFICIOS.
profits not distributed during business year that are added to the following year's ac counts‖ reduction in insurance premiums im plemented when the profits of the insuranc company permit.
ACUMULACIÓN DE DELITOS.
joinder of crimes. Occurs when there is more than one accused, more than one crime, or a combination of both.
ACUMULACIÓN DE FUNCIONES.
combination of two or more administrative functions or positions (in one person). Accumulation of salaries for combined functions is usually prohibited.
ACUMULACIÓN DE INDEMNIZACIONES.
cumulative indemnification, receipt of reimbursement for the same harm from various sources.
ACUMULACIÓN DE PENAS.
accumulation of sentences; total sum of the punishment for the crimes a criminal has committed.
ACUMULACIÓN DE PROCESOS.
See ACUMULACIÓN DE AUTOS.
ACUMULACIÓN DEL POSESORIO Y DEL PETITORIO.
joinder of an ACCIÓN PETITORIA and an ACCIÓN POSESORIA.
ACUMULADO.
adj, accumulated; attributed, imputed; tried jointly.
ACUMULAR.
v, to accrue; to try jointly two or more actions; to unite, join, combine; to impute (a crime).

CUMULATIVAMENTE.
adv, cumulatively. Used to refer to a judge who knows the facts of a lawsuit to the exclusion of other judges, due to his having dealt with the matter in a preliminary hearing. See A PREVENCIÓN.

CUÑAR.
v, to coin, mint (money).

CUSABLE.
adj, indictable, impeachable, accusable.

CUSACIÓN.
f, accusation, charge, impeachment, indictment ‖ the act of informing a judge of a crime in order that it be investigated and a penalty be imposed ‖ arraignment.

CUSACIÓN FALSA.
false accusation, criminal act of falsely accusing another of a criminal act. The party who is falsely accused may revoke gifts given the accuser and the accuser becomes ineligible to inherit from the party accused.

CUSACIÓN FISCAL.
criminal indictment filed after hearing initial evidence.

CUSACIÓN MALICIOSA.
malicious accusation.

CUSADO.
m, defendant, accused ‖ adj, accused.

CUSADOR.
m, accuser, complainant, prosecutor. In principle neither criminals nor judges may bring criminal complaints ‖ however, the latter may do so in their non-judicial capacity. A party may not accuse his spouse with a few limited exceptions.

CUSAR.
v, to accuse, incriminate, charge, denounce ‖ to indict, impeach, inform on ‖ to arraign ‖ to prosecute.

CUSAR A MUERTE.
to accuse of a capital crime.

CUSAR UNA GANANCIA.
to show a profit.

CUSAR UNA PÉRDIDA.
to show a loss.

CUSAR POR GRAN JURADO.
to indict.

CUSAR RESULTADOS.
to show results.

CUSATIVO.
See ACUSATORIO.

ACUSATORIO.
adj, accusatory, accusing, incriminating.

ACUSE DE RECIBO.
m, acknowledgement of receipt.

ACHACAR.
v, to attribute, impute statements or actions (usually criminal).

ACHAQUE.
m, indisposition, illness ‖ pretext, excuse ‖ fine or penalty for breaking livestock laws ‖ spurious lawsuit or legal action instigated in order to obtain money for agreement not to continue litigation.

ACHAQUERO.
m, judge who imposes fine or penalty for breaking livestock laws.

ACHOCAR.
v, to injure (with sticks or stones) ‖ to hurl against a wall ‖ to hoard money.

ACHURAR.
v, to stab, maim, or kill someone with a blade.

"AD ABSURDUM".
See "AB ABSURDUM".

" AD CAUTELAM".
as a precaution.

"AD ABUNDATIORUM CAUTELUM".
for greater security or caution.

"AD EFFECTUM VIDENDI".
for the purpose of having it in view or at hand.

"AD EXEMPLUM".
for example.

"AD FINEM".
ad finem ‖ to the end.

AD HOC.
ad hoc ‖ for this, for this case.

AD HÓMINEM.
ad hominem, to the person, of personal character.

"AD HONOREM".
gratuitously, for free ‖ for honor.

"AD HUC SUB JUDICE LIS EST".
the action is still under the jurisdiction of the court or sub judice.

AD IMPOSIBILIA NEMO TENETUR.
No one is obligated to do the impossible.

"AD INFINITUM".
ad infinitum, without limit, indefinitely.

"AD INQUIRENDUM".
for the purpose of inquiring ‖ judicial order commanding an inquiry, preliminary proceeding, or legal action to begin.

"AD INTERIM".
for the interim or time being, in the meantime.

"AD JUDICIUM".
to a judgment, to a court.

AD LÍBITUM.
at pleasure, at will.

AD LÍTEM.
ad litem, for the duration of the lawsuit, during the lawsuit.

"AD LITERAM".
to the letter, verbatim, literal.

"AD MANUM".
by secretary or scribe or clerk.

"AD MENSURAM".
according to measurement, to measure ‖ pursuant to the conditions or circumstances.

"AD NUTUM".
at one's choice or pleasure.

"AD PEDEM LITTERAE".
to the letter, textually.

AD PERPÉTUAM.
forever, in perpetuity, for eternity.

"AD PROBATIONEM".
as evidence or proof. Refers to evidence which goes to prove the existence of something, not its validity.

AD QUEM.
to which, for which. Used to indicate judge or tribunal which will hear an appeal of a lower court decision.

AD REFERÉNDUM.
subject to approval of a higher or competent authority.

"AD REM".
to the thing. Used to refer to express right that one has to the thing.

"AD ROGATIO".
See ARROGACIÓN.

"AD SOLEMNITATEM".
refers to a formality necessary for the validity of a transaction as opposed to those required to prove a transaction.

"AD USUM".
according to habit or use ‖ in accord with customs or practice.

AD VALÓREM.
ad valorem, according to the value, for the value.

ADACTO.
adj, forged, obligated ‖ subjugated.

ADAGIO.
m, adage, saying ‖ proverb.

ADATAR.
v, to date ‖ to credit.

ADDICTIO IN DIEM.
See ADICCIÓN A DIE.

ADDICTUS.
adj, adjudicated, judged.

ADEHALA.
f, extra, bonus (attached to a salary a emolument) ‖ tip, extra.

ADELANTACIÓN.
See ADELANTAMIENTO.

ADELANTADAMENTE.
adv, with anticipation, in advance, beforeh

ADELANTADO.
m, emissary from Spain who obtained r over certain property in New World ‖ adj vanced, civilized ‖ early, advance.

ADELANTAR.
v, to move forward, advance ‖ to accele speed up, hurry (an action). Refers comm to early payments.

ADEMPLIO.
See ADEMPRIBIO.

ADEMPRIBIO.
m, communal pasture land owned by tw more towns.

ADENCIÓN.
f, ademption, dispossession, seizure ‖ the a thing.

ADÉSPOTA.
m, he who refuses to admit the authorit another.

ADEUDAR.
v, to owe ‖ to debit.

ADEUDARSE.
v, to go into debt.

ADEUDO.
m, debt, obligation, debit ‖ customs duty.

ADHERIR.
v, to stick, seal ‖ to concur, agree with, s port, join, adhere to (a decision or opinion

ADHERIRSE.
v, to join. Used to refer to action of non-ap lant party joining the appellant in the appe

ADHESIÓN.
f, adhesion, sticking ‖ assent given to a th party's action ‖ undisputed acceptance of c tractual terms set unilaterally ‖ collaborat or cooperation with another ‖ act of vol

ering for the army or joining a band.

HESIÓN PROCESAL.
e TERCERÍA COADYUVANTE.

HESIVO.
lj, concurring, agreeing ‖ related to adheren-
or adhesion.

IADO.
lj, appointed ‖ fixed at a precise moment or
te in time.

IAR.
to set, appoint (a date).

ICCIÓN A DIE.
temporary order, provisional order effective
ntil a certain day ‖ agreement to release
ller from sales contract (for a better offer).

ICCIÓN IN DIEM.
e ADICCIÓN A DIE.

ICIÓN.
addition ‖ adding ‖ footnote ‖ check, bill (in
restaurant or hotel).

ICIÓN
E LA HERENCIA.
cceptance by heir of the inheritance. May be
xpress or implied.

ICIÓN DE NOMBRE.
ddition of name. In many countries, there are
ws which regulate which of the parent's last
ames may be used by the child.

ICIONAL.
lj, additional, extra, complementary, bonus.
sed in tax law and legislation to refer to ad-
tional clauses or laws.

IMPLEMENTO.
, compliance with a condition imposed by
gislation or judicial decree.

IR LA HERENCIA.
, to accept the inheritance.

JETIVO.
dj, adjective. Refers to a norm, precept, or
ody of law which regulates procedural law
nd practice.

JUDICACIÓN.
adjudication ‖ award.

JUDICACIÓN DE HERENCIA.
djudication of inheritance. Must be reques-
d by one or all of the heirs depending on the
ivisibility of the good.

JUDICACIÓN DE QUIEBRA.
djudication of a bankruptcy.

JUDICACIÓN DE TERRITORIOS.
djudication of national boundaries.

ADJUDICACIÓN EN PAGO.
See DACIÓN EN PAGO.

ADJUDICACIÓN PROCESAL.
judgment, judicial award or decision.

ADJUDICADOR.
m, awarder, adjudicator, judge, person with
power and position to adjudicate matters.

ADJUDICAR.
v, to adjudicate, award (a thing to someone) ‖
to award a thing in auction to the highest bidder ‖ to adjudicate questionable legal rights.

ADJUDICAR EL CONTRATO.
to award the contract.

ADJUDICATARIO.
m, awardee, grantee, successful bidder.

ADJUDICATIO.
m, adjudication, award to one of the litigants.

ADJUDICATIVO.
adj, adjudicative, deciding.

ADJUDICATURA.
f, litigation, trial dispute, legal action.

ADJUNCIÓN.
f, addition, adjunction ‖ type of accession unit-
ing two pieces of personal property of different owners, such that they form one, but
are able to be separated later.

ADJUNTAR.
v, to enclose ‖ to attach. Used to refer to sending of bills or samples with letter.

ADJUNTO.
m, one of several judges who make up a tribunal ‖ adj, enclosed, attached, accompanying
‖ herewith.

ADMINICULAR.
v, to provide additional proof, corroborate.

ADMINÍCULO.
f, corroboration, additional proof.

ADMINISTRACIÓN.
m, administration, governance of things, fulfillment of employment obligations or position
‖ employment of administrator ‖ administrative office building ‖ administrator's office.

ADMINISTRACIÓN ACTIVA.
governmental administration ‖ government
action to comply with laws, promote public interests and resolve problems.

ADMINISTRACIÓN
ACCESORIA.
ancillary administration.

ADMINISTRACIÓN CENTRAL.
central administration ‖ federal government.

ADMINISTRACIÓN CONSULTIVA.
advisory administration ‖ body of advisors.
ADMINISTRACIÓN CONTENCIOSA.
act of judicially resolving administrative law conflicts.
ADMINISTRACIÓN CON TESTAMENTO ANEXO.
administration with will attached.
ADMINISTRACIÓN DE BIENES DEL AUSENTE.
administration of property of an absentee.
ADMINISTRACIÓN DE IMPUESTOS.
tax administration ‖ tax collector's office.
ADMINISTRACIÓN DE JUSTICIA.
administration of justice.
ADMINISTRACIÓN DE LA COSA COMÚN.
administration of jointly owned thing (by one person, all owners, or an outside administrator).
ADMINISTRACIÓN DE LA HERENCIA.
estate administration (prior to the division of the estate).
ADMINISTRACIÓN DE LA QUIEBRA.
bankruptcy receivership ‖ administration of the affairs of the bankrupt's estate (by an administrator or creditors).
ADMINISTRACIÓN DE LA SOCIEDAD.
corporate or partnership administration. See SOCIEDAD.
ADMINISTRACIÓN DE LA SOCIEDAD CONYUGAL.
administration of marital community or community property.
ADMINISTRACIÓN DE LA SUCESIÓN.
administration of the decedent's estate.
ADMINISTRACIÓN DELIBERANTE.
state organs which resolve issues but do not enforce the resolutions.
ADMINISTRACIÓN JUDICIAL.
judicial administration or receivership ‖ administration or receivership pursuant to judicial appointment.
ADMINISTRACIÓN LEGAL.
receivership pursuant to law.
ADMINISTRACIÓN PÚBLICA.
public administration.
ADMINISTRADO.
adj, administered, governed by another ‖ subject to jurisdiction of administrative tribunals.
ADMINISTRADOR.
m, administrator ‖ curator, guardian, one who

directs and manages the goods or busines
another ‖ one who works in government
ministration.
ADMINISTRADOR CONCURSAL.
trustee in bankruptcy.
ADMINISTRADOR DE BIENES DE ENEMIGOS.
custodian of alien property (usually du
time of war).
ADMINISTRADOR DE CONTRIBUCIONES.
tax collector.
ADMINISTRADOR JUDICIAL.
receiver or trustee or administrator wh
judicially chosen to manage a particular t
or estate.
ADMINISTRADOR LEGAL.
administrator (by law) ‖ one whose posi
derives from law (e.g. father relative to p
perty of his minor children).
ADMINISTRAR.
v, to administrate, manage, care for, regu
use of (goods) ‖ to enjoy a government p
tion or employment ‖ to govern, rule,
ministrate.
ADMINISTRAR UN JURAMENTO.
to administer an oath.
ADMINISTRAR JUSTICIA.
to administer justice.
ADMINISTRATIVO.
m, administrative employee, one who work
the administration of business (as oppose
a technician or executive) ‖ adj, adminis
tive, pertaining to the administration of go
‖ pertaining to government administration
ADMISIBILIDAD.
f, admissibility.
ADMISIBLE.
adj, admissible, able to be admitted, acce
able (re legal arguments or bases of appea
ADMISIÓN.
f, admission, confession ‖ acceptance ‖ acc
tance of payment ‖ acceptance of new part
‖ admission of evidence or complain
process prior to the final proceeding in wh
judge determines compliance with cert
legal formalities.
ADMISIÓN COMPLETA.
full admission.
ADMISIÓN CONCOMITANTE.
incidental admission.

OMISIÓN DE PARTE.
admission by a party.
OMISIÓN DE SENTENCIA.
confession of judgment.
OMISIÓN DESVENTAJOSA.
admission against interest.
OMISIÓN DIRECTA.
express or direct admission.
OMISIÓN IMPLÍCITA.
tacit or implied admission.
OMISIÓN PLENARIA.
full admission.
OMISIÓN PROCESAL.
judicial or in-court admission.
OMISIÓN TEMPORARIA.
temporary importation.
OMITIR.
, to admit, concede ‖ to authorize the lawsuit
to proceed ‖ to receive ‖ to permit (to enter)
to accept.
OMITIR UN RECLAMO.
to allow a claim.
OMONICIÓN.
, admonition, warning, reminder ‖ cross-complaint (by defendant).
OLESCENCIA.
, adolescence. Used to refer to issues of
emancipation and marital capacity.
OLESCENTE.
n, f, adolescent ‖ adj, adolescent.
OPCIÓN.
, adoption ‖ social or legal act by which child,
not otherwise one's own, is accepted as such ‖
act of adopting a resolution, agreement, or
measure ‖ act of following an opinion, decision, or doctrine.
OPCIÓN DE EXPÓSITOS.
adoption of foundlings by institution. Lasts
only until child reaches majority and may be
revoked at will.
OPCIÓN DE HECHO.
de facto adoption.
OPCIÓN LEGITIMADORA.
adoption to legitimize children born out of
wedlock.
OPCIÓN
MENOS PLENA.
simple or incomplete adoption ‖ adoption of
spouse's natural or adopted offspring.
OPCIÓN PLENA.
full adoption. Refers to adoption of children

born to common law spouses and by widows
or widowers.
ADOPCIÓN SIMPLE.
See ADOPCIÓN MENOS PLENA.
ADOPTACIÓN.
f, adoption.
ADOPTADO.
m, foundling who is adopted ‖ adj, adopted.
ADOPTADOR.
See ADOPTANTE.
ADOPTANTE.
m, adopter, person who adopts child naturally
born to others.
ADOPTAR.
v, to adopt, accept ‖ to pass ‖ to accept as one's
own.
ADOPTAR UN ACUERDO.
to pass a resolution.
ADOPTIVO.
m. son or daughter by adoption ‖ adopting
parent (rare) ‖ adj, adoptive ‖ adopted.
ADOR.
m, time allotted to use water in system where
water is shared.
ADQUIRENTE.
m, f, acquirer, one who becomes owner or
proprietor of something ‖ purchaser, buyer.
ADQUIRENTE A TÍTULO GRATUITO.
recipient of a gift, donee.
ADQUIRENTE A TÍTULO ONEROSO.
purchaser for value.
ADQUIRENTE DE BUENA FE.
good faith purchaser.
ADQUIRENTE SIN PREVIO
CONOCIMIENTO.
purchaser without (prior) notice.
ADQUIRIDO.
adj, acquired.
ADQUIRIDOR.
See ADQUIRENTE.
ADQUIRIR.
v, to acquire (ownership of property) ‖ to attain (by hard work) ‖ to obligate oneself.
ADQUIRIR POR TÍTULO DE
COMPRA.
to acquire by purchase.
ADQUISICIÓN.
f, acquisition. Includes purchase, gift, in-
heritance, etc.
ADQUISICIÓN A TÍTULO GRATUITO.
acquisition by gift or donation.

ADQUISICIÓN A TÍTULO ONEROSO.
purchase for value.

ADQUISICIÓN A TÍTULO SINGULAR.
acquisition pursuant to a specific bequest of specific property.

ADQUISICIÓN A TÍTULO UNIVERSAL.
acquisition pursuant to general bequest or a percentage thereof.

ADQUISICIÓN DE BUENA FE.
good faith acquisition, acquisition in which the acquirer believes that the thing is owned by the transferor.

ADQUISICIÓN DE COSAS.
acquisition of chattels.

ADQUISICIÓN DE DERECHOS.
acquisition of rights.

ADQUISICIÓN DE LA HERENCIA.
acquisition of the decedent's estate (by inheritance) ‖ incorporation of all or part of the property of one into estate of other as a result of the latter's acceptance.

ADQUISICIÓN DE MALA FE.
bad faith acquisition, acquisition in which the acquirer knows that the transferor does not own the good.

ADQUISICIÓN DE NOMBRE.
obtaining of a name.

ADQUISICIÓN DERIVADA.
derivative acquisition.

ADQUISICIÓN DERIVATIVA.
acquisition by transfer of title.

ADQUISICIÓN ORIGINARIA.
acquisition by original creation.

ADQUISICIÓN ORIGINAL.
original acquisition.

ADQUISICIÓN PROCESAL.
third party testimony. Used to refer to proof offered by one party which works to the benefit of other parties to the action.

ADQUISITIVO.
adj, acquisitive, able to acquire.

ADROLLERO.
m, shyster, cheat, person who buys or sells fraudulently.

ADSCRIBIR.
v, to assign, appoint (person to a position temporarily).

ADSCRIPCIÓN.
f, temporary assignment.

ADUANA.
f, customs house, customs ‖ customs department.

ADUANAR.
v, to register with customs house ‖ to pay du at customs house.

ADUANERO.
m, customs official ‖ adj, customs.

ADUCCIÓN DE PRUEBAS.
f, presentation of proof, production of evidence (in trial).

ADUCIR.
v, to present or produce (evidence) ‖ to argue

ADUEÑARSE.
v, to become legal owner of something ‖ to take physical but not legal ownership.

ADÚLTERA.
f, adulteress ‖ adj, adulterous.

ADULTERACIÓN.
f, adulteration ‖ falsification ‖ the act of making impure or false.

ADULTERACIÓN DE DOCUMENTOS.
falsification of documents.

ADULTERAR.
v, to adulterate ‖ to falsify ‖ to commit adultery.

ADULTERINO.
adj, adulterine, adulterous ‖ causing adulter ‖ resulting from, pertaining to, or of adulter ‖ falsified, false, forged.

ADULTERIO.
m, adultery (between two married persons or between a married person and an unmarried person).

ADÚLTERO.
m, f, adulterer (if male), adulteress (if female ‖ adj, adulterous.

ADULTA.
f, (female) adult.

ADULTO.
m, grown-up, adult ‖ (male) adult ‖ adj, adult

ADVENIMIENTO DEL PLAZO.
m, maturity of a term or time period.

ADVENTICIO.
adj, accidental, adventitious.

ADVERACIÓN.
f, certification ‖ attestation, affirmation, confirmation ‖ certification of the authenticity of statements not made before a public notary.

ADVERADO.
adj, attested ‖ witnessed ‖ certified.

VERSARIO.
1, adversary ‖ adj, adversarial, adverse.

VERTENCIA.
warning, admonition ‖ notice ‖ recommen-
ation ‖ reminder or notice from a govern-
ental authority (regarding the law or an
rder, etc.) ‖ advice.

VERTIR.
, to warn ‖ to recommend ‖ to remind or give
otice ‖ to advise ‖ to observe.
ee ADVERTENCIA.

VOCACIÓN.
, support, protection ‖ practice of law.

VOCADO.
ee ABOGADO.

RONÁUTICO.
dj, aeronautic.

ROPUERTO.
n, airport, landing strip.

ANAR.
, to steal, rip off.

ECCIÓN.
, act of pledging or mortgaging or encumber-
ng ‖ charge, assessment, fee.

ECCIÓN
E BIENES.
, encumbering or pledging or mortgaging of
oods.

ECTABLE.
dj, able to be encumbered.

ECTACIÓN.
, assignment (to a post or position) ‖ designa-
ion of means for a specific end ‖ imposition of
lien or encumbrance ‖ appropriation.

ECTAR.
, to add to, unite ‖ to simulate, feign ‖ to im-
ose a lien or encumbrance on, pledge, en-
umber ‖ to allocate, earmark, assign.

ECTO.
n, affection ‖ adj, earmarked, designated to
arry out services or functions for determined
nds ‖ pledged, encumbered.

ERENTE.
dj, encumbered ‖ subject to tenancy in com-
non.

ERICIÓN.
, act of assaying and sealing weights and
neasures ‖ office of weights and measures.

ERIR.
, to assay scales and weights and measures to
ssure their accuracy and legality.

AFERRADOR.
m, constable.

"AFFECTUS MARITALIS".
m, marital love or affection. Refers to state of
marital relationship.

AFIANZADO.
adj, bonded, guaranteed ‖ on bail, on bond.

AFIANZADO PARA DERECHOS ADUANEROS.
bonded for purposes of customs duties, cus-
toms-bonded.

AFIANZADO PARA RENTAS INTERIORES.
bonded for purposes of internal revenue taxes.

AFIANZADOR.
m, bondsman, guarantor.

AFIANZAMIENTO.
m, act of bonding, guaranteeing ‖ bond,
guaranty.

AFIANZAR.
v, to bond, guarantee (another's obligation) ‖
to back, support.

AFIDAVIT.
m, affidavit.

AFIDUCIAR.
v, to guarantee, to assure.

AFILIACIÓN.
f, membership, affiliation, association ‖ adoption ‖ entry into an association or party.

AFILIADO DEL GREMIO.
m, union member. May be one of four types:
FUNDADORES (founding) ‖ ACTIVOS (active
members) ‖ HONORARIOS (honorary members) ‖ PROTECTORES (distinguished members).

AFILIADO DEL SINDICATO.
See AFILIADO DEL GREMIO.

AFILIAR.
v, to become a member, affiliate, join ‖ to
admit a person as a member.

AFILIARSE.
v, to affiliate oneself.

AFINCAR.
v, to acquire farms ‖ to establish oneself in a
place.

AFINIDAD.
f, affinity, relationship, kinship.

AFIRMACIÓN.
f, affirmation ‖ verbal or written affirmance ‖
legal statement or declaration or deposition ‖
legal affirmation of rights to a territory.

AFIRMADOR.
m, affirmant ‖ adj, affirming.
AFIRMANTE.
m, affirmant ‖ adj, affirmative.
AFIRMAR.
v, to affirm, ratify ‖ to swear to, aver ‖ to proclaim a right to ‖ to make annual payment for services.
AFIRMAR BAJO JURAMENTO.
to swear to, state under oath.
AFIRMARSE.
v, to ratify, stand firmly by that said or done.
AFIRMATIVA.
f, affirmation, proposition or opinion indicating assent.
AFIRMATIVO.
adj, affirmative, positive.
AFITAR.
v, to mark farm boundaries with stones or markers.
AFORADO.
m, person or entity possessing a privilege or exemption ‖ adj, appraised (for tax purposes) ‖ taken to court ‖ rented, leased ‖ privileged, subject to privilege or exemption.
AFORADOR.
m, appraiser, assessor.
AFORAGE.
m, official price fixed for sale of beverages ‖ price of bribe payable to government authority.
AFORAR.
v, to appraise, value ‖ to gage ‖ estimate.
AFORISMO.
m, aphorism, adage, saying.
AFORO.
m, appraisal, evaluation (for tax and customs purposes) ‖ legal capacity (of persons to enter a public site).
AFORO DE BUQUES.
ship appraisal (for taxing ship registration).
AFRANCAR.
v, to emancipate, free a slave.
AFRENTA.
f, affront, insult ‖ shame, dishonor.
AFUCIAR.
v, to obligate (by agreement).
AFUFA.
f, flight, evasion.
AGARRAR.
v, to take, grab.

AGARROTADO.
adj, executed by blows (as capital pun§ ment).
AGARROTAR.
v, to execute as capital punishment.
AGAVILLAR.
v, to rob as part of a gang ‖ to band togetl
AGENCIA.
f, agency (in all senses) ‖ branch ‖ bureau fice.
AGENCIA DE COLOCACIONES.
employment agency.
AGENCIA DE NEGOCIOS.
business or commercial agency or brokera§
AGENCIA FISCAL.
tax agent, internal revenue agent.
AGENCIAR.
v, to negotiate, facilitate ‖ to perform § quirements) ‖ to achieve an end.
AGENCIARSE.
v, to obtain (something, a place, employm§ etc.).
AGENTE.
m, agent, factor, intermediary, representa ‖ agent for a foreign corporation.
AGENTE ADMINISTRADOR.
managing agent.
AGENTE COMERCIAL.
See AGENTE DE COMERCIO.
AGENTE DE CIRCULACIÓN.
traffic policeman.
AGENTE DE COMERCIO.
middleman ‖ commercial agent or interr diary, broker.
AGENTE DE LA ADMINISTRACIÓN.
government official.
AGENTE DE LA AUTORIDAD.
officer of the peace, police officer.
AGENTE DE LA FUERZA PÚBLICA.
civil guard, civil defense officer (comm sioned to keep public order) ‖ police office
AGENTE DE PLAZA.
local representative.
AGENTE DE POLICÍA.
police officer.
AGENTE DE RETENCIÓN.
withholding agent.
AGENTE DE TRANSFERENCIA.
transfer agent ‖ stock transfer agent.
AGENTE DEL FISCO.
See AGENTE FISCAL.

NTE DEL GOBIERNO.
ernment agent, federal agent or repre-
tative ‖ representative of the executive
nch ‖ union representative charged with
otiating with government.

NTE DIPLOMÁTICO.
ernment diplomat.

NTE EJECUTIVO.
rney charged with enforcing the tax laws
behalf of the government.

NTE ESPECIAL.
cial agent.

NTE FIDUCIARIO.
stee, fiduciary agent.

NTE FINANCIERO.
al or financial agent.

NTE FISCAL.
agent, internal revenue agent ‖ prosecutor,
ernment attorney ‖ district attorney.

NTE GENERAL.
eral agent.

NTE INCULPABLE.
ocent agent.

NTE RETENEDOR.
hholding agent.

NTES AUXILIARES DE MERCIO.
sons operating with traders (e.g. brokers,
tioneers, warehousemen, factors, common
riers).

NTES CONSULARES.
sular officers or agents.

NTES DE ADUANAS.
toms agents.

NTES DE CAMBIO Y BOLSA.
ck brokers.

NTES DE NEGOCIOS.
siness or commercial agents or brokers.

NTES DE SEGUROS.
urance brokers.

RMANAMIENTO.
practice whereby surviving spouse receives
entirety of deceased spouse's estate, in-
ding all community and individual property
ohabitation.

NAR.
o deal (in things of little value).

O.
speculation, hoarding, cornering the mar-
t ‖ raise in price resulting from fluctuations
market ‖ agio, profit margin.

AGIOTAJE.
m, abusive speculation ‖ profit made from
changes in the price of money, goods, or commercial paper ‖ usury.

AGIOTISTA.
m, usurer ‖ profiteer ‖ he who benefits from
AGIO or AGIOTAJE.

AGITACIÓN.
f, agitation ‖ political agitation.

AGITADOR.
m, agitator, subversive.

AGITAR.
v, to agitate, create public instability ‖ to wave
a white flag in order to ask for assistance (from
authority or enemy).

AGNACIÓN.
f, agnation, male kinship through father's side.

AGNADO.
m, agnate, male related by agnation.

AGNATICIO.
adj, agnatic, related by way of father's lineage.

AGNICIÓN.
f, recognition of having paid the laudemium
fee for an emphyteusis leasehold, which payment is made with money and under the name
of another.

AGOBIAR.
v, to impose a double penalty (without justification).

AGONÍA.
f, agony.

AGOSTADOR.
m, squanderer (of another's goods).

AGRA.
m, country property or farm under cultivation.

AGRACIAR.
v, to decorate, honor ‖ to pardon, exempt.

AGRAFIA.
f, agraphia, loss of memory (of a document) ‖
physical inability to write.

AGRARIO.
m, public defender of agricultural interests ‖
adj, agrarian, pertaining to agriculture.

AGRAVACIÓN.
f, aggravation, worsening. Used to refer to increase of criminal liability due to circumstances.

AGRAVACIÓN DE DELITOS COMUNES.
aggravation of common crimes ‖ system by
which militia are charged with a higher offense
for commission of a civil crime.

AGRAVACIÓN DE LA PENA.
increased punishment or sanction.
AGRAVAMIENTO.
See AGRAVACIÓN.
AGRAVANTE.
m, aggravating circumstance ‖ adj, aggravating.
AGRAVANTE CALIFICADA.
aggravating circumstances of habitual criminality ‖ increase in punishment due to repeated criminality.
AGRAVANTEMENTE.
adv, aggravatingly ‖ with a charge or tax.
AGRAVAR.
v, to offend ‖ to injure ‖ to impose a tax or charge.
AGRAVATORIO.
adj, aggravating ‖ requiring a new judicial order ‖ requiring compliance with prior order.
AGRAVIADO.
m, injured or wronged party ‖ appellant ‖ adj, injured, wronged ‖ offended.
AGRAVIADOR.
m, violator, offender ‖ tort-feasor.
AGRAVIANTE.
m, offender, injurer ‖ adj, injuring, offending.
AGRAVIAR.
v, to injure, damage, wrong, offend.
AGRAVIO.
m, injury, offense, insult ‖ lower court error (complained of on appeal).
AGRAVIO A LA PERSONA.
personal tort.
AGRAVIO CIVIL.
civil injury.
AGRAVIO MALICIOSO.
malicious mischief.
AGRAVIO MARÍTIMO.
maritime tort.
AGRAVIO MATERIAL.
physical or material damage or injury.
AGRAVIO MORAL.
emotional injury ‖ pain and suffering ‖ non-physical and non-economic and non-commercial damage.
AGRAVIO PROCESABLE.
actionable wrong or tort.
AGRAVIO PROTERVO.
wanton injury.
AGRAVIOSO.
adj, tortious, injurious ‖ insulting.

AGREDIR.
v, to intentionally assault, attack.
AGREGADO.
m, attache ‖ person given a position with having been properly named thereto ‖ added, additional.
AGREGADO COMERCIAL.
commercial attache ‖ high-level governm representative responsible for commercial fairs with other countries.
AGREGADO DIPLOMÁTICO.
diplomatic attache, junior diplomat (wh starting his/her career).
AGREGADURÍA.
f, position, function or office of a diplomat
AGREGAR.
v, to incorporate, add.
AGREMIACIÓN.
f, affiliation (with a union).
AGREMIACIÓN DE LAS PROFESIONES LIBERALES.
affiliation with professional organization order to be able to carry out professional tivities).
AGREMIADO.
m, union member ‖ adj, unionized.
AGREMIAR.
v, to unionize.
AGRESIÓN.
f, aggression, attack ‖ offense, insult, provo tion ‖ invasion. May be legal or illegal.
AGRESIÓN FÍSICA.
physical aggression.
AGRESIÓN MORAL.
aggression or attack upon emotions and sp of a person.
AGRESIÓN MUTUA.
bilateral aggression.
AGRESIÓN SIMPLE.
simple battery or aggression.
AGRESOR.
m, aggressor, assailant, attacker.
AGRUPACIÓN.
f, group assembly ‖ meeting ‖ associatior group.
AGRUPACIÓN DE FINCAS.
act of merging legal ownership of two or mo adjoining pieces of property owned by t same party into one. This is done at the R Estate Registry upon request.

GRUPACIÓN HORIZONTAL.
horizontal combination.

GRUPACIÓN TEMPORAL DE EMPRESAS.
joint venture (of corporations) ‖ association of several companies which maintain their distinct entities, but act as one for determined purposes. Formed by contract.

GRUPACIÓN VERTICAL.
vertical combination.

GRUPAMIENTO.
See AGRUPACIÓN.

GUA.
n, water.

GUAR ACCIONES.
v, to water stock.

GUAS JURISDICCIONALES.
jurisdictional waters.

GUAS TERRITORIALES.
territorial waters.

GUINALDO.
m, year-end bonus (for employees).

HIJADA.
f, god-daughter.

HIJADO.
m, god-child ‖ god-son.

HOGAR.
v, to drown ‖ to suffocate ‖ to smother ‖ to bother, oppress.

HORCADURA.
f, hanging.

HORCAMIENTO.
See AHORCADURA.

HORCAR.
v, to hang (a person).

HORCARSE.
v, to hang oneself.

HORRO.
m, savings ‖ saving.

ISLACIONISMO.
m, isolationism.

ISLAMIENTO.
m, isolation.

JENO.
adj, foreign ‖ strange ‖ another's, belonging to another.

JUAR.
m, household goods and clothing ‖ trousseau.

JUSTADOR DE DERECHOS.
m, liquidator.

JUSTADOR DE RECLAMACIONES.
m, claims adjuster.

AJUSTAR.
v, to adjust, settle ‖ to arrange ‖ to determine or fix a lump sum rate for a service ‖ to negotiate ‖ to reconcile.

AJUSTAR CUENTA.
to settle accounts.

AJUSTARSE.
v, to come to an agreement or settlement or reconciliation.

AJUSTE.
m, agreement, contract, transaction ‖ settlement, accord ‖ arrangement ‖ liquidation of debt, closing of account ‖ negotiation ‖ negotiated price ‖ reconciliation.

AJUSTE DE TRABAJO.
piecework rate.

AJUSTES.
m, act of agreeing on dowry and other issues of marriage.

AJUSTICIADO.
m, executed criminal (pursuant to judicial order).

AJUSTICIAR.
v, to execute (a person).

AL CONTADO.
adj, cash. Refers to payment at time of purchase.

AL CONTRARIO.
to the contrary.

AL CORRIENTE.
adj, current ‖ on time, punctual, up to date. Refers to timely payments.

AL DESCUBIERTO.
adj, short, insufficient, having inadequate funds available. Used to describe payment of a bill of exchange against an overdrawn account.

AL FIADO.
on credit.

AL OÍDO.
secretly, said to a persons ear.

AL PIE DE LA FÁBRICA.
ex factory, at place of manufacture. Usually in reference to the value of merchandise.

AL PIE DE LA LETRA.
to the letter, textually.

AL PIE DE LA OBRA.
ex works ‖ at the work site. Usually in reference to the value of merchandise.

AL PORTADOR.
adj, bearer, to the holder.

AL TANTO DE ALGO.
informed, up to date, in the know.
AL UNÍSONO.
adv, unanimously.
AL USADO.
adj, customary, as accustomed. Refers to method of payment.
AL USO.
adj, according to trade or commercial usage.
ALARGAR EL PLAZO.
to extend a term or time period.
ALARGAR LA MECHA.
to increase a salary or payment ‖ to delay a transaction or other matter for one's own convenience.
ALBACEA.
m, executor (if male), executrix (if female).
ALBACEA AUXILIAR.
subexecutor.
ALBACEA CONSULAR.
consular executor or executrix ‖ consul who is named to represent legatees who are citizens of the consul's nation in probate proceedings.
ALBACEA DATIVO.
court-appointed executor of an intestate's estate.
ALBACEA DEFINITIVO.
permanent executor.
ALBACEA ESPECIAL.
special executor.
ALBACEA MANCOMUNADO.
joint executor, co-executor.
ALBACEA PROVISIONAL.
temporary executor.
ALBACEA SUCESIVO.
substituted executor.
ALBACEAZGO.
m, executorship, position of executor of an estate.
ALBALÁ.
m, f, document ‖ royal grant.
ALBANA.
See AUBANA.
ALBARÁN.
m, "for rent" or "for lease" sign ‖ also see ALBALÁ.
ALBOROQUE.
m, token or drink between a buyer and seller to seal a transaction.

ALBEDRÍO.
m, free will ‖ unwritten legal custom, pre dent.
ALBINAGIA.
See AUBANA.
ALBOROTADOR.
m, rioter, agitator.
ALBOROTARSE.
to riot.
ALBOROTO.
m, disturbance ‖ riot.
ALBOROTOS POPULARES.
civil commotion.
ALCABALA.
f, sales tax (payable by both buyer and selle
ALCABALATORIO.
m, sales tax code ‖ physical area in whict sales tax has to be paid.
ALCABALERO.
m, sales tax collector.
ALCAHUETAR.
v, to pimp ‖ to induce a woman to prostitu herself.
ALCAHUETE.
m, pimp, panderer, procurer.
ALCAIDE.
m, governor or warden of a prison ‖ jailer.
ALCAIDÍA.
f, wardenship, jailer's job.
ALCALDADA.
f, abuse of mayor's authority.
ALCALDE.
m, mayor ‖ magistrate.
ALCALDE DE BARRIO.
district mayor ‖ in large cities, person who ac as mayor in a part of the city.
ALCALDE DE LA MAR.
mayor of islands or coastal areas (usually n med by military authorities).
ALCALDE LETRADO.
magistrate who is a lawyer.
ALCALDE MAYOR.
mayor ‖ judge who is a lawyer.
ALCALDE MUNICIPAL.
mayor.
ALCALDE PEDANEO.
village mayor (who is designated by a sup rior).
ALCALDESA.
f, mayoress ‖ wife of a mayor.

LCALDÍA.
f, mayoralty, position of mayor ‖ mayor's office ‖ city hall.

LCANCE.
m, reach, arm's length ‖ scope ‖ intelligence, capability ‖ capacity, ability ‖ net liability.

LCISTA.
m, bull market (slang) ‖ person who plays the stock market expecting it to rise ‖ adj, bull (market).

LCOHOLISMO.
m, alcoholism.

LCOHÓLICO.
m, alcoholic ‖ adj, alcoholic.

LCURNIA.
f, lineage.

LDEA.
f, hamlet, village, unincorporated town.

LEATORIO.
adj, aleatory, uncertain, contingent upon luck.

LEGABLE.
adj, pleadable, able to be alleged.

LEGACIÓN.
f, allegation, accusation ‖ plea, defense ‖ argument, contention.

LEGACIÓN DE BIEN PROBADO.
summing up.

LEGACIÓN DE CULPABILIDAD.
plea of guilty.

LEGACIÓN DE INOCENCIA.
plea of not guilty.

LEGACIÓN EN DERECHO.
special allegation in appeals in which written statements are substituted for oral statements.

LEGACIÓN FALSA.
false allegation.

LEGACIÓN FICTICIA.
See ALEGACIÓN FALSA.

LEGACIÓN PRIVILEGIADA.
privileged plea.

LEGACIONES.
pleadings ‖ plural of ALEGACIÓN.

LEGADOR.
m, person who uses false or improper proof or argument.

LEGAR.
v, to allege, contend, state, claim, aver ‖ to cite (law, cases, etc) ‖ to give final argument, sum up.

ALEGATO.
m, pleading, written argument, brief, legal position, plea, affirmation, declaration ‖ final argument, summary statement.

ALEGATO DE AGRAVIOS.
notice of appeal including the bases for such appeal.

ALEGATO DE BIEN PROBADO.
final argument, summing up.

ALEGATO DE CONCLUSIONES.
See ALEGATO DE BIEN PROBADO.

ALEGATO DE RÉPLICA.
reply brief.

ALEGATO SUPLIMENTAL.
supplemental plea.

ALEGATOS DE INSTANCIA.
pleadings.

ALEVE.
adj, dishonest ‖ treacherous.

ALEVOSÍA.
f, perfidy, treachery.

ALEVOSO.
adj, treacherous, perfidious.

ALFILERES.
m, personal expenses of a woman ‖ pin money.

ALFOZ.
m, county, district, borough.

ALGUACIL.
m, officer of the court, marshall, bailiff ‖ police, warrant officer.

ALGUACIL MAYOR.
sheriff.

ALHAJA.
f, gem, jewel ‖ jewelry ‖ valued thing or person.

ALIADO.
m, alley ‖ adj, allied.

ALIANZA.
f, agreement, pact, treaty ‖ alliance, union ‖ affinity by marriage.

ALIAR.
v, to agree ‖ to ally, join together.

ALIAS.
m, alias.

ALÍCUOTA.
f, aliquot ‖ part contained in the whole an exact number of times.

ALIENABLE.
adj, alienable.

ALIENACIÓN.
f, alienation, transfer, sale.

ALIENADO.
m, insane person ‖ adj, insane ‖ sold, transfered.

ALIENAR.
v, to alienate, transfer, sell.

ALIENISTA.
m, doctor who specializes in mental health. May be an expert in guardianship proceeding, criminal cases, etc.

ALIGERAR.
v, to lighten (obligations, burdens) ‖ to shorten, accelerate.

ALIJAMIENTO.
m, loss due to jettisoning cargo to avoid danger.

ALIJAR.
v, to jettison ‖ to unload (a ship of cargo).

ALIJO.
m, unloading (of a ship) ‖ contraband goods.

ALIJO FORZOSO.
jettison.

ALIMENTADOR.
m, provider, person who pays a food allowance.

ALIMENTANTE.
See ALIMENTADOR.

ALIMENTAR.
v, to provide food, feed ‖ to pay alimony or maintenance.

ALIMENTARIO.
m, one who is legally maintained or provided for or paid alimony.

ALIMENTISTA.
See ALIMENTARIO.

ALIMENTOS.
m, food ‖ maintenance ‖ alimony ‖ allowance, support (pursuant to will, contract, divorce decree, etc.).

ALIMENTOS PROVISIONALES.
alimony pendente lite.

ALINDAR.
v, to delimit boundaries by markers.

ALISTADO.
m, volunteer (for military).

ALISTAMIENTO.
m, registration ‖ enlistment, recruitment.

ALIVIO.
m, defense attorney (slang).

ALMA DEL TESTADOR.
Literally, soul of the testator ‖ testator's will or implied desires. Used to refer to the desire to

donate an estate to the poor (barring any h or legatees), which is implied at times.

ALMACÉN.
m, warehouse ‖ store.

ALMACÉN ADUANERO.
customs warehouse.

ALMACÉN AFIANZADO.
bonded warehouse.

ALMACÉN GENERAL DE DEPÓSITO.
public warehouse. Used in maritime law.

ALMACENADOR.
See ALMACENERO.

ALMACENAJE.
m, storage or warehouse charge or fee.

ALMACENERO.
m, warehouse keeper ‖ shop owner, groce

ALMACENISTA.
m, warehouse owner ‖ shop owner, groce

ALMIRANTAZGO.
m, admiralty ‖ maritime or admiralty cou airport or port tax.

ALMONEDA.
f, public auction, sale ‖ family sale.

ALNADA.
f, stepdaughter.

ALNADO.
m, stepchild ‖ stepson.

ALOCUCIÓN.
f, speech, address.

ALODIAL.
adj, allodial.

ALODIO.
m, allodium, land held in fee simple absolu

ALOGADOR.
m, renter, lessee.

ALOJAMIENTO.
m, lodgings ‖ billeting, quartering (of milit

ALOJAR.
v, to put up, lodge ‖ to quarter, billet.

ALONGAR.
v, to lengthen, prolong, extend.

ALQUILABLE.
adj, rentable, leasable (in cities).

ALQUILADOR.
m, lessor, landlord, hirer ‖ tenant, less hiree.

ALQUILANTE.
m, tenant, lessee, hiree.

ALQUILAR.
v, to rent, to lease.

UILARSE.
» hire one's services ‖ to be for rent.

UILER.
rental or lease payment ‖ act of renting, ing.

UILER DEL TERRENO.
und rent.

A.
ocument of induction into active military ice ‖ certificate of good health (given to a viously-ill person) ‖ statement declaring : a person is a taxpayer ‖ adj, high.

A CORTE DE JUSTICIA.
gh court of justice.

A MAR.
gh seas.

A TRAICIÓN.
gh treason.

AS PARTES CONTRATANTES.
gh contracting parties.

ERABLE.
, alterable, ambulatory.

ERACIÓN.
lteration, adulteration, change, modifica-n ‖ dispute, disagreement ‖ disturbance, nmotion.

ERACIÓN DE LA PAZ.
ach of the peace.

ERACIÓN DEL ORDEN.
: ALTERACIÓN DE LA PAZ.

ERADOR.
provocateur (of riots, disturbances).

ERAR.
o alter, change, modify, adulterate ‖ to se a breach of the peace.

ERCACIÓN.
ltercation, dispute, fight.

ERCADO.
: ALTERCACIÓN.

ERCAR.
o fight, quarrel.

ERNACIÓN.
riendly agreement ‖ competition, rivalry.

ERNANCIA.
ommunication, dealing ‖ alternation.

ERNAR.
o alternate (jobs, work).

ERNATIVA.
lternative, option.

ERNATIVO.
, alternative ‖ alternating.

ALUCINACIÓN.
f, hallucination ‖ trickery.

ALUMBRAMIENTO.
m, discovery of subterranean waters ‖ birth,

ALUVIÓN.
m, alluvion. Refers to means of acquiring property deposited by river.

ALZA.
f, rise, increase (in stock market).

ALZADA.
f, appeal.

ALZADO.
n. person who declares bankruptcy with hidden assets ‖ robbery, theft ‖ adj, fraudulently bankrupt.

ALZAMIENTO.
m, higher bid (at an auction) ‖ rebellion ‖ absconding ‖ concealment of assets by a bankrupt.

ALZAMIENTO DE BIENES.
fraudulent bankruptcy ‖ hiding assets of a bankrupt.

ALZAR.
v, to bring an administrative appeal ‖ to appeal ‖ to raise, to increase.

ALZAR EL PRECIO.
to increase or raise the price, up the price.

ALZARSE.
v, to bring a fraudulent bankruptcy proceeding ‖ to go fraudulently bankrupt ‖ to rebel ‖ to appeal ‖ to abscond.

ALLANAMIENTO.
m, search (of premises under court order) ‖ abide by (a judicial decision) ‖ breaking and entering ‖ trespass, unlawful entry ‖ answer of "nolo contedere" to the remedies of a complaint (e.g. agreeing to comply with the remedy requested).

ALLANAMIENTO A LA DEMANDA.
acquiescence to opposing litigant's claim.

ALLANAMIENTO A LA SENTENCIA.
agreement to abide by a judicial decision.

ALLANAMIENTO DE DOMICILIO.
trespass, unlawful entry (of a building) ‖ refusal to leave a building.

ALLANAMIENTO DE MORADA.
See ALLANAMIENTO DE DOMICILIO.

ALLANAR.
v, to authorize a governmental entry (of premises) ‖ to trespass, break and enter ‖ to enter and search ‖ to raid ‖ to settle, adjust.

ALLANARSE.
v, to capitulate, yield, acquiesce to the opponent's claim ‖ to abide by a judicial decision.

ALLEGADO.
m, relative, close friend ‖ person who lives on another's property at the expense of another ‖ adj, near, close.

AMA.
f, housewife ‖ female head of household ‖ proprietress ‖ type of household help (e.g. governess, etc.) ‖ woman with household help.

AMA DE CASA.
f, housewife ‖ female head of household.

AMALGAMA.
f, mixture, amalgam, merger.

AMANCEBADO.
m, person who lives with another out of wedlock.

AMANCEBAMIENTO.
m, concubinage.

AMANTE.
m, f, lover ‖ adulterer ‖ adj, loving.

AMANUENSE.
m, clerk, secretary ‖ notary's clerk, amanuensis.

AMARTILLAR.
v, to secure an agreement or business deal.

AMAYORAZGAR.
v, to form an estate to be inherited by first born.

AMBIGÜEDAD.
f, ambiguity.

AMBIGÜEDAD LATENTE.
latent ambiguity.

AMBIGÜEDAD PATENTE.
patent or obvious ambiguity.

AMBIGUO.
adj, ambiguous.

ÁMBITO ESPACIAL DE LA LEY.
m, territorial prescriptive jurisdiction ‖ spatial applicability of the law.

ÁMBITO PERSONAL DE LA LEY.
m, prescriptive jurisdiction over the parties.

ÁMBITO TEMPORAL DE LA LEY.
m, period of time during which a law is in effect. Usually from publication to repeal except where retroactive.

AMBOS EFECTOS.
m, both purposes. Used in appeals to refer to the dual effect of demanding the review and suspension of the lower court decision.

AMBULATORIO.
adj, ambulatory, movable ‖ changeable, ceptible to change.

AMELGAR.
v, to mark a farm's boundaries.

AMENAZA.
f, threat.

AMENAZADOR.
m, threatener ‖ adj, threatening.

AMENAZAR.
v, to threaten.

AMIGABLE COMPONEDOR.
m, friendly mediator chosen by both parti(a dispute.

AMILLARAMIENTO.
m, tax assessment.

AMILLARAR.
v, to determine goods to be taxable.

AMISTOSO.
adj, amicable, friendly.

AMNESIA.
f, amnesia.

AMNISTÍA.
f, amnesty.

AMNISTÍA INCONDICIONAL.
absolute or unconditional amnesty.

AMNISTÍA IMPROPIA.
general amnesty ‖ amnesty which is suppc to benefit those accused of political crimes which is also applied to common criminals

AMNISTÍA PROPIA.
political amnesty, that which is applicable applied to those accused of political cri only.

AMNISTIAR.
v, to grant amnesty ‖ to pardon.

AMO.
m, male head of household ‖ head of fami proprietor ‖ possessor ‖ influential man ‖ n with household help.

AMO DE CASA.
m, householder ‖ male head of household.

AMOJONAMIENTO.
m, demarcation, act of surveying or mark boundaries.

AMOJONAR.
v, to mark boundaries ‖ to survey and deli with markers.

AMONEDACIÓN.
f, minting, coining.

)NEDAR.
o mint, coin.

)NESTACIÓN.
dmonition, order ‖ warning ‖ publication of arriage) banns.

ONESTACIONES MATRIMONIALES.
irriage banns.

ONESTAR.
o warn ‖ to admonish ‖ to advise ‖ to re-
ire, order ‖ to publish (marriage) banns.

ORTIZABLE.
i, amortizable, payable, redeemable ‖ de-
eciable.

ORTIZACIÓN.
depreciation, reduction in value of property
imortization, extinguishment or redemption
a charge. Used to refer to long term debts.

ORTIZACIÓN CIVIL.
moval of goods from common use by person
corporations.

ORTIZACIÓN DE EMPRÉSTITOS.
ncellation or payment of loans.

ORTIZACIÓN DE LA DEUDA
JBLICA.
tirement of the public debt or government
curities by the State.

ORTIZACIÓN DE LAS ACCIONES.
purchase of corporate shares by corpora-
on.

ORTIZAR.
to amortize ‖ to redeem ‖ to refund ‖ to
polish.

OTINADO.
, rioter, rebel ‖ adj, rebellious ‖ mutinous ‖
otous.

OTINADOR.
, rioter.

OTINAR.
to incite to riot ‖ to provoke public disorder
to mutiny.

OTINARSE.
to riot ‖ to mutiny.

OVIBLE.
dj, movable ‖ transferrable.

OVILIDAD.
transferability ‖ removability.

IPARA.
attachment of personal property.

IPARAR.
, to protect, defend ‖ to support ‖ to fulfill
gal requirements to mine state-owned pro-

perty ‖ to attach personal property ‖ to pardon
‖ to hold harmless ‖ to vouch for, guarantee.

AMPARARSE.
v, to get protection, relief ‖ to protect oneself.

AMPARO.
m, defense ‖ defender ‖ summary proceeding
which serves to guarantee constitutional rights
‖ protection, shelter ‖ aid, support, backing ‖
relief ‖ exemption ‖ pardon ‖ mining right.

AMPARO SOCIAL.
social security.

AMPLIACIÓN.
f, increase, extension ‖ extension of due date.

AMPLIACIÓN DE CRÉDITO.
authorization to incur an expenditure in excess
of the state budget ‖ increase of amount of
loan.

AMPLIACIÓN
DE LA DEMANDA.
amended complaint ‖ second complaint which
complements the first and adds new claims,
additional damages, or demands for property
based on the same cause of action.

AMPLIACIÓN DE LA HIPOTECA.
extension of mortgage to cover future advances or additional security to compensate loss in
value of original mortgage ‖ filing or registration of such an extension.

AMPLIACIÓN DEL PLAZO.
extension of stipulated term.

AMPLIFICACIÓN.
f, development (of an idea or proposition) ‖
amplification.

AMPLIFICAR.
v, to enlarge, amplify, extend ‖ to develop.

AMPLIAR.
See AMPLIFICAR.

ANAL.
m, digest ‖ compilation ‖ adj, anal.

ANALFABETO.
m, illiterate, illiterate person ‖ ignorant person
‖ adj, illiterate.

ANÁLOGAMENTE.
adv, by analogy, analogously, similarly.

ANALOGÍA.
f, analogy.

ANALOGÍA JURÍDICA.
f, resolution of a case based on rules applicable
to analogous legal relationships or concepts.

ANALOGÍA LEGAL.
f, resolution of a case based on rules contained

in analogous code law or statutes. Type of ANALOGÍA JURÍDICA.

ANALÓGICO.
See ANÁLOGO.

ANÁLOGO.
adj, analogous ‖ similar.

ANARQUÍA.
f, anarchy.

ANATA.
f, yearly income or yield or pay.

ANATEMA.
f, anathema.

ANATOCISMO.
m, anatocism ‖ compound interest ‖ agreement to pay compound interest. Usually considered to be usurious.

ANCESTRAL.
adj, ancestral.

ANCIANIDAD.
f, old age.

ANCLAJE.
m, anchorage ‖ anchorage fee.

ANDADOR.
m, ministerial messenger, courier.

ANDAR CON EL TIEMPO.
v, to adjust oneself to the circumstances or situation.

ANDAR MANGA POR HOMBRO.
v, to lack order in government affairs.

ANDRONA.
f, small space (in which construction is prohibited).

ANEJO.
m, town or village annexed to another ‖ adj, annexed, added to.

ANEXAR.
v, to annex, add, join, incorporate.

ANEXIDADES.
adj, adjuncts, accessories, appurtenances ‖ rights or things, which are united or added to principal thing.

ANEXIÓN.
f, annexation. Used to refer to property incorporated by government.

ANGARIA.
f, angary, destruction or use of property of a neutral nation by a hostile nation when property is found in the latter's territory ‖ forced service (of invalid or neutral party to carry arms or baggage).

ANGUSTIAS MENTALES.
f, mental anguish, pain and suffering.

ÁNIMO.
m, animo, animus, intention, intent.

ÁNIMO CRIMINAL.
criminal intent.

ÁNIMO DE DONAR.
intent to give or donate.

ÁNIMO DE LUCRO.
desire or intention to make money or profit (from a certain act or business).

ÁNIMO DE REVOCAR.
intention to revoke.

ANIMOSIDAD.
f, animosity, hate ‖ aversion.

"ANIMUS".
m, animus, intention, disposition, mind, desire.

"ANIMUS DOMINI".
intent to own.

"ANIMUS SOLVENDI".
intent to fulfill an obligation or pay a debt.

"ANIMUS POSSIDENDI".
animus possidendi, intent to possess.

"ANNATA".
See ANATA.

ANOMALÍAS FÍSICAS.
f, physical anomalies.

ANÓMALO.
adj, anomalous.

ANÓNIMO.
m, anonymous letter or article ‖ adj, anonymous ‖ not related to an individual person. Used in corporate law to describe types of companies (See SOCIEDAD ANÓNIMA).

ANOTACIÓN.
f, annotation, note, comment ‖ inscription, registration, filing ‖ entry.

ANOTACIÓN CONTABLE.
accounting entry.

ANOTACIÓN DE CRÉDITOS.
filing of security interest (to perfect interest).

ANOTACIÓN DE LA DEMANDA.
filing of complaint which affects real property ‖ type of provisional lis pendens.

ANOTACIÓN DE LA SENTENCIA.
filing of judgment lien pertaining to real property with the Real Property Registry.

ANOTACIÓN DE EMBARGO.
filing of writ of attachment in relevant registry.

OTACIÓN DE LEGADO.
ing in relevant registry of contested interest decedent's property (by legatees).

OTACIÓN DE LITIS.
ing of a lis pendens.

OTACIÓN DE SECUESTRO.
ing of writ of attachment and levy.

OTACIÓN EN REGISTRO ÚBLICO.
ing with public registry (of act or right).

OTACIÓN PREVENTIVA.
rovisional filing to protect legal interests in roperty ‖ provisional property registration. May occur during litigation.

IOTAR.
, to register, file, inscribe (in a public registry).

ITAGONISMO.
1, antagonism.

ITE.
rep, before ‖ in front of, in the presence of ‖ n view of, in light of.

ITE LA SALA.
1 open court.

ITE LÍTEM.
nte litem, before litigation, before suit filed.

ITE MÍ.
efore me (used by witnesses, notaries, etc. to ndicate their act of witnessing).

ITECEDENTE.
dj, antecedent, preceding, prior.

ITECEDENTES.
n, background, prior history, record.

ITECEDENTES CRIMINALES.
iee ANTECEDENTES PENALES.

ITECEDENTES DE POLICÍA.
police record.

ITECEDENTES PENALES.
criminal record or history.

ITECESOR.
n, predecessor, progenitor ‖ predecessor, prior officeholder ‖ adj, prior, previous.

ITECONTRATO.
n, preliminary agreement.

ITEDATA.
f, antedating, predating, affixation of an earlier date.

ITEDATAR.
v, to antedate, predate.

ITEDICHO.
adj, aforesaid, above-mentioned, aforenamed, aforementioned.

ANTEDIQUE.
m, pre-port area.

ANTEFECHAR.
v, to antedate, predate.

ANTEFIRMA.
f, title placed before signature at end of legal instrument.

ANTEJUICIO.
m, preliminary hearing to assure existence of probable cause or to bring criminal charges against a judge or judicial officer.

ANTEMENCIONADO.
adj, aforesaid, aforementioned.

ANTENACIDO.
m, premature child, preemie ‖ adj, prematurely born.

ANTENUPCIAL.
adj, pre-nuptial, antenuptial.

ANTEPAGAR.
v, to pre-pay, pay in advance.

ANTEPASADO.
m, ancestor ‖ adj, prior in time, previous thereto.

ANTEPONER.
v, to prefer, give preference to.

ANTEPROCESAL.
adj, pre-trial, occurring before trial.

ANTEPROYECTO.
m, draft, preliminary plan. Used to refer to draft legislation or preliminary work.

ANTEPROYECTO DE CONTRATO.
first draft of contract.

ANTERIORIDAD.
f, precedence, priority (in time) ‖ In patent law, prior art, knowledge and techniques which exist or have been invented prior to a given point in time (usually at the time of a new invention).

ANTERIORMENTE.
adv, previously, formerly, heretofore.

ANTES CITADO.
adj, before-cited, aforementioned.

ANTES ESCRITO.
adj, above-written, before-written.

ANTES MENCIONADO.
adj, aforenamed, aforementioned.

ANTICIPACIÓN.
f, anticipation ‖ prepayment ‖ charging before due ‖ preference ‖ prior position ‖ act of doing something prior to its due performance.

ANTICIPADO.
adj, advance. Used in reference to payments.
ANTICIPAR.
v, to advance, hasten ‖ to anticipate ‖ to pay in advance.
ANTICIPO.
m, advance payment ‖ act of paying in advance ‖ anticipation.
ANTICIPO DE FONDOS.
advance payment of money, advance.
ANTICIPO DE HERENCIA.
intervivos gift (as part of eventual inheritance).
ANTICONSTITUCIONAL.
adj, unconstitutional.
ANTICRESIS.
f, antichresis, transfer by debtor to creditor of right to the fruits of real property, the proceeds of which are applied first against the interest and then against the principal of debt ‖ contract by which aforementioned transfer occurs. Right may only be granted by owner of real estate or party who has rights to the fruits of such property.
ANTICRESISTA.
m, antichresis creditor. See ANTICRESIS.
ANTICRÉTICO.
adj, antichretic. See ANTICRESIS.
ANTIGÜEDAD.
f, years of service, period of employment, seniority ‖ period of existence (in corporations and partnerships) ‖ antiquity.
ANTIGUO.
adj, ancient.
ANTIJURIDICIDAD.
f, illegality, unlawfulness.
ANTIJURÍDICO.
adj, illegal, unlawful, contrary to law.
ANTILEGAL.
adj, unlawful, illegal, against the law.
ANTILOGÍA.
adj, illogical, contradiction (between two legal texts).
ANTINOMIA.
f, antinomy ‖ apparent or real contradiction or inconsistency between two propositions or laws.
ANTIPARLAMENTARIO.
m, person or idea opposed to parliamentary form of government ‖ adj, unparliamentary, opposed to parliamentary custom.

ANTÍPOCA.
f, writing which acknowledges a rental o leasehold.
ANTIPOCAR.
v, to acknowledge in writing a leasehold an the obligation to pay rent thereon ‖ to obligat oneself again to what had been suspended.
ANTIPROFESIONAL.
adj, unprofessional.
ANTIRREGLAMENTARIO.
adj, done or said against a rule or regulation against orders.
ANTISEMITISMO.
m, anti-semitism.
ANTISOCIAL.
adj, anti-social ‖ against labor laws.
ANTONOMASIA.
f, antonomasia. Use of a proper name insteac of an appellative ‖ to meet certain condition o have certain quality in the most perfect way.
ANTOR.
m, person from whom stolen goods are pur chased in good faith.
ANTORÍA.
f, right of recovery against seller of stole goods.
ANTROPOLOGÍA.
f, anthropology.
ANTROPOLOGÍA CRIMINAL.
criminal anthropology.
ANUALIDAD.
f, annual charge, yearly payment ‖ annuity. May be FIJA (fixed) or VARIABLE (floating); ANTICIPADA (anticipated) or VENCIDA (matured).
ANUALIDAD ACUMULADA.
accumulated annuity.
ANUALIDAD CIERTA.
annuity certain.
ANUALIDAD CONDICIONAL.
contingent or conditional annuity.
ANUALIDAD DE SUPERVIVENCIA.
survivorship annuity.
ANUALIDAD INCONDICIONAL.
annuity certain, unconditional annuity.
ANUALIDAD ORDINARIA.
ordinary annuity.
ANUENCIA.
f, consent.
ANUENTE.
adj, consenting, agreeing.

ULABILIDAD.
voidability.
ULABLE.
dj, voidable, capable of annulment ‖ cancell-ble.
ULACIÓN.
annulment, nullification, invalidation, abro-ation (of a contract, treaty, privilege or will) ‖ xtinguishment, vacation ‖ defeasance ‖ voidance.
ULACIÓN DE LA INSTANCIA.
ismissal of a case.
ULADO.
dj, voided, annulled, nullified, cancelled, brogated, vacated, quashed, set aside, defea-ed, invalidated ‖ abated ‖ disaffirmed.
ULAR.
, to void, annul, cancel, abrogate ‖ to vacate, everse, quash, set aside ‖ to defeat, invalidate to abate ‖ to disaffirm.
ULATIVO.
dj, nullifying, annulling, able to void or annul.
UNCIO.
n, notice, announcement ‖ edict, proclama-ion.
UNCIO JUDICAL.
ublic notice (of a judicial decision, printed ublicly).
VERSO.
n, face of a document.
ADIDO.
n, allonge ‖ extension, addition, supplement ‖ dj, added.
ADIR.
, to add, incorporate ‖ to increase, augment ‖ o complement.
O.
n, year.
O CALENDARIO.
alendar year.
O CIVIL.
alendar year (of 365 or 366 days).
O COMÚN.
ordinary year (of 365 days).
O CONTINUO.
alendar year.
O CONTRIBUTIVO.
tax year, year as defined for tax purposes.
O DE LUTO.
first year of widowhood (during which remar-riage is prohibited).

AÑO DE VIUDEDAD.
See AÑO DE LUTO.
AÑO ECONÓMICO.
fiscal year.
AÑO FINANCIERO.
fiscal year, financial year.
AÑO FISCAL.
fiscal year.
AÑO GRAVABLE.
taxable year, tax year.
AÑO IMPOSITIVO.
tax year.
AÑO JUDICIAL.
judicial year, period of year during which courts are in session. In many countries, courts are not in session during all twelve months.
AÑO JURÍDICO.
legal year, year as defined for legal purposes.
AÑO MUERTO.
grace period of a year prior to which payment begins.
AÑO SOCIAL.
See AÑO ECONÓMICO.
APADRINAR.
v, to be godfather or godparent.
APALABRAR.
v, to talk someone into agreeing to something ‖ to agree orally, make an oral contract ‖ to agree beforehand.
APARCERÍA.
f, sharecropping ‖ farm partnership (by which one party invests the property and the other the labor, the fruits of which are divided among the partners).
APAREJADA EJECUCIÓN.
See EJECUCIÓN APAREJADA.
APARENTE.
adj, apparent ‖ open and notorious.
APARIENCIA.
f, appearance ‖ likelihood, probability ‖ con-jecture ‖ similarity ‖ simulation.
APARIENCIA DE TÍTULO.
apparent title, color of title.
APARTADO.
m, section, article (of statute or decree) ‖ pa-ragraph ‖ post-office box.
APARTADO DE CORREOS.
m, post office box ‖ special delivery mail.
APARTAMENTO.
m, separation, division ‖ isolation ‖ retirement ‖ withdrawal of action or appeal.

APARTARSE.
v, to withdraw, desist, terminate, drop.
APÁTRIDA.
f, stateless person ‖ adj, stateless.
APEAR.
v, to survey, mark boundaries.
APELABLE.
adj, appealable, subject to appeal (e.g. decisions).
APELACIÓN.
f, appeal ‖ legal recourse challenging prior decision ‖ written request to appeal lower court decision. Approval of APELACIÓN is a prerequisite to EXPRESIÓN DE AGRAVIOS.
APELACIÓN ACCESORIA.
See APELACIÓN ADHESIVA.
APELACIÓN ADHESIVA.
type of appeal filed by losing party with the consent of winning party.
APELACIÓN CON AMBOS EFECTOS.
See EFECTOS DE LA APELACIÓN.
APELACIÓN CON EFECTO DEVOLUTIVO.
appeal which does not enjoin enforcement of judgment.
APELACIÓN CON EFECTO SUSPENSIVO.
appeal which enjoins enforcement of judgment.
APELACIÓN DEL INTERDICTO.
appeal of an injunction.
APELACIÓN DESIERTA.
appeal withdrawn or dropped.
APELACIÓN INCIDENTAL.
See APELACIÓN ADHESIVA.
APELACIÓN LIMITADA.
See APELACIÓN PARCIAL.
APELACIÓN PARCIAL.
limited appeal.
APELADO.
m, appellee, respondent ‖ decision subject to appeal ‖ adj, appealed ‖ pertaining to an appellee.
APELADOR.
See APELANTE.
APELANTE.
m, appellant.
APELAR.
v, to appeal (a lower sentence).
APELAR A LOS PIES.
to flee, split.
APELLIDO.
m, surname, family name, last name.

APEO.
m, survey and demarcation of propert documentation of survey and demarcation
APERCIBIDO.
adj, warned, cautioned.
APERCIBIMIENTO.
m, warning, caution.
APERCIBIR.
v, to warn, caution ‖ to judicially require cc pliance with a court order ‖ to furnish, p vide.
APEROS.
m, work tools, equipment.
APERSONADO.
m, litigant, party to an action.
APERSONAMIENTO.
m, appearance.
APERSONARSE.
v, to appear ‖ to become party to an action
APERTURA.
f, opening, act of opening ‖ beginning.
APERTURA DE ASAMBLEA.
calling (the meeting) to order, opening meeting or session.
APERTURA DE AUDIENCIA.
pre-trial conference ‖ opening of trial or cou
APERTURA DE CRÉDITO.
opening of a line of credit ‖ granting of a loa
APERTURA DE LA CORRESPONDENCL
opening mail or correspondence.
APERTURA DE LA SUCESIÓN.
initiation of probate proceeding.
APERTURA DE LAS LICITACIONES.
See APERTURA DE LAS PROPUESTAS.
APERTURA DE LAS PROPUESTAS.
opening of bids.
APERTURA DE LIBROS.
opening of the books to take inventory or f accounting ‖ (initial) opening of the boo used in business.
APERTURA DEL JUICIO ORAL.
opening of oral trial.
APERTURA DEL TESTAMENTO.
reading or opening of a will.
APIADARSE.
v, to pardon, grant amnesty ‖ to pity, take p on, have pity for (something or someone).
APLAZABLE.
adj, postponable, able to be delayed.
APLAZADA.
f, extension of time.

LAZADO.
adj, deferred ‖ subject to a term ‖ flunked, failed (an examination).

LAZAMIENTO.
m, deferment, postponement ‖ fixing of a new term ‖ suspension ‖ summoning ‖ adjournment ‖ continuance.

LAZAR.
v, to defer, postpone ‖ to suspend ‖ to summon.

LICACIÓN.
application (of a law) ‖ enforcement (of a law) ‖ adjudication of property rights ‖ imposition of penalties or sanctions.

LICAR.
v, to apply, employ, use ‖ to impose a punishment or penalty ‖ to allocate, adjudicate, or award property rights ‖ to enforce a law.

LICAR UN IMPUESTO.
to impose a tax.

OCA.
f, apocha, written acknowledgement of payment, receipt.

ÓCRIFO.
adj, supposed, assumed ‖ false ‖ imitated.

ODERADO.
n, party who is empowered, attorney, agent, proxy, representative ‖ adj, empowered.

ODERADO GENERAL.
general agent ‖ managing partner.

ODERADO JUDICIAL.
attorney, legal representative.

PODERADO ESPECIAL.
special agent.

PODERADO SINGULAR.
See APODERADO ESPECIAL.

PODERAMIENTO.
n, empowerment, authorization ‖ power, authority ‖ power of attorney ‖ taking of possession, appropriation.

PODERAR.
v, to empower ‖ to give possession.

PODERARSE.
v, to take possession ‖ to become owner.

PODO.
m, nickname.

PÓGRAFO.
m, apograph, transcript, copy (of original writing).

PÓLIDO.
See APÁTRIDA.

APOLOGÍA DEL DELITO.
f, advocating of criminal behavior.

APORTACIÓN.
f, contribution ‖ dowry ‖ presentation of documents or proof together with writing or allegation ‖ withholding (from pay) for retirement.

APORTAR.
v, to contribute (to a corporation) ‖ to bring (a dowry) ‖ to present documents ‖ to arrive into port ‖ to have money withheld (from pay for retirement).

APORTAR FONDOS.
to finance, furnish funds.

APORTE.
m, contribution, payment.

APORTE JUBILATORIO.
payment made into a pension fund.

APOSTAR.
v, to bet.

APOSTILLA.
f, footnote, annotation, short note of explanation, apostille.

APOYAR LA MOCIÓN.
v, to second the motion.

APRECIABLE.
adj, appreciable, considerable ‖ estimable, able to be appraised.

APRECIACIÓN.
f, appreciation, increase (in value) ‖ estimation, calculation (of value).

APRECIACIÓN DE LAS PRUEBAS.
judicial evaluation or weighing of evidence ‖ hearing to determine the authenticity of evidence (in criminal and civil law).

APRECIADOR.
m, appraiser ‖ adj, grateful, appreciative.

APRECIAR.
v, to appraise, value ‖ to appreciate, increase in value.

APREHENDER.
v, to apprehend, catch, capture, seize ‖ to perceive, conceive (without forming a judgment) ‖ to attach.

APREHENSIÓN.
f, apprehension, capture, seizure ‖ arrest or detention of accused.

APREHENSOR.
m, apprehender, person who apprehends something or someone.

APREMIAR.
v, to compel compliance with something (by a

judicial authority) ‖ to penalize, impose a surtax (for late payment) ‖ to order or urge a party to act in a suit ‖ to dun, collect a bill.

APREMIAR EL PAGO.
to compel payment.

APREMIO.
m, court order, judicial decision ‖ surtax, late charge ‖ grilling, pressure used to obtain a confession ‖ judicial order to require parties to file their writs without delay ‖ legal proceeding for purposes of debt collection (usually tax collection).

APREMIO ILEGAL.
illegal pressure (used by official to seek a confession from a prisoners). Constitutes a crime.

APREMIO JUDICIAL.
collection proceeding.

APREMIO PERSONAL.
collection proceeding against personal property.

APREMIO REAL.
sale of attached real property.

APRENDIZ.
m, f, trainee, apprentice.

APRENDIZAJE.
m, training, learning ‖ apprenticeship ‖ training period ‖ education period.

APRESAMIENTO.
m, capturing (e.g. of a foreign shipment).

APRESAMIENTO DE BUQUE.
seizure of ship and its cargo.

APRESAR.
v, to seize contraband ‖ to capture a ship ‖ to take prisoner, imprison.

APRIETO.
m, conflict, difficulty, trouble.

APRIORISMO.
m, a priori reasoning.

APRISIONAR.
v, to imprison.

APROBACIÓN.
f, approval ‖ acceptance, conformity, assent ‖ ratification.

APROBACIÓN DE CRÉDITO.
credit approval.

APROBACIÓN DE CUENTA.
approval of an accounting.

APROBACIÓN DE ESTATUTOS.
formal approval of the bylaws (of a corporation).

APROBAR.
v, to approve ‖ to accept, assent ‖ to rat confirm.

APRONTAR.
v, to comply with an obligation punctually ‖ deliver goods or money promptly ‖ to ma ready, prepare.

APROPIABLE.
adj, approvable, acceptable.

APROPIACIÓN.
f, appropriation ‖ acquisition.

APROPIACIÓN ILÍCITA.
conversion, illegal taking.

APROPIACIÓN IMPLÍCITA.
constructive conversion.

APROPIACIÓN INDEBIDA.
misappropriation, conversion.

APROPIACIÓN VIRTUAL.
See APROPIACIÓN IMPLÍCITA.

APROPIADO.
m, appropriated property ‖ adj, appropria ‖ appropriate, fitting, proper, suitable.

APROPIADOR.
m, appropriator ‖ thief.

APROPIAR.
v, to appropriate.

APROPIARSE.
v, to convert ‖ to appropriate, take possessi of (something).

APROVECHAMIENTO.
m, utilization, development ‖ use ‖ enjoyme (of benefits) ‖ exploitation, abuse.

APROVECHAMIENTO DE AGUAS.
right to use public waters ‖ economic use water.

APROVECHAMIENTOS COMUNES.
right to use fields, water, woods and simil things in common with others of a village province.

APROVECHAR UN DERECHO.
to exercise a right.

APROVECHARSE.
v, to take advantage of, abuse.

APTITUD.
f, aptitude.

APTITUD LEGAL.
legal competency.

APTO.
m, person who exercises a legal right ‖ adj, a suitable ‖ capable.

PUD.
in the book of, in the work of.

PUD ACTA.
apud acta, in the same record, in the same file ‖ among the recorded proceedings.

PUESTA.
f, bet, wager.

PUNTAMIENTO.
m, notation, entry ‖ case summary, extract.

PUÑALADO.
adj, stabbed, killed by stabbing.

PUÑALAR.
v, to stab.

PURO.
m, haste ‖ collection action.

QUEL A QUIEN PUEDA INTERESAR.
whom it may concern.

QUÍ DENTRO.
herein.

QUIESCENCIA.
f, acquiescence, consent (whether express or implied, conditional or unconditional).

RANCEL.
m, tariff, official charge ‖ law, norm of official charges ‖ fee.

ARANCEL ADUANERO.
schedule of customs duties.

ARANCEL DE ADUANA.
See ARANCEL ADUANERO.

ARANCEL CONSULAR.
list of consular fees.

ARANCEL DE CORREDORES.
list of brokers' commissions.

ARANCEL DE EXPORTACIÓN.
export duties.

ARANCEL DE IMPORTACIÓN.
import duties.

ARANCEL DE HONORARIOS.
fee schedule.

ARANCEL DE PROCURADORES.
schedule of attorney's fees.

ARANCEL DE RENTA.
See ARANCEL FISCAL.

ARANCEL FISCAL.
revenue tariff.

ARANCEL JUDICIAL.
schedule of court costs.

ARANCEL NOTARIAL.
schedule of notary's fees.

ARANCELARIO.
adj, tariff, related to tariffs.

ARBITRABLE.
adj, arbitrable.

ARBITRACIÓN.
f, arbitration.

ARBITRADOR.
m, arbitrator, arbiter, arbitrager.

ARBITRAJE.
m, arbitration ‖ arbitration hearing ‖ arbitrage.

ARBITRAJE COMERCIAL.
commercial arbitration (i.e. of business disputes).

ARBITRAJE COMPULSIVO.
compulsory arbitration.

ARBITRAJE CONVENCIONAL.
non-compulsory arbitration, arbitration at request of parties.

ARBITRAJE DE CAMBIO.
arbitrage.

ARBITRAJE DE DERECHO.
arbitration (decided by lawyers based on law).

ARBITRAJE EXTRAJUDICIAL.
out-of-court arbitration.

ARBITRAJE FORZOSO.
compulsory arbitration.

ARBITRAJE INDUSTRIAL.
industrial or labor arbitration.

ARBITRAJE INTERPUESTO.
See ARBITRAJE OBLIGATORIO.

ARBITRAJE JUDICIAL.
arbitration pursuant to rules of court procedure.

ARBITRAJE LABORAL.
labor or industrial arbitration.

ARBITRAJE NECESARIO.
compulsory arbitration.

ARBITRAJE OBLIGATORIO.
obligatory arbitration.

ARBITRAJE VOLUNTARIO.
See ARBITRAJE CONVENCIONAL.

ARBITRAJISTA.
m, f, arbitrator.

ARBITRAL.
adj, arbitral, pertaining to arbitration or arbitrage.

ARBITRAMENTO.
m, arbitrament, arbitration award or decision ‖ ability to issue an arbitral award.

ARBITRAMIENTO.
See ARBITRAMENTO.

ARBITRAR.
v, to arbitrate ‖ to engage in arbitrage.
ARBITRAR FONDOS.
to raise money.
ARBITRARIAMENTE.
adv, arbitrarily ‖ by arbitration.
ARBITRARIEDAD.
f, arbitrariness ‖ unjust or illegal action.
ARBITRARIO.
adj, arbitral ‖ arbitrary.
ARBITRIO.
m, arbitrament, discretion ‖ tax, fee ‖ recourse, expedient.
ARBITRIO JUDICIAL.
judicial discretion ‖ judicial decision.
ARBITRIOS.
m, municipal or provincial taxes or charges ‖ means, resources.
ARBITRISTA.
m, promoter of unsound financial plans ‖ con artist ‖ sham politician.
ÁRBITRO.
m, arbitrator, referee, arbiter, umpire, arbitration judge.
ÁRBITRO DE DERECHO.
arbitrator, referee, umpire ‖ judge or lay person who acts as an arbitrator and is bound by legal principles.
ÁRBITRO EXTRAJUDICIAL.
non-judicial arbitrator ‖ out-of-court arbitrator.
ÁRBITRO PROFESIONAL.
professional arbitrator.
ÁRBITRO PROPIETARIO.
regular arbitrator.
ÁRBITRO REEMPLAZANTE.
alternate arbitrator.
ARCHIVERO.
m, file clerk, person in charge of files ‖ archivist.
ARCHIVISTA.
m, file clerk ‖ archivist ‖ registrar.
ARCHIVISTA GENERAL.
clerk of the documents of deceased or retired notaries.
ARCHIVO.
m, file.
ARGUCIA.
f, specious argument, sophistry.

ARGÜIR.
v, to argue, dispute ‖ to prove ‖ to allege, accuse ‖ to deduce, reason.
ARGUMENTADOR.
m, arguer, person who argues ‖ adj, argumentative.
ARGUMENTACIÓN.
f, argumentation, argument.
ARGUMENTAR.
v, to argue.
ARGUMENTATIVO.
adj, argumentative.
ARGUMENTO.
m, argument.
ARISTOCRACIA.
f, aristocracy.
ARISTÓCRATA.
m, f, aristocrat.
ARMA.
m, arm, weapon ‖ strong argument ‖ branch of the army ‖ troops, army.
ARMA ALEVOSA.
weapon which when used leaves the other party defenseless.
ARMA BLANCA.
bladed weapon.
ARMA MORTÍFERA.
deadly weapon.
ARMADA.
f, armada ‖ navy.
ARMADOR.
m, ship owner.
ARMADOR-FLETADOR.
ship lessee.
ARMAMENTO.
m, armaments, weapons ‖ naval supplies.
ARMAMENTO EN CORSO.
See PATENTE DE CORSO.
ARMAR.
v, to outfit ‖ to arm ‖ to supply.
ARMISTICIO.
m, armistice.
ARQUEO.
m, tonnage ‖ surveying (of ships) ‖ accounting, audit (of cash) ‖ appraisal of assets.
ARQUEO DE BUQUES.
capacity, measure of capacity (of a ship) determination of (ship's) tonnage.
ARQUEO DE FONDOS.
public accounting, audit of public treasury (generally by surprise).

ARQUETIPO.
n, archetype ‖ original from which copies are made.

ARRAIGADO.
n, person released on bond ‖ adj, released on bond ‖ landed, owning real state ‖ acculurated, settled (in a place).

ARRAIGAR.
, to put up or place bond or bail (for purpose of guaranteeing payment of costs in case suit filed by a foreigner is lost) ‖ to acquire real estate.

ARRAIGO.
n, act of providing bond (to guarantee payment of costs if suit filed by a foreigner is lost) acquisition of real estate ‖ wealth in real property.

ARRAIGO EN JUICIO.
placement of bond or guaranty (to guarantee payment of costs if suit filed by a foreigner is lost) ‖ obligation to place said bond or guaranty.

ARRAS.
, security, pledge ‖ down payment, earnest money ‖ dowry, money given as security of intent to wed ‖ gift of 13 coins given by bridegroom to bride upon marriage.

ARRASTRAR EL PLEITO.
, to interfere in a case pending in lower court (by superior court).

ARRASTRAR LOS AUTOS.
, to try an action pending in one court, before another court

ARREBATO.
n, fury, fit, heat of passion ‖ surprise.

ARREGLADO.
adj, neat, orderly ‖ fixed, taken care of ‖ agreed upon, arranged.

ARREGLADOR DE AVERÍA.
average surveyor or adjuster.

ARREGLAR.
v, to arrange, fix up, take care of ‖ to repair damage or destruction.

ARREGLAR UNA CAUSA.
to settle a case.

ARREGLAR UNA CUENTA.
to settle an account.

ARREGLAR UNA RECLAMACIÓN.
to adjust a claim.

ARREGLARSE.
v, to compromise ‖ to settle, come to an agreement.

ARREGLO.
m, arrangement, pact, accord, understanding ‖ reconciliation, resolution of conflict, settlement ‖ rule, order.

ARREGLO DE AVERÍA.
average adjustment.

ARREGLO EXTRAJUDICIAL.
out-of-court settlement.

ARRENDABLE.
adj, rentable, leasable.

ARRENDACIÓN.
See ARRENDAMIENTO.

ARRENDADO.
m, rented premises, leasehold ‖ adj, rented, leased (re. real property).

ARRENDADOR.
m, lessor, landlord ‖ (less commonly) tenant, lessee, renter, hirer ‖ purchaser of stolen goods.

ARRENDADOR A LA PARTE.
sharecropper.

ARRENDAMIENTO.
m, lease, rental ‖ act of leasing, renting ‖ lease contract, rental contract ‖ services contract ‖ price of lease or rental. May be used in reference to things, real property, or services.

ARRENDAMIENTO A TIEMPO.
time charter.

ARRENDAMIENTO DE OBRA.
See LOCACIÓN DE OBRA.

ARRENDAMIENTO DE SERVICIOS.
service contract ‖ employment, hire.

ARRENDAR.
v, to lease, rent, let ‖ to hire.

ARRENDAR A DIENTE.
to rent publicly-owned land for purpose of grazing cattle.

ARRENDATARIO.
m, lessee, tenant, leaseholder ‖ adj, renting, leasing.

ARRENDATICIO.
m, base rent ‖ adj, lease, leasing, pertaining to renting or rent (payment).

ARREPENTIMIENTO ACTIVO.
m, spontaneous repentance or apology or confession.

ARREPENTIMIENTO ESPONTÁNEO.
See ARREPENTIMIENTO ACTIVO.

ARREPENTIRSE.
v, to repent, regret ‖ to reconsider, withdraw ‖ to revoke (an agreement).

ARRESTADO.
m, arrested person, prisoner ‖ adj, arrested, imprisoned ‖ bold, daring.

ARRESTAR.
v, to arrest ‖ to imprison ‖ to impose a military punishment.

ARRESTO.
m, arrest ‖ imprisonment.

ARRESTO ILEGAL.
false arrest or imprisonment.

¡ARRIBA LAS MANOS!
Raise your hands! (words used by robbers).

ARRIENDO.
m, rental, lease, hire ‖ also see ARRENDAMIEN-TO.

ARROGAR.
v, to arrogate.

ARROGARSE.
v, to usurp.

ARROJAR.
v, to expel, throw out (e.g. of an association) ‖ to throw out or away ‖ to hurl.

ARRUMAJE.
m, stowage of a ship.

ARSENAL.
m, arsenal.

ARTE.
m, f, art ‖ craft ‖ skill, ability ‖ astuteness ‖ profession, occupation, trade.

ARTE ANTERIOR.
prior art.

ARTESANO.
m, artisan, craftsman.

ARTICULADO.
m, series of articles, clauses, or paragraphs ‖ sections of a statute.

ARTICULAR.
v, to divide into articles ‖ to form, formulate ‖ to question.

ARTÍCULO.
m, article (in all senses) ‖ interrogatory, question of an interrogatory ‖ incidental question.

ARTÍCULO DEL CONTRATO.
clause of the contract ‖ contract clause.

ARTÍCULO DE MUERTE.
articulo mortis, at the point of death.

ARTÍCULO DE PREVIO PRONUNCIAMIENTO.
dilatory exception.

ARTÍCULO DE PREVIO Y ESPECIAL PRONUNCIAMIENTO.
initial objection or demurrer which stops judicial proceeding until it is resolved.

ARTÍCULO DE PRIMERA NECESIDAD.
article which is necessary to sustain life (‖ necessary food items, clothing, etc.).

ARTÍCULO INHIBITORIO.
peremptory exception.

ARTÍCULO MORTIS.
See IN ARTÍCULO MORTIS.

ARTÍCULO PATENTADO.
patented product.

ARTÍCULO PROPIETARIO.
See ARTÍCULO PATENTADO.

ARTÍCULOS DE PREVIO PRONUNCIAMIENTO.
dilatory defenses, pleas which tend to delay suspend criminal proceedings. May be bas on improper jurisdiction, res judicata, stati of limitations, amnesty or pardon, lack proper authorization to bring charges, etc.

ARTIFICIO.
m, artifice, ruse ‖ skill.

ARTIMAÑAS LEGALES.
f, legal stratagems.

ASALARIADO.
m, wage-earner, salaried worker ‖ adj, sa ried.

ASALTADOR.
See ASALTANTE.

ASALTANTE.
m, assailant, attacker ‖ adj, assaulting, attac ing.

ASALTAR.
v, to assault, attack.

ASALTO.
m, assault, attack ‖ armed robbery.

ASAMBLEA.
f, meeting, reunion, congress ‖ assembly, pc tical body (such as senate or house of repr sentatives).

ASAMBLEA CONSTITUTIVA.
organizational meeting.

ASAMBLEA CONSTITUYENTE.
constitutional convention.

ASAMBLEA CONSULTIVA.
advisory body.

AMBLEA DE ACREEDORES.
'editors' meeting (in bankruptcy proceed-
gs).
AMBLEA DELIBERANTE.
:presentatives' meeting (at any political
vel).
AMBLEA
XTRAORDINARIA.
)ecial meeting. Most corporate by-laws de-
gnate meetings as ordinary or special and
aaintain different quorum and voting requi-
:ments accordingly.
)pposed to ASAMBLEA ORDINARIA.
AMBLEA LEGISLATIVA.
ieeting of both houses of parliament or con-
ress or legislature (for special purposes or
ecisions) ‖ legislature.
AMBLEA MUNICIPAL.
iunicipal council, board of aldermen.
AMBLEA NACIONAL.
ongress, national legislative body ‖ special
)ngressional session (to elect a president, for
)ecial agreements, etc.).
AMBLEA ORDINARIA.
egular meeting. Most corporate by-laws
esignate meetings as ordinary or special and
aaintain different quorum and voting re-
uirements accordingly.
)pposed to ASAMBLEA EXTRAORDINARIA.
AMBLEA PLENARIA.
ill meeting.
AMBLEÍSTA.
ו, member of council or political body ‖ one
rho attends or speaks at a meeting, reunion,
r congress.
CENDENCIA.
ancestry, parentage.
CENDIENTE.
ו, ancestor, forefather ‖ adj, ascending,
ising.
EGURACIÓN.
, insurance contract ‖ insurance.
EGURABLE.
idj, insurable.
EGURADO.
ו, the insured, insured or covered party ‖ adj,
isured, assured.
EGURADOR.
ו, insurer, assurer, insurance carrier or com-
)any, underwriter ‖ adj, insuring, assuring,
afeguarding.

ASEGURADORES CONTRA INCENDIOS.
fire underwriters.
ASEGURADORES CONTRA RIESGOS
MARÍTIMOS.
marine underwriters.
ASEGURADORES DE CRÉDITO.
credit underwriters.
ASEGURAMIENTO.
m, act of insuring or assuring.
ASEGURAMIENTO DE BIENES
LITIGIOSOS.
temporary lien on property during trial.
ASEGURAMIENTO DE COSA ASEGURADA.
double insurance.
ASEGURAMIENTO DE LA PRUEBA
PERICIAL.
deposition of an expert witness, taking expert
testimony before trial.
ASEGURANZA.
f, insurance.
ASEGURAR.
v, to insure, underwrite ‖ to insure, guarantee
‖ to protect, secure ‖ to affirm, aver.
ASEGURARSE.
v, to take out insurance, carry insurance ‖ to
reassure oneself.
ASEGURO.
m, insurance ‖ assurance.
ASENTAMIENTO.
m, recording, accession ‖ industrial or business establishment ‖ attachment, seizure.
ASENTAMIENTO JUDICIAL.
attachment, seizure (of goods, for failure to
appear or to answer a complaint).
ASENTAR.
v, to attach or seize goods pursuant to court
order for failure to appear or answer a complaint ‖ to make an entry.
ASENTIMIENTO.
m, consent, assent (to contract or act) ‖ acceptance.
ASENTIR.
v, to consent, assent (to a contract) ‖ to acquiesce.
ASENTISTA.
m, supplier who contracts with the government or public to furnish goods.
ASERCIÓN.
f, assertion, affirmation.
ASERTÓRICO.
adj, assertory, tending to affirm..

ASERTORIO.

See JURAMENTO ASERTORIO.

ASESINAR.

v, to assassinate, murder.

ASESINATO.

m, assassination, murder. May be by treachery, drowning, fire, poison, or explosion, with premeditation, for payment, with extreme brutality, etc. Murder of family member is PARRICIDIO.

ASESINO.

m, murderer, assassin ‖ adj, homicidal, murderous.

ASESOR.

m, legal adviser or advisor (to a judge or law tribunal) ‖ advisor, consultant, counsel, counsellor ‖ insurance adjuster ‖ adj, counselling, advising ‖ advisory.

**ASESOR
DE MENORES.**

guardian ad litem ‖ legal counsel to advise court in matters related to minors.

ASESOR JURÍDICO.

counsel, legal adviser, counselor.

ASESOR LEGAL

See ASESOR JURÍDICO.

ASESOR LETRADO.

legal counsel ‖ in-house counsel (to a publicly held corporation or government owned corporation).

ASESORADO.

m, judge or lay tribunal which is advised by a legal advisor ‖ adj, advised, informed.

ASESORAMIENTO.

m, advice, counsel, act of counselling.

ASESORAR.

v, to advise, counsel.

ASESORARSE.

v, to seek advice ‖ to get advice ‖ to take (someone's) advice ‖ to take an advisor (by law judge).

ASESORÍA.

f, position of counsellor or advisor or consultant or assessor ‖ office of such person ‖ fee paid such person ‖ advice, consultation.

ASEVERACIÓN.

f, affirmation, averment.

ASEVERACIÓN FALSA.

false affirmation.

ASEVERAR.

v, to aver, assert, affirm.

ASEVERATIVO.

adj, affirmative.

ASIENTO.

m, seat (of tribunal) ‖ peace treaty ‖ entry, annotation (in a ledger or a public registry) ‖ provisions contract (for military troop) ‖ prudence, good judgment.

ASIENTO DE PRESENTACIÓN.

registration of a mortgage in a real estate registry.

ASIENTO DEL JUZGADO.

judge's bench, the bench.

ASIENTO PRINCIPAL DE LOS NEGOCIOS.

principal place of business.

ASIGNACIÓN.

f, salary, payment ‖ allowance ‖ quota, appropriation.

ASIGNACIÓN FAMILIAR.

payment in addition to salary which is related to the number of members in the employee's family.

ASIGNACIÓN PRENATAL.

payment in addition to salary paid to a pregnant woman.

ASIGNADO.

m, wages paid in kind ‖ adj, destined, determined ‖ subordinate, additional.

ASIGNAR.

v, to assign, allot ‖ to destine ‖ to fix, establish ‖ to name, designate, appoint.

ASIGNATARIO.

m, beneficiary, legatee.

ASILADO.

m, asylee, refugee (in an embassy or similar refuge) ‖ person committed to an asylum or home (for the poor, elderly, etc.).

ASILAMIENTO.

m, granting of asylum or refuge.

ASILAR.

v, to grant asylum or refuge ‖ to place in an asylum or home.

ASILO.

m, asylum ‖ juvenile institution ‖ institution.

ASILO DIPLOMÁTICO.

diplomatic asylum (granted by embassies usually to heads of state who have been deposed).

ASILO FAMILIAR.

homestead right.

ASILO POLÍTICO.

political asylum (usually granted to persons

accused or convicted of political crimes).

ASISTENCIA.
f, aid, assistance, relief ‖ attendance ‖ payment made to jurors and witnesses for their services.

ASISTENCIA A LA VEJEZ.
social security assistance for the elderly.

ASISTENCIA CONYUGAL.
marital support ‖ non-monetary spousal assistance.

ASISTENCIA FAMILIAR.
family support.

ASISTENCIA JURÍDICA.
legal advice or aid ‖ legal services.

ASISTENCIA MARÍTIMA.
help at sea, assistance to vessels in need.

ASISTENCIA MÉDICA.
medical care or assistance.

ASISTENCIA RECÍPROCA.
mutual aid or help.

ASISTENCIA SOCIAL.
welfare ‖ social welfare, public assistance (to students, soldiers, orphans, prisoners, etc.). May be funded privately, publicly, or by a combination of both.

ASISTENCIAL.
adj, social service, pertaining to relief or social service.

ASISTENCIAS.
f, allowance ‖ welfare payment.

ASISTENTE.
m, assistant ‖ attendee, person present at a meeting.

ASISTIR.
v, to aid, assist, help ‖ to attend, be present ‖ to carry out a proceeding.

ASISTIR A UNA REUNIÓN.
to attend a meeting.

ASOCIACIÓN.
m, association ‖ collaboration ‖ not-for-profit or non-profit organization.

ASOCIACIÓN DE PRÉSTAMOS PARA EDIFICACIÓN.
building and loan association.

ASOCIACIÓN DEL RENGLÓN.
trade association.

ASOCIACIÓN DELICTIVA.
See ASOCIACIÓN ILÍCITA and DELITOS EN BANDA.

ASOCIACIÓN DENUNCIABLE.
partnership at will.

ASOCIACIÓN EN PARTICIPACIÓN.
See SOCIEDAD ACCIDENTAL.

ASOCIACIÓN GREMIAL.
labor union, trade association.

ASOCIACIÓN ILEGAL.
illegal association, illegal combination, association prohibited by law.

ASOCIACIÓN ILÍCITA.
criminal association, conspiracy. Divided into immoral conspiracy (whose purpose is to commit crimes which are mala in se) and delinquent conspiracy (that which is mala prohibita).

ASOCIACIÓN MERCANTIL.
business organization or corporation or association.

ASOCIACIÓN NO PECUNARIA.
non-profit or not-for-profit organization.

ASOCIACIÓN OBRERA.
labor or trade union.

ASOCIACIÓN PATRONAL.
employer's association.

ASOCIACIÓN PROFESIONAL.
professional organization or corporation or association ‖ trade association.

ASOCIACIÓN PROFESIONAL OBRERA.
trade union.

ASOCIACIÓN SINDICAL.
labor or trade union.

ASOCIACIÓN VOLUNTARIA.
voluntary association.

ASOCIADO.
m, associate ‖ partner, co-partner ‖ member, affiliate ‖ adj, associated, related ‖ united.

ASOCIARSE.
v, to join, associate oneself with ‖ to become a partner of ‖ to organize a corporation.

ASOCIO.
m, company, corporation, association.

ASONADA.
f, protest, demonstration. Rebellion and sedition are types of ASONADA.

ASTUCIA.
f, astuteness ‖ shrewdness, cunning. In criminal law, its existence aggravates the severity of a crime.

ASUETO.
m, day off ‖ partial day off.

ASUMIR.
v, to assume, suppose ‖ to assume (power, responsibilities) ‖ to assume (a debt).

ASUNCIÓN.
f, assumption (of power, position, responsibilities) ‖ assumption (of a debt without novation).

ASUNCIÓN DE CRÉDITO.
assumption of a loan (by a new creditor without novation).

ASUNCIÓN DE DEUDA.
assumption of a debt, or indebtedness (by a new debtor without novation). ASUNCIÓN differs from novation, in that novation extinguishes the original obligation in favor of a new obligation. ASUNCIÓN implies that the original obligation is transferred to the new debtor without releasing the prior debtor.

ASUNCIÓN DE HIPOTECA.
assumption of the mortgage (and all related obligations).

ASUNCIÓN DEL RIESGO.
assumption of risk.

ASUNTO.
m, matter, affair, business ‖ lawsuit, case, proceeding ‖ one who assumes power or a duty or position.

ASUNTO CONTENCIOSO.
matter in dispute or in litigation.

ASUNTO INCIDENTAL.
collateral or incidental issue.

ASUNTO PENDIENTE.
pending or unfinished business.

ATACABLE.
adj, contestable, refutable.

ATACAR.
v, to attack, assault ‖ to violate a right ‖ to insult, offend, impugn ‖ to contradict, challenge, rebut, contest.

ATADO DE PIES Y MANOS.
unable to act, hands and feet tied, lacking freedom.

ATAQUE.
m, attack, assault.

ATAQUE A MANO ARMADA.
assault with a weapon.

ATAQUE PARA COMETER ASESINATO.
assault with intent to murder.

ATAR LAS MANOS.
to tie one's hands.

ATASCARSE.
v, to lack elements (to continue an allegation) ‖ to get stuck.

ATENCIÓN.
f, attention ‖ abuse of authority, illegal procedure.

ATENCIONES.
f, matters, affairs, business ‖ kindnesses, courtesies, plural of ATENCIÓN.

ATENDER.
v, to take care of, attend to ‖ to approve (a request, petition or request) ‖ to carry out a function.

ATENDER EL COMPROMISO.
to meet the obligation or engagement or duty.

ATENDER LA DEUDA.
to provide debt service ‖ to meet a debt.

ATENERSE.
v, to follow, comply, abide by (with a law or order) ‖ to settle (an obligation ‖ to observe.

ATENTADO.
m, attempt, (criminal) assault ‖ attack ‖ aggression ‖ threat ‖ illegality, illegal procedure ‖ abuse of authority (by government officials) ‖ adj, threatened ‖ discreet, judicious, moderate.

ATENTADO A LA VIDA.
attempt to kill.

ATENTADO CONTRA EL PUDOR.
indecent exposure ‖ indecency. May be a crime.

ATENTADO CONTRA LA AUTORIDAD.
aggression or intimidation against a government or public authority (by disobedience, resistance, or contempt). Includes resisting arrest and contempt of court.

ATENTAR.
v, to attempt to commit (a criminal act) ‖ to perpetrate (a crime) ‖ to physically attack a person representing the government or other authority.

ATENTATORIO.
adj, illegal, unlawful ‖ related to attempt.

ATENUACIÓN.
f, mitigation, extenuation.

ATENUADO.
adj, mitigated, extenuated.

ATENUANTE.
m, extenuating or mitigating circumstance ‖ adj, mitigating, extenuating.

ATENUANTE CALIFICADO.
special mitigating circumstance (which applies if certain conditions are met). In criminal law,

these serve to reduce criminal responsibility (e.g. minority, etc.).

ATENUAR.
v, to mitigate, extenuate, reduce (the seriousness of the punishment or crime.)

ATESORAMIENTO.
m, hoarding ‖ act of taking money or property out of circulation.

ATESORAR.
v, to treasure, hoard, save.

ATESTACIÓN.
f, declaration, deposition, testimony (of a witness) ‖ statement ‖ affidavit.

ATESTACIÓN POR NOTARIO PÚBLICO.
notarization ‖ testimony by a public notary.

ATESTADO.
m, sworn statement, affidavit ‖ certificate, certification ‖ adj, witnessed, sworn to, certified.

ATESTAR.
See ATESTIGUAR.

ATESTAR FALTA DE PAGO.
to certify or note payment.

ATESTAR LA FIRMA.
to witness the signature.

ATESTIGUAR
v, to testify, be witness to ‖ to be deposed, attest ‖ to certify.

ATESTIGUACIÓN.
f, testimony, deposition ‖ affidavit (written) ‖ sworn statement.

ATINADO.
adj, relevant, pertinent, correct.

ATÍPICO.
adj, atypical.

ATORMENTADOR.
m, tormenter ‖ executioner.

ATORMENTAR.
v, to torment.

ATRACADOR.
m, robber, stick-up man or woman.

ATRACAR.
v, to assault ‖ to stick-up, hold-up, rob (in a populated area).

ATRACCIÓN.
f, attraction.

ATRACO.
m, robbery, stick-up, hold-up ‖ assault.

ATRASADO.
adj, in arrears, behind, delinquent, late (with payments) ‖ (mentally) backward, slow.

ATRASADO DE PAGO.
in default, in arrears.

ATRASADOS.
m, delinquent debtors ‖ businessmen who don't pay their debts on time.

ATRASO.
m, delay (in obligation).

ATRASOS.
m, arrears.

ATRIBUCIÓN.
f, power, ability, attribution ‖ position, function.

ATRIBUIR.
v, to attribute or ascribe to.

ATRIBUIR JURISDICCIÓN.
to extend or define jurisdiction of judge.

ATROCIDAD.
f, atrocity ‖ extreme cruelty ‖ extraordinary excess.

ATROPARSE.
v, to assemble in troops ‖ to lose order ‖ to ride roughshod over, become undisciplined ‖ to offend a woman's honor ‖ to rape.

ATROPELLAR.
v, to violate, break ‖ to disregard, violate (e.g. the law) ‖ to run over ‖ to treat arbitrarily to trample or step on or over ‖ to abuse ‖ to offend a woman's honor ‖ to ride or run roughshod over.

ATROPELLO.
m, running down (a person or thing, by a vehicle) ‖ rape ‖ abuse, arbitrary treatment ‖ violation (of a law).

AUBANA.
f. appropriation by a sovereign of property owned by a foreigner who has died.

AUDICIÓN DE ALEGATOS.
interlocutory proceeding.

AUDICIÓN DE AVENIMIENTO.
conciliation proceeding, settlement conference.

AUDICIÓN DE JUZGAMIENTO.
hearing at which judgment is issued.

AUDIENCIA.
f, hearing, trial, audience ‖ courtroom, court ‖ tribunal, court ‖ jurisdictional district ‖ day or date of hearing or trial ‖ district over which court has jurisdiction.

AUDIENCIA DE CONCILIACIÓN.
settlement hearing, pre-trial conference (held to try to reconcile parties).

AUDIENCIA DE LOS GRADOS.
hearing.
AUDIENCIA EN JUSTICIA.
court hearing.
AUDIENCIA PROVINCIAL.
high provincial court.
AUDIENCIA TERRITORIAL.
high court with jurisdiction over given territory.
AUDITOR.
m, auditor, person who audits ‖ judge, judge advocate ‖ legal advisor (to a judge).
AUDITORÍA.
f, position of auditor ‖ judge advocate ‖ legal advisor ‖ courtroom or office of auditor or judge advocate or legal advisor ‖ accounting firm or office ‖ audit.
AUSENCIA.
f, absence (without leaving a representative and without explanation). May be cause to declare the absentee presumed dead.
AUSENCIA CON PRESUNCIÓN DE FALLECIMIENTO.
absence which leads to a legal presumption of death.
AUSENTE.
m, absentee ‖ missing person ‖ person who is in absentia ‖ adj, absent.
AUSENTISMO.
m, absenteeism ‖ practice of residing in a place removed from one's property.
AUTARQUÍA.
f, autarchy ‖ economic self-sufficiency (of a nation).
AUTÉNTICA.
f, certified copy (of an order or other document). See AUTÉNTICO.
AUTENTICACIÓN.
f, authentication.
AUTENTICAR.
v, to authenticate, certify (the copy of a document).
AUTENTICIDAD.
f, authenticity.
AUTÉNTICO.
adj, authentic, genuine ‖ certified.
AUTENTIFICAR.
to authenticate.
AUTO.
m, decree (of judge), decision, ruling ‖ writ, warrant ‖ car, automobile.

AUTO ACORDADO.
Supreme Court ruling (in which all its br█ ches or justices participate).
AUTO ALTERNATIVO.
alternative writ.
AUTO APELABLE.
appealable decision.
AUTO DE AVOCACIÓN.
writ of certiorari
AUTO DE CASACIÓN.
writ of error. See CASACIÓN.
AUTO DE COMPARECENCIA.
summons (to appear in court).
AUTO DE DEFICIENCIA.
deficiency order.
AUTO DE DETENCIÓN.
warrant of arrest.
AUTO DE EJECUCIÓN.
writ of execution.
AUTO DE EMBARGO.
writ of attachment.
AUTO DE ENJUICIAMIENTO.
judgment, decision.
AUTO DE ESTAR A DERECHO.
judicial order to defendant to appear, pay, comply with judicial decision.
AUTO DE EXPROPIACIÓN.
decision ordering expropriation.
AUTO DE INDAGACIÓN.
writ of inquiry.
AUTO DE MANDAMUS.
writ of mandamus.
AUTO DE OFICIO.
decision or order issued sua sponte.
AUTO DE PAGO.
official demand for payment.
AUTO DE POSESIÓN.
writ of possession.
AUTO DE PRISIÓN.
incarceration order ‖ order to imprison duri█ or after criminal trial ‖ warrant for arrest.
AUTO DE PROCEDER.
order to proceed.
AUTO DE PROCESAMIENTO.
order to bind over, and indictment or inform█ tion. This implies formal charges.
AUTO DE PROVIDENCIA.
temporary restraining order, temporary i█ junction, temporary mandatory writ.
AUTO DE PRUEBA.
order to produce evidence.

TO DE QUIEBRA.
claration of bankruptcy.
TO DE REIVINDICACIÓN.
it to replevin.
TO DE RESTITUCIÓN.
it of restitution.
TO DE REVISIÓN.
it of review.
TO DE SOBRESEIMIENTO.
quittal of criminal charges (at any stage of
e proceeding, for failure of proof or other
asons).
TO DE SUSTANCIACIÓN.
der to proceed.
TO DEFINITIVO.
ial decision or ruling.
TO EJECUTIVO.
it of execution.
TO INHIBITORIO.
it of prohibition.
TO INTERLOCUTORIO.
terlocutory order.
TO PARA MEJOR PROVEER.
cision issued to better the course of pro-
edings.
TO PERENTORIO.
eremptory writ.
TO PREPARATORIO.
it issued prior to or in preparation of judg-
ent.
TO PROVISIONAL.
mporary writ.
TOACUSACIÓN.
self-accusation ‖ confession ‖ admission (of
uilt).
TOCALUMNIA.
false self-incrimination (e.g. of a crime one
as not committed)
TOCOMPOSICIÓN.
out-of-court settlement (includes arbitra-
ons and simple settlements).
TOCONTRATO.
contract between one party acting on his
wn behalf and that same party acting on be-
alf of another party.
TOCOPIAR.
o copy a document.
TOCRACIA.
autocracy.
TODEFENSA.
representation pro se, pro se defense (in a

trial) ‖ self-defense (in criminal law, may be a
legitimate defense).
AUTODENUNCIA.
f, self-accusation ‖ confession ‖ admission (of
guilt).
AUTODESPIDO.
f, resignation (of employment). May be VO-
LUNTARIO (voluntary) or FORZOSO (forced).
AUTODETERMINACIÓN DE LOS
PUEBLOS.
f, self-determination (of citizens to choose go-
vernment).
AUTOEJECUTABLE.
adj, self-executing.
AUTOGOBIERNO.
See DESCENTRALIZACIÓN ADMINISTRATIVA,
AUTARQUÍA and AUTONOMÍA.
AUTÓGRAFO.
m, autograph.
AUTOINCRIMINACIÓN.
f, self-incrimination.
AUTOLESIÓN.
f, self-inflicted injury.
AUTOMUTILACIÓN.
f, self-mutilation.
AUTONOMÍA.
f, autonomy ‖ independence ‖ self-gover-
nance.
AUTONOMÍA
DE LA VOLUNTAD.
free will ‖ contractual freedom.
AUTONOTIFICACIÓN.
f, service by a party in interest.
AUTOPSIA.
f, autopsy.
AUTOR.
m, author, principal, active party (of a crime)
‖ author (of literature).
AUTOR MATERIAL.
party who actually carries out physical acts
which constitute a crime.
AUTORÍA PENAL.
f, criminal participation, authoring of a crime.
AUTORIDAD.
f, authority.
AUTORIDAD AMPLIA.
full authority.
AUTORIDAD COMPETENTE.
competent authority.
AUTORIDAD COMPLETA.
See AUTORIDAD AMPLIA.

AUTORIDAD DE DISPOSICIÓN.
power of disposition.
AUTORIDAD DE LA COSA
JUZGADA.
force and effect of judicial decision.
AUTORIDAD DE REVOCACIÓN.
power of revocation.
AUTORIDAD JUDICIAL.
judicial authority.
AUTORIDAD MARITAL.
authority of husband (in relation to his wife).
AUTORIDADES.
f, authorities.
AUTORIDADES ADUANERAS.
customs authorities.
AUTORIDADES CONSTITUIDAS.
established authorities.
AUTORIDADES DE SANIDAD.
health authorities.
AUTORIDADES EDILICIAS.
municipal authorities.
AUTORIDADES JURÍDICAS.
legal authorities.
AUTORIDADES POLICIALES.
police authorities.
AUTORIZACIÓN.
f, authorization ‖ written document granting authority or approval or consent ‖ certification or witnessing of public document by special notary public or court officer or other public official.
AUTORIZACIÓN AMPLIA.
full authority.
AUTORIZACIÓN APARENTE.
apparent authority.
AUTORIZACIÓN DE COMPRA.
authority to purchase.
AUTORIZACIÓN DE LIBROS.
approval or legalization of a new set of books (e.g. corporate or accounting) by public authority.
AUTORIZACIÓN DE PAGO.
authority to pay.
AUTORIZACIÓN ESPECIAL.
special authority.
AUTORIZACIÓN EXPRESA.
express authority.
AUTORIZACIÓN GENERAL.
general authority.
AUTORIZACIÓN IMPLÍCITA.
implied authority.

AUTORIZACIÓN JUDICIAL.
judicial authority ‖ judicial authorization permission (e.g. required to allow otherwi incompetent individuals to act).
AUTORIZACIÓN LEGISLATIVA.
legislative authority or authorization (e.g. certain executive acts).
AUTORIZACIÓN LIMITADA.
limited authority.
AUTORIZACIÓN MARITAL.
marital authorization or permission (grant by a husband such that his wife may carry o certain acts).
AUTORIZACIÓN NO LIMITADA.
unlimited authority.
AUTORIZACIÓN PARA CONTRAER
MATRIMONIO.
judicial order permitting those not otherwi so allowed, to marry.
AUTORIZACIÓN PARA LAS PERSONAS
ABSTRACTAS.
government authorization of any form of leg entity. Includes certification of incorporatio
AUTORIZACIÓN PATERNA.
parental or paternal authorization (such th children may carry out certain acts).
AUTORIZACIÓN POR
IMPEDIMENTO.
authority by estoppel.
AUTORIZACIÓN REAL.
actual authority.
AUTORIZACIÓN UNILATERAL.
unilateral authority.
AUTORIZAR.
v, to authorize, empower ‖ to permit, conse ‖ to certify, witness ‖ to authenticate, legali (a document by a special notary public, cou clerk, or other public official).
AUTORRESPONSABILIDAD.
f, responsibility for one's own acts.
AUTOS.
m, plural of AUTO ‖ court file ‖ sum of the di ferent elements which make up a criminal c civil action. Usually called PROCESO in crim nal actions, and AUTOS in civil actions.
AUTOS PARA SENTENCIA.
judicial pronouncement that evidentiary po tion of trial is closed and that the judge is co sidering his judgment.
AUXILIAR.
n, f, assistant ‖ adj, helping, auxiliary, assistan

XILIARES.
, f, assistants ‖ helpers, aides.

XILIARES DE LA JUSTICIA.
sistants of justice (whether public officials or ɔt).

XILIATORIA.
order of a superior court to compel comiance with the decree of a lower court or ɔurt of another jurisdiction.

AL.
, aval, act of being surety (on promissory ɔtes and bills of exchange).

AL ABSOLUTO.
ill guaranty or surety. See AVAL.

AL LIMITADO.
nited guaranty or surety. ɛe AVAL.

ALAR.
to be surety on a promissory note or draft.

ALISTA.
a, surety of promissory note or draft.

ALORAR.
to value, appraise.

ALUACIÓN.
valuation, appraisal ‖ evaluation.

ALUADOR.
a, appraiser.

ALUAR.
, to value, appraise ‖ to evaluate.

ALÚO.
a, valuation, assessment, appraisal.

ALÚO CATASTRAL.
ppraisal of real estate.

ALÚO CERTIFICADO.
ertified appraisal.

ALÚO FISCAL.
ppraisal for purposes of taxation.

ALÚO PREVENTIVO.
xpert appraisal of value or damage for evienciary purposes on a later court action.

ALÚO SUCESORIO.
ppraisal of a decedent's estate.

ALLAR.
, to close up a farm with obstacles or barriers.

E NEGRA.
, shyster lawyer.

ENENCIA.
, agreement, accord, settlement, compromie.

ENIDOR.
n, mediator, arbitrator, reconciler.

AVENIMIENTO.
m, agreement, mediation, understanding, arrangement.

AVENIR.
v, to reconcile, bring to terms ‖ to arbitrate.

AVENIRSE.
v, to agree ‖ to settle, become reconciled.

AVENTURA.
f, adventure, risk.

AVENTURERO.
m, adventurer.

AVERÍA.
f, deterioration, damage, destruction ‖ detriment, loss ‖ (maritime) average.

AVERÍA COMÚN.
general or gross average.

AVERÍA GRUESA.
See AVERÍA COMÚN.

AVERÍA MENOR.
minor or petty average.

AVERÍA ORDINARIA.
See AVERÍA MENOR.

AVERÍA PEQUEÑA.
See AVERÍA MENOR.

AVERÍA SIMPLE.
See AVERÍA PARTICULAR.

AVERIADO.
adj, deteriorated, damaged ‖ destroyed ‖ damaged in attempt to save persons or cargo on a boat ‖ subject to maritime average.

AVERIAR.
v, to cause deterioration, damage, or destruction ‖ to cause damage in attempt to save person or cargo on a boat ‖ to cause maritime average.

AVERÍAS COMUNES.
general average (which benefits all people on board or their cargo).

AVERÍAS GRUESAS.
See AVERÍAS COMUNES.

AVERÍAS PARTICULARES.
simple average (which does not benefit all people on board or their cargo).

AVERÍAS SIMPLES.
See AVERÍAS PARTICULARES.

AVERIGUACIÓN DEL DELINCUENTE.
interrogation of the accused.

AVERIGUAR.
v, to inquire.

AVIAR.
v, to loan money to miners or cattle ranchers

or farmers ‖ to finance the expenses of a mine ‖ to equipor fit out ‖ to finance, advance money to.

AVIESO.
adj, malicious.

AVISAR.
v, to notify, advise ‖ to give notice ‖ to warn, forewarn, to counsel.

AVISO.
m, notice, announcement ‖ advertisement ‖ warning, precaution ‖ formal notice ‖ news.

AVISO DE COMPARECENCIA.
notice of appearance.

AVISO DE PROTESTO.
notice of protest.

AVISO DE RECHAZO.
notice of dishonor.

AVISO EMPLAZATORIO.
summons to appear.

AVISO JUDICIAL.
judicial notice.

AVISO OPORTUNO.
fair warning, due notice.

AVISO RAZONABLE.
reasonable notice.

AVOCACIÓN.
f, transfer or removal of a case from a lower court to a superior court.

AVOCAR.
v, to request removal of a case from a lower court to a superior court ‖ to remove case from a lower court (upon order of a superior court).

AVOCARSE AL CONOCIMIENTO.
to take the case over.

AVULSIÓN.
f, avulsion, that carried by river from property of one person to that of another. One of the means of acquiring property.

AXIOLOGÍA JURÍDICA.
See ESTIMATIVA JURÍDICA.

AXOVAR.
v, to inherit property (by wife) which is in alienable until she has children.

AYUDANTE.
m, f, assistant, helper, aide ‖ alternate, substitute, second.

AYUNTAMIENTO.
m, municipal or city council ‖ town hall, city hall ‖ sexual intercourse ‖ city government.

AZAR.
m, chance ‖ fortune ‖ misfortune ‖ also see CASO FORTUITO.

AZOTAR.
v, to whip, flog, thrash.

B

BACHILLER EN LEYES.
m, bachelor in law (a lower degree, which used to precede the degree which licensed one to practice law; no longer in use).

BAGAJE.
m, baggage, equipment.

BAHÍA.
f, bay.

BAJA.
f, decrease (in value) ‖ going out of business (for tax purposes) ‖ statement to tax authorities of going out of business ‖ drop or withdrawal from a list or organization ‖ absence or loss of a soldier in the military.

BAJAR
AL SEPULCRO.
to die.

BAJAR LA MANO.
to lower the price of something.

BAJAR LOS OJOS.
to be ashamed ‖ to obey ‖ to capitulate, give up.

BAJISTA.
m, stock exchange speculator (who profits from the fall of prices), bear ‖ person who causes stock prices to fall for later gain.

BAJO APECIBIMIENTO.
duly warned, under penalty.

BAJO CONTRATO.
under contract.

BAJO EL PIE.
at one's feet ‖ humiliated ‖ beaten ‖ under dictatorship or foreign rule.

BAJO FIANZA.
on bail or bond. Used in reference to accused who are able to leave jail upon placing a financial guaranty.

BAJO JURAMENTO.
on or under (sworn) oath.

BAJO MANO.
secretly, clandestinely, under the table.

BAJO OBLIGACIÓN.
under obligation.

BAJO PALABRA.
on one's word ‖ on one's own recognizance.

BAJO PENA DE.
under penalty of.

BAJO PROTESTA.
under protest.

BAJO SELLO.
under seal.

BAJO SU PALABRA.
on his or her word, on his or her personal recognizance, on his or her word of honor.

BALANCE.
m, balance sheet, ledger ‖ scales ‖ balances balance.

BALANCE COMERCIAL.
balance of trade, trade balance.

BALANCE DE APERTURA.
opening or beginning balance sheet.

BALANCE DE CAJA.
cash flow sheet.

BALANCE DE CONTABILIDAD.
balance sheet.

BALANCE DE FUSIÓN.
consolidated balance sheet (re: mergers).

BALANCE DE LIQUIDACIÓN.
balance sheet for purposes of liquidating a business.

BALANCE DE RESULTADOS.
profit and loss statement.

BALANCE DE SITUACIÓN.
balance sheet.

BALANCE FISCAL.
balance sheet for tax purposes.
BALANCE GENERAL CONSOLIDADO.
consolidated balance sheet.
BALANCE IMPOSITIVO.
balance sheet for tax purposes.
BALANCE PROVISORIO.
temporary or interim balance sheet.
BALANCE SIMULADO.
fraudulent balance sheet.
BALANCE TENTATIVO.
draft or tentative balance sheet.
BALANCEADOR.
m, examiner of accounts, person who examines a company to prepare its accounts and take inventory.
BALANCETE.
m, temporary balance sheet.
BALANZA.
f, judgment, estimate, comparison ‖ balance (g. of payments).
BALANZA COMERCIAL.
trade balance, balance of trade.
BALANZA DE COMERCIO.
See BALANZA COMERCIAL.
BALANZA DE INTERCAMBIO.
balance of trade, trade balance.
BALANZA DE MERCANCÍAS.
balance of trade, trade balance.
BALANZA DE PAGOS.
balance of payments.
BALOTA.
f, ballot.
BALOTAJE.
m, voting by ballot ‖ election run-off.
BANAS.
f, banns (of matrimony).
BANCA.
f, banking ‖ bank ‖ bankers' meeting.
BANCA CENTRAL.
central banking.
BANCA DE SUCURSALES.
branch banking.
BANCA DE INVERSIONES.
investment banking.
BANCA DE INVERSIONISTAS.
See BANCA DE INVERSIONES.
BANCABLE.
adj, bankable ‖ negotiable ‖ tolerable.
BANCADA.
f, party affiliation in legislature or congress.

BANCARIO.
adj, banking, related to banks.
BANCARROTA.
f, bankruptcy.
BANCO.
m, bank ‖ jail ‖ bench ‖ money changer's bench or table.
BANCO AGRÍCOLA.
agricultural loan bank.
BANCO CAPITALIZADOR.
bank for capitalization of savings.
BANCO CENTRAL.
central bank.
BANCO COMERCIAL
commercial bank.
BANCO COOPERATIVO.
cooperative bank, coop bank.
BANCO DE AHORROS.
savings bank.
BANCO DE AHORRO POR ACCIONES.
joint-stock savings bank.
BANCO DE BANCOS.
central bank.
BANCO DE CAPITALIZACIÓN.
See BANCO CAPITALIZADOR.
BANCO DE COMERCIO.
See BANCO COMERCIAL.
BANCO DE CRÉDITO AGRÍCOLA.
farm or agricultural loan bank.
BANCO DE CRÉDITO INMOBILIARIO.
mortgage bank.
BANCO DE EMISIÓN.
bank of issue ‖ issuing bank ‖ opening bank.
BANCO DE EMISIÓN DE VALORES.
issuing bank, banking institution which acts as an intermediary for the issue of corporate stocks and bonds.
BANCO DE EMISIÓN Y DESCUENTO.
reserve bank, commercial bank which discounts, receives deposits, opens current accounts, and makes loans and transfers.
BANCO DE INVERSIÓN.
investment bank.
BANCO DE LOS ACUSADOS.
dock, defendant's seat in court.
BANCO DEL ESTADO.
government or state bank.
BANCO DE LIQUIDACIÓN.
clearing house.
BANCO EMISOR.
See BANCO DE EMISIÓN.

BANCO ESTATAL.
government bank ‖ state bank.
BANCO FIDUCIARIO.
trust company.
BANCO HIPOTECARIO.
real estate mortgage bank.
BANCO INDUSTRIAL.
industrial development bank.
BANCO MUNDIAL.
World Bank.
BANCO MUTUALISTA DE AHORRO.
mutual savings bank.
BANCO NACIONAL.
government bank, national bank (authorized by federal government to operate throughout country).
BANCO PARTICULAR.
private or unincorporated bank.
BANCO PRIVADO.
See BANCO PARTICULAR.
BANCO REGIONAL.
regional bank, local bank.
BANDA.
f, gang, group of three or more person for criminal purposes.
BANDA CRIMINAL.
gang or band of delinquents or criminals.
BANDERA.
f, flag, banner ‖ standard ‖ colors (of troops).
BANDERA NACIONAL.
national flag.
BANDIDAJE.
m, banditry.
BANDIDO.
m, bandit, outlaw, highwayman (usually in unpopulated areas).
BANDO.
m, faction, party ‖ decree, proclamation, public mandate (from higher authority) ‖ law.
BANDOLERISMO.
m, banditry.
BANDOLERO.
m, highwayman.
BANQUERO.
m, owner or head of a bank ‖ banker.
BANQUILLO.
m, dock, defendant's seat (at criminal trial).
BANQUILLO DE LOS TESTIGOS.
witness stand.
BANQUILLO DEL ACUSADO.
dock, defendant's seat.

BARATERÍA.
f, fraud, fraudulent sale or purchase ‖ crime c judge who is bribed ‖ barratry, maritim fraud, fraud by ship captain and crew to th prejudice of insurance company or shipper c ship owner.
BARATERÍA DE CAPITÁN Y MARINEROS.
barratry of captain and crew (of a ship).
BARATERÍA DE PATRÓN.
barratry of the master (of a ship).
BARATERO.
m, person who commits barratry, barrator grafter, briber.
BARATO.
m, tip given by a winning better to thos around him or her ‖ sale, special offer of good at a low price ‖ adj, cheap
BARCAJE.
m, ship transport or transportation ‖ price c such transportation or transport.
BARCO.
m, ship, vessel, boat.
BAREMO.
m, adjusted accounts book.
BARÓN.
m, baron.
BARONÍA.
f, barony.
BARRA.
f, public audience which attends meetings o select bodies ‖ public, courtroom (of court at tendees).
BARRACA.
f, warehouse, storehouse.
BARRAGANA.
f, concubine, companion (recognized by law to be entitled to certain rights).
BARRAGANERÍA.
f, concubinage.
BARRAGANÍA.
f, condition of being a concubine.
BARRAQUERO.
m, owner or manager of a warehouse.
BARRAS AVIADAS.
shares of a partner who furnishes no capita (e.g. in a mining venture).
BARRAS AVIADORAS.
shares of a partner who furnishes capital (e.g in a mining venture).

BARRIO.
n, district, quarter ‖ area, section ‖ suburb, outskirts.

BASE.
, basis, foundation (of a principle) ‖ base.

BASE DE COSTO.
cost basis.

BASE DE EFECTIVO.
cash basis.

BASE IMPONIBLE.
tax basis or base.

BASE IMPOSITIVA.
See BASE IMPONIBLE.

BASE LIQUIDABLE.
tax base less deductions.

BASE NAVAL.
naval base.

BASES.
f, terms and conditions ‖ fundamentals ‖ grounds, bases.

BASES CONVENCIONALES PLURALES DE TRABAJO.
contractual rules and regulations regarding work conditions agreed upon by an employer or group of employers and the representative(s) of the employees.

BASES
DE LA ACCIÓN.
grounds of action, theory of the case.

BASES DE TRABAJO.
rules or conditions of work.

BASTANTEAR.
v, to officially acknowledge as valid the credentials of an attorney to represent a client in an action.

BASTANTEO.
m, official acceptance of the credentials of an attorney to represent a client in an action ‖ document to such effect.

BASTANTERO.
m, official who reviews the validity of the credentials of an attorney to represent a client in an action.

BASTARDEAR.
v, to falsify, alter ‖ to bastardize.

BASTARDEO.
f, bastardy.

BASTARDÍA.
f, bastardy, illegitimacy.

BASTARDO.
m, bastard, illegitimate offspring.

BASTÓN.
m, stick, cane ‖ truncheon.

BASTONERO.
m, person who carries a BASTÓN.

BATELES.
m, gang of ruffians or thieves.

BAUTISMO.
m, baptism.

BAUTIZO.
m, baptism, act of baptizing.

BEBIDAS ALCOHÓLICAS.
alcoholic beverages.

BEBIDAS NOCIVAS.
toxic beverages.

BELICISMO.
m, bellicosity, aggressiveness, militarism, propensity to go to war.

BELIGERANCIA.
f, belligerence ‖ right to fight (war) on equal terms.

BELIGERANTE.
m, adj, belligerent (e.g. country in a war).

BENEFICENCIA.
f, beneficence ‖ welfare or do-good organization ‖ relief ‖ free medical assistance.

BENEFICIADO.
m, beneficiary (of a charity or kindness) ‖ adj, benefited.

BENEFICIAR.
v, to benefit ‖ to exploit, develop, cultivate ‖ to sell stocks and bonds below par ‖ to process ‖ to sell commercial paper at a discount.

BENEFICIARIA.
f, beneficiary.

BENEFICIARIO.
m, beneficiary, person who benefits ‖ payee.

BENEFICIARIO CONDICIONAL.
conditional or contingent beneficiary.

BENEFICIARIO DE PREFERENCIA.
preference beneficiary.

BENEFICIARIO EN EXPECTIVA.
future beneficiary.

BENEFICIARIO EVENTUAL.
See BENEFICIARIO CONDICIONAL.

BENEFICIO.
m, benefit ‖ gain, profit ‖ payment of a benefit ‖ cultivation or other work (on land) ‖ mining, extraction of minerals ‖ earnings of a business ‖ improvements.

BENEFICIO DE ABDICACIÓN.
right of a widow to renounce all rights to her

husband's property (thus also escaping liability for his debts).

BENEFICIO DE BANDERA.
right to a decrease in fees payable by a vessel due to the type of merchandise carried.

BENEFICIO DE CESIÓN DE ACCIONES.
right of subrogation to creditor's rights held by a co-guarantor upon paying a creditor ‖ right to assignment of action on a debt against co-guarantors, held by guarantor who pays creditor.

BENEFICIO DE COMPETENCIA.
right of a debtor to pay when he reasonably can afford to do so. Usually must be granted to certain debtors who are relatives or partners of the creditor or who are debtors in good faith.

BENEFICIO DE EXCARCELACIÓN.
right to be released on bail.

BENEFICIO DE EXCUSIÓN.
right of excussio ‖ right of guarantor to demand that creditor exhaust his remedies against the principal debtor, before seeking payment from guarantor.

BENEFICIO DE INVENTARIO.
right of inventory, right of heir to request the taking of a formal inventory of the decedent's property before accepting the inheritance.

BENEFICIO DE LITIGAR SIN GASTOS.
right to sue without paying filing fee.

BENEFICIO DE ORDEN.
benefit of discussion ‖ preference, priority.

BENEFICIO DE POBREZA.
right of indigent to bring or defend an action without having to pay filing fee or attorney's fees.

BENEFICIO DE RESTITUCIÓN.
restitutio in integrum, right of restitution.

BENEFICIO POR MUERTE.
death benefit.

BENEFICIO TRIBUTABLE.
taxable gain or profit.

BENEFICIOS A TRIBUTAR.
taxable profits.

BENEFICIOS ACUMULADOS.
undivided profits, earned surplus.

BENEFICIOS DE INDEMNIZACIÓN.
indemnity benefits.

BENEFICIOS EXTRAORDINARIOS.
excess profits.

BENEFICIOS IMPONIBLES.
taxable profits.

BENEFICIOS POR ACCIDENTE.
accident benefits.

BENEFICIOS POR INCAPACIDAD.
disability benefits.

BENEFICIOSO.
beneficial ‖ profitable.

BEODEZ.
f, drunkenness, intoxication.

BEODO.
m, drunkard ‖ adj, intoxicated.

BICAMERAL.
adj, bicameral, that which follows a govern mental system whereby two houses carry ou legislative functions.

BIEN.
m, benefit, utility ‖ thing, good ‖ adj, good.

BIEN COMÚN.
common good, common welfare.

BIEN DE FAMILIA
See BIEN DE LA FAMILIA

BIEN DE LA FAMILIA.
homestead ‖ recognition of right of family to real property for purpose of living and essen tial needs, without right to mortgage, transfer etc.

BIEN JURÍDICO.
legally protected interest.

BIEN PÚBLICO.
public good, public welfare.

BIENES.
m, property (real or personal, tangible or in tangible) ‖ assets ‖ estate ‖ goods.

BIENES AB INTESTATO.
intestate's estate.

BIENES ABANDONADOS.
abandoned property ‖ goods which have been left or real property which has not been visited or cared for.

BIENES ACCESORIOS.
accessions. May be JURIDICA (by law), DE DESTINO (by dint of its purpose or use), MATE-RIAL (by physical attachment, e.g. fixture).

BIENES ACENSUADOS.
property which has been subjected to a CENSO.

BIENES ADVENTICIOS.
adventitious property ‖ property of eldest son who is under parental control, which property is acquired through his own efforts or through

gift or devise other than from his father. The property belongs to the son but the parents have the right to use it.

BIENES ALODIALES.
alodial property ‖ property free from liens or other encumbrances.

BIENES ANTIFERNALES.
property which a husband settles on his wife.

BIENES APORTADOS AL MATRIMONIO.
separate spousal property ‖ property owned by each spouse prior to marriage.

BIENES CASTRENSES.
son's property acquired while in military service. Includes that given by parents upon departure for the military, booty, property inherited from a companion, etc.

BIENES COLACIONABLES.
property which must be returned to an estate in probate because their prior transfer violated the inheritance laws.

BIENES COMUNALES.
community goods, goods belonging to a municipality available for community use.

BIENES COMUNES.
communal property ‖ public property ‖ property belonging to no one individual but to the public in general (e.g. light, air, rain water, etc.) ‖ community property (of husband and wife).

BIENES CONSUMIBLES.
consumables ‖ property which can not be used without destroying it.

BIENES CONTRACTUALES.
contractual goods, goods which may be the subject matter of a contract.

BIENES CORPORALES.
corporal goods.

BIENES CUASICASTRENSES.
children's goods (earned from public position or a profession).

BIENES DE ABOLENGO.
inherited goods.

BIENES DE ABOLORIO.
See BIENES DE ABOLENGO.

BIENES DE APROVECHAMIENTO COMÚN.
property for communal use (e.g. common pasture, trees, etc.).

BIENES DE BENEFICENCIA.
chattels of a charitable organization.

BIENES DE CADA UNO DE LOS CÓNYUGES.
separate property (of married couple).

BIENES DE CAPITAL.
capital assets, capital goods, goods of production.

BIENES DE CONSUMO.
consumer goods, property which satisfies a human need, convenience or desire.

BIENES DE DOMINIO PRIVADO.
private property.

BIENES DE DOMINIO PÚBLICO.
public property, property owned by government.

BIENES DE FORTUNA.
property, wealth, assets.

BIENES DE HERENCIA.
decedent's estate.

BIENES DE INGRESOS ENTORPECIDOS.
See BIENES IGNORADOS.

BIENES DE LA SOCIEDAD CONYUGAL.
community property, marital estate.

BIENES DE LA SUCESIÓN.
property of estate of a decedent.

BIENES DE MANOS MUERTAS.
See MANOS MUERTAS.

BIENES DE MENORES.
property of minors ‖ minor children's property.

BIENES DE PRODUCCIÓN.
capital goods.

BIENES DE PROPIEDAD PRIVADA.
private property (whether owned by persons or entities or the government if the property is not open to public use).

BIENES DE PROPIOS.
See BIENES COMUNALES.

BIENES DE SERVICIO PÚBLICO.
local governmental property, property owned by local governments and their subsidiary entities.

BIENES DE USO PÚBLICO.
public property ‖ property available for public use.

BIENES DEL ESTADO.
government property, state property. May be owned by the province (BIENES DE USO PÚBLICO or BIENES DE LOS ESTADOS PROVINCIALES) or nation (BIENES DE DOMINIO PÚBLICO or BIENES DEL ESTADO NACIONAL.

BIENES DEL MARIDO.

husband's property, separate property of husband over which the wife has no property rights.

BIENES DEL QUEBRADO.

bankrupt's estate, property which is available to satisfy creditors' claims.

BIENES DIVISIBLES.

divisible property, property which by its nature is not harmed by division into two or more parts.

BIENES DOMINIALES.

See BIENES DOMINICALES.

BIENES DOMINICALES.

governmental goods or property.

BIENES DOTALES.

dowry.

BIENES DURABLES.

durable goods, goods which continue to function under prolonged use.

BIENES DURADEROS.

See BIENES DURABLES.

BIENES EMBARGADOS.

attached property, property subject to attachment or judicial lien (may be lien lis pendens or a final judgment lien).

BIENES ENAJENABLES.

alienable property, transferable property.

BIENES ENFITÉUTICOS.

goods which are given in ENFITEUSIS.

BIENES EXTRADOTALES.

paraphernal property.

BIENES FISCALES.

public property, property of the State.

BIENES FORALES.

leasehold property or estate ‖ leasehold.

BIENES FUNGIBLES.

fungible goods.

BIENES FUTUROS.

future goods, future acquired goods or property.

BIENES GANANCIALES.

marital estate, property which is earned or purchased by both the husband and the wife during marriage ‖ community property, property of conjugal partnership.

BIENES GRAVADOS.

property over which there is an encumbrance, covenant, or tax.

BIENES HEREDITARIOS.

inherited property.

BIENES HIPOTECABLES.

mortgageable property. There are three ty of mortgageable property: real property ch tels which must be registered ‖ real prope which is transferable ‖ mixed property.

BIENES HIPOTECADOS.

mortgaged property.

BIENES IGNORADOS.

goods which have been overlooked or hidd during the dissolution of a marriage and th must be distributed later ‖ unknown prope property of which a person is unaware he is owner.

BIENES INALIENABLES.

inalienable property, property which is transferable.

BIENES INCORPORALES.

incorporeal or intangible goods.

BIENES INDIVISIBLES.

indivisible property (e.g. an animal, buildi etc.).

BIENES INDIVISOS.

indivisible goods.

BIENES INEMBARGABLES.

unattachable property. This consists of thin that are absolutely necessary for owner's su sistence or occupation, similar to those i cluded in homestead exemptions.

BIENES INCORPORALES.

intangible assets.

BIENES INCORPOREOS.

See BIENES INCORPORALES.

BIENES INMATERIALES.

intangible goods.

BIENES INMOVILIZADOS.

fixed assets.

BIENES INMUEBLES.

real property, real estate, real assets. This i cludes among other things land, building roads and thing fixed to those things and times, trees and plants attached to the eart fixtures; statues, reliefs, pictures, etc. attache to a building; machines, instruments etc, th are directly necessary for the use of the pr perty; animal pens; documents which ent real property rights.

BIENES LIBRES.

unencumbered property, property which free and clear of all obligations ‖ tax-exem property.

ES LITIGIOSOS.
erty the ownership of which is in litigation.

ES MANCOMUNADOS.
munal property.

ES MOBILIARIOS.
ables ‖ personal property.

ES MOSTRENCOS.
, waif property, property claimed by no
or everyone.

ES MUEBLES.
onal property, chattels, personalty, mov-
s, movable property. This includes any-
g which is not BIENES INMUEBLES.

ES NO CONSUMIBLES.
-consumable goods.
BIENES CONSUMIBLES).

ES NO DURADEROS.
-durable goods.
BIENES DURABLES.

ES NO FUNGIBLES.
-fungible goods.

ES NO HIPOTECABLES.
-mortgageable goods.
BIENES HIPOTECABLES.

ES NULLIUS.
perty without an owner.

ES PARAFERNALES.
aphernal property, separate property
ch a wife brings with her upon marriage,
rt from her dowry.

ES PATRIMONIALES.
perty inherited by son from parents or
ndparents ‖ public property not open to
lic use ‖ private property.

ES POR HEREDAR.
editaments, property that may be inhe-
d.

ES PRESENTES.
perty in possession ‖ presently-existing
ds.

ES PRINCIPALES.
cipal goods.
posed to BIENES ACCESORIOS.

ES PRIVADOS
L ESTADO.
ernment property, property owned by the
ernment in its private capacity. This in-
des national land without owner; mines;
f property; goods of persons who die intes-
; places of war ‖ public works; unidentified
wrecks.

BIENES PRIVATIVOS.
private property ‖ separate property of a husband and wife.

BIENES
PROFECTICIOS.
property obtained by child as interest or profit
on property held or administered by parents
on his behalf.

BIENES PROPIOS.
separate property of husband and wife ‖
private unencumbered property ‖ private property owned free and clear.

BIENES PÚBLICOS.
public property ‖ property owned by a city, a
province or a nation.

BIENES RAÍCES.
real estate or property.

BIENES REALES.
real estate or property.

BIENES RELICTOS.
inherited property.

BIENES RESERVABLES.
inalienable property, property held subject to
condition that it not be transferred ‖ property
being held legally for someone else.

BIENES RESERVATIVOS.
See BIENES RESERVABLES.

BIENES RESERVATORIOS.
See BIENES RESERVABLES.

BIENES SEDIENTES.
real property.

BIENES SEMOVIENTES.
animals which are mobile.

BIENES
SEPULCRALES.
burial property.

BIENES SITIOS.
See BIENES INMUEBLES.

BIENES SITOS.
See BIENES INMUEBLES.

BIENES SOCIALES.
corporate property, partnership property.

BIENES SUCESORIOS.
assets of the estate of decedent.

BIENES TRONCALES.
estate of a descendent who dies without offspring, which property does not pass to normal
heirs, but to blood relatives. Usually limited to
real estate.

BIENES VACANTES.
real estate with no known owner.

BIENES VINCULADOS.
property which must be kept in the family, which may not be sold.
BIENES Y SERVICIOS.
goods and services.
BIENESTAR.
m, welfare.
BIENESTAR SOCIAL.
social welfare.
BIENHECHURÍA.
f, improvements (to real estate).
BIENQUERENCIA.
f, good will.
BIGAMIA.
f, bigamy ‖ bigamous marriage. Usually deemed to be a crime.
BÍGAMO.
m, bigamist ‖ person who marries a widow or widower.
BILATERAL.
adj, bilateral (in contract and international law).
BILATERALIDAD DEL PROCESO.
duality or plurality or parties in a case.
BILLETE.
m, bill, banknote ‖ promissory note ‖ note ‖ ticket.
BILLETE DE BANCO.
bill, banknote ‖ bearer or order paper issued by a bank, which doesn't collect interest.
BÍNUBO.
m, twice-married person, person who has married a second time ‖ adj, twice-married, pertaining to a second marriage.
BIPARTIDISMO.
bipartisanism, political system involving two parties.
BISABUELA.
f, great-grandmother.
BISABUELO.
m, great-grandfather.
BISNIETA.
f, great-granddaughter.
BISNIETO.
m, great-grandchild ‖ great-grandson.
BITÁCORA.
See CUADERNO DE BITÁCORA.
BLANCAS.
f, whites, white women ‖ adj, white.
BLANCO.
m, ballot which is left blank or unused, i.e.

which, after use, does not indicate vote blank ‖ legal (re. taxes).
BLANQUEO DE CAPITALES.
m, tax whitewash, government agreeme accept late tax payments, without imp any penalty.
BLASFEMIA.
f, blasphemy.
BLOQUEADO.
adj, blocked, blockaded, obstructed ‖ frc
BLOQUEAR.
v, to block, obstruct, blockade ‖ to freez
BLOQUEAR FONDOS.
to freeze assets.
BLOQUEO.
m, blockade, obstruction.
BLOQUEO ARMADO.
armed blockade.
BLOQUEO EN EL PAPEL.
paper blockade.
BOCHINCHE.
m, riot, civil disturbance.
BOCHINCHERO.
m, rioter.
BODA.
f, wedding, marriage ceremony.
BODEGA.
f, warehouse, storehouse ‖ hold (of a sh grocery store ‖ cellar.
BOICOT.
m, boycott.
BOICOTEO.
See BOICOT.
BOICOTEAR.
v, to boycott.
BOLETA.
f, ticket, slip ‖ sales slip, proof of sale ‖ pe license ‖ free pass ‖ merchant's receipt ‖ ti (of a traffic infraction) ‖ rough draft of a blic writing given to special notary public ‖ lot ‖ certificate.
BOLETA BANCARIA.
certificate of deposit.
BOLETA DE CITACIÓN.
judicial notice ‖ summons.
BOLETA DE COMPARENDO.
See BOLETA DE CITACIÓN.
BOLETA DE CONSIGNACIÓN.
certificate of deposit.
BOLETA DE DEPÓSITO.
deposit slip ‖ certificate of deposit.

LETA DE GARANTÍA.
rtificate of deposit to guarantee performan-
e of a contract.

LETÍN.
, bulletin, credit note ‖ license, permit (to
ork or for a company) ‖ voucher for lodg-
gs.

LETÍN JUDICIAL.
w report, official publication of judicial
ecisions and court edicts.

LETÍN OFICIAL.
overnment reporter, official publication of
egislation passed, regulations, and other noti-
es of a legal nature ‖ official gazette.

LETO.
a, ticket ‖ preliminary contract.

LETO DE CARGA.
ill of lading.

LETO DE COMPRAVENTA.
reliminary sales contract.

LETO DE EMPEÑO.
awn ticket.

LETO PAPELETA ELECTORAL.
allot, voting ballot.

LSA.
, money, wealth ‖ bourse, stock exchange,
tock market.

LSA DE COMERCIO.
tock exchange, stock market, bourse.

LSA DE TRABAJO.
ee AGENCIA DE COLOCACIONES.

LSÍN.
n, black-market stock exchange, exchange of
tocks not legally authorized ‖ over the coun-
er stock exchange.

ONIFICACIÓN.
, discount, reduction ‖ bonus (of employee's
alary).

ONIFICACIÓN TRIBUTARIA.
ax rebate.

ONISTA.
n, f, bondholder.

ONO.
m, bond ‖ voucher, certificate ‖ bonus.

ONO DE AHORRO.
savings bond.

ONO DE CAJA.
short term government note, treasury bill ‖
certificate of time deposit.

ONO DE CONSOLIDACIÓN.
funding bond ‖ consolidated bond.

BONO DE CONVERSIÓN.
refunding bond.

BONO DE CRÉDITO TERRITORIAL.
bond of a mortgage bank.

BONO DE FUNDADOR.
bond issued to a promoter for services.

**BONO DE INTERÉS
POR SOBREUTILIDADES.**
income bond.

**BONO DE OBLIGACIÓN
PREFERENTE.**
prior-lien bond.

BONO DE OPCIÓN.
bond carrying the right to subscribe for stock.

BONO DE PARTICIPACIÓN.
See ACCIONES DE GOCE.

BONO DE PRENDA.
note issued for loan against goods in warehouse.

BONO DE PRIMERA HIPOTECA.
first-mortgage bond.

BONO DE RENDIMIENTOS.
income bond.

BONO DE RENTA PERPETUA.
perpetual bond.

BONO DE TESORERÍA.
government bond, treasury bill.

BONO FISCAL.
government bond, exchequer bond.

BONO HIPOTECARIO.
mortgage bond ‖ bond of a mortgage bank.

BONO INMOBILIARIO.
real-estate bond.

BONO NOMINATIVO.
registered bond.

BONO PARTICIPANTE.
bond with participation in profits in addition to
fixed interest.

BONO REDIMIBLE.
callable bond.

BONO RETIRABLE.
See BONO REDIMIBLE.

BONO SOBRE EQUIPO.
equipment-trust note, equipment bond.

BONO TALONARIO.
coupon bond.

BONOS DEL TESORO.
treasury bonds.

BORDEAR EL PRESIDIO.
to beg to be caught (in a criminal act), beg for
punishment.

BORRADOR.
m, rough draft, rough copy ‖ eraser ‖ merchant's daily record.

BORRADOR DE ACUERDO.
rough draft of agreement.

BORRADURA.
f, erasure ‖ deletion.

BORRAR.
v, to erase, delete ‖ to expunge.

BORRÓN.
m, blotch, smudge ‖ rough draft ‖ erasure.

BORRÓN
Y CUENTA NUEVA.
wiping the slate clean, expungement (of crimes).

BOTÍN.
m, booty, spoils of war.

BRACEROS CONTRATADOS.
contract labor.

BRAZO.
m, arm ‖ branch (of the law).

BRAZOS.
m, laborers.

BREVE.
m, paper brief ‖ adj, brief.

BUEN COMPORTAMIENTO.
m, good behavior.

BUEN NOMBRE.
m, good name or reputation.

BUEN PADRE
DE FAMILIA.
literally, good family man. Used to refer to a standard of care which would be expected of a diligent father ‖ similar to the standard of the reasonable man using ordinary care.

BUENA CONDUCTA.
f, good behavior, activity unrelated to any criminality or criminals or convicts or gambling or drinking or women of low repute.

BUENA FAMA.
f, good name or reputation.

BUENA FE.
f, honor ‖ good faith, bona fide (owner).

BUENA GUARDA.
f, safekeeping.

BUENA PAGA.
f, good credit.

BUENA PRO.
Expression used to formally award a bid or government contract.

BUENAS COSTUMBRES.
f, mores, moral conventions (of society), moral customs.

BUENOS OFICIOS.
m, mediation, (in a dispute between two parties or nations in conflict) ‖ good offices.

BUFETE.
m, law firm, law office ‖ clientele (of a law firm) ‖ desk.

BUQUE.
m, ship.

BURDEL.
m, house of prostitution, bordello, brothel whorehouse.

BURGO.
m, hamlet, village, town.

BURGOMAESTRE.
m, mayor.

BURGUÉS.
m, villager, inhabitant of a hamlet ‖ bourgeois(e), member of the middle class ‖ adj, belonging to a town, village, or hamlet ‖ bourgeois.

BURGUESÍA.
f, bourgeoisie.

BUROCRACIA.
f, bureaucracy.

BURÓCRATA.
m, f, bureaucrat.

BUROCRÁTICO.
adj, bureaucratic.

BURSÁTIL.
adj, pertaining to the stock exchange or stock exchange transactions.

BUSCA.
f, search, hunt ‖ perquisite.

BUSCÓN.
m, petty thief.

BUSCONA.
f, prostitute, whore.

C

CABAL.
adj, according to exact weight or measurement ‖ just perfect ‖ ended, complete ‖ honest.

CABALERO.
m, second-born son (with no right to inherit father's estate).

CABALLERO.
m, gentleman ‖ sir.

CABECERA.
f, capital of a county or district (includes county seat) ‖ heading.

CABECERO.
m, lessee, tenant (who subleases to another) ‖ head of household ‖ tenant who collect rents for landlord.

CABECILLA.
m, leader, spokesperson ‖ rebel leader ‖ captain of rebel forces ‖ gang leader, ringleader.

CABER RECURSO.
v, to include or allow the right of appeal.

CABEZA.
f, head ‖ capital (of state, province, etc.) ‖ mayor, person who presides over a meeting, community, town ‖ chapter heading (of a legal writing) ‖ person legally registered as dead ‖ head of cattle.

**CABEZA
DE CASA.**
head of household or family.

**CABEZA
DE FAMILIA.**
head of household.

CABEZA DE PROCESO.
introductory document (of a criminal proceeding), document which starts or opens a criminal procedure.

CABEZA DE SENTENCIA.
preamble to judicial decision. Includes name of parties, matter in dispute, etc.

CABEZA DE TESTAMENTO.
preamble to will (usually includes name of testator, testator's marital status, state of physical and mental health, religion, and fact that he is writing the will of his own free volition).

CABEZA MAYOR.
horse or mule or ox.

CABEZA MENOR.
goat or sheep or pig.

CABEZALERA.
f, executrix (of will).

CABEZALERO.
m, executor (of will) ‖ rent collector ‖ head leaseholder of a multi-leasehold estate who collects rents and pays them to the landlord.

CABIDA.
f, expanse or measurements of a lot or piece of land.

CABILDANTE.
m, city council member, city councilor.

CABILDEAR.
v, to lobby ‖ to discuss (a matter) at a meeting.

CABILDERO.
m, lobbyist, political intriguer.

CABILDO.
m, town hall, city council ‖ municipal council ‖ city council meeting.

CABLES SUBMARINOS.
underwater cables.

CABO.
m, corporal ‖ captain (mil) ‖ chapter, paragraph.

CABOTAJE.
m, coastal navigation or sailing ‖ tax imposed

upon vessel sailing by sight of coast ‖ coastal shipping.

ABOTAJE AÉREO.
domestic air traffic.

ABREVACIÓN.
f, right of taker of a CENSO to obtain the recognition of the tenant of an ENFITEUSIS that the land and improvements are subject to a CENSO.

ACIQUISMO.
m, domination and influence of a CACIQUE.

ACIZ.
m, Turkish lawyer or jurist ‖ interpreter of legal principles of Koran.

ACO.
m, thief, pickpocket ‖ criminal

ACOGAMIA.
f, elopement, marriage entered into secretly. May be illegal.

ACHEAR.
v, to search suspects ‖ to frisk (for arms).

ACHETERO.
m, stiletto, short and pointed knife.

ACHORILLO.
m, small pistol.

ADALSO.
m, scaffold, hangman's scaffold.

ADÁVER.
m, cadaver, corpse, body.

ADENA.
f, chain (e.g. of stores, events, etc.).

ADENA DE TÍTULO.
chain of title.

CADENA PERPETUA.
life imprisonment.

CADENA TEMPORAL.
imprisonment temporary.

CADETE.
m, military cadet ‖ trainee, apprentice ‖ office boy.

CADUCABLE.
adj, forfeitable ‖ voidable.

CADUCAR.
v, to become void, be null (a law, rule, will, contract, etc.) ‖ to lapse, expire (a right, recourse, etc.) ‖ to be without valid passport or legal document (due to its expiration) ‖ to be forfeited.

CADUCIDAD.
f, lapsing, expiration, nullity (of right, recourse, etc.) ‖ invalidity (of will, contract, etc. due to lapsing).

CADUCIDAD DE LA CONCESIÓN.
lapsing of concessionaire's right (e.g. due to failure to have begun work).

CADUCIDAD DE LA FIANZA.
forfeiture of a bond.

CADUCIDAD DE LA HIPOTECA.
lapsing of the mortgage filing.

CADUCIDAD DE LA INSTANCIA.
nonsuit ‖ constructive abandonment of legal suit (for failure to prosecute for a period of time).

CADUCIDAD DE LAS LEYES.
expiration of statutes or laws.

CADUCIDAD DE LAS OBLIGACIONES.
lapsing of duties.

CADUCIDAD DE LOS ASIENTOS DEL REGISTRO.
lapsing of registration in the real property registry. Period of time after which lapse occurs depends on whether it is a marginal note, mere annotation, temporary filing, true filing, etc.

CADUCIDAD DE LOS LEGADOS.
invalidity of legacy (for failure to comply with testamentary conditions).

CADUCIDAD DE LOS TESTAMENTOS.
invalidity of will (for failure to comply with legal formalities, incapacity of heir, etc.)

CADUCIDAD DE MARCAS.
lapse of trademark registration (due to passage of time, lack of use, or failure to pay trademark tax or fees).

CADUCIDAD DE PATENTES.
lapse of patent registration (due to passage of time, lack of use, or failure to pay patent tax or fees).

CADUCIDAD LABORAL.
expiration of statute of limitations pertaining to labor law claim.

CADUCO.
adj, lapsed, expired ‖ no longer valid.

CAER.
v, to fall (in all senses) ‖ to lose (a job, favor, a fortune, etc.) ‖ to be in error ‖ to fall due ‖ to win, come into luck ‖ to receive (property) ‖ to give oneself to another ‖ to fall within (a class or definition) ‖ to surrender, give up.

CAER EN COMISO.
to be forfeited.

CAER EN MANOS DE ALGUIEN.
to be kidnapped ‖ to be under someone's power or control ‖ to fall into the hands of ‖ to find oneself subject to some one else's discretion ‖ to be arrested or detained.

CAER EN MORA.
to become delinquent, fall in arrears (on a debt).

CAÍDA.
f, fall, drop.

CAÍDA DE UNA CASA.
bankruptcy of a concern.

CAÍDO.
adj, due, matured ‖ fallen.

CAÍDOS.
m, arrears ‖ perquisites ‖ graft.

CAJA.
f, box ‖ safe, strong box (in hotels, banks, etc.) ‖ central post office ‖ cash box, till ‖ fund.

CAJA DE AHORROS.
savings bank.

CAJA DE CAUDALES.
safe ‖ safe-deposit box.

CAJA DE COMPENSACIÓN.
equalization fund ‖ clearing house.

CAJA DE CONVERSIÓN.
office to exchange foreign currency. Usually governmental.

CAJA DE CRÉDITO AGRARIO.
farm or agricultural loan bank.

CAJA DE DEPÓSITOS.
savings bank ‖ public depository (of goods, seized pursuant to judicial order).

CAJA DE GARANTÍA.
public fund which serves to guaranty something ‖ workers' compensation fund (used to compensate workers' on-the-job injuries).

CAJA DE JUBILACIÓN.
government social security fund ‖ entity charged with managing such funds ‖ special fund kept by companies, unions, etc. for distinct purposes, such as benefits ‖ retirement or pension fund.

CAJA DE MATERNIDAD.
maternity-leave fund (for workers on maternity leave).

CAJA DE PENSIÓN.
See CAJA DE JUBILACIÓN.

CAJA DE PREVISIÓN.
See CAJA DE JUBILACIÓN.

CAJA DE RECLUTAMIENTO.
recruitment division (of military).

CAJA DE RESISTENCIA.
strike fund.

CAJA DE SEGURIDAD.
safe deposit box ‖ safety deposit box.

CAJA DOTAL.
pension fund.

CAJA FISCAL.
national treasury.

CAJA MARÍTIMA.
workers' compensation fund for mercha marine.

CAJA MUTUA DE AHORROS.
mutual savings bank.

CAJA RECAUDADORA.
tax collector's office.

CAJA RURAL.
small farm loan bank.

CAJILLA DE SEGURIDAD.
safe or safety deposit box.

CALABOZO.
m, jail, prison, cell.

CALABOZO JUDICIAL.
jail.

CALAMIDAD.
f, calamity, great misfortune ‖ disgrace.

CALCULACIÓN.
infraction, infringement (of laws, regulations

CALENDARIO.
m, calendar ‖ agenda, schedule ‖ court cale der, docket, trial docket.

CALENDARIO JUDICIAL.
court calendar.

CALETA.
f, thief (who steals by boring through a wall) porters' union, longshoremen's union.

CALIBRE.
m, caliber.

CALICATA.
f, mining or petroleum exploration.

CALIDAD.
f, quality ‖ way of being, manner ‖ characte condition, state ‖ contractual condition or co venant ‖ requirements for a job pertaining t personal data (e.g. age, sex, marital statu etc.).

CALIDAD DE LA PENA.
quality or degree of punishment.

CALIDAD DEL DELITO.
quality or seriousness of the crime.

CALIFICACIÓN.
f, judgment, opinion ‖ characterization of a criminal action by prosecuting and defense attorneys ‖ grade, mark (e.g. from school).

CALIFICACIÓN DE CONDUCTA.
evaluation of bankrupt's degree of responsibility (i.e. fraudulent, negligent, nonnegligent).

CALIFICACIÓN DE LA QUIEBRA.
judicial determination of the bankrupt's degree of fault (i.e. whether the bankruptcy was caused fraudulently, negligently, or nonnegligently).

CALIFICACIÓN DEL DELITO.
classification of the crime before the sentencing judge in order for him or her to impose the proper sentence ‖ evaluation of facts and applicable law and punishment with respect to an accused. Results in an ESCRITO DE CALIFICACIÓN (legal conclusions) which both parties formulate upon entering into a PLENARIO.

CALIFICACIÓN REGISTRAL.
proof of title to real property ‖ title search and history, evaluation, examination, and proof of the legality of documents and titles registered with the Real Estate Registry, performed prior to filing.

CALIFICADO.
adj, qualified, competent (argument or proof) ‖ qualified, conditional ‖ aggravated, subject to a more severe penalty.

CALIFICAR.
v, to evaluate a crime ‖ to determine the facts, the guilty party, the applicable law, and the punishment ‖ to test noble birth ‖ to judge, rate, classify, pass judgment on (qualities and facts) ‖ to certify ‖ to authorize ‖ to grade, mark (e.g. students' exams).

CALIGRAFÍA.
f, handwriting, calligraphy, penmanship.

CALÍGRAFO EXPERTO.
See CALÍGRAFO PERITO.

CALÍGRAFO PERITO.
handwriting expert.

CALUMNIADOR.
m, slanderer, defamer ‖ adj, slandering, defaming.

CALUMNIAR.
v, to slander, defame, cast aspersions.

CALUMNIA.
f, slander, defamation.

CALUMNIOSO.
adj, slanderous, defamatory, calumnious.

CALLAR.
v, to remain silent ‖ to keep something secret.

CÁMARA.
f, chamber ‖ legislative chamber of house (e.g. of representatives) ‖ board ‖ room.

CÁMARA ALTA.
senate, upper house of bicameral legislature or parliament.

CÁMARA ARBITRAL.
arbitration board, board of arbitration.

CÁMARA BAJA.
house of representatives ‖ chamber of deputies ‖ lower house of bicameral legislature or parliament.

CÁMARA COMPENSADORA.
(bank) clearing house.

CÁMARA DE ALQUILERES.
landlord-tenant court, tribunal which resolves formal and informal disputes regarding urban rentals.

CÁMARA DE APELACIÓN.
court of appeals.

CÁMARA DE COMPENSACIÓN.
(bank) clearing house ‖ commercial paper court ‖ tribunal which resolves disputes involved in banking compensation.

CÁMARA DE DIPUTADOS.
house of representatives ‖ chamber of deputies. See CÁMARA BAJA.

CÁMARA DE LOS COMUNES.
house of commons.

CÁMARA DE LOS LORES.
house of lords.

CÁMARA DE REPRESENTANTES.
house of representatives. See CÁMARA BAJA.

CÁMARA DE SENADORES.
senate. See CÁMARA ALTA.

CÁMARA LETAL.
death chamber, gas chamber.

CÁMARA MUNICIPAL.
city council.

CÁMARAS DE COMERCIO, NAVEGACIÓN, INDUSTRIA.
Chambers of Commerce, Navigation, Industry (private promotional organizations).

CÁMARAS JUDICIALES.
courts of appeal, appellate courts.

CÁMARAS LEGISLATIVAS.
legislative chambers (i.e. house and senate, house of lords and house of commons).

CAMARILLA.
f, power group, coterie which influences government decisions (especially regarding public business decisions) ‖ lobby, lobbying group.

CAMARISTA.
m, judge, appellate judge ‖ council member ‖ minister of King's Council.

CAMBALACHE.
m, exchange or swap of things of little value.

CAMBIADOR.
m, money-changer ‖ person who exchanges or swaps.

CAMBIAL.
f, bill of exchange, draft.

CAMBIAL DOMICILIADA.
domiciled bill.

CAMBIAR.
v, to exchange, vary, modify ‖ to exchange, swap ‖ to change (e.g. money) ‖ to negotiate.

CAMBIAR UNA LETRA.
to negotiate a bill.

CAMBIARIO.
adj, exchange, pertaining to exchange (usually money or negotiable instruments).

CAMBIO.
m, change, transformation ‖ variation, alteration ‖ exchange ‖ small change ‖ premium (payable on negotiable instruments) ‖ exchange house ‖ money changer ‖ exchange (of foreign currencies) ‖ exchange rate ‖ price fluctuation (of precious metals) ‖ quotation price (of stocks).

CAMBIO A CORTO PLAZO.
short exchange, short-sight exchange.

CAMBIO A LA PAR.
real par, exchange when the nominal value equals market value ‖ exchange of currency on a one-for-one basis (e.g. one balboa for one dollar) ‖ exchange of currency when the market rate is equal to a fixed official rate.

CAMBIO A LA PAR COMERCIAL.
exchange at the real or commercial rate.

CAMBIO A LA VISTA.
at sight exchange.

CAMBIO A TÉRMINO.
foreign exchange futures.

CAMBIO DE CONTRABANDO.
black-market exchange.

CAMBIO DE LA LIBRA.
sterling exchange.

CAMBIO DE NOMBRE.
name change.

CAMBIO DE RESIDENCIA.
change of residence.

CAMBIO DIRECTO.
direct exchange (between two parties).

CAMBIO DIRIGIDO.
controlled exchange.

CAMBIO EXTERIOR.
foreign exchange ‖ foreign trade.

CAMBIO EXTRANJERO.
See CAMBIO EXTERIOR.

CAMBIO FLOTANTE.
floating exchange rate.

CAMBIO INDIRECTO.
exchange of currency (through a third country or party).

CAMBIO LIBRE.
currency exchange on free market ‖ exchange rate on free market.

CAMBIO LOCAL.
exchange of money by the issuance of a draft against a domestic drawee.

CAMBIO MERCANTIL.
exchange carried out through merchants (not directly from producer to buyer).

CAMBIO NEGRO.
black market exchange (of money) ‖ illegal changing of money.

CAMBIO OFICIAL.
official exchange rate (designated by government).

CAMBIO REAL.
See CAMBIO A LA PAR.

CAMBIO SOCIAL.
change of articles of incorporation (e.g. corporate purposes, organization, activities, termination date, etc.).

CAMBIOS DE ENTREGA.
foreign-exchange futures.

CAMBISTA.
m, money changer, money broker ‖ banker.

CAMINO.
m, road, path ‖ ways, means ‖ procedure (to achieve an end).

CAMINO DE SERVIDUMBRE.
easement, right-of-way.

CAMINO DERECHO.
lawful means ‖ straight and narrow path.
CAMINO PÚBLICO.
public pathway.
CAMIÓN DE POLICÍA.
patrol wagon.
CAMIONERO AFIANZADO.
bonded trucker.
CAMPAÑA.
f, campaign ‖ ship's cruise ‖ duration or period
of employment (usually in terms of years) ‖
(business) year.
CAMPO.
m, camp ‖ field (in all senses) ‖ army or group
or party in political or military campaigns.
CAMPO DE CONCENTRACIÓN.
concentration camp.
CANALLA.
m, riffraff, bum ‖ gangster.
CANALLA ORGANIZADA.
gangsterism.
CANCELABLE.
adj, voidable, annullable, cancelable.
CANCELACIÓN.
f, cancellation ‖ annulment (of a public document, a registration of an obligation, etc.).
**CANCELACIÓN DE ANTECEDENTES
PENALES.**
expungement (of criminal record). May occur
if convict does not commit another crime after
serving sentence.
CANCELACIÓN DE ASIENTOS.
cancellation of registration or entry or filing on
books or in a registry.
CANCELACIÓN DE HIPOTECAS.
cancellation of the mortgage (on real property).
**CANCELACIÓN EN EL REGISTRO DE LA
PROPIEDAD.**
express cancellation of a title entry in real
property registry. May be total or partial.
CANCELAR.
v, to cancel, annul, void ‖ to revoke ‖ to discharge ‖ to expunge, abolish ‖ to pay, settle,
pay off.
CANCELAR UN CHEQUE.
to cancel a check.
CANCELAR LA FACTURA.
to pay or cancel a bill or invoice.
CANCILLER.
m, chancellor, head of state ‖ ambassador ‖

consul employee ‖ Minister of Foreign Affairs,
Secretary of State.
CANCILLERÍA.
f, Foreign Office (G.B.), department of state,
State Department (U.S.), governmental office
which is responsible for diplomatic action ‖
chancery ‖ chancellorship.
CANDADO.
m, predating clause (of a legislative bill), clause which fixes the effective date of the proposal at an earlier date.
CANDIDATO.
m, candidate.
CANGALLAR.
v, to steal minerals (from mines).
CANJE.
m, exchange, barter ‖ conversion (of negotiable instruments) ‖ clearing (of checks).
CANJE DE PRISIONEROS.
exchange of prisoners of war or hostages.
CANJEABLE.
adj, exchangeable, convertible.
CANJEAR.
v, to exchange, barter ‖ to convert (negotiable
instruments) ‖ to clear checks.
CANON.
m, canon, rule, norm, model ‖ precept ‖ rent,
lease payment (for farms) ‖ royalty payment.
**CANON
DE ARRENDAMIENTO.**
rent rate or payment.
CANON DE SUPERFICIE.
mining royalty, payment made for mining license.
CANTAR LA PALINODIA.
to retract something publicly.
CANTIDAD.
f, quantity, amount ‖ sum.
CANTIDAD ALZADA.
agreed sum or amount.
CANTIDAD DETERMINADA.
fixed amount.
CANTIDAD GARANTIZADA.
guaranteed amount.
CANTIDAD ILÍQUIDA.
unliquidated or undetermined amount.
CANTIDAD INDETERMINADA.
sum uncertain.
CANTIDAD LÍQUIDA.
liquid money ‖ liquid assets ‖ amount liquidated.

CANTÓN.
m, canton, district.

CAPACIDAD.
f, capacity ‖ space ‖ legal capacity ‖ legal qualification ‖ legal competency ‖ legal standing ‖ capacity (of ship).

CAPACIDAD CIVIL.
legal capacity ‖ legal competency.

CAPACIDAD CONTRIBUTIVA.
taxpaying capacity or ability.

CAPACIDAD DE ACTUAR.
See CAPACIDAD DE EJERCICIO.

CAPACIDAD DE DELINCUENCIA.
ability or predilection for delinquency or criminality.

CAPACIDAD DE DERECHO.
legal capacity ‖ legal capacity to possess a right or be subject to an obligation.

CAPACIDAD DE EJERCICIO.
capacity or ability to act.

CAPACIDAD DE HECHO.
legal capacity (of a person to exercise his or her legal rights independent of other persons).

CAPACIDAD DE LA MUJER CASADA.
legal capacity of a married woman. In some legal systems, marriage limits a woman's legal capacity and rights.

CAPACIDAD DE OBRAR.
See CAPACIDAD DE HECHO.

CAPACIDAD DE LAS PERSONAS JURÍDICAS.
legal capacity of legal entities.

CAPACIDAD DEL MENOR.
legal competency of a minor ‖ legal capacity of a minor.

CAPACIDAD FINANCIERA.
financial standing, credit rating.

CAPACIDAD JURÍDICA.
legal standing ‖ also see CAPACIDAD DE DERECHO.

CAPACIDAD LEGAL.
legal capacity (to possess or exercise designated rights).

CAPACIDAD PARA ARRENDAR.
capacity to grant a leasehold or rental.

CAPACIDAD PARA CELEBRAR ACTOS JURÍDICOS.
competency or capacity to enter into legal transactions.

CAPACIDAD PARA COMPRAR Y VENDER.
capacity to buy and sell.

CAPACIDAD PARA CONTRAER MATRIMONIO.
marital capacity, capacity to marry.

CAPACIDAD PARA CONTRATAR.
capacity to contract.

CAPACIDAD PARA DONAR.
capacity to give or donate.

CAPACIDAD PARA HIPOTECAR.
capacity to mortgage (one's property).

CAPACIDAD PARA LA TUTELA.
capacity to be guardian.

CAPACIDAD PARA OBLIGARSE.
capacity to obligate oneself.

CAPACIDAD PARA SER PARTE.
competency to be party to a lawsuit.

CAPACIDAD PARA SUCEDER.
capacity to inherit.

CAPACIDAD PARA TESTAR.
capacity to make a will.

CAPACIDAD PENAL.
criminal competency, competency to stand criminal trial (considering age, mental capacity, etc.).

CAPACIDAD PLENA.
full authority.

CAPACIDAD POLÍTICA.
right to exercise civil rights (e.g. of assembly meeting, petition, demonstration, free press, voting, etc.).

CAPACIDAD PROCESAL.
standing, legal capacity (to be party to a suit) ‖ capacity to sue and be sued.

CAPACIDAD SINDICAL.
capacity to be a union member.

CAPACIDAD TESTIFICAL.
capacity to act as a witness.

CAPACITACIÓN.
f, training, preparation, instruction.

CAPACITAR.
v, to empower, delegate, commission ‖ to train, qualify, prepare.

CAPARRA.
f, earnest money (if re real estate) ‖ down payment, pledge money.

CAPASUELDO.
m, discount for advance payment.

CAPAZ.
adj, capable, able, competent (either legally or otherwise).

CAPITACIÓN.
f, capitation ‖ head tax assessment ‖ per capita revenue assessment, poll tax assessment.

APITAL.
, capital city (of a nation, province, state) ‖ m, capital, wealth, principal ‖ wealth brought by husband to marriage ‖ adj, principal, major, primary, fundamental ‖ capital.
APITAL ACCIONARIO.
capital corresponding to stock.
APITAL ANTECEDENTE.
starting or original capital.
APITAL AUTORIZADO.
authorized capital.
APITAL CIRCULANTE.
operating or working capital.
APITAL COMANDITARIO.
capital of limited partner.
APITAL COMPUTABLE.
accountable capital.
APITAL CONGELADO.
frozen capital ‖ capital which has been attached by judicial or administrative order.
APITAL CUBIERTO.
paid-up capital.
APITAL DE LA SOCIEDAD CONYUGAL.
community property.
APITAL DE ROTACIÓN.
See CAPITAL CIRCULANTE.
APITAL DE USO.
capital goods.
APITAL DECLARADO.
stated or declared capital (of corporations).
APITAL DESEMBOLSADO.
issued capital.
APITAL DISPONIBLE.
disposable or free capital.
APITAL EFECTIVO.
See CAPITAL DESEMBOLSADO.
APITAL EN ACCIONES.
capital corresponding to issued stock.
APITAL EN GIRO.
operating or working capital.
APITAL ESCRITURADO.
See CAPITAL DECLARADO.
APITAL EXTRANJERO.
foreign capital.
APITAL FIJO.
fixed capital.
APITAL FUNDACIONAL.
beginning or original capital.
APITAL IMPRODUCTIVO.
non-working capital.

CAPITAL INICIAL.
initial or original capital (investment).
CAPITAL INMOBILIARIO.
capital in real property (which is leasable).
CAPITAL INMOVILIZADO.
See CAPITAL FIJO.
CAPITAL INTEGRADO.
paid-up capital.
CAPITAL LÍQUIDO.
net worth ‖ liquid assets.
CAPITAL MOBILIARIO.
capital in personal property.
CAPITAL NETO.
net worth.
CAPITAL NOMINAL.
See CAPITAL DECLARADO.
CAPITAL PRIVADO.
private capital or investment.
CAPITAL PRODUCTIVO.
working capital.
CAPITAL PROPIO.
equity capital.
CAPITAL PÚBLICO.
governmental capital ‖ capital belonging to government.
CAPITAL REALIZABLE.
See CAPITAL DISPONIBLE.
CAPITAL SOCIAL.
capital stock ‖ capital of a partnership ‖ nominal capital.
CAPITAL SUSCRITO.
subscribed capital.
CAPITAL VARIABLE.
variable capital. Opposed to stated capital.
CAPITALISMO.
m, capitalism.
CAPITALISTA.
m, f, capitalist ‖ owner of capital ‖ adj, capitalist.
CAPITALIZABLE.
adj, able to be capitalized (in corporations).
CAPITALIZACIÓN.
f, capitalization ‖ compounding (of interest to capital).
CAPITALIZACIÓN DE INTERESES.
See ANATOCISMO.
CAPITALIZACIÓN DE UTILIDADES.
capitalization of earnings or profits.
CAPITALIZAR.
v, to capitalize ‖ to compound (interest to principal).

CAPITÁN DE BUQUE.
ship captain.
CAPITÁN GENERAL.
commander-in-chief (of the armed forces).
CAPITIS DIMINUTIO.
m, diminished (legal) capacity, capitis diminutio.
CAPITULACIÓN.
f, capitulation, surrender ‖ agreement, settlement, pact.
CAPITULACIONES MATRIMONIALES.
antenuptial agreement or settlement ‖ marriage articles.
CAPITULACIONES DE MATRIMONIO.
See CAPITULACIONES MATRIMONIALES.
CAPITULADO.
m, governor or mayor who surrenders ‖ agreement to surrender ‖ adj, capitulated, surrendered.
CAPITULANTE.
m, surrenderor, capitulator ‖ accuser (of local authority) ‖ adj, capitulating.
CAPITULAR.
v, to capitulate, surrender ‖ to make an agreement or settlement or pact to negotiate a surrender ‖ to impeach ‖ to file charge of malfeasance.
CAPITULEAR.
v, to lobby.
CAPITULEO.
m, lobbying.
CAPITULERO.
m, lobbyist ‖ politician.
CAPÍTULO.
m, chapter ‖ title, item, heading ‖ meeting, assembly ‖ municipal council ‖ charge ‖ accusation.
CAPÍTULO DE CULPAS.
charges of malfeasance.
CAPTACIÓN.
f, understanding, comprehension ‖ reception, hearing (of sound) ‖ diversion ‖ winning of confidence, affection, or goodwill.
CAPTATORIA.
See INSTITUCIÓN CAPTATORIA.
CAPTURA.
f, capture, apprehension, seizure, arrest.
CARÁCTER.
m, character ‖ condition ‖ type, sort, species, genre ‖ personal qualities or characteristics (e.g. age, sex, etc.).

CARÁCTER PÚBLICO.
governmental function ‖ public character.
CÁRCEL.
f, jail, prison, dungeon.
CÁRCEL ESTATAL.
state prison.
CÁRCEL FEDERAL.
federal prison.
CÁRCEL PRIVADA.
prison where person(s) are held by private individuals under no color of legal right (e.g. f... purposes of retribution or for ransom).
CARCELAJE.
m, incarceration, imprisonment ‖ forced detention ‖ fee paid upon leaving prison.
CARCELERÍA.
f, forced detention (not necessarily in a prison) ‖ bail.
CARCELARIO.
adj, prison, jail, pertaining to prison or jail.
CARCELERO.
m, jailer, jail keeper, warden.
CAREAR.
v, to confront, bring face to face (to haste... truth finding process) ‖ to match, compar... check.
See CAREO.
CAREO.
m, confrontation of two witnesses or defer... dants with contradictory evidence in order t... evaluate the truthfulness of testimony (unde... court order).
CAREO DE TESTIGOS.
confrontation of witnesses.
CARESTÍA.
f, scarcity of food and other necessities ‖ in... flated prices (regarding goods and services o... general consumption).
CARGA.
f, load, cargo, freight ‖ charge, duty, tax ‖ bur... den, obligation, duty ‖ liability ‖ encumbranc... ‖ condition.
CARGA CONCEJIL.
obligation or tax imposed on all neighborhoo... residents.
CARGA DE JUSTICIA.
government obligation to indemnify the hol... ders of abolished legal interests.
CARGA DE LA AFIRMACIÓN.
burden of proof (to support statements made).

RGA DE LA CERTEZA.
urden of proof.
RGA DE LA DEMANDA.
bligation regarding the filing of suit.
RGA DE LA HERENCIA.
harge payable by a decedent's estate.
RGA DE LA PRUEBA.
urden of proof.
RGA DE BUQUES.
hip's cargo ‖ loading of cargo onto a ship.
RGA DE PAGO.
aying cargo (e.g. cargo, passengers, corres-
ondence).
RGA
EL FIDUCIARIO.
rustee's duties.
RGA DEL SEGURO.
bligation to insure.
RGA EN LA DONACIÓN.
ondition attached to a gift requiring inaction
r action by the donee.
RGA IMPOSITIVA.
ax burden.
RGA MÁXIMA.
naximum weight and size (of cargo).
RGA PERSONAL.
ersonal condition (requiring action or inac-
ion) ‖ personal debt.
RGA PROCESAL.
ondition of parties to an action (in order to
btain certain procedural benefits).
RGA PÚBLICA.
bligation owed to government (e.g. federal
ax).
RGA REAL.
eal property tax ‖ condition attached to real
state (requiring action or inaction).
RGA TRIBUTARIA.
See CARGA IMPOSITIVA.
RGA VECINAL.
ee CARGA CONCEJIL.
RGADILLAS.
, accrued interest, accumulated interest.
RGADOR.
n, shipper, carrier ‖ loader, conveyer.
RGAMENTO.
n, load, cargo, lading.
RGAR LA MANO.
, to overprice, overcharge ‖ to insist on the ef-
ectiveness of something ‖ to treat severely (in
rder to repress or as a habit).

CARGAREME.
m, receipt, proof of money received ‖ deposit
voucher.
CARGARSE.
v, to obligate oneself ‖ to take on an obligation
‖ to kill, murder ‖ to accept a debit.
CARGAS DE FAMILIA.
family expenses, expenses of a person whose
maintenance falls on the family.
CARGAS DE LA HERENCIA.
debts and costs of a decedent's estate.
CARGAS DE LA SOCIEDAD CONYUGAL.
See CARGAS DEL MATRIMONIO.
CARGAS DE LAS FINCAS.
expenses of a farm or rural property ‖ real
property encumbrance.
CARGAS DEL MATRIMONIO.
marital expenses ‖ expenses of maintaining
marital property.
CARGAS SOCIALES.
indirect labor costs (e.g. social security, medical expenses, etc).
CARGO.
m, position, commission, office, post ‖ debit,
total due ‖ charge, accusation ‖ clause which
imposes an extraordinary obligation ‖ affirmative obligation ‖ receipt and time stamped at
the bottom of legal documents by court clerks.
CARGO CONSOLIDADO.
omnibus count.
CARGO DE CONFIANZA.
office of trust ‖ fiduciary position.
CARGO DE LA PRUEBA.
burden of proof.
CARGO FIDUCIARIO.
fiduciary position.
CARGOS PÚBLICOS.
public offices (whether obligatory or voluntary).
CARGOS JUDICIALES.
charges, accusations (in a civil, criminal or administrative lawsuit) ‖ judicial offices, judicature.
CARICARILLO.
m, step-sisters and brothers (resulting from a
marriage of widow and widower)
CARNAL.
adj, blood, full ‖ related by blood ‖ sexual.
CARNÉ.
m, identification (document or card) ‖ membership card.

CARNÉ PROFESIONAL.
m, professional membership card ‖ identification document

CARPETA.
f, case file, file, folder ‖ document, bill, invoice.

CARRERA CRIMINAL.
f, criminal career.

CARRERA JUDICIAL.
judicial career ‖ judicial training or preparation.

CARRO CELULAR.
patrol wagon.

CARTA.
f, letter ‖ writ of a higher court ‖ written constitution, charter (of a nation) ‖ public document.

CARTA ABIERTA.
open letter ‖ draft for unlimited amount.

CARTA ACOMPAÑATORIA.
letter of transmittal.

CARTA ACORDADA.
court warning (issued by a higher court to advise a lower court of its failure to comply with its duties).

CARTA BLANCA.
carte blanche, unlimited power, full powers.

CARTA CERTIFICADA.
certified or registered letter.

CARTA COMERCIAL.
business letter.

CARTA CONFIDENCIAL.
confidential or personal letter.

CARTA CONFIRMATORIA.
confirming or confirmatory letter.

CARTA CONSTITUCIONAL.
constitutional charter (of a nation) ‖ articles of incorporation ‖ charter.

CARTA CONSTITUTIVA.
corporate charter.

CARTA CONTRATO.
letter agreement ‖ contract arrived at by mail.

CARTA CREDENCIAL.
credentials ‖ letter of credentials ‖ diplomatic or ambassadorial credentials.

CARTA DE AVISO.
notice.

CARTA DE AUTORIZACIÓN.
letter of authority.

CARTA DE CITACIÓN.
See CÉDULA DE CITACIÓN.

CARTA DE CIUDADANÍA.
naturalization papers, citizenship identification document (of naturalized citizen).

CARTA DE COMISIÓN.
delegation of special authority to a lower judge by superior court.

CARTA DE COMPROMISO.
letter of undertaking.

CARTA DE CRÉDITO.
bearer draft ‖ letter of credit.

CARTA DE CRÉDITO A PLAZO.
time letter of credit.

CARTA DE CRÉDITO A LA VISTA.
sight letter of credit.

CARTA DE CRÉDITO AUXILIAR.
ancillary letter of credit.

CARTA DE CRÉDITO CIRCULAR.
circular letter of credit.

CARTA DE CRÉDITO CONFIRMADO IRREVOCABLE.
confirmed irrevocable letter of credit.

CARTA DE CRÉDITO SIMPLE.
simple letter of credit.

CARTA DE CREENCIA.
credentials ‖ letter of credentials.

CARTA DE DERECHOS.
bill of rights.

CARTA DE DOTE.
dowry letter ‖ letter which details woman's dowry.

CARTA DE EMBARQUE.
bill of lading.

CARTA DE EMPLAZAMIENTO.
See CÉDULA DE EMPLAZAMIENTO.

CARTA DE ESPERA.
moratorium or extension letter, letter granting debtor an extension of time in which to pay.

CARTA DE GARANTÍA.
letter of guaranty.

CARTA DE GRACIA.
sale with agreement of repurchase.

CARTA DE INTENCIÓN.
letter of intent.

CARTA DE LEGOS.
See AUTO DE LEGOS.

CARTA DE MAR.
ship's papers, sea letter.

CARTA DE NATURALEZA.
See CARTA DE NATURALIZACIÓN.

CARTA DE NATURALIZACIÓN.
naturalization papers or certificate.

CARTA DE PAGO.
receipt of payment ‖ acquittance.
CARTA DE PAGO Y LASTO.
receipt (of payment) and transfer of creditor's rights (to third party who pays on debtor's behalf).
CARTA DE PERSONERÍA.
power of attorney.
CARTA DE POBREZA.
certificate of indigence.
CARTA DE PORTE.
bill of lading ‖ shipping agreement or contract.
CARTA DE PORTE A LA ORDEN.
order bill of lading.
CARTA DE PORTE AÉREO.
air waybill or bill of lading.
CARTA DE PORTE NOMINATIVA.
straight bill of lading.
CARTA DE PRIVILEGIO.
franchise, concession.
CARTA DE PROCURACIÓN.
See CARTA DE PERSONERÍA.
CARTA DE RECOMENDACIÓN.
letter of recommendation.
CARTA DE TRANSMISIÓN.
transmittal or cover letter.
CARTA DE TRANSPORTE AÉREO.
air waybill or bill of lading.
CARTA DE TUTORÍA.
letter of guardianship.
CARTA DE VENTA.
bill of sale, public document issued to prove a sales contract.
CARTA EJECUTORIA.
final sentence or judgment or decision ‖ document containing a final sentence or judgement or decision.
CARTA FIANZA.
letter of guarantee.
CARTA FORERA.
judicial or administrative decision or letter granting a privilege, exemption, or immunity ‖ judicial provision to allow one to bring suit within period of one year.
CARTA FUNDAMENTAL.
constitution, charter.
CARTA MISIVA.
letter, missive.
CARTA ORDEN.
writ (issued by a higher court to a lower judge, official or court) ‖ written order.

CARTA ORDEN DE CRÉDITO.
See CARTA DE CRÉDITO.
CARTA ORGÁNICA.
articles of incorporation (e.g. of a corporation).
CARTA PLOMADA.
letter or document sealed with lead.
CARTA PODER.
power of attorney or proxy (granted by letter).
CARTA PRECARIA.
real estate title (granted on basis of adverse possession for at least 30 years).
CARTA PUEBLA.
document which divides up land and grants such divisions to new settlers.
CARTA RECEPTORIA.
order or warrant to investigate ‖ search warrant.
CARTA RECREDENCIAL.
letter which is given by an ambassador or other minister to host government, upon relinquishing post.
CARTA REGISTRADA CON ACUSE DE RECIBO.
registered letter with receipt requested.
CARTA ROGATORIA.
letters rogatory.
CARTA TESTAMENTARIA.
letters testamentary.
CARTEL.
m, cartel, group monopoly. May be: DE PRECIOS (to fix prices) ‖ DE CONDICIONES (to set conditions of sale) ‖ DE CLIENTELA (to divide market) ‖ DE VENTA (to set price or percentage of market) ‖ DE COMPRA (to purchase together) ‖ DE LIMITACIÓN (to limit production).
CARTERA.
f, cabinet ministry, office of minister ‖ official identification document or book ‖ list of assets ‖ record, portfolio ‖ right to commission held by commissioned agent.
CARTERA DACTILAR.
record of fingerprints.
CARTERA DE COLOCACIONES.
portfolio.
CARTERA DE HACIENDA.
ministry of the treasury.
CARTERISTA.
m, pickpocket ‖ purse snatcher.

CARTILLA MILITAR.
f, draft registration document, military service papers.
See LIBRETA DE ENROLAMIENTO.

CARTULAR.
adj, of record, related to negotiable instruments.

CARTULARIO.
m, court clerk, notary public ‖ archivist ‖ registry, book of records ‖ adj, related to negotiable instruments.

CASA.
f, firm ‖ trading or commercial house ‖ house, home.

CASA DE AYUNTAMIENTO.
city or town hall.

CASA BANCARIA.
bank, banking house.

CASA CAMBIARIA.
money-exchange office.

CASA CENTRAL.
main or home office.

CASA CONSISTORIAL.
city hall.

CASA DE ACEPTACIONES.
acceptance house.

CASA DE AMONEDACIÓN.
mint.

CASA DE BANCA.
See CASA BANCARIA.

CASA DE BENEFICENCIA.
poorhouse ‖ hospital for the poor ‖ asylum.

CASA DE CITAS.
See CASA DE PROSTITUCIÓN.

CASA DE COMERCIO.
commercial business, business, firm.

CASA DE CONTRATACIÓN.
stock or commodity exchange.

CASA DE CORRECCIÓN.
reformatory.

CASA DE CORREOS.
post office.

CASA DE CUSTODIA.
low security prison, detention center.

CASA DE DEPÓSITO.
warehouse.

CASA DE DETENCIÓN.
jail, detention center (for those awaiting sentence)

CASA DE EMPEÑOS.
pawnshop.

CASA DE EXPÓSITOS.
orphanage.

CASA DE GOBIERNO.
president's house ‖ presidential estate.

CASA DE JUEGO.
gambling house or parlor, gaming establishment.

CASA DE LENOCINIO.
See CASA DE PROSTITUCIÓN.

CASA DE LIQUIDACIÓN.
clearing house.

CASA DE MONEDA.
mint, government manufacturer of monies, tax stamps, postal stamps, state lottery tickets, etc.

CASA DE PROSTITUCIÓN.
house of prostitution, whorehouse.

CASA DE RENTA.
rental house or property.

CASA DE TOLERANCIA.
house of prostitution or whorehouse where such activity is not considered to be strictly illegal.

CASA DEL PUEBLO.
town hall (in small villages) ‖ socialist party or union hall.

CASA EN COMÚN.
condominium property.

CASA HABITACIÓN.
right to board (given as emolument in certain fields of employment) ‖ residence, dwelling.

CASA HABITADA.
inhabited house.

CASA MATRIZ.
headquarters, main office, home office ‖ parent corporation.

CASA PATERNA.
parental home.

CASA SOLARIEGA.
homestead.

CASABLE.
adj, marriageable ‖ subject to CASACIÓN.

CASACIÓN.
f, repeal or nullification of a court decision made by the highest courts of the nation, exclusively on substantive grounds of interpretation and application of the law.

CASADA.
f, married woman (whether or not subsequently divorced or widowed).

CASADO.
m, married man ‖ adj, married.
CASADERO.
adj, of marriageable age.
CASAMIENTO.
m, marriage, wedding ‖ matrimony.
CASAMIENTO A SOBRE BIENES.
family agreement whereby two married couples, one of which is barren, agree to will their property to the other.
CASAMIENTO CONSENSUAL.
common-law marriage, marriage by simple agreement.
CASAMIENTO MORGANÁTICO.
morganatic marriage, marriage between a person of nobility and an untitled person.
CASAMIENTO POR ACUERDO Y COHABITACIÓN.
common-law marriage.
CASAMIENTO PUTATIVO.
putative marriage ‖ marriage which is void or voidable although entered into in good faith.
CASAR.
v, to marry, wed ‖ to void or annul or repeal a lower court ruling.
CASARSE.
v, to marry, get married.
CASI-CONTRATO.
m, quasi-contract.
CASO.
m, case, event ‖ case, lawsuit, legal action, question.
CASO DE LA LEY.
case or circumstance or contingency foreseen by the law.
CASO FORTUITO.
force majeure, act of God.
CASO INCIERTO.
force majeure, act of God, chance.
CASO OMISO.
casus omissus, contingency not covered by law.
CASO PENSADO.
premeditated action.
CASO PERDIDO.
hopeless case.
CASTIDAD.
f, abstention, celibacy (if unmarried or widowed or divorced) ‖ fidelity (in a marriage).
CASTIGABLE.
adj, punishable ‖ able to be fined.

CASTIGADOR.
m, punisher ‖ adj, punishing, punitive.
CASTIGAR.
v, to punish, chastise, impose a penalty, penalize ‖ to reduce, diminish (a budget, expense) ‖ to charge off, write off.
CSTIGO.
m, penalty, fine, punishment ‖ charge-off, write-off ‖ correction, amendment, depreciation.
CASTIGO CORPORAL.
corporal punishment.
CASTIGO EJEMPLAR.
punishment which serves as a public example.
CASTIGO MAYOR.
serious or severe punishment.
CASTRACIÓN.
f, castration.
CASUAL.
f, judicial order or decree to avoid attempts ‖ adj, casual ‖ accidental, occasional.
CASUALIDAD.
f, chance, coincidence.
CASUS BELLI.
m, casus belli, cause or reason or motive for war.
CATASTRAL.
adj, pertaining to CATASTRO.
CATASTRO.
m, real estate registry ‖ cadastre ‖ plat, plat map ‖ real estate survey.
CATÁSTROFE.
f, catastrophe.
CÁTEDRA.
f, department or faculty or school (in a university) ‖ (university) chair, professor's chair ‖ lectern ‖ professorship.
CATEDRÁTICO.
m, professor, person who holds a CÁTEDRA.
CATEGORÍA PROFESIONAL.
professional category, rating within a profession ‖ categories of professionals.
CAUCIÓN.
f, caution, precaution ‖ warning ‖ surety, guaranty, security, pledge ‖ bond, bail, bail bond.
CAUCIÓN DE ARRAIGO.
See FIANZA DE ARRAIGO.
CAUCIÓN DE BUENA CONDUCTA.
bail bond, bail, bond (of an accused).

CAUCIÓN DE CONDUCTA.
See CAUCIÓN DE BUENA CONDUCTA.

CAUCIÓN DE DAÑO INMINENTE.
construction bond, given by a party to his or her neighbor to indemnify the neighbor for any damage which may result from construction.

CAUCIÓN DE FIDELIDAD.
fidelity bond.

CAUCIÓN DE INDEMNIDAD.
indemnity bond.

CAUCIÓN DE LICITADOR.
bid bond.

CAUCIÓN DE RATO.
plaintiff's bond (or of attorney).

CAUCIÓN JURATORIA.
personal recognizance ‖ sworn agreement to comply with an obligation. Used in civil procedure where no bond is set.

CAUCIÓN PARA COSTAS.
bond placed for the payment of costs.

CAUCIÓN PERSONAL.
personal guaranty (of a third party).

CAUCIÓN PROCESAL.
pendente lite bond. May be DE ARRAIGO, DE CONDUCTA, DE RATO or an EMBARGO PREVENTIVO.

CAUCIÓN REAL.
security interest in property.

CAUCIONABLE.
adj, bailable.

CAUCIONAR.
v, to bail, bond, guarantee, pledge, secure, pledge ‖ to place bail.

CAUDAL.
m, wealth, estate, fortune, property.

CAUDAL HEREDITARIO.
decendent's estate.

CAUDAL RELICTO.
decendent's estate.

CAUDAL SOCIAL.
assets of a business association.

CAUDALES PÚBLICOS.
public assets ‖ state property held in money, securities, and similarly liquid assets.

CAUDILLAJE.
m, rule or governance or leadership by a caudillo.

CAUDILLISMO.
See CAUDILLAJE.

CAUDILLO.
m, caudillo, chief ‖ leader (at war) ‖ leader

CAUSA.
f, cause, cause of action ‖ origin ‖ action, la suit, case ‖ trial, litigation ‖ prosecution ‖ le basis of civil obligation (e.g. contract, tort, et ‖ purpose of an act or transaction, purpose entering into a contract (usually, but not ways, the equivalent of consideration).

CAUSA ACTUAL.
instant case.

CAUSA ADECUADA.
adequate or sufficient (contractual) consi ration.

CAUSA AJUSTADA.
See CAUSA ARREGLADA.

CAUSA ARREGLADA.
settled case.

CAUSA CIVIL.
civil lawsuit.

CAUSA CONCURRENTE.
concurrent cause ‖ concurrent case.

CAUSA CONOCIDA Y TERMINADA.
case heard and concluded.

CAUSA CONTINUA.
continuing consideration. See CAUSA.

CAUSA CONTINUADA.
continued lawsuit.

CAUSA CRIMINAL.
criminal lawsuit.

CAUSA DE ALMIRANTAZGO.
suit in admiralty.

CAUSA DE DIVORCIO.
divorce case.

CAUSA DE HONOR.
criminal lawsuit pertaining to victim's honor

CAUSA DE IMPUNIDAD.
basis of criminal immunity.

CAUSA DE INCULPABILIDAD.
basis for criminal excuse based on lack of i tent to commit crime and lack of negligence

CAUSA DE INIMPUTABILIDAD.
basis for criminal excuse based on lack capacity or the fact that the act is not imp table to defendant.

CAUSA DE INSOLVENCIA.
act of bankruptcy.

CAUSA DE JUSTIFICACIÓN.
basis of justification or excuse (of a crime).

CAUSA DE LA OBLIGACIÓN.
legal basis of civil liability ‖ purpose of enterir

nto a contract (usually, but not always, the equivalent of consideration).

AUSA DEL CONTRATO.
purpose of entering into a contract (usually, but not always, the equivalent of consideration).

AUSA DETERMINANTE.
decisive or main cause.

AUSA EFICIENTE.
principal cause.

AUSA ENJUICIADA.
case on or in trial.

AUSA EXIPIENDI.
grounds of exception.

AUSA EXPRESA.
express consideration. See CAUSA.

AUSA FIN.
purpose, end purpose. Similar to contractual consideration.

AUSA FINAL.
purpose, end purpose.

AUSA GRATUITA.
gratuitous consideration. See CAUSA.

AUSA ILÍCITA.
Illicit purpose of a contract, contractual purpose which is immoral, goes against the public welfare, or is illegal.

AUSA IMPRACTICABLE.
impossible consideration.

AUSA INADECUADA.
inadequate or insufficient consideration.

AUSA INDIRECTA.
remote cause, causa remota.

AUSA INMEDIATA.
See CAUSA PRÓXIMA.

AUSA INSUFICIENTE.
See CAUSA INADECUADA.

AUSA JUSTIFICADA.
just cause.

AUSA LÍCITA.
licit purpose, purpose which is moral, legal, and is in accord with the public welfare.

AUSA NOMINAL.
nominal consideration. See CAUSA.

AUSA NULA.
void basis, legal basis of civil liability which is void, illegal purpose ‖ purpose of entering a contract which is illegal.

AUSA ONEROSA.
valuable or good consideration. See CAUSA.

CAUSA PASADA.
past consideration. See CAUSA.

CAUSA POR EFECTUARSE.
executory consideration. See CAUSA.

CAUSA PRESENTE.
instant cause.

CAUSA PROBABLE.
probable cause.

CAUSA PRÓXIMA.
proximate cause.

CAUSA PÚBLICA.
public welfare.

CAUSA RAZONABLE.
reasonable consideration. See CAUSA

CAUSA REMOTA.
remote cause.

CAUSA SIMULADA.
fabricated or sham purpose (of a contract). See CAUSA DEL CONTRATO.

CAUSA SOBREVINIENTE.
supervening cause.

CAUSA SUFICIENTE.
adequate consideration. See CAUSA ‖ sufficient cause.

CAUSA TÁCITA.
implied consideration. See CAUSA.

CAUSA VALIOSA.
good or valuable consideration. See CAUSA.

CAUSADO.
See ACTO CAUSADO.

CAUSAHABIENTE.
m, assignee ‖ subrogee, successor ‖ legatee, heir ‖ recipient of another's right.

CAUSAL.
f, cause, motive ‖ adj, causal.

CAUSAL DE DIVORCIO.
grounds for divorce.

CAUSAL DE RECUSACIÓN.
grounds for challenge.

CAUSALES DE CASACIÓN.
bases for annulment (of a judgment).

CAUSALIDAD.
f, causality ‖ cause.

CAUSANTE.
m, assignor, subrogor ‖ predecessor ‖ taxpayer ‖ testator ‖ author, originator, one who causes.

CAUSAR.
v, to cause, produce an effect ‖ to sue.

CAUSAR ESTADO.
to definitively end a case.

CAUSAR IMPUESTO.
to be subject to tax.
CAUSAR INTERESES.
to bear interest.
CAUSAS APLAZADAS.
adjourned cases.
CAUSAS DE AGRAVACIÓN.
See CIRCUNSTANCIAS AGRAVANTES.
CAUSAS DE ATENUACIÓN.
See CIRCUNSTANCIAS ATENUANTES.
CAUSAS DE INIMPUTABILIDAD.
circumstances by which an accused is judged to be not responsible (e.g. minority).
CAUSAS DE IRRESPONSABILIDAD.
circumstances or conduct by which someone is deemed not to be liable (e.g. self-defense).
CAUSAS DE LA GUERRA.
causes of war.
CAUSATIVO.
adj, causative.
CAUSÍDICO.
adj, forensic, concerning lawsuit.
CAUTELA.
f, precaution, caution, care, reserve ‖ guaranty, bond. Usually used relative to a matter in litigation.
CAUTELA SOCINIANA.
testamentary clause whereby the property due the legal heir is encumbered, in exchange for which he may receive additional different benefits. The legal heir must choose between taking the encumbered property and the additional benefits together, and taking the property which is legally due him without encumbrances but without the additional benefits.
CAUTELAR.
v, to protect, safeguard ‖ adj, protecting, safeguarding, precautionary. Used to describe orders preventing damage to something or someone.
CAUTELARSE.
v, to take precautions.
CAUTIVERIO.
m, state of being captured or in captivity.
CAUTIVO.
m, captive, prisoner, prisoner with war ‖ adj, captive, imprisoned.
CAUTO.
adj, sage, wise, astute, prudent.

CECA.
f, mint, place where money is coined ‖ coin.
CEDENTE.
m, assignor, conveyor, transferor, grantor endorser.
CEDER.
v, to assign, give, transfer, convey (a right another for consideration or not) ‖ to con promise, cede, give in, capitulate ‖ to ma concessions ‖ to abandon, leave, relinquish.
CEDIBLE.
adj, transferable, assignable.
CEDIDO.
adj, assigned, transferred.
CÉDULA.
f, slip of paper ‖ citation, notice (issued by judicial official) ‖ notice of meeting, summo to a meeting ‖ personal identification doc ment ‖ document which confirms an oblig tion, especially a debt ‖ certificate ‖ offici document ‖ order ‖ bond.
CÉDULA ANTE DIEM.
summons to a meeting of the membersh scheduled for the following day.
CÉDULA DE ADUANA.
customs permit.
CÉDULA DE BANCO.
negotiable instrument or certificate of depos issued by a bank.
CÉDULA DE CAMBIO.
bill of exchange.
CÉDULA DE CAPITALIZACIÓN.
certificate issued by a BANCO CAPITALIZADO
CÉDULA DE CITACIÓN.
summons, subpoena.
CÉDULA DE CIUDADANÍA.
citizenship document or papers.
CÉDULA DE DILIGENCIAS.
order from higher court to lower court re questing factual investigation of matter.
CÉDULA DE DIVIDENDO.
dividend coupon.
CÉDULA DE EMPADRONAMIENTO.
registration certificate.
CÉDULA DE EMPLAZAMIENTO.
summons, subpoena.
CÉDULA DE FUNDADOR.
bond issued to a promoter for services rende red.
CÉDULA DE IDENTIDAD.
personal identification document.

ÉDULA DE NOTIFICACIÓN.
official notice of a cause of action, legal procedure or judgment.

ÉDULA DE PRIVILEGIO DE INVENCIÓN.
letters patent.

ÉDULA DE REQUERIMIENTO.
writ, order.

ÉDULA DE SUBSCRIPCIÓN.
subscription warrant.

ÉDULA DE TESORERÍA.
treasury bond or note.

ÉDULA FISCAL.
taxpayer's identification document.

ÉDULA HIPOTECARIA.
bond guaranteed by mortgage.

ÉDULA INMOBILIARIA.
mortgage certificate ‖ real-estate bond.

ÉDULA PERSONAL.
identification document.

ÉDULA TESTAMENTARIA.
codicil (to a will).

EDULAR.
v, to enlist, enroll, register.

ÉDULAS BENEFICIARIAS.
See CÉDULAS PREFERENTES.

ÉDULAS DE EMISIÓN.
See CÉDULAS PREFERENTES.

ÉDULAS DE INVERSIÓN.
investment securities.

ÉDULAS PREFERENTES.
founders' preferred shares (usually, with special powers).

CEDULACIÓN.
f, registration, filing ‖ publication ‖ inscription.

CEDULÓN.
m, edict, decree (posted on door of residence of fugitive from justice) ‖ public notice.

CELADOR DE PRISIONES.
m, jailer, warden.

CELDA.
f, cell.

CELDA DE CASTIGO.
cell for special punishment.

CELDA DE PAGO.
paid cells (sometimes available for political prisoners).

CELEBRACIÓN.
f, celebration ‖ execution, signing (of a document) ‖ praise.

CELEBRACIÓN DE MATRIMONIOS ILEGALES.
celebration of a de facto marriage ‖ celebration of a civil marriage which is null and void for failure to be carried out by a person with proper authority to marry.

CELEBRACIÓN DEL MATRIMONIO.
marriage ceremony ‖ civil or religious ceremony in which two parties declare their consent to marry before a governmental or religious authority ‖ marriage preparations ‖ wedding celebration.

CELEBRAR.
v, to celebrate ‖ to enter into (an agreement) ‖ to execute ‖ to hold (a meeting) ‖ to carry out.

CELEBRAR ACTOS.
to carry out actions or acts.

CELEBRAR ASAMBLEA.
to hold a meeting.

CELEBRAR ELECCIONES.
to hold elections.

CELEBRAR NEGOCIOS.
to carry out or transact business.

CELEBRAR UN ACUERDO.
to enter into or make an agreement.

CELEBRAR UN CONTRATO.
to make or enter into a contract.

CELEBRAR UN JUICIO.
to hold a trial.

CELEBRAR UN MATRIMONIO.
to solemnize a marriage.

CELEBRAR UNA AUDIENCIA.
to hold a hearing.

CELEBRAR UNA ELECCIÓN.
to hold an election.

CELEBRAR UNA ENTREVISTA.
to hold an interview.

CELEBRAR UNA JUNTA.
to hold a meeting.

CELEBRAR UNA SUBASTA.
to have an auction.

CELEBRAR UNA VISTA.
to hold a hearing.

CELESTINA.
f, bawd, madam, woman procurer.

CELIBATO.
m, celibacy, chastity ‖ bachelorhood.

CÉLIBE.
adj, celibate ‖ unmarried, unwed.

CEMENTERIO.
m, cemetery.
CENSAR.
v, to take a census ‖ to make a tax list (of residents).
CENSARIO.
m, person who pays a CENSO.
CENSATARIO.
m, taxpayer (based on land ownership), real estate taxpayer ‖ pledger ‖ lessee ‖ one who pays an annuity out of his estate.
CENSISTA.
m, census-taker ‖ tax assessor.
CENSO.
m, census ‖ tax, real estate or property tax ‖ leasehold, lease ‖ contract whereby an annuity is paid by the owner of property which has been mortgaged or pledged to secure payments made for money borrowed or property purchased. This obligation runs with the land.
CENSO COMÚN.
annuity contract secured by pledge of all property owned by a given person.
CENSO CONSIGNATIVO.
contract whereby an annuity is paid by the owner of property which has been mortgaged or pledged to secure payments for money loaned ‖ lease contract whereby the lessee agrees to make the payments out of the money received from the property.
CENSO DE BIENES.
inventory.
CENSO DE CONTRIBUYENTES.
tax roll or taxpayer list.
CENSO DE POBLACIÓN.
population census.
CENSO DE POR VIDA.
life annuity contract, CENSO imposed for the life of a person.
CENSO DE RIQUEZA.
inventory of property owned.
CENSO ELECTORAL.
voting list.
CENSO ENFITÉUTICO.
annuity contract made in exchange for use of land.
CENSO FRUCTUARIO.
annuity contract which is paid by transferring that produced on certain real estate to the creditor.

CENSO GRACIOSO.
annuity contract given gratuitously which runs with the land or is payable from fruits of the land.
CENSO IRREDIMIBLE.
irredeemable CENSO.
CENSO MIXTO.
CENSO with additional personal guaranty of payer.
CENSO PECUNIARIO.
CENSO which is payable in a predetermined amount of money.
CENSO PERPETUO.
perpetual CENSO.
CENSO PERSONAL.
annuity contract which runs with the person, not with the land. Opposed to CENSO REAL.
CENSO REAL.
true CENSO, annuity contract which runs with the land not with the person. Opposed to CENSO PERSONAL.
CENSO REDIMIBLE.
redeemable CENSO.
CENSO RESERVATIVO.
sale of real property which is subject to payment of annual payments secured by a CENSO on the property.
CENSO TEMPORAL.
CENSO for limited period of time.
CENSO VITALICIO.
See CENSO DE POR VIDA.
CENSOR.
m, censor, critic.
CENSUAL.
adj, pertaining to CENSO.
CENSUALISTA.
m, annuitant ‖ recipient of an annuity or CENSO.
CENSUARIO.
m, payer of a CENSO.
CENSURADOR.
m, censor, censurer, critic ‖ adj, censorious, critical.
CENSURA.
f, censure ‖ censorship ‖ position of censor ‖ decision or judgment of a censor.
CENSURAR.
v, to censure, criticize ‖ to judge a work or thing.
CENTRALIZACIÓN ADMINISTRATIVA.
f, administrative centralization.

CENTRALIZACIÓN POLÍTICA.
f, political centralization ‖ executive and legis-
ative centralization.

CEREMONIA.
f, ceremony ‖ formalization ‖ protocol, formality.

CEREMONIAL.
m, book or document in which ceremonies are
reported ‖ protocol ‖ adj, ceremonial.

CERRADO.
m, enclosed or fenced-in garden ‖ adj, closed,
hidden ‖ protected ‖ restricted, reserved ‖
obscure ‖ narrow-minded, obstinate.

CERRAR UNA CUENTA.
to close or liquidate an account.

CERTEZA.
f, certainty.

CERTEZA LEGAL.
legal certainty.

CERTIFICABLE.
adj, certifiable.

CERTIFICACIÓN.
f, certification, attestation, sworn declaration ‖
testimonial or documentary proof of the truth
of an issue ‖ registration or certification (of
mail sent).

CERTIFICACIÓN DE AGENTE DE BOLSA.
stock broker's certificate.

CERTIFICACIÓN DE CARGAS.
certificate of real estate encumbrances ‖
abstract of encumbrances prepared by Real
Property Registry.

CERTIFICACIÓN DE DOMINIO.
title, title papers, certificate of title, certificate
of ownership (of federal state and municipal
governments and other public entities).

CERTIFICACIÓN DE SERVICIOS.
certification of work being performed ‖ proof
of services being rendered.

CERTIFICACIÓN DEL REGISTRO CIVIL.
certification or official authorization of the
Civil Registry.

CERTIFICACIÓN DEL REGISTRO DE LA
PROPIEDAD.
certificate of title. May be LITERALES (stating
the entries registered); or EN RELACIÓN (stating what needs to be done for a valid entry to
be registered).

CERTIFICADO.
m, certificate (e.g. to practice a profession) ‖
certified or registered mail ‖ certificate, war-

rant ‖ declaration, affidavit of a special notary
public (as to the truth of the matter before
him) ‖ adj, certified ‖ registered ‖ attested to.

CERTIFICADO CATASTRAL.
certificate of real estate filing.

CERTIFICADO DE ACCIONES.
stock certificate.

CERTIFICADO DE ADEUDO.
certificate of indebtedness.

CERTIFICADO DE ADICIÓN.
certificate of patent improvement.

CERTIFICADO DE AVALÚO.
appraisal certificate or statement.

CERTIFICADO DE AVERÍAS.
average statement.

CERTIFICADO DE BUENA
CONDUCTA.
letter or certificate of good conduct (issued by
the police).

CERTIFICADO DE CAMBIO.
exchange certificate.

CERTIFICADO DE CIUDADANÍA.
citizenship papers.

CERTIFICADO DE CONSTITUCIÓN.
certificate of (corporate) incorporation.

CERTIFICADO DE DEFUNCIÓN.
death certificate.

CERTIFICADO DE DEPÓSITO.
certificate of deposit, deposit slip ‖ warehouse
deposit document ‖ warrant ‖ bond note.

CERTIFICADO DE DIVISAS.
foreign exchange certificate.

CERTIFICADO DE MATRIMONIO.
marriage certificate.

CERTIFICADO DE NACIMIENTO.
birth certificate.

CERTIFICADO DE NATIMUERTO.
stillbirth certificate.

CERTIFICADO DE NECESIDAD.
certificate of necessity.

CERTIFICADO DE ORIGEN.
certificate of origin (of a ship or good).

CERTIFICADO DE PROPIEDAD.
ownership certificate ‖ deed (re: real estate).

CERTIFICADO DE PROTESTO.
certificate of protest.

CERTIFICADO DE SESIÓN.
minutes of a meeting.

CERTIFICADO DE TRABAJO.
certificate of work performed, proof of services rendered.

CERTIFICADO DEL TESORO.
treasury note.
CERTIFICADO DE UTILIDAD PÚBLICA.
certificate of public convenience or use.
CERTIFICADO PRENUPCIAL.
certificate of pre-marital medical examination.
CERTIFICAR.
v, to certify ‖ to register (mail) ‖ to attest, bear witness, swear to.
CERTIFICAR UNA FIRMA.
to witness or certify a signature.
CERTIFICATORIO.
adj, certificatory, certifying.
CESACIÓN.
f, cessation, discontinuance ‖ suspension ‖ end, finale ‖ abandonment.
CESACIÓN DE HOSTILIDADES.
cessation of or end or halt to hostilities.
CESACIÓN DE LA ACCIÓN.
dropping or discontinuance of legal action.
CESACIÓN DE PAGOS.
suspension of payments. See SUSPENSIÓN DE PAGOS. Constitutes an act of bankruptcy.
CESACIÓN DEL BENEFICIO DE INVENTARIO.
cessation of rights implicit in BENEFICIO DE INVENTARIO. May occur by express renunciation of inheritor, or as a result of hiding assets, improper sale or gift of property, or the improper encumbering of property.
CESACIÓN DEL PROCEDIMIENTO.
discontinuance of legal proceedings.
CESANTE.
m, dismissed government employee ‖ adj, unemployed, jobless ‖ dismissed, laid off.
CESANTÍA.
f, dismissal or severance of a government employee ‖ severance pay.
CESE.
m, discontinuance, cessation.
CESIBILIDAD.
f, transferability, alienability, disposability, assignability.
CESIBLE.
adj, transferable, alienable, disposable, assignable.
CESIÓN.
f, transfer, alienation, disposal, assignment, conveyance ‖ concession, grant.
CESIÓN ACTIVA.
assignment of a right.

CESIÓN CONTRACTUAL DE BIENES.
voluntary assignment of property.
CESIÓN DE ACCIONES.
transfer of shares ‖ transfer of rights or claims
CESIÓN DE BIENES.
abandonment or assignment for benefit o creditors, general assignment by contract o court order.
CESIÓN DE LA CLIENTELA.
transfer of good will (with an agreement not t compete in surrounding area) ‖ transfer c clients (of business).
CESIÓN DE CRÉDITOS.
assignment of credit or claim to monies owed (which may occur with or without debtor' consent) ‖ extension of credit.
CESIÓN DE CRÉDITOS LITIGIOSOS.
assignment of claim in litigation.
CESIÓN DE DERECHOS.
assignment of rights.
CESIÓN DE DERECHOS Y ACCIONES.
assignment of right and actions.
CESIÓN DE DESPACHO.
transfer of a law firm.
CESIÓN DE TERRITORIO.
transfer of territory of one nation to another.
CESIÓN DE TÍTULOS MERCANTILES.
assignment of negotiable instrument (by creditor).
CESIÓN DE ARRENDAMIENTO.
assignment of lease.
CESIÓN DE CRÉDITO HIPOTECARIO.
assignment of loan secured by a mortgage.
CESIÓN DE SALARIO.
assignment of employee's wages to a creditor.
CESIÓN DE SUELDO.
See CESIÓN DE SALARIO.
CESIÓN GENERAL.
general assignment.
CESIÓN HEREDITARIA.
transfer of inheritance.
CESIÓN JUDICIAL DE BIENES.
assignment of property by court order.
CESIÓN LIBRE.
absolute assignment conveyance.
CESIÓN PASIVA.
transfer of a debt.
CESIÓN POR PLANTACIÓN.
temporary transfer of land for cultivation (which land, after a period of years, is retransferred in part to the original owner, the

emainder staying with the cultivator/trans-
eree).

SIÓN PRO TANTO.
ssignment pro tanto.

SIÓN SIN CONDICIONES.
ee CESIÓN LIBRE.

SIÓN VOLUNTARIA.
oluntary assignment.

SIONARIO.
a, assignee, transferee, grantee.

SIONARIO CONJUNTO O
ANCOMUNADO.
oassignee, joint assignee.

SIONARIO DE BIENES DEL
ALLIDO.
ssignee of a property of a bankrupt estate.

SIONARIO
E DERECHO.
ssignee in law.

SIONARIO DE HECHO.
ssignee in fact.

SIONISTA.
a, assignor, grantor, transferor.

A.
bbreviation of COMPAÑÍA (company).

CLO ECONÓMICO.
n, business cycle.

EGO.
n, adj, blind.

ENCIA PROCESAL.
, science of civil procedure.

ENCIAS JURÍDICAS.
, jurisprudence, science of law.

ERRE.
n, zipper ‖ closure ‖ closing-up ‖ (employer)
ock-out, shut-down of industry or business
or economic reasons or labor-related pro-
olems.

ERRE DEL REGISTRO DE LA
PROPIEDAD.
closing hour of the real estate registry ‖ refusal
o register (in the real estate registry.)

ERRE PATRONAL.
ock-out (by employer).

RCUITO.
n, circuit ‖ judicial circuit.

RCUITO JUDICIAL.
udicial circuit ‖ circuit court.

RCUITO PROMISCUO.
circuit court (which tries both civil and criminal cases).

CIRCULACIÓN.
f, circulation (of money, securities, goods) ‖
traffic.

CIRCULACIÓN DE LIBROS OBSCENOS.
circulation of obscene books or materials, act
of publishing or manufacture or reproduction
or exhibition of, or otherwise trafficking, in
obscene books, images or other objects.

CIRCULANTE.
m, currency ‖ adj, circulating.

CIRCULAR.
f, order or regulation (usually issued by a
governmental entity) ‖ letter, communication
‖ notice, warning ‖ v, to circulate, move ‖ to
circulate (goods, documents, etc.)

CIRCUNSCRIPCIÓN.
f, district (electoral, administrative, etc.) ‖
limitation, circumscription.

CIRCUNSCRIPCIÓN JUDICIAL.
judicial district.

CIRCUNSTANCIAL.
adj, circumstantial.

CIRCUNSTANCIAS.
f, circumstances.

CIRCUNSTANCIAS AGRAVANTES.
aggravating circumstances (in criminal law).

CIRCUNSTANCIAS ATENUANTES.
extenuating circumstances (in criminal law).

CIRCUNSTANCIAS EXIMENTES.
justifying or exculpatory circumstances.

CIRCUNSTANCIAS MODIFICATIVAS.
modifying circumstances, circumstances
which change the treatment of a case.

CIRCUNVENCIÓN DE MENORES.
See ABUSO DE MENORES.

CISMA.
m, schism, division ‖ discord, dissension.

CITA.
f, meeting ‖ date, appointment ‖ citation, cite,
reference ‖ subpoena, summons.

CITACIÓN.
f, citation, cite, reference ‖ summons, subpoena ‖ notice of a meeting ‖ quotation.

CITACIÓN A COMPARECER.
summons to appear ‖ subpoena.

CITACIÓN A JUICIO.
(court) summons.

CITACIÓN A LICITADORES.
call for bids, invitation to bidders.

CITACIÓN ANTE DIEM.
notice the day prior to something.

CITACIÓN DE REMATE.
notice of public sale, public auction notice (issued under judicial order).

CITACIÓN PARA SENTENCIA.
summons (of the plaintiff and defendant) to hear judgment.

CITACIÓN POR EDICTO.
service by publication.

CITACIÓN Y EMPLAZAMIENTO.
summons.

CÍTANSE OPOSITORES.
objections called for.

CÍTANSE POSTORES.
bids invited.

CITAR.
v, to cite, refer to ‖ to summon, subpoena ‖ to give notice (of a meeting) ‖ to make an appointment, date or engagement ‖ to quote.

CITAR A COMPARENDO.
to summon to appear.

CITAR A JUNTA.
to call a meeting.

CITAR A UNO PARA ESTRADOS.
to summon a party in default by public notice.

CITATORIA.
f, summons, subpoena, citation.

CITATORIO.
adj, pertaining to a summons or subpoena or citation.

CIUDAD.
f, city, town.

CIUDADANÍA.
f, citizenship, nationality ‖ people, citizens.

CIUDADANO.
m, citizen.

CIUDADANO NATIVO.
native citizen.

CIUDADANO POR NACIMIENTO.
See CIUDADANO NATIVO.

CIUDADANO POR NATURALIZACIÓN.
naturalized citizen.

CIUDADANO POR OPCIÓN.
person who is born abroad and later chooses the nationality of one of his parents.

CIVIL.
m, citizen ‖ member of National Guard ‖ adj, civil (as opposed to religious, military, criminal, public or governmental).

CIVILISTA.
m, attorney who specializes in civil law ‖ adj, specializing in or pertaining to civil law.

CIVISMO.
m, civic conscience, patriotism.

CLAN.
m, clan, tribe ‖ group.

CLANDESTINIDAD.
f, secrecy, clandestinity, surreptitiousness.

CLANDESTINO.
adj, clandestine, secret.

CLARO.
adj, true, evident, clear.

CLASE.
f, class ‖ type, kind ‖ level, degree ‖ rank (school) class, lesson ‖ lecture hall, classroor ‖ class, lecture, lesson ‖ totality of non-com missioned officers or soldiers who are induc ted into military service in a given year.

CLASE SOCIAL.
social class or level or rank.

CLASES PASIVAS.
non-working class or group of persons, class o people who receive income without workin; (e.g. retirees, disabled persons).

CLASIFICACIÓN.
f, classification.

CLASIFICACIÓN DE BUQUES.
classification of ships or vessels.

CLASIFICACIÓN DE GRAVÁMENES.
marshaling or prioritization of liens.

CLASIFICAR.
v, to classify, sort, grade, rate.

CLASIFICAR BIENES.
to marshal assets.

CLAUSTRO.
m, council made up of the rector or dean, pro fessors and graduates of a given university.

CLAUSTRO MATERNO.
womb.

CLÁUSULA.
f, clause, article (of a contract, regulation, law. etc).

CLÁUSULA A LA ORDEN.
order clause, clause which makes commercia paper negotiable with the words "to the order of".

CLÁUSULA ACCESORIA.
clause of secondary importance ‖ additional agreement (e.g. guaranty).

CLÁUSULA ACCIDENTAL.
accessory clause ‖ clause which is not necessary for contractual validity.

CLÁUSULA AD CAUTELAM.
testamentary clause which invalidates all prior wills.
CLÁUSULA AMARILLA.
yellow-dog clause (in employment contracts).
CLÁUSULA AMBIGUA.
ambiguous clause.
CLÁUSULA ANTIRRENUNCIA.
antiwaiver clause.
CLÁUSULA ARBITRARIA.
arbitrary clause.
CLÁUSULA AUTÓNOMA.
unrelated article (in a law).
CLÁUSULA BELGA DEL ATENTADO.
Literally, Belgian clause of attempt, clause whereby an attempted homicide or assassination of a foreign head of state or member of his family is not considered to be a political crime for purposes of extradition. If it were deemed to be a political crime, such would usually prohibit extradition.
CLÁUSULA CONMINATORIA.
penalty clause (contract).
CLÁUSULA C.&.F.
cost and freight clause (contract).
CLÁUSULA C.I.F.
cost, insurance and freight clause (contract).
CLÁUSULA CODICILAR.
codicil (to a will).
CLÁUSULA COMPROMIŠARIA.
See CLÁUSULA COMPROMISORIA.
CLÁUSULA COMPROMISORIA.
arbitration clause ‖ clause by which the parties agree to submit disputes to arbitration.
CLÁUSULA DE ARBITRAJE FORZOSO.
compulsory arbitration clause.
CLÁUSULA DE ARREPENTIMIENTO.
rescission clause.
CLÁUSULA DE ATRIBUCIÓN.
jurisdiction clause, choice of jurisdiction clause, clause by which the parties agree to the jurisdiction of the court which shall settle any disputes.
CLÁUSULA DE CADUCIDAD.
expiration or termination clause.
CLÁUSULA DE CELIBATO.
celibacy clause ‖ clause requiring the employee to waive his salary if he or she gets married.
CLÁUSULA DE CONFIANZA.
clause naming executor or executrix.

CLÁUSULA DE CONSTITUTO.
clause acknowledging that possession of property is held on behalf of another person.
CLÁUSULA DE DESCUBIERTO.
deductible clause (insurance).
CLÁUSULA DE ENCADENAMIENTO.
exclusivity clause, clause which ensures long-term exclusivity of distribution to certain clients through a series of short term contracts ‖ tying clause.
CLÁUSULA DE ESCAPE.
escape clause.
CLÁUSULA DE ESQUIROL.
See CLÁUSULA AMARILLA.
CLÁUSULA DE ESTILO.
customary clause, clause which is included due to the custom, law, or practice of a country.
CLÁUSULA DE EXCLUSIÓN SINDICAL.
closed shop clause.
CLÁUSULA DE EXCLUSIVA.
exclusive territory clause, clause which limits area in which buyer may resell goods purchased.
CLÁUSULA DE EXCLUSIVIDAD SINDICAL.
closed shop clause.
CLÁUSULA DE FRANCO FÁBRICA.
ex-factory clause.
CLÁUSULA DE INALIENABILIDAD.
non-transfer clause, clause by which the transferee is prohibited from conveying the property.
CLÁUSULA DE INDIVISIÓN.
non-division clause, clause by which the transferee is prohibited from dividing the property.
CLÁUSULA DE IRRESPONSABILIDAD.
clause excluding liability.
CLÁUSULA DE MEJOR COMPRADOR.
better price clause ‖ clause by which a sales contract is voided if a better price for the same product is found within a specific time.
CLÁUSULA DE NACIÓN MAS FAVORECIDA.
most-favored-nation clause.
CLÁUSULA DE NO COMPETENCIA.
non-competition clause.
CLÁUSULA DE NO NEGOCIABILIDAD.
clause which prohibits negotiability.
CLÁUSULA DE PAGO A MEJOR FORTUNA.
clause allowing obligor to comply when he or

she is in an economic position to do so. See BENEFICIO DE COMPETENCIA.

CLÁUSULA DE PAGO CUANDO EL DEUDOR QUIERA.
clause allowing obligor to comply when he or she wishes to.

CLÁUSULA DE PAGO CUANDO EL DEUDOR PUEDA.
clause requiring obligor to comply when he or she is first able to.
See BENEFICIO DE COMPETENCIA.

CLÁUSULA DE PRECARIO.
loan clause ‖ clause which indicates that the transfer is a loan at will, and that the true owner can repossess it any time.

CLÁUSULA DE REPOSICIÓN.
repossession clause.

CLÁUSULA DE RESERVA DEL DOMINIO.
See PACTO DE RESERVA DE DOMINIO.

CLÁUSULA DE SALVEDAD.
saving clause.

CLÁUSULA DE VALOR EN CUENTA.
for-value clause (in negotiable instruments), clause which creates a presumption that the maker or drafter has received value for the negotiable instrument.

CLÁUSULA DE VALOR ORO.
gold clause (in which the rate is tied to the price of gold).

CLÁUSULA DE VALOR RECIBIDO.
value received clause, clause which indicates that the maker or drafter of a negotiable instrument has received value.

CLÁUSULA DE VIUDEDAD.
clause prohibiting marriage (after death of one of the spouses).

CLÁUSULA DEROGATIVA.
clause in a will declaring invalid any subsequent will.

CLÁUSULA DEROGATORIA.
nullifying article.
See also CLÁUSULA AD CAUTELUM.

CLÁUSULA ESENCIAL.
clause essential to a valid contract.

CLÁUSULA EX ... .
delivery clause.

CLÁUSULA F.A.S.
free along side clause.

CLÁUSULA FIDEICOMISARIA.
clause creating a FIDEICOMISO in a will.

CLÁUSULA F.O.B.
free on board clause.

CLÁUSULA F.O.R.
free on railway clause.

CLÁUSULA F.O.T.
free on train clause.

CLÁUSULA LEONINA.
unconscionable clause. Usually applied to business association contracts.

CLÁUSULA LIBERATORIA.
clause which determines when and how an obligation will be extinguished.

CLÁUSULA LIBRE DE AVERÍAS.
(insurance) exclusion clause for minor damage.

CLÁUSULA LIBRE DE HOSTILIDADES.
(insurance) exclusion clause for war and other hostilities.

CLÁUSULA MONETARIA.
floating rate clause.

CLÁUSULA NEUTRA.
neutral clause, clause which adopts law of other agreement (in collective bargaining agreements).

CLÁUSULA ORO.
gold payment clause, clause requiring payment in gold.

CLÁUSULA PENAL.
penalty clause.

CLÁUSULA PREVISIONAL.
clause creating fringe social security benefits for employees.

CLÁUSULA POTESTATIVA.
clause which may or may not be included in a contract ‖ see CONDICIÓN POTESTATIVA.

CLÁUSULA PRINCIPAL.
principal clause, clause of greatest importance to the contract.

CLÁUSULA PROHIBITIVA.
prohibitive clause, negative condition (in will or other transfer).

CLÁUSULA RESCISORIA.
rescission or termination clause ‖ clause which rescinds a contract.

CLÁUSULA RESOLUTIVA.
See CLÁUSULA RESOLUTORIA.

CLÁUSULA RESOLUTORIA.
cancellation or breach of contract clause, clause which states that the contract is rescinded if one of the parties breaches the contract.

CLÁUSULA SALARIAL.
salary or payment clause (in employment contract).

CLÁUSULA SEGÚN AVISO.
clause requiring drawer to inform payor of the obligation to pay a draft.

CLÁUSULA SIN AVISO.
clause stating that the obligation to pay the draft does not depend on notice.

CLÁUSULA SIN COMPROMISO.
clause making an offer revocable or non-binding.

CLÁUSULA SINDICAL.
union clause, clause which is required by a union related to such union's rights.

CLÁUSULA SOCINIANA.
See CAUTELA SOCINIANA.

CLÁUSULAS DE ESTILO.
customary or standard clauses.

CLAUSULADO.
m, series of clauses.

CLAUSURA.
f, closing session (of court, congress, meetings) ‖ closure of a business.

CLAUSURA DE SESIONES.
adjournment.

CLAUSURA MERCANTIL.
suspension of business ‖ business closure.

CLEMENCIA.
f, clemency.

CLEPTOMANÍA.
f, kleptomania.

CLEPTOMANÍACO.
See CLEPTÓMANO.

CLEPTÓMANO.
m, kleptomaniac.

CLIENTE.
m, client, customer.

CLIENTELA.
f, clientele ‖ protection, patronage.

COACCIÓN.
f, coercion, compulsion, duress, pressure.

COACCIÓN EN EL MATRIMONIO.
coercion to marry.

COACCIÓN EN LOS CONTRATOS.
contractual duress.

COACCIÓN EN LOS TESTAMENTOS.
testamentary duress, duress to sign a will.

COACCIONAR.
v, to compel, coerce, pressure.

COACREEDOR.
m, joint creditor.

COACTIVO.
adj, coercive, compelling.

COACTOR.
m, co-plaintiff, joint plaintiff ‖ tax collector ‖ bid collector at auction.

COACUSADO.
m, co-defendant, joint defendant (in a criminal action) ‖ adj, jointly accused. May be charged with same or different crimes which arise out of the same act.

COACUSADOR.
m, joint complainant, co-complainant (in a criminal case) ‖ co-counsel (for the prosecution, either in accusatory or prosecuting phase).

COACUSAR.
v, to accuse jointly.

COADJUTOR.
m, assistant, helper.

COADMINISTRADOR.
m, co-administrator.

COADYUVANTE.
m, third party (to an action). May be either third party defendant or third party plaintiff.

COADYUVAR.
v, to contribute, assist, help ‖ to join (a plaintiff or a defendant in ongoing litigation).

COAFIANZAMIENTO.
m, joint or co-bonding, bonding with another ‖ co-guaranteeing.

COALBACEA.
m, f, co-executor (male), co-executrix (female). May be MANCOMUNADO (joint), SUCESIVO (successive) or SOLIDARIO (joint and several).

COAGENTE.
m, joint agent.

COALICIÓN.
m, coalition, alliance, union, confederation (e.g. of people, businesses, nations, etc.).

COARRENDADOR.
m, joint lessor, joint landlord, co-lessor.

COARRENDATARIO.
m, co-lessee, co-tenant, joint tenant.

COARTACIÓN.
f, limitation, restriction.

COARTADA.
f, alibi.

COARTAR.
v, to limit, restrict (e.g. liberties, rights).
COASEGURADOR.
m, co-insurer.
COASEGURO.
m, double insurance, insurance of two or more policies regarding the same risk.
COASOCIADO.
m, partner, associate ‖ adj, associated.
COASOCIAR.
v, to associate with.
COAUTOR.
m, co-author ‖ accomplice, collaborator ‖ accessory.
COAVALISTA.
m, f, co-guarantor.
COBARDÍA.
f, cowardice.
COBRABILIDAD.
f, collectibility.
COBRABLE.
adj, collectable, recoverable (either because the debt has matured or because the debtor is solvent even if the debt is not mature).
COBRADERO.
See COBRABLE.
COBRADOR.
m, collection agent, bill collector ‖ bank teller ‖ payee.
COBRADOR DE IMPUESTOS.
tax collector.
COBRANZA.
f, collection, recovery (of monies owed) ‖ exaction ‖ cashing (of a check, etc.).
COBRAR.
v, to collect, recover, recoup, retrieve ‖ to acquire, obtain ‖ to charge, bill ‖ to cash (a check).
COBRO.
m, collection, recovery (of a debt), recoupment ‖ acquisition.
COBRO DE LO INDEBIDO.
unjust enrichment, improper receipt (of money or things) ‖ receipt of something by error.
COCESIONARIO.
m, co-assignee ‖ joint assignee.
COCIENTE ELECTORAL.
m, electoral proportion, number of votes necessary to elect a person to office.

CODELINCUENCIA.
f, partnership in crime ‖ complicity.
CODELINCUENTE.
m, partner in crime. May be an accesso before the fact, accomplice, or accessory aft the fact.
CODEMANDADO.
m, co-respondent, co-defendant, joint defe dant.
CODEUDOR.
m, joint debtor.
CODICILIO.
See CODICILO.
CODICILO.
m, codicil ‖ last wishes (made prior to or aft a will, with fewer formalities, to add to, su tract from, or clarify will). Frequently not e forceable.
CODIFICACIÓN.
f, codification.
CODIFICADOR.
m, codifier ‖ codification, digest ‖ adj, codif ing.
CODIFICADOR ARANCELARIO.
schedule of customs duties.
CODIFICAR.
v, to codify.
CÓDIGO.
m, code, digest (of laws, regulations, etc).
CÓDIGO AERONÁUTICO.
aviation code.
CÓDIGO ALIMENTARIO.
code regulating the production, manufactur and sale of foodstuffs.
CÓDIGO CIVIL.
civil code (covers personal rights, propert rights, non-commercial contracts, torts, famil law, wills, and estates).
CÓDIGO DE ADUANAS.
customs code.
CÓDIGO DE CIRCULACIÓN.
See CÓDIGO DEL CAMINO.
CÓDIGO DE COMERCIO.
commercial code (covers business and som corporate law, bankruptcy, business associa tions, insurance and occasionally admiralt law).
CÓDIGO DE CONSTRUCCIONES.
See CÓDIGO DE EDIFICACIÓN.
CÓDIGO DE EDIFICACIÓN.
building code.

DIGO DE ENJUICIAMIENTO.
le of trial procedure.
DIGO DE ÉTICA PROFESIONAL.
le of professional ethics.
DIGO DE JUSTICIA MILITAR.
litary code of justice.
DIGO DE JUSTINIANO.
stinian code.
DIGO DE LA FAMILIA.
mestic relations code.
DIGO DE LAS QUIEBRAS.
nkruptcy law.
DIGO DE TRÁNSITO.
hicular traffic code.
DIGO DE POLICÍA.
lice regulation code.
DIGO DE PROCEDIMIENTO CIVIL.
de of civil procedure.
DIGO DE PROCEDIMIENTO NAL.
de of criminal procedure.
DIGO DE PRUEBAS.
w of evidence.
DIGO DEL AIRE.
traffic code.
DIGO DEL CAMINO.
affic rules.
DIGO DEL TRABAJO.
bor code.
DIGO EN LO CIVIL.
e CÓDIGO DE PROCEDIMIENTO CIVIL.
DIGO EN LO PENAL.
e CÓDIGO DE PROCEDIMIENTO PENAL.
DIGO FISCAL.
x code.
DIGO FUNDAMENTAL.
nstitution, organic law (of a state or nation).
DIGO LABORAL.
bor code.
DIGO MARÍTIMO.
aritime or admiralty code.
DIGO MERCANTIL.
mmercial code.
DIGO MILITAR.
ilitary code.
DIGO NAPOLEÓNICO.
ode Napoleon, Napoleonic Code.
DIGO PENAL.
iminal or penal code.
DIGO PROCESAL CIVIL.
de of civil procedure.

CÓDIGO PROCESAL PENAL.
code of criminal procedure.
CODIRECTOR.
m, co-director, associate director.
COEFICIENTE DE CRIMINALIDAD.
m, crime rate ‖ rate of crime.
COEMITENTE.
m, co-issuer, co-drawer.
COENCAUSADO.
m, joint defendant, co-defendant.
COERCER.
v, to restrain.
COERCIBLE.
adj, coercible.
COERCIÓN.
f, coercion, restraint.
COERCITIVO.
adj, coercive ‖ restraining.
COESPOSA.
f, woman married to a man who has another wife or wives.
COEXISTENCIA PACÍFICA.
peaceful co-existence.
COFIADOR.
m, co-surety.
COFIDUCIARIO.
m, co-trustee, joint trustee.
COFIRMANTE.
m, f, cosigner.
COFRADÍA.
f, brotherhood, association ‖ trade-union.
COGER EN LA TRAMPA.
to catch in the act ‖ to set up, lay a trap (to obtain evidence of criminal activity).
COGESTIÓN.
See PARTICIPACIÓN EN LA DIRECCIÓN DE LAS EMPRESAS.
COGIRADOR.
m, co-maker ‖ co-drawer.
COGNACIÓN.
f, cognation ‖ blood relationship through female line.
COGNADO.
m, cognate ‖ blood relative (through female line).
COGNATICIO.
adj, cognatic.
COGNICIÓN.
f, knowledge, cognition ‖ notice, cognizance, recognition.

COGNICIÓN JUDICIAL.
judicial notice or recognition.
COGNICIÓN LIMITADA.
limited jurisdiction.
COGNITIVO.
adj, cognitive.
COHABITACIÓN.
f, cohabitation ‖ sexual intercourse.
COHABITAR.
v, to cohabit, live together ‖ to have sexual intercourse.
COHECHADOR.
m, briber, suborner.
COHECHAR.
v, to suborn, bribe, pay off ‖ to corrupt.
COHECHO.
m, subornation, bribery, corruption, graft.
COHEREDAR.
v, to inherit jointly (with others).
COHEREDERO.
m, co-inheritor, joint heir, co-heir.
COHEREDERO DEL AUSENTE.
co-heir of heir who is not present.
COHEREDERO DEL DONATARIO.
co-heir who is also a donee.
COIMA.
f, graft, bribery, pay-off ‖ concubine.
COIMEAR.
v, to bribe, graft.
COIMERO.
m, grafter, briber.
COINCIDENCIA DE LA VOLUNTAD.
f, meeting of the minds.
COINQUILINO.
m, co-tenant, co-lessee, joint tenant.
COINTERESADO.
m, partner, associate, jointly-interested party ‖ adj, jointly interested.
COITO.
m, carnal knowledge, coitus.
COLABORACIÓN.
f, collaboration, cooperation (especially on literary or scientific work).
COLACIÓN.
f, collation, arrangement and organization ‖ bestowal (of university degree) ‖ comparison (of things) ‖ attribution (of something to someone) ‖ parish jurisdiction.
COLACIÓN DE BIENES.
hotchpotch, hodgepodge ‖ hotchpot, return of goods distributed by the deceased to heirs

prior to his death, in order that distribution the estate occur in accord with the law.
COLACIONABLE.
adj, returnable pursuant to hotchpot rul susceptible to hotchpotch.
COLACIONAR.
v, to collate.
COLATERAL.
m, collateral relative ‖ adj, collateral.
COLATERAL ORDINARIO.
relatives consisting of aunts, uncles, gre aunt and uncles, cousins (in law of wills and tates).
COLATERAL PRIVILEGIADO.
relatives composed of brothers and sisters a their descendants (in law of wills and estate
COLECCIÓN.
f, collection.
COLECCIÓN LEGISLATIVA.
federal register, official or private publicati of laws.
COLECTA.
f, collection, receipts ‖ fund raising campai
COLECTAR.
v, to collect (bills, money, etc.).
COLECTIVA E INDIVIDUALMENTE.
adv, joint and severally.
COLECTIVIDAD.
f, collectivity ‖ community, group of pers united in purpose or interest.
COLECTIVISMO.
m, collectivism, social movement in favor collective action and ownership.
COLECTIVO.
m, bus ‖ adj, collective, joint.
COLECTOR.
m, collector.
COLECTOR DE DERECHOS ADUANEROS.
customs duties collector.
COLECTOR DE CONTRIBUCIONES.
See COLECTOR DE IMPUESTOS.
COLECTOR DE IMPUESTOS.
tax collector.
COLECTOR DE RENTAS INTERNAS.
internal revenue or tax collector.
COLECTOR FISCAL.
tax collector.
COLECTURÍA.
f, revenue collector's office.

COLEGA.
n, f, associate, colleague (in a law firm, school, church, etc).

COLEGATARIO.
n, collegatary, joint legatee.

COLEGIACIÓN.
, organization of a professional group ‖ incorporation of a professional organization ‖ act of joining a professional organization.

COLEGIADO.
n, member of a professional organization ‖ tribunal consisting of more than one judge ‖ adj, joined together in a group.

COLEGIARSE.
, to join a professional organization.

COLEGIO.
n, professional organization ‖ college ‖ secondary school.

COLEGIO DE ABOGADOS.
bar association, lawyers' organization. Membership may be mandatory or voluntary.

COLEGIO DE PROCURADORES.
association of solicitors ‖ bar association.

COLEGIO ELECTORAL.
electoral college.

COLEGISLACIÓN.
f, bicameral legislation, legislation requiring approval of both legislative houses.

COLEGISLADOR.
m, member of the same legislative chamber ‖ adj, co-legislative, pertaining to the duality of consent of the chambers of a bicameral congress.

COLÉRICAMENTE.
angrily, ab irato.

COLGADO.
adj, strangled, hung, suspended ‖ pending.

COLGAR.
v, to hang ‖ to suspend ‖ to impute, accuse ‖ to depend (upon some independent thing or person).

COLIGACIÓN.
f, union, confederation ‖ alliance ‖ tie, link ‖ formation of union, confederation, etc..

COLIGARSE.
v, to form an association or union or group.

COLINDANTE.
m, adjoining property, neighboring land ‖ adj, adjoining, adjacent, touching, abutting.

COLINDAR.
v, to adjoin, abut.

COLISIÓN.
f, collision ‖ opposition ‖ clash, conflict.

COLISION DE DERECHOS Y DEBERES.
conflict of rights and duties. This occurs when two or more rights or duties cannot be carried out at the same time.

COLITIGANTE.
m, f, co-litigant (whether plaintiff or defendant).

COLOCACIÓN.
f, employment, work ‖ job, post, position ‖ placing, placement ‖ location, place.

COLONIA.
f, colony ‖ settlement.

COLONIZACIÓN.
f, colonization, settlement (of land) ‖ placement of agricultural workers.

COLONO.
m, rural lessee ‖ farm tenant ‖ rural settler.

COLOR.
m, color ‖ pretext, motive, excuse (for having taken an action) ‖ character, nature.

COLUDIR.
v, to collude, conspire.

COLUSIÓN.
f, collusion.

COLUSOR.
m, colluder.

COLUSORIO.
adj, collusive.

COLLERA.
f, chain gang, chain of prisoners.

COMADRE.
f, god-mother ‖ mother of child with respect to the god-mother ‖ god-mother of child with respect to the child's mother.

COMANDANCIA.
f, command, position and power of a commander ‖ territory or district within a commander's jurisdiction ‖ headquarters, office or building of a commander.

COMANDANTE.
m, commander, commanding officer ‖ major.

COMANDATARIO.
m, co-agent, (with joint or several liability).

COMANDITA.
f, type of limited partnership (which is registered). Partnership in which active members are liable for the obligations beyond their investment and may manage the partnership and in which passive members are liable only

to the extent of their investment and may not manage the partnership.

COMANDITA POR ACCIONES.
limited share partnership. See COMANDITA.

COMANDITA SIMPLE.
limited partnership.
See COMANDITA.

COMANDITADO.
m, general partner ‖ managing partner.

COMANDITAR.
v, to invest money as a limited or silent partner in a COMANDITA.

COMANDITARIO.
m, silent or limited partner ‖ adj, silent, limited.

COMARCA.
f, region, district, territorial division.

COMBINACIÓN.
f, combination ‖ cartel.

COMBINACIÓN VERTICAL.
vertical combination.

COMBINAR.
v, to combine, merge ‖ to form a cartel.

COMBLEZA.
f, concubine.

COMBLEZADO.
m, concubine's husband, cuckold.

COMBLEZO.
m, married woman's lover.

COMENTADOR.
m, commentator.

COMENTARIO.
m, comment, commentary ‖ legal comment, explanation.

COMENTARISTA.
m, f, commentator.

COMERCIABILIDAD.
f, marketability.

COMERCIABLE.
adj, marketable, salable.

COMERCIAL.
adj, commercial, business, mercantile, pertaining to commerce.

COMERCIALISTA.
f, m, lawyer or scholar who specializes in commercial lawyer (includes business lawyer) ‖ adj, related to commercial law.

COMERCIALIZAR.
v, to commercialize, promote, market.

COMERCIANTE.
f, m, merchant, dealer, trader, businessman.

COMERCIANTE ACCIDENTAL.
businessman operating without being properly established.

COMERCIANTE ALMACENISTA.
middleman, jobber ‖ wholesaler.

COMERCIAR.
v, to trade, market, deal.

COMERCIO.
m, commerce, trade, business ‖ business actor ‖ business establishment, commerce house, store ‖ commercial sector (of a city).

COMERCIO AL POR MAYOR.
wholesale business.

COMERCIO AL POR MENOR.
retail business.

COMERCIO BANCARIO.
banking, banking business.

COMERCIO DE ALTURAS.
See COMERCIO DE ULTRAMAR.

COMERCIO DE COMISIÓN.
commission business.

COMERCIO DE EXPORTACIÓN.
export business.

COMERCIO DE IMPORTACIÓN.
import business.

COMERCIO DE ULTRAMAR.
overseas trade.

COMERCIO EXTERIOR.
foreign trade, export-import business.

COMERCIO FRANCO.
free trade, duty free commerce.

COMERCIO INTERESTATAL.
interstate commerce.

COMERCIO INTERIOR.
domestic trade.

COMERCIO MARÍTIMO.
maritime commerce or trade.

COMERCIO SEXUAL.
sexual intercourse ‖ illegal sexual intercourse or dealings ‖ sexual commerce ‖ sex business.

COMERCIO TERRESTRE.
ground trade or commerce, commerce which is by neither sea nor air.

COMESTIBLE.
adj, edible.

COMESTIBLES.
m, food, foodstuffs.

COMETER.
v, to commit (e.g. an error or crime) ‖ to perpetrate (a crime) ‖ to empower, entrust ‖ to give a commercial commission.

COMETER ASESINATO.
to commit murder.

COMETER PLEITO.
to agree or contract to something subject to guaranties.

COMETER SUICIDIO.
to commit suicide.

COMETIDO.
m, commission, charge, duty, assignment ‖
adj, committed.

COMICIAL.
adj, comitial, concerning elections.

COMICIO.
m, election board or commission ‖ group or body of voters ‖ election poll.

COMICIOS.
m, elections, polls.

COMICIOS GENERALES.
general election.

COMICIOS PRIMARIOS.
primary election.

COMIENZO DE EJECUCIÓN.
m, first criminal action in the perpetration of a crime ‖ beginning of the performance of an obligation

COMISAR.
v, to forfeit ‖ to confiscate.

COMISARÍA.
f, station, headquarters ‖ police headquarters ‖ office of commissioner ‖ jail, temporary holding in commissioner's office.

COMISARÍA DE POLICÍA.
police station.

COMISARIO.
m, chief ‖ shareholder's representative. See SÍNDICO.

COMISARIO DE AVERÍAS.
average surveyor.

COMISARIO DE COMERCIO.
trade commissioner.

COMISARIO DE PATENTES.
commissioner of patents.

COMISARIO DE POLICÍA.
police chief ‖ marshall of the court ‖ judicial official charged with maintaining order.

COMISARIO DE QUIEBRA.
trustee in bankruptcy, judge-selected party to represent, intervene or investigate a bankruptcy.

COMISARIO TESTAMENTARIO.
testamentary representative or trustee, per-

son to whom a testator unconditionally delegates the authority to distribute the estate.

COMISIÓN.
f, commission ‖ fee ‖ agency ‖ committee ‖ commission (e.g. of a crime) ‖ assignment ‖ percentage fee (based on sales) ‖ order, mandate.

COMISIÓN ASESORA.
consulting or advisory board.

COMISIÓN DE AGENTE.
agent fee.

COMISIÓN DE COBRO.
collection fee or commission.

COMISIÓN DE COMPROMISO.
commitment fee.

COMISIÓN DE CONTROL DE CAMBIOS.
foreign exchange control board.

COMISIÓN DE DELITO.
commission of a crime.

COMISIÓN DE DIVISAS.
foreign exchange control board.

COMISIÓN DE ENCUESTA.
fact-finding or investigative board.

COMISIÓN DE INDAGACIÓN.
See COMISIÓN DE ENCUESTA.

COMISIÓN DE HIGIENE.
board of health.

COMISIÓN DE MEDIOS Y ARBITRIOS.
ways and means commission.

COMISIÓN DE SERVICIO PÚBLICO.
public service commission.

COMISIÓN DE VIGILANCIA.
control committee ‖ creditors' committee which is designated to review the actions of a bankrupt, or of a receiver or trustee in bankruptcy.

COMISIÓN DIRECTIVA.
executive committee.

COMISIÓN EJECUTIVA.
See COMISIÓN DIRECTIVA.

COMISIÓN GESTORA.
See COMISIÓN DIRECTIVA.

COMISIÓN MERCANTIL.
commercial or mercantile commission ‖ contract granting a mercantile commission. See COMISIONISTA.

COMISIÓN PARITARIA.
labor-management board or committee, board of employers and employees.

COMISIÓN ROGATORIA.
letter rogatory (between courts of different jurisdictions).

COMISIONES PARLAMENTARIAS.
parliamentary or congressional or legislative committees.

COMISIONADO.
m, agent, proxy, representative ‖ commissioner ‖ adj, commissioned.

COMISIONADO MUNICIPAL.
temporary municipal school superintendent (appointed by the executive branch). Sometimes called COMISIONADO.

COMISIONAR.
v, to commission ‖ to give a commission to.

COMISIONISTA.
m, commission agent, agent.

COMISO.
m, confiscation (of prohibited merchandise) ‖ seizure, sequestration ‖ loss, forfeiture.

COMISORIO.
adj, valid and binding for a specified period of time or until a certain date.
See PACTO COMISORIO.

COMITÉ.
m, committee, commission.

COMITÉ ADMINISTRADOR.
managing or administrative committee.

COMITÉ CONJUNTO.
joint committee.

COMITÉ CONSULTIVO.
advisory or consulting board.

COMITÉ DE AFOROS.
board of appraisers.

COMITÉ DE AGRAVIOS.
grievance committee.

COMITÉ DE EMPRESA.
business committee, board of a business made up of its president or directors and elected representatives of the personnel to promote the purposes of the business.

COMITÉ DE FIDUCIARIOS.
board of trustees.

COMITÉ DE HUELGA.
strike committee.

COMITÉ DIRECTIVO.
managing or executive committee.

COMITÉ EJECUTIVO.
executive committee.

COMITÉ PARITARIO.
labor dispute board, board to resolve labor disputes which is made up of representatives of labor and management and a president appointed by the government.

COMITÉ PLANEADOR.
planning board.

COMITENTE.
m, principal, party who commissions ‖ shipper, party who ships goods on consignment.

COMITIR.
v, to name a consignment agent.

COMMORIENCIA.
f, simultaneous death.

COMODANTE.
m, gratuitous bailer ‖ gratuitous lender of a good which is to be used in a certain way and for a certain purpose for a term.

COMODAR.
v, to lend or bail gratuitously.

COMODATARIO.
m, gratuitous bailee ‖ borrower of a good, at no charge, to be used in certain way and for a certain purpose, for a term.

COMODATO.
m, commodatum agreement, gratuitous bailment (for benefit of bailee) ‖ contract by which non-fungible item is loaned for a term at no charge.

COMODATORIO.
adj, pertaining to commodatum.

COMPADRAZGO.
m, emotional or spiritual relationship between a god-father of a child and his or her parents.

COMPADRE.
m, god-father ‖ relationship of god-father to actual father of the child.

COMPAÑERO DE TRABAJO.
fellow worker.

COMPAÑÍA.
f, unit ‖ company ‖ informal business association of various persons for the same purpose.
See also SOCIEDAD.

COMPAÑÍA ANÓNIMA.
stock company or corporation.

COMPAÑÍA ARMADORA.
shipping company.

COMPAÑÍA ASOCIADA.
affiliate or associated company.

COMPAÑÍA CAPITALIZADORA.
See BANCO CAPITALIZADOR.

COMPAÑÍA CERRADA.
close corporation.

COMPAÑÍA CIVIL.
civil corporation.
COMPAÑÍA COLECTIVA.
partnership.
COMPAÑÍA COMANDITARIA.
limited partnership.
COMPAÑÍA CONTROLADORA.
controlling company, company which has control over another company. A parent company.
COMPAÑÍA DE AFIANZAMIENTO.
bonding company.
COMPAÑÍA DE CAPITALIZACIÓN.
See BANCO CAPITALIZADOR.
COMPAÑÍA DE CRÉDITO TERRITORIAL.
real estate mortgage bank or company.
COMPAÑÍA DE FIANZAS.
See COMPAÑÍA FIADORA.
COMPAÑÍA DE FIDEICOMISO.
type of trust company. See FIDEICOMISO.
COMPAÑÍA DE INVERSIONES.
See COMPAÑÍA INVERSIONISTA.
COMPAÑÍA DE RENTAS.
See COMPAÑÍA INVERSIONISTA.
COMPAÑÍA DE RESPONSABILIDAD LIMITADA.
limited-liability company.
COMPAÑÍA DE SEGUROS MUTUALES.
mutual insurance company.
COMPAÑÍA DE TRANSPORTE.
common carrier, transportation company.
COMPAÑÍA DE UTILIDAD PÚBLICA.
public-utility company ‖ public service corporation.
COMPAÑÍA DOMINADA.
controlled company.
COMPAÑÍA EN COMANDITA.
See SOCIEDAD EN COMANDITA.
COMPAÑÍA EN NOMBRE COLECTIVO.
general partnership.
COMPAÑÍA FIADORA.
bonding company.
COMPAÑÍA FIDUCIARIA.
trust company.
COMPAÑÍA FILIAL.
sister company ‖ subsidiary or controlled company.
COMPAÑÍA FINANCIERA.
finance or financial company.
COMPAÑÍA INVERSIONISTA.
investment company.

COMPAÑÍA MATRIZ.
parent company.
COMPAÑÍA MERCANTIL.
business association.
COMPAÑÍA OPERADORA.
operating company.
COMPAÑÍA POR ACCIONES.
stock company.
COMPAÑÍA PROPIETARIA.
proprietary company.
COMPARADO.
adj, compared ‖ comparative.
COMPARECENCIA.
f, appearance (before an authority). May occur in person or in writing.
COMPARECENCIA CONDICIONADA.
conditional appearance.
COMPARECENCIA EN GENERAL.
general appearance.
COMPARECENCIA EN JUICIO.
court appearance, appearance in an action (in person or by a legal representative, within specified time period).
COMPARECENCIA ESPECIAL.
special appearance.
COMPARECENCIA NOTARIAL.
documentary evidence which a special public notary attests to in a legal action or matter.
COMPARECENCIA OBLIGATORIA.
compulsory or obligatory appearance.
COMPARECENCIA PARA SENTENCIA.
(court) appearance for sentencing ‖ appearance for decision or judgment or ruling.
COMPARECENCIA VOLUNTARIA.
voluntary appearance.
COMPARECER.
v, to appear, present oneself (personally or by representative) ‖ to appear (in court).
COMPARECER PARA OBJETO ESPECIAL.
to appear specially, make a special appearance.
COMPARECER SIN LIMITACIONES.
to appear generally, make a general appearance.
COMPARECIENTE.
m, party making an appearance (in court).
COMPARENDO.
m, summons to appear ‖ subpoena.
COMPARICIÓN.
f, summons to appear ‖ subpoena ‖ appearance.

COMPARTE.
f, co-litigant, joint party.
COMPATERNIDAD.
See COMPADRAZGO.
COMPATIBILIDAD.
f, compatibility.
COMPATIBILIDAD DE BENEFICIOS EN DERECHO LABORAL.
compatibility of simultaneous or alternating employment or services in two or more jobs.
COMPATIBLE.
adj, consistent ‖ suitable ‖ compatible.
COMPELER.
v, to compel, oblige ‖ to constrain.
COMPENDIAR.
v, to summarize, synthesize, condense.
COMPENDIO.
m, extract ‖ summary, condensation, synthesis (oral or written) ‖ compendium, digest, abstract.
COMPENSABLE.
adj, compensable, able to be compensated ‖ repairable, recoverable.
COMPENSACIÓN.
f, compensation, reparation, recovery, recompense, indemnification ‖ equalization ‖ set-off.
COMPENSACIÓN BANCARIA.
(bank) clearing ‖ set-off of debits and credits between two banks to determine true balance.
COMPENSACIÓN CON EL ESTADO.
set-off of government accounts. May be prohibited if one account arises from taxes.
COMPENSACIÓN DE ALIMENTOS.
set-off of an alimony payment against another obligation owed by the recipient of alimony.
COMPENSACIÓN DE COSTOS.
payment of (court) costs.
COMPENSACIÓN DE INJURIAS.
cancellation of legal rights arising out of mutual insults.
COMPENSACIÓN EXTRAORDINARIA.
overtime pay.
COMPENSACIÓN MERCANTIL.
clearing ‖ set-off of debits and credits between commercial companies.
COMPENSACIÓN PARCIAL.
partial set-off.
COMPENSACIÓN POR ACCIDENTES DE TRABAJO.
workmen's compensation.

COMPENSACIÓN POR PARO.
unemployment compensation.
COMPENSACIÓN TOTAL.
total set-off.
COMPENSAR.
v, to set off, balance, equalize, to compensate repair, indemnify.
COMPENSATIVO.
adj, compensatory, countervailing ‖ offsetting
COMPENSATORIO.
See COMPENSATIVO.
COMPETENCIA.
f, jurisdictional capacity or competency venue ‖ competition, rivalry.
COMPETENCIA DE JURISDICCIÓN.
jurisdictional conflict.
COMPETENCIA DESLEAL.
unfair trade, illegal competition.
COMPETENCIA EXCEPCIONAL.
special jurisdiction.
COMPETENCIA EXCLUSIVA.
exclusive jurisdiction.
COMPETENCIA ILÍCITA.
illegal competition.
COMPETENCIA MATERIAL.
subject matter jurisdiction.
COMPETENCIA NECESARIA.
compulsory jurisdiction.
COMPETENCIA NEGATIVA.
refusal to take jurisdiction (by two or more courts).
COMPETENCIA ORIGINARIA.
original jurisdiction.
COMPETENCIA POR TERRITORIO.
territorial jurisdiction.
COMPETENCIA POSITIVA.
jurisdictional or venue conflict (between two or more courts which assert jurisdiction over a matter).
COMPETENCIA PRINCIPAL.
general jurisdiction.
COMPETENTE.
adj, legally qualified or competent ‖ capable, able ‖ applicable, appropriate.
COMPETER.
v, to pertain to, concern ‖ to be incumbent upon ‖ to have jurisdiction over.
COMPETIR.
v, to compete, vie.

COMPILACIÓN.
f, compilation, code (of laws) ‖ codification, collection (of laws).

COMPILADOR.
m, compiler, codifier ‖ reporter.

COMPLEMENTO DE LEGÍTIMA.
legal action of a legal heir to require return and legal distribution of the estate to which he or she is legally entitled when the will provides for less than the legal proportion.

CÓMPLICE.
f, accomplice (to a crime) ‖ accessory (to a crime if he or she participates secondarily in criminal act).

CÓMPLICE EN LA QUIEBRA.
accomplice to fraud in a bankruptcy.

CÓMPLICE ENCUBRIDOR.
accessory after the fact.

CÓMPLICE INSTIGADOR.
accessory before the fact.

CÓMPLICE NECESARIO.
principal accomplice, accomplice without whom crime could not be committed.

CÓMPLICE SECUNDARIO.
secondary accomplice, accomplice whose actions are not essential to the commission of a crime.

COMPLICIDAD.
f, complicity ‖ indirect and non-essential assistance or cooperation before or during a crime.

COMPLOT.
m, plot ‖ conspiracy.

COMPLOTADO.
m, conspirator.

COMPLOTAR.
v, to conspire, plot.

COMPLOTARSE.
v, to plot, conspire.

COMPONEDOR.
m, mediator.

COMPONENDA.
f, pact or agreement of questionable legality ‖ arbitration.

COMPONENTE.
m, component ‖ member (of a group).

COMPONER.
v, to arbitrate, mediate ‖ to settle, agree ‖ to settle (out of court) ‖ to compose, make up, make out ‖ to repair.

COMPONIBLE.
adj, arbitrable, reconcilable.

COMPOS MENTIS.
sound of mind, compos mentis.

COMPOSICIÓN.
f, settlement, agreement ‖ capitulation ‖ adjustment.

COMPOSICIÓN PROCESAL.
out-of-court settlement.

COMPOSTURA.
f, settlement, agreement ‖ treaty, contract ‖ adultering substance ‖ repair (of something).

COMPRA.
f, purchase, acquisition ‖ purchasing, buying.

COMPRA Y VENTA.
See COMPRAVENTA.

COMPRABLE.
adj, purchasable, able to be purchased legally ‖ bribable, subject to subornation.

COMPRADOR.
m, buyer, purchaser, acquirer, vendee. May be of MALA FE (buyer in bad faith) or BUENA FE (buyer in good faith).

COMPRADOR INOCENTE.
innocent purchaser, purchaser in good faith.

COMPRAR.
v, to purchase, buy, acquire ‖ to suborn, bribe.

COMPRAVENTA.
f, sales contract ‖ bargain and sale. Refers to both the contract and act.

COMPRAVENTA A CRÉDITO.
time sale, credit sale, credit purchase, installment sale.

COMPRAVENTA A ENSAYO.
purchase on approval, trial purchase, purchase conditioned on buyer's approval.

COMPRAVENTA A PRUEBA.
See COMPRAVENTA A ENSAYO.

COMPRAVENTA A LA VISTA.
See COMPRAVENTA AL CONTADO.

COMPRAVENTA A PLAZOS.
time or credit or installment sale, credit purchase.

COMPRAVENTA A TÉRMINO.
purchase on account ‖ purchase with payment in full at a later date ‖ purchase with delivery at a later date.

COMPRAVENTA AL CONTADO.
cash purchase, cash and carry purchase in which payment and delivery occur simultaneously.

COMPRAVENTA CON RESERVA DE DOMINIO.
type of purchase-lease whereby the buyer pays installments on property the title to which he obtains upon payment of the final installment. During the payment period the seller maintains legal title.

COMPRAVENTA DE COSA AJENA.
conversion (by sale), sale of another's goods.

COMPRAVENTA DE COSA FUERA DE COMERCIO.
sale of prohibited goods (e.g. public property).

COMPRAVENTA DE COSA FUTURA.
futures contract ‖ purchase of future goods.

COMPRAVENTA DE HERENCIA.
sale of inheritance. If unvested, it is null; if vested, it is assignable and transferable.

COMPRAVENTA FORZOSA.
forced sale ‖ judicial sale (against owner's wishes).

COMPRAVENTA MERCANTIL.
purchase for resale.

COMPRAVENTA MERCANTIL SOBRE MUESTRAS.
purchase of samples for resale.

COMPRAVENTA SOLEMNE.
formalized purchase-sale ‖ sale which is subject to formalities.

COMPROBABLE.
adj, verifiable, demonstrable.

COMPROBACIÓN.
f, proof, verification ‖ check (of copy with original) ‖ confirmation.

COMPROBACIÓN DE LA DEUDA.
proof of debt.

COMPROBANTE.
m, voucher, receipt ‖ proof, evidence ‖ adj, verifying, substantiating.

COMPROBANTE DE ADEUDO.
proof of debt.

COMPROBANTE DE VENTA.
bill of sale.

COMPROBAR.
v, to verify, prove, confirm ‖ to check (one thing against another) ‖ to accredit.

COMPROBATORIO.
adj, proving, substantiating, verifying, confirming.

COMPROMETEDOR.
adj, compromising.

COMPROMETER.
v, to submit to arbitration ‖ to expose to danger, risk ‖ to obligate or bind another.

COMPROMETERSE.
v, to obligate or bind oneself to something (unilaterally- or bilaterally) ‖ to make an appointment ‖ to become engaged (to marry).

COMPROMETIDO.
adj, engaged (to be married) ‖ obligated, bound ‖ busy ‖ involved in an uncertain case ‖ subject to a certain risk ‖ promised.

COMPROMISARIO.
m, arbitrator, mediator, umpire ‖ electors delegate ‖ adj, arbitrating, mediating.

COMPROMISO.
m, promise, word of honor, unilateral commitment ‖ difficulty, predicament ‖ engagement (to marry) ‖ engagement, appointment, date ‖ compromise, arbitration, settlement ‖ electoral delegation or college.

COMPROMISO ARBITRAL.
arbitration clause ‖ agreement to submit a dispute to arbitration.

COMPROMISO COLATERAL.
collateral agreement or engagement.

COMPROMISO DE VENTA.
letter of intent to sell ‖ unilateral promise to sell, offer ‖ bilateral promise to sell and buy.

COMPROMISO EVENTUAL.
contingent or conditional liability.

COMPROMISO POLÍTICO.
electoral delegation of power by voters to elected officials such that the latter may appoint or elect lesser officials ‖ political compromise or settlement.

COMPROMISO PROCESAL.
arbitration agreement, agreement to arbitrate in case of dispute.

COMPROMISORIO.
adj, pertaining to an arbitration or promise or predicament or engagement or delegation.

COMPULSA.
f, examination and verification of documents ‖ comparison or check of a document with another document or other writing which has been judicially authenticated ‖ authenticated copy of a document or pleading.

COMPULSAR.
v, to compare (documents) ‖ to make authenticated copies ‖ to compel.

COMPULSIÓN.
f, compulsion.

COMPULSIVO.
m, writ || adj, compulsive || compelling.
COMPULSO.
adj, compulsory, required, obligatory.
COMPULSORIO.
m, court order requiring the issuance of a COMPULSA (i.e. the copy of a document).
COMPURGACIÓN.
f, exculpation || refutation (of criminal charges or civil claims).
COMPURGADOR.
m, compurgator, witness or character witness for the defense.
COMPUTABLE.
adj, calculable, computable.
COMPUTACIÓN DE GRADOS.
f, determination of familiar relationship by degrees.
COMPUTAR.
v, to compute, calculate || to count.
CÓMPUTO DE PLAZOS.
m, calculation of time periods or terms (e.g. MES refers to 30 days, DÍA refers to 24 hours, etc.).
CÓMPUTO DE SERVICIOS.
m, calculation of period of employment (for retirement benefits).
COMÚN.
adj, common, usual, ordinary, general || common, communal, shared, public || vulgar || frequent, habitual || of civil jurisdiction.
COMUNA.
f, municipality.
COMUNAL.
adj, communal, common.
COMUNERO.
m, tenant in common, joint tenant, person who holds joint and indivisible rights || communal property owner || joint property owner.
COMUNICACIÓN.
f, communication || dispatch || telephone call || transmission || document, letter || revelation, discovery (something unknown or secret) || disclosure || demonstration or transfer of proof and documentary evidence by one party in litigation to another.
COMUNICACIÓN DE CONFIANZA.
See COMUNICACIÓN PRIVILEGIADA.
COMUNICACIÓN JUDICIAL.
judicial communication (of information, requests, or notification).

COMUNICACIÓN PRIVILEGIADA.
privileged communication.
COMUNICACIÓN RESERVADA.
confidential information.
COMUNICADO.
m, communicator || letter to the editor, public letter || public notice, communique, official announcement || adj, communicated.
COMUNICAR.
v, to communicate || to inform, advise, tell, announce || to transmit, send.
COMUNIDAD.
f, community || association || joint ownership.
COMUNIDAD DE AGUAS.
water association (organized to distribute water rights and use, and impose penalties for misuse).
COMUNIDAD DE BIENES.
communal property || joint ownership || tenancy in common, joint tenancy by the entirety || community property.
COMUNIDAD DE INTERÉS.
common interests.
COMUNIDAD DE PASTOS.
communal pasture, common.
COMUNIDAD DE REGANTES.
See COMUNIDAD DE AGUAS.
COMUNIDAD EN MANCOMÚN.
tenancy in common || joint tenancy (of real property).
COMUNIDAD HEREDITARIA.
community of heirs.
COMUNIDAD INCIDENTAL.
joint tenancy pursuant by law.
COMUNIDAD LEGAL.
legal community.
COMUNIDAD LEGAL CONTINUADA.
community property (in relation to agricultural, livestock, industrial or business endeavors).
COMUNIDAD PROINDIVISO.
joint tenancy || tenancy in common.
COMUNIDAD SOLIDARIA.
community of several joint tenancies (re: real property).
COMUNÍQUESE.
let it be know, know all men.
COMUNISMO.
m, communism.
COMUNISTA.
m, f, communist || adj, communist.

CON FRANCA MANO.
with a free hand, freely, liberally.
CON LAS MANOS EN LA MASA.
(caught) red-handed or in flagrante delicto or in the act.
CONATO.
m, propensity, tendency ‖ effort, endeavor, attempt ‖ (criminal) attempt, attempted crime.
CONCAUSA.
f, joint cause (which, together with another, results in an effect).
CONCEBIDO.
adj, conceived ‖ born ‖ born and living after 24 hours.
CONCEDENTE.
m, grantor ‖ adj, granting, conceding.
CONCEDER.
v, to grant, concede (a thing or right) ‖ to award (a bid).
CONCEDER UNA COMISIÓN.
to grant a commission.
CONCEDER CRÉDITO.
to extend credit, grant a loan.
CONCEDER UNA PATENTE.
to grant a patent.
CONCEDER UN PRÉSTAMO.
to grant or make a loan.
CONCEJAL.
m, city council member, alderman ‖ adj, open, public.
CONCEJALA.
f, female city council member, alderwoman.
CONCEJALÍA.
f, position of councilman or councilwoman or alderman.
CONCEJIL.
adj, pertaining to a CONCEJO ‖ municipal ‖ council, pertaining to a council ‖ pertaining to a council meeting.
CONCEJO.
m, city council, town-council, board of aldermen ‖ municipality ‖ city council meeting ‖ town hall, city hall.
CONCEJO ABIERTO.
residents' meeting.
CONCENTRACIÓN.
f, concentration ‖ mass.
CONCENTRACIÓN DE ACCIONES.
concentration of shares (in one person).
CONCENTRACIÓN DE EMPRESAS.
corporate or business merger or consolidation.

CONCENTRACIÓN HORIZONTAL.
horizontal combination (re: antitrust).
CONCENTRACIÓN INDUSTRIAL.
market concentration (re: antitrust).
CONCENTRACIÓN PARCELARIA.
combination of small agricultural plots (for economic purposes).
CONCENTRACIÓN VERTICAL.
vertical combination (re: antitrust).
CONCEPCIÓN.
f, conception (of life or a plan).
CONCERTADO.
adj, concerted ‖ arranged ‖ agreed.
CONCERTAR.
v, to contract, to agree ‖ to settle, close, conclude (a deal) ‖ to agree upon ‖ to coordinate.
CONCERTAR UN CONTRATO.
to make a contract.
CONCERTAR UN PRÉSTAMO.
to negotiate a loan.
CONCESIBLE.
adj, grantable.
CONCESIÓN.
f, concession ‖ authorization, permission ‖ licence ‖ franchise ‖ public franchise, concession ‖ allowance ‖ rebate.
CONCESIÓN ADMINISTRATIVA.
government franchise or concession or license.
CONCESIÓN DE CRÉDITO.
extension of credit or of a loan.
CONCESIÓN DE SERVICIOS PÚBLICOS.
concession or grant or licensing of public services.
CONCESIÓN INMOBILIARIA.
long-term real estate lease (usually for a period of at least twenty years at the end of which the owner must reimburse the lessee for improvements made thereto by lessee).
CONCESIÓN REAL.
See CONCESIÓN ADMINISTRATIVA.
CONCESIONARIO.
m, licensee, franchisee, concessionaire, grantee (especially governmental) ‖ adj, concessionary.
CONCESIONARIO DE LA PATENTE.
patentee.
CONCESIONARIO EXCLUSIVO.
See CONCESIONARIO ÚNICO.
CONCESIONARIO ÚNICO.
exclusive agent or licensee.

ONCESIVO.
adj, grantable.

ONCIENCIA.
f, conscience, integrity ‖ justice, equity.

ONCIENCIA JURÍDICA.
conscience of the court (to apply legal norms justly and equitably) ‖ public conscience (of what is just and legal).

ONCIERTO.
m, agreement, contract, settlement, pact ‖ transaction ‖ conspiracy, plot (to commit a crime) ‖ (musical) concert.

ONCIERTO DE VOLUNTADES.
meeting of the minds.

ONCIERTO ECONÓMICO.
revenue-sharing agreement between state and federal governments (by which taxes collected by the federal government are returned to the state) ‖ agreement regarding business or economic matters.

ONCILIACIÓN.
f, conciliation, reconciliation, settlement ‖ pretrial settlement.

ONCILIACIÓN LABORAL.
labor arbitration ‖ strike arbitration (with or without government involvement).

ONCILIACIÓN SINDICAL.
See CONCILIACIÓN LABORAL.

ONCILIADOR.
m, conciliator, reconciler.

ONCILIATIVO.
adj, conciliatory.

ONCILIAR.
m, council member ‖ v, to reconcile, mediate ‖ to achieve a reconciliation or settlement ‖ to reconcile (accounting books) ‖ adj, council, pertaining to a council.

ONCILIO.
m, council ‖ council decrees or resolutions or agreements.

CONCLUIR.
v, to conclude, end, terminate ‖ to draft or formulate CONCLUSIONES ‖ to end an allegation (see ALEGATO).

CONCLUSIÓN.
f, conclusion, end, termination ‖ determination ‖ charges, allegation ‖ conclusion of a trial.

CONCLUSIÓN ALTERNATIVA.
alternative criminal allegation or sentence (offered by the defense or prosecutor).

CONCLUSIÓN DEL SUMARIO.
end of preliminary hearing in criminal action. Criminal trials are often divided into two parts. The first (SUMARIO) consists of consideration of the evidence by a judge who has the power to acquit but not to condemn. The second phase (PLENARIO) consists of a consideration of the evidence gathered by the judge of the SUMARIO and any additional evidence gathered during the PLENARIO, which consideration will then permit the judge to make a final determination regarding guilt or innocence.

CONCLUSIÓN DEFINITIVA.
final statement, closing argument (in which the final criminal charges are submitted for consideration) ‖ final decision.

CONCLUSIÓN PROVISIONAL.
pre-trial criminal charges, criminal allegations submitted before trial.

CONCLUSIÓN PROVISORIA.
provisional decision.

CONCLUSIONES.
f, charges, proposed findings (submitted by the prosecutor or plaintiff attorney, and the defense attorney).

CONCLUSIONES DE DERECHO.
conclusions of law.

CONCLUSIONES DE HECHO.
findings of fact.

CONCLUSIVO.
adj, final, concluding.

CONCLUSO.
adj, concluded, closed (case), awaiting sentence.

CONCLUYENTE.
adj, conclusive, determining.

CONCOMITANTE.
adj, concomitant, concurrently.

CONCORDANCIA.
f, conformity ‖ related provision.

CONCORDAR.
v, to agree, be in accord ‖ to total up, tally.

CONCORDATARIO.
adj, relating to an agreement or accord (e.g. with creditors).

CONCORDATO.
m, debtor reorganization plan. Upon request of a debtor whether before or after declaration of bankruptcy, a judge may call a meeting of creditors, at which the debtor's financial

situation will be discussed and the reorganization plan put forth in order to forestall a bankruptcy. The plan is approved by a vote of the creditors and then ratified by the court.

CONCUBINA.
f, concubine.

CONCUBINARIO.
m, man who lives with a concubine ‖ adj, pertaining to concubinage.

CONCUBINATO.
m, concubinage ‖ common-law marriage.

CONCÚBITO.
m, sexual intercourse.

CONCULCADOR.
m, violator ‖ adj, infringing.

CONCULCAR.
v, to infringe, violate.

CONCURRENCIA.
f, meeting, gathering ‖ attendance ‖ equality (of rights) ‖ competition, rivalry ‖ competitors (as a whole) ‖ concurrence.

CONCURRENCIA DE ACCIONES.
joinder of lawsuits.

CONCURRENCIA DE CRÉDITOS.
simultaneous action of creditors against debtor who is in bankruptcy.

CONCURRENCIA DE NORMAS.
concurrence of legal rules applicable to a case.

CONCURRENCIA DESLEAL.
See COMPETENCIA DESLEAL.

CONCURRENTE.
m, attender, attendee ‖ competitor, rival ‖ adj, concurrent, simultaneous.

CONCURRIR.
v, to meet, gather ‖ to compete ‖ to attend ‖ to concur (in an opinion or decision).

CONCURRIR A UNA LICITACIÓN.
to participate in a bidding.

CONCURRIR UNA REUNIÓN.
to attend a meeting.

CONCURSADO.
m, insolvent, bankrupt, person or business in bankruptcy or insolvency proceedings ‖ adj, insolvent, bankrupt.

CONCURSAL.
adj, bankruptcy.

CONCURSANTE.
m, competitor, rival ‖ candidate ‖ party who participates in insolvency proceedings ‖ attendee, one who takes a part in a meeting ‖ bidder.

CONCURSAR.
v, to declare bankruptcy, file an insolvency petition ‖ to compete, participate in a competition.

CONCURSO.
m, meeting, assembly ‖ concurrence (of circumstances) ‖ aid, cooperation, assistance bidding, licitation ‖ insolvency or bankruptcy proceeding ‖ competition.

CONCURSO CIVIL.
bankruptcy proceeding regulated by a civil code.

CONCURSO COMERCIAL.
bankruptcy proceeding regulated by a commercial code.

CONCURSO CULPABLE.
bankruptcy proceeding in which the debtor is proven to have been negligent.

CONCURSO DE ACCIONES.
concurrence of more than one mutually exclusive rights.

CONCURSO DE ACREEDORES.
meeting of creditors to approve an insolvent's plan of reorganization.

CONCURSO DE CIRCUNSTANCIAS.
coincidence of criminal acts (such that a judge must weigh the criminality of each actor).

CONCURSO DE COMPETENCIA.
competitive bidding.

CONCURSO DE DEBERES.
See CONCURSO DE DERECHOS.

CONCURSO DE DELINCUENTES.
joint delinquency or criminality ‖ preparation and commission of a crime by various criminals.

CONCURSO DE DELITOS.
coincidence of multiple criminal offenses.

CONCURSO DE DERECHOS.
concurrence of rights and obligations of various people in a given set of facts.

CONCURSO DE LEYES.
See CONFLICTO DE LEYES ‖ plurality of applicable criminal code provisions to a given set of facts.

CONCURSO DE PRECIOS.
See CONCURSO DE COMPETENCIA.

CONCURSO FRAUDULENTO.
bankruptcy in which the debtor is proven to have acted fraudulently.

CONCURSO IDEAL.
plurality of applicable criminal code provisions to a given set of facts.

CONCURSO NECESARIO.
involuntary bankruptcy.
CONCURSO NEGLIGENTE.
negligent or non-fraudulent bankruptcy.
CONCURSO PREVENTIVO.
type of CONCURSO DE ACREEDORES held prior
to court order of debtor's bankruptcy.
CONCURSO PÚBLICO.
public bidding or licitation.
CONCURSO PUNIBLE.
criminal insolvency. May be either negligent or
fraudulent insolvency.
CONCURSO REAL.
combination of series of related criminal acts
resulting in a penalty less severe than the
mere summation of penalties of the independent crimes).
CONCURSO RESOLUTORIO.
type of CONCURSO DE ACREEDORES held after
court order of debtor's bankruptcy.
CONCURSO Y CONSENTIMIENTO.
advice and consent.
CONCUSIÓN.
f, extortion (by a public official or judge).
CONCUSIONARIO.
m, extortionist, extortioner.
See CONCUSIÓN.
CONCHABAR.
v, to hire help (usually for menial labor).
CONCHABARSE.
v, to plot, scheme, plan an illegal act ‖ to agree
to provide menial labor or to be a servant.
CONCHABO.
See CONTRATO DE ENGANCHE.
CONDADO.
m, county, district, shire.
CONDAL.
adj, count, pertaining to a count. See CONDE.
CONDE.
m, count, earl.
CONDENA.
f, punishment, penalty, sentence (in criminal
law) ‖ testimony read by court clerk from sentence ‖ jail or prison term.
CONDENA A MUERTE.
death sentence.
CONDENA ACCESORIA.
accessory punishment, punishment additional
to confinement.
CONDENA ACUMULATIVA.
cumulative sentence.

CONDENA COMÚN.
civil sentence against a soldier.
CONDENA CONDICIONAL.
sentence which allows the criminal to be free
on parole.
CONDENA DE FUTURO.
judgment with stay of execution.
CONDENA EN COSTAS.
order to pay court costs and attorney's fees of
opposing side (in judgment).
CONDENA EN SUSPENSO.
suspended sentence.
CONDENA JUDICIAL.
judicial sentence.
CONDENA PERPETUA.
life sentence.
CONDENA VITALICIA.
See CONDENA PERPETUA.
CONDENABLE.
adj, condemnable ‖ reprehensible.
CONDENACIÓN.
f, condemnation, reprobation, censure ‖ sentence, punishment, penalty (of a criminal).
CONDENADO.
n, convict, person who is condemned or convicted ‖ adj, condemned, censured ‖ sentenced ‖ convicted.
CONDENADO MILITAR.
person convicted by military court.
CONDENADOR.
m, condemnor ‖ sentencer, convicter ‖ adj,
censuring ‖ convicting, sentencing ‖ condemnatory.
CONDENAR.
v, to sentence, convict, condemn ‖ to condemn, censure.
CONDENAR EN CORTE.
to convict.
CONDENAR EN COSTAS.
to asses costs against.
See CONDENA EN COSTAS
CONDENARSE.
v, to condemn oneself ‖ to incriminate oneself.
CONDENATORIO.
adj, condemnatory.
CONDICIÓN.
f, condition, stipulation (in contract or judgment) covenant ‖ proviso ‖ state, condition ‖
quality, class.
CONDICIÓN AFIRMATIVA.
affirmative condition (to do something).

CONDICIÓN CALLADA.
See CONDICIÓN TÁCITA.

CONDICIÓN CAPTATORIA.
dependant condition.

CONDICIÓN CASUAL.
casual condition ‖ condition dependant on chance, contingent condition.

CONDICIÓN CIERTA.
possible condition.

CONDICIÓN COMPATIBLE.
consistent or compatible condition.

CONDICIÓN CONDICIONADA.
testamentary condition which is expressly conditioned on its legality and enforceability.

CONDICIÓN CONJUNTA.
copulative condition, condition which requires the fulfillment of various acts before a right can be enjoyed or an obligation can become effective.

CONDICIÓN CONTRARIA A LAS BUENAS COSTUMBRES.
immoral condition.

CONDICIÓN CONSTITUTIVA.
essential condition.

CONDICIÓN CONVENIBLE.
condition which may be included in a contract.

CONDICIÓN COPULATIVA.
copulative condition.

CONDICIÓN CUMPLIDA.
condition which has been fulfilled (for any reason).

CONDICIÓN DE DERECHO.
condition which implies or restricts or enlarges legal rights.

CONDICIÓN DE HECHO.
condition dependent on an event external to the parties.

CONDICIÓN DE PLAZO.
temporary condition, condition which exists for a term.

CONDICIÓN DEPENDIENTE.
dependent condition.

CONDICIÓN DESCONVENIBLE.
repugnant condition, condition which is repugnant to the contract of which it is a part.

CONDICIÓN DESHONESTA.
See CONDICIÓN CONTRARIA A LAS BUENAS COSTUMBRES.

CONDICIÓN DISYUNTIVA.
disjunctive condition ‖ alternative condition, (such that fulfillment of one of several acts

constitutes compliance with the condition.

CONDICIÓN DIVISIBLE.
condition which permits partial compliance.

CONDICIÓN EN EL MATRIMONIO.
marital condition, condition in marriage.

CONDICIÓN EN LA HERENCIA.
testamentary condition.

CONDICIÓN EN LA LEGÍTIMA.
testamentary condition which restricts the rights of those who are, by law, required to inherit a certain percentage. Usually unenforceable.

CONDICIÓN EN LAS OBLIGACIONES.
See OBLIGACIÓN CONDICIONAL.

CONDICIÓN EN LAS SUSTITUCIONES.
condition upon replacement legatees.

CONDICIÓN EN LOS LEGADOS.
See LEGADO CONDICIONAL.

CONDICIÓN EN LOS TESTAMENTOS.
testamentary condition.

CONDICIÓN EVENTUAL.
condition dependent on a fortuitous event or an act of a third party.

CONDICIÓN EXPRESA.
express condition.

CONDICIÓN EXTINTIVA.
extinguishing condition.

CONDICIÓN ILEGAL.
See CONDICIÓN ILÍCITA.

CONDICIÓN ILÍCITA.
unlawful condition, condition against the law or morality.

CONDICIÓN IMPLÍCITA.
implied condition.

CONDICIÓN IMPOSIBLE.
impossible condition, condition which is impossible to fulfill. Includes those which are factually and legally impossible to fulfill (e.g. illegality).

CONDICIÓN IMPOSIBLE DE DERECHO.
legally impossible condition.

CONDICIÓN IMPOSIBLE DE HECHO.
factually or physically impossible condition.

CONDICIÓN INCIERTA.
uncertain condition, condition the fulfillment of which is uncertain.

CONDICIÓN INCOMPATIBLE.
repugnant condition.

CONDICIÓN INDEPENDIENTE.
independent condition.

CONDICIÓN INDIVISIBLE.
compulsory condition, condition which requires total fulfillment.

CONDICIÓN INMORAL.
immoral condition.

CONDICIÓN LEGAL DE LAS PERSONAS.
legal status of persons.

CONDICIÓN LÍCITA.
lawful condition (i.e. not against the law or morality).

CONDICIÓN MIXTA.
mixed condition, condition which depends partly on external events and partly on one's will.

CONDICIÓN NECESARIA.
necessary condition, condition which is required for the contract to be enforceable (e.g. price, amount).

CONDICIÓN NEGATIVA.
negative condition.

CONDICIÓN POSIBLE.
possible condition.

CONDICIÓN POSITIVA.
positive condition, condition which depends upon a positive act being carried out.

CONDICIÓN POTESTATIVA.
condition the fulfillment of which depends upon the action of a given party.

CONDICIÓN PRECEDENTE.
condition precedent.

CONDICIÓN PRECISA.
See CONDICIÓN EXPRESA.

CONDICIÓN PREVIA.
See CONDICIÓN PRECEDENTE.

CONDICIÓN PROHIBIDA.
prohibited condition.

CONDICIÓN PURA.
condition the fulfillment of which does not depend at all upon the action of a given party.

CONDICIÓN RESOLUTORIA.
condition subsequent, resolutory condition, dissolving condition ‖ condition which once fulfilled, operates to revoke the obligation, restoring the thing to the state prior to obligation.

CONDICIÓN RESTRICTIVA.
restrictive or negative condition.

CONDICIÓN RETROACTIVA.
retroactive condition.

CONDICIÓN SINE QUA NON.
indispensable condition, condition sine qua non.

CONDICIÓN SUBSECUENTE.
condition subsequent.

CONDICIÓN SUCESIVA.
successive condition, condition which has to be performed prior to a second one (both performed by the same party)

CONDICIÓN SUPERFLUA.
superfluous condition, condition which reiterates legal requirements.

CONDICIÓN SUSPENSIVA.
condition precedent.

CONDICIÓN SUPUESTA.
implied condition.

CONDICIÓN TÁCITA.
implied condition.

CONDICIÓN TORPE.
indecent condition ‖ condition which requires fulfillment of immoral sexual relations.

CONDICIÓN ÚNICA.
single or sole condition.

CONDICIÓN VOLUNTARIA.
See CONDICIÓN POTESTATIVA.

CONDICIONADO.
m, conditions terms ‖ adj, conditioned ‖ conditional.

CONDICIONAL.
adj, conditional.

CONDICIONALMENTE.
adv, conditionally, provisionally, qualifiedly.

CONDICIONAR.
v, to condition, qualify, to impose a condition.

CONDICIONES CONCURRENTES.
concurrent conditions.

CONDICIONES DE PAGO.
terms or conditions of payment.

CONDICIONES DE VENTA.
terms or conditions of sale.

CONDOMINIO.
m, joint ownership ‖ tenancy in common, joint tenancy.

CONDOMINIO POR CONFUSIÓN DE LÍMITES.
joint tenancy caused by borders of land becoming confused.

CONDOMINIO POR INDIVISIÓN FORZOSA.
joint ownership or tenancy in common by reason of the fact that it is impossible to reasonably divide the property in question.

CONDÓMINO.
m, joint owner. Includes joint tenant and tenant in common.

CONDONACIÓN.
f, release or extinction (of a debt), remission ‖ pardon (of death sentence). May be EXPRESA (express) or TÁCITA (implied); TOTAL (total) or PARCIAL (partial).

CONDONANTE.
adj, releasing, forgiving ‖ pardoning.

CONDONAR.
v, to pardon (e.g. a criminal sentence) ‖ to forgive, release, extinguish (a debt or obligation), to remit.

CONDUCCIÓN.
f, guide, orientation ‖ transportation, conveyance ‖ agreement regarding price and salary ‖ governance or management of a town or business ‖ conduct, comportment, behavior ‖ driving.

CONDUCENTE.
adj, conducive ‖ instrumental, leading (toward) ‖ pertinent, relevant.

CONDUCTA.
f, transportation, conveyance ‖ management ‖ guidance, direction ‖ government, power ‖ conduct, comportment, behavior.

CONDUCTA INDEBIDA.
f, misconduct.

CONDUCTOR.
m, conductor, person involved in CONDUCCIÓN ‖ driver ‖ transporter.

CONDUEÑO.
m, co-owner, joint owner, joint tenant.

CONEXIDADES.
f, incidental rights.

CONEXIÓN.
f, relationship, connection ‖ tie.

CONEXIÓN DE CAUSAS.
joinder of actions ‖ interrelationship or interdependency of two or more related actions which may be joint.

CONEXO.
adj, related.

CONFABULACIÓN .
f, conspiracy, plot ‖ confab, confabulation, meeting.

CONFABULADOR.
m, conspirator.

CONFABULARSE.
v, to conspire, plot.

CONFEDERACIÓN.
f, federation, association, confederation ‖ union, community (of nations).

CONFEDERACIÓN DE SINDICATOS.
trade union federation or confederation or alliance.

CONFEDERACIÓN PATRONAL.
employers' association.

CONFERENCIA.
f, conference, meeting, discussion ‖ talk, lecture ‖ communication, telephone conversation ‖ congress, assembly ‖ pool, syndicate, cartel.

CONFERENCIAR.
v, to consult ‖ to confer, discuss ‖ to hold a conference.

CONFERIR.
v, to confer, award ‖ to hold a meeting, confer ‖ to check, compare.

CONFERIR PODERES.
to empower, confer powers on.

CONFESABLE.
adj, able to be confessed (before judge) ‖ licit, honorable.

CONFESADO.
m, confession, admission ‖ confessor, penitent ‖ adj, confessed, admitted.

CONFESANTE.
m, party in interest who confesses or admits something in court; confessing.

CONFESAR.
v, to confess, admit ‖ to testify.

CONFESAR DE PLANO.
to make a full confession.

CONFESIÓN .
f, confession ‖ admission ‖ testimony ‖ admission against interest. May be JUDICIAL (in court) or EXTRAJUDICIAL (out-of-court); EXPRESA (express) or TÁCITA (implied); SIMPLE (full) or CALIFICADA (qualified); CIVIL (civil) or PENAL (criminal).

CONFESIÓN CIVIL.
admission, civil confession, confession in a non-criminal action.

CONFESIÓN COMPLEJA.
related admission or confession, admission related, but made separately from another.

CONFESIÓN CONDICIONAL.
qualified confession.

CONFESIÓN DE DOTE.
dowry the delivery of which is proven by

husband's admission or by DOCUMENTO PRIVADO (as opposed to a DOCUMENTO PÚBLICO).

CONFESIÓN DE LA DEUDA.
admission or confession of indebtedness.

CONFESIÓN DEL DELITO.
criminal confession.

CONFESIÓN DIVIDIDA.
qualified confession (in which the qualification pertains to only part of the confession).

CONFESIÓN DIVISIBLE.
See CONFESIÓN INDIVIDUA.

CONFESIÓN EN JUICIO.
signed declaration or statement (of a civil defendant of answers to set questions about the facts of the case).

CONFESIÓN EN PLEITOS CON EL ESTADO.
confession in actions involving the State. Must follow a different procedure in order to be admissible.

CONFESIÓN EN PLENO TRIBUNAL.
judicial or in-court confession.

CONFESIÓN EN SEGUNDA INSTANCIA.
admission made on appeal (when in the trial no admission had been made on the issue).

CONFESIÓN ESPONTÁNEA.
voluntary confession.

CONFESIÓN EXPRESA.
express admission.

CONFESIÓN EXTRAJUDICIAL.
out-of-court admission or confession, confession which is made outside the confines of legal procedures and without the requisite formalities.

CONFESIÓN FICTA.
tacit admission, admission by silence.

CONFESIÓN IMPLÍCITA.
implied confession.

CONFESIÓN INDIVIDUA.
qualified confession (in which the qualification pertains to the confession as a whole).

CONFESIÓN INVOLUNTARIA.
involuntary confession.

CONFESIÓN JUDICIAL.
judicial confession ‖ deposition ‖ reply to interrogatories.

CONFESIÓN POR ESCRITO.
written confession or admission.

CONFESIÓN PROVOCADA.
See CONFESIÓN INVOLUNTARIA.

CONFESIÓN SIMPLE.
full confession or admission ‖ admission or confession of facts (vs. motives).

CONFESIÓN TÁCITA.
See CONFESIÓN IMPLÍCITA.

CONFESIÓN VERBAL.
oral confession. The record may be signed by the party confessing or if he or she refuses, by the judge's clerk.

CONFESIONAL.
adj, confessional, related to admissions or confessions.

CONFESO.
m, confessor, one who confesses or admits or acknowledges ‖ party in civil action who admits.

CONFESORIA.
See ACCIÓN CONFESORIA.

CONFIABLE.
adj, reliable, trustworthy.

CONFIADOR.
m, credulous person ‖ trusting person.

CONFIANZA.
f, confidence (in all sense) ‖ trust.

CONFIAR.
v, to trust ‖ to entrust, charge.

CONFIDENCIAL .
adj, confidential, secret, private.

CONFIDENTE.
m, f, informer, rat, squealer ‖ confidant (if male), confidante (if female) ‖ adj, trustworthy, trusty.

CONFINACIÓN.
f, confinement.

CONFINADO.
m, parolee with limitation on movement ‖ prisoner ‖ adj, confined.

CONFINAMIENTO.
m, confinement ‖ restricted parole (regarding movement); confinement of parolee to restricted area ‖ deportation, exile.

CONFINAMIENTO REUNIDO.
imprisonment with others.

CONFINAMIENTO SOLITARIO.
solitary confinement, isolation (in prison).

CONFINAR.
v, to confine, imprison ‖ to parole to a certain limited area ‖ to limit (boundaries).

CONFIRMACIÓN.
f, confirmation, acknowledgement ‖ proof,

evidence ‖ repetition, corroboration ‖ ratification or reaffirmation of a defective legal act.

CONFIRMACIÓN DE ACTOS JURÍDICOS.
approval or confirmation of legal acts or transactions which would be considered void in the absence of such confirmation ‖ confirmation of a lower court decision by an appellate court.

CONFIRMACIÓN DE SENTENCIA.
affirmance of judgement.

CONFIRMAR.
v, to confirm (in all senses) ‖ to corroborate ‖ to verify, prove ‖ to ratify, affirm (e.g. a voidable contract).

CONFIRMATORIO.
adj, confirming, affirming, reaffirming, ratifying.

CONFISCABLE.
adj, subject to confiscation, expropriation, or taking.

CONFISCACIÓN.
f, confiscation ‖ expropriation ‖ condemnation, taking.

CONFISCAR.
v, to confiscate, expropriate ‖ to condemn.

CONFISCATORIO.
adj, confiscatory.

CONFLICTO.
m, conflict, opposition, dispute, war, battle, combat ‖ struggle, difficult situation ‖ antagonism.

CONFLICTO DE ATRIBUCIONES.
conflict of power ‖ conflict of venue ‖ conflict of two or more judges who believe that they have the authority to hear and resolve a dispute ‖ conflict of governmental entities (regarding jurisdiction).

CONFLICTO DE COMPETENCIA.
See CUESTIÓN DE COMPETENCIA.

CONFLICTO DE DERECHOS.
conflict of different legal rights.

CONFLICTO DE EVIDENCIA.
conflict of evidence.

CONFLICTO DE JURISDICCIÓN.
conflict of jurisdiction.

CONFLICTO DE LEYES.
conflict of laws.

CONFLICTO DE PODERES.
conflict of powers (between the executive, judicial or legislative branches of government).

CONFLICTO INTERSINDICAL.
conflict or dispute which arises betwee unions.

CONFLICTO JURISDICCIONAL.
jurisdictional conflict.

CONFLICTO JURISPRUDENCIAL.
conflict of precedent, conflict of lines « decisions.

CONFLICTOS DEL TRABAJO.
labor disputes, labor-management conflict May be INDIVIDUALES (individual) or COLE« TIVOS (collective); DE DERECHOS relative ı the law) or DE INTERESES (relative to woı conditions or pay).

CONFORMADO.
adj, approved, ratified ‖ satisfied.

CONFORMAR.
v, to adjust, adapt, conform.

CONFORMARSE.
v, to agree to.

CONFORME.
m, approval (of a superior) ‖ written approva (in judicial or administrative files) ‖ acknov ledgment ‖ acceptance ‖ adj, agreed, aı proved, ok, okay ‖ in conformance, in agree ment ‖ in order.

CONFORME A DERECHO.
in accord with the law, legal.

CONFORME A LO ALEGADO Y PROBADO
in accord with the evidence proved.

CONFORMES DE TODA CONFORMIDAD«
m, similarity of the facts and law of two cases

CONFORMIDAD.
f, equality, similarity, likeness ‖ approval, ac ceptance ‖ consent.

CONFRONTA.
f, comparison, checking.

CONFRONTAR.
v, to confront, to be face to face ‖ to compare check, verify ‖ to confine, limit.

CONFUSIÓN.
f, confusion, confusio, mingling, interminglin, (of assets), disorder ‖ merger ‖ confusion obscurity (of a text) ‖ turbulence, perplexity jail, cell, prison ‖ extinction of an obligatioı due to merger of creditor and debtor in onı person.

CONFUSIÓN DE BIENES.
confusion of goods.

CONFUSIÓN DE COSAS.
confusion or confusio (of goods).

CONFUSIÓN DE DERECHOS.
extinguishment of rights due to the merger of debtor and creditor in the same person.

CONFUSIÓN DE DEUDAS.
merger or confusion of debts.

CONFUSIÓN DE LÍMITES.
See CONDOMINIO POR CONFUSIÓN DE LÍMITES.

CONFUSIÓN DE PATRIMONIOS.
confusion of property or estates.

CONFUSIÓN DE SERVIDUMBRES.
merger of easements (in an owner of both a dominant and a servient estate).

CONFUTACIÓN.
f, refutation, confutation.

CONFUTAR.
v, to refute, disprove, invalidate, rebut, negate.

CONGELACIÓN.
f, freezing (of assets or prices).

CONGELACIÓN DE FONDOS.
freezing of assets.

CONGELACIÓN DE PRECIOS.
freezing of prices.

CONGREGACIÓN.
f, congregation || meeting.

CONGRESAL.
m, f, member of a parliamentary or political or scientific conference or congress.

CONGRESISTA.
m, f, congressman or congresswoman || person who attends a congress or convention of arts, sciences, literature, or economy || delegate to a political convention.

CONGRESO.
m, congress, convention, meeting || congress (of a nation) || congress building, capitol.

CONGRESO CONSTITUYENTE.
constitutional congress.

CONGRESOS INTERNACIONALES.
international congresses or conferences or meetings or conventions.

CONGRUENCIA.
f, conformity (e.g. of questions and answers, judgment and complaint), congruity.

CONGRUENTE.
adj, congruous, fitting || in agreement (with) || convenient, opportune.

CONGRUENTEMENTE.
adv, congruously, aptly, fittingly.

CONJETURA.
f, conjecture || circumstantial evidence.

CONJUEZ.
m, associate judge || one of several justices judging a case || provisional or alternate judge.

CONJUNCIÓN.
f, union, conjunction || political alliance || means of acquiring property by accession.

CONJUNTIVA.
f, type of OBLIGACION MÚLTIPLE.

CONJUNTO.
m, ally, friend || mixture, confusion || totality, whole entirety || adj, mixed, confused || joint, common || conjunctive.

CONJURA.
f, conspiracy, plot (against the head of State or government).

CONJURACIÓN.
See CONJURA.

CONJURADO.
m, conspirator, co-conspirator || adj, conspiring, plotting.

CONJURADOR.
m, conspirator.

CONJURAMENTAR.
v, to swear in, administer an oath.

CONJURAMENTARSE.
v, to take the oath (to take a certain action at a later point in time).

CONJURAR.
v, to conspire, plot.

CONMINACIÓN.
f, admonition, warning, threat (e.g. of a judge or other authority to tell the truth) || judgment || judicial order with express punishment for failure to comply.

CONMINADOR.
m, admonisher, person who warns or threatens.

CONMINAR.
v, to threaten, warn, (with sanctions by one with authority) || to admonish to tell the truth (by a judge to an accused) || to issue a court order with express punishment for failure to comply.

CONMINATORIO.
m, threat, admonishment || adj, threatening, admonishing.

CONMONITORIO.
m, note from a superior judge admonishing a lower court judge || record, report.

CONMOCIÓN CIVIL.
civil commotion.

CONMUTACIÓN.
f, exchange || commutation.
CONMUTACIÓN DE IMPUESTOS.
commutation of taxes.
CONMUTACIÓN DE LA PENA.
commutation of criminal sentence.
CONMUTACIÓN DE LA SENTENCIA.
See CONMUTACIÓN DE LA PENA.
CONMUTACIÓN IMPOSITIVA.
See CONMUTACIÓN DE IMPUESTOS.
CONMUTAR.
v, to exchange || to commute (a criminal sentence).
CONMUTATIVO.
adj, exchangeable. Used to refer to a contract the fulfillment of which is not dependant upon chance.
CONNIVENCIA.
f, connivance || confabulation || complicity || participation in a crime.
CONNUBIO.
See MATRIMONIO.
CONOCEDOR.
m, expert (without a degree) || connoisseur || adj, expert.
CONOCENCIA.
See CONFESIÓN EN JUICIO.
CONOCER.
v, to know, have knowledge of || to be familiar with || to understand || to have visited (e.g. a place or city).
CONOCER DE.
to take cognizance of.
CONOCER DE INSTRUCCIÓN.
to hear or try a criminal case.
CONOCER DE LA APELACIÓN.
to hear the appeal.
CONOCER DE NUEVO.
to retry or rehear.
CONOCER DE UN PLEITO.
to judge a case, be a judge in an action.
CONOCER DE UNA CAUSA.
to hear or try a case.
CONOCIBLE.
adj, able to be tried || knowable.
CONOCIMIENTO.
m, knowledge, intelligence, understanding || warning, notice; confession, acknowledgment || ocean bill of lading, maritime letter which acts as a bill of lading || hearing, cognizance || voucher || bill of lading.

CONOCIMIENTO A LA ORDEN.
order bill of lading.
CONOCIMIENTO ACUMULATIVO.
concurrent jurisdiction.
CONOCIMIENTO AL PORTADOR.
bearer bill of lading.
CONOCIMIENTO DE ALMACÉN.
warehouse receipt || dock warrant.
CONOCIMIENTO DE CARGA.
See CONOCIMIENTO DE EMBARQUE.
CONOCIMIENTO DE CAUSA.
hearing of a case || knowledge of the reason (for something).
CONOCIMIENTO DE EMBARQUE.
bill of lading.
CONOCIMIENTO DE FAVOR.
accommodation bill of lading.
CONOCIMIENTO DE PRIMERA MANO.
See CONOCIMIENTO ORIGINAL.
CONOCIMIENTO DEL TESTADOR.
personal acquaintance with testator || testator's knowledge (of someone or something).
CONOCIMIENTO JUDICIAL.
judicial notice or knowledge.
CONOCIMIENTO LIMPIO.
clean bill of lading.
CONOCIMIENTO ORIGINAL.
personal knowledge.
CONOCIMIENTO PERSONAL.
personal knowledge.
CONOCIMIENTO REAL.
actual knowledge.
CONOCIMIENTO Y CREENCIA.
knowledge and belief.
CONQUISTA.
f, conquest || community property earned during marriage.
CONSANGUINEO.
m, blood relation, kin || adj, consanguineous.
CONSANGUINIDAD.
f, consanguinity.
CONSANGUINIDAD COLATERAL.
collateral consanguinity.
CONSANGUINIDAD LINEAL.
lineal consanguinity.
CONSECUENCIA.
f, consequence, effect, result || consistency, conformity.
CONSECUENCIA DE HECHOS JURÍDICOS.
consequence of a legal event || doctrine in civil

law which determines the liability of an actor for the consequence, based on whether it was INMEDIATA (normal and ordinary result); MEDIATA (abnormal and out of the ordinary); or CASUAL (unforeseeable).

CONSEJERO.
m, advisor, consultant ‖ attorney, lawyer, counsel ‖ council member, member of a board ‖ adj, advisory.

CONSEJERO JURÍDICO.
legal counsel.

CONSEJERO LEGAL.
See CONSEJERO JURÍDICO.

CONSEJEROS DIRECTORES.
directors.

CONSEJO.
m, judgment, decision ‖ advice ‖ board, council ‖ supreme court ‖ board of directors (e.g. of a corporation).

CONSEJO ADMINISTRATIVO.
See CONSEJO DE ADMINISTRACIÓN.

CONSEJO CONSULTIVO.
consulting or advisory board.

CONSEJO DE ADMINISTRACIÓN.
board of directors, directorate ‖ administrative board.

CONSEJO DE CONCILIACIÓN Y ARBITRAJE.
board of labor arbitration.

CONSEJO DE DIRECCIÓN.
board of directors.

CONSEJO DE EMPRESA.
See CONTROL OBRERO.

CONSEJO DE ESTADO.
council of state.

CONSEJO DE FÁBRICA.
industrial board, board organized to deal with a wide variety of matters concerning an industry (e.g. health and safety, improved production, etc.).

CONSEJO DE FAMILIA.
guardianship court (for minors or those otherwise unable to represent themselves) ‖ meeting to resolve family matters.

CONSEJO DE GABINETE.
See CONSEJO DE MINISTROS.

CONSEJO DE GESTIÓN.
See CONTROL OBRERO.

CONSEJO DE GOBIERNO.
council of state.

CONSEJO DE GUERRA.
council of war.

CONSEJO DE INCAUTACIÓN.
board of receivers (in bankruptcy or winding up proceedings).

CONSEJO DE INSPECCIÓN.
See CONSEJO DE VIGILANCIA.

CONSEJO DE MINISTROS.
cabinet, council of ministers ‖ board of controllers.

CONSEJO DE SEGURIDAD.
security council.

CONSEJO DE VIGILANCIA.
committee that watches the actions of the management on behalf of the interests of the stockholders. See COMISARIO and SÍNDICO.

CONSEJO EJECUTIVO.
executive board.

CONSEJO PATERNO.
parental advice (needed for certain legal acts) ‖ parental consent.

CONSEJO REUNIDO.
supreme court of military justice sitting en banc.

CONSEJO SUPREMO DE JUSTICIA MILITAR.
supreme court of military justice.

CONSENSO.
m, assent, consent, consensus, agreement.

CONSENSUAL.
adj, consensual.

CONSENTIDO.
m, judgment which is not appealed ‖ adj, consented to.

CONSENTIMIENTO.
m, consent, agreement, acquiescence.

CONSENTIMIENTO DEL OFENDIDO.
consent of the victim. Usually changes nature of the crime.

CONSENTIMIENTO DEL PACIENTE.
patient's consent.

CONSENTIMIENTO ESCRITO.
written consent.

CONSENTIMIENTO EXPRESO.
express consent.

CONSENTIMIENTO IMPLÍCITO.
implied consent.

CONSENTIMIENTO MATRIMONIAL.
marital consent, consent to be married (manifested by a man and woman).

CONSENTIMIENTO PARA ADOPTAR.
consent to adopt (of adoptee).

CONSENTIMIENTO PARA CONTRAER MATRIMONIO.
consent to marry (e.g. of parents, or others legally responsible).

CONSENTIMIENTO PARA EMANCIPAR.
consent to emancipation (of child by parents).

CONSENTIMIENTO PARA LEGITIMAR.
consent to legitimate illegitimate children (by spouse).

CONSENTIMIENTO PRESUNTO.
constructive consent.

CONSENTIMIENTO TÁCITO.
implied consent.

CONSENTIR.
v, to consent, acquiesce, agree ‖ to accept (e.g. an offer), to obligate oneself ‖ to authorize.

CONSERVACIÓN.
f, custodianship, guardianship ‖ resistance, maintenance, care, conservation.

CONSERVACIÓN DE COSA AJENA.
care of another's property.

CONSERVADOR.
m, conservator, custodian, guardian, warden, curator ‖ adj, conservative ‖ conserving, preserving.

CONSIDERACIÓN.
f, consideration (of thought), deliberation ‖ respect ‖ reason, motive.

CONSIDERANDO.
m, whereas clause, legal reason ‖ v, considering, whereas, in consideration of

CONSIDERANDOS.
m, legal bases, foundations or reasons (supporting a law, regulation, decision, etc.).

CONSIGNACIÓN.
f, consignment ‖ destination (of location of a thing) ‖ earmarking (of funds by a treasurer to cover specified debts) ‖ written doctrine, opinion, judgment ‖ deposit ‖ dispatch (of goods) ‖ court deposit ‖ remittance, payment.

CONSIGNACIÓN EN PAGO.
deposit in payment of a debt.

CONSIGNACIÓN JUDICIAL.
judicial deposit.

CONSIGNADOR.
m, consignor.

CONSIGNAR.
v, to consign, dispatch ‖ to earmark ‖ to write a doctrine, opinion, or judgment ‖ to deposit ‖ to pay ‖ to make an appropriation ‖ to hold for trial ‖ to remand.

CONSIGNATARIO.
m, consignee, recipient ‖ depositary ‖ creditor who manages a debtor's farm, per contract, until debt is paid ‖ dockside representative of a ship owner who takes care of the administrative and custom's arrangements of freight and passengers ‖ trustee.

CONSILIARIO.
m, advisor ‖ corporate counsel ‖ counselor.

CONSOCIO.
m, partner, co-partner, associate, fellow partner (in a partnership) ‖ accomplice.

CONSOLIDACIÓN.
f, consolidation, solidity ‖ conversion of a floating debt to a term obligation ‖ funding (of a political party or government) ‖ recovery from another by the owner of the right to use property ‖ merger in one person of different rights pertaining to property.

CONSOLIDACIÓN DE FINCAS.
merger of two or more pieces of real estate.

CONSOLIDACIÓN HORIZONTAL.
horizontal combination.

CONSOLIDACIÓN VERTICAL.
vertical combination.

CONSOLIDAR.
v, to consolidate, bring together (e.g. property) ‖ to merge, combine ‖ to consolidate a servient and dominant estate by merger of rights and obligations in the same person ‖ to fund or convert a floating debt (to fixed and long term ‖ to support, back ‖ to strengthen.

CONSORCIADO.
adj, syndicated, pooled, merged.

CONSORCIAL.
adj, pertaining to a syndicate, consortium, pool, or merger.

CONSORCIO.
m, consortium, association of businesses such that they are managed with a common purpose, but maintain their individuality ‖ organization of condominium co-proprietors which is a separate legal entity) ‖ exploitation of public resources.

CONSORCIO BANCARIO.
bank syndicate.

CONSORCIO DE COPROPIETARIOS.
organization of co-proprietors of a condominium (to decide matters concerning the condominium).

CONSORCIO DE REASEGURO.
reinsurance pool.
CONSORTE.
m, spouse.
CONSORTES.
m, co-litigants (whether defendant or plaintiff) ‖ co-defendants ‖ spouses ‖ accomplices.
CONSPIRACIÓN.
f, conspiracy, plot.
CONSPIRADOR.
m, conspirator.
CONSPIRAR.
v, to conspire, plot.
CONSTANCIA.
f, perseverance ‖ exactitude, certainty (of fact) ‖ written proof or evidence.
CONSTANCIA DE DEUDA.
evidence of indebtedness.
CONSTANCIA ESCRITA.
written proof, record, or evidence.
CONSTANCIA NOTARIAL.
notary's attestation, notarial proof.
CONSTANCIAS.
f, records ‖ vouchers.
CONSTANCIAS JUDICIALES.
judicial records.
CONSTANTE EL MATRIMONIO.
during the marriage.
CONSTAR.
v, to be certain or clear ‖ to show, demonstrate ‖ to be evident ‖ to be recorded (in a book or writing) ‖ to integrate, to be constituted of various parts.
CONSTATAR.
v, to prove ‖ to affirm, verify.
CONSTE POR EL PRESENTE DOCUMENTO.
know all men by these presents.
CONSTITUCIÓN.
f, formation, constitution ‖ constitution of a government or corporation ‖ form of government ‖ regulation, order, norm ‖ incorporation.
CONSTITUCIÓN CONSUETUDINARIA.
unwritten constitution.
CONSTITUCIÓN CRIMINAL.
criminal tendencies.
CONSTITUCIÓN DE LA DOTE.
formation and delivery of the dowry.
CONSTITUCIONAL.
adj, constitutional.

CONSTITUCIONALIDAD.
f, constitutionality.
CONSTITUCIONALISMO.
m, constitutionalism, legal organization of a society pursuant to a constitution which is the highest law of the land.
CONSTITUIR.
v, to constitute, form, compose ‖ to found, create, establish ‖ to impose an obligation ‖ to appoint, depute.
CONSTITUIR QUÓRUM.
to constitute a quorum.
CONSTITUIR UNA SOCIEDAD.
to found or organize a company.
CONSTITUIRSE EN.
v, to take on, assume (e.g. an obligation or position).
CONSTITUIRSE EN OBLIGACIÓN.
to obligate or bind oneself ‖ to promise.
CONSTITUIRSE FIADOR.
v, to make oneself liable, vouch for, guaranty
CONSTITUIRSE POR.
See CONSTITUIRSE EN.
CONSTITUTIVO.
adj, essential ‖ constitutive.
CONSTITUTO.
m, leaseback ‖ transfer of title of a good to another with possession remaining in seller.
CONSTITUTO POSESORIO.
transfer of title of a good to another with the seller remaining in possession.
CONSTITUYENTE.
m, f, constituent ‖ adj, constituent, component ‖ establishing ‖ constitutional, pertaining to the right to constitute or establish.
CONSTREÑIMIENTO.
m, constraint, compulsion.
CONSTREÑIR.
v, to constrain, compel.
CONSTRUCCIÓN.
f, construction ‖ building, erection ‖ building, edifice ‖ art or science of construction.
CONSUEGRO.
m, relationship between mothers- and fathers-in law of a couple.
CONSUETA.
f, norms, customary rules, custom, practice.
CONSUETUDINARIO.
adj, customary, habitual.
CONSUETUDO.
See COSTUMBRE.

CÓNSUL.
m, consul ‖ judge of a commercial court.

CONSULADO.
m, consulate ‖ republican government ‖ consulship ‖ jurisdiction of consul ‖ consulate, building of consulate.

CONSULAJE.
m, consular fee.

CONSULAR.
adj, consular.

CONSULTA.
f, judgment (which requires an expert) ‖ legal advice ‖ legal opinion ‖ legal consultation or inquiry ‖ consultation, meeting (on legal point) ‖ advisory opinion ‖ inquiry.

CONSULTAR.
v, to consult, seek advice ‖ to inquire ‖ to opine, issue an advisory opinion ‖ to advise ‖ to consider, study.

CONSULTIVO.
m, advisory vote ‖ technical or expert body ‖ consultants' group ‖ adj, consultative ‖ advisory.

CONSULTOR.
m, consultant, advisor.

CONSULTOR JURÍDICO.
legal advisor.

CONSULTORIO.
m, law firm, lawyer's office ‖ professional's office.

CONSUMACIÓN.
f, consummation, end, termination, completion ‖ achievement of desired ends.

CONSUMACIÓN DEL DELITO.
consummation of a crime.

**CONSUMACIÓN DEL
MATRIMONIO.**
consummation of a marriage ‖ first sexual intercourse after marriage.

CONSUMADO.
adj, ended, concluded ‖ achieved ‖ unchangeable, consummate.

CONSUMAR.
v, to carry out (to the letter) ‖ to fulfill, complete ‖ to commit (a crime) ‖ to consummate (e.g. a marriage).

CONSUMAR EL MATRIMONIO.
to consummate the marriage.

CONSUMIBLE.
adj, consumed as a consequence of its first use.

CONSUMICIÓN.
f, consumption.

CONSUMIDO.
adj, consumed.

CONSUMIR.
v, to consume ‖ to eat ‖ to expend, spend ‖ tc destroy ‖ to extinguish.

CONSUMO.
m, consumption.

CONTABILIDAD.
f, accounting, accountancy.

CONTABLE.
m, accountant, book keeper ‖ adj, countable, computable ‖ accounting, related to accountancy.

CONTADO.
See AL CONTADO.

CONTADOR.
m, accountant, book keeper ‖ counter ‖ auditor ‖ cashier ‖ court appointed accountant (to liquidate an account) ‖ money-table.

CONTADOR AUTORIZADO.
certified public accountant (U.S.) ‖ chartered accountant (G.B.).

CONTADOR DIPLOMADO.
See CONTADOR AUTORIZADO.

CONTADOR FISCAL.
government tax or revenue officer, tax man.

CONTADOR JUDICIAL.
court-appointed auditor or accountant.

CONTADOR PARTIDOR.
accountant who acts as executor of an estate.

CONTADOR PERITO.
accountant who acts as an expert witness.

CONTADOR PÚBLICO.
certified or chartered public accountant ‖ public accountant.

**CONTADOR
TESTAMENTARIO.**
executor (designated by the deceased).

CONTADURÍA.
f, accountancy ‖ accountant's office and post ‖ accounting office.

**CONTAGIO DE ENFERMEDADES
VENÉREAS.**
transmission or communication of venereal diseases.

CONTANTE.
adj, cash.

CONTAR A UNO CON LOS MUERTOS.
to count someone as dead ‖ to scorn.

CONTENCIÓN.
f, dispute, contention ‖ litigation, lawsuit.
CONTENCIOSO.
adj, contentious, contested ‖ contradictory ‖ disputed, litigious.
CONTENCIOSO ADMINISTRATIVO.
related to administrative litigation (brought before a judge who deals with administrative matters).
CONTENDER.
v, to contend, argue, dispute ‖ to litigate, demand (of another) ‖ to fight, battle.
CONTENEDOR.
m, fighter, warrior ‖ litigant ‖ opponent ‖ container ‖ adj, containing ‖ holding back, restraining ‖ retaining.
CONTENIDO.
m, contents (of the law) ‖ extent of an obligation ‖ adj, contained ‖ restrained, temperate ‖ retained.
CONTENTA.
f, endorsement ‖ certificate of solvency ‖ release (of a debt by a creditor).
CONTESTABLE.
adj, litigable ‖ debatable, disputable, subject to dispute or agreement or contention ‖ able to be answered.
CONTESTACIÓN.
f, answer, reply, response ‖ dispute, contention ‖ affirmation or negation (to a judge's question).
CONTESTACIÓN A LA DEMANDA.
reply or plea or answer to a complaint.
CONTESTAR.
v, to answer, reply, respond ‖ to confess, swear before a witness, to swear on oath ‖ to confirm, prove, corroborate.
CONTESTAR EL PLEITO.
to answer the complaint.
CONTESTAR LA DEMANDA.
to answer the complaint.
CONTESTE.
adj, in accord or agreement with ‖ confirming (e.g. other witness's testimony. See TESTIGO CONTESTE.
CONTEXTO.
m, context.
CONTEXTUAL.
adj, contextual.
CONTIENDA.
f, lawsuit, litigation, case, dispute.

CONTIENDA INTERSINDICAL.
labor representation dispute, litigation between labor unions to represent workers.
CONTINENCIA DE LA CAUSA.
f, continuity of action, cohesion of litigation.
Occurs when lawsuits pertain to the same litigants, subject matter, and type of action, or to the same litigants and subject matter, or to the same subject matter and type of action, or to the same cause of action, or to the same type of action and litigants.
CONTINGENCIA.
f, contingency ‖ possibility ‖ risk.
CONTINGENCIA SOCIAL.
risk which is usually covered by governmental social security plan.
CONTINGENTE.
m, contingency, possibility ‖ quota, quantity of goods subject to import, export ‖ contingent (of troops) ‖ quota or part ‖ adj, contingent.
CONTINUACIÓN.
f, continuance ‖ continuation.
CONTINUAR.
v, to continue.
CONTINUIDAD.
f, continuity, uninterrupted state.
CONTINUO.
adj, continuous, permanent, continuing.
CONTRA.
f, difficulty, obstacle, inconvenience (in business) ‖ disadvantage; political opposition ‖ m, argument, reasoning (against a plan) ‖ con, negative ‖ prep, against, opposed to.
CONTRA EL ORDEN PÚBLICO.
against public policy, against the peace.
CONTRA LA PREPONDERANCIA DE LA PRUEBA.
against the weight or preponderance of the evidence.
CONTRA LEY.
against the law, illegal.
CONTRA TODO RIESGO.
against all risks.
CONTRAAFIANZAR.
v, to guarantee a mortgage or pledge ‖ to assure the payment of a guarantor or surety.
CONTRAASIENTO.
m, credit entry corresponding to debit (or vice versa).
CONTRAAPELACIÓN.
f, cross appeal.

CONTRAAPELAR.
v, to cross-appeal.
CONTRAAVISO.
m, contradictory and superseding notice.
CONTRABANDEAR.
v, to smuggle.
CONTRABANDEO.
m, smuggling.
CONTRABANDISTA.
m, black marketeer (to avoid taxes) ‖ smuggler (import or export).
CONTRABANDO.
m, contraband ‖ smuggling or selling or production of prohibited goods.
CONTRABANDO DE GUERRA.
war contraband.
CONTRACAMBIO.
m, exchange ‖ re-exchange, expense of undergoing a second exchange (in banking).
CONTRACTUAL.
adj, contractual.
CONTRADECLARACIÓN.
f, counterdeclaration, counteraffidavit.
CONTRADEMANDA.
f, counterclaim, reconvention.
CONTRADEMANDANTE.
m, f, counterclaimant ‖ crossplaintiff.
CONTRADEMANDAR.
v, to counterclaim.
CONTRADENUNCIA.
f, counterclaim ‖ counteraccusation.
CONTRADICCIÓN.
f, contradiction, negation ‖ opposition.
CONTRADICTOR.
m, contradictor ‖ opposition.
CONTRADICTORIA.
f, contradictory proposition.
CONTRADICTORIAMENTE.
adv, contradictorily.
CONTRADICTORIO.
m, adversarial action ‖ adj, contradictory.
CONTRADOCUMENTO.
m, document which opposes the effect of or contradicts another document.
CONTRAENDOSAR.
v, to re-indorse, return a draft to the person who indorsed it by means of endorsement.
CONTRAENDOSO.
m, re-endorsement, return of a draft to prior endorser by means of endorsement.

CONTRAER.
v, to contract, assume ‖ to obligate oneself ‖ to carry out (a legal obligation).
CONTRAER MATRIMONIO.
to marry, wed, get married.
CONTRAER UNA DEUDA.
to incur a debt.
CONTRAER UNA OBLIGACIÓN.
to incur an obligation.
CONTRAER DOMICILIO.
to become domiciled (somewhere).
CONTRAER MATRIMONIO.
to marry.
CONTRAER PARENTESCO.
to become a relative of someone else.
CONTRAESCRITURA.
f, specially notarized document which opposes the effect of another specially notarized document.
CONTRAESPIONAJE.
m, counterespionage.
CONTRAESTADÍA.
f, overstay (of a ship at an unloading berth).
CONTRAESTIPULACIÓN.
f, clause in an agreement used to the detriment of third parties or to avoid certain charges.
CONTRAFIADO.
m, indemnified, person who is indemnified.
CONTRAFIADOR.
m, indemnifier, person who indemnifies..
CONTRAFIANZA.
f, indemnity bond ‖ back bond.
CONTRAFUERO.
m, violation or infringement of a privilege.
CONTRAGARANTÍA.
f, counterguaranty.
CONTRAGIRO.
m, redraft.
CONTRAHACER.
v, to imitate ‖ to forge, falsify ‖ to counterfeit ‖ to pirate, plagiarize.
CONTRAHECHO.
adj, counterfeit, forged, falsified ‖ deformed, defective (regarding humans).
CONTRAINTERROGAR.
v, to cross-examine.
CONTRAINTERROGATORIO.
m, cross-examination.
CONTRAINSTRUMENTO.
See CONTRADOCUMENTO.

CONTRALOR.
m, comptroller, auditor, accounts examiner.
CONTRAMARCA.
f, countermark (on coins) ‖ second mark or brand, e.g. on animals, etc. ‖ right to impose a tax or charge a fee, thus placing a mark on the items for which tax has been paid.
CONTRAPARTE.
f, opposing party, adversary (to an action) ‖ counterpart.
CONTRAPARTIDA.
f, credit entry corresponding to debit (or vice versa).
CONTRAPETICIÓN.
f, counterclaim ‖ cross-motion.
CONTRAPOSICIÓN.
f, opposition.
CONTRAPRESTACIÓN.
f, consideration (in a contract) ‖ price.
CONTRAPRESTACIÓN INSUFICIENTE.
inadequate consideration.
CONTRAPROBANZA.
f, counterproof, counter-evidence.
CONTRAPROBAR.
v, to refute ‖ to disprove.
CONTRAPRODUCENTE.
adj, counterproductive.
CONTRAPROPOSICIÓN.
f, counteroffer, counter-proposal ‖ counter-motion.
CONTRAPROPUESTA.
f, counteroffer, counter-proposal.
CONTRAPROTESTO.
m, defense against a claim of a dishonored draft, that the drawer already paid an authorized person.
CONTRAPRUEBA.
f, second proof (of a book being published) ‖ conflicting evidence, counterevidence.
CONTRAPROYECTO.
m, substitute plan or draft ‖ change of plans ‖ legislative bill introduced by the executive, the majority of the legislature, or a special commission which opposes another bill.
CONTRAQUERELLA.
f, counterclaim by a party who has been accused in a QUERELLA.
CONTRARIAR.
v, to contradict, oppose ‖ to resist ‖ to impede, disturb.

CONTRARIO.
m, other party to a suit, adversary ‖ adj, opposite, contrary; unenforceable, adverse ‖ bad.
CONTRARIO A LA PRUEBA.
against the preponderance of the evidence.
CONTRARREGISTRO.
m, reappraisal of the documents or goods subject to restriction or tax by a customs or tax office.
CONTRARRÉPLICA.
f, rejoinder ‖ defendant's answer to plaintiff's replication.
CONTRARREPLICAR.
v, to draft a rejoinder.
CONTRARREQUERIR.
v, to join a co-guarantor (in an action) ‖ to bring a third party action against a co-guarantor.
CONTRARRESTAR.
v, to offset, set off ‖ to oppose.
CONTRARREVOLUCIÓN.
f, counterrevolution.
CONTRASEGURO.
m, re-insurance ‖ premium deposit insurance, retrievable premium insurance, insurance which insures the payment of pre-existing insurance.
CONTRASELLAR.
to counterseal.
CONTRASELLO.
m, counterseal, second seal.
CONTRASENTIDO.
m, absurdity.
CONTRASTE.
m, contrast ‖ dispute ‖ resistance, opposition ‖ assaying, public weighing of monies ‖ public assayer, public inspector of weights and measures.
CONTRATA.
f, contract, pact, agreement ‖ public registration of an agreement; public contract (between the government and a private party).
CONTRATA A LA GRUESA.
bottomry bond.
CONTRATA DE ARRIENDO.
lease.
CONTRATA DE FLETAMENTO.
charter party.
CONTRATABLE.
adj, able to be contracted ‖ subject to contract.

CONTRATACIÓN.

f, contract, agreement, pact ‖ commerce, business ‖ act of contracting ‖ contractual writing and payment, making of a contract.

CONTRATACIÓN COLECTIVA.

collective bargaining.

CONTRATACIÓN DIRECTA.

public contract (made without benefit of public bid).

CONTRATACIÓN LIBRE.

open-shop contract.

CONTRATACIÓN PREFERENTE.

modified closed shop contract (which requires preferential hiring of union members).

CONTRATACIÓN SEMILIBRE.

modified closed shop contract which allows the employer to hire non-union workers as long as they join the union within a specified time.

CONTRATADO.

m, contract worker, independent contractor ‖ adj, contracted.

CONTRATANTE.

m, contractor, contracting party, covenantee, covenanter ‖ hirer ‖ adj, contracting.

CONTRATAR.

v, to contract, make a contract for ‖ to hire, employ, engage.

CONTRATISTA.

m, f, contractor (with the government) ‖ contractor, independent contractor.

CONTRATO.

m, contract, agreement, pact.

CONTRATO A CORRETAJE.

general contract pursuant to which work is sublet.

CONTRATO A COSTO MÁS HONORARIO.

cost-plus contract.

CONTRATO A FAVOR DE TERCERO.

third party beneficiary contract, contract in favor of a third party.

CONTRATO A LA GRUESA.

bottomry bond.

CONTRATO A PRECIO GLOBAL.

lump-sum contract.

CONTRATO A PRECIOS UNITARIOS.

unit-price contract.

CONTRATO A SUMA ALZADA.

See CONTRATO A PRECIO GLOBAL.

CONTRATO A TÍTULO GRATUITO.

gratuitous contract.

CONTRATO A TÍTULO ONEROSO.

onerous contract, contract in which both parties have obligations to fulfill.

CONTRATO ABIERTO.

non-exclusive contract, contract which permits other parties to contract pursuant to the same terms.

CONTRATO ABSTRACTO.

contract which sets forth the obligations, but not the consideration for which the obligations are incurred.

CONTRATO ACCESORIO.

accessory contract.

CONTRATO ADMINISTRATIVO.

government contract (with administrative body). Includes public works contract, public services contract, concessions contract, etc.

CONTRATO AL MEJOR POSTOR.

contract to the highest bidder.

CONTRATO ALEATORIO.

hazardous contract, aleatory contract.

CONTRATO ANTENUPCIAL.

antenuptial agreement ‖ antenuptial settlement.

CONTRATO ATÍPICO.

atypical contract, contract which is not a traditionally denominated contract. See CONTRATO INNOMINADO.

CONTRATO BILATERAL.

bilateral contract.

CONTRATO CAUTELAR.

security agreement.

CONTRATO CIVIL.

civil contract, contract the terms of which are regulated by a civil code.

CONTRATO COLECTIVO DE ENGANCHE.

labor contract through an agent.

CONTRATO COLECTIVO DE TRABAJO.

collective bargaining agreement.

CONTRATO COMPLEJO.

contract which contains elements of different types of contract.
See CONTRATO INNOMINADO.

CONTRATO CON CLÁUSULA PENAL.

contract with a penalty clause.

CONTRATO CONDICIONAL.

conditional contract ‖ contract containing a condition.

CONTRATO CONJUNTO.

joint contract.

CONTRATO CONMUTATIVO.
commutative contract ‖ certain contract.

CONTRATO CONSENSUAL.
consensual contract.

CONTRATO CONSIGO MISMO.
See AUTOCONTRATO.

CONTRATO DE ADHESIÓN.
adhesion contract, contract of adhesion.

CONTRATO DE ADMINISTRACIÓN.
management contract.

CONTRATO DE AGENCIA.
agency agreement ‖ dealership contract.

CONTRATO DE AHORRO.
straight annuity contract, annuity certain.

CONTRATO DE AJUSTE.
seamen's contract, employment contract for ship's crew (on a trip basis).

CONTRATO DE APARCERÍA.
See APARCERÍA.

CONTRATO DE APRENDIZAJE.
apprenticeship agreement.

CONTRATO DE ARRENDAMIENTO.
lease, rental contract (of things).

CONTRATO DE ARRENDAMIENTO DE OBRAS.
See CONTRATO DE LOCACIÓN DE OBRA.

CONTRATO DE ARRENDAMIENTO DE SERVICIOS.
See CONTRATO DE LOCACIÓN DE SERVICIOS.

CONTRATO DE BENEFICENCIA.
gratuitous contract (for altruistic principles).

CONTRATO DE CAMBIO.
contract whereby one party agrees to pay a sum certain to the other party on behalf of a third party ‖ contract underlying the issuance of a draft ‖ contract for the exchange of foreign currency ‖ commutative contract, contract for valuable consideration which does not imply a permanent relationship between the parties.

CONTRATO DE CAPITALIZACIÓN.
"lottery annuity" contract, special annuity contract by which one party makes monthly payments to another, such that the other will pay an annuity at the end of the agreed term, or earlier if the policy holder is picked by lottery at an earlier time.

CONTRATO DE CESIÓN DE CRÉDITOS.
contract to assign an account, loan assignment contract. When the account is assigned for a

price, the law of sales applies; if it is assigned gratuitously, the law of gifts applies.

CONTRATO DE COLABORACIÓN EMPRESARIA.
type of joint venture, registered association of two or more companies for a specific purpose of joint interest. See AGRUPACIONES DE COLABORACIÓN and UNIONES TRANSITORIAS DE EMPRESA.

CONTRATO DE COMISIÓN.
commission contract.

CONTRATO DE COMODATO.
gratuitous bailment contract.

CONTRATO DE COMPAÑÍA MERCANTIL.
commercial partnership or incorporation agreement, contract whereby two persons invest effort and property, to carry out commercial activities and share in the profits.

CONTRATO DE COMPRA Y VENTA.
See CONTRATO DE COMPRAVENTA.

CONTRATO DE COMPRAVENTA.
sales or buy-sell or purchase agreement.

CONTRATO DE COMPROMISO.
arbitration agreement regarding a specific dispute; agreement whereby two or more parties agree to submit a definite dispute to the arbitration of a third party who they have voluntarily chosen.

CONTRATO DE CONCHABO.
employment contract.

CONTRATO DE CONDOMINIO.
agreement for joint tenancy or tenancy in common. See CONDOMINIO.

CONTRATO DE CORRETAJE.
brokerage contract ‖ contract whereby the CORREDOR (broker) agrees to search out business opportunities with third parties for the PRINCIPAL (principal).

CONTRATO DE CUADRILLA.
farm labor contract of a group of migrant farm workers.

CONTRATO DE CUENTA CORRIENTE BANCARIA.
contract for a bank account.

CONTRATO DE CUENTA CORRIENTE MERCANTIL.
contract for a commercial account.

CONTRATO DE CUSTODIA.
bailment contract, contract to bail goods to another party for their safekeeping, with or without payment.

CONTRATO DE DEPÓSITO.
bailment contract.
CONTRATO DE DOBLE.
repurchase agreement, contract whereby one party buys property from a second party and sells it back immediately. Although it involves two sales, it is treated as one transaction. There are three types: cash purchase and sale in the same month or the month following; purchase at the end of one month with sale in the following month; cash purchase and sale at other specified dates.
CONTRATO DE DONACIÓN.
donation agreement.
CONTRATO DE EDICIÓN.
publishing contract, contract between writer and publisher.
CONTRATO DE EJECUCIÓN DIFERIDA.
contract to be performed at a given moment in the future.
CONTRATO DE EJECUCIÓN INSTANTÁNEA.
contract which is performed simultaneously to the contracting.
CONTRATO DE EJECUCIÓN SUCESIVA.
contract to be performed over a given period of time.
CONTRATO DE EMBARCO.
See CONTRATO DE EMBARQUE.
CONTRATO DE EMBARQUE.
seaman's employment contract.
CONTRATO DE EMPEÑO.
pawn contract.
CONTRATO DE EMPLEO.
See CONTRATO DE TRABAJO.
CONTRATO DE EMPRESA.
independent contractor contract ‖ contract entered into in the normal course of business.
CONTRATO DE ENCADENAMIENTO.
exclusive dealing agreement, contract which requires a purchase of a product or service to buy exclusively from specified seller ‖ tying agreement.
CONTRATO DE ENFITEUSIS.
emphyteusis contract, contract for long term lease of real estate which requires the lessee to make improvements and pay an annual rental and which permits the lessee to transfer his rights by sale or donation.
CONTRATO DE ENGANCHE.
temporary employment contract of workers

who are contracted to work away from thei residences.
CONTRATO DE ENROLAMIENTO.
employment contract.
CONTRATO DE EQUIPO.
contract with a group of workers which grou as a whole is responsible for executing the work.
CONTRATO DE ESTABILIDAD.
price-control agreement. State agreemen with private parties by which certain prices are frozen and others are freed in order to en hance price stability.
CONTRATO DE FIANZA.
surety or guarantor agreement.
CONTRATO DE FIDEICOMISO.
trust agreement.
CONTRATO DE FIDUCIA.
trust agreement.
CONTRATO DE FLETAMENTO.
charter agreement, freight-charter agreemen ‖ shipping agreement.
CONTRATO DE GARANTÍA.
security agreement ‖ guarantor agreement.
CONTRATO DE HIPOTECA.
mortgage agreement.
CONTRATO DE INTENCIÓN.
letter of intent.
CONTRATO DE JUEGO.
bet, betting agreement.
CONTRATO DE LOCACIÓN.
type of contract which may be DE COSA or DE OBRA, or DE SERVICIOS (see below).
CONTRATO DE LOCACIÓN DE COSA.
rental or lease agreement pertaining to goods.
CONTRATO DE LOCACIÓN DE OBRA.
construction contract, building contract, contract by which one party agrees to construct or manufacture a thing.
CONTRATO DE LOCACIÓN DE SERVICIOS.
services contract, contract by which one party agrees to provide services to another.
CONTRATO DE MANDATO.
See MANDATO.
CONTRATO DE MUTUO.
type of temporary loan agreement by which goods are given to another for consumption pursuant to an agreement that goods of the same type and amount will be returned later.

CONTRATO DE OBRAS.
public works contract. Concluded by private
or public bid or by direct contract.
CONTRATO DE OPCIÓN.
option contract, firm offer. May be: OPCIÓN
DIRECTA (option contract entered into in
one's own name) or OPCIÓN MEDIADORA (option contract entered into by an agent on behalf of another).
CONTRATO DE PALABRA.
oral contract, gentlemen's agreement.
CONTRATO DE PASAJE.
common carrier contract, public transportation agreement. Usually regulated by the law
of common carriers.
CONTRATO DE PERMUTA.
barter agreement, agreement to exchange
goods.
CONTRATO DE PRENDA.
pledge or chattel mortgage agreement.
CONTRATO DE PRÉSTAMO.
loan agreement.
CONTRATO DE PRÉSTAMO DE
USO.
bailment agreement.
CONTRATO DE PRUEBA.
conditional employment contract (for a trial
or probation period) ‖ contract prior to a final
employment contract which provides the conditions under which a provisional employee
works ‖ agreement for purposes of testing
something.
CONTRATO DE PURA
BENEFICENCIA.
gift, donation agreement.
CONTRATO DE RENTA DE RETIRO.
retirement annuity or income contract.
CONTRATO DE RENTA VITALICIA.
life annuity agreement.
CONTRATO DE REPRESENTACIÓN.
production contract ‖ license agreement (to
produce a theatrical or musical work) ‖ agency
agreement.
CONTRATO DE RETROVENDENDO.
See CONTRATO DE RETROVENTA.
CONTRATO DE RETROVENTA.
repurchase agreement ‖ contract by which the
seller agrees to repurchase the thing sold upon
the occurrence of a stipulated condition.
CONTRATO DE SEGURO.
insurance agreement or contract.

CONTRATO DE SOCIEDAD.
partnership agreement ‖ incorporation agreement.
CONTRATO DE SUMINISTRO.
provisions or supply contract ‖ requirements
contract to supply government with goods.
CONTRATO DE TAREA.
task work contract, contract work.
CONTRATO DE TRABAJO.
employment contract, work agreement. Regulated by special legislation pertaining to
employment contracts.
CONTRATO DE TRACTO SUCESIVO.
See CONTRATO DE EJECUCIÓN SUCESIVA.
CONTRATO DE TRANSPORTE.
transportation agreement ‖ shipping agreement.
CONTRATO DE VENTA CONDICIONAL.
conditional sales contract.
CONTRATO DERIVADO.
subcontract ‖ secondary contract ‖ contract
which amplifies upon a primary contract.
CONTRATO DIRIGIDO.
contract which in large part is subject to government regulation.
CONTRATO DIVISIBLE.
divisible contract ‖ severable contract.
CONTRATO EN NOMBRE AJENO.
power of attorney or proxy agreement.
CONTRATO ENFITÉUTICO.
See CONTRATO DE ENFITEUSIS.
CONTRATO ENTRE AUSENTES.
contract created without being face to face
(e.g. via mail, telephone, telegram, etc.).
CONTRATO ESCRITO.
written contract.
CONTRATO ESTIMATORIO.
consignment sale contract, contract whereby
one party agrees to try to sell a good for another on condition that he or she be permitted
to keep the excess over an estimated value of
the good, and that good be returnable if sale is
not completed.
CONTRATO EXPRESO.
express contract.
CONTRATO EXTINTIVO.
nullifying contract, contract which repeals the
rights and obligations set forth in a prior contract.
CONTRATO FALSO.
See CONTRATO FINGIDO.

CONTRATO FIDUCIARIO.
trust agreement or indenture ‖ fiduciary agreement.

CONTRATO FINGIDO.
simulated contract.

CONTRATO FORMAL.
specialty or special agreement, contract which requires certain formalities in order to be valid.

CONTRATO FORZOSO.
contract required by law (e.g. a party is legally required to contract insurance).

CONTRATO GRATUITO.
See CONTRATO A TÍTULO GRATUITO.

CONTRATO ILÍCITO.
illegal contract, unlawful contract. Because such contract is null, ab initio, there is no obligation to perform. Formation of an illegal contract may also be a crime.

CONTRATO IMPLÍCITO.
implied contract.

CONTRATO INDIVIDUAL DE TRABAJO.
individual employment contract (i.e. with each employee individually).

CONTRATO INDIVISIBLE.
indivisible contract.

CONTRATO INFORMAL.
simple contract.

CONTRATO INNOMINADO.
unnamed or innominate contract, contract which lacks any special nomination or classification in the law. Contracts which fill definitional requirements set forth in codes are NOMINADOS (named); those which do not fulfill all requirements are INNOMINADOS (unnamed).

CONTRATO INSTANTÁNEO.
See CONTRATO DE EJECUCIÓN INSTANTÁNEA.

CONTRATO INTERNACIONAL.
international contract, contract between two or more persons of different countries. May be private-private, government-government or private-government.

CONTRATO "INTUITU PERSONAE".
personal contract ‖ contract based on a person's personal relationship or skill or judgment or character. Such a contract is non-assignable.

CONTRATO JUDICIAL.
contract of record, contract which by law requires the approval of a judge to be valid ‖

court ordered "contract" which requires t transfer of goods from one party to anothe regardless of the owner's consent ‖ agreeme between parties to continue the lawsu through decision ‖ agreement between parti to modify procedural aspects of a lawsuit. Al see TRANSACCIÓN.

CONTRATO JUSTO DE FLETAMENTO.
clean charter.

CONTRATO LEONINO.
unconscionable contract.

CONTRATO LÍCITO.
legal contract, lawful agreement.

CONTRATO LITERAL.
written contract.

CONTRATO LUCRATIVO.
See CONTRATO A TÍTULO ONEROSO.

CONTRATO MATRIMONIAL.
pre-nuptial agreement ‖ marriage settlemen

CONTRATO MERCANTIL.
commercial contract, contract regulated the commercial code. Usually due to one the parties acting as a merchant or the subjec matter being commercial.

CONTRATO MIXTO.
See CONTRATO COMPLEJO.

CONTRATO MÚLTIPLE.
mixed contract, contract which combines th qualities of various contracts identified in th codes.
See CONTRATO INNOMINADO.

CONTRATO NO SOLEMNE.
simple contract, contract requiring no lega formalities.

CONTRATO NOMINADO.
identifiable contract, contract identified anc described in a code. Opposed to CONTRATC INNOMINADO.

CONTRATO NORMATIVO.
contract which creates rules to regulate the fu ture conduct of the parties (e.g. collective bar gaining agreement).

CONTRATO NOTARIAL.
notarized contract, clerk-certified contract contract signed before a NOTARIO domestical ly, or before a consul or embassy if abroad. See NOTARIO.

CONTRATO NOTARIZADO.
See CONTRATO NOTARIAL.

CONTRATO NUPCIAL.
See CONTRATO MATRIMONIAL.

CONTRATO ONEROSO.
See CONTRATO A TÍTULO ONEROSO.

CONTRATO PARTIBLE.
divisible or severable contract.

CONTRATO PERFECTO.
enforceable or valid contract.

CONTRATO PIGNORATICIO.
pledge agreement.

CONTRATO PLURILATERAL.
multilateral contract. May be either joint or joint and several.

CONTRATO POR ADHESIÓN.
See CONTRATO DE ADHESIÓN.

CONTRATO POR CONCHABO.
See CONTRATO DE ENGANCHE.

CONTRATO POR CORREO.
mail-order contract ‖ letter contract, contract formed by an offer and acceptance sent by mail.

CONTRATO POR CORRESPONDENCIA.
See CONTRATO POR CORREO.

CONTRATO POR CUENTA DE QUIEN CORRESPONDE.
special contract for the benefit of an undetermined third party. This contract obliges one party to care for property during the period that true owner is not yet determined.

CONTRATO POR EQUIPO.
labor contract (entered into collectively by employees).

CONTRATO POR PERSONA A NOMBRAR.
contract by which the person, whose services are essential to the contract, is left unnamed until a later date.

CONTRATO PRELIMINAR.
preliminary contract, contract which sets forth, among other things, the terms of negotiation for and general framework of a later contract.

CONTRATO PREPARATORIO.
See CONTRATO PRELIMINAR.

CONTRATO PRESUNTO.
implied contract.
See CUASICONTRATO.

CONTRATO PRINCIPAL.
main contract, contract which is separate and independent, to which a subcontract usually is tied.

CONTRATO PRIVADO.
private agreement, contract regulated by non-

public law; simple contract, contract entered into without formalities.

CONTRATO PÚBLICO.
public contract, contract regulated by public law or public policy ‖ special contract, specialty, contract entered into with formalities.

CONTRATO REAL.
real contract, contract which requires the delivery of something to be valid (in addition to mere consent and capacity).

CONTRATO REMUNERATORIO.
contract in which a service is delivered in exchange for a payment which amount is left to the unilateral decision of the recipient of services (e.g. tips).

CONTRATO REVOCATIVO.
revocatory or nullifying contract, contract which revokes a prior contract.

CONTRATO SIMPLE.
See CONTRATO INFORMAL.

CONTRATO SIMULADO.
contract which attempts to hide the true purpose of the parties (e.g. to avoid taxes, etc.). Usually accompanied by a side agreement, either oral or written, in which the true purpose is set forth.

CONTRATO SINALAGMÁTICO.
bilateral contract.

CONTRATO SINDICAL.
collective bargaining agreement.

CONTRATO SOBRE SERVICIOS PÚBLICOS.
public service contract.

CONTRATO SOBREENTENDIDO.
See CONTRATO IMPLÍCITO.

CONTRATO SOCIAL.
social pact or agreement (between the citizenry and government in order that the latter be empowered to govern) ‖ contract which creates a business association ‖ partnership agreement.

CONTRATO SOLEMNE.
special contract, specialty, contract entered into with formalities.

CONTRATO SUCESIVO.
installment contract ‖ contract which requires periodic fulfillment of obligations.

CONTRATO SUI GENERIS.
sui generis contract.
See CONTRATO INNOMINADO.

CONTRATO TÁCITO.
implied contract.

CONTRATO TÍPICO.
typical contract, contract which is denominated pursuant to code law and which is not combined with other types.
See CONTRATO INNOMINADO.

CONTRATO UNILATERAL.
unilateral contract.

CONTRATO USURARIO.
usurious contract ‖ see also CONTRATO DE MUTUO and PRÉSTAMO.

CONTRATO VERBAL.
parol contract, oral agreement.

CONTRATO VERDADERO.
express contract, contract the purpose and terms of which are expressly stated.

CONTRATO-LEY.
union contract which is passed into law for an entire trade or industry.

CONTRAVALOR.
m, collateral.

CONTRAVENCIÓN.
f, contravention ‖ breach, infraction, violation of minor municipal ordinance or rules (frequently penalized by administrative penalties) ‖ violation, transgression (e.g. of contract, law, etc.), infraction.

CONTRAVENIR.
v, to violate, infringe, transgress ‖ to breach.

CONTRAVENTA.
f, purchase back, repurchase (by seller). See CONTRATO DE RETROVENTA.

CONTRAVENTOR.
m, contravenor ‖ breacher, violator ‖ transgressor.

CONTRAYENTE.
m, f, fiancee, betrothed party ‖ contracting party.

CONTRIBUCIÓN.
f, contribution, participation ‖ portion ‖ tax, levy, charge; assessment.

CONTRIBUCIÓN DE AVERÍA.
average contribution.

CONTRIBUCIÓN DE HERENCIA.
estate tax.

CONTRIBUCIÓN DE INMUEBLE.
See CONTRIBUCIÓN INMOBILIARIA.

CONTRIBUCIÓN DE MEJORAS.
proportional distribution of expenses among recipients of a benefit when voluntary contributions are inadequate ‖ improvements assessment.

CONTRIBUCIÓN DE SANGRE.
military service.

CONTRIBUCIÓN DIRECTA.
direct tax, levy imposed directly on persons.

CONTRIBUCIÓN ELECTORAL.
poll tax.

CONTRIBUCIÓN ESPECIAL.
extraordinary tax applicable under unusual circumstances, such as war (e.g. special capital gains tax, levy imposed on the value which private property has increased as a consequence of public works or services).

CONTRIBUCIÓN FISCAL.
national tax.

CONTRIBUCIÓN INDIRECTA.
indirect tax, levy imposed on production, sales, or consumption.

CONTRIBUCIÓN INDUSTRIAL.
professional services tax ‖ levy imposed on the service of a professional (e.g. attorney).

CONTRIBUCIÓN INMOBILIARIA.
real estate tax.

CONTRIBUCIÓN NOTARIAL.
notary's fee.

CONTRIBUCIÓN SOBRE BENEFICIOS EXTRAORDINARIOS.
excess-gains tax.

CONTRIBUCIÓN SOBRE INGRESO.
income tax.

CONTRIBUCIÓN SOBRE LA PROPIEDAD.
property tax.

CONTRIBUCIÓN SOBRE TRANSMISIÓN DE BIENES.
transfer tax.

CONTRIBUCIÓN SOBRE UTILIDADES.
income tax ‖ type of income tax imposed on capital gains, earnings, interest, dividends, etc.

CONTRIBUCIÓN TERRITORIAL.
real property or real estate tax (based on estimated sale value, value of products yielded by the land, value of potential productivity, etc.).

CONTRIBUCIÓN ÚNICA.
nonrecurrent tax.

CONTRIBUIR.
v, to pay taxes ‖ to voluntarily provide an amount (for a specified purpose) ‖ to help, cooperate ‖ to contribute.

CONTRIBUTARIO.
m, taxpayer ‖ usufructuary ‖ contributor.

CONTRIBUTIVO.
adj, contributing, pertaining to contributions ‖ tax, pertaining to taxes.

CONTRIBUYENTE.
See CONTRIBUTARIO.

CONTRINCANTE.
m, opposition, competitor, rival, adversary (in litigation).

CONTROL.
m, control.

CONTROL DE CAMBIOS.
(foreign) exchange control. There is usually an official rate set by the government and sometimes an unofficial black market rate to purchase money in violation of the exchange controls.

CONTROL OBRERO.
employee control or inspection or observance of a business (especially regarding compliance with legal and contractual norms). Distinguished from COGESTIÓN or PARTICIPACIÓN EN LA DIRECCIÓN DE LAS EMPRESAS which imply workers actual participation and responsibility in management.

CONTROLADO.
adj, controlled ‖ submitted for inspection.

CONTROLAR.
v, to control, exercise control ‖ to inspect, examine, assess ‖ to intervene, to register ‖ to watch over ‖ to govern, rule, dominate, direct, guide ‖ to approve ‖ to suspend ‖ to restrict.

CONTROVERSIA.
f, controversy, dispute (between nations or persons) ‖ lawsuit dispute, litigation.

CONTROVERTIBLE.
adj, controvertible, subject to question ‖ debatable ‖ actionable.

CONTROVERTIDO.
adj, controverted, debated, argued ‖ litigated.

CONTROVERTIR.
v, to controvert, argue, debate, discuss ‖ to litigate.

CONTUBERNAL.
m, cohabitant, one who shares a house and food with another.

CONTUBERNIO.
m, cohabitation, habitation with another ‖ illegal or immoral cohabitation, concubinage ‖

conspiracy, collusion, complicity (for illegal purpose).

CONTUMACIA.
f, non-appearance (in court), active or passive refusal to appear in court when summoned ‖ default, contumacy ‖ contempt of court. See REBELDÍA.

CONTUMAZ.
m, person who has failed to appear in court when summoned ‖ adj, obstinate, stubborn ‖ non-appearing, contumacious.

CONTUMAZMENTE.
adv, contumaciously ‖ obstinately, stubbornly.

CONTUMELIA.
f, insult, offense (spoken directly to the person) ‖ defamation spoken directly to the person).

CONVALIDACIÓN.
f, confirmation ‖ validation (of something invalid), legal action of making valid what was, theretofore, invalid.

CONVALIDACIÓN DE MATRIMONIO.
revalidation of marriage (which was null due to lack of real consent).

CONVALIDAR.
v, to confirm ‖ to validate, revalidate.

CONVENCER.
v, to convince, prove, persuade.

CONVENCIMIENTO.
m, conviction, belief ‖ persuasion ‖ proof.

CONVENCIÓN.
f, convention, custom ‖ meeting of city representatives or council member ‖ agreement, pact, convention. In private law, CONVENCIÓN of the parties is necessary to form a contract and a contract is, in a way, equivalent to a CONVENCIÓN.

CONVENCIÓN COLECTIVA DE TRABAJO.
See CONTRATO COLECTIVO DE TRABAJO.

CONVENCIÓN CONSTITUYENTE.
constitutional convention.

CONVENCIÓN DE TRABAJO.
labor agreement.

CONVENCIÓN INTERNACIONAL.
international agreement (to carry out a plan of mutual interest). Usually less formal and for ends less political than those of a treaty.

CONVENCIÓN MATRIMONIAL.
prenuptial agreement (regarding economic organization of marital couple).

CONVENCIONAL.
m, privilege (granted by convention) ‖ convention participant, delegate ‖ adj, conventional ‖ agreed, contractual, by agreement.

CONVENCIONISTA.
m, f, delegate, convention participant.

CONVENIDO.
m, defendant ‖ adj, agreed.

CONVENIO.
m, agreement, pact, treaty, entente, contract ‖ pool, entente, settlement.

CONVENIO COLECTIVO DE TRABAJO.
collective bargaining agreement.

CONVENIO COMERCIAL.
trade agreement.

CONVENIO CONCURSAL.
creditors' agreement (re: insolvency or bankruptcy).

CONVENIO CONDICIONADO.
conditional agreement.

CONVENIO DE COMERCIO RECÍPROCO.
reciprocal trade agreement.

CONVENIO DE FIDEICOMISO.
trust agreement.

CONVENIO DE GARANTÍA.
warranty agreement ‖ guaranty or surety agreement.

CONVENIO ENTRE DEUDOR Y ACREEDORES.
reaffirmation agreement ‖ debtor-creditor agreement (which involves a composition or an extension, or both) for the benefit of a debtor in bankruptcy. If the debtor fulfills the terms of such agreement, he is discharged.

CONVENIO ESCRITO.
written agreement.

CONVENIO EXPRESO.
express agreement.

CONVENIO IMPLÍCITO.
implied agreement.

CONVENIO INTERNACIONAL.
international agreement or treaty (between one or more governments, most frequently pertaining to non-political matters).

CONVENIO MAESTRO.
See CONVENIO PATRÓN.

CONVENIO PATRÓN.
master agreement.

CONVENIO VERBAL.
oral agreement.

CONVENIR.
v, to agree (in opinion or judgment) ‖ to meet, convene, gather (in a place) ‖ to pertain to, correspond ‖ to be useful or worthwhile ‖ to cohabit.

CONVENIRSE.
v, to come to an agreement, make a deal ‖ to be in accordance with; to reconcile oneself ‖ to convene.

CONVERSIÓN.
f, conversion ‖ transformation (of a void act into a legal one by ratification) ‖ change, modification ‖ replacement of paper money for coin ‖ reduction (in the rate of interest).

CONVERSIÓN DE ANOTACIONES PREVENTIVAS.
transformation or conversion of temporary lien to a permanent lien. The effective date of such registration is often that of the preliminary lien.

CONVERSIÓN DE LA DEUDA PÚBLICA.
conversion or novation of public debt instruments for other instruments.

CONVERTIBILIDAD.
f, convertibility (of foreign currency).

CONVERTIBLE.
adj, convertible, subject to conversion.

CONVERTIDO.
adj, converted, changed, transformed.

CONVERTIR.
v, to convert, change, transform. May refer to religious, political, moral or monetary conversion.

CONVICCIÓN.
f, conviction, certainty

CONVICTO.
m, convict, person who has been convicted under the law ‖ adj, convicted.

CONVINCENTE.
adj, convincing, persuasive.

CONVIVENCIA CONYUGAL.
f, marital co-habitation. Refers to the material and spiritual union of the couple.

CONVOCACIÓN.
f, convocation, public call or calling.

CONVOCAR.
v, to summon, call ‖ to convoke, convene, call together.

CONVOCAR A LICITACIÓN.
to call for bids.

CONVOCAR DE NUEVO.
to reconvene.
CONVOCAR UNA SESIÓN.
to call a meeting.
CONVOCATORIA.
f, decree (private or public) ‖ notice (of a meeting) ‖ summons (of a court).
CONVOCATORIA DE ACREEDORES.
petition to call creditors' meeting (before a judge, by a debtor's creditor, for the purpose of forestalling a debtor's bankruptcy). As a consequence of the CONVOCATORIA, the creditors will vote on a plan which the debtor proposes in order to extend the payment periods or to lower the level of payments. Upon an affirmative vote the plan must be approved by the court.
CONVOCATORIA PARA PROPUESTAS.
call for bids.
CONYÚDICE.
m, co-judge. See CONJUEZ.
CONYUGAL.
adj, conjugal, marital, pertaining to married couple, matrimonial, connubial.
CONYUGALMENTE.
adv, conjugally, matrimonially.
CÓNYUGE.
f, m, spouse. Spouses have reciprocal duties to live together, to be faithful, to help each other. Usually the husband and wife have different rights and duties as toward each other.
CÓNYUGE CULPABLE.
errant or culpable spouse (in a divorce) ‖ spouse whose actions has caused the divorce. The spouse loses the right to the marital estate, and to the custody of the children in proportion to the misconduct (except that the wife usually remains in custody of very young children).
CÓNYUGE FIDUCIARIO.
executor or executrix to distribute the estate of the decedent spouse. If the party remarries, he or she loses his or her right to be executor or executrix.
CÓNYUGE INOCENTE.
innocent spouse or party in a divorce case ‖ spouse whose actions do not give rise to an action for divorce. The spouse maintains the right to custody of the children and to the earnings of the errant spouse.

CÓNYUGE SOBREVIVIENTE.
See CÓNYUGE SUPÉRSTITE.
CÓNYUGE SUPÉRSTITE.
surviving spouse. The survivor has the right to a set percentage of the decedent's estate, regardless of the will.
CONYUGECIDA.
m, f, husband or wife who murders his or her spouse.
CONYUGECIDIO.
m, murder of a husband or wife by his or her spouse.
CONYUNTA.
contract by which a beast of burden is loaned for a period (usually one year), in consideration for which the borrower feeds and cares for the animal. Owner may reserve the right to use the animal for a few days each year.
COOBLIGACIÓN.
f, co-obligation, joint obligation ‖ obligation by which two or more obligors are jointly liable.
COOBLIGADO.
m, co-obligor, joint obligor ‖ guarantor, surety.
COOPERACIÓN.
f, cooperation ‖ collaboration, collective activity on a common enterprise.
COOPERACIÓN CRIMINAL.
aiding and abetting, criminal assistance or cooperation; consists of abetting in some way but for which the crime would not have been accomplished.
COOPERACIÓN DELICTIVA.
See COOPERACIÓN CRIMINAL.
COOPERATIVA.
f, cooperative ‖ cooperative corporation, co-op ‖ co-operative association ‖ voluntary association of people for business purposes the profits of which are distributed in accord with the degree of the person's non-monetary participation. May or may not be incorporated as a civil or business corporation. May be FAMILIAR (between family members) or DE VENTA LIBRE (open to non-family members); POPULAR or DE OBREROS (employees' cooperative) or DE COMERCIANTES (business cooperative); COLECTIVA (profits re-invested), INDIVIDUAL (benefits distributed among members), or MIXTA (a combination of the prior two) ‖ adj, cooperative.

COOPERATIVA DE ARRENDAMIENTO.
real estate leasing cooperative.
COOPERATIVA DE CONSUMO.
consumers' cooperative or co-op.
COOPERATIVA DE CRÉDITO.
credit cooperative or co-op.
COOPERATIVA DE PRODUCTORES.
producers' co-operative or co-op.
COOPERATIVISMO.
m, doctrine and movement in favor of economic and social cooperation and of cooperatives.
COOPERATIVISTA.
m, cooperative member, co-op member ‖ adj, cooperative, pertaining to co-operatives.
COOPERATIVO.
adj, cooperative, pertaining to cooperatives.
COPAR.
v, to corner, monopolize.
COPARTICIPACIÓN.
f, joint participation, co-participation ‖ co-partnership, partnership.
COPARTÍCIPE.
m, joint owner, joint tenant ‖ co-partner ‖ accomplice, partner (in crime) ‖ adj, joint, co-.
COPIA.
f, copy, duplicate ‖ transcript.
COPIA AUTENTICADA.
certified copy.
COPIA AUTORIZADA.
certified copy.
COPIA CARBÓN.
carbon copy.
COPIA CERTIFICADA.
certified copy ‖ office copy.
COPIA EN LIMPIO.
See COPIA LIMPIA.
COPIA FIEL.
true copy.
COPIA LEGALIZADA.
certified copy (of a document) ‖ legalized copy.
COPIA LIMPIA.
clean copy.
COPIADOR DE CARTAS.
type of book for the copying of letters required by law to be kept by businesses.
COPOSEEDOR.
m, joint possessor.
COPOSESOR.
See COPOSEEDOR.

COPOSESIÓN.
f, joint possession.
COPROPIEDAD.
f, joint tenancy, tenancy in common ‖ join ownership, co-ownership. See CONDOMINIO.
COPROPIETARIO.
m, joint tenant, tenant in common, join owner, co-owner.
CÓPULA.
f, sexual intercourse, coitus.
CÓPULA CARNAL.
See CÓPULA.
CORONA.
f, crown.
CORONEL.
m, colonel.
CORPORACIÓN.
f, legal entity ‖ corporation (no longer used) ‖ trade association ‖ trade union ‖ association, group ‖ public corporation.
CORPORACIONES DE OFICIOS.
professional organizations or associations ‖ guilds, trade unions, etc.
CORPORAL.
adj, corporal, corporeal, bodily ‖ material, real.
CORPORALIDAD.
f, corporeality.
CORPORATIVAMENTE.
adj, corporately.
CORPORATIVISMO.
m, system of socio-political organization made up of groups or associations of persons based on their common interests. The same interests organization of persons in groups
CORPORATIVO.
adj, corporate, pertaining to a corporation.
CORREAL.
See OBLIGACIÓN SOLIDARIA.
CORREALIDAD.
See OBLIGACIÓN SOLIDARIA.
CORRECCIÓN.
f, amendment ‖ improvement ‖ censure, reproach, reprimand, correction ‖ punishment, penalty (of courts and others) ‖ repression.
CORRECCIÓN DISCIPLINARIA.
disciplinary punishment (imposed by a superior for an error committed by a subordinate) ‖ judicial punishment for non-criminal contempt of court or negligence in legal proce-

dure imposed upon individuals, legal representatives, judges, and other judicial functionaries (except prosecuting attorneys).

CORRECCIONAL.
m, correctional institution, juvenile reformatory ‖ adj, corrective, correctional.

CORRECCIONALISMO.
m, penal system the basis of which is to modify criminal behavior through education.

CORRECTIVO.
m, sanction, penalty (usually for minor crimes or infractions), corrective ‖ adj, corrective.

CORREDOR.
m, broker, intermediary, middleman (usually in commercial agreements) ‖ stock broker.

CORREDOR DE CAMBIOS.
note and (foreign) exchange broker, middleman who negotiates commercial paper, money loans, or foreign exchange agreements, who determines the rate of interest, and who determines what guarantees are needed.

CORREDOR DE COMERCIO.
merchandise broker. Usually guarantees the identity and legal capacity of the parties, reviews the agreement for mistakes or misunderstandings, delivers certified copies of the contracts to the parties, and maintains professional secrecy regarding the proceedings. May also function as notary public if so qualified and documentation needs notarization.

CORREDOR DE OREJA.
See CORREDOR DE CAMBIOS.

CORREDOR INTÉRPRETE DE BUQUES.
licensed shipping agent. Must translate shipping documents and interpret for ship's captain, negotiate shipping contracts and maritime insurance, and represent the captain at trial.

CORREDURÍA.
f, brokerage, profession of broker ‖ broker's fee or commission ‖ accusation, denunciation.

CORREGIDOR.
m, magistrate ‖ mayor.

CORREGIDOR DE POLICÍA.
police commissioner.

CORREIDAD.
f, criminal relationship which unites two or more persons who have been accused of the same crime.

CORREO.
m, mail, post, correspondence ‖ postal service ‖ post office ‖ courier, mail boy ‖ accomplice or co-actor who acts as a courier for other criminals; accessory (to a crime) ‖ mail boat or plane.

CORREO CERTIFICADO.
registered mail.

CORRER.
v, to run ‖ to elapse ‖ to expire, run out (e.g. time, statute of limitations) ‖ to lease, rent ‖ to auction ‖ to fall or be due (in terms of money) ‖ to be exposed to, run (a risk).

CORRER EL PLAZO.
to have the time period running.

CORRER EL TÉRMINO.
to have the term run or be close to expiration.

CORRER EL TIEMPO.
to have the time pass or run.

CORRER LAS PAGAS.
to receive payment for services not rendered due to sickness, accident, or other permitted leave ‖ to be current in distributing salaries ‖ to be current in paying debts.

CORRER OBLIGACIÓN.
to be obligated.

CORRER POR MANO DE UNO.
to be in charge of something ‖ to depend on another for the resolution of something.

CORRESPONDENCIA.
f, correspondence, mail, post ‖ reciprocity.

CORRESPONDENCIA CERTIFICADA.
registered mail.

CORRESPONDENCIA REGISTRADA.
registered mail.

CORRESPONSAL.
m, f, correspondent ‖ merchant to whom another merchant grants authority to represent him in his commercial affairs ‖ letter-writer.

CORRETAJE.
m, brokerage ‖ broker's fee or commission for services rendered.

CORRETAJE MATRIMONIAL.
marriage brokerage, matchmaking service. Contracts of such services usually are legally accepted and enforceable.

CORRIENTE.
adj, standard, normal (in commerce) ‖ current, running.

CORRIGENDO.
m, convict, inmate (of a correctional institution).

CORROBORACIÓN.
f, corroboration, confirmation, ratification || reiteration (of an order).

CORROBORAR.
v, to corroborate, confirm, ratify || to reiterate.

CORROBORATIVO.
adj, corroborating.

CORROMPER.
v, to corrupt, pervert || to bribe, fix || to seduce (e.g. a woman).

CORROMPIDO.
adj, corrupt, corrupted || crooked, dishonest.

CORRUPCIÓN.
f, corruption, perversion, vice || bribery || seduction || depravity.

CORRUPTELA.
f, abuse of power || corruption || excessive tolerance (of subordinate) || abuse of rules || malpractice.

CORRUPTIBILIDAD.
f, corruptibility.

CORRUPTIBLE.
adj, corruptible, able to be perverted || bribable || perishable.

CORRUPTOR.
m, corruptor, perverter || briber.

CORSO.
See PATENTE DE CORSO.

CORTABOLSAS.
m, pickpocket, petty thief (of things on one's person).

CORTE.
f, court (of justice), tribunal || monarch's residence || national capital || small service for which one is paid || parliament.
Also see TRIBUNAL.

CORTE DE APELACIÓN.
court of appeals, appeals or appellate court.

CORTE DE CASACIÓN.
court of cassation. See CASACIÓN.

CORTE DE DISTRITO.
district court.

CORTE DE JUICIOS ORDINARIOS.
court of common pleas.

CORTE DE JUSTICIA.
court of justice.

CORTE DE POLICÍA.
police court.

CORTE DE SUCESIONES.
probate court.

CORTE DEL ALMIRANTAZGO.
admiralty court.

CORTE EN LO CIVIL.
civil court.

CORTE INTERNACIONAL DE JUSTICIA.
International Court of Justice.

CORTE MARCIAL.
court martial, military court.

CORTE MUNICIPAL.
municipal court.

CORTE NOCTURNA.
night court.

CORTE PERMANENTE DE JUSTICIA INTERNACIONAL.
Permanent Court of International Justice.

CORTE PLENA.
full court.

CORTE SUPERIOR.
superior court.

CORTE SUPREMA.
supreme court.

CORTE SUPREMA DE JUSTICIA.
Supreme Court (of a nation).

CORTES.
parliamentary or congressional session.

CORTES CONSTITUYENTES.
constitutional conventions.

CORTES ORDINARIAS.
congressional or parliamentary session to deal with ordinary or non-constitutional matters. Opposed to CORTES CONSTITUYENTES.

CORTESÍA.
f, courtesy, politeness || gift, favor || grace, generosity || grace period, extension of term for payment or credit term.

CORTESÍA INTERNACIONAL.
comity of nations.

CORTO DE MEDIOS.
short, short on money.

COSA.
f, chose, res || thing, object. COSA is a term of variable definition depending on the specific legal system. Among others, it may refer to any tangible object subject to valuation or to any tangible object regardless of susceptibility to valuation. Also see COSAS.

COSA ABANDONADA.
abandoned thing, chose that has been expressly or implicitly deserted by its owner or posses-

sor without intention to transfer it to another. The first party to exercise ownership rights over the thing is its true owner, with the exception of works of art.

COSA ACCESORIA.
res accessoria, accessory chose, accessory, accession, thing that is united to or dependant upon a principal thing. COSA ACCESORIA either cannot exist without the principal thing or, if truly independent, must in some way serve or complement the other thing.

COSA AJENA.
another's thing, chose of another person.

COSA ASEGURADA.
insured good.

COSA CIERTA.
proven thing, thing which exists, thing certain.

COSA COMÚN.
thing which is common to all and which belongs to no one, whether jointly or individually.

COSA CONSUMIBLE.
consumable, consumable item.

COSA CORPORAL.
corporeal thing, res corporeal, thing which can be perceived by the senses.

COSA DE DIOS.
act of God.

COSA DE NADIE.
res nullius, property of nobody.

COSA DETERMINADA.
specified thing, COSA CIERTA which has been duly individualized and identified.

COSA DIVISIBLE.
divisible thing.

COSA EN EL COMERCIO.
any thing which can be the object of private legal transactions.

COSA EN POSESIÓN.
chose in possession.

COSA ESPECÍFICA.
specific thing.

COSA FUERA DEL COMERCIO.
any thing which cannot be the object of a private legal transaction. This includes those which are prohibited by law, and those the transfer of which is encumbered by intervivos transfers or wills.

COSA FRUCTÍFERA.
fructiferous or fruit bearing thing.

COSA FUNGIBLE.
fungible good, res fungible.

COSA FUTURA.
See BIENES FUTUROS.

COSA GENÉRICA.
generic or indefinite thing.

COSA GRAVADA.
encumbered thing, object which is used to guaranty an obligation.

COSA HIPOTECADA.
mortgaged thing.

COSA HURTADA.
stolen thing, res furtiva.

COSA ILÍCITA.
illegal thing ‖ thing the legal transfer of which is prohibited ‖ infraction, misdemeanor.

COSA IMPOSIBLE.
impossible act (philosophically, physically, or morally).

COSA INALIENABLE.
See BIENES INALIENABLES.

COSA INCIERTA.
uncertain or unproven thing, something the existence of which has not been proven ‖ doubtful thing ‖ something not yet in existence.

COSA INCORPORAL.
incorporeal thing, res non-corporeal, thing which cannot be perceived by the senses.

COSA INDETERMINADA.
unspecified or generic thing.

COSA INDIVISIBLE.
indivisible thing, thing which would be destroyed by division. If co-owners of a COSA INDIVISIBLE are unable to agree upon its division or use, it must be sold; the price is then divided among the owners.

COSA INMATERIAL.
See BIENES INMATERIALES.

COSA INMUEBLE.
real property, real estate, res immobiles, immovable. Synonymous with BIEN INMUEBLE.

COSA JUZGADA.
res judicata, matter decided, thing decided by a court which has issued a final decision against which there is virtually no recourse. In order for the decision to have effect in other actions, the parties, thing, cause of action, and capacity of the parties must be the same in both actions.

COSA LÍCITA.
legal thing, thing the transfer of which is legal ‖ action which is not prohibited.

COSA LITIGIOSA.
subject of litigation, matter in dispute, res litigiosae; property which is the subject of litigation.

COSA MUEBLE.
chattel, movable thing, res mobiles. The concept of a COSA MUEBLE is more limited than that of personal property in that only the latter includes intangible property and rights.

COSA NO CONSUMIBLE.
See BIENES NO CONSUMIBLES.

COSA PERDIDA.
lost thing, thing about which the owner, possessor, or holder does not know the location. A finder of a lost thing must return it to its owner, possessor, or holder if he knows who it is. However, a finder of a lost thing usually must be compensated in accord with the value of the thing.

COSA PRINCIPAL.
principal thing, thing which needs no other thing to exist.

COSA PRIVADA.
private property.

COSA PROPIA.
one's own property.

COSA ROBADA.
See COSA HURTADA.

COSA SUSCEPTIBLE DE POSESIÓN.
property which legally may be subject to possession.

COSAS.
f, goods ‖ plural of COSA.

COSAS EN TRÁNSITO.
goods in transit.

COSECHA.
f, yield, harvest, crop.

COSTA.
f, cost, price ‖ coast.

COSTAS.
f, court costs, costs. Includes not only the filing fees, but also the fees payable to lawyers and other personnel in an action. Usually payable by the losing party, even in criminal actions.

COSTE.
m, cost, price, expense ‖ cost of living expenses, minimum expense necessary to maintain a typical two parent, two child home. Includes costs of household furniture and wares, housing, food, clothing, education, etc.

COSTEAR.
v, to pay for, finance.

COSTO.
m, payment in kind (for salary) ‖ cost, expense, price. In this sense, COSTE is used in Spain, and COSTO in Latin America.

COSTO DE LA VIDA.
cost of living. See COSTE.

COSTO DE VIDA.
See COSTO DE LA VIDA.

COSTUMBRE.
f, custom, practice ‖ routine, habit. COSTUMBRE may be GENERAL (national), LOCAL (district), or PARTICULAR (personal or group).

COSTUMBRES.
f, customs, mores.

COTEJO.
m, confrontation, comparison, contrast ‖ comparison of documents, comparative examination of documents to determine their authenticity, the exactitude of the copy, and similarity of the signature. Documents which both parties agree to, publicly sworn writings, judicially approved documents, etc. are admissible for the purposes of COTEJO.

COTEJO DE LETRAS.
expert examination of handwriting (between different documents or different parts of the same document).

COTIZACIÓN.
f, quote, quotation (of a price) ‖ bid. May or may not be enforceable.

COTIZAR.
v, to bid, quote (in a stock exchange or market).

COTO.
m, plot with boundary markers ‖ hunting grounds ‖ boundary, border ‖ boundary marker ‖ agreement to price-fix ‖ price, rate, tariff.

CREDENCIAL.
f, identification ‖ credential.

CREDENCIALES.
f, credentials (to identify a person's qualifications); credentials (for a foreign minister or a public employee).

CREDIBILIDAD.
f, credibility.

CRÉDITO.
m, reputation, standing, renown, personal credit ‖ payment, installment ‖ right to receive

a thing (usually money) ‖ loan, credit ‖ accommodation ‖ claim.
CRÉDITO A SOLA FIRMA.
unsecured credit.
CRÉDITO ABIERTO.
See APERTURA DE CRÉDITO and LETRA ABIERTA.
CRÉDITO ACTIVO.
active debt, loan (viewed from the vantage of creditor).
CRÉDITO ACTIVO DE LA HERENCIA.
claims on behalf of a decedent's estate against third parties.
CRÉDITO AL DESCUBIERTO.
unsecured credit or loan (usually granted on the basis of the borrower's solvency, good name, and history of timely payments).
CRÉDITO ANTICRÉTICO.
loan or credit secured by an ANTICRESIS.
CRÉDITO BANCARIO.
bank credit or loan (includes credit extended by other non-bank financial institutions) ‖ confidence in a bank (or other financial institution).
CRÉDITO CAMBIARIO.
right of collection in favor of a payee of a negotiable instrument.
CRÉDITO CIERTO.
existing debt.
CRÉDITO COMERCIAL.
commercial credit or loan.
CRÉDITO COMÚN.
loan or credit granted by an ACREEDOR COMÚN.
CRÉDITO CONFIRMADO.
confirmed credit or loan.
CRÉDITO CONSUNTIVO.
loan for purposes of consumption (versus production).
CRÉDITO DE ACEPTACIÓN.
acceptance credit.
CRÉDITO EXIGIBLE.
liquid debt, loan which is payable or collectible.
CRÉDITO EXTRAORDINARIO.
extraordinary budget item, extra budget which is approved apart from ordinary governmental budget, to cover unforeseen expenditures ‖ credit or loan granted under extraordinary circumstances.

CRÉDITO HIPOTECARIO.
mortgage loan or credit, mortgage. Transferrable to third parties if debtor is notified, and the transfer is made in a public writing usually filed with the real estate registry. Enjoys preference in a debtor reorganization or bankruptcy.
CRÉDITO INCOBRABLE.
bad or unrecoverable debt.
CRÉDITO LÍQUIDO.
liquidated debt.
CRÉDITO LITIGIOSO.
disputed debt (in litigation), doubtful debt ‖ debt in litigation.
CRÉDITO MERCANTIL.
commercial credit, merchants' credit.
CRÉDITO NO ENDOSABLE.
non-endorsable or non-negotiable loan (because of non-endorsability).
CRÉDITO ORDINARIO.
line item (in an ordinary government budget) ‖ ordinary debt, unprivileged debt.
CRÉDITO PASIVO.
passive debt, debt owed (viewed from the vantage of debtor).
CRÉDITO PASIVO DE LA HERENCIA.
claims against a decedent's estate by third parties.
CRÉDITO PERSONAL.
personal credit.
CRÉDITO PIGNORATICIO.
loan secured by a pledge. Enjoys privilege in a debtor reorganization or bankruptcy.
CRÉDITO PRENDARIO.
See CRÉDITO PIGNORATICIO.
CRÉDITO PRIVADO.
private loan (e.g. both debtor and creditor are private parties).
CRÉDITO PRIVILEGIADO.
privileged debt, debt payable before others in case of debtor reorganization or bankruptcy.
CRÉDITO PRODUCTIVO.
loan for purposes of production.
CRÉDITO PÚBLICO.
public or national debt.
CRÉDITO QUIROGRAFARIO.
unsecured credit.
CRÉDITO REAL.
secured loan or debt ‖ good credit, credit which is likely to be paid.

CRÉDITO REFACCIONARIO.
construction or repair loan, loan granted for the purpose of manufacturing or repairing goods. Enjoys a privilege in case of debtor reorganization or bankruptcy.

CRÉDITO SIMPLE.
loan or credit granted by an ACREEDOR SIMPLE.

CRÉDITO SOLIDARIO.
loan or credit granted by ACREEDORES SOLIDARIOS.

CREÍBLE.
adj, credible.

CREMACIÓN.
f, cremation.

CREMATÍSTICA.
f, political economy ‖ pecuniary interest (from a business transaction).

CRETINISMO.
m, cretinism, imbecility.

CRIADO.
m, domestic help or servant.

CRIATURA.
f, newly-born, newly-born child ‖ fetus ‖ creature.

CRIMEN.
m, crime, felony, major criminal offense ‖ fault. In criminal law, CRIMEN refers to more serious criminal transgressions, usually penalized by the death sentence or long prison terms.

CRIMEN CAPITAL.
capital crime, crime for which the penalty is death.

CRIMEN DE GUERRA.
war crime, violation of the laws of war.

CRIMEN PASIONAL.
crime of passion.

CRIMEN POLÍTICO.
political crime.

CRIMINAL.
f, m, criminal, offender ‖ felon (if serious) ‖ delinquent (if less serious) ‖ adj, criminal, felonious, delinquent.

CRIMINAL DE GUERRA.
war criminal, person who violates laws of war.

CRIMINAL HABITUAL.
habitual criminal, recidivist.

CRIMINAL REINCIDENTE.
See CRIMINAL HABITUAL.

CRIMINALIDAD.
f, criminality ‖ crime, total volume of crimes.

CRIMINALISTA.
m, criminologist, criminalist, penologist ‖ criminal attorney or lawyer.

CRIMINALÍSTICA.
f, criminology, study of crime to determine who committed the crime and when, where, and how it was committed.

CRIMINALIZAR.
v, to make a crime out of a previously legal act ‖ to transfer a case from the civil courts to the criminal courts ‖ to lead another into a life of crime.

CRIMINALMENTE.
adv, criminally.

CRIMINOGENIA.
f, study of crime as a pathological aberration.

CRIMINOLOGÍA.
f, criminology, penology, science of the study of crime.

CRIOLLO.
m, Creole ‖ child born outside of Europe to European parents ‖ Black child born in the Americas ‖ person born in the Americas of European ancestry.

CRISIS.
f, crisis ‖ critical moment.

CRISIS ECONÓMICA.
economic crisis.

CRISIS FINANCIERA.
financial crisis.

CRISIS LABORAL.
labor crisis.

CRISIS MINISTERIAL.
cabinet crisis, cabinet reorganization.

CRONOLOGÍA.
f, chronology, sequence of events.

CRUEL.
adj, cruel.

CRUELDAD.
f, cruelty.

CRUELDAD MENTAL.
mental cruelty.

CRUZ DEL MATRIMONIO.
cross of marriage, obligations and duties of marriage.

CRUZ ROJA.
Red Cross.

CRUZARSE DE MANOS.
to cross one's arms ‖ to remain inactive ‖ to strike.

CUADERNO DE BITÁCORA.
m, (ship's) logbook.

CUADERNO DE PRUEBA.
file of proof ‖ file in which all the evidence is collected in an action involving contested facts.

CUADRIENIO LEGAL.
m, the four years following obtaining legal majority. During this period the law usually allows the adult to exercise only some of the acts previously prohibited.

CUADRILLA.
f, gang or band of (four or more) criminals ‖ group of workers, work gang ‖ squad.

CUANTÍA.
f, amount, quantity, quanta ‖ amount of the demand less costs (which may determine the jurisdiction of a court) ‖ importance.

CUARENTENA.
f, quarantine.

CUARTA ACCIÓN.
f, action of employee against employer for recovery of damages, for sickness or accident, or for professional risks.

CUARTEL.
m, quarter, zone, district, area ‖ quarters, barracks.

CUARTEL DE POLICÍA.
police station.

CUARTO.
m, room ‖ chamber ‖ each of the branch of one's family through one's grandparents ‖ quarter ‖ adj, fourth, quarter.

CUASICONTRACTUAL.
adj, quasi-contractual.

CUASICONTRATO.
m, quasi-contract, quasi-contractus.

CUASIDELITO.
m, unintentional tort ‖ act or omission which unintentionally causes damage to another through carelessness, imprudence, or want of skill.

CUASIDELICTUAL.
adj, unintentionally tortious, related to CUASIDELITO.

CUASIJUDICIAL.
adj, quasi-judicial.

CUASINEGOCIABLE.
adj, quasi-negotiable.

CUASIPOSESIÓN.
f, possession of rights and other incorporeal property.

CUASIPÚBLICO.
adj, quasi-public, semi-public.

CUASIRRENTA.
f, quasi-rent, income in excess of costs from goods which are not reproducible in the short run (e.g heavy machinery).

CUASITRADICIÓN.
f, transfer of documents which represent the alienation of rights and other incorporeal property.

CUASIUSUFRUCTO.
m, quasi usufruct, right to use and enjoy a consumable thing. Opposed to true usufruct. CUASIUSUFRUCTO requires the return of goods similar in type to those given in USUFRUCTO.

CUATRERISMO.
m, livestock theft or rustling.

CUATRERO.
m, livestock thief or rustler.

CUATRO QUINTOS.
m, four-fifths portion (of a decedent's estate to which the descendants are entitled in some civil law jurisdictions).

CUBIERTA DE ACTUACIONES.
f. cover page of an action brought in military court.

CUBRIR.
v, to cover ‖ to pay ‖ to hide ‖ to pretend ‖ to cover up ‖ to defend, represent.

CUBRIR EL EXPEDIENTE.
to fulfill all the requirements ‖ to appear to fulfill all the requirements.

CUBRIR LA CUENTA.
to cover the account.

CUBRIRSE.
v, to cover or pay a debt ‖ to cover oneself.

CUBRIRSE CON LAS ÓRDENES.
to cover oneself or excuse oneself by stating that one is or was acting under orders from a superior.

CUENTA.
f, count, calculation, counting ‖ account, bill, check ‖ (accounting) statement ‖ explanation, reason, accounting ‖ obligation, duty, charge.

CUENTA ACREEDORA.
positive balance (of an account).
CUENTA AJENA.
another's account ‖ another's behalf.
CUENTA AUXILIAR.
adjunct account.
CUENTA CONJUNTA.
joint account.
CUENTA CONVENIDA.
account stated.
CUENTA CORRIENTE.
commercial account, current or open account.
CUENTA CORRIENTE BANCARIA.
checking account. May be AL DESCUBIERTO
(with right to overdraw) or CON PROVISIÓN DE
FONDOS (without right to overdraw).
**CUENTA CORRIENTE
MERCANTIL.**
commercial checking account ‖ commercial
account or running balance between merchants.
CUENTA DE CAPITAL.
capital account.
CUENTA DE COSTAS.
account of (court) costs.
CUENTA DE CRÉDITO.
credit or loan account.
CUENTA DE GANANCIAS Y PÉRDIDAS.
profit and loss statement or account.
**CUENTA DE LA ADMINISTRACIÓN DE
LA HERENCIA.**
account of an administrator or executor or executrix regarding a decedent's estate.
CUENTA DE REGRESO.
protest charges.
CUENTA DE RESACA.
protest charges (of a dishonored bill of exchange against the maker of the bill).
CUENTA DE TUTELA.
trust account ‖ guardianship account.
CUENTA DE VENTA.
bill of sale.
CUENTA DEUDORA.
account with a negative balance ‖ account payable.
CUENTA FIDUCIARIA.
trust account.
CUENTA INCOBRABLE.
bad debt.
CUENTA JUDICIAL.
debt being collected through litigation.

CUENTA JURADA.
account for litigation-related fees and expenses. There is a special process for collection
which requires that the person who wishes to
collect swear that the account is due and
owing.
CUENTA LIQUIDADA.
liquidated or settled account.
CUENTA MALA.
bad debt.
CUENTA PARTICIONAL.
account for division (of something).
CUENTA SIMULADA.
pro forma account.
**CUENTA SUJETA A
PREAVISO.**
notice account, account subject to prior notice.
CUENTACORRENTISTA.
m, holder of a current account (either commercial or bank account).
CUENTAS DE ORDEN.
memoranda accounts.
CUENTAS EN PARTICIPACIÓN.
type of joint venture.
See SOCIEDAD ACCIDENTAL and SOCIEDAD EN
PARTICIPACIÓN.
CUERDA FLOJA.
f, papers that are not part of court record but
are in the file.
CUERDO.
adj, sane, sound, reasonable.
CUERPO.
m, body (of laws, people, etc.) ‖ corps (military, consular, etc.), party.
CUERPO DE BIENES.
total assets.
CUERPO DE DISCIPLINA.
disciplinary body.
CUERPO DE ESCRITURA.
brief writing provided in camera at the request
of other party for the purpose of comparing
handwriting.
CUERPO DE LA HERENCIA.
corpus of a decedent's estate.
CUERPO DE LEYES.
See CUERPO LEGAL.
CUERPO DE POLICÍA.
See CUERPO POLICÍACO.
CUERPO DE VIGILANCIA PARTICULAR.
body of private guard, bodyguard, or police.

CUERPO DEL DELITO.
corpus delicti, proof of crime including not only the victim, but the instruments of the crime, and virtually all other physical evidence of the crime ‖ positive fact of commission of crime.

CUERPO DEL DERECHO.
See CUERPO LEGAL.

CUERPO DIPLOMÁTICO.
diplomatic corps.

CUERPO ELECTORAL.
electorate, electoral body.

CUERPO JURÍDICO DE LA ARMADA.
judicial body of the armed forces.

CUERPO LEGAL.
body of laws, corpus juris ‖ code.

CUERPO LEGISLATIVO.
legislative body.

CUERPO MUNICIPAL.
municipal body or entity.

CUERPO POLICÍACO.
police force.

CUESTIÓN.
f, question ‖ matter, issue, affair ‖ doubt ‖ dispute, controversy; problem, conflict.

CUESTIÓN ARTIFICIAL.
artificial or feigned issue. See CUESTIÓN.

CUESTIÓN COLATERAL.
collateral issue or matter.
See CUESTIÓN.

CUESTIÓN DE COMPETENCIA.
conflict of venue between two courts or judges. May be POSITIVA (both courts take the case) or NEGATIVA (neither court takes the case.)

CUESTIÓN DE CONFIANZA.
request for a vote of confidence.

CUESTIÓN DE DERECHO.
issue in law, question of law. See CUESTIÓN.

CUESTIÓN DE HECHO.
question of fact. See CUESTIÓN.

CUESTIÓN DE JURISDICCIÓN.
See CONFLICTO DE JURISDICCIÓN.

CUESTIÓN DE PROCEDIMIENTO.
point of order, question of procedure.

CUESTIÓN DE PURO DERECHO.
question of law. If case rests on this alone, it may lead to a summary judgment due to lack of factual dispute.

CUESTIÓN EN DISPUTA.
matter in issue or controversy. See CUESTIÓN.

CUESTIÓN ESPECIAL.
special issue. See CUESTIÓN.

CUESTIÓN FABRICADA.
sham or fictitious issue.
See CUESTIÓN.

CUESTIÓN GENERAL.
general issue. See CUESTIÓN.

CUESTIÓN PREJUDICIAL.
question which must be resolved by a court before another court may hear the case (e.g. question of whether a debtor is legally bankrupt before bankruptcy proceeding may be held).

CUESTIÓN PREVIA.
matter precedent (which must be resolved prior to resolution of main action) ‖ administrative issue (which may have effect upon criminal matter). See CUESTIÓN.

CUESTIÓN SOCIAL.
See PROBLEMA SOCIAL.

CUESTIÓN SUSTANCIAL.
factual or substantial question or issue or controversy. See CUESTIÓN.

CUESTIONABLE.
adj, questionable, doubtful, dubious.

CUESTIONAR.
v, to question, interrogate ‖ to doubt ‖ to debate, discuss, dispute.

CUESTIONARIO.
m, questionnaire ‖ interrogatory.

CUIDADO.
m, care, caution ‖ fear, preoccupation, worry ‖ charge, care, custody.

CULPA.
f, fault, failing ‖ blame ‖ culpability, guilt negligence, liability. In civil law, CULPA is the unintentional lack of due diligence, for which the actor is civilly liable in tort. In criminal law CULPA is the violation of a law without intent or malice, for a reason that could or should have been avoided. May be IN FACIENDO (positive action) or IN OMITTENDO (omission).

CULPA CIVIL.
non- criminal liability or negligence.
See CULPA.

CULPA CON PREVISIÓN.
See CULPA CONSCIENTE.

CULPA CONCURRENTE.
joint fault (of actor and victim), comparative negligence. In such cases, the actor must compensate the victim only for the amount by

which the percentage of fault of the victim exceeds the percentage of fault of the actor.

CULPA CONSCIENTE.
foreseen fault.

CULPA CONTRACTUAL.
contractual failure (whether negligent or intentional) which results in breach ‖ contractual negligence which results in breach.

CULPA CUASIDELICTUAL.
tortious negligence ‖ liability or fault caused by CUASIDELITO (i.e. carelessness or imprudence or want of skill).

CULPA DE LA VÍCTIMA.
comparative negligence.
See CULPA CONCURRENTE.

CULPA DELICTUAL.
voluntary act or omission resulting in the violation of a law or regulation and which constitutes a tort.

CULPA ESTRICTAMENTE DICHA.
ordinary fault, fault caused by imprudence, negligence, or lack of skill or care.

CULPA EXTRACONTRACTUAL.
tortious negligence or liability, non-contractual (and non-criminal) liability or negligence. fault which causes a non-contractual violation of a right. See CULPA.

CULPA GRAVE.
See CULPA LATA.

CULPA "IN CONTRAHENDO".
See CULPA PRECONTRACTUAL.

CULPA INCONSCIENTE.
unforeseen (criminal) fault.

CULPA LATA.
gross fault, lata culpa ‖ lack of the most basic due diligence of a careful person to avoid harm.

CULPA LEVE.
ordinary fault, levis culpa ‖ lack of attention or care of an ordinary reasonable person.

CULPA LEVÍSIMA.
slight fault, levissima culpa ‖ lack of diligence resulting in an omission of an ordinary reasonable person.

CULPA MORAL.
See RESPONSABILIDAD MORAL.

CULPA NO DOLOSA.
unintentional culpability, fault which results without intent to case harm.

CULPA OBJETIVA.
See RESPONSABILIDAD OBJETIVA.

CULPA PENAL.
criminal negligence. May be either DOLO (gross fault, fault committed with intent) or CULPA ESTRICTAMENTE DICHA (ordinary fault, fault caused by imprudence, negligence, or lack of skill or care).

CULPA POR ABSTENCIÓN.
fault due to omission, negligent omission.

CULPA PRECONTRACTUAL.
pre-contractual negligence or liability.

CULPA PROFESIONAL.
professional fault or negligence.

CULPA SUBJETIVA.
negligence determined on the basis of factual carelessness, imprudence or want of skill. Opposed to violation or law which constitutes negligence.

CULPABILIDAD.
f, culpability, liability ‖ guilt.

CULPABLE.
f, m, responsible or guilty party, culprit ‖ adj, culpable, liable; guilty.

CULPABLEMENTE.
adv, culpably.

CULPACIÓN.
f, accusation ‖ confession.

CULPADAMENTE.
adv, culpably.

CULPADO.
m, author (of a crime) ‖ culprit ‖ adj, accused, charged.

CULPAR.
v, to blame, accuse, attribute blame ‖ to find guilty.

CULPARSE.
v, to blame oneself, confess.

CULPOSO.
adj, culpable ‖ guilty (in terms of crimes which involve intent).

CULTO.
m, cult ‖ rite ‖ religion ‖ adj, polite, cultured, refined ‖ learned, educated.

CULTURA.
f, culture (in all senses) ‖ education, refinement ‖ civilization.

CÚMPLASE.
m, literally, an order to be obeyed. Words placed at the foot of a law upon publication to indicate that the law is to have full force and effect.

CUMPLIDOR.
m, person who fulfills an obligation(s) ‖ adj, reliable, trustworthy.

CUMPLIMIENTO.
m, fulfillment, performance ‖ satisfaction (of an obligation); term of military service ‖ expiration, maturity ‖ completion.

CUMPLIMIENTO DE LA CONDENA.
service of the (criminal) sentence.

CUMPLIMIENTO DE LA LEY.
compliance with the law.

CUMPLIMIENTO DE LA OBLIGACIÓN.
contractual performance ‖ performance of an obligation.

CUMPLIMIENTO DE LAS PENAS.
satisfaction of the (judicial) sanctions.

CUMPLIMIENTO DE UN DEBER.
fulfillment of a duty or order. In criminal law fulfillment of an order may serve to excuse an otherwise illegal act.

CUMPLIMIENTO ESPECÍFICO.
specific performance.

CUMPLIMIENTO MATERIAL.
material performance.

CUMPLIMIENTO PARCIAL.
partial performance.

CUMPLIMIENTO PROCESAL.
compliance with the rules of procedure.

CUMPLIR.
v, to carry out, perform, fulfill, execute ‖ to discharge ‖ to satisfy ‖ to reach (a certain age) ‖ to expire, mature ‖ to finish (military service) ‖ to serve (a criminal sentence).

CUMPLIR CON ESPECIFICACIONES.
to meet specifications.

CUMPLIR DE PALABRA.
to promise, but not to carry out.

CUMPLIR EL PEDIDO.
to fill the order.

CUMPLIR LA PALABRA.
to carry out one's promises.

CUMPLIR LA PRUEBA.
to pass the test.

CUMPLIR UNA SENTENCIA.
to serve a sentence.

CUMPLIRSE EL PLAZO.
to mature (in terms of a term) ‖ to lapse (in terms of a term).

CUMULATIVO.
adj, cumulative.

CUÑADA.
f, sister-in-law, sister of a husband or wife relative to the spouse of the husband or wife.

CUÑADO.
m, brother-in-law, brother of a husband or wife relative to the spouse of the husband or wife.

CUOTA.
f, quota, share, portion allotment (of an inheritance, business, corporation, etc.) ‖ (import or export) quota ‖ installment, installment payment ‖ contribution ‖ fee, commission.

CUOTA CONTRIBUTIVA.
tax rate ‖ tax assessment.

CUOTA DE IMPORTACIÓN.
import quota.

CUOTA DE IMPUESTO.
tax rate.

CUOTA DE RETRIBUCIÓN.
rate of return.

CUOTA EN AVERÍA GRUESA.
general average contribution.

CUOTA IMPONIBLE.
taxable value.

CUOTA LITIS.
(lawyer's) contingent fee. Also see PACTO DE CUOTA LITIS.

CUOTA MORTUORIA.
death benefit.

CUOTA OBREROPATRONAL.
assessment for workmen's social security paid by employer.

CUOTA VIUDAL.
usufructuary portion of surviving spouse.

CUPO.
m, share or quota of service or tax (owed by each town or city) ‖ import, export, or production quota ‖ share of recruits which each town must send to do military service.

CUPÓN.
m, coupon, document attached to certain instruments which when torn off accompany the payment of installments or against which payments are paid.

CUPÓN DE ACCIÓN.
dividend coupon.

CUPÓN DE DEUDA.
coupon cut from a bond.

CUPÓN DE DIVIDENDO.
dividend coupon.

CURADOR.

m, curator ‖ administrator ‖ trustee ‖ conservator ‖ guardian, legal guardian. Also see TUTOR. The spouse is the CURADOR for his/her incapacitated spouse's estate. Adult sons are the CURADOR of their parents' estate. Parents are the CURADOR for their unmarried children. CURADOR'S are equally responsible for the children of his or her initial charge.

CURADOR AD HOC.

curator ad hoc, special judicial guardian named when the initial CURADOR has interests opposed to that of his charge.

CURADOR AD LITEM.

curator ad litem, guardian ad litem (selected by a judge to protect the interests of a minor, an absent party, or an otherwise incapacitated party).

CURADOR DE BIENES.

curator bonis ‖ administrator, conservator, curator of goods until they can be given to the person who owns them.

CURADOR DE INCAPACES.

guardian of an adult who is an invalid or mentally ill. Sometimes called TUTOR.

CURADOR DE LA HERENCIA.

administrator of a decedent's estate, executrix (female), executor (male). This CURADOR must perform an inventory witnessed by a notary public and two witnesses.

CURADOR DEL AUSENTE.

administrator of the estate of a disappeared person or an absentee. This CURADOR is designated by a judge and is required to administer the property of the disappeared party on his behalf.

CURADOR NATURAL.

natural guardian (father or mother).

CURADOR PARA EL CASO.

guardian ad hoc.

CURADURÍA.

f, position of guardian or curator or trustee (i.e guardianship, curatorship, trusteeship).

CURANDERISMO.

m, illegal practice of medicine ‖ witch doctoring.

CURANDERO.

m, quack doctor.

CURATELA.

f, guardianship of estates of adults who ar legally unable to care for their property.

CURATELA DATIVA.

guardianship decided by the court.

CURATELA LEGÍTIMA.

legal guardianship, guardianship determine by law.

CURATELA TESTAMENTARIA.

guardianship (named by parents in a will, t administer the estate of their invalid, mentall ill, or deaf and dumb and illiterate children).

CURIA.

f, bar, body of legal professionals ‖ tribuna court.

CURIAL.

m, officer of the court, court clerk ‖ attorney lawyer.

CURSO.

m, course (of a lawsuit).

CURSO DE CAMBIO.

rate of exchange (of credit instruments o moneys) ‖ body of stock exchange transac tions.

CURSO FORZOSO.

legal tender, currency which must by law b accepted.

CURSO LEGAL.

legal tender or currency.

CURSO NORMAL DE LOS NEGOCIOS.

ordinary course of business.

CUSTODIA.

f, custody ‖ guardianship, custodianship guard ‖ care, protection ‖ deposit

CUSTODIA LEGIS.

legal custody.

CUSTODIAL.

adj, custodial.

CUSTODIAR.

v, to guard, watch ‖ to have custody of or ove ‖ to care for, take care of, protect.

CUSTODIO.

m, custodian, guardian, watchman ‖ depossitary ‖ adj, custodial, guardian.

CZAR.

See ZAR.

CH

CHACRA.
f, small farm.
CHALÁN.
m, sharp or astute merchant ‖ horse-trader.
CHALANEAR.
v, to be a sharp or cunning business man or woman.
CHANCILLER.
See CANCILLER.
CHANTAJE.
m, blackmail ‖ extortion.
CHANTAJISTA.
m, blackmailer ‖ extortioner.
CHARTISMO.
See CARTISMO.
CHEQUE.
m, check.
CHEQUE A LA ORDEN.
order check, check payable to the order of.
CHEQUE AL PORTADOR.
bearer check, check payable to the bearer.
CHEQUE CERTIFICADO.
certified check.
CHEQUE CIRCULAR.
bank money order, cashier's check.
CHEQUE CRUZADO.
check for deposit only (which is indicated by two parallel lines drawn across its text).
CHEQUE CRUZADO GENERAL.
check for deposit only in any bank.
See CHEQUE CRUZADO.
CHEQUE CRUZADO ESPECIAL.
check for deposit only in a specified bank.
See CHEQUE CRUZADO.
CHEQUE DE CAJA.
cashier's check.

CHEQUE DE GERENCIA BANCARIA.
See CHEQUE DE CAJA.
CHEQUE DE VIAJE.
See CHEQUE DE VIAJERO.
CHEQUE DE VIAJERO.
traveller's check.
CHEQUE DOCUMENTADO.
documentary check, check payable against presentment of documents.
CHEQUE DOMICILIADO.
domiciled check, check which is payable only at a certain bank.
CHEQUE IMPUTADO.
check for the payment of a specific debt (which is so indicated on the check).
CHEQUE PARA ACREDITAR EN CUENTA.
check for deposit only (which is so indicated by words to such effect).
CHEQUE POSTAL.
postal money order.
CHEQUE SIN FONDOS.
bad check, check written against insufficient funds.
CHEQUE VISADO.
See CHEQUE CERTIFICADO.
CHICANA.
f, legal chicanery, lawyers' dilatory tactics ‖ woman born in the United States of Mexican parents ‖ woman born in Mexico of American parents ‖ woman born in Mexico of Mexican parents who has lived the majority of her life in the United States.
CHICANO.
m, man born in the United States of Mexican parents ‖ man born in Mexico of American parents ‖ man born in Mexico of Mexican

parents who has lived the majority of his life in the United States.

CHOFER.
m, chauffeur.

CHOFER PARTICULAR.
private chauffeur.

CHOQUE.
m, crash, collision ‖ automobile accident ‖ accident involving vehicles, planes, or vessels ‖ fight ‖ quarrel ‖ clash, conflict, (unfortunate) encounter ‖ battle ‖ war ‖ (physical or emotional) shock.

CHOZNO.
m, great-great-great grandson ‖ great-great-great grandchild.

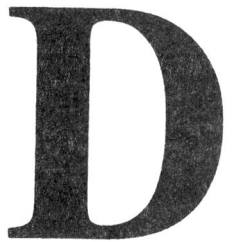

DACIÓN.

f, giving, surrender, act of giving ‖ delivery ‖ datio (not used in Anglo-American law).

DACIÓN DE ARRAS.

payment of earnest money.

DACIÓN EN PAGO.

thing in lieu of payment, voluntary delivery by a debtor and acceptance by a creditor of a chose, in lieu of fulfillment of the agreed obligation.

DACTILAR.

adj, digital, finger, pertaining to fingers.

DACTILOGRAMA.

m, fingerprint, dactylogram.

DACTILOSCOPÍA.

f, dactyloscopy, identification (of persons) by fingerprint.

DACTILOSCÓPICO.

adj, dactyloscopic.

DACTILOSCOPISTA.

m, f, fingerprint expert.

DÁDIVA.

f, gift, present, dation ‖ donation, contribution, grant ‖ thing given pursuant to volition (i.e not obligatory).

DÁDIVAS A FUNCIONARIOS PÚBLICOS.

bribery of public servants ‖ gifts to public officials (which cannot be classified as bribery).

DADOR.

m, giver, grantor ‖ donor, contributor ‖ drawer, maker (of commercial paper).

DADOR DE PRÉSTAMO.

lender, creditor.

DADOR DE TRABAJO.

employer.

DAMA.

f, woman ‖ lady ‖ mistress, concubine.

"DAMNATIO".

criminal sentence (no longer used).

DAMNIFICADO.

m, injured party, victim ‖ adj, injured, damaged.

DAMNIFICADOR.

m, injurer.

DAMNIFICAR.

v, to injure, damage.

" DAMNUM ABSQUE INJURIA".

damnum absque injuria, non-actionable damage.

"DAMNUM EMERGENS".

See DAÑO EMERGENTE.

DAÑADO.

adj, bad, perverse ‖ damaged, spoiled (food) ‖ injured.

DAÑADOR.

m, injurer, damager.

DAÑAR.

v, to injure, damage, harm (in any way) ‖ to mistreat ‖ to let spoil ‖ to spoil, go bad.

DAÑINO.

adj, damaging, injurious, harmful ‖ corrupting, pernicious.

DAÑO.

m, damages ‖ nuisance ‖ compensation recoverable in court for damage or harm suffered ‖ damage, injury, loss, harm ‖ mistreatment. Daño may result in civil and/or criminal liability.

DAÑO AQUILIANO.

quasi-delictual damage, damage which results from carelessness, imprudence, or lack of skill.

DAÑO CAUSADO A LOS INTERESES DEL PATRONO.

damage or loss to employer's interests. If

caused by negligence or intentional employee conduct, employee may be liable.

DAÑO CAUSADO POR ANIMALES.
injury or loss caused by animals. Owner of the animal(s) may be liable.

DAÑO CAUSADO POR COSAS INANIMADAS.
injury or loss caused by inanimate objects. Owner or guardian or user may be liable.

DAÑO CAUSADO POR HECHO AJENO.
injury or loss caused by acts of a third party. A party different from the actor may be liable depending upon the relationship between the two (e.g. parent-child, employer-employee, etc.).

DAÑO CORPORAL.
bodily harm, personal injury, physical damage (to one's person).

DAÑO CIERTO.
sum-certain damages ‖ damages which are not speculative.damages may be certain even though their amount cannot be precisely determined at a given time.

DAÑO DIRECTO.
direct damages.

DAÑO EMERGENTE.
damages resulting from contractual breach of debtor ‖ physical damage to personal property.

DAÑO EVENTUAL.
speculative damages.

DAÑO FORTUITO.
damage resulting from force majeure.

DAÑO IMPREVISTO.
unforeseeable injury ‖ injury resulting from force majeure.

DAÑO INDIRECTO.
consequential damages.

DAÑO IRREPARABLE.
irreparable harm ‖ harm resulting from an unappealable interlocutory order.

DAÑO MATERIAL.
physical damage.

DAÑO MORAL.
injury caused to one's honor, reputation, affections, or sentiments by another's negligence or intentional acts ‖ pain and suffering and/or emotional distress.

DAÑO PARTICULAR.
injury to an individual's rights (where no general rights of society are involved).

DAÑO PATRIMONIAL.
See DAÑO MATERIAL.

DAÑO PERSONAL.
personal injury, bodily harm, physical damage (to one's person); personal injury, injury caused to oneself or one's personal rights.

DAÑO POTENCIAL.
See DAÑO EVENTUAL.

DAÑO RESARCIBLE.
recoverable or compensable damages.

DAÑO UNIVERSAL.
damage to society's rights. Opposed to DAÑO PARTICULAR.

DAÑOS ANTICIPADOS.
prospective damages.

DAÑOS CAUSADOS POR ANIMALES.
injuries or loss caused by animals. Owner of the animal(s) may be liable.

DAÑOS CAUSADOS POR COSAS INANIMADAS.
injuries or loss caused by inanimate objects. Owner or guardian or user may be liable.

DAÑOS CAUSADOS POR HECHO AJENO.
injuries or loss caused by acts of a third party. A party different from the actor may be liable depending upon the relationship between the two (e.g. parent-child, employer-employee, etc.).

DAÑOS COMPENSATORIOS.
compensatory damages.

DAÑOS CONTINUOS.
continuing damages.

DAÑOS CONVENCIONALES.
stipulated damages, damages agreed to by contract.

DAÑOS E INTERESES.
damages plus interest ‖ damages caused by a debtor's failure to timely pay, plus the resulting loss of interest.

DAÑOS EFECTIVOS.
actual damages.

DAÑOS EJEMPLARES.
exemplary or punitive damages, smart money.

DAÑOS ESPECIALES.
See DAÑOS INDIRECTOS.

DAÑOS ESPECULATIVOS.
speculative damages.

DAÑOS GENERALES.
general damages.

DAÑOS ILÍQUIDOS.
unliquidated damages.

DAÑOS INDIRECTOS.
indirect or special damages.
DAÑOS INMEDIATOS.
proximate or direct damages.
DAÑOS INMODERADOS.
excessive damages.
DAÑOS INTERNACIONALES.
damages incurred by one country and caused by another.
DAÑOS NO DETERMINADOS.
unliquidated damages.
DAÑOS NO LIQUIDADOS.
See DAÑOS NO DETERMINADOS.
DAÑOS NOMINALES.
nominal damages.
DAÑOS PECUNIARIOS.
monetary damages.
DAÑOS PUNITIVOS.
vindictive or exemplary or punitive damages, smart money.
DAÑOS REMOTOS.
remote damages.
DAÑOS SOBREVENIDOS.
subsequent damages.
DAÑOS Y PERJUICIOS.
Literally, damages and losses ‖ damages, compensation for damage or loss.
DAÑOSO.
adj, damaging, injurious, prejudicial ‖ harmful.
DAR.
v, to give, transmit, transfer ‖ to give, donate, make a gift ‖ to delive ‖ to bestow (a position or title) ‖ to offer (employment) ‖ to apply, dispose ‖ to permit, authorize ‖ to produce, occur ‖ to incur ‖ to declare.
DAR A CONOCER.
to make known.
DAR A CRÉDITO.
to loan, lend (without guarantee) ‖ to sell on credit (without further guarantee).
DAR AUDIENCIA.
to hold a hearing or trial.
DAR AVISO.
to give notice.
DAR CARPETAZO.
to set aside, shelve ‖ to conclude (a matter), consider (a matter) closed.
DAR CONOCIMIENTO.
to serve ‖ to serve notice ‖ to report ‖ to make known.

DAR CRÉDITO.
to believe, trust (in a person or occurrence) ‖ to grant a credit.
DAR CUENTA.
to report, inform ‖ to account for, justify ‖ to render an account.
DAR DE BAJA.
to cancel, eliminate, charge off.
DAR DE MANO.
to leave something or someone ‖ to stop or suspend work.
DAR DERECHO DE UNO.
to obligate someone to do something through court-order.
DAR EL SÍ.
to give one's approval or yes or okay to something ‖ to agree to something ‖ to agree to sexual intercourse or marriage.
DAR EN ARRIENDO.
to lease, rent, let.
DAR EN PRENDA.
to pledge, give pursuant to a pledge.
DAR EXPEDIENTE.
to expedite.
DAR FE.
to swear to, attest, witness, certify.
DAR FIANZA.
to give bond or bail, bond.
DAR LA FIRMA.
to empower a representative (to carry on business dealings).
DAR LA PALABRA.
to give someone the floor (to speak at a meeting).
DAR LA RAZÓN A.
to agree or side with.
DAR LAS NOVEDADES.
to give an update (on the news).
DAR LECTURA.
to read, have read.
DAR MUERTE.
to put to death ‖ to murder, assassinate ‖ to kill in war.
DAR OBEDIENCIA.
to recognize someone as one's superior and to obey orders.
DAR ÓRDENES.
to give orders, order.
DAR PALABRA Y MANO.
to give one's hand in marriage ‖ to give one's word.

DAR PARTE.
to notify, inform, advise ‖ to offer membership or participation (in a company or transaction).

DAR PODER.
to empower ‖ to give a proxy or a power of attorney.

DAR POR CONCLUSO.
to be ready to issue sentence ‖ to close, consider finished.

DAR POR NULO.
to void or nullify (an action, transaction, or agreement) ‖ to make ineffective.

DAR POR QUITO.
to declare innocent or free of obligation.

DAR POR RECIBIDO.
to acknowledge receipt.

DAR POR TERMINADO.
to adjourn (e.g. a meeting).

DAR POR VENCIDO.
to make or cause to become due and payable.

DAR PRESTADO.
to lend.

DAR PRÓRROGA.
to grant an extension (in time), extend a term.

DAR SU PALABRA.
to give one's word, promise orally.

DAR TIERRA.
to bury, inter.

DAR UN VEREDICTO.
to return a verdict.

DAR VISTA.
to require a litigant to take a position about a matter (e.g. to answer a request made by the opposing party) ‖ to hold a hearing ‖ to open a record for inspection.

DARSE.
v, to exchange, give to one another ‖ to surrender, give in ‖ to dedicate oneself (to something).

DARSE A MERCED.
to unconditionally capitulate, give up, surrender.

DARSE LAS MANOS.
to collaborate ‖ to associate, unite, join together ‖ to reconcile ones' differences.

DARSE POR CITADO.
to accept a summons.

DARSE POR NOTIFICADO.
to accept service.

DATA.
f, date and place (at which an event occurred or a document or contract is signed) ‖ (accounting) entry or item.

DATAR.
v, to date, indicate the date and place.

"DATIO".
See DACIÓN.

"DATIO IN SOLITUM".
See DACIÓN EN PAGO.

DATIVO.
m, judicially-appointed legal guardian of a minor or an incompetent ‖ judicially-appointed administrator or executor or executrix (of a decedent's estate).

DATO.
m, document, instrument ‖ to make or post an accounting entry ‖ datum, information.

DATOS.
data, information.

"DE AUDITU".
on hearsay.

DE BIEN ESSE.
provisionally.

"DE CUJUS".
from whom one claims. Used to distinguish decedent from one who inherits.

DE DERECHO.
de jure.

DE FACTO.
See DE HECHO.

DE FUERO.
de jure.

DE GRACIA.
adj, gratis, free ‖ de gratia, as a favor ‖ grace (e.g. period).

DE HECHO.
de facto ‖ arbitrarily ‖ in fact, really, actually. Used to designate a government which takes power without legal right. Opposed to DE JURE or DE DERECHO.

DE JURE.
See DE DERECHO.

DE LA MANO Y PLUMA.
from the hand of, hereby signed by. Used to identify a true signature of the purported person.

DE MALAS.
with twisted intention ‖ disposed to hurt or denigrate.

DE MANCOMÚN.
adv, jointly.

DE MANO A MANO.
directly, personally.
DE MENOS.
short, less.
DE OCASIÓN.
second-hand, used ‖ at a bargain or reduced-price.
DE OCULTIS.
clandestinely ‖ in hiding ‖ carefully.
DE OFICIO.
officially, under authority, pursuant to law ‖ by administrative initiative ‖ sua sponte. Used to refer to court-appointed attorneys and to decisions or orders made by a judge, at his own instance.
DE OÍDAS.
on hearsay.
DE ORDENANZA.
obligatory.
DE PERSONA A PERSONA.
personally, directly ‖ alone (between two people).
DE PLENO DERECHO.
by law, exclusively. Refers to legal relationship which arises by reason of law only.
DE PRESTADO.
precarious, revocable ‖ as a loan ‖ on loan.
DE PRIMERA MANO.
from the first seller ‖ from the manufacturer ‖ first-hand ‖ from the source ‖ original.
DE PÚBLICO Y NOTARIO.
public knowledge, well-known facts ‖ judicially recognizable facts, facts of which court may take judicial notice.
DE QUOTA LITIS.
See PACTO DE QUOTA LITIS.
DE SANA MENTE.
of sound mind, sane.
DE SEGUNDA MANO.
from the second or last seller ‖ second-hand, used ‖ copied.
DE TRÁNSITO.
in transit, travelling ‖ temporary, not permanent.
DE TURNO.
on duty.
DE VISTA.
on personal knowledge ‖ having actually seen the matter in question. Opposed to DE OÍDAS or "DE AUDITU".

DE VISU.
See DE VISTA.
DEAMBULAR.
v, to be fugitive ‖ to ramble, roam.
DEBATE.
m, debate, controversy, discussion. Used legislatively.
DEBATIR.
v, to discuss, debate, argue.
DEBE.
m, debit ‖ debt, unpaid loan ‖ position of debtor.
DEBELACIÓN.
f, armed victory, conquest by war.
DEBENTURE.
m, debenture, bond.
DEBENTURISTA.
m, f, holder of debentures.
DEBER.
m, debt, monetary obligation ‖ duty, obligation ‖ v, to owe, be in debt (to a party) ‖ to have to.
DEBER DE ASISTENCIA.
duty of assistance. In domestic relations, includes duty of physical and emotional support. In reference to emergencies, refers to the duty to render assistance. In labor law, refers to the duty to comply with duties of employment, especially in terms of hours of work.
DEBER DE COHABITACIÓN.
duty of cohabitation. Refers to marital duty to reside in the same home and to have sexual relations.
DEBER DE FIDELIDAD.
See FIDELIDAD CONYUGAL.
DEBER DE OBEDIENCIA.
duty of obedience. Refers in military and administrative law, to duty owed by subordinate to his superior ‖ in domestic relations, refers to duty of wife to husband, and of children to their parents.
DEBER DE SOCORRO.
duty of support (in domestic relations) ‖ duty to render emergency assistance.
DEBER JURÍDICO.
legal duty or obligation. Opposed to moral duty. May be ABSOLUTO (absolute) or RELATIVO (relative); RELIGIOSO (owed to God), SOCIAL (owed to another), or PERSONAL (owed to oneself); POSITIVO (to act) or NEGATIVO (to refrain from action) ‖ PERPETUO (permanent) or TEMPORAL (temporary); EXIGIBLE (legally

binding) or NO EXIGIBLE (not legally binding);
COERCIBLE (enforceable) or INCOERCIBLE
(unenforceable).

DEBERES.
m, duties, obligations.

DEBERES DEL HOMBRE Y DEL CIUDADANO.
See DECLARACIÓN DE LOS DERECHOS DEL
HOMBRE Y DEL CIUDADANO.

DEBERES IMPOSITIVOS.
tax obligations.

DEBERES JUDICIALES.
judicial duties.

DEBERES PROCESALES.
procedural requirements or obligations.

DEBIDA DELIBERACIÓN.
due consideration.

DEBIDA DILIGENCIA.
due diligence.

DEBIDAMENTE.
adv, duly, properly ‖ justly.

DEBIDAMENTE JURAMENTADO.
duly sworn.

DEBIDO.
adj, owed, due ‖ owing ‖ corresponding ‖
legal, licit ‖ past participle, owing (to), due
(to), because (of).

DEBIDO AVISO.
due notice.

DEBIDO PROCEDIMIENTO DE LEY.
See DEBIDO PROCEDIMIENTO LEGAL.

DEBIDO PROCEDIMIENTO LEGAL.
due process of law.

DEBIDO PROCESO.
due process.

DEBIL MENTAL.
adj, feebleminded.

DEBILIDAD MENTAL.
f, mental deficiency, retardation, feeblemin-
dedness.

DEBITAR.
v, to debit.

DEBITAR DE MÁS.
to overdebit.

DÉBITO.
m, debit ‖ debt.

DÉBITO CONYUGAL.
obligation of each spouse to the other to participate in sexual intercourse.

DÉCADA.
f, decade, period of ten years ‖ period of ten
days.

DECADENCIA.
f, decadence ‖ lapsing, depression, slump.

DECAER.
v, to fall ‖ to lapse.

DECALVACIÓN.
f, shaving of the head.

DECALVAR.
v, to shave (the hair of a person as punishment).

DECANO.
m, dean ‖ president (of a professional association) ‖ senior member (of an organization).

DECAPITACIÓN.
f, beheading, decapitation.

DECENCIA.
f, decency ‖ honesty, rectitude ‖ dignity, propriety.

DECESO.
m, death (whether legal or natural).

DECIDIR.
v, to decide, come to a decision, determine,
find, form a judgment ‖ to settle, resolve.

DECIR.
m, testimony, statement ‖ saying, aphorism,
maxim ‖ v, to say, state, tell ‖ to testify, show ‖
to affirm, assure ‖ to opine, express an opinion
‖ to name, call.

DECIR DE AGRAVIO.
to request an explanation or excuse.

DECIR UNA PALABRA.
See HABLAR UNA PALABRA.

DECISIÓN.
f, decision, opinion, judgment ‖ finding ‖ verdict ‖ resolution, determination ‖ substantive
law or rule ‖ strength of character.

DECISORIO.
adj, decisive, definitive ‖ final ‖ convincing.

DECLARABLE.
adj, declarable, able to be stated or declared.

DECLARACIÓN.
f, statement, declaration ‖ communication,
manifestation (of something otherwise not
known) ‖ finding, determination, conclusion
(of a judge) ‖ publication, communication ‖
sworn statement or testimony (includes depositions, interrogatories, questions, examination in court, etc.). In criminal law, the defendant's answer is called DECLARACIÓN
INDAGATORIA ‖ in civil law, the defendant's
answers to interrogatories are called CONFE-
SIÓN EN JUICIO.

DECLARACIÓN ABSTRACTA.
statement of intent or will (but not the cause or basis from which it derives).
DECLARACIÓN ARANCELARIA.
customs declaration.
DECLARACIÓN DE ADUANA.
See DECLARACIÓN ARANCELARIA.
DECLARACIÓN DE AUSENCIA.
(judicial) determination of (a person's) absence or disappearance.
DECLARACIÓN DE BIENES.
accounting, statement of property owned.
DECLARACIÓN DE CONCURSO.
declaration of insolvency or bankruptcy.
DECLARACIÓN DE CONTRIBUCIÓN SOBRE INGRESOS.
income tax return.
DECLARACIÓN DE CULPABILIDAD.
confession ‖ guilty plea.
DECLARACIÓN DE DERECHOS.
bill of rights.
DECLARACIÓN DE DERECHOS Y GARANTÍAS.
bill of (constitutional rights).
DECLARACIÓN DE ENTRADA.
See DECLARACIÓN ARANCELARIA.
DECLARACIÓN DE FALLECIMIENTO.
See DECLARACIÓN DE MUERTE DE AUSENTE.
DECLARACIÓN DE GUERRA.
declaration of war.
DECLARACIÓN DE HEREDEROS.
See DECLARATORIA DE HEREDEROS.
DECLARACIÓN DE IMPUESTOS.
See DECLARACIÓN FISCAL.
DECLARACIÓN DE INCAPACIDAD.
finding of incompetency ‖ adjudication of incompetency. Judicial decision required in order to name a guardian for mentally insane, mentally retarded, or deaf-mute.
DECLARACIÓN DE INCONSTITUCIONALIDAD.
declaration or statement of unconstitutionality.
DECLARACIÓN DE INDEPENDENCIA.
Declaration of Independence.
DECLARACIÓN DE INOCENCIA.
plea of not guilty or innocence.
DECLARACIÓN DE MUERTE DE AUSENTE.
(judicial) certification or declaration of presumptive death.

DECLARACIÓN DE NEUTRALIDAD.
affirmation of neutrality.
DECLARACIÓN DE NULIDAD.
annulment ‖ declaration of voidness.
DECLARACIÓN DE OFICIO.
sua sponte judicial decision.
DECLARACIÓN DE QUIEBRA.
(judicial) determination of bankruptcy or pronouncement of bankruptcy. Determination made upon proof that the debtor is a merchant, that he has ceased to pay his debts as they come due, and that he is insolvent. See QUIEBRA.
DECLARACIÓN DE REBELDÍA.
finding of non-appearance, judicial decision made upon a party's failure to appear after having been summoned. Requisite to permit a case to proceed where the defendant has failed to appear.
DECLARACIÓN DE RECHAZO.
notice of dishonor.
DECLARACIÓN DE RENTA.
income tax return.
DECLARACIÓN DE TESTIGOS.
witnesses' testimony of statements (made upon written or oral deposition).
DECLARACIÓN DE VOLUNTAD.
manifestation of consent. Required for all valid acts which create, transfer, modify. or terminate rights or obligations. May be EXPRESA (express) or TÁCITA (implied).
DECLARACIÓN EN COMISIÓN.
(temporary) executive suspension of power and duties of government official.
DECLARACIÓN EXPRESA.
See DECLARACIÓN DE VOLUNTAD.
DECLARACIÓN FALSA.
false testimony ‖ false statement, lie (made with knowledge of its falseness).
DECLARACIÓN FISCAL.
tax return or statement.
DECLARACIÓN INDAGATORIA.
signed declaration or statement (of a criminal defendant from the unsworn answers to questions about the facts of the case).
DECLARACIÓN JUDICIAL.
testimony or statement made upon deposition of the parties and their witnesses (in civil and criminal actions) ‖ judicial finding or conclusion or determination, court order ‖ favorable decision (of judge).

DECLARACIÓN JURADA.
sworn statement, affidavit, deposition.

DECLARACIÓN PATRIMONIAL.
asset statement (required of persons for tax purposes and of public officials upon assuming their position, against which their wealth and possible later corruption will be compared).

DECLARACIÓN PROCESAL.
See DECLARACIÓN JUDICIAL.

DECLARACIÓN RECEPTICIA.
notice which is legally binding only upon receipt by the other party.

DECLARACIÓN TÁCITA.
See DECLARACIÓN DE VOLUNTAD.

DECLARADO.
adj, declared, stated ‖ manifested, communicated.

DECLARADOR.
m, declarant, deponent ‖ witness ‖ affiant.

DECLARANTE.
m, f, party making statement for governmental administrative purposes ‖ declarant, deponent ‖ witness ‖ affiant. May be a party or nonparty witness.

DECLARAR.
v, to declare, state, say, communicate ‖ to swear to, testify ‖ to find, conclude, determine, decide ‖ to confess.

DECLARARSE.
v, to tell secrets to ‖ to confess ‖ to adopt a new political position.

DECLARATIVO.
adj, declaratory, explanatory.

DECLARATORIA.
f, statement, declaration ‖ adj, declaratory.

DECLARATORIA DE HEREDEROS.
determination of the heirs of a decedent (whether by will or intestate succession).

DECLARATORIA DE JURISDICCIÓN.
procedure to maintain jurisdiction over a case. Used to stay interference of a judge in a case over which he has no jurisdiction.

DECLARATORIA DE POBREZA.
declaration of indigence ‖ plea of poverty (made in order to obtain free legal assistance in both criminal and civil actions).

DECLARATORIO.
adj, declaratory.

DECLINAR.
v, to decline ‖ to refuse (jurisdiction).

DECLINATORIA.
f, jurisdictional plea, motion to challenge jurisdiction, declinatory exception ‖ court refusal of jurisdiction.

DECLINATORIA DE JURISDICCIÓN.
See DECLINATORIA.

DECOMISAR.
v, to confiscate, seize (under authority of law).

DECOMISO.
m, confiscation, seizure (of instruments of a crime or products under authority of law) ‖ damage, loss (pursuant to contract penalty clause) ‖ right to repossess ‖ confiscated goods ‖ also see COMISO.

DECORO.
m, decorum ‖ respect, consideration ‖ honor.

DECRETAR.
v, to decree, order ‖ to state ‖ to resolve, decide.

DECRETO.
m, decree, resolution, order, sentence ‖ writ, warrant ‖ note (in the margin of a document) ‖ executive order, proclamation, resolution (of the executive branch).

DECRETO DE URGENCIA.
emergency law (issued by executive branch) ‖ emergency decree or order (issued by a de facto government).

DECRETO DELEGADO.
m, executive orders or decrees which are issued pursuant to a delegation of power from another branch of the government.

DECRETO JUDICIAL.
order, decision, sentence (issued by judicial branch).

DECRETO LEY.
executive order or proclamation. Frequently, such an order is issued by the executive branch which is meant to have the effect of law despite the fact that the legislative branch has not issued it.

DECRETO REGLAMENTARIO.
regulation, regulatory order (issued by a minister or secretary, pursuant to law).

DECURSAS.
f, rents in arrears, lease payments past due (on land in CENSO).

DEDUCCIÓN.
f, deduction, inference.

DEDUCIR.
v, to deduce, infer, conclude ‖ to derive ‖ to

conclude, draw a conclusion ‖ to subtract, deduct (e.g. from a decedent's estate that portion which by law belongs to another) ‖ to litigate, bring a lawsuit.

DEFECTO.
m, defect, fault, physical imperfection ‖ lack, absence ‖ shortage.

DEFECTO DE FORMA.
procedural error (of a judge). May permit retrial or the setting aside of a decision.

DEFECTO LEGAL.
legal defect, non-fulfillment of legal requisites ‖ defective complaint (due to lack of clarity, omission, or other procedural error).

DEFECTO EN TÍTULOS INSCRIBIBLES.
defective public instrument (which lacks one of the requisites of a public instrument).

DEFECTOS INSUBSANABLES.
inexcusable defects (which prohibit title registration of real estate at the real estate record office). May be due to defect in form, legal prohibition of transfer, or other disability of the registrar to record the transfer.

DEFECTOS OCULTOS.
hidden defects (e.g. of a product).

DEFECTOS SUBSANABLES.
excusable defects (which affect an instrument's validity, but do not result in a complete nullity). Registrar may not record a document with such defects but may, upon request, record a temporary registration.

DEFENDER.
v, to defend, protect, shelter ‖ to save ‖ to prohibit, impede ‖ to defend (in an action).

DEFENDERSE.
v, to defend oneself (e.g. at trial) ‖ to contradict (e.g. falsehoods, inconsistencies).

DEFENDIBLE.
adj, defensible, defendable.

DEFENDIDO.
m, defendant ‖ adj, defended, protected.

DEFENSA.
f, defense, act of defending ‖ shelter ‖ aid ‖ defender, defense attorney ‖ defense in a civil action ‖ (written) answer, plea (to a criminal complaint).

DEFENSA CIVIL.
civil defense (re: armed forces).

DEFENSA DE HECHO.
self-defense.

DEFENSA EN JUICIO.
(right to) defense at trial pursuant to due process. Usually guaranteed by constitution.

DEFENSA LEGÍTIMA.
See LEGÍTIMA DEFENSA.

DEFENSA NACIONAL.
national defense.

DEFENSA POR POBRE.
indigent's (right to) legal counsel. In both criminal and civil litigation.

DEFENSA PREVIA.
preliminary written defense filed by defense attorney within the first days of initial interrogation of an accused.

DEFENSA PUTATIVA.
alleged self-defense.

DEFENSIVA.
f, defensive, defensive position ‖ adj, defensive, protective.

DEFENSIVO.
m, defense, protection ‖ adj, defensive, protective.

DEFENSOR.
m, defense counsel or attorney, defense, counsel for the defense ‖ defender, person who acts in legitimate defense of a person ‖ defender, protector.

DEFENSOR DE CONFIANZA.
private defense counsel (i.e. attorney chosen by defendant). Opposed to DEFENSOR DE OFICIO.

DEFENSOR DE LOCOS Y PRÓDIGOS.
guardian for incompetent persons.

DEFENSOR DE MENORES.
guardian ad litem of minors ‖ curator or conservator of minors. May be a guardian over minor's rights and interests only, or over the minor, also.

DEFENSOR DE OFICIO.
court-appointed defense counsel, public defender. Appointed for indigent defendants.

DEFENSOR DE POBRES Y AUSENTES.
public defender (for poor people and absentees), court official whose permanent function is to represent indigent defendants and those who cannot be located for trial.

DEFENSOR JUDICIAL.
court-appointed attorney ‖ attorney who carries out legal functions upon judicial request (includes guardian ad litem, curator, conservator) ‖ trial attorney, legal counsel at trial ‖

defense attorney, counsel for the defendant.

DEFENSORÍA.
, position or function of defender in civil or criminal trial; office of public defender (as an institution).

DEFENSORIO.
n, written apology.

DEFERIDO.
See JURAMENTO DEFERIDO.

DEFICIENCIA.
, deficiency || defect, fault.

DEFICIENCIA MENTAL.
See DEBILIDAD MENTAL.

DEFICIENTE.
adj, deficient, defective, faulty || incomplete.

DEFICIENTE MENTAL.
n, retardate, retarded person, mentally retarded person.

DÉFICIT.
n, deficit || shortage.

DEFINICIÓN.
, definition || decision, determination, resolution (e.g. of a conflict or lawsuit).

DEFINIMIENTO.
n, final order, judgment (of a tribunal) || pardon (of a murderer by relatives of victim).

DEFINITIVAMENTE.
adv, finally, definitively, decisively.

DEFINITIVO.
adj, decisive, definitive, conclusive || unappealable, final.

DEFLACIÓN.
, deflation.

DEFORMACIÓN DEL ROSTRO.
facial disfigurement.

DEFRAUDACIÓN.
, defrauding, fraud || fraudulent tax evasion.

DEFRAUDADOR.
n, defrauder || tax evader, party who fraudulently fails to pay tax.

DEFUNCIÓN.
, death.

DEGENERACIÓN.
, degeneration.

DEGOLLACIÓN.
, beheading, decapitation.

DEGRADACIÓN.
degradation || privation of a dignity, demotion (from a position) || social degradation.

DEGRADAR.
v, to degrade || to demote.

DEGÜELLO.
m, beheading.

DEJACIÓN.
omission || carelessness || transfer, abandonment, renunciation (e.g. of a right to property).

DEJADEZ.
f, abandonment || neglect, negligence (re: obligations).

DEJADO DE LA MANO DE DIOS.
abandoned, not taken care of || left by the hand of God. Used in reference to criminals who are involved in heinous crimes or sins or to persons or things that are abandoned or not taken care of.

DEJAR.
v, to leave || to let || to abandon, go away || to name, appoint (a person to a position) || to lend || to bequeath (by will).

DEJAR EN EL SITIO.
to kill suddenly or instantly.

DEJE DE CUENTA.
See ABANDONO DE MERCADERÍAS.

DELACIÓN.
f, delatio, denunciation, accusation (of a crime to an authority).

DELATOR.
m, accuser, informer, delator || adj, informing, accusing.

DELEGACIÓN.
f, delegation, transfer (e.g. of authority) || authorization of an agent, transfer of rights || delegation (to a substitute) || office or position of delegate || delegation, body of delegates || novation (of an obligation) || delegation of authority (by a judge to deal with a matter).

DELEGACIÓN DE CRÉDITO.
novation, contractual assignment by creditor. Requires consent of the debtor and old and new creditors.

DELEGACIÓN DE DEUDA.
novation, contractual assignment by debtor. Requires consent of the creditor and old and new debtors. May be PERFECTA (total) which frees the old debtor or a separate liability owed to the old creditor, or IMPERFECTA (partial) whereby the old debtor still remains liable to the old creditor under a separate obligation.

DELEGACIÓN IMPERFECTA.
DELEGACIÓN in which the original obligor con-

tinues to be joint obligor (i.e. where there is not a full release).

DELEGACIÓN PERFECTA.
DELEGACIÓN in which the original obligor is released in full.

DELEGADO.
m, agent ‖ delegate, representative, substitute ‖ assignee (of a DELEGACIÓN DE DEUDA or DELEGACIÓN DE CRÉDITO) ‖ adj, delegated ‖ assigned ‖ transferred ‖ substituted.

DELEGADOS OBREROS.
employee or worker representatives (on committees or meetings of the employer).

DELEGADOS SINDICALES.
union representatives (on committees or meetings of the employer).

DELEGANTE.
m, principal ‖ assignor (of a DELEGACIÓN DE DEUDA or DELEGACIÓN DE CRÉDITO) ‖ party or group which empowers delegate.

DELEGAR.
v, to delegate, authorize (e.g. an agent, delegate, representative); to assign.
See DELEGACIÓN.

DELETÉREO.
adj, poisonous, deadly.

DELIBERACIÓN.
f, deliberation (e.g. of a court or tribunal).

DELIBERADAMENTE.
adv, deliberately.

DELIBERANTE.
adj, deliberating ‖ voting, with right to vote.

DELIBERAR.
v, to deliberate, consider.

DELICTIVO.
adj, criminal, delinquent.

DELINCUENCIA.
f, delinquency, criminality ‖ crime, misdemeanor.

DELINCUENCIA DE MENORES.
juvenile delinquency.

DELINCUENTE.
m, delinquent, criminal offender ‖ the accused, party accused of a crime (whether or not guilty).

DELINCUENTE HABITUAL.
habitual criminal or offender.

DELINCUENTE POLÍTICO.
political criminal.

DELINCUENTE PROFESIONAL.
professional criminal.

DELINCUENTE SEXUAL.
sex offender, party convicted of sex crimes.

DELINQUIR.
v, to commit a crime or misdemeanor.

DELIRANTE.
See LOCURA CRÓNICA DELIRANTE.

DELITO.
m, offense, violation of law ‖ crime, felony (serious), misdemeanor (if less serious) ‖ inte tional tort.

DELITO A DISTANCIA.
crime committed from a location physical distant from the victim.

DELITO ABERRANTE.
crime in which an unusual or extraordina chain of causation is involved ‖ aberrant c heinous crime.

DELITO AERONÁUTICO.
crime related to aeronautics and air travel.

DELITO AGOTADO.
crime the effects of which have come to pas in full (i.e. no further injury or damage wi occur as a result of the crime).

DELITO CALIFICADO.
aggravated crime, crime committed subject t an aggravating circumstance set forth by statu te.

DELITO CASUAL.
unpremeditated crime.

DELITO CIVIL.
intentional tort (which may or may not be, ad ditionally, a crime).

DELITO COLECTIVO.
group crime, crime involving more than on party.

DELITO COMETIDO EN AUDIENCIA.
offense committed in court or in trial.

DELITO COMETIDO POR EL TRABAJADOR.
offense committed by an employee (whethe related to work or not).

DELITO COMPLEJO.
crime which in itself constitutes two or more crimes or a crime which facilitates a furthe crime.

DELITO COMÚN.
common crime, violation of law set forth in the penal code. Opposed to DELITO ESPECIAL.

DELITO CONCURRENTE.
simultaneous crime, crime which is carried ou

by the same actor, independent of but substantially at the same time as other crimes.

DELITO CONEXO.
related crime, crime which facilitates the commission of other related crimes.

DELITO CONSUMADO.
fully completed crime (whether or not the result was that desired).

DELITO CONTINUADO.
continuous crime.

DELITO CONTINUO.
See DELITO PERMANENTE.

DELITO CUALIFICADO.
See DELITO CALIFICADO.

DELITO CULPOSO.
crime which results from negligent or imprudent conduct.

DELITO DE ACCIÓN.
See DELITO DE COMISIÓN.

DELITO DE ACCIÓN PRIVADA.
crime which may be prosecuted by private action only.

DELITO DE ACCIÓN PÚBLICA.
crime against public order which may only be prosecuted by the government.

DELITO DE COMISIÓN.
crime of commission (i.e. involving an affirmative act).

DELITO DE COMISIÓN POR OMISIÓN.
crime of failing to fulfill a duty, which failure results in a legal injury.

DELITO DE DAÑO.
category of crime which results in legal injury. Opposed to DELITO DE PELIGRO.

DELITO DE INSTANCIA PRIVADA.
crime which may only be prosecuted if the victim or the victim's family or representative require it, but which is then prosecuted by the government.

DELITO DE LA MUCHEDUMBRE.
crime committed by a group or mass of people.
See MUCHEDUMBRE DELINCUENTE.

DELITO DE OLVIDO.
crime of omission resulting from having forgotten to act when required.

DELITO DE OMISIÓN.
crime of omission.

DELITO DE OPINIÓN.
crime carried out by stating one's opinion (e.g. defamation).

DELITO DE PELIGRO.
crime of endangerment. Category of crime which refers to creation of danger of legal injury.

DELITO DEPENDIENTE DE INSTANCIA PRIVADA.
See DELITO DE INSTANCIA PRIVADA.

DELITO DEPORTIVO.
sports injury which amounts to a crime.

DELITO DOLOSO.
intentional crime, crime committed with malice aforethought.

DELITO ESPECIAL.
(non-criminal) statutory crime, violation of a statute or code other than the penal code.

DELITO FISCAL.
tax crime, violation of tax laws.

DELITO FLAGRANTE.
crime discovered in flagrante.

DELITO FORMAL.
offense which need not produce actual harm in order to be a crime.
Opposed to DELITO MATERIAL.

DELITO FRUSTRADO.
unsuccessful crime, criminal action in which all the elements of the crime have been fulfilled, except the intended legal injury.

DELITO IMPERFECTO.
attempted crime.
Opposed to DELITO PERFECTO.

DELITO IMPOSIBLE.
impossible crime, crime which physically cannot be carried out (e.g. attempted murder by poisoning someone with a substance which one believes, albeit erroneously, to be poiso-nous).

DELITO INSTANTÁNEO.
instantaneous crime, crime which is committed the moment the act occurs. Opposed to DELITO PERMANENTE.

DELITO INTENCIONAL.
intentional crime, crime committed with malice aforethought.

DELITO INTENTADO.
See DELITO TENTADO.

DELITO INVOLUNTARIO.
involuntary crime, crime committed without intent, due to force majeure or due to coercion by another.

DELITO MATERIAL.
offense which must produce actual harm in order to be a crime.

DELITO MILITAR.
military offense or crime.
DELITO NOMINADO.
named crime, crime which is designated speci-
fically by name in a code or statute.
DELITO ORGANIZADO.
organized crime.
DELITO PASIONAL.
See CRIMEN PASIONAL.
DELITO PERFECTO.
crime which is fully carried out and successful.
DELITO PERMANENTE.
continuing crime, crime which takes place
over a period of time.
Opposed to DELITO INSTANTÁNEO.
DELITO POLÍTICO.
political crime.
DELITO POR IMPRUDENCIA.
See DELITO CULPOSO.
DELITO PRETERINTENCIONAL.
crime the result of which exceeds the actor's
intent.
DELITO PRIVADO.
See DELITO DE ACCIÓN PRIVADA ‖ see also
DELITO DE INSTANCIA PRIVADA.
DELITO PÚBLICO.
See DELITO DE ACCIÓN PÚBLICA.
DELITO PUTATIVO.
putative crime, act which the author mistaken-
ly believes to be a crime.
DELITO REITERADO.
repeated crime.
DELITO SIMPLE.
single crime, act which is punishable as one offense alone.
DELITO TENTADO.
attempt, attempted crime.
DELITOS CONTRA EL ESTADO CIVIL.
crimes against the marriage laws (e.g. crimes
of SUPRESIÓN DEL ESTADO CIVIL (concealment of one's true marital status), SUPOSI-
CIÓN DE ESTADO CIVIL (claim of a false marital
status), and MATRIMONIOS ILEGALES (fraudulent marriages).
DELITOS CONTRA EL HONOR.
torts or crimes against another's honor (e.g.
defamation, invasion of privacy).
**DELITOS CONTRA EL ORDEN
PÚBLICO.**
crimes against the public order (e.g. rebellion,
sedition, resisting arrest, disorderly conduct).

**DELITOS CONTRA LA
ADMINISTRACIÓN DE JUSTICIA.**
crimes against the administration of justice
(e.g. abuse of authority, fraudulent use of
stamps and documents, perjury).
**DELITOS CONTRA LA
ADMINISTRACIÓN PÚBLICA.**
crimes against the governmental administration (e.g. acceptance of bribes, disobedience
of public officers, malfeasance).
**DELITOS CONTRA
LA FE PÚBLICA.**
crimes involving public instruments (e.g. falsification of money or credit instruments,
commercial or industrial fraud).
DELITOS CONTRA LA HONESTIDAD.
sex crimes (e.g. adultery, rape, statutory rape,
corruption of a minor).
DELITOS CONTRA LA LIBERTAD.
crimes against an individual's rights or freedoms (e.g. interference with individual rights
such as right to work, freedom of association,
freedom of press).
DELITOS CONTRA LA PROPIEDAD.
property crimes, crimes against property.
**DELITOS CONTRA LA SALUD
PÚBLICA.**
crimes against public health (e.g. selling con-
taminated food).
**DELITOS CONTRA LA SEGURIDAD DE
LA NACIÓN.**
crimes against national security (e.g. treason).
DELITOS CONTRA LA VIDA.
crimes against life (e.g. murder, abortion, homicide).
DELITOS CONTRA LAS PERSONAS.
crimes against persons (e.g. abandonment,
dueling, crimes against life).
**DELITOS CONTRA LOS BIENES DE LA
NACIÓN.**
offenses against public or federal property.
**DELITOS CONTRA LOS PODERES
PÚBLICOS Y EL ORDEN
CONSTITUCIONAL.**
See REBELIÓN and SEDICIÓN.
DELITOS ELECTORALES.
electoral crimes, crimes involving election
fraud.
DELITOS EN BANDA.
group crimes, crimes committed by three or
more persons.

DELITOS QUE COMPROMETEN LA PAZ Y LA DIGNIDAD DE LA NACIÓN.
crimes or offenses which compromise the peace and dignity of the nation.

DEMAGOGIA.
f, demagogy.

DEMAGOGO.
m, demagogue.

DEMANDA.
f, complaint, petition ‖ demand, request ‖ question ‖ order (of merchandise).

DEMANDA ALTERNATIVA.
complaint for alternative relief.

DEMANDA ANALÍTICA.
See DEMANDA ALTERNATIVA.

DEMANDA CONDICIONADA.
complaint conditioned on the decision of another case.

DEMANDA DE APELACIÓN.
bill of appeal, appeal.

DEMANDA DE DAÑOS Y PERJUICIOS.
complaint for damages.

DEMANDA DE IMPUGNACIÓN.
exception ‖ objection.

DEMANDA DE NULIDAD.
complaint requesting the nullification of some act or decision.

DEMANDA DE POBREZA.
request for permission to file suit without paying court costs.

DEMANDA DECLARATIVA.
petition for declaratory judgement.

DEMANDA EN JUICIO HIPOTECARIO.
bill of foreclosure, complaint to foreclose on a mortgage.

DEMANDA GRADUADA.
See DEMANDA ALTERNATIVA.

DEMANDA INCIDENTAL.
incidental or related complaint.

DEMANDA JUDICIAL.
judicial complaint.

DEMANDA PLURAL.
complaint based on several grounds.

DEMANDA PRINCIPAL.
principal complaint or demand.

DEMANDA SIMPLE.
short form complaint.

DEMANDA SUCESIVA.
subsequent complaint.

DEMANDA SUPLEMENTARIA.
supplemental complaint.

DEMANDADA.
f, defendant.

DEMANDADO.
m, defendant, respondent, the defense ‖ adj, sued ‖ demanded, requested ‖ questioned ‖ ordered.

DEMANDADOR.
See DEMANDANTE.

DEMANDADOR POR AUTO DE CASACIÓN.
plaintiff in error.

DEMANDANTE.
m, plaintiff, claimant, complainant, petitioner, prosecution.

DEMANDAR.
v, to complain, petition, sue, file suit against ‖ to demand, request ‖ to question ‖ to order (goods).

DEMANDAR EN JUICIO.
to sue.

DEMARCACIÓN.
f, demarcation, delineation (e.g. of boundaries, jurisdiction).

DEMENCIA.
f, insanity, dementia, loss of judgment or reason.

DEMENTE.
m, insane person ‖ adj, insane, demented.

DEMÉRITO.
m, demerit.

DEMOCRACIA.
f, democracy.

DEMOCRACIA DIRECTA.
direct democracy (without resort to representatives, etc.).

DEMOCRACIA ECONÓMICA Y SOCIAL.
economic and social democracy (exclusive of political democracy).

DEMOCRACIA INDUSTRIAL.
industrial democracy, employee participation in the management and profits of a company.

DEMOCRACIA POLÍTICA.
political democracy.

DEMOCRACIA POPULAR.
popular democracy. Used to describe political system in the Soviet Republics and satellite countries.

DEMOCRACIA REPRESENTATIVA.
representative democracy, democracy carried out by representatives.

DEMOCRACIA SEMIDIRECTA.
quasi-direct democracy, democracy which in part involves the people directly and in part is carried out via their representatives.

DEMÓCRATA.
m, f, democrat, person who supports a democratic form of government; democrat, person who supports a political party denominated as democrat ‖ adj, democratic ‖ democrat.

DEMOGRAFÍA.
f, demography.

DEMORA.
f, delay, lateness, tardiness.

DEMORAR.
v, to delay, be late ‖ to remain ‖ to hold (illegally, by police).

DEMOROSO.
adj, overdue, late, in default.

DEMOSTRABLE.
adj, provable, demonstrable.

DEMOSTRACIÓN.
f, demonstration, proof ‖ showing.

DEMOSTRAR.
v, to prove, demonstrate, show.

DEMOSTRATIVO.
adj, demonstrative.

DENEGACIÓN.
f, denial ‖ negation, negative ‖ refusal.

DENEGACIÓN COMPLETA.
general denial.

DENEGACIÓN DE AUXILIO.
refusal to aid. May be a tort of ABUSO DE AUTORIDAD.

DENEGACIÓN DE JUSTICIA.
abuse of justice, judicial crime of refusal to apply the law.

DENEGACIÓN GENERAL.
See DENEGACIÓN COMPLETA.

DENEGAR.
v, to negate ‖ to refuse, deny.

DENEGATORIO.
adj, rejecting, denying.

DENOMINACIÓN.
f, denomination ‖ naming ‖ name.

DENOMINACIÓN COMERCIAL.
firm name ‖ trade name.

DENUNCIA.
f, denunciation, accusation (to the competent authorities of an illegal act) ‖ announcement ‖ advice, notice ‖ notice of termination of a treaty ‖ presentment ‖ filing a claim for public land ‖ police report. May be obligatory (as with officers of the court or police), or prohibited (as with certain family members), but it is usually voluntary.

DENUNCIA DE ACCIDENTE.
accident report.

DENUNCIA DE EXTRAVÍO.
notice of loss.

DENUNCIA DEL CONTRIBUYENTE.
income-tax return.

DENUNCIA FALSA.
malicious prosecution ‖ false accusation.

DENUNCIABLE.
adj, able to be terminated ‖ able to be denounced.

DENUNCIACIÓN.
See DENUNCIA.

DENUNCIADO.
m, accused party, accused ‖ adj, stated, declared ‖ accused.

DENUNCIADOR.
m, accuser, denouncer ‖ declarant.

DENUNCIANTE.
m, f, informer, informant, denouncer, accuser ‖ person who files a report ‖ claimant of a mine, person who has a mining claim.

DENUNCIAR.
v, to denounce, accuse ‖ to file a formal accusation, file a police report ‖ to give notice ‖ to communicate ‖ to formally promulgate ‖ to repudiate an obligation or contract ‖ to proclaim, announce ‖ to give notice of termination (of a treaty) ‖ to file a mining claim.

DENUNCIAR DATOS.
to provide information.

DENUNCIAR UN CONVENIO.
to denounce an agreement or treaty.

DENUNCIAR UN SALDO.
to show a balance.

DENUNCIAR UNA MINA.
to file a mining claim.

DENUNCIO.
m, denouncement ‖ request for a mining claim registration. See DENUNCIA.

DEONTOLOGÍA JURÍDICA.
f, professional responsibility, legal ethics.

DEPARTAMENTO.
m, territorial division (in a building, vehicle, land, etc.); district, section ‖ ministry, department (of government), administrative office ‖

apartment, flat ‖ jurisdiction of a captain of the Navy ‖ compartment. In some countries DEPARTAMENTO is equivalent to a county or province.

DEPENDENCIA.
f, dependency (of persons or nations, or organization) ‖ sub-office ‖ branch office ‖ agency.

DEPENDIENTE.
m, agent, representative (commercially) ‖ dependent person or thing ‖ adj, dependent, subordinate ‖ inferior (hierarchically).

DEPENDIENTE DE COMERCIO.
business assistant or agent.

DEPONENTE.
f, m, deponent, declarant, witness ‖ depositor, bailer.

DEPONER.
v, to testify, give witness, declare on oath before a judge ‖ to depose, remove from office ‖ to affirm, assure ‖ to put aside.

DEPORTACIÓN.
f, banishment, deportation ‖ penal sanction of expulsion from society. May be SIMPLE (with considerable freedom within specified territorial limits) or EN RECINTO FORTIFICADO (with additional physical limitations placed on personal rights).

DEPOSICIÓN.
f, deposition, testimony, declaration on oath before a judge ‖ surrender (in a fight or battle) ‖ deposition, removal from office, dethronement ‖ dismissal, firing, cashiering (from work).

DEPOSITANTE.
m, depositor, bailer.

DEPOSITAR.
v, to deposit.

DEPOSITARIA.
f, depository, deposit ‖ treasurer ‖ position or function of depositary.

DEPOSITARIO.
m, depositary, bailee, trustee, party responsible for the care and keeping of thing(s) of others.

DEPOSITARIO ADMINISTRADOR.
bailee, trustee. Usually has more responsibilities than a simple DEPOSITARIO in terms of management of property.

DEPOSITARIO JUDICIAL.
receiver ‖ court appointed bailee or trustee.

DEPÓSITO.
m, deposit, deposited item ‖ store ‖ deposit, down payment ‖ deposit, warehouse, depository ‖ delivery (of a thing for the care and keeping by another) ‖ bailment contract ‖ trust agreement, contract for the care and keeping of a thing by another. May be MOBILIARIO (personal property) or INMOBILIARIO (real property); GRATUITO (gra-tuitous), or ONEROSO or REMUNERADO (remunerative).

DEPÓSITO A LA VISTA.
demand deposit.

DEPÓSITO A PLAZO.
time deposit.

DEPÓSITO A TÉRMINO.
See DEPÓSITO A PLAZO.

DEPÓSITO ACCIDENTAL.
involuntary bailment.

DEPÓSITO ADUANERO.
customs deposit or warehouse ‖ customs deposit.

DEPÓSITO AFIANZADO.
bonded warehouse.

DEPÓSITO BANCARIO.
bank deposit.

DEPÓSITO CIVIL.
gratuitous bailment, gratuitous deposit (of real or personal property).

DEPÓSITO COMERCIAL.
See DEPÓSITO MERCANTIL.

DEPÓSITO CONVENCIONAL.
See DEPÓSITO VOLUNTARIO.

DEPÓSITO DE AHORROS.
savings deposit.

DEPÓSITO DE CADÁVERES.
morgue.

DEPÓSITO DE GIRO.
demand deposit.

DEPÓSITO DE MENORES E INCAPACES.
temporary institutionalization of minors and the incapacitated (until a guardian can be appointed).

DEPÓSITO DE PERSONAS.
custody of individuals for their protection ‖ placement of persons in homes for their care and custody.

DEPÓSITO EFECTIVO.
actual bailment.

DEPÓSITO EN AVERÍA GRUESA.
general-average deposit.

DEPÓSITO EN PAGO.
court deposit in payment of debt.
DEPÓSITO EXTRAJUDICIAL.
See DEPÓSITO VOLUNTARIO.
DEPÓSITO GRATUITO.
gratuitous deposit or bailment.
DEPÓSITO IRREGULAR.
irregular deposit, deposit whereby the thing deposited may be returned in kind.
DEPÓSITO JUDICIAL.
court-ordered deposit or sequestration.
DEPÓSITO LEGAL.
See DEPÓSITO NECESARIO.
DEPÓSITO MERCANTIL.
bailment ‖ commercial deposit. Law may require that the deposit of things be with a bank or deposit company, or with a factor; or that the deposit be a result of a commercial transaction; or that both parties be merchants.
DEPÓSITO NECESARIO.
legal deposit, deposit required by law ‖ necessary deposit, deposit made because of some urgent need.
Opposed to DEPÓSITO VOLUNTARIO.
DEPÓSITO REGULAR.
regular deposit, deposit whereby the thing deposited must be returned in specie.
DEPÓSITO SUJETO A PREAVISO.
deposit in notice account.
DEPÓSITO VOLUNTARIO.
consensual deposit arising by reason of no special need.
DEPRAVACIÓN.
f, depravity, vice, corruption.
DEPRAVADO.
m, depraved or corrupt person, degenerate ‖ adj, depraved, corrupt; degenerate.
DEPRAVADOR.
See DEPRAVADO.
DEPRECIABLE.
adj, depreciable.
DEPRECIACIÓN.
f, depreciation.
DEPRECIACIÓN EXCESIVA.
over-depreciation.
DEPRECIAR.
v, to depreciate (the value of something).
DEPREDACIÓN.
f, depredation ‖ piracy, theft of a boat or airplane or of the things located thereon ‖

abuse of power through corruption or fraud ‖ vandalism, plundering.
DEPRESIÓN ECONÓMICA.
f, depression, economic depression.
DEPRESIVO.
adj, depressing, depressive, tending to depress.
DEPRETERICIÓN.
See PRETERICIÓN.
DERECHO.
m, right, freedom ‖ law ‖ privilege, franchise, benefit ‖ adj, straight ahead ‖ right (vs. left).
DERECHO A DESEMPEÑAR CARGOS PÚBLICOS.
right to hold office.
DERECHO A LA COSA.
See "JUS AD REM".
DERECHO A LA HUELGA.
right to strike.
DERECHO A LA INTIMIDAD.
right to privacy.
DERECHO A LA PROPIA IMAGEN.
right to reproduce one's own image.
DERECHO A LA VIDA.
right to life.
DERECHO A SUFRAGIO.
right to vote.
DERECHO A TRABAJAR.
right to work.
DERECHO ABSOLUTO.
absolute or unrestricted right ‖ right in rem, right against the world.
DERECHO ACCESORIO.
secondary right, right which is secondary to another right.
DERECHO ADJETIVO.
adjective or procedural law.
DERECHO ADMINISTRATIVO.
administrative law, law which pertains in any way to public administration.
DERECHO ADMINISTRATIVO DEL TRABAJO.
law applicable to public agencies which deal with labor matters.
DERECHO ADQUIRIDO.
vested right.
DERECHO AERONÁUTICO.
aeronautic or aviation law.
DERECHO AGRARIO.
agriculture law, law which regulates the par-

ties, activities, and legal relationships arising from agricultural activities.

DERECHO AJENO.
third party right.

DERECHO AL HONOR.
right to one's honor (e.g. right against defamation).

DERECHO AL NOMBRE.
right to one's name. Pertains to first and last name.

DERECHO AL TRABAJO.
See DERECHO A TRABAJAR.

DERECHO ANGLOAMERICANO.
Anglo-American law.

DERECHO ANTECEDENTE.
antecedent or prior right.

DERECHO APARENTE.
apparent right.

DERECHO ASTRONÁUTICO.
law of outer space.

DERECHO BANCARIO.
banking law.

DERECHO BURSÁTIL.
law which pertains to securities and stock exchanges.

DERECHO CAMBIARIO.
right pertaining to a negotiable instrument ‖ law regulating foreign exchange.

DERECHO CANÓNICO.
ecclesiastical law, law spiritual, canon law.

DERECHO CAUSÍDICO.
law pertaining to specific cases or situations.

DERECHO CESÁREO.
Roman law consisting of constitutions, edicts, decrees and orders issued by the Roman Emperors.

DERECHO CIENTÍFICO.
doctrine, legal commentary made up of the works and opinions of legal writers.

DERECHO CIVIL.
civil law ‖ civil law, Roman law ‖ civil law (as opposed to military law, ecclesiastical law, commercial law, criminal law, or common law) ‖ law contained in or pertaining to the CÓDIGO CIVIL of a nation, law which regulates the rights and obligations of persons, families, personal and real property, contracts, torts, wills, trusts, estates, family relations, and name and legal status of persons. The classification of DERECHO CIVIL is distinct from DERECHO

MERCANTIL, LABORAL, etc. in that it regulates basic personal matters.

DERECHO COLECTIVO DEL TRABAJO.
union law, labor law (as it pertains to workers' collective activities), law which regulates the relationships between employers and trade unions.

DERECHO COMERCIAL.
See DERECHO MERCANTIL.

DERECHO COMO VOTANTE.
voter's right, right to vote.

DERECHO COMPARADO.
comparative law.

DERECHO COMÚN.
national law, federal law ‖ civil law (as opposed to labor law, commercial law, etc) ‖ general law, law applicable to everyone.

DERECHO CONDICIONAL.
conditional right.

DERECHO CONSTITUCIONAL.
constitutional law.

DERECHO CONSTITUIDO.
See DERECHO POSITIVO.

DERECHO CONSTITUYENTE.
right to establish a nation's constitution.

DERECHO CONSUETUDINARIO.
customary law, law based on custom and usage.

DERECHO CONSULAR.
consular fee.

DERECHO CONYUGAL.
right of consortium ‖ marital or spousal right.

DERECHO CORPORATIVO.
trade union law, guild union law ‖ labor law (as it pertains to labor unions).

DERECHO CRIMINAL.
See DERECHO PENAL.

DERECHO DE ABSTENCIÓN.
right to abstain (from deciding something.) In election law, refers to the right not to vote. In procedural law, refers to a judge's right to recuse him or herself from a case. In commercial law, refers to creditor's right to abstain from voting in issues pertaining to a bankruptcy in which he or she is involved. In civil law, it refers to an heir's right to refuse his or her interest.

DERECHO DE ACCESIÓN.
See ACCESIÓN.

DERECHO DE ACRECER.
right of accession (from he who cannot or does

not want to receive his interest) ‖ right of co-heirs to interest in a decedent's estate, which interest has been renounced by co-heir ‖ right to exercise purchase option over stock which has not been purchased by the other share-holders pursuant to their right of first refusal.

DERECHO DE ADMISIÓN.
right to admission ‖ written statement in which an establishment's right to refuse admission is set forth.

DERECHO DE AGREMIACIÓN.
right to form or join a labor union.

DERECHO DE ALZADA.
See DERECHO DE APELACIÓN.

DERECHO DE AMPARO.
right to file a JUICIO DE AMPARO.

DERECHO DE ANGARIA.
See ANGARIA.

DERECHO DE ANTENA.
right to locate antennae, or send or receive transmissions by antenna.

DERECHO DE APELACIÓN.
right of appeal.

DERECHO DE APOYO.
right to build something touching or leaning against a neighbor's property.

DERECHO DE ASILO.
right of asylum.

DERECHO DE ASISTENCIA.
right to aid and assistance (of allies) ‖ right to attend (performances or meetings) ‖ right to public trial.

DERECHO DE ASISTENCIA JUDICIAL.
right to legal assistance.

DERECHO DE ASOCIACIÓN.
right of association ‖ right of self-organization.

DERECHO DE AUBANA.
See AUBANA.

DERECHO DE AUTODETERMINACIÓN.
right of sovereignty, right of self-determination.

DERECHO DE AUTOR.
copyright, authorship rights.

DERECHO DE BOSQUE.
timber right.

DERECHO DE CAPITACIÓN.
poll tax.

DERECHO DE CAPTURA.
right to enemies' ships and private cargo taken during war.

DERECHO DE CIRCULACIÓN.
See LIBERTAD DE CIRCULACIÓN.

DERECHO DE CLIENTELA.
goodwill.

DERECHO DE COALICIÓN.
See DERECHO DE FEDERACIÓN.

DERECHO DE COMERCIAR.
See LIBERTAD DE COMERCIAR.

DERECHO DE CONSERVACIÓN.
right to retain property (held by another, upon breach of a contract).

DERECHO DE CONSUMICIÓN.
cover charge.

DERECHO DE CORRECCIÓN.
right of an author to have his works corrected (after publication of an error) ‖ right (of parents or guardians) to discipline children.

DERECHO DE CRÉDITO.
credit, property or monies owed ‖ creditor's right.

DERECHO DE CRÍTICA.
right to criticize (as a form of freedom of speech).

DERECHO DE DEFENSA.
right to intervene (in litigation) ‖ right of self-defense (of a person or a nation).

DERECHO DE DELIBERAR.
right to deliberate, right of an heir to consider whether to accept or renounce his/her interest.

DERECHO DE DESPIDO.
right to discharge.

DERECHO DE DIRECCIÓN.
right to control (an employee, maintained by employer).

DERECHO DE DISPONER.
right to dispose of property.

DERECHO DE DIVIDIR.
right of partition (of joint tenants).

DERECHO DE DOMINIO.
right of fee simple ownership. Opposed to DERECHO DE USO, DERECHO DE HABITACIÓN, etc.

DERECHO DE ENFITEUSIS.
See ENFITEUSIS.

DERECHO DE ENTRADA.
import duty or tax ‖ right of entry.

DERECHO DE EXPORTACIÓN.
export duty.

DERECHO DE EXPULSIÓN.
right to deport (aliens).

DERECHO DE EXTRANJERÍA.
law regulating the rights and obligations of aliens.

DERECHO DE FAMILIA.
domestic relations or family law.

DERECHO DE FEDERACIÓN.
right to organize.

DERECHO DE FORMA.
See DERECHO ADJETIVO.

DERECHO DE GENTES.
jus gentium, international law.

DERECHO DE GUERRA.
law of war.

DERECHO DE HABITACIÓN.
right of habitation.

DERECHO DE HOGAR SEGURO.
homestead right.

DERECHO DE HUELGA.
right to strike.

DERECHO DE IMPORTACIÓN.
import tax or duty ‖ right to import (something).

DERECHO DE IMPOSICIÓN.
taxing power.

DERECHO DE IMPRESIÓN.
copyright.

DERECHO DE INMUNIDAD.
right to immunity ‖ see also INMUNIDAD PARLAMENTARIA.

DERECHO DE INSOLVENCIA.
bankruptcy law.

DERECHO DE LAS OBLIGACIONES.
law of obligations, law applicable to contract, tort, or other private legal obligations.

DERECHO DE LAS SUCESIONES.
law of successions, law of wills and (decedents') estates.

DERECHO DE LEGÍTIMA DEFENSA.
See DERECHO DE DEFENSA and LEGÍTIMA DEFENSA.

DERECHO DE LOS NEGOCIOS.
commercial or business law.

DERECHO DE LOS RIESGOS DEL TRABAJO.
workman's compensation law.

DERECHO DE MINAS.
mining right ‖ mining law.

DERECHO DE MONEDAJE.
seigniorage.

DERECHO DE MONTE.
See DERECHO DE BOSQUE.

DERECHO DE NAVEGACIÓN.
maritime law, law regulating navigation ‖ admiralty law.

DERECHO DE NO RESPONDER.
right to silence (of an accused).

DERECHO DE PASO.
right of way, right of access (of a servient estate over a dominant estate).

DERECHO DE PASTOS.
right to pasture animals on another's property.

DERECHO DE PATENTE.
patent right.

DERECHO DE PATRONATO.
right of patronage.

DERECHO DE PERMANENCIA.
right to remain, right of continued occupancy.

DERECHO DE PERSECUCIÓN.
creditor's right to attach his or her debtor's assets (even when the assets are held by third parties).

DERECHO DE PESCA.
fishing rights, right to fish.

DERECHO DE PETICIÓN.
right to petition (a government).

DERECHO DE PREFERENCIA.
preferential creditor's right over rights of other creditors ‖ also see DERECHO DE PRELACIÓN.

DERECHO DE PRELACIÓN.
right of first refusal, preferential right.

DERECHO DE PRIMOGENITURA.
right of primogeniture or a first born.

DERECHO DE PRIORIDAD.
right of pre-emption.

DERECHO DE PROPIEDAD.
property rights.

DERECHO DE PROPIEDAD LITERARIA.
copyright.

DERECHO DE RECURSO.
right of appeal.

DERECHO DE RECUSACIÓN.
right to challenge.

DERECHO DE REDENCIÓN.
right of redemption.

DERECHO DE REGRESO.
See ACCIÓN CAMBIARIA.

DERECHO DE REPETICIÓN.
right of repetition, right to reclaim money paid or goods transferred by mistake.

DERECHO DE RÉPLICA.
right to reply to published opinions.

DERECHO DE REPRESENTACIÓN.
right to representation (corresponding to minors and incapacitated persons) ‖ (principal's) right of representation (in agency relationship) ‖ right of child to receive in the stead of his or her deceased parent(s) an estate which parent(s) would have inherited from their family had the parent(s) been alive.

DERECHO DE REPRODUCCIÓN.
See DERECHO DE IMPRESIÓN.

DERECHO DE RESCATE.
See DERECHO DE REDENCIÓN.

DERECHO DE RESISTENCIA.
right to object, right of resistance (to oppression).

DERECHO DE RESISTENCIA A LA OPRESIÓN.
right to resist oppression. See RESISTENCIA A LA OPRESIÓN.

DERECHO DE RESOLUCIÓN.
right of termination (of an agreement, etc.).

DERECHO DE RETENCIÓN.
type of lien which grants the right to retain property until debts related to the property are paid by owner (e.g. mechanic's lien, construction lien, etc.).

DERECHO DE RETRACTO.
See RETRACTO.

DERECHO DE REUNIÓN.
type of right of association, right to meet. Applies especially to demonstrations.

DERECHO DE SERVIDUMBRE.
right of easement, easement rights, right of passage.

DERECHO DE SINDICALIZACIÓN.
right to organize or unionize.

DERECHO DE SUFRAGIO.
See SUFRAGIO.

DERECHO DE SUPERFICIE.
surface rights, right to use the surface of real property.

DERECHO DE TANTEO.
See TANTEO.

DERECHO DE TRABAJO.
See DERECHO DEL TRABAJO.

DERECHO DE TRÁNSITO.
freedom of passage, freedom to travel.

DERECHO DE USO.
right of use ‖ right to use (a thing owned by another).

DERECHO DE VECINDAD.
law applicable to relations between neighbors.

DERECHO DE VÍA.
right of way.

DERECHO DE VISITA.
right to inspect or search, inspection right (e.g. of a nation at war over the ships of a neutral nation to assure that they are not carrying contraband for the enemy, or of a nation to inspect cargo to assure that no contraband enters national territory) ‖ right of inspection (of peace or occupation forces) ‖ visitation rights, right of or to visitation (i.e. of divorced parents to visit their children).

DERECHO DE VOTAR.
See DERECHO ELECTORAL.

DERECHO DEL CONTRATO.
contract law, law applicable to a contract.

DERECHO DEL TRABAJO.
labor or employment law ‖ industrial relations law.

DERECHO DIPLOMÁTICO.
law of diplomacy (i.e. regulating conduct of diplomats).

DERECHO DISCIPLINARIO.
right to discipline (without resort to the law, e.g. parental punishment of children, army punishment of errant soldiers, etc.).

DERECHO DISCIPLINARIO DEL TRABAJO.
right to discipline employees ‖ law applicable to the right to discipline employees.

DERECHO DIVINO.
divine right ‖ religious law.

DERECHO DOCTRINAL.
See DERECHO CIENTÍFICO.

DERECHO ECLESIÁSTICO.
See DERECHO CANÓNICO.

DERECHO ECONÓMICO.
business law.

DERECHO ELECTORAL.
right to vote.

DERECHO ESCRITO.
written law (as opposed to tradition or custom).

DERECHO ESPACIAL.
law of the skies ‖ law of space.

DERECHO ESPECIAL.
law which regulates conduct pertaining to special activities or conduct (i.e. conduct not regu-

lated by DERECHO CIVIL) ‖ local law, law which is not national law.

DERECHO ESTRICTO.
law applied strictly regardless of considerations of equity.

DERECHO EVENTUAL.
conditional right.

DERECHO EXPRESO.
written law.

DERECHO EXTRANJERO.
foreign law.

DERECHO EXTRAPATRIMONIAL.
right without economic value.

DERECHO FACULTATIVO.
elective right, right which is not mandatory, nor legally required (e.g. the right to marry).

DERECHO FIJO.
fixed tax or fee.

DERECHO FINANCIERO.
public finance law, law regulating a nation's right to collect and disburse monies, to go into debt, etc.

DERECHO FISCAL.
tax law. Forms part of DERECHO FINANCIERO.

DERECHO FORAL.
local traditional law applicable in some parts of Spain as contrasted with civil code law. This distinction emanates from the ancient regional division of Spain such that in certain areas general DERECHO CIVIL did not apply.

DERECHO FORMAL.
See DERECHO ADJETIVO.

DERECHO FUNDAMENTAL.
constitutional law ‖ fundamental right.

DERECHO FUTURO.
future interest or right.

DERECHO HEREDITARIO.
law of successions, law of inheritance, law of wills and decedents' estates ‖ right to take by inheritance.

DERECHO HIPOTECARIO.
law of mortgages, mortgage law (regarding real property); real property law ‖ right of a mortgagee.

DERECHO IMPUGNATORIO.
right of objection.

DERECHO INDEMNIZATORIO.
right to indemnity.

DERECHO INDIVIDUAL DEL TRABAJO.
law applicable to employment and related matters.

DERECHO INDUSTRIAL.
law which deals not only with DERECHO DEL TRABAJO, but with all other laws which might affect an industry ‖ see also DERECHO DEL TRABAJO.

DERECHO INMOBILIARIO.
real property or real estate law.

DERECHO INTELECTUAL.
intellectual property right.

DERECHO INTERNACIONAL.
international law.

DERECHO INTERNACIONAL DEL TRABAJO.
international labor law.

DERECHO INTERNACIONAL PRIVADO.
international private law, conflict of laws, law which regulates the laws which are to be applied to private individuals and entities in cases with international elements.

DERECHO INTERNACIONAL PÚBLICO.
international law, international public law, international law which regulates the relations between nations and other public entities.

DERECHO INTERNO.
municipal law ‖ national law, law applicable within a given nation.

DERECHO INTERPLANETARIO.
law of outer space.

DERECHO JUDICIAL.
law governing courts and judges ‖ judge-made or case law.

DERECHO JURISPRUDENCIAL.
judge-made or case law.

DERECHO JUSTICIAL.
law of procedure.

DERECHO LABORAL.
labor law.

DERECHO LABORAL CONSTITUCIONAL.
constitutional labor law.

DERECHO LEGAL.
statutory law.

DERECHO LÍQUIDO.
uncontested and liquidated right.

DERECHO LITIGIOSO.
contested right, right subject to litigation.

DERECHO MARCARIO.
trademark law ‖ trademark right.

DERECHO MARÍTIMO.
maritime or admiralty law.

DERECHO MATERIAL.
See DERECHO SUBSTANTIVO.
DERECHO MATRIMONIAL.
marital law, law pertaining to the rights and
obligation of a husband or wife.
DERECHO MERCANTIL.
commercial law, mercantile law, law merchant
or mercantile; business law.
DERECHO MILITAR.
military law.
DERECHO MINERO.
mining law.
DERECHO MOBILIARIO.
personal property law.
DERECHO MONETARIO.
law which regulates the manufacture, value,
circulation and exchange of money.
DERECHO MUNICIPAL.
municipal law ‖ law which regulates cities,
towns ‖ law which regulates counties, etc.
DERECHO NACIONAL.
national law (vs. international law).
DERECHO NATURAL.
natural law (as opposed to positive law) ‖ na-
tural right.
DERECHO NO ESCRITO.
unwritten law.
**DERECHO NORMATIVO
LABORAL.**
law applicable to collective bargaining.
DERECHO NOTARIAL.
law applicable to notaries public and special
notaries public. See NOTARIO PÚBLICO and
ESCRIBANO.
DERECHO OBJETIVO.
law, objective law.
Opposed to DERECHO SUBJETIVO.
DERECHO OBLIGACIONAL.
See DERECHO DE LAS OBLIGACIONES.
DERECHO OBRERO.
labor law.
DERECHO ORGÁNICO.
organic or fundamental or constitutional law.
DERECHO PARLAMENTARIO.
rules of parliamentary procedure, law ap-
plicable to the internal functioning of a parlia-
ment or congress or legislature.
DERECHO PARTICULAR.
privilege, franchise.
DERECHO PATRIMONIAL.
property law.

DERECHO PATRIO.
law of a particular country.
DERECHO PENAL.
criminal or penal law.
**DERECHO PENAL
INTERNACIONAL.**
international criminal law.
DERECHO PERSONAL.
law regulating relationship between two or
more people. Includes domestic relations,
obligations, contracts, etc.
Opposed to DERECHO REAL.
DERECHO PERSONALÍSIMO.
personal right which is inalienable and truly
personal, (e.g. honor, liberty, etc.).
DERECHO POLÍTICO.
political science ‖ law which regulates governmental entities (e.g. national constitution).
DERECHO POSITIVO.
positive law ‖ positive right.
DERECHO POTESTATIVO.
See DERECHO FACULTATIVO.
DERECHO PREFERENTE.
prior claim.
DERECHO PREMIAL.
right to an award (for heroic, noble or bene-
volent behavior).
DERECHO PRENDARIO.
pledge or chattel mortgage ‖ rights derived
therefrom.
DERECHO PRETORIO.
judge-made or case law.
DERECHO PRIMARIO.
basic right, antecedent right.
DERECHO PRIVADO.
private law. Opposed to DERECHO PÚBLICO.
DERECHO PROCESAL.
procedural law.
**DERECHO PROCESAL
ADMINISTRATIVO.**
law of administrative procedure, law which
regulates administrative procedure.
DERECHO PROCESAL CIVIL.
law of civil procedure.
DERECHO PROCESAL DE TRABAJO.
procedural law applicable to labor law matters.
DERECHO PROCESAL INTERNACIONAL.
international procedural law.
DERECHO PROCESAL MILITAR.
military procedural law.

DERECHO PROCESAL PENAL.
law of criminal procedure.
DERECHO PROHIBITIVO.
law which imposes a prohibition ‖ prohibitively high import duty.
DERECHO PROPORCIONAL.
proportional import duty.
DERECHO PÚBLICO.
public law.
DERECHO REAL.
law regulating rights over real property ‖ in rem right ‖ right pertaining to tangible property. Opposed to DERECHO PERSONAL.
DERECHO REAL DE GARANTÍA.
in rem right pertaining to guaranties of tangible property.
DERECHO RITUAL.
See DERECHO RITUARIO.
DERECHO RITUARIO.
law of procedure.
DERECHO ROMANO.
Roman law.
DERECHO RURAL.
agricultural law, law which pertains to agricultural activities.
DERECHO SINDICAL.
labor relations or labor law (as it pertains to the rights of employees to organize collectively).
DERECHO SOCIAL.
labor law, law which tends to protect and improve the rights of the worker ‖ societal rights, rights emanating from being a part of a society.
DERECHO SUBJETIVO.
subjective right (opposed to DERECHO OBJETIVO) ‖ right which requires that the holder instigate action for its protection (e.g. creditor's rights as opposed to rights which can be protected by the state without intervention of interested parties, e.g. right to vote).
DERECHO SUBSIDIARIO.
See DERECHO SUPLETORIO.
DERECHO SUBSTANCIAL.
See DERECHO SUBSTANTIVO.
DERECHO SUBSTANTIVO.
substantive law ‖ substantive right.
DERECHO SUCESORIO.
See DERECHO DE LAS SUCESIONES.
DERECHO SUPERIOR.
prior claim or right.

DERECHO SUPLETORIO.
law which is applied in absence of applicable code or statute ‖ law which applies when the parties to a contract are silent as to a matter.
DERECHO TRANSITORIO.
law applicable for limited period of time.
DERECHO TRIBUTARIO.
See DERECHO FISCAL.
DERECHO TUTELAR.
law regulating the rights of minors.
DERECHO USUAL.
customary law.
DERECHO VIGENTE.
law in effect.
DERECHO VITALICIO.
right to life estate, right existing for life of person.
DERECHOHABIENTE.
successor, beneficiary ‖ holder of a right.
DERECHOS.
See DERECHO ‖ laws, combination of principles, precepts and rules which regulate a given society ‖ tariff, fee, charge, duty, tax ‖ tariffs, fees, charges, duties, taxes ‖ fees (paid certain professionals).
DERECHOS ABSOLUTOS.
absolute rights.
DERECHOS ADUANEROS.
See DERECHOS DE ADUANA.
DERECHOS AJUSTABLES.
flexible or adjustable tariffs.
DERECHOS AL VALOR.
ad valorem duties.
DERECHOS ARANCELARIOS.
legal fees (of court assistants or other public officers, for their work) ‖ customs duties.
DERECHOS CIVILES.
civil rights.
DERECHOS CONSULARES.
consular fees.
DERECHOS DE ADUANA.
customs duties.
DERECHOS DE AUTOR.
authorship rights, copyright, rights of author ‖ royalties (from copyright).
DERECHOS DE ENTRADA.
import duties.
DERECHOS DE EXCLUSIVIDAD.
exclusive rights.
DERECHOS DE EXPORTACIÓN.
export duties.

DERECHOS DE FÁBRICA.
right to manufacture ‖ manufacturing royalties.
DERECHOS DE GUARDA.
custodian's fees ‖ licensee's rights.
DERECHOS DE LA PERSONALIDAD.
personal rights, human rights, right to life, liberty, ownership, security, and to resist oppression.
DERECHOS DE PATENTE.
patent royalties ‖ patent rights.
DERECHOS DE PROPIEDAD.
property rights.
DERECHOS DE PROTECCIÓN.
See DERECHOS PROTECTORES.
DERECHOS DE REPRESALIA.
retaliatory tariffs.
DERECHOS DE SALIDA.
See DERECHOS DE EXPORTACIÓN.
DERECHOS DE SALVADOR.
See DERECHOS DE SALVAMENTO.
DERECHOS DE SALVAMENTO.
salvage money.
DERECHOS DE SECRETARÍA.
fees of court clerk.
DERECHOS DE SELLO.
stamp taxes.
DERECHOS DE SUBSCRIPCIÓN.
stockholder preemptive rights, stock rights.
DERECHOS DE SUCESIÓN.
inheritance taxes.
DERECHOS DE TERCEROS.
rights of third parties.
DERECHOS DE TIMBRE.
stamp taxes.
DERECHOS DEL HOMBRE Y DEL CIUDADANO.
See DECLARACIÓN DE LOS DERECHOS DEL HOMBRE Y DEL CIUDADANO.
DERECHOS DEL TRABAJADOR.
employees' rights, workers' rights.
DERECHOS EQUITATIVOS.
equitable rights.
DERECHOS ESENCIALES.
basic rights.
DERECHOS ESTATALES.
government fees, duties, or taxes.
DERECHOS EXPECTATIVOS.
expectant rights.
DERECHOS FLEXIBLES.
See DERECHOS AJUSTABLES.

DERECHOS FUNDAMENTALES DE LOS ESTADOS.
fundamental rights of nations (in international law).
DERECHOS HUMANOS.
human rights.
DERECHOS IMPOSITIVOS.
duties, taxes.
DERECHOS INDIVIDUALES.
individual rights (which cannot be governmentally restricted, e.g. right to life, liberty, judicial fairness, freedom of thought, work, expression, association, movement, right of defense against accusations).
DERECHOS INHERENTES A LA PERSONA.
See DERECHO PERSONALÍSIMO.
DERECHOS INNATOS.
natural rights (e.g. right to life, personal safety, association, right to defend against accusations).
DERECHOS JUBILATORIOS.
pension rights.
DERECHOS JUDICIALES.
court costs.
DERECHOS LIMITADOS.
qualified rights.
DERECHOS NATURALES.
See DERECHOS INNATOS.
DERECHOS PARA RENTA PÚBLICA.
revenue tariffs.
DERECHOS PERSONALES.
personal rights (emanating from an obligation).
DERECHOS POLÍTICOS.
constitutional rights (pertaining to public functions) ‖ political rights.
DERECHOS PORTUARIOS.
port duties.
DERECHOS PROTECTORES.
protective duties.
DERECHOS RELATIVOS.
relative rights.
DERECHOS REPARADORES.
remedial rights.
DERECHOS RESERVADOS.
reserved rights.
DERECHOS RESTITUTORIOS.
See DERECHOS REPARADORES.
DERECHOS RIBEREÑOS.
riparian rights.

DERECHOS SECUNDARIOS.
secondary rights.
DERECHOS SINDICALES.
union rights, rights of a union.
DERECHOS SUCESORIOS.
inheritance or death taxes.
DERECHOS VARIABLES.
See DERECHOS AJUSTABLES.
DERECHOS Y ACCIONES.
rights and actions.
DERECHOS Y GARANTÍAS.
constitutional rights and guarantees (regarding personal freedoms).
"DERELICTIO".
abandonment.
DEROGABLE.
adj, voidable, repealable.
DEROGACIÓN.
f, repeal, abolition, derogation, annulment ‖ partial reform (of a law). May be EXPRESA (express) or TÁCITA (implied).
DEROGADO.
adj, repealed, abolished, nullified, voided ‖ reformed.
DEROGAR.
v, to repeal, abolish, derogate, void, annul, nullify ‖ to reform.
DEROGATORIO.
adj, repealing, abolishing, voiding, annulling, nullifying.
DERRAMA.
f, tax distribution or apportionment ‖ extraordinary tax.
DERRAMAR.
v, to apportion or distribute tax burden among residents of a town.
DERRELICTO.
m, derelict, abandoned ship.
DERRIBAR.
v, to demolish ‖ to knock down ‖ to dethrone ‖ to overthrow.
DERROCAMIENTO.
m, coup, coup d'etat, overthrow.
DERROCAR.
v, to dethrone, overthrow (a king) ‖ to overthrow (a government).
DERROCHE.
m, extravagance, superfluous expense.
DERROTA.
f, permission to pasture cattle after harvest ‖ defeat .

DESACATAR.
v, to be disrespectful, commit contempt ‖ to commit or be guilty of crime of DESACATO.
DESACATO.
m, contempt (of public authority) ‖ crime o insulting, threatening, or injuring a publi functionary.
DESACATO A LA CORTE.
See DESACATO AL TRIBUNAL.
DESACATO AL TRIBUNAL.
contempt of court.
DESACATO CIVIL.
civil contempt.
DESACATO CRIMINAL.
criminal contempt.
DESACONSEJAR.
v, to advise against.
DESACUERDO.
m, disagreement, discrepancy, discord ‖ lacl of agreement (between partners, allies or deci sions).
DESADEUDAR.
v, to free from debt ‖ to remove a lien.
DESADEUDARSE.
v, to pay one's debts; to free oneself from debt
DESAFIANZAR.
v, to release the bond or surety.
DESAFÍO.
m, challenge ‖ rivalry, competition ‖ provoca tion.
DESAFORAR.
v, to deprive of privilege or right.
DESAFUERO.
m, deprivation of privilege (especially witl regard to right to special jurisdiction) ‖ unlaw ful act ‖ misdemeanor, violation.
DESAGRAVIAR.
v, to indemnify, compensate, redress ‖ to re pair.
DESAGRAVIO.
m, reparation (of physical or emotional dama ge) ‖ compensation, indemnification; redress
DESAGUISADO.
m, offense, injury ‖ adj, unjust ‖ illegal.
DESAHOGADO.
adj, unencumbered ‖ wealthy, well-to-do.
DESAHUCIADOR.
m, dispossessor.
DESAHUCIAR.
v, to evict (a tenant) ‖ to lose hope (of recovery of health).

DESAHUCIO.

m, eviction, dispossession (of a tenant by landlord for failure to comply with terms of lease or the law) ‖ loss of hope (e.g. that an ill person will recover) ‖ discharge, dismissal ‖ severance pay ‖ notice of discharge or of resignation or of termination of lease.

DESALOJAMIENTO.

m, dispossession, eviction.

DESALOJAR.

to dispossess, evict ‖ to vacate, move out.

DESALOJO.

m, eviction, dispossession (of a tenant by landlord for failure to comply with terms of lease or the law).

DESALOJO DEL TRABAJADOR.

eviction of worker from employer-provided lodgings.

DESALOJO FÍSICO.

actual eviction.

DESALOJO IMPLÍCITO.

See DESALOJO VIRTUAL.

DESALOJO VIRTUAL.

constructive eviction.

DESALQUILAR.

v, to quit, vacate (rented premises) ‖ to evict (a tenant) ‖ to be vacant (of tenants).

DESAMORTIZACIÓN.

f, return to circulation of that which was in disuse. Usually applied to real property which is held without being used.

DESAMORTIZAR.

to disentail.

DESAMPARAR.

v, to abandon (a person or thing in need of assistance or protection) ‖ to absent oneself (from a place) ‖ to give up or drop an appeal.

DESAMPARO.

m, abandonment, desertion.

DESAPARECER.

v, to disappear.

DESAPARECIDO.

m, disappeared person or thing ‖ person missing in action ‖ adj, disappeared.

ESAPARICIÓN.

f, disappearance, absence without notification ‖ voluntary hiding ‖ flight ‖ kidnap ‖ loss of a quality; nullity or prescription of a right ‖ triumph over an inconvenience or difficulty.

DESAPODERAR.

v, to dispossess ‖ to dethrone, remove from power or office ‖ to cancel power of attorney.

DESAPOSESIONAR.

v to dispossess (usually without a superior right).

DESAPRISIONAR.

v, to release, set free (prisoners).

DESAPROBAR.

v, to disallow ‖ to disapprove, condemn.

DESAPROPIARSE.

v, to abandon, divest oneself (of property).

DESAPROPIO.

m, transfer of property.

DESARCHIVAR.

v, to take documents or files out of a filing system.

DESARMAR.

v, to unarm, disarm (an enemy or a suspect).

DESARMARSE.

v, to disarm (oneself).

DESARROLLAR.

v, to develop, grow.

DESARROLLO.

m, development, evolution ‖ growth.

DESARROLLO ECONÓMICO.

economic development.

DESASEGURAR.

v, to cancel insurance.

DESASOCIAR.

v, to dissolve an association ‖ to remove a partner or member.

DESASTRE.

m, disaster.

DESATENDER.

v, to disregard, neglect ‖ to default, dishonor.

DESATESORAR.

v, to spend savings or liquid assets.

DESAUTORIZACIÓN.

f, withdrawal of authority.

DESAUTORIZADO.

adj, unauthorized.

DESAUTORIZAR.

v, to revoke power or authority ‖ to withdraw a loan or other line of credit ‖ to revoke unauthorized statement (made by another).

DESAVENENCIA.

f, disagreement, opposition (of opinions), discord.

DESAVENIRSE.

v, to disagree, quarrel, fight.

DESBLOQUEAR.

v, to unfreeze assets (usually of funds held in a

belligerent country) ‖ to lift a blockade.
DESBLOQUEO.
m, unfreezing, unblocking, freeing (e.g. of blocked funds or loans or commerce, etc.).
DESCABALAR.
v, to pilfer, remove (part of something) ‖ to make incomplete.
DESCALIFICAR.
v, to disqualify ‖ to withdraw authorization.
DESCAMINO.
m, contraband.
DESCANSO.
m, rest ‖ break, work break.
DESCANSO SEMANAL.
legal right to weekly period of rest (usually at least 24 hours per week).
DESCAPITALIZACIÓN.
f, decapitalization ‖ partial or total loss of business capital.
DESCARGA.
f, act of unloading (of freight) ‖ discharge (of a firearm).
DESCARGAR.
v, to unload (freight) ‖ to fire, discharge (a firearm) ‖ to free, discharge, release (from an obligation) ‖ to hit violently ‖ to clear, exonerate.
DESCARGARSE.
v, to leave, resign, quit (employment) ‖ to free oneself from the responsibilities of a position ‖ to exculpate oneself ‖ to explain away or answer criminal charges.
DESCARGO.
m, (bookkeeping) entry ‖ unloading ‖ answer, explanation (to an accusation or charge) ‖ compliance, satisfaction, release (with the demands of justice) ‖ acquittal.
DESCARGO EN QUIEBRA.
discharge in bankruptcy.
DESCARGUE.
m, unloading (of freight).
DESCASAMIENTO.
m, annulment of a marriage ‖ divorce.
DESCASAR.
v, to separate (re concubines) ‖ to annul a marriage.
DESCENDENCIA.
f, descendants ‖ lineage.
DESCENDIENTE.
m, descendant.
DESCENTRALIZACIÓN.
f, decentralization (of governmental authori-

ty) ‖ decentralization (of jurisdiction authority).
DESCONFIANZA.
f, lack of confidence, mistrust, distrust ‖ suspicion.
DESCONFIAR.
v, to mistrust, distrust ‖ to suspect.
DESCONFORMAR.
v, to object to ‖ to dissent, disagree.
DESCONFORME.
m, disagreement ‖ adj, disagreeing.
DESCONFORMIDAD.
f, dissent, objection ‖ disagreement, lack of agreement.
DESCONOCER.
v, to fail to recognize (a person) ‖ to ignore something ‖ to disavow, disown, disclaim, repudiate ‖ to attack legal status. Opposed to RECONOCER.
DESCONTABLE.
adj, discountable ‖ eligible.
DESCONTADOR.
m, payee of a discounted bill.
DESCONTANTE.
See DESCONTADOR.
DESCONTAR.
v, to discount, reduce (in price) ‖ to discount (a negotiable instrument).
DESCRÉDITO.
m, discredit, defamation ‖ devaluation.
DESCRIPCIÓN.
f, description.
DESCUBIERTO.
m, shortage ‖ overdraft ‖ adj, uncovered.
DESCUBRIMIENTO.
m, discovery.
DESCUBRIR.
v, to discover ‖ to uncover a crime ‖ to file a criminal complaint ‖ to identify the author of a crime and ask where he is to be found.
DESCUENTO.
m, discount, reduction ‖ discount (of negotiable instruments), sale of negotiable instruments before their maturity date ‖ spread, amount by which a discounted negotiable instrument is reduced.
DESCUENTO COMERCIAL.
discount calculated on the nominal value.
DESCUENTO DE CAJA.
discount for early payment or cash payment.

DESCUENTO DE PRONTO PAGO.
See DESCUENTO DE CAJA.

DESCUENTO RACIONAL.
discount calculated on the actual value.

DESCUIDADO.
adj, careless, negligent.

DESCUIDERO.
m, pickpocket.

DESCUIDO.
m, carelessness, lack of care, negligence ‖ omission ‖ inadvertence.

DESCUIDO CULPABLE.
culpable neglect.

DESCUIDO DOLOSO.
intentional neglect.

DESDE EL LLANO.
outside the government, from the government opposition.

DESDE EL VIENTRE DE LA MADRE.
from conception to birth ‖ from birth.

DESECHAR.
v, to discard ‖ to reject ‖ to dismiss, nonsuit ‖ to vote down.

DESEMBARCAR.
v, to unload (passengers or cargo from a ship).

DESEMBARGAR.
v, to release (e.g. an attachment or garnishment or lien).

DESEMBARGO.
m, lifting of an order of seizure or attachment.

DESEMEJANZA.
f, dissimilarity.

DESEMPEÑAR.
v, to redeem or recover from or get something out of hock or pledge ‖ to fill or comply with (requirements) ‖ to carry out a function or position.

DESEMPLEO.
m, unemployment.

DESEMPLEO FRICCIONAL.
frictional unemployment, unemployment resulting from a change of activity or location at the worker's instigation.

DESENCANTARAR.
v, to draw names out of a ballot box in an election ‖ to withdraw a name from a list of candidates. See INSACULACIÓN.

DESENCARCELAR.
v, to free (a prisoner).

DESERCIÓN.
f, desertion (of a country, a ship, military service, or employment) ‖ treason ‖ abandonment of an appeal after it has been properly filed ‖ forfeiture.

DESERCIÓN DE RECURSOS.
abandonment of appeal ‖ abandonment or forfeiture of right of appeal.

DESERTAR.
v, to desert ‖ to abandon ‖ to forfeit.

DESERTAR LA APELACIÓN.
to abandon the appeal.

DESERTOR.
m, deserter.
See DESERCIÓN.

DESERVICIO.
m, breach of obligation to perform a service.

DESESTIMACIÓN.
f, denial of a motion or complaint.

DESESTIMACIÓN DE LA PERSONALIDAD SOCIETARIA.
piercing the corporate veil.

DESESTIMAR.
v, to underestimate (a request) ‖ to deny or overrule or dismiss or reject motions or objections of one or both of the parties (by a judge).

DESESTIMATORIO.
adj, rejecting, denying.

DESFALCADOR.
m, embezzler ‖ defaulter.

DESFALCAR.
v, to embezzle, take or use property for which one is curator, trustee, etc.

DESFALCO.
m, embezzlement. May be APROPRIACIÓN INDEBIDA (conversion by misappropriation), ESTAFA (theft by fraud), MALVERSACIÓN DE CAUDALES PÚBLICOS (embezzlement of public monies).

DESFIGURAR.
v, to disfigure (a face) ‖ to distort (the truth, facts, etc.).

DESFLORACIÓN.
f, deflowering, defloration (of a virgin). May be consensual or non-consensual.

DESFLORAR.
v, to deflower, have intercourse with a virgin.

DESGLOSAR.
v, to remove notes from a document ‖ to remove a page or document from a court file, leaving a copy of the original or a notation to

certify the removal ‖ to separate sheets from the file.

DESGLOSE.
m, removal of pages or documents from a court file.

DESGRACIA.
f, misadventure, mishap, accident ‖ disgrace.

DESGRAVACIÓN.
f, tax reduction, tax benefit.

DESGRAVAR.
v, to reduce import duties or taxes imposed on goods ‖ to remove a lien, disencumber.

DESHABITADO.
m, uninhabited. Used in penal law, as to distinguish theft from an uninhabited structure from theft from an inhabited structure.

DESHACER.
v, to undo ‖ to destroy ‖ to wear away ‖ to rout, vanquish (an enemy) ‖ to rescind a contract ‖ to nullify a contract ‖ to modify or change an agreement or negotiation ‖ to cancel, annul.

DESHACER EL CONTRATO.
to rescind or cancel a contract.

DESHEREDACIÓN.
f, disinheritance. See INDIGNIDAD PARA SUCEDER and PRETERICIÓN.

DESHEREDADO.
m, disinherited heir ‖ party who voluntarily renounces all right to his inheritance.

DESHEREDAMIENTO.
See DESHEREDACIÓN.

DESHEREDAR.
v, to disinherit ‖ to deprive a party (who by law should or would otherwise inherit) of his inheritance, whether by will or by law.

DESHIPOTECAR.
v, to cancel a mortgage ‖ to pay off a mortgage.

DESHONESTIDAD.
f, dishonesty, lack of honesty.

DESHONESTO.
adj, dishonest ‖ unchaste.

DESHONOR.
m, dishonor ‖ loss or lack of honor.

DESHONRAR.
v, to dishonor.

DESHONROSO.
adj, dishonest, dishonorable.

DESIDIA.
f, negligence ‖ laziness ‖ carelessness.

DESIERTO.
m, bidding or auction in which no one participates ‖ deserted place (used in criminal law to describe location of a crime as an aggravating or attenuating circumstance) ‖ adj, deserted.

DESIGNADO.
m, designated party or thing ‖ adj, designated.

DESIGNAR.
v, to designate, name ‖ to cite, indicate.

DESIGUAL.
adj, unequal ‖ dissimilar, different ‖ varying ‖ unjust. Used to describe the injustice which favoritism brings.

DESIGUALAR.
v, to make unequal ‖ to distribute an estate unequally between heirs who should inherit equally.

DESINSACULACIÓN.
f, initial jury selection by random drawing (of names or numbers from a box) ‖ other types of selection by similar methods.

DESINSACULAR.
v, to draw names or numbers of persons to serve in the judicial system.

DESINTERESADAMENTE.
adv, disinterestedly, altruistically.

DESINVERSIÓN.
f, disinvestment.

DESINVESTIDURA.
f, disqualification.

DESISTIMIENTO.
m, abandonment of crime ‖ voluntary dismissal or discontinuance or abandonment of an action or other legal proceeding. May be EXPRESO (express) or TÁCITO (implied).

DESISTIMIENTO DE LA ACCIÓN.
abandonment of action.

DESISTIMIENTO DE LA DEMANDA.
See DESISTIMIENTO DE LA ACCIÓN.

DESISTIMIENTO DEL RECURSO.
abandonment of appeal.

DESISTIR.
v, to desist, abandon (a crime or a legal proceeding) ‖ to waive (a right).

DESISTIRSE DE LA DEMANDA.
to abandon the action.

DESLEAL.
adj, disloyal, traitorous, false ‖ seditious ‖ unfair.

DESLIGAR.
v, to free (from an obligation) ‖ to unravel (a matter).

DESLINDAR.
v, to demarcate, delimit, determine and mark the boundaries of property ‖ to delineate or clarify the terms of an issue.

DESLINDE.
m, property survey ‖ demarcation (of property). See AMOJONAMIENTO.

DESLINDE Y AMOJONAMIENTO.
survey and demarcation of boundaries.

DESMANDAR.
v, to revoke a power of attorney or an agency ‖ to give a counterorder ‖ to deprive of a legacy.

DESMEDRO.
m, damage, injury, prejudice, deterioration ‖ degeneration, decadence.

DESMEMBRAR.
v, to dismember ‖ to divide, separate.

DESMEMBRARSE.
to dissolve, disassociate ‖ to become divided ‖ to secede.

DESMENTIR.
v, to accuse of lying ‖ to disprove, prove false ‖ to conceal ‖ to contradict, deny (a statement of another).

DESMILITARIZAR.
v, to demilitarize ‖ to make civilian.

DESMONETIZAR.
v, to demonetize, take money (especially coinage) out of circulation.

DESNACIONALIZAR.
v, to take citizenship away ‖ to denationalize, end the status of independent nation ‖ to denationalize, give back to the private sector that which was nationalized.

DESNATURALIZADO.
adj, denaturalized, deprived of citizenship (after having been naturalized in another country) ‖ unnatural. Used to describe family members who fail to fulfill their legal or moral obligations regarding the family.

DESNATURALIZAR.
v, to denaturalize, deprive of citizenship ‖ to require expatriation ‖ to deform, pervert, degenerate ‖ to change, denature (a thing).

DESNATURALIZARSE.
v, to renounce one's citizenship or nationality in favor of another.

DESOBEDIENCIA.
f, disobedience ‖ breaking of laws, regulations, orders ‖ non-compliance with order or duties.

DESOBEDIENCIA DE LA AUTORIDAD.
disobedience of authority.

DESOBEDIENCIA MILITAR.
disobedience of military authority.

DESOBLIGAR.
v, to relieve from duty ‖ to release or free from obligation.

DESOCUPACIÓN.
f, unemployment, lack of work ‖ ejectment, eviction.

DESOCUPACIÓN ESTACIONAL.
seasonal unemployment.

DESOCUPACIÓN FORZOSA.
involuntary unemployment, unemployment which exists despite the capability and desire of a person to work.

DESOCUPADO.
adj, unemployed ‖ idle ‖ not busy, not working ‖ unoccupied, free.

DESOCUPAR.
v, to vacate ‖ to dispossess ‖ to evict.

DESOCUPAR JUDICIALMENTE.
to dispossess ‖ to evict, in both cases by means of the court.

DESOCUPARSE.
v, to quit a job ‖ to finish one's work, be free.

DESOLLAR.
v, to skin ‖ to injure.

DESORDEN.
m, disorder, anarchy, chaos ‖ mutiny, sedition ‖ riot ‖ irregularity (in the proceedings).

DESORDEN PÚBLICO.
breach of the peace ‖ disorderly conduct. Usually considered to be a crime, but varies greatly in different jurisdictions.

DESORGANIZACIÓN.
f, disorganization. May refer to lack of order of method in private or public corporations.

DESPACHANTE.
m, clerk ‖ customs agent.

DESPACHANTE DE ADUANAS.
customs agent.

DESPACHAR.
v, to dispatch, send (a message or correspondence) ‖ to settle a matter quickly ‖ to decide an action ‖ to sell (goods) ‖ to evict, eject ‖ to kill ‖ to give birth.

DESPACHO.

m, sending off, dispatch ‖ conclusion of a matter ‖ message, letter, correspondence ‖ office (for business) ‖ law office ‖ judge's chambers ‖ file ‖ commission, title or appointment to a position ‖ sale of commercial goods ‖ store or shop ‖ governmental dispatch, official message; signature of the head of state, ministers, or other public authorities ‖ court order, writ (to do or prohibit something) ‖ order to a subordinate judge or tribunal ‖ shipment.

DESPACHO ADUANAL.

customhouse clearance.

DESPACHO DE ADUANA.

See DESPACHO ADUANAL.

DESPACHO DE EXHORTOS.

book in which receipt of letters rogatory are noted by trial court judges.

DESPACHO ORDINARIO.

ordinary (judicial) proceeding. Opposed to extraordinary judicial proceeding.

DESPALMAR.

v, to rob by violence or force.

DESPEDIR.

v, to fire, dismiss, let go (an employee) ‖ to throw (something).

DESPEDIRSE.

v, to quit, resign (employment).

DESPEJAR
LA SALA.

v, to clear the courtroom.

DESPIDO.

m, firing, dismissal, discharge (from employment). May be INJUSTIFICADO (without legal justification) or JUSTIFICADO (legally justificable).

DESPIDO INDIRECTO.

resignation (from employment by employee due to breach of employment contract). Usually refers to forced resignation.

DESPIDO LABORAL.

See DESPIDO.

DESPIDO PUNITIVO.

discharge for cause.

DESPIGNORAR.

v, to release a pledge.

DESPOBLADO.

m, unpopulated and uncultivated area ‖ adj, unpopulated.

DESPOJANTE.

m, f, deforcer, despoiler.

DESPOJAR.

v, to despoil, rob ‖ to evict, dispossess by force ‖ to use and enjoy property of another by force ‖ to take pursuant to court order goods possessed by one party for return to their rightful owner.

DESPOJO.

m, bounty (of victors), plunder ‖ action or judgment which transfers goods to their rightful owner ‖ action for conversion ‖ forceful eviction ‖ dispossession. Usually of tenant, but may be of owner.

DESPOJOS.

m, residue, leftovers ‖ low value minerals ‖ corpse, cadaver ‖ usable rubble from a building which has been torn down.

DESPOSADO.

m, recently married person ‖ handcuffed prisoner.

DESPOSAR.

v, to marry, wed.

DESPOSEER.

v, to dispossess ‖ to seize (another's property) ‖ to evict.

DESPOSEERSE.

v, to disown (property), renounce rights of ownership.

DESPOSEIMIENTO.

m, dispossession, ouster ‖ divestiture.

DESPOSORIO.

See DESPOSORIOS.

DESPOSORIOS.

m, vows (of marriage), marriage vows, promise to marry.

DESPOTISMO.

m, despotism, tyranny, autocracy ‖ government of an absolute ruler who establishes, nullifies, or modifies laws pursuant to his personal convenience ‖ absolute or limitless authority ‖ abuse of authority ‖ ability, or rank.

DESPRECIO DEL OFENDIDO.

m, contempt for the age, sex, or dignity of the victim. Refers in criminal law to an aggravating circumstance.

DESTAJISTA.

m, f, pieceworker ‖ jobber.

DESTAJO.

See TRABAJO A DESTAJO.

DESTIERRO.

m, exile, banishment (from a designated territory, temporarily or permanently). Used as a criminal punishment, usually for political crimes.

DESTINAR.
v, to destine ‖ to designate, assign (a person to a job).

DESTINATARIO.
m, addressee, consignee.

DESTINO.
m, destination ‖ work, employment, occupation ‖ establishment, institution or place of work ‖ public employment given freely in return for a favor, and for which little actual work is expected.

DESTITUCIÓN.
f, deprivation (of one's property) ‖ removal, discharge, dismissal (from public employment or office as punishment) ‖ abandonment, destitution.

DESTITUIR.
v, to deprive ‖ to discharge.

DESTRONAMIENTO.
m, dethroning, deposition, deposal.

DESTRUCCIÓN.
f, destruction, ruin, devastation ‖ deterioration ‖ abusive consumption (of goods) ‖ refutation (of an argument).

DESUETUDO.
disuse ‖ longstanding non-application of a rule.

DESUSO.
m, disuse.

DESVALIJAR.
v, to rob (the contents of a suitcase) ‖ to assault, rob ‖ to defraud, swindle (by trick or deceit).

DESVALIJO.
m, robbery.

DESVEDAR.
v, to lift or revoke a prohibition.

DESVIACIÓN.
f, deviation ‖ vice.

DESVIACIÓN JURÍDICA.
deviation from the proper use of the law.

DESVINCULAR.
v, to disentail.

DETALLAR.
v, to itemize, detail.

DETALLES.
m, particulars ‖ details.

DETECTIVE.
m, detective.

DETECTIVISMO.
m, detective service.

DETECTOR DE MENTIRAS.
m, lie detector.

DETENCIÓN.
f, restraint ‖ detention, deprivation of liberty ‖ provisional arrest ‖ stop, halt ‖ lateness ‖ detainer, distraint.

DETENCIÓN DE LA SENTENCIA.
arrest of judgment.

DETENCIÓN ILEGAL.
illegal detention or restraint (by government).

DETENCIÓN MALICIOSA.
malicious arrest.

DETENCIÓN POR ORDEN VERBAL.
parol arrest.

DETENCIÓN PREVENTIVA.
preventive arrest or detention.

DETENCIÓN VIOLENTA.
forcible detainer or restraint.

DETENER.
v, to retain, reserve ‖ to detain, delay ‖ to arrest ‖ to distrain ‖ to restrain.

DETENER EL PAGO.
to stop or delay payment.

DETENTACIÓN.
f, unlawful detainer (of real or personal property) ‖ lawful holding (of property or position).

DETENTADOR.
m, person who unlawfully detains (real or personal property) ‖ person who lawfully holds property or position.

DETENTAR.
v, to hold or retain, against the law, that which does belongs to another ‖ to hold (property or position legally).

DETERIORO.
m, deterioration ‖ detriment ‖ damage, loss.

DETERMINACIÓN.
f, determination ‖ resolution, conclusion ‖ resolve.

DETRIMENTO.
m, detriment ‖ deterioration, loss, partial destruction ‖ weakness (of health) ‖ prejudice ‖ psychological or emotional injury.

DEUDA.
f, debt, indebtedness, debt owing, obligation (usually, to pay money) ‖ (criminal) guilt ‖ female kin, close female relative.

DEUDA A CORTO PLAZO.
See DEUDA A PLAZO BREVE.
DEUDA A LARGO PLAZO.
long-term debt.
DEUDA A PLAZO BREVE.
short-term debt.
DEUDA ALIMENTARIA.
See DEUDA ALIMENTICIA.
DEUDA ALIMENTICIA.
obligation of support (in terms of subsistence). Usually used to describe the obligation of parents to children, etc.
DEUDA AMORTIZABLE.
amortizable debt.
DEUDA CONSOLIDADA.
consolidated debt.
DEUDA EN GESTIÓN.
debt being collected by legal means.
DEUDA EXTERIOR.
foreign debt, external debt ‖ debt incurred abroad and payable in foreign currency.
DEUDA EXTERNA.
See DEUDA EXTERNA.
DEUDA FLOTANTE.
floating debt.
Opposed to DEUDA CONSOLIDADA.
DEUDA ILÍQUIDA.
unliquidated debt.
DEUDA IMPOSITIVA.
tax liability.
DEUDA INCOBRABLE.
bad debt.
DEUDA INTERIOR.
local debt, government debt incurred locally and payable in local currency.
DEUDA LÍQUIDA.
liquidated debt.
DEUDA MALA.
See DEUDA INCOBRABLE.
DEUDA MANCOMUNADA.
joint debt, jointly-held debt. Opposed to DEUDA MANCOMUNADA Y SOLIDARIA.
**DEUDA MANCOMUNADA
Y SOLIDARIA.**
joint and severally held debt, obligation for which debtors are held liable individually and jointly.
DEUDA PERPETUA.
perpetual debt.
DEUDA POR JUICIO.
judgment debt.

DEUDA PRIVILEGIADA.
preferred or privileged debt.
DEUDA PÚBLICA.
public debt, government debt incurred locally or abroad.
DEUDA QUIROGRAFARIA.
unsecured debt.
DEUDA SOLIDARIA.
See DEUDA MANCOMUNADA Y SOLIDARIA.
DEUDA VENCIDA.
matured debt.
DEUDAS HEREDITARIAS.
decedent's debts.
DEUDAS MORTUARIAS.
expenses of illness that led to death and burial or decedent.
DEUDOR.
m, debtor ‖ obligor ‖ adj, indebted.
DEUDOR ALIMENTARIO.
person who owes alimony or support payment.
DEUDOR ALIMENTICIO.
See DEUDOR ALIMENTARIO.
DEUDOR CONCORDATARIO.
bankrupt who has made an agreement with his creditors.
DEUDOR EN MORA.
See DEUDOR MOROSO.
DEUDOR HIPOTECARIO.
mortgagor.
DEUDOR MANCOMUNADO.
joint debtor.
DEUDOR MOROSO.
delinquent debtor.
DEUDOR POR JUICIO.
judgment debtor.
DEUDOR PRENDARIO.
debtor of a debt secured with a pledge or chattel mortgage.
DEUDOR SOLIDARIO.
joint and several debtor.
DEUDOS.
m, relatives, kindred, kin.
DEVALUACIÓN.
f, devaluation (of money).
DEVENGAR.
v, to accrue interest ‖ to be entitled to receive moneys (for services, work, etc.).
DEVENGO.
m, amount earned or due or accrued.
DEVIEDO.
m, prohibition, injunction.

DEVOLUCIÓN.
f, restitution, return, devolution ‖ refusal ‖ tax refund ‖ uncollectible document returned to owner. Used commercially to refer to the right of the buyer to return a good in certain situations. Used in tax law to the return of tax paid, to taxpayers.

DEVOLUCIÓN DE IMPUESTO.
tax refund.

DEVOLUTIVO.
adj, returnable, able to be returned. Used in procedural law, to refer to the effect of sending a lower court decision to an appellate court.

DEVOLVER.
v, to return ‖ to refund ‖ to remit, remand.

DÍA.
m, day.

DÍA ARTIFICIAL.
natural day, period of time made up of the solar day and night ‖ artificial day, period of time during which the sun is above the horizon.

DÍA CIERTO.
day certain.

DÍA CIVIL.
civil day, day starting and ending at midnight.

DÍA COLENDO.
See DÍA FESTIVO.

DÍA DADO.
given day ‖ day certain.

DÍA DE COMPARECENCIA.
appearance day.

DÍA DE CORTESÍA.
day of grace.

DÍA DE CUTIO.
See DÍA DE TRABAJO.

DÍA DE DESCANSO.
day of rest (usually Sunday).

DÍA DE FIESTA.
See DÍA FESTIVO.

DÍA DE GRACIA.
day of grace.

DÍA DE HACIENDA.
See DÍA DE TRABAJO.

DÍA DE INDULTO.
day of pardon. Refers to day, usually a civil or religious holiday, used to pardon those sentenced to death, etc.

DÍA DE TRABAJO.
working day.

DÍA DE VACANCIA.
day when courts are not in session.

DÍA FERIADO.
non-working day ‖ also see DÍA FESTIVO.

DÍA FESTIVO.
holiday.

DÍA HÁBIL.
working or business day.

DÍA HÁBIL ADMINISTRATIVO.
working day for governmental activities.

DÍA HÁBIL JUDICIAL.
juridical day.

DÍA INCIERTO.
day uncertain, day the occurrence of which remains uncertain.

DÍA INHÁBIL.
non-working day ‖ non-juridical day.

DÍA LABORABLE.
See DÍA DE TRABAJO.

DÍA NATURAL.
natural day ‖ day measured from sunrise to sunset ‖ calendar day.

DÍA NO LABORABLE.
non-working day.

DÍA ÚTIL.
See DÍA HÁBIL.

DIACRÍTICO.
adj, distinguishing, distinctive.

DIARIO.
m, daily newspaper, daily, journal ‖ daybook, daily expense book ‖ book of original entry of deeds for record‖ adj, daily.

DIARIO DE NAVEGACIÓN.
ship's log book.

DÍAS Y HORAS HÁBILES.
juridical days and hours.

DICCIONARIO.
m, dictionary.

DICENTE.
m, f, speaker, declarer, deponent ‖ saying.

"DICTA TESTIUM".
witness's testimony.

DICTADOR.
m, dictator.

DICTADURA.
f, dictatorship.

DICTADURA SINDICAL.
Literally, union dictatorship ‖ acts of the union leadership requiring the adherence of membership to a determined policy or expulsion from the union or similar penalty.

DICTAMEN.
m, opinion, letter of an attorney in a case, usually in writing ‖ opinion, advice ‖ opinion, judgment, decision (of court).

DICTAMEN DE AUDITORÍA.
auditor's certificate or opinion.

DICTAMEN JUDICIAL.
judicial decision.

DICTAMEN PERICIAL.
expert's opinion.

DICTAMINAR.
v, to pass judgment, give an opinion ‖ to rule, issue a decision.

DICTAR.
v, to dictate ‖ to issue, promulgate (a law) ‖ to issue a verdict, decision.

DICTAR FALLO.
to pronounce judgment.

DICTAR LA SENTENCIA.
to sentence ‖ to issue a (judicial) decision.

DICTAR PROVIDENCIA.
See DICTAR FALLO.

DICTAR SENTENCIA.
See DICTAR FALLO.

DICTAR UN AUTO.
to issue a writ.

DICTAR UN DECRETO.
to issue a decree.

DICTAR UNA OPINIÓN.
to render or issue an opinion.

DICTÓGRAFO.
m, dictograph.

"DICTUM".
aphorism, saying, adage ‖ witness's testimony ‖ dictum ‖ adj, stated, said.

DICHO.
m, saying ‖ opinion ‖ rumor ‖ adj, said, stated, declared (may be in writing) ‖ written, set forth.

DIES A QUO.
dies a quo, day from which.

DIETA.
f, salary of a legislator or congressman ‖ diet, congress ‖ remuneration for carrying out functions away from official residence. Usually of a judge or other public official ‖ daily stipend for carrying out a commission.

DIETA DE TESTIGO.
witness' fee.

DIFAMACIÓN.
f, defamation, libel.

DIFAMACIÓN CRIMINAL.
criminal libel.

DIFAMACIÓN ESCRITA.
libel, written defamation.

DIFAMACIÓN ORAL.
slander, oral defamation.

DIFAMACIÓN VERBAL.
See DIFAMACIÓN ORAL.

DIFAMAR.
v, to defame ‖ to libel ‖ to slander.

DIFAMATORIO.
adj, libelous, calumnious.

DIFERIR.
v, to defer, postpone, adjourn, put over ‖ to extend, prolong, delay.

DIFUNTO.
m, deceased, decedent ‖ adj, deceased, dead, late.

DIGESTO.
m, digest, compilation of laws ‖ Roman digest, Justinian digest.

DIGITALES.
f, fingerprints.

DIGNATARIO.
m, official ‖ officer.

DIGNIDAD.
f, dignity ‖ merit, excellence ‖ decorum ‖ honorific position.

DIGNIDAD DEL OFENDIDO.
victim's dignity. Offense to a victim's dignity is considered to be an aggravating circumstance in criminal law.

DIGNO DE CONFIANZA.
reliable, worthy of confidence.

DILACIÓN.
f, delay.

DILACIÓN DELIBERATORIA.
time period for answering complaint.

DILACIÓN PROBATORIA.
See DILACIÓN DELIBERATORIA.

DILAPIDACION.
f, prodigality, waste of property.

DILATAR.
v, to defer, delay ‖ to extend ‖ to postpone.

DILATORIO.
adj, dilatory, delaying.

DILIGENCIA.
f, care, zeal ‖ diligence (in legal and moral obligations), promptness ‖ speed ‖ matter, business ‖ enforcement or performance of a

ruling ‖ proceeding of a judge's clerk in a civil trial ‖ step, measure.

DILIGENCIA DE EMBARGO.
attachment proceedings.

DILIGENCIA DE EMPLAZAMIENTO.
service of summons.

DILIGENCIA DE LANZAMIENTO.
dispossession or ejectment proceedings.

DILIGENCIA DE PRUEBA.
taking of evidence.

DILIGENCIA EXTRAORDINARIA.
unusual care ‖ extraordinary proceeding.

DILIGENCIA NORMAL.
See DILIGENCIA ORDINARIA.

DILIGENCIA ORDINARIA.
ordinary diligence or care.

DILIGENCIA PROCESAL.
court proceeding.

DILIGENCIA PROPIA.
due diligence or care.

DILIGENCIA RAZONABLE.
reasonable diligence or care.

DILIGENCIA SIMPLE.
ordinary diligence or care.

DILIGENCIA SUMARIA.
summary proceeding.

DILIGENCIAS DEL PROTESTO.
measure taken to protest a note or draft.

DILIGENCIAS JUDICIALES.
judicial proceedings.

DILIGENCIAS PARA MEJOR PROVEER.
actions to be taken pursuant to court order to facilitate the rapid adjudication of a case or to clarify existing evidence or to obtain additional evidence. May be ordered by a court after the parties have presented their case, in order to add to or clarify the evidence.

DILIGENCIAS PRELIMINARES.
all actions preliminary to trial, pre-trial proceedings. Usually includes discovery, naming of guardian ad litem, measuring of property, etc.

DILIGENCIAS PREPARATORIOS DEL JUICIO.
See DILIGENCIAS PRELIMINARES.

DILIGENCIAS PROBATORIAS.
evidentiary proceeding or hearing.

DILIGENCIADOR.
m, business representative or agent ‖ negotiator.

DILIGENCIAR.
to conduct, carry through, prosecute ‖ to serve (process).

DILIGENCIERO.
m, agent, representative.

DILIGENTE.
adj, diligent, careful ‖ prompt, speedy ‖ industrious.

DILOGÍA.
f, ambiguity ‖ double meaning.

DIMISIÓN.
f, resignation, quitting, retirement (by an employee of a position).

DIMITIR.
v, to resign, quit, retire from (employment) ‖ to leave (a thing) ‖ to abandon.

DINASTÍA.
f, dynasty.

DINERO.
m, money ‖ wealth, fortune.

DIPLOMA.
m, diploma (issued by an academic institution).

DIPLOMACIA.
f, diplomacy.

DIPLOMADO.
m, professional person ‖ adj, licensed.

DIPLOMÁTICO.
m, diplomat ‖ diplomacy ‖ adj, diplomatic.

DIPSOMANÍA.
f, dipsomania, alcoholism.

DIPUTACIÓN.
f, congressional delegation ‖ delegation, committee ‖ post of congressman, representative, or member of Parliament and duration thereof ‖ congressional matter or business.

DIPUTADO.
m, delegate, representative, deputy ‖ congressman, representative, member of house of representatives.

DIPUTADO PROPIETARIO.
regular member of a board.

DIPUTADO SUPLENTE.
alternate member of a board.

DIPUTAR.
v, to deputize ‖ to appoint, delegate, empower ‖ to designate.

DIRECCIÓN.
f, address ‖ residence, domicile ‖ direction, act of directing ‖ course, direction ‖ precept, norm, rule ‖ guidance ‖ management, directorate ‖ directorship ‖ direction of traffic.

DIRECCIÓN DEL PROCESO.
management of trial, power given to courts

over the procedure to be followed in a case. May be FORMAL (following normal and usual procedures) or MATERIAL (following special procedures for judicial economy and in order to prevent contradictory or moot decisions).

DIRECCIÓN GENERAL.
general management. Refers to higher authorities in the public administration or quasi-governmental corporations.

DIRECTIVA.
f, management, board of directors or governors, directorate (of a union or other corporation) ‖ policy, guideline.

DIRECTIVO.
m, director, member of a board of directors ‖ adj, directors' or director's ‖ managerial ‖ executive.

DIRECTO.
adj, direct ‖ straight ‖ straight ahead ‖ effective. Meaning is highly dependent upon the noun which it complements.

DIRECTOR.
m, director, member of a board of directors ‖ agent, representative (of a commercial company).

DIRECTOR GENERAL.
general director (of the DIRECCIÓN GENERAL).

DIRECTORIO.
m, directorate, board of directors ‖ adj, directory, directive.

DIRECTORIOS ENCADENADOS.
interlocking directorates.

DIRECTORIOS ENTRELAZADOS.
interlocking directorates.

DIRIGENTE SINDICAL.
m, member of the governing body of a labor union.

DIRIGIR.
v, to direct, manage ‖ to address (e.g. correspondence to someone).

DIRIGIRSE AL BANQUILLO.
to take the (witness) stand.

DIRIGIRSE AL TRIBUNAL.
to address the court.

DIRIGISMO.
m, government control of economic and social activities.

DIRIGISMO ESTATAL.
government intervention (e.g. in business).

DIRIGISMO OFICIAL.
See DIRIGISMO ESTATAL.

DIRIMENTE.
m, impediment to marriage, circumstance, fact or situation which makes a valid marriage impossible ‖ magistrate (or other party) who annuls a marriage.

DIRIMIR.
v, to settle, adjust ‖ to annul, declare void.

DISCERNIMIENTO.
m, judicial appointment, empowerment of a person by a judge (e.g. appointment of a guardian, conservator, etc.).

DISCERNIR.
v, to appoint (a party to a position or function, by a judge) ‖ to swear in.

DISCIPLINA.
f, discipline, observance of laws and regulations.

DISCIPLINARIO.
adj, disciplinary.

DISCONFORME.
adj, dissenting, objecting, not in agreement.

DISCONFORMIDAD.
f, dissent, objection ‖ opposition, disapproval, disagreement, nonconformity, difference.

DISCONTINUO.
adj, intermittent, discontinuous.

DISCORDIA.
f, discord, opposition ‖ difference of opinions, decisions or judgments ‖ split decision, variance of opinion (of judges sitting on a tribunal, which results in a majority voting against a given decision).

DISCORDANCIA.
f, difference ‖ dissent, disagreement.

DISCRECIÓN.
f, discretion.

DISCRECIONAL.
adj, discretionary.

DISCRIMINACIÓN.
f, discrimination.

DISCULPA.
f, excuse, apology ‖ pretext ‖ satisfaction of damage.

DISCULPAR.
v, to exonerate, excuse, exculpate ‖ to apologize.

DISCURSO.
m, speech, statement ‖ conversation ‖ discourse ‖ oration ‖ reasoning, power to reason ‖ reflection, meditation ‖ space or duration or flow of time.

DISCURSO AL JURADO.
statement to the jury.
DISCURSO DE INFORME.
summing up ‖ statement to the jury.
DISCUSIÓN.
f, discussion, debate.
DISCUSIÓN DE LA PRETENSIÓN.
defendant's denial.
DISCUTIBLE.
adj, debatable, controvertible ‖ arguable.
DISCUTIR.
v, to discuss ‖ to debate ‖ to argue about.
DISENSO.
m, dissension, dissent ‖ negation ‖ waiver of a contracting party.
DISENTIR.
v, to disagree with, dissent, differ.
DISFRAZ.
m, costume ‖ cover, pretense. May be an aggravating circumstance in a crime.
DISFRUTAR.
v, to enjoy.
DISFRUTE.
m, satisfaction, enjoyment ‖ use ‖ benefit ‖ possession.
DISIDENCIA.
f, dissidence, discrepancy ‖ disagreement, dissent.
DISIDENTE.
m, dissenter ‖ adj, dissident, dissenting.
DISIMULACIÓN.
f, dissimulation, hiding ‖ pretense, false appearance.
DISIMULO.
See DISIMULACIÓN.
DISOLUCIÓN.
f, dissolution, separation ‖ termination (of a contract) ‖ resolution, conclusion ‖ liquidation.
DISOLUCIÓN DE LA SOCIEDAD CONYUGAL.
separation of marital property.
DISOLUCIÓN DE LAS PERSONAS JURÍDICAS.
dissolution of legal entities.
DISOLUCIÓN DE SOCIEDADES.
dissolution of business associations.
DISOLUCIÓN DEL MATRIMONIO.
marital dissolution. May be NATURAL (due to death), LEGAL (divorce or separation) or ESPECIAL (nullity).

DISOLVER.
v, to dissolve, separate ‖ to undo ‖ to destroy ‖ to negotiate a contract ‖ to resolve (a doubt or suspicion).
DISOLVER LA REUNIÓN.
to adjourn the meeting.
DISPARO DE ARMA DE FUEGO.
m, discharge of a firearm. May be a crime.
DISPENSA.
f, dispensation, exemption (from the law) ‖ document of dispensation.
DISPENSA DE EDAD.
exemption from marital age limitations.
DISPENSABLE.
adj, excusable ‖ able to be exempted ‖ dispensable, not requisite.
DISPENSACIÓN.
f, exemption ‖ dispensation ‖ pardon.
DISPENSAR.
v, to excuse, exempt ‖ to absolve.
DISPONER.
v, to dispose ‖ to order ‖ to arrange for, prepare.
DISPONIBILIDAD.
f, availability ‖ available resources.
DISPONIÉNDOSE.
provided that.
DISPONIBLE.
adj, available, free ‖ liquid, demandable.
DISPOSICIÓN.
f, disposition ‖ requirement, specification ‖ order, mandate ‖ decision, resolution (of a court) ‖ power to dispose (of personal property) ‖ disposal, distribution of a decedent's estate pursuant to will ‖ provision, rule ‖ proviso ‖ clause (within a law).
DISPOSICIÓN DE ÚLTIMA VOLUNTAD.
last will and testament, will, testament.
DISPOSICIONES.
f, arrangements ‖ plural of DISPOSICIÓN.
DISPOSICIONES DISCRECIONALES.
discretionary provision, DISPOSICIÓN which leaves discretion (e.g.to a judge).
DISPOSICIONES LEGALES.
statutory clauses.
DISPOSICIONES PROCESALES.
rules of procedure, procedural clauses.
DISPOSICIONES SUSTANTIVAS.
substantive law provisions or clauses.
DISPOSICIONES TRANSITORIAS.
temporary provisions.

DISPOSICIONES TRIBUTARIAS.
tax rules.

DISPOSITIVO.
m, device ‖ adj, dispositive.

DISPUTA.
f, dispute ‖ argument.

DISPUTA OBRERA.
labor dispute.

DISPUTABLE.
adj, disputable, controvertible ‖ arguable.

DISPUTAR.
v, to dispute, question ‖ to debate ‖ to compete or contend for.

DISTANCIA.
f, distance ‖ difference, inequality ‖ discrepancy.

DISTINGUIR.
v, to distinguish ‖ to mark, indicate ‖ to estimate.

DISTRACCIÓN.
f, misappropriation ‖ distraction ‖ fraud.

DISTRACCIÓN DE FONDOS.
misappropriation of funds.

DISTRACTO.
m, mutual rescission (of a contract).

DISTRAER.
v, to divert, misappropriate ‖ to distract.

DISTRITO.
m, district, region, area.

DISTRITO ADUANERO.
customs district.

DISTRITO FEDERAL.
federal district.

DISTRITO IMPOSITIVO.
tax district.

DISTRITO JUDICIAL.
judicial district.

DISYUNTIVO.
adj, disjunctive, containing an alternative.

DITA.
f, guarantor, surety, person who guarantees payment ‖ debt ‖ guaranty, surety.

DIVÁN.
m, divan, Turkish congress.

DIVIDENDO.
m, dividend.

DIVIDENDO ACUMULATIVO.
cumulative dividend.

DIVIDENDO ATRASADO.
late dividend, dividend in arrears.

DIVIDENDO CASUAL.
See DIVIDENDO OCASIONAL.

DIVIDENDO DE BIENES.
property dividend ‖ dividend in kind.

DIVIDENDO DE CAPITAL.
capital dividend.

DIVIDENDO DE LIQUIDACIÓN.
liquidating dividend.

DIVIDENDO EN ACCIONES.
stock dividend.

DIVIDENDO EN ESPECIE.
See DIVIDENDO DE BIENES.

DIVIDENDO EN PAGARES.
scrip dividend.

DIVIDENDO OCASIONAL.
irregular dividend.

DIVIDENDO PREFERENCIAL.
See DIVIDENDO PREFERENTE.

DIVIDENDO PREFERENTE.
preferred dividend, dividend issued to preferred stockholders.

DIVIDENDO PROVISIONAL.
See DIVIDENDO PROVISORIO.

DIVIDENDO PROVISORIO.
interim dividend.

DIVIDUO.
adj, divisible.

DIVISA.
f, insignia, emblem ‖ termination of a business ‖ devise, part of a father's estate which corresponds to each of his children ‖ foreign exchange ‖ national currency ‖ slogan ‖ devise.

DIVISAS A LA VISTA.
demand (foreign) exchange.

DIVISIBILIDAD.
f, divisibility.

DIVISIBLE.
adj, divisible, severable.

DIVISIÓN.
f, division, separation, partition ‖ distribution ‖ discord, enmity.

DIVISIÓN DE LA HERENCIA.
distribution of a decedent's estate ‖ action for distribution of a decedent's estate.

DIVISIÓN DE LA COSA COMÚN.
partition of a thing held in common.

DIVISIÓN DEL TRABAJO.
division of labor.

DIVORCIAR.
v, to divorce.

DIVORCIO.
m, divorce.
DIVORCIO CONTENCIOSO.
contested divorce.
DIVORCIO EN REBELDÍA.
divorce granted in absentia (of one of the parties).
DIVORCIO POR CAUSA.
fault based divorce, divorce for cause.
DIVULGACIÓN.
f, publication ‖ disclosure, revelation.
DOBLE.
m, traitor ‖ stock transaction which consists of buying or selling stock at one price for selling or repurchase at a different price the following month or period ‖ adj, double ‖ insincere.
DOBLE NACIONALIDAD.
double nationality.
DOBLE TRIBUTACIÓN.
double taxation.
DOBLE VÍNCULO.
dual relationship. Refers in law of successions, to the relationship of child to both the mother and father.
DOCENTE.
m, f, teacher, professor ‖ adj, teaching, educational, pertaining to education.
DOCTOR.
m, doctor, physician ‖ attorney, lawyer ‖ doctor, person who has received a doctoral degree ‖ degree of doctor.
DOCTOR EN DERECHO.
doctor of laws, juris doctor.
DOCTORADO.
m, doctoral studies ‖ doctoral degree ‖ doctorate.
DOCTRINA.
f, doctrine ‖ theses and opinions of legal scholars.
DOCTRINA LEGAL.
legal doctrine ‖ judicial construction regarding a given law.
DOCTRINAL.
adj, doctrinal.
DOCTRINARIO.
adj, doctrinal, doctrinaire.
DOCTRINAS SINDICALES.
union doctrines or theories.
DOCUMENTACIÓN.
f, documentation ‖ document ‖ documents ‖ written proof or justification ‖ personal iden-

tification ‖ instruction or information regarding a scientific problem.
DOCUMENTACIÓN COMPROBATORIA.
supporting documents or proof ‖ vouchers.
DOCUMENTACIÓN DE LA AERONAVE.
aircraft's papers, aircraft registration papers.
DOCUMENTACIÓN DEL BUQUE.
ship's papers.
DOCUMENTACIÓN JUSTIFICADA.
See DOCUMENTACIÓN COMPROBATORIA.
DOCUMENTADOR.
m, court clerk.
DOCUMENTADOR PÚBLICO.
notary public.
DOCUMENTAL.
adj, documentary, regarding documents.
DOCUMENTAR.
v, to document, provide proof or evidence (of something) ‖ to prepare a document(s).
DOCUMENTAR UNA DEUDA.
to give a note or other evidence of indebtedness.
DOCUMENTO.
m, document, writing ‖ written proof, evidence ‖ instrument.
DOCUMENTO A LA ORDEN.
order paper.
DOCUMENTO AL PORTADOR.
bearer paper.
DOCUMENTO ANÓNIMO.
unsigned document.
DOCUMENTO AUTÉNTICO.
certified document, certified writing, notarized document. Refers to writings which have been sworn to before a public official authorized to attest to not only the veracity of the signature of the document, but its substance as well.
DOCUMENTO AUTÓGRAFO.
personally signed document.
DOCUMENTO CAMBIARIO.
bill of exchange.
DOCUMENTO COMERCIAL.
commercial paper.
DOCUMENTO CON UNA SOLA FIRMA.
single-name paper.
DOCUMENTO CONSTITUTIVO.
incorporation papers.
DOCUMENTO CREDITORIO.
credit instrument.

DOCUMENTO DE COMERCIO.
See DOCUMENTO COMERCIAL.
DOCUMENTO DE CONSTITUCIÓN.
See DOCUMENTO CONSTITUTIVO.
DOCUMENTO DE CRÉDITO.
credit instrument.
DOCUMENTO DE GIRO.
draft, bill of exchange.
DOCUMENTO DE TRÁNSITO.
bill of lading.
DOCUMENTO DE TRANSMISIÓN.
transfer deed ‖ bill of sale.
DOCUMENTO DE VENTA.
bill of sale.
DOCUMENTO DECLARATIVO.
statement, document that states something.
DOCUMENTO DISPOSITIVO.
dispositive document.
DOCUMENTO EJECUTIVO.
See TÍTULO EJECUTIVO.
DOCUMENTO FORMAL.
document which meets certain formal requirements.
DOCUMENTO HETERÓGRAFO.
document prepared by someone other than its signer.
DOCUMENTO JUSTIFICATIVO.
supporting document.
DOCUMENTO MANCOMUNADO.
joint or two-name paper.
DOCUMENTO NEGOCIABLE.
negotiable instrument.
DOCUMENTO NOTARIAL.
notarial document, document of a notary public.
DOCUMENTO PRIVADO.
private writing. Refers to documents and papers, witnessed or not, which are not sworn to before any public official.
Opposed to DOCUMENTO PÚBLICO.
DOCUMENTO PROBATORIO.
evidentiary document, document that may serve as evidence.
DOCUMENTO PÚBLICO.
certified document, certified writing, notarized document; writing which has been sworn to before a special notary public, judicial clerk, or other public official authorized to certify documents, facts, statements of intent, and dates. Includes ESCRITURA PÚBLICA.
DOCUMENTO SIMPLE.
document without special formalities.

DOCUMENTO SOLEMNE.
document which meets certain formal requirements needed for its validity.
DOCUMENTO TRANSMISIBLE.
negotiable instrument.
DOCUMENTOS OTORGADOS EN EL EXTRANJERO.
documents which have been issued abroad (either by authorities of the foreign government or by consular officers located abroad).
DOLARIZAR.
v, to change a monetary system to one based on the United States dollar.
DOLO.
m, lie, fraud, trick (to induce another party to enter into a contract or other legal relationship) ‖ malicious failure to fulfill obligations ‖ mens rea.
DOLO CAUSANTE.
fraud in the inducement of another party to enter into a contract. Usually allows the defrauded party to void or rescind the contract.
DOLO CIVIL.
tortious fraud ‖ tortious intent.
DOLO DE ÍMPETU.
unpremeditated criminal intent. Opposed to DOLO DE PROPÓSITO.
DOLO DE PROPÓSITO.
premeditated criminal intent.
Opposed to DOLO DE ÍMPETU.
DOLO INCIDENTAL.
immaterial fraud.
DOLO NEGATIVO.
deceitful withholding of information.
DOLO PENAL.
criminal intent.
DOLO POSITIVO.
positive acts of deceit which induce something (e.g. a contract).
DOLOSO.
adj, fraudulent.
DOMESTICADO.
adj, domesticated ‖ obedient.
DOMÉSTICO.
adj, domestic ‖ national, internal (as opposed to foreign).
DOMICILIAR.
v, to domicile.
DOMICILIARSE.
v, to take up residence, domicile oneself.

DOMICILIARIO.
adj, domiciliary.
DOMICILIO.
m, domicile ‖ place where, for legal purposes, one lives. Implies not only residence in the place, but intent to live there.
DOMICILIO ACCIDENTAL.
temporary residence.
DOMICILIO AD LITEM.
domicile chosen for the purposes of litigation.
DOMICILIO COMERCIAL.
business address, commercial domicile ‖ corporate domicile; corporate headquarters, place where the principal activity of a business is carried out. For commercial companies, the corporate domicile is located at the address indicated in the articles of incorporation or where the management or administration is. Companies with various branches, have a DOMICILIO ESPECIAL at each branch, for local transactions.
DOMICILIO CONSTITUIDO.
legal residence ‖ domicile of choice.
DOMICILIO CONVENCIONAL.
domicile of choice.
DOMICILIO CONYUGAL.
matrimonial domicile ‖ place chosen by the husband, where the married couple is domiciled, even if the couple is separated.
DOMICILIO DE HECHO.
de facto domicile.
DOMICILIO DE ORIGEN.
domicile of origin, natural domicile.
DOMICILIO DE LAS PERSONAS MORALES.
corporate domicile.
DOMICILIO ESPECIAL.
residence determined for special legal purposes (e.g. legal notice, etc.).
DOMICILIO FISCAL.
domicile for tax purposes.
DOMICILIO LEGAL.
necessary domicile, legal domicile, domicile set by law.
DOMICILIO MUNICIPAL.
domestic domicile.
DOMICILIO NACIONAL.
national domicile.
DOMICILIO NECESARIO.
necessary domicile.

DOMICILIO REAL.
de facto or actual domicile ‖ principal place of residence and activities.
DOMICILIO SOCIAL.
main office ‖ corporate domicile.
DOMICILIO VERDADERO.
true domicile ‖ domicile of choice.
DOMINANTE.
adj, dominant ‖ predominant.
DOMINAR.
v, to dominate, repress, subject ‖ to exercise ownership rights (over something) ‖ to exercise power or influence (over someone).
DOMINICAL.
adj, proprietary, ownership ‖ Sunday, pertaining to Sunday.
DOMINIO.
m, dominion, power, control (to use and dispose of property) ‖ ownership ‖ right of ownership ‖ property, domain ‖ command, mastery ‖ profound knowledge (of a subject or language) ‖ dominion (of a nation over territory) ‖ self-government ‖ area of influence ‖ dominion, territorial possession which acts autonomously, but is subject to the rule of a mother country ‖ pure and simple ownership over property (including fee simple ownership).
DOMINIO ABSOLUTO.
fee simple, freehold.
DOMINIO AÉREO.
air space (over which a person or nation can exercise ownership rights).
DOMINIO DEL ESTADO.
state property, property of the nation.
DOMINIO DIRECTO.
legal ownership ‖ ownership over property, the use and enjoyment of which has been given to another.
DOMINIO DURANTE LA VIDA.
life estate.
DOMINIO EMINENTE.
eminent domain (of government over private property) ‖ also see DOMINIO ÚTIL.
DOMINIO FISCAL.
government ownership.
DOMINIO FLUVIAL.
riparian ownership.
DOMINIO IMPERFECTO.
conditional ownership, non-fee simple owner-

ship ‖ ownership which is subject to the obligation to return to the legal owner or transfer to others upon the occurrence of an event or passage of time ‖ right of conditional ownership.

DOMINIO LACUSTRE.
lake ownership, lake domain. Usually state owned.

DOMINIO MARÍTIMO.
government maritime ownership.

DOMINIO PERFECTO.
unlimited and unconditional ownership.

DOMINIO PLENO.
fee simple.

DOMINIO POR TIEMPO FIJO.
estate for years.

DOMINIO REVOCABLE.
conditional ownership, ownership subject to condition subsequent.

DOMINIO SIMPLE.
fee simple.

DOMINIO SUPREMO.
eminent domain.

DOMINIO TERRESTRE.
state ownership of real property near national borders.

DOMINIO TERRITORIAL.
ownership of land.

DOMINIO ÚTIL.
right to usufruct, right to use and enjoy property ‖ useful ownership, usufruct.

DOMINIO VITALICIO.
life estate, ownership for life.

DON.
m, gift, donation ‖ ability ‖ title of respect used before first name of men.

DONACIÓN.
f, donation, gift ‖ agreement to donate. Agreements to donate are considered to be enforceable contracts in many civil law countries.

DONACIÓN "ANTE NUPTIAS".
pre-nuptial gift (between the betrothed).

DONACIÓN CON CARGO.
conditional gift, gift given subject to agreement that the receiver use the gift in a certain way or fulfill another obligation.

DONACIÓN DE BIENES FUTUROS.
gift of future goods ‖ gift of goods over which the donor has no existing legal right. Usually prohibited by law.

DONACIÓN DE PADRES A HIJOS.
parental gift to children.

DONACIÓN DIRECTA.
contractual gift, contract for the donation of a gift which requires the consent of donor and donee ‖ direct donation, gift given directly between donor and donee.
Opposed to DONACIÓN INDIRECTA.

DONACIÓN EN VIDA.
inter vivos gift.

DONACIÓN INDIRECTA.
gift which is given regardless of the consent of the donee ‖ indirect donation, gift given through a third party.
Opposed to DONACIÓN DIRECTA.

DONACIÓN INOFICIOSA.
gift which takes property from those who have the legal right to receive a certain proportion of property under the laws of inheritance

DONACIÓN MANUAL.
hand-delivered gift.

DONACIÓN ONEROSA.
conditional gift, gift which requires the donee to perform an act of value lesser than that of the gift given.

DONACIÓN POR CAUSA DE MUERTE.
causa mortis gift.

DONACIÓN POR RAZÓN DE MATRIMONIO.
wedding gift. May be between spouses or by third parties.

DONACIÓN PURA.
gift arising out of pure generosity of spirit ‖ unconditional gift. Opposed to DONACIÓN ONEROSA.

DONACIÓN REMUNERATORIA.
compensatory gift, gift arising out of desire to compensate someone for something for which the donee could legally require payment. Some authors consider this to be a form of compensation, rather than gift.

DONACIÓN SUB-MODO.
See DONACIÓN CON CARGO.

DONACIONES MUTUAS.
reciprocal gifts, gifts given between two or more persons at the same time.

DONADOR.
m, donator, donor.

DONANTE.
m, donor, giver.

DONAR.
v, to donate, contribute, give.

DONATARIO.
m, donee, recipient.

DONATIVO.
m, donation, gift, contribution.

DONCELLA.
f, female virgin.

DORSO.
m, reverse side of back of a document.

DOTACIÓN.
f, dowry ‖ endowment ‖ crew ‖ personnel.

**DOTACIÓN DE
BUQUE.**
See TRIPULACIÓN.

DOTACIÓN PURA.
pure endowment.

DOTAL.
adj, dotal, referring to dowry.

DOTANTE.
m, donor ‖ adj, donating, endowing.
See DOTAR.

DOTAR.
v, to donate to a dowry ‖ to endow a foundation or other beneficent institution ‖ to provide, furnish ‖ to man a ship with the crew and furnish supplies needed for a journey ‖ to staff a public office or private business with employees, and to assign their functions and salaries ‖ to give a benefit to something.

DOTE.
f, dowry ‖ endowment ‖ capability, talents.

DOTE ADVENTICIA.
dowry given by mother or her family.

DOTE CONFESADA.
agreed dowry, dowry contract which is written or to which the parties agree.

DOTE ENTREGADA.
dowry which has been delivered and for which there is a written contract.

DOTE PROFECTICIA.
dowry given by father or his family.

DOTE PROMETIDA.
promised dowry.

DOY FE.
witnessed, attested to, certified, I attest to, I certify, I hereby witness. Term standardly used by notaries, ESCRIBANOS, and court clerks, located directly prior to the signature, to demonstrate his or her certification of the contents of the document.

DRACONIANO.
adj, Draconian, excessively severe.

DRAGOMÁN.
m, interpreter ‖ expert who explains and advises regarding the means of operation.

DROGA.
f, drug ‖ debt ‖ trick, fraud.

DROGAR.
v, to drug.

DROGARSE.
v, to drug oneself, inject or consume a drug.

**"DUARUM CIVITUM ESSE,
NOSTRO JURE CIVILE
NEMO POTEST."**
No one can have double nationality.

DUBITABLE.
See DUDABLE.

DUDA.
f, doubt, uncertainty, question.

DUDA RAZONABLE.
reasonable doubt.

DUDABLE.
adj, doubtful.

DUDOSO.
adj, dubious ‖ questionable.

DUELISTA.
m, duelist, dueler, participant in a duel ‖ scrapper, fighter.

DUELO.
m, duel ‖ pain, grief, sorrow, unhappiness ‖ mourning.

DUEÑA.
f, female property owner ‖ woman of the house, female head of household.

DUEÑO.
m, male property owner, title holder to property ‖ independent person ‖ man of the house, male head of household.

DUEÑO MATRICULADO.
registered owner.

DUEÑO SIN RESTRICCIONES.
absolute owner.

DÚPLICA.
f, rejoinder, defendant's second answer (to plaintiff's replication).

DUPLICACIÓN.
f, duplication.

DUPLICADO.
m, duplicate dispatch ‖ copy, duplicate ‖ adj, copied, duplicated.

DUPLICAR.
v, to duplicate ‖ to file a defendant's second answer. See DÚPLICA.

DUPLICIDAD.
f, duplicity.
DUQUE.
m, duke.
DUQUESA.
f, duchess ‖ wife of a duke.
"DURA LEX, SED LEX".
Although the law is harsh, the law it is.

DURACIÓN.
f, duration, length ‖ life.
DURACIÓN DE PENAS.
f, length of sentence.
DURACIÓN DE LA PATENTE.
term of a patent.
DURANTE AUSENCIA.
durante absentia, during the absence.

"... E HIJO".
and Son. Often used in corporate names which are based on the name of a person.

"... E HIJOS".
and Sons. See "... E HIJO".

EBRIEDAD.
f, inebriation. May constitute an excuse to crime.

EBRIO.
m, drunkard ‖ adj, intoxicated, drunk.

EBRIO HABITUAL.
habitual drunkard, alcoholic.

ECLESIÁSTICO.
m, priest, clergyman ‖ adj, ecclesiastic, related to the Church.

ECOLOGÍA.
f, ecology ‖ environment ‖ study of ecology or environment.

ECOLÓGICO.
adj, ecological.

ECONOMATO.
m, bailee ‖ deposit, warehouse (of essential goods for general public or for a special purpose).

ECONOMATO LABORAL.
workers' cooperative or co-op or cooperative store.

ECONOMÍA.
f, economy ‖ economics ‖ administration of goods ‖ economy, saving, thrift ‖ cheapness ‖ scarcity ‖ economy, structure of organisms and institutions.

ECONOMÍA AGRARIA.
study of agricultural management ‖ agricultural management ‖ agricultural economics.

ECONOMÍA AGRÍCOLA.
See ECONOMÍA AGRARIA.

ECONOMÍA APLICADA.
applied economics ‖ study of applied economics.

ECONOMÍA DIRIGIDA.
organized or directed economy, economy organized pursuant to a governmental plan.

ECONOMÍA INTERVENIDA.
See ECONOMÍA DIRIGIDA.

ECONOMÍA PLANIFICADA.
planned economy.

ECONOMÍA POLÍTICA.
political economy, economics, study of the production, circulation, distribution, and consumption of resources.

ECONOMÍA PROCESAL.
procedural or judicial economy. Refers to the principle that attempts to save time and/or money in judicial administration.

ECONOMÍA SOCIAL.
See ECONOMÍA POLÍTICA.

ECONÓMICO.
adj, economic, economical ‖ cheap ‖ well-administered.

ECONOMISTA.
m, f, economist.

ECONOMIZAR.
v, to economize, save.

ECÓNOMO.
m, trustee (of an incompetent) ‖ guardian (of an incompetent).

ECHADA.
adj, expelled, thrown out ‖ thrown, cast.

ECHAR.
v, to throw, cast ‖ to throw out, get rid of ‖ to dismiss, discharge ‖ to drop from membership ‖ to lock, lock up, bolt ‖ to impose a tax or duty ‖ to attribute, impute, ascribe ‖ to start a busi-

ness ‖ to bet, play (money) ‖ to do accounts, make an accounting ‖ to guess, calculate ‖ to give notice, advise ‖ to decide ‖ to follow a certain path ‖ to follow a certain profession ‖ to overthrow, demolish institutions or propositions ‖ to condemn, sentence.

ECHAR AL MAR.
to jettison (into the sea).

ECHAR BANDO.
to publish a decree, edict, or proclamation.

ECHAR LA CUENTA.
to calculate accounts ‖ to estimate, approximate (an expense).

ECHAR LA MANO.
to arrest, catch, detain (someone).

ECHAR SUERTES.
to draw lots ‖ to divide by lots.

ECHAR TIERRA A
UN ASUNTO.
to cover up or bury something.

ECHAZÓN.
f, jettison ‖ act of jettisoning or throwing (from a ship).

EDAD.
f, age ‖ life, life span, lifetime. Used in reference to capacity of persons in many areas of the law.

EDAD LEGÍTIMA.
age of majority.

EDECÁN.
m, aide-de-camp ‖ military chief of presidential honor guard.

EDICIÓN.
f, issue, edition (of a book or writing).

EDICIÓN OFICIAL.
official edition, first publication of a law or regulation usually in a public record (e.g. Federal Register).

EDICTO.
m, executive order ‖ decree, edict, proclamation (issued by some authority) ‖ public notice or summons (issued by a judge).

EDICTO EMPLAZATORIO.
summons to appear.

EDICTOS JUDICIALES.
notification of a judicial summons (of an unknown defendant or a defendant whose domicile is unknown, by publication in a private or public record).

EDICTOS MATRIMONIALES.
banns (of marriage).

EDIFICACIÓN.
f, building, construction.

EDIFICACIÓN, SIEMBRA Y PLANTACIÓN.
construction, sowing, and planting. Refers to the three means of accession.

EDIFICACIÓN EN PREDIO AJENO.
construction on another's real estate. Usually belongs to the owner of the real estate.

EDIFICACIÓN FORZOSA.
required urban development, construction of buildings in a city as required by law (e.g. to alleviate housing shortages).

EDIFICADO.
m, improved farmland ‖ farm upon which a building has been constructed, built-up area ‖ adj, built ‖ built up ‖ built upon.

EDIFICIO DE LOS TRIBUNALES.
courthouse.

EDIFICIO PÚBLICO.
m, public building, government building. Includes local, provincial, and national offices, universities, and museums. Implies public access.

EDIL.
m, city or town councilman, alderman.

EDILA.
f, city councilwoman, town councilwoman, alderwoman.

EDILICIO.
adj, civic, municipal.

EDITOR.
m, publisher.

EDUCIR.
v, to deduce, conclude, come up with conclusions.

EFECTIVAMENTE.
adv, in reality, truly.

EFECTIVAR.
v, to cash, negotiate ‖ to collect.

EFECTIVO.
adj, existing, real, true ‖ permanent (position, job, etc.) ‖ cash ‖ money.

EFECTO.
m, effect, consequence, result ‖ end, purpose, intent, objective ‖ impression, effect ‖ merchandise, commercial good ‖ chattel ‖ commercial paper, negotiable document.

EFECTO CAMBIARIO.
bill of exchange.

EFECTO COMUNICANTE.
See EFECTO EXTENSIVO.

EFECTO DE COMPLACENCIA.
accommodation bill.
EFECTO DECLARATIVO.
declaratory effect. Said of some legal acts when the result is merely to confirm the existing or pre-existing status of something.
EFECTO DEVOLUTIVO.
effect of appeal process in sending court file to appellate court (with no stay of decision).
EFECTO EXTENSIVO.
co-extensive effect. Describes the impact of testimony of one litigant on another litigant's case.
EFECTO LEGAL.
legal effect.
EFECTO LIBERATORIO DEL PAGO.
releasing effect of payment, effect which payment of an obligation has of extinguishing all further obligations.
EFECTO RETROACTIVO.
retroactive effect (of laws, regulations, etc.).
EFECTO SIMPLEMENTE DEVOLUTIVO.
non-staying effect, effect (of an appeal) which does not have the effect of staying a lower court decision.
EFECTO SUSPENSIVO.
staying effect, effect (of an appeal) which has the effect of staying a lower court decision.
EFECTOS.
m, goods, things, chattels ‖ plural of EFECTO.
EFECTOS AL PORTADOR.
bearer paper.
EFECTOS CIVILES.
consequences produced in civil law (of certain acts or status, e.g. birth, contracts, etc.).
EFECTOS COTIZABLES.
listed securities or commodities.
EFECTOS DE COMERCIO.
commercial goods, merchandise ‖ commercial paper, negotiable instruments.
EFECTOS DE CORTESÍA.
accommodation paper.
EFECTOS DE DIFÍCIL COBRO.
negotiable instruments which are difficult to collect.
EFECTOS DE LA APELACIÓN.
legal consequences of an appeal (on the order or decision of the lower court). May be EFECTO DEVOLUTIVO or EFECTO SUSPENSIVO.

EFECTOS DE LA DEMANDA.
legal consequences of complaint. Implies that the complaint has been filed (see ESCRITO DE DEMANDA) and that the running of an applicable statute of limitations has been interrupted and that certain rights to litigate are thenceforth transferable to heirs of plaintiff, etc.
EFECTOS DE LA GUERRA.
legal consequences of war.
EFECTOS DE LAS OBLIGACIONES.
legal consequences of obligations ‖ legal consequences of debts.
EFECTOS DE LAS PENAS.
consequences of sentencing (on freedom, life, etc.).
EFECTOS DE LOS CONTRATOS.
legal consequences of contracts.
EFECTOS DEL DELITO.
legal consequences of an offense. May refer to consequences either in criminal or tort law.
EFECTOS DEL MATRIMONIO.
legal consequences of marriage.
EFECTOS DESATENDIDOS.
dishonored bills.
EFECTOS DOCUMENTARIOS.
documentary negotiable instruments.
EFECTOS EXTRANJEROS.
foreign negotiable instruments.
EFECTOS FINANCIEROS.
finance bills.
EFECTOS JURÍDICOS.
legal purposes or ends ‖ legal effects.
EFECTOS NEGOCIABLES.
negotiable instruments.
EFECTOS PASIVOS.
bills payable.
EFECTOS PERSONALES.
personal property ‖ personal effects.
EFECTOS PÚBLICOS.
government-issued obligations or securities ‖ securities or obligations issued by foreign governments (if approved by the government where they are being negotiated).
EFECTOS REDESCONTABLES.
eligible paper for rediscount purposes.
EFECTOS TIMBRADOS.
stamped paper or documents.
EFECTUAR.
v, to fulfill, carry out, comply with.

EFECTUAR COBROS.
to collect (money, debts, etc.).
EFECTUAR UN PAGO.
to make a payment.
EFECTUAR UNA REUNIÓN.
to hold a meeting.
EFECTUAR UNA VENTA.
to make a sale.
EFICACIA.
f, efficacy, effectiveness ‖ validity ‖ power, influence ‖ force.
EFICACIA DEL ORDEN JURÍDICO.
effectiveness of legal decision, degree to which a decision or order achieves its ends.
EFICACIA PROBATORIA.
value as evidence, probative value (usually, in court).
EFICAZ.
adj, effective.
EFICAZMENTE.
adv, efficiently ‖ effectively ‖ with the desired effect.
EFRACCIÓN.
f, physical breaking (through certain objects such as a wall, roof, etc.). May be an aggravating factor in criminal law.
EFUGIO.
m, evasion ‖ means to avoid a difficulty.
EGRESADO.
m, graduate ‖ adj, graduated (from a school, college, or university).
EGRESAR.
v, to graduate, leave after finishing one's studies.
EGRESO.
m, expenditure, expense ‖ exit.
EJECUCIÓN.
f, execution ‖ performance, fulfillment ‖ compliance (with an order) ‖ means of carrying (something) out ‖ carrying out ‖ enforcement (of a judgment) ‖ attachment ‖ imposition of the death penalty ‖ summary proceedings (for payment of a debt) ‖ judgment ‖ levy, attachment ‖ foreclosure.
EJECUCIÓN APAREJADA.
statutory summary proceedings request, request for summary proceedings the basis of which is expressly contemplated in the law.
EJECUCIÓN CAPITAL.
See EJECUCIÓN DE LA PENA CAPITAL.

EJECUCIÓN COACTIVA.
foreclosure.
EJECUCIÓN COLECTIVA.
joint action (of various creditors against one debtor) ‖ group execution, execution of a group of criminals.
EJECUCIÓN CONCURSAL.
enforcement in bankruptcy proceedings.
EJECUCIÓN DE ALQUILERES.
summary legal proceedings to allow a landlord to collect rent in arrears.
EJECUCIÓN DE HIPOTECA.
mortgage foreclosure.
EJECUCIÓN DE LA PENA CAPITAL.
imposition of capital punishment ‖ carrying out the death penalty.
EJECUCIÓN DE LA PENA DE MUERTE.
See EJECUCIÓN DE LA PENA CAPITAL.
EJECUCIÓN DE LAS COSTAS.
payment of costs (of execution of judgment). Usually determined in the judgment itself.
EJECUCIÓN DE LAS PENAS.
execution of a criminal sentence, carrying out of a criminal sentence.
EJECUCIÓN DE LOS TRATADOS INTERNACIONALES.
performance of international treaties.
EJECUCIÓN DE MUERTE.
See EJECUCIÓN DE LA PENA CAPITAL.
EJECUCIÓN DE SENTENCIAS.
execution of a sentence or judgment or final order.
EJECUCIÓN DE SENTENCIAS DICTADAS POR TRIBUNALES EXTRANJERAS.
execution of foreign judgments.
EJECUCIÓN DEFINITIVA.
final process.
EJECUCIÓN EN REBELDÍA.
execution of a default judgment.
EJECUCIÓN FORZOSA.
execution of a judgment and other documents which may be executed as if they were a judgment.
EJECUCIÓN HIPOTECARIA.
mortgage foreclosure.
EJECUCIÓN INDIVIDUAL.
foreclosure by a sole creditor.
EJECUCIÓN PROCESAL.
execution of judgment.

EJECUCIÓN PROCESAL PENAL.
execution of a criminal sentence, carrying out of a criminal sentence.

EJECUCIÓN SUMARÍSIMA.
summary execution (of a judgment or document of a similar nature) ‖ summary execution without separate trial.

EJECUCIÓN VOLUNTARIA.
voluntary compliance with judgment, voluntary execution.

EJECUTABLE.
adj, workable ‖ practicable ‖ enforceable ‖ able to be executed.

EJECUTADO.
m, debtor whose goods have been subject to an action of execution ‖ executed criminal, convicted person who is put to death ‖ adj, executed, carried out, performed ‖ complied with.

EJECUTANTE.
m, executant, person who performs or executes something ‖ creditor who demands payment of a debt through summary legal proceedings.

EJECUTAR.
v, to execute, perform, carry out, realize ‖ to demand payment of a debt through summary legal proceedings ‖ to execute (a person).

EJECUTAR BIENES.
to foreclose on property.

EJECUTAR UN AJUSTE.
to work out an adjustment or a settlement.

EJECUTAR UN CONTRATO.
to perform a contract.

EJECUTAR UN PEDIDO.
to fill an order.

EJECUTAR UNA HIPOTECA.
to foreclose on a mortgage.

EJECUTIVAMENTE.
adv, quickly, promptly ‖ summarily, expeditiously ‖ efficiently.

EJECUTIVIDAD.
f, right of foreclosure or execution ‖ immediate applicability.

EJECUTIVO.
m, the executive, executive branch ‖ executive (of a corporation) ‖adj, rapid, prompt, efficient ‖ executory, final, immediately applicable (refers to court orders) ‖ summary (used to describe summary proceeding to ca-

rry out a judgment, etc. or a debt instrument which is the basis of such a proceeding).

EJECUTIVO FEDERAL.
federal executive, federal executive branch,

EJECUTOR.
m, executor, performer, doer ‖ executioner.

EJECUTOR TESTAMENTARIO.
executor (of a will).

EJECUTORA TESTAMENTARIA.
f, executrix.

EJECUTORIA.
f, final sentence or judgment or decision ‖ document containing a final sentence or judgment or decision ‖ executorship, position of executor or executrix ‖ writ of execution.

EJECUTORIAR.
v, to obtain a favorable judgment (which can be executed) ‖ to have a judgment become res judicata ‖ to prove the existence of facts and things.

EJECUTORIO.
adj, executory ‖ final, irrevocable ‖ immediately applicable.

EJEMPLAR.
m, example ‖ sample, model, specimen ‖ original (from which copies are made) ‖ copy (made from original) ‖ adj, exemplary ‖ precedent, antecedent.

EJEMPLAR DE FIRMA.
sample of a signature.

EJEMPLAR DUPLICADO.
duplicate copy.

EJEMPLARIDAD.
f, quality of being exemplary ‖ quality of being a deterrent example (e.g. a criminal sentence).

EJERCER.
v, to practice law ‖ to put into practice ‖ to practice (a profession).

EJERCER EL COMERCIO.
to engage in commerce.

EJERCER LA ABOGACÍA.
to practice law.

EJERCER UN DERECHO.
to exercise a right.

EJERCER UNA ACCIÓN.
to bring an action.

EJERCER UNA PROFESIÓN.
to practice a profession ‖ to work at a trade.

EJERCICIO.
m, practice, carrying out (of a profession) ‖ exercise (of a right) ‖ fiscal year ‖ business year

‖ each one of the tests taken (to be given a professorship) ‖ budget cycle, accounting period. Usually a year.

EJERCICIO CONTABLE.
fiscal year.

EJERCICIO DE ACCIONES.
prosecution of lawsuits.

EJERCICIO DE DERECHOS.
exercise or assertion of rights.

EJERCICIO ECONÓMICO.
fiscal year.

EJERCICIO FINANCIERO.
See EJERCICIO CONTABLE.

EJERCICIO ILEGAL DE LA MEDICINA.
illegal practice of medicine.

EJERCICIO IMPOSITIVO.
tax year.

EJERCICIO LEGÍTIMO DE UN DERECHO.
legal use of a right. The possession of a right does not necessarily imply the legality of its use is legal.

EJERCICIO PROFESIONAL.
practice of a profession.

EJERCICIO SOCIAL.
See EJERCICIO ECONÓMICO.

EJERCITABLE.
adj, enforceable.

EJERCITAR.
v, to practice, exercise ‖ to train.

EJERCITAR UN DERECHO.
to exercise a right.

EJERCITAR UN JUICIO.
to sue, bring suit.

EJERCITAR UNA ACCIÓN.
to bring suit, sue.

EJÉRCITO.
m, armed forces.

EJÉRCITO MERCENARIO.
mercenaries, armed forces made up of mercenaries.

EJÉRCITO NACIONAL.
national armed forces ‖ armed forces made up exclusively of national citizens.

EJÉRCITO PERMANENTE.
permanent forces ‖ national guard.

EJÉRCITO REVOLUCIONARIO.
revolutionary forces.

EJERCITORIA.
f, maritime action (against the owner of a ves-

sel for the debts incurred by the captain fc provisions and repairs).

ÉJIDO.
m, common grazing pasture (of villagers cor tiguous to the village) ‖ common land given t the government to a group of persons to far and use, but which is not susceptible to div sion, transfer, mortgage, etc.

ELABORACIÓN.
f, production, preparation and manufactui (of a product) ‖ plot, scheme ‖ drafting or fo mulation of a legislative bill or draft bill.

ELABORAR.
v, to elaborate ‖ to prepare, make, manufa ture (a product) ‖ to draft, discuss, and a; prove (a legislative bill or legal text).

ELECCIÓN.
f, election ‖ selection, preference, choice ‖ e ercise of right to vote.

ELECCIÓN DIRECTA.
direct election or voting, election by dire vote.

ELECCIÓN EN LAS OBLIGACIONES.
choice of duties. Refers to right of obligor « obligee to carry out one of a variety of oblig tions (including failure to perform).

ELECCIÓN EN LOS LEGADOS.
selection of property distribution betwee heirs.

ELECCIÓN GENERAL.
general election. Usually one in which sen tors, deputies or congressmen, and governo are elected.

ELECCIÓN INDIRECTA.
indirect elections, elections in which the ele tors vote for representatives who then vote a final election.

ELECCIÓN PARCIAL.
special election (to fill a vacancy caused ! death, etc.).

ELECCIONES.
f, elections.

ELECTIVO.
m, elected position ‖ elected person ‖ a« elective.

ELECTO.
adj, elect (e.g. "president-elect").

ELECTOR.
m, elector, voter.

ELECTORADO.
m, electorate.

ELECTORAL.
adj, electoral, pertaining to elections or electors.
ELECTROCUCIÓN.
f, electrocution.
ELEGIBILIDAD.
f, eligibility ‖ legal capacity to be elected.
ELEGIBLE.
adj, eligible
ELEGIR.
v, to elect, vote on ‖ to select, choose, prefer ‖ to designate or name by election.
ELEVAR.
v, to elevate ‖ to raise ‖ to promote.
ELEVAR A INSTRUMENTO PÚBLICO.
to convert into a public document.
ELEVAR A LEY.
to enact or pass a law.
ELEVAR AL TRIBUNAL.
to take to court.
ELEVAR EL PROCESO.
to refer to a higher court ‖ to appeal a case.
ELEVAR EL RECURSO.
to appeal ‖ to file a motion.
ELEVAR EN CONSULTA A LA CORTE SUPREMA.
to take a case to the Supreme Court.
ELEVAR PARTE.
to make a report.
ELEVAR UNA MEMORIA.
to submit a report.
ELEVAR UNA RECLAMACIÓN.
to make a claim.
ELIMINACIÓN.
f, elimination, exclusion ‖ expulsion ‖ death, extermination.
ELUCIDACIÓN.
f, elucidation, explanation, clarification.
ELUDIR IMPUESTOS.
to avoid taxes.
ELUSIÓN.
f, avoidance.
EMANCIPACIÓN.
f, emancipation. May be POR MATRIMONIO DEL MENOR (by marriage), POR LA MAYOR EDAD (by reaching the age of majority), POR CONCESIÓN DEL PADRE O MADRE (by agreement of one of the parents).
EMANCIPADO.
m, emancipated person ‖ liberated territory ‖ adj, emancipated.

EMANCIPADOR.
m, person who frees or liberates ‖ parent who emancipates his or her minor child.
EMANCIPAR.
v, to emancipate, free, liberate.
EMANCIPARSE.
v, to liberate or free oneself ‖ to start one's own business (after having worked for another).
EMBAJADA.
f, ambassadorship ‖ residence of ambassador ‖ embassy ‖ staff of embassy ‖ diplomatic message.
EMBAJADOR.
m, ambassador ‖ emissary, representative, messenger.
EMBARAZADA.
f, pregnant woman ‖ adj, pregnant.
EMBARAZAR.
v, to impregnate, make pregnant ‖ to impede, make difficult.
EMBARAZO.
m, difficulty, obstacle, impediment ‖ pregnancy ‖ state of pregnancy.
EMBARCACIÓN.
f, embarkation ‖ ship, vessel, boat.
EMBARGABLE.
adj, susceptible to attachment and garnishment (re: property).
EMBARGADO.
m, debtor subject to a legal attachment or garnishment ‖ garnishee, person whose property is attached or garnished ‖ country to which an embargo has been applied ‖ adj, attached, garnished ‖ obstructed, impeded; embargoed ‖ seized.
EMBARGADOR.
m, creditor who requests the imposition of a attachment or garnishment ‖ garnishor ‖ court which has imposed an attachment or garnishment ‖ country which has imposed an embargo.
EMBARGAR.
v, to impede, obstruct, make difficult ‖ to embargo, seize ‖ to attach, garnish.
EMBARGO.
m, impediment, obstacle, difficulty ‖ embargo, seizure ‖ attachment ‖ garnishment.
EMBARGO DE ARMAS.
arms embargo, prohibition of the export of armaments, munitions, and other articles of war.

EMBARGO DE BUQUES.
sequestration of vessels ‖ embargo of vessels, prohibition that ships leave harbor ‖ attachment of vessels.

EMBARGO DE GUERRA.
war embargo.

EMBARGO DE HABERES.
garnishment (of a salary).

EMBARGO DE PENSIONES.
garnishment (of a pension).

EMBARGO PRECAUTORIO.
See EMBARGO PREVENTIVO.

EMBARGO PREVENTIVO.
pre-judgment attachment or garnishment.

EMBARGO PROVISIONAL.
temporary garnishment or attachment.

EMBARGO PROVISORIO.
See EMBARGO PROVISIONAL.

EMBARGO SUBSECUENTE.
post-judgment attachment or garnishment.

EMBAUCADOR.
m, cheat, swindler ‖ chiseler, chintz.

EMBAUCAR.
v, to cheat, swindle, trick.

EMBLEMA COMERCIAL.
m, commercial symbol.

EMBRIAGUEZ.
f, drunkenness. May constitute an excuse to a crime.

EMBUSTE.
m, fraud, trick.

EMBUSTERÍA.
f, trickery, fraud.

EMBUSTERO.
m, crook, cheat.

EMERGENCIA.
f, emergency.

EMERGENTE.
adj, emergent.

EMIGRACIÓN.
f, emigration.

EMIGRADO.
m, emigrant, emigre ‖ adj, emigrated.

EMIGRANTE.
m, emigrant, emigre.

EMIGRAR.
v, to emigrate (to work, to live, or to escape persecution).

EMINENTE.
adj, eminent, high, elevated ‖ outstanding.

EMISARIO.
m, emissary.

EMISIBLE.
adj, issuable.

EMISIÓN.
f, emission ‖ television or radio or telegraphic broadcast ‖ offering, issuance (of securities).

EMISIÓN CONSOLIDADA.
consolidated bond issuance.

EMISIÓN DE ACCIONES.
stock issuance.

EMISIONISMO.
m, unlimited issue of paper money.

EMISOR.
m, issuer.

EMITENTE.
m, f, drawer of a check or bill.

EMITIR.
v, to issue, put forth, emit (something) ‖ to put into circulation (bills, coins, etc.) ‖ to issue, make a public offering (of securities) ‖ to express (an opinion).

EMITIR UN CHEQUE.
to draw or write a check.

EMITIR EL FALLO.
to issue a judgment.

EMITIR UNA OPINIÓN.
to express an opinion.

EMOCIÓN VIOLENTA.
f, heat of passion. May be considered to be a mitigating circumstance in criminal law.

EMOLUMENTO.
m, emolument.

EMPADRONAMIENTO.
m, census ‖ census-taking ‖ registration (of a legal status).

EMPADRONAR.
v, to take a census of ‖ to register (a legal status).

EMPALAR.
v, to impale.

EMPAREDAMIENTO.
m, confinement (to a space which provides no room for movement and without communication).

EMPAREDAR.
v, to confine (to a space which provides no room for movement and without communication).

EMPARENTAR.
v, to become a family member.

EMPATAR.
v, to tie (re: votes) ‖ to equal.
EMPECER.
v, to damage, injure ‖ to prevent ‖ to obstruct.
EMPEÑADO.
adj, pledged, pawned.
EMPEÑAR.
v, to pledge, pawn ‖ to secure, to undertake.
EMPEÑARSE.
v, to become indebted, go into debt ‖ to insist on a position or opinion ‖ to start (an argument or war).
EMPEÑO.
m, strong desire or aspiration ‖ goal, end, purpose ‖ tenacity ‖ patron, protector ‖ commitment, gentlemen's agreement ‖ heavily indebted situation ‖ pawn, pledge ‖ pledge contract ‖ pawnshop.
EMPEZAR A REGIR.
v, to take effect.
EMPERADOR.
m, emperor.
EMPIRISMO JURÍDICO.
legal empiricism, position that the only source of legal knowledge is sensory or experiential.
EMPLAZADOR.
m, process server of summons, summons server.
EMPLAZAMIENTO.
m, summons, call ‖ fixing of a time period (in a lawsuit during which period the parties must fulfill a certain act) ‖ site, location.
EMPLAZAMIENTO A HUELGA.
strike call.
EMPLAZAMIENTO POR EDICTO.
summons by publication.
EMPLAZAR.
v, to place, locate ‖ to summons, call (someone to explain something) ‖ to summon, issue a summons (to appear in court) ‖ to subpoena (a witness).
EMPLEADA.
f, female employee.
EMPLEADO.
m, male employee ‖ adj, employed ‖ used.
EMPLEADO PÚBLICO.
public employee, public servant.
EMPLEADOR.
m, employer.
EMPLEAR.
v, to employ ‖ to give work to (a person) ‖ to

use, utilize ‖ to consume, spend ‖ to apply.
EMPLEO.
m, occupation, activity ‖ work, occupation ‖ position ‖ use, application ‖ consumption, expense ‖ monetary investment.
EMPLEO PROVECHOSO.
gainful employment.
EMPLEO TOTAL.
full employment (either nationally or worldwide) ‖ total employment.
EMPRESA.
f, plan, project ‖ enterprise ‖ undertaking ‖ business, firm, company ‖ association created to carry out a specified commercial activity or purpose.
EMPRESA COLECTIVA.
partnership.
EMPRESA COMÚN.
common or joint enterprise ‖ joint venture.
EMPRESA CONDUCTORA.
common carrier.
EMPRESA CONJUNTA.
common or joint enterprise, joint venture.
EMPRESA DE DEPÓSITO EN SEGURIDAD.
safety-deposit or safe-deposit company.
EMPRESA DE ECONOMÍA MIXTA.
See SOCIEDAD DE ECONOMÍA MIXTA.
EMPRESA DE EXPLOTACIÓN.
operating company.
EMPRESA DE FIANZAS.
bonding company.
EMPRESA DE SERVICIOS PÚBLICOS.
public utility company.
EMPRESA DE TRANSPORTE AFIANZADA.
bonded carrier.
EMPRESA DE TRANSPORTE PARTICULAR.
private carrier.
EMPRESA DE TRANSPORTE POR AJUSTE.
contract carrier.
EMPRESA DE UTILIDAD PÚBLICA.
public utility company.
EMPRESA ESPECULATIVA.
commercial enterprise, business.
EMPRESA ESTATAL.
state utility company.
EMPRESA FIADORA.
bonding or surety company.

EMPRESA FILIAL.
subsidiary, subsidiary enterprise.
EMPRESA FISCAL.
government enterprise.
EMPRESA LUCRATIVA.
commercial enterprise.
EMPRESA MUNICIPAL.
municipal utility company.
EMPRESA NO LUCRATIVA.
nonprofit or not-for-profit organization.
EMPRESA OPERADORA.
operating company.
EMPRESA PORTEADORA.
common carrier.
EMPRESA SUBSIDIARIA.
subsidiary enterprise or company.
EMPRESA TENEDORA.
holding company.
EMPRESA VERTICAL.
vertical combination.
EMPRESARIO.
m, entrepreneur || impresario || employer ||
businessman, contractor, concessionaire ||
person who is head of a business which carries
out an economic activity organized for the
purpose of production or the sale of goods or
services.
EMPRESTAR.
v, to lend, loan.
EMPRÉSTITO.
m, loan or advance or credit || loan contract ||
government loan.
EMPRÉSTITO A LA GRUESA.
bottomry.
EMPRÉSTITO CON GARANTÍA.
secured or guaranteed loan.
EMPRÉSTITO DE CONSUMO.
See CONTRATO DE MUTUO.
EMPRÉSTITO DE GUERRA.
war loan.
EMPRÉSTITO DE RENTA PERPETUA.
perpetual loan.
EMPRÉSTITO DE USO.
type of gratuitous bailment contract by which
goods are loaned free of charge to another for
temporary use to be returned at the end of a
given period.
EMPRÉSTITO FORZOSO.
forced loan.
EN ATRASO.
in arrears.

EN AUSENCIA.
in absentia.
EN BLANCO.
in blank, without writing, not filled in || un-
defined (e.g. to powers).
EN CAMBIO.
on the other hand || in exchange.
EN COBRANZA.
in process of collection || subject to collection.
EN COMISO.
forfeited.
EN CONDICIONES.
duly || in good condition.
EN CONTRARIO.
on the contrary, to the contrary.
EN CUANTO HA LUGAR.
pursuant to law || acceptable.
EN CUOTAS.
in installments or payments.
EN DESCUBIERTO.
unpaid || overdrawn || lacking sufficient funds.
EN ESPECIE.
in kind.
EN FE.
in good faith.
EN FE DE LO CUAL.
in witness whereof.
EN FIANZA.
on bail or bond. Used in reference to accused
who are able to leave jail upon placing a finan-
cial guaranty.
EN FIDEICOMISO.
in trust.
EN FIRME.
firm (offer or bid) || irrevocable and on a date
certain || confirmed (information) || definitive,
final || unconditional.
EN FLAGRANTE.
in flagrante delicto.
**EN FRAUDE
DE ACREEDORES.**
to defraud creditors.
EN GESTIÓN.
in process, under negotiation || in process of
collection by legal means.
EN LA CUERDA FLOJA.
in a court file (which is loosely sewn together
with a cord or thread to permit easy examination). Court files may be physically tied together by such a cord to show their separate but
related nature.

EN LA FUENTE.
at the source.

EN MASA.
en masse, together, as a block.

EN MI NOMBRE Y EN LUGAR DE MÍ.
in my name ‖ in my place ‖ in my stead.

EN MORA.
overdue, in arrears.

EN NEGOCIACIÓN.
in negotiation ‖ under discussion.

EN NOMBRE AJENO.
on behalf of, in the name of (a third party).

EN NOMBRE DE.
on behalf of, in the name of.

EN NÚMEROS Y EN LETRAS.
in figures and in words.

EN ORDEN.
in order, orderly.

EN PAGO.
in payment ‖ in satisfaction.

EN PERSONA.
in person ‖ present.

EN PIE.
on one's feet, standing ‖ respectfully ‖ in effect ‖ in force.

EN PRENDA.
in pledge, as a pledge or guaranty ‖ in hock or pawn.

EN PRÉSTAMO.
as a loan (usually short-term) ‖ on loan (from a library) ‖ on trial (re: products).

EN REBELDÍA.
in default, having failed to appear (in court) ‖ in rebellion.

EN RELACIÓN.
closed to new evidence, to which no new evidence may be submitted. Used to refer to appeals ‖ in relation to.

EN SUBSTANCIA.
in essence, in brief, briefly, in a nutshell.

EN SUMA.
in summary, in brief.

EN SUSPENSO.
deferred, postponed ‖ stayed.

EN TELA DE JUICIO.
in litigation, under judicial consideration (when the outcome is uncertain).

EN TÉRMINO.
in time, within the term or period.

EN TRÁNSITO.
in transit, en route.

EN TRES PAGAS.
comment made of a bad debtor referring to the fact that he pays in one of three ways: late, inadequately, or never.

EN VENTA.
for sale.

EN VIGENCIA.
in force and effect.

EN VIGOR.
in force and effect.

EN VIRTUD DE.
by virtue of.

EN VOZ.
verbally ‖ orally.

ENAJENABLE.
adj, transferable, alienable.

ENAJENACIÓN.
f, transfer, alienation.

ENAJENACIÓN
DE EFECTOS.
alienation of affections.

ENAJENACIÓN EN FRAUDE
DE ACREEDORES.
transfer to defraud creditors.

ENAJENACIÓN FORZOSA.
forced transfer, transfer of property against the will of the owner for legal reason ‖ expropriation ‖ condemnation.

ENAJENACIÓN MENTAL.
insanity.

ENAJENADO.
m, insane person ‖ adj, alienated (property) ‖ insane.

ENAJENADOR.
m, transferor, alienor.

ENAJENANTE.
See ENAJENADOR.

ENAJENAR.
v, to transfer ownership ‖ to grant a right ‖ to go insane or crazy.

ENCABEZAMIENTO.
m, leadership ‖ inscribing, listing, registration (of taxpayers, etc.) ‖ per capita tax distribution ‖ heading, caption (e.g. of a will, a judgment, a notarized document). Usually includes the name of the party issuing it, where it has been drafted and to what it refers.

ENCABEZAR.
v, to inscribe, list, register (taxpayers, etc.) ‖ to head a list (of persons) ‖ to lead ‖ to draft a heading or caption.

ENCADENACIÓN.
See ENCADENAMIENTO.
ENCADENADO.
adj, enchained.
ENCADENADURA.
See ENCADENAMIENTO.
ENCADENAMIENTO.
m, enchainment ‖ connection, relationship, nexus ‖ chain of events.
ENCADENAR.
v, to chain, restrict movement ‖ to connect, link, tie together (events, ideas, etc.).
ENCAJE.
m, bank reserves (in cash or other liquid assets required by Central Bank) ‖ reserve, reserves.
ENCAJE BANCARIO.
bank reserves (in cash or other liquid assets required by Central Bank).
ENCAJE EXCEDENTE.
excess reserves.
ENCAJE LEGAL.
legal reserve.
ENCAJE METÁLICO.
reserve in specie. See ENCAJE.
ENCALLADURA.
f, grounding, running aground, foundering (of a boat).
ENCALLAR.
v, to run aground, founder.
ENCANALLAMIENTO.
m, perversion, degeneracy ‖ corruption.
ENCANALLAR.
v, to pervert, corrupt.
ENCAÑONADO.
adj, at gun point.
ENCARCELACIÓN.
f, imprisonment, confinement, incarceration.
ENCARCELACIÓN ILEGAL.
false imprisonment.
ENCARCELAMIENTO.
See ENCARCELACIÓN.
ENCARCELADO.
adj, jailed, imprisoned, incarcerated, confined.
ENCARCELAR.
to jail, incarcerate, imprison, confine ‖ to take to prison.
ENCARECIMIENTO.
m, increase (in prices or cost of living).
ENCARGADO.
m, agent, representative ‖ temporary replacement (of a superior) ‖ adj, in charge.

ENCARGADO DE CASA DE RENTA.
building janitor.
ENCARGADO DE NEGOCIOS.
charge d'affaires, charge des affaires.
ENCARGAR.
v, to entrust, charge ‖ to recommend, advise to dispose of ‖ to order.
ENCARGARSE.
v, to assume a position of trust.
ENCARGO.
m, entrustment ‖ request ‖ order (to do something) ‖ position, post, office ‖ order (for merchandise) ‖ purchase (by an agent) ‖ commission, assignment.
ENCARGO DE CONFIANZA.
trust, confidential assignment.
ENCARPETAR.
v, to defer, shelve ‖ to file.
ENCARTAR.
v, to banish (a criminal who has failed to appear) ‖ to include (in a company, etc.) ‖ to summon by means of publication or other public notice ‖ to register, enroll ‖ to sentence ‖ to proscribe, prohibit, ban.
ENCAUSABLE.
adj, indictable.
ENCAUSADO.
m, defendant (usually criminal).
ENCAUSAR.
v, to bring criminal charges, file a criminal complaint, prosecute.
ENCIERRO.
m, enclosure, confinement ‖ prison, jail ‖ cell
ENCINTA.
adj, pregnant.
ENCOMENDAR.
v, to commission, entrust ‖ to commend.
ENCOMENDERO.
m, commissioner, person who carries out orders of another.
ENCOMIENDA.
f, commission, agency, post ‖ commandership ‖ protection, custody ‖ commendation, praise ‖ postal parcel.
ENCOMIENDA POSTAL.
postal parcel.
ENCONTRAR UNA MINA.
to discover a mine ‖ to find a gold mine (figuratively).
ENCUBIERTA.
adj, fraudulent ‖ hidden, concealed.

ENCUBIERTAMENTE.
adv, secretly, clandestinely, deceitfully || fraudulently || reservedly.

ENCUBRIDOR.
m, accessory after the fact || type of accomplice who aids and abets a person who has committed a crime by participating in the benefits of the crime or by hiding the criminal tools or the criminal himself.

ENCUBRIMIENTO.
m, hiding, concealment, harboring || aiding and abetting after the fact, participation in a crime after it has occurred.

ENCUBRIMIENTO ACTIVO.
active concealment.

ENCUBRIR.
v, to hide, conceal || to harbor || to pretend || to aid and abet (a criminal after the fact).

ENCUESTA.
f, inquiry, investigation, inquest || public opinion poll or survey.

ENDEUDADO.
adj, indebted.

ENDEUDARSE.
v, to go into debt || to acknowledge an obligation.

ENDOGAMIA.
f, inbreeding, prohibition to marry outside a determined social nucleus.

ENDORSAR.
See ENDOSAR.

ENDORSATARIO.
See ENDOSATARIO.

ENDORSO.
See ENDOSO.

ENDOSABLE.
adj, endorsable.

ENDOSADO.
m, endorsee, indorsee || adj, endorsed, indorsed.

ENDOSADOR.
See ENDOSANTE.

ENDOSANTE.
m, f, endorser (e.g. who transfers commercial paper).

ENDOSAR.
v, to indorse, endorse (e.g. commercial paper).

ENDOSATARIO.
m, indorsee, endorsee (e.g. to whom commercial paper is transferred).

ENDOSE.
m, indorsement, endorsement (e.g. of commercial paper).

ENDOSO.
m, indorsement, endorsement || action of endorsement.

ENDOSO A LA ORDEN DEL PORTADOR.
bearer endorsement.

ENDOSO AL COBRO.
endorsement granting a power of attorney for collection purposes.

ENDOSO ABSOLUTO.
absolute endorsement.

ENDOSO ANTEDATADO.
pre-dated endorsement.

ENDOSO ANTERIOR.
prior endorsement || previous endorsement.

ENDOSO CALIFICADO.
qualified endorsement.

ENDOSO CESIÓN.
endorsement. Opposed to ENDOSO DE FAVOR.

ENDOSO COMPLETO.
See ENDOSO REGULAR.

ENDOSO CONDICIONAL.
qualified or conditional endorsement.

ENDOSO DE FAVOR.
accommodation endorsement, endorsement by an accommodation party.

ENDOSO DE GARANTÍA.
See ENDOSO DE FAVOR.

ENDOSO DE REGRESO.
endorsement to a prior party.

ENDOSO EN BLANCO.
blank endorsement.

ENDOSO EN GARANTÍA.
endorsement as guarantor.

ENDOSO EN PRENDA.
endorsement to pledge an instrument.

ENDOSO EN PROCURACIÓN.
endorsement to grant power of attorney.

ENDOSO EN PROPIEDAD.
endorsement to transfer title.

ENDOSO ESPECIAL.
special endorsement.

ENDOSO FALSIFICADO.
forged endorsement.

ENDOSO IMPERFECTO.
See ENDOSO IRREGULAR.

ENDOSO IRREGULAR.
improperly executed endorsement, endorsement which does not fulfill all of the require-

ments regarding the transfer of commercial paper.

ENDOSO LIMITADO.
See ENDOSO CONDICIONAL.

ENDOSO PERFECTO.
legal endorsement, endorsement which fulfills all legal requirements regarding endorsements.

ENDOSO POR ACOMODAMIENTO.
accommodation endorsement.

ENDOSO REGULAR.
full endorsement. Usually must contain date, name of person to whom the paper is endorsed, special words such as "VALOR RECIBIDO", "ENTENDIDO" or "EN CUENTA", and the signature of the endorser.

ENDOSO PLENO.
full endorsement.

ENECHADO.
m, foundling ‖ adj, abandoned.

ENEMIGO.
m, enemy, adversary ‖ adj, enemy, hostile.

ENEMIGO JURADO.
sworn enemy.

ENERGÍA.
f, energy ‖ power, force.

ENERGÍA ATÓMICA.
atomic energy.

ENFERMEDAD.
f, illness, sickness, disease.

ENFERMEDAD ACCIDENTE.
type of on-the-job illness or disease (usually does not result directly from the work itself, but requires compensation by the employer).

ENFERMEDAD CONTAGIOSA.
contagious disease.

ENFERMEDAD DEL TRABAJO.
on-the-job illness. Includes ENFERMEDAD ACCIDENTE, ENFERMEDAD INCULPABLE, and ENFERMEDAD PROFESIONAL. May require compensation by employer.

ENFERMEDAD INCULPABLE.
illness, sickness, disease (which is not caused by employee fault). May require compensation by employer.

ENFERMEDAD INDUSTRIAL.
occupational disease.

ENFERMEDAD MENTAL.
mental illness.

ENFERMEDAD PROFESIONAL.
occupational or work-related disease or illness

(which is the natural and probable result of the work being carried out). Usually requires compensation by employer.

ENFERMEDAD VENÉREA.
venereal disease.

ENFITEUSIS.
f, emphyteusis. Contract between owner of land and tenant, by which tenant may enjoy use, and dispose of his right in the property usually for a long period of time or permanently, in exchange for rent. Prohibited in some jurisdictions.

ENFITEUTA.
f, m, emphyteuta, tenant who holds property in ENFITEUSIS.

ENFITÉUTICO.
adj, emphyteuticus, of or pertaining to ENFITEUSIS.

ENFRENTAMIENTO.
m, confrontation.

ENFRENTAR.
v, to confront.

ENGANCHE.
m, voluntary enlistment (e.g. for the armed forces).

ENGANCHE DE TRABAJADORES.
contracting of workers for work elsewhere.

ENGAÑADO.
m, tricked person ‖ adj, tricked, fooled, deceived ‖ cheated ‖ cuckolded.

ENGAÑAR.
v, to trick, deceive, fool ‖ to cheat ‖ to lie ‖ to be unfaithful (in a marriage).

ENGAÑO.
m, trick, deception, swindle ‖ marital infidelity ‖ mistake, error.

ENGAÑOSO.
m, deceiver, cheater, con man ‖ liar ‖ adj, false ‖ misleading, deceptive ‖ fraudulent.

ENGENDRAR.
v, to procreate, reproduce ‖ to produce, cause originate.

ENGENDRO.
m, fetus ‖ deformed newborn.

ENGRILLAR.
v, to shackle ‖ to imprison, take prisoner.

ENGRILLETAR.
v, to put shackles on.

ENJUAGUE.
m, dirty business, illegal means to get something not otherwise obtainable.

ENJUICIABLE.
adj, chargeable, indictable, triable ‖ suspicious, presumably guilty.
ENJUICIADO.
m, defendant, accused ‖ adj, on trial.
ENJUICIAMIENTO.
m, rules of legal procedure ‖ procedure, legal procedure ‖ judgment ‖ sentence ‖ prosecution ‖ suit, lawsuit ‖ trial.
ENJUICIAMIENTO CIVIL.
civil procedure ‖ civil trial ‖ civil lawsuit.
ENJUICIAMIENTO CRIMINAL.
criminal procedure ‖ criminal trial ‖ criminal prosecution.
ENJUICIAMIENTO DEL MAGISTRADO.
trial or prosecution of the judge (for incompetence or malfeasance).
ENJUCIAMIENTO MALICIOSO.
malicious prosecution.
ENJUICIAMIENTO MILITAR.
military trial.
ENJUICIAMIENTO PENAL.
See ENJUICIAMIENTO CRIMINAL.
ENJUICIAR.
v, to examine, discuss, and resolve a problem ‖ to prosecute (a case) ‖ to file, bring (an action) ‖ to try a case ‖ to judge, sentence.
ENJURAR.
v, to transfer a right.
ENLACE.
m, tie, nexus, connection ‖ union ‖ marriage, wedding ‖ lineage.
ENLEGAJAR.
v, to prepare a file ‖ to add a document to a file.
ENLOQUECER.
v, to go crazy or insane ‖ to make someone go insane.
ENMENDADOR.
m, corrector, rectifier ‖ compensator ‖ amender.
ENMENDADURA.
See ENMIENDA.
ENMENDAMIENTO.
See ENMIENDA.
ENMENDAR.
v, to correct, rectify ‖ to indemnify, compensate, redress (for damage done) ‖ to amend (e.g. a constitution) ‖ to correct a faulty decision of a lower court (upon request of one of the parties).

ENMIENDA.
f, correction, rectification (of an error) ‖ indemnification, compensation, redress ‖ amendment, modification (e.g. of a law, decision, regulation, constitution, etc.) ‖ rehabilitation (of a criminal) ‖ correction of a faulty lower court decision.
ENREDARSE LA MADEJA.
to have new problems arise in a case ‖ to confuse (a matter).
ENRIQUECIMIENTO SIN CAUSA.
m, unjust enrichment.
ENROLADO.
m, enlisted person (in armed forces).
ENROLAMIENTO.
m, enlistment, inscription.
ENROLAR.
v, to enlist, sign up ‖ to list on (a vessel).
ENSAÑAMIENTO.
m, intentional aggravation of crime.
ENSAÑAR.
v, to irritate, anger, infuriate.
ENSAÑARSE.
v, to aggravate a crime intentionally ‖ to act cruelly to a party who has surrendered.
ENSAY.
m, testing (of metals prior to minting).
ENSAYE.
See ENSAY.
ENSAYO.
m, testing (of a thing) ‖ instruction, teaching ‖ attempt ‖ See also ENSAY.
ENSEÑANZA.
f, teaching, education ‖ instruction ‖ doctrine, theory ‖ warning ‖ example ‖ experience ‖ guidance.
ENSERES.
m, household goods ‖ work tools or instruments or implements.
ENSORDECER.
v, to cause deafness ‖ to become deaf.
ENTABLAR.
v, to bring, file, initiate (an action).
ENTABLAR ACCIÓN.
to bring or file suit.
ENTABLAR DEMANDA.
to file a complaint ‖ to bring suit.
ENTABLAR DENUNCIA.
to accuse ‖ to file a police report.
ENTABLAR EJECUCIÓN.
to start an executive proceeding.

ENTABLAR JUICIO HIPOTECARIO.
to start a foreclosure proceeding.
ENTABLAR NEGOCIACIONES.
to open negotiations.
ENTABLAR PLEITO.
to bring or file or initiate a lawsuit.
ENTABLAR QUERELLA.
to file a private accusation in a criminal proceeding.
ENTABLAR RECLAMACIÓN.
to file a claim.
ENTABLAR UN PROTESTO.
to protest.
ENTABLE DE PARTIDA.
m, registration of a baptismal, marriage or death certificate (at a later point in time).
ENTE.
m, entity, organism ‖ a being.
ENTE AUTÁRQUICO.
independent governmental entity, organism of the state that is permitted to act independently.
ENTE AUTÓNOMO.
See ENTE AUTÁRQUICO.
ENTE DE EXISTENCIA JURÍDICA.
See ENTE JURÍDICO.
ENTE JURÍDICO.
legal entity.
ENTE MORAL.
See ENTE JURÍDICO.
ENTENDER EN.
to have jurisdiction over.
ENTERADO.
m, government approval ‖ approval of the government of a death sentence issued by a military court ‖ adj, aware.
ENTERO.
m, payment or delivery of money (usually to public offices) ‖ adj, whole, complete.
ENTERRAR.
v, to bury, put underground (a person or property) ‖ to bury, shelve, place on the back burner (a file, etc.).
ENTIDAD.
f, entity, body, organism ‖ being ‖ institution, establishment, company, organization. May be an individual or a corporation or partnership.
ENTIDAD ANÓNIMA.
stock company.
ENTIDAD ASEGURADORA.
insurance carrier or company.

ENTIDAD BANCARIA.
banking house.
ENTIDAD COMERCIAL.
business concern.
ENTIDAD CONTABLE.
accounting entity.
ENTIDAD DE DERECHO PRIVADO.
private company.
ENTIDAD DE DERECHO PÚBLICO.
public company.
ENTIDAD JURÍDICA.
legal entity.
ENTIDAD LEGAL.
See ENTIDAD JURÍDICA.
ENTIDAD LOCAL MENOR.
unincorporated village or town (which is not recognized as an independent municipality due to its small population).
ENTIDAD POLÍTICA.
political entity or body.
ENTIDAD PRIVADA.
private entity.
ENTIDAD SINDICAL.
labor union.
ENTIDAD SOCIAL.
association.
ENTIERRO.
m, burial, interment ‖ grave ‖ funeral ‖ buried treasure ‖ theft of buried treasure.
ENTRADA.
f, (physical) entry, entrance ‖ entry (which increases corporate assets) ‖ monthly or yearly salaries or payments, etc. ‖ invasion (of troops) ‖ entry (as a member or partner in a corporation or group) ‖ first days of a month or year ‖ admission, admittance ‖ cash receipts ‖ deposit ‖ down payment.
ENTRADA A CAJA.
cash receipts.
ENTRADA POR SALIDA.
entry which is both a debit and credit in accounting books ‖ matter which has equivalent pros and cons.
ENTRADA Y REGISTRO EN LUGAR CERRADO.
right and ability of an authority to enter a place and inspect it as part of pre-trial investigation.
ENTRADAS Y SALIDAS.
access easement, right-of-way ‖ income and expenses.

ENTRADAS.
f, income, revenue ‖ receipts ‖ entries.
ENTRADAS BRUTAS.
gross income or receipts.
ENTRADAS DE EXPLOTACIÓN.
operating revenue.
ENTRADAS DE OPERACIÓN.
See ENTRADAS DE EXPLOTACIÓN.
ENTRADAS NETAS.
net income.
ENTRAR.
v, to enter (e.g. a building, a family by marriage, a profession, etc.) ‖ to begin (a year, month, etc.) ‖ to invade, occupy.
ENTRAR A LA PARTE.
to participate (in something which may produce profits or losses).
ENTRAR EN VIGOR.
to become effective, come into effect.
ENTRAR EN VOZ.
to answer, file an answer.
**ENTRE LA VIDA
Y LA MUERTE.**
between life and death.
ENTRE SÍ.
inter se, among themselves.
ENTRE VIVOS.
inter vivos.
ENTREDICHO.
m, prohibition, injunction ‖ argument, discussion.
ENTREGA.
f, delivery, handing over (of a thing or person) ‖ receipt ‖ submission, capitulation ‖ treason ‖ delivery, transfer (of possession) ‖ delivery, payment (of a monthly payment, etc.).
ENTREGA A CUENTA.
received on account. Refers to money paid against an account which has not been liquidated.
ENTREGA DE AUTOS.
delivery of court files (to a party for temporary use).
ENTREGA DE CHEQUE SIN PROVISIÓN DE FONDOS.
delivery of check written against insufficient funds, delivery of a bad check. May be a crime.
ENTREGA DE GIRO SIN PROVISIÓN DE FONDOS.
delivery of draft written against insufficient funds, delivery of a bad draft. May be a crime.

ENTREGA DE LA COSA VENDIDA.
delivery of property sold, transfer of the property sold. Must be such that the property is free of all other possessory rights.
ENTREGA EFECTIVA.
actual delivery.
ENTREGA MATERIAL.
See ENTREGA REAL.
ENTREGA REAL.
actual delivery.
ENTREGA SIMBÓLICA.
constructive delivery.
ENTREGABLE.
adj, deliverable ‖ transferable.
ENTREGADERO.
See ENTREGABLE.
ENTREGADO.
m, thing or person which has been delivered ‖ adj, delivered, transferred.
ENTREGADO EN COMODATO.
bailed ‖ loaned or lent pursuant to a COMODATO.
ENTREGADOR.
m, deliverer ‖ transferor.
**ENTREGADOR DE
LA CITACIÓN.**
process server.
ENTREGAMIENTO.
m, delivery, action of delivering ‖ act of providing assistance or information about person (to police, kidnappers, etc.).
ENTREGAR.
v, to deliver, give, transfer (a thing) ‖ to place, turn over (something or someone) into the hands of another (for their disposal) ‖ to transfer (right of possession) ‖ to commit treason ‖ to fail to defend properly ‖ to give up.
ENTREGAR EN MANO.
to hand deliver, deliver personally. Used re correspondence.
ENTREGARSE.
v, to surrender, give up ‖ to capitulate ‖ to dedicate oneself entirely to an activity or business ‖ to become responsible for (someone or something).
ENTRELINEAR.
v, to write between the lines. In notarized documents this is sometimes permitted.
ENTRELÍNEAS.
f, result of interlineation, that written between the lines.

ENTRERRENGLONADURA.
f, interlineation. See ENTRELÍNEAS.

ENTRERRENGLONAR.
See ENTRELINEAR.

ENTRETENIMIENTO.
m, maintenance, support ‖ expenses of preservation and repair ‖ entertainment.

ENTRONCAR.
v, to demonstrate a person's relationship to another family ‖ to pertain to a family by reason of common ancestor ‖ to become related to another family.

ENTUERTO.
m, wrong, injury, offense.

ENUMERACIÓN.
f, enumeration.

ENUMERAR.
v, to enumerate.

ENUNCIACIÓN.
f, enunciation, statement, declaration.

ENUNCIAR.
v, to enunciate, state, declare.

ENUNCIATIVO.
adj, declaratory, enunciative.

ENVENENADO.
adj, poisoned ‖ embittered, enraged.

ENVENENAMIENTO.
m, poisoning ‖ death by poisoning.

ENVENENAMIENTO DE AGUAS.
pollution of drinking water.

ENVENENAMIENTO PROFESIONAL.
act of person who kills by poison as a profession ‖ contamination in the work place (which results in illnesses in workers).

ENVENENAR.
v, to poison ‖ to kill by poison ‖ to accuse.

ENVENENARSE.
v, to become embittered ‖ to poison oneself.

ENVIADO.
m, messenger, delivery boy (without power of agency) ‖ envoy ‖ disciplinary or punitive transfer ‖ adj, sent, transmitted.

ENVIADO DIPLOMÁTICO.
diplomatic envoy.

ENVIADO ESPECIAL.
special envoy (of a political message).

ENVIADO EXTRAORDINARIO.
diplomatic envoy, envoy extraordinary.

ENVIAR.
v, to send, dispatch, mail, ship, transmit ‖ to fire off.

ENVICIAR.
v, to corrupt, pervert.

ENVICIARSE.
v, to become corrupted or addicted to (e.g. alcohol, gambling).

ENVILECER.
v, to dump (goods), offer goods at lower than cost ‖ to devalue (e.g. money).

ENVIUDAR.
v, to become a widow or widower.

ENVOLVER.
v, to package, pack, wrap ‖ to run circles around ‖ to astound, floor (with accusations, questions and charges).

EPIDEMIA.
f, epidemic.

EPÍGRAFE.
m, epigraph, inscription ‖ title, name, label ‖ caption, heading.

EPIQUEYA.
f, interpretation of the laws according to the circumstances of the times, places, things and people.

EPÍSTOLA.
f, epistle, letter, missive.

EPISTOLAR.
adj, pertaining to correspondence.

ÉPOCA.
f, period, time, era.

ÉPOCA DE PAGO.
due date.

EQUIDAD.
f, equity, equality ‖ natural law ‖ moderation in the prices of things sold or contract conditions.

EQUILIBRIO.
m, equilibrium.

EQUILIBRIO DE PODERES.
balance of powers.

EQUILIBRIO ECONÓMICO.
economic stability (e.g. income adequate to meet expenses ‖ supply equal to demand; credits equal to debits).

EQUIPAR.
v, to equip, supply (often a vessel) ‖ to give, provide (usually household goods).

EQUIPO.
m, equipment ‖ provision or gift of personal items ‖ woman's dowry ‖ team (e.g. of workers or of sportsmen).

EQUITATIVAMENTE.
equitably, fairly, justly.
EQUITATIVO.
adj, equitable, just, fair.
EQUIVALENTE.
adj, equivalent.
EQUIVALER.
v, to be equal ‖ to have equal or similar (use or value) ‖ to be equivalent ‖ to have the same effect.
EQUIVOCACIÓN.
f, error, mistake.
EQUIVOCADAMENTE.
adv, wrongly, mistakenly, by error.
EQUÍVOCAMENTE.
adv, equivocally, ambiguously.
EQUIVOCAR.
v, to confuse, mistake.
EQUIVOCARSE.
v, to err, be mistaken, be in error.
EQUÍVOCO.
m, error, mistake ‖ ambiguity ‖ equivocation ‖ adj, equivocal.
ERA.
f, era.
ERARIO.
m, national treasury ‖ public funds ‖ exchequer.
'ERGA OMNES".
with respect to everyone, against the world. Refers to types of rights.
EROGACIÓN.
f, distribution (of property or money) ‖ expenses (especially of government or corporations).
EROGAR.
v, to distribute (e.g. property or money).
ERRATA.
f, erratum.
ERROR.
m, error, mistake ‖ falsehood, untruth ‖ consent made under fraud or mistake (usually nullifies consent).
ERROR ACCIDENTAL.
incidental error, immaterial mistake, mistake which does not nullify consent.
ERROR COMÚN.
common error.
ERROR DE CÁLCULO.
miscalculation, error in calculation.

ERROR DE DERECHO.
mistaken belief about the law or custom.
ERROR DE HECHO.
factual mistake.
ERROR DE PLUMA.
clerical error.
ERROR DETERMINANTE.
See ERROR ESENCIAL.
ERROR EN EL DERECHO PENAL.
criminal mistake. Refers to mistake in fact (e.g. attempt perpetrated on the wrong person) and mistake of law (e.g. belief that actions are not criminal).
ERROR EN EL DERECHO PROCESAL.
erroneous legal procedure, mistake in the legal procedure of an action.
ERROR EN EL MATRIMONIO.
marriage based on mistaken identity or personality of one of the spouses.
ERROR EN EL NOMBRE DEL HEREDERO.
mistaken name of an heir. Usually not grounds for invalidation of bequest.
ERROR EN EL OBJETO.
mistake in legal purpose of a transaction. Usually constitutes a material error, which nullifies consent.
ERROR EN EL PAGO.
mistaken payment, payment to a wrong party.
ERROR EN LA PERSONA.
mistaken identity (of a person). May invalidate transaction.
ERROR ESENCIAL.
material mistake, mistake which is essential to the legal action or relationship.
ERROR EXCUSABLE.
excusable error.
ERROR GROSERO.
gross error or mistake.
ERROR IN JUDICANDO.
substantive judicial error, judicial error in applying substantive law.
ERROR IN PROCEDENDO.
procedural judicial error, judicial error in applying procedural law.
ERROR INEXCUSABLE.
inexcusable error.
ERROR INSIGNIFICANTE.
immaterial mistake or error.

ERROR JUDICIAL.
judicial error, any error of a judge or tribunal in an action.
ERROR PERJUDICIAL.
prejudicial error.
ERROR REPONIBLE.
reversible error.
ERROR SOBRE LA COSA.
error about the nature or identity of a thing.
ES DECIR.
namely, id est ‖ that is to say.
ESBIRRO.
m, lower ranking court officer ‖ constable, police officer.
ESCABECHAR.
v, to kill violently.
ESCABEL.
m, defendant's chair.
ESCALA.
f, stopover, port of call ‖ classification, scale, gradation ‖ proportion, scale.
ESCALA DE LAS PENAS.
classification of criminal sanctions or punishments.
ESCALAFÓN.
m, hierarchical listing of armed forces personnel (with their length of service, rank, and job) ‖ listing of jobs and their salaries.
ESCÁNDALO PÚBLICO.
m, public disorder ‖ public scandal. May be a crime, but the activity which constitutes this crime varies from country to country. May also be grounds for divorce in some jurisdictions.
ESCALADOR.
m, burglar ‖ climber ‖ adj, climbing.
ESCALAMIENTO.
m, scaling ‖ breaking and entering, the entering of an enclosed place by means other than a proper entrance.
ESCALAR.
v, to break into, enter forcibly ‖ to climb ‖ to scale.
ESCAMOTAR.
See ESCAMOTEAR.
ESCAMOTEADOR.
m, swindler ‖ pickpocket.
ESCAMOTEAR.
v, to swindle, trick, cheat ‖ to pickpocket.
ESCAMOTEO.
m, swindling ‖ trickery ‖ filching, swiping.

ESCAPAR.
v, to escape, run away, save oneself ‖ to hide oneself from (enemies, creditors) ‖ to liberate, save (from harm, work, etc.).
ESCAPAR POR LA TANGENTE.
to respond evasively ‖ to go off on a tangent ‖ to get off on an excuse.
ESCARAMUZA.
f, quarrel, fight (of little importance).
ESCARMIENTO.
m, punishment (to stop reoccurrence of act or to serve as a lesson), object lesson, experience which serves as a deterrent.
ESCISIÓN.
n, corporate break-up (including spin-offs, split-ups, and split-offs).
ESCISIÓN PROCESAL.
partial removal of a cause, separation of causes of action from one into two actions due to their separate nature.
Opposed to ACUMULACIÓN DE ACCIONES and ACUMULACIÓN DE AUTOS.
ESCLARECIMIENTO.
m, clarifying notice ‖ clarification (of a crime, criminals, or other facts).
ESCLAVITUD.
f, slavery.
ESCLAVIZAR.
v, to enslave ‖ to deprive of rights ‖ to impose a tyranny.
ESCLAVO.
m, slave.
ESCRIBA.
m, scribe ‖ lawyer and legal interpreter in Hebraic law.
ESCRIBANÍA.
f, office of a court clerk or of a court secretary ‖ office of a notary public ‖ position of ESCRIBANO ‖ office of an ESCRIBANO.
ESCRIBANO.
m, special notary ‖ judicial assistant. Sometimes referred to as a NOTARIO. The ESCRIBANO is an officer of the court (in the sense that an attorney is) who retypes and certifies certain legal documents (e.g. real estate contracts, expert witnesses testimony) and witnesses documents. He works under license of the government, and usually must have completed extensive studies after having become an attorney. An ESCRIBANO's certification may verify having witnessed the signature of the

signatory or, additionally, may verify the truth of the facts included in the document being signed. The ESCRIBANO who works as a judicial assistant certifies court documents among others and otherwise assists in court related matters.

ESCRIBANO DE MARINA.
maritime registrar ‖ notary who certifies those documents which maritime law requires.

ESCRIBANO DE REGISTRO.
special notary, public clerk who is authorized to witness and certify certain documents which are specially registered in a registry pursuant to law. Type of ESCRIBANO PÚBLICO.

ESCRIBANO MAYOR DE GOBIERNO.
notary general, public official who swears the president-elect and ministers into office and acts as an ESCRIBANO for the president and other ministers.

ESCRIBANO PÚBLICO.
special notary who witnesses documents, but does not act as a judicial assistant ‖ term used in some countries for ESCRIBANO.

ESCRIBANO SECRETARIO.
special court clerk, judge's assistant who provides judge with a daily report on the state of the case before him, organizes and cares for the court files, certifies legal documents and statements, and serves as a court file clerk. Sometimes called ACTUARIO or SECRETARIO.

ESCRIBIENTE.
m, f, clerk.

ESCRIBIENTE NOTARIAL.
notary's clerk.

ESCRITO.
m, document, writing, manuscript ‖ book ‖ composition ‖ petition, allegation, accusation ‖ bill, written request to a judge ‖ adj, written.

ESCRITO DE ACUSACIÓN.
bill of indictment (usually in a military court), prosecutor's written charges (usually in the second phase of a military trial).

ESCRITO DE AGRAVIOS.
appeal, bill of appeal.

ESCRITO DE AMPLIACIÓN.
amended complaint, complaint written subsequent to the original with additional allegations.

ESCRITO DE CALIFICACIÓN.
criminal information, indictment, criminal complaint which emanates from a preliminary hearing.

ESCRITO DE CONCLUSIÓN.
final brief (submitted in a declaratory judgment action) ‖ written summary of conclusions (submitted in a declaratory judgment action) in lieu of oral argument.

ESCRITO DE CONCLUSIONES.
See ESCRITO DE CONCLUSIÓN.

ESCRITO DE CONCLUSIONES PROVISIONALES.
indictment (in a military court) submitted immediately after the preliminary hearing.

ESCRITO DE CONTESTACIÓN A LA DEMANDA.
answer or reply (to a complaint).

ESCRITO DE DEFENSA.
answer (to a military complaint).

ESCRITO DE DEMANDA.
complaint. Includes summary of facts and law upon which it is based.

ESCRITO DE DÚPLICA.
See DÚPLICA.

ESCRITO DE INSTRUCCIÓN EN LAS APELACIONES.
appellate brief.

ESCRITO DE INTERPOSICIÓN DEL RECURSO DE CASACIÓN.
written appeal (submitted to a court of cassation).

ESCRITO DE OPOSICIÓN DEL EJECUTADO.
answer (to a complaint in a JUICIO EJECUTIVO).

ESCRITO DE PRESENTACIÓN.
initial brief.

ESCRITO DE RECUSACIONES.
brief including challenges.

ESCRITO DE RÉPLICA.
See RÉPLICA.

ESCRITO DE REPOSICIÓN.
petition or request for consideration.

ESCRITO INDISCIPLINADO.
publication which itself violates military discipline. Constitutes a serious offense.

ESCRITOS DE CONCLUSIÓN.
final pleadings.

ESCRITOS DIPLOMÁTICOS.
diplomatic notes or messages.

ESCRITOR.
m, writer, author ‖ author of an ESCRITO.

ESCRITORIO.
m, office (of bankers, notary publics, etc.) ‖ desk.

ESCRITURA.
f, action of writing ‖ writing, document, manuscript ‖ written work ‖ handwriting ‖ legal instrument, document in which an obligation, a contract, or other statement is set forth and signed ‖ legal instrument or document entered into before an ESCRIBANO (e.g. a deed).

ESCRITURA A TÍTULO GRATUITO.
gratuitous deed.

ESCRITURA ADICIONAL.
supplemental or additional instrument, document which is physically separate from another but complementary to it.

ESCRITURA CONSTITUTIVA.
articles of association or incorporation.

ESCRITURA CORRIDA.
longhand.

ESCRITURA DE CANCELACIÓN.
document cancelling a debt.

ESCRITURA DE CESIÓN.
deed of assignment.

ESCRITURA DE COMPRAVENTA.
deed ‖ bill of sale.

ESCRITURA DE CONCORDATO.
creditors' agreement with bankrupt.

ESCRITURA DE CONSTITUCIÓN.
See ESCRITURA CONSTITUTIVA.

ESCRITURA DE CONSTITUCIÓN DE HIPOTECA.
mortgage deed.

ESCRITURA DE CONVENIO.
specialty contract.

ESCRITURA DE DONACIÓN.
deed of gift.

ESCRITURA DE EMISIÓN DE BONOS.
bond indenture.

ESCRITURA DE ENAJENACIÓN.
transfer title or document.

ESCRITURA DE FIDEICOMISO.
trust indenture.

ESCRITURA DE FUNDACIÓN.
articles of association or incorporation.

ESCRITURA DE HIPOTECA.
mortgage deed.

ESCRITURA DE NACIMIENTO.
birth certificate.

ESCRITURA DE PLENO DOMINIO.
fee simple deed.

ESCRITURA DE PRÉSTAMO E HIPOTECA.
loan and mortgage document.

ESCRITURA DE PROPIEDAD.
title deed.

ESCRITURA DE REFORMA.
amendment document.

ESCRITURA DE SATISFACCIÓN.
document cancelling debt.

ESCRITURA DE SEGURO.
insurance policy.

ESCRITURA DE SOCIEDAD.
See ESCRITURA SOCIAL.

ESCRITURA DE TRASPASO.
transfer deed.

ESCRITURA DE VENTA.
bill of sale ‖ deed.

ESCRITURA FIDUCIDARIA.
trust deed.

ESCRITURA GUARENTIGIA.
public document whereby the parties agree to judicial execution for subsequent failure to comply with judgment.

ESCRITURA HIPOTECARIA.
See ESCRITURA DE HIPOTECA.

ESCRITURA MATRIZ.
original instrument, original of a contract or other document registered with a special notary who certifies the signatures of the parties and witnesses thereto.

ESCRITURA NOTARIAL.
notarized document, instrument executed before and certified by a notary public.

ESCRITURA PRIVADA.
unnotarized document, writing which has not been witnessed and recorded by a special notary public. Valid only as between the parties. See ESCRIBANO.

ESCRITURA PÚBLICA.
notarized document, writing which has been witnessed and recorded by a special notary public. Valid evidence between the parties and as to third parties. Type of DOCUMENTO PÚBLICO. The following usually must be ESCRITURAS PÚBLICAS to be fully effective between the parties or as to third parties: deeds, real estate contracts, leases for periods exceeding 6 months, marriage and dowry agreements, transfer or repudiation or renunciation of inheritances or community property, authoriza-

tion to marry or litigate or administer property, etc. See ESCRIBANO.

ESCRITURA SELLADA.
sealed instrument or writing.

ESCRITURA SOCIAL.
partnership agreement ‖ articles of incorporation.

ESCRITURA TRASLATIVA DE DOMINIO.
deed, transfer document.

ESCRITURAR.
v, to notarize or witness or certify and register (as or with a special notary public).

ESCRITURARIO.
adj, notarial, pertaining to records of official notary.

ESCRUTADOR.
m, inspector, examiner, person who scrutinizes.

ESCRUTAR.
v, to scrutinize ‖ to count votes.

ESCRUTINIO.
m, scrutiny, close examination ‖ vote or ballot count (in elections).

ESCRUTIÑADOR.
m, scrutineer, vote or ballot counter ‖ scrutinizer.

ESCUELA.
f, school (of thought) ‖ school, place of learning.

ESCUELA CORRECCIONAL.
reform school, reformatory.

ESCUELA DE DERECHO.
law school.

ESENCIAL.
adj, essential ‖ indispensable.

ESFERA DE INFLUENCIA.
f, sphere of influence.

ESPACIO.
m, space, area, dimension ‖ volume, capacity ‖ time period, passage of time, lapse of time.

ESPACIO AÉREO.
air space.

ESPACIO VITAL.
personal space, vital space needed by persons or groups of persons to live.

ESPECIALIDAD.
f, specialty.

ESPECIE.
f, species ‖ fact, case, matter, business ‖ proposition, information ‖ pretext, excuse ‖ military unrest ‖ rumor.

ESPECIFICACIÓN.
f, production, creation (of a new object from other things) ‖ specification.

ESPECIFICACIONES.
f, specifications, specs.

ESPECULACIÓN.
f, speculation ‖ profiteering. See AGIO.

ESPERA.
f, wait, delay ‖ stay ‖ term, period (granted by a judge to a debtor to do something, pay something, or present proof ‖ grace period (granted by creditors to debtors for payment after debt has become due) ‖ (trial) recess, time delay (granted for the arrival of witnesses, parties, etc.).

ESPERANZA.
f, hope ‖ desire, wish ‖ expectancy ‖ expectation ‖ prospects.

ESPERANZA DE VIDA.
life expectancy.

ESPÍA.
m, f, spy, secret agent.

ESPÍA DOBLE.
double agent.

ESPIADO.
m, person or thing that is spied upon ‖ accused party ‖ adj, spied-on.

ESPIAR.
v, to spy, be a secret agent.

ESPIONAJE.
m, espionage, act of spying.

ESPONSALES.
m, engagement, mutual promise to marry.

ESPOSA.
f, wife ‖ spouse.

ESPOSAR.
v, to handcuff (a prisoner).

ESPOSAS.
f, handcuffs.

ESPOSO.
m, husband ‖ spouse.

ESPURIO.
m, illegitimate child, bastard ‖ adj, spurious.

ESQUILMAR.
v, to swindle, cheat, trick ‖ to exploit ‖ to harvest ‖ to impoverish.

ESQUIROL.
m, strike-breaker, scab.

ESQUIZOFRENIA.
f, schizophrenia.

ESTABILIDAD.

f, stability, security ‖ permanence, duration. Used to refer to right of employee to employment security.

ESTABILIDAD ABSOLUTA.

permanent job security, guarantee of permanent employment (or, if dismissed, indemnification for future lost earnings until retirement). Type of ESTABILIDAD EN EL EMPLEO.

ESTABILIDAD DURABILIDAD.

See ESTABILIDAD RELATIVA.

ESTABILIDAD EN EL EMPLEO.

job security (such that the employee may not be dismissed without cause or indemnification).

ESTABILIDAD GREMIAL.

job security for union representatives, protection against dismissal for employees who represent unions.

ESTABILIDAD PERDURABILIDAD.

See ESTABILIDAD ABSOLUTA.

ESTABILIDAD RELATIVA.

relative job security, guarantee of temporary employment (or, if dismissed, indemnification paid for number of years worked, in relation to the level of salary). Type of ESTABILIDAD EN EL EMPLEO.

ESTABILIDAD SINDICAL.

See ESTABILIDAD GREMIAL.

ESTABLECER.

v, to establish, found ‖ to enact.

ESTABLECER IMPUESTOS.

to impose taxes.

ESTABLECIMIENTO.

m, establishment, store, shop, commercial business ‖ factory, workshop, plant ‖ charitable organization, foundation ‖ organization dedicated to education, culture, philanthropy, recreation, or patriotism ‖ establishment, foundation, thing, or place that is established ‖ order, resolution.

ESTABLECIMIENTO DE SERVIDUMBRES POR DESTINO DEL DUEÑO.

establishment by implication of an affirmative easement over property sold to another. This results not by express agreement but by the conduct of the original owner of the property over which the easement exists.

ESTABLECIMIENTO MILITAR.

military division (dedicated to one type of work) ‖ military installation.

ESTABLECIMIENTOS PENALES.

m, correctional or penal institutions.

ESTACA.

f, stake ‖ continuous mining concession.

ESTACIÓN DE POLICÍA.

f, police station.

ESTADÍA.

f, stay ‖ period of time which a vessel remains in dock.

ESTADÍSTICA.

f, statistic.

ESTADO.

m, state ‖ condition (e.g. of a person) ‖ hierarchical groupings within a society (e.g. military state, church state) ‖ marital status ‖ nation, country; nation-state ‖ political administrative department of a nation ‖ public administration (of government) ‖ state, (territorial, semi-autonomous division of a nation) ‖ ministry of finance (of a nation) ‖ government ‖ report statement.

ESTADO BANCARIO.

bank statement.

ESTADO CIVIL.

marital or legal status.

ESTADO CON FINES CONTRIBUTIVOS.

tax statement, statement for tax purposes.

ESTADO CONDENSADO.

condensed balance sheet.

ESTADO CONSTITUCIONAL.

constitutional government, government that is based on a constitution.

ESTADO CONTABILÍSTICO.

balance sheet.

ESTADO DE CONCURSO.

state of bankruptcy.

ESTADO DE CONTABILIDAD.

balance sheet.

ESTADO DE DERECHO.

government of laws, government which is governed by law.

ESTADO DE EMERGENCIA.

state of emergency, condition of nation which interrupts the normal functioning of a nation and places constitutional institutions in danger.

ESTADO DE GANANCIAS Y PÉRDIDAS.

income statement ‖ profit-and loss statement

ESTADO DE GUERRA.

state of war.

ESTADO DE INDIVISIÓN.
undivided condition, condition of undivided estate or property.

ESTADO DE LIQUIDACIÓN.
state of liquidation ‖ liquidation statement.

ESTADO DE NECESIDAD.
extenuating circumstance (that offense was committed to avoid more serious harm). Constitutes an excuse to crime.

ESTADO DE PAZ.
state of peace.

ESTADO DE PELIGROSIDAD.
See PELIGROSIDAD.

ESTADO DE RESULTADOS.
earnings or income statement.

ESTADO DE SITIO.
state of siege ‖ governmental proclamation called against a threat to public order which suspends personal constitutional guarantees and increases the authority of the executive.

ESTADO DE SITUACIÓN.
general balance sheet ‖ general accounting statement.

ESTADO DEL ACTIVO Y PASIVO.
assets and liabilities statement.

ESTADO FEDERAL.
federal state, federation ‖ nation made up of various states or provinces which possess a separate government, legislation, and a degree of administrative autonomy.

ESTADO FINANCIERO.
financial statement ‖ balance sheet.

ESTADO INTERMEDIO.
interim statement.

ESTADO LEGAL.
legal status ‖ marital status.

ESTADO MILITAR.
military state, government of martial law.

ESTADO NACIONAL.
nation state ‖ federal government.

ESTADO POSESORIO.
state or condition of possession.

ESTADO SOBERANO.
sovereign state.

ESTADO TAPÓN.
buffer state.

ESTADO TOTALITARIO.
totalitarian state.

ESTADOS BAJO MANDATO Y ADMINISTRACIÓN FIDUCIARIA.
states under trusteeship.

ESTADOS NEUTRALIZADOS.
neutral states or nations.

ESTADOS SEMISOBERANOS.
quasi-sovereign states or nations.

ESTADOS SOBERANOS.
sovereign states or nations.

ESTADOS UNIDOS.
united states. Often but not always used to refer to the United States of America.

ESTADOS UNIDOS DE AMÉRICA.
United States of America.

ESTADOS VASALLOS.
See ESTADOS SEMISOBERANOS.

ESTAFA.
f, fraud, generic term for crimes which cause loss of property by trickery or deceit.

ESTAFA PROCESAL.
fraud against the opposing party by means of mutilation, substitution, or secretion of court papers, or by similar procedural deceit.

ESTAFADOR.
m, defrauder, swindler, perjurer.

ESTAFAR.
v, to defraud ‖ to swindle, cheat, trick ‖ to default, welsh.

ESTALLAR.
v, to break out, start (e.g. war) ‖ to blow up (e.g. bombs).

ESTAMPILLA.
f, stamp.

ESTAMPILLA DE TIMBRE NACIONAL.
documentary stamp.

ESTAMPILLA FISCAL.
revenue or tax stamp.

ESTANCO.
m, state monopoly (either managed or licensed by the state) ‖ store where state-controlled goods are sold ‖ limitation or prohibition on the production, manufacture, or sale of goods.

ESTANQUERO.
m, retailer of goods pursuant to a government license (e.g. tobacco).

ESTAR A DERECHO.
v, to appear at trial or in court (either in person or through an attorney or other representative) ‖ to be legal, in accord with the law.

ESTAR A JUZGADO Y SENTENCIADO.
to be before the court for judgment.

ESTAR A LA MUERTE.
to be on death's doorstep, at death's door.

ESTAR A MATAR.
to hate, abhor ‖ to be deadly enemies with, be at knife point (figuratively) ‖ to bring about international tensions.

ESTAR ALGO EN MANO DE UNO.
to have a decision in another's hands.

ESTAR AMARRADO AL PALO.
to be chained to a stick ‖ to be prisoner.

ESTAR CON EL PIE EN EL ESTRIBO.
to be about to take off (on a trip) ‖ to be about to die.

ESTAR EN BUEN USO.
to be in good condition.

ESTAR EN SESIÓN.
to be in meeting or session.

ESTATAL.
m, f, administrative agent of the state ‖ adj, state ‖ of the state, pertaining to the state ‖ subject to state jurisdiction ‖ state, state-owned.

ESTATISMO.
m, statism.

ESTATUIDO.
adj, provided ‖ enacted.

ESTATUIR.
v, to enact ‖ to stipulate, provide.

ESTATUTARIO.
adj, statutory ‖ by-law, pertaining to by-laws.

ESTATUTO.
m, statute, law, regulation, ordinance ‖ rule (with the force of law imposed by governing body) ‖ constitution ‖ obligation, duty ‖ norm (regulating international jurisdictional competence) ‖ rule(s) applicable to a given profession.

ESTATUTO DE LOS PARTIDOS POLÍTICOS.
platform of a political party ‖ rules applicable to political parties.

ESTATUTO FORMAL.
jurisdictional statute (which regulates procedural conflict of laws) ‖ law of procedure.

ESTATUTO ORGÁNICO.
organic or fundamental law.

ESTATUTO PERSONAL.
jurisdictional statute (which regulates conflict of laws in matters of nationality, legal status, etc. of persons) ‖ national law ‖ personal law, law which regulates persons and personal rights ‖ personal law, law which is applicable on the basis of one's nationality.

ESTATUTO REAL.
property law, law which regulates property law which is applicable on the basis of the location of a property or right.

ESTATUTOS.
m, by-laws (of a corporation) ‖ plural of ESTATUTO.

ESTATUTOS DE SOCIEDADES.
by-laws (of a business association). Usually must be approved by a competent government authority.

ESTATUTOS PROFESIONALES.
labor law (pertaining to a specific profession industry, occupation). Includes laws, regulations and other rules.

ESTATUTOS SOCIALES.
See ESTATUTOS DE SOCIEDADES.

ESTELIONATO.
m, stellionate, type of fraud consisting of contracting in bad faith regarding property which belongs to another party or regarding encumbered property as if it were free of all encumbrances. Usually a crime.

ESTERILIDAD.
f, sterility ‖ infertility (in either a man or woman).

ESTERILIZACIÓN.
f, sterilization. Used to be a criminal sanction

ESTIGMA.
m, stigma ‖ brand (used to mark slaves) ‖ innate physiological characteristic of a criminal (much disputed).

ESTILAR.
v, to draft, draw up.

ESTILO.
m, style ‖ form, method.

ESTILO CALIGRÁFICO.
handwriting.

ESTIMACIÓN.
f, estimation ‖ valuation, evaluation, appraisal

ESTIMAR.
v, to estimate, appraise, evaluate ‖ to esteem

ESTIMATIVA JURÍDICA.
f, judgment regarding the value of law (e. fairness, effectiveness, etc.).

ESTIMATIVO.
adj, estimated, appraised.

ESTIMATORIA.
See ACCIÓN ESTIMATORIA.

ESTIPENDIO.
m, stipend ‖ salary, pay for services rendered

ESTIPULACIÓN.
f, oral agreement || contract, agreement || stipulation, condition || clause.

ESTIPULACIÓN A CARGO DE TERCERO.
contract clause which obligates a non- contracting party. Usually considered to be void, unless later ratified.

ESTIPULACIÓN A FAVOR DE TERCERO.
contract or clause in favor of third party beneficiary.

ESTIPULACIÓN CONDICIONADA.
condition, conditional clause.

ESTIPULACIÓN "POST MORTEM".
causa mortis condition, clause which makes the death of one or both of the parties a condition precedent.

ESTIPULANTE.
m, f, stipulator, contractor, party who stipulates (usually, to a clause in favor of third party beneficiaries) || adj, stipulating.

ESTIPULAR.
v, to stipulate, agree, contract.

ESTIRPE.
f, stirpes || family tree || lineage, ancestry || heirs, successors.

ESTORBO PÚBLICO.
m, common nuisance.

ESTRADO.
m, dais, platform, stand.

ESTRADO DE TESTIGOS.
witness stand.

ESTRADOS.
m, courtrooms, hearing rooms || location in a court-house where summons by public notice is posted.

ESTRAGO.
m, major or serious damage or destruction.

ESTRANGULAR.
v, to strangle.

ESTRECHAR A PREGUNTAS.
to put someone on the hot seat, question under pressure.

ESTRECHAR LOS TÉRMINOS.
to shorten the term or period.

ESTRICTAMENTE.
adv, strictly, to the letter of the law.

ESTRICTO.
adj, strict, rigorous || close || totally in accord with the law.

ESTRUCTURA.
f, building, structure.

ESTRUCTURA DEL CAPITAL.
capital structure.

ESTUDIAR DERECHO.
v, to study law.

ESTUDIO.
m, study || investigation, research || law office or firm || lawyer's office.

ESTUPEFACIENTE.
m, narcotic which causes loss of senses.

ESTUPRADOR.
m, statutory rapist, person who commits statutory rape.

ESTUPRAR.
v, to commit statutory rape.

ESTUPRO.
m, statutory rape, sexual intercourse with a consenting female (usually) between the ages of 12 and 15.

ÉTICA.
f, ethics.

ÉTICA DE LOS NEGOCIOS.
business ethics.

ÉTICA PROFESIONAL.
professional ethics.

ÉTICO.
adj, ethical, moral.

ETIOLOGÍA CRIMINAL.
f, study of the causes of criminal conduct.

ETIOLOGÍA DEL DELITO.
See ETIOLOGÍA CRIMINAL.

ETNOLOGÍA JURÍDICA.
f, legal ethnology, study of the evolution of law among peoples.

EUNUCO.
m, eunuch.

EUTANASIA.
f, euthanasia.

EVACUACIÓN DE LA POBLACIÓN CIVIL.
f, evacuation of civilians (during war).

EVACUADO.
m, evacuee, evacuated person || adj, evacuated.

EVACUAR.
v, to evacuate || to leave, vacate || to carry out, perform.

EVACUAR LA RESPUESTA.
to answer, file an answer.

EVACUAR LAS DILIGENCIAS.
to comply with the formalities.

EVACUAR UN ENCARGO.
to carry out an order or assignment or commission.

EVACUAR UN INFORME.
to make a report.

EVACUAR UN NEGOCIO.
to liquidate a business.

EVACUAR UNA PROTESTA.
to file a protest.

EVACUAR PROTESTO.
to protest (note or draft).

EVACUAR PRUEBA.
to provide proof or evidence.

EVACUAR UN TRASLADO.
to answer a court's request to state one's position about a given matter which is part of the proceeding.

EVADIDO.
m, fugitive ‖ escapee ‖ person who escapes from enemy to fight in opposing army ‖ adj, evaded.

EVADIR.
v, to evade, dodge.

EVADIR IMPUESTOS.
to evade taxes.

EVADIRSE.
v, to abscond, escape, take off.

EVALUACIÓN.
f, evaluation ‖ estimation ‖ valuation, appraisal ‖ assessment.

**EVALUACIÓN DE
LOS DAÑOS.**
appraisal of damages.

EVALUAR.
v, to appraise, assess, value, rate.

EVASIÓN.
f, evasion ‖ flight, escape (from army, prison, etc.). May be a crime.

EVASIÓN DE CAPITALES.
capital flight, exportation of capital. May be a crime.

EVASIÓN DE DIVISAS.
evasion or flight of foreign exchange.

**EVASIÓN DE
PRISIONEROS.**
escape of prisoners (usually in war).

EVASIÓN DEL IMPUESTO.
tax evasion.

EVASIÓN FISCAL.
tax evasion, failure to declare income or illegal reduction of income in violation of tax law.

EVASIVA.
f, evasion (e.g. of response to interrogation) ‖ evasive answer.

EVASIVO.
adj, evasive.

EVASOR.
m, evader (e.g. tax).

EVENTO.
m, event, happening, occurrence ‖ accident ‖ chance ‖ contingency.

EVENTUAL.
adj, eventual ‖ contingent ‖ extra (payment in addition to salary) ‖ fortuitous.

EVENTUALIDAD.
f, eventuality ‖ possibility ‖ event.

EVENTUALIDAD DEL MAR.
perils of the sea.

EVICCIÓN.
f, eviction, ejection ‖ dispossession, ouster ‖ disturbance or total conversion of one's right to quiet enjoyment of property.

EVICCIÓN EN EL ARRENDAMIENTO.
tenant eviction ‖ disturbance or total conversion of one's right to quiet enjoyment of leased property.

EVICCIÓN EN LA COMPRAVENTA.
dispossession of property purchased ‖ repossession (of personal property purchased) ‖ foreclosure (of real property purchased) ‖ disturbance or total conversion of one's right to quiet enjoyment of purchased property.

EVIDENCIA.
f, evidence, proof.

EVIDENCIA CIRCUNSTANCIAL.
circumstantial evidence.

EVIDENCIA POR REFERENCIA.
hearsay evidence.

EVIDENCIAL.
adj, evidentiary.

EVIDENCIAR.
v, to make evident ‖ to prove.

EVIDENTE.
adj, evident ‖ proven, evidenced ‖ demonstrated.

EVITABLE.
adj, avoidable.

EVITAR.
v, to avoid, evade ‖ to dodge ‖ to impede ‖ to abstain.

"EX CONTRACTU".
ex contractu, from contract.

"EX LEGE".
according to law.
"EX NUNC".
henceforth, from now on, from this time forth.
EX OFFICIO.
ex officio, by virtue of one's position or office.
EX PARTE.
ex parte.
EX POST FACTO.
ex post facto, after the fact.
"EX TUNC".
from then on, from that time forth ‖ from the beginning.
EXACCIÓN.
f, imposition, levying, exaction (e.g. of taxes).
EXACCIÓN ILEGAL.
illegal exaction ‖ extortion.
EXACTOR.
m, tax collector.
EXAGERACIÓN.
f, exaggeration.
EXAMEN.
m, examination (e.g. of witnesses) ‖ (educa-- tional) test, exam ‖ inspection, search ‖ questioning, interrogation ‖ investigation, inquiry, inquisition.
EXAMEN DE TESTIGOS.
examination of witnesses. Includes depositions and in court examination of witnesses.
EXAMEN PERICIAL.
examination of an expert witness (by a judge regarding an expert's report).
EXAMEN PRENUPCIAL.
pre-marital medical exam of betrothed couple.
EXAMINADOR.
m, examiner.
EXAMINADOR BANCARIO.
bank examiner.
EXAMINAR.
to examine, inspect ‖ to investigate ‖ to search.
EXCARCELACIÓN.
f, freeing or release of a prisoner.
EXCARCELAR.
v, to release (from prison) ‖ to free, set free.
EXCAUTIVO.
m, ex-convict, ex-con.
EXCEDENCIA.
f, excess, surplus ‖ situation of an employee of officer who retains his or her position without the duties normally pertaining thereto.

EXCEDENTE.
m, absentee, public official who is temporarily absent from position ‖ surplus, overage, excess ‖ adj, excessive ‖ improper, beyond the rules or norm.
EXCEDENTE DE CAPITAL.
capital surplus.
EXCEDENTE DE EXPLOTACIÓN.
current or trading profits.
EXCEDENTE REPARTIBLE.
surplus which may be distributed.
EXCEDENTE SIN CONSIGNAR.
unappropriated surplus.
EXCEDENTES.
m, surplus goods.
EXCEPCIÓN.
f, exception ‖ motion ‖ privilege ‖ exemption (e.g. from military service) ‖ demurrer ‖ defense which, without denying the basis of the action, is put forth to delay or negate it ‖ criminal plea, defense (which does not deny the facts alleged, e.g. a justification or an excuse).
EXCEPCIÓN COHERENTE.
personal defense.
EXCEPCIÓN CONTRARIA.
alternative defense ‖ contradictory defense.
EXCEPCIÓN DE ARRAIGO.
motion for plaintiff to place a bond sufficient to cover the costs inherent in the complaint required of a plaintiff who has no property and is a non-resident in the country in which he is bringing suit.
EXCEPCIÓN DE COMPROMISO PREVIO.
defense or motion to dismiss based on previous accord or settlement.
EXCEPCIÓN DE COSA JUZGADA.
motion to dismiss or defense of res judicata, exceptio rei judicatae (if in civil law) ‖ motion to dismiss or defense of prohibition against double jeopardy (if in criminal law).
EXCEPCIÓN DE DEFECTO LEGAL.
special demurrer ‖ motion to dismiss or defense based on failure to state a claim upon which relief may be granted.
EXCEPCIÓN DE DEMANDA INSUFICIENTE.
defense or motion to dismiss based on the insufficiency of the complaint.

EXCEPCIÓN DE DERECHO.
demurrer ‖ motion to dismiss or defense based on law (vs. facts).

EXCEPCIÓN DE DINERO NO ENTREGADO.
motion to dismiss or defense based on money not paid.

EXCEPCIÓN DE DIVISIÓN.
motion to dismiss or defense based on non-joinder of an indispensable party (by a guarantor against a creditor when there is more than one guarantor).

EXCEPCIÓN DE EXCUSIÓN.
defense of excussio, guarantor's defense that the creditor has failed to exhaust his remedies against the principal debtor.

EXCEPCIÓN DE FALTA DE ACCIÓN.
motion to dismiss or defense based on failure to state a claim upon which relief may be granted.

EXCEPCIÓN DE FALTA DE CUMPLIMIENTO.
motion to dismiss or defense based on the failure of the other party to perform (e.g. an obligation).

EXCEPCIÓN DE FALTA DE PERSONALIDAD.
motion to dismiss or defense based on lack of standing to sue or the failure to name the proper party-defendant or the fact that the attorney representing the plaintiff is not legally qualified to do so.

EXCEPCIÓN DE FALTA DE PERSONERÍA.
See EXCEPCIÓN DE FALTA DE PERSONALIDAD.

EXCEPCIÓN DE HECHO.
exceptio in factum, motion to dismiss or defense based on fact (vs. law).

EXCEPCIÓN DE INCOMPETENCIA.
jurisdictional plea, motion to dismiss or defense alleging lack of jurisdiction of venue of court.

EXCEPCIÓN DE JURISDICCIÓN.
See EXCEPCIÓN DE INCOMPETENCIA.

EXCEPCIÓN DE LA INCAPACIDAD DE LA PARTE.
motion to dismiss or defense based on lack of proper standing.

EXCEPCIÓN DE LITISPENDENCIA.
motion to dismiss or defense based on the fact that the claims are already being litigated in another suit.

EXCEPCIÓN DE NULIDAD.
motion to dismiss or defense based on the voidness of a legal instrument or transaction.

EXCEPCIÓN DE OSCURIDAD.
motion to dismiss or defense based on the failure of the pleading to allege facts with sufficient definiteness.

EXCEPCIÓN DE PRESCRIPCIÓN.
motion to dismiss or defense based on the statute of limitations having run.

EXCEPCIÓN DECLARATIVA.
declaratory exception or plea.

EXCEPCIÓN DECLINATORIA.
foreign plea, jurisdictional plea, motion to dismiss or defense alleging lack of jurisdiction or venue of court.

EXCEPCIÓN DILATORIA.
dilatory plea, exceptio dilatoria, plea which tends to postpone or suspend trial on the merits. Includes EXCEPCIÓN: DE JURISDICCION, DE DEFECTO LEGAL, DE LITISPENDENCIA, and DE FALTA DE PERSONALIDAD.

EXCEPCIÓN ESPECIAL.
special exception or defense.

EXCEPCIÓN GENERAL.
general denial or defense.

EXCEPCIÓN "NON ADIMPLETI CONTRACTUS".
motion to dismiss or defense based on breach of a contractual condition precedent.

EXCEPCIÓN PERENTORIA.
peremptory exception or plea, exceptio peremptoria; motion to dismiss or defense based on failure to state a claim upon which relief may be granted. Opposed to EXCEPCIÓN DILATORIA.

EXCEPCIÓN PERSONAL.
exceptio in personam, personal defense.

EXCEPCIÓN PROCESAL.
exception or motion to dismiss based on procedural defect.

EXCEPCIÓN PROCURATORIA.
motion to dismiss or defense based on lack of representation.

EXCEPCIÓN REAL.
exceptio in rem, non-personal defense or exception.

EXCEPCIÓN SUPERVENIENTE.
defense or motion to dismiss which is raised after trial has started.

EXCEPCIÓN SUSTANCIAL.
demurrer ‖ motion to dismiss or defense based on a point of substantive law.

EXCEPCIÓN TEMPORAL.
See EXCEPCIÓN DILATORIA.

EXCEPCIONABLE.
adj, demurrable ‖ able to be defended ‖ subject to a motion to dismiss.

EXCEPCIONANTE.
m, party who files defense or motion to dismiss or exception.

EXCEPCIONAR.
v, to plead, defend (against a complaint) ‖ to except, exclude.

EXCEPCIONES EN LO PENAL.
See ARTÍCULOS DE PREVIO PRONUNCIAMIENTO.

EXCEPTIO VERITATIS".
defense or motion to dismiss based on truth of the defamatory statement (to action based on defamation).

EXCEPTUAR.
v, to except ‖ to exclude ‖ to exempt.

EXCESO.
m, excess, overage, surplus ‖ crime, offense.

EXCESO DE EXPLOTACIÓN.
current of trading profits.

EXCESO DE PÉRDIDA.
excess loss.

EXCESO DE SEGURO.
overinsurance.

EXCESO DE SINIESTRALIDAD.
excess loss.

EXCESO DE UTILIDADES.
excess profits.

EXCITACIÓN A LA REBELIÓN.
n, incitement to riot or rebel. Constitutes a crime.

EXCITACIÓN PARA LA REBELIÓN.
See EXCITACIÓN A LA REBELIÓN.

EXCLUSIÓN.
f, exclusion ‖ prohibition ‖ dismissal, expulsion.

EXCLUSIÓN SINDICAL.
See CLÁUSULA DE EXCLUSIÓN SINDICAL or CLÁUSULA DE EXCLUSIVIDAD SINDICAL.

EXCLUSIVA.
f, monopoly ‖ exclusive license or privilege ‖ basis for refusing a position or employment.

EXCLUSIVIDAD EN EL CONTRATO DE TRABAJO.
f, exclusivity of employment contract, state of employment which requires the employee to work for one employer exclusively.

EXCLUSIVIDAD LABORAL.
f, exclusive employment, work which prohibits the employee from working for another employer at the same time.

EXCLUSIVO.
adj, exclusive.

EXCLUYENTE.
f, justification, excuse ‖ adj, justifying, excusing, exculpatory, excluding, exclusive.

EXCULPAR.
v, to exculpate, excuse.

EXCULPARSE.
v, to be exculpated, be excused.

EXCUSA.
f, excuse ‖ motive. May be: PERENTORIA (excuse which totally exonerates the accused) or ATENUANTE (excuse which lessens the severity of the crime).

EXCUSA ABSOLUTORIA.
absolute excuse, excuse which results in absolution from criminal punishment.

EXCUSA DE TUTELA Y PROTUTELA.
excuse from compliance with guardianship obligations.

EXCUSA JUDICIAL.
excuse from acting as military defense attorney.

EXCUSACIÓN.
f, excuse ‖ recusal sua sponte, self-disqualification from a case by the judge.

EXCUSADO.
m, person who is excused or pardoned ‖ adj, exempt (from punishment, taxes, etc.) ‖ adj, excused ‖ exempted.

EXCUSADOR.
m, person who excuses or pardons.

EXCUSAR.
v, to excuse ‖ to exempt ‖ to pardon.

EXCUSARSE.
v, to disqualify or excuse oneself.

EXCUSIÓN.
f, excussio, right to require a creditor to exhaust all remedies against debtor before proceeding against the guarantor.

EXCUSIÓN DE BIENES.
legal action to proceed against the goods of the principal debtor before proceeding against those of the guarantor.

EXÉGESIS.
f, interpretation of law.
EXEGÉTICA.
f, literal interpretation ‖ legal interpretation pursuant to text of statute.
EXENCIÓN.
f, privilege, immunity (usually legal) ‖ exception, excuse ‖ exemption (from taxes, obligations, etc.) ‖ deferment (from military service).
EXENCIÓN ARANCELARIA.
exemption from customs duties.
EXENCIÓN CONTRIBUTIVA.
tax exemption.
EXENCIÓN FISCAL.
tax exemption.
EXENCIÓN JUDICIAL.
exemption from carrying out judicial posts (pertaining to superior military officers).
EXENCIÓN PERSONAL.
personal exemption.
EXENCIÓN POR PERSONAS A CARGO.
exemption for dependents.
EXENCIÓN TRIBUTARIA.
See EXENCIÓN CONTRIBUTIVA.
EXENTAR.
v, to exempt, excuse.
EXENCIONAR.
See EXENTAR.
EXENTO.
adj, exempt ‖ excused ‖ immune ‖ privileged.
EXENTO DE CONTRIBUCIÓN.
tax-exempt.
EXENTO DE DERECHOS.
duty-free.
EXENTO DE IMPUESTOS.
tax-exempt.
EXEQUÁTUR.
m, exequatur, certificate issued by a government to a foreign consul which recognizes his or her official status and right to perform duties.
EXHEREDACIÓN.
f, disinheritance.
EXHEREDAR.
v, to disinherit.
EXHIBICIÓN.
f, exhibition, exposition ‖ discovery ‖ production.
EXHIBICIÓN DE DOCUMENTOS.
production of documents (in litigation, to

refer to and check their authenticity).
EXHIBICIÓN DE LA COSA DEMANDADA.
production of the res.
EXHIBICIÓN DE LOS LIBROS DEL REGISTRO.
disclosure of the books of a public registry.
EXHIBICIÓN DEL TÍTULO POR EL POSEEDOR.
display of title of ownership. Refers to obligation incumbent upon possessor.
EXHIBICIONES DESHONESTAS.
public indecency, lewdness (such that it will be seen by others). Usually a crime.
EXHIBICIONISTA.
f, m, exhibitionist.
EXHIBIR.
v, to show, demonstrate ‖ to display, exhibit ‖ to produce documents or property (in litigation).
EXHORTAR.
v, to exhort ‖ to issue letters rogatory.
EXHORTO.
m, letters rogatory, formal request from one court to another. May be MANDATORIO or CARTA ORDEN (mandatory upon the other court), or SUPLICATORIO (requesting).
EXHUMACIÓN.
f, exhuming, exhumation.
EXHUMAR.
v, to exhume. May be a crime.
EXIGENCIA.
f, demand, requirement, exigency ‖ requirement.
EXIGIBLE.
adj, payable ‖ demandable, exigible.
EXIGIR.
v, to demand, require ‖ to levy, charge, or require payment (e.g. of a tax).
EXILIADO.
adj, exiled.
EXILIAR.
v, to exile (a person).
EXILIO.
m, exile ‖ expatriation ‖ place of exile.
EXIMENTE.
f, exempting or exonerating circumstance ‖ exemption ‖ adj, justifying, exculpatory, excusing ‖ exempting.
EXIMIR.
v, to exempt, exonerate.

EXIMIR DE DERECHOS.
exempt from duties.
EXISTENCIA.
f, existence ‖ life ‖ human life.
EXISTENCIA DE LAS PERSONAS.
existence of persons. May be VISIBLE (physical) or IDEAL (legal).
EXISTENCIAS.
f, stock, goods or products which have been reserved for consumption, use, or trade.
EXOGAMIA.
f, practise of marrying outside one's family, race, or territory.
EXONERACIÓN.
f, exoneration, excuse, exception, release.
EXONERAR.
v, to exonerate, exculpate ‖ to acquit, absolve ‖ to release, discharge ‖ to dismiss, remove.
EXONERAR DE IMPUESTOS.
to exempt from taxes.
EXONERAR DE RESPONSABILIDAD.
to free from liability.
EXORBITANTE.
adj, exorbitant.
EXORDIO.
m, exordium, introductory part of a speech, preamble.
EXPATRIACIÓN.
f, expatriation.
EXPECTANTE.
adj, expectant (e.g. condition or right or obligation that is fairly certain to arise in the future).
EXPECTATIVA.
f, expectation, expectancy.
EXPECTATIVA DE VIDA.
life expectancy.
EXPEDICIÓN.
f, dispatch of an order or decree ‖ remittance, shipment, consignment.
EXPEDICIÓN DE ADUANAS.
customhouse clearance.
EXPEDIDOR.
m, shipper ‖ forwarder ‖ maker, drawer.
EXPEDIENTE.
m, file (pertaining to a given matter) ‖ friendly action, proceeding which is not contentious ‖ non-contentious administrative action ‖ recourse, means (to resolve certain difficulties).
EXPEDIENTE DE APREMIO.
proceeding for collection.

EXPEDIENTE DE CONSTRUCCIÓN.
file regarding a request for a building permit.
EXPEDIENTE JUDICIAL.
court file (on a particular case).
EXPEDIENTE EN APELACIÓN.
record on appeal.
EXPEDIR.
v, to attend to (matters) ‖ to issue (e.g. a decision or resolution) ‖ to ship, remit, forward ‖ to facilitate, expedite ‖ to send, transmit (messages, telegrams, etc.).
EXPEDIR DISPOSICIONES.
to issue or hand down decisions.
EXPEDIR SENTENCIA.
to pronounce judgment, issue a decision.
EXPEDIR UN AUTO.
to issue a writ or other type of judicial pronouncement.
EXPEDIR UN CHEQUE.
to write or draw a check.
EXPEDIR UNA FACTURA.
to make out a bill or invoice.
EXPEDIR UNA ORDEN JUDICIAL.
to issue a judicial writ or order.
EXPEDIR UNA PATENTE.
to issue a patent.
EXPEDIR UNA RESOLUCIÓN.
to issue a decision.
EXPENDEDOR.
m, dealer, retail merchant, seller, vendor ‖ adj, spending.
EXPENDER.
v, to spend, expend ‖ to sell on commission ‖ to sell, handle, retail, deal in ‖ to circulate counterfeit money in small amounts.
EXPENDICIÓN DE MONEDA FALSA.
f, circulation of counterfeit money.
EXPENSAS.
f, expenses, costs.
EXPENSAS EN EL DIVORCIO.
litigation costs of divorce.
EXPERTICIA.
f, expertise, skill ‖ expert testimony ‖ expert advice ‖ expert appraisal.
EXPERTO.
m, expert.
EXPERTO EN HUELLAS DIGITALES.
fingerprint expert.
EXPERTO TRIBUTARIO.
tax expert.

EXPIAR.
v, to atone for.

EXPIRAR.
v, to expire, lapse ‖ to die.

EXPLICABLE.
adj, explainable, explicable.

EXPLICATIVO.
adj, explanatory.

EXPLÍCITO.
adj, explicit.

EXPLOTACIÓN.
f, exploitation ‖ use, employment ‖ abuse.

EXPLOTACIÓN DE INCAPACES.
See DEFRAUDACIÓN DE INCAPACES.

EXPLOTACIÓN DE UNA PATENTE.
use of a patent.

EXPLOTACIÓN FISCAL.
government use or operation.

EXPLOTAR.
v, to exploit, use, employ ‖ to extract minerals ‖ to exploit, abuse.

EXPOLIACIÓN.
f, extortion or illegal imposition of taxes and commissions.

EXPOLIAR.
v, to despoil, plunder.

EXPONENTE.
m, f, person who explains or expounds or exposes ‖ adj, explanatory.

EXPONER.
v, to show, set forth, demonstrate ‖ to reveal, expose ‖ to explain or interpret the meaning of something ‖ to declare, expound, explain ‖ to expose, jeopardize.

EXPORTACIÓN.
f, exportation.

EXPORTADOR.
m, exporter.

EXPORTAR.
v, to export.

EXPOSICIÓN.
f, exposition, exhibit, show ‖ explanation, clarification, interpretation ‖ risk, danger ‖ written petition (presented to a governmental authority), libel ‖ statement.

EXPOSICIÓN DE MOTIVOS.
purposes article (at the beginning of legislation), preliminary recitals.

EXPOSICIÓN DE NIÑOS.
abandonment of children.

EXPÓSITO.
m, foundling, abandoned newborn ‖ adj, abandoned.

EXPOSITOR.
m, commentator, exhibitor ‖ adj, expository.

EXPRESAMENTE.
adv, expressly, explicitly.

EXPRESAR.
v, to state, tell, express ‖ to show, depict.

EXPRESAR AGRAVIOS.
to plead.

EXPRESIÓN DE AGRAVIOS.
f, written bases of appeal filed with appellate court upon approval by lower court of simple right of appeal.

EXPRESO.
adj, express, clear, evident, patent, detailed ‖ intentional, voluntary.

EXPROMISIÓN.
f, means of carrying out a novation with or without debtor's knowledge or consent.

EXPROPIABLE.
adj, subject to expropriation or condemnation.

EXPROPIACIÓN.
f, expropriation, condemnation.

EXPROPIACIÓN FORZOSA.
expropriation, condemnation.

EXPROPIACIÓN ILEGAL.
illegal expropriation, taking.

EXPROPIACIÓN JUDICIAL.
judicial condemnation (of property).

EXPROPIADO.
m, party who has had property expropriated or condemned ‖ adj, expropriated.

EXPROPIADOR.
m, expropriator, condemner.

EXPROPIANTE.
See EXPROPIADOR.

EXPROPIAR.
v, to expropriate, condemn ‖ to take (as in a governmental taking).

EXPULSAR.
v, to expel, eject.

EXPULSIÓN.
f, expulsion, ejection ‖ dismissal ‖ exclusion ‖ deportation.

EXPULSIÓN DE EXTRANJEROS.
deportation of foreigners.

EXPURGAR.
v, to expunge, censor (printed material).

EXTENDER.
v, to authorize (e.g. a writing, resolution, etc.) ‖ to extend, expand (e.g. jurisdiction, law, etc.) ‖ to execute (e.g. an instrument) ‖ to prolong, extend.
EXTENDER EL PLAZO.
to extend the term.
EXTENDER LAS ACTAS.
to write up the minutes.
EXTENDER LOS ASIENTOS.
to make the entries ‖ to record the filings.
EXTENDER UN CONTRATO.
to draw up a contract.
EXTENDER UN CHEQUE.
to draw or write a check.
EXTENDER UNA PATENTE.
to issue a patent.
EXTENSIBLE.
adj, extendible.
EXTENSIÓN.
f, extension ‖ size, scope, range ‖ duration.
EXTENSIÓN DE LA HIPOTECA.
extension of property subject to the mortgage (usually, to all natural accessions, improvements, etc.).
EXTENSIÓN DE LAS PENAS.
duration of the (criminal) sentence.
EXTENSIÓN DEL PLAZO.
extension of the term.
EXTERMINAR.
v, to exterminate ‖ to devastate (by armed force).
EXTINCIÓN.
f, extinction, cessation, termination, disappearance (of species things, etc.) ‖ paying off, liquidation ‖ annulment ‖ extinguishment.
EXTINCIÓN DE ACCIONES.
termination of right to bring civil proceeding.
EXTINCIÓN DE DERECHOS.
termination of legal rights.
EXTINCIÓN DE LA ACCIÓN PENAL.
termination of right to bring a criminal action. May be due to the death of the accused, amnesty, the running of the statute of limitations, or the withdrawal of the complaint.
EXTINCIÓN DE LAS PENAS.
termination of punishment. May be due to the death of the accused, amnesty, the running of the statute of limitations, or the withdrawal of the complaint.

EXTINCIÓN DE LOS CONTRATOS.
termination of contracts. May be produced by nullification, rescission, revocation, or agreement of the parties.
EXTINGUIR.
v, to extinguish, end, terminate, expire ‖ to annul ‖ to pay off.
EXTINGUIRSE.
v, to expire, lapse.
EXTINTIVO.
adj, extinguishing, with power to extinguish (e.g. a right).
EXTORNAR.
v, to give a rebate (on an insurance policy upon its modification).
EXTORNO.
m, rebate, refund, drawback (e.g. on an insurance policy upon its modification).
EXTORSIÓN.
f, extortion, blackmail.
EXTORSIONADOR.
m, extortioner, extortionist.
EXTORSIONAR.
v, to blackmail, extort money.
EXTORSIONISTA.
m, f, extortionist, blackmailer.
EXTORSIVO.
adj, extortionate ‖ blackmail, related to blackmail.
EXTRACARTULAR.
adj, not on the record, unofficial ‖ not included in a negotiable instrument.
EXTRACONTABLE.
adj, not shown in the books.
EXTRACONTRACTUAL.
adj, extra-contractual, ex-contractu ‖ tortious, related to torts.
EXTRACTA.
f, true copy of a publicly-recorded document.
EXTRACTO.
m, summary, synthesis (of a writing) ‖ excerpt ‖ summary (of an administrative legal proceeding) ‖ title abstract or history, summary of a title of ownership registered in the public registry ‖ statement of (financial) account.
EXTRACTO DE BALANCE.
condensed balance sheet.
EXTRACTO DE CUENTA.
statement of account.
EXTRACTO DE LA LITIS.
record of the case.

EXTRADICIÓN.
f, extradition.
EXTRAJUDICIAL.
adj, extrajudicial.
EXTRAJUDICIALMENTE.
adv, extrajudicially, privately, by private agreement.
EXTRAJURÍDICO.
adj, extralegal.
EXTRALIMITACIÓN.
f, abuse of right or another's trust.
EXTRALIMITACIÓN DE MANDO.
military abuse of authority.
EXTRAMATRIMONIAL.
adj, extramarital.
EXTRANJERÍA.
n, alienage, status of being a foreigner, law which regulates foreigners.
EXTRANJERO.
m, foreigner, alien, person from foreign country ‖ adj, foreign.
EXTRANJERO ENEMIGO.
enemy alien.
EXTRAÑAMIENTO.
m, exile.
EXTRAÑAR.
v, to exile, banish.
EXTRAÑO.
m, foreigner, alien ‖ adj, foreign, alien ‖ strange.

EXTRAOFICIAL.
adj, unofficial.
EXTRAPETICIÓN.
f, motion for ruling on matter outside the confines of the case.
EXTRAPROCESAL.
adj, out-of-court.
EXTRATERRITORIAL.
adj, extraterritorial.
EXTRATERRITORIALIDAD.
f, extraterritoriality.
EXTRATRIBUTARIO.
adj, not for the purposes of taxation.
EXTRAVÍO.
m, loss (of something) ‖ harm, injury.
EXTREMISTA.
m, f, extremist ‖ adj, extremist.
EXTREMO.
m, extreme, end ‖ fact alleged by one the parties ‖ adj, extreme, terminal, last.
EXTREMOS DE LA ACCIÓN.
m, factual requirements of a claim, factual allegations which must be set forth to prove a claim upon which relief can be granted;
EXTREMOS DE LA DEMANDA.
m, factual requirements of the complaint.
EXTREMOS DE LA EXCEPCIÓN.
grounds of defense or objection or motion.
EXTRÍNSECO.
adj, extrinsic.

FÁBRICA.
f, factory, plant ‖ building.

FABRICACIÓN DE MONEDA FALSA.
f, manufacture of counterfeit money.

FABRICADO.
adj, fabricated, made-up ‖ manufactured.

FACCIÓN.
f, faction ‖ rebel group, gang, band ‖ act of war.

FACCIÓN DE TESTAMENTO.
testamentary capacity.

FACILITACIÓN AL ENEMIGO.
f, aiding the enemy.

FACILITAR INFORMES.
v, to furnish information.

"FACTO".
See HECHO.

FACTOR.
m, author, factor, maker ‖ railway freight clerk ‖ general agent, commercial agent, i.e. person who is charged with the administration of the business of a merchant which requires a special power of agency.

FACTORAJE.
m, agency.

FACTORES DEL DELITO.
factors which cause a crime to occur (e.g. personal and environmental elements which had an impact upon the criminal).

FACTORÍA.
f, agency ‖ agent's offices ‖ factory, industrial complex.

FACTURA.
f, invoice, bill, charge slip.

FACTURA COMERCIAL.
commercial invoice.

FACTURA COMÚN.
invoice. Opposed to FACTURA CONFORMADA.

FACTURA CONFORMADA.
invoice approved by payor.

FACTURA CONSULAR.
consular invoice.

FACTURA DE VENTA.
bill of sale.

FACTURAR.
v, to invoice, bill, charge ‖ to register freight (for railway travel).

FACTURERO.
m, invoice book.

FACTURISTA.
m, invoice clerk.

FACULTAD.
f, ability, capability ‖ faculty (of a university) ‖ power, right ‖ license, permission.

FACULTAD DE DERECHO.
law school.

FACULTAD DE DISPONER.
right of disposal (of goods).

FACULTAD DE IR AL PARO.
right to strike.

FACULTAD DE JUZGAR.
power to judge or decide.

FACULTAD DE NOMBRAR.
power of appointment or name.

FACULTAD DE OPTAR.
right to decide.

FACULTAD DE TESTAR.
testamentary capacity.

FACULTAD DISCRECIONAL.
See PODER DISCRECIONAL.

FACULTAD POLICIAL.
police power.

FACULTAD PROCESAL.
procedural right.
FACULTADES CONCURRENTES.
See PODERES CONCURRENTES.
FACULTADES DELEGADAS.
See PODERES DELEGADOS.
FACULTADES EXTRAORDINARIAS.
See PODERES EXTRAORDINARIOS.
FACULTADES REGLADAS.
See ACTO REGLADO.
FACULTADES RESERVADAS.
See PODERES RESERVADOS.
FACULTAR.
v, to empower, authorize, grant a power or
right.
FACULTATIVO.
adj, pertaining to a right or power ‖ optional.
FALACIA.
f, fallacy ‖ fraud, trickery, deceit.
FALANGISMO.
m, Falangism, Falange movement.
FALAZ.
m, defrauder, liar, deceiver ‖ adj, fallacious,
false, deceiving.
FALENCIA.
f, (manifest) lie, open deceit ‖ mistake, defect
‖ insolvency, commercial bankruptcy.
FALSA DENUNCIA.
false accusation (of a crime). Usually a crime
in itself.
FALSA INDICACIÓN DE PROCEDENCIA.
false labelling regarding the manufacture of
the goods.
FALSA PRUEBA.
false evidence. Includes false alibi or witness
or testimony, etc.
FALSAMENTE.
adv, falsely, deceitfully.
FALSARIO.
m, falsifier, liar ‖ false witness ‖ perjurer.
FALSAS APARIENCIAS.
false pretenses.
FALSAS NOTICIAS.
false information. May constitute a crime.
FALSEAR.
See FALSIFICAR.
FALSEDAD.
f, treason, disloyalty, duplicity ‖ trick, fraud ‖
falsehood, lie ‖ misrepresentation.
FALSEDAD DE DOCUMENTOS.
evidentiary falsehood, documentary evidence

in which untruths are intentionally put forth a
truths.
FALSEDAD FRAUDULENTA.
fraudulent misrepresentation.
FALSEDAD IDEOLÓGICA.
documentary evidence in which facts are fal
sified. Opposed to FALSEDAD MATERIAL.
FALSEDAD IMPORTANTE.
material misrepresentation.
FALSEDAD INCULPABLE.
innocent misrepresentation.
FALSEDAD INOCENTE.
See FALSEDAD INCULPABLE.
FALSEDAD JUSTICIABLE.
actionable misrepresentation.
FALSEDAD MATERIAL.
falsification or alteration of document.
FALSEDAD NEGLIGENTE.
negligent misrepresentation.
FALSÍA.
f, falseness, duplicity.
FALSIFICACIÓN.
f, falsification, adulteration, forgery (of ev
dence, money, documents, etc.).
FALSIFICACIÓN DE CHEQUES.
check forgery (either by signing the signatur
of the true maker or by increasing the amou
of the check).
FALSIFICACIÓN DE DOCUMENTOS.
falsification of documents (whether private o
public).
**FALSIFICACIÓN
DE MARCAS.**
trademark infringement.
FALSIFICACIÓN DE MONEDA.
counterfeiting or forging of currency.
**FALSIFICACIÓN
DE PATENTES.**
patent infringement.
**FALSIFICACIÓN DE SELLOS, TIMBRES
Y MARCAS.**
forgery of stamps, postal stamps, and offici
letterhead, issued by the government.
FALSIFICADO.
adj, falsified, forged.
FALSIFICADOR.
m, forger, falsifier ‖ counterfeiter.
FALSIFICADOR DE MONEDA.
counterfeiter.
FALSIFICAR.
v, to falsify, forge, counterfeit.

FALSO.
adj, false, untrue ‖ counterfeit, supposed ‖ deceptive.
FALSO COBRO.
m, return commission charged for uncollectible document.
FALSO PRETEXTO.
m, false pretense.
FALSO TESTIMONIO.
m, perjury, false testimony ‖ false evidence.
FALSO TÍTULO.
m, fraudulent title to property. Used to refer to crime of using a falsified title to property to commit fraud.
FALTA.
f, lack, omission ‖ defect ‖ flaw ‖ failure, breach ‖ fault, error ‖ infraction, violation, offense ‖ shortage.
FALTA DE ACEPTACIÓN.
nonacceptance ‖ refusal.
FALTA DE ASISTENCIA.
(employment) absenteeism.
FALTA DE AVISO.
failure to notify.
FALTA DE CAPACIDAD.
lack of legal capacity or competency.
FALTA DE CAUSA.
lack of (contractual) consideration.
See CAUSA.
FALTA DE COMPETENCIA.
improper venue or jurisdiction.
FALTA DE CUMPLIMIENTO.
failure to perform or comply, noncompliance, nonperformance, nonfulfillment, nonfeasance.
FALTA DE DISCIPLINA.
lack of discipline.
FALTA DE EJECUCIÓN.
See FALTA DE CUMPLIMIENTO.
FALTA DE ENTREGA.
nondelivery.
FALTA DE INTENCIÓN.
lack of intent.
FALTA DE JURISDICCIÓN.
lack of jurisdiction.
FALTA DE JUSTIFICACIÓN.
lack of justification ‖ lack of justifying defense.
FALTA DE MANUTENCIÓN.
nonsupport.
FALTA DE PAGO.
failure to pay, nonpayment.

FALTA DE PARTES.
lack of proper joinder of parties.
FALTA DE PERSONALIDAD.
lack of standing ‖ lack of proper legal representation.
FALTA DE PERSONERÍA.
See FALTA DE PERSONALIDAD.
FALTA DE PREAVISO.
lack of prior notice (e.g. of employment dismissal).
FALTA DE PROVOCACIÓN.
failure to provoke. To justify crime on grounds of self-defense, accused must prove his failure to provoke attack.
FALTA DE PRUEBA.
lack of evidence ‖ lack of persuasive evidence.
FALTA DE PUNTUALIDAD.
lateness, tardiness. Usually grounds for dismissal.
FALTA DE TRABAJO.
lack of work or employment.
FALTA DE USO.
lack of use, nonuse.
FALTA DE VIGILANCIA.
lack of due care.
FALTA DISCIPLINARIA.
breach of discipline.
FALTA GRAVE.
major or serious offense.
FALTA LEVE.
minor offense.
FALTANTE.
m, defaulting or non-appearing party, person who fails to appear in court ‖ lack, non-existence ‖ adj, lacking.
FALTAR.
v, to fail, breach ‖ to lack ‖ to be absent ‖ to default, fail to appear (in court) ‖ to be short, be lacking.
FALTAS.
f, minor offenses or infractions of the law.
FALTAS EN EL PROCEDIMIENTO.
procedural errors.
FALTAS INSUBSANABLES.
See DEFECTOS INSUBSANABLES.
FALTAS SUBSANABLES.
See DEFECTOS SUBSANABLES.
FALTO.
adj, defective, lacking ‖ scarce.
FALLA.
f, failure, breakdown ‖ defect, fault.

FALLA DE CAUSA.
failure of consideration.
FALLA EN CAJA.
cash shortage.
FALLAR.
v, to issue or render a decision or judgment or sentence ‖ to sentence, decide (a case), rule ‖ to judge ‖ to err, make a mistake, to fail, break down ‖ to be lacking.
FALLAR SIN LUGAR.
to dismiss.
FALLECIMIENTO.
m, death.
FALLIDO.
m, adj, bankrupt, insolvent.
FALLIDO CULPABLE.
bankrupt due to negligence.
FALLIDO FRAUDULENTO.
fraudulent bankrupt.
FALLIDO REHABILITADO.
discharged bankrupt.
FALLO.
m, arbitration award ‖ error, mistake ‖ sentence, judgment, decision, ruling, opinion, finding, verdict. Usually refers to final decision.
FALLO ADMINISTRATIVO.
executive order.
FALLO ARBITRAL.
arbitration award.
FALLO CONDENATORIO.
(criminal) conviction.
FALLO CONDICIONADO.
conditional judgment.
FALLO DE CULPABILIDAD.
See FALLO CONDICIONADO.
FALLO DEL JURADO.
jury verdict.
FALLO DEFINITIVO.
final judgment or sentence or decision or ruling.
FALLO JUDICIAL.
judicial decision or ruling.
FALLO PLENARIO.
plenary decision ‖ decision of several legally identical cases heard by the various courts in a certain chamber together, such that the decision has the effect of precedence in future cases decided by courts of that chamber and lower courts. Only another FALLO PLENARIO pertaining to the same issues may overrule a prior FALLO PLENARIO.

FALLO SIMULADO.
See FALLO FABRICADO.
FAMA.
f, fame ‖ reputation, name ‖ common knowledge ‖ commonly held opinion or belief ‖ good name or reputation.
FAMA PÚBLICA.
public reputation.
FAMILIA.
m, family (usually including several degrees of relations).
FAMILIA ADOPTIVA.
adoptive family (includes adopting parents and adopted child).
FAMILIA
DE ORIGEN.
natural parents (of adopted child).
FAMILIA ESTRICTA.
family (consisting of parents and children).
FAMILIA EXTENSA.
extended family.
FAMILIA ILEGÍTIMA.
illegitimate family, family created without benefit of marriage.
FAMILIA LABORAL.
domestic work carried out by a family or group of related persons.
FAMILIA MATRIARCAL.
matriarchal family.
FAMILIA NATURAL.
natural family ‖ de facto family, family created without benefit of marriage.
FAMILIA PATRIARCAL.
patriarchal family.
FAMILIAR.
m, family characteristic ‖ relation ‖ close friend ‖ servant, help ‖ adj, family, pertaining to the family ‖ familiar, known ‖ domestic.
FAMULATO.
m, position or post of a domestic servant.
FAMULICIO.
m, theft (by or with the help of a domestic servant).
FANÁTICO.
m, fanatic ‖ fan ‖ adj, fanatical.
FANATISMO.
m, fanaticism.
F.A.S.
See CLÁUSULA F.A.S.
FASCISMO.
m, fascism.

FATAL.
adj, fatal, deadly ‖ obligatory ‖ inevitable, unavoidable.

FATIGA.
f, fatigue, tiredness ‖ extraordinary work ‖ bother, suffering.

FAVOR.
m, favor ‖ help, assistance, aid ‖ honor, grace ‖ kindness ‖ sexual favor ‖ accommodation.

FAVORECEDOR.
m, endorser of an accommodation bill ‖ helper ‖ client, customer ‖ adj, favoring, helping.

FAVORECIDO.
m, maker of an accommodation bill ‖ winner in any drawing of lots; adj, favored.

FE.
f, belief ‖ faith, confidence, credence ‖ confirmation ‖ authentication, certification, affirmation (of the truth of a document) ‖ certificate, testimonial (of the truth of a document) ‖ solemn oath.

FE CONYUGAL.
fidelity, confidence of marital fidelity.

FE DE CONOCIMIENTO.
verification of the parties (by a special notary public in public documents), confirmation by a notary that the parties signing a public document are who they say they are. May be confirmed by personal knowledge or by witnesses.

FE DE ERRATAS.
list of errata, notice of misprints.

FE DE LIVORES.
special public notary's statement to describe the details of a death, injury, etc.

FE DE SOLTERÍA.
certificate of bachelorhood, certificate that one has not been married before.

FE DE VIDA.
certificate of existence, certificate that a person is or was alive at a given moment.

FE DE VIUDEDAD.
certificate of widowhood, certificate that one was widowed and has not remarried.

FE NOTARIAL.
authority which a notary's certification holds.

FE PROVISIONAL.
temporary presumption of truth (of an impugned document).

FE PÚBLICA.
legal authority (granted notary publics, judicial clerks, stock brokers, special notary pu-

blics (ESCRIBANOS), consuls, and other functionaries to authenticate or certify the authenticity of documents).

FE PÚNICA.
bad faith.

FECUNDACIÓN.
f, fertilization, insemination.

FECUNDACIÓN ARTIFICIAL.
artificial insemination.

FECHA.
f, date, day.

FECHA CIERTA.
date for which there is sufficient evidentiary proof as to be effective as against third parties.

FECHA DE REGISTRO.
date of record ‖ date of registration or filing.

FECHA DE VALOR.
effective date.

FECHA DE VIGENCIA.
See FECHA DE VALOR.

FECHA EFECTIVA.
effective date.

FECHA UT RETRO.
See FECHA UT SUPRA.

FECHA UT SUPRA.
aforementioned date.

FECHAR.
v, to date (e.g. a document).

FECHO.
adj, done, executed, carried out ‖ issued.

FECHORÍA.
f, malfeasance, misdeed.

FEDATARIO.
m, person authorized to authenticate documents pursuant to FE PÚBLICA (e.g. county clerk).

FEDERACIÓN.
f, federation, union, alliance, association ‖ federal state.

FEDERAL.
m, federal party ‖ adj, federal, pertaining a federation ‖ national, pertaining to national powers (versus state powers).

FEDERALISMO.
m, federalism.

FEDERALIZAR.
v, to federalize (from a non-federal status, e.g. making a provincial city into a federal entity, such as Washington, D.C.).

FEDERAR.
v, to federate, confederate.

FEDERARSE.
v, to join together in a federation ‖ to form an association.

FEHACIENTE.
adj, credible ‖ evidencing, certifying, attesting ‖ authentic, true, convincing. Said of documents which meet the rules of evidence for submission.

FELÓN.
m, evil or wicked person ‖ felon, criminal ‖ adj, wicked, evil ‖ felonious.

FELONA.
f, female FELÓN.

FELONÍA.
f, treachery, disloyalty ‖ felony.

FEMINISMO.
m, feminism.

FERIA.
f, holiday, public holiday, special day off from work (during the work week) ‖ legal holiday or holidays. Many South American nations enjoy a month of legal holidays starting on or near December 25.

FERIA JUDICIAL.
legal holiday.

FERIADO.
m, day of rest, day off ‖ days on which the organs of justice do not function and which are not computed within judicial time period.

FERIADO NACIONAL.
national or public or bank holiday.

FERROCARRIL.
m, train, railroad.

FESTIVIDAD.
f, festivity ‖ also see DÍA FESTIVO.

FETICIDA.
f, m, person who kills a fetus (e.g. mother herself or another person ‖ adj, feticidal.

FETICIDIO.
m, feticide, abortion.

FETICHISMO.
m, fetishism, sexual arousal deriving from objects.

FETO.
m, fetus.

FEUDALISMO.
m, feudalism.

FIABLE.
adj, responsible, trustworthy.

FIADO.
m, person under bond ‖ adj, purchased on credit or on time payments.

FIADOR.
m, bondsman, bailsman ‖ surety (if jointly liable with person primarily liable) ‖ guarantor (if secondarily liable after person who is primarily liable).

FIADOR CIVIL.
bondsman or guarantor or surety (see FIADOR) of obligation regulated by a civil code. See FIADOR.

FIADOR COMERCIAL.
FIADOR who guaranties a commercial transaction. See FIADOR.

FIADOR JUDICIAL.
judgment bondsman or bailsman (of a criminal, criminally accused or party who has lost a civil action).

FIADOR LEGAL.
party who must post a legal bond or guaranty. See FIADOR.

FIADOR MANCOMUNADO.
co-surety, joint surety. See FIADOR.

FIADOR MERCANTIL.
See FIADOR COMERCIAL.

FIADOR SOLIDARIO.
surety. See FIADOR.

FIANZA.
f, bond, bail, guaranty, security, pledge, collateral ‖ guaranty, bond contract.

FIANZA A LAS RESULTAS DEL JUICIO.
judgment bond, bond posted to guaranty payment of a monetary liability or obligation resulting from a judicial decision.

FIANZA CARCELARIA.
criminal bail.

FIANZA COMERCIAL.
See FIANZA MERCANTIL.

FIANZA CONFORME A LA LEY.
statutory bond.

FIANZA CONVENCIONAL.
voluntary bond or guaranty (posted by a person who is not required to do so by law).

FIANZA DE ADUANA.
customs bond.

FIANZA DE ALMACÉN.
warehouse bond.

FIANZA DE APELACIÓN.
appeal bond.

IANZA DE ARRAIGO.
court bond (posted by plaintiff pursuant to an EXCEPCIÓN DE ARRAIGO).
IANZA DE AVERÍAS.
average bond.
IANZA DE CONSERVACIÓN.
maintenance bond.
IANZA DE CONTRATISTA.
contract bond.
IANZA DE CUMPLIMIENTO.
performance bond. Includes supply and construction bond.
IANZA DE DECLARACIÓN ÚNICA.
single-entry bond.
IANZA DE DEMANDADO.
defendant's bond.
IANZA DE DEPÓSITO.
warehouse bond.
IANZA DE DERECHO.
appearance bond.
IANZA DE DESEMBARQUE.
landing bond.
IANZA DE EMBARGO.
attachment bond.
IANZA DE ENTREDICHO.
injunction bond.
IANZA DE EXPORTACIÓN.
export bond.
IANZA DE FIDELIDAD.
fiduciary bond.
IANZA DE GARANTÍA.
surety bond.
IANZA DE LICITADOR.
bid bond.
IANZA DE LITIGANTE.
court bond.
IANZA DE MANUTENCIÓN.
maintenance bond.
IANZA DE NEUTRALIDAD.
neutrality bond.
IANZA DE PAGO.
payment bond.
IANZA DE POSTURA.
bid bond.
IANZA DE SUBASTADOR.
auctioneer's bond.
IANZA DEL PROCESADO EN LIBERTAD.
penal or criminal bond (posted to guaranty appearance of defendant in court).
IANZA EN AVERÍA GRUESA.
general average bond.

FIANZA ESPECIAL.
special bail, bail above or to the action.
FIANZA GENERAL.
general bond (posted to guaranty not only the principal obligation, but the incidental obligations, etc.).
FIANZA HIPOTECARIA.
mortgage.
FIANZA JUDICIAL.
judicial bond, judicially-imposed bond or guaranty.
FIANZA LEGAL.
legal bond, legal guaranty, one required by law.
FIANZA MANCOMUNADA.
joint bond.
FIANZA MERCANTIL.
performance bond or guaranty of commercial transaction.
FIANZA NOTARIAL.
bond granted before a notary public.
FIANZA PARTICULAR.
personal surety.
FIANZA PERSONAL.
See FIANZA PARTICULAR.
FIANZA PIGNORATICIA.
pledge, chattel mortgage.
FIANZA PRENDARIA.
See FIANZA PIGNORATICIA.
FIANZA REIVINDICATORIA.
replevin bond.
FIANZA SIMPLE.
common bail.
FIANZA SOLIDARIA.
surety or suretyship bond ‖ surety contract.
FIANZA VOLUNTARIA.
See FIANZA CONVENCIONAL.
FIAR.
v, to assure, guaranty ‖ to bond, place bond, or bail for ‖ to sell on credit or on time.
FIAT.
m, fiat.
FICCIÓN.
f, fiction ‖ falsity ‖ invention.
FICCIÓN DE DERECHO.
legal fiction.
FICCIÓN JURÍDICA.
See FICCIÓN DE DERECHO.
FICCIÓN LEGAL.
See FICCIÓN DE DERECHO.

FICTA.
See CONFESIÓN FICTA.
FICTICIO.
adj, fictitious.
FICTO.
adj, constructive ‖ fictitious.
FICHA DACTILOSCÓPICA.
record of fingerprints.
FIDEDIGNO.
adj, trustworthy.
FIDEICOMISARIO.
m, trustee ‖ trust beneficiary ‖ representative
of debenture holders ‖ executor (male), exe-
cutrix (female) ‖ adj, trust.
FIDEICOMISARIO JUDICIAL.
judicial trustee.
FIDEICOMISO.
m, trust ‖ trusteeship.
FIDEICOMISO ACTIVO.
active trust.
FIDEICOMISO CARITATIVO.
charitable trust.
FIDEICOMISO CIVIL.
See FIDEICOMISO.
FIDEICOMISO COMERCIAL.
business trust.
FIDEICOMISO CONDICIONAL.
contingent or conditional trust.
FIDEICOMISO CONSERVATORIO.
testamentary trust.
FIDEICOMISO DE BENEFICENCIA.
See FIDEICOMISO PÚBLICO.
**FIDEICOMISO DE FONDOS
DEPOSITADOS.**
funded trust.
FIDEICOMISO DE PENSIONES.
pension trust.
FIDEICOMISO DE SEGURO DE VIDA.
life-insurance trust.
FIDEICOMISO DEFINIDO.
direct or express trust.
FIDEICOMISO DIRECTO.
See FIDEICOMISO DEFINIDO.
FIDEICOMISO DISCRECIONAL.
discretionary trust.
FIDEICOMISO EXPRESO.
See FIDEICOMISO DEFINIDO.
FIDEICOMISO FAMILIAR.
testamentary trust.
FIDEICOMISO FORMALIZADO.
executed or perfect trust.

FIDEICOMISO FORZOSO.
trust required by law.
FIDEICOMISO IMPLÍCITO.
implied trust.
FIDEICOMISO IMPUESTO.
trust required by law.
FIDEICOMISO MÚLTIPLE.
multiple trust.
**FIDEICOMISO PARA
LOS PRÓDIGOS.**
spendthrift trust.
FIDEICOMISO PARTICULAR.
private trust.
FIDEICOMISO PERPETUO.
perpetual trust.
FIDEICOMISO POR FORMALIZAR.
executory trust.
**FIDEICOMISO POR
PRESUNCIÓN LEGAL.**
See FIDEICOMISO PRESUNTO.
FIDEICOMISO PRESUNTO.
constructive trust.
FIDEICOMISO PRIVADO.
See FIDEICOMISO PARTICULAR.
FIDEICOMISO PÚBLICO.
public trust.
FIDEICOMISO PURO.
simple trust.
FIDEICOMISO SIMPLE.
See FIDEICOMISO PURO.
FIDEICOMISO RESULTANTE.
resulting trust.
FIDEICOMISO SECRETO.
secret trust.
**FIDEICOMISO SIN DEPÓSITO
DE FONDOS.**
unfunded trust.
FIDEICOMISO SINGULAR.
private trust.
FIDEICOMISO SOBRENTENDIDO.
implied trust.
FIDEICOMISO TESTAMENTARIO.
testamentary trust.
FIDEICOMISO UNIVERSAL.
trust covering an entire estate.
FIDEICOMISO VOLUNTARIO.
voluntary trust.
FIDEICOMITENTE.
m, trustor, settler, cestui que trust.
FIDELIDAD.
f, fidelity, faithfulness.

FIDELIDAD CONYUGAL.
marital fidelity.

FIDUCIA.
See CONTRATO FIDUCIARIO.

FIDUCIARIO.
m, trustee ‖ type of trustee who is viewed as a first heir to hold property under stated conditions for a second heir (the beneficiary) ‖ fiduciary ‖ adj, fiduciary.

FIEL.
m, faithful spouse ‖ religious believer ‖ official charged with assuring compliance with orders, laws, or regulations ‖ adj, faithful (to the truth or the original document), accurate ‖ loyal, faithful.

FIEL CONTRASTE.
public inspector of weights and measures.

FIEL COPIA.
f, true copy.

FIEL CUMPLIMIENTO.
m, faithful performance or observance.

FIELATO.
m, position and office of public inspector (especially if municipal) ‖ excise tax collection office.

FIGURA DE DELITO.
f, legal definition or elements of crime or offense.

FIGURA DELICTIVA.
See FIGURA DE DELITO.

FIGURA PENAL.
See FIGURA DE DELITO.

FIJACIÓN DE PRECIOS.
f, price fixing (between companies) ‖ setting of maximum prices (by government).

FIJAR.
v, to fix ‖ to assess, determine.

FIJAR LOS DAÑOS Y PERJUICIOS.
to assess damages.

FILIACIÓN.
f, filiation, relationship between parents and children. May be ADOPTIVA (by adoption); DE DERECHO (by law); DE HECHO (illegitimate; biological); DESCONOCIDA (unknown); ILEGÍTIMA (illegitimate) ‖ LEGÍTIMA (legitimate); MATERNA (maternal); PATERNA (paternal).

FILIAL.
adj, filial.

FILICIDA.
f, m, filicide, parent who murders his or her child.

FILICIDIO.
m, filicide, killing of child (by parent).

FILIGRANA.
f, watermark (on paper).

FILÍPICA.
f, invective.

FILOSOFÍA DEL DERECHO.
f, jurisprudence ‖ philosophy of law.

FIN.
m, end, finale, termination, conclusion ‖ death ‖ end, purpose, objective, object.

FIN DE LA EXISTENCIA DE LAS PERSONAS JURÍDICAS.
termination of artificial persons. May occur by decision of members or by law.

FIN DE LA EXISTENCIA DE LAS PERSONAS VISIBLES.
death of natural persons.

FIN DEL PROCESO.
(chronological) end of the proceedings ‖ purpose of the proceedings.

FINADO.
m, dead person ‖ adj, deceased.

FINAL.
m, final, end, conclusion ‖ adj, final, end ‖ ending, concluding.

FINANCIACIÓN.
f, financing.

FINANCIAMIENTO.
m, financing, action of financing.

FINANCIAR.
v, to finance.

FINANCIERA.
f, finance company ‖ adj, finance, financial, pertaining to finance.

FINANCIERO.
m, financier ‖ adj, finance, financial, pertaining to finance. Usually used to refer to Ministry of Finance, stock market, banking, or big industry.

FINANZAS.
f, finances.

FINANZAS PÚBLICAS.
public finances ‖ public resources and income collected by the government.

FINAR.
v, to die.

FINCA.
f, estate of real property (whether urban or rural) ‖ plot (of land) ‖ farm.

FINCA COLINDANTE.
contiguous or neighboring property.

FINCA RÚSTICA.
rural property.

FINCA URBANA.
urban property.

FINCAR.
v, to acquire real estate ‖ to base, found (e.g. an argument).

FINES DEL MATRIMONIO.
purposes of or reasons for marriage.

FINIQUITAR.
v, to extinguish (a debt) ‖ to close (an account) ‖ to issue a writing which extinguishes a debt).

FINIQUITO.
m, extinction, release (of a debt) ‖ closing of an account ‖ quittance, release, acquittance, writing which extinguishes a debt.

FIRMA.
f, signature (of first and last name) ‖ firm, company, business ‖ firm name.

FIRMA A RUEGO.
signature of a document or contract on behalf of a person who, due to incapacity, cannot sign.

FIRMA COMERCIAL.
commercial firm, company, business ‖ firm signature.

FIRMA DE FAVOR.
accommodation endorsement.

FIRMA DE LETRADO.
attorney's signature, signature of a practicing attorney who is a member of the bar association.

FIRMA EN BLANCO.
signature of an uncompleted document.

FIRMA ENTERA.
complete signature (consisting of the full name of the signer).

FIRMA FALSIFICADA.
falsified signature, forged signature. Usually a crime.

FIRMA MEDIA.
partial signature.

FIRMA RECONOCIDA.
signature legally recognized by signatory.

FIRMA SANCIONADA.
authorized signature.

FIRMA SOCIAL.
See RAZÓN SOCIAL.

FIRMADA.
adj, signed.

FIRMADO DE PROPIO PUÑO.
See FIRMADO DE PUÑO.

FIRMADO DE PUÑO.
personally signed.

FIRMADO Y SELLADO POR.
signed and sealed by, under the hand and sea of.

FIRMADOR.
See FIRMANTE.

FIRMANTE.
m, signer, signatory ‖ maker (of a document

FIRMANTE CONJUNTO.
cosigner.

FIRMANTE POR ACOMODACIÓN.
accommodation maker or endorser.

FIRMAR.
v, to sign, execute.

FIRME.
adj, final (e.g. decision or sentence from whic there is no further recourse).

FIRMÓN.
See ABOGADO FIRMÓN.

FISCAL.
m, prosecutor, prosecuting attorney, state attorney, government attorney ‖ governme representative ‖ election supervisor ‖ adj, fi cal, pertaining to public treasury or funds financial ‖ prosecution, prosecuting, pertai ing to the prosecutor ‖ auditor ‖ controller.

FISCAL DE CÁMARA.
state's attorney on appeal, attorney who re resents the government before the appe courts.

FISCAL DE CUENTAS.
auditor.

FISCAL DE DISTRITO.
district attorney.

FISCAL DE ESTADO.
state's attorney (designated to defend ar protect state property and interests).

FISCAL GENERAL.
attorney general.

FISCAL TOGADO.
judge advocate (before the higher courts military justice).

FISCALÍA.
f, government attorney's office ‖ inspector

office ‖ controller or auditor's office ‖ district attorney or prosecutor's office ‖ position, function, and office of a FISCAL.

FISCALISTA.
adj, pertaining to the treasury.

FISCALIZACIÓN.
f, control, supervision ‖ investigation, inspection.

FISCALIZADOR.
m, inspector ‖ adj, investigating.

FISCALIZAR.
v, to act as state's attorney ‖ to criticize, judge ‖ to inspect ‖ to control.

FISCO.
m, public or national treasury ‖ state treasury.

FISCO MUNICIPAL.
city government ‖ city treasury.

FÍSICO.
adj, physical.

FLAGELACIÓN.
f, flagellation.

FLAGRANTE.
adj, flagrant.

FLAGRANTE DELITO.
flagrante delicto.

FLETADOR.
m, freighter, charterer.

FLETAMENTO.
m, charter contract (for a vessel or part thereof).

FLETAMENTO A PLAZO.
See FLETAMENTO POR TIEMPO.

FLETAMENTO CON OPERACIÓN POR CUENTA DEL ARRENDADOR.
gross charter.

FLETAMENTO CON OPERACIÓN POR CUENTA DEL ARRENDATARIO.
net charter.

FLETAMENTO POR TIEMPO.
time charter.

FLETAMENTO POR VIAJE REDONDO.
voyage charter.

FLETAMIENTO.
See FLETAMENTO.

FLETANTE.
m, ship owner who charters to a charterer.

FLETAR.
v, to charter (a vessel or part thereof to ship goods or persons) ‖ to freight, affreight.

FLETE.
m, cargo, shipment ‖ transportation ‖ freight

or transportation charge or rate ‖ (ship) chartering fee ‖ charter price ‖ freight.

FLETE BRUTO.
gross freight.

FLETE EVENTUAL.
freight contingency, collectible freight.

FLETE MARÍTIMO.
ocean freight.

FLETE NETO.
net freight.

FLETERO.
m, freight carrier ‖ also see FLETADOR.

FLEXIBLE.
adj, flexible ‖ tolerant, indulgent ‖ agreeing ‖ easily reformed (re constitutions).

FLOTA.
f, merchant marine or navy ‖ navy fleet, naval flotilla.

FLOTAR
UN EMPRÉSTITO.
v, to float a loan.

FLUVIAL.
adj, fluvial, river.

F.M.I.
See FONDO MONETARIO INTERNACIONAL.

F.O.B.
See CLÁUSULA F.O.B.

"FOEDUS".
m, alliance, league ‖ pact, treaty.

FOJA.
f, sheet, leaf (of paper).

FOLIAR.
v, to number (the leaves of a file, book, etc.).

FOLIO.
m, leaf, folio (of a book, file, etc.).

FOMENTAR.
v, to found, organize ‖ to develop ‖ to excite ‖ to foster, encourage, promote.

FOMENTO.
m, development ‖ fostering, encouragement ‖ promotion.

FONDEO.
m, inspection of ship's cargo.

FONDO.
m, fund ‖ question of law (in contrast to procedural question).

FONDO AMORTIZANTE.
sinking fund.

FONDO COMÚN.
general fund (of a corporation, derived from shareholder investments).

FONDO COMÚN DE INVERSIÓN.
mutual fund, mutual investment fund which invests in a variety of securities on the part of its investors.

FONDO DE AMORTIZACIÓN.
sinking fund.

FONDO DE CAMBIOS.
fund for control of foreign exchange.

FONDO DE COMERCIO.
going concern ‖ commercial establishment (inclusive of all property and rights, whether tangible or intangible).

FONDO DE CONVERSIÓN.
See FONDO DE CAMBIOS.

FONDO DE ESTABILIZACIÓN.
equalization fund, stabilization fund.

FONDO DE GARANTÍA.
guaranty fund ‖ worker compensation fund (for compensation which a company must pay for illness or injury of a worker).

FONDO DE IGUALIZACIÓN.
See FONDO DE ESTABILIZACIÓN.

FONDO DE LA CUESTIÓN.
merits of the case ‖ heart of the matter.

FONDO DE PREVISIÓN.
pension fund ‖ contingency fund ‖ reserve fund.

FONDO DE RESERVA.
reserve fund (for payment of normal dividends and other payments). Set aside within the corporation.

FONDO ESPECIAL.
special fund.

FONDO JUBILATORIO.
pension fund.

FONDO MUTUALISTA.
mutual fund.

FONDO RESERVADO.
reserve fund.

FONDO SOCIAL.
See CAPITAL SOCIAL.

FONDO MONETARIO INTERNACIONAL.
International Monetary Fund.

FONDOS.
m, funds, accounts ‖ coins, bills of exchange, securities, and negotiable instruments.

FONDOS BLOQUEADOS.
blocked or frozen funds.

FONDOS CONGELADOS.
See FONDOS BLOQUEADOS.

FONDOS DE AMORTIZACIÓN.
sinking fund ‖ amortization reserve (set aside to pay a debt) ‖ repair fund (set aside to pay for repair of property).

FONDOS DE FIDEICOMISO.
See FONDOS FIDUCIARIOS.

FONDOS DEL CONCURSO.
bankruptcy estate, bankrupt's property.

FONDOS DISPONIBLES.
disposable capital or funds, monies of a corporation or partnership which are at its immediate disposal.

FONDOS FIDUCIARIOS.
trust funds.

FONDOS LÍQUIDOS.
liquid funds ‖ dividend appropriations fund (of a corporation), reserve payable to shareholders ‖ capital payable to shareholders upon dissolution.

FONDOS PÚBLICOS.
government assets, public funds (inclusive of money and securities and outstanding obligations) ‖ government securities and obligations.

FORAJIDO.
m, outlaw, fugitive from justice.

FORAL.
adj, pertaining to FUERO ‖ pertaining to provincial or local law (in contrast to national law) ‖ descriptive of property over which emphyteusis rights have been granted.

FORENSE.
adj, forensic ‖ legal, juridical.

FORERO.
m, owner of property leased pursuant to emphyteusis contract ‖ type of leaseholder who uses property pursuant to an emphyteusis contract ‖ adj, pertaining to FUERO ‖ jurisdictional ‖ venue, pertaining to venue ‖ statutory, code ‖ customary, pertaining to custom or usage.

FORMA.
f, form, procedure (as opposed to substance) ‖ means or method of proceeding (in an action or contract or other legal act) ‖ expression of the will of the parties.

FORMA DE LOS ACTOS JURÍDICOS.
legal formalities (to be observed in legal acts). Refers to necessity of witnesses, special notary public, etc.

FORMA ESPECIAL.
procedure or formalities established by a contract or a private legal document.
FORMA LEGAL.
legal formalities or procedure (required by a particular transaction). Opposed to FORMA LIBRE.
FORMA LIBRE.
unregulated procedure, procedure in which no formalities are legally required. See FORMA LEGAL.
FORMACIÓN DE CAUSAS.
m, initiation of a criminal complaint.
FORMACIÓN DE LAS LEYES.
f, enactment procedure ‖ establishment of laws.
FORMACIÓN PROFESIONAL.
f, professional education and training (usually technical or scientific).
FORMAL.
adj, procedural, pertaining to form or procedure (as opposed to substance) ‖ express (as opposed to implicit) ‖ formal.
FORMALIDAD.
f, dependability ‖ formality, formal requirement of a legal transaction ‖ punctuality, timeliness, punctual compliance ‖ requirement (of a contract or other legal act) ‖ red tape, legal procedure or formalities (in a lawsuit, etc.).
FORMALIDADES.
f, formalities.
FORMALISMO.
m, formalism.
FORMALIZAR.
v, to observe legal procedure or formalities ‖ to formalize (e.g. by marriage, etc.).
FORMALIZAR PROTESTO.
to protest.
FORMAR.
v, to form ‖ to draw up ‖ to fashion ‖ to educate, raise.
FORMAR EXPEDIENTE A ALGUIEN.
to initiate an administrative investigation (e.g. into suspicious behavior of employee).
FORMAR PARTIDO.
to form a political party ‖ to request or induce persons to act in a certain way.
FORMAR PROCESO.
to bring suit.

FORMAR SUMARIO.
to formally start a preliminary investigation.
FORMAS DE GOBIERNO.
forms of government.
FORMAS DE LOS CONTRATOS.
legal formalities (to be observed in executing contracts).
FORMAS DE LOS TESTAMENTOS.
legal formalities (to be observed in executing wills).
FORMAS DE MATRIMONIO.
forms of marriage procedures.
FORMAS LEGALES.
legal procedure, procedure established by law.
FORMAS PROCESALES.
legal procedure pertaining to litigation.
FORMAS SOLEMNES.
legal or formal requisites (for validity of an act).
FÓRMULA.
f, formula ‖ settlement proposal ‖ settlement agreement ‖ settlement clause ‖ slate (of candidate).
FÓRMULA DE PROPUESTA.
proposal.
FORMULAR.
v, to formulate, draw up (e.g. a charge or accusation, or the terms of a power of attorney, etc.) ‖ to file a complaint or petition.
FORMULAR CARGOS.
to bring charges.
FORMULAR DENUNCIA.
to file an accusation or complaint.
FORMULAR OPOSICIÓN.
to object.
FORMULAR UN REPARO.
to file an objection.
FORMULAR UNA RECLAMACIÓN.
to file a claim.
FORMULARIO.
m, procedural code book ‖ form, questionnaire ‖ adj, formalistic, pursuant to form or formalities.
FORMULARIO DE CONTRATO.
contract form.
FORMULARIO DE PROPUESTA.
bidding blank, proposal form.
FORMULARIO TIMBRADO.
stamped form ‖ stamped paper.
FORMULARIO VALORADO.
See FORMULARIO TIMBRADO.

FORMULISMO.
m, formalism, red tape, exaggerated formality.
FORNICACIÓN.
f, fornication.
FORNICADOR.
m, fornicator.
FORO.
m, trial bar, entirety of trial attorneys ‖ association of trial attorneys ‖ emphyteusis contract or right ‖ forum ‖ lease, rental ‖ leasehold.
FORTUITO.
adj, fortuitous ‖ also see CASO FORTUITO.
FORTUNA DE MAR.
f, navy property (includes vessels, cargo, and other accessories) ‖ uninsured maritime risks, maritime risks which the shipping owner or transporter does not insure against ‖ legal responsibility of the ship owner for maritime risks.
"FORUM ARRESTI".
forum arresti. Refers in maritime law to forum which will judge a case of piracy in open waters between ships of different nationalities: usually where the vessel is attached or makes its first port of call.
FORZADAMENTE.
adv, forcibly.
FORZADO.
m, prisoner sentenced to forced labor ‖ adj, obligatory ‖ coerced, forced.
FORZADOR.
m, rapist ‖ coercer, forcer.
FORZAR.
v, to force, coerce (e.g. an action) ‖ to break, force (e.g. a door) ‖ to take by force (e.g. in battle) ‖ to rape (e.g. a woman).
FORZOSO.
adj, obligatory, compulsory ‖ inexcusable ‖ against the law.
FRACASAR.
v, to fail, be unsuccessful.
FRACASO.
m, failure, ruin.
FRACTURA.
f, breaking (into a structure). Constitutes an element of crime of ROBO.
FRAGANTE.
See FLAGRANTE.
FRAGUAR.
v, to falsify ‖ to plot, scheme.

FRAGUAR UNA FIRMA.
to forge a signature.
FRANCO.
m, leave of absence ‖ adj, free, no charge ‖ exempt ‖ privileged ‖ tax- or duty-free.
FRANCO A BORDO.
See CLÁUSULA F.O.B.
FRANCO AL COSTADO VAPOR.
See CLÁUSULA F.A.S.
FRANCO BORDO.
free board certificate.
FRANCO DE DERECHOS.
duty-free.
FRANCO EN ALMACÉN.
ex warehouse.
FRANCO EN EL MUELLE.
free on dock, ex quay.
FRANCO FUERA DEL BUQUE.
free alongside, ex ship.
FRANCO SOBRE RIELES.
free on cars, F.O.B. cars.
FRANCO SOBRE VAGÓN.
See FRANCO SOBRE RIELES.
FRANQUEAR.
v, to exempt, except (e.g. from taxes, duties, charges, etc) ‖ to free (e.g. from impediments, problems) ‖ to emancipate (a slave) ‖ to pay postal fees (for transmittal of correspondence or packages).
FRANQUEO.
m, postage.
FRANQUICIA.
f, franchise ‖ grant, privilege ‖ exempt losses, losses which are not paid by an insurance policy because they fall within the insurance deductible ‖ percentage payable on insured maritime losses ‖ postal fees ‖ exemption from payment of certain fees and charges (usually customs duties).
FRANQUICIA ADUANERA.
exemption from customs duties.
FRANQUICIA ARANCELARIA.
exemption from customs duties.
FRANQUICIA DE VOTO.
franchise to vote.
FRANQUICIA IMPOSITIVA.
tax exemption.
FRANQUICIA TRIBUTARIA.
tax exemption.
FRATRICIDA.
m, f, person who kills his brother or sister.

FRATRICIDIO.
m, fratricide.
FRAUDE.
m, fraud ‖ abuse of confidence. Usually deemed to be a crime.
FRAUDE A LA LEY.
fraudulent evasion of applicable law (e.g. change of the apparent location of a document's execution or of an action to avoid compliance with otherwise applicable law).
FRAUDE DE ACREEDORES.
debtor fraud (against creditors). Usually treated separately in civil and commercial law.
FRAUDE ELECTORAL.
electoral or voting or election fraud.
FRAUDE PROCESAL.
fraud committed by use of legal procedure. Includes among others: perjury, evidentiary fraud, wrongful use of civil proceedings, abuse of process, etc.
FRAUDES AL COMERCIO Y LA INDUSTRIA.
commercial or industrial fraud (to cause increases or decreases in the price of goods, securities, etc. through making false statements in the offer of securities, making fraudulent contracts or agreements in restraint of trade, spreading false commercial information, etc).
FRAUDULENCIA.
f, fraudulence.
FRAUDULENTAMENTE.
adv, fraudulently.
FRAUDULENTO.
adj, fraudulent.
FRENTE.
f, forehead ‖ front ‖ facade (of a building) ‖ adv, opposite ‖ in front of.
FRENTE.
m, front, line of fire ‖ name of some political parties and movements ‖ top margin of a letter or document ‖ face of a document.
FRENTE OBRERO.
employers' group or association.
FRÍVOLO.
adj, trivial ‖ frivolous.
FRONTERA.
f, border, boundary (between countries) ‖ frontier.
FRONTERA ARTIFICIAL.
artificially designated border (without respect to geographical or traditional political boundaries).
FRONTERA CONVENCIONAL.
conventional border, border established by treaty.
FRONTERA NATURAL.
natural boundary or border.
FRUCTUOSO.
adj, successful, profitable, productive.
FRUSTRACIÓN.
f, frustration ‖ criminal attempt, commission of all the acts necessary to commit a crime which for other reasons does not occur. See DELITO TENTADO and DELITO FRUSTRADO.
FRUSTRADO.
adj, frustrated.
FRUTOS.
m, fruits (of labor), products. May be NATURALES (agricultural and animal products and animal offspring), INDUSTRIALES (manu-factured goods) or CIVILES (periodic income from property, etc.).
FRUTOS CAÍDOS.
fallen fruits, fruits which have fallen from the tree or plant.
FRUTOS DEL PAÍS.
national products, domestic commodities.
FRUTOS E INTERESES.
fruits and interest.
FRUTOS INDUSTRIALES.
industrial products.
FRUTOS MANIFIESTOS.
fruits which are easily visible.
FRUTOS NACIDOS.
germinated fruits.
FRUTOS NATURALES.
natural fruits, fruits of the land.
FRUTOS PENDIENTES.
hanging fruits, fruits which have not yet fallen from the tree or plant.
FRUTOS PERCIBIDOS.
harvested fruits.
FUEGO.
m, fire (in all senses) ‖ heat ‖ heat of passion ‖ hearth.
FUEGO PERJUDICIAL.
hostile or unfriendly fire.
FUENTE.
f, source.
FUENTE CONFIABLE.
reliable source of information.

FUENTE DE GANANCIA.
source of profit or income.
FUENTE DE INGRESOS.
source of income.
FUENTE FIDEDIGNA.
reliable source.
FUENTE INFORMATIVA.
source of information.
FUENTE PRODUCTORA.
source of supply.
FUENTE RENTÍSTICA.
source of revenue.
FUENTES DE LAS OBLIGACIONES.
f, bases of obligations. May be DELITOS (intentional torts); CUASI-DELITOS (unintentional torts); CONTRATOS (contracts); CUASI-CONTRACTOS (quasi-contracts); LEYES (laws).
FUENTES DEL DERECHO.
principles or foundations or origins of positive law. Includes constitutions, treaties, statutes, usage, judicial precedence, etc.
FUENTES JURÍDICAS.
sources of the law.
FUERA DE AUDIENCIA.
out of court.
FUERA DE LA LEY.
outside the law (such that the actor may be detained by anyone).
FUERA DE DUDA RAZONABLE.
beyond a reasonable doubt.
FUERA DE JUICIO.
extrajudicial.
FUERA DE LITIGIO.
extrajudicial
FUERA DE LUGAR.
out of place, uncalled for.
FUERA DE MATRIMIONO.
out of wedlock ‖ outside the marriage.
FUERA DE ORDEN.
out of order.
FUERA DE RAZÓN.
unreasonable.
FUERA DE TÉRMINO.
untimely, late.
FUERA DE TIEMPO.
past the expiration or maturity date, late, delayed.
FUERO.
m, jurisdiction ‖ forum ‖ venue ‖ tribunal ‖ privilege, exemption ‖ code (of laws), statute book ‖ customs and usages which become

common law ‖ entirety of privileges (granted a person by reason of his position or employment) ‖ letters or documents which grant privileges or exemptions.
FUERO ACTIVO.
right to be heard before specialized courts.
FUERO AUXILIAR.
ancillary jurisdiction.
FUERO CIVIL.
civil jurisdiction, jurisdiction of civil courts and judges.
FUERO COMERCIAL.
commercial jurisdiction.
FUERO COMPETENTE.
competent jurisdiction (determined either by choice of the parties or by law).
FUERO COMÚN.
general jurisdiction.
FUERO CONCURRENTE.
concurrent jurisdiction.
FUERO DE ATRACCIÓN.
ancillary jurisdiction (e.g. jurisdiction of bankruptcy court over matter ancillary to its original jurisdiction).
FUERO DE ELECCIÓN.
choice of jurisdiction (in a contract).
FUERO DE LAS SUCESIONES.
probate jurisdiction.
FUERO DE LOS CONCURSOS.
bankruptcy jurisdiction ‖ bankruptcy court.
FUERO DEL CONTRATO.
See FUERO DE ELECCIÓN.
FUERO DEL TRABAJO.
jurisdiction of labor tribunal.
FUERO ESPECIAL.
special jurisdiction, jurisdiction of specialized courts.
Opposed to FUERO ORDINARIO.
FUERO EXCLUSIVO.
exclusive jurisdiction.
FUERO LABORAL.
See JURISDICCIÓN LABORAL.
FUERO MILITAR.
privilege of military personnel and officers to be judged by military courts ‖ jurisdiction of military courts.
FUERO MUNICIPAL.
municipal code (of city ordinances).
FUERO ORDINARIO.
ordinary jurisdiction, jurisdiction of ordinary courts. Opposed to FUERO ESPECIAL.

FUERO PASIVO.
right to trial (of detained persons).

FUERO PERSONAL.
jurisdiction of courts over defendant based on his domicile.

FUERO POR CONEXIÓN.
See FUERO DE ATRACCIÓN.

FUERO SINDICAL.
right to employment security for union representatives (such that they may not be dismissed or relocated by their employer without due cause).

FUERZA.
f, force ‖ violence, intimidation ‖ power ‖ military unit.

FUERZA ARMADA.
army ‖ any branch of the armed forces ‖ member of the armed forces.

FUERZA CANCELATORIA.
legal tender.

FUERZA COERCITIVA.
coercion.

FUERZA DE COSA JUZGADA.
See AUTORIDAD DE LA COSA JUZGADA.

FUERZA DE LEY.
Literally, force of law ‖ legal enforcement.

FUERZA EJECUTIVA.
judicial power to expedite (see JUICIO EJECUTIVO) ‖ executory authority, authority of judicial decisions that authorize execution of judgment ‖ authority of higher public administrative authorities.

FUERZA EN LAS COSAS.
(use of) force against inanimate objects.

FUERZA IRRESISTIBLE.
irresistible force.

FUERZA LEGAL.
force of law.

FUERZA LIBERATORIA.
power to free or release ‖ power of currency to be used as legal tender to fulfill monetary obligations.

FUERZA MAYOR.
force majeure, act of God.

FUERZA PROBATORIA.
evidentiary weight, value as evidence.

FUERZA PÚBLICA.
police power ‖ (internal) law enforcement forces.

FUERZAS ARMADAS.
army ‖ armed forces.

FUERZAS EXTRAÑAS.
outside forces.

FUGA.
f, flight, escape. May constitute an element of a crime.

FUGA AL ENEMIGO.
flight toward the enemy. Element of treason.

FUGA DE CAPITALES.
capital flight (to another country), clandestine exportation of money.

FUGARSE.
v, to flee, escape, take flight, abscond.

FUGITIVO.
m, fugitive ‖ adj, fugitive ‖ brief ‖ passing, transitory.

FULLERÍA.
f, swindling, cheating.

FULLERO.
m, crook, swindler.

FUNCIÓN.
f, function (in all senses) ‖ job, occupation ‖ attributions ‖ work, job ‖ performance, show ‖ function, public meeting, or show attended by many persons ‖ operation.

FUNCIÓN SOCIAL.
social purpose, function in society.

FUNCIONARIO.
m, functionary, official.

FUNCIONARIO FISCAL.
financial officer or official.

FUNCIONARIO JUDICIAL.
judicial official, officer of the court.

FUNCIONARIO PÚBLICO.
public functionary or official. May or may not be paid, but usually has a position of some degree of authority.

FUNDABILIDAD.
f, sustainability.

FUNDACIÓN.
f, foundation, not-for-profit organization, non-profit corporation ‖ foundation, basis, principle ‖ founding, establishment.

FUNDADAMENTE.
adv, with good reason ‖ upon a sound basis.

FUNDADO.
adj, well-founded, sound.

FUNDADOR.
m, founder, incorporator ‖ organizer, promoter.

FUNDAMENTAL.
adj, fundamental.

FUNDAMENTALMENTE.
adv, fundamentally.

FUNDAMENTAR.
v, to establish a basis ‖ to reason, discuss ‖ to state the RESULTANDOS and CONSIDERANDOS (bases) of a judgment.

FUNDAMENTO.
m, foundation, origin ‖ reason, motive, explanation.

FUNDAMENTO JURÍDICO.
legal foundation, main legal purpose, or reason.

FUNDAR.
v, to found, establish, create ‖ to support, base ‖ to create an estate or foundation ‖ to endow.

FUNDAR UN AGRAVIO.
to state the legal bases of appeal (i.e. the alleged error(s)).

FUNDAR RECURSO.
to state the legal foundation of an appeal.

FUNDIR.
v, to merge, join, unite ‖ to cast ‖ to smelt.

FUNDIRSE.
v, to go bankrupt, fail ‖ to merge, unify, join together (groups or corporations).

FUNDO.
m, estate ‖ rural property.

FUNDO DOMINANTE.
dominant estate.

FUNDO MADERERO.
timberland.

FUNDO MINERO.
mining property.

FUNDO SIRVIENTE.
servient estate.

FUNGIBILIDAD.
f, fungibility.

FUNGIBLE.
adj, fungible.

FUNGIR.
v, to substitute ‖ to act (e.g. as a substitute).

FUSILAMIENTO.
m, execution by firing squad.

FUSILAR.
v, to execute a person by firing squad ‖ to plagiarize.

FUSIÓN.
f, corporate merger.

FUSIÓN HORIZONTAL.
horizontal merger (of competing companies).

FUSIÓN VERTICAL.
vertical merger (of companies).

FUSIONAR.
v, to merge (corporations or partnerships) ‖ to unite interests.

FUSTIGACIÓN.
f, strong censure.

FUTURO.
m, future ‖ adj, future.

G

GABARRO.
m, accounting error or mistake ‖ obligation or duty connected with the receipt of a thing.

GABELA.
f, generic term for all taxes or payments made to the state ‖ tax, charge.

GABELA DE CONSUMO.
excise tax.

GABINETE.
m, president's cabinet, cabinet (of executive branch).

GACETA.
f, gazette ‖ official governmental publication (in which laws, executive orders, rules, etc. are published).

GAJE.
m, salary, pay, wages.

GANADO.
m, livestock ‖ adj, achieved, won ‖ beaten.

GANADOR.
m, winner.

GANANCIA.
f, benefit ‖ profit, gain ‖ earnings ‖ acquisition of goods.

GANANCIA BRUTA.
gross profit.

GANANCIA EN BRUTO.
See GANANCIA BRUTA.

GANANCIA EN OPERACIONES.
operating profit.

GANANCIA LÍQUIDA.
See GANANCIA NETA.

GANANCIA NETA.
net profit.

GANANCIAL.
adj, profit, pertaining to profit ‖ community, pertaining to community property.

GANANCIALES.
m, community estate, property in marriage ‖ adj, community, pertaining to property acquired during marriage.

GANANCIALES IGNORADOS.
deemed community property, property deemed to be part of the community property of a marital estate, although it was not acquired until after the dissolution of the marriage.

GANANCIAS.
f, profits ‖ earnings ‖ winnings.

GANANCIAS A DIVIDIR.
undivided profits.

GANANCIAS DE CAPITAL.
capital gains.

GANANCIAS ESPERADAS.
anticipated profits.

GANANCIAS EVENTUALES.
fortuitous profits (not due to work or improvements).

GANANCIAS EXCESIVAS.
excess profits.

GANANCIAS EXTRAORDINARIAS.
extraordinary profits.

GANANCIAS GRAVABLES.
taxable profits.

GANANCIAS NO DISTRIBUIDAS.
See GANANCIAS A DIVIDIR.

GANANCIAS PARA REPARTIR.
See GANANCIAS A DIVIDIR.

GANANCIAS SEGÚN LOS LIBROS.
profits on the books.

GANANCIAS PREVISTAS.
anticipated profits.

GANANCIAS Y PÉRDIDAS.
profit and loss ‖ profits and losses.

GANANCIOSO.
adj, lucrative, profitable ‖ winning.

GANAR.
v, to earn ‖ to win ‖ to acquire, obtain ‖ to achieve (an end).

GANAR DINERO.
to make money ‖ to earn money.

GANAR INTERÉS.
to earn interest.

GANAR TIEMPO.
to catch up ‖ to save time ‖ to delay one thing in order to do some other related thing.

GANAR UN PLEITO.
to win a suit.

GANAR VECINDAD.
to establish legal residence.

GANARSE LA VIDA.
to earn one's living.

GANGA.
f, bargain, deal.

GANGSTERISMO.
m, gangsterism.

GARANTE.
m, guarantor, warrantor, bondsman, surety, guarantee.

GARANTÍA.
f, bond, bail ‖ guaranty ‖ pledge, security ‖ guarantee, guaranty contract ‖ warranty.

GARANTÍA DE CRÉDITO.
guaranty of a loan.

GARANTÍA DE FIRMA.
guaranty of a drawer's signature (on a negotiable instrument, by means of witnesses of payee who recognize the signature).

GARANTÍA DE PERSONA.
proof of bearer's identity (re: negotiable instrument).

GARANTÍA DE PETICIÓN.
right to petition (the government).

GARANTÍA EVENTUAL.
conditional guaranty.

GARANTÍA FLOTANTE.
floating security interest, security interest in a variable group of assets.

GARANTÍA HIPOTECARIA.
mortgage security, guaranty secured by a mortgage on real estate.

GARANTÍA INCONDICIONAL.
absolute guaranty.

GARANTÍA MANCOMUNADA.
joint guaranty.

GARANTÍA PERSONAL.
personal guaranty.

GARANTÍA PIGNORATICIA.
See PRENDA.

GARANTÍA PRENDARIA.
pledge, chattel mortgage, security interest.

GARANTÍA PROCESAL.
bond for court costs, procedural right.

GARANTÍA REAL.
security, guaranty secured by security interest in real or personal property.

GARANTÍA SOLIDARIA.
joint and several guaranty.

GARANTÍAS CONCURRENTES.
concurrent guaranties.

GARANTÍAS CONSTITUCIONALES.
constitutional guaranties, civil rights, individual rights.

GARANTÍAS ESCRITAS.
written warranties.

GARANTÍAS IMPLÍCITAS.
implied warranties.

GARANTÍAS PROCESALES.
right to procedural due process ‖ procedural guaranties or rights (in litigation).

GARANTIR.
v, to guaranty, bond.

GARANTIZADO.
m, object of a guaranty ‖ adj, guarantied ‖ warranted.

GARANTIZADOR.
m, guarantor, surety.

GARANTIZAR.
v, to guarantee, warrant.

GARROTE.
m, garrote, instrument to impose capital punishment by strangulation.

GASTAR.
v, to spend, expend (money) ‖ to use, consume.

GASTO.
m, expense, cost ‖ expenditure, outlay ‖ spending.

GASTOS.
m, costs, expenses, expenditures ‖ outflow, expenses.

GASTOS A REPARTIR.
undistributed expenses.

GASTOS ADMINISTRATIVOS.
administrative expenses. Includes salaries of office workers and executive staff.

GASTOS ADUANALES.
customs expenses.

GASTOS CAUSÍDICOS.
litigation costs. Includes court costs, attorneys' fees, and all other expenses of litigation.

GASTOS CONSTANTES.
See GASTOS FIJOS.

GASTOS CONTENCIOSOS.
costs of litigation, litigation expenses.

GASTOS DE ADMINISTRACIÓN.
costs of administration, administrative costs (of managing property).

GASTOS DE CAPITAL.
capital expenses.

GASTOS DE CONSERVACIÓN.
maintenance costs, costs of keeping property in good repair.

GASTOS DE CONSTITUCIÓN.
organization starting expenses.

GASTOS DE DEPÓSITO.
expenses of bailment or deposit or warehousing. See DEPÓSITO.

GASTOS DE DESARROLLO.
See GASTOS DE FOMENTO.

GASTOS DE ESCRITURACIÓN.
costs of fulfilling requirements for the transfer of property. Includes filing fee, notary public charges, etc.

GASTOS DE EXPLOTACIÓN.
operating expenses.

GASTOS DE FOMENTO.
development costs.

GASTOS DE FUNCIONAMIENTO.
operating expenses.

GASTOS DE INICIACIÓN.
organization or starting expenses.

GASTOS DE JUSTICIA.
See GASTOS CAUSÍDICOS.

GASTOS DE OPERACIÓN.
operating costs.

GASTOS DE ORGANIZACIÓN.
starting costs ‖ organizational expenses.

GASTOS DE PROTESTO.
protest charges.

GASTOS DE PURO LUJO.
expenditures for pure luxuries (exclusively for personal comfort, adornment, or show).

GASTOS DE RECTIFICACIÓN REGISTRAL.
expenses of changing a registration at the real estate registry. Court usually determines who will pay.

GASTOS DE REPATRIACIÓN.
repatriation costs, costs of returning (e.g. a prisoner) to his prison, country, encampment, etc.

GASTOS DE REPRESENTACIÓN.
expenses of representation (for which money in addition to salary is paid, to a head of state, national ministers, diplomats, etc.).

GASTOS DE ÚLTIMA ENFERMEDAD.
costs of (a person's) final illness before death. Usually privileged in terms of other creditors.

GASTOS FIJOS.
fixed costs.

GASTOS FINANCIEROS.
finance charges ‖ financial expenses.

GASTOS FUNERARIOS.
funeral costs.

GASTOS GENERALES.
general expenses, overhead.

GASTOS INDIRECTOS.
indirect costs.

GASTOS JUDICIALES.
court costs and other official fees of litigation ‖ expense budget of judiciary ‖ also see GASTOS CAUSÍDICOS.

GASTOS JURÍDICOS.
legal expenses.

GASTOS LEGALES.
See GASTOS JURÍDICOS.

GASTOS NECESARIOS.
necessary expenses. Includes, among others, real property tax surcharges, mortgages which are registered upon taking possession, and monies and materials invested in necessary improvements.

GASTOS ORDINARIOS.
ordinary and reasonable expenses.

GASTOS PREPARATORIOS.
development costs.

GASTOS PÚBLICOS.
public spending ‖ national, state (or provincial), or municipal spending ‖ public debt.

GASTOS SUNTUARIOS.
See GASTOS DE PURO LUJO.

GASTOS ÚTILES.
useful expenditures (spent on property). In contrast to those for pure maintenance or those of pure luxury.

GEMELO.
m, twin (individually). See MELLIZO.

GENEALOGÍA.
f, genealogy.

GENERACIÓN.
f, generation (in all sense) ‖ procreation ‖ impregnation, insemination.

GENERAL.
m, general (in armed forces) ‖ adj, general, common, usual, frequent ‖ superior ‖ ordinary, normal.

GENERALATO.
m, generalship ‖ entirety of generals (from one or more nations or during one or more time periods).

GENERALES DE LA LEY.
See PREGUNTAS GENERALES DE LA LEY.

GENERALIDAD.
f, generality ‖ majority ‖ vagueness ‖ community property of a town.

GENERALÍSIMO.
m, commander in chief (usually, during time of war).

GÉNERO.
m, type, sort, class ‖ genre ‖ species ‖ gender ‖ merchandise, goods.

GENOCIDIO.
m, genocide.

GENTES.
f, foreign people ‖ peoples ‖ people.

GENTILES.
m, gentiles.

GEOPOLÍTICA.
f, geopolitics ‖ science of geopolitics ‖ adj, geopolitical.

GERENCIA.
f, management ‖ managership, position, office, and duration of a manager.

GERENTE.
m, manager.

GESTACIÓN.
f, gestation, duration of pregnancy.

GESTIÓN.
f, administration, performance (of a function) ‖ job ‖ step, action, measure, maneuver ‖ negotiation ‖ handling, management.

GESTIÓN CONJUNTA.
cooperative management or administration (of workers in a business).

GESTIÓN DE NEGOCIOS AJENOS.
handling of the affairs of a person who is absent (without his or her knowledge and without having received legal authority).

GESTIÓN JUDICIAL.
legal measure ‖ judicial proceeding.

GESTIÓN OFICIOSA.
officiousness.

GESTIÓN PROCESAL.
court proceeding.

GESTIONAR.
v, to take steps or measures (to accomplish an end) ‖ to arrange for, negotiate, handle, deal with.

GESTIONAR UN EMPRÉSTITO.
to arrange a loan.

GESTIONAR EL PAGO.
to demand payment.

GESTIONAR EN JUICIO.
to litigate.

GESTIONAR EN NOMBRE DE.
to act in the name of.

GESTIONAR FONDOS.
to raise money.

GESTIONAR UNA PATENTE.
to apply for a patent.

GESTOR.
m, negotiator, arranger ‖ promoter ‖ agent, representative ‖ manager, administrator, general partner, active partner ‖ shareholder active in company management ‖ adj, promoting ‖ negotiating.

GESTOR DE NEGOCIOS AJENOS.
person who manages or protects the interest of another person (without his or her knowledge and without having received legal authority).

GESTOR JUDICIAL.
legal representative, attorney.

GESTOR OFICIOSO.
one who acts for another without authority.

GINECOCRACIA.
f, gynecocracy, government by women.

GIRADO.
m, drawee ‖ adj, drawn.

GIRADOR.
m, drawer, maker.

GIRANTE.
See GIRADOR.

GIRAR.
v, to send, remit, transfer ‖ to write, draw (commercial paper) ‖ to do business, trade ‖ to turn, spin.

GIRAR A CARGO DE.
to draw against.

GIRAR DINERO.
to withdraw cash.
GIRAR EN DESCUBIERTO.
to overdraw.
GIRAR LA CUENTA.
to make out and send the bill or account (to the client).
GIRAR UN CHEQUE.
to write or draw a check.
GIRAR UN OFICIO.
to issue a judicial communication.
GIRO.
m, remittance, transfer of money (through a bank, post office or telegraph) ‖ turnover ‖ transfer of money in the form of commercial paper ‖ draft, bill of exchange ‖ line of business.
GIRO A PLAZO.
time draft or bill of exchange.
GIRO A LA VISTA.
sight or demand draft.
GIRO BANCARIO.
bank draft or bill of exchange or money order ‖ banking business.
GIRO COMERCIAL.
commercial or trade draft ‖ commercial business.
GIRO DE CAMBIO A PLAZO.
time draft.
GIRO DE CORTESÍA.
See GIRO DE FAVOR.
GIRO DE FAVOR.
accommodation paper.
GIRO DOCUMENTARIO.
documentary draft or bill of exchange.
GIRO EN DESCUBIERTO.
overdraft, drawing a check against insufficient funds.
GIRO POSTAL.
money-order (sent through the post office).
GIRO TELEGRÁFICO.
wire transfer.
GLOSA.
f, glossa, explanation, interpretation of a difficult or obscure text ‖ footnote, annotation (which makes reference to a mortgage, obligation, etc.) ‖ observation, notation regarding an entry in an account.
GLOSADOR.
m, annotator ‖ legal commentator (usually member of a school of legal commentators).

GLOSAR.
v, to write glossas or explanations ‖ to footnote, annotate.
GNOSEOLOGÍA JURÍDICA.
f, jurisprudence.
GOBERNABLE.
adj, governable.
GOBERNACIÓN.
f, government ‖ governorship, management ‖ territory ‖ governorship, office of governor, governor's office ‖ governor's jurisdiction.
GOBERNADOR.
m, governor, person who governs ‖ (state, provincial) governor ‖ (city) mayor ‖ (executive) minister or secretary.
GOBERNANTE.
m, governor, ruler, person who governs ‖ adj, governing, ruling.
GOBERNANTES.
governing body of managers or directors.
GOBERNAR.
v, to govern, rule ‖ to order (pursuant to authority) ‖ to direct, guide.
GOBIERNO.
m, government ‖ ministry, cabinet (of executive ministers or secretaries) ‖ administration (of government) ‖ governorship ‖ state or province (ruled by a governor) ‖ government house ‖ term of office (of a governor) ‖ control ‖ management, direction.
GOBIERNO DE FACTO.
de facto government.
GOBIERNO DE HECHO.
See GOBIERNO DE FACTO.
GOBIERNO DE JURE.
legal government, legally elected government, government de jure.
GOBIERNO EN EL DESTIERRO.
government in exile.
GOBIERNO FEDERAL.
federal government.
GOBIERNO PARLAMENTARIO.
parliamentary government.
GOBIERNO PRESIDENCIALISTA.
presidential government.
See PRESIDENCIALISMO.
GOBIERNO REPRESENTATIVO.
representative government.
GOBIERNO TÍTERE.
puppet government or regime, figurehead government.

GOCE.
m, enjoyment.
GOLPE.
m, coup d'etat ‖ hit, knock, blow. May be punishable as a crime.
GOLPE DE ESTADO.
coup d'etat, overthrow of the government.
GOLPEAR.
v, to hit, knock.
GOLPISTA.
m, person who is in favor of coup d'etat ‖ adj, characteristic of such person.
GOZAR.
v, to enjoy ‖ to have possession ‖ to have a right to ‖ to have sexual intercourse.
GOZAR DE UN DERECHO.
to have a right.
GOZAR DE UN VOTO.
to have a right to vote.
GOZAR DE UNA REBAJA.
to receive a discount.
GOZAR DE UNA RENTA.
to receive an income.
GOZAR INTERESES.
to draw interest.
GRACIA.
f, executive pardon (of a criminal) ‖ gift ‖ grace period granted (a debtor) ‖ forgiveness of (a debt) ‖ privilege.
GRACIOSO.
adj, gratuitous, free ‖ liberal ‖ amusing, funny.
GRADACIÓN.
f, gradation ‖ classification ‖ preferences (of debts in a bankruptcy).
Also see GRADUACIÓN DE LA PENA.
GRADO.
m, degree, title (obtained from an educational institution) ‖ level, stage (of a lawsuit) ‖ degree (of a crime).
GRADO DE PENA.
degree of punishment. Usually maximum, normal, or minimum.
GRADUACIÓN.
f, classification ‖ ranking, grading ‖ graduation (e.g. from school) ‖ division of levels or categories ‖ order ‖ rank.
GRADUACIÓN DE ACREEDORES.
f, order and act of classifying creditors' preferences (in a bankruptcy).

GRADUACIÓN DE CRÉDITOS.
f, order and act of classifying preferences (of debts in a bankruptcy).
GRADUACIÓN DE LA PENA.
f, imposition of punishment where a statute imposes an indeterminate sentence.
GRAN POTENCIA.
f, major power (re: nations).
GRANJERÍA.
f, profits from farming ‖ raising and sale of livestock ‖ profits, gain.
GRATIFICACIÓN.
f, bonus or extra compensation (for unusual services rendered) ‖ fee.
GRATIFICAR.
v, to pay a bonus (for extra work).
GRATIS.
adj, free, gratis ‖ gratuitous.
GRATUIDAD.
f, gratuitousness.
GRATUITO.
adj, free, gratis ‖ gratuitous ‖ unfounded, without basis (re allegations, arguments, etc.).
GRAVADO.
adj, taxed.
GRAVAMEN.
m, charge, obligation ‖ real property lien or encumbrance ‖ tax.
GRAVAMEN CANCELADO.
See GRAVAMEN LIQUIDADO.
GRAVAMEN DE ADUANA.
customs duty.
GRAVAMEN DE VALORIZACIÓN.
improvement assessment.
GRAVAMEN DEL TIMBRE.
stamp tax.
GRAVAMEN EQUITATIVO.
equitable tax.
GRAVAMEN ESPECÍFICO.
specific tax.
GRAVAMEN FISCAL.
tax.
GRAVAMEN GENERAL.
general tax.
GRAVAMEN IRREPARABLE.
irreparable harm. Refers to harm which causes an interlocutory order to be immediately appealable.
GRAVAMEN LIQUIDADO.
tax which has been paid.

GRAVAMEN SUCESORIO.
estate or inheritance tax.
GRAVAR.
v, to assess ‖ to mortgage, encumber, pledge ‖ to tax.
GRAVE.
adj, serious. Used in reference to crimes, punishments, etc.
GRAVEDAD DE LAS PENAS.
f, importance or seriousness of the punishment.
GRAVOSO.
adj, expensive ‖ grievous, offensive ‖ onerous.
GREMIAL.
adj, union or guild, pertaining to unions or trade unions or guilds.
GREMIALISMO.
m, trade unionism ‖ excessive influence of trade unions.
GREMIALISTA.
f, m, supporter of trade unions or unions ‖ union leader.
GREMIALIZAR.
v, to unionize.
GREMIO.
m, trade union, union, guild ‖ group of persons who belong to the same profession or have the same skill.
GRILLETES.
m, shackles.
GRILLO.
m, shared shackles (such that the legs of two prisoners are coupled).
GRITOS SUBVERSIVOS.
m, subversive or anti-government cries or shouts (e.g. "death to the ..." or "long live ....").
GRUESA VENTURA.
See PRÉSTAMO A LA GRUESA.
GRUPO.
m, group ‖ block.
GRUPO DE SOCIEDADES.
business group ‖ corporate family, group of independent but related corporations.
GRUPO PARLAMENTARIO.
block, parliamentary or congressional block, party members in parliamentary or congressional houses.
GRUPO REBELDE.
rebel group (in the military).
GRUPOS DE INTERESES.
interest groups, lobbies.

GRUPOS DE PRESIÓN.
pressure or interest groups.
GUARDA.
m, f, guardianship, custodianship ‖ care, custody ‖ guardian, custodian, steward, curator, conservator ‖ compliance, observance (of the law).
GUARDADOR.
m, guardian.
GUARDAR.
v, to care for ‖ to conserve, act as guardian or custodian or steward or curator or conservator ‖ to comply with or observe (the law) ‖ to save.
GUARDAR DECISIÓN.
to reserve decision.
GUARDIA.
f, guard ‖ protection, custody ‖ police force.
GUARDIÁN.
m, custodian ‖ guardian ‖ policeman.
GUARENTIGIO.
adj, characteristic of a consent judgment, contract, or other authorization to enforce an agreement as if it had been ordered by a court.
GUBERNAMENTAL.
adj, governmental.
GUBERNATIVAMENTE.
adv, governmentally.
GUBERNATIVO.
m, person who is detained to maintain public order and administrative authority ‖ adj, governmental, pertaining to government ‖ gubernatorial.
GUERRA.
f, war.
GUERRA CIVIL.
civil war.
GUERRA DE NERVIOS.
war of nerves ‖ cold war (between countries).
GUERRA DE PRECIOS.
price war.
GUERRA DE TARIFAS.
See GUERRA DE PRECIOS.
GUERRA FRÍA.
See GUERRA DE NERVIOS.
GUERREAR.
v, to wage war, fight (with arms).
GUERRERO.
m, fighter.

GUERRILLA.

f, guerilla ‖ guerilla forces, band lead by rebel leader.

GUERRILLA RURAL.

rural guerilla forces.

GUERRILLA URBANA.

urban guerilla forces.

GUERRILLERO.

m, member of a guerilla group.

GUÍA.

f, guide ‖ special permit or clearance or permission or exemption (granted to allow the trading of certain restricted products) ‖ document which has the aforementioned effect ‖ way bill ‖ bill of lading.

GUÍA AÉREA.

air waybill or bill of lading.

GUÍA DE CARGA.

waybill, manifest.

GUÍA DE CARGA AÉREA.

air waybill.

GUÍA DE DEPÓSITO.

warehouse receipt or certificate.

GUÍA DE EMBARQUE.

ship's receipt ‖ ship's bill of lading.

GUÍA DE ENCOMIENDA.

parcel receipt.

GUÍA DE EXPORTACIÓN.

export permit ‖ export waybill.

GUÍA DE INTERNACIÓN.

import permit.

GUÍA DE TRASPORTE.

waybill.

GUIAR.

v, to guide ‖ to advise, counsel ‖ to drive (e.g. a car).

GUIAR UN PLEITO.

to conduct a lawsuit.

GUIAR SIN LICENCIA.

to drive without a license.

GUILDA.

f, guild.

GUILLOTINA.

f, guillotine.

GUILLOTINAR.

v, to guillotine ‖ to cut off further discussion (of a law, etc. in congress).

H

HÁBEAS CORPUS.
m, habeas corpus, right of all citizens who are detained or are held prisoner by government to appear immediately and in public before a judge or tribunal which after a hearing, will decide whether or not the arrest was legal and whether the prisoner must be set free or kept in custody.

HABEMOS CONFITEN TEM REUM".
We have a prisoner who has confessed. Finally, the prisoner has confessed.

HABER.
m, estate, property, assets, capital ‖ wealth ‖ soldier's wages ‖ credit ‖ liabilities (for accounting purposes) ‖ salary ‖ credit balance ‖ v, to have.

HABER CONYUGAL.
community property, marital estate. For certain purposes, may include separate property of spouses.

HABER HEREDITARIO.
decedent's estate ‖ distributable decedent's estate, decedent's estate reduced by estate claims (e.g. debts, taxes, etc.).

HABER JUBILATORIO.
pension.

HABER LUGAR.
to lie, be admissible.

HABER MONEDADO.
money.

HABER POR CONFESO.
to deem a confession made (for legal purposes)

HABER SOCIAL.
corporate capital ‖ assets of a business association.

HABERES.
property, assets ‖ wages ‖ resources.

HABIENDO PROTESTADO JURAMENTO.
being duly sworn.

HÁBIL.
adj, competent (e.g. to testify, marry, etc.) ‖ working (day).

HABILITACIÓN.
f, authorization or qualification of a person otherwise incompetent ‖ employee profit sharing, worker participation in the profits ‖ authorization ‖ sharing ‖ financing.

HABILITACIÓN DE BANDERA.
government authorization allowing foreigners to trade in a nation's harbors.

HABILITACIÓN DE DÍAS Y HORAS INHÁBILES.
authorization of a judge to treat as juridical days and hours those days and hours which are otherwise not. Used to prevent prejudice to the parties.

HABILITACIÓN DE EDAD.
See EMANCIPACIÓN.

HABILITACIÓN PARA COMPARECER EN JUICIO.
legal authorization to allow an otherwise incompetent person (e.g. due to age or family relationship) to participate in a lawsuit.

HABILITACIÓN PARA RECOBRAR LA NACIONALIDAD.
authorization to recover lost nationality.

HABILITADO.
m, judicial assistant who is authorized to replace a judicial secretary or clerk ‖ employee who shares in the profits of a business ‖ official who handles money, paymaster ‖ representative ‖

adj, legally competent ‖ authorized to do something otherwise not permitted.

HABILITAR.

v, to authorize, make competent (to do something otherwise not permitted) ‖ to validate ‖ to enable, qualify ‖ to recognize as competent ‖ to grant legal emancipation of a minor ‖ to authorize the carrying out of legal acts on nonjuridical days ‖ to hand over the administration of an estate of bankrupt to him ‖ to share corporate or business profits with employees thereof ‖ to equip, fit out ‖ to give a share in the profits or a business.

HABILITAR LOS LIBROS.

to attach revenue stamps to the books as required.

HABILITARSE.

v, to make funds available (for a certain purpose).

HABITABILIDAD.

f, habitability.

HABITABLE.

adj, habitable.

HABITACIÓN.

f, habitation, dwelling ‖ residence ‖ domicile ‖ right of habitation.

HABITANTE.

m, inhabitant ‖ resident, dweller.

HABITAR.

v, to inhabit, reside, live in (e.g. a house or an area).

HABITUALIDAD PENAL.

f, habitual criminality.

HACEDERO.

adj, feasible, practicable. doable.

HACENDÍSTICO.

adj, fiscal.

HACER.

v, to make ‖ to do.

HACER ACTO DE PRESENCIA.

to be present, attend.

HACER BALANCE.

to balance an account ‖ to draw up a balance sheet.

HACER BANCARROTA.

to go bankrupt, go into bankruptcy.

HACER CAPAZ.

to enable, qualify.

HACER CESIÓN.

to assign, transfer, make an assignment or transfer.

HACER CONSTAR.

to show, demonstrate ‖ to put into record.

HACER CONTRABANDO.

to smuggle.

HACER CUMPLIR.

to enforce ‖ to make (someone) comply or fulfill.

HACER DERECHO.

See ESTAR A DERECHO.

HACER DILIGENCIA.

to take measures.

HACER EFECTIVO.

to cash, negotiate, collect.

HACER EL VACÍO.

to ostracize ‖ to make apparent one's disapproval or lack of agreement regarding government or other action.

HACER EMPEÑO.

to pawn.

HACER ESTRADOS.

to hear a case.

HACER FE.

to certify ‖ to prove sufficiently.

HACER JURAMENTO.

to take an oath.

HACER LA GUERRA.

to make war.

HACER LAS PARTES.

to distribute (an inheritance, community property, etc.).

HACER LUGAR.

to justify, support ‖ to approve.

HACER MAL A ALGUIEN.

to prejudice someone's interests ‖ to injure or offend someone.

HACER MELLA.

to persuade, convince ‖ to have a penalty take effect ‖ to damage or cause loss.

HACER NOTIFICAR.

to notify.

HACER PAGO.

to pay ‖ to fulfill, satisfy (an obligation).

HACER PARTES.

to divide (something in order to distribute to different persons), partition.

HACER PRENDA.

to take in pledge or pawn.

HACER PROTESTAR.

to protest (e.g. a draft).

HACER QUIEBRA.

to file or go into bankruptcy.

HACER RESPONSABLE.
to hold responsible.

HACER SABER.
to advise, notify ‖ to make known.

HACER SU NEGOCIO.
to profit from a situation.

HACER TRANCE.
to seize (pursuant to law).

HACER UN EMPRÉSTITO.
to make a loan.

HACER UNA LIBRANZA.
to issue or draw a bill of exchange.

HACER USO DE LA PALABRA.
to take the floor.

HACER VALER.
to enforce, put into affect ‖ to assert.

HACER VIDA.
to cohabit as husband and wife ‖ to follow or have a certain type of life (e.g. that of a politician or criminal, etc.).

HACERSE A LA MAR.
to put out to sea ‖ to be on the high seas.

HACERSE GARANTE DE.
to become surety for.

HACERSE PRESENTE.
to appear, make an appearance ‖ to attend, be present, be in attendance.

HACERSE RICO.
to get rich.

HACIENDA.
f, finance ‖ estate, property, capital, assets ‖ wealth ‖ (ministry of) finance or treasury ‖ work, plant ‖ stock farm, cattle ranch ‖ livestock ‖ cattle.

HACIENDA COMERCIAL.
See FONDO DE COMERCIO.

HACIENDA PARTICULAR.
private property.

HACIENDA PÚBLICA.
national wealth, public assets ‖ (department of) public finance (whether state/provincial, national or municipal).

HÁGASE SABER.
let it be known, know all men.

HALLADOR.
m, finder.

HALLARSE EN ESTADO DE PLEITO.
v, to be part of or party to litigation.

HALLAZGO.
m, discovery, finding (of a thing or person) ‖ found property.

HAMPÓN.
m, gangster.

HASTA NUEVA ORDEN.
(valid) until new orders are given.

HECHO.
m, fact ‖ act, action, deed, actus ‖ event ‖ work ‖ business ‖ matter subject to litigation ‖ adj, done, made.

HECHO AJENO.
act of another person or resulting from outside influence.

**HECHO CONTRARIO
A LA LEY.**
illegal act.

HECHO DE ENEMIGOS.
act of public enemy.

HECHO DE GUERRA.
act of war.

HECHO DE LA COSA.
act caused by a thing. Damage usually attributable to owner.

HECHO DE LOS ANIMALES.
act caused by an animal. Damage usually attributable to owner.

HECHO FABRICADO.
false fact.

HECHO JURÍDICO.
legally significant phenomenon, event or situation ‖ phenomenon, event, or situation which gives rise to, modifies, transfers, preserves, or extinguishes a legal right or duty.

HECHO NOTORIO.
notorious or well-known fact, common knowledge. May or may not need to be proven.

HECHO NUEVO.
new fact, materially new fact to litigation (which arises or comes to light after the initiation of the lawsuit). Introduction into evidence usually limited.

HECHO TANGIBLE.
physical fact.

HECHOS ADMINISTRATIVOS.
administrative acts, acts which are carried out by the government administration.

HECHOS ESENCIALES.
essential facts.

HECHOS JUSTIFICATIVOS.
justifying or excusing facts, facts which serve to excuse or justify an otherwise criminal act.

HECHOS LITIGIOSOS.
facts in dispute, contested facts.

HECHOS NEGATIVOS.
negative facts, HECHO JURÍDICO which is an abstention or omission.

HECHOS PERTINENTES.
pertinent facts.

HECHOS POSITIVOS.
positive facts, HECHO JURÍDICO which is an affirmative phenomenon, event, or situation.

HECHOS PROBADOS.
proven facts, facts which are determined to be true or accurate by a judge or tribunal.

HECHOS PROCESALES.
procedurally significant act or event, act or event which gives rise to, modifies, or extinguishes a procedural right ‖ procedural acts.

HECHOS SOBREVENIDOS.
events which occur or come to light after the commencement of litigation.

HEGEMONÍA.
n, hegemony.

HEREDABLE.
adj, inheritable.

HEREDAD.
f, estate, farm, plot.

HEREDAD AJENA.
farm or rural property belonging to another.

HEREDAD CERRADA.
enclosed property, property without means of egress.

HEREDAD DOMINANTE.
dominant estate (re: easements).

HEREDAD MATERNA.
maternal estate.

HEREDAD PATERNA.
paternal estate.

HEREDAD RESIDUAL.
remainder, residual or remainingestate.

HEREDAD RESIDUARIA.
See HEREDAD RESIDUAL.

HEREDAD SIRVIENTE.
servient estate (re: easements).

HEREDAD YACENTE.
inheritance in abeyance.

HEREDADO.
m, real property owner ‖ inheritor, heir ‖ adj, inherited ‖ landed, owning property.

HEREDAMIENTO.
m, tenement, landed property ‖ bequest, gift, endowment.

HEREDAR.
v, to inherit, take by will or by intestate succession ‖ to name heirs.

HEREDERO.
m, heir (if intestate succession) ‖ devisee, legatee (if testamentary succession) ‖ farm owner, heritor ‖ adj, inheriting.

HEREDERO AB INTESTATO.
heir, intestate successor.

HEREDERO ABSOLUTO.
unconditional heir, heir who receives subject to no conditions.

HEREDERO ADOPTIVO.
heir by adoption.

HEREDERO ANÓMALO.
irregular heir, party who receives despite not having been named as heir (e.g. state, religious order, etc.).

HEREDERO APARENTE.
See HEREDERO PUTATIVO.

HEREDERO BENEFICIARIO.
heir beneficiary, heir who accepts the inheritance pursuant to INVENTARIO.
See A BENEFICIO DE INVENTARIO.

HEREDERO COLATERAL.
heir collateral.

HEREDERO CONDICIONAL.
conditional heir, heir who receives subject to fulfillment of condition(s). May be a CONDICIÓN SUSPENSIVA (condition precedent) or a CONDICIÓN RESOLUTORIA (condition subsequent).

HEREDERO CONVENCIONAL.
heir conventional, contractual heir.

HEREDERO DEL REMANENTE.
remainderman, residuary legatee.

HEREDERO EN EXPECTATIVA.
heir expectant.

HEREDERO EN LÍNEA RECTA.
lineal heir.

HEREDERO FIDEICOMISARIO.
beneficiary of a testamentary trust.

HEREDERO FIDUCIARIO.
testamentary trustee ‖ fiduciary heir.

HEREDERO FORZOSO.
forced heir, heir who by law cannot be excluded.

HEREDERO GRAVADO.
life estate heir, heir with a life estate.

HEREDERO INCIERTO.
uncertain heir, heir whose identity is uncertain

due to ambiguity of names, terms, or incomplete designation.

HEREDERO INSTITUIDO.
heir testamentary.

HEREDERO IRREGULAR.
See HEREDERO ANÓMALO.

HEREDERO LEGAL.
heir at law, legal heir.

HEREDERO LEGITIMARIO.
legal heir.

HEREDERO LEGÍTIMO.
See HEREDERO LEGITIMARIO.

HEREDERO LIBRE.
See HEREDERO ABSOLUTO.

HEREDERO NECESARIO.
See HEREDERO FORZOSO.

HEREDERO PARTICULAR.
legatee.

HEREDERO POR CONSANGUINIDAD.
heir of the blood.

HEREDERO POR ESTIRPE.
heir per stirpes.

HEREDERO PÓSTUMO.
posthumous heir, heir born after the decedent's death.

HEREDERO PRESUNTO.
heir who may inherit if the heir conditional does not fulfill the condition.
See HEREDERO CONDICIONAL.

HEREDERO PRETERIDO.
legal heir who is omitted from the will. May request a nullification of the will.

HEREDERO PROPIETARIO.
heir to legal title (but not use) of property. Opposed to HEREDERO USUFRUCTUARIO.

HEREDERO PURO Y SIMPLE.
heir who accepts the inheritance without benefit of an inventory. See A BENEFICIO DE INVENTARIO.

HEREDERO PUTATIVO.
putative heir, person who appears to be the rightful heir to property but due to special circumstances does not usually inherit.

HEREDERO RESERVATARIO.
heir with a future interest, heir with a reversionary or remainder interest.

HEREDERO SINGULAR.
heir of specific devise or legacy, heir of property which has been specifically identified.

HEREDERO SUBSTITUTO.
substitute heir, heir who receives due to ano-

ther's inability to receive or refusal of the estate.

HEREDERO TESTAMENTARIO.
heir testamentary (or by pre-nuptial agreement). Opposed to HEREDERO LEGITIMARIO.

HEREDERO ÚNICO.
sole heir.

HEREDERO UNIVERSAL.
heir of general legacy or devise ‖ universal heir.

HEREDERO USUFRUCTUARIO.
heir of use and enjoyment (but not legal title) to property.
Opposed to HEREDERO PROPIETARIO.

HEREDERO VOLUNTARIO.
See HEREDERO TESTAMENTARIO.

HEREDEROS EXTRAÑOS.
heirs that are neither HEREDEROS NECESARIOS nor HEREDEROS SUYOS.

HEREDEROS NECESARIOS.
legal heirs that may not be excluded by the testator.

HEREDEROS SUYOS.
children, grandchildren, and great-grandchildren of a person at the time that the will is written.

HEREDITABLE.
adj, inheritable.

HEREDITARIO.
adj, hereditary ‖ pertaining to inheritances.

HERENCIA.
f, inheritance, decedent's estate ‖ heredity ‖ hereditaments ‖ estate.

HERENCIA ADVENTICIA.
inheritance of a BIEN ADVENTICIO.

HERENCIA CONJUNTA.
parcenary, joint inheritance.

HERENCIA CRIMINAL.
criminal pre-disposition which is inherited from parent.

HERENCIA DE PARTE ALÍCUOTA.
general estate or inheritance, legacy or devise by which person receives a percentage or share of the decedent's estate.

HERENCIA FORZOSA.
(part of) estate which legally must be distributed to certain persons (e.g. children, wife).

HERENCIA FUTURA.
future estate, inheritance which one is eventually to receive from a person who is still alive.

HERENCIA LEGÍTIMA.
inheritance by legal heirs (usually by intestacy). Refers to portion distributed to legal heirs.

HERENCIA PROFECTICIA.
inheritance by child who is still under parental control in respect and consideration of the child's parent.

HERENCIA VACANTE.
escheat, inheritance without heirs.

HERENCIA YACENTE.
inheritance of estate of which the heir testamentary or legal heir has not yet taken possession.

HERIDA.
f, wound, injury, lesion. May be physical or emotional ‖ adj, wounded, injured, hurt.

HERIDO.
m, injured person ‖ adj, wounded injured, hurt.

HERIR.
v, to injure, hurt, wound ‖ to offend.

HERMANA.
f, sister.

HERMANASTRA.
f, step-sister.

HERMANASTRO.
m, step-brother.

HERMANDAD.
f, brotherhood, relationship between brothers ‖ sisterhood, relationship between sisters ‖ sorority ‖ fraternity, brotherhood ‖ alliance, society, league, confederation.

HERMANO.
m, brother.

HERMANO BASTARDO.
illegitimate brother.

HERMANOS.
m, brothers ‖ brothers and sisters ‖ brothers or sisters.

HERMANOS BILATERALES.
See HERMANOS GERMANOS.

HERMANOS CARNALES.
See HERMANOS GERMANOS.

**HERMANOS DE
DOBLE VÍNCULO.**
See HERMANOS GERMANOS.

HERMANOS GEMELOS.
twin brothers.

HERMANOS GERMANOS.
sibling, brothers or brother(s) and sister(s) of the same mother and father ‖ brother, member of an order or religion.

HERMANOS UNILATERALES.
half brothers, half brothers and sisters.

"HIC ET NUNC".
here and now.

HIGIENE PÚBLICA.
f, public hygiene ‖ public health.

**HIGIENE Y SEGURIDAD
EN EL TRABAJO.**
work health and safety, health and safety at work. Usually a responsibility of employer.

HIJA.
f, daughter.

HIJASTRA.
f, step-daughter.

HIJASTRO.
m, step-son ‖ step-child.

HIJO.
m, son ‖ child.

HIJO ADOPTIVO.
adopted child or son.

HIJO ADULTERINO.
illegitimate child or son resulting from adultery.

HIJO BASTARDO.
See HIJO ILEGÍTIMO.

HIJO DE BENDICIÓN.
See HIJO LEGÍTIMO.

HIJO DE CRIANZA.
adopted child.

HIJO DE FAMILIA.
minor, minor child or son (under parental control).

HIJO DE LA CUNA.
foundling, abandoned child.

HIJO DE PADRE DESCONOCIDO.
child or son born of an unknown father.

HIJO EMANCIPADO.
emancipated child or son ‖ child who has reached the age of majority or has been granted emancipation by his parents.

HIJO ESPURIO.
See HIJO BASTARDO.

HIJO EXTRAMATRIMONIAL.
illegitimate child or son, son or child born out of wedlock.

HIJO ILEGÍTIMO.
illegitimate child or son ‖ bastard.

HIJO INCESTUOSO.
child or son resulting from incest.

HIJO LEGITIMADO.
legitimated child or son, child or son born to unmarried parents who subsequently marry and who thus becomes a legitimate child.
HIJO LEGÍTIMO.
legitimate child or son, child conceived to parents after marriage.
HIJO MANCER.
prostitute's child or son.
HIJO NATURAL.
natural child or son, illegitimate child or son (of persons who were free to marry).
HIJO NATURAL RECONOCIDO.
natural child or son who has been legally acknowledged by parents as their offspring.
HIJO PÓSTUMO.
posthumously-born child or son, child born after the death of the father.
HIJO RECONOCIDO.
natural child or son who is legally recognized by one or both of the parents.
HIJO SACRÍLEGO.
child or son born to a woman and a priest.
HIJUELA.
f, accessory, subordinate thing ‖ part of estate to be inherited by each heir ‖ document given to each heir, in which the property received by him or her is listed.
HIPNOTISMO.
m, hypnotism.
HIPOTECA.
f, mortgage (of real property). Deemed to be an interest in rem.
HIPOTECA ABSTRACTA.
See HIPOTECA INDEPENDIENTE.
HIPOTECA AÉREA.
aircraft mortgage or lien.
HIPOTECA AERONÁUTICA.
See HIPOTECA AÉREA.
HIPOTECA CERRADA.
closed mortgage.
HIPOTECA COLECTIVA.
blanket mortgage.
HIPOTECA CONVENCIONAL.
See HIPOTECA VOLUNTARIA.
HIPOTECA DE BIENES INMUEBLES.
chattel mortgage, security interest in personal property.
HIPOTECA DE LA HIPOTECA.
Literally, mortgage of the mortgage, security

in a mortgage (held by a creditor of mortgagee).
HIPOTECA EN PRIMER GRADO.
first mortgage.
HIPOTECA EN PRIMER LUGAR.
See HIPOTECA EN PRIMER GRADO.
HIPOTECA EN SEGUNDO GRADO.
second or junior mortgage.
HIPOTECA ESPECIAL.
special mortgage, mortgage over specified property. Virtually all mortgages are now special mortgages.
HIPOTECA EXPRESA.
registered mortgage, mortgage filed with the real estate registry. Without registration the mortgage is ineffective against third parties. Opposed to HIPOTECA TÁCITA.
HIPOTECA GENERAL.
general mortgage, blanket mortgage, mortgage over all of debtor's property without greater specification. No longer valid.
HIPOTECA INDETERMINADA.
open-end mortgage.
HIPOTECA LEGAL.
legal mortgage, statutory mortgage, mortgage which is implied by law. May not need to be registered to be perfected.
HIPOTECA NAVAL.
ship mortgage or lien, mortgage of a vessel.
HIPOTECA POSTERIOR.
junior or second mortgage.
HIPOTECA PRECEDENTE.
first or prior or underlying mortgage.
HIPOTECA PRENDARIA.
chattel mortgage ‖ pledge.
HIPOTECA PRINCIPAL.
first mortgage.
HIPOTECA SECUNDARIA.
See HIPOTECA POSTERIOR.
HIPOTECA SUPERIOR.
See HIPOTECA PRECEDENTE.
HIPOTECA TÁCITA.
tacit or implied mortgage, mortgage which does not have to be registered in order to have effect against third parties. Opposed to HIPOTECA EXPRESA. Type of HIPOTECA LEGAL.
HIPOTECA VOLUNTARIA.
conventional mortgage, mortgage imposed as a result of a voluntary contract. Opposed to statutory mortgage.

HIPOTECABLE.
adj, mortgageable, able to be mortgaged.
HIPOTECADO.
adj, mortgaged.
HIPOTECANTE.
m, f, mortgager.
HIPOTECAR.
v, to mortgage ‖ to obtain a mortgage on.
HIPOTECARIO.
adj, mortgage, pertaining to mortgages.
HIPÓTESIS.
f, hypothesis.
HIPOTÉTICO.
adj, hypothetical.
HISTERIA.
f, hysteria ‖ hysterics.
HISTORIA DEL DERECHO.
f, history of law, study of the historical development of law.
HISTORIAL.
m, record, history ‖ background ‖ adj, historical ‖ historic.
HISTORICISMO JURÍDICO.
m, juridical historicism, theory that the development of law is based on historical developments. Opposed to theory of natural law.
HITO.
m, boundary marker or post.
HOGAR.
m, home ‖ family.
HOJA.
f, page, leaf.
HOJA SELLADA.
stamped leaf or page or sheet of paper.
HOJA TIMBRADA.
See HOJA SELLADA.
HOLÓGRAFO.
m, holograph ‖ manuscript ‖ adj, holographic, hand-written.
HOMBRE.
m, man, male ‖ mankind.
HOMBRE BUENO.
honest and upstanding man ‖ arbitrator, referee, arbiter.
HOMBRE DE PAJA.
straw man, front man.
HOMICIDA.
m, f, killer, murderer, person guilty of homicide ‖ adj, homicidal.
HOMICIDIO.
m, murder, killing ‖ homicide. May be VOLUN-

TARIO (voluntary) or INVOLUNTARIO (involuntary).
HOMICIDIO ACCIDENTAL.
See HOMICIDIO CASUAL.
HOMICIDIO CALIFICADO.
aggravated homicide, homicide aggravated by circumstances of killing (e.g. relationship between victim and actor).
HOMICIDIO CASUAL.
involuntary manslaughter.
HOMICIDIO CONSUMADO.
consummate homicide.
HOMICIDIO CUALIFICADO.
See HOMICIDIO CALIFICADO.
HOMICIDIO CULPABLE.
manslaughter, unintentional homicide (which is neither justifiable nor excusable).
HOMICIDIO CULPOSO.
See HOMICIDIO CULPABLE.
HOMICIDIO DOLOSO.
murder, intentional homicide.
HOMICIDIO EN RIÑA TUMULTUARIA.
murder or homicide resulting from a brawl such that the author is not able to be determined.
HOMICIDIO FRUSTRADO.
attempted murder which (due to independent causes) does not injure or kill.
HOMICIDIO INCULPABLE.
justifiable homicide.
HOMICIDIO INTENTADO.
attempted murder (which does not result in death).
HOMICIDIO INVOLUNTARIO.
See HOMICIDIO CASUAL.
HOMICIDIO NECESARIO.
homicide by necessity.
HOMICIDIO PIADOSO.
euthanasia.
HOMICIDIO POR NEGLIGENCIA.
negligent homicide.
HOMICIDIO PREMEDITADO.
murder, premeditated murder.
HOMICIDIO PRETERINTENCIONAL.
manslaughter (in which the actor wishes to injure, not kill).
HOMICIDIO-SUICIDIO.
m, aiding and abetting a suicide.
HOMOLOGACIÓN.
f, homologation, finality of arbitral award resulting from passage of statutory period after

decision without objection by the parties, or from approval by a court or other competent authority ‖ judicial approval of parties' acts required in order to be effective ‖ approval, confirmation, consent.

HOMOLOGAR.
v, to approve, consent, confirm ‖ to make an arbitral award final by the passage of statutory period without objection by the parties, or by the approval by a court or other competent authority ‖ to issue written approval of parties' acts ‖ to proceed before a higher administrative authority to obtain requisite approval of an agreement, etc.

HOMOLOGATORIO.
adj, approving, confirming, consenting.

HOMOSEXUAL.
f, m, homosexual ‖ adj, homosexual.

HOMOSEXUALIDAD.
f, homosexuality.

HONESTAMENTE.
adv, honestly, honorably.

HONESTIDAD.
f, honesty ‖ modesty ‖ decency.

HONESTO.
adj, honest ‖ decent, chaste ‖ modest ‖ just, fair, reasonable.

HONOR.
m, honor.

HONORABILIDAD.
f, honor ‖ good reputation or repute ‖ honesty.

HONORABLE.
adj, honorable.

HONORABLEMENTE.
adv, honorably.

HONORARIO.
m, honorarium ‖ adj, honorary.

HONORARIO CONDICIONAL.
contingent fee.

HONORARIO DEFINIDO.
fixed or set fee.

HONORARIO FIJO.
See HONORARIO DEFINIDO.

HONORARIOS.
m, fees, remuneration, stipend, salary (usually used in reference to compensation for professional services).

**HONORARIOS DE
LOS DIRECTORES.**
directors' fees or honorarium.

HONORES.
m, position, employment, position ‖ rank, dignity ‖ privileges or status or position granted as an honor (which may or may not accompany a special dignity).

HONORÍFICO.
adj, honorific.

HONORIS CAUSA.
for honor, because of honor ‖ honorarily.

HONRA.
f, honor.

HONRADEZ.
f, honesty, integrity, rectitude.

HONRADO.
adj, honest ‖ honorable, reputable ‖ upstanding.

HONRAR.
v, to honor, respect ‖ to meet (e.g. one's obligations).

HORA.
f, hour ‖ time.

HORARIO DE TRABAJO.
f, work schedule.

HORAS EXTRAORDINARIAS.
f, overtime, extra hours.

HORAS HÁBILES.
judicial office hours, hour during which judicial offices are open for service. May differ between civil and criminal courts.

HORAS INHÁBILES.
non-working hours for judicial offices, hours during which judicial offices are closed for service.

HORCA.
f, gallows.

HOSPITALIZACIÓN.
f, hospitalization.

HOSTIL.
adj, hostile.

HOSTILIDAD.
f, hostility, enmity.

HOSTILIDADES.
f, hostilities (between enemies, nations, etc.).

HUELGA.
f, strike, labor strike, work strike.

HUELGA DE BRAZOS CAÍDOS.
sit-down strike, strike in which workers refuse to work but remain on the employer's premises.

HUELGA DE BRAZOS CRUZADOS.
See HUELGA DE BRAZOS CAÍDOS.

HUELGA DE HAMBRE.
hunger strike.
HUELGA DE OCUPACIÓN.
See HUELGA DE BRAZOS CAÍDOS.
HUELGA DE SOLIDARIDAD.
sympathy strike, strike to show solidarity with another union which is striking.
HUELGA GENERAL.
general strike (of all union workers).
HUELGA ILEGAL.
illegal strike.
HUELGA PASIVA.
See HUELGA DE BRAZOS CAÍDOS.
HUELGA PATRONAL.
lock-out.
HUELGA POLÍTICA.
political strike ‖ labor strike against a company to pressure it to lobby the government to change a policy or law ‖ labor strike used to pressure the government to change a policy or law.
HUELLA DACTILAR.
f, fingerprint.
HUELLA DIGITAL.
See HUELLA DACTILAR.
HUÉRFANO.
m, orphan ‖ person abandoned by mother or father or both.
HUIDA.
f, escape, flight.
HUIDA DE CAPITALES.
capital flight.
HUIDERO.
m, escapee, fugitive ‖ adj, fugitive.
HUIDO.
See HUIDERO
HUJIER.
See UJIER.
HUMANO.
m, human, human being ‖ adj, human, humanitarian ‖ humane.
HURTADO.
adj, stolen, robbed.
HURTADOR.
m, thief, robber.
HURTAR.
v, to commit larceny, burgle ‖ to steal, thieve.

HURTARSE.
v, to abscond, take off, steal away.
HURTO.
m, larceny, burglary ‖ theft, stealing. This crime usually consists of the unauthorized possession or use of property of another for personal gain, without use of force or violence.
HURTO CALAMITOSO.
larceny during a disaster (e.g. fire, earthquake, etc.). Usually an aggravating circumstance.
HURTO CALIFICADO.
aggravated larceny. Usually consists of theft of specified types of things (e.g. livestock, tools of the trade, etc.), or under specified circumstances (e.g. during a public disorder, etc.), or by certain means (e.g. false keys or by climbing, etc.).
HURTO CON CIRCUNSTANCIAS AGRAVANTES.
aggravated larceny or burglary.
HURTO CUALIFICADO.
See HURTO CALIFICADO.
HURTO DE AUTOMOTORES.
automobile theft ‖ joy riding, theft of a car for pleasure.
HURTO DE USO.
type of larceny for temporary use, whether it be the prohibited use of property otherwise legally in one's possession, or the unauthorized use of something of another.
HURTO DEFRAUDACIÓN.
sale of stolen goods (which constitutes theft).
HURTO DOMÉSTICO.
larceny or theft committed by a servant or other domestic help.
HURTO FAMÉLICO.
larceny caused by hunger or other basic need. May be a justification.
HURTO FAMULARIO.
See HURTO DOMÉSTICO.
HURTO MAYOR.
grand larceny.
HURTO MENOR.
petty larceny.
HURTO RURAL.
larceny committed in the country (usually of agricultural products or animals).

ICONOCLASTA.
f, m, iconoclast ‖ adj, iconoclastic.
IDEAL.
adj, ideal ‖ legal.
ÍDEM.
pron, the same.
IDENTIDAD.
f, sameness ‖ identity.
IDENTIDAD DE ACCIÓN.
See CONTINENCIA DE LA CAUSA.
IDENTIDAD DE CAUSA.
quality of sameness of a present case with that which has already been heard.
IDENTIDAD DE COSAS.
See CONTINENCIA DE LA CAUSA.
IDENTIDAD DE LETRAS.
See COTEJO DE LETRAS.
IDENTIDAD DE PERSONA.
See IDENTIDAD PERSONAL.
IDENTIDAD DE OBJETO.
identical nature of the claim, quality of being the same claim as that of a prior lawsuit.
IDENTIDAD DE PARTES.
identical parties, quality of being the same parties as those of a prior lawsuit.
IDENTIDAD DEL IMPUTADO.
identity of the accused ‖ recognition or identification of the accused (by witnesses to a crime).
IDENTIDAD DEL LITIGIO.
See CONTINENCIA DE LA CAUSA.
IDENTIDAD PERSONAL.
coincidence of persons (between the person appearing in court and the person summoned to appear) ‖ personal identity ‖ heir who is vested with the rights and obligations of the decedent.

IDENTIFICABLE.
adj, identifiable.
IDENTIFICACIÓN.
f, identification, identification documents or papers, I.D. ‖ identification (of persons or property) ‖ criminal identification procedure (of an accused).
IDENTIFICACIÓN DE ACUSADOS.
identification of the accused or offenders.
IDENTIFICACIÓN DE DELINCUENTES.
identification of the accused or offenders.
IDENTIFICACIÓN DEL CADÁVER.
identification of the (dead) body or cadaver.
IDENTIFICADOR.
m, identifier.
IDENTIFICAR.
v, to identify.
IDEOLOGÍA.
f, ideology.
IDIOCIA.
See IDIOTEZ.
IDIOTA.
m, idiot ‖ adj, idiotic.
IDIOTEZ.
f, idiocy, severe mental incapacity.
IDIOTISMO.
m, idiocy, severe mental incapacity.
IDOLATRÍA.
f, idolatry ‖ adoration.
IDONEIDAD.
f, aptness, capability, sufficiency, suitability.
IDÓNEO.
adj, apt, capable, suitable, competent, sufficient ‖ legally competent.
IGNORADO.
adj, unknown, ignored.

IGNORANCIA.
f, ignorance, lack of knowledge or information ‖ unawareness.
IGNORANCIA DE ARMISTICIO.
ignorance of armistice.
IGNORANCIA DE DERECHO.
ignorance of the law.
IGNORANCIA DE LA LEY.
See IGNORANCIA DE DERECHO.
IGNORANCIA DEL DERECHO.
See IGNORANCIA DE DERECHO.
IGNORANCIA INEXCUSABLE.
inexcusable ignorance (e.g. of one's duty or function).
IGNORANTE.
m, ignorant person ‖ adj, ignorant, unlearned ‖ uninformed, unaware.
IGNORAR.
v, to ignore ‖ to be uneducated.
IGUAL.
adj, equal, same, identical.
IGUALA.
f, compromise, settlement ‖ compensation made as part of a settlement ‖ contingency fee (charged by a lawyer based on recovery) ‖ fee, retainer ‖ services contract.
IGUALAR.
v, to make equal, equalize, adjust ‖ to give equal treatment, not to differentiate ‖ to treat or judge impartially ‖ to compromise, settle, agree ‖ to bequeath equal legacies.
IGUALDAD.
f, equality.
IGUALDAD ANTE LA LEY.
equality under the law, equality in the eyes of the law, equal protection of the laws.
IGUALDAD ANTE EL IMPUESTO.
See IGUALDAD FISCAL.
IGUALDAD DE TRATO ENTRE TRABAJADORES.
equal treatment of workers.
IGUALDAD FISCAL.
tax equality. Refers to the principle that he who earns or has more should pay more tax.
IGUALDAD FRENTE A LA LEY.
See IGUALDAD ANTE LA LEY.
IGUALDAD PROCESAL.
procedural equality (between parties in litigation).
IGUALITARIO.
adj, equitable, egalitarian.

ILEGAL.
adj, illegal, unlawful ‖ illicit ‖ illegitimate.
ILEGALIDAD.
f, illegality.
ILEGALMENTE.
adv, illegally.
ILEGISLABLE.
adj, unable to be legislated (e.g. regulation of thoughts or feelings, etc.).
ILEGITIMAR.
v, to make illegitimate ‖ to be unaware of the illegality.
ILEGITIMIDAD.
f, illegitimacy ‖ illegality.
ILEGÍTIMO.
adj, illegitimate ‖ illegal ‖ false.
ILÍCITO.
adj, illicit, unlawful, illegal.
ILICITUD.
f, illicitness, illegality.
ILIMITADO.
adj, unlimited.
ILÍQUIDO.
adj, unliquidated (e.g. account, funds) ‖ illiquid.
IMAGEN.
f, image ‖ figure, representation ‖ appearance.
IMBÉCIL.
f, m, imbecile ‖ adj, imbecile.
IMBECILIDAD.
ı, imbecility.
IMBELE.
adj, defenseless, unable to fight or defend oneself.
IMITACIÓN.
f, imitation, copy.
IMITACIÓN DE MARCA.
trademark passing off.
IMITACIÓN DE NOMBRE COMERCIAL.
trade name passing off.
IMITADO.
adj, imitated ‖ false, spurious.
IMITAR.
v, to imitate, copy, counterfeit.
IMPAGABLE.
adj, unpayable.
IMPAGADO.
adj, unpaid.
IMPAGO.
m, unpaid person ‖ adj, unpaid.

MPARCIAL.
adj, impartial, unbiased, neutral.
MPARCIALIDAD.
f, impartiality, neutrality.
MPEDIDO.
adj, disabled (person), maimed ‖ disqualified.
MPEDIMENTO.
m, obstacle, hindrance, impediment, difficulty ‖ disability ‖ impediment to a valid marriage ‖ estoppel.
IMPEDIMENTO ABSOLUTO.
absolute impediment.
IMPEDIMENTO DIRIMENTE.
impediment to a valid marriage.
IMPEDIMENTO IMPEDIENTE.
prohibitive impediment ‖ impediment which prohibits marriage.
IMPEDIMENTO LEGAL.
legal impediment.
MPEDIR.
v, to impede, make difficult, frustrate ‖ to estop.
MPEDITIVO.
adj, impeding, frustrating.
MPENSA.
f, expense, expenditure ‖ necessary and useful expense or expenditure.
MPERATIVO LEGAL.
m, legal imperative or requirement.
MPERDONABLE.
adj, irremissible ‖ unforgivable, unpardonable.
MPERFECTO.
adj, defective, faulty, imperfect ‖ incomplete.
MPERIALISMO.
m, imperialism.
MPERICIA.
f, want of skill or experience or knowledge in a profession or trade.
MPERIO.
m, empire ‖ status of emperor ‖ reign of emperor ‖ imperium, judicial authority, right to adjudge and to have the judgment carried out.
MPERIO DE
LA LEY.
rule of law (such that not only private persons, but governing bodies are subject to the law).
MPERSONAL.
adj, impersonal.
MPERTINENCIA.
f, impertinence.

IMPERTINENTE.
adj, impertinent.
ÍMPETU.
m, impetus, impulse.
ÍMPETU DE IRA.
See IMPULSO DE IRA.
ÍMPETU DE PÁNICO.
See IMPULSO DE PÁNICO.
IMPIGNORABLE.
adj, not able to be pledged.
IMPLANTAR.
v, to implant ‖ to start, establish, set up.
IMPLICAR.
v, to implicate.
IMPLÍCITO.
adj, implicit, tacit.
IMPONENTE.
m, depositor (in a bank account) ‖ contributor ‖ investor ‖ adj, obliging, obligating ‖ imposing.
IMPONER.
v, to obligate ‖ to assess, impose (e.g. taxes, duties) ‖ to inspire (e.g. fear, respect) ‖ to invest (money) ‖ to deposit (e.g. funds in a bank account) ‖ to inform, teach.
IMPONER CONTRIBUCIONES.
to assess or impose taxes.
IMPONER IMPUESTOS.
See IMPONER CONTRIBUCIONES.
IMPONER UNA MULTA.
to impose a fine.
IMPONIBILIDAD.
f, taxability.
IMPONIBLE.
adj, taxable, dutiable, subject to levy or assessment.
IMPORTABLE.
adj, importable, able to imported.
IMPORTACIÓN.
f, importation ‖ imports, imported goods.
IMPORTACIÓN INVISIBLE.
invisible importation, importation of funds from the export of services or use of services domestically by foreigners.
IMPORTACIÓN LIBRE DE DERECHOS.
duty-free importation ‖ duty-free import or goods.
IMPORTADOR.
m, importer ‖ adj, importing.
IMPORTANTE.
adj, important ‖ material ‖ weighty.

IMPORTUNAR.
v, to bother, harass ‖ to demand payment.
IMPOSIBILIDAD.
f, impossibility ‖ disability.
IMPOSIBILIDAD DE
LAS OBLIGACIONES.
impossibility of complying with legal obligations (due to legal or physical disability).
IMPOSIBILIDAD DE PAGO.
(legal or physical) impossibility of payment.
IMPOSIBILIDAD MATERIAL.
physical impossibility.
IMPOSIBILIDAD MORAL.
relative impossibility.
IMPOSIBILITADO.
m, person who cannot comply (with something) ‖ adj, disabled, invalid.
IMPOSIBILITAR.
v, to impede ‖ to prohibit ‖ to veto ‖ to make impossible ‖ to disable.
IMPOSIBLE.
adj, impossible.
IMPOSICIÓN.
f, imposition ‖ duty, obligation ‖ tax, levy, assessment ‖ contribution.
IMPOSICIÓN DE COSTAS.
judicial assessment of the costs of litigation on one of the parties.
IMPOSICIÓN DEL PATRIMONIO.
capital levy.
IMPOSICIÓN DE LA RENTA.
income taxation.
IMPOSICIÓN FISCAL.
taxation.
IMPOSICIÓN PROGRESIVA.
progressive taxation.
IMPOSICIÓN REAL.
real property taxation.
IMPOSICIÓN REGRESIVA.
regressive taxation.
IMPOSICIÓN SOBRE CAPITALES.
capital taxation.
IMPOSITIVO.
adj, tax, pertaining to taxes or taxation.
IMPOSTERGABLE.
adj, unable to be postponed.
IMPOSTOR.
m, impostor, impersonator ‖ defamer, one who accuses falsely; defrauder, swindler.
IMPOSTURA.
f, imposture ‖ false accusation, defamation,

slander (if oral), libel (if written) ‖ lie ‖ impersonation ‖ false pretense.
IMPOTENCIA.
f, impotence ‖ powerlessness, lack of power inability.
IMPOTENTE.
m, impotent man, sterile woman ‖ adj, impotent.
IMPRACTICABLE.
adj, impracticable.
IMPREMEDITACIÓN.
f, lack of premeditation.
IMPREMEDITADO.
adj, unpremeditated.
IMPRENTA.
f, press ‖ printing ‖ print shop ‖ print.
IMPRESCINDIBLE.
adj, essential, absolutely necessary, indispensable ‖ legally indispensable.
IMPRESCRIPTIBILIDAD.
f, imprescriptibility, inability to be taken away.
IMPRESCRIPTIBLE.
adj, imprescribable, imprescriptible, not subject to prescription.
IMPRESIÓN.
f, impression, print ‖ fingerprint.
IMPRESIONES DACTILARES.
fingerprints.
IMPRESIONES DIGITALES.
See IMPRESIONES DACTILARES.
IMPRESTABLE.
adj, unloanable, unlendable.
IMPREVISIBILIDAD.
f, unforeseeability.
IMPREVISIBLE.
adj, unforeseeable.
IMPREVISIÓN.
f, improvidence, lack of foresight.
IMPREVISOR.
m, person who lacks foresight or constantly fails to use due care; adj, lacking in foresight.
IMPREVISTO.
adj, unforeseen.
IMPREVISTOS.
m, unapproved expenditures (by the government), expenses not provided for in the government budget.
IMPROCEDENCIA.
f, inopportuneness ‖ unlawfulness, illegality lack of basis or foundation ‖ invalidity of document, proof, recourse, etc.

IMPROCEDENTE.
adj, unlawful, illegal ‖ baseless, unfounded ‖ inadmissible; inopportune.

IMPRODUCTIVO.
adj, unproductive, unfruitful.

IMPROPIO.
adj, foreign, alien ‖ inappropriate, unsuitable, unfitting.

IMPRORROGABILIDAD.
f, unextendibility, unpostponability ‖ inability to stay the running of a statute of limitations or extend a given due date.

IMPRORROGABLE.
adj, unextendible (in time).

IMPRUDENCIA.
f, imprudence ‖ lack of due care ‖ type of inexcusable negligence for lack of due care. Used in both criminal and tort law.

IMPRUDENCIA CONCURRENTE.
contributory negligence or lack of due care.

IMPRUDENCIA CRIMINAL.
criminal negligence or lack of due care.

IMPRUDENCIA CULPABLE.
culpable negligence or lack of due care.

IMPRUDENCIA PROFESIONAL.
type of professional negligence (for lack of due care) ‖ breach of duty of due care by a professional. In labor law, it refers to a workers' negligent conduct which results in injury to himself.

IMPRUDENCIA SIMPLE.
type of simple negligence which, although no regulation or law is broken, results in criminal damage.

IMPRUDENCIA TEMERARIA.
reckless negligence.

IMPRUDENTE.
f, m, imprudent person ‖ adj, imprudent, negligent ‖ indiscreet.

IMPRUDENTEMENTE.
adv, imprudently.

IMPÚBER.
adj, impuberate, under the age of 12 in females and 14 in males. The law usually prohibits marriage of such children.

IMPUBERTAD.
f, pre-puberty.

IMPUDICIA.
f, indecency, lewdness.

IMPUESTO.
m, tax, duty, charge, levy, fee, assessment ‖ impost, imposition.

IMPUESTO A LA HERENCIA.
See IMPUESTO SUCESORIO.

IMPUESTO A LA TRANSFERENCIA DE TÍTULOS VALORES.
securities turnover or securities transfer tax.

IMPUESTO A LAS GANANCIAS.
income tax.

IMPUESTO A LAS RENTAS.
income tax.

IMPUESTO A LAS TRANSACCIONES.
excise tax.

IMPUESTO A LAS UTILIDADES.
See IMPUESTO A LAS RENTAS.

IMPUESTO A LAS VENTAS.
sales tax.

IMPUESTO A LOS BENEFICIOS ADICIONALES.
excess gains or excess profits tax.

IMPUESTO A LOS BENEFICIOS EXTRAORDINARIOS.
excess gains or excess profits tax.

IMPUESTO A LOS BENEFICIOS EVENTUALES.
capital gains tax.

IMPUESTO A LOS CAPITALES.
capital stock tax, tax on amount of property represented by stock held by individual.

IMPUESTO A LOS COMBUSTIBLES.
gas tax.

IMPUESTO A LOS PREDIOS.
land tax.

IMPUESTO A LOS RÉDITOS.
income tax.

IMPUESTO ADICIONAL.
surtax.

IMPUESTO ADUANAL.
duty, customs duty or tax.

IMPUESTO ARANCELARIO.
See IMPUESTO ADUANAL.

IMPUESTO AL CONSUMO.
consumption tax ‖ excise tax.

IMPUESTO AL PATRIMONIO NETO.
net worth tax, tax on net worth of a person.

IMPUESTO AL VALOR AGREGADO.
value added tax, VAT. Usually paid by buyer and deductible from taxes payable upon resale.

IMPUESTO BÁSICO.
basic tax.
IMPUESTO COMPLEMENTARIO.
surtax.
IMPUESTO DE AUSENTISMO.
absentee tax, tax imposed on absentees.
IMPUESTO DE CAPITACIÓN.
head or poll tax.
IMPUESTO DE DERECHOS REALES.
real estate transfer tax.
IMPUESTO DE ESTAMPILLADO.
stamp tax.
IMPUESTO DE HERENCIAS.
inheritance tax.
IMPUESTO DE INMUEBLES.
real estate tax.
IMPUESTO DE INTERNACIÓN.
import tax or duty.
IMPUESTO DE JUSTICIA.
court tax. See GASTOS CAUSÍDICOS.
IMPUESTO DE LEGADO.
inheritance tax.
IMPUESTO DE MEJOR.
improvement assessment.
IMPUESTO DE PRIVILEGIO.
franchise tax or assessment.
IMPUESTO DE PATRIMONIO.
capital tax or levy.
IMPUESTO DE SELLOS.
stamp tax.
IMPUESTO DE SOLTERÍA.
tax imposed on unmarried persons.
IMPUESTO DE SUCESIÓN.
inheritance tax.
IMPUESTO DE SUPERPOSICIÓN.
surtax.
IMPUESTO DE TESTAMENTARÍA.
See IMPUESTO DE SUCESIÓN.
IMPUESTO DE TIMBRES.
stamp tax.
IMPUESTO DE TRANSFERENCIA.
transfer tax.
IMPUESTO DE VALORIZACIÓN.
real estate improvement tax or levy.
IMPUESTO DIRECTO.
direct tax.
IMPUESTO ELECTORAL.
poll tax.
IMPUESTO ESTATAL.
state tax or levy.

IMPUESTO EXTRAORDINARIO.
surtax.
IMPUESTO FISCAL.
federal tax.
IMPUESTO HEREDITARIO.
inheritance tax.
IMPUESTO INDIRECTO.
indirect tax.
IMPUESTO INDIVIDUAL SOBRE LA RENTA.
individual income tax.
IMPUESTO INMOBILIARIO.
real estate tax.
IMPUESTO NORMAL.
See IMPUESTO ORDINARIO.
IMPUESTO ORDINARIO.
ordinary tax, tax which is regularly paid to th
national treasury.
Opposed to IMPUESTO EXTRAORDINARIO.
IMPUESTO PARA PREVISIÓN SOCIAL.
social security tax.
IMPUESTO PATRIMONIAL.
capital tax.
IMPUESTO POR CABEZA.
head tax, poll tax.
IMPUESTO PORTUARIO.
port tax or fee or charge.
IMPUESTO PREDIAL.
real property tax.
IMPUESTO PROGRESIVO.
progressive tax.
IMPUESTO PROPORCIONAL.
proportional tax.
IMPUESTO REAL.
real property tax.
IMPUESTO REGRESIVO.
regressive tax.
IMPUESTO SOBRE BENEFICIOS.
profits tax.
IMPUESTO SOBRE BENEFICIOS EXTRAORDINARIOS.
excess profits tax.
IMPUESTO SOBRE BIENES.
property tax.
IMPUESTO SOBRE COMPRAVENTA.
sales tax.
IMPUESTO SOBRE CONCESIONES.
franchise tax.
IMPUESTO SOBRE DIVERSIONES.
amusement tax.

IMPUESTO SOBRE DONACIONES.
gift tax.
IMPUESTO SOBRE EL INCREMENTO DE PATRIMONIO.
capital gains tax.
IMPUESTO SOBRE EL INGRESO.
income tax.
IMPUESTO SOBRE EL LUJO.
luxury tax.
IMPUESTO SOBRE ENTRADAS.
admissions tax.
IMPUESTO SOBRE ESPECTÁCULOS.
See IMPUESTO SOBRE ENTRADAS.
IMPUESTO SOBRE EXCESO DE GANANCIAS.
excess profits tax.
IMPUESTO SOBRE FRANQUICIAS.
franchise tax.
IMPUESTO SOBRE INGRESOS DE SOCIEDADES.
corporate (or other business association) income tax.
IMPUESTO SOBRE INGRESOS INDIVIDUALES.
individual income tax.
IMPUESTO SOBRE LAS SOCIEDADES.
See IMPUESTO SOBRE INGRESOS DE SOCIEDADES.
IMPUESTO SOBRE LOS INGRESOS BRUTOS.
gross revenue tax.
IMPUESTO SOBRE PRODUCCIÓN.
production tax.
IMPUESTO SOBRE RIQUEZA MUEBLE.
personal property tax.
IMPUESTO SOBRE TRANSFERENCIAS.
transfer tax.
IMPUESTO SOBRE TRANSMISIONES.
See IMPUESTO SOBRE TRANSFERENCIAS.
IMPUESTO SOBRE UTILIDADES EXCESIVAS.
excess profits tax.
IMPUESTO SOBRE VENTAS.
sales tax.
IMPUESTO SUCEDÁNEO.
substitute tax, tax in lieu of a different tax.
IMPUESTO SUCESORIO.
inheritance or estate tax.
IMPUESTO SUNTUARIO.
luxury tax.

IMPUESTO TERRITORIAL.
land tax, real estate tax.
IMPUESTO ÚNICO.
single tax ‖ one-time tax.
IMPUESTOS ILEGALES.
unauthorized taxes, monies illegally collected as a tax.
IMPUESTOS INTERNOS.
excise taxes.
IMPUESTOS NACIONALES.
national or federal taxes.
IMPUESTOS RETENIDOS.
taxes withheld, withholding taxes.
IMPUGNABILIDAD.
f, refutability, ability to be impugned ‖ vulnerability.
IMPUGNABLE.
adj, impugnable, refutable, able to be contested ‖ attackable.
IMPUGNACIÓN.
m, impugnment, refutation, objection, contradiction ‖ attack.
IMPUGNACIÓN EN EL CONCORDATO.
objection or challenge to a reorganization plan of a debtor in bankruptcy. Usually includes all forms of non-affirmation (e.g. non-participation, affirmative objection, etc.).
IMPUGNACIÓN EN LA QUIEBRA.
challenge by the bankrupt, trustee, or creditor against another creditor's claim filed in the bankruptcy.
IMPUGNACIÓN PROCESAL.
procedural challenge or objection.
IMPUGNADOR.
m, impugner, refuter, contradictor ‖ attacker ‖ adj, impugning, refuting, contradicting.
IMPUGNAR.
v, to impugn, refute, contradict, take exception to ‖ to attack ‖ to challenge (an action or position of another party) ‖ to request the nullification of something ‖ to deem an action to be unlawful.
IMPUGNAR POR NULIDAD.
to challenge as null and void.
IMPUGNAR UN TESTAMENTO.
to challenge or contest a will.
IMPUGNATIVO.
adj, impugning.
IMPUGNATORIO.
See IMPUGNATIVO.

IMPULSAR.
v, to activate, give impulse to ‖ to impel, drive.
IMPULSIÓN.
f, impulsion, impulse.
IMPULSIVIDAD.
f, impulsiveness.
IMPULSIVO.
adj, impulsive.
IMPULSO.
See IMPULSIÓN.
IMPULSO DE IRA.
heat of anger. May be considered to be an extenuating circumstance in criminal law.
IMPULSO DE PÁNICO.
state of panic. May be considered to be an extenuating circumstance in criminal law.
IMPULSO DE PARTE.
request or instance of a party (to a lawsuit).
IMPULSO PROCESAL.
prosecution of or activity in a lawsuit which moves a case forward.
IMPULSOS DE PERVERSIDAD BRUTAL.
See HOMICIDIO CALIFICADO.
IMPUNE.
adj, unpunished.
IMPUNEMENTE.
adv, with impunity, without punishment.
IMPUNIDAD.
f, impunity.
IMPURIFICAR.
v, to purge a country of political undesirables or opponents ‖ to adulterate ‖ to make impure ‖ to dirty, stain.
IMPUTABILIDAD.
f, imputability ‖ causal relationship between the actor and the criminal act.
IMPUTABLE.
adj, imputable.
IMPUTACIÓN.
f, imputation, attribution ‖ charge, accusation ‖ charge, application (e.g. of a sum of money).
IMPUTACIÓN DEL PAGO.
application of payment (to one of several accounts owed by one debtor to one creditor). Right of debtor.
IMPUTADO.
m, person subject to a criminal procedure without beinyet formally accused or indicted ‖ adj, imputed.

IMPUTADOR.
m, accuser ‖ adj, attributing ‖ charging, accusing.
IMPUTAR.
v, to impute, attribute ‖ to charge, accuse ‖ to charge, apply (monies to a specific account).
"IN ABSENTIA".
in absentia, absent, not present. Usually re court appearance.
IN ARTÍCULO MORTIS.
at the hour of death, in articulo mortis.
"IN CAPITA".
per capita.
"IN DUBIS, ABSTINE".
In doubtful cases, abstain from decision.
"IN DUBIS, FAVORABILIOR PARS EST ELIGENDA".
In doubtful cases, choose the most favorable.
"IN DUBIO, PRO OPERARIO".
In doubtful cases, decide in favor of the worker.
"IN DUBIO, PRO POSSESSORE".
In doubtful cases, decide in favor of the possessor.
"IN DUBIO, PRO REO".
In doubtful cases, decide in favor of the accused.
IN EXTREMIS.
in extremis.
"IN FRAGANTI".
in flagrante, in the act, flagrantly.
"IN ITINERE".
on the way, during the journey, in itinere, on the way to or from work.
"IN LIMINE LITIS".
at the start of a lawsuit, preliminary to litigation.
"IN MEMÓRIAM".
in memory (of).
"IN PARI CAUSA, MELIOR EST CAUSA POSSIDENTIS".
In equal cases, the possessor should be preferred.
IN PÉCTORE.
Literally, in the breast ‖ under reservation. Refers to a decision taken but not announced.
IN RE.
in re.
"IN SITU".
at the place or site.

IN SÓLIDUM.
in solido, in solidum, as a whole, jointly.
See OBLIGACIÓN SOLIDARIA.
IN STATU QUO.
as the status quo.
"IN STIRPES".
in stirpes.
IN VOCE.
out loud ‖ orally. Used to refer to oral rather than written processes.
INABROGABLE.
adj, not able to be abrogated ‖ irrevocable, indefeasible.
INACCIÓN.
f, inaction ‖ omission.
INACEPTABLE.
adj, unacceptable.
INACEPTADO.
adj, unaccepted, not accepted.
INACTUABLE.
adj, not actionable.
INACUMULATIVO.
adj, noncumulative.
INADMISIBILIDAD.
f, inadmissibility ‖ summarily dismissable. Used to refer to cause of action which should be dismissed on procedural grounds.
INADMISIBLE.
adj, inadmissible, incompetent (e.g. evidence).
INADMISIÓN.
f, nonadmission, rejection.
INADOPTABLE.
adj, unadoptable.
INALIENABILIDAD.
f, inalienability, untransferability.
INALIENABLE.
adj, inalienable, untransferable.
INAMOVIBLE.
adj, unremovable (e.g. from office).
INAMOVILIDAD.
f, undismissability, unremovability (e.g. of certain employees except for specified cause).
INAPELABILIDAD.
f, unappealability, finality ‖ definitiveness.
INAPELABLE.
adj, unappealable sentence or judgement (by law, prescription or agreement of the parties) ‖ adj, unappealable, final ‖ definitive.
INAPLAZABLE.
adj, undeferrable, not able to be postponed.

INAPLICABILIDAD.
f, inapplicability.
INAPLICABLE.
adj, inapplicable, irrelevant.
INAPRECIABLE.
adj, inestimable, inappreciable (in value).
INASISTENCIA.
f, absence, nonattendance, failure to attend.
INASISTENTE.
f, m, absentee ‖ adj, absent, not present.
INATACABLE.
adj, incontestable, irrefutable ‖ unattackable.
"INAUDITA ALTERA PARS".
The other party unheard. Used to refer to the principle that a judge cannot decide without hearing the opposing party, unless that party fails to appear.
INCAPACIDAD.
f, incapacity ‖ legal incapacity, legal lack of qualification, legal incompetency ‖ incompetence, ineptitude ‖ disability.
INCAPACIDAD ABSOLUTA.
absolute legal incapacity ‖ total permanent disability.
INCAPACIDAD ABSOLUTA PERMANENTE.
See INCAPACIDAD PERMANENTE TOTAL.
INCAPACIDAD ABSOLUTA TEMPORAL.
See INCAPACIDAD PERMANENTE TOTAL.
INCAPACIDAD CIVIL.
express legal incapacity (by law or judgment).
INCAPACIDAD DE DERECHO.
legal lack of capacity or inability to be a party.
INCAPACIDAD DE EJERCICIO.
factual incapacity ‖ inability to exercise a legal right requiring appointment of legal representative or aid.
INCAPACIDAD DE HECHO.
factual incapacity, inability to exercise a legal right requiring appointment of legal representative or aid.
INCAPACIDAD DEL SORDOMUDO.
lack of (legal) capacity of a deaf and dumb person. May occur in some countries if the person is unable to read and write.
INCAPACIDAD DEL TRABAJADOR.
employee disability.
INCAPACIDAD FÍSICA.
physical disability.
INCAPACIDAD JURÍDICA.
See INCAPACIDAD LEGAL.

INCAPACIDAD LABORAL.
inability to work, work disability.
INCAPACIDAD LEGAL.
legal incompetence or lack of capacity. May be total or partial.
INCAPACIDAD MENTAL.
mental disability.
INCAPACIDAD NATURAL.
lack of legal capacity due to physical problem ‖ physical inability (to carry out legal acts without assistance, e.g. inability of syphilitics to marry, etc.).
INCAPACIDAD PARA CASARSE.
incompetence or lack of capacity to marry.
INCAPACIDAD PARA COMERCIAR.
incompetence or lack of capacity to carry out business.
INCAPACIDAD PARA CONTRATAR.
incompetence or lack of capacity to contract.
INCAPACIDAD PARA SUCEDER.
incompetence or lack of capacity to inherit.
INCAPACIDAD PARA TRABAJAR.
work disability.
INCAPACIDAD PARCIAL.
partial disability or incompetence.
INCAPACIDAD PARTICULAR.
personal disability.
INCAPACIDAD PENAL.
See INIMPUTABILIDAD.
INCAPACIDAD PERMANENTE.
permanent disability.
INCAPACIDAD PERMANENTE TOTAL.
total permanent disability.
INCAPACIDAD TEMPORARIA TOTAL.
temporary total disability.
INCAPACIDAD PERPETUA.
permanent disability or incompetence.
INCAPACIDAD POLÍTICA.
lack of capacity to exercise rights pertaining to politics (e.g. voting, running for office, etc.).
INCAPACIDAD PROCESAL.
procedural incompetence.
INCAPACIDAD RELATIVA.
See INCAPACIDAD PARCIAL.
INCAPACIDAD TOTAL.
total disability or incapacity.
INCAPACIDAD TRANSITORIA.
temporary disability.
INCAPACITADO.
m, person who is disabled or incapacitated or legally incapacitated or unqualified or minor ‖

adj, disabled, incapacitated ‖ legally incapacitated or unqualified ‖ underage, minor.
INCAPACITAR.
v, to deprive of legal capacity ‖ to prohibit from certain activities ‖ to disqualify.
INCAPACITARSE.
v, to become disabled.
INCAPAZ.
f, m, incompetent, incapable or unable person ‖ adj, incompetent, incapable, inept, unable.
INCAUTACIÓN.
f, seizure, attachment ‖ sequestration, confiscation, impoundment ‖ expropriation, taking ‖ repossession.
INCAUTAMENTE.
adv, without caution.
INCAUTAR.
v, to attach, seize ‖ to confiscate, expropriate, condemn.
INCAUTARSE.
v, to seize, attach ‖ to sequester, confiscate, impound ‖ to expropriate, take ‖ to repossess.
INCENDIAR.
v, to set fire to, burn.
INCENDIARIO.
m, arsonist ‖ adj, incendiary.
INCENDIARISMO.
m, arson.
INCENDIO.
m, fire ‖ conflagration.
INCENDIO DOLOSO.
See INCENDIO MALICIOSO.
INCENDIO INTENCIONAL.
intentional fire ‖ also see INCENDIO MALICIOSO.
INCENDIO MALICIOSO.
arson.
INCENDIO MARÍTIMO.
maritime fire.
INCENDIO PREMEDITADO.
intentional fire ‖ also see INCENDIO MALICIOSO.
INCENDIO Y OTROS ESTRAGOS.
arson resulting in the commission of another crime. Used in criminal law.
INCENTIVACIÓN.
f, industrial work incentive, industrial incentive whereby increased production is rewarded by bonuses.
INCENTIVO.
m, incentive.

INCESIBLE.
adj, inalienable, untransferable.
INCESTAR.
v, to commit incest.
INCESTO.
m, incest, sexual relations between persons whose marriage would be prohibited by law.
INCESTUOSO.
adj, incestuous.
INCIDENCIA.
f, incidence ‖ occurrences or events of a trial.
INCIDENCIA DEL IMPUESTO.
incidence of taxation.
INCIDENTAL.
adj, incidental ‖ secondary.
INCIDENTALMENTE.
adv, incidentally.
INCIDENTE.
m, incident, occurrence, event, happening ‖ altercation ‖ question ‖ incidental proceeding or motion ‖ adj, incidental.
INCIDENTE DE NULIDAD.
incidental proceeding or motion to nullify a transaction or proceeding.
INCIDENTE DE POBREZA.
incidental proceeding to determine if party should be relieved of court costs on grounds of poverty ‖ motion requesting aforementioned proceeding.
INCIDENTE DE PREVIO Y ESPECIAL PRONUNCIAMIENTO.
incidental proceeding to stay the main litigation, which is decided by interlocutory order ‖ motion requesting aforementioned proceeding.
INCIDENTE EN CASACIÓN.
incidental proceeding which is decided by a court of cassation ‖ motion requesting aforementioned proceeding. See CASACIÓN.
INCIDENTE EN PIEZA SEPARADA.
incidental proceeding which does not stay the main litigation and is decided by interlocutory order ‖ motion requesting aforementioned proceeding.
INCIDENTE EN PRIMERA INSTANCIA.
incidental proceeding which is decided by interlocutory order of the judge in the main litigation ‖ motion requesting aforementioned proceeding.
INCIDENTE EN SEGUNDA INSTANCIA.
incidental proceeding which is decided by in-

terlocutory order of an appellate judge who is not the judge of the main litigation ‖ motion requesting aforementioned proceeding.
INCIDENTEMENTE.
adv, incidentally.
INCIDENTES DE PREVIO Y ESPECIAL PRONUNCIAMIENTO.
questions which must be settled before trial can proceed.
INCIERTO.
adj, untrue, false ‖ uncertain.
INCINERACIÓN.
f, incineration.
INCINERAR.
v, to incinerate, burn.
INCIPIENTE.
adj, incipient.
INCISO.
m, clause ‖ paragraph ‖ subsection.
INCITACIÓN.
f, stimulus, impulse ‖ provocation.
INCITADOR.
m, inciter, provocateur, agitator.
INCITAMENTO.
See INCITACIÓN.
INCITAMIENTO.
See INCITACIÓN.
INCITAR.
v, to incite, provoke, agitate ‖ to induce.
INCLUIR.
v, to include ‖ to incorporate ‖ to contain ‖ to enclose.
INCLUSA.
f, home for foundlings.
INCLUSIÓN.
f, inclusion ‖ incorporation ‖ enclosure.
INCLUSIÓN POR REFERENCIA.
inclusion or incorporation by reference.
INCLUSO.
adv, including.
INCOACIÓN.
f, initiation, commencement (e.g. of a criminal act or intent).
INCOADO.
adj, inchoate ‖ commenced, initiated, begun ‖ filed (re: a complaint).
INCOAR.
v, to initiate, commence, begin ‖ to initiate a criminal act ‖ to file a criminal lawsuit.
INCOBRABLE.
adj, unrecoverable, uncollectible.

INCOERCIBLE.
adj, uncoercible.
INCOMPARECENCIA.
f, failure to appear (when summoned), non-appearance.
INCOMPARECENCIA DEL ACUSADO.
failure of the accused to appear.
INCOMPARENCIA.
See INCOMPARECENCIA.
INCOMPATIBILIDAD.
f, incompatibility ‖ contradiction. Used to refer to marital relations and the inability to carry out certain functions or positions concurrently with others, etc.
INCOMPATIBILIDAD DE PRECEPTOS LEGALES.
incompatibility of legal principles.
INCOMPATIBLE.
adj, incompatible.
INCOMPENSABLE.
adj, unable to be compensated.
INCOMPETENCIA.
f, incompetence, inability, ineptness ‖ incompetency, lack of legal competence or capacity ‖ lack of jurisdiction or venue.
INCOMPETENCIA ABSOLUTA.
absolute jurisdictional incompetency of a court to hear a case (e.g. criminal court hearing a civil matter).
INCOMPETENCIA MATERIAL.
lack of legal competency of a court to hear a matter due to lack of jurisdiction over the thing.
INCOMPETENCIA PERSONAL.
lack of legal competency of a court to hear a matter due to lack of jurisdiction over the person.
INCOMPETENCIA RELATIVA.
relative jurisdictional incompetency of a court to hear a case. Arises in those cases in which court has jurisdiction but not venue over the case.
INCOMPETENTE.
adj, incompetent, inept, incapable, unqualified, unfit ‖ lacking legal competence or capacity ‖ unauthorized.
INCOMPLETO.
adj, incomplete.
INCOMUNICABLE.
adj, secret, reserved ‖ illegible.

INCOMUNICACIÓN.
f, deprivation of communication ‖ isolation ‖ solitary confinement.
INCOMUNICADO.
adj, incommunicado.
INCOMUNICAR.
v, to isolate, deprive of communication ‖ to submit to solitary confinement.
INCONCILIABLE.
adj, contradictory, incompatible.
INCONCLUSO.
adj, unfinished.
INCONCLUYENTE.
adj, inconclusive.
INCONCUSO.
unquestionable, undeniable ‖ incontrovertible, incontestable.
INCONDICIONADO.
See INCONDICIONAL.
INCONDICIONAL.
adj, unconditional, noncontingent ‖ absolute.
INCONDUCENTE.
adj, useless, inadequate.
INCONDUCIVO.
adj, irrelevant ‖ immaterial.
INCONDUCTA.
f, bad behavior.
INCONEXO.
adj, unrelated ‖ irrelevant.
INCONFESABLE.
adj, unspeakable, not able to be confessed.
INCONFIRMADO.
adj, unconfirmed.
INCONFORME.
adj, dissenting ‖ not in agreement.
INCONGRUENCIA.
f, incongruity, inconsistency.
INCONGRUENTE.
adj, incongruent.
INCONMUTABLE.
adj, immutable, unchangeable ‖ unexchangeable.
INCONSCIENCIA.
f, unconsciousness ‖ unawareness ‖ serious irresponsibility. Used in civil law to nullify agreements, and in criminal law to mitigate or justify offense.
INCONSCIENTE.
f, m, unconscious ‖ thoughtless person ‖ adj unconscious ‖ unaware ‖ seriously irresponsible. See INCONSCIENCIA.

INCONSECUENCIA.
f, contradiction, inconsistency ‖ disloyalty ‖ illogic reasoning.
INCONSECUENTE.
adj, inconsistent, changeable.
INCONSTITUCIONAL.
adj, unconstitutional.
INCONSTITUCIONALIDAD.
f, unconstitutionality.
INCONTESTABILIDAD.
f, incontestability, incontrovertibility, undisputability.
INCONTESTABLE.
adj, incontestable, incontrovertible, indisputable, undisputable.
INCONTESTACIÓN.
See ARTÍCULO DE INCONTESTACIÓN.
**INCONTESTACIÓN
A LA DEMANDA.**
failure to answer complaint.
INCONTESTADO.
adj, unanswered ‖ uncontroverted, uncontested.
INCONTINENCIA.
f, incontinence ‖ lack of restraint ‖ inability to hold one's water ‖ excessive or improper sexuality, drunkenness, etc.
INCONTINUO.
adj, interrupted, discontinuous, disconnected.
INCONTROVERTIBLE.
adj, incontrovertible, incontestable, indisputable, irrefutable.
INCORPORABLE.
adj, able to be incorporated or joined.
INCORPORACIÓN.
f, incorporation (into), joining (e.g. a group, army, etc.).
Also see ACCESIÓN.
**INCORPORACIÓN POR
REFERENCIA.**
incorporation by reference.
INCORPORAL.
adj, intangible, incorporeal.
INCORPORAR.
v, to incorporate (into), join ‖ to merge ‖ to unite ‖ to annex (e.g. territory) ‖ to mobilize (e.g. battalion during wartime).
INCORPORARSE.
v, to incorporate (e.g. oneself into a group, movement) ‖ to stand at attention ‖ to line up ‖ to join (e.g. the armed forces).

INCORPÓREO.
adj, incorporeal, intangible.
INCORREGIBILIDAD.
f, incorrigibility.
INCORREGIBLE.
adj, incorrigible.
INCORRUPCIÓN.
f, honesty, honor.
INCORRUPTIBILIDAD.
f, incorruptibility.
INCORRUPTIBLE.
adj, incorruptible.
INCORRUPTO.
adj, uncorrupted, not corrupt ‖ virginal, chaste.
INCREDIBILIDAD.
f, incredibility, unbelievability.
INCREDULIDAD.
f, incredulity.
INCREMENTAR.
v, to increase, augment ‖ to develop.
INCREMENTO.
m, increase, augment.
INCRIMINACIÓN.
f, incrimination.
INCRIMINAR.
v, to incriminate.
INCULPABILIDAD.
f, innocence, lack of guilt. Used in civil and criminal law.
INCULPABLE.
adj, innocent, not guilty ‖ guiltless.
INCULPACIÓN.
f, accusation, charge, denunciation ‖ imputation ‖ censure.
INCULPADO.
m, defendant, accused person, the accused ‖ adj, innocent, without guilt.
INCULPAR.
v, to inculpate, denounce, accuse.
INCULPATORIO.
adj, incriminating, inculpatory.
INCUMBENCIA.
f, faculty, power ‖ duty obligation.
INCUMBIR.
v, to be incumbent upon, the duty of.
INCUMPLIDO.
adj, unfulfilled ‖ defaulted.
INCUMPLIMIENTO.
m, breach, nonfulfillment, default, non-compliance, failure to comply (usually by omission rather than by commission) ‖ disobedience.

INCUMPLIMIENTO CON ANTICIPACIÓN.
anticipatory breach of contract.
INCUMPLIMIENTO DE CONDICIÓN.
breach of condition.
INCUMPLIMIENTO DE CONTRATO.
breach of contract.
INCUMPLIMIENTO DE DEBERES.
breach of duty, negligence.
INCUMPLIMIENTO DE PROMESA MATRIMONIAL.
breach of promise (to marry).
INCUMPLIMIENTO DE ÓRDENES.
disobedience of orders, failure to comply with orders.
INCUMPLIMIENTO IMPLÍCITO.
implied breach of contract.
INCUMPLIR.
v, to breach, fail to comply, default ‖ to disobey.
INCURABLE.
adj, incurable.
INCURIA.
f, negligence, carelessness.
INCURRIR.
v, to err, commit a mistake or offense ‖ to incur (e.g. expenses).
INCURRIR EN UNA DEUDA.
to incur a debt.
INCURRIR EN MORA.
to be late in a payment.
INCURRIR EN UNA MULTA.
to become liable for a fine.
INCURRIR EN RESPONSABILIDAD.
to become (civilly) liable (for something).
INCURSO.
adj, included (in the litigation) ‖ falling within (e.g. a rule, regulation) ‖ liable.
INDAGACIÓN.
f, investigation ‖ criminal inquest or investigation.
INDAGADO.
m, investigated person ‖ person who has made a statement in a criminal inquest ‖ adj, investigated.
INDAGADOR.
m, investigator, interrogator, examiner. Usually applied in criminal matters.
INDAGAR.
v, to inquire ‖ to examine, interrogate ‖ to investigate.

INDAGATORIA.
See DECLARACIÓN INDAGATORIA.
INDAGATORIO.
adj, investigative, investigatory.
INDEBIDAMENTE.
adv, unnecessarily, not required ‖ unduly, improperly ‖ illegally, illicitly.
INDEBIDO.
adj, illicit, illegal ‖ undue, unjust, improper ‖ unnecessary, not required.
INDECENCIA.
f, indecency ‖ obscenity.
INDECENTE.
adj, indecent ‖ obscene, lewd.
INDECISIÓN.
f, indecision.
INDECISO.
adj, undecided, doubtful.
INDECISORIO.
See JURAMENTO INDECISORIO.
INDECLINABLE.
adj, mandatory, obligatory, requisite ‖ unwaivable.
INDECORO.
m, morals offense ‖ adj, indecorous.
INDEFENDIBLE.
adj, defenseless, indefensible.
INDEFENSIBLE.
See INDEFENDIBLE.
INDEFENSIÓN.
f, lack of defense or protection ‖ state of being undefended.
INDEFENSO.
adj, defenseless, without defense.
INDELEGABLE.
adj, undelegable.
INDELIBERACIÓN.
f, lack of deliberation or premeditation.
INDELIBERADAMENTE.
adv, without deliberation or premeditation ‖ rashness.
INDELIBERADO.
adj, undeliberated, unpremeditated, undeliberate.
INDEMNE.
adj, indemnified, compensated ‖ unharmed, undamaged.
INDEMNIDAD.
f, indemnity, insurance, bond (against damages and losses) ‖ state of being unharmed, undamaged.

INDEMNIZABLE.
adj, indemnifiable, compensable ‖ repairable ‖ able to be subrogated.
INDEMNIZACIÓN.
f, indemnification, compensation ‖ repair ‖ subrogation.
INDEMNIZACIÓN COMPENSATORIA.
compensatory damages, indemnification.
INDEMNIZACIÓN DE DAÑOS Y PERJUICIOS.
See DAÑOS Y PERJUICIOS.
INDEMNIZACIÓN DE PERJUICIOS.
See DAÑOS Y PERJUICIOS.
INDEMNIZACIÓN DE PREAVISO.
See INDEMNIZACIÓN POR FALTA DE PREAVISO.
INDEMNIZACIÓN DOBLE.
double damages.
INDEMNIZACIÓN EN LA FIANZA.
subrogation for the guarantee. Includes the total amount of the debt, legal interest, incidental expenses, consequential damages and losses.
INDEMNIZACIÓN INSIGNIFICANTE.
insignificant or nominal damages.
INDEMNIZACIÓN JUSTA.
just or adequate damages.
INDEMNIZACIÓN OBRERA.
workman's compensation.
INDEMNIZACIÓN POR ACCIDENTE.
compensation for accident injuries, accident benefits.
INDEMNIZACIÓN POR ANTIGÜEDAD.
indemnification for termination of employment based on seniority of employee.
INDEMNIZACIÓN POR CESANTÍA.
See INDEMNIZACIÓN POR DESPIDO.
INDEMNIZACIÓN POR DESAHUICIO.
See INDEMNIZACIÓN POR DESPIDO.
INDEMNIZACIÓN POR DESPIDO.
indemnification for unjustified firing (of employee).
INDEMNIZACIÓN POR ENFERMEDAD.
sickness benefits.
INDEMNIZACIÓN POR FALTA DE PREAVISO.
indemnification for unjustified firing (of employee) without prior notice.
INDEMNIZACIÓN POR FALLECIMIENTO DEL TRABAJADOR.
employee death benefits ‖ indemnification for employee death (resulting from natural causes).
INDEMNIZACIÓN POR MUERTE.
death benefits.
INDEMNIZACIÓN RAZONABLE.
See INDEMNIZACIÓN JUSTA.
INDEMNIZADO.
m, indemnified or compensated person ‖ indemnitee ‖ adj, indemnified, compensated.
INDEMNIZADOR.
m, indemnifier, compensator ‖ indemnitor
INDEMNIZAR.
v, to indemnify, compensate ‖ to repay ‖ to subrogate (a guarantor).
INDEMNIZATORIO.
adj, indemnifying, compensating.
INDEPENDENCIA.
f, independence, freedom, liberty, autonomy.
INDEPENDENCIA ECONÓMICA.
economic independence or freedom.
INDEPENDENCIA JUDICIAL.
judicial autonomy or independence ‖ judicial impartiality.
INDEPENDERSE.
See INDEPENDIZARSE.
INDEPENDIZARSE.
v, to become independent, become emancipated.
INDEPENDIENTE.
f, m, unmarried adult who lives alone ‖ independent, member of an independent party ‖ adj, independent ‖ emancipated ‖ sovereign, autonomous ‖ impartial ‖ unaffiliated (e.g. politically).
INDEPENDIENTEMENTE.
adv, independently, autonomously ‖ separately.
INDEROGABLE.
adj, unrepealable ‖ not able to be superseded.
INDETERMINABLE.
adj, undeterminable, indeterminable.
INDETERMINADAMENTE.
adv, indeterminately ‖ doubtfully ‖ without coercion or prohibition.
INDETERMINADO.
adj, undetermined ‖ indeterminate, indefinite.
INDEX.
See ÍNDICE.
INDICACIÓN.
f, indication.
INDICACIÓN DE PROCEDENCIA.
indication of place of origin or manufacture.

INDICAR.
v, to indicate, express ‖ to instruct.

ÍNDICE.
m, index (of chapters) ‖ index, rate ‖ indication, sign ‖ list.

ÍNDICE DE CRIMINALIDAD.
crime rate, rate of crime.

ÍNDICES DEL REGISTRO DE LA PROPIEDAD.
lists (of real estate and owners) maintained by a real estate registry.

ÍNDICES NOTARIALES.
lists and statistics maintained by special public notaries.
See NOTARIO PÚBLICO.

INDICIADO.
m, criminal suspect ‖ adj, suspect.

INDICIAR.
v, to indicate, signal ‖ to suspect.

INDICIO.
m, indicium ‖ indication, sign ‖ conjecture, suspicion ‖ presumption ‖ circumstantial evidence (upon which criminal accusation is based).

INDICIO CLARO.
clear or irrebutable or conclusive presumption or circumstantial evidence.

INDICIO DE PRUEBA.
scintilla or trace of evidence.

INDICIO DUDOSO.
inconclusive or rebuttable presumption or circumstantial evidence.

INDICIO GRAVE.
See INDICIO CLARO.

INDICIO INDUDABLE.
See INDICIO CLARO.

INDICIO OSCURO.
See INDICIO DUDOSO.

INDICIO REMOTO.
See INDICIO DUDOSO.

INDICIO VIOLENTO.
See INDICIO VEHEMENTE.

INDICIO VEHEMENTE.
very strong circumstantial evidence which incriminates.

INDIGENCIA.
f, indigence.

INDIGENTE.
m, indigent ‖ adj, indigent, poor, needy.

INDIGNIDAD.
f, indignity.

INDIGNIDAD PARA SUCEDER.
disqualification from inheritance ‖ action which disqualifies a person from inheritance (e.g. murdering testator).

INDIGNO.
adj, undignified ‖ unmeritorious ‖ unqualified (to inherit).

INDILIGENCIA.
f, carelessness, lack of care or diligence ‖ negligence.

INDIRECTAMENTE.
adv, indirectly.

INDIRECTO.
adj, indirect ‖ irregular.

INDISCIPLINA.
f, lack of discipline ‖ rebellion, sedition.

INDISCIPLINADO.
adj, undisciplined.

INDISCRECIÓN.
f, indiscretion.

INDISCRETAMENTE.
adv, indiscreetly.

INDISCRETO.
m, indiscreet person ‖ adj, indiscreet.

INDISCULPABLE.
adj, inexcusable ‖ unjustifiable.

INDISCUTIBLE.
adj, incontrovertible, unquestionable ‖ indisputable, not open to discussion.

INDISOLUBILIDAD.
f, indissolubility.

INDISOLUBILIDAD DEL MATRIMONIO.
indissolubility of a marriage.

INDISOLUBLE.
adj, indissoluble.

INDISPENSABLE.
adj, indispensable, inexcusable, necessary, requisite.

INDIVIDUAL.
adj, individual ‖ personal, private.

INDIVIDUALISMO.
m, individualism.

INDIVIDUALIZACIÓN DE LA PENA.
f, adaptation of the punishment to the individual.

INDIVIDUALIZADO.
adj, individualized.

INDIVIDUALIZAR.
v, to individualize.

INDIVIDUALMENTE.
adv, individually, personally.

INDIVIDUO.
m, individual, person ‖ member ‖ adj, individual ‖ indivisible.

INDIVISIBILIDAD.
f, indivisibility.

INDIVISIBILIDAD ABSOLUTA.
absolute indivisibility (due to nature of the thing,e.g. an animal).

INDIVISILIBIDAD ACTIVA.
joint and indivisible right to assets (by creditors).

INDIVISILIBIDAD CONVENCIONAL.
indivisibility arising out of a contract.

INDIVISIBILIDAD DE LA CONFESIÓN.
indivisibility of a confession. Used to refer to principle that a judge must take a confession as a whole not merely believe those parts which are prejudicial to the defendant.

INDIVISILIBIDAD EN LA COMPRAVENTA.
indivisibility of a property being sold. Refers to the principle that an agreement by one of the owners to sell property owned by more than one person imposes the obligation to sell on the other owners.

INDIVISILIBIDAD EN LAS OBLIGACIONES.
See OBLIGACIÓN INDIVISIBLE.

INDIVISILIBIDAD PASIVA.
joint and several liability (re: obligations).

INDIVISIBILIDAD RELATIVA.
partial or relative indivisibility, indivisibility for certain purposes and divisibility for others.

INDIVISIBLE.
adj, indivisible.

INDIVISIBLEMENTE.
adv, indivisibly.

INDIVISIÓN.
f, indivision ‖ co-ownership (of property between two or more persons).

INDIVISIÓN DE LA HERENCIA.
indivision of the decedent's estate, state during which an estate is in probate and remains undivided.

INDIVISIÓN FORZOSA.
legal prohibition against partition.

INDIVISIÓN HEREDITARIA.
indivision of a decedent's estate, state of a decedent's property prior to distribution.

INDIVISIÓN TEMPORAL.
temporary prohibition against partition.

INDIVISO.
adj, undivided.

INDOCUMENTADO.
m, person who lacks identification papers or proper documentation ‖ adj, undocumented.

INDUBITABLE.
adj, undoubted, doubtless.

INDUCCIÓN.
f, inducement (especially to criminal act) ‖ induction (re: logic).

INDUCIDO.
adj, induced ‖ person who has been induced.

INDUCIR.
v, to induce, instigate, provoke ‖ to infer, induce.

INDUCTOR.
m, inducer ‖ person who has induced another (usually to act criminally).

INDULTADO.
m, person who has been pardoned or granted amnesty ‖ adj, pardoned.

INDULTAR.
v, to pardon, grant amnesty, grant a reprieve ‖ to commute (a sentence).

INDULTO.
m, pardon, amnesty, reprieve ‖ commutation of sentence ‖ commutation of death sentence ‖ privilege or licence to do the prohibited.

INDULTO GENERAL.
general amnesty or pardon.

INDULTO INTERNACIONAL.
type of international "pardon" granted to ships found in enemy waters such that they may be abandoned to the enemy within a given period of time without being captured as such.

INDUSTRIA.
f, industry ‖ work.

INDUSTRIA AGRARIA.
agricultural industry.

INDUSTRIA DE GUERRA.
defense industry.

INDUSTRIA EN CIERNES.
See INDUSTRIA NACIENTE.

INDUSTRIA FORESTAL.
forestry industry.

INDUSTRIA NACIENTE.
infant industry.

INDUSTRIAL.
m, industrialist, manufacturer ‖ adj, industrial.

INDUSTRIALISMO.
m, industrialism.

INÉDITO.
adj, unpublished.
INEFICACIA.
f, inefficacy ‖ inefficiency.
INEFICACIA DE LOS CONTRATOS.
inefficacy of a contract (due to its invalidity,
voidness, voidability, unenforceability, or rescission).
INEFICACIA JURÍDICA.
lack of legal effect.
INEFICAZ.
adj, ineffective ‖ inoperative.
INEFICIENTE.
adj, inefficient.
INEJECUCIÓN.
f, non-performance, failure to perform or carry out.
INEMBARGABILIDAD.
f, unseizability, unattachability.
INEMBARGABLE.
adj, not attachable or garnishable.
INENAJENABILIDAD.
See INANIENABILIDAD.
INENAJENABLE.
adj, inalienable, untransferable.
INEPTITUD.
f, ineptitude, incompetence.
INEPTO.
adj, inept, incompetent.
INEQUÍVOCO.
adj, unequivocal, certain, unambiguous.
INESTABILIDAD.
f, instability ‖ insecurity.
INEVITABLE.
adj, inevitable, unavoidable.
INEXCUSABLE.
adj, inexcusable ‖ unjustifiable, unpardona-
ble.
INEXISTENCIA.
f, lack, non-existence.
**INEXISTENCIA DE LOS ACTOS
JURÍDICOS.**
non-existence of legal interests.
INEXISTENCIA DEL MATRIMONIO.
non-existence of the marriage.
INEXISTENTE.
adj, non-existent, lacking ‖ null.
INFALIBILIDAD.
f, infallibility.
INFAMACIÓN.
f, defamation, calumny.

INFAMADOR.
m, dishonorer, defamer.
INFAMANTE.
adj, defamatory, calumnious.
INFAMAR.
v, to defame, dishonor.
INFAMATORIO.
See INFAMANTE.
INFAME.
f, m, scoundrel, vile or evil person ‖ adj, lack
ing in honor ‖ infamous.
INFAMIA.
f, infamy, dishonor, discredit ‖ vileness, evil.
INFANCIA.
f, infancy. Usually deemed to be from birth t
seven years of age.
INFANTICIDA.
f, m, person who has killed an infant.
INFANTICIDIO.
infanticide.
INFECUNDIDAD.
See ESTERILIDAD.
INFERENCIA.
f, inference, implication.
INFERENCIA LEGAL.
legal inference.
INFERENCIA LÓGICA.
logical conclusion or inference.
INFERIOR.
m, person of inferior rank ‖ adj, inferior ‖ l
wer ‖ of lesser quality.
INFIDELIDAD.
f, infidelity, disloyalty, unfaithfulness.
INFIDELIDAD CONYUGAL.
marital infidelity or unfaithfulness.
INFIDENCIA.
f, disloyalty ‖ breach of trust or of a duty of s
crecy.
See ABUSO DE CONFIANZA.
INFIDENTE.
adj, disloyal.
INFIEL.
f, m, infidel ‖ unfaithful or disloyal persor
adulterer ‖ adj, unfaithful ‖ disloyal ‖ inacc
rate, inexact.
INFILTRACIÓN.
f, infiltration (e.g. of political parties).
INFIRMACIÓN.
See INVALIDACIÓN.
INFLACIÓN.
f, inflation.

INFLACIÓN ABIERTA.
uncontrolled inflation (by government).
INFLACIÓN GALOPANTE.
galloping inflation.
INFLACIÓN REPRIMIDA.
controlled inflation.
INFLACIÓN REPTANTE.
creeping inflation.
INFLIGIR.
v, to inflict, impose.
INFLUENCIA.
f, influence ‖ power, authority.
INFLUENCIA INDEBIDA.
undue influence.
INFLUIR.
v, to influence, exercise authority or power.
INFLUJO.
See INFLUENCIA.
INFLUYENTE.
f, m, influential person ‖ adj, influential.
INFORMACIÓN.
f, information, knowledge ‖ judicial or legal interrogation or inquest or investigation (of a crime or other matter) ‖ expert's opinion or report issued by a consulting body or other expert regarding area of expertise ‖ oral allegations, allegations made orally.
INFORMACIÓN AD PERPETUAM.
declaratory judgment hearing, hearing to determine the status of certain events or things.
INFORMACIÓN DE ABONO.
supporting testimony, testimony given by witnesses in a criminal trial as to the truthfulness of statements made in a preliminary hearing by other witnesses who are not available at time of trial.
INFORMACIÓN DE "COMMODO E INCOMMODO".
type of environmental impact hearing regarding certain proposed construction, usually of a public nature.
INFORMACIÓN DE CRÉDITO.
credit check or investigation or report.
INFORMACIÓN DE DOMINIO.
special hearing to register real estate in real estate registry when proof of proper title is lacking, based on right of possession.
See INFORMACIÓN POSESORIA.
INFORMACIÓN DE POBREZA.
indigence hearing, hearing to demonstrate indigent status in order to be exempted from

paying court costs. See BENEFICIO DE LITIGAR SIN GASTOS.
INFORMACIÓN DE VITA ET MORIBUS.
information about the history and habits of a person who wishes to obtain a position or status ‖ police record.
INFORMACIÓN EN DERECHO.
See PAPEL EN DERECHO.
INFORMACIÓN PARA DISPENSA DE LEY.
exemption hearing. Refers to hearing to determine whether a person should be exempted from fulfilling legal requirement (e.g. exemptions to military induction, prohibitions to marrying).
INFORMACIÓN PARA PERPETUA MEMORIA.
See INFORMACIÓN AD PERPETUAM.
INFORMACIÓN PARLAMENTARIA.
congressional or parliamentary inquiry ‖ congressional or parliamentary hearing ‖ congressional information service.
INFORMACIÓN POSESORIA.
special hearing to determine who is in actual possession of real property ‖ special hearing to register real estate in a real estate registry when proof of proper title is lacking, based on actual possession.
See INFORMACIÓN DE DOMINIO.
INFORMACIÓN SUMARIA.
judicial investigative hearing. Usually brief and less formal.
INFORMADOR.
m, informer, informant ‖ advisor or investigator (to whom special investigative power is granted in a legal proceeding).
INFORMALIDAD.
f, informality.
INFORMALMENTE.
adv, informally.
INFORMANTE.
m, informer, informant ‖ advisor or investigator (to whom special investigative power is granted in a legal proceeding).
INFORMAR.
v, to inform, communicate, give information to, brief (someone on something) ‖ to file an INFORME ‖ to advise ‖ to opine, adjudge ‖ to give an expert opinion, report on.
INFORMATIVO.
adj, informative.

INFORME.

m, notice, information, communication ‖ opinion, decision, judgment (of a judge, court, or expert) ‖ oral hearing or trial (of an attorney) ‖ statistical or historical data ‖ report.

INFORME CREDITICIO.

credit report.

INFORME DE CRÉDITO.

See INFORME CREDITICIO.

INFORME EN ESTRADOS.

plea before the court.

INFORME FISCAL.

government minister's report, report prepared by a government ministry at the request of a judge in a criminal trial.

INFORME "IN VOCE".

oral hearing, oral trial. This is an exception to the general rule in civil law that litigation is carried out by submission of written motions and evidence.

INFORME PERICIAL.

expert's report or opinion (either written or oral).

INFORME SOBRE ACCIDENTE.

accident report.

INFORMES.

See PRUEBA DE INFORMES.

INFORMES FALSOS.

(intentionally) false reports regarding the armed forces of one's own country or an enemy country.

INFRA.

infra.

"INFRA PETITA".

less than requested. Used to refer to a sentence in which an accused is sentenced to a term less than that requested.

INFRACCIÓN.

f, infraction, violation, criminal offense, crime (includes both misdemeanors and felonies) ‖ breach.

INFRACCIÓN DE ARMISTICIO.

breach of a truce or armistice.

INFRACCIÓN DE LEY.

violation of law.

INFRACCIÓN DE POLICÍA.

violation of regulations promulgated by the police.

INFRACCIÓN DE REGLAMENTOS.

violation of regulations.

INFRACCIÓN GRAVE.

serious violation of a law or rule or regulation.

INFRACCIÓN PENAL.

criminal violation.

INFRACCIÓN TRIBUTARIA.

violation of the tax laws. They may be SIMPLE (simple) for violations of a procedural nature, DE OMISIÓN (of omission) for failure to provide accurate information or other omissions, or DE DEFRAUDACIÓN (fraudulent) for seriously fraudulent acts.

INFRACTOR.

m, violator, transgressor, criminal.

INFRAESTRUCTURA.

f, infrastructure.

INFRAHUMANO.

adj, subhuman.

INFRAPETICIÓN.

See "INFRA PETITA".

INFRASCRIPTO.

adj, undersigned ‖ written hereafter.

INFRASCRITO.

See INFRASCRIPTO.

INFRASEGURO.

m, underinsurance, insurance for less than full value.

INFRINGIR.

v, to infringe, transgress ‖ to disobey, violate.

INGENUIDAD.

f, condition of being born free (versus into slavery) ‖ sincerity, ingenuousness ‖ innocence, candor.

INGENUO.

m, free man (versus slave) ‖ adj, ingenuous, naive ‖ candid, sincere.

INGERENCIA.

See INJERENCIA.

INGRATAMENTE.

adv, ungratefully.

INGRATITUD.

f, ingratitude, ungratefulness. May be cause to revoke gifts, etc.

INGRATO.

m, ingrate ‖ adj, ungrateful ‖ disagreeable ‖ difficult.

INGRESAR.

v, to enroll, enter (e.g. a school or university) ‖ to be nominated to an academic position or chair.

INGRESO.

m, entrance, enrollment, admission ‖ entry ‖

entrance examination ‖ inclusion, incorporation ‖ income, receipts.
INGRESO BRUTO.
gross income.
INGRESO IMPONIBLE.
taxable income.
INGRESO NETO.
net income.
INGRESO TRIBUTABLE.
taxable income.
INGRESOS.
m, income, receipts, revenue ‖ earnings.
INGRESOS DE EXPLOTACIÓN.
operating revenue.
INGRESOS FINANCIEROS.
financial income or revenue.
INGRESOS INTERIORES.
internal revenue.
**INGRESOS
PER CÁPITA.**
per capita income.
INHÁBIL.
adj, unqualified ‖ incapacitated, unable, inept
‖ off, non-working (e.g. days, hours).
INHABILIDAD.
f, inability, ineptitude ‖ incapacity.
INHABILITACIÓN.
f, incapacitation, disablement, disability ‖ disqualification (for certain positions or types of
jobs), ineligibility ‖ disbarment.
INHABILITACIÓN ABSOLUTA.
complete disqualification ‖ disbarment (of a
lawyer). Refers to a type of punishment or
sanction for an offence.
INHABILITACIÓN ESPECIAL.
suspension, limited disqualification, disqualification for a limited period of time (usually
6 to 12 years) ‖ suspension (of a lawyer) ‖ disqualification from practising a specific profession or activity.
**INHABILITACIÓN PARA
CARGO PÚBLICO.**
ineligibility for public office or governmental
position.
INHABILITANTE.
See LEY INHABILITANTE.
INHABILITAR.
v, to disqualify, make ineligible ‖ to disbar (if a
lawyer).
INHABITABLE.
adj, uninhabitable, unlivable.

INHABITADO.
adj, uninhabited.
INHERENTE.
adj, inherent ‖ inseparable.
INHIBICIÓN.
f, inhibition ‖ abstention ‖ prohibition, obstacle ‖ temporary restraining order preventing
a debtor from encumbering or selling property.
INHIBIR.
v, to inhibit ‖ to prohibit a judge from hearing
a case over which he has no jurisdiction.
INHIBIRSE.
v, to restrain oneself ‖ to disqualify oneself or
withdraw from a case as a judge (e.g. for lack
of jurisdiction).
INHIBITORIA.
f, motion or hearing to request that a case be
dismissed for lack of jurisdiction (without prejudice to bring the suit in a proper tribunal). ‖
restraining order requiring a judge to dismiss
a case for lack of jurisdiction.
INHIBITORIA DE JURISDICCIÓN.
See INHIBITORIA.
INHIBITORIO.
adj, inhibitory.
INHONESTO.
adj, dishonest ‖ indecent.
INHONORAR.
v, to dishonor.
INHUMACIÓN.
f, burial, interment.
INHUMACIÓN ILEGAL.
illegal burial.
INHUMANAMENTE.
adv, inhumanely.
INHUMANIDAD.
f, inhumanity ‖ cruelty.
INICIACIÓN.
f, initiation.
INICIAL.
f, initial, first letter of a word ‖ adj, initial.
INICIAR.
v, to initiate ‖ to corrupt ‖ to commence.
INICIAR UNA ACCIÓN.
to file a lawsuit, bring an action.
INICIAR EL JUICIO.
to start the trial, open the case.
INICIAR LA SESIÓN.
to open the meeting ‖ to open court ‖ to open
the hearing.

INICIARSE.
v, to begin (e.g. a profession).

INICIATIVA.
f, initiative ‖ right to present an initiative ‖ exercise of right to present an initiative.

INICIATIVA DE LEY.
bill, proposed law.

INICIATIVA EN LA FORMACIÓN DE LAS LEYES.
executive or congressional initiative, executive or congressional right to propose new legislation.

INICIATIVA POPULAR.
initiative, popular initiative, citizen's right to propose new legislation.

INICUO.
adj, inequitable, unjust, unfair.

INIMPUTABILIDAD.
f, unaccusability, unindictability (e.g. of an insane person).

ININTELIGIBLE.
adj, unintelligible ‖ undecipherable.

ININTERRUMPIDO.
adj, uninterrupted.

INITIO.
See "AB INITIO".

INJERENCIA.
f, intervention, interference ‖ interjection.

INJERIR.
v, to introduce, insert (a thing into another) ‖ to interject, mention.

INJURIA.
f, defamation (either slander or libel) through words which are injurious to the good name or reputation but which do not include accusations of criminality ‖ injury, damage ‖ wrong, offense ‖ insult ‖ damage, loss.

INJURIA CIVIL.
tortious or actionable defamation. Opposed to INJURIA PENAL. See INJURIA.

INJURIA LABORAL.
violation of labor contract which is deemed to be sufficiently serious as to warrant the termination of the employer-employee relationship.

INJURIA PENAL.
criminal defamation, defamation which amounts to a crime. Opposed to INJURIA CIVIL. See INJURIA.

INJURIADOR.
m, offender ‖ injuring or damaging party ‖ adj, offensive, abusive ‖ injuring.

INJURIAR.
v, to offend, insult ‖ to damage, injure, cause injury or damage ‖ to prejudice.

INJURIAS A LA AUTORIDAD.
type of contempt of authority, defamation to the state or its officers or representatives thereof.

INJURIAS EN EL EXTRANJERO.
See INJURIAS POR ESCRITO.

INJURIAS EN JUICIO.
type of contempt of court, insults in the course of litigation.

INJURIAS ENCUBIERTAS.
implied insults, insults made by means of allegory, allusions. They become INJURIAS MANIFIESTAS if the offender fails to provide another interpretation.

INJURIAS GRAVES.
serious defamation. Used in both criminal and civil law.

INJURIAS LEVES.
minor defamation, defamation which is not serious. Used in both criminal and civil law.

INJURIAS MANIFIESTAS.
express insults. As opposed to INJURIAS ENCUBIERTAS.

INJURIAS POR ESCRITO.
libel, written defamation.

INJURIAS RECÍPROCAS.
reciprocal defamation.

INJURIAS VERBALES.
slander, oral defamation.

INJURIOSO.
adj, injurious ‖ defamatory ‖ offensive, insulting.

INJUSTAMENTE.
adv, unjustly, unfairly ‖ illegally, unlawfully ‖ unreasonably.

INJUSTICIA.
f, injustice.

INJUSTICIA NOTORIA.
manifest injustice.

INJUSTIFICABLE.
adj, unjustifiable, inexcusable.

INJUSTIFICADAMENTE.
adv, unjustifiably, inexcusably ‖ unreasonably

INJUSTIFICADO.
adj, unjustified, unexcused, unwarranted ‖ unproven.

INJUSTO.
adj, unjust, unfair.

INMADUREZ.
f, immaturity.
INMATERIAL.
adj, immaterial, intangible, incorporeal.
INMATERIALIDAD.
f, immateriality, intangibility.
INMATRICULACIÓN.
f, registration, filing, inscription. Used to describe filing of title papers with real property registry.
INMEDIACIÓN.
f, immediacy ‖ procedure by which a judge requires parties and non-parties to appear before him in order that he better evaluate the claims.
INMEDIATAMENTE.
adv, immediately.
INMEDIATO.
adj, immediate.
INMIGRACIÓN.
f, immigration.
INMIGRANTE.
f, m, immigrant.
INMIGRAR.
v, to immigrate.
INMIGRATORIO.
adj, immigration, pertaining to immigration.
INMINENCIA.
f, imminence.
INMINENTE.
adj, imminent.
INMOBILIARIA.
f, real estate broker.
INMOBILIARIO.
adj, real property, concerning real property.
INMODERADO.
adj, immoderate, excessive,
INMOLACIÓN.
f, immolation.
INMORAL.
adj, immoral ‖ indecent ‖ illicit.
INMORALIDAD.
f, immorality ‖ dishonor ‖ indecency, obscenity.
INMOTIVADO.
adj, without motive ‖ unmotivated.
INMÓVIL.
adj, immobile.
INMOVILIDAD.
f, immobility.
INMOVILIZACIÓN.
f, immobilization.

INMOVILIZACIONES.
nonliquid investments.
INMOVILIZAR.
v, to immobilize.
INMUEBLE.
m, real estate, real property ‖ adj, immovable.
INMUEBLE DOTAL.
real estate given as part of a dowry.
INMUEBLE ENFITÉUTICO.
property held under emphyteusis.
INMUEBLE POR ACCESIÓN.
accession to real estate (inclusive of some accessories which are not physically attached thereto).
See INMUEBLE POR ACCESIÓN FÍSICA
and INMUEBLE POR ACCESIÓN MORAL.
INMUEBLE POR ACCESIÓN FÍSICA.
accession physically attached to real estate.
INMUEBLE POR ACCESIÓN MORAL.
accession or accessory which is integral to real estate and is not physically attached thereto (e.g. keys to a house, fish in a pond, farm tools, animals used for cultivation).
INMUEBLE POR SU CARÁCTER REPRESENTATIVO.
document or instrument which pertains to real estate. Considered to be real property in se.
INMUEBLE POR SU NATURALEZA.
real estate due to its inherent nature (i.e. land, what lies beneath, and all parts thereof which are solid or liquid).
INMUNE.
adj, immune ‖ free ‖ exempt.
INMUNIDAD.
f, immunity.
INMUNIDAD BÉLICA.
immunity during wartime, protection from the ravages of war.
INMUNIDAD DISCIPLINARIA.
immunity of labor union officials from disciplinary action.
INMUNIDAD FISCAL.
tax exemption.
INMUNIDAD JUDICIAL.
immunity of attorneys to charges of defamation arising out of litigation.
INMUNIDAD PARLAMENTARIA.
parliamentary or congressional immunity, immunity of senators and deputies or congressmen from criminal liability (with express exceptions).

INMUNIDAD PROFESIONAL.
professional immunity, immunity from criminal liability which arises out of the practise of certain professions.

INMUNIDADES CONSULARES.
consular immunity. Consists of immunity of consular offices and documents from search or seizure, and consular personnel from certain criminal liability and procedure, granted by the host country.

INMUNIDADES Y PRIVILEGIOS DIPLOMÁTICOS.
diplomatic immunities and privileges. Consists of exemption of ambassador from taxes, and immunity of embassy offices and documents from search or seizure, and diplomatic corps from certain criminal liability and procedure, granted by the host country.

INMUTABILIDAD DEL LITIGIO.
inability to amend the complaint or claim.

INNATO.
adj, innate.

INNAVEGABILIDAD.
f, unseaworthiness (of vessel).

INNAVEGABLE.
adj, unseaworthy (vessel) ‖ unnavigable (waters).

INNECESARIO.
m, unnecessary formality ‖ adj, unnecessary, volitional ‖ unnecessary, superfluous.

INNEGABLE.
adj, undeniable, irrebuttable, incontrovertible.

INNOCUO.
adj, innocuous.

INNOMINADO.
adj, anonymous ‖ unnamed ‖ with no express name. Used to distinguish contracts which are expressly classified by name (NOMINADOS) and those which are not (INNOMINADOS).

INNOVACIÓN.
f, innovation ‖ change, modification ‖ move.

INNOVAR.
v, to innovate ‖ to change, alter, modify ‖ to move (something).

INOBSERVANCIA.
f, nonobservance, non-compliance.

INOBSERVANCIA JUSTIFICABLE.
excusable non-compliance or nonobservance.

INOCENCIA.
f, innocence.

INOCENTE.
adj, innocent, not guilty.

INOCUO.
See INNOCUO.

INOFENSIVO.
adj, inoffensive ‖ impotent.

INOFICIOSIDAD.
f, lack of legal right. Used to refer to person who fails to bequeath property which pursuant to law is due the legal heir.
See LEGADO FORZOSO.

INOFICIOSO.
adj, inefficient ‖ ineffective, not operable ‖ extralegal (re: bequests which exceed that permitted by law).

INOPONIBILIDAD.
f, ineffectiveness (of legal actions as against specified persons) ‖ inability to raise a defense or demand a right.

INQUILINATO.
f, rental home ‖ rental, lease (usually of a residence) ‖ right to rent or lease ‖ rental or lease payment ‖ rental or lease contract.

INQUILINO.
m, tenant, renter, lessee (usually of a residence) ‖ sharecropper.

INQUIRIDOR.
m, investigator, inquirer, questioner.

INQUIRIR.
v, to question, inquire, ask ‖ to investigate.

INQUISICIÓN.
f, inquiry ‖ inquest ‖ investigation, inquisition ‖ search.

INQUISIDOR.
See INQUIRIDOR.

INQUISITIVO.
adj, inquisitive.

INQUISITORIO.
See INQUISITIVO.

INSACULACIÓN.
f, placing of names in a box or urn such that later they will be drawn by lot ‖ balloting, voting by ballot.

INSACULAR.
v, to ballot, vote by ballot.

INSALUBRIDAD.
f, unhealthiness, lack of sanitation.

INSANABLE.
adj, incurable.

INSANIA.
f, insanity.

INSANO.
m, insane person ‖ adj, insane, crazy.

INSATISFECHO.
adj, unsatisfied.

INSCRIBIBLE.
adj, registrable, able to be filed or recorded (in a registry).

INSCRIBIR.
v, to inscribe, register (something) ‖ to enroll (someone) ‖ to file, record (property ownership with a real estate registry).

INSCRIBIRSE.
v, to enroll, sign up.

INSCRIPCIÓN.
f, act of registration or filing or inscription ‖ enrollment ‖ record entry, record, entry ‖ recording, filing, registration.

INSCRIPCIÓN CONCISA.
summary recording or registration, summary of that contained in the principal registration or recording.

INSCRIPCIÓN CONSTITUTIVA.
real estate filing (used exclusively to constitute, modify, transfer, or terminate rights in real property).

INSCRIPCIÓN DE ACTAS DE NOTORIEDAD.
recording of open possession, registration of intent to gain adverse possession to property.

INSCRIPCIÓN DE ACTOS Y CONTRATOS CON PRECIO.
recording of contracts for value.

INSCRIPCIÓN DE ACTOS Y CONTRATOS DE LA CASADA.
recording of contracts entered into by a wife. In some countries contracts which require a husband's consent may only be recorded with annotation that such consent is lacking if such is the case.

INSCRIPCIÓN DE AERONAVES.
registration of airplane ownership.

INSCRIPCIÓN DE BIENES DE LA COMUNIDAD CONYUGAL.
registration of community property.

INSCRIPCIÓN DE BIENES DEL ESTADO.
registration of government-owned real estate.

INSCRIPCIÓN DE BUQUES.
ship ownership registration, registration of vessels.

INSCRIPCIÓN DE DERECHO REAL SOBRE FINCA NO INSCRIPTA.
recording of interest in unregistered real property.

INSCRIPCIÓN DE LA CESIÓN DEL CRÉDITO HIPOTECARIO.
recording of the termination of a mortgage.

INSCRIPCIÓN DE LA HERENCIA.
See INSCRIPCIÓN DEL DERECHO HEREDITARIO.

INSCRIPCIÓN DE LA POSESIÓN.
possessory filing, recording of possession (of property). Possession filings alone (versus ownership) are usually not permitted. See INFORMACIONES POSESORIAS.

INSCRIPCIÓN DE LA TRASLACIÓN DEL DOMINIO.
recording of transfer of ownership.

INSCRIPCIÓN DE LAS CONCESIONES ADMINISTRATIVAS.
recording of governmental licenses.

INSCRIPCIÓN DE LAS SOCIEDADES.
corporate filing, recording of incorporation of a commercial enterprise.

INSCRIPCIÓN DE LOS COMERCIANTES.
business filing of sole proprietorship, recording of sole proprietorship.

INSCRIPCIÓN DECLARATIVA.
elective or non-obligatory filing of transfer of ownership.

INSCRIPCIÓN DEL DERECHO HEREDITARIO.
registration of a successory interest.

INSCRIPCIÓN DESTRUIDA.
registration records destroyed by deliberate acts such as war, etc.

INSCRIPCIÓN EN EL REGISTRO CIVIL.
registration in the vital statistics registry.

INSCRIPCIÓN EN EL REGISTRO DE LA PROPIEDAD.
filing in a real estate registry (of ownership and other rights and interests related thereto).

INSCRIPCIÓN EN EL REGISTRO MERCANTIL.
filing with the business or commercial registry.

INSCRIPCIÓN ESPECIAL.
special filing in a real estate registry. Occurs when the data recorded differs from that required by law.

INSCRIPCIÓN FACULTATIVA.
See INSCRIPCIÓN VOLUNTARIA.

INSCRIPCIÓN MARÍTIMA.
enlistment in the naval draft.
INSCRIPCIÓN OBLIGATORIA.
obligatory registration or filing.
INSCRIPCIÓN
VOLUNTARIA.
elective or non-obligatory filing regarding real property.
INSCRIPTO.
See INSCRITO.
INSCRITO.
adj, of record ‖ registered, filed, recorded ‖ registered or filed or recorded document or instrument.
INSEMINACIÓN.
f, insemination.
INSEPERABILIDAD.
f, inseparability.
INSEPERABLE.
adj, inseparable.
INSERCIÓN.
f, insertion. May be used to describe the publication of a statement in a newspaper as required by a judicial decision.
INSERCIÓN OBLIGATORIA.
legal notice, obligatory publication ‖ publication of a statement in a newspaper as required by law or by judicial or administrative decision.
INSIDIA.
f, insidiousness ‖ snare, trap ‖ malicious trick or artifice or trickery.
INSIDIOSO.
m, malicious trickster ‖ traitor ‖ insidious person ‖ adj, insidious.
INSIGNIA.
f, insignia ‖ sign.
INSIGNIFICANCIA.
f, insignificance.
INSIGNIFICANTE.
adj, insignificant.
INSINUACIÓN.
f, insinuation, intimation ‖ petition, claim, motion ‖ presentation of a DOCUMENTO PÚBLICO to a court or judge for his approval and signature ‖ public certification or documentation before an officer of the court of acts done or things delivered ‖ public certification or authentication of documents or instruments ‖ presentation of evidence that a bequest which exceeds legal requirements was not made under duress.

INSINUAR.
v, to insinuate ‖ to make or file an INSINUACIÓN.
ÍNSITO.
adj, inherent, innate, inborn.
INSOLUBLE.
adj, insoluble, unsolvable, without solution.
INSOLUTO.
adj, pending ‖ unpaid, not paid.
INSOLUTUMDACIÓN.
f, giving in payment, datio in solutum.
INSOLVENCIA.
f, insolvency, inability to pay one's debts.
INSOLVENCIA CULPABLE.
negligent bankruptcy, bankruptcy due to negligence.
INSOLVENCIA EN LA
COMPRAVENTA.
insolvency of purchaser (during purchase).
INSOLVENCIA EN LA FIANZA.
insolvency of guarantor or surety.
INSOLVENCIA EN LA SOCIEDAD.
insolvency of partner in a partnership or certain corporations.
INSOLVENCIA EN LAS
OBLIGACIONES.
insolvency of obligor.
INSOLVENCIA EN LAS SUCESIONES.
insolvency of heir (in the case that there are estate debts to pay).
INSOLVENCIA FRAUDULENTA.
fraudulent insolvency. Usually criminal.
INSOLVENTE.
adj, insolvent ‖ unable to pay one's debts.
INSOSTENIBLE.
adj, unsustainable ‖ untenable.
INSPECCIÓN.
f, inspection, examination ‖ post of inspector office or locale of inspector ‖ jurisdiction of inspector.
INSPECCIÓN DEL TRABAJO.
work-site inspection ‖ administrative agency charged with enforcement of labor laws.
INSPECCIÓN JUDICIAL.
judicial inspection or visual inspection by judge (of evidence).
INSPECCIÓN OCULAR.
on-site inspection (carried out by judge in presence of the parties or witnesses).
INSPECCIONAR.
v, to inspect, examine (something).

INSPECTOR.
m, inspector. Title used to describe police, military, tax, labor, etc. inspectors.
INSPECTOR GENERAL.
inspector general, chief inspector.
INSPECTORÍA.
f, enforcement corps of inspector ‖ jurisdiction of inspector.
INSTALACIÓN.
f, installation, establishment ‖ taking charge (of a job or post).
INSTALAR.
v, to install, establish.
INSTALARSE.
v, to establish oneself (e.g. in a job or position).
INSTANCIA.
f, petition, plea, request, demand ‖ insistence ‖ instance ‖ rebuttal ‖ jurisdictional level or stage.
INSTANCIA DE ARBITRAJE.
arbitration proceedings.
INSTANCIA DE OFICIO.
beginning or continuation of a suit sua sponte.
INSTANCIA DE PARTE AGRAVIADA.
petition of the injured party ‖ procedure by which criminal action is instigated by victim, not by state.
INSTANCIA DILATORIA.
dilatory plea.
INSTANCIA PRIVADA.
See DELITO DEPENDIENTE DE INSTANCIA PRIVADA.
INSTANTÁNEO.
adj, instantaneous.
INSTANTE.
m, instant, instance ‖ petitioner.
INSTAR.
v, to request, petition, demand, plead ‖ to bring a summary proceeding ‖ to instigate ‖ to prosecute (an action).
INSTIGACIÓN.
f, instigation, incitation ‖ criminal abetting.
INSTIGACIÓN A COMETER DELITOS.
criminal instigation ‖ instigation to commit a crime.
INSTIGACIÓN A LA REBELIÓN.
instigation to rebel.
INSTIGACIÓN AL DUELO.
provocation to duel.
INSTIGACIÓN AL SUICIDIO.
aiding and abetting a suicide.

INSTIGACIÓN Y AYUDA AL SUICIDIO.
instigating and abetting a suicide.
INSTIGADOR.
m, instigator, inciter, provocateur.
INSTIGAR.
v, to instigate, incite, provoke ‖ to abet.
INSTITOR.
m, factor.
INSTITUCIÓN.
f, institution ‖ establishment, company ‖ foundation ‖ principal state entity ‖ designation of legatees ‖ principal areas or branches of the law.
INSTITUCIÓN CAPTATORIA.
testamentary condition that legatee will bequeath property to testator or other specific person. Usually void.
INSTITUCIÓN CONTRACTUAL.
gift conditioned upon death of donee. Usually revocable.
INSTITUCIÓN DE HEREDERO.
designation of legatees and their rights and obligations (by testator).
INSTITUCIONAL.
adj, institutional ‖ constitutional.
INSTITUCIONALIZACIÓN.
f, institutionalization.
INSTITUCIONES.
f, institutions, principles or norms of a science ‖ constitutional entities of state.
INSTITUCIONES ARMADAS.
armed forces.
INSTITUIDO.
m, named legatee ‖ adj, named, appointed, designated, established.
INSTITUIR.
v, to institute, found, begin, start, establish.
INSTITUTO.
m, institute, building ‖ institution, norm, rule ‖ corporation, establishment, organism ‖ institute, school.
INSTITUTO ARMADO.
armed force, branch of the armed forces.
INSTITUTO DE EMISIÓN.
issuing bank.
INSTITUTO FINANCIERO.
finance institution.
INSTITUYENTE.
m, f, founder ‖ adj, establishing, founding.
INSTRUCCIÓN.
f, instruction, teaching ‖ doctrine, norm, rule

‖ warning, order ‖ type of probable cause proceeding (in which the evidence is gathered in order that the judge determine whether or not there is cause to warrant a trial). This is the first stage of a criminal trial. Sometimes called a SUMARIO. See PLENARIO.

INSTRUCCIÓN AL JURADO.
instruction to the jury.

INSTRUCCIÓN CÍVICA.
civic education, teaching of constitution and the basic principles of a nation's institutions.

INSTRUCCIÓN CRIMINAL.
preliminary criminal proceeding.

INSTRUCCIÓN DE CAUSA.
preparation of the case.

INSTRUCCIÓN DEL SUMARIO.
proceeding to bring forth evidence (to determine both civil and criminal liability).

INSTRUCCIÓN MILITAR.
military education or instruction.

INSTRUCCIÓN PENAL.
type of probable cause proceeding (in which the evidence is gathered in order that the judge determine whether or not there is cause to warrant a trial). This is the first stage of a criminal trial. Sometimes called a SUMARIO. See PLENARIO.

INSTRUCCIÓN PÚBLICA.
public education.

INSTRUCCIÓN SUMARIA.
preliminary criminal proceeding.

INSTRUCCIONES.
f, orders (given to military or diplomatic corps) ‖ instructions, regulatory rules.

INSTRUCTIVO.
adj, instructive.

INSTRUCTOR.
m, instructor, teacher, professor ‖ prosecutor ‖ judge in a probable cause hearing. See INSTRUCCIÓN PENAL.

INSTRUIDO.
adj, instructed ‖ expert.

INSTRUIR.
v, to instruct, teach ‖ to inform ‖ to gather evidence in criminal trial. See INSTRUCCIÓN.

INSTRUIR SUMARIO.
to carry out preliminary criminal proceedings.

INSTRUIR UN EXPEDIENTE.
to collect all the facts pertaining to a matter, hear the parties and witnesses and make the appropriate decision.

INSTRUMENTAL.
adj, instrumental.

INSTRUMENTAL CIVIL.
possession of real estate which was transferred by means of written document.

INSTRUMENTO.
m, instrument ‖ document, writing, instrument ‖ means ‖ proof.

INSTRUMENTO AL PORTADOR.
bearer instrument.

INSTRUMENTO AUTÉNTICO.
authenticated writing, document which has been issued and authorized by a public officer.

INSTRUMENTO CONSTITUTIVO.
articles of incorporation or partnership agreement.

INSTRUMENTO DE TÍTULO.
document of title.

INSTRUMENTO DE VENTA.
bill of sale.

INSTRUMENTO EJECUTIVO.
See TÍTULO EJECUTIVO.

INSTRUMENTO PRIVADO.
See DOCUMENTO PRIVADO.

INSTRUMENTO PÚBLICO.
See DOCUMENTO PÚBLICO.

INSTRUMENTOS DE CRÉDITO.
credit instruments ‖ negotiable instruments.

INSTRUMENTOS DE TRABAJO.
tools of the trade, work tools.

INSTRUMENTOS DEL DELITO.
instruments or tools of the crime.

INSTRUMENTOS LIBERATORIOS.
legal tender.

INSTRUMENTOS NEGOCIABLES.
commercial paper ‖ negotiable instruments.

INSUBORDINACIÓN.
f, insubordination.

INSUBORDINADO.
m, insubordinate person or group ‖ adj, insubordinate.

INSUBORDINAR.
v, to incite to insubordination.

INSUBORDINARSE.
v, to rebel, be insubordinate.

INSUBSANABLE.
adj, irreparable.

INSUBSISTENCIA.
f, inexistence ‖ derogation ‖ nullity, voidness

NSUBSISTENTE.
adj, that which has disappeared or been lost or consumed || void, null.

NSUBSTITUIBLE.
adj, irreplaceable, unsubstitutable.

NSUFICIENCIA.
f, insufficiency, scarcity || ineptitude, inability.

NSUFICIENCIA DE LA PRUEBA.
insufficiency of the evidence.

NSUFICIENCIA DE LAS LEYES.
legal loophole, gap in the law, area where the law does not regulate or regulate adequately.

NSUFICIENTE.
adj, insufficient.

NSULTAR.
v, to insult, offend (by word or by deed).

NSULTO.
m, insult, offense || accident.

NSULTO A CENTINELA.
insulting a (military) sentry.

NSUMISIÓN.
f, disobedience, rebellion || resistance (to an invasion) || desire for independence.

NSUMISO.
m, disobedient or rebellious person || adj, undisciplined, disobedient, rebellious.

NSUMO.
m, input || consumption.

NSUPERABLE.
adj, unimprovable, insuperable.

NSURGENTE.
m, insurgent, rebel || adj, insurgent.

NSURRECCIÓN.
f, insurrection, rebellion.

NSURRECCIONAR.
v, to instigate rebellion or insurrection (against the government).

NSURRECCIONARSE.
v, to rebel (against the government).

NSURRECTO.
adj, rebellious, seditious.

NTANGIBLE.
adj, intangible.

NTEGRACIÓN.
f, integration, incorporation || assimilation || payment (of corporate capital by shareholders).

NTEGRANTES.
m, members || partners || constituents.

NTEGRAR.
v, to integrate || to make up, form part of || to reimburse, repay.

INTEGRIDAD.
f, integrity || completeness, wholeness.

INTEGRIDAD FÍSICA.
See DERECHO DE LA INTEGRIDAD FÍSICA.

INTEGRIDAD MORAL.
See DERECHO DE LA INTEGRIDAD MORAL.

INTELECTUAL.
f, m, intellectual person || adj, intellectual.

INTELIGENCIA.
f, intelligence.

INTELIGIBLE.
adj, intelligible.

INTEMPERANCIA.
f, intemperance.

INTEMPESTIVAMENTE.
adv, ill-timed || without due or proper notice. Used to refer to dismissals from work.

INTENCIÓN.
f, intention, goal, aim, end || criminal intent.

INTENCIÓN CRIMINAL.
criminal purpose or intent.

INTENCIÓN DE LOS CONTRATANTES.
intent of the contracting parties.

INTENCIÓN FRAUDULENTA.
fraudulent purpose.

INTENCIÓN LEGISLATIVA.
legislative intent.

INTENCIONADAMENTE.
adv, intentionally (usually toward an evil end).

INTENCIONADO.
adj, intended, deliberate.

INTENCIONAL.
adj, intentional, deliberate. In criminal law, will often affect degree of guilt.

INTENCIONALIDAD.
f, intent.

INTENCIONALMENTE.
adv, intentionally, purposefully.

INTENDENCIA.
f, jurisdiction or post or office of an INTENDENTE || quartermaster service of armed forces || office of the mayor.

INTENDENTE.
m, superintendent || quartermaster general of armed forces || mayor.

INTENDENTE DE POLICÍA.
superintendent of police, police chief.

INTENTAR.
v, to try, attempt || to try to enforce a right.

INTENTAR CONTRADEMANDA.
to file a counterclaim or cross-claim.

INTENTAR DEMANDA.
to file an action, bring suit.
INTENTO.
m, intent, aim, purpose, intention.
INTER VIVOS.
adj, inter vivos.
INTERACCIÓN.
f, interaction.
INTERCALACIÓN.
f, intercalation, insertion.
INTERCALAR.
v, to insert, add to, intercalate.
INTERCAMBIAR.
v, to exchange ‖ to interchange.
INTERCAMBIO.
m, exchange ‖ interchange.
INTERCEPTACIÓN.
f, interception.
**INTERCEPTACIÓN DE
LA CORRESPONDENCIA.**
interception of correspondence.
INTERCEPTAR.
v, to intercept.
INTERCESIÓN.
f, intercession.
"INTERCESSIO".
f, intercession (of superior court judges to oppose the decisions of other judges).
INTERDEPENDENCIA.
f, interdependence.
INTERDICCIÓN.
f, prohibition, interdiction ‖ deprivation of civilian rights (e.g. as a result of serious criminality).
INTERDICCIÓN CIVIL.
legal deprivation of civilian rights or deprivation of right to practice profession, suspension from position (e.g. as a result of serious criminality).
INTERDICCIÓN JUDICIAL.
legal deprivation of civilian rights or deprivation of right to practice profession, suspension from position (e.g. as a result of incapacity of a mental defective person).
INTERDICCIÓN LEGAL.
See INTERDICCIÓN CIVIL.
INTERDICTO.
m, prohibition, injunction ‖ person who is subject to an INTERDICCIÓN CIVIL ‖ injunction hearing, temporary restraining order hearing.
INTERDICTO DE ADQUIRIR.
motion to obtain an injunction ordering that

possession of something be turned over to the petitioner ‖ hearing to decide aforementioned motion ‖ injunction or other order resulting therefrom.
INTERDICTO DE DESPOJO.
See INTERDICTO DE RECOBRAR.
INTERDICTO DE NO INNOVAR.
motion to obtain an injunction (to any change in the status quo) ‖ hearing to decide aforementioned motion ‖ injunction or other order resulting therefrom.
INTERDICTO DE OBRA NUEVA.
motion to obtain an injunction against further construction (of a structure) ‖ hearing to decide aforementioned motion ‖ injunction or other order resulting therefrom.
**INTERDICTO DE OBRA
RUINOSA.**
motion to obtain an injunction ordering the repair of something which threatens property or persons ‖ hearing to decide aforementioned motion ‖ injunction or other order resulting therefrom.
INTERDICTO DE RECOBRAR.
motion to obtain an order for the immediate return of something taken by violence or clandestine means ‖ special summary hearing to decide aforementioned motion ‖ injunction or other order resulting therefrom.
INTERDICTO DE RETENER.
motion to obtain an injunction or restraining order prohibiting interference with possession or ownership ‖ special summary hearing to decide aforementioned motion ‖ injunction or other order resulting therefrom.
INTERDICTO DEFINITIVO.
permanent or final injunction.
INTERDICTO EXHIBITORIO.
motion to produce (property which is the subject of litigation) ‖ hearing to decide aforementioned motion ‖ restraining order or injunction or other order resulting therefrom.
INTERDICTO PREVENTIVO.
temporary restraining order (to prevent harm) preventive injunction.
INTERDICTO PROHIBITORIO.
negative injunction, injunction prohibiting action.
INTERDICTO PROVISORIO.
temporary restraining order ‖ temporary injunction.

INTERÉS.
m, interest ‖ benefit, profit, earnings.
INTERÉS ASEGURABLE.
insurable interest.
INTERÉS COMPENSATORIO.
compensation or indemnification for loss of use of monies for a given period of time.
INTERÉS COMPUESTO.
compound interest.
INTERÉS COMÚN.
common or joint interest.
INTERÉS CONVENCIONAL.
contractual or conventional interest, interest agreed upon by contract. Often may exceed the legal rate but may not be usurious.
INTERÉS DE DEMORA.
interest charged for a late payment.
INTERÉS DE GRACIA.
See INTERÉS DE DEMORA.
INTERÉS DE MORA.
interest for late payment.
INTERÉS DE PLAZA.
current or going rate of interest.
INTERÉS DEMORADO.
See INTERÉS DE DEMORA.
INTERÉS DOMINANTE.
controlling interest.
INTERÉS EN LA CAUSA.
legal interest in the cause of action or litigation. May be DIRECTO (direct) or INDIRECTO (indirect).
INTERÉS GENERAL.
general interest (as against an individual's interest).
INTERÉS ILÍCITO.
illegal interest (of military personnel in contracts, etc.).
INTERÉS JUDICIAL.
(monetary) interest which runs from the start of a lawsuit.
INTERÉS LEGAL.
legal interest (as determined by law).
INTERÉS LUCRATIVO.
interest charged on a loan (of money).
INTERÉS LUCRATORIO.
See INTERÉS LUCRATIVO.
INTERÉS MAYORITARIO.
majority interest.
Opposed to INTERÉS MINORITARIO.
INTERÉS MINORITARIO.
minority interest.

Opposed to INTERÉS MAYORITARIO.
INTERÉS MORATORIO.
late payment charge, interest payable on late payment as penalty.
INTERÉS PENAL.
See INTERÉS PUNITORIO.
INTERÉS PREDOMINANTE.
See INTERÉS DOMINANTE.
INTERÉS PRIVADO.
private interest.
INTERÉS PROCESAL.
See INTERÉS EN LA CAUSA.
INTERÉS PÚBLICO.
public interest.
INTERÉS PUNITORIO.
interest paid as penalty (for any breach of contract). See INTERÉS MORATORIO.
INTERÉS RETRASADO.
interest in arrears.
INTERÉS SIMPLE.
simple interest.
INTERÉS USURARIO.
usury, usurious interest.
INTERESADO.
m, party in interest, interested party ‖ contracting party ‖ party, party to litigation ‖ adj, interested.
INTERESAR.
v, to have interest (in something) ‖ to associate (oneself) ‖ to participate in a business or company for profit.
INTERESARSE.
v, to be interested.
INTERESES.
m, plural of INTERÉS ‖ interests, fortune, possessions, property ‖ interests (e.g. of the nation).
INTERESES A PROPORCIÓN.
interest paid proportionally (vis-à-vis principal).
INTERESES ACCIONARIOS.
stockholdings ‖ interest or dividends paid on capital stock.
INTERESES ATRASADOS.
interest in arrears.
INTERESES CREADOS.
vested interests.
INTERESTADAL.
See INTERESTATAL.
INTERESTADUAL.
See INTERESTATAL.

INTERESTATAL.
adj, interstate.

INTERFECTO.
m, murder victim ‖ adj, murdered.

INTERFERENCIA.
f, interference.

INTERFERIR.
v, to interfere.

INTERFOLIAR.
v, to insert writings in a folder or set of documents.

ÍNTERIN.
m, interim.

INTERINAMENTE.
adv, temporarily, momentarily.

INTERINARIO.
See INTERINO.

INTERINAR.
v, to work as an INTERINO.

INTERINATO.
m, position of temporary worker ‖ also see INTERINIDAD.

INTERINIDAD.
f, temporariness ‖ duration of temporary or substitute work.

INTERINO.
m, temporary worker, temp, substitute ‖ adj, temporary, provisional, pro tem, pro tempore ‖ acting, interim.

INTERIOR.
m, interior or middle or non-costal portion (of a country) ‖ provincial part of a country ‖ adj, internal ‖ domestic, national ‖ civil (e.g. war) ‖ interior, not the capital (e.g. provinces) ‖ local.

INTERIORMENTE.
adv, domestically, nationally ‖ internally ‖ inwardly.

INTERLINEACIÓN.
m, interlineation, writing between the lines.

INTERLINEAR.
v, to interlineate, write between the lines.

INTERLOCUTORIAMENTE.
adv, interlocutorily.

INTERLOCUTORIO.
adj, interlocutory.

INTERMEDIAR.
v, to intermediate, mediate.

INTERMEDIARIO.
m, intermediary ‖ middleman ‖ adj, intermediary.

INTERMEDIO.
m, meantime, meanwhile, interim, interval ‖ intermission.

INTERNACIÓN.
f, (civil or criminal) commitment (of a person to an institution, e.g. hospital, jail), confinement ‖ internment, detention, imprisonment.

INTERNACIONAL.
adj, international.

INTERNACIONALES OBRERAS.
f, international workers, organizations.

INTERNACIONALISMO.
m, internationalism.

INTERNACIONALISTA.
f, m, internationalist, lawyer who specializes in international law.

INTERNACIONALIZACIÓN.
f, internationalization (of a previously national matter) ‖ submission to the authority of various nations or an international body.

INTERNACIONALIZAR.
v, to internationalize (a previously national matter) ‖ to submit to the authority of various nations or an international body.

INTERNADO.
m, committed or confined person (e.g. to a hospital) ‖ boarding home or school ‖ adj, committed ‖ hospitalized.

INTERNAMENTE.
adv, internally, domestically.

INTERNAMIENTO.
See INTERNACIÓN.

INTERNAR.
v, to commit, confine (to an institution) ‖ to intern, detain, imprison ‖ to import ‖ to send to a concentration or work camp.

INTERNO.
adj, interior ‖ local ‖ national.

INTERNUNCIO.
m, envoy.

INTERPARLAMENTARIO.
adj, interparliamentary, between parliaments, interlegislative.

INTERPELACIÓN.
f, request for help or protection ‖ judicial order to pay a debt, or to comply with an obligation or order, or to answer a question truthfully (in civil law) ‖ parliamentary question, formal question posed by a member of parliament to the cabinet about the latter's actions ‖ summons ‖ citation ‖ examination.

INTERPELACIÓN JUDICIAL.
judicial order at the request of a creditor to his obligor for payment of a debt or to comply with an obligation.

INTERPELADO.
m, person who receives a judicial order to pay a debt, or to comply with an obligation or order, or to answer a question truthfully (in civil law).

INTERPELANTE.
m, person who causes the issuance of a judicial order to pay a debt, or to comply with an obligation or order, or to answer a question truthfully (in civil law) ‖ person who poses a parliamentary question.

INTERPELAR.
v, to request help or protection ‖ to examine, question, interrogate ‖ to threaten a debtor or other obligor with his breach ‖ to formulate parliamentary questions to a minister of a cabinet.

INTERPONER.
v, to file a claim or motion or appeal ‖ to appoint a mediator ‖ to interpose, intervene ‖ to bring (an action), file (a complaint).

INTERPONER DEMANDA CONTENCIOSA.
to bring (an action), file (a complaint).

INTERPONER RECURSO DE APELACIÓN.
to appeal, file an appeal.

INTERPOSICIÓN.
f, intervention ‖ mediation ‖ interference.

INTERPÓSITA PERSONA.
f, mediator, intermediary, go-between ‖ agent who acts (improperly) to further his own interests.

INTERPRETABLE.
adj, subject to interpretation ‖ able to be interpreted.

INTERPRETACIÓN.
f, interpretation ‖ explanation ‖ clarification.

INTERPRETACIÓN AMPLIA.
See INTERPRETACIÓN EXTENSIVA.

INTERPRETACIÓN ANALÓGICA.
interpretation by analogy.

INTERPRETACIÓN AUTÉNTICA.
authentic interpretation, interpretation by the author of the matter under consideration (e.g. in laws, by legislator).

INTERPRETACIÓN DE LA DEMANDA.
interpretation of a complaint.

INTERPRETACIÓN DE LA LEY LABORAL.
interpretation of labor law.

INTERPRETACIÓN DE LA LEY PENAL.
interpretation of criminal law.

INTERPRETACIÓN DE LAS LEYES.
interpretation of the law, statutory interpretation.

INTERPRETACIÓN DE LAS SENTENCIAS.
See ACLARACIÓN DE SENTENCIA.

INTERPRETACIÓN DE LOS HECHOS.
interpretation of the facts.

INTERPRETACIÓN DE LOS TESTAMENTOS.
testamentary interpretation, interpretation of wills.

INTERPRETACIÓN DECLARATIVA.
explanation, clarification.

INTERPRETACIÓN DEL CONTRATO.
interpretation of the contract.

INTERPRETACIÓN DOCTRINAL.
doctrinal interpretation, interpretation in accord with legal doctrine or jurisprudence.

INTERPRETACIÓN ESTRICTA.
See INTERPRETACIÓN RESTRICTIVA.

INTERPRETACIÓN EXTENSIVA.
extensive interpretation, liberal interpretation.

INTERPRETACIÓN GRAMATICAL.
strict or close or literal interpretation, interpretation limited to the strict sense of the words.

INTERPRETACIÓN HISTÓRICA.
historical interpretation, interpretation of the words in light of the times in which the writing occurred.

INTERPRETACIÓN JUDICIAL.
See INTERPRETACIÓN USUAL.

INTERPRETACIÓN LEGISLATIVA.
legislative interpretation.

INTERPRETACIÓN LITERAL.
literal or close interpretation.

INTERPRETACIÓN LÓGICA.
logical interpretation.

INTERPRETACIÓN RAZONABLE.
reasonable interpretation.

INTERPRETACIÓN RESTRICTIVA.
restrictive interpretation.

INTERPRETACIÓN RESTRINGIDA.
close or restrictive interpretation.

INTERPRETACIÓN SISTEMÁTICA.
interpretation in the context of the general area of the law involved.

INTERPRETACIÓN TÉCNICA.
technical interpretation.

INTERPRETACIÓN USUAL.
usual or customary interpretation.

INTERPRETADOR.
m, interpreter (of legal texts).

INTERPRETAR.
v, to interpret, explain, clarify ‖ to translate.

INTERPRETATIVO.
adj, interpretative ‖ useful for interpretation.

INTÉRPRETE.
f, m, (oral) interpreter (of speaker of another language) ‖ person who interprets the law.

INTERPUESTA PERSONA.
See INTERPÓSITA PERSONA.

INTERREGNO.
m, interregnum, lapse between the reigns of sovereign when there is no government.

INTERREGNO PARLAMENTARIO.
parliamentary interregnum, period of time between parliamentary sessions.

INTERROGACIÓN.
f, interrogation, inquisition ‖ question, query, inquiry . See INTERROGATORIO.

INTERROGADO.
m, person under interrogation ‖ adj, interrogated.

INTERROGADOR.
m, interrogator.

INTERROGANTE.
m, question, inquiry, query, interrogation ‖ doubtful question or problem ‖ adj, interrogating, inquiring.

INTERROGAR.
v, to interrogate, question (especially in criminal cases).

INTERROGATIVO.
adj, questioning, interrogating.

INTERROGATORIO.
m, interrogatory ‖ interrogatories, series of questions which are usually, but not always, written.

INTERROGATORIO CRUZADO.
cross-examination (of witnesses).

INTERROGATORIO DIRECTO.
direct examination (of witnesses).

INTERROGATORIO DE PRISIONEROS.
interrogation of accused party (either written or oral). Pertains to rules regarding prisoners of war.

INTERRUMPIR.
v, to interrupt, suspend, temporarily cease ‖ to interrupt (someone).

INTERRUPCIÓN.
f, interruption, suspension ‖ obstacle, impediment ‖ interruption (of person or communication).

INTERRUPCIÓN DE LA PRESCRIPCIÓN.
tolling of statue of limitations ‖ interruption of prescriptive period of possession. May be NATURAL (factual) based on the possessor having lost actual possession for a period of time ‖ or CIVIL (legal) based on the fact that the true owner has filed a complaint objecting to the possession.

INTERRUPTIVO.
See ACTO INTERRUPTIVO.

INTERRUPTOR.
m, interrupter, person who interrupts ‖ circuit breaker.

INTERVALO.
m, interval.

INTERVALO CLARO.
See INTERVALO LÚCIDO.

INTERVALO LÚCIDO.
lucid interval or moment.

INTERVALO SOSPECHOSO.
suspicious interval, period of time which coincides with commission of a criminal act for which the accused has no alibi.

INTERVALOS DEL DERECHO.
legal time periods, periods of time which have legal effect.

INTERVENCIÓN.
f, intervention, participation ‖ intervention, imposition of authority ‖ intervention, mediation, intercession ‖ audit (of accounts) ‖ auditor's office ‖ custom's inspection ‖ foreign intervention ‖ personal attendance or presence (for a legal act) ‖ federal intervention in provincial or state affairs ‖ voluntary acceptance and payment by a third party of a dishonored draft ‖ court-ordered inspection of correspondence or other communication (e.g. telephone conversations).

INTERVENCIÓN ARMADA.
armed intervention (of one nation in territory of another).

NTERVENCIÓN DE ACREEDORES EN LA PARTICIÓN.
intervention of creditors (or heirs) in the distribution of a decedent's estate.

NTERVENCIÓN DE TERCERO.
See TERCERÍA.

NTERVENCIÓN DIPLOMÁTICA.
diplomatic intervention (between nations), diplomatic pressure.

NTERVENCIÓN ECONÓMICA.
economic intervention.

NTERVENCIÓN EN LA LETRA DE CAMBIO.
voluntary acceptance and payment by a third party of a dishonored draft.

NTERVENCIÓN FEDERAL.
federal intervention in provincial or state affairs.

NTERVENCIÓN FORZOSA.
compulsory intervention.

NTERVENCIÓN INTERNACIONAL.
international intervention.

NTERVENCIÓN JUDICIAL DE BIENES.
See ASEGURAMIENTO DE BIENES LITIGIOSOS, DEPÓSITO JUDICIAL, and PROHIBICIÓN DE INTERVENCIÓN JUDICIAL EN LAS TESTAMENTARIAS.

NTERVENCIÓN NECESARIA.
See INTERVENCIÓN FORZOSA.

NTERVENCIÓN OFICIAL.
diplomatic intervention (which is made public).

NTERVENCIÓN PACÍFICA.
peaceful intervention ‖ mediation, arbitration.

NTERVENCIÓN POLÍTICA.
political intervention (of federal government in affairs of state or provincial governments).

NTERVENCIÓN VOLUNTARIA.
voluntary intervention.

NTERVENCIONISMO INTERNACIONAL.
m, international interventionism.

NTERVENIDO.
m, country or party which is subject to INTERVENCIÓN ‖ party whose telephone is being tapped ‖ adj, subject to INTERVENCIÓN.

NTERVENIDOR.
See INTERVENTOR.

NTERVENIR.
v, to intervene, participate ‖ to intervene (as a third party plaintiff) ‖ to debate (in parliament) ‖ to mediate, arbitrate, intercede ‖ to approve an agreement between other parties ‖ to audit (accounts) ‖ to voluntarily accept and pay a dishonored draft on behalf of the maker ‖ to perform a customs inspection ‖ to intervene (in the affairs of other nations, or of provinces or states by federal government) ‖ to order inspection of correspondence or other communication (e.g. telephone conversations) ‖ to control, supervise.

INTERVENIR EL PAGO.
to stop payment (e.g. on a check).

INTERVENIR EN JUICIO.
to join, intervene in an action.

INTERVENIR JUDICIALMENTE.
to place under court control or supervision.

INTERVENTOR.
m, intervener, person or government which intervenes (see INTERVENIR) ‖ collaborator, party ‖ third party plaintiff ‖ customs inspector ‖ controller, inspector, auditor ‖ receiver ‖ trustee.

INTESTADA.
f, intestate's estate.

INTESTADO.
m, intestate, person who dies intestate ‖ intestate's estate ‖ adj, intestate.

INTESTATO.
See AB INTESTATO and ABINTESTATO.

ÍNTIMA CONVICCIÓN.
f, closely-held belief or conviction.

INTIMACIÓN.
f, notification ‖ warning ‖ notice ‖ special notice, extraordinary order.

INTIMACIÓN A LA PERSONA.
personal demand.

INTIMACIÓN A REBELDES Y SEDICIOSOS.
demand for surrender to rebels.

INTIMACIÓN DE PAGO.
demand for payment.

INTIMACIÓN JUDICIAL DE PAGO.
court order to pay.

INTIMACIÓN PARA DETENER UN BUQUE.
demand to inspect or detain a ship (during time of war).

INTIMAR.
v, to intimate ‖ to become intimate ‖ to warn, caution ‖ to give notice, notify ‖ to require, oblige ‖ to threaten.

INTIMATORIO.
adj, threatening, cautioning ‖ notificatory or notifying (of requirement to comply).

INTIMIDACIÓN.
f, intimidation. In civil law, use of INTIMIDA-CIÓN may nullify legal acts ‖ in crimi-nal law, may be a crime.

INTIMIDACIÓN DE LOS JUECES.
intimidation of judges. Court orders resulting from INTIMIDACIÓN DE LOS JUECES have no legal effect.

INTIMIDACIÓN PÚBLICA.
causing public disorder, inspiring public fear, intimidation of the public. Usually a crime.

INTIMIDAD.
f, intimacy, privacy. May require the taking of evidence in a closed or private hearing.

INTIMIDAR.
v, to intimidate, inspire fear.

INTOXICACIÓN.
f, intoxication, poisoning.

"INTRA VIRES HAEREDITATIS".
under the power of inheritance. Refers to the character of the actions of the legatee in answering for debts of the estate.

INTRAESTATAL.
adj, intrastate.

INTRANSFERIBLE.
adj, inalienable, untransferable, nontransferable.

INTRANSMISIBLE.
adj, inalienable, untransferable, nontransferable.

INTRASMISIBLE.
See INTRANSMISIBLE.

INTRIGA.
f, intrigue.

INTRODUCCIÓN.
f, introduction, insertion ‖ entry, penetration ‖ introduction, preface ‖ importation.

INTRODUCCIÓN DE BILLETES Y TÍTULOS FALSOS.
importation of counterfeit bills and commercial paper (from abroad). Usually a crime.

INTRODUCCIÓN DE MONEDA FALSA.
importation of counterfeit money (from abroad). Usually a crime.

INTRODUCIR.
v, to introduce, insert ‖ to cause to enter or penetrate ‖ to import.

INTRUSARSE.
v, to encroach ‖ to take or seize illegally.

INTRUSIÓN.
f, intrusion ‖ usurpation of a position, post, or

profession ‖ appropriation of real estat (without legal right).

INTRUSISMO.
m, act of usurping positions, post, or profes sion (without legal right). Usually a crime.

INTRUSO.
m, intruder, penetrator ‖ appropriator (of rea estate) ‖ usurper ‖ illegitimate monarch ‖ ad intrusive, usurping.

"INTUITU PECUNIAE".
for pecuniary reasons, for money.

"INTUITU PERSONAE".
for personal considerations, based on person qualifications.

INUNDACIÓN.
f, flood, flooding, inundation.

INUNDAR.
v, to flood, inundate.

INÚTIL.
adj, useless ‖ superfluous, unnecessary ‖ ir valid.

INUTILIDAD.
f, incapacity ‖ inability ‖ uselessness ‖ i validity.

INUTILIDAD FÍSICA.
physical incapacity.

INUTILIDAD POR LESIONES.
inability (of victim) to work due to injuries. I criminal law, usually an aggravating circum tance.

INUTILIZACIÓN.
f, act of making something useless ‖ disabl ment, act of disabling.

INUTILIZACIÓN DE DOCUMENTOS.
suppression or destruction of public docu ments. May be a crime if it results in injury damage.

INUTILIZACIÓN PARA EL SERVICIO MILITAR.
act of disabling for purposes of military se vice. If intentionally caused, usually a crime.

INUTILIZADO.
adj, destroyed, injured ‖ unused ‖ useless.

INUTILIZAR.
v, to deprive of utility.

INUTILIZARSE.
v, to injure, damage ‖ to destroy.

INVALIDACIÓN.
f, invalidation, nullification ‖ derogation ‖ m tual rescission (of a contract).

INVALIDAR.
v, to invalidate, nullify, void, annul ‖ to derogate ‖ to quash ‖ to mutually rescind (a contract).

INVALIDEZ.
f, legal invalidity, nullity, voidness ‖ physical invalidity or disability.

INVALIDEZ ABSOLUTA.
total disability.

INVALIDEZ DEFINITIVA.
permanent disability.

INVALIDEZ LABORAL.
work disability or impairment (for employment purposes). May be FÍSICA (physical), PROFESIONAL (professional), or GENERAL (general).

INVALIDEZ PARCIAL.
See INVALIDEZ RELATIVA.

INVALIDEZ PERMANENTE.
permanent disability or impairment.

INVALIDEZ PROVISIONAL.
temporary disability or impairment.

INVALIDEZ PROVISORIA.
temporary disability.

INVALIDEZ RELATIVA.
partial disability.

INVALIDEZ TOTAL.
See INVALIDEZ ABSOLUTA.

INVALIDEZ TRANSITORIA.
See INVALIDEZ PROVISORIA.

INVÁLIDO.
m, invalid (person) ‖ adj, invalid, null, void, without effect ‖ disabled, sick ‖ rescinded.

INVASIÓN.
f, invasion ‖ intrusion.

INVASIÓN DE DERECHOS.
infringement or invasion of rights.

INVENCIÓN.
f, invention.

INVENDIBLE.
adj, unsalable.

INVENTAR.
v, to invent ‖ to falsify.

INVENTARIO.
m, stock, inventory ‖ bulk inventory ‖ act of taking inventory ‖ inventory list.

INVENTARIO DE BIENES DE LOS HIJOS.
inventory of property of children. When the parents use or administrate the goods of their children, they must take INVENTARIO DE BIENES DE LOS HIJOS.

INVENTARIO DE BIENES DEL AUSENTE.
inventory of property of an absentee.

INVENTARIO DE BIENES DEL MENOR.
inventory of property of a minor. The guardian of a minor must take INVENTARIO DE BIENES DEL MENOR.

INVENTARIO DE BIENES RESERVABLES.
inventory of decedent's estate (by a widow upon remarriage).

INVENTARIO EN EL USUFRUCTO.
inventory of property used pursuant to usufruct.

INVENTARIO EN LA SOCIEDAD DE GANANCIALES.
inventory of marital property or estate.

INVENTARIO EN LAS SOCIEDADES.
inventory of corporate or partnership property.

INVENTARIO EN TESTAMENTARIAS Y ABINTESTATOS.
inventory of decedent's estate (whether intestate or testate).

INVENTARIO FÍSICO.
physical inventory.

INVENTARIO GENERAL.
general inventory.

INVENTARIO REAL.
See INVENTARIO FÍSICO.

INVENTO.
m, invention.

INVENTO LABORAL.
employee invention, invention discovered by employee while at work.

INVENTOR.
m, inventor, discoverer.

INVERSIÓN.
f, investment ‖ alteration, change, transposition.

INVERSIÓN DE LA PRUEBA.
transfer of the burden of proof.

INVERSIÓN DOMINANTE.
controlling interest.

INVERSIÓN NETA.
net investment.

INVERSIÓN SEXUAL.
homosexuality.

INVERSIONISTA.
f, m, investor.

INVERSO.
adj, inverse, opposite.

INVERSOR.
m, investor.

INVERTIDO.
m, homosexual ‖ adj, inverted ‖ invested (property).

INVERTIR.
v, to invest ‖ to invert.

INVESTIDURA.
f, investiture.

INVESTIGABLE.
adj, susceptible to investigation.

INVESTIGACIÓN.
f, investigation, inquiry.

INVESTIGACIÓN DE LA MATERNIDAD.
investigation of maternity.

INVESTIGACIÓN DE LA PATERNIDAD.
investigation of paternity.

INVESTIGACIÓN DE TÍTULO.
title search.

INVESTIGACIÓN DEL DELITO.
investigation of the crime.

INVESTIGADOR.
m, investigator.

INVESTIGAR.
v, to investigate.

INVESTIR.
v, to vest (a person with a position), confer upon.

INVIOLABILIDAD.
f, inviolability.

INVIOLABILIDAD DE LA CORRESPONDENCIA.
inviolability of correspondence.

INVIOLABILIDAD DE LA DEFENSA EN JUICIO.
absolute right to defense at trial.

INVIOLABILIDAD DE LA PROPIEDAD.
inviolability of property, absolute right to ownership of property.

INVIOLABILIDAD DEL DOMICILIO.
inviolability of domicile or home, absolute right against unwarranted entry into one's domicile.

INVIOLABILIDAD PARLAMENTARIA.
absolute right against prosecution for acts of legislator acting in his character as such.

INVIOLABLE.
adj, inviolate, inviolable, immune.

INVOCACIÓN.
f, invocation, request for help ‖ allegation or list of reasons, laws or customs.

INVOCAR.
v, to invoke, request help or a favor ‖ to rely upon a law or other norm, cite a legal text.

INVOLUNTARIAMENTE.
adv, involuntarily, unconsciously.

INVOLUNTARIEDAD.
f, involuntariness.

INVOLUNTARIO.
adj, involuntary, unconscious ‖ forced, obligatory.

IPSO FACTO.
ipso facto, by the mere fact.

IPSO JURE.
ipso jure, by the operation of the law itself.

IR A LA BANCARROTA.
to go bankrupt, go into bankruptcy. May be either FORTUITA (non-negligent), CULPOSA (negligent), or FRAUDULENTA (fraudulent).

IR A LA MANO A UNO.
to contain or restrain someone.

IR A LA PAR.
to divide the profits evenly or in equal shares

IR A LA PARTE.
to be financially interested in a business.

IR A LA QUIEBRA.
to go bankrupt, go into bankruptcy.

IR POR SU MANO.
to drive pursuant to the legal direction of traffic.

IRA.
f, ire, anger.

IRRAZONABLE.
adj, unreasonable.

IRRECONCILIABLE.
adj, irreconcilable.

IRRECUPERABLE.
adj, unrecoverable, unable to be recouped uncollectible.

IRRECURRIBLE.
See SENTENCIA IRRECURRIBLE.

IRRECUSABLE.
adj, unchallengeable, unimpeachable, not subject to challenge (e.g. personal qualifications of a judge).

IRREDIMIBLE.
adj, irredeemable ‖ untransferable (re: exchanges of prisoners).

IRREEMPLAZABLE.
adj, unreplaceable.

IRREFORMABLE.
adj, unchangeable, untransformable.

IRREFUTABLE.
adj, irrefutable.
IRREGULAR.
adj, irregular, contrary to rule ‖ exceptional ‖ abnormal ‖ of questionable morality or legality.
IRREGULARIDAD.
f, irregularity.
IRREGULARIDAD ADMINISTRATIVA.
administrative abuse of authority.
IRREIVINDICABLE.
adj, not actionable.
IRRELEVANTE.
adj, irrelevant.
IRREMEDIABLE.
adj, irremediable, without solution.
IRREMISIBLE.
adj, unpardonable, unforgivable.
IRREMPLAZABLE.
See IRREEMPLAZABLE.
IRRENUNCIABILIDAD.
f, non-renounceability, inability to renounce.
IRRENUNCIABLE.
adj, not able to be renounced or waived.
IRREPARABLE.
adj, irreparable, irremediable.
IRREPRIMIBLE.
adj, irrepressible.
IRREPROCHABLE.
adj, irreproachable.
IRRESCINDIBLE.
adj, not subject to rescission, unrescindable.
IRRESISTIBLE.
adj, irresistible.
IRRESOLUBLE.
adj, unsolvable, insoluble.
IRRESOLUCIÓN.
f, irresolution, indecision, lack of resolution.
IRRESOLUTO.
adj, irresolute.
IRRESPETUOSO.
adj, disrespectful.
IRRESPONSABILIDAD.
f, irresponsibility.
IRRESPONSABILIDAD CIVIL.
exemption or immunity from civil liability.

IRRESPONSABILIDAD PENAL.
exemption or immunity from criminal liability.
IRRESPONSABLE.
adj, irresponsible.
IRRETRACTABLE.
adj, not subject to retraction.
IRRETROACTIVIDAD.
f, non-retroactivity. Used to refer to principle that neither criminal nor civil laws can have ex-post facto effect.
IRRETROACTIVIDAD PENAL.
penal non-retroactivity. Used to refer to principle opposing ex-post facto criminal laws.
IRREVERSIBLE.
adj, irreversible.
IRREVOCABILIDAD.
f, irrevocability, inability to revoke.
IRREVOCABLE.
adj, irrevocable.
IRRITABLE.
adj, irritable ‖ voidable, able to be annulled.
IRRITAR.
v, to irritate, anger ‖ to void, annul.
ÍRRITO.
adj, invalid ‖ void, null.
IRROGACIÓN.
f, cause of damage or injury ‖ cause of new expenditures.
IRROGAR.
v, to cause, incur.
IRROGAR GASTOS.
to incur expenses.
IRROGAR PERJUICIO.
to incur damage.
IRRUMPIR.
v, to break (into a place with violence).
IRRUPCIÓN.
f, invasion, attack ‖ breaking (into a place with violence).
ISLA.
f, island.
ÍTEM.
m, item ‖ article ‖ furthermore, also, moreover.
"ITER CRIMINIS".
the stages of the crime, process of the crime.

JACTANCIA.
f, jactitation, slander of title, false claim to legal right or obligation due.
See JUICIO DE JACTANCIA.

JEFA.
f, (female) director or chief or boss, female who is in charge of an organization or institution.

JEFATURA.
f, directorship, post of chief or director ‖ office or building of chief or director ‖ direction of chief or director ‖ headquarters.

JEFATURA DE POLICÍA.
police headquarters.

JEFE.
m, (male) director or chief or boss ‖ commander ‖ man who is in charge of an organization or institution ‖ leader.

JEFE DE ESTADO.
head of state, sovereign, e.g. king, president, prime minister.

JEFE DE FAMILIA.
head of family. Usually but not always the husband.

JEFE DE GOBIERNO PROVISIONAL.
head of a provisional government.
See GOBIERNO PROVISIONAL.

JEFE DE MISIÓN.
head of the ambassadorial mission.

JEFE DEL ESTADO.
See JEFE DE ESTADO.

JEFE MILITAR.
military chief of staff ‖ chief of staff of ground forces, chief of staff of army.

JEFE NAVAL.
military chief of staff ‖ chief of staff of navy.

JEFE POLÍTICO.
political leader, leader of a political movement.

JEFE PROVISIONAL DEL ESTADO.
temporary head of state, provisional head of state.

JERARQUÍA.
f, hierarchy, category.

JERÁRQUICAMENTE.
adv, hierarchically, pursuant to hierarchy.

JERÁRQUICO.
adj, hierarchic, hierarchical.

JERGA.
f, jargon, lingo ‖ special language used within certain professions.

JORNADA.
f, occasion, circumstance ‖ death, passing away ‖ work day or week (in hours) ‖ journey, trip.

JORNADA DE TRABAJO.
work day (in hours), daily work hours ‖ work week (in hours), weekly work hours.

JORNAL.
m, day's or daily pay or wages.

JORNALERO.
m, day laborer ‖ laborer ‖ manual laborer.

JUBILACIÓN.
f, retirement ‖ act of retirement ‖ retirement pay ‖ retirement benefits.

JUBILACIÓN DE VEJEZ.
old-age pension.

JUBILACIÓN POR ANCIANIDAD.
See JUBILACIÓN DE VEJEZ.

JUBILACIÓN POR INVALIDEZ.
retirement due to disability ‖ disability pension.

JUBILADO.

m, retiree, retired person ‖ pensioner ‖ adj, retired.

JUBILADO SIN JUBILACIÓN.

retirement without retirement benefits. Refers to lapse of time which may occur between actual retirement and the commencement of retirement benefits.

JUBILAR.

v, to retire (someone) ‖ to give a pension.

JUBILARSE.

v, to retire voluntarily ‖ to request retirement ‖ to retire with a pension.

JUBILATORIO.

adj, retirement, pertaining to retirement.

"JUDEX".

judex, judge ‖ expert, expert witness ‖ censor ‖ critic.

"JUDICATIO".

trial, litigation ‖ matter in litigation.

"JUDICATUM".

res judicata.

"JUDICATUM NEGARE".

to disagree with a judgment.

"JUDICATUM SOLVERE".

to pay costs ‖ to obey an adverse judgment.

JUDICATURA.

f, judicature ‖ judgeship ‖ term of office of judge.

JUDICIAL.

adj, judicial, pertaining to litigation.

JUDICIALMENTE.

adv, judicially ‖ in litigation ‖ before the court or judge ‖ by order of a court or judge ‖ litigiously, contentiously.

JUDICIARIO.

adj, judicial.

"JUDICIUM".

judicium ‖ trial, litigation, hearing ‖ sentence, decision, judgment, award, verdict ‖ accusation ‖ defense ‖ courtroom.

JUECES DE CONCIENCIA.

jurors.

JUECES DEL PUEBLO.

See JUECES DE CONCIENCIA.

JUECES POPULARES.

See JUECES DE CONCIENCIA.

JUEGO.

m, game ‖ gambling ‖ bet, gamble ‖ wager ‖ set (of things) ‖ flexibility, movement.

JUEGO DE AZAR.

game of chance.

JUEGO PÚBLICO.

(legal) gambling house, bookmaking establishment.

JUEGOS PROHIBIDOS.

prohibited games (e.g. games of chance).

JUEZ.

m, judge, justice ‖ arbitrator ‖ arbiter.

JUEZ A QUO.

judge of a lower court whose decision has been appealed.

JUEZ AD QUEM.

judge on appeal, judge to whom one argues a judgment on appeal.

JUEZ ADMINISTRATIVO.

administrative judge.

JUEZ ARBITRADOR.

arbitrator, arbiter, referee, umpire (chosen by the parties or a third party).

JUEZ ÁRBITRO.

arbitrator or arbiter or referee or umpire chosen by third party; also see JUEZ ARBITRADOR.

JUEZ ASOCIADO.

associate judge.

JUEZ AVENIDOR.

arbitrator.

JUEZ CANTONAL.

district court or county court judge.

JUEZ CIVIL.

civil court judge ‖ inferior court judge with jurisdiction over civil disputes. See DERECHO CIVIL.

JUEZ CIVIL Y CRIMINAL.

inferior court judge with jurisdiction over criminal and civil disputes.

JUEZ COMPETENTE.

competent judge, judge with jurisdiction over a case.

JUEZ COMPROMISARIO.

arbitrator.

JUEZ CONCILIADOR.

mediator, conciliator (used to avoid recourse to the courts).

JUEZ CORRECCIONAL.

judge of misdemeanors and lesser infractions of the law.

JUEZ CRIMINAL.

criminal court judge.

JUEZ DE ADUANAS.

customs court judge.

JUEZ DE ALZADA.
appeals court judge, appellate judge.
JUEZ DE APELACIONES.
See JUEZ DE ALZADAS.
JUEZ DE AVENENCIA.
See JUEZ AVENIDOR.
JUEZ DE CIRCUITO.
circuit court judge.
JUEZ DE COMERCIO.
commercial court judge, judge with jurisdiction over matters regulated by the commercial code. See DERECHO COMERCIAL.
JUEZ DE COMPETENCIA.
judge who decides jurisdictional conflicts.
JUEZ DE DERECHO.
judge who applies the law in a case (but does not determine the facts). Opposed to JUEZ DE HECHO.
JUEZ DE DISTRITO.
district court or county court judge.
JUEZ DE FALTAS.
lower court judge who has jurisdiction over minor municipal infractions.
JUEZ DE FONDO.
trial judge ‖ judge who decides questions of law.
JUEZ DE HECHO.
judge who determines the facts of a given case (but does not apply the law to the facts). Opposed to JUEZ DE DERECHO.
JUEZ DE INSTRUCCIÓN.
judge who has jurisdiction over an the initial factual stage of a criminal trial. See INSTRUCCIÓN.
JUEZ DE LA CAUSA.
trial judge, judge who hears a case.
JUEZ DE LETRAS.
See JUEZ LETRADO.
JUEZ DE LO CIVIL.
civil court judge.
JUEZ DE LO CRIMINAL.
criminal court judge.
JUEZ DE MENORES.
juvenile court judge.
JUEZ DE PAZ.
justice of the peace, magistrate.
JUEZ DE POLICÍA.
police judge or magistrate.
JUEZ DE PRIMERA INSTANCIA.
court of the first instance, lower court judge.

JUEZ DE QUIEBRA.
bankruptcy court judge.
JUEZ DE SÍ MISMO.
one's own judge.
JUEZ DE TURNO.
judge whose is sitting or presently working.
JUEZ DEL CRIMEN.
criminal court judge.
JUEZ DEL TRABAJO.
labor court judge.
JUEZ ESPECIAL.
judge who has jurisdiction over special matters (e.g. impeachment proceedings) ‖ special criminal court investigator who is to prepare a criminal matter to be heard by another judge ‖ special civil court judge appointed by the parties who has the power of issuing a binding decision.
JUEZ EXHORTADO.
judge who receives letters rogatory.
JUEZ EXHORTANTE.
judge who issues letters rogatory.
JUEZ EXTRAORDINARIO.
See JUEZ ESPECIAL.
JUEZ FEDERAL.
federal court judge.
JUEZ INCOMPETENTE.
judge without jurisdiction over a case.
JUEZ INFERIOR.
judge of a lower court whose decision has been appealed ‖ lower or trial court judge. See JUEZ SUBORDINADO.
JUEZ INSTRUCTOR.
judge in charge of preliminary stage of criminal proceedings.
JUEZ INTERINO.
judge pro tempore, judge pro tem.
JUEZ LEGO.
lay judge, judge who lacks legal training or is not an attorney.
JUEZ LETRADO.
judge who is an attorney.
JUEZ MENOR.
magistrate ‖ justice of the peace.
JUEZ MILITAR.
court-martial judge, military court judge.
JUEZ MIXTO.
judge who hears both criminal and civil matters.
JUEZ MUNICIPAL.
municipal court judge.

JUEZ DE ALZADA.
appeals court judge, appellate judge.

JUEZ DE APELACIONES.
See JUEZ DE ALZADAS.

JUEZ DE AVENENCIA.
See JUEZ AVENIDOR.

JUEZ DE CIRCUITO.
circuit court judge.

JUEZ DE COMERCIO.
commercial court judge, judge with jurisdiction over matters regulated by the commercial code. See DERECHO COMERCIAL.

JUEZ DE COMPETENCIA.
judge who decides jurisdictional conflicts.

JUEZ DE DERECHO.
judge who applies the law in a case (but does not determine the facts). Opposed to JUEZ DE HECHO.

JUEZ DE DISTRITO.
district court or county court judge.

JUEZ DE FALTAS.
lower court judge who has jurisdiction over minor municipal infractions.

JUEZ DE FONDO.
trial judge ‖ judge who decides questions of law.

JUEZ DE HECHO.
judge who determines the facts of a given case (but does not apply the law to the facts). Opposed to JUEZ DE DERECHO.

JUEZ DE INSTRUCCIÓN.
judge who has jurisdiction over an the initial factual stage of a criminal trial. See INSTRUCCIÓN.

JUEZ DE LA CAUSA.
trial judge, judge who hears a case.

JUEZ DE LETRAS.
See JUEZ LETRADO.

JUEZ DE LO CIVIL.
civil court judge.

JUEZ DE LO CRIMINAL.
criminal court judge.

JUEZ DE MENORES.
juvenile court judge.

JUEZ DE PAZ.
justice of the peace, magistrate.

JUEZ DE POLICÍA.
police judge or magistrate.

JUEZ DE PRIMERA INSTANCIA.
court of the first instance, lower court judge.

JUEZ DE QUIEBRA.
bankruptcy court judge.

JUEZ DE SÍ MISMO.
one's own judge.

JUEZ DE TURNO.
judge whose is sitting or presently working.

JUEZ DEL CRIMEN.
criminal court judge.

JUEZ DEL TRABAJO.
labor court judge.

JUEZ ESPECIAL.
judge who has jurisdiction over special matters (e.g. impeachment proceedings) ‖ special criminal court investigator who is to prepare a criminal matter to be heard by another judge ‖ special civil court judge appointed by the parties who has the power of issuing a binding decision.

JUEZ EXHORTADO.
judge who receives letters rogatory.

JUEZ EXHORTANTE.
judge who issues letters rogatory.

JUEZ EXTRAORDINARIO.
See JUEZ ESPECIAL.

JUEZ FEDERAL.
federal court judge.

JUEZ INCOMPETENTE.
judge without jurisdiction over a case.

JUEZ INFERIOR.
judge of a lower court whose decision has been appealed ‖ lower or trial court judge. See JUEZ SUBORDINADO.

JUEZ INSTRUCTOR.
judge in charge of preliminary stage of criminal proceedings.

JUEZ INTERINO.
judge pro tempore, judge pro tem.

JUEZ LEGO.
lay judge, judge who lacks legal training or is not an attorney.

JUEZ LETRADO.
judge who is an attorney.

JUEZ MENOR.
magistrate ‖ justice of the peace.

JUEZ MILITAR.
court-martial judge, military court judge.

JUEZ MIXTO.
judge who hears both criminal and civil matters.

JUEZ MUNICIPAL.
municipal court judge.

the other is public, and which is based on administrative law.

JUICIO CONTRADICTORIO.
contradictory case, action in which remedy or demand opposes or contradicts remedy or demand in another action ‖ also see JUICIO CONTENCIOSO.

JUICIO CORRECCIONAL.
misdemeanor case, criminal trial or proceeding in which the accusation involves a misdemeanor.

JUICIO CRIMINAL.
criminal case ‖ criminal trial or proceeding ‖ action or trial regarding an ACCIÓN PENAL.

JUICIO CRIMINAL CONTRA JUECES O MAGISTRADOS.
criminal case or proceeding brought against judges or magistrates for malfeasance.

JUICIO DE ABINTESTATO.
intestacy proceeding.

JUICIO DE ALIMENTOS.
alimony hearing or proceeding, action to obtain alimony payment (whether from a divorced or married person).

JUICIO DE AMIGABLES COMPONEDORES.
arbitration (submitted voluntarily by the parties to an arbitrator who is a not necessarily an attorney; usually not subject to substantive or procedural rules).

JUICIO DE AMPARO.
proceeding or trial regarding constitutional guarantees. See AMPARO.

JUICIO DE APELACIÓN.
appellate hearing ‖ appellate proceeding.

JUICIO DE APREMIO.
See APREMIO.

JUICIO DE ÁRBITROS.
See JUICIO ARBITRAL.

JUICIO DE AVENENCIA.
arbitration proceedings.

JUICIO DE CALUMNIA.
defamation proceeding or trial, case or trial involving INJURIA or CALUMNIA.

JUICIO DE COGNICIÓN.
full adversary proceeding or trial.

JUICIO DE CONCILIACIÓN.
settlement hearing. Usually pre-trial and is a formal stage in litigation in which both parties meet in the presence of a judge.

JUICIO DE CONCURSO DE ACREEDORES.
See CONCURSO DE ACREEDORES. May be VO-

LUNTARIO or PREVENTIVO (held at the request of the debtor) or INVOLUNTARIO (at the request of the creditors).

JUICIO DE CONSIGNACIÓN.
hearing to place disputed property or money in escrow.

JUICIO DE CONVOCATORIA DE ACREEDORES.
See CONVOCATORIA DE ACREEDORES.

JUICIO DE DERECHO.
trial in which matters of law are at issue ‖ stage in criminal trial after a jury has entered a guilty verdict, in which matters of law are addressed by the lawyers. Purpose is to determine the sentence and the remedy.

JUICIO DE DESAHUCIO.
eviction hearing, ejectment proceeding, proceeding for ouster.

JUICIO DE DESALOJO.
See JUICIO DE DESAHUCIO.

JUICIO DE DESLINDE.
See DESLINDE and JUICIO DE MENSURA.

JUICIO DE DESPIDO.
trial regarding employee discharge.

JUICIO DE DISENSO.
proceeding at which legal opposition to marriage is heard.

JUICIO DE DIVORCIO.
divorce proceedings ‖ divorce (suit).

JUICIO DE EJECUCIÓN.
See JUICIO EJECUTIVO.

JUICIO DE EMBARGO.
attachment or garnishment proceedings.

JUICIO DE ENAJENACIÓN FORZOSA.
condemnation proceedings.

JUICIO DE EXEQUÁTUR.
hearing to challenge enforceability of a foreign judgment.

JUICIO DE EXPERTOS.
proceeding in which expert witnesses are used ‖ expert testimony.

JUICIO DE FALTAS.
misdemeanor case, type of criminal proceeding resulting from commission of a FALTA (often heard in a police court).

JUICIO DE HERENCIA VACANTE.
See HERENCIA VACANTE or JUICIO DE ABINTESTATO.

JUICIO DE INJURIA.
See JUICIO DE CALUMNIA.

JUICIO DE INQUISICIÓN.
inquest ‖ judicial inquiry.
JUICIO DE INSANIA.
incompetency proceeding, competency proceeding (to determine the sanity of a person).
JUICIO DE INSOLVENCIA.
insolvency proceedings ‖ also see JUICIO DE QUIEBRA.
JUICIO DE JACTANCIA.
action of jactitation, type of proceeding for injury caused by defamation or making false claim which prejudices another's rights.
JUICIO DE LANZAMIENTO.
dispossession or ouster or ejectment proceedings.
JUICIO DE LITISEXPENSAS.
hearing regarding allocation of court costs.
JUICIO DE MAYOR CUANTÍA.
proceeding or trial to hear large claim.
JUICIO DE MENOR CUANTÍA.
small claims trial, proceeding to hear small claim.
JUICIO DE MENSURA, DESLINDE Y AMOJONAMIENTO.
case of boundary, boundary suit, declaratory judgment hearing for the determination of boundaries.
JUICIO DE MÍNIMA CUANTÍA.
See JUICIO VERBAL.
JUICIO DE NOVO.
trial de novo, new trial.
JUICIO DE NULIDAD.
proceeding for annulment or to declare something void.
JUICIO DE PERITOS.
See JUICIO DE EXPERTOS.
JUICIO DE PRIMERA INSTANCIA.
inferior court trial or proceeding, trial court proceeding.
JUICIO DE PURO DERECHO.
trial in which solely matters of law are at issue.
JUICIO DE QUIEBRA.
bankruptcy proceeding in which the debtor is or is not declared bankrupt.
JUICIO DE RESPONSABILIDAD.
civil suit for damages.
JUICIO DE SEGUNDA INSTANCIA.
appeals hearing, appellate trial.
See APELACIÓN and SEGUNDA INSTANCIA.
JUICIO DE SUCESIÓN.
See JUICIO SUCESORIO.

JUICIO DE TERCERA INSTANCIA.
See TERCERA INSTANCIA.
JUICIO DE TESTAMENTARÍA.
probate proceeding.
JUICIO DE TRABAJO.
labor law action or proceeding.
JUICIO DECLARATIVO.
declaratory judgment proceeding or case.
JUICIO DECLARATORIO.
See JUICIO DECLARATIVO.
JUICIO DEL TRABAJO.
labor trial ‖ trial involving an employer-employee conflict.
JUICIO DIVISORIO.
partition proceeding ‖ case requesting the remedy of partition between co-owners.
JUICIO EJECUTIVO.
executory proceeding or process ‖ execution, supplementary proceeding (to execute on a judgment) ‖ proceeding in a criminal trial in which an executory order is issued ‖ proceeding for enforcement of judgment.
JUICIO EN REBELDÍA.
trial or proceeding in absentia, proceeding in which defendant has failed to appear in or abandons an action.
JUICIO ESCRITO.
trial by evaluation exclusively of written evidence submitted. Opposed to JUICIO ORAL.
JUICIO EXTRAORDINARIO.
See JUICIO SUMARIO.
JUICIO FENECIDO.
case in which a final order has been issued and carried out ‖ case which has been dismissed ‖ case which has been dismissed for failure to prosecute. See CADUCIDAD DE LA INSTANCIA.
JUICIO GENERAL.
See JUICIO UNIVERSAL.
JUICIO HIPOTECARIO.
See EJECUCIÓN HIPOTECARIA.
JUICIO INTESTADO.
intestacy proceeding.
JUICIO MILITAR.
court marshall, court marshall proceeding, trial within the jurisdiction of the military tribunals.
JUICIO ORAL.
oral proceeding or trial (i.e. one carried out before the judge orally) ‖ criminal trial or proceeding during which evidence is offered orally.

JUICIO ORDINARIO.
full trial, non-expedited trial.
Opposed to JUICIO SUMARIO.

JUICIO PARTICULAR.
See JUICIO SINGULAR.

JUICIO PENAL.
See JUICIO CRIMINAL.

JUICIO PETITORIO.
petitory proceeding or trial, in rem proceeding or trial.

JUICIO PLENARIO.
type of possessory hearing in which matters of law, or law and fact are in dispute ‖ also see JUICIO ORDINARIO.

JUICIO POLÍTICO.
impeachment proceeding or trial, proceeding to impeach a president, vice-president, cabinet ministers, or members of the Supreme Court or other courts for malfeasance or misfeasance ‖ political trial.

JUICIO POR DELITOS DE IMPRENTA.
type of criminal trial for felonies or misdemeanors pertaining to printed publications.

JUICIO POR JURADO.
jury trial.

JUICIO POSESORIO.
type of possessory proceeding limited to disputes over the acquisition, retention, or regaining of possession (either physical or legal) of a thing.

JUICIO REIVINDICATORIO.
See REIVINDICATORIO.

JUICIO SECUNDARIO.
ancillary suit or action.

JUICIO SIN DEMANDADO.
trial with a John or Jane Doe as defendant.

JUICIO SINGULAR.
proceeding or trial in which rights of an individual question or thing are involved. Opposed to JUICIO UNIVERSAL.

JUICIO SOBRE LOS MÉRITOS.
trial on the merits.

JUICIO SUCESORIO.
probate hearing to determine the heirs or legatees of a decedent, the payment of the estate obligations, and the distribution of property. May be either a JUICIO DE TESTAMENTARÍA or JUICIO DE ABINTESTATO.

JUICIO SUMARIO.
type of summary hearing in which matters regarding possession of property are in dispu-

te ‖ summary or expedited proceeding. Opposed to JUICIO ORDINARIO.

JUICIO SUMARIO MILITAR.
expedited court martial (during peace time).

JUICIO SUMARÍSIMO.
specially expedited summary proceeding.

JUICIO TESTAMENTARIO.
testamentary proceeding ‖ probate hearing or proceeding (when there are minors or other persons who lack legal capacity, but who have an interest in the will which is opposed by third parties, and when the legatees of age are unable to agree on a private division of the estate).

JUICIO UNIVERSAL.
proceeding in which all the assets of a person are under the court's scrutiny. They are divided into two types: decedents' estates and bankruptcy.

JUICIO VERBAL.
trial which is simplified, expedited, and carried out orally, except for the initial complaint.

JUICIOS ACUMULADOS.
consolidated actions ‖ joined actions.

JUNTA.
f, gathering, assembly ‖ meeting, session ‖ group, council, board, board of directors ‖ tribunal ‖ junta, provisional military government ‖ entirety ‖ entire, whole.

JUNTA ADMINISTRATIVA.
administrative board.

JUNTA ARBITRAL.
arbitration board.

JUNTA ASESORA.
See JUNTA CONSULTIVA.

JUNTA CONSULTIVA.
consulting board, administrative council.

JUNTA DE ACCIONISTAS.
shareholders' or stockholders' meeting.

JUNTA DE ACREEDORES.
creditors' meeting for the purpose of evaluating a rescheduling or modification of their credits, proposed by the debtor.

JUNTA DE ARBITRAJE.
See JUNTA ARBITRAL.

JUNTA DE COMERCIO.
board of trade, chamber of commerce.

JUNTA DE CONCILIACIÓN.
arbitration board.

JUNTA DE DIRECCIÓN.
board of governors.

JUNTA DE DIRECTORES.
board of directors.
JUNTA DE ELECCIONES.
See JUNTA ELECTORAL.
JUNTA DE GOBIERNO.
provisional government ‖ board of governors ‖ board of directors.
JUNTA DE PLANIFICACIÓN.
See JUNTA PLANIFICADORA.
JUNTA DE REVISIÓN.
board of review ‖ auditing group or board.
JUNTA DE SÍNDICOS.
board of trustees.
JUNTA DIRECTIVA.
board of directors.
JUNTA ELECTORAL.
meeting of voters ‖ board of poll booth watchers ‖ electoral board, board to control the legality of elections.
JUNTA ESPECIAL.
special meeting.
JUNTA GENERAL DE ACCIONISTAS.
general shareholders' meeting ‖ general meeting of shareholders (of a SOCIEDAD ANÓNIMA to vote on matters which pursuant to the bylaws are deemed to be ordinary).
JUNTA GENERAL ORDINARIA.
See JUNTA GENERAL DE ACCIONISTAS.
JUNTA PLANIFICADORA.
planning group or board or commission.
JUNTA SINDICAL.
board of directors (of a trade union).
JUNTAR MERIENDAS.
to join forces.
JUNTO.
adj, together.
JURA.
f, oath, promise ‖ act of swearing.
JURA DE LA BANDERA.
act of swearing allegiance to the national flag (e.g. by its soldiers.)
"JURA NOVIT CURIA".
The judge knows the law. Implies that the parties merely need to set forth the facts of the case in order for a dispute to be resolved and that the judge is responsible for finding and applying the correct law.
JURADO.
m, jury ‖ juror, juryman, member of a jury ‖ member of a board which awards bids or similar competitions ‖ person who has given

an oath upon taking a position (e.g. interpreters, expert witnesses) ‖ adj, sworn, promised.
JURADO DE ENJUICIAMIENTO.
tribunal to try a judge's malfeasance or misfeasance.
JURADO ESPECIAL.
special jury.
JURADO ORDINARIO.
common or ordinary jury.
JURADO SUPLENTE.
alternate juror.
JURADURÍA.
f, position of juror ‖ jury service ‖ office of a judge or examiner.
JURAMENTAR.
v, to swear to, take an oath.
JURAMENTARSE.
v, to take an oath, promise under oath ‖ to swear oneself to something.
JURAMENTO.
m, oath (either affirming or negating something).
JURAMENTO AFIRMATIVO.
See JURAMENTO ASERTORIO.
JURAMENTO ASERTÓRICO.
See JURAMENTO ASERTORIO.
JURAMENTO ASERTORIO.
affirmative oath.
JURAMENTO DE CARGO.
oath of office.
JURAMENTO DE DECIR LA VERDAD.
oath to tell the truth ‖ witness's oath.
JURAMENTO DE FIDELIDAD.
oath of allegiance.
JURAMENTO DE LOS INTÉRPRETES.
interpreters' oath (to interpret accurately and thoroughly).
JURAMENTO DE LOS TESTIGOS.
witnesses' oath (to tell the truth).
JURAMENTO DECISORIO.
harmonious testimony, testimony which is not subject to being weighed by a judge because it is given in deference to the opposing party.
JURAMENTO DEFERIDO.
See JURAMENTO DECISORIO.
JURAMENTO ESTIMATORIO.
sworn appraisal ‖ also see JURAMENTO SUPLETORIO.
JURAMENTO INDECISORIO.
indecisive testimony, testimony which is

weighed by the judge against the other party's evidence.

JURAMENTO JUDICIAL.
judicial oath, judges' oath of office ‖ oath administered by judge in trial. See JURAMENTO DECISORIO.

JURAMENTO POLÍTICO.
presidential or vice-presidential oath of office.

JURAMENTO PROFESIONAL.
professional oath (to perform one's profession or position faithfully).

JURAMENTO PROMISORIO.
testimony corroborating a promise, contract, or act.

JURAMENTO REFERIDO.
testimony by reference to testimony of other party (rather than by direct response).

JURAMENTO SOLEMNE.
solemn oath.

JURAMENTO SUPLETORIO.
supplementary testimony, testimony of parties which is requested by a judge to supplement testimony which is in some way inadequate.

JURAR.
v, to swear to, take an oath ‖ to promise ‖ to take an oath of office ‖ to give testimony under oath ‖ to swear, blaspheme.

JURAR EL CARGO.
to take the oath of office.

JURAR EN FALSO.
to commit perjury, perjure oneself.

JURE.
See DE DERECHO.

JURICIDAD.
See JURIDICIDAD.

JURÍDICAMENTE.
adv, legally, juridically, lawfully, according to law ‖ by legal means ‖ by means of court ‖ before a court or judge.

JURIDICIDAD.
f, lawfulness, legality, affirmative tendency in favor of the rule of law (i.e. to resolve social or political problems by strict application of the law).

JURÍDICO.
adj, juridical, legal, lawful ‖ pertaining to the law ‖ pursuant to law.

JURÍDICO-LABORAL.
adj, pertaining to labor law.

JURÍDICO MILITAR.
m, member of the legal branch of the military ‖ adj, pertaining to military law.

"JURIS ET DE JURE".
of law and of right, by total and absolute right ‖ irrebuttable. Used to describe an irrebuttable presumption which operates to disallow submission of any adverse evidence.

"JURIS TANTUM".
of law until controverted ‖ rebuttable. Used to describe a rebuttable presumption in favor of a fact until proven otherwise.

JURISCONSULTO.
m, jurist, jurisconsult, legal expert ‖ lawyer, attorney.

JURISDICCIÓN.
f, jurisdiction ‖ venue. JURISDICCIÓN refers in the strict sense to the power of the court to adjudicate cases. It commonly includes the common law concepts of both venue and jurisdiction. Jurisdiction in common law practice is used to describe the inherent power of the court to hear cases and refers implicitly to 1) the physical boundaries within which a court is competent to hear disputes, and 2) the subject matter over which it has authority to hear and adjudicate disputes. Venue indicates the county or city within which a court with jurisdiction may hear and adjudicate cases. Wherever the term JURISDICCIÓN is used herein it may, depending on the circumstances, refer to venue or to jurisdiction or to both, although throughout the definitions the term "jurisdiction" alone will be used.

JURISDICCIÓN ACUMULATIVA.
concurrent jurisdiction, jurisdiction over a case initially shared with another court. See JURISDICCIÓN.

JURISDICCIÓN ADMINISTRATIVA.
administrative jurisdiction, jurisdiction of administrative bodies and courts. See JURISDICCIÓN.

JURISDICCIÓN CASTRENSE.
military jurisdiction, jurisdiction of the military courts. See JURISDICCIÓN.

JURISDICCIÓN CIVIL.
civil jurisdiction, jurisdiction over civil matters. Opposed to JURISDICCIÓN CRIMINAL. See JURISDICCIÓN.

JURISDICCIÓN COMERCIAL.
jurisdiction over commercial acts or contracts. See JURISDICCIÓN.

JURISDICCIÓN COMPETENTE.
proper jurisdiction or venue.
See JURISDICCIÓN.
JURISDICCIÓN COMÚN ORDINARIA.
general jurisdiction, jurisdiction over ordinary matters (i.e. matters which are not subject to special jurisdiction). See JURISDICCIÓN.
JURISDICCIÓN CONTENCIOSA.
jurisdiction over a case in which there is a dispute. See JURISDICCIÓN.
JURISDICCIÓN CONTENCIOSO-ADMINISTRATIVA.
jurisdiction to review the final decisions of administrative bodies and courts.
See JURISDICCIÓN.
JURISDICCIÓN CONVENCIONAL.
agreed upon jurisdiction ‖ jurisdiction agreed upon by the parties either prior to the dispute (e.g. by contract), or after the dispute (e.g. to submit to jurisdiction of an arbitrator).
See JURISDICCIÓN.
JURISDICCIÓN COORDINADA.
concurrent jurisdiction. See JURISDICCIÓN.
JURISDICCIÓN CORRECCIONAL.
type of criminal jurisdiction over minor criminal matters (similar to jurisdiction over misdemeanor cases). See JURISDICCIÓN.
JURISDICCIÓN CRIMINAL.
criminal jurisdiction, jurisdiction over criminal matters. See JURISDICCIÓN.
JURISDICCIÓN DE PRIMERA INSTANCIA.
original jurisdiction. See JURISDICCIÓN.
JURISDICCIÓN DELEGADA.
jurisdiction exercised by a court over a specific matter or for limited period of time by delegation from a higher court. See JURISDICCIÓN.
JURISDICCIÓN DISCIPLINARIA.
disciplinary jurisdiction, jurisdiction over minor criminal infractions.
See JURISDICCIÓN.
JURISDICCIÓN EN APELACIÓN.
appellate jurisdiction. See JURISDICCIÓN.
JURISDICCIÓN ESPECIAL.
special or limited jurisdiction.
See JURISDICCIÓN.
JURISDICCIÓN EXCEPCIONAL.
jurisdiction exercised by a TRIBUNAL DE EXCEPCIÓN. See JURISDICCIÓN.
JURISDICCIÓN EXTRAORDINARIA.
See JURISDICCIÓN ESPECIAL.

JURISDICCIÓN FEDERAL.
federal jurisdiction, jurisdiction over federal matters. See JURISDICCIÓN.
JURISDICCIÓN FORZOSA.
mandatory jurisdiction, jurisdiction which cannot be declined by the court or changed by the parties. See JURISDICCIÓN.
JURISDICCIÓN GENERAL.
general jurisdiction. See JURISDICCIÓN.
JURISDICCIÓN IMPRORROGABLE.
territorial jurisdiction which is not subject to extension. In civil law, jurisdiction of courts over civil law matters may sometimes be extended beyond the territorial limitations originally considered; in criminal law, jurisdiction is usually unextendible.
See JURISDICCIÓN.
JURISDICCIÓN JUDICIAL.
judicial or court jurisdiction.
See JURISDICCIÓN.
JURISDICCIÓN LABORAL.
jurisdiction over labor law matters.
See JURISDICCIÓN.
JURISDICCIÓN LIMITADA.
limited jurisdiction, jurisdiction over a particular case or proceeding, or a particular phase thereof. See JURISDICCIÓN.
JURISDICCIÓN MARÍTIMA.
admiralty jurisdiction. See JURISDICCIÓN.
JURISDICCIÓN MERCANTIL.
See JURISDICCIÓN COMERCIAL.
JURISDICCIÓN MILITAR.
military court jurisdiction, jurisdiction of military courts, tribunals, and counsels.
See JURISDICCIÓN.
JURISDICCIÓN ORDINARIA.
general jurisdiction. Opposed to JURISDICCIÓN ESPECIAL. See JURISDICCIÓN.
JURISDICCIÓN ORIGINAL.
original jurisdiction. See JURISDICCIÓN.
JURISDICCIÓN PENAL.
criminal jurisdiction, jurisdiction over (all) criminal matters. See JURISDICCIÓN.
JURISDICCIÓN PLENA.
full jurisdiction, jurisdiction to become acquainted with, to hear, to decide, and to execute the judgment of a case.
See JURISDICCIÓN.
JURISDICCIÓN PREVENTIVA.
jurisdiction which is taken where there is concurrent jurisdiction. See JURISDICCIÓN.

JURISDICCIÓN PRIVATIVA.
exclusive jurisdiction. See JURISDICCIÓN.
JURISDICCIÓN PRIVILEGIADA.
See JURISDICCIÓN ESPECIAL.
JURISDICCIÓN PROPIA.
statutory or legal jurisdiction over a case (as opposed to that chosen by the parties).
See JURISDICCIÓN.
JURISDICCIÓN PRORROGADA.
jurisdiction over a matter which the court would not otherwise have, but for the agreement of the parties to grant it such jurisdiction.
See JURISDICCIÓN.
JURISDICCIÓN SOBRE LA SUCESIÓN.
probate jurisdiction, jurisdiction over the probate of a decedent's estate.
See JURISDICCIÓN.
JURISDICCIÓN SUPERIOR.
appellate jurisdiction. See JURISDICCIÓN.
JURISDICCIÓN TERRITORIAL.
territorial jurisdiction. See JURISDICCIÓN.
JURISDICCIÓN VOLUNTARIA.
jurisdiction over case in which there is no dispute between the parties (opposed to JURISDICCIÓN CONTENCIOSA) ‖ also see JURISDICCIÓN PRORROGADA.
JURISDICCIONAL.
adj, jurisdictional.
JURISPERITO.
m, (non-practicing) legal expert.
JURISPRUDENCIA.
f, jurisprudence, case law, interpretation of the law by judges. Depending on the country, JURISPRUDENCIA may not include all judge-made law, but only those decisions emanating from the courts of CASACIÓN or, sometimes, the Supreme Court.
JURISPRUDENCIA INTERPRETIVA.
court decisions which interpret the law.
JURISPRUDENCIA JUDICIAL.
court decisions ‖ judge-made law.
JURISPRUDENCIA PROCESAL.
decisions of the law of procedure.
JURISPRUDENCIA SENTADA.
established legal precedence.
JURISPRUDENCIAL.
adj, related to court decisions.
JURISTA.
m, jurist.
JURO.
m, right of perpetual ownership.

"JUS".
jus ‖ right ‖ law.
"JUS ABUTENDI".
jus abutendi, absolute right ‖ right to transfer property.
"JUS AD REM".
jus ad rem, right over a thing.
"JUS ALTIUS NON TOLLENDI".
right that limits a neighbor's height of construction.
"JUS CIVILE".
jus civile.
"JUS COMMERCII".
right to trade or transact business.
"JUS CONNUBII".
right to marry.
"JUS FRUENDI".
right to the fruits or products.
"JUS GENTIUM".
jus gentium, law of nations, international law.
"JUS IN RE".
See "JUS AD REM".
"JUS LABORIS".
right to nationality based on work or employment in a country. Also known as the Garay Doctrine.
"JUS POSSESSIONIS".
jus possessionis, right of possession in fact (not necessarily as a result of ownership).
"JUS POSSIDENDI".
jus possidendi, right to possess (as a result of ownership).
"JUS PREFERENDI".
law of choice.
"JUS SANGUINIS".
jus sanguinis, law of the blood. Used to describe principle upon which nationality of child is determined by the nationality of the parents.
"JUS SOLI".
jus soli. Used to describe principle upon which nationality of child is determined by the place of birth.
"JUS SUFRAGII".
jus sufragii, right to vote.
"JUS UTENDI".
jus utendi, right to use property.
"JUS VARIANDI".
right to change or modify terms of an employment contract.
JUSFILOSOFÍA.
f, philosophy of law.

JUSTA CAUSA.
f, just cause, reasonable cause (in contract law and international relations) ‖ justified cause (in criminal law).

JUSTICIA.
f, justice, equity, reason ‖ judicial branch (of government), judiciary ‖ criminal judge or tribunal ‖ death sentence ‖ police, authorities ‖ jurisdiction.

JUSTICIA CIVIL.
general jurisdiction over civil matters ‖ civil courks.

JUSTICIA COMÚN.
common courts.

JUSTICIA CONMUTATIVA.
commutative justice.

JUSTICIA CRIMINAL.
criminal jurisdiction ‖ criminal courts.

JUSTICIA DE PAZ.
magistrate's courts, small claims courts.

JUSTICIA DEL TRABAJO.
labor courts.

JUSTICIA FEDERAL.
federal courts ‖ federal jurisdiction.

JUSTICIA MILITAR.
military justice ‖ justice administered in accord with the code of military justice ‖ military judiciary ‖ military justice code.

JUSTICIA ORDINARIA.
ordinary courts ‖ ordinary jurisdiction.

JUSTICIA SOCIAL.
social justice.

JUSTICIABLE.
adj, justiciable.

JUSTICIERO.
adj, fair, just, equitable ‖ strict.

JUSTIFICABLE.
adj, justifiable, excusable.

JUSTIFICACIÓN.
f, justification, excuse ‖ just cause ‖ legal excuse or justification ‖ proof, evidence, verification ‖ explanation.

JUSTIFICACIÓN DE CUENTAS.
explanation of accounts ‖ justification of accounts.

JUSTIFICACIÓN DE LAS AVERÍAS.
proof or verification of maritime average.

JUSTIFICACIÓN DE LOS CONTRATOS MERCANTILES.
admissible or competent evidence of commercial contracts.

JUSTIFICADAMENTE.
adv, justifiably, excusably ‖ exactly, precisely.

JUSTIFICADO.
adj, justified, excused ‖ proven ‖ according to law ‖ justly ‖ excusable.

JUSTIFICANTE.
m, justifier, person who puts forth an excuse or justification ‖ proof, voucher ‖ excuse, absolver ‖ adj, justifying.

JUSTIFICAR.
v, to justify (in all meanings) ‖ to put forth an excuse or justification ‖ to pardon, excuse ‖ to prove (evidence) ‖ to show innocence (of a suspect).

JUSTIFICARSE.
v, to prove one's innocence ‖ to justify one's actions.

JUSTIFICATIVO.
m, voucher ‖ document which proves or justifies something ‖ adj, justifying, excusing, justificatory.

JUSTIPRECIACIÓN.
f, (action of) appraisal or valuation.

JUSTIPRECIADOR.
m, appraiser.

JUSTIPRECIAR.
v, to appraise, value, estimate, evaluate. Often refers to expert's appraisal.

JUSTIPRECIO.
m, appraisal, valuation, estimate, evaluation.

JUSTO.
adj, just, fair, equitable ‖ legal, according to law ‖ reasonable, honorable, proper ‖ impartial ‖ exactly, precisely ‖ innocent ‖ morally upstanding.

JUSTO PRECIO.
reasonable or fair price.

JUSTO SALARIO.
fair and reasonable salary. Refers to the doctrine of establishing a reasonable salary, maintaining an equilibrium between the employee's needs and the employer's ability to pay.

JUSTO TÍTULO.
legitimate title (to property). Refers to principle that determines whether a person possesses or has acquired title legitimately (e.g. in good faith).

JUVENIL.
adj, juvenile.

JUZGADO.
m, tribunal, court ‖ judges who together

decide a case ‖ courtroom ‖ judiciary, judicature ‖ judgeship, position of judge ‖ adj, decided, determined, adjudged, judged.

JUZGADO CENTRAL.
central court with jurisdiction over all criminal, administrative and labor matters throughout a nation.

JUZGADO CORRECCIONAL.
correctional court ‖ magistrate's court.

JUZGADO CRIMINAL.
criminal court.

JUZGADO DE ADUANAS.
customs court.

JUZGADO DE CIRCUITO.
circuit court.

JUZGADO DE CIRCULACIÓN.
traffic court.

JUZGADO DE DISTRITO.
district court ‖ district court judge. Either criminal or civil.

JUZGADO DE GUARDIA.
court which is in session during hours and days when ordinary court is not in session, e.g. night court.

JUZGADO DE INSTRUCCIÓN.
court which hears preliminary criminal proceedings. See INSTRUCCIÓN.

JUZGADO DE JURISDICCIÓN ORIGINAL.
court of the first instance.

JUZGADO DE LETRAS.
court of the first instance.

JUZGADO DE LO CIVIL.
civil court.

JUZGADO DE LO PENAL.
See JUZGADO CRIMINAL.

JUZGADO DE NOCHE.
night court.

JUZGADO DE PAZ.
court of a judge of the peace.

JUZGADO DE PRIMERA INSTANCIA.
trial court, court of the first instance, lower court ‖ jurisdiction of a trial court judge ‖ trial courtroom or building in which trial courts are located.

JUZGADO DE RELACIONES FAMILIARES.
court of domestic relations.

JUZGADO DE SUSTANCIACIÓN.
trial court.

JUZGADO DE TRABAJO.
labor court.

JUZGADO EN LO CRIMINAL.
See JUZGADO CRIMINAL.

JUZGADO FEDERAL.
federal court.

JUZGADO INSTRUCTOR.
See JUZGADO DE INSTRUCCIÓN.

JUZGADO MAYOR.
higher court.

JUZGADO MENOR.
lower court.

JUZGADO MUNICIPAL.
municipal court.

JUZGADOR.
m, judge, person who adjudges ‖ trial judge ‖ adj, judging.

JUZGAMIENTO.
m, action of judging ‖ judgment ‖ sentence, decision.

JUZGAMIENTO DEL JEFE DE ESTADO.
prosecution of the head of state.

JUZGAR.
v, to adjudge, decide ‖ to administer justice ‖ to consider, ponder ‖ to judge, pass judgment on ‖ to hear a case.

KAISER.
German emperor.
"KARTELL".
See CARTEL.
"KIBUTZ".
kibbutz.

KILO.
See KILOGRAMO.
KILOGRAMO.
m, kilogram.
KILÓMETRO.
m, kilometer.

L.A.B..
See CLÁUSULA F.O.B..

LABERINTO.
m, labyrinth ‖ difficult investigation or procedure.

LABOR.
f, labor, work.

LABORABLE.
adj, workable ‖ working (e.g. day).

LABORAL.
adj, labor, regarding work or labor ‖ employment.

LABORALISTA.
m, labor lawyer, specialist in labor law.

LABORATORIO.
m, laboratory.

LABOREAR.
v, to work (something) ‖ to work or excavate (a mine).

LABOREO.
m, cultivation (of the earth) ‖ working (of a mine).

LABORIOSIDAD.
f, industriousness, application to work.

LABORIOSO.
adj, laborious, arduous, difficult ‖ industrious, dedicated (to work).

LABORISMO.
m, labor movement.

LABORISTA.
m, member of labor party or movement ‖ adj, labor or worker's (party).

LABRADÍO.
See LABRANTÍO.

LABRADOR.
m, peasant, farm worker, farm-hand.

LABRANTÍO.
m, farmland.

LABRAR.
v, to work farmland ‖ to carry out a profession ‖ to lease rural property ‖ to construct, build ‖ to issue a written statement which may have legal consequences (e.g. a statement upon inspection) ‖ to draw up (a document).

LABRIEGO.
m, farm-hand, farm worker, peasant.

LACERACIÓN.
f, laceration, lesion.

LACERADO.
adj, cut ‖ offended.

LACERAR.
v, to lacerate, cut ‖ to injure, wound, damage, hurt ‖ to prejudice (someone or thing) ‖ to save, pinch pennies ‖ to suffer, tolerate.

LACRAR.
v, to seal with sealing wax.

LACRE.
m, sealing wax.

LACREAR.
See LACRAR.

LACTANCIA.
f, lactation or nursing period.

LADRÓN.
m, thief, person who commits HURTO or ROBO.

LADRÓN CUATRERO.
thief of livestock, livestock rustler.

LADRONA.
f, female thief.

LADRONEAR.
v, to be a professional thief.

LADRONERA.
f, thieve's den or hideout ‖ thievery, burglary, larceny.

LADRONERÍA.
f, overpricing.

LADRONICIO.
m, theft, larceny.

LADRONZUELO.
m, petty thief or larcenist, small-time burglar ‖ juvenile burglar.

LAGO.
m, lake.

LAGUNA.
f, lagoon, small lake ‖ legal loophole, area unregulated by law ‖ gap, hiatus, omission, blank space (of a text).

LAGUNAS DEL DERECHO.
See LAGUNAS LEGALES.

LAGUNAS LEGALES.
legal loopholes, areas unregulated by legal norms.

LAICISMO.
m, laicism.

LAICO.
adj, lay, secular.

"LAISSEZ FAIRE".
laissez faire.

LANCHADA.
f, maximum load of a boat, launch, lighter, or barge.

LANZAMIENTO.
m, throw ‖ launch, launching ‖ thrust ‖ beginning of an activity ‖ eviction or dispossession under court order ‖ launching (of a new product).

LANZAR.
v, to hurl, throw, launch ‖ to thrust ‖ to commence or begin an activity ‖ to evict or dispossess under court order ‖ to launch (e.g. a new product) ‖ to free ‖ to spread a rumor.

LANZAR MANOS EN UNO.
to catch, arrest.

LAPIDACIÓN.
f, lapidation, stoning (to death).

LAPIDAR.
v, to stone to death.

LAPSO.
m, lapse, time period, space (in time) ‖ lapse, mistake, error ‖ negligence, fault.

LAPSO DE ESPERA.
waiting period ‖ period during which a person must wait to receive insurance or social welfare benefits.

LARGA.
f, procrastination (in order to get the other party to stop its activity).

LARGAR.
v, to abandon, leave ‖ to free, place at liberty ‖ to unfurl.

LARGAS.
See LARGA.

LASCIVIA.
f, lasciviousness, lewdness.

LASCIVO.
adj, lascivious, lewd.

LASTIMADO.
adj, injured, hurt.

LASTIMADURA.
f, injury, wound, sore.

LASTO.
m, receipt or bill against a party who is paying on behalf of another.

LASTRAR.
v, to ballast ‖ to weigh (something) down.

LASTRE.
m, ballast ‖ judgment.

LATAMENTE.
adv, broadly, amply.

LATENTE.
adj, latent, hidden.

LATERAL.
adj, lateral ‖ oblique ‖ collateral (in lineage).

LATIFUNDIO.
m, latifundium, large piece of rural property owned by one person.

LATIFUNDIO NATURAL.
naturally formed latifundium, latifundium formed out of necessity in order to compensate for the poor quality of the land.
See LATIFUNDIO.

LATIFUNDIO SOCIAL.
LATIFUNDIUM which is economically successful and well-exploited, but which creates social problems.

LATIFUNDISMO.
m, ownership of large rural estates by sole persons ‖ theory or movement supporting the aforementioned ownership.

LATIFUNDISTA.
m, owner of a LATIFUNDIO.

LATO.
adj, broad ‖ liberal.

"LATO SENSU".
latu sensu, broadly, liberally.

LATROCINAR.
v, to be a thief.

LATROCINIO.
m, theft, larceny ‖ taking by theft or deceit. Includes HURTO and ROBO.

LAUDAR.
v, to issue an arbitration decision ‖ to decide a dispute extra- judicially.

LAUDEMIO.
m, laudemeo, amount paid by the emphyteuta to the fee simple owner when the emphyteusis is transferred.

LAUDO.
m, laudum, award, arbitrament ‖ judgment, decision.

LAUDO ARBITRAL.
arbitration award or arbitrament issued pursuant to a voluntary arbitration agreement.

LAUDO DE AMIGABLES COMPONEDORES.
arbitration award which is not necessarily determined by the rules of law, but by fairness and equity.

LAUDO HOMOLOGADO.
court approved arbitration award.

"LE MORT SAISIT LE VIF".
(French legal expression, occasionally used in Spanish). Death gives possession to the living. Refers to the doctrine that a successor receives (at least, theoretically) from the moment of the decedent's passing.

LEALTAD.
f, loyalty ‖ faithfulness, fidelity ‖ allegiance.

"LEASING".
leasing, renting. Adopted from English terminology and thus varies in legal meaning greatly from jurisdiction to jurisdiction, and may or may not include the option to purchase the leased property at the end of the contract term.

LECTIVO.
adj, school or university days, days which are open for educational purposes.

LECTOR.
m, reader ‖ professor.

LECTURA.
f, reading.

LECTURA DE ACUSACIÓN.
reading of the accusation (at the arraignment hearing).

LECTURA DE LA DECLARACIÓN.
reading of any statement made by a witness or party.

LECTURA DE LAS LEYES PENALES.
reading of the criminal laws.

LECTURA DE LOS DOCUMENTOS PÚBLICOS.
reading of certified documents.

LECTURA DEL TESTAMENTO.
reading of the will.

LECHO.
m, bed ‖ river bed.

LECHO CONYUGAL.
marital bed.

LECHO MARINO.
marine bed, ocean floor.

LEGACÍA.
f, legate's post ‖ legateship ‖ jurisdiction of legate.

LEGACIÓN.
f, legation ‖ embassy ‖ office or building of legation ‖ legate's staff.

LEGADO.
m, representative, delegate ‖ head representative of a legation ‖ testamentary gift ‖ devise (if real estate) ‖ legacy, bequest (if personal property).

LEGADO A LOS POBRES.
testamentary gift to the poor.

LEGADO A PARIENTES INDETERMINADOS.
testamentary gift to unspecified relatives.

LEGADO A TÍTULO SINGULAR.
specific testamentary gift, testamentary gift of specified property.

LEGADO A TÍTULO UNIVERSAL.
general testamentary gift, testamentary gift of property as a whole.

LEGADO ALTERNATIVO.
alternative testamentary gift, testamentary gift in the alternative of two or more things.

LEGADO ANUAL.
testamentary gift of an annuity.

LEGADO CAUSAL.
testamentary gift in which the reason for the gift is specified.

LEGADO CON DEMOSTRACIÓN.
testamentary gift in which the gift is identified by certain characteristics which are in fact irrelevant.

LEGADO CONDICIONAL.
conditional testamentary gift.

LEGADO DE ALIMENTOS.
testamentary gift of necessities (i.e. food,

clothing, housing, education, and medical care).

LEGADO DE BENEFICIENCIA.
charitable testamentary gift.

LEGADO DE BIENES PERSONALES.
legacy, bequest.

LEGADO DE BIENES RAÍCES.
devise.

LEGADO DE CANTIDAD.
testamentary gift by reference to specific weight, number, or size of a class of things (e.g. money).

LEGADO DE CORAZÓN.
donation of a heart (upon death).

LEGADO DE CÓRNEA.
donation of a cornea (upon death).

LEGADO DE COSA ACCESORIA.
testamentary gift of a property which is secondary to a principal gift.

LEGADO DE COSA AJENA.
testamentary gift of another person's property.

LEGADO DE COSA CIERTA.
specific testamentary gift, testamentary gift of specifically identified property.

LEGADO DE COSA DETERMINADA.
See LEGADO DE COSA CIERTA.

LEGADO DE COSA EMPEÑADA.
See LEGADO DE COSA GRAVADA.

LEGADO DE COSA ESPECIFICADA.
See LEGADO DE COSA CIERTA.

LEGADO DE COSA FUERA DE COMERCIO.
testamentary gift of property which cannot be the subject of commercial transactions (e.g. bodily parts).

LEGADO DE COSA FUNGIBLE.
testamentary gift of a fungible good.

LEGADO DE COSA GENÉRICA.
See LEGADO DE COSA INDETERMINADA.

LEGADO DE COSA GRAVADA.
testamentary gift of property regarding which a security interest or mortgage has been granted.

LEGADO DE COSA HIPOTECADA.
See LEGADO DE COSA GRAVADA.

LEGADO DE COSA INDETERMINADA.
testamentary gift of a good specified only in generic terms (e.g. bicycle, necklace).

LEGADO DE COSA POSEÍDA EN COMÚN.
testamentary gift of jointly-held property.

LEGADO DE COSA PRINCIPAL.
testamentary gift of a principal piece of property and of all property accessory to it.

LEGADO DE COSA PROPIA DEL HEREDERO.
testamentary gift to heir of heir's property.

LEGADO DE COSA PROPIA DEL LEGATARIO.
testamentary gift to legatee of legatee's property.

LEGADO DE COSA PROPIA DEL TESTADOR.
testamentary gift of property owned by the testator.

LEGADO DE CRÉDITO.
testamentary gift of the right to monies owed the testator.

LEGADO DE CUERPO CIERTO.
See LEGADO DE COSA CIERTA.

LEGADO DE DEMOSTRACIÓN.
See LEGADO CON DEMOSTRACIÓN.

LEGADO DE DEUDA.
testamentary gift of a debt of the testator.

LEGADO DE EDUCACIÓN.
testamentary gift to provide for the education of certain persons.

LEGADO DE ELECCIÓN.
See LEGADO ALTERNATIVO.

LEGADO DE LIBERACIÓN.
testamentary gift of forgiving a debt.

LEGADO DE OPCIÓN.
See LEGADO ALTERNATIVO.

LEGADO DE PARTE ALÍCUOTA.
general testamentary gift by reference to a portion or part of the decedent's estate.

LEGADO DE PENSIÓN.
testamentary gift of a pension.

LEGADO DE PERDÓN DE DEUDA.
See LEGADO DE LIBERACIÓN.

LEGADO DE RENTA VITALICIA.
testamentary gift of a life annuity.

LEGADO DE TODA LA HERENCIA.
testamentary gift of the entire estate.

LEGADO DE UN PREDIO.
devise, testamentary gift of real property.

LEGADO DE UNA CASA.
devise of a house.

LEGADO DE UNA HACIENDA.
devise of a farm or ranch.

LEGADO DE USUFRUCTO.
testamentary gift of the right to USUFRUCTO.

LEGADO DEL QUINTO.
general testamentary gift of one fifth of the estate.

LEGADO DOBLE.
testamentary gift of two or more pieces of property.

LEGADO EN LUGAR DE LEGÍTIMA.
testamentary gift of specific property to the relatives who by law must inherit a given proportion of a decedent's estate, which gift is made in lieu of the share.

LEGADO ESPECÍFICO.
specific bequest or devise.

LEGADO FORZOSO.
testamentary gift to persons and in amounts as required by law. In most civil law countries, a decedent's estate must be distributed in specific proportions to specified members of the decedent's family.

LEGADO GRATUITO.
unconditional testamentary gift.

LEGADO INCONDICIONAL.
unconditional bequest or legacy or devise.

LEGADO LEGAL.
testamentary gift which by law must be granted (e.g. support to the pregnant widow, matrimonial bed).

LEGADO MODAL.
See LEGADO ONEROSO.

LEGADO ONEROSO.
testamentary gift conditioned on the performance of certain acts or the abstention therefrom.

LEGADO PURO Y SIMPLE.
See LEGADO GRATUITO.

LEGADO REMANANTE.
remainder property (of a bequest or devise).

LEGADO REPETIDO.
testamentary gift which grants the same thing to two or more persons.

LEGADO SINGULAR.
See LEGADO A TÍTULO SINGULAR ‖ also see LEGADO DE COSA CIERTA ‖ also see LEGADO DE CORAZÓN.

LEGADO TEMPORAL.
testamentary gift which designates the time upon which the gift is granted or ends.

LEGADO UNIVERSAL.
testamentary gift of all of one's estate to one person alone.

LEGADO VOLUNTARIO.
voluntary testamentary gift.
Opposed to LEGADO FORZOSO.

LEGAJO.
m, court file ‖ file ‖ bundle or bunch of papers.

LEGAJO DE SENTENCIA.
judgment docket, civil or criminal docket.

LEGAL.
adj, legal, lawful ‖ legitimate, licit.

LEGALIDAD.
f, legality, legitimacy, lawfulness ‖ political structure of a nation pursuant to the constitution.

LEGALISMO.
m, legality, legal technicality ‖ rule of law.

LEGALISTA.
f, m, legal stickler, person who unduly favors narrow or literal interpretation of law.

LEGALÍSTICO.
adj, legalistic.

LEGALIZACIÓN.
f, legalization ‖ authentication or attestation or certification or verification of signatures or of the legal capacity of the persons who have signed a document ‖ act of authenticating or attesting or certifying or verifying signatures or the legal capacity of the persons who have signed a document.

LEGALIZAR.
v, to legalize ‖ to legitimate ‖ to authenticate, legalize.

LEGALMENTE.
adv, legally, lawfully, according to law.

LEGAMENTE.
adv, ignorantly.

LEGAR.
v, to bequeath, leave, grant (by will) ‖ to send as a legate ‖ to deputize, delegate.

LEGATARIO.
m, beneficiary, testamentary donee ‖ legatee (of personal property) ‖ devisee (of real property).

LEGATARIO DE ALIMENTOS.
beneficiary of a (testamentary) maintenance allowance.

LEGATARIO DE BIENES RAÍCES.
devisee.

LEGATARIO DE BIENES PERSONALES.
legatee.

LEGISLABLE.
adj, able to be regulated by legislation.

LEGISLACIÓN.
f, legislation, body of positive laws.
LEGISLACIÓN COMPARADA.
comparative law.
LEGISLACIÓN DE FONDO.
substantive law.
LEGISLACIÓN DE TRABAJO.
See LEGISLACIÓN OBRERA.
LEGISLACIÓN DEL TRABAJO.
labor law ‖ labor legislation.
LEGISLACIÓN DELEGADA.
body of executive orders issued pursuant to powers expressly granted by the legislative branch.
LEGISLACIÓN JUDICIAL.
judge-made law.
LEGISLACIÓN OBRERA.
labor law.
LEGISLACIÓN SECUNDARIA.
rule-making pursuant to legislation.
LEGISLADOR.
m, legislator ‖ adj, legislative.
LEGISLAR.
v, to legislate ‖ to issue orders or rules or regulations.
LEGISLATIVO.
adj, legislative.
LEGISLATURA.
f, legislature ‖ provincial legislature ‖ legislative session or term.
LEGISLATURA EXTRAORDINARIA.
special session of the legislature or congress.
LEGISPERITO.
m, legal expert.
LEGISTA.
m, lawyer, attorney ‖ professor of law or jurisprudence ‖ law student.
LEGÍTIMA.
f, legitime, portion of inheritance which by law must be granted to certain specified relative (e.g. children, spouse) ‖ adj, legitimate, real.
LEGÍTIMA DE LOS ASCENDIENTES LEGÍTIMOS.
legitime of legitimate ascendants.
LEGÍTIMA DE LOS ASCENDIENTES NATURALES.
legitime of natural ascendants.
See ASCENDIENTES NATURALES.
LEGÍTIMA DE LOS DESCENDIENTES LEGÍTIMOS.
legitime of legitimate descendants.

LEGÍTIMA DE LOS HIJOS ILEGÍTIMOS.
legitime of illegitimate children.
LEGÍTIMA DE LOS HIJOS LEGITIMADOS.
legitime of the legitimated children.
LEGÍTIMA DE LOS HIJOS LEGÍTIMOS.
legitime of the legitimate children.
LEGÍTIMA DE LOS HIJOS NATURALES RECONOCIDOS.
legitime of illegitimate but recognized children.
LEGÍTIMA DEFENSA.
legitimate defense, criminal excuse of personal defense or defense of relatives or others.
LEGÍTIMA DEFENSA DE BUENA FE.
See DEFENSA PUTATIVA.
LEGÍTIMA DEFENSA DE EXTRAÑOS.
criminal excuse of defense of others.
LEGÍTIMA DEFENSA DE PARIENTES.
legitimate defense of relatives.
LEGÍTIMA DEFENSA IMAGINARIA.
See DEFENSA PUTATIVA.
LEGÍTIMA DEFENSA OPINADA.
See DEFENSA PUTATIVA.
LEGÍTIMA DEFENSA PROPIA.
legitimate self-defense.
LEGÍTIMA DEFENSA SUBJETIVA.
See DEFENSA PUTATIVA.
LEGÍTIMA DEL CÓNYUGE VIUDO.
legitime of the widowed spouse.
LEGÍTIMA DESIGNADA.
designated legitime, legitime which is express set forth in a will which grants at least the legal minimum of an inheritance to those entitle thereto.
LEGÍTIMA ESTRICTA.
legal legitime, amount of inheritance (e. one-third in Spain) which must be distribute to certain specified relatives.
LEGÍTIMA LARGA.
legitime ab intestato, legitime which is given legal heirs when there is no will.
LEGITIMACIÓN.
f, legal standing ‖ legitimation ‖ justification proof of the truth of a matter ‖ ability or a thority to carry out a position.
LEGITIMACIÓN ADOPTIVA.
legitimation by adoption.
LEGITIMACIÓN EN LA CAUSA.
legal standing.
LEGITIMACIÓN PARA OBRAR.
See LEGITIMACIÓN PROCESAL.

LEGITIMACIÓN PROCESAL.
legal standing.

LEGITIMADO.
m, legitimated person ‖ legitimation by law ‖ adj, legitimated.

LEGÍTIMAMENTE.
adv, legitimately ‖ lawfully, legally ‖ pursuant to law or justice ‖ by right.

LEGITIMAR.
v, to legitimize, legitimate ‖ to justify or prove the legitimacy of something or someone ‖ to recognize the legitimacy of something or someone.

LEGITIMARIO.
m, legal legatee or devisee, person who by law must inherit a given portion of a decedent's estate ‖ adj, pertaining to a legitime.

LEGITIMIDAD.
f, legitimacy ‖ legality, conformity with the law ‖ character of a legitimate child ‖ authenticity, genuineness.

LEGÍTIMO.
adj, legitimate ‖ legal, lawful ‖ true, authentic, genuine.

LEGO.
m, layman ‖ lay judge ‖ adj, characteristic of non-Church property ‖ unknowledgeable, ignorant ‖ illiterate ‖ profane ‖ lay, secular.

LEGULEYO.
m, pettifogger, derogatory term for lawyer who is less interested in justice than in legal technicalities.

LENGUA.
f, language ‖ tongue.

LENGUA EXTRANJERA.
foreign language.

LENGUA MATERNA.
mother tongue.

LENIDAD.
f, leniency, weakness.

LENOCINIO.
m, pandering, procuring ‖ pimping.

LENÓN.
m, panderer ‖ pimp.

LEONERA.
f, gambling casino or house.

LEONERO.
m, owner of a gambling house.

LEONINO.
adj, one-sided, unfair, abusive ‖ unconscionable.

LESA MAJESTAD.
leze or lese majesty, crime against the sovereign.

LESA PATRIA.
types of crimes which threaten national security.

LESBIANA.
f, lesbian ‖ adj, lesbian.

LESBIANISMO.
m, lesbianism.

LESIÓN.
f, lesion, wound ‖ injury (for which the injurer may be guilty of crime or liable in tort) ‖ loss suffered by one of the parties to a sales contract due to an unfair price obtained by overreaching or unconscionability.

LESIÓN CORPORAL.
bodily or personal injury.

LESIÓN DE TRABAJO.
occupational or on-the-job injury.

LESIÓN EN EL DERECHO MERCANTIL.
pecuniary loss suffered in a commercial transaction.

LESIÓN EN LAS PARTICIONES.
loss suffered due to the improper distribution of a decedent's estate.

LESIÓN EN LOS CONTRATOS.
economic loss suffered by reason of an unequal contract.

LESIÓN ENORME.
loss suffered by one of the parties to a contract due to an unfair price obtained by overreaching or unconscionability.

LESIÓN ENORMÍSIMA.
loss suffered by one of the parties to a contract due to an extremely unfair price obtained by overreaching or unconscionability.

LESIÓN JURÍDICA.
legally recognized or compensable injury.

LESIÓN LABORAL.
injury suffered by an employee due to the imposition of unconscionable or inappropriate conditions of the work contract ‖ on-the-job injury.

LESIÓN MORTAL.
fatal injury.

LESIÓN NO MORTAL.
non-fatal injury.

LESIONADO.
m, injured person ‖ adj, injured.

LESIONADOR.
m, injurer, damager ‖ adj, injuring, damaging.
LESIONAR.
v, to injure, damage, wound, hurt ‖ to damage, cause loss or damage ‖ to cause prejudice.
LESIONES.
f, injury, injuries, damage ‖ wounds ‖ loss ‖ prejudice.
LESIONES DEPORTIVAS.
sports injuries.
LESIONES EN RIÑA.
injuries resulting from a brawl or fight.
LESIONES GRAVES.
serious injuries. Usually includes such injuries as blindness, imbecility, impotency, loss of an eye or limb, physical deformities, or other injury which incapacitates one for work for more than ninety days.
LESIONES GRAVÍSIMAS.
extraordinarily serious injuries. Usually includes castration or other serious mutilation.
LESIONES LEVES.
slight injuries. Includes injuries which incapacitate one for work from one to fifteen days.
LESIONES LEVÍSIMAS.
insignificant injuries. Includes injuries which cause no loss of work.
LESIONES MENOS GRAVES.
less-serious injuries. Includes injuries which incapacitate one for work for from fifteen to thirty days.
LESIONES VOLUNTARIAS.
self-inflicted injuries. Usually to avoid complying with a duty, such as military service.
LESIVO.
adj, injurious, detrimental, harmful.
LETAL.
adj, lethal, deadly.
LETRA.
f, draft, bill of exchange ‖ letter (in all meanings) ‖ handwriting.
LETRA A PLAZO.
time bill or draft.
LETRA A DÍA FIJO.
See LETRA A PLAZO.
LETRA A LA VISTA.
See LETRA A PRESENTACIÓN.
LETRA A PRESENTACIÓN.
sight draft or bill.
LETRA A TÉRMINO.
See LETRA A PLAZO.

LETRA ABIERTA.
open letter of credit, letter of credit for an undesignated amount.
LETRA ACEPTADA.
accepted draft or bill.
LETRA BANCARIA.
bank draft, banker's draft.
LETRA CAMBIARIA.
See LETRA DE CAMBIO.
LETRA DE ACOMODACIÓN.
accommodation bill.
LETRA DE BANCO.
See LETRA BANCARIA.
LETRA DE CAMBIO.
bill of exchange, draft, credit instrument by which one party orders another party to pay a third party.
LETRA DE CAMBIO A DÍA FIJO.
bill of exchange payable on a designated date.
LETRA DE CAMBIO A DÍAS FECHA.
bill of exchange payable x days from the date of issue.
LETRA DE CAMBIO A DÍAS VISTA.
bill of exchange payable x days from presentment.
LETRA DE CAMBIO A LA VISTA.
sight draft, bill of exchange payable on sight.
LETRA DE CAMBIO A MESES FECHA.
bill of exchange payable x months from the date of issue.
LETRA DE CAMBIO A MESES VISTA.
bill of exchange payable x months from presentment.
LETRA DE CAMBIO ACEPTADA.
accepted bill of exchange.
LETRA DE CAMBIO AL PORTADOR.
bearer bill of exchange.
LETRA DE CAMBIO DOCUMENTADA.
documentary bill of exchange.
LETRA DE CAMBIO DOMICILIADA.
domiciled bill of exchange.
LETRA DE CAMBIO EN PAGO DE DEUDAS.
bill of exchange for payment of bills.
LETRA DE CAMBIO ENDOSADA.
indorsed bill of exchange.
LETRA DE CAMBIO EXTRANJERA.
foreign bill of exchange.
LETRA DE CAMBIO EXTRAVIADA.
missing or lost bill of exchange.

LETRA DE CAMBIO IMPERFECTA.
irregular bill of exchange, draft which does not fulfill all of the requirements thereto.

LETRA DE CAMBIO NO DOMICILIADA.
non-domiciled bill of exchange.

LETRA DE CAMBIO PERDIDA.
See LETRA DE CAMBIO EXTRAVIADA.

LETRA DE CAMBIO PERJUDICADA.
bill of exchange which the drawer fails to accept or dishonor within legal period.

LETRA DE CAMBIO PROTESTADA.
dishonored bill of exchange.

LETRA DE CAMBIO SEGUNDA.
substitute bill of exchange (for one that was lost, stolen, or destroyed).

LETRA DE CAMBIO VENCIDA.
payable bill of exchange, draft which is due.

LETRA DE CRÉDITO.
letter of credit.

LETRA DE LA LEY.
letter of the law, precise reading of the statute.

LETRA DE RECAMBIO.
See RECAMBIO.

LETRA DE RESACA.
See RESACA.

LETRA LIMPIA.
clean bill of exchange.

LETRA MENUDA.
ruse, trickery ‖ sagacity ‖ small print.

LETRA MUERTA.
blue laws, laws which are dead letter (i.e are still in effect but which are neither complied with nor enforced).

LETRA NO ATENDIDA.
dishonored bill of exchange.

LETRA PERJUDICADA.
bill of exchange not presented when due.

LETRA PROTESTADA.
protest bill, protested bill of exchange.

LETRA RECHAZADA.
dishonored bill.

LETRADA.
f, female attorney ‖ wife or an attorney ‖ literate woman.

LETRADO.
m, male attorney ‖ attorney ‖ adj, learned, erudite.

LETRADO ASESOR.
See LETRADO CONSULTOR.

LETRADO CONSULTOR.
judge's legal advisor (who is an attorney),

lawyer who is a legal advisor of a law judge.

LETRADO CRIMINALISTA.
criminal lawyer, lawyer who defends criminals.

LETRAS PATENTES.
letters patent ‖ public edict under seal pertaining to an important matter.

LETRERO.
m, billboard.

LEVA.
f, military recruitment or draft ‖ act of raising anchor.

LEVADOR.
m, thief who flees immediately after a crime ‖ astute thief.

LEVANTADO.
adj, elevated, lifted ‖ rebellious, under insurrection.

LEVANTADOR.
m, agitator, insurrectionist ‖ illegal bookmaker or bookie ‖ adj, rebellious, seditious, in revolt.

LEVANTAMIENTO.
m, act of raising or lifting ‖ act of raising oneself up ‖ rebellion, uprising, revolt, insurrection ‖ adjustment of accounts ‖ end of sequestration period ‖ lifting of a lien.

LEVANTAR.
v, to raise, lift ‖ to build, construct ‖ to establish, found ‖ to give impetus to ‖ to raise (one's voice) ‖ to increase ‖ to raise (prices) ‖ to rebel, revolt ‖ to recruit or enlist (persons into military service) ‖ to liberate ‖ to lift a fine or sentence ‖ to impute falsely ‖ to free, liberate ‖ to unload cargo from ships.

LEVANTAR CAPITAL.
to raise capital.

LEVANTAR EL EMBARGO.
to release an attachment or embargo.

LEVANTAR EL SITIO.
to lift or raise the siege ‖ to resist or fight a proposal.

LEVANTAR LA GARANTÍA.
to release a guaranty.

LEVANTAR LA MANO.
to threaten to hit, raise one's hand to ‖ to raise one's hand (in an auction) ‖ to halt (a vehicle).

LEVANTAR LA MANO DE UNA PERSONA.
to abandon a person ‖ to withdraw protection for someone.

LEVANTAR LA SESIÓN.
to adjourn a meeting, call a meeting to a close.

LEVANTAR LAS MANOS.
to raise one's hands. Used as a sign of surrender or lack of resistance, or to request the right to speak at a meeting. Also used to take a hand vote.

LEVANTAR UN ACTA.
to write or draw up a summary of something (e.g. minutes, agreement, inventory).

LEVANTAR UN PAGARÉ.
to pay off a promissory note.

LEVANTAR UN PROTESTO.
to issue a notice of protest.

LEVANTARSE.
v, to get up, arise ‖ to rebel, revolt ‖ to start a revolution (for independence) ‖ to recuperate lost strength, wealth, or position.

LEVANTISCO.
m, advocator of military uprisings or lack of discipline ‖ adj, turbulent.

LEVE.
adj, light ‖ unimportant, not serious.

LEVEMENTE.
adv, lightly, unimportantly, not seriously ‖ with little injury.

LEX.
f, lex, law.

LEX FORI.
lex fori, law of the forum.

LEX GENERALIS.
See LEY GENERAL.

LEX LOCI.
lex loci, law of the place.

LEX LOCI CELEBRATIONIS.
lex loci celebrationis, law of the place where the transaction was formed.

LEX LOCI CONTRACTUS.
lex loci contractus, law of the place where the contract was made.

LEX LOCI EXECUTIONIS.
lex loci executionis, law of the place where the transaction must be carried out.

LEX LOCI SOLUTIONIS.
law of the place of payment or performance.

LEX NON SCRIPTA.
unwritten law.

LEX REI SITAE.
lex rei sitae, law of the place where the thing is located.

LEX SCRIPTA.
written law.

LEY.
f, law ‖ positive law ‖ statute ‖ rule, norm, precept ‖ body of laws ‖ rule of conduct ‖ rule, regulation, ordinance ‖ order, decree, mandate ‖ fidelity, loyalty ‖ requirements, conditions (of a transaction) ‖ religion, character, weight or size ‖ metal alloy.

LEY ADJETIVA.
adjective or procedural law. Opposed to LEY SUBSTANTIVA.

LEY ADMINISTRATIVA.
administrative statute.

LEY AGRARIA.
agrarian statute, statute pertaining to the exploitation, ownership, and development of agricultural lands.

LEY ANTERIOR.
prior or previous law.

LEY ANUAL.
annual budget (of a nation).

LEY ATRIBUTIVA.
law which confers a right or attribute on a person or sector of society ‖ law which changes jurisdiction of administrative organisms.

LEY BÁSICA.
See LEY FUNDAMENTAL.

LEY CAMBIARIA.
law of commercial paper or negotiable instruments.

LEY CIVIL.
civil law, law which regulates the rights of persons and establishes the form and effect of private agreements ‖ civil code ‖ civil law, as opposed to criminal law, public law, military law, or religious law ‖ civil statute.

LEY COERCITIVA.
law which punishes pernicious acts.

LEY COMERCIAL.
commercial law ‖ commercial statute.

LEY COMÚN.
law in effect in two or more countries ‖ civil law when it is applied equally to all inhabitants of a nation without special jurisdiction.

LEY CONSTITUCIONAL.
constitutional law ‖ national constitution ‖ law which is constitutional ‖ statute which amends constitution.

LEY CONTRIBUTIVA.
tax law.

LEY DE BASES.
law which provides basic precepts, norms, or

principles, in order that the executive power determine the details.

EY DE DEFENSA SOCIAL.
public defense law, law whose purpose is to protect morals and other standards of society.

EY DE DERECHO PRIVADO.
positive norms of DERECHO PRIVADO.

EY DE DERECHO PÚBLICO.
positive norms of DERECHO PÚBLICO.

EY DE EDIFICACIÓN.
building code.

EY DE EMERGENCIA.
emergency statute or order. Usually temporary.

EY DE ENJUICIAMENTO CIVIL.
law of civil procedure.

EY DE ENJUICIAMENTO CRIMINAL.
law of criminal procedure.

EY DE EXCEPCIÓN.
See LEY DE EMERGENCIA.

EY DE FUGAS.
practice justifying the murder of a prisoner by claiming that he or she was trying to escape.

EY DE LA LEGISLATURA.
legislative act or law.

EY DE LA OFERTA Y LA DEMANDA.
law of supply and demand.

EY DE LA SILLA.
law that employers must provide chairs with backs for employees who work in sitting position.

EY DE LEYES.
national constitution ‖ law regulating the promulgation, effect, and other procedural aspects of the law.

EY DE MINAS.
mining statute.

EY DE ORDEN PRIVADO.
statute which deals with private matters. See ORDEN PRIVADO.

EY DE ORDEN PÚBLICO.
statute which deals with public matters. See ORDEN PÚBLICO.

EY DE PATENTES.
patent statute.

EY DE POLICÍA.
municipal statute which exists to keep the peace.

EY DE PRESCRIPCIÓN.
statute of limitations.

LEY DE PRESUPUESTOS.
budget ‖ budget statute.

LEY DE PROCEDIMIENTO.
procedural law.

LEY DE PROPIEDAD INDUSTRIAL.
industrial property statute.

LEY DE PROPIEDAD INTELECTUAL.
intellectual property statute.

LEY DE QUIEBRAS.
bankruptcy law.

LEY DE SEGURIDAD.
national security law or order.

LEY DE SOCIEDADES.
law of business associations (including corporate and partnership law).

LEY DECLARATIVA.
written statute which sets forth that which previously had been mere custom ‖ also see LEY INTERPRETIVA.

LEY-DECRETO.
order issued by the executive branch which has the effect of law (includes executive order).

LEY DEL CONTRATO.
force of law which terms of contract have as between the parties.

LEY DEL DEPORTE.
statute pertaining to sports.

LEY DEL EMBUDO.
unequal or unfair treatment by government.

LEY DEL ENCAJE.
court ruling which ignores legal precepts. Subject to being overruled.

LEY DEL FORO.
See LEX FORI.

LEY DEL LUGAR.
See LEX LOCI.

LEY DEL LUGAR DE LA COSA.
See LEX REI SITAE.

LEY DEL LUGAR DEL CONTRATO.
See LEX LOCI CONTRACTUS.

LEY DEL PABELLÓN.
law of the ship's nationality.

LEY DEL TALIÓN.
biblical axiom which makes the punishment fit the crime (i.e. an eye for an eye, a tooth for a tooth).

LEY DEL TIMBRE.
stamp-tax law.

LEY DEL TRABAJO.
labor law statute.

LEY DEL TRIBUNAL.
See LEX FORI.

LEY DEROGADA.
repealed statute (either by express repeal or by subsequent conflicting statute).

LEY DIRECTA.
statute which expressly permits or prohibits something (e.g. age of majority, importation of specific goods, etc.).

LEY DISPOSITIVA.
law which regulates general situations or transactions to which the parties have not previously agreed.

LEY ELECTORAL.
statute pertaining to voting and candidature, election statute.

LEY EN BLANCO.
statute which imposes a sanction without describing in detail the subject matter to which it applies.

LEY EN EL ESPACIO.
See ÁMBITO ESPACIAL DE LA LEY.

LEY EN EL TIEMPO.
See ÁMBITO TEMPORAL DE LA LEY.

LEY ESCRITA.
written law.

LEY ESPECIAL.
special statute, statute which pertains to a specific area of the law (e.g. mining, water, or intellectual property rights).

LEY ESTADUAL.
state statute ‖ state law, law promulgated by a state within a nation.

LEY ESTATAL.
federal statute ‖ federal law.

LEY "EX POST FACTO".
ex post facto law. Type of retrospective law.

LEY EXTRANJERA.
foreign law, law of another nation.

LEY EXTRATERRITORIAL.
extraterritorial law, law which is applicable outside the territory of the promulgating nation.

LEY FEDERAL.
See LEY ESTATAL.

LEY FISCAL.
tax law.

LEY FORMAL.
statute.

LEY FUNDAMENTAL.
constitution (of a nation).

LEY GENERAL.
statute which is equally applicable to all inhabitants and citizens of a nation.

LEY HIPOTECARIA.
law of mortgages.

LEY IMPERATIVA.
obligatory statute, statute which must be followed (regardless of the will of the parties).

LEY IMPERFECTA.
law which provides no sanction for violation thereof.

LEY INCONSTITUCIONAL.
unconstitutional statute.

LEY INDIRECTA.
law which protects rights indirectly through prohibition of acts contrary to those rights.

LEY INHABILITANTE.
statute which determines a person's capacity to act.

LEY INJUSTA.
inequitable or unjust law.

LEY INTERPRETATIVA.
statute which is to clarify doubts or deficiencies in a law.

LEY IRREFORMABLE.
immutable law, law which cannot be amended.

LEY IRRETROACTIVA.
prospective law, law with no retroactive effect.

LEY JUDICIAL.
law pertaining to the judiciary ‖ judge-made law.

LEY MARCIAL.
martial law.

LEY MERCANTIL.
commercial law or statute.

LEY MODIFICATIVA.
amendatory statute, statute which amends law which repeals or amends.

LEY MUNICIPAL.
municipal statute.

LEY NACIONAL.
national law, law of a nation ‖ law of nationality.

LEY NATURAL.
natural law.
Opposed to LEY POSITIVA.

LEY NEGATIVA.
law which prohibits ‖ law which revokes or repeals a prior law without replacing it with another law.

LEY NO ESCRITA.
unwritten law, custom.
LEY NOTARIAL.
statute which pertains to NOTARIO (S).
LEY ÓMNIBUS.
omnibus statute, statute which pertains to a variety of different areas of the law.
LEY ORDINARIA.
statute which provides no privileges or exceptions.
LEY ORGÁNICA.
statute which regulates administrative entities or other public bodies ‖ organic law ‖ constitution, charter.
LEY PARTICULAR.
special law, law which pertains to one person or class of persons.
LEY PASAJERA.
temporary statute, statute which has temporary effect. Opposed to LEY PERMANENTE.
LEY PENAL.
criminal statute.
LEY PERFECTA.
law which proscribes or permits certain activity and as well provides a sanction for its violation.
LEY PERMANENTE.
permanent statute. Opposed to LEY PASAJERA.
LEY PERMISIVA.
law which neither orders nor prohibits, but simply permits activities.
LEY PERPETUA.
See LEY PERMANENTE.
LEY PERSONAL.
special law.
LEY POLÍTICA.
constitution of a nation ‖ legal norms which regulate the relations between a government and its citizenry ‖ law pertaining to political organization and election of the executive and legislative branches ‖ law related to organization of political parties.
LEY POSITIVA.
positive law ‖ law in effect.
LEY PRIMERA.
primary statute which is subsequently amended or repealed.
LEY PRIVADA.
special law.
LEY PROCESAL.
procedural or adjective law ‖ procedural statute. Opposed to LEY SUBSTANTIVA.

LEY PROHIBITIVA.
prohibitive law, law which proscribes or prohibits.
LEY PROVINCIAL.
provincial law, law of the provinces ‖ provincial statute.
LEY PUNITIVA.
punitive statute.
LEY REMUNERATIVA.
remunerative statute, law which establishes payment for public service.
LEY REPARADORA.
remedial statute.
LEY RETROACTIVA.
retroactive law.
LEY SINGULAR.
special law, law which pertains to one person or class of persons.
LEY SUBSTANTIVA.
substantive law ‖ substantive statute. Opposed to LEY ADJETIVA or LEY PROCESAL.
LEY SUNTUARIA.
sumptuary statute, statute which limits or taxes purchases of luxuries.
LEY SUPLETORIA.
supplementary law which regulates previously unregulated areas within a law ‖ also see LEY DISPOSITIVA.
LEY SUPREMA.
supreme law ‖ constitution of a nation.
LEY TÁCITA.
implied law (derived from custom or from express law).
LEY TERRITORIAL.
law which applies territorially, regardless of the citizenship of the person.
LEY TRANSITORIA.
See LEY PASAJERA.
LEY UNIFORME.
uniform law ‖ treaty which has been ratified by different countries.
LEY URGENTE.
emergency statute (passed to resolve an immediate problem of a public nature).
LEY VIGENTE.
law in effect.
**LEYES DE
LA GUERRA.**
laws of war.
LEYES DE PREVISIÓN.
social security laws.

LEYES DE RESIDENCIA.
immigration statutes (usually used to determine the legality of resident aliens).

LEYES DEL MERCADO.
laws of the market or marketplace ‖ laws of supply and demand.

LEYES DEL PAÍS.
law of the land.

LEYES DEFECTAS.
See LAGUNAS DEL DERECHO.

LEYES IMPOSITIVAS.
tax laws.

LEYES LABORALES.
labor laws.

LEYES OBRERAS.
See LEYES LABORALES.

LEYES MILITARES.
military statutes, statutes pertaining to the military.

LEYES REFUNDIDAS.
See LEYES REVISADAS.

LEYES REVISADAS.
revised statutes.

LEYES TRIBUTARIAS.
tax laws.

LIBELAR.
v, to petition, file a complaint, bring suit ‖ to libel.

LIBELISTA.
m, author of libelous materials.

"LIBELLIO".
copier ‖ bookseller ‖ also see ESCRIBANO.

LIBELO.
m, petition, demand, complaint ‖ libel.

LIBELO FAMOSO.
serious libel, libel which expressly attacks a person's honor or reputation.

LIBELO INFAMATORIO.
See LIBELO FAMOSO.

LIBERACIÓN.
f, act of liberating or freeing, liberation ‖ quittance, note indicating payment in full ‖ agreement not to demand full payment ‖ discharge of a debt or other obligation ‖ exemption (e.g. from taxes) ‖ redemption of a mortgage.

LIBERACIÓN CONDICIONAL.
parole, conditional freedom (of a prisoner).

LIBERACIÓN DE GRAVÁMENES INSCRITOS.
clearing title, freeing title from encumbrances. Includes redemption of a mortgage.

LIBERACIÓN DE OBLIGACIONES.
discharge of obligations or duties.

LIBERACIÓN DE PRISIONEROS.
liberation or freeing of prisoners. May be FOR ZOSA (by force); GRACIOSA (spontaneou concession); PECUNIARIA (for money); REC PROCA (reciprocal); or EXIGIDA (required b the conqueror at the end of a war).

LIBERACIÓN INTERPRETATIVA EN LOS CONTRATOS.
discharge (either partial or total) of an obligc as a result of obscure or inadequate contrac tual clauses which appear to violate the law.

LIBERACIÓN POR ERROR.
discharge of obligor by error.

LIBERADO.
m, liberated or released person ‖ adj, libera ted, freed, released ‖ exempt, exempted ‖ di charged (from an obligation) ‖ cancelled, e: tinguished ‖ paid-up.

LIBERADOR.
m, liberator ‖ adj, liberating.

LIBERAL.
m, f, liberal ‖ member of a liberal political pa ty ‖ adj, liberal.

LIBERALIDAD.
f, generosity, altruism ‖ altruistic gift or se vice.

LIBERALIDAD ANTIFAMILIAR.
gifts made out of the estate which the leg heirs should rightfully inherit.

LIBERALIDADES MUTUALES.
See DONACIONES MUTUAS.

LIBERALISMO.
m, liberalism. May refer to economic or poli cal or social liberalism, and may not be tran lated in political terms from country to count (i.e. LIBERALISMO in one country may ha quite the opposite meaning in another cou try).

LIBERALMENTE.
adv, liberally ‖ generously ‖ quickly.

LIBERAR.
v, to free, liberate (a person or territory) ‖ exempt or discharge someone from an oblig tion ‖ to issue.

LIBERAR ACCIONES.
to issue stock or shares.

LIBERAR DE DERECHOS.
to exempt from duties.

LIBERAR DE RESPONSABILIDAD.
to free from liability.
LIBERARSE.
v, to free oneself from obligations ‖ to liberate a territory.
LIBERATORIO.
adj, freeing, liberating, discharging, exempting.
LIBERTAD.
f, freedom ‖ liberty ‖ independence ‖ privilege, franchise, license ‖ abuse ‖ exemption from obligations ‖ excessive familiarity ‖ right ‖ constitutional rights ‖ widowhood ‖ unmarried status.
LIBERTAD A PRUEBA.
probation, conditional release.
LIBERTAD ACADÉMICA.
academic freedom.
LIBERTAD BAJO CAUCIÓN.
See LIBERTAD BAJO FIANZA.
LIBERTAD BAJO FIANZA.
release or discharge (from prison) on bail.
LIBERTAD BAJO PALABRA.
release or discharge (from prison) on one's personal recognizance.
LIBERTAD CAUCIONAL.
See LIBERTAD BAJO FIANZA.
LIBERTAD CIVIL.
body of civil liberties.
LIBERTAD CONDICIONAL.
prison parole.
LIBERTAD CONTRACTUAL.
freedom of contract.
LIBERTAD DE ACCIÓN.
freedom of decision.
LIBERTAD DE AMAR.
right to love (in the way one wishes).
LIBERTAD DE ASOCIACIÓN.
freedom or right of association.
LIBERTAD DE BANCOS.
right to establish banks.
LIBERTAD DE CÁTEDRA.
academic freedom.
LIBERTAD DE CIRCULACIÓN.
freedom of movement.
LIBERTAD DE CIRCULACIÓN ECONÓMICA.
freedom of commerce. Used in constitutions to refer to the right to interstate or interprovince trade without the imposition of tariffs.
LIBERTAD DE COALICIÓN.
right of association.

LIBERTAD DE COMERCIAR.
right to trade or carry out business.
LIBERTAD DE COMERCIO E INDUSTRIA.
freedom of commerce and industry ‖ freedom of trade and industry.
LLIBERTAD DE CONCIENCIA.
freedom of thought.
LIBERTAD DE CONTRATAR.
See LIBERTAD CONTRACTUAL.
LIBERTAD DE CULTOS.
freedom of religion or worship.
LIBERTAD DE ELEGIR MAESTRO.
right to chose one's own teacher.
LIBERTAD DE ENSEÑANZA.
right to teach (one's own beliefs).
LIBERTAD DE ESPÍRITU.
lack of prejudice or preconception ‖ atheism ‖ spiritual strength ‖ freedom of thought.
LIBERTAD DE EXPRESION.
freedom of expression (both in word and thought).
LIBERTAD DE IMPRENTA.
freedom of the press.
LIBERTAD DE INDUSTRIA.
right to work ‖ right to engage in economic activities.
LIBERTAD DE LA PERSONA.
See LIBERTAD EXTERIOR.
LIBERTAD DE LA PROPIEDAD.
right to own property.
LIBERTAD DE LOS MARES.
freedom of the seas.
LIBERTAD DE NAVEGACIÓN.
freedom or right to navigate (e.g. international or national waters).
LIBERTAD DE NO TRABAJAR.
right not to work.
LIBERTAD DE OPINIÓN.
See LIBERTAD DE PALABRA.
LIBERTAD DE PACTAR.
freedom of contract.
LIBERTAD DE PALABRA.
freedom of speech.
LIBERTAD DE PENSAMIENTO.
freedom of thought.
LIBERTAD DE PETICIÓN.
right to petition.
LIBERTAD DE PRENSA.
freedom of the press.
LIBERTAD DE REUNIÓN.
freedom of assembly.

LIBERTAD DE SOBREVUELO INOFENSIVO.
right to non-offensive or benign flight over foreign airspace.

LIBERTAD DE TESTAR.
freedom to grant by will.

LIBERTAD DE TRABAJAR.
See LIBERTAD DE TRABAJO.

LIBERTAD DE TRABAJO.
right to work (in the profession of choice) ‖ freedom to work (without joining a union).

LIBERTAD DE TRÁNSITO.
See LIBERTAD DE CIRCULACIÓN.

LIBERTAD DE VIENTRES.
(literally) freedom of the womb ‖ free birth. Used to refer to the right to be born free (even if the mother is a slave).

LIBERTAD EXTERIOR.
personal rights and freedoms. Includes freedom of movement, religion, press, speech, association, assembly, demonstration, petition, to own property, and to work.

LIBERTAD INDIVIDUAL.
civil rights ‖ individuals' right to dispose of his or her property as desired.

LIBERTAD INDUSTRIAL.
See LIBERTAD DE INDUSTRIA.

LIBERTAD JURÍDICA.
legal freedom (to exercise or not personal rights and freedoms).

LIBERTAD PERSONAL.
See LIBERTAD INDIVIDUAL.

LIBERTAD POLÍTICA.
political freedom.

LIBERTAD PROFESIONAL.
See LIBERTAD DE COMERCIO E INDUSTRIA and LIBERTAD DE TRABAJO.

LIBERTAD PROVISIONAL.
parole pending criminal sentencing.

LIBERTAD RELIGIOSA.
religious freedom.

LIBERTAD SIN FIANZA.
release or discharge on one's personal recognizance.

LIBERTAD SINDICAL.
right to form a union ‖ right to belong or not to a union.

LIBERTAD VIGILADA.
freedom of movement under supervision ‖ parole under supervision.

LIBERTADO.
m, freed person ‖ adj, placed at liberty, freed ‖ emancipated ‖ free.

LIBERTADOR.
m, liberator ‖ adj, liberating, freeing.

LIBERTAR.
v, to free, liberate ‖ to emancipate ‖ to discharge (an obligation) ‖ to lift a lien or other encumbrance ‖ to save from harm ‖ to acquit, exonerate.

LIBERTARIO.
m, anarchist ‖ extreme defender of freedom ‖ enemy of the state.

LIBERTARSE.
v, to achieve or obtain freedom ‖ to emancipate oneself ‖ to escape.

LIBERTICIDA.
adj, that which attacks freedom.

LIBERTINAJE.
m, abuse of freedom, licentiousness.

LIBERTINO.
m, libertine ‖ adj, ingenuous ‖ free.

LIBRADO.
m, drawee (of a draft) ‖ adj, issued; drawn.

LIBRADOR.
m, drawer (of a draft).

LIBRAMIENTO.
m, order of payment of money or delivery of something, signed by a company treasurer or administrator or other qualified person ‖ deliverance.

LIBRANCISTA.
m, issuer of a LIBRAMIENTO ‖ holder of a LIBRAMIENTO.

LIBRANTE.
See LIBRADOR.

LIBRANZA.
f, draft, bill of exchange ‖ order of payment (which does not fulfill all the requisites of a draft).

LIBRAR.
v, to save, rescue ‖ to place hope or trust in ‖ to give birth ‖ to expel placenta during birth ‖ to issue a judicial, executive, administrative, or other type of order ‖ to liberate, rescue from captivity ‖ to issue or send bills of exchange or drafts, checks, or other order of payment ‖ to draw on an account ‖ to deliver something.

LIBRAR SENTENCIA.
to pronounce judgment, issue a decision.

LIBRE.
adj, free ‖ sovereign ‖ autonomous ‖ exempt, excused ‖ unattached ‖ available ‖ dishonest, licentious ‖ insubordinate ‖ absolved, innocent ‖ free of obligations or liens.

LIBRE A BORDO.
free on board.

LIBRE AL COSTADO.
free alongside.

LIBRE ALBEDRÍO.
free will.

LIBRE ARBITRIO.
See LIBRE ALBEDRÍO.

LIBRE CAMBIO.
free trade.

LIBRE CIRCULACIÓN DE LOS TRABAJADORES.
freedom of movement for workers. Refers to freedom of movement between nations (which, for instance, workers within the European Community enjoy).

LIBRE COMERCIO.
free or unrestricted trade.

LIBRE COMPETENCIA.
freedom of competition, free market.

LIBRE CONVICCIÓN.
absolute freedom of choice which a judge enjoys in evaluating the evidence which has been seen and heard.

LIBRE DE CONTRIBUCIÓN.
tax-free.

LIBRE DE DERECHOS.
duty-free.

LIBRE DE GASTOS.
free of charges.

LIBRE DE GRAVAMEN.
free and clear, free from encumbrances or duties of taxes.

LIBRE DE IMPUESTO.
tax-free ‖ tax-exempt.

LIBRE PLÁTICA.
pratique, admission of a ship into port after a health inspection.

LIBRECAMBIO.
See LIBRE CAMBIO.

LIBRECAMBISMO.
m, economic doctrine favoring free exchange.

LIBRETA.
f, official document in which certain data may be noted.(e.g. marital status, identity) ‖ booklet, notebook.

LIBRETA CÍVICA.
personal identity document (for women). Also serves as voter registration card.

LIBRETA DE AHORRO.
savings book.

LIBRETA DE CASAMIENTO.
document showing marriage, divorces, children born of that marriage, etc. ‖ marriage certificate.

LIBRETA DE ENROLAMIENTO.
personal identity document (for men). May also serve as the equivalent of the American selective service card and voter registration card.

LIBRETA DE MATRIMONIO.
See LIBRETA DE CASAMIENTO.

LIBRETA DE TRABAJO.
work document (issued by the government to authorize a person to work in certain specified fields).

LIBRO.
m, book ‖ principal section or division of codes, laws, or other lengthy works ‖ register.

LIBRO AMARILLO, AZUL (or any other color).
white paper, official government publication informing the public on foreign policy and other similar matters.

LIBRO COPIADOR.
letter book, book in which copies of correspondence of a business are kept.

LIBRO DE ACCIONES.
stock certificate register (for nominative shares).

LIBRO DE ACCIONISTAS.
See LIBRO DE ACCIONES.

LIBRO DE ACTAS.
minutes book.

LIBRO DE ALTA Y BAJA.
daily register of number of personnel.

LIBRO DE ASIENTO.
memo or memorandum book.

LIBRO DE ASIENTO ORIGINAL.
book in which the original entry or filing was made.

LIBRO DE ASISTENCIA A ASAMBLEAS.
meeting attendance book.

LIBRO DE CAJA.
cash receipt book, cash book.

LIBRO DE CARGAMENTOS.
register in which receipt and delivery of ship's cargo is entered.

LIBRO DE CONDENAS CONDICIONALES.
book in which a list of criminals granted suspended sentences is kept.
LIBRO DE CONTABILIDAD.
account book.
LIBRO DE CUENTA Y RAZÓN.
See LIBRO DE CONTABILIDAD.
LIBRO DE CUENTAS AJUSTADAS.
informal account record book.
LIBRO DE DERECHO.
law book.
LIBRO DE FAMILIA.
See LIBRO DE LA FAMILIA.
LIBRO DE FILIACIÓN.
register of births (usually kept by the state).
LIBRO DE INCAPACITADOS.
register of names of persons lacking legal capacity, deceased persons, and persons in absentia.
LIBRO DE INVENTARIOS Y BALANCES.
inventory and balance book.
LIBRO DE LA FAMILIA.
official family register, document in which marriage of two persons, children resulting therefrom, and deaths within such family are noted.
LIBRO DE MATRÍCULA.
employee register (of a company).
LIBRO DE MINUTAS.
See LIBRO DE ACTAS.
LIBRO DE NAVEGACIÓN.
See DIARIO DE NAVEGACIÓN.
LIBRO DE PRIMERA ENTRADA.
See LIBRO DE ASIENTO ORIGINAL.
LIBRO DE QUEJAS.
complaint book. May or may not be required by law.
LIBRO DE ROL.
document which sets forth the names of ship captain, officers, and sailors, the ports of departure and destination, the salaries of personnel and advances thereon, and the signatures of all employees.
LIBRO DE SENTENCIAS.
judgment docket.
LIBRO DE TEXTO.
official textbook, textbook required by government.
LIBRO DE TRABAJO.
register of days and overtime worked.

LIBRO DE VOTOS RESERVADOS.
register of dissenting opinions of a tribunal. See VOTO RESERVADO.
LIBRO DIARIO.
See LIBROS DE COMERCIO.
LIBRO MAESTRO.
selective service registry book ‖ also see LIBRO MAYOR.
LIBRO MAYOR.
ledger, account ledger.
LIBRO TALONARIO.
stub book.
LIBROS.
m, account books, accounts, books.
LIBROS DE A BORDO.
See DOCUMENTACIÓN DEL BUQUE.
LIBROS DE COMERCIO.
commercial books, books kept by businesses whether for convenience or by law. Consist of DIARIO (diary, daily journal, daybook), LIBROS DE INVENTARIOS Y BALANCES or DE INVENTARIOS (general account book), COPIADOR DE CARTAS (letter book), and LIBRO MAYOR (ledger).
LIBROS DE LAS CASAS DE PRÉSTAMOS.
pawnshop books which document receipt of pawned property.
LIBROS DE LOS AGENTES COLEGIADOS.
register of agents who are required by law to be members of a professional association (e.g. stockbrokers, commercial agents).
LIBROS DE NAVEGACIÓN.
navigation books (required by law).
LIBROS DE NAVEGACIÓN AÉREA.
air navigation books (required by law).
LIBROS DE SOCIEDADES MERCANTILES.
corporate books, books kept by corporations whether for convenience or by law. They consist of LIBROS DE COMERCIO and LIBRO DE ACTAS.
LIBROS DEL REGISTRO CIVIL.
birth, marriage, death, and citizenship record books.
LIBROS DEL REGISTRO DE LA PROPIEDAD
real estate register, real property registry.
LIBROS DEL REGISTRO MERCANTIL.
records of registration of all business ventures and other commercial matters the registration of which is required by law.
LIBROS FACULTATIVOS.
records or books not required by law.

LIBROS OBLIGATORIOS.
records or books required by law.
LIBROS PROHIBIDOS.
prohibited books ‖ censored books.
LIBROS SINDICALES.
union books (of a variety of types).
LICENCIA.
f, license (in all its meanings) ‖ consent ‖ liberty ‖ discharge ‖ permission, authorization ‖ lack of discipline ‖ degree (in education) ‖ abuse of freedom ‖ right ‖ leave of absence (from work).
LICENCIA ABSOLUTA.
full discharge (from the military service).
LICENCIA AUTORIZADA.
authorized leave (from work).
LICENCIA DE ALIJO.
unloading permit.
LICENCIA DE ARMAS.
license to bear arms.
LICENCIA DE CAMBIO.
exchange permit (e.g. foreign currency).
LICENCIA DE CAZA.
license to bear arms to hunt ‖ hunting license.
LICENCIA DE CONDUCTOR.
driver's license.
LICENCIA DE CONSTRUCCIÓN.
building permit.
LICENCIA DE FABRICACIÓN.
manufacturing license.
LICENCIA DE GUIAR.
driver's license.
LICENCIA DE IMPORTACIÓN.
import license.
LICENCIA DE PATENTE.
patent license.
LICENCIA DIARIA EN PREAVISO.
legal right to paid leave of two hours at the beginning or end of each work day during the pretermination period of PREAVISO (ending a work contract), to look for work.
LICENCIA EXCLUSIVA.
exclusive license.
LICENCIA GRATUITA.
gratuitous license.
LICENCIA JUDICIAL.
judicial consent to enter into certain transactions which consent must be obtained by minors, and other persons who lack legal capacity.

LICENCIA MARITAL.
husband's consent which must be obtained by a wife in order for her to enter into certain transactions.
LICENCIA MATRIMONIAL.
marriage license ‖ consent by third parties to marry. May be FAMILIAR or PATERNA (parental consent) or ESTATAL or SUPERIOR (state consent).
LICENCIA PARA ABRIR ESTABLECIMIENTOS.
license to open businesses.
LICENCIA PARA CASARSE.
marriage license.
LICENCIA PARA CONTRAER MATRIMONIO.
See LICENCIA MATRIMONIAL.
LICENCIA PARA EDIFICAR.
building permit.
LICENCIA PATERNA.
parental consent.
LICENCIA PROFESIONAL.
professional license, license to practise a profession.
LICENCIA REMUNERADA.
onerous license, license for remuneration.
LICENCIA SIMPLE.
simple license ‖ non-exclusive license.
LICENCIA TEMPORAL.
temporary authorized leave of absence (from work or military).
LICENCIABLE.
m, soldier who is about to be discharged ‖ soldier who having completed his service remains therein due to unusual circumstances ‖ adj, able to be licensed or consented to or authorized or discharged ‖ sentenced to prison when person is releasable.
LICENCIADO.
m, licensee ‖ licentiate ‖ freed person ‖ released prisoner ‖ fully discharged soldier ‖ attorney, lawyer, person who is licensed to practice law ‖ person who is competent in some academic area ‖ person who is licensed to practice some profession which requires such license ‖ adj, freed ‖ licensed. In some countries, a LICENCIADO has obtained a type of university degree (see LICENCIATURA), which is all that is needed in order to practice as an attorney or doctor of medicine and other similar professions (i.e. no other certification process occurs).

LICENCIADO EN DERECHO.
attorney, lawyer, person who is licensed to practice law.

LICENCIAMIENTO.
m, graduation ‖ military discharge or leave (either full or temporary).

LICENCIAMIENTO DE PENADOS.
release of prisoners (upon completion of their sentence or upon early parole).

LICENCIANTE.
m, licensor.

LICENCIAR.
v, to license ‖ to permit, give permission, allow ‖ to grant a license (especially to practice law) ‖ to grant a type of university degree (see LICENCIADO) ‖ to grant a full military discharge.

LICENCIARSE.
v, to obtain a type of university degree (see LICENCIATURA) ‖ to become perverted or licentious.

LICENCIATURA.
f, licensee ‖ type of university degree obtained after having successfully completed a somewhat lengthy period of study in a certain field. May be considered equivalent to a bachelor's degree or a master's in certain cases or a juris doctorate in the case of law. University studies which must be completed to obtain a degree of this same name.

LICENCIOSAMENTE.
adv, licentiously.

LICENCIOSO.
adj, licentious ‖ perverted ‖ free.

LICITACIÓN.
f, licitation, bid, bidding ‖ public auction.

LICITADOR.
m, bidder (at an auction or in a bid).

LÍCITAMENTE.
adv, legally, lawfully, legitimately ‖ justly.

LICITANTE.
See LICITADOR.

LICITAR.
v, to bid (at an auction or licitation) ‖ to offer more than the going price (usually in a closed bid) ‖ to auction, take bids.

LÍCITO.
adj, legal, lawful, legitimate ‖ just ‖ moral.

LICITUD.
f, lawfulness, legitimacy ‖ justness.

LID.
f, combat, battle ‖ fight ‖ dispute, controversy, argument ‖ trial by duel.

LÍDER.
m, leader ‖ chief, head (usually of a political party or other social group).

LIDERATO.
m, leadership ‖ exercise of leadership responsibilities.

LIDERAZGO.
See LIDERATO.

LIDERAZGO DE PRECIOS.
price leadership (of one or two businesses within a market).

LIDIA.
f, battle, fight ‖ opposition.

LIDIADOR.
m, combatant, fighter ‖ bull fighter ‖ opposition ‖ litigant.

LIDIAR.
v, to battle, combat, fight ‖ to oppose ‖ to bother, be a nuisance ‖ to make fun of someone ‖ to litigate.

LIGA.
f, tie, relationship ‖ alliance, league ‖ mixture alloy, compound ‖ amount of copper used in minting coins ‖ pact.

LIGA DE LAS NACIONES.
League of Nations.

LIGAMEN.
m, marital ties, legal effect of marriage ‖ impediment to marriage resulting from the existence of a prior undissolved marriage.

LIMITACIÓN.
f, limitation ‖ restriction, impediment ‖ border.

LIMITACIÓN DE LA LIBERTAD CONTRACTUAL.
limitations in law on freedom to contract.

LIMITACIÓN DE LOS PRECIOS.
See PRECIO MÁXIMO.

LIMITACIONES DEL DOMINIO.
legal limitations regarding property ownership rights.

LIMITADAMENTE.
adv, with limitations, limitedly.

LIMITADO.
adj, limited, with limits ‖ slow, with limited understanding.

LIMITAR.
v, to limit, confine ‖ to border, have a commo

border ‖ to place limits on ‖ to restrict ‖ to impede ‖ to set the maximum jurisdiction, authority, or rights of something.

LIMITARSE.
v, to restrict or limit expenses ‖ to reduce one's activities.

LIMITATIVO.
adj, limiting, restrictive.

LÍMITE.
m, border, boundary (e.g. between countries, provinces) ‖ limitation ‖ end, termination, finish ‖ the extreme, outside limit (of something).

LÍMITES DEL DOMINIO.
physical and legal limits of property ownership. Includes LIMITACIONES DEL DOMINIO.

LIMÍTROFE.
adj, bordering, conterminous, adjoining.

LIMOSNA.
f, alms, gift to the poor.

LIMPIO DE MANOS.
with clean hands, honorable, upright.

LINAJE.
m, lineage (both ascending and descending) ‖ class or condition of something.

LINCHAMIENTO.
m, lynching.

LINCHAR.
v, to lynch ‖ to punish without benefit of judicial sentence.

LINDE.
m, limit, border, boundary ‖ property line.

LINDERO.
m, limit, boundary, border ‖ property line ‖ adj, bordering, conterminous, adjoining.

LÍNEA.
f, line (in all meanings) ‖ route ‖ class, species ‖ series (of persons or things) ‖ equator ‖ lineage, branch.

LÍNEA AÉREA.
airline ‖ air route ‖ airborne cable or line.

LÍNEA ASCENDENTE.
ascending lineage or line.

LÍNEA COLATERAL.
collateral lineage or line. Includes siblings, aunts and uncles, nieces and nephews, and cousins.

LÍNEA DE AGUA.
water-line (on a boat).

LÍNEA DE CAMBIO DE FECHA.
date-line.

LÍNEA DE CARGA.
water-line of loaded ship.

LÍNEA DE CARGA MÁXIMA.
deep-water line.

LÍNEA DE FLOTACIÓN.
See LÍNEA DE AGUA.

LÍNEA DE NAVEGACIÓN.
shipping line or route ‖ maritime shipping company. See LÍNEA DE AGUA.

LÍNEA DE PLIMSOLL.
See LÍNEA DE CARGA MÁXIMA.

LÍNEA DE TRAVIESO.
See LÍNEA COLATERAL.

LÍNEA DESCENDENTE.
descending lineage or line.

LÍNEA DIRECTA.
straight or direct line ‖ direct call (by telephone).

LÍNEA DURA.
hard line or position.

LÍNEA FEMENINA.
ascending and descending female lineage.

LÍNEA FÉRREA.
railway line ‖ railroad company ‖ rail, track ‖ hard line.

LÍNEA FLUVIAL.
river navigation route.

LÍNEA MASCULINA.
ascending and descending male lineage.

LÍNEA MATERNA.
ascending maternal lineage.

LÍNEA PATERNA.
ascending paternal lineage.

LÍNEA RECTA.
straight line ‖ honor, propriety ‖ direct line (in parentage).

LÍNEA TELEFÓNICA.
telephone line.

LÍNEA TELEGRÁFICA.
telegraph line.

LÍNEA TRANSVERSAL.
See LÍNEA COLATERAL.

LÍNEA VON KARMAN.
von Karman line, boundary between national airspace and international airspace (i.e. outer space).

LINEAL.
adj, lineal ‖ pertaining to family lineage.

LÍNEAS DE COMUNICACIONES.
lines of communication.

LINGOTE.
m, ingot.

"LIQUET".
See "NON LIQUET".

LIQUIDABLE.
adj, able to be liquidated. See LIQUIDACIÓN.

LIQUIDACIÓN.
f, liquidation ‖ settlement (of accounts) ‖ winding up (e.g. of a company) ‖ termination ‖ extermination, killing ‖ account presented to judge showing notary fees, fees, interest, and other pertinent costs ‖ clearance sale, sale.

LIQUIDACIÓN DE AVERÍAS.
liquidation of ship's average.

LIQUIDACIÓN DE CONDENA.
calculation of condemned criminal's sentence (considering time already served) ‖ document containing aforementioned calculation.

LIQUIDACIÓN DE LA DOTE.
liquidation of the wife's dowry (upon separation of the marital estate).

LIQUIDACIÓN DE LA HERENCIA.
See PARTICIÓN DE LA HERENCIA.

LIQUIDACIÓN DE LA SOCIEDAD CIVIL.
liquidation, winding up of a SOCIEDAD CIVIL (upon dissolution).

LIQUIDACIÓN DE LA SOCIEDAD COMERCIAL.
liquidation, winding up of a SOCIEDAD COMERCIAL (upon dissolution).

LIQUIDACIÓN DE LA SOCIEDAD CONYUGAL.
liquidation or partition of the marital community.

LIQUIDACIÓN DE LA SOCIEDAD DE GANANCIALES.
separation of marital property (upon the dissolution or annulment of a marriage).

LIQUIDACIÓN DE LA SUCESIÓN.
probate proceeding in which assets and debts of a decedent's estate and the rights of heirs and legatees are settled and distributed.

LIQUIDACIÓN FORZOSA.
forced liquidation.

LIQUIDADO.
m, thing which has been liquidated or finished or done or killed ‖ adj, liquidated ‖ finished, done ‖ killed.

LIQUIDADOR.
m, trustee in bankruptcy ‖ liquidator ‖ receiver. May be either judicial or otherwise.

LIQUIDADOR JUDICIAL.
court-appointed liquidator ‖ receiver.

LÍQUIDAMENTE.
adv, with a fixed amount of money ‖ with cash.

LIQUIDAR.
v, to liquidate ‖ to wind up, dissolve ‖ to settle (accounts) ‖ to spend totally ‖ to end, finish (something) ‖ to kill ‖ to sell at an extraordinarily low price ‖ to clear out stock.

LIQUIDAR UN GIRO.
to honor or pay a draft.

LIQUIDAR UN NEGOCIO.
to liquidate a business.

LIQUIDAR UNA CUENTA.
to settle an account ‖ to liquidate an account.

LIQUIDEZ.
f, liquidity.

LÍQUIDO.
m, net account ‖ adj, net, clear ‖ liquid ‖ liquidated.

LÍQUIDO IMPONIBLE.
net amount subject to tax, net taxable amount.

LISAMENTE.
adv, plainly, without interpretation.

LISIADO.
m, maimed or injured or disabled person ‖ adj, maimed, injured, disabled (by accident or criminal action).

LISIADURA.
f, action of maiming or injuring ‖ injury, disablement.

LISIAR.
v, to maim, injure, disable (especially if this results in visible injury).

LISO Y LLANO.
adj, easy, that which presents no difficulties ‖ unlimited, without restrictions.

LISTA.
f, list ‖ inventory ‖ catalogue ‖ list of candidates ‖ roll-call.

LISTA DE CORREOS.
general delivery office ‖ general delivery.

LISTA DE JURADOS.
jury list.

LISTA DE LITIGIOS.
calendar of cases, trial docket.

LISTA DE PASAJEROS.
passenger list.

LISTA DE PERITOS Y TESTIGOS.
witness list (inclusive of ordinary and expert witnesses).

LISTA DE PLEITOS.
See LISTA DE LITIGIOS.
LISTA ELECTORAL.
list of candidates.
LISTA NEGRA.
blacklist.
LISTAR.
v, to list ‖ to include on a list.
LISTERO.
m, roll keeper, roll taker.
LISTO.
adj, ready.
LISTO DE MANOS.
m, capable of thievery ‖ person who takes advantage of benefits improperly.
LITE.
m, litigation.
LITE PENDENTE.
lite pendente.
LITERAL.
adj, literal, to the letter, textual.
LITERALIDAD.
f, literalness.
LITERALMENTE.
adv, literally.
LITERARIO.
adj, literary ‖ imaginative, fictional.
LITERATO.
m, writer ‖ fiction writer ‖ adj, cultured, well-read.
LITERATURA.
f, literature ‖ bibliography.
LITERATURA JURÍDICA.
legal writings including texts or treatises.
LITIGACIÓN.
f, litigation, action of litigating.
LITIGADOR.
m, litigant.
LITIGANTE.
m, litigant.
LITIGANTE VENCEDOR.
successful party (in a a lawsuit).
LITIGANTE VENCIDO.
losing party (in a lawsuit).
LITIGAR.
v, to litigate ‖ to argue or dispute (something) ‖ to oppose a complaint.
LITIGIO.
m, litigation ‖ controversy, dispute ‖ trial, hearing.

LITIGIOSO.
m, matter in dispute, subject of litigation ‖ adj, litigious, contentious.
LITIS.
f, lawsuit, case.
"LITIS CONTESTATIO".
f, litis constestio, answer or response (to a complaint) which rejects the claims stated therein.
LITIS EXPENSAS.
See LITISEXPENSAS.
LITISCONSORCIAL.
pertaining to joinder or joint litigation.
LITISCONSORCIO.
m, joinder, condition of being joint litigants. May be ACTIVO (if there are several joint plaintiffs) or PASIVO (if there are several joint defendants).
LITISCONSORCIO NECESARIO.
necessary joinder.
LITISCONSORTE.
joint litigant (either defendant or plaintiff).
LITISCONTESTACIÓN.
f, answer or response (to a complaint) which rejects the claims stated therein. If written it is called the CONTESTACIÓN A LA DEMANDA.
LITISEXPENSAS.
f, costs and expenses of litigation ‖ legal determination of party to bear costs and expenses of litigation.
LITISPENDENCIA.
f, lawsuit pending judicial decision ‖ litispendence, period of time during which a case is pending ‖ same cause of action pending in another court.
LITORAL.
m, coast ‖ shore ‖ adj, littoral ‖ coastal.
LO PROMETIDO ES DEUDA.
That which was promised is due.
LO ÚLTIMO.
final or last offer ‖ the worst ‖ the latest.
LOC.CIT.
See LOCO CITATO.
LOCA.
f, female lunatic, insane woman ‖ whore ‖ adj, crazy ‖ zany.
LOCACIÓN.
f, hire, rental ‖ lease. Includes: LOCACIÓN DE COSAS (renting of personal or real property or lease although not always a lease which provides and option to purchase) ‖ LOCACIÓN DE

LOCACIÓN DE SERVICIOS (employment or hiring out of services) ‖ LOCACIÓN DE OBRA (building, construction or manufacturing agreements or other agreements for the supply of works).

LOCACIÓN DE CAPITALES.
loan with interest.

LOCACIÓN DE COSAS.
rental or hire or lease of goods.

LOCACIÓN DE FINCAS RÚSTICAS.
lease of a farm or other rural property.

LOCACIÓN DE FINCAS URBANAS.
lease of urban property.

LOCACIÓN DE OBRAS.
See CONTRATO DE LOCACIÓN DE OBRA and LOCACIÓN.

LOCACIÓN DE SERVICIOS.
See CONTRATO DE LOCACIÓN DE SERVICIOS and LOCACIÓN.

LOCACIÓN-GERENCIA.
lease of a business, contract by which an owner of a business rents it to another for a term, at the other's risk.

LOCACIÓN-VENTA.
hire-purchase, lease (with option to purchase at the end of the lease term).

LOCACIÓN Y CONDUCCIÓN.
locatio-conductio, hire (of services or goods) by the hirer to the renter.

LOCADOR.
m, hirer, lessor ‖ landlord (if pertaining to land) ‖ contractor, employer

LOCADOR DE SERVICIOS.
employer.

LOCAL.
m, local ‖ site, situs, location ‖ locale, business establishment, premises ‖ adj, municipal, provincial, or regional (as opposed to national) ‖ local.

LOCALES
DE TRABAJO.
work sites, work places.

LOCALIDAD.
f, locality ‖ town, place, locale ‖ ticket (which permits one to be seated in a theater, etc.).

LOCALIZACIÓN.
f, act of locating, location.

LOCALIZAR.
v, to locate ‖ to confine to certain limits.

LOCATARIO.
m, lessee, renter ‖ tenant (if pertaining to land).

LOCATIVO.
adj, rental, lease, hire, related to hiring, leasing, or renting.

LOCO.
m, lunatic, insane person, mentally ill person ‖ adj, foolish, unwise ‖ stupid.

LOCO CITATO.
at the designated place.

LOCO DE ATAR.
raving lunatic.

LOCO PERENNE.
permanently insane person or lunatic.

LOCUCIÓN.
f, locution ‖ sentence ‖ phrase.

LOCURA.
f, insanity, mental illness, lunacy.

LOCURA CRIMINAL.
criminal insanity, insanity which causes one to commit a crime.

LOCURA MORAL.
mental illness which prevents person from being able to discern right from wrong.

"LOCUS".
locus, place, site ‖ position, situation ‖ passage, fragment (from a text) ‖ family ‖ time, occasion, opportunity ‖ country ‖ farm ‖ burial.

"LOCUS DELICTI".
locus delicti.

"LOCUS REGIT ACTUM".
locus regit actum, legal transactions are regulated by the law of the place in which they are executed.

LOGIA.
f, lodge ‖ Freemason's lodge.

LOGRAR.
v, to achieve, obtain ‖ to enjoy, possess.

LOGREAR.
v, to be a lender of money ‖ to profiteer.

LOGRERÍA.
f, money lending ‖ usury ‖ profiteering.

LOGRERO.
m, usurer, person who lends money usuriously ‖ money lender ‖ profiteer ‖ adj, usurious.

LOGRO.
m, attainment, achievement ‖ profit ‖ usury, excessive interest.

LOGUER.
m, lease or rental payment.

LOGUERO.
m, price of a lease or rental.

LONGEVIDAD.

f, longevity.

"LONGI TEMPORIS PRAESCRIPTIO".

f, acquisition of title by adverse possession ‖ acquisition of prescriptive rights after a passage of a long period of time, e.g. twenty years.

"LONGISSIMI TEMPORIS PRAESCRIPTIO".

f, acquisition of title by adverse possession ‖ acquisition of prescriptive rights after a passage of a very long period of time, e.g. thirty years.

LONJA.

f, commercial exchange, public building where merchants meet to buy and sell.

LOQUERO.

m, guard in a hospital for the mentally ill.

LOS MÍOS.

family ‖ family and friends ‖ fellow party members ‖ compatriots ‖ fellow believers or followers.

LOTE.

m, lot, portion ‖ lot, parcel (of land).

LOTEO.

m, parcelling, division (of land).

LOTERÍA.

f, lottery, raffle.

LOTERÍA NO AUTORIZADA.

unauthorized lottery.

LOTERO.

m, owner of a lottery agency ‖ seller of lottery tickets.

LUCES.

f, lights ‖ progress ‖ intelligence.

LUCES DE SITUACIÓN.

night position light (of a ship or vessel).

LUCES Y SEÑALES AÉREAS.

lights and signals (of airplanes).

LUCIDEZ.

f, lucidity.

LUCIDEZ MENTAL.

mental lucidity.

LÚCIDO.

adj, lucid

LUCRAR.

v, to make a profit, profit.

LUCRARSE.

v, to enrich oneself.

LUCRATIVO.

adj, lucrative, money making.

LUCRATORIO.

adj, lucrative.

LUCRO.

m, profit, gain ‖ interest, return on money.

LUCRO BRUTO.

gross profit.

LUCRO CESANTE.

lost profits (e.g. due to the debtor's failure to pay).

LUCRO ESPERADO.

anticipated profits.

LUCRO LÍQUIDO.

net profit ‖ profit obtained from the resale of something.

LUCRO NACIENTE.

profit made from borrowed funds or assets.

LUCROS Y DAÑOS.

profit and loss.

LUCROSO.

adj, profitable, lucrative.

LUCHA.

f, fight, battle ‖ war ‖ struggle ‖ dispute ‖ effort ‖ adversity.

LUCHA CONTRA LA POBREZA.

war against poverty.

LUCHA DE CLASES.

class struggle, conflict between the classes.

LUGAR.

m, place, site, spot ‖ location ‖ position, employment ‖ text, passage, fragment of a writing ‖ time ‖ occasion, opportunity ‖ cause, motive ‖ space, position on a list.

LUGAR DE LOS HECHOS.

locus delicti.

LUGAR DE PAGO.

place of payment.

LUGAR DE TRABAJO.

place of work, work place.

LUGAR DEL DELITO.

locus delicti.

LUGAR DEL SELLO.

place of the seal.

LUGAR EN LOS CONTRATOS.

locus contractus.

LUGAR HABITADO.

inhabited place.

LUGAR INSALUBRE.

unsanitary or unhealthy place.

LUGAR NO HABITADO.

uninhabited place.

LUGAR PÚBLICO.
public place. May be either EXTERIOR (outside) or INTERIOR (inside).

LUGAR Y FECHA.
place and date, place and time.

LUGARES COMUNES.
platitudes, commonplace thoughts or ideas.

LUGARTENIENCIA.
f, lieutenancy.

LUGARTENIENTE.
m, lieutenant ‖ second in command.

LUJO.
m, luxury.

LUJURIA.
f, lechery, lust.

LUMIA.
f, whore.

LUNÁTICO.
m, lunatic ‖ adj, lunatic.

"LUPA".
f, whore, prostitute.

LUPANAR.
m, house of prostitution, whorehouse.

LUSTRO.
m, period of five years.

LUTO.
m, mourning, bereavement ‖ clothes and other signs of mourning.

LUTO DE LA VIUDA.
widow's mourning clothes.

LUXACIÓN.
f, dislocation.

LUZ.
f, light.

"LYMPHATICUS".
m, raving maniac.

LYNCH.
See LINCHAR.

LLAMADA.

f, call ‖ telephone call ‖ request or offer to work (which is sometimes required in order to emigrate) ‖ reference number or mark (to a footnote) ‖ signal, gesture (to distract someone).

LLAMADA A LICITACIÓN.

call for bids.

LLAMADA A PROPUESTAS.

call for bids ‖ call for proposals.

LLAMADA EN GARANTÍA.

placing on notice of a third party of a suit pending for which he may be potentially liable.

LLAMADO.

m, see LLAMADA ‖ adj, recruited, inducted into the military ‖ mobilized.

LLAMADOR.

m, caller.

LLAMAMIENTO.

m, convocation, summoning ‖ summons, citation ‖ requirement ‖ call for help ‖ induction into military service.

LLAMAMIENTO A JUICIO.

summons to court ‖ indictment.

LLAMAMIENTO A LA SUCESIÓN.

See VOCACIÓN HEREDITARIA.

LLAMAMIENTO A LICITACIÓN.

call for bids.

LLAMAMIENTO DE AUTOS.

judicial order requesting all pertinent files regarding a given case in order to issue a decision.

LLAMAR.

v, to call ‖ to summons ‖ to call, name ‖ to telephone, call ‖ to call (a meeting, for help, attention ‖ to recruit, induct into military service.

LLAMAR A CONCURSO.

to call for bids.

LLAMAR A JUICIO.

to summon to court ‖ to bring to trial.

LLAMAR A JUNTA.

to call a meeting.

LLAMAR AL ORDEN.

to call to order.

LLAMAR AUTOS.

to subpoena records.

LLAMAR AUTOS PARA SENTENCIA.

to close the evidentiary period prior to issuing a decision.

LLAMARSE.

v, to be named, be called.

LLAMARSE A LA PARTE.

to request one's share (of something).

LLANO.

m, guarantor who may not decline jurisdiction ‖ adj, simple, moderate ‖ flat.

LLAVE.

f, key (in all meanings).

LLAVE HALLADA.

lost key (which is found by the non-owner). Use of such key is considered to be an aggravating circumstance in the case of theft.

LLAVE SUSTRAÍDA.

misappropriated or stolen key. Use of such key is considered to be an aggravating circumstance in the case of theft.

LLAVERO.

m, keeper of the keys.

LLAVES FALSAS.

keys obtained for illegal purposes (including skeleton keys, lock picking instruments used in order to burgle a house, keys stolen from the true owner).

LLEGADA.

f, arrival ‖ adj, arrived.

LLEGAR.

v, to arrive, reach ‖ to land ‖ to achieve (a hope) ‖ to amount to, reach (a certain price) ‖ to meet ‖ to ascend, rise.

LLEGAR A UN ACUERDO.

to arrive at or come to an agreement.

LLEVADERO.

adj, tolerable.

LLEVANZA.

f, rental, leasing.

LLEVAR.

v, to carry, transport ‖ to take ‖ to transfer ‖ to wear, carry, have on oneself ‖ to cut off, sever ‖ to tolerate, suffer, bear ‖ to induce, persuade ‖ to obtain, achieve ‖ to manage, keep (books, etc.) ‖ to win ‖ to have been (living) ‖ to yield, produce ‖ to lease, rent.

LLEVAR A EFECTO.

to put into effect, make effective.

LLEVAR A PROTESTO.

to protest.

LLEVAR A REMATE.

to put up for auction, take to auction.

LLEVAR A TÉRMINO.

to do, carry out, complete, finish.

LLEVAR FECHA DE.

to bear the date of.

LLEVAR INTERESES.

to bear interest.

LLEVAR LA CUENTA.

to keep track or account of.

LLEVAR LA FIRMA DE OTRO.

to represent a business.

LLEVAR LA MEJOR PARTE.

to get the best of, have the upper hand (in a competitive or belligerent situation).

LLEVAR LA PALABRA.

to speak for, be spokesperson for.

LLEVAR LA PEOR PARTE.

to get the worst of, be in a losing position.

LLEVAR LA VOZ CANTANTE.

to set forth a group's proposal ‖ to govern, rule ‖ to call the shots, manage.

LLEVAR SU MANO.

to drive pursuant to the legal direction of traffic.

LLEVAR UN PLEITO.

to conduct a lawsuit.

LLEVAR UN REGISTRO.

to keep a record or filing.

LLEVARSE.

v, to carry, transport (with one) ‖ to steal, burgle ‖ to move (at the expiration of a lease term) ‖ to be (a number of) years older than another ‖ to get along (with someone).

LLEVARSE A ALGUIEN POR DELANTE.

See LLEVARSE ALGO.

LLEVARSE ALGO.

to run roughshod over ‖ to lack due respect ‖ to steal.

LLEVARSE LA PALMA.

to be victorious, carry the day.

LLEVARSE LA TRAMPA UNA COSA.

to fail, break down, fall through (relative to a business or other venture).

LLUVIA.

f, rain ‖ abundance, shower.

MACANA.
f, mess, problem ‖ merchandise which is difficult to sell ‖ lie, fib.
MACERELO.
m, quarrelsome person, troublemaker.
MÁCULA.
f, stain, blotch, blemish, blot ‖ trick.
MACULAR.
v, to stain, blemish ‖ to dishonor, defame.
MACUQUERO.
m, person who steals minerals from abandoned mines.
MACUTENO.
m, thief, pickpocket.
MACHACAR.
v, to smash, hit violently ‖ to crush ‖ to insist repeatedly.
MACHACONERÍA.
f, irritating insistence.
MACHETAZO.
m, blow of a machete.
MACHETE.
m, machete.
MACHUCADURA.
f, blow, contusion ‖ wound.
MACHUCAR.
v, to wound by crushing or smashing.
MADAMA.
f, madame (of a house of prostitution) ‖ Mrs., missus.
MADEJA.
f, intrigue, imbroglio, affair.
MADERO.
m, lumber used for construction ‖ embarkation.
MADRASTRA.
f, step-mother.

MADRE.
f, mother ‖ mother, sister (in religion) ‖ old woman ‖ source ‖ most important element or part ‖ womb.
MADRE ADOPTIVA.
adoptive mother.
MADRE ADULTERINA.
woman who has a child by a man to whom she is not married ‖ married woman who has a child by a man who is not her husband.
MADRE DE FAMILIA.
woman who is head of the house.
MADRE DE LECHE.
wet nurse.
MADRE DESCONOCIDA.
unknown mother.
MADRE ILEGÍTIMA.
woman who has a child by a man who is not married to her at the time of birth.
MADRE INCESTUOSA.
woman who has a child through incest.
MADRE NATURAL.
natural mother.
MADRE PATRIA.
motherland, mother country ‖ Spain (as used in Spanish-American countries).
MADRE POLÍTICA.
mother-in-law ‖ step-mother.
MADRE PUTATIVA.
putative mother.
MADRE SACRÍLEGA.
Literally, sacrilegious mother ‖ woman who has a child by a priest ‖ nun who bears a child.
MADRE TRABAJADORA.
working mother or mother-to-be.
MADRE VIUDA.
widowed mother.

MADRIGADA.
f, woman who is married for the second time.

MADRINA.
f, god-mother.

MADRINAZGO.
m, god-motherhood.

MAESTRA.
f, female teacher or professor || teacher's wife.

MAESTRA DE ESCUELA.
female school teacher.

MAESTRA DE PRIMERA ENSEÑANZA.
female primary school teacher.

MAESTRA DE PRIMERAS LETRAS.
female school teacher.

MAESTRAJE.
m, mastership of embarkations.

MAESTRAL.
adj, pertaining to MAESTRE || masterly.

MAESTRAMENTE.
adv, skillfully, adroitly || perfectly.

MAESTRANZA.
f, arsenal || arms repair shop || employees who work in arms repair shop.

MAESTRE.
m, master of a cavalry || chief, head.

MAESTRÍA.
f, profession of teaching || teacher's certificate || status or level of a teacher || ruse, trick || remedy.

MAESTRO.
m, male teacher or professor || principal || expert, experienced person || master, lead, head or lead or principal person in a vocation.

MAESTRO ARUAÑÓN.
builder of hydraulic works.

MAESTRO DE ARTES Y OFICIOS.
master of arts and trades.

MAESTRO DE ESCUELA.
male school teacher.

MAESTRO DE OBRAS.
construction foreman (of a building or houses).

MAESTRO DE PRIMERA ENSEÑANZA.
male primary school teacher.

MAESTRO DE PRIMERAS LETRAS.
male school teacher.

MAESTRO EN LEYES.
master of law || jurist || Ll. M.

MAESTRO MAYOR.
director of public works || construction foreman.

MAFIA.
f, Italian Mafia || mafia, gang || trick.

MAFIOSO.
m, mafioso, gang member || member of the Italian Mafia || immoral person.

MAGANCERÍA.
f, trick, fraud.

MAGANCÉS.
m, traitor, disloyal person || adj, injuring.

MAGANCIA.
f, trick, fraud.

MAGAÑA.
f, trick, fraud, ruse.

MAGIA.
f, magic.

MÁGICO.
m, witch, magician || adj, magical, marvelous || attractive, seductive.

"MAGISTERIA POTESTAS".
sovereignty || sovereign power.

MAGISTERIAL.
adj, teaching, pertaining to teaching.

MAGISTERIO.
m, teaching || profession of teacher || teaching certificate || post of teacher || staff of teachers in a given area.

MAGISTRADO.
m, head, chief (in government) || Minister of Justice, equivalent in U.S. to Attorney General || in Spain, Supreme Court justice or civil court judge.

MAGISTRADO CONSULAR.
See JUEZ CONSULAR.

MAGISTRADO PONENTE.
member of a multi-judge court who writes the court's opinion.

MAGISTRADO REVISOR.
member of a multi-judge court who revises the court's opinion.

MAGISTRADO SUPLENTE.
judge pro tem, judge pro tempore, judge who replaces judges who are absent.

MAGISTRAL.
adj, magisterial || masterly, brilliant, outstanding.

MAGISTRATURA.
f, position, functions, and term of a judgeship || total judiciary in a nation.

MAGISTRATURA DEL TRABAJO.
labor judiciary.

MAGISTRATURA TUTELAR DE MENORES.
court for guardianship of minors.

MAGNATE.
m, magnate.

MAGNICIDIO.
m, assassination of the head of State or other public figure.

MAGNÍFICO.
adj, magnificent ‖ yes, means of expressing consent to something.

MAGNITUD.
f, magnitude.

MAGO.
m, magician.

MAGULLADURA.
f, contusion caused by a blow with an object.

MAGULLAR.
v, to batter, bash.

MAJADERÍA.
f, stupidity ‖ foolishness ‖ absurd reproach or accusation.

MAL.
m, evil ‖ illegality, dishonesty ‖ injury, offense, prejudice, harm ‖ crime, misdemeanor, felony ‖ adj, bad ‖ wrong, unjust, improper, insufficient, evil, incorrect ‖ adv, wrongly, unjustly ‖ improperly ‖ insufficiently ‖ with difficulty ‖ badly, evilly ‖ incorrectly.

MAL A MAL.
by force ‖ against one's wishes.

MAL BICHO.
unscrupulous person ‖ perverse person.

MAL ENGENDRO.
juvenile delinquent, J.D. ‖ rapscallion.

MAL INMINENTE.
proximate injury or damage (to life, limb or property). Constitutes an element of intimidation (as a cause for nullification of certain acts) and may be an element in the criminal excuse of ESTADO DE NECESIDAD.

MAL INNECESARIO.
unnecessary harm ‖ unnecessary evil. May be an aggravating circumstance in criminal law.

MAL MAYOR.
greater harm ‖ greater evil.

MAL MENOR.
lesser harm ‖ lesser evil.

MAL NACIDO.
illegitimate child ‖ perverse person.

MAL NOMBRE.
bad reputation, ill fame.

MAL RECADO.
bad act ‖ carelessness.

MALA ACCIÓN.
punishable action ‖ bad act.

MALA BARATA.
abandonment of goods.

MALA CONDUCTA.
misconduct, improper or bad conduct.

MALA FAMA.
bad reputation.

MALA FE.
bad faith ‖ disloyally ‖ fraud, dolus, deceit.

MALA FIRMA.
illegible signature ‖ person with bad or no credit.

MALA PAGA.
bad payor, person who does not pay in a timely fashion ‖ insolvent person.

MALA PRESA.
party who violates international agreements regarding the taking of vessels.

MALA SOCIEDAD.
bad company.

MALA VIDA.
the bad life.

MALA VOLUNTAD.
bad intention, evil intent.

MALA VOZ.
unfavorable opinion (about someone's reputation).

MALABARISTA.
m, f, cunning thief.

MALACONSEJADA.
f, person who is given bad advice ‖ adj, badly advised.

MALAMENTE.
adv, badly ‖ in a bad situation.

MALANDANZA.
f, bad luck.

MALAS ARTES.
bad or improper means.

MALAS COMPAÑÍAS.
bad company.

MALAS COSTUMBRES.
bad conduct or habits, action which is against the law or good morals or work ethics, etc.

MALAS LENGUAS.
evil tongues, bad mouthers.

MALASANGRE.
f, bad blood ‖ f, m, vengeful person.

MALAVENTURA.
f, misfortune, disgrace.

MALBARATADOR.
m, person who sells for under cost ‖ spend-thrift, squanderer, wastrel.

MALBARATAR.
v, to sell under cost ‖ to go to the dogs, ruin oneself ‖ to throw away a fortune.

MALBARATO.
m, waste ‖ sale at under cost.

MALCASADO.
m, marital partner who fails to fulfill marital duties.

MALCASAR.
v, to marry badly (for any reason).

MALCASO.
m, treason ‖ infamy ‖ punishable action.

MALCONTENTO.
m, discontent ‖ adj, discontented (person).

MALCRIADO.
m, spoiled person ‖ badly raised person ‖ adj, spoiled.

MALCRIAR.
v, to spoil ‖ to raise (a child) badly.

MALDAD.
f, malice, bad intent, perfidity, bad faith, evil, wickedness.

MALDADOSAMENTE.
adv, maliciously, wickedly, with malice or bad intent.

MALDADOSO.
adj, malicious, wicked.

MALDECIDO.
adj, perverse, wicked.

MALDECIMIENTO.
m, personal attack.

MALDECIR.
v, to speak badly of ‖ to defame ‖ to censure.

MALDICIÓN.
f, curse ‖ damnation.

MALDISPUESTO.
m, person who is unprepared ‖ adj, unpre-pared ‖ prejudicial (to someone) ‖ contrary (person) ‖ organized against the law.

MALDITAMENTE.
adv, very badly or wickedly.

MALDITO.
adj, perverse, wicked ‖ with bad conduct ‖ cheap (person) ‖ of very poor quality ‖ damned.

MALEADOR.
See MALEANTE.

MALEANTE.
m, person with a bad background ‖ dangerous

subject or person ‖ hoodlum ‖ ex-convict, excon.

MALEAR.
v, to corrupt, pervert ‖ to injure something ‖ to let go to ruin.

MALEARSE.
v, to become corrupt or perverted ‖ to be in bad company ‖ to do things illegally.

MALEDICENCIA.
f, defamation, slander ‖ denigration, bad-mouthing.

MALEFICIAR.
v, to prejudice or hurt.

MALEFICIO.
m, curse, evil spell ‖ charm, spell ‖ evil which occurs as a result of spells.

MALÉFICO.
adj, harmful.

MALENTENDIDO.
m, misunderstanding ‖ disagreement.

MALESTAR.
m, general malaise ‖ uneasiness, disquiet, dis-content ‖ political discontent.

MALÉVOLAMENTE.
adv, malevolently.

MALEVOLENCIA.
f, malevolence.

MALÉVOLO.
adj, malevolent.

MALFORMACIÓN.
f, congenital defect.

MALGASTADOR.
m, spendthrift, squanderer.

MALGASTAR.
v, to squander money ‖ to waste time.

MALHABLADO.
adj, obscene or blasphemous (person).

MALHADADO.
adj, unhappy or unfortunate (person).

MALHECHO.
m, misdeed, bad action ‖ stupid act ‖ person with a physical defect ‖ adj, badly done.

MALHECHOR.
m, delinquent, hoodlum ‖ habitual criminal bandit ‖ temporary guerilla fighter.

MALHERIDO.
adj, critically wounded or injured (person).

MALHERIR.
v, to wound or injure critically.

MALICIA.
f, bad intention, malice ‖ fraud ‖ propensity t behave badly ‖ duplicity.

MALICIADOR.
m, person who suspects another.

MALICIAR.
v, to suspect || to corrupt.

MALICIOSO.
adj, malicious, suspicious.

MALIGNAR.
v, to corrupt || to spoil || to do evil to something || to malign.

MALIGNIDAD.
f, perversity || propensity or tendency to do evil.

MALIGNO.
adj, malignant, bad, evil, wicked, malicious.

MALINTENCIONADO.
m, person with bad intentions || adj, with bad intentions.

MALMANDADO.
adj, disobedience || reluctant, unwillingly obedient (person).

MALMARIDADA.
f, unfaithful wife || adj, unfaithful.

MALMETER.
v, to sell lower than cost || to squander || to estrange.

MALMIRADO.
adj, disliked || discredited.

MALO.
see MAL.

MALOCA.
f, raid into or from Indian territory.

MALOGRAMIENTO.
See MALOGRO.

MALOGRAR.
v, to miss or lose an opportunity.

MALOGRARSE.
v, to be frustrated (at something) || to fail to achieve (something).

MALOGRO.
m, failure || frustration || interruption or non-completion of a promising venture.

MALÓN.
m, Indian raid, surprise Indian attack.

MALOQUEAR.
v, to raid (carried out by Indians).

MALOS ANTECEDENTES.
bad reputation || criminal records (kept by police).

MALOS TRATOS.
mistreatment || abuse || bad treatment or dealings (between family members) || bad relationship or feelings (between family members) || lack of due respect.

MALOS USOS.
See USO MALO.

MALPARADO.
adj, injured, damaged, impaired (person).

MALPARANZA.
f, frustration || prejudice || situation which ends in failure.

MALPARAR.
v, to mistreat || to leave in a lurch.

MALPARIR.
v, to abort, have an abortion.

MALPARTO.
m, abortion || premature birth || stillbirth.

MALPENSADO.
m, pessimist, negative person || adj, malicious, suspicious.

MALQUERENCIA.
f, ill will || hatred, hate.

MALQUERER.
v, to hate, bear ill will || to maintain illicit sexual relations.

MALQUISTAR.
v, to make an enemy, alienate, estrange.

MALROTADOR.
m, spendthrift.

MALROTAR.
v, to squander money.

MALSANO.
adj, harmful to health || noxious.

MALSONANTE.
adj, offensive.

MALTRABAJA.
f, m, idler, loafer, someone who fails to perform employee's duties .

MALTRATAMIENTO.
See MALOS TRATOS.

MALTRATAR.
v, to treat badly || to insult, injure || to defame || to hit || to injure || to let go to ruin.

MALTRATO.
See MALOS TRATOS.

MALTRATO A INFERIOR.
mistreatment of a subordinate || abuse of authority.

MALTRATO A SUPERIOR.
insulting an officer.

MALTRATO INJUSTIFICADO.
abuse of military orders.

MALTRECHO.
m, victim of mistreatment ‖ injured person ‖ adj, injured, hurt, damaged.
MALTUSIANISMO.
m, Malthusianism.
MALUM IN SE.
malum in se.
MALUM PROHIBITUM.
malum prohibitum.
MALVADAMENTE.
adv, maliciously ‖ unjustly.
MALVADO.
m, evil person ‖ adj, of bad intent ‖ perverse.
MALVAR.
v, to corrupt ‖ to prostitute oneself.
MALVENDER.
v, to sell at a loss.
MALVERSACIÓN.
f, misappropriation or embezzlement.
MALVERSACIÓN DE CAUDALES PÚBLICOS.
embezzlement of public monies. Usually a crime.
MALVERSADOR.
m, embezzler (of public monies).
MALVERSAR.
v, to embezzle, misappropriate (public monies).
MALVIVIR.
v, to live badly (economically, socially and personally).
MAMA.
f, mama, mother, mom, mum.
MAMANDURRIA.
f, sinecure, salary given for little effort.
MAMAR.
v, to get something without due effort ‖ to fall into a trap ‖ to suckle.
MAMPORRO.
m, light blow, cuff, tap.
MANANTIAL.
m, spring (of a river) ‖ source, origin.
MANAR.
v, to spring forth (water or some other liquid) ‖ to abound.
MANCAMIENTO.
m, injury to one or both hands ‖ lack, privation.
MANCAR.
v, to injure or completely remove a hand.
MANCEBA.
f, concubine, mistress.

MANCEBÍA.
f, house of prostitution, whorehouse, brothel ‖ licentious life ‖ cohabitation with a mistress ‖ pimping.
MANCEBO.
m, youth ‖ single man ‖ employee ‖ pharmacist's assistant ‖ shop assistant or clerk.
MANCELLAR.
See MANCILLAR.
MANCELLOSO.
adj, malicious, malignant ‖ dishonorable.
MANCER.
See HIJO MANCER.
MANCILLADO.
adj, dishonored.
MANCILLAMIENTO.
m, sexual dishonor or humiliation ‖ falling into a licentious lifestyle or vice.
MANCILLAR.
v, to dishonor, deprive of honor ‖ to cause emotional damage.
MANCIPACIÓN.
f, transfer of goods or rights ‖ also see COMPRAVENTA.
MANCIPAR.
v, to enslave ‖ to become slave.
MANCO.
m, person who lacks one or both hands or arms ‖ adj, handless, armless, defective.
MANCOMUNADAMENTE.
adv, jointly.
MANCOMUNADO.
m, object of joint liability ‖ adj, joint.
MANCOMUNADA Y SOLIDARIAMENTE.
joint and severally.
MANCOMUNAR.
v, to unite, bring persons together for a certain purpose ‖ to unite forces, join efforts ‖ to join resources (for a business) ‖ to obligate two or more people jointly to carry out a transaction, pay a debt, do or abstain from doing something.
MANCOMUNARSE.
v, to unite, associate oneself with others ‖ to obligate oneself jointly.
MANCOMUNIDAD.
f, joint liability, quality of a joint obligation ‖ contract between two or more debtors and one or more creditors. May be SIMPLE or A PRORRATA (each debtor is liable for a pro rata portion of the obligation) or SOLIDARIA O

TOTAL (each debtor is primarily liable for fulfilling the obligation in full).

MANCOMUNIDAD A PRORRATA.
joint liability for a debt on a pro rata basis.

MANCOMUNIDAD SIMPLE.
See MANCOMUNIDAD A PRORRATA.

MANCOMUNIDAD SOLIDARIA.
joint and several liability.

MANCOMUNIDAD TOTAL.
See MANCOMUNIDAD SOLIDARIA.

MANCHA.
f, birthmark ‖ spot, blemish, blot, blotch (on the body) ‖ dishonor.

MANCHAR.
v, to stain, spot ‖ to dishonor, embarrass.

MANDA.
f, offer to exchange (one thing for another) ‖ testamentary gift (which may be LEGADO [simple gift] or FIDEICOMISO [in form of trust]).

MANDA FORZOSA.
See LEGADO FORZOSO.

MANDADERO.
m, messenger boy ‖ representative.

MANDADO.
m, order, mandate ‖ task which is carried out in a place different from that where it is ordered ‖ adj, sent ‖ established ‖ ordered.

MANDAMIENTO.
m, order from a superior to a subordinate ‖ basic or fundamental rule or principle ‖ writ of mandamus, written judicial order demanding or directing that certain action be taken.

MANDAMIENTO AFIRMATIVO.
mandatory injunction.

MANDAMIENTO COMPULSORIO.
type of subpoena duces tecum requiring that certain documents be verified or that specified public documents be brought to a judicial hearing.

MANDAMIENTO DE ARRESTO.
order or warrant of arrest.

MANDAMIENTO DE DESALOJO.
order of ejectment or ouster.

MANDAMIENTO DE EJECUCIÓN.
writ of execution.

MANDAMIENTO DE EMBARGO.
writ of attachment. May be either PREVENTIVO (pre-judgment attachment) or EJECUTIVO (pursuant to a writ of execution).

MANDAMIENTO DE PRISIÓN.
warrant of arrest ‖ criminal sentence, order directing detention of criminal for a given period of time.

MANDAMIENTO DE REGISTRO.
search warrant.

MANDAMIENTO FINAL.
final or permanent injunction.

MANDAMIENTO JUDICIAL.
order of execution, judicial order demanding that a decision or other order be carried out.

MANDAMIENTO PERPETUO.
permanent injunction.

MANDAMIENTO PRECEPTIVO.
mandatory injunction.

MANDAMIENTO PROVISIONAL.
preliminary injunction ‖ temporary restraining order.

MANDAMIENTOS JUDICIALES PARA EL REGISTRO DE LA PROPIEDAD.
judicial writ ordering the real estate registry to carry out some act within its jurisdiction.

MANDAMUS.
mandamus.

MANDANTE.
m, person who confers a power upon another to act on his behalf. Includes principal ‖ adj, constituent, mandatory.

MANDAR.
v, to order ‖ to impose a regulation or rule or order ‖ to grant, leave, bequeath, devise (pursuant to a will) ‖ to offer ‖ to promise ‖ to govern, rule ‖ to grant a position or commission ‖ to remit, send ‖ to grant a power.

MANDAR PAGAR.
to order payment, order that someone pay a bill.

MANDATARIO.
m, president, commander in chief (of a nation) ‖ person who, pursuant to a written power, acts on behalf of another. Includes agent, factor, representative ‖ mandatary ‖ attorney, delegate ‖ broker, agent.

MANDATARIO EN EL MATRIMONIO.
proxy or attorney in a marriage by proxy.

MANDATARIO EN LA COMPRAVENTA.
agent for one of the parties in a sale.

MANDATARIO EN LA POSESIÓN.
agent who exercises possession for his principal.

MANDATARIO GENERAL.
general agent.

MANDATARIO JUDICIAL.
attorney ‖ judicial representative.

MANDATARIO REAL Y VERDADERO.
true and lawful attorney.

MANDATARIO SINGULAR.
special agent.

MANDATARIO SUBSTITUTO.
agent of an agent.

MANDATO.
m, order, mandate ‖ precept ‖ disposition ‖ prohibition, injunction, writ ‖ charge, commission ‖ representation ‖ power of attorney ‖ voters' mandate (power of representation which elected congressmen and similar representatives are implicitly granted) ‖ term of office ‖ presidential term of office ‖ agency.

MANDATO "AD JUDICIA".
See MANDATO JUDICIAL.

MANDATO "AD NEGOTIA".
See MANDATO EXTRAJUDICIAL.

MANDATO "ALIENA GRATIA".
agency for the benefit of a third party ‖ power of attorney pertaining thereto.

MANDATO APARENTE.
apparent or ostensible agency ‖ power of attorney pertaining thereto.

MANDATO CIVIL.
agency regulated by DERECHO CIVIL ‖ power of attorney pertaining thereto.
See DERECHO CIVIL.

MANDATO COLECTIVO.
collective agency, agency in which there is more than one agent and/or principal ‖ power of attorney pertaining thereto.

MANDATO CONDICIONAL.
conditional agency (regarding its effectiveness, its revocation, or its performance) ‖ power of attorney pertaining thereto.

MANDATO CONJUNTO.
type of agency which requires the agents to act together in order for the act to be valid ‖ power of attorney pertaining thereto.

MANDATO CONVENCIONAL.
simple agency, agency in fact (as opposed to that implied by law) ‖ power of attorney pertaining thereto.

MANDATO CRIMINAL.
mandate to commit a crime.

MANDATO DE HECHO.
de facto agency ‖ power of attorney pertaining thereto.

MANDATO DE PAGO.
order of payment, payment order, order to a third party to pay ‖ agency for payment ‖ power of attorney pertaining thereto.

MANDATO DELEGABLE.
delegable agency ‖ power of attorney pertaining thereto.

MANDATO DISTRIBUTIVO.
agency which in one agreement assigns different duties to different agents ‖ power of attorney pertaining thereto.

MANDATO DOMÉSTICO.
agency of a wife to contract on behalf of the marital community ‖ power of attorney pertaining thereto.

MANDATO ESCRITO.
written agency ‖ power of attorney pertaining thereto.

MANDATO ESPECIAL.
special agency, agency for a specific purpose ‖ power of attorney pertaining thereto.

MANDATO EXPRESO.
express agency ‖ power of attorney pertaining thereto.

MANDATO EXTRAJUDICIAL.
agency for non-litigious matters ‖ power of attorney pertaining thereto. Opposed to MANDATO JUDICIAL or "AD JUDICIA".

MANDATO FACULTATIVO.
agency which grants a degree of discretion to agent in the transactions to be carried out ‖ power of attorney pertaining thereto.

MANDATO GENERAL.
general agency ‖ power of attorney pertaining thereto.

MANDATO GRATUITO.
gratuitous agency, agency for which agent is not paid ‖ power of attorney pertaining thereto.

MANDATO ILÍCITO.
illegal agency ‖ agency granted outside the legal structures ‖ agency to carry out an illegal purpose ‖ power of attorney pertaining thereto.

MANDATO IMPERATIVO.
limited agency, agency which grants no discretion to agent in the transactions to be carried out ‖ power of attorney pertaining thereto.

MANDATO INTERLOCUTORIO.
interlocutory order ‖ temporary injunction.

MANDATO INTERNACIONAL.
mandate or power to administrate over certain territories.

MANDATO IRREVOCABLE.
irrevocable agency ‖ power of attorney pertaining thereto.

MANDATO JUDICIAL.
agency for judicial matters ‖ power of attorney pertaining thereto. Opposed to MANDATO EXTRAJUDICIAL or "AD NEGOTIA".

MANDATO LEGISLATIVO.
electoral mandate ‖ power of attorney pertaining thereto.

MANDATO MANCOMUNADO.
joint agency, agency in which the agents are jointly liable ‖ power of attorney pertaining thereto. See MANCOMUNADO.

MANDATO MERCANTIL.
agency for purposes of DERECHO MERCANTIL ‖ power of attorney pertaining thereto. See DERECHO MERCANTIL.

MANDATO ONEROSO.
See MANDATO RETRIBUIDO.

MANDATO PARA CONTRAER MATRIMONIO.
power of attorney to carry out a marriage by proxy ‖ proxy pertaining thereto.

MANDATO PARTICULAR.
agency for a specific matter ‖ power of attorney pertaining thereto.

MANDATO PENAL.
See MANDATO CRIMINAL.

MANDATO PERSONAL.
personal agency ‖ power of attorney pertaining thereto.

MANDATO PRESUNTO.
implied agency ‖ power of attorney pertaining thereto.

MANDATO PROCESAL.
power of attorney for legal matters.

MANDATO RETRIBUIDO.
remunerative agency (i.e. agent is paid for his services ‖ power of attorney pertaining thereto.

MANDATO REVOCABLE.
revocable agency ‖ power of attorney pertaining thereto.

MANDATO SOLIDARIO.
agency for which the agents have joint and

several liability ‖ power of attorney pertaining thereto.

MANDATO SUCESIVO.
agency which names more than one agent, but which requires them to act consecutively, not simultaneously ‖ power of attorney pertaining thereto.

MANDATO TÁCITO.
implied agency ‖ power of attorney pertaining thereto.

MANDATO VERBAL.
oral agency ‖ power of attorney pertaining thereto.

MANDATORIO.
adj, mandatory, obligatory.

MANDO.
m, power, authority (over subordinates, whether legal or merely factual) ‖ authority of executive branch ‖ federal government ‖ military chief ‖ command.

MANDÓN.
m, person with propensity to abuse authority or power ‖ mine foreman ‖ imperious or domineering person.

MANDRACHE.
m, public gambling house.

MANDRACHERO.
m, gambler.

MANDRACHO.
See MANDRACHE.

MANDUCATORIA.
f, food, sustenance.

MANEAR.
See MANEJAR.

MANEJABLE.
adj, easy to use ‖ easy to drive ‖ docile, obedient, manageable.

MANEJAR.
v, to direct, administrate ‖ to rule, govern ‖ to order ‖ to drive ‖ to conduct or behave oneself (in a certain fashion).

MANEJO.
m, governance, administration, direction ‖ authority ‖ comportment, manner ‖ intrigue, machination ‖ driving, control (of a vehicle).

MANERA.
f, manner, way, form ‖ procedure, method ‖ system, style ‖ kind, sort, type.

MANERAS.
f, manners, customs, habits.

MANFERIDOR.
m, assay of weights and measures (carried out by a public official).

MANFERIR.
v, to assay weights, measures, coins, etc.

MANFLA.
f, concubine ‖ house of prostitution, bordello ‖ woman with whom one has illegal sexual relations.

MANFLOTA.
f, house of prostitution.

MANGA.
f, broadest part of a ship's beam.

MANGA ANCHA.
leniency, excessive tolerance.

MANGANILLO.
m, trick, ruse, fraud.

MANGAR.
v, to beg ‖ to steal ‖ to rob.

MANGAS.
f, benefits, profits ‖ extras, bonuses.

MANGO.
m, handle ‖ bill (of money).

MANGÓN.
m, retailer ‖ second-hand dealer.

MANGONEADA.
f, ruse, trick, fraud.

MANGONEAR.
v, to use excessive influence or be unscrupulous ‖ to profit from graft or other improper activity while in public office.

MANGONEO.
m, abuse of authority or influence while in public office, graft.

MANGONERO.
m, person who abuses his authority or influence while in public office.

MANÍA.
f, mania, obsession, fixation ‖ insanity ‖ ill will.

MANÍA PERSECUTORIA.
paranoia.

MANÍACO.
See MANIÁTICO.

MANIATAR.
v, to handcuff, manacle ‖ to tie (someone's hands) together.

MANIÁTICO.
m, maniac, obsessive person ‖ insane or crazy person ‖ adj, maniacle, obsessive ‖ crazy.

MANIBLAJ.
f, m, whorehouse servant.

MANICOMIO.
m, informal term for mental hospital ‖ insan or lunatic asylum, mad or crazy house.

MANICORTO.
m, tightwad.

MANIDA.
f, place of abode or residence.

MANIFACTURA.
See MANUFACTURA.

MANIFESTACIÓN.
f, manifestation, declaration (either written c oral) ‖ publication ‖ discovery, revelation confidence ‖ notification, communication sign, evidence, indication ‖ demonstratio public meeting, political rally.

MANIFESTACIÓN DE HERENCIA.
type of public probate document which ev dences the appearance of heirs, a literal co of the will, list of estate property, and certa parts of the law of wills. Must be signed by tv witnesses.

MANIFESTACIÓN DE LA VOLUNTAD.
manifestation of consent or desire.

MANIFESTACIÓN DE LOS LIBROS DEL REGISTRO.
public availability and display of the books the Real Estate Registry.

MANIFESTACIÓN DE VOLUNTAD MATRIMONIAL.
manifestation (offered before a public auth rity) of consent to marry.

MANIFESTACIÓN NAVAL.
naval confrontation of warships in territor waters of another country.

MANIFESTACIÓN POLÍTICA.
political demonstration or rally ‖ governme tal statement regarding politics.

MANIFESTACIONES NO PACÍFICAS.
non-peaceful demonstrations (usually pol cal).

MANIFESTADOR.
m, declarant, person who makes a stateme or declaration ‖ discoverer ‖ informer, accuse

MANIFESTANTE.
m, political demonstrator

MANIFESTAR.
v, to state, declare, manifest ‖ to make kno ‖ to publish, reveal ‖ to discover ‖ to confes to give testimony or evidence ‖ to refer ‖ show, demonstrate ‖ to communicate, noti

MANIFESTATIVO.
adj, susceptible to being shown or expressed or demonstrated.
MANIFIESTA.
adj, manifest.
MANIFIESTA TORPEZA.
obvious or manifest negligence ‖ manifestly tortious conduct.
MANIFIESTAMENTE.
adv, manifestly, evidently, clearly.
MANIFIESTO.
m, manifest, sea-letter (maritime law) ‖ testimony of a ship captain before a judge ‖ public statement or declaration ‖ manifesto, political manifesto ‖ government justification of action (usually of war or other similar measures) ‖ adj, evident, patent, clear, manifest ‖ discovered ‖ undeniable ‖ visible.
MANIFIESTO COMUNISTA.
Communist Manifesto.
MANIFIESTO DE EMBARQUE.
ship's manifest.
MANIGERO.
m, foreman of farm workers ‖ contractor of farm hands.
MANILARGO.
m, crook, robber, light-fingered person ‖ groper, man who takes indecent liberties with women ‖ adj, open-handed, generous.
MANILLA.
f, handcuff, manacle.
MANIOBRA.
f, handwork, work that is done by hand ‖ machination, maneuver‖ handling (of business).
MANIOBRAR.
v, to do hand work ‖ to maneuver, handle (a car, plane, etc. in tight spots) ‖ to conspire, be involved in an intrigue.
MANIPULACIÓN.
f, manipulation (of someone or something) ‖ handling.
MANIPULAR.
v, to manipulate ‖ to handle.
MANIPULEO.
m, special handling of certain affairs ‖ interference ‖ handling of goods.
MANIRROTO.
adj, m, spendthrift ‖ prodigal.
MANIVACÍO.
adj, empty-handed, tight-fisted.

MANO.
f, hand ‖ direction of traffic ‖ persons meeting for a special purpose ‖ means, element of obtaining a certain end ‖ person who carries something out or performs ‖ skill, ability ‖ government, rule ‖ help, assistance ‖ collaboration, backing, support ‖ punishment.
MANO ARMADA.
See A MANO ARMADA.
MANO DE HIERRO.
Literally, hand of steel ‖ hard-hand, big stick, tyranny, repression.
MANO DE JUSTICIA.
hand of justice.
MANO DE OBRA.
manual labor ‖ labor ‖ labor costs ‖ workforce (in the market).
MANO DERECHA.
right hand.
MANO DURA.
strong discipline ‖ cruel repression.
MANO FUERTE.
sheriff, martial, officer of the court who executes judicial orders. See MANO DURA.
MANO IZQUIERDA.
left hand.
MANO MUERTA.
See MANOS MUERTAS.
MANOS.
f, hands ‖ hands, manual labor.
MANOS LARGAS.
ready-fisted person, scrapper, brawler ‖ playboy.
MANOS LIBRES.
Literally, free hands ‖ person who owns property subject to no liens or incumbrances ‖ income obtained at a secondary job, moonlighting income.
MANOS LIMPIAS.
clean hands ‖ honesty, rectitude, integrity ‖ pay for extra hours.
MANOS MUERTAS.
dead hands ‖ owner of property (usually real property) who may not transfer it in any fashion.
MANOS PUERCAS.
illegal profits obtained from a position.
MANOSEAR.
v, to fondle, touch, handle, paw.
MANOSEO.
m, fondling, touching, handling, pawing.

MANOTADA.
f, slap ‖ blow, punch (with the hand).
MANOTAZO.
See MANOTADA.
MANOTEADO.
See MANOTADA.
MANOTEO.
See MANOTADA.
MANOTÓN.
See MANOTADA.
MANQUEDAD.
f, handlessness ‖ armlessness ‖ lack ‖ defect.
MANQUERA.
See MANQUEDAD.
MANSALVA.
adj, insurance, regarding insurance ‖ without any risk.
MANSO.
adj, meek, mild.
MANTENCIÓN.
see MANUTENCIÓN.
MANTENEDOR.
m, maintainer ‖ defender ‖ provider.
MANTENENCIA.
f, maintenance ‖ provision ‖ conservation, sustenance ‖ food.
MANTENER.
v, to maintain, provide for, support ‖ to conserve, sustain ‖ to defend, protect ‖ to support, uphold ‖ to maintain, keep up.
MANTENER LA PALABRA.
to keep an offer open over a period of time ‖ to persevere.
MANTENERSE.
v, to provide for, maintain oneself.
MANTENIDA.
f, kept woman, concubine.
MANTENIDO.
m, gigolo.
MANTENIENTE.
adj, with all one's might or strength.
MANTENIMIENTO.
m, maintenance, maintaining (of things, people, rights) ‖ support ‖ conservation (of things) ‖ defense, protection ‖ upkeep.
MANTENIMIENTO DE FAMILIA.
family maintenance or support.
MANTENIMIENTO DEL ORDEN PÚBLICO.
maintaining public order.

"MANU MILITARI".
by military force ‖ by armed force, violently ‖ with full force.
MANUABLE.
adj, manageable, handleable.
MANUAL.
m, manual ‖ appointment book ‖ notebook ‖ rough draft diary ‖ adj, manual ‖ hand-made.
MANUFACTURA.
f, manufactured good ‖ hand-made product ‖ machine-made product ‖ factory ‖ industry.
MANUFACTURACIÓN.
f, manufacturing.
MANUFACTURAR.
v, to manufacture, make ‖ to produce by mechanical means.
MANUFACTURERO.
adj, manufacturing, pertaining to manufactured goods.
MANUMISIÓN.
f, manumission, freeing of a slave ‖ release from one's power.
MANUMISO.
m, freed slave.
MANUMISOR.
m, person who frees a slave.
"MANUMISSIO".
See MANUMISIÓN.
MANUMITIR.
v, to emancipate, free from slavery ‖ to grant a release from one's power.
"MANUS".
manus, hand ‖ power.
MANUSCRIBIR.
v, to write by hand. Required in many countries for purposes of specially notarized documents, etc.
MANUSCRITO.
m, manuscript, book written by hand ‖ adj, hand written, written by hand.
MANUTENCIÓN.
f, food ‖ sustenance ‖ support ‖ expenses of feeding ‖ conservation ‖ defense ‖ protection of the possession.
MANUTENER.
v, to maintain, support (by law).
MANUVACÍO.
See MANIVACÍO.
MANZANA.
f, apple ‖ block (of houses or buildings).

MANZANA DE LA DISCORDIA.
bone of contention, heart of the discord or conflict.

MAÑA.
f, habit, mannerism.

MAÑANA.
f, morning, period before noon ‖ m, tomorrow ‖ future ‖ adv, tomorrow.

MAÑAS.
f, bad habits.

MAÑEAR.
v, to manage with skill or astuteness.

MAÑERÍA.
f, infertility, barrenness ‖ trick.

MAÑERO.
m, surety ‖ delegate for payment ‖ adj, astute ‖ tricky ‖ manageable, easy, facile.

MAÑOSAMENTE.
adv, skillfully, ably, with skill or ability ‖ cunningly, craftily.

MAÑOSO.
adj, skillful ‖ crafty, cunning.

MAÑUELAS.
f, cunning or crafty person.

MAOÍSMO.
m, Maoism.

MAPA.
m, map.

MAQUIAVÉLICO.
adj, Machiavellian.

MAQUIAVELISMO.
m, Machiavellianism.

MÁQUINA.
f, machine ‖ enormous building.

MÁQUINA DE ESCRIBIR.
typewriter.

MÁQUINA INFERNAL.
Literally, infernal machine ‖ home-made bomb.

MAQUINACIÓN.
f, machination ‖ conspiracy, plot.

MAQUINACIONES PARA ALTERAR LOS PRECIOS.
conspiracy to fix prices.

MAQUINADOR.
m, machinator, plotter, conspirator.

MAQUINAL.
adj, machine, pertaining to machines ‖ mechanical, automatic.

MAQUINALMENTE.
adv, without deliberation ‖ thoughtlessly ‖ unconsciously.

MAQUINAR.
v, to plot, conspire ‖ to fix prices.

MAQUINARIA.
f, machinery ‖ art of constructing machines, mechanics.

MAQUINISMO.
m, mechanization ‖ use of machines.

MAQUINISTA.
f, m, machinist, mechanic ‖ inventor of machines.

MAQUINISTA NAVAL.
naval mechanic or machinist.

MAR.
m, sea, ocean ‖ tide ‖ seas, oceans.

MAR ADYACENTE.
territorial or jurisdictional waters ‖ littoral waters.

MAR ANCHA.
open sea, high seas.

MAR EPICONTINENTAL.
epicontinental waters.

MAR JURISDICCIONAL.
See MAR ADYACENTE.

MAR LIBRE.
high seas.

MAR LITORAL.
See MAR ADYACENTE.

MAR TERRITORIAL.
See MAR ADYACENTE.

MARACA.
f, prostitute.

MARAÑA.
f, mess, entanglement ‖ lie, trick ‖ loose woman.

MARAÑAR.
v, to entangle ‖ to become entangled.

MARASMO.
m, stoppage, paralyzation of activities ‖ inactivity, apathy.

MARBETE.
m, label ‖ railway luggage identification tag or label.

MARCA.
f, trademark, brand ‖ mark ‖ branding, marking ‖ stamp, brand.

MARCA COLECTIVA.
collective trademark.

MARCA COMERCIAL.
See MARCA DE FÁBRICA.

MARCA DE COMERCIO.
See MARCA DE FÁBRICA.

MARCA DE FÁBRICA.
trademark, brand.
MARCA DE GANADO.
livestock brand.
MARCA DE MATRÍCULA AÉREA.
sign or mark which indicates the registration of an airplane in a country.
MARCA DE NACIONALIDAD AÉREA.
registration mark of an airplane.
MARCA DE POPA.
tail marking on a plane (indicating the name and nationality of the plane).
MARCA DE CALIDAD.
official approval as to quality.
MARCA FIGURATIVA.
symbol representative of a trademark.
MARCA INDUSTRIAL.
See MARCA DE FÁBRICA.
MARCA POLÍTICA.
political border (of a province or nation).
MARCA REGISTRADA.
registered trademark.
MARCADO.
adj, marked ‖ marked, pronounced ‖ disposed, ordered.
MARCADOR.
m, marker, brander, person who marks or brands.
MARCAR.
v, to take a ship's bearings ‖ to label ‖ to indicate, show ‖ to point out, emphasize ‖ to brand ‖ to make a signal ‖ to put a tail markings on a plane.
MARCARIO.
adj, pertaining to trademarks.
MARCIAL.
adj, martial, pertaining to war ‖ bellicose ‖ gallant, valiant.
MARCHA.
f, march ‖ departure ‖ transfer from one point to another ‖ round-trip ‖ road ‖ speed, velocity (of a vehicle) ‖ functioning, progress ‖ motion, function, operation.
MARCHA ATRÁS.
decadence ‖ reverse ‖ retraction.
MARCHAMAR.
v, to stamp goods which have been subject to customs inspection.
MARCHAMERO.
m, customs official who stamps goods as inspected.

MARCHAMO.
m, customs stamp of inspection.
MARCHANTE.
m, merchant, vendor ‖ trafficker, trader ‖ client ‖ regular client ‖ adj, commercial, mercantile.
MARCHAR.
v, to walk, march ‖ to travel ‖ to depart ‖ to start, go (in terms of a car) ‖ to proceed, progress ‖ to function, operate.
MARCHARSE.
v, to leave a place ‖ to abdicate, renounce.
MARE MÁGNUM.
m, confusion, disorder, chaos.
MAREA.
f, tide (of the oceans) ‖ sea shore.
MAREADOR.
m, counterfeit money changer, changer of counterfeit money for legal tender.
MAREAJE.
m, mariner's profession, seamanship ‖ nautical science, art of navigation ‖ ship's route.
MAREANTE.
m, seaman, mariner, navigator.
MAREAR.
v, to navigate, sail ‖ to helm a ship ‖ to sell, retail ‖ to send merchandise ‖ to bother, irritate, irk ‖ to be seasick ‖ to be dizzy.
MAREJADA.
f, agitation, discontent ‖ groundswell.
MAREMÁGNUM.
See MARE MÁGNUM.
MAREO.
m, dizziness ‖ seasickness ‖ bother, irritation, annoyance.
MARES
Y LAGOS INTERIORES.
landlocked lakes or seas.
MARETA.
f, agitation ‖ grumbling, murmuring (of a mass of people).
MARFUZ.
adj, lying, false ‖ repudiated.
MARGEN.
m, margin ‖ border, extremity ‖ coastal zone ‖ opportunity, occasion ‖ margin (of profit) ‖ profit (of a business).
MARGEN DE FLUCTUACIÓN.
margin of fluctuation or change (especially used in terms of the margin of fluctuation over or under the official exchange rate).

MARGINAL.
m, writings or notes in the margins of a document or book ‖ adj, marginal.

MARGINALIDAD.
f, marginality, living on or outside the margin of a social class.

MARGINAR.
v, to leave to the side ‖ to neglect someone ‖ to note in the margin (e.g. of books) ‖ to require the services of, collaborate ‖ to relegate, postpone.

MARICA.
m, homosexual ‖ pansy.

MARICÓN.
See MARICA.

MARIDABLE.
adj, marital, conjugal, matrimonial.

MARIDAJE.
m, marital ties or bonds ‖ union, tie, nexus (between things).

MARIDAR.
v, to marry, wed ‖ to live in matrimony ‖ to have sexual relations.

MARIDO.
m, husband, married man ‖ male consort.

MARIDO FINGIDO.
man who pretends to be a husband to an unwitting woman.

MARIGUANA.
See MARIHUANA.

MARIHUANA.
f, marijuana, marihuana.

MARIJUANA.
see MARIHUANA.

MARIMONERA.
f, quarrel, spat.

MARINA.
f, coast, seashore, shoreline ‖ seamanship ‖ navy ‖ naval personnel ‖ fleet ‖ flotilla ‖ naval forces ‖ merchant marine ‖ marine sciences ‖ adj, marine, naval.

MARINA DE GUERRA.
fleet of war ships ‖ navy.

MARINA MERCANTE.
merchant marine.

MARINAJE.
m, ship's crew, sailors.

MARINAR.
v, to set sail ‖ to put crew on board ‖ to take a ship.

MARINEAR.
v, to be a sailor.

MARINERADO.
adj, manned, outfitted (in terms of a ship's crew).

MARINERAJE.
See MARINERÍA.

MARINERAR.
v, to outfit a ship with necessary crew.

MARINERÍA.
f, seamanship ‖ group of sailors ‖ ship's crew.

MARINERO.
m, mariner, sailor, seaman ‖ navy man ‖ adj, naval, pertaining to the navy ‖ easily handled, seaworthy, well-balanced (in terms of a ship).

MARINESCO.
adj, pertaining to professional seamen.

MARINO.
m, nautical expert, navigator ‖ adj, marine, pertaining to the sea or naval war or navy.

MARIPOSEAR.
v, to flit about, be indecisive about one's future.

MARIPOSÓN.
See MARICA.

MARIQUITA.
See MARICA.

MARISCAL.
m, marshal (in the military).

MARISCAL DE CAMPO.
camp marshal.

MARISCALATO.
m, marshalcy ‖ rank of marshal ‖ body of all marshals of a country.

MARISCANTE.
m, thief, robber.

MARISCAR.
v, to steal, thieve, burgle.

MARISCO.
m, thief, robber, burglar.

MARISMA.
f, marsh ‖ salt-marsh.

MARITAL.
adj, marital, conjugal, matrimonial.

MARÍTIMO.
adj, maritime, concerning navigation ‖ pertaining to ocean-going commerce ‖ naval ‖ nautical ‖ coastal.

MARÍTIMOTERRESTRE.
adj, pertaining to the coastal or littoral areas.

MAROMERO.
m, political opportunist.

MARQUÉS.
m, marquis.

MARQUETA.
See DERECHO DE PERNADA.

MARRAJO.
m, astute person ‖ wily person, shark ‖ adj, wily, sly.

MARRAR.
v, to lack ‖ to err ‖ to go astray, deviate (from proper conduct).

MARRO.
m, lack, fault ‖ mistake, error.

MARTILLAR.
v, to oppress ‖ to torment, torture ‖ to hammer ‖ to sell at auction.

MARTILLERO.
m, auctioneer.

MARTILLERO JUDICIAL.
judicial auctioneer, auctioneer who carries out judicial auctions.

MARTILLO.
m, hammer ‖ persecutor, oppressor ‖ tormentor, torturer ‖ exterminator ‖ auction house or room.

MARXISMO.
m, Marxism.

MÁS ADELANTE.
farther ‖ further ‖ hereinafter.

MASA.
f, mass ‖ humanity ‖ the masses or people ‖ estate, totality of property (used in reference to wills, bankruptcies, and corporations).

MASA DE BIENES.
estate, totality of property.

MASA DE LA HERENCIA.
See MASA HEREDITARIA.

MASA DE LA QUIEBRA.
bankruptcy estate, bankrupt's estate, estate in bankruptcy.

MASA DE LAS PRUEBAS.
totality of the evidence.

MASA FALLIDA.
See MASA DE LA QUIEBRA.

MASA HEREDITARIA.
decedent's estate.

MASA SOCIAL.
social masses (of people) ‖ corporate assets.

MASACRAR.
v, to massacre, kill, slaughter.

MASACRE.
f, massacre.

MÁSCARA.
f, mask, costume ‖ pretext, excuse.

MASCULINIDAD.
f, masculinity.

MASCULINO.
adj, masculine, male ‖ manly.

MASÓN.
m, Mason, Freemason.

MASONERÍA.
f, Masonry.

MASOQUISMO.
m, masochism.

MASOQUISTA.
f, m, masochist.

MATADERO.
m, slaughterhouse ‖ dirty or exhausting job.

MATAMIENTO.
m, suicide ‖ murder.

MATANTE.
m, killer, murderer ‖ slaughterer ‖ adj, killing

MATANZA.
f, murder, killing ‖ slaughter, massacre slaughtering.

MATANZA INÚTIL.
killing of soldiers who have surrendered Usually considered to be a crime.

MATANZAS COLECTIVAS.
mass killings or murders.

MATAR.
v, to kill, murder ‖ to exhaust, crush ‖ to extin guish ‖ to destroy, annihilate. This include patricide, matricide, homicide, fratricide, i fanticide, abortion, assassination, etc.

MATARSE.
v, to commit suicide, kill oneself ‖ to kill on self working, work excessively.

MATASELLOS.
m, post office cancelling stamp.

MATATÍAS.
m, usurer ‖ loan shark ‖ exploiter.

"MATER FAMILIAS".
mother of the family, woman of the hous hold.

MATERIA.
f, matter, activity, business ‖ substance, co tents ‖ object ‖ cause, motive ‖ subject, top theme ‖ adj, material, physical, not abstract

MATERIA DE AUTOS.
See MATERIA DE REGISTRO.

MATERIA DE ESTADO.
activity of the State.
MATERIA DE REGISTRO.
matter of record, matter which is in the court record.
MATERIA IMPOSITIVA.
tax matter.
MATERIA MONETARIA.
monetary or money matter.
MATERIA PRIMA.
raw material.
MATERIAL.
m, material || substance || equipment (needed for a work) || adj, material, regarding matter || mundane, ordinary || physical.
MATERIAL INCOMBUSTIBLE.
non-combustible material.
MATERIAL NUCLEAR.
nuclear matter or substance.
MATERIAL PROCESAL.
subject matter of a suit.
MATERIALES.
m, materials || equipment, supplies.
MATERIALES DE CONSTRUCCIÓN.
construction materials, materials of construction.
MATERIALIDAD.
f, materiality.
MATERIALISMO.
m, materialism.
MATERIALISMO HISTÓRICO.
m, historical materialism || materialistic interpretation or conception of history.
MATERIALIZAR.
v, to materialize || to firm up, make concrete || to carry out a project || to put into practise.
MATERIALMENTE.
adv, materially.
MATERIAS CORROSIVAS.
corrosive materials.
MATERIAS INFLAMABLES.
inflammables, inflammable substances.
MATERNAL.
adj, maternal.
MATERNALMENTE.
adv, maternally.
MATERNIDAD.
f, maternity hospital || maternity, motherhood. May be LEGÍTIMA (legitimate) or ILEGÍTIMA (illegitimate).

MATERNIDAD NATURAL.
motherhood of an illegitimate child (fathered by either a married or unmarried man).
MATERNO.
adj, maternal, pertaining to the mother || mother (in reference to native language).
MATÓN.
m, bully.
MATONISMO.
m, bullying, overbearing, domineeringly threatening.
MATRERO.
m, highwayman || shrewdness, cunning || fugitive from justice (who hides in the mountains) || shrewd or cunning person.
MATRIARCADO.
m, matriarchy.
MATRIARCAL.
adj, matriarchal.
MATRICIDA.
f, m, matricide, person who kills his/her mother.
MATRICIDIO.
m, matricide, murder of one's mother.
MATRÍCULA.
f, register, list, roster, roll (in a registry) || listing, registration, inscription (on a list usually of professionals or students); matriculation, entrance, enrollment (in a university) || registration number of a vehicle || matriculation certificate || matriculation fee.
MATRÍCULA DE AERONAVES.
airplane registration || airplane registration certificate and letters.
MATRÍCULA DE AUTOMOTORES.
automobile registration || automobile registration certificate.
MATRÍCULA DE BUQUES.
ship registration, register of merchant ships.
MATRÍCULA DE COMERCIO.
business register, register where all persons engaged in business must be registered.
MATRÍCULA DE LOS COMERCIANTES.
See MATRÍCULA DE COMERCIO.
MATRÍCULA DE MAR.
seamen's register || enlistment of seamen.
MATRICULADO.
m, enlisted seaman || adj, matriculated, inscribed, enlisted, registered.
MATRICULADOR.
m, registrar, matriculator.

MATRICULAR.
v, to matriculate, enlist, enroll, register.

MATRICULARSE.
v, to enlist or register or enroll oneself ‖ to order or request another to register on one's behalf ‖ to sign up for a pedagogical course or the relevant examination.

MATRIMONIAL.
adj, matrimonial, pertaining to matrimony, married life, or the spouses.

MATRIMONIALMENTE.
adv, matrimonially.

MATRIMONIAR.
v, to marry, wed.

MATRIMONIARSE.
v, to marry, get married, wed.

MATRIMONIO.
m, marriage, matrimony ‖ married couple.

MATRIMONIO A PRUEBA.
temporary or trial cohabitation to determine whether or not to marry.

MATRIMONIO A YURAS.
See MATRIMONIO CLANDESTINO.

MATRIMONIO ADOLESCENTE.
child marriage, marriage between a female of 15 to 17 years of age and a male of 17 to 19 years of age.

MATRIMONIO APARENTE.
common law or non-formalized marriage . See MATRIMONIO PUTATIVO.

MATRIMONIO ATENTADO.
marriage invalid due to defect or other impediment.

MATRIMONIO CANÓNICO.
religious marriage, church wedding, marriage performed pursuant to requirements of the Church. In most civil law countries, a religious marriage has no legal effect and a civil marriage must take place as well or in its stead.

MATRIMONIO CIVIL.
civil marriage, civil wedding, wedding performed before a government official pursuant to State law. In most civil law countries this is the only form of legal marriage, as the separate marriages carried out by Church officials have no legal effect. In most common law countries, church weddings serve to marry a couple for all civil legal purposes.

MATRIMONIO CLANDESTINO.
elopement.

MATRIMONIO CON LA OFENDIDA.
marriage of a raped woman to her rapist. In many civil law countries a woman who has been raped or deflowered as a minor has the option of requiring the offender to marry her, in which case the offense becomes unpunishable.

MATRIMONIO CON SEPARACIÓN DE BIENES.
marriage in which the spouses continue to hold their estates separately. May occur VOLUNTARIAMENTE (by agreement), COMO SANCIÓN PENAL (as a criminal punishment), or JUDICIALMENTE (by court order).

MATRIMONIO CONCERTADO Y NO CELEBRADO.
marriage agreed upon but not carried out.

MATRIMONIO CONSENSUAL.
common-law marriage.

MATRIMONIO CONSUMADO.
consummated marriage.

MATRIMONIO DE HECHO.
See MATRIMONIO CONSENSUAL.

MATRIMONIO DE LA MANO IZQUIERDA
See MATRIMONIO MORGANÁTICO.

MATRIMONIO DE MIXTA RELIGIÓN.
marriage between persons of different faiths.

MATRIMONIO DE OPINIÓN.
See MATRIMONIO PUTATIVO.

MATRIMONIO DE REPUTACIÓN.
See MATRIMONIO PUTATIVO.

MATRIMONIO DEL MILITAR.
military marriage. May be subject to differen or less strict requirements.

MATRIMONIO EN AERONAVE.
marriage performed in an airplane.

MATRIMONIO EN BUQUE.
ship-board marriage.

MATRIMONIO EN EL EXTRANJERO.
foreign marriage, marriage performed outside the country of citizenship of one or both of the parties.

MATRIMONIO ENTRE PERSONAS DE RAZAS DISTINTAS.
(racially) mixed marriage.

MATRIMONIO ILEGAL.
illegal marriage, marriage performed in violation of the law. May result in the nullity of the marriage and in the imposition of crimina sanctions.

MATRIMONIO IN ARTÍCULO MORTIS.
marriage in articulo mortis, marriage under imminent fear of death of one or both of the parties. May be performed subject to fewer formalities.

MATRIMONIO IN EXTREMIS.
See MATRIMONIO IN ARTÍCULO MORTIS.

MATRIMONIO INEXISTENTE.
See INEXISTENCIA DEL MATRIMONIO.

MATRIMONIO INSTAURADO.
once putative marriage the disabilities of which have been cured.

MATRIMONIO LEGÍTIMO.
legal marriage || legal wedding, wedding which is carried out pursuant to law.

MATRIMONIO MORGANÁTICO.
morganatic marriage, marriage between persons of different social positions.

MATRIMONIO NATURAL.
See MATRIMONIO CONSENSUAL.

MATRIMONIO NULO.
null marriage.

MATRIMONIO POLÍGAMO.
polygamous marriage.

MATRIMONIO POR PODER.
marriage by power of attorney, marriage by proxy.

MATRIMONIO PUTATIVO.
putative marriage, marriage celebrated despite a nullifying impediment.

MATRIMONIO RATO.
unconsummated marriage.

MATRIMONIO SECRETO.
secret marriage, secret wedding.

MATRIMONIO SIN RÉGIMEN DETERMINADO DE BIENES.
marriage in which there has been no prior property agreement between the couple.

MATRIMONIO TEMPORAL.
See MATRIMONIO A PRUEBA || dissolved marriage.

MATRIZ.
f, headquarters || head office, main office || original, principal, chief || checkbook stub.

MATRONA.
f, matron || mother of the family || mid-wife || female inspector who carries out body searches on women when required.

MATRONÍMICO.
adj, derived from the name of the maternal side of the family.

MATURRANGA.
f, street walker || trickery.

MATUTE.
m, black market goods, products sold in violation of law || smuggling.

MATUTEAR.
v, to sell on the black market || to smuggle.

MATUTERO.
m, smuggler, black-market dealer.

MATUTINO.
adj, morning, pertaining to the morning.

MAULA.
m, useless object || fraud, trick || cheat || adj, informal || negligent || lazy.

MAULERO.
m, trickster, defrauder.

MÁXIMA.
f, maxim, principle, axiom || saying.

MÁXIMAS DE EXPERIENCIA.
principles arising out of judgments which are similar.

MÁXIMAS PROCESALES.
procedural principles.

MÁXIMO.
m, maximum, extreme, limit, highest || highest price || adj, maximum, extreme, limit.

MÁXIMUM.
m, maximum, extreme limit, highest || highest price.

MAYOR.
m, boss, superior || chief executive || name of certain court officers (e.g. chief clerk) || major (in the Armed Forces) || adj, great, major || older (person), middle-aged || greater, bigger, larger || largest, biggest || main, principal || adult, of age.

MAYOR CUANTÍA.
major claim || plenary lawsuit (carried out without prescribing time periods or other procedural restrictions). Usually this is used in cases in which the amount of money is high or matter in question is important. Opposed to MENOR CUANTÍA.

MAYOR DE EDAD.
of age, adult.

MAYOR EDAD.
adulthood, majority || old or older age.

MAYOR GENERAL.
major general (of Armed Forces).

MAYOR VALÍA.
increase in value (due to extraneous circumstances).

MAYORA.
major's wife.

MAYORAL.
m, hospital administrator ‖ mayor (of a town).

MAYORAZGA.
f, first born female (who enjoys the rights of primogeniture) ‖ female heir (who enjoys the rights of primogeniture) ‖ wife of a MAYORAZGO. See MAYORAZGO.

MAYORAZGO.
m, first born male (who enjoys the rights of primogeniture) ‖ primogeniture ‖ estate inherited by first born ‖ owner of such estate. Although this institution was once in frequent use, it has fallen into distinct disfavor, and in most countries has been replaced by a system of inheritance which is more equitable to all of the children in a family.

MAYORAZGO ALTERNATIVO.
life estate granted to primogeniture and upon his death to another son.

MAYORAZGO DE AGNACIÓN ARTIFICIAL.
primogeniture estate granted to person who is not a first born male but is so named.

MAYORAZGO DE AGNACIÓN ARTIFICIOSA.
See MAYORAZGO DE AGNACIÓN ARTIFICIAL.

MAYORAZGO DE AGNACIÓN FINGIDA.
See MAYORAZGO DE AGNACIÓN ARTIFICIAL.

MAYORAZGO DE AGNACIÓN RIGUROSA.
primogeniture estate which is granted to first born male exclusively.

MAYORAZGO DE AGNACIÓN VERDADERA.
See MAYORAZGO DE AGNACIÓN RIGUROSA.

MAYORAZGO DE FEMINEIDAD.
primogeniture estate which is granted to females exclusively.

MAYORAZGO DE MASCULINIDAD.
primogeniture estate which is granted to males exclusively.

MAYORAZGO DE SEGUNDOGENITURA.
estate which is granted from second born to second born.

MAYORAZGO ELECTIVO.
estate which permits the owner to chose his or her heir.

MAYORAZGO INCOMPATIBLE.
primogeniture estate which is incompatible with the inheritance of another estate.

MAYORAZGO PERPETUO.
perpetual estate of primogeniture, estate which may only be granted to a first-born, except in the case that there is no off-spring, in which case the estate may be granted to anyone.

MAYORAZGO REGULAR.
ordinary primogeniture. This implies transmission first to the eldest son, then to his eldest son or barring this to his eldest daughter, and barring this to the second-born son and his off-spring.

MAYORAZGO SALTUARIO.
de facto holder of an estate of primogeniture, by reason of his having all the qualities required of a primogeniture except that of being first born.

MAYORAZGO TEMPORAL.
primogeniture estate subject to conditions, after which the estate is held without limitation.

MAYORAZGUISTA.
f, person who writes about primogeniture, regarding its historical, social, legal and economic aspects.

MAYORDOMEAR.
v, to administrate, rule, govern (e.g. a thing or estate).

MAYORDOMÍA.
f, position, functions, office of MAYORDOMO ‖ administration, government.

MAYORDOMO.
m, mayordomo, owner of an estate ‖ foreman, overseer (e.g. of an estate, house, ranch) ‖ member of a group which is to administer the spending of funds ‖ brother (of a brotherhood).

MAYORES.
m, grandparents ‖ forefathers ‖ elders.

MAYORÍA.
f, quality of being greater ‖ adult ‖ majority, adulthood ‖ majority (of votes or persons) ‖ office of MAYOR ‖ generality ‖ predominant public opinion.

MAYORÍA ABSOLUTA.
absolute majority (of votes) (i.e. over 50%)

MAYORÍA CALIFICADA.
qualified majority (i.e. requiring more than 50%).

MAYORÍA DE CANTIDAD.
majority in number (taking into account the interest of each voter).
MAYORÍA DE DOS TERCIOS.
majority of two-thirds.
MAYORÍA DE EDAD.
adulthood, majority.
MAYORÍA RELATIVA.
relative majority (i.e. although not over 50%, that which received the most votes).
MAYORÍA SILENCIOSA.
silent majority.
MAYORIDAD.
f, majority, adulthood ‖ superiority.
MAYORISTA.
m, wholesaler, wholesale.
MAYORITARIO.
m, majority ‖ adj, majority, pertaining to a majority.
MAYORMENTE.
adv, majorly, principally ‖ especially ‖ much.
MAYÚSCULA.
f, capital letter ‖ capital (letter) ‖ adj, enormous, large (especially as applied to blunders or mistakes).
MAZADA.
f, blow, hit (with a mace or club).
MAZAGATOS.
m, difficult situation ‖ quarrel, fight, row.
MAZAZO.
See MAZADA.
MAZMORRA.
f, dungeon, underground cell or enclosure.
MAZO.
m, bulk sale goods ‖ group of goods which are sold together ‖ bother, pest.
MAZORCA.
f, despotic government ‖ persons who form a despotic government.
MAZORQUERO.
m, member of a despotic government or a tyranny.
"MEA CULPA".
mea culpa, due to my fault.
MECÁNICO.
adj, mechanical ‖ low, disdainful ‖ involuntary, automatic.
MECANISMO.
m, mechanism ‖ organization, system.
MECANOGRAFÍA.
f, typewriting, typing.

MECANOGRAFIAR.
v, to type, write by typewriter.
MECHERA.
f, shoplifter.
MEDALLA.
f, medal, medallion.
MEDIA FIRMA.
signature of last name only.
MEDIA GANANCIA.
sharecropping by which the sharecropper gives half of the produce to the owner during the term of the agreement.
MEDIA HERMANA.
half-sister.
MEDIA PARTE.
half (of a whole) ‖ advance of half of the salary or pay.
MEDIA SANCIÓN.
passage of bill in a bicameral congress, by one chamber.
MEDIA VIDA.
50% depreciation ‖ half life ‖ prolonged dedication to something ‖ lengthy stay in a place where one was not born.
MEDIA VUELTA.
U-turn ‖ turn-about ‖ retreat, fall back ‖ change of mind or opinions.
MEDIACIÓN.
f, conciliation, mediation ‖ intercession ‖ complicity ‖ assistance as a third party to a contract ‖ pimping.
MEDIACIÓN INTERNACIONAL.
international mediation of a conflict.
MEDIACIÓN LABORAL.
labor mediation. Describes state of affairs between informal attempts at reconciliation and formal arbitration, reconciliation and arbitration.
MEDIACIÓN MERCANTIL.
middleman work, work of commissioned intermediary who assists in arranging or putting together commercial transactions, but does not act as their agent.
MEDIADO.
m, person who has half of something.
MEDIADOR.
m, mediator ‖ middleman ‖ conciliator, reconciler ‖ commissioned agent ‖ accomplice ‖ pimp ‖ international negotiator or mediator.
MEDIANERA.
See PARED MEDIANERA.

MEDIANERÍA.
f, dividing or common wall (between two houses or buildings || joint ownership of a partition or dividing wall.

MEDIANERO.
m, each of the owners of a dividing wall || person who divides agricultural produce with another person by halves || middle-class person || adj, situated in the middle || owned by neighbors. See MEDIADOR.

MEDIANTE.
adj, intervening || interceding || adv, by means of, through.

MEDIANTE ESCRITURA.
by a written instrument || by deed.

MEDIAR.
v, to do half of something || to have time pass || to intercede, plead || to reconcile || to mediate (e.g. in an international conflict).

MEDIAS PALABRAS.
insinuation || insincere or incomplete statement.

MEDIAS TINTAS.
half-way, wishy-washy.

MEDIATAMENTE.
adv, indirectly || distantly (in time).

MEDIATIZAR.
v, to give up sovereignty of a lesser state to a foreign state.

MEDIATO.
adj, related in time or space (although not closely). Opposed to INMEDIATO (immediate).

MEDIBLE.
adj, measurable || appraisable, able to be valued.

MÉDICA.
f, female doctor or physician || wife of a doctor or physician.

MEDICAMENTO.
m, medicine, remedy.

MEDICINA.
f, medicine, science of medicine || medicine, remedy.

MEDICINA DEL TRABAJO.
work medicine, science of medicine which deals with work-related health problems.

MEDICINA FORENSE.
forensic medicine.

MEDICINA LEGAL.
forensic medicine.

MEDICINAL.
adj, medicinal || medical, pertaining to medicine.

MEDICINANTE.
m, quack, witch doctor || medical intern (i.e. student who without being a full doctor, practices medicine || may or may not be legal).

MEDICIÓN.
f, measurement.

MÉDICO.
m, doctor, physician || adj, pertaining to doctors.

MÉDICO DE APELACIÓN.
specialist, consulting doctor.

MÉDICO DE CABECERA.
family doctor.

MÉDICO FORENSE.
forensic doctor || coroner.

MÉDICO LEGISTA.
expert in medical law.

MEDICUCHO.
m, unskilled doctor.

MEDIDA.
f, measure, step || act of measuring || determination of measurement || measurer, object used to measure || precaution || limit, moderation.

MEDIDA CAUTELAR.
interim or precautionary measure (in a case, e.g. preliminary injunction, order of sequestration).

MEDIDA DE FUERZA.
forceful means, means of force || strike.

MEDIDA DE LOS DAÑOS.
measure of damages.

MEDIDA SUPERFICIAL DE LAS FINCAS.
measurement of property.

MEDIDAMENTE.
adv, carefully, with moderation or caution.

MEDIDAS CAUTELARES.
See MEDIDAS CONSERVATIVAS.

MEDIDAS CONSERVATIVAS.
precautionary measures or steps , measures to preserve something during the pendency of a legal action. Includes, among others, INVENTARIO, FIANZA, CAUCIÓN, GARANTÍA, RESERVA, RETENCIÓN, EMBARGO, DEPÓSITO, RESERVA DE DERECHO, HIPOTECA, PRENDA, CLÁUSULA PENAL.

MEDIDAS DE PREVISIÓN.
precautionary measure (in a case, e.g. preliminary injunction, order of sequestration).

MEDIDAS DE SEGURIDAD.
security measures.
MEDIDAS EDUCATIVAS.
See MEDIDAS TUTELARES.
MEDIDAS JURÍDICAS.
See MEDIDAS LEGALES.
MEDIDAS LEGALES.
legal measures or steps.
**MEDIDAS PARA
MEJOR PROVEER.**
See DILIGENCIAS PARA MEJOR PROVEER.
MEDIDAS PREVENTIVAS.
preventive measures or steps.
MEDIDAS PROTECTORAS.
See MEDIDAS TUTELARES.
**MEDIDAS
TUTELARES.**
measures or steps regarding guardianship (taken in order to prevent or stop on-going juvenile delinquency).
MEDIDO.
adj, measured || subject to limits.
MEDIDOR.
m, person who measures || surveyor || measuring apparatus or device.
**MEDIDOR DE
TIERRAS.**
surveyor.
MEDIERÍA.
f, sharecropping.
MEDIERO.
m, person who divides agricultural produce with another person by halves || also see TERCERÍA.
MEDIO.
m, center || recourse, element || procedure || means || moderation || social status || social sector || adj, half, fifty percent || average, mean || twin.
MEDIO FLETE.
half shipload || half freight || half rate.
MEDIO HERMANO.
half brother.
MEDIO LUTO.
final stage of mourning.
MEDIO SOCIAL.
social status.
MEDIO TÉRMINO.
See TÉRMINO MEDIO.
MEDIOS.
m, means || steps || economic resources.

MEDIOS COMPULSORIOS.
requisite or compulsory legal means || requisite or compulsory legal steps.
MEDIOS DE COMUNICACIÓN.
means of communication || media.
MEDIOS DE DERECHO.
legal mean || legal steps.
MEDIOS DE PRUEBA.
means of proof. Includes, among others, INSPECCIÓN OCULAR, CONFESIÓN, TESTIMONIO, INFORME PERICIAL, DOCUMENTO PÚBLICO, DOCUMENTO PRIVADO, PRESUN-CIÓN, INDICIO, ANTECEDENTE (DE REGISTROS PÚBLICO), ATESTADO.
MEDIOS DE PUBLICIDAD.
publicity, means of publicizing || advertising media.
MEDIOS DE VIDA.
means of existence || means of livelihood.
MEDIOS ECONÓMICOS.
financial resources || financial means.
MEDIOS FRAUDULENTOS.
false pretenses.
MEDIOS LEGALES.
legal steps or measure || legal means.
MEDIOS Y ARBITRIOS.
ways and means.
MEDIQUILLO.
m, quack, unqualified doctor.
MEDIR.
v, to measure || to compare.
MEDIRSE.
v, to limit oneself || to compete with, rival (someone).
MEDRANA.
f, fear, fright.
MEDRAR.
v, to grow animals or plants || to improve one's fortune || to progress.
MEDRO.
m, growth, betterment, increase, progress.
MEDROSO.
adj, fearful, scared || timid.
MÉDULA DEL DERECHO.
f, essential element of law.
MEFISTOFÉLICO.
adj, Mephistophelean, demonic || perverse.
MEGALOMANÍA.
f, megalomania.
MEJOR.
m, best || adj, better, superior.

MEJOR COMPRADOR.
See PACTO DE MEJOR COMPRADOR.

MEJOR FORTUNA.
better fortune.

MEJOR POSTOR.
winning bidder, highest (or lowest) bidder.

MEJOR PROVEER.
See DILIGENCIAS PARA MEJOR PROVEER.

MEJORA.
f, benefit, advantage ‖ improvement ‖ progress ‖ benefit, advantage ‖ higher bid ‖ support and basis of an appeal ‖ increase in price ‖ bequest of more than that legally prescribed to those who by law must receive a proportion of an inheritance.

MEJORA DE APELACIÓN.
appeal setting forth its bases.

MEJORA DE PERTENENCIAS.
development of mining claims.

MEJORA DEL EMBARGO.
expansion of the terms of a writ of attachment, for failure of the prior writ to adequately cover the judgment or loan in full.

MEJORA HEREDITARIA.
bequest in excess of that given to others ‖ bequest of more than that legally prescribed to those who by law must receive a proportion of an inheritance ‖ those goods taken from the TERCIO DE MEJORA and given in addition to a person who by law must inherit a given proportion.

MEJORA INOFICIOSA.
illegal bequest (in that it exceeds that legally allowed).
See HEREDERO FORZOSO.

MEJORA PATRIMONIAL.
economic benefit.

MEJORA PERMANENTE.
permanent improvement.

MEJORA TÁCITA.
bequest of more than that legally prescribed to those who by law must receive a proportion of an inheritance, without expressing that such proportion has been exceeded.

MEJORADO.
m, person who receives a MEJORA HEREDITARIA ‖ adj, improved, bettered ‖ progressed ‖ increased ‖ outbid.

MEJORADOR.
m, person who improves something or makes an improvement (e.g. a patent).

MEJORANTE.
See MEJORADOR.

MEJORAMIENTO.
m, betterment, improvement ‖ act of bettering or improving.

MEJORAR.
v, to improve, better ‖ to progress ‖ to increase ‖ to recover one's health ‖ to outbid, raise or up (a bid) ‖ to better one's social, economic, or professional position ‖ to bequeath a MEJORA HEREDITARIA.

MEJORAR UN EMBARGO.
to extend an attachment or garnishment to additional property.

MEJORAS.
f, improvements (to a house or thing for its preservation, betterment or otherwise). May be NECESARIAS (indispensable), ÚTILES (useful), or VOLUNTARIAS (voluntary).

MEJORÍA.
f, progress, advancement ‖ improvement in health ‖ superiority.

MELANCOLÍA.
f, melancholy.

MELANCÓLICO.
m, melancholic person ‖ adj, melancholic.

MELLA.
f, prejudice ‖ impression, notch.

MELLAR.
v, to cause damage or injury.

MELLIZO.
m, twin ‖ adj, twin (brother or sister).

MEMBRETE.
m, letterhead (paper) ‖ name and address (whether at the bottom or the top of the paper) ‖ memorandum or note of something which includes only the most important of the document referred to.

MEMORANDO.
See MEMORÁNDUM.

MEMORÁNDUM.
m, memorandum ‖ diary, date book, memo book ‖ memorandum, less formal diplomatic communication.

MEMORIA.
f, memory ‖ fame, glory, celebrity ‖ reputation, name, opinion ‖ commemoration ‖ annual report (of a corporation) ‖ study, dissertation ‖ type of inventory ‖ expense report codicil (of a will).

MEMORIA ANUAL.
annual report (of a corporation).
MEMORIA DE ACCIDENTE.
accident report.
**MEMORIA DE
LOS MUERTOS.**
reputation of the dead.
MEMORIA ELECTRÓNICA.
electronic memory.
MEMORIA TESTAMENTARIA.
codicil (of a will).
MEMORIAL.
m, legal brief provided an appellate court ‖ document requesting something and providing the reasons and bases therefore ‖ notebook ‖ official bulletin or newsletter which is issued regularly, but not with frequency.
MEMORIAS.
f, memoirs.
MENAJE.
m, household furniture and housewares.
MENCIÓN.
f, mention (of a person or thing).
MENCIÓN REGISTRAL.
reference or mention or annotation of real or personal property in a real estate registry filing pertaining to different personal or real property.
MENCIONAR.
v, to mention, indicate ‖ to name, refer to.
MENDACIDAD.
f, mendacity, habit of lying ‖ lying.
MENDACIO.
m, lie ‖ error ‖ errata.
MENDICIDAD.
f, mendacity, mendicancy.
MENDIGANTE.
m, mendicant, beggar.
MENDIGAR.
v, to beg.
MENDIGO.
m, beggar ‖ pauper, indigent.
MENDIGUEZ.
m, begging.
MENDOSO.
m, liar ‖ adj, mistaken.
MENEAR.
v, to manage, rule, govern ‖ to direct an establishment ‖ to take care of a matter.
MENEARSE.
v, to proceed with extreme diligence.

MENESTER.
m, need or lack (of something) ‖ occupation, position ‖ duty, charge.
MENESTEROSO.
m, beggar ‖ pauper, indigent ‖ adj, needy, poor, impoverished.
MENGANO.
m, Joe Blow ‖ any Tom, Dick, or Harry.
MENGUA.
f, consumption, use ‖ lessening, diminution ‖ decadence ‖ lack of something (necessary to be whole or right) ‖ necessity, misery ‖ scarcity ‖ dishonor, discredit, disgrace.
MENGUADAMENTE.
adv, without honor ‖ with cowardice.
MENGUADO.
adj, cowardly ‖ timid, shy ‖ stupid, foolish ‖ stingy, miserly.
MENGUAMIENTO.
See MENGUA.
MENGUANTE.
m, decadence, decrease, diminution ‖ adj, decreasing, diminishing.
MENGUAR.
v, to diminish, lessen.
MENOR.
m, minor, underage person ‖ adj, smaller, lesser ‖ fewer, reduced ‖ inferior ‖ younger.
MENOR ADULTO.
young adult, adolescent. Usually a person between the 14 and 21 years of age.
MENOR COMERCIANTE.
businessman who is under the age of 18 or under 21, depending on the legal system .
MENOR CUANTÍA.
small claim, litigation of a smaller amount which permits summary proceedings to be used.
**MENOR
DE EDAD.**
minor, underage person.
MENOR EDAD.
minority ‖ young age.
MENOR EMANCIPADO.
emancipated minor, minor who is not legally subject to parental control.
MENOR IMPÚBER.
minor below the age of puberty.
MENOR NO EMANCIPADO.
minor who is legally subject to parental control.

MENORIDAD.
f, minority.

MENOS.
adj, less, minor ‖ least, fewest.

MENOSCABADOR.
m, person who diminishes or deteriorates (something).

MENOSCABAR.
v, to reduce, diminish ‖ to deteriorate ‖ to damage ‖ to discredit, dishonor, defame.

MENOSCABO.
m, reduction, diminution, decrease ‖ deterioration ‖ damage ‖ discredit, dishonor, defamation.

MENOSPRECIO.
m, undervaluation, underrating ‖ contempt, scorn.

MENOSPRECIO DE MERCANCÍAS.
disparagement of merchandise.

"MENS REA".
mens rea.

MENSAJE.
m, (oral) message ‖ dispatch ‖ communication ‖ communication between two chambers of a congress or parliament.

MENSAJERA.
f, errand girl.

MENSAJERÍA.
f, message service ‖ private or informal postal or courier service.

MENSAJERO.
m, messenger ‖ errand boy.

MENSUAL.
adj, monthly, by month ‖ for a month.

MENSUALIDAD.
f, monthly salary or wage ‖ monthly allowance.

MENSUALIZACIÓN.
f, conversion to a salary paid by month.

MENSUALMENTE.
adv, each month, monthly ‖ by months.

MENSURA.
f, measurement.

MENSURADOR.
m, surveyor ‖ measurer, person who measures.

MENSURAR.
v, to measure ‖ to consider, judge.

MENTAL.
adj, mental, intellectual, psychological, abstract.

MENTALIDAD.
f, mentality.

MENTALMENTE.
adv, mentally.

MENTAR.
v, to name, cite, mention.

MENTECATEZ.
f, mental deficiency, stupidity.

MENTIDO.
adj, lying, tricking ‖ deceptive, false.

MENTIR.
v, to lie ‖ to pretend ‖ to trick ‖ to falsify ‖ to break a promise or agreement.

MENTIRA.
f, lie, deception, falsehood, falsification ‖ trick, fiction.

MENTIROSAMENTE.
adv, falsely, deceitfully.

MENTIROSO.
m, liar, fibber ‖ adj, false, untrue.

MENTIS.
m, flat denial (of an accusation or affirmation).

MENUDAMENTE.
adv, in detail.

MENUDO.
m, coin, coinage ‖ adj, in detail ‖ small ‖ of little importance.

MEQUETREFE.
m, meaningless or useless person ‖ adj, useless.

MERCA.
f, purchase.

MERCACHIFLE.
m, peddler.

MERCADANTE.
See MERCADER.

MERCADEAR.
v, to trade, deal, do business.

MERCADEO.
m, commerce, trade, business ‖ marketing.

MERCADER.
m, merchant, vendor, businessman, trader.

MERCADER DE CALLE.
street vendor.

MERCADER DE GRUESO.
wholesaler.

MERCADERA.
f, female merchant or vendor or trader ‖ businesswoman ‖ wife of a merchant.

MERCADERÍA.
f, merchandise, goods, products, wares.

MERCADO.
m, market ‖ market-place ‖ merchandising ‖ merchants in a market ‖ item purchased ‖ purchasing country.

MERCADO A TÉRMINO.
futures market.

MERCADO ABIERTO.
free or open market.

MERCADO AL CONTADO.
cash market.

MERCADO COMÚN.
common market.

MERCADO COMÚN EUROPEO.
European Common Market.

MERCADO DE CAPITALES.
capital market, long-term loan market.

MERCADO DE COMPRADORES.
buyers' market.

MERCADO DE CRÉDITO.
credit or loan or debt market.

MERCADO DE DESCUENTO.
discount market.

MERCADO DE DINERO.
money market ‖ short-term loan market.

MERCADO DE DIVISAS.
foreign exchange market.

MERCADO DE MERCANCÍAS.
goods and products market.

MERCADO DE TRABAJO.
labor market.

MERCADO DE VALORES.
stock market.

MERCADO DE VENDEDORES.
sellers' market.

MERCADO NEGRO.
black market.

MERCADO PARALELO.
parallel market, market which evades governmental restrictions.

MERCADOS Y FERIAS.
markets and fairs.

MERCANCÍA.
f, merchandise, goods, wares ‖ product which can be sold ‖ commerce ‖ commercial sale.

MERCANCÍAS.
f, freight-train ‖ plural of MERCANCÍA.

MERCANCÍAS Y SERVICIOS.
goods and services.

MERCANTE.
m, buyer ‖ vender, merchant ‖ mercantile ‖ merchant ship.

MERCANTE ARMADO.
merchant ship which is armed as a warship.

MERCANTIL.
adj, mercantile, commercial ‖ lucrative ‖ regulated by commercial law.

MERCANTILISMO.
m, mercantilism.

MERCANTILISTA.
specialist in commercial law ‖ supporter of mercantilism.

MERCANTILIZAR.
v, to commercialize (especially a profession not otherwise subject to trading) ‖ to promote trade.

MERCANTIVO.
adj, mercantile, commercial.

MERCAR.
v, to purchase, buy (with money) ‖ to trade.

MERCED.
f, compensation (for work) ‖ wage ‖ mercy ‖ rental payment ‖ favor, help, assistance ‖ benefit ‖ grant, gift.

MERCED DE TIERRAS.
land grant.

MERCENARIO.
m, salaried worker ‖ field hand, farm worker ‖ day worker ‖ mercenary ‖ adj, mercenary ‖ venal, purchasable.

MERCERÍA.
f, commerce in insignificant goods ‖ notions ‖ notions store.

MERCERO.
m, notions merchant ‖ notions store owner.

MERCHANTE.
m, door-to-door salesman ‖ merchant ‖ adj, mercantile.

MERCHANTERÍA.
f, commercial deal.

MERECEDOR.
adj, meritorious, deserving (of something).

MERECER.
v, to merit, deserve ‖ to be worth.

MERECIDAMENTE.
adv, deservedly.

MERECIDO.
adj, merited, deserved (punishment).

MERETRICIO.
m, sexual intercourse with a prostitute ‖ adj, pertaining to prostitutes.

MERETRIZ.
f, prostitute, whore.

MERIDIANO.
m, meridian ‖ adj, mid-day, pertaining to mid-day.

MÉRITO.
m, merit, attribute ‖ value, worth (of things).

MÉRITO EJECUTIVO.
right of execution.

MÉRITO PROBATORIO.
value as proof or evidence, probative value.

MÉRITO PROCESAL.
basis of claim, grounds.

MERITORIAMENTE.
adv, on its merits, meritoriously.

MERITORIO.
m, meritorious person ‖ adj, meritorious.

MÉRITOS DE LA CAUSA.
See MÉRITOS DEL PROCESO.

MÉRITOS DE LOS AUTOS.
See MÉRITOS DEL PROCESO.

MÉRITOS DEL PROCESO.
merits of the case.

MERMA.
f, shrinkage, loss, diminution (due to natural causes) ‖ petty theft.

MERMAR.
v, to diminish, shrink (due to natural causes ‖ to reduce a legal right or interest.

MERO.
adj, mere.

MERO IMPERIO.
power of sovereign to punish criminals.

MERODEADOR.
m, marauder ‖ outlaw (in rural areas).

MERODEAR.
v, to maraud, plunder, sack.

MERODEO.
m, theft in rural areas ‖ marauding, plundering, sacking.

MES.
m, month ‖ monthly payment.

MES NATURAL.
natural month, month counted from date to date.

MESA.
f, table ‖ chairmanship of a corporation or meeting.

MESA DE ENTRADAS.
receptionist for a governmental department (for the purpose of receiving correspondence and legal documents and delivering it to the proper office).

MESA DE VOTACIÓN.
polling station or place.

MESA DIRECTIVA.
board of directors.

MESA EJECUTIVA.
board of governors or directors ‖ executive board.

MESA ELECTORAL.
polling or voting station ‖ persons who are charged with receiving and counting votes to assure against election fraud.

MESA ESCRUTADORA.
See MESA ELECTORAL.

MESA RECEPTORA.
See MESA ELECTORAL.

MESA REDONDA.
Literally, round table ‖ round table discussion ‖ persons who meet to discuss a given matter (without regard to hierarchy).

MESADA.
f, monthly payment (whether for work, rent, etc.).

MESOCRACIA.
f, government by the middle class ‖ bourgeoisie.

MESTIZO.
m, mestizo ‖ adj, mestizo.

METAFÍSICA.
f, metaphysics ‖ adj, metaphysical ‖ excessively abstract or subtle.

METÁLICO.
m, cash ‖ adj, metallic ‖ cash.

METEDOR.
m, introducer, incorporator ‖ smuggler.

METEDURÍA.
f, contraband.

METER.
v, to put, place ‖ to introduce ‖ to smuggle to invest (capital) ‖ to place money, bet ‖ trick ‖ to spend.

**METER LA MANO
EN UNA COSA.**
to interfere (in something) ‖ to steal from.

METER LA MANO HASTA EL CODO.
to be up to your ears in something ‖ to steal impetuously.

METER PRENDAS.
to take part in a business.
METERSE.
v, to go into debt ‖ to intrude ‖ to injure at gun-point ‖ to enter, follow a career or profession.
MÉTODO.
m, method, procedure, conduct ‖ personal habit ‖ order.
MÉTODO COMPARATIVO.
comparative method (of examining law).
MÉTODO DE INTERPRETACIÓN.
interpretative method, method of interpretation.
MÉTODO EXEGÉTICO.
method of legal interpretation and analysis based on statutory texts.
MÉTODO HISTÓRICO.
historical method (of viewing the development of law and its interpretation).
MÉTODO JURÍDICO.
legal method, the totality of logical procedures used in order to research the causes and purposes of law, to understand and interpret its sources, to structure the law books, and to teach and spread positive law.
MÉTODOS DE COLABORACIÓN EN LA EMPRESA.
systems of employee-employer relationships (e.g. employee shareholdership, managerial participation, etc.).
METRÓPOLI.
f, metropolis, main city ‖ capital ‖ mother country (with respect to her colonies).
METROPOLITANO.
m, subway ‖ adj, metropolitan.
MEZCLA.
f, mixture ‖ aggregation.
MEZCLADO.
adj, mixed.
MEZCLAR.
v, to mix, incorporate, unite, join ‖ to make an enemy ‖ to stir ‖ to confuse concepts.
MEZCLARSE.
v, to intermarry ‖ to mix, introduce oneself into the company of others ‖ to participate in a matter ‖ to meddle, interfere.
MIEDO.
m, fear, fright, apprehension. May nullify consent (in contracts) or may excuse action (in criminal law).

MIEDO CERVAL.
tremendous or intense fear.
MIEDO INSUPERABLE.
overwhelming fear, fear which is not able to be overcome.
MIEMBRO.
m, member (in all its meanings) ‖ part ‖ associate.
MIEMBRO CONSTITUYENTE.
founding member.
MIEMBRO DEL CONGRESO.
congressman or congresswoman.
MIEMBRO DE LA FIRMA.
member of the firm.
MIEMBRO FUNDADOR.
See MIEMBRO CONSTITUYENTE.
MIEMBRO NATO.
member ex officio.
MIEMBRO ORIGINARIO.
See MIEMBRO CONSTITUYENTE.
MIEMBRO PRINCIPAL.
See MIEMBRO TITULAR.
MIEMBRO PROPIETARIO.
See MIEMBRO TITULAR.
MIEMBRO SUBROGANTE.
See MIEMBRO SUPLENTE.
MIEMBRO SUPLENTE.
alternate member.
MIEMBRO TITULAR.
regular member.
Opposed to MIEMBRO SUPLENTE.
MIEMBRO VIRIL.
penis.
MIEMBRO VITALICIO.
life member.
MIGRACIÓN.
f, immigration ‖ (international) migration.
MIGRACIÓN INTERNA.
internal migration, migration within a country.
MILICIA.
f, militia ‖ military service ‖ science of educating military troops.
MILICO.
m, soldier or military officer. (der.)
MILITANTE.
f, m, militant ‖ activist, political party activist, union member, member of an association ‖ adj, militant.
MILITAR.
m, member of armed forces, soldier ‖ adj, military, pertaining to the military ‖ warlike, mar-

tial, related to war ‖ v, to serve in the armed forces ‖ to fight, make war on ‖ to be a militant member (of a party, union etc.) ‖ to militate.

MILITARA.
f, wife or widow or daughter of a member of the armed forces.

MILITARADA.
f, military uprising or activity. (der.)

MILITARISMO.
m, militarism.

MILITARISTA.
m, militarist.

MILITARIZACIÓN.
f, militarization ‖ submission of workers to the jurisdiction of the military during times of war or other extreme circumstances.

MILITARIZACIÓN DE LOS TRABAJADORES.
mobilization or militarization of the workers (during times of war or other extreme circumstances) such that some of their labor rights (such as the right to strike) are restricted.

MILITARIZAR.
v, to militarize.

MILITARMENTE.
adv, militarily.

MILITARÓN.
m, soldier or member of the armed forces ‖ desire to militarize society. (der.)

MILITAROTE.
m, hawkish member of the armed forces. (der.)

MINA.
f, mine ‖ underground passage, mine shaft ‖ mining rights ‖ mining lease ‖ girl, chick, doll.

MINERAJE.
m, working or exploitation of a mine.

MINERAL.
m, mineral ‖ adj, mineral.

MINERÍA.
f, mining ‖ science of mining ‖ totality of persons who are involved in mining (from miners to mine operators) ‖ totality of mines of a nation or area.

MINERISTA.
m, (mining) prospector.

MINERO.
m, miner ‖ adj, mining.

MINGA.
f, contract to work on holidays in exchange for liquor ‖ work performed for another by a group of person who are paid communally.

MINGACO.
m, work performed for another by a group of person who are paid communally.

MINIFUNDIO.
m, small farmstead.

MINIFUNDISMO.
m, use of the land pursuant to a MINIFUNDIO system.

MINIFUNDISTA.
f, m, small farm owner ‖ adj, pertaining to MINIFUNDIO.

MÍNIMO.
m, minimum, minimum limit ‖ adj, minimum ‖ minimal ‖ smaller ‖ inferior ‖ minuscule ‖ minimum.

MÍNIMUM.
m, minimum, minimum limit.

MINISTERIAL.
m, supporter or a public minister or government ‖ adj, ministerial, pertaining to a governmental ministry.

MINISTERIALISMO.
m, doctrine of supporting the government in power ‖ tendency of supporting the government in power.

MINISTERIALMENTE.
adv, ministerially.

MINISTERIO.
m, ministry, (government) department totality of ministries or federal departments position and term of government minister or department secretary ‖ presidential cabinet building and offices of minister or department secretary ‖ position, employment, occupation office ‖ destination, use (of something).

MINISTERIO DE AERONÁUTICA.
Department or Ministry of Aviation.

MINISTERIO DE AGRICULTURA.
Department or Ministry of Agriculture.

MINISTERIO DE ASUNTOS EXTERIORES.
Department or Ministry of Foreign Affairs.

MINISTERIO DE AVIACIÓN.
See MINISTERIO DE AERONÁUTICA.

MINISTERIO DE COMERCIO.
Department or Ministry of Commerce or Trade.

MINISTERIO DE COMUNICACIONES.
Department or Ministry of Communication

MINISTERIO DE DEFENSA NACIONAL.
Department or Ministry of National Defense.
MINISTERIO DE ECONOMÍA.
Department or Ministry of the Economy.
MINISTERIO DE EDUCACIÓN.
Department or Ministry of Education.
MINISTERIO DE EJÉRCITO.
Department or Ministry of the Army.
MINISTERIO DE ESTADO.
Department or Ministry of State.
MINISTERIO DE FINANZAS.
Department or Ministry of Finance.
MINISTERIO DE FOMENTO.
Department or Ministry of Development.
MINISTERIO DE GRACIA Y JUSTICIA.
Department or Ministry of Justice.
MINISTERIO DE GUERRA.
Department or Ministry of War or Defense.
MINISTERIO DE HACIENDA.
Treasury Department ‖ Treasury.
**MINISTERIO DE INDUSTRIA
Y COMERCIO.**
Department or Ministry of Industry and Trade.
**MINISTERIO DE INFORMACIÓN
Y TURISMO.**
Department or Ministry of Information and Tourism.
MINISTERIO DE INSTRUCCIÓN PÚBLICA.
Department or Ministry of Public Education.
MINISTERIO DE JUSTICIA.
Department or Ministry of Justice.
MINISTERIO DE LA GUERRA.
See MINISTERIO DE GUERRA.
MINISTERIO DE LA VIVIENDA.
Department or Ministry of Public Housing.
MINISTERIO DE MARINA.
Department or Ministry of Navy, Navy Department.
MINISTERIO DE OBRAS PÚBLICAS.
Department or Ministry of Public Works.
**MINISTERIO DE RELACIONES
EXTERIORES.**
State Department, Foreign Office, Department or Ministry of Foreign Affairs.
MINISTERIO DE SALUD PÚBLICA.
Department or Ministry of Public Health.
MINISTERIO DE SANIDAD.
See MINISTERIO DE SALUD PÚBLICA.
MINISTERIO DE TRABAJO.
Department or Ministry of Labor.

MINISTERIO DE TRANSPORTES.
Department or Ministry of Transportation.
MINISTERIO DEL AIRE.
See MINISTERIO DE AERONÁUTICA.
MINISTERIO DEL INTERIOR.
Department of the Interior, Home Office.
MINISTERIO DEL TRABAJO.
Department or Ministry of Labor.
MINISTERIO FISCAL.
Justice Department, Attorney's General Office (at a federal level) ‖ State Attorney's General Office (at a state level).
MINISTERIO PÚBLICO.
See MINISTERIO FISCAL.
MINISTERIO PÚBLICO DE MENORES.
office responsible for defending minors and others who are legally incapacitated.
MINISTERIO PÚBLICO DEL TRABAJO.
state attorney's office in charge of defending the public interest in labor law cases.
MINISTERIO PUPILAR.
(government) department for the protection of the rights of minors and others who lack effective legal representation.
MINISTERIO RELÁMPAGO.
minister who resigns for failure to receive congressional or parliamentary approval.
MINISTRA.
f, female government minister ‖ wife of a government minister.
MINISTRABLE.
adj, capable of acting as minister.
MINISTRACIÓN.
f, ministration ‖ exercise of a position ‖ service ‖ occupation, employment, position.
MINISTRADOR.
m, government minister or secretary ‖ professional ‖ adj, professional, pertaining to a person who practices a profession.
MINISTRANTE.
m, government minister or secretary ‖ medical doctor ‖ adj, administering.
MINISTRAR.
v, to be a government minister or secretary ‖ to carry out the office of government minister or secretary ‖ to serve, carry out a position ‖ to supply, provide, furnish (money, etc.)
MINISTRIL.
m, minor court officer (e.g. bailiff).
MINISTRO.
m, cabinet minister or secretary ‖ judge ‖ mes-

senger, representative ‖ diplomat, diplomatic envoy ‖ aides or assistants within the Justice Department ‖ person who carries out something (of his own free will).

MINISTRO DEL PODER EJECUTIVO.
cabinet minister.

MINISTRO DEL TRIBUNAL.
judge, magistrate.

MINISTRO DELEGADO.
deputy or assistant minister.

MINISTRO PLENIPOTENCIARIO.
minister plenipotentiary.

MINISTRO SECRETARIO.
cabinet minister.

MINISTRO SIN CARTERA.
minister without portfolio, cabinet member without a designated department.

MINORACIÓN.
f, lessening, diminishment, reduction, lowering.

MINORAR.
v, to reduce, cut, diminish, lessen, lower ‖ to make smaller.

MINORITARIO.
adj, minority.

MINORÍA.
f, minority ‖ state of being under the age of majority ‖ minority, number or group which numbers less than 50% of the whole. May be ABSOLUTA (absolute) or RELATIVA (relative).

MINORÍA DE EDAD.
minority, state of being under the age of majority.

MINORÍA NACIONAL.
national minority (in terms of race, religion, language, etc.).

MINORIDAD.
f, minority, state of being under the age of majority.

MINORIDAD PENAL.
minority for purposes of criminal law.

MINORISTA.
m, retailer ‖ retail merchandise.

MINUCIA.
f, minutia.

MINUCIOSIDAD.
f, meticulousness.

"MINUS PETITIO".
complaint which (due to error) demands less than that permitted by law.

MINUTA.
f, summary, minute ‖ rough draft or copy (e.g. of a contract, will) on which notes are made for the final copy ‖ rough draft of an order or other document ‖ original copy of an order or other communication (usually kept as record) ‖ notation, note, reminder ‖ list of persons or things that form part of something ‖ attorney's billing or bill (sent to a client).

MINUTA RUBRICADA.
rough draft of an order or other document signed by a minister or other public official.

MINUTAR.
v, to prepare a rough draft or copy ‖ to summarize a contract.

MINUTARIO.
m, special notarial ledger in which the rough copies or summaries of contracts, will, etc. are recorded.

MINUTAS.
f, minutes of a meeting.

MIRAMIENTO.
m, respect, consideration, circumspection.

MIRAR.
v, to look ‖ to intend ‖ to consider, examine ‖ to inquire into ‖ to protect ‖ to concern oneself with.

MISERABLE.
adj, miserable, cheap ‖ poor ‖ ruinous.

MISERABLEMENTE.
adv, miserably, cheaply ‖ ruinously ‖ poorly.

MISEREAR.
v, to be cheap or miserly.

MISERIA.
f, misery ‖ misadventure, calamity ‖ poverty ‖ avarice ‖ meanness.

MISERICORDIA.
f, mercy, compassion.

MÍSERO.
See MISERABLE.

MISIÓN.
f, mission ‖ building of diplomatic mission.

MISIÓN DIPLOMÁTICA.
diplomatic mission.

MISIVA.
See CARTA MISIVA.

MISIVO.
m, missive, letter.

MITAD.
f, half,

MITIGACIÓN.
f, mitigation.
MITIGADOR.
m, mitigator || adj, mitigating.
MITIGAR.
v, to mitigate, moderate.
MITIGATIVO.
adj, mitigating.
MITIGATORIO.
adj, mitigating.
MITÍN.
m, meeting || political meeting or rally.
MIXTI FORI.
mixed forum || forum in which crimes of both a secular and ecclesiastic nature may be heard.
MOBILIARIO.
m, household furniture || adj, mobile, movable || pertaining to personal property.
MOBILIARIO Y EQUIPO.
furniture and fixtures.
MOBILIARIO Y ÚTILES.
See MOBILIARIO Y EQUIPO.
MOBLAJE.
m, household furniture and goods.
MOCIÓN.
f, motion, movement || acceptance of a suggestion or proposal || (parliamentary) motion || tendency, inclination.
MOCIÓN PARA LEVANTAR LA SESIÓN.
motion to adjourn the meeting.
MOCIONANTE.
m, person who makes a motion or proposal.
MOCIONAR.
v, to make or present a motion || to propose.
MODALIDADES.
f, varieties, types.
MODELO.
m, model, sample || original (of something) || standard || blank form.
MODELO DE FÁBRICA.
industrial model.
MODELO DE LA FIRMA.
sample of a signature, specimen signature.
MODELO IMPRESO.
blank form.
MODELO INDUSTRIAL.
industrial model.
MODERACIÓN.
f, moderation.
MODERADAMENTE.
adv, moderately, with moderation.

MODERADO.
adj, moderate.
MODERADOR.
m, head of state || person who acts with moderation.
MODERAR.
v, to act with moderation, moderate, regulate.
MÓDICO.
adj, moderate || cheap.
MODIFICABLE.
adj, modifiable || amendable.
MODIFICACIÓN.
f, modification, change, innovation, reform || moderation, amendment, correction, addition || nullification, abrogation || counter-order.
MODIFICACIÓN DE DERECHOS.
modification or restriction or amplification of legal rights.
MODIFICAR.
v, to modify, change, transform, reform || to amend, correct || to nullify, abrogate.
MODIFICATIVO.
adj, modifying || nullifying.
MODIFICATORIO.
See MODIFICATIVO.
MODO.
m, means, method.
MODO DE CONTAR LOS INTERVALOS DEL DERECHO.
means of determining legal periods or terms.
MODOS DE ADQUIRIR.
means of acquiring property.
"MODUS FACENDI".
modus operandi.
"MODUS OPERANDI".
modus operandi.
MODUS VIVENDI.
modus vivendi.
MOHATRA.
m, fraud, fraudulent deal || usury.
MOHATRAR.
v, to defraud || to charge usuriously.
MOJAR.
v, to stab || to enter a piece of property || to meddle in a matter.
MOJÓN.
m, boundary stone or marker || landmark.
MOJONA.
f, surveying, delineating boundaries || rental paid for beverages imbibed in a drinking establishment.

MOJONACIÓN.
f, survey, boundary delineation.
MOJONAR.
v, to place boundary stones or markers.
MOJONERA.
f, site of boundary stone or marker, landmark site.
MOLDE.
m, mold ‖ model, sample.
MOLER.
v, to mill ‖ to bother ‖ to mistreat.
MOLESTAR.
v, to bother, annoy ‖ to irritate ‖ to tire ‖ to anger ‖ to take advantage of.
MOLESTIA.
f, bother, irritation, annoyance ‖ discomfort.
MOLESTIA PÚBLICA.
public nuisance.
MOLIMIENTO.
m, bother, perturbation.
MOLLAR.
adj, easily fooled or persuaded ‖ of little effort and great use.
MOMENTANEO.
adv, momentarily ‖ immediately, instantaneously.
MOMENTO.
m, moment.
MOMIFICAR.
v, to mummify.
MONARQUÍA.
f, monarchy.
MONEDA.
f, coin, coinage ‖ money, specie ‖ currency ‖ wealth.
MONEDA AMONEDADA.
See MONEDA METÁLICA.
MONEDA BLOQUEADA.
blocked currency.
MONEDA CONTANTE Y SONANTE.
See MONEDA METÁLICA.
MONEDA CONTROLADA.
controlled or managed currency.
MONEDA CORRIENTE.
legal currency, currency.
MONEDA CORTADA.
coin which has been cut.
MONEDA DE CUENTA.
unit of account (used for accounting purposes).

MONEDA DE CURSO LEGAL.
See MONEDA LEGAL.
MONEDA DE FUERZA LIBERATORIA.
See MONEDA LEGAL.
MONEDA DE PODER LIBERATORIO.
See MONEDA LEGAL.
MONEDA DÉBIL.
unstable or weak currency.
MONEDA DIRIGIDA.
See MONEDA CONTROLADA.
MONEDA DIVISIONARIA.
divisional or fractional coin, coin which is a part or fraction of the legal tender of a country.
MONEDA EXTRANJERA.
foreign currency.
MONEDA FALSA.
counterfeit or fake money.
MONEDA FIDUCIARIA.
fiduciary money, currency the extrinsic value of which is greater than its intrinsic value.
MONEDA FUERTE.
stable or strong currency.
MONEDA LEGAL.
legal currency, legal tender.
MONEDA LEGÍTIMA.
legal currency, legal tender.
MONEDA METÁLICA.
coin, coinage, specie.
MONEDA NACIONAL.
national currency, legal tender of a nation.
MONEDA SONANTE.
specie.
MONEDA TRABUCANTE.
overweight coin.
MONEDAJE.
m, coinage.
MONEDERÍA.
f, mintage, minting.
MONEDERO.
m, mint, manufacturer of coins.
MONEDERO FALSO.
counterfeiter, manufacturer of counterfeit coins ‖ passer of counterfeit money.
MONETARIO.
m, coinage, totality of coins ‖ adj, monetary.
MONETIZACIÓN.
f, monetization.
MONETIZAR.
v, to mint ‖ to monetize.

MONGOLISMO.
m, mongolism.

MONICIÓN.
f, admonition.

MONIPODIO.
m, deal or contract for illegal purposes.

MONISMO.
m, monism, doctrine which holds that international and national law are one and the same because the validity of one depends on the other.

MONITORIO.
adj, monitory.

MONOCRACIA.
m, government of one sole authority (e.g. monarchy, dictatorship).

MONOGAMIA.
f, monogamy.

MONÓGAMO.
adj, monogamous || married one time.

MONOGRAFÍA.
f, monograph.

MONOMANÍA.
f, monomania || dominant concern.

MONOMETALISMO.
m, monometallism.

MONOPÓLICO.
adj, monopolistic.

MONOPOLIO.
m, monopoly.

MONOPOLIO DE HECHO.
de facto monopoly, monopoly resulting from natural or market factors.

MONOPOLIO FISCAL.
government monopoly.

MONOPOLIO LEGAL.
monopoly established by law.

MONOPOLIO NATURAL.
natural monopoly.

MONOPOLISTA.
m, monopolist, monopolizer || adj, monopolistic.

MONOPOLÍSTICO.
adj, monopolistic.

MONOPOLIZACIÓN.
f, monopolization.

MONOPOLIZADOR.
m, monopolist, monopolizer || adj, monopolizing.

MONOPOLIZAR.
v, to monopolize, corner.

MONSTRUO.
m, monster.

MONSTRUOSIDAD.
f, monstrosity, deformity || atrocity, cruelty.

MONSTRUOSO.
adj, monstrous, enormous, immense.

MONTA.
f, importance or significance of something || amount of various parts of an account.

MONTANTE.
m, amount, sum, total amount of an account or other obligation.

MONTANTE CIERTO.
sum certain.

MONTANTEAR.
v, to intermediate, reconcile (e.g. disputes) || to be bossy, abuse one's authority by throwing one's weight around.

MONTE.
m, amount || mountain || impediment, obstacle || forest.

MONTE DE PIEDAD.
pawnshop || national pawnshop.

MONTE DE UTILIDAD PÚBLICA.
public forest, forest protected by law for public purposes.

MONTE PÍO.
See MONTEPÍO.

MONTEPÍO.
m, widows' or orphans' pension fund, fund made up of members' contributions to pay for widowers or orphans of the group || public or private assistance office (which administers such funds) || pension || pawnshop.

MONTO.
m, amount, sum, total.

MONTONERA.
f, rural guerilla group.

MONTONERO.
m, rural guerrilla, rural guerrilla fighter || fighter, warrior || person who, unable to fight alone, provokes a fight when he is surrounded by friends and supporters.

MONUMENTO.
m, monument || historical document || element of proof || artistic, literary, or scientific work || mausoleum.

MOQUETE.
m, punch || punch in the nose.

MOQUETEAR.
v, to punch || to punch in the nose.

MORA.
f, delay ‖ lateness, tardiness ‖ delinquency (in payment).

"MORA ACCIPIENDI".
See MORA DEL ACREEDOR.

MORA DEL ACREEDOR.
delay or delinquency of obligee in accepting the obligor's payment.

MORA DEL DEUDOR.
delay or delinquency of obligor in complying with his obligations.

MORA EN EL DEPÓSITO.
delay in the return of an item deposited.

MORA EN LA DONACIÓN.
delay in delivery of a promised gift.

MORA EN LA DOTE.
delay in the delivery of a dowry.

MORA EN LAS OBLIGACIONES MERCANTILES.
delay in commercial obligations.

"MORA EX CONTRACTU".
contractual delay or delinquency, delay or delinquency arising out of the terms of a contract.

"MORA EX LEGE".
delay or delinquency arising out of the terms of law.

"MORA EX PERSONA".
delay or delinquency caused by a person.

"MORA EX RE".
delay or delinquency caused by a thing or related to the delivery of a thing ‖ delay or delinquency which occurs automatically as a result of the expiration of a term, without request of or notification by the creditor.

MORA PROCESAL.
procedural delay (in litigation).

"MORA SOLVENDI".
See MORA DEL DEUDOR.

MORADA.
f, house, home, habitation, dwelling ‖ residence ‖ domicile.

MORADOR.
m, dweller, inhabitant ‖ resident ‖ domiciliary ‖ lessee ‖ guest.

MORAL.
f, ethics ‖ morals ‖ pain and suffering ‖ adj, moral ‖ decent ‖ honorable ‖ abstract, nonphysical.

MORAL DEL INTERÉS.
See UTILITARISMO.

MORAL PÚBLICA.
public morals or ethics.

MORALIDAD.
f, morality.

MORAR.
v, to dwell, reside ‖ to be domiciled ‖ to be a neighbor ‖ to stay.

MORATORIA.
f, moratorium ‖ extension of time.

MORATORIA JUDICIAL.
judicially imposed suspension of procedures (e.g. bankruptcy procedures).

MORBIDEZ.
f, sickness ‖ sick rate, percentage of sick people in a given time and place ‖ sensuality.

MÓRBIDO.
adj, morbid, sick, sickly, unwholesome.

MORBOSA.
adj, sick, ill ‖ pertaining to an illness ‖ able to produce illness.

MORBOSIDAD.
f, morbidity ‖ total number of sick people at a given time and place.

MORDAZA.
f, gag.

MORDER.
v, to bite ‖ to spend little by little ‖ to embezzle in small amounts ‖ to defame, criticize.

MORDER UNO EL PALO.
to be forced to sell at giveaway prices.

MORDIDA.
f, bribe.

MORDIDO.
adj, embezzled ‖ reduced.

MORDISCO.
m, action of effect of MORDER.

"MORES".
mores, customs, conduct.

MORGANÁTICO.
See MATRIMONIO MORGANÁTICO.

MORGUE.
f, morgue.

MORIBUNDO.
m, duying person ‖ adj, moribund, dying.

MORIGERACIÓN.
f, ordered life ‖ moderation of habits, temperance ‖ limitation, reduction.

MORIGERADO.
adj, temperate, moderate.

MORIR.
v, to die ‖ to end, be extinguished.

MORIR CIVILMENTE.
to be legally dead (i.e. considered dead for civil law purposes) although physically alive.

MORIRSE.
v, to die.

MOROSAMENTE.
adv, with delay, tardily || slowly.

MOROSIDAD.
f, lateness, tardiness || delay, delinquency || (contractual) default (due to delinquency).

MOROSO.
adj, slow, late, tardy || delinquent, in default (in complying with obligations due to delinquency) || negligent.

MORRADA.
f, slap.

MORTALDAD.
See MORTALIDAD.

MORTALIDAD.
f, mortality (in all its meanings).

MORTALMENTE.
adv, mortally, fatally.

MORTANDAD.
f, slaughter (due to epidemic, war, etc.) || death toll, mortality rate.

MORTÍFERO.
adj, lethal, deadly, fatal.

MORTIFICACIÓN.
f, mortification.

MORTIFICAR.
v, to subdue, mortify || to annoy, irritate, rile.

MORTINATO.
m, prenatal death.

MORTIS CAUSA.
mortis causa, due to the death of.

MORTUARIO.
m, funeral || adj, pertaining to death.

MOS".
use, practice || conduct, comportment || custom, habit,

MOSTRAR.
v, to show, exhibit || to explain || to prove, convince || to reveal, make known.

MOSTRARSE.
v, to show oneself to be.

MOSTRARSE PARTE.
to make an appearance, appear (in a lawsuit). Usually is performed by submission of a pleading.

MOSTRENCO.
See BIENES MOSTRENCOS.

MOTAR.
v, to steal, thieve.

MOTE.
m, alias || nickname || ambiguous phrase.

MOTEJADOR.
m, name caller.

MOTEJAR.
v, to call names.

MOTEL.
m, motel.

MOTETE.
m, nickname || disgrace, dishonor.

MOTÍN.
m, mutiny, rebellion, sedition, insurrection || uprising, riot || collective civil disobedience.

MOTÍN DE PRISIONEROS.
prisoner riot or uprising.

MOTÍN MILITAR.
mutiny or military uprising.

MOTIVACIÓN.
f, motivation.

MOTIVADAMENTE.
adv, with motivation || justifiably, with basis or foundation.

MOTIVADO.
adj, motivated || justified, reasoned.

MOTIVAR.
v, to motivate || to found, base (e.g. a decision, plan).

MOTIVO.
m, motive || cause || adj, moving.

MOTIVO FUNDADO.
probable cause || good or sound reason || sound motive.

MOTIVO INDIRECTO.
remote cause || indirect reason.

MOTOR.
m, motor || cause, motive.

MOTORISTA.
m, motorist.

MOTRIL.
m, shop boy.

"MOTU PROPRIO".
voluntarily, on one's own || freely || spontaneously, of one's own free will.

MOVEDURA.
f, movement || miscarriage.

MOVER.
v, to move, transfer || to incite, induce || to persuade, invite or require || to alter || to abort, have a miscarriage.

MOVERSE.
v, to change one's position ‖ to proceed with care.

MOVIBLE.
adj, movable ‖ changeable.

MOVIDO.
m, miscarriage, abortion.

MÓVIL.
m, motive, cause, reason ‖ adj, mobile ‖ changeable.

MOVILIDAD.
f, mobility ‖ condition of being very mobile.

MOVILIDAD LABORAL.
mobility of work force.

MOVILIDAD VERTICAL.
vertical mobility (e.g. socially, professionally).

MOVILIZACIÓN.
f, mobilization ‖ war mobilization, war effort.

MOVILIZACIÓN DE LOS TRABAJADORES.
mobilization of the workers.

MOVILIZACIÓN INTEGRAL.
wartime mobilization. Includes military, industrial, economic mobilization.

MOVILIZADO.
adj, mobilized.

MOVILIZAR.
v, to mobilize.

MOVIMIENTO.
m, movement, motion ‖ change of position ‖ activity ‖ alteration, change ‖ political movement.

MOVIMIENTO COOPERATIVO.
co-operative movement, socio-political movement which encourages co-operatives.

MOVIMIENTO DE MASAS.
movement of the masses.

MOVIMIENTO DE OPINIÓN.
social group which maintains a given opinion.

MOVIMIENTO FEMINISTA.
feminist movement.

MOVIMIENTO MILITAR.
military movement.

MOVIMIENTO SINDICAL.
labor union movement ‖ trade union movement.

MOVIMIENTO SOCIAL.
social movement.

MOVIMIENTO SUBVERSIVO.
subversive movement.

MOYANA.
f, lie ‖ fraud, trick.

MOZA.
f, prostitute ‖ waitress ‖ maid ‖ young girl ‖ single woman.

MOZA DE FORTUNA.
prostitute.

MOZA DE PARTIDO.
prostitute.

MOZCORRA.
f, prostitute.

MUCHEDUMBRE DELINCUENTE.
f, mob, mass or crowd or group which does criminal acts (without preplanning).

MUDADA.
f, transfer, action of moving.

MUDANZA.
f, transfer, action of moving, movement ‖ volatility, emotional inconsistency ‖ notable change in status.

MUDAR.
v, to move, transfer ‖ to vary, change ‖ to leave one thing for another ‖ to relieve (e.g. a person on guard duty).

MUDAR DE MANOS.
to transfer ownership, to change hands.

MUDARSE.
v, to adopt another way of life ‖ to move (e.g. house) ‖ to move away, leave ‖ to change one's clothes.

MUDEZ.
f, muteness ‖ silence.

MUDO.
m, mute person ‖ adj, mute, dumb ‖ reserved silent ‖ speechless.

MUDO VOLUNTARIO.
person who refuses to speak.

MUEBLAJE.
m, furniture.

MUEBLAR.
v, to furnish.

MUEBLES.
m, furniture.

MUEBLES POR SITIOS.
personal property for real estate. Used in relation to extending or restricting marital property rights.

MUEBLES Y ÚTILES.
furniture and fixtures.

MUELLAJE.
m, wharfage, dockage, charge for using dock wharf.

MUELLE.
m, wharf, dock, pier ‖ (train) platform ‖ adj, delicate ‖ sensual, voluptuous.

MUERTE.
f, death ‖ end, extinction ‖ destruction, ruin, desolation ‖ cessation of an activity ‖ death sentence.

MUERTE A MANO ARMADA.
murder with a weapon.

MUERTE ACCIDENTAL.
accidental death.

MUERTE APARENTE.
apparent death, state in which the signs of life are imperceptible.

MUERTE CIVIL.
civil death.

MUERTE DEL ACUSADO.
death of the accused or (criminal) defendant.

MUERTE DEL CÓNYUGE.
death of the spouse.

MUERTE DEL IMPUTADO.
See MUERTE DEL ACUSADO.

MUERTE DEL TRABAJADOR.
employee's death (due to a work accident or work- related illness).

MUERTE NATURAL.
natural death, death due to natural causes.

MUERTE PRESUNTA.
presumptive death.

MUERTE SENIL.
death due to old-age.

MUERTE SIMULTÁNEA.
simultaneous death.

MUERTE VIOLENTA.
violent death, death due to external forces.

MUERTO.
m, dead person ‖ corpse, cadaver, remains ‖ adj, dead, deceased ‖ killed ‖ lifeless, inactive ‖ paralyzed ‖ exhausted ‖ unproductive ‖ inefficient ‖ above water (on ships) ‖ amortized ‖ killed in action.

MUERTO EN COMBATE.
killed in action.

MUESCA.
f, brand (e.g. on an animal).

MUESTRA.
f, model, guide ‖ sample, specimen ‖ shop sign ‖ indication, sign, signal.

MUESTRA POSTAL.
sample for purposes of postal inspection.

MUESTRARIO.
m, sample catalogue.

MUEVEDO.
m, aborted fetus.

MUJER.
f, woman ‖ wife, female spouse or mate.

MUJER CASADA.
married woman, woman married pursuant to law ‖ wife ‖ common-law wife ‖ missus, Mrs.

MUJER CIUDADANA.
female citizen.

MUJER COMERCIANTE.
female merchant.

MUJER COMÚN.
mistress of two or more men ‖ prostitute ‖ wife who is also a mistress.

MUJER DE GOBIERNO.
governess.

MUJER DE LA VIDA AIRADA.
prostitute.

MUJER DE PUNTO.
prostitute.

MUJER DE SU CASA.
housewife ‖ good housewife.

MUJER DEL ARTE.
prostitute.

MUJER DEL DEUDOR.
wife of the debtor or obligor.

MUJER DEL PARTIDO.
prostitute.

MUJER ENCINTA.
pregnant woman.

MUJER ILEGÍTIMA.
woman who lives with a man without being legally married to him. May be concubine, mistress, or adulteress.

MUJER PÚBLICA.
prostitute.

MUJER SOLTERA.
single or unmarried woman.

MUJER TRABAJADORA.
working woman.

MUJERIEGO.
m, womanizer ‖ effeminate man ‖ group of women.

MUJERIL.
adj, pertaining to women ‖ effeminate.

MUJERZUELA.
f, prostitute.

MULA.
f, trickery, fraud.

MULTA.
f, fine, pecuniary penalty (for violation of the law).

MULTA CONVENCIONAL.
contractual penalty.

MULTA DISCIPLINARIA.
disciplinary fine (military justice).

MULTA FISCAL.
tax penalty or fine.

MULTA GUBERNATIVA.
administrative penalty.

MULTA PENAL.
criminal penalty or fine.

MULTABLE.
adj, able to be fined or penalized.

MULTAR.
v, to fine, impose a fine, penalize.

MULTICAMERALISMO.
m, multicamaralism.

MULTILATERAL.
adj, multilateral.

MULTIMILLONARIO.
m, multimillionaire.

MULTIPARA.
f, mother of more than one child at a single birth (e.g. mother of twins) ‖ mother of more than one child.

MULTIPARTIDISMO.
m, political system with many parties.

MÚLTIPLE.
adj, multiple, various, numerous, many.

MULTIPLICIDAD DE ACCIONES.
f, multiplicity of actions or lawsuits.

MUNICIONES.
f, ammunition, munitions.

MUNICIPAL.
m, city policeman ‖ adj, municipal, pertaining to a town, city, municipality.

MUNICIPALIDAD.
f, town or city hall ‖ town or city council ‖ municipality ‖ town, city ‖ township ‖ county ‖ municipal government.

MUNICIPALIZACIÓN DE SERVICIOS.
f, municipalization of services.

MUNICIPALIZAR.
v, to make a city own or be responsible for, municipalize (e.g. a service).

MUNÍCIPE.
m, resident of a town ‖ city councilperson.

MUNICIPIO.
m, city, town ‖ municipality, municipal cor-
poration ‖ town or city council ‖ municipal district ‖ town or city hall.

MUNIDO.
adj, having or possessing a tool or instrument.

MUNIFICENCIA.
f, munificence.

MUNÍFICO.
adj, munificent, liberal (with money), generous.

MUNÍSCULO.
m, small gift, token, token gift.

MUÑECA.
f, doll ‖ boundary marker or stone ‖ wrist.

MURAL.
m, mural ‖ adj, pertaining to a wall.

MURALLA.
f, rampart, thick protective wall.

MURCIAR.
v, to steal, thieve, burgle.

MURCIO.
m, thief, burglar, robber.

MURMULLO.
m, murmur.

MURMURACIÓN.
f, malicious gossip, bad-mouthing.

MURMURACIÓN CONTRA EL SERVICIO.
grumbling or complaining about military duties or other aspects of military service.

MURMURACIÓN CONTRA EL SUPERIOR.
grumbling or complaining about one's superior.

MURMURADOR.
m, gossiper, complainer, grumbler.

MURMURAR.
v, to murmur ‖ to gossip ‖ to complain (behind a person's back), grumble.

MURO.
m, wall.

MURO MEDIANERO.
common or party wall.

MUTABILIDAD.
f, mutability, variability.

MUTABLE.
adj, changeable, variable, mutable.

MUTACIÓN.
f, change, variation, mutation ‖ transfer, ceding.

MUTACIÓN DE CAUCE.
change of river-bed (which may result in acquisition of property).

MUTACIÓN SOCIAL.
social change.

MUTATIS MUTANDIS.
mutatis mutandis.

MUTILACIÓN.
f, mutilation ‖ disfigurement ‖ suppression.

MUTILACIÓN CRIMINAL.
mutilation which is a crime.

MUTILADO.
m, disfigured person ‖ adj, mutilated ‖ disfigured.

MUTILADO DE GUERRA.
war-injured, war invalid.

MUTILADOR.
m, mutilator (either the person or the instrument responsible for the action).

MUTILAR.
v, to mutilate (something or someone).

MUTILARSE.
v, to mutilate oneself.

MUTILO.
See MUTILADO.

MUTISMO.
m, spontaneous silence ‖ forced silence ‖ muteness.

MUTUAL.
f, mutual company. See MUTUALIDAD ‖ adj, mutual, reciprocal.

MUTUALIDAD.
f, mutuality, reciprocity ‖ mutual insurance company, not-for- profit insurance company ‖ mutual benefit company ‖ mutual benefit.

MUTUALISMO.
m, mutualism movement, social movement of mutual aid and benefit or mutual organizations.

MUTUALISTA.
m, supporter of mutualism movement ‖ member of a MUTUALIDAD.

MUTUAMENTE.
adv, mutually, reciprocally.

MUTUANTE.
m, creditor, loaner, lender.

MUTUARIO.
See MUTUATARIO.

MUTUATARIO.
m, borrower ‖ adj, mutuary.

MUTUO.
m, mutuum, type of loan agreement by which a lender lends money or things upon agreement that the borrower will return an equal number, type, and quality of such things at the end of the contract, with or without interest ‖ adj, mutual.

MUTUO AUXILIO.
mutual aid, reciprocal material or spiritual assistance. See MUTUO.

MUTUO CIVIL.
mutuum regulated by a civil code. See MUTUO.

MUTUO CONSENTIMIENTO.
mutual consent or agreement.

MUTUO DISENSO.
mutual termination of a contract or other act. See MUTUO.

MUTUO DISENSO CONYUGAL.
uncontested divorce, mutual termination of a marriage. See MUTUO.

MUTUO DISENSO EN LAS OBLIGACIONES.
mutual termination of obligations. See MUTUO.

MUTUO GRATUITO.
gratuitous mutuum. See MUTUO.

MUTUO MERCANTIL.
mutuum regulated by commercial law. See MUTUO.

MUTUO ONEROSO.
onerous mutuum. See MUTUO.

MUTUO PIGNORATICIO.
mutuum secured by a pledge or chattel mortgage or other security interest. See MUTUO.

N

NABO.
See EMBARGO.

NACEDERO.
m, spring, river source.

NACER.
v, to be born || to descend (e.g. from a family) || to come or originate from || to spring from || to infer, deduce || to save oneself from serious danger.

NACIDO.
adj, born || natural, innate || appropriate, apt, proper.

NACIDO FUERA DEL MATRIMONIO.
born out of wedlock, (born) illegitimate.

NACIMIENTO.
m, birth, act of being born || (river) source or spring || beginning, origin, start || place in the family order, relationship to siblings.

NACIMIENTO DE PERSONAS ABSTRACTAS.
establishment of artificial persons (which takes place upon their legal authorization).

NACIMIENTO EN AERONAVE.
birth on board an airplane.

NACIMIENTO EN BUQUE.
birth on board ship.

NACIMIENTO SIMULTÁNEO.
multiple birth.

NACIÓN.
f, nation, country, state || ethnic group, group of people of the same ethnic group which usually speaks the same language || race, group of people of the same racial group which usually speaks the same language.

NACIÓN CAUTIVA.
nation dominated by another power.

NACIÓN EN ARMAS.
country at war.

NACIÓN MÁS FAVORECIDA.
most favored nation.

NACIONAL.
m, national, native, domestic || member of the national guard or militia || adj, national, domestic.

NACIONALIDAD.
f, nationality, citizenship.

NACIONALIDAD AÉREA.
nationality of an airplane, country in which an airplane is registered.

NACIONALIDAD DE LA AERONAVE.
See NACIONALIDAD AÉREA.

NACIONALIDAD DEL BUQUE.
nationality of the ship.

NACIONALIDADES.
f, principle of international law that any nation has the right to establish itself as an independent state.

NACIONALISMO.
m, nationalism, patriotism || nationalistic political movement. Opposed to provincial or state movements, or to the actions of other nations. Also see NAZISMO.

NACIONALISMO ECONÓMICO.
economic nationalism.

NACIONALISTA.
f, m, nationalistic person || adj, nationalist, nationalistic.

NACIONALIZACIÓN.
f, nationalization (of property or activities) || naturalization (of persons) || intervention of one nation into the affairs of another || provision of services to the national government.

NACIONALIZAR.
v, to naturalize || to nationalize || to import by paying a duty.

NACIONALIZARSE.
v, to be naturalized ‖ to be nationalized.
NACIONALMENTE.
adv, nationally.
NACIONALSOCIALISMO.
See NAZISMO.
NACIONES UNIDAS.
United Nations.
NADERÍA.
f, a nothing ‖ insignificant injury.
NADIE.
no one ‖ a no one.
NAO.
f, ship, vessel.
NAONATO.
m, one born on board ship.
NARCOANÁLISIS.
m, narcoanalysis, exploration of a person's subconscious by means of drugs.
NARCÓTICO.
m, narcotic ‖ adj, narcotic.
NARRACIÓN.
m, narration, information, description ‖ exposition of the facts. Requisite part of criminal allegations.
NARRAR.
v, to relate, narrate, tell ‖ to set forth (facts).
N.A.S.A.
National Aeronautics and Space Organization (ORGANIZACIÓN NACIONAL DE AERONÁUTICA Y DEL ESPACIO DE LOS EE.UU.) The English initials are often used in Spanish.
"NASCITURUS".
nasciturus, he who is yet to be born.
NATA.
f, the principal, the most select.
NATAL.
adj, natal ‖ native ‖ birthday.
NATALICIO.
m, birthday ‖ celebration of birthday ‖ adj, pertaining to one's birthday.
NATALIDAD.
f, birth rate.
NATALIDAD DIRIGIDA.
planned parenthood.
NATIVO.
m, native, person who is native-born ‖ adj, native ‖ spontaneous ‖ born, natural, innate ‖ domestic.
NATO.
adj, born ‖ innate.

NATURA.
f, nature ‖ natural order.
NATURAL.
adj, natural ‖ native.
NATURALEZA.
f, nature (of a thing or person) ‖ universal order ‖ tendency, inclination ‖ instinct ‖ right to be considered as a native of a town ‖ naturalization ‖ genre, type ‖ parentage, family ties.
NATURALEZA DE LAS OBLIGACIONES.
fundamental character of obligations. May be DE DAR (to give), DE HACER (to do something), or DE NO HACER (not to do something).
NATURALEZA HUMANA.
human nature.
NATURALIDAD.
f, naturalness ‖ nationality, citizenship ‖ spontaneity ‖ birthright of citizen.
NATURALIZACIÓN.
f, naturalization.
NATURALIZAR.
v, to naturalize ‖ to adopt the local customs.
NATURALIZARSE.
v, to become or be naturalized.
NATURALMENTE.
adv, naturally.
NAUFRAGAR.
v, to be shipwrecked, sink, go down ‖ to go to rack and ruin.
NAUFRAGIO.
m, shipwreck, sinking ‖ ruin, ruination.
NÁUFRAGO.
m, shipwreck victim.
NAUTA.
m, mariner, sailor, seaman.
NÁUTICA.
f, art and science of navigation ‖ profession of a sailor.
NÁUTICO.
adj, nautical, pertaining to navigation or the art and science of navigation ‖ naval, maritime, marine.
NAVAJA.
f, knife.
NAVAJADA.
f, gash or cut of a knife, slice.
NAVAJEAR.
v, to gash, cut, slice (with a knife).
NAVAL.
adj, naval, pertaining to navigation or the Navy ‖ maritime, marine ‖ seafaring ‖ sea.

NAVE.
f, ship, vessel, boat ‖ passenger or cargo carrying vessel.

NAVE DE CARGA.
cargo ship, freighter.

NAVE ESPACIAL.
spaceship.

NAVEGABILIDAD.
f, navigability.

NAVEGABLE.
adj, navigable.

NAVEGACIÓN.
f, navigation ‖ science and art of navigation ‖ duration of navigation ‖ profession of a sailor.

NAVEGACIÓN A LA SIRGA.
navigation by towline.

NAVEGACIÓN A LA VELA.
navigation by sail.

NAVEGACIÓN A VAPOR.
navigation by steam.

NAVEGACIÓN AÉREA.
air navigation, transportation by air.

NAVEGACIÓN ASTRONÓMICA.
See NAVEGACIÓN DE ALTURA.

NAVEGACIÓN COSTANERA.
See NAVEGACIÓN DE CABOTAJE.

NAVEGACIÓN DE ALTA MAR.
navigation on the high seas.

NAVEGACIÓN DE ALTURA.
See NAVEGACIÓN DE ALTA MAR.

NAVEGACIÓN DE CABOTAJE.
coastal navigation.

NAVEGACIÓN DE CAZA ESCOTA.
short sea journey.

NAVEGACIÓN DE GOLFO.
See NAVEGACIÓN DE ALTURA.

NAVEGACIÓN DE GRAN CABOTAJE.
sea navigation (without crossing an ocean).

NAVEGACIÓN EN CONSERVA.
navigation by group.

NAVEGACIÓN EN CONVOY.
navigation in convoy.

NAVEGACIÓN FLUVIAL.
inland navigation ‖ river navigation.

NAVEGACIÓN IMPROPIA.
See NAVEGACIÓN DE CABOTAJE.

NAVEGACIÓN INTERIOR.
See NAVEGACIÓN FLUVIAL.

NAVEGACIÓN LACUSTRE.
lake navigation.

NAVEGACIÓN MARÍTIMA.
sea navigation.

NAVEGACIÓN PRÁCTICA.
See NAVEGACIÓN DE CABOTAJE.

NAVEGACIÓN PROPIA.
See NAVEGACIÓN DE ALTURA.

NAVEGACIÓN SUBMARINA.
submarine navigation.

NAVEGACIÓN SUPERMARINA.
marine navigation (on the waters).

NAVEGADOR.
m, navigator, sailor, seaman.

NAVEGANTE.
m, person who is on board ship either as passenger or sailor.

NAVEGAR.
v, to navigate, steer ‖ to go by ship or airplane ‖ to fly ‖ to travel.

NAVIERO.
m, ship owner ‖ ship supplier or purveyor, person who supplies ship with provisions ‖ adj, shipping, pertaining to navigation or ships.

NAVIERO GESTOR.
m, voluntary representative of a merchant ship or merchant ship owners' association.

NAVÍFRAGO.
m, cause of shipwrecks.

NAVÍO.
m, ship (over 500 tons in weight).

NAVÍO DE CARGA.
merchant ship, freighter.

NAVÍO DE GUERRA.
warship.

NAVÍO DE RECREO.
recreational boat.

NAVÍO DE TRANSPORTE.
vessel used to transport goods, troops, livestock, provisions and munitions.

NAVÍO MERCANTE.
merchant ship, freighter.

NAVÍO MERCANTIL.
merchant ship, freighter.

NAVÍO PARTICULAR.
merchant ship, freighter.

NAZI.
m, Nazi.

NAZISMO.
m, Nazism, National Socialist Party.

NEANIOCRACIA.
f, government of young people.

NEBULÓN.
m, hypocrite.

NEBULOSO.
adj, cloudy, unclear ‖ suspicious ‖ difficult.

NECESARIAMENTE.
adv, necessarily, inevitably.

NECESARIO.
adj, necessary ‖ determined, inevitable ‖ obligatory, required.

NECESIDAD.
f, necessity, need ‖ unavoidable causation, irresistible impulse ‖ determinism ‖ poverty, misery, want.

NECESIDAD EXTREMA.
urgent or extreme need (which may serve to justify otherwise illegal acts) ‖ deathly need (of assistance).

NECESIDAD FÍSICA.
See NECESIDAD NATURAL.

NECESIDAD NATURAL.
physical necessity.

NECESIDAD PARTICULAR.
private or individual need.
Opposed to government needs.

NECESIDAD PÚBLICA.
public necessity or convenience or need.

NECESIDAD RACIONAL DEL MEDIO EMPLEADO.
reasonable need for the means used.

NECESITAR.
v, to need, necessitate ‖ to have a need for, lack ‖ to require.

NECIO.
m, stupid or ignorant person ‖ adj, stupid, ignorant.

NECROCOMIO.
m, morgue.

NECROFILIA.
f, necrophilia.

NECROFILOMANÍA.
See NECROFILIA.

NECROFOBIA.
f, necrophobia, serious fear of death.

NECROLOGÍA.
f, necrology ‖ death statistics ‖ obituary ‖ list of dead.

NECROMANÍA.
f, necromania, mental illness which consists of the desire to enter cemeteries and disturb the graves.

NECRÓPOLIS.
f, necropolis, important cemetery.

NECROPSIA.
f, necropsy, autopsy, postmortem physical examination.

NECROSCOPIA.
See NECROPSIA.

NEFANDARIO.
m, sodomite ‖ homosexual.

NEFANDO.
adj ‖ abominable, repulsive, degenerate ‖ homosexual.

NEFARIO.
adj, nefarious, perverse ‖ abominable, despicable.

NEFASTO.
adj, unlucky.

NEGABLE.
adj, deniable, controvertible, refutable, able to be negated.

NEGACIÓN.
f, negation, denial, negative ‖ refusal ‖ prohibition ‖ act or position of neither confessing not negating an accusation ‖ total lack ‖ excuse.

NEGACIÓN DE DERECHO.
denial of a question of law.

NEGACIÓN DE HECHO.
denial of a question of fact.

NEGACIÓN DEL ACUSADO.
denial of the accused, defendant's denial.

NFGADO.
adj, denied ‖ useless, inept.

NEGADOR.
m, person or thing that denies or negates something.

NEGANTE.
m, f, denier, negator, person who denies or negates.

NEGAR.
v, to negate, deny ‖ to refuse ‖ to prohibit ‖ to say no to ‖ to oppose ‖ to impede, disturb, make difficult ‖ to abandon (e.g. an idea, movement) ‖ to hide (e.g. the truth) ‖ to fail to recognize the existence of something.

NEGARSE.
v, to excuse oneself ‖ to be opposed to something ‖ to disobey ‖ to resist.

NEGATIVA.
f, negative ‖ denial, negation, refusal ‖ rejection ‖ declaration that something is false ‖ adj, negative.

NEGATIVA A DECLARAR.
resistance to giving testimony before a judge or other court official.
NEGATIVA A FIRMAR.
resistance to signing (e.g. sworn testimony, contracts).
NEGATIVA COARTADA.
special denial.
NEGATIVA DE CALIDAD.
denial regarding characteristics (of a person or thing).
NEGATIVA DE DERECHO.
denial of the legality of a transaction or conduct or procedure.
NEGATIVA DE HECHO.
factual denial, denial of fact.
NEGATIVA INDEFINIDA.
general denial.
NEGATIVAMENTE.
adv, negatively ‖ disloyally ‖ contradictorily.
NEGATIVO.
m, accused who does not confess ‖ witness who denies ‖ adj, negative ‖ contradictory ‖ unfavorable, adverse ‖ contrary ‖ amoral ‖ immoral.
NEGATORIA.
See ACCIÓN NEGATORIA.
NEGLIGENCIA.
f, negligence, omission of care that should otherwise be given to matters ‖ lack of due care ‖ neglect ‖ abandonment ‖ lack of attention or application, carelessness.
NEGLIGENCIA COMPARATIVA.
comparative negligence.
NEGLIGENCIA CONCURRENTE.
joint or concurrent negligence.
NEGLIGENCIA CONJUNTA.
joint negligence.
NEGLIGENCIA CONTRIBUYENTE.
contributory negligence.
NEGLIGENCIA CRASA.
gross negligence.
NEGLIGENCIA CRIMINAL.
criminal negligence.
NEGLIGENCIA CULPABLE.
culpable negligence.
NEGLIGENCIA DEL MARIDO ADMINISTRADOR.
negligence of the husband as administrator of his earnings and his wife's dowry.

NEGLIGENCIA EN EL ABORDAJE.
negligence which causes a collision between ships.
NEGLIGENCIA EN LA SOCIEDAD.
corporate or partnership negligence (by an agent thereof).
NEGLIGENCIA GRAVE.
gross negligence.
NEGLIGENCIA INCIDENTAL.
collateral negligence.
NEGLIGENCIA INEXCUSABLE.
inexcusable negligence.
NEGLIGENCIA MILITAR.
military negligence (e.g. in carrying out orders).
NEGLIGENCIA PROCESAL.
failure to move a case forward, want of activity in a case (either by the parties or the court).
NEGLIGENCIA SOBREVINIENTE.
supervening negligence.
NEGLIGENCIA SUBSECUENTE.
subsequent negligence.
NEGLIGENCIA TEMERARIA.
gross negligence.
NEGLIGENTE.
m, negligent person ‖ adj, negligent, careless ‖ imprudent.
NEGLIGENTEMENTE.
adv, negligently, carelessly ‖ imprudently.
NEGOCIABILIDAD.
f, negotiability.
NEGOCIABLE.
adj, negotiable, transferable ‖ endorsable, indorsable ‖ transferable to bearer.
NEGOCIACIÓN.
f, commercial deal or transaction ‖ commerce ‖ transfer, cession ‖ endorsement, indorsement ‖ discount of stock ‖ purchase or sale (on the open market or on the stock exchange) ‖ negotiation (between countries) ‖ exchange of prisoners.
NEGOCIACIONES INCOMPATIBLES CON EL EJERCICIO DE FUNCIONES PÚBLICAS.
business matters which are incompatible with public office or government employment.
NEGOCIACIONES PROHIBIDAS.
prohibited transactions (e.g. prohibited for civil servants).
NEGOCIADO.
m, illegal transaction involving state funds or

the help of public officers ‖ adj, negotiated ‖ business.

NEGOCIADOR.
m, negotiator ‖ merchant ‖ international negotiator.

NEGOCIAL.
adj, pertaining to negotiations ‖ transactional, pertaining to transactions.

NEGOCIAR.
v, to negotiate ‖ to deal in, buy and sell, trade, do business in ‖ to indorse, endorse (negotiable instruments) ‖ to discount ‖ to corrupt, suborn.

NEGOCIAR DOCUMENTOS.
to discount negotiable instruments.

NEGOCIAR UN EMPRÉSTITO.
to negotiate a loan.

NEGOCIAR UN GIRO.
to negotiate a draft.

NEGOCIO.
m, business, occupation, activity, work, employment ‖ business, trade ‖ negotiation ‖ pretension ‖ treatment ‖ profit or benefit of a transaction ‖ undue or illegal profit ‖ place of business, shop, commercial establishment.

NEGOCIO ABSTRACTO.
abstract transaction, transaction in which the purpose of the business has been separated from the transaction in question and is irrelevant to its validity (e.g. the issuance of a negotiable instrument re the purposes for which it is issued).

NEGOCIO AJENO.
business of others, foreign business (but in which one may be involved).

NEGOCIO CON
EL EXTRANJERO.
foreign trade or commerce.

NEGOCIO DE AUTORIZACIÓN.
transaction by proxy upon the principal's authorization.

NEGOCIO EXTRAORDINARIO.
(extraordinary) matter the execution of which requires the grant of a special power to an agent from the corporation or principal in question.

NEGOCIO FIDUCIARIO.
fiduciary transaction.

NEGOCIO FUTURO.
future profit (from a business venture) ‖ future deal or transaction.

NEGOCIO JURÍDICO.
legal transaction, deal, or matter which ten to change, create, preserve, transfer, or te minate legal rights.

NEGOCIO ORDINARIO.
(ordinary) matter the execution of which do not require the grant of a special power.

NEGOCIO PROCESAL.
declaration or conduct to change, create, terminate legal proceedings.

NEGOCIO PROPIO.
personal business ‖ matters which the perso involved take care of.

NEGOCIO REDONDO.
beneficial business deal.

NEGOCIOSO.
adj, careful in business ‖ diligent.

NEGRO.
adj, black ‖ illegal, underground, black (e market) ‖ contraband ‖ hidden ‖ bad.

NEMINE DISCREPANTE.
without discrepancies or contradiction without opposition ‖ unanimously.

NEMOFOBIA.
f, antagonistic attitude toward established r les and regulations.

NEOFETO.
m, eight- or nine-week old fetus.

NEÓFITO.
m, neophyte, recent convert ‖ beginner.

NEOLÓGICO.
adj, pertaining to neologism.

NEOLOGISMO.
m, neologism.

NEÓLOGO.
m, neologist.

NEONATAL.
adj, pertaining to newborns.

NEPOTISMO.
m, nepotism.

NERVIO.
m, nerve ‖ energy, force.

NERVIOSIDAD.
f, nervousness ‖ fear.

NERVIOSISMO.
See NERVIOSIDAD.

NERVIOSO.
adj, nervous ‖ strong, vigorous ‖ fearful ‖ u comfortable ‖ irritated.

NERVOSIDAD.
See NERVIOSIDAD.

ETO.
n, net profits or earnings (after expenses) ‖ adj, net, liquid ‖ pure, clean, genuine ‖ remaining.

EUMA.
n, statement of will through gestures and signs.

EURÓLOGO.
n, neurologist.

EURÓPATA.
n, f, neurotic person, neurotic.

EUROSIS.
f, neurosis.

EURÓTICO.
n, neurotic person ‖ adj, neurotic.

EUTRAL.
n, neutral state or nation ‖ adj, neutral, impartial ‖ indifferent.

EUTRALIDAD.
f, neutrality, impartiality ‖ indifference ‖ international neutrality.

EUTRALIDAD ABSOLUTA.
absolute neutrality (as between nations).

EUTRALIDAD ACCIDENTAL.
temporary neutrality (as between nations).

EUTRALIDAD ACTIVA.
See NEUTRALIDAD ARMADA.

EUTRALIDAD AÉREA.
neutrality in the air (as between nations).

EUTRALIDAD ARMADA.
armed neutrality (as between nations).

EUTRALIDAD CONVENCIONAL.
stipulated neutrality (as between nations).

EUTRALIDAD MARÍTIMA.
neutrality on the seas (as between nations).

EUTRALIDAD NATURAL.
natural neutrality (which arises out of the rule that no nation is required to participate in war).

EUTRALIDAD OBLIGATORIA.
negotiated neutrality (as between nations).

EUTRALIDAD PERPETUA.
permanent neutrality (as between nations).

EUTRALIDAD RELATIVA.
relative neutrality prohibiting participation in a war but reserving the right to trade.

EUTRALIDAD VOLUNTARIA.
voluntary neutrality (as between nations).

EUTRALISMO.
n, neutralism.

NEUTRALISTA.
m, supporter of neutralism.

NEUTRALIZABLE.
adj, neutralizable.

NEUTRALIZACIÓN.
f, neutralization ‖ offset.

NEUTRALIZADO.
adj, neutralized.

NEUTRALIZAR.
v, to become neutral ‖ to declare a state of neutrality ‖ to neutralize.

NEUTRALIZARSE.
v, to be neutralized, declare neutrality.

NEUTRALMENTE.
adv, neutrally.

NEUTRO.
m, neuter ‖ adj, neutral, impartial ‖ indifferent.

NEXO.
m, nexus, tie, link.

NEXO MUTUO.
alliance, reciprocal ties (between two groups or persons).

NEXO SOCIAL.
social nexus.

"NEXUM".
m, nexus, tie, link.

NIDO.
m, nest ‖ den (of thieves) ‖ origin, cause.

NIETASTRA.
f, daughter of step-child, step-grand-daughter.

NIETASTRO.
m, child of step-child, step-grandchild ‖ son of step-child, step grand-son.

NIETA.
f, granddaughter.

NIETO.
m, grandchild ‖ grandson ‖ great-grandchild or son.

NIETO DE EXTRANJERO.
second-generation child, grandchild of an immigrant.

NIGROMANCIA.
f, necromancy, black magic.

NIGROMANTE.
m, person who believes in or practices black magic.

NIHILISMO.
m, nihilism.

NINFÓMANA.
f, nymphomaniac.

NINFOMANÍA.
f, nymphomania.

NINGUNO.
m, not one or any ‖ adj, no, not any, none ‖ null, ineffective, void.

NIÑEZ.
f, childhood, life until seven years of age ‖ beginning.

NIÑA.
f, girl ‖ little girl, girl child until seven years of age ‖ female adolescent ‖ naive or inexperienced person ‖ unmarried woman.

NIÑO.
m, boy ‖ little boy, boy child until seven years of age ‖ male adolescent ‖ naive or inexperienced person ‖ unmarried male or person.

NÍQUEL.
m, money ‖ property ‖ nickel (metal).

NIVEL.
m, level (in all meanings) ‖ quality of being horizontal ‖ height ‖ equality, equivalency ‖ stage ‖ position.

NIVEL DE VIDA.
standard of living, economic level (of a country, etc.).

NIVEL PROFESIONAL.
professional ability or level.

NIVEL SOCIAL.
social level or class or position.

NIVELAR.
v, to level, even out ‖ to make equal ‖ to prepare, equip.

NO APARENTE.
See SERVIDUMBRE NO APARENTE.

NO APTO.
not apt or fit or appropriate (e.g. for certain ages).

NO BELICOSO.
non-violent, pacifist.

NO BELIGERANCIA.
non-belligerence, neutrality.

NO COMBATIENTE.
non-combatant ‖ civilian, person who does not take up arms in time of war.

NO CONSUMIBLE.
non-consumable.

NO CULPABLE.
not guilty.

NO DAR.
See OBLIGACIÓN DE NO DAR.

NO DECIR.
See OBLIGACIÓN DE NO DECIR.

NO DECIR PALABRA.
to not breathe a word, keep silent (about something) ‖ to not oppose ‖ to fail to give adequate reasons or explanations.

NO ESCRITO.
See DERECHO NO ESCRITO.

NO ESTAR EN ESTADO DE PLEITO.
to not be able to litigate.

NO EXIGIBILIDAD DE OTRA CONDUCTA.
theory in criminal law that where a criminal could not have acted differently, punishment cannot be imposed for having acted illegally.

NO FUNGIBLE.
See BIENES NO FUNGIBLES.

NO HA LUGAR.
unfounded, unbased. Expression used to describe judicial decisions denying a complaint or answer or motion.

NO HACER.
See OBLIGACIÓN DE NO HACER.

NO HIPOTECABLES.
See BIENES NO HIPOTECABLES.

NO INNOVAR.
v, to not change or innovate. Used to refer to procedural obligation not to change conduct or a state or situation following an injunction to that effect.

NO INTERVENCIÓN.
non-intervention.

NO LUCRATIVO.
non-profit, not-for-profit ‖ not profitable.

NO NEGOCIABLE.
unnegotiable ‖ non-negotiable (in all its meanings).

NO SOLEMNE.
See CONTRATO NO SOLEMNE.

NO TENER PRECIO.
to be invaluable or priceless ‖ to be worthless

NO TENER VUELTA DE HOJA.
to have no other response or objection ‖ to be undeniable.

NO USO.
non-use, disuse.

NO VENIR EN ESTADO DE PLEITO.
to not be able to litigate.

NOBLE.
adj, noble ‖ loyal ‖ excellent ‖ illustrious ‖ honorable, estimable.

NOBLEZA.
f, nobility ‖ excellence ‖ loyalty.

NOCIBLE.
adj, noxious ‖ prejudicial.

NOCIVIDAD.
f, noxiousness, harmfulness.

NOCIVO.
adj, noxious, harmful ‖ prejudicial ‖ offensive ‖ bad.

NOCTURNAL.
See NOCTURNO.

NOCTURNALIDAD.
f, aggravating circumstance of having committed a crime at night.

NOCTURNIDAD.
See NOCTURNALIDAD.

NOCTURNINO.
See NOCTURNO.

NOCTURNO.
adj, night, pertaining to night ‖ nocturnal.

NOCHE.
f, night, nighttime ‖ period of time from sunset to dawn ‖ darkness, obscurity ‖ death penalty.

NOINTERCURSO.
m, free trade (in terms of commercial transactions between warring nations).

NOLICIÓN.
f, unwillingness.

NOLUNTAD.
f, lack of volition, unwillingness.

NÓMADA.
f, m, nomad ‖ nomadic family or person.

NÓMADE.
See NÓMADA.

NOMADISMO.
m, nomadic state.

NOMBRADO.
m, appointee ‖ adj, famous, well-known ‖ named, mentioned ‖ appointed, placed in a position.

NOMBRAMIENTO.
m, naming, giving a name ‖ appointment (of a person for a position), naming ‖ dispatch, decree, or other order admitting (a person) to practice a profession ‖ election ‖ commission ‖ nomination.

NOMBRAMIENTO DE ÁRBITROS EN EL CONTRATO DE SEGURO.
naming of arbitrators pursuant to an insurance contract.

NOMBRAMIENTO DE CURADORES EJEMPLARES.
court appointment of guardians for the mentally ill, the deaf and dumb, and those persons who lack legal capacity.

NOMBRAMIENTO DE CURADORES PARA BIENES.
court appointment of trustee of property (usually in a will).

NOMBRAMIENTO DE CURADORES PARA PLEITOS.
court appointment of public defender.

NOMBRAMIENTO DE PERITOS EN EL CONTRATO DE SEGURO.
naming of experts pursuant to an insurance contract.

NOMBRAMIENTOS ILEGALES.
improper nomination or appointment (of persons to administrative positions, to which they are not legally entitled).

NOMBRAR.
v, to name ‖ to mention, cite, refer to ‖ to call roll ‖ to appoint ‖ to admit to practice ‖ to honor ‖ to nominate.

NOMBRAR NUEVAMENTE.
to reappoint.

NOMBRE.
m, name ‖ last name ‖ first name ‖ fame ‖ infamy, notoriety, celebrity ‖ reputation ‖ power, authority ‖ alias ‖ nickname.

NOMBRE COLECTIVO.
name given to a COMPAÑÍA COLECTIVA ‖ name of general partners (in a SOCIEDAD EN COMANDITA).

NOMBRE COMERCIAL.
trade or commercial name ‖ business or company or firm name.

NOMBRE DE BAUTISMO.
See NOMBRE DE PILA.

NOMBRE DE COMERCIO.
See NOMBRE COMERCIAL.

NOMBRE DE FÁBRICA.
trade name.

NOMBRE DE FAMILIA.
last or family name.

NOMBRE DE GUERRA.
pseudonym, assumed name ‖ false or fictitious name.

NOMBRE DE LA MUJER CASADA.
married name, last name of a married woman.

**NOMBRE DE LA MUJER
DIVORCIADA.**
last name of a divorced woman.
NOMBRE DE PILA.
first name, Christian or baptismal name, fore-
name, given name.
NOMBRE FICTICIO.
See NOMBRE DE GUERRA.
NOMBRE IMAGINARIO.
pen name, nom de plume.
NOMBRE INDIVIDUAL.
See NOMBRE DE PILA.
NOMBRE PROPIO.
See NOMBRE DE PILA.
NOMBRE SOCIAL.
company or firm name.
NOMBRE SUPUESTO.
assumed name, pseudonym, alias.
NOMENCLADOR.
m, nomenclature ‖ list, catalogue (of persons,
cities, etc.).
"NOMEN".
m, name.
NOMENCLATOR.
See NOMENCLADOR.
NOMENCLATURA.
See NOMENCLADOR.
NÓMINA.
f, list of personnel and their respective jobs ‖
relationship between persons and their res-
pective names ‖ list of things (e.g. inventory).
NOMINACIÓN.
f, nomination ‖ naming, appointment ‖ election.
NOMINADO.
m, appointee, nominee ‖ elected person ‖ adj,
appointed, named.
Also see CONTRATO NOMINADO.
NOMINADOR.
m, appointer, nominator, namer ‖ electorate.
NOMINAL.
adj, nominal ‖ pertaining to a name ‖ nominal
‖ honorary.
NOMINALMENTE.
adv, nominally, in name only.
NOMINAR.
v, to name, appoint, designate ‖ to nominate ‖
to elect.
NOMINATIVO.
adj, nominative ‖ nominative, bearing a name
‖ registered (e.g. stock).

NOMOLOGÍA.
f, nomology, the science of laws.
NOMÓLOGO.
m, nomologist ‖ jurist.
NON.
adj, odd, uneven (number) ‖ no.
"NON ADIMPLETI CONTRACTUS".
See EXCEPTIO NON ADIMPLETI CONTRACTUS.
"NON BIS IN IDEM".
non bis in idem, no two trials for the same cause of action ‖ no double jeopardy.
"NON NUMERATA PECUNIA."
See EXCEPTIO NON NUMERATA PECUNIA.
**"NON PLUS JURIS
AD ALIUM TRANSFERRE POTEST
QUAM IPSE HABET".**
one cannot transfer more rights than what one
has.
NONATO.
m, child born via Caesarean operation ‖ child
born immediately prior to mother's death ‖
adj, unborn, non-existent.
NORMA.
f, norm, rule of conduct, standard ‖ practice ‖
legal norm ‖ organic body of law ‖ precept ‖
personal criteria ‖ guideline.
NORMA CORRIENTE.
current practice.
NORMA DE VALOR.
measure of value.
NORMA FUNDAMENTAL.
fundamental rule or norm.
NORMA JURÍDICA.
legal rule (contained in law as a whole).
NORMA LEGAL.
legal rule ‖ positive law ‖ statutory rule (contained in statutes).
**NORMA MÁS FAVORABLE
AL TRABAJADOR.**
the rule most favorable to the employee. Applicable in doubtful cases.
NORMA MORAL.
moral rule.
NORMA PENAL EN BLANCO.
broad criminal rule which allows the executive
branch to determine the exact nature of the illegal conduct punished under such rule (e.g. a
provision punishing the violation of environmental regulations, whatever they may be).
NORMA PROCESAL.
procedural rule.

NORMA SOCIAL.
social norm or rule or standard.

NORMACIÓN.
f, normative tendency ‖ group of norms.

NORMAL.
adj, normal ‖ natural, ordinary ‖ habitual, usual ‖ average ‖ pursuant to norm or rule or guideline.

NORMALIDAD.
f, normality ‖ normalcy ‖ adaptation of a norm ‖ custom.

NORMALIZACIÓN.
f, normalization.

NORMALIZAR.
v, to normalize ‖ to put in order ‖ to adjust or adapt to a norm ‖ to return or bring back to normal (e.g. after a war, uprising).

NORMALMENTE.
adv, normally, habitually.

NORMAS CONTABLES.
accounting practices or standards.

NORMAS DE ELECCIÓN.
rules which apply pursuant to the parties' choice.

NORMAS DE INTEGRACIÓN.
rules of legal construction.

NORMAS DE TRABAJO.
work rules.

NORMAS DEL PROCEDIMIENTO.
procedural rules.

NORMAS SOCIOLÓGICAS.
sociological rules.

NORMATIVO.
adj, normative.

NOS.
m, (the royal) we ‖ us.

NOSOCOMIO.
m, hospital.

NOTA.
f, note ‖ notation, annotation ‖ signal, sign ‖ objection (e.g. to an argument, doctrine) ‖ commentary (e.g. to a legal writing or judicial decision) ‖ censure ‖ grade or classification of a tribunal or professor who examines persons ‖ abstract, case summary ‖ notation in books of special notary public ‖ inventory ‖ diplomatic note.

NOTA DESFAVORABLE.
dishonorable mention (in a military service record).

NOTA DIPLOMÁTICA.
diplomatic note or dispatch.

NOTA EN DERECHO CIVIL.
note or notation in a private document (which under civil law may or may not have legal effect desired).

NOTA MARGINAL.
marginal note, margin reference (used in real estate and other civil registries to refer to a main registration or filing).

NOTA NOTARIAL.
notarial annotation (in a document).

NOTA OFICIOSA.
official notice or communication (from government) ‖ official comment (to public rumors regarding who is in power).

NOTA PROCEDIMENTAL.
procedural summary of the factual and legal bases of an appeal.

NOTA REGISTRAL.
registration annotation, filing notation (used in real estate and other civil registries to alter or cancel a prior filing).

NOTA VERBAL.
verbal note, oral diplomatic communication.

NOTABLES.
m, notables, worthies, dignitaries, pillars of society.

NOTACIÓN.
See ANOTACIÓN.

NOTAR.
v, to note, mark ‖ to observe, note ‖ to annotate, make notes or annotations ‖ to summarize ‖ to discredit, defame ‖ to censure, condemn.

NOTARÍA.
f, notary's office ‖ position and functions of a notary. See NOTARIO.

NOTARIADO.
m, career and profession of a notary ‖ body of notaries (e.g. in a country) ‖ adj, notarized, certified by a notary. See NOTARIO.

NOTARIAL.
adj, notarial.

NOTARIATO.
m, certificate of notary ‖ appointment of notary ‖ practice of a notary (in accord with his or her appointment).

NOTARIO.
m, notary, notary public, public notary, public officer whose work is to administer oaths and

witness out-of-court documents. In some countries.

NOTARIO.
is equivalent to ESCRIBANO.

NOTARIO AUTORIZANTE.
witnessing or attesting notary.

NOTARIO FEDANTE.
witnessing or attesting notary.

NOTARIO MAYOR.
federal notary, notary with powers to certify births, deaths, marriages and other matter relating to civil status.

NOTARIO PÚBLICO.
notary public, public notary, notary.

NOTAS.
f, notes ‖ body of notarial annotations ‖ plural of NOTA.

NOTICIA.
f, notice ‖ notification ‖ news ‖ idea, notion ‖ communication, data, information.

NOTICIA DE RECHAZO.
notice of dishonor.

NOTICIA FALSA.
false or imprecise information ‖ false news.

NOTICIA FAMILIAR.
information pertaining to the life and death of family members.

NOTICIAR.
v, to notify ‖ to inform, communicate or give news.

NOTICIERO.
m, news reporter, newsman ‖ news, news bulletin ‖ adj, news.

NOTICIÓN.
m, sensational news ‖ scoop.

NOTICIOSO.
m, person who is up to date on the news.

NOTIFICACIÓN.
f, notification ‖ service of process ‖ document which gives notice ‖ official notification of a decision ‖ notice (of something via a notary).

NOTIFICACIÓN DE APELACIÓN.
notice of appeal.

NOTIFICACIÓN DE LA DEMANDA.
service of the complaint.

NOTIFICACIÓN DE LOS ACTOS CIVILES.
notification or notice of civil acts. See ACTO CIVIL. In order for certain actions to have legal effect, the interested parties must be notified.

NOTIFICACIÓN DEL AUTO DE PRISIÓN.
notification of the decision to imprison.

NOTIFICACIÓN DEL PROTESTO.
notification of protest due to dishonor of a negotiable instrument.

NOTIFICACIÓN EN EL EXPEDIENTE.
notification by filing notice in the court file.

NOTIFICACIÓN EN ESTRADOS.
type of service or notice by publication consisting of placing a notice at court (due to the fact that the defendant has failed to appear).

NOTIFICACIÓN EN REBELDÍA.
See NOTIFICACIÓN EN ESTRADOS.

NOTIFICACIÓN IMPLÍCITA.
implied notice.

NOTIFICACIÓN PERSONAL.
personal service.

NOTIFICACIÓN POR CÉDULA.
notice by written service.

NOTIFICACIÓN POR EDICTOS.
notice or service by publication (due to the fact that the defendant has failed to appear).

NOTIFICACIÓN POR EXPEDIENTE.
notice by means of an entry in the court file.

NOTIFICACIÓN POR NOTA.
See NOTIFICACIÓN EN EL EXPEDIENTE.

NOTIFICACIÓN PRESUNTA.
implied service.

NOTIFICACIÓN PREVENTIVA.
service of notice of intention.

NOTIFICACIÓN PREVIA.
prior notice.

NOTIFICACIÓN REGISTRAL.
notification by filing with the real estate registry.

NOTIFICADOR.
m, notifier ‖ process server.

NOTIFICANTE.
m, court or judge who issues a notice of decision ‖ adj, notifying.

NOTIFICAR.
v, to notify ‖ to issue a judicial or notarial notice ‖ to serve.

NOTIFICAR UN AUTO.
to serve a writ or warrant or order.

NOTIFICAR UNA CITACIÓN.
to serve a summons or subpoena.

NOTIFICATIVO.
adj, notifying.

NOTO.
adj, notified, published ‖ notorious, known.

NOTORIAMENTE.
adv, notoriously, publicly, manifestly.

NOTORIEDAD.
f, notoriety, publicity ‖ evidence ‖ fame, celebrity ‖ knowledge.

NOTORIEDAD DE DERECHO.
constructive notoriety, notoriety declared or presumed by the law.

NOTORIEDAD DE HECHO.
actual notoriety, notoriety based on evidence produced regarding its existence.

NOTORIO.
adj, notorious, evident, public.

NOVACIÓN.
f, novation, substitution of debtor or creditor by another person or changing the purpose or conditions of the contract.

NOVACIÓN OBJETIVA.
type of novation in which the purpose or conditions of the contract are changed.

NOVACIÓN SUBJETIVA.
type of novation in which a third party replaces the original creditor or debtor.

NOVACIÓN TÁCITA.
implied novation.

NOVAR.
v, to substitute by novation.

NOVATO.
m, novice ‖ apprentice, beginner ‖ new person.

NOVEDAD.
f, news ‖ novelty, innovation ‖ alteration, change, development ‖ pregnancy ‖ surprise.

NÓVEL.
adj, new, novel ‖ beginning.

NOVELA.
f, novel ‖ fiction, lie.

NOVELAR.
v, to write or publish a literary novel ‖ to fictionalize history ‖ to lie, invent.

NOVENARIO.
m, period of nine days of mourning (during which the heir may not be forced to accept or reject the inheritance).

NOVENTA Y NUEVE AÑOS.
m, ninety-nine years. Usually a legal limit on lease terms.

NOVIA.
f, girlfriend ‖ fiancee, engaged woman ‖ bride, recently married woman.

NOVIAZGO.
m, betrothal, engagement to be married ‖ courtship.

NOVIO.
m, boyfriend ‖ fiance, engaged man ‖ groom, bridegroom, recently married man.

NÚBIL.
adj, nubile.

NUBILIDAD.
f, nubility, marriageability ‖ marriageable age, age at which one becomes physically capable of marriage.

NUDA PROPIEDAD.
f, bare ownership, bare right of ownership.

NUDISMO.
m, nudism.

NUDO.
m, knot ‖ adj, bare, simple ‖ nude.

NUDO EN LA GARGANTA.
a knot in the throat.

NUDO PROPIETARIO.
bare owner, property owner without other right (e.g. of use or habitation).

NUERA.
f, daughter-in-law (whether widowed or not).

NUEVA AUDIENCIA.
f, rehearing.

NUEVO.
adj, new, recent ‖ unused ‖ different, distinct ‖ added ‖ novel ‖ beginning.

NUEVO DERECHO.
new law.

NUEVO ESTADO.
new nation.

NUEVO JUICIO.
new hearing, trial de novo.

NUEVO MUNDO.
New World (i.e. North and South America vis à vis Europe).

NUGATORIO.
m, deceiver ‖ adj, nugatory, deceiving ‖ ineffective ‖ invalid.

NULAMENTE.
adv, invalidly ‖ voidly ‖ without legal force or effect.

NULIDAD.
f, nullity, invalidity ‖ lack of force or effect ‖ incapacity ‖ ineptitude ‖ useless person ‖ nonexistence ‖ absolute illegality.

NULIDAD AB INITIO.
nullity from the start.

NULIDAD ABSOLUTA.
absolute nullity ‖ absolute lack of legal force or effect ‖ nullity which may be alleged or

raised or claimed by any party. Opposed to NULIDAD RELATIVA.

NULIDAD COMPLETA.
complete or total nullity.
Opposed to NULIDAD PARCIAL.

NULIDAD DE FONDO.
fundamental or basic nullity.

NULIDAD DE LA COMPRAVENTA.
voidness of sales.

NULIDAD DE LA DONACIÓN.
voidness of a gift.

NULIDAD DE LA POSESIÓN.
voidness of possession.

NULIDAD DE LA SOCIEDAD CIVIL.
non-existence of a civil corporation (due to legal defect of incorporation).
See SOCIEDAD CIVIL.

NULIDAD DE LA SOCIEDAD MERCANTIL.
non-existence of a commercial corporation (due to legal defect of incorporation).
See SOCIEDAD MERCANTIL.

NULIDAD DE LAS ACTUACIONES.
ineffectiveness of the pleadings or other procedural steps.

NULIDAD DE LAS ANOTACIONES PREVENTIVAS.
voidness or ineffectiveness of the filings in a real estate registry.
See ANOTACIÓN PREVENTIVA.

NULIDAD DE LAS NEGOCIACIONES MERCANTILES.
voidness of commercial dealings.

NULIDAD DE LOS ACTOS.
voidness or nullity of illegal acts.

NULIDAD DE LOS ACTOS DE LA CASADA.
voidness of a married woman's actions.

NULIDAD DE LOS CONTRATOS.
voidness of contracts (for failure of one of the essential elements of the contract).

NULIDAD DE LOS DOCUMENTOS PRIVADOS.
voidness or ineffectiveness of private instruments or documents.

NULIDAD DE LOS PROCEDIMIENTOS.
invalidity of the proceedings.

NULIDAD DE LOS TESTAMENTOS.
invalidity or failure of testaments or wills.

NULIDAD DE PLENO DERECHO.
absolute nullity.

NULIDAD DEL MATRIMONIO.
nullity or voidness of the marriage.

NULIDAD EN LA QUIEBRA.
voidness of acts or contracts of bankrupt after the effective date of bankruptcy.

NULIDAD IMPLÍCITA.
implied nullity.

NULIDAD INTRÍNSECA.
intrinsic nullity.

NULIDAD LEGAL.
legal invalidity or nullity, voidness which occurs by law. Opposed to that voided by judicial action.

NULIDAD MANIFIESTA.
patent voidness, voidness evident on the face of the document or apparent from the circumstances of the transaction.

NULIDAD PARCIAL.
partial nullity or voidness.

NULIDAD PROCESAL.
procedural voidness or nullity.

NULIDAD RELATIVA.
nullity which may only be alleged or claimed by a party in interest.
Opposed to NULIDAD ABSOLUTA.

NULIDAD SUSTANTIVA.
substantive invalidity or nullity.

NULIDAD TOTAL.
total nullity or invalidity.

NULIDAD VIRTUAL.
implied nullity.

NULIFICAR.
v, to nullify, annul, void ‖ to invalidate.

NULO.
adj, null, void, invalid ‖ ineffective ‖ fundamentally defective ‖ illegal, prohibited ‖ incapable, worthless, inept.

NULLIUS.
See BIEN NULLIUS.

"NULLUM CRIMEN, NULLA POENA SINE PRAEVIA LEGE."
No crime or punishment without prior law. Refers to prohibition of ex post facto laws.

NUMERABLE.
adj, numerable, countable.

NUMERACIÓN.
f, numeration, numbering.

NUMERAL.
m, combination of ship's identifying flags ‖ adj, number, pertaining to numbers.

NUMERAR.
v, to number ‖ to count ‖ to mark with numbers ‖ to express by number.

NUMERARIO.
m, cash ‖ coin ‖ adj, numerical.

NUMÉRICAMENTE.
adv, numerically ‖ individually.

NUMÉRICO.
adj, numerical.

NÚMERO.
m, number ‖ class, type, category ‖ number, group.

NUMO.
m, money.

NUMULARIO.
m, banker ‖ usurer ‖ adj, pertaining to money.

NUNCIO.
m, messenger ‖ deliverer ‖ nuncio, papal ambassador.

"NUNCUPATIO".
oral statement ‖ also see NUNCUPATIVO.

NUNCUPATIVO.
adj, nuncupative, oral. Used in reference to wills and testaments.

NUNCUPATORIO.
adj, nuncupative, written.

NUPCIAL.
adj, nuptial, pertaining to wedding or marriage.

NUPCIALIDAD.
f, nuptiality, marriage rate.

NUPCIAS.
f, wedding, marriage ‖ marriage ceremony and celebration.

NUPTUAL.
adj, nuptial.

NUTRIDO.
adj, fed ‖ nourished.

NUTRIMENTO.
m, nutriment, nourishment ‖ food ‖ cause, stimulus.

Ñ

ÑA.
f, mam, madam ‖ missus.

ÑAFITEAR.
v, to thieve, steal.

ÑAFLE.
See ÑIFLE.

ÑAGAZA.
f, decoy, ruse ‖ trick, snare.

ÑAÑA.
f, older sister or grandmother or aunt (who cares for younger children in the family ‖ minor or fictitious ailment.

ÑAÑO.
m, older brother ‖ close or intimate friend.

ÑAPA.
f, promotional gift, special gift given by merchants to clients to induce them to return ‖ tip ‖ extra, bonus.

ÑAUSA.
adj, blind.

ÑERVOSO.
adj, nervous ‖ neurotic.

ÑIFLE.
m, ruse used in court by obligor in which he or she denies or misunderstands the allegations to such an extent that the court declares him or her mentally deficient or otherwise incompetent and relieves the person of liability.

ÑIFRERÍAS.
f, bad treatment.

ÑO.
m, master ‖ mister.

ÑOR.
m, mister.

ÑUCO.
m, father-in-law.

ÑUDO.
m, knot.

ÑUÑI.
f, mother-in-law.

O

OBEDECER.
v, to obey ‖ to comply with the authorities ‖ to carry out one's duties.

OBEDECIBLE.
adj, obeyable (e.g. order that is not illegal).

OBEDECIMIENTO.
m, obedience.

OBEDIENCIA.
f, obedience ‖ compliance ‖ submission (to an order).

OBEDIENCIA CIEGA.
blind or unquestioning obedience.

OBEDIENCIA CONYUGAL.
See OBEDIENCIA DE LA MUJER.

OBEDIENCIA DE LA MUJER.
wifely obedience, obedience owed by the wife to her husband.

OBEDIENCIA DE LOS HIJOS.
obedience owed by minor children to their parents.

OBEDIENCIA DE LOS PUPILOS.
obedience owed by ward to his guardian.

OBEDIENCIA DEBIDA.
due obedience, obedience owed by a subordinate to his superior. Frequently used to refer to the obedience of personnel within the military hierarchy.

OBEDIENCIA FILIAL.
See OBEDIENCIA DE LOS HIJOS.

OBEDIENCIA JERÁRQUICA.
hierarchical obedience, obedience owed by a subordinate to his superior.

OBEDIENCIA LABORAL.
compliance of employee with the duties of employment.

OBEDIENTE.
m, obedient person ‖ adj, obedient, docile.

ÓBITO.
m, death, passing, demise.

OBITORIO.
m, morgue.

OBITUARIO.
m, obituary ‖ death registry.

OBJECIÓN.
f, objection, argument posed in opposition ‖ difficulty relative to the validity or effectiveness of a norm, thesis, proposition, etc. ‖ observation.

OBJECIÓN DENEGADA.
objection overruled.

OBJETANTE.
m, objector, objecting party ‖ opposition ‖ contradictor ‖ adj, objecting.

OBJETANTE DE CONCIENCIA.
conscientious objector (in the military).

OBJETAR.
v, to object ‖ to oppose, contradict ‖ to argue ‖ to observe ‖ to pose doubts.

OBJETIVAMENTE.
adv, objectively ‖ impartially.

OBJETIVAR.
v, to attribute external existence to ideas or processes.

OBJETIVIDAD.
f, objectivity ‖ impartiality.

OBJETIVISMO JURÍDICO.
m, legal objectivism,

OBJETIVO.
m, end, purpose, objective ‖ intention ‖ adj, objective, external ‖ pertaining to an object ‖ impartial, disinterested, dispassionate.

OBJETIVO MILITAR.
military objective.

OBJETIVO POLÍTICO.
political objective ‖ purposes of war.

OBJETO.
m, object, thing ‖ material thing ‖ matter, business ‖ end, purpose, objective, intention ‖ subject, subject matter.

OBJETO CIERTO.
concrete object, material thing.

OBJETO DE LA OBLIGACIÓN.
subject matter of an obligation.

OBJETO DEL ACTO JURÍDICO.
subject matter of a legal act.
See ACTO JURÍDICO.

OBJETO DEL CONTRATO.
subject matter of a contract.

OBJETO DEL DERECHO.
subject matter of law or to which the law pertains (e.g. persons, things and legal actions) ‖ subject matter of a right.

**OBJETO MATERIAL
DEL DELITO.**
corpus delicti which is a thing, subject matter of the crime.

OBJETO PERDIDO.
lost object or thing.

OBJETO SOCIAL.
corporate purpose.

OBJETO SOCIETARIO.
See OBJETO SOCIAL.

OBJETOR DE CONCIENCIA.
See OBJETANTE DE CONCIENCIA.

OBJETOS DE PRISIONEROS.
personal effects of prisoners.

OBLICUO.
adj, oblique ‖ indirect, figurative.
See ACCIÓN OBLICUA.

OBLIGABLE.
adj, obligational, that which may be the object of an obligation.

OBLIGACIÓN.
f, obligation, duty ‖ legal duty imposed by law or contract to act or refrain from acting.

OBLIGACIÓN A DÍA.
See OBLIGACIÓN A PLAZO.

OBLIGACIÓN A PLAZO.
future obligation or duty fixed by a date or term certain.

OBLICACIÓN A PRORRATA.
See OBLIGACIÓN MANCOMUNADA.

OBLIGACIÓN A TÉRMINO.
See OBLIGACIÓN A PLAZO.

OBLIGACIÓN ACCESORIA.
accessory obligation or duty, obligation or duty which is secondary to a primary obligation.

OBLIGACIÓN ALIMENTARIA.
See OBLIGACIÓN ALIMENTICIA.

OBLIGACIÓN ALIMENTICIA.
obligation to pay alimony ‖ obligation or duty to provide for another. Usually used to refer to the obligation of parents to provide for their children (inclusive of housing, food and clothing).

OBLIGACIÓN ALTERNATIVA.
alternative obligation or duty.

OBLIGACIÓN AMBULATORIA.
obligation or duty which runs with the land.

OBLIGACIÓN AMORTIZABLE.
amortizable obligation, obligation based on time-payments.

OBLIGACIÓN APLAZADA.
See OBLIGACIÓN A PLAZO ‖ obligation or duty regarding which the creditor has granted an extension of time in which to comply ‖ obligation or duty which is in default.

OBLIGACIÓN AUTÓNOMA.
separate or autonomous obligation or duty, obligation or duty which has no relationship to another.

**OBLIGACIÓN BAJO CONDICIÓN
RESOLUTORIA.**
type of conditional obligation or duty which is subject to a condition subsequent.

**OBLIGACIÓN BAJO CONDICIÓN
SUSPENSIVA.**
type of conditional obligation or duty which is subject to a condition precedent.

OBLIGACIÓN BILATERAL.
bilateral obligation or duty, obligation which imposes duties on both parties.

OBLIGACIÓN CIVIL.
legally enforceable obligation or duty ‖ duty or obligation which is regulated by a civil code.

OBLIGACIÓN COLECTIVA.
See OBLIGACIÓN MANCOMUNADA.

OBLIGACIÓN COMPUESTA.
multiple obligation or duty, one which is composed of more than one duty or obligation either in the alternative or conjunctively.

OBLIGACIÓN COMÚN.
non-preference obligation, type of obligation which enjoys no privilege or preference in fulfillment.

OBLIGACIÓN CON CLÁUSULA PENAL.
obligation or duty with a penalty clause.
OBLIGACIÓN CONDICIONAL.
conditional obligation or duty.
OBLIGACIÓN CONJUNTA.
See OBLIGACIÓN CONJUNTIVA.
OBLIGACIÓN CONJUNTIVA.
conjunctive obligation.
OBLIGACIÓN CONTRACTUAL.
contractual obligation. In contrast to obligations imposed by law, tort, quasi-contract, etc.
OBLIGACIÓN CORREAL.
See OBLIGACIÓN SOLIDARIA.
OBLIGACIÓN CORRELATIVA.
type of obligation which is related to another obligation.
OBLIGACIÓN CREDITICIA.
enforceable loan obligation.
OBLIGACIÓN CUASICONTRACTUAL.
quasi-contractual obligation.
See CUASICONTRACTO.
OBLIGACIÓN CUASIDELICTUOSA.
quasi-delictual obligation. See CUASIDELITO.
OBLIGACIÓN DE BUENA FE.
obligation or duty of good faith.
OBLIGACIÓN DE COMERCIO.
See OBLIGACIÓN MERCANTIL.
OBLIGACIÓN DE CONSERVACIÓN.
duty of preservation (of a thing deposited with a non-owner). Usually rests on a bailee.
OBLIGACIÓN DE DAR.
duty to turn over (property, by transfer or return of ownership, use, tenancy, etc.).
OBLIGACIÓN DE DAR CANTIDAD DE COSAS.
duty to turn over a quantity of things (e.g. things which are able to be counted, measured, or weighed).
OBLIGACIÓN DE DAR COSA CIERTA.
duty to turn over a specified piece of property.
OBLIGACIÓN DE DAR COSA INCIERTA.
duty to turn over an unspecified piece of property.
OBLIGACIÓN DE DAR SUMA DE DINERO.
duty to turn over a sum certain (of money).
OBLIGACIÓN DE ENTREGA.
duty to deliver.
OBLIGACIÓN DE ESTRICTO DERECHO.
obligation or duty regarding which there is a law which regulates compliance or interpretation thereof.

OBLIGACIÓN DE GUARDA.
parental duty (of non-abandonment of offspring).
OBLIGACIÓN DE HACER.
duty to act, affirmative duty, obligation to do something.
OBLIGACIÓN DE INFORMACIÓN.
duty to warn and instruct (e.g. buyer about property being sold).
OBLIGACIÓN DE MEDIOS.
obligation related to the means used to achieve a given end.
Opposed to OBLIGACIÓN DE RESULTADO.
OBLIGACIÓN DE NO DAR.
duty not to turn over (property).
OBLIGACIÓN DE NO DECIR.
duty not to inform or to say something.
OBLIGACIÓN DE NO HACER.
duty not to act, negative duty, obligation not to do something.
OBLIGACIÓN DE PROBAR.
burden of proof, obligation of proving something.
OBLIGACIÓN DE PRUDENCIA Y DILIGENCIA.
type of duty of due care to use prudence and diligence.
OBLIGACIÓN DE REPARACIÓN.
duty to indemnify or of indemnification.
OBLIGACIÓN DE RESTITUCIÓN.
duty of returning a thing (in its original condition on the given date).
OBLIGACIÓN DE RESULTADO.
obligation related to the ends desired. Opposed to OBLIGACIÓN DE MEDIOS.
OBLIGACIÓN DE SEGURIDAD.
type of duty of due care to proceed with safety.
OBLIGACIÓN DE TRACTO SUCESIVO.
term obligation or duty. Opposed to OBLIGACIÓN DE TRACTO ÚNICO.
OBLIGACIÓN DE TRACTO ÚNICO.
obligation or duty which can be fulfilled at one time. As opposed to OBLIGACIÓN DE TRACTO SUCESIVO.
OBLIGACIÓN DECLARADA POR SENTENCIA.
obligation imposed by court order or arbitral award.
OBLIGACIÓN DELICTUOSA.
obligation or duty emanating from a criminal act ‖ obligation to indemnify for voluntary breach of a duty to act or not to act.

OBLIGACIÓN DETERMINADA.
See OBLIGACIÓN DE RESULTADO.
OBLIGACIÓN DISYUNTA.
See OBLIGACIÓN ALTERNATIVA.
OBLIGACIÓN DISYUNTIVA.
See OBLIGACIÓN ALTERNATIVA.
OBLIGACIÓN DIVISIBLE.
divisible obligation.
OBLIGACIÓN ENERVADA.
See OBLIGACIÓN NATURAL.
OBLIGACIÓN ESPECÍFICA.
determinate obligation or duty.
OBLIGACIÓN EX LEGE.
legal or statutory obligation, obligation which derives directly from the law, a statute, or a code. In contrast to those which arise out of agreement between parties.
OBLIGACIÓN EXTRACONTRACTUAL.
non-contractual obligation (e.g. statutory, tort, quasi-contract, and criminal).
OBLIGACIÓN FACULTATIVA.
obligation which allows the obligor to substitute another action for the required performance. The nature and existence of the obligation is determined on the basis of the principal or original performance.
OBLIGACIÓN GENÉRICA.
obligation to provide a specific number of things which have not been specifically identified.
OBLIGACIÓN ILÍCITA.
illegal obligation or duty, obligation or duty whose purpose is illegal. May refer to either a contract as a whole or a clause in a contract.
OBLIGACIÓN ILÍQUIDA.
non-monetary obligation.
OBLIGACIÓN IMPERFECTA.
unenforceable obligation.
OBLIGACIÓN IMPOSIBLE.
impossible obligation, obligation which is impossible or totally absurd to perform.
OBLIGACIÓN INCUMPLIDA.
unfulfilled obligation or duty.
OBLIGACIÓN INDIVIDUAL.
obligation in which there is one obligor and one obligee.
OBLIGACIÓN INDIVISIBLE.
indivisible obligation.
OBLIGACIÓN INMORAL.
immoral obligation or duty.

OBLIGACIÓN LEGAL.
legal obligation, obligation established by statute ‖ licit obligation, obligation whose purpose is legal or licit.
OBLIGACIÓN LÍCITA.
licit obligation, obligation whose purpose is legal or licit.
OBLIGACIÓN LÍQUIDA.
monetary obligation.
OBLIGACIÓN LITERAL.
written obligation or duty.
OBLIGACIÓN MANCOMUNADA.
joint obligation, obligation in which there is more than one debtor or creditor or both.
OBLIGACIÓN MERCANTIL.
commercial obligation, obligation which emanates from a commercial transaction.
OBLIGACIÓN MIXTA.
type of obligation emanating from both civil and natural obligations. See OBLIGACIÓN CIVIL and OBLIGACIÓN NATURAL.
OBLIGACIÓN MODAL.
obligation which involves the delivery of a thing and a service.
OBLIGACIÓN MORAL.
moral or natural obligation, obligation not enforceable at law.
OBLIGACIÓN MÚLTIPLE.
See OBLIGACIÓN COMPUESTA.
OBLIGACIÓN NATURAL.
natural or moral obligation, obligation not enforceable at law.
OBLIGACIÓN NEGATIVA.
duty not to act, negative duty, obligation to abstain from doing something.
OBLIGACIÓN NULA.
null obligation, void obligation (due to its nonexistence, illegality, impossibility of purpose, lack of capacity, defect, etc.).
OBLIGACIÓN PATRIMONIAL.
obligation regarding tangible or intangible property.
OBLIGACIÓN PECUNIARIA.
monetary obligation.
OBLIGACIÓN PENAL.
See OBLIGACIÓN DELICTUOSA.
OBLIGACIÓN PERFECTA.
perfect obligation, obligation which fulfills all legal requirements for its enforcement.
OBLIGACIÓN PERSONAL.
personal obligation, obligation resting upon a

person ‖ obligation entailing the personal services of a specific individual.

OBLIGACIÓN PERSONALÍSIMA.
obligation entailing the personal services of a specific individual.

OBLIGACIÓN PLURAL.
obligation which involves a variety of obligors or obligees or subject matters.

OBLIGACIÓN POR CULPA.
obligation emanating from an act of negligence.

OBLIGACIÓN POR NEGLIGENCIA.
See OBLIGACIÓN POR CULPA.

OBLIGACIÓN POSIBLE.
obligation which is possible to fulfill.

OBLIGACIÓN POSITIVA.
affirmative or positive duty, duty to act, obligation to act.

OBLIGACIÓN POTESTATIVA.
obligation the performance of which is voluntary on the part of the obligor.

OBLIGACIÓN PRINCIPAL.
principal obligation.

OBLIGACIÓN PRIVILEGIADA.
preferred obligation, obligation with priority of performance over others.

OBLIGACIÓN PROFESIONAL.
professional obligation or duty.

OBLIGACIÓN PURA Y SIMPLE.
simple obligation, unconditional obligation or duty.

OBLIGACIÓN PUTATIVA.
putative or apparent obligation, obligation which contracted in good faith is lacking a valid purpose or subject matter and therefore is only apparent.

OBLIGACIÓN REAL.
obligation which pertains to real property. Opposed to OBLIGACIÓN PERSONAL.

OBLIGACIÓN SIMPLE.
obligation which is composed of one obligation or duty to act or abstain from acting. Opposed to OBLIGACIÓN COMPUESTA.

OBLIGACIÓN SIMPLEMENTE MANCOMUNADA.
obligation in which each obligor is responsible for his or her portion of the obligation. Opposed to OBLIGACIÓN SOLIDARIA.

OBLIGACIÓN SIN CONVENIO.
non-contractual obligation or duty.

OBLIGACIÓN SINALAGMÁTICA.
unilateral obligation which may change into a bilateral obligation.

OBLIGACIÓN SOLIDARIA.
joint and several obligation, obligation which binds each and all of the obligors for the obligation in full.
Opposed to OBLIGACIÓN MANCOMUNADA.

OBLIGACIÓN SUBSIDIARIA.
See OBLIGACIÓN ACCESSORIA.

OBLIGACIÓN TRANSMISIBLE.
assignable obligation.

OBLIGACIÓN TRIBUTARIA.
tax obligation.

OBLIGACIÓN UNILATERAL.
unilateral obligation.

OBLIGACIÓN VOLUNTARIA.
consensual obligation, obligation which is voluntarily entered into.

OBLIGACIONAL.
adj, obligational, pertaining to obligations.

OBLIGACIONES.
plural of OBLIGACIÓN ‖ family obligations ‖ social obligations or duties.

OBLIGACIONES AL PORTADOR.
bearer negotiable instruments or securities.

OBLIGACIONES COMERCIALES.
See OBLIGACIONES MERCANTILES.

OBLIGACIONES CONEXAS.
related obligations.

OBLIGACIONES DE COMPAÑÍAS MERCANTILES.
obligations of commercial companies.

OBLIGACIONES DEL TESORO.
treasury bonds (of the government).

OBLIGACIONES ENTRE MARIDO Y MUJER.
marital obligations.

OBLIGACIONES HIPOTECARIAS.
obligations guaranteed by mortgages.

OBLIGACIONES INHERENTES A LA PERSONA.
personal obligations which arise out of family or other personal relationships.

OBLIGACIONES INHERENTES A LA POSESIÓN.
obligations resulting from the possession of real estate.

OBLIGACIONES MERCANTILES.
obligations regulated by commercial law ‖ securities, negotiable instruments.

OBLIGACIONES RECÍPROCAS.
reciprocal obligations.
OBLIGACIONISTA.
f, m, obligee (of commercial obligation) ‖ holder of negotiable instruments.
OBLIGADO.
m, obligor ‖ debtor (in terms of monetary obligations) ‖ adj, obligated.
OBLIGANTE.
adj, obligatory, obliging.
OBLIGAR.
v, to obligate, oblige ‖ to compel, impel ‖ to require ‖ to place a lien on goods for the payment of a debt or the fulfillment of an obligation.
OBLIGARSE.
v, to obligate oneself ‖ to undertake, bind oneself to (an obligation).
OBLIGATIVO.
adj, obligatory.
OBLIGATORIAMENTE.
adv, obligatorily, mandatorily.
OBLIGATORIEDAD.
f, character of being obligatory or mandatory.
OBLIGATORIO.
adj, obligatory, compulsory, required, mandatory.
OBRA.
f, work (e.g. of art) ‖ product ‖ building under construction ‖ means, power ‖ book ‖ artisan's work ‖ fortification ‖ repairs ‖ action, activity ‖ work, labor.
OBRA ANÓNIMA.
anonymous work.
OBRA ARTÍSTICA.
work of art, artistic work.
OBRA CIENTÍFICA.
scientific work.
OBRA CINEMATOGRÁFICA.
cinematographic work.
OBRA DE ARTE.
work of art.
OBRA DE CARIDAD.
charity work.
OBRA DE FÁBRICA.
factory work.
OBRA DE MANO.
handiwork, hand-made good.
OBRA DRAMÁTICA.
play, drama, piece to be played in a theater.

OBRA INÉDITA.
unpublished work.
OBRA LITERARIA.
literary work.
OBRA MAESTRA.
masterpiece.
OBRA MANUAL.
manual labor.
OBRA MUERTA.
mortal sin ‖ upperworks, freeboard, superstructure of a ship.
OBRA MUSICAL.
musical piece or work.
OBRA NUEVA.
new construction or building (on new or old foundations).
OBRA PIADOSA.
charitable work.
OBRA POR PIEZAS.
piecework.
OBRA PÓSTUMA.
posthumously published work.
OBRA RUINOSA.
work or building in a state of ruin.
OBRA SEUDÓNIMA.
work published under a pseudonym.
OBRA SOCIAL.
social work ‖ social service.
OBRA VIVA.
quickwork, the substructure of a ship.
OBRADA.
f, day's work.
OBRADOR.
m, worker ‖ workshop, repair shop.
OBRAJERO.
m, work boss.
OBRAR.
v, to work, labor ‖ to do ‖ to cause (an effect) ‖ to build, construct.
OBRAJE.
m, manufacture, production ‖ work imposed upon Indians by colonialists.
OBRAS BENÉFICAS.
charitable or charity work.
OBRAS COMPLETAS.
complete works (of an artist or author).
OBRAS PÚBLICAS.
public works ‖ department of public works.
OBREPCIÓN.
f, obreption, obtaining something from a public authority by fraud or misrepresentation.

OBRERISMO.
m, labor movement ‖ workers, labor ‖ false show of concern for the workers in order to obtain their support.

OBRERA.
f, working woman.

OBRERO.
m, worker, laborer ‖ manual laborer, workman ‖ adj, working, laboring.

OBRERO MILITAR.
civilian who works for military industry.

OBSCENIDAD.
f, obscenity ‖ obscene thing ‖ lasciviousness, lewdness.

OBSCENO.
adj, obscene ‖ lewd, lascivious.

OBSCURANTISMO.
m, obscurantism, systematic opposition to teaching and progress relative to culture and political rights.

OBSCURIDAD.
f, darkness ‖ lack of clarity ‖ obscurity, humble background ‖ ignorance ‖ unintelligible text or passage ‖ confusion caused by lack of information or news.

OBSCURIDAD DE LAS LEYES.
lack of statutory clarity which creates confusion.

OBSCURIDAD DE LOS CONTRATOS.
lack of contractual clarity.

OBSCURO.
adj, dark ‖ lacking clarity ‖ obscure ‖ ignorant ‖ doubtful, uncertain ‖ unintelligible ‖ confusing ‖ dangerous ‖ black.

OBSECRACIÓN.
f, plea, prayer, supplication.

OBSECUENCIA.
f, submission, obedience.

OBSECUENTE.
adj, docile, submissive ‖ obedient ‖ tolerant.

OBSEQUIADOR.
m, gift giver ‖ donor.

OBSEQUIAR.
v, to give ‖ to donate ‖ to pay special attentions to ‖ to seduce (e.g. a woman).

OBSEQUIO.
m, act of donating or giving ‖ donation ‖ gift ‖ seduction (e.g. of a woman).

OBSEQUIUM".
donation, gift ‖ service ‖ duty, obligation.

OBSERVACIÓN.
f, observation ‖ examination or analysis of a matter ‖ observance, compliance (with an order) ‖ objection, misgiving.

OBSERVADO.
m, thing under examination or observation ‖ adj, observed ‖ complied with ‖ objected to.

OBSERVADOR.
m, observer ‖ adj, observant.

OBSERVADOR-PARTÍCIPE.
participant-observer, observer who is also a participant.

OBSERVANCIA.
f, observance of, compliance with (something) ‖ obedience ‖ respect, deference.

OBSERVAR.
v, to observe, watch, examine ‖ to spy ‖ to comply with, carry out (something) ‖ to obey ‖ to object (to something).

OBSESIÓN.
f, obsession.

OBSESIONAR.
v, to provoke an obsession.

OBSESIVO.
adj, obsessive.

OBSESO.
m, obsessive person, obsessed person ‖ adj, obsessed.

OBSIDIONAL
adj, under siege, related to a place or city under siege.

OBSOLESCENCIA.
f, obsolescence.

OBSOLESCENTE.
adj, becoming obsolete.

OBSOLETO.
adj, obsolete.

OBSTACULIZAR.
v, to impede ‖ to obstruct, place obstacles in the way, make (something) difficult.

OBSTÁCULO.
m, obstacle, impediment, obstruction ‖ hindrance, difficulty.

OBSTAR.
v, to impede ‖ to contradict, object, refute ‖ to oppose.

OBSTANTIVO.
See ACTO OBSTANTIVO.

OBSTRUCCIÓN.
f, obstruction, impediment, obstacle ‖ parliamentary disruption.

OBSTRUCCIONISMO.
m, obstructionism ‖ parliamentary or congressional filibustering.

OBSTRUCTOR.
m, obstructor, person or thing which obstructs.

OBSTRUIR.
v, to obstruct ‖ to oppose (an action) ‖ to impede, stop ‖ to refuse the adoption of certain steps ‖ to filibuster (a discussion).

OBTEMPAR.
v, to obey ‖ to accept, assent.

OBTENCIÓN.
f, acquisition, attainment, achievement.

OBTENER.
v, to obtain, acquire ‖ to attain, achieve.

OBTESTACIÓN.
f, obtestation, supplication.

OBTUSO.
m, obtuse.

OBVIAR.
v, to obviate, avoid ‖ to resolve problems or difficulties ‖ to facilitate.

OBVIO.
adj, obvious.

OBYECTO.
m, objection, opposition ‖ answer.

OCASIÓN.
f, occasion, occurrence ‖ opportunity, chance ‖ danger, risk ‖ reason, cause.

OCASIÓN PRÓXIMA.
proximate cause.

OCASIÓN REMOTA.
remote cause.

OCASIONADAMENTE.
adv, for a given reason or motive.

OCASIONADO.
adj, occasioned ‖ damaged ‖ irritating, annoying, displeasing ‖ risky, dangerous.

OCASIONAL.
adj, occasional, not habitual ‖ causing ‖ accidental.

OCASIONALMENTE.
adv, occasionally ‖ contingently.

OCASIONAR.
v, to occasion, be the cause or motive ‖ to endanger ‖ to excite, provoke. Used generally to refer to a bad consequence.

OCCIDENTAL.
adj, occidental, western, pertaining to the west.

OCCIDENTE.
m, the west ‖ western countries.

OCCISIÓN.
f, violent death.

OCCISO.
m, person who dies by violent means.

OCIAR.
v, to idle or laze about ‖ to quit work.

OCIO.
m, idleness, inaction ‖ unemployment ‖ spare or free time, after-work hours, leisure ‖ stopping of work ‖ break (from work).

OCIOS.
m, pastime interests, hobbies, activities pursued in spare time.

OCIOSIDAD.
f, state of person who does not want to, cannot, or does not have to work ‖ inactivity, inaction ‖ rest ‖ laziness, idleness.

OCIOSO.
m, idler, lazy person ‖ unemployed person ‖ adj, unnecessary, useless ‖ unobligated ‖ without benefit.

OCLOCRACIA.
f, government of the multitude or mob, mob rule.

OCTAVILLA.
f, an eighth of a sheet of paper ‖ flier, leaflet.

OCULAR.
adj, ocular, eye, pertaining to the eye ‖ also see TESTIGO OCULAR and INSPECCIÓN OCULAR.

OCULTACIÓN.
f, concealment, cover-up ‖ hiding, secretion ‖ subterfuge, deception.

OCULTACIÓN DE BIENES.
concealment of property.

OCULTACIÓN DE BIENES HEREDITARIOS.
concealment of property of a decedent's estate.

OCULTACIÓN DE DELINCUENTES.
aiding and abetting criminals by disguising or hiding them or giving them a new appearance.

OCULTACIÓN DE IDENTIDAD.
concealment of one's identity.

OCULTACIÓN DE NOMBRE.
concealment of name, refusal to given one's name.

OCULTACIÓN DE TESTAMENTO.
concealment of a will.

OCULTADOR.
m, concealer, hider ‖ secretor.

OCULTAMENTE.
adv, secretly ‖ secretively ‖ without warning.

OCULTAR.
v, to hide, cover-up, conceal ‖ to deceive ‖ to shut-up.

OCULTARSE.
v, to hide (oneself), go into hiding ‖ to undergo a change of name and abode.

OCULTISMO.
m, occultism.

OCULTISTA.
f, m, occultist ‖ adj, pertaining to occultism.

OCULTO.
adj, hidden ‖ unknown ‖ covered up.

OCULUM PRO OCULO, DENTEM PRO DENTE".
An eye for an eye, a tooth for a tooth.

OCUPABLE.
adj, employable ‖ occupiable, habitable.

OCUPACIÓN.
f, occupation, habitation ‖ possession, occupancy ‖ control (over a thing) ‖ work, employment ‖ profession, job ‖ filling up, occupancy.

OCUPACIÓN BÉLICA.
non-aggressive occupation by the military.

OCUPACIÓN DE DOCUMENTOS MILITARES.
(improper) possession of military papers.

OCUPACIÓN DE ESTABLECIMIENTOS.
occupation or possession of business establishments (by the workers to halt the ordinary course of business).

OCUPACIÓN DE PAÍS ENEMIGO.
See OCUPACIÓN DE TERRITORIO ENEMIGO.

OCUPACIÓN DE PROPIEDADES.
occupation of real property (e.g. by an army).

OCUPACIÓN DE TERRITORIO ENEMIGO.
occupation of enemy territory.

OCUPACIÓN LEGAL.
legal occupation (of the military).

OCUPACIÓN MILITAR.
military occupation.

OCUPACIÓN TEMPORAL.
temporary possession of or entry onto property of another.

OCUPADA.
adj, busy, occupied ‖ pregnant.

OCUPADO.
adj, occupied ‖ busy ‖ taken, conquered ‖ in use ‖ reserved.

OCUPADOR.
m, occupier ‖ possessor ‖ holder.
See OCUPANTE.

OCUPANTE.
m, occupier ‖ conqueror ‖ occupying (force) ‖ property being occupied.

OCUPAR.
v, to occupy, possess ‖ to seize ‖ to conquer, take ‖ to take possession of something ‖ to take (e.g. a position or employment) ‖ to receive a primogeniture estate ‖ to give work to ‖ to give reason to think ‖ to bother, disturb ‖ to inhabit, live in.

OCUPARSE.
v, to work on some activity ‖ to carry out a job ‖ to study a matter ‖ to see to something, take responsibility for a matter.

OCURRENCIA.
f, occurrence, happening, event, incident.

OCURRENCIA DE ACREEDORES.
meeting of creditors.

OCURRENCIAS NOTABLES.
noteworthy events ‖ part of a ship's log in which injuries suffered by a vessel and related information are set forth.

OCURRIR.
v, to occur, happen ‖ to appear ‖ to appeal to a judge or court.

O.E.A.
(ORGANIZACIÓN DE ESTADOS AMERICANOS).
Organization of American States.

O.T.A.N.
(ORGANIZACIÓN DEL TRATADO DEL ATLÁNTICO NORTE). N.A.T.O. National Atlantic Treaty Organization.

ODIAR.
v, to hate.

ODIO.
m, hatred.

ODIOSAMENTE.
adv, hatefully, with hatred.

ODIOSIDAD.
f, hatefulness.

ODIOSO.
adj, hateful ‖ repulsive.

OFENDER.
v, to offend ‖ to hurt, wound, mistreat ‖ to injure ‖ to insult.

OFENDER LOS OJOS.
to scandalize, shock the eyes || to displease || to hurt one's eyes (with light, changes, etc.).

OFENDERSE.
v, to take offense, feel insulted.

OFENDÍCULO.
m, obstacle, impediment.

OFENDIDO.
m, offended or injured person || victim || adj, offended.

OFENSA.
f, offense, insult, defamation || wound, injury, damage || lack of due respect. May be an attenuating or aggravating circumstance.

OFENSA A LA AUTORIDAD.
lack of due respect to public authority. Usually an aggravating circumstance or a category of crimes, including inter alia, resisting arrest, insubordination, rebellion.

OFENSA A LAS BUENAS COSTUMBRES.
See OFENSAS A LA MORAL and OFENSAS AL PUDOR.

OFENSA CUALIFICADA A LA VÍCTIMA.
offense to the victim. Usually an aggravating circumstance in which a criminal insults the sex, age, or dignity of the victim.

OFENSA GRAVE.
serious offense. The seriousness of a crime is attenuated if committed in revenge of an OFENSA GRAVE.

OFENSAS A LA MORAL.
crimes against or of morality. Usually includes such crimes as pederasty and swearing.

OFENSAS A LA RELIGIÓN.
religious offenses or crimes.

OFENSAS AL PUDOR.
crimes against decency. Usually includes such crimes as rape and other sexual offenses.

OFENSIVA.
adj, offensive.

OFENSIVAMENTE.
adv, offensively.

OFENSIVO.
adj, offensive (person) || aggravating || prejudicial, injurious.

OFENSOR.
m, offender, offending person.

OFERENTE.
m, offerer.

OFERTA.
f, (contractual) offer || bid, tender || proposal

|| promise to give, do, carry out, or comply with something || offer, steal, give-away || gift || supply.

OFERTA CON RESERVAS.
conditional offer.

OFERTA DE TRABAJO.
offer of employment, job offer || labor supply.

OFERTA MERCANTIL.
offer of sale of commercial goods (whether retail or wholesale).

OFERTAR.
See OFRECER.

"OFFICIUM".
office, position || duty, charge.

OFICIAL.
m, office worker, clerk || official || worker, workman || master worker || (military) officer || (administrative) official || officer of the court, court employee || adj, official || public || formal.

OFICIAL CIVIL.
public employee || office worker.

OFICIAL DE ADMINISTRACIÓN.
administrative worker in the Armed Forces.

OFICIAL DE JUSTICIA.
officer of the court, court employee.

OFICIAL DE SECRETARÍA.
ministry official, officer of a government ministry or department.

OFICIAL DEL EJÉRCITO.
army officer.

OFICIAL GENERAL.
major general of one of the armed forces || general officer.

OFICIAL LETRADO.
public officer with a law degree.

OFICIAL PÚBLICO.
notary public, special notary public.
See ESCRIBANO.

OFICIALÍA.
f, administrative or judicial official's position or post || clerkship.

OFICIALIDAD.
f, character of being official || body of officer of armed forces, army, unit, etc.

OFICIALISMO.
m, officialism, tendency and opinion found in the government in power || tendency of government in power to reward party members.

OFICIALISTA.
f, m, member or supporter of the governing party.

OFICIALIZAR.

v, to make official (what was not theretofore official).

OFICIALMENTE.

adv, officially ‖ according to the government.

OFICIAR.

v, to give notice of, notify of (a decision or other official matter, in writing) ‖ to act as, act in the capacity of ‖ to send OFICIOS.
See OFICIO.

OFICINA.

f, office ‖ department or office of the public administration.

OFICINA DE COLOCACIÓN OBRERA.

employment office (whether private or public).

OFICINAS PÚBLICAS.

public offices or departments, governmental offices or departments.

OFICINESCO.

m, bureaucracy, red tape ‖ adj, pertaining to offices (whether public or private) ‖ bureaucratic.

OFICINISTA.

f, m, office worker, bureaucrat ‖ person who occupies an office.

OFICIO.

m, occupation, work ‖ craft, trade, skilled work ‖ position, post, job, office ‖ written communication or notice (from a governmental office) ‖ written communication (intra-governmental regarding position or post) ‖ office (site) ‖ prejudicial action ‖ beneficial step.

OFICIO DE REPÚBLICA.

elected position within the provincial or municipal administration.

OFICIO JUDICIAL.

right of judges and courts to act sua sponte ‖ written communication from a judge or court.

OFICIO PÚBLICO.

public office, post, position (within the public administration).

OFICIOSAMENTE.

adv, diligently ‖ officiously.

OFICIOSIDAD.

f, diligence ‖ superfluous step ‖ officiousness, interference.

OFICIOSO.

adj, officious, meddlesome, interfering ‖ diligent, careful ‖ active ‖ laborious ‖ efficient ‖ descriptive efforts to reconcile belligerent nations ‖ unofficial, non-definitive, character of communication which does not grant a position ‖ quasi-official (newspaper which is the government mouthpiece without directly admitting such).

OFRECEDOR.

m, offerer.

OFRECER.

v, to offer ‖ to bid ‖ to promise ‖ to obligate oneself ‖ to give (something) ‖ to manifest, show ‖ to dedicate to someone .

OFRECERSE.

v, to offer oneself.

OFRECIENTE.

m, offerer.

OFRECIMIENTO.

m, offer ‖ promise ‖ proposal ‖ dedication.

OFRECIMIENTO DE PAGO.

offer of payment (by debtor to creditor) ‖ firm offer to pay in advance.

OFUSCACIÓN.

f, obfuscation, confusion.

OÍDA.

f, hearing, effect of hearing.
See TESTIGOS DE OÍDAS.

OÍDO.

m, ear ‖ hearing, sense of hearing ‖ adj, heard.

OÍR.

v, to hear, listen ‖ to hear (a plea, etc) ‖ to understand ‖ to attend (a university class) ‖ to admit (parties' proof, allegations, etc. by judge).

OÍR, VER Y CALLAR.

to mind your own business.

OJEADA.

f, scan ‖ visual recognition ‖ glance, summary inspection.

OJERIZA.

f, hatred, enmity ‖ ill will.

OJO.

m, eye ‖ Be careful!

OJO ALERTA.

Beware!. Be careful!. Watch out!

OJO AVISOR.

See OJO ALERTA.

OJOS QUE TE VIERON IR.

Reference to opportunities lost forever.

OLEODUCTO.

m, oil or petroleum pipeline.

OLFATEAR.

v, to sniff, smell || to be curious (about something) || to question.

OLIGARCA.

f, m, oligarch.

OLIGARQUÍA.

f, oligarchy.

OLIGÁRQUICO.

m, oligarch || adj, oligarchical.

OLÓGRAFO.

m, holograph, manuscript || adj, hand-written, holographic.

OLVIDADO.

adj, forgotten, left behind || lost.

OLVIDO.

m, loss of memory || amnesia || lack of memory || pardon || amnesty || negligence, lack of care || abandonment, desertion.

OMECILLO.

m, homicide.

OMISIBLE.

adj, able to be omitted.

OMISIÓN.

f, omission || abstention || failure to carry out duties or orders || carelessness, neglect.

OMISIÓN DE DEBERES.

failure to carry out duties or obligations.

OMISIÓN DE DENUNCIA.

failure to report a crime. May be deemed to be a crime.

OMISIÓN DE HEREDEROS.

omission of heirs at law.

OMISIÓN DE INCORPORACIÓN.

away without leave (from the armed forces).

OMISIÓN DE PRESENTACIÓN.

failure to register for the draft.

OMISIÓN DE SALUDO.

failure to salute (an officer).

OMISIÓN DOLOSA.

intentional omission or neglect.

**OMISIÓN EN
LAS OBLIGACIONES.**

breach by omission, failure to carry out duties or obligations || failure to act as an obligation or duty.

OMISIÓN EN LO CIVIL.

civil omission, omission which is regulated by the Civil Code.

OMISIÓN EN LO PENAL.

criminal omission, omission which amounts to a crime.

OMISIÓN EN LO PROCESAL.

procedural omission or abstention, omission (either intentional or unintentional) of a trial procedure.

**OMISIÓN EN
LOS CONTRATOS.**

contractual omission, failure to expressly stipulate regarding a given contractual issue || contractual breach by omission.

OMISO.

m, person who fails to perform an obligation or duty || adj, omitted || omission || neglected, uncared for.

OMITIR.

v, to omit, abstain || to fail to care for || to breach a duty by omission.

OMNÍMODAMENTE.

adv, in any case, all embracingly, totally.

OMNÍMODO.

adj, all embracing, totally, unlimitedly.

OMNIPOTENCIA.

f, omnipotence || governmental absolutism || imperialism.

OMNIPOTENTE.

f, m, omnipotent person || adj, omnipotent.

ONEROSO.

adj, onerous, burdensome || bothersome, uncomfortable || that which imposes a tax or charge or other obligation.

Opposed to LU-CRATIVO or GRATUITO.

See LUCRATIVO and GRATUITO.

ONTOLOGÍA JURÍDICA.

f, legal ontology.

O.N.U.

f, (ORGANIZACIÓN DE LAS NACIONES UNIDAS) U.N., United Nations Organization.

"ONUS PROBANDI".

burden of proof.

**"ONUS PROBANDI
INCUMBIT ACTORI".**

The burden of proof rests on the alleging party.

OPCIÓN.

f, option, election, selection, choice || right to choose || right to a post or position.

OPCIÓN DE COMPRA.

purchase option.

OPCIÓN DE NACIONALIDAD.

right to choose one's nationality.

OPCIÓN DEL HEREDERO.

right of heir to accept or reject the inheritance

OPCIÓN DEL LEGATARIO.

right of legatee to accept of reject a specific bequest or devise.

OPCIÓN Y CÚMULO.

option of a party whose contractual rights have been breached to choose between being compensated pursuant to contractual or extracontractual remedies or to join the two types of remedies.

OPCIONAL.

adj, optional.

"OPE LEGIS".

by reason of the law ‖ legal effect which takes place without any conduct or declaration from the interested parties.

OPERACIÓN.

f, (surgical) operation ‖ working (of something) ‖ maneuver (of armed forces) ‖ execution (of an action) ‖ operation on the stock market ‖ sales contract (of goods) ‖ transaction, deal, operation ‖ banking transaction or operation ‖ loan.

OPERACIÓN A CUBIERTO.

stock exchange transaction in which the parties obligations are covered.

OPERACIÓN A LA VISTA.

See OPERACIÓN AL CONTADO.

OPERACIÓN A PLAZO.

term market transaction.

OPERACIÓN A TÉRMINO.

See OPERACIÓN A PLAZO.

OPERACIÓN A VOLUNTAD.

stock exchange transaction in which the agreed term may be modified at will by one of the parties.

OPERACIÓN AL CONTADO.

market transaction for cash.

OPERACIÓN BANCARIA.

banking transaction, banking operation.

OPERACIÓN CESÁREA.

caesarian operation.

OPERACIÓN CON OPCIÓN.

market transaction with option to rescind their consent within a given period of time.

OPERACIÓN DE BOLSA.

stock exchange transaction.

OPERACIÓN DE CAMBIO.

exchange of foreign currency, foreign currency transaction.

OPERACIÓN DE CRÉDITO.

credit transaction.

OPERACIÓN EN DESCUBIERTO.

transaction in which the parties' obligations are not covered by other transactions or assets which limit the risk of performance of such obligation.

OPERACIÓN EN FIRME.

firm market transaction, market transaction which is not subject to rescission.

OPERACIÓN QUIRÚRGICA.

surgical operation.

OPERAR.

v, to operate, work, have effect on ‖ to maneuver ‖ to operate (on someone) ‖ to deal in the stock market ‖ to make credit transaction ‖ to deal in, trade.

OPERARIO.

m, worker, manual laborer.

OPERATIVO.

m, operation, operative ‖ adj, operative, effective ‖ efficient.

OPERATIVOS.

m, operatives, military operations.

"OPERAE".

personal services.

OPINANTE.

m, opiner, person who opines.

OPINAR.

v, to form an opinion, opine ‖ to examine the reasons and arguments regarding something.

OPINIÓN.

f, opinion, judgment, belief, conception ‖ (judicial) judgment, decision.

OPINIÓN COLECTIVA.

collective or group opinion.

OPINIÓN DE LOS AUTORES.

majority opinion of legal writers.

OPINIÓN DE LOS JURISCONSULTOS.

majority opinion of the jurists.

OPINIÓN PÚBLICA.

public opinion.

OPINIONES CONSULTIVAS.

advisory opinions.

OPIO.

m, opiate ‖ opium.

OPISTOGRAFÍA.

f, writing on both sides of a page.

OPONER.

v, to oppose, object to ‖ to argue against ‖ to confront ‖ to resist, counteract.

OPONERSE.

v, to impede ‖ to contradict ‖ to impugn ‖ to

deny ‖ to resist, defend oneself ‖ to confront someone ‖ to compete for a position.

OPONIBILIDAD.
f, quality of right or defense to oppose ‖ quality of a transaction which creates rights against third parties.

OPONIBLE.
adj, opposable ‖ quality of an argument or objection or excuse, etc. used to impede or oppose another.

OPORTUNAMENTE.
adv, opportunely, conveniently.

OPORTUNIDAD.
f, opportunity, chance.

OPORTUNISMO.
m, opportunism.

OPORTUNISTA.
f, m, opportunist.

OPORTUNO.
adj, opportune, convenient ‖ beneficial ‖ timely.

OPOSICIÓN.
f, opposition ‖ impediment, obstacle ‖ incompatibility ‖ contradiction ‖ resistance ‖ opposing argument ‖ verbal attack ‖ defense ‖ contradictory opinion ‖ hatred, enmity.

OPOSICIÓN ADMINISTRATIVA.
competition for a public position (for a university seat, administrative office, etc.).

OPOSICIÓN AL MATRIMONIO.
opposition to marriage (by those who must give their consent thereto) ‖ legal impediment or obstacle to marriage.

OPOSICIÓN EN EL CONCURSO CIVIL.
hearing to call for opposition to the bankruptcy of a non-commercial debtor (by a creditor).

OPOSICIÓN EN LA QUIEBRA.
hearing to call for opposition to the bankruptcy of a commercial debtor (by a creditor).

OPOSICIÓN POLÍTICA.
political opposition.

OPOSICIÓN PROCESAL.
opposition to an action occurring in a legal proceeding.

OPOSICIONISTA.
f, m, pertaining to opposition ‖ political opponent.

OPOSITOR.
m, candidate running in a competition for a

public position ‖ government opposition ‖ opponent ‖ adj, opposing.

OPRESIÓN.
m, oppression, tyranny ‖ subjection ‖ affliction.

OPRESIVO.
adj, oppressive.

OPRESOR.
m, oppressor, oppressive person, tyrant ‖ adj oppresive.

OPRIMIR.
v, to pressure ‖ to subjugate, oppress ‖ to bother ‖ to abuse power, tyrannize ‖ to enslave.

OPROBIAR.
v, to dishonor ‖ to vilify, revile ‖ to defame.

OPROBIO.
m, infamy, shame ‖ ignominy ‖ dishonor vilification.

OPROBIOSO.
m, person who causes infamy, shame, dishonor, vilification, etc ‖ adj, infamous, shameful, ignominious ‖ vilifying.

OPTANTE.
m, chooser, decider, person who opts.

OPTAR.
v, to opt, select, decide, elect, choose.

OPTATIVO.
adj, optional, pertaining to an option ‖ subject to election.

ÓPTIMO.
m, optimum ‖ adj, optimal, unbeatable ‖ optimum.

OPUESTAMENTE.
adv, with opposition ‖ oppositely ‖ contradictorily.

OPUESTO.
adj, opposing, contrary, contradictory, adverse ‖ enemy ‖ opposite.

"OPUS".
m, hand work ‖ literary work ‖ building construction ‖ industry, artifice.

OPÚSCULO.
m, very short work.

ORAL.
adj, oral, parol ‖ mouth to mouth (re. tractions, tales, etc.).

ORALIDAD.
See JUICIO ORAL.

ORALMENTE.
adv, orally.

ORATORIA.
f, oration, discourse, speech ‖ oratory.
ORATORIA FORENSE.
forensic oratory, in-trial oratory.
ORATORIA POLÍTICA.
political oratory.
ORATORIO.
m, place where orations are given ‖ adj, oratorical.
ORDEN.
f, m, order ‖ command ‖ branches of government ‖ endorsement ‖ order (to a subordinate) ‖ court order ‖ order, commission, post ‖ order of competing creditors ‖ right of FIADOR that the creditor proceed first against the debtor ‖ levels of courts to which one may have recourse ‖ rule, norm ‖ situation, state ‖ class, group, category ‖ good disposition, proportion ‖ public order, normality ‖ relation between things ‖ series ‖ religious order ‖ military order.
ORDEN COMPULSORIA.
compulsory order.
ORDEN DE COMPARECENCIA.
summons, order to appear.
ORDEN DE DETENCIÓN.
order of detention.
ORDEN DE EMBARGO.
writ of execution, sequestration order, seizure order.
ORDEN DE ENTREGA.
delivery order.
ORDEN DE LOS PRIVILEGIOS SOBRE BIENES.
order of liens or security interest (in goods).
ORDEN DE PRISIÓN.
order of imprisonment (whether pending or after trial).
ORDEN DE SUCEDER.
order of descent, order in which heirs or legatees are to receive.
ORDEN DEL DÍA.
(fem.) daily orders.
ORDEN DEL DÍA.
(masc.) agenda (of a meeting).
ORDEN DEL SERVICIO.
military order.
ORDEN DE AUDIENCIAS.
schedule of hearings.
ORDEN ESCRITA.
written order.

ORDEN JERÁRQUICO.
hierarchical order.
ORDEN JURÍDICO.
legal order, totality of legal norms ‖ totality of sources of law.
ORDEN MILITAR.
military order.
ORDEN MORAL.
order of morality, totality of ideas and opinions, institutions, customs, traditions regarding morals.
ORDEN PÚBLICO.
public order ‖ state of a nation during times of normality ‖ totality of norms which maintain public order (including criminal statutes, marriage and divorce laws, etc.) ‖ public policy ‖ ordre public.
ORDEN PÚBLICO INTERNACIONAL.
overriding public interest in international matters ‖ public international order, totality of those norms which are so essential to a nation's institutions that they must be applied over foreign norms or laws even when the rules of private international law would dictate otherwise (e.g. in the case of polygamous marriage).
ORDEN SOCIAL.
social order.
ORDEN SUCESORIO.
See ORDEN DE SUCEDER.
ORDEN VERBAL.
oral order, order transmitted by words.
ORDENACIÓN.
f, arrangement, disposition, distribution ‖ rule, norm ‖ command ‖ harmony, accounting or auditor's office ‖ payment or paymaster's office.
ORDENACIÓN BANCARIA.
administrative rules regulating banks, banking law.
ORDENACIÓN DE PAGOS.
national or provincial accounting office.
ORDENADAMENTE.
adv, in an orderly fashion, with order ‖ pursuant to an order or sequence ‖ without violence or confusion.
ORDENADO.
adj, ordered ‖ pursuant to an order ‖ peaceful, orderly.

ORDENADOR.
m, person who establishes order ‖ paymaster, paymaster general ‖ computer.

ORDENAMIENTO.
m, order, organization, system ‖ command ‖ law ‖ body of laws ‖ official determination regarding the sources of law ‖ code of laws or regulations.

ORDENANCISMO.
m, attitude and state of excessive orderliness.

ORDENANCISTA.
f, m, martinet, person overly devoted to order.

ORDENANZA.
m, f, order, method, system ‖ command, disposition ‖ internal rules regulating the military ‖ ordinance ‖ military orderly ‖ body of pertinent concepts ‖ orderly ‖ ordinance, statute, law ‖ rules enacted by a county or city.

ORDENANZA LABORAL.
labor law as set forth in ministerial orders.

ORDENANZAS.
f, body of military commands ‖ plural of OR-DENANZA

ORDENANZAS LOCALES.
local ordinances and law. Includes ORDENAN-ZAS MUNICIPALES.

ORDENANZAS MUNICIPALES.
municipal ordinances or regulations or rules.

ORDENAR.
v, to order, give orders ‖ to require with authority ‖ to re-establish legal order out of chaos ‖ to establish order, arrange.

ORDENATORIO.
See ORDENADOR.

ORDINARIAMENTE.
adv, ordinarily, habitually, commonly ‖ frequently ‖ rudely, uncouthly.

ORDINARIEZ.
f, rudeness ‖ vulgarity ‖ bad manners.

ORDINARIO.
m, daily household expenses ‖ ordinary judge (opposed to special judge) ‖ adj, ordinary, habitual, common, usual ‖ plebeian, common, vulgar ‖ ordinary mail ‖ normal (proceeding or procedure).

ORFANDAD.
f, the condition of an orphan ‖ orphan's pension ‖ abandonment.

ORGÁNICO.
adj, organic ‖ organizational ‖ pertaining to an organism ‖ harmonic ‖ organic, pertaining to

the constitution and the functioning of institutions.

ORGANISMO.
m, organism ‖ series of law, regulations, customs, uses, etc. which regulate an institution or social group ‖ body, entity, organization, institution.

ORGANISMO AUTÓNOMO.
autonomous entity (created by law but independent of the government).

ORGANISMOS ESPECIALIZADOS.
specialized organizations (created within the United Nations).

ORGANIZACIÓN.
f, organization, society, group of organized persons ‖ order ‖ establishment, institution (of something) ‖ reform ‖ structure.

ORGANIZACIÓN CONTABLE.
accounting department ‖ body of accounting rules and procedures.

ORGANIZACIÓN CRIMINAL.
mafia, criminal association or gang.

ORGANIZACIÓN DE EMPRESA.
business organization or structure.

ORGANIZACIÓN DE LAS NACIONES UNIDAS.
United Nations Organization.

ORGANIZACIÓN DE LOS ESTADOS AMERICANOS.
Organization of American States.

ORGANIZACIÓN JUDICIAL.
law of judicial procedure, body of rules and regulations which regulate the administration of justice in a given country.

ORGANIZACIÓN MÁS REPRESENTATIVA.
union which is the most representative (of a given profession or trade).

ORGANIZACIÓN MILITAR.
military structure.

ORGANIZACIÓN MUNDIAL DE LA SALUD.
International Health Organization.

ORGANIZACIÓN NO GUBERNAMENTAL.
non-governmental organization.

ORGANIZACIÓN SOCIAL.
social structure or organization.

ORGANIZADO.
adj, organized, prepared ‖ organic.

ORGANIZADOR.
m, organizer.

ORGANIZARSE.
v, to organize, order.

ÓRGANO.
m, organ (in all its meanings) || agency, organ, branch, part (of a body or entity) || means || person who carries out something or achieves an end || organism, entity, institution.

ORIENTACIÓN.
f, orientation || guidance || information || bearings.

ORIENTACIÓN PROFESIONAL.
guidance in choosing a profession or trade.

ORIENTADOR.
m, guidance counsellor.

ORIENTAL.
adj, oriental, easterly || Uruguayan.

ORIENTAR.
v, to orient, guide || to direct || to get one's bearings || to inform.

ORIENTE.
m, the east || birth, origin.

ORIFICIO.
m, orifice.

ORIGEN.
m, origin, source, root, start, beginning || mother country || motive, cause || ancestors, roots.

ORIGINAL.
m, original or authentic work, work not copied or plagiarized, imitated, adapted or translated || the original, authentic or original document || court where case was first heard || first copy of a document registered with a special notary public || adj, original, beginning || strange, unusual || new, novel, ingenious.

ORIGINALIDAD.
f, originality.

ORIGINALMENTE.
adv, originally || pursuant to the original.

ORIGINAR.
v, to originate, case || to produce, provoke.

ORIGINARIO.
adj, original || means of acquiring property which do not require the transfer of property (e.g., prescription, occupation, etc.).

ORILLAR.
v, to resolve , arrange (something difficult) || to avoid a risk || to border on something, be close to.

ORIUNDEZ.
f, origin || ancestors || mother country.

ORIUNDO.
adj, originating (from a place, person or thing).

ORO.
m, gold.

ORO DE LEY.
standard gold.

ORTODOXIA.
f, orthodoxy.

ORTOTANASIA.
See HOMICIDIO PIADOSO.

ORTOGRAFÍA.
f, spelling.

OSTENSIBLE.
adj, ostensible, patent, clear || apparent (opposed to real).

OSTENSIÓN.
f, manifestation.

OSTENTACIÓN.
f, ostentation || manifestation.

OSTENTAR.
v, to show, manifest || to show off, flaunt.

OTEAR.
v, to observe, watch from a height.

OTORGADO.
adj, authorized.

OTORGADOR.
m, grantor, person who grants.

OTORGAMIENTO.
m, grant, license, authorization, permission || consent || act of executing an instrument || will, testament, testamentary grant || notarial solemnity and signature || offer, promise || contract.

OTORGAMIENTO DE CONTRATO SIMULADO.
consent to a false contract. May be deemed to be a crime.

OTORGAMIENTO NOTARIAL.
notarial authorization (of a document or writing). Usually includes the fact that the parties have entered into the act of their own free will, and the notarial solemnity and signature.

OTORGANTE.
m, grantor, authorizer || acceptor || offerer, promisor || contracting party.

OTORGAR.
v, to grant || to consent, agree to, accept || to offer, promise, stipulate || to give || to execute (an instrument) || to award.

OTORGO.
See OTORGAMIENTO.

OTRO.
adj, other, another ‖ different ‖ new ‖ equal.

OTROSÍ.
adv, in addition to, additionally. Used in litigation to add something omitted in a previous writing.

OYENTE.
m, auditor, unenrolled student who audits a class.

P

PABELLÓN.
m, national flag ‖ ship's colors or flag of nationality ‖ pavilion.

PABELLÓN ENEMIGO.
national flag of enemy nation's ship.

PABELLÓN NEUTRAL.
national flag of neutral nation's ship.

PACIENCIA.
f, patience.

PACIFICACIÓN.
f, pacification ‖ peace, tranquility ‖ submission ‖ peace treaty.

PACIFICADOR.
m, peacemaker, pacifier ‖ reconciler.

PACÍFICAMENTE.
adv, peacefully.

PACIFICAR.
v, to re-establish peace ‖ to impose peace ‖ to reconcile ‖ to submit to.

PACÍFICO.
m, Pacific Ocean ‖ adj, peaceful, tranquil ‖ without contradiction or opposition.

PACIFISMO.
m, pacifism.

PACOTILLA.
f, goods taken on board a ship by captain or crew free of charge ‖ group of commercial goods ‖ small business.

PACTA".
agreements ‖ engaged (to be married).

"PACTA SUNT SERVANDA".
agreements must be carried out.

PACTAR.
v, to agree upon or to contract ‖ to make a bilateral contract ‖ to stipulate.

PACTO.
m, agreement, contract, pact ‖ treaty clause.

PACTO ACCESORIO.
accessory contract, contract which is accessory to principal contract.

PACTO ADICIONAL.
subsequent contract which modifies, clarifies, or rescinds the original contract.

PACTO AGREGADO.
See PACTO ADICIONAL.

PACTO AMBIGUO.
ambiguous contract.

PACTO ANTICRÉTICO.
loan agreement which is repaid by the products or fruits of an item placed in pledge. See ANTICRESIS.

PACTO COLECTIVO DE CONDICIONES DE TRABAJO.
collective bargaining agreement.

PACTO COMISORIO.
contractual clause which allows for rescission for breach of contract.

PACTO COMISORIO EN LA ANTICRESIS.
loan agreement which is repaid by the products or fruits of an item placed in pledge, but which allows the creditor to keep the pledged item in case of breach of contract. See ANTICRESIS.

PACTO COMISORIO EN LA COMPRAVENTA.
sales contract which stipulates that the agreement is revoked if the price is not paid or other obligations performed before a given period of time.

PACTO COMISORIO EN LA PRENDA.
loan agreement which provides that the creditor may keep the item given in pledge in case of breach of contract.

PACTO COMPROMISORIO.
arbitration clause.

PACTO CONTRA LEY.
illegal contract or contractual clause.

PACTO CONVENIDO.
accessory agreement ‖ covenant, contractual clause.

PACTO DE ADICIÓN.
sales contract by which the buyer stipulates that if the seller is able to better the buyer's purchase price, the seller may rescind the contract and obtain the return of the good for resale to a second buyer.

PACTO DE ARREPENTIMIENTO.
contract whereby a right is waived.

PACTO DE ASISTENCIA RECÍPROCA.
reciprocal assistance agreement.

PACTO DE CABALLEROS.
gentlemen's agreement.

PACTO "DE CONTRAHENDO".
pre-pact, agreement preparatory to an international treaty.

PACTO DE CUOTALITIS.
contingent fee agreement (between an attorney and client).

PACTO DE FAMILIA.
marriage agreement.

PACTO DE HIPOTECA.
mortgage agreement or contract (in which the mortgagee is not the seller of the property).

PACTO DE JORNADA MAYOR.
overtime agreement, contract by which an employee agrees to work overtime.

PACTO DE LA LEY COMISORIA.
See PACTO COMISORIO.

PACTO DE MEJOR COMPRADOR.
See PACTO DE ADICIÓN.

PACTO DE NO AGRESIÓN.
non-aggression treaty (between nations).

PACTO DE NO ENAJENAR.
agreement not to transfer (something).

PACTO DE NO PEDIR.
See PACTUM DE NON PETENDO.

PACTO DE NO PRESTAR LA EVICCIÓN.
clause by which seller expressly excludes warranty of quiet enjoyment of good.

PACTO DE PREFERENCIA.
clause in a contract by which a potential seller grants a potential buyer a right of preference over other buyers if a good is to be sold.

PACTO DE REMISIÓN.
See PACTUM DE NON PETENDO.

PACTO DE RESERVA DE DOMINIO.
contract with a security interest, contract b which the seller of property is permitted to te minate the contract, and retake possession fc breach of contract by buyer.

PACTO DE RESERVA DE HIPOTECA.
mortgage agreement, agreement by which th seller of real estate retains a mortgage on th property sold.

PACTO DE RETRAER.
See PACTO DE RETROVENTA.

PACTO DE RETRO.
See PACTO DE RETROVENTA.

PACTO DE RETROEMENDO.
See PACTO DE REVENTA.

PACTO DE RETROVENTA.
repurchase clause, contractual clause by whic the seller reserves the right to require the b yer to sell back the good sold.

PACTO DE REVENTA.
repurchase clause, contractual clause by whic the buyer reserves the right to require the s ller to purchase back the good sold.

PACTO DE SANGRE.
blood pact, pact solemnized by a blood ritua

PACTO DE SEÑALAMIENTO DE DÍA.
See PACTO DE ADICIÓN.

PACTO DE SUCESIÓN FUTURA.
agreement to make a will (in favor of som one).

PACTO DE SUCESIÓN MUTUA.
agreement to make mutual wills (each in fav of the other).

PACTO DE VENTA A SATISFACCIÓN DE COMPRADOR.
clause by which a sales contract may be re cinded if the object of the sale is not to the b yer's satisfaction.

PACTO EN CONTRARIO.
agreement the terms of which differ fro those set forth in the law which is to govern the parties are silent on the matter.

PACTO ESPECIAL.
agreement with terms different from tho commonly set forth in agreements of such kin See PACTO EN CONTRARIO.

PACTO FEDERAL.
interstate or interprovince agreement, agre

ment between various states or provinces pursuant to the constitution.

PACTO LEGÍTIMO.
legal agreement. See PACTO EN CONTRARIO.

PACTO LEONINO.
See CLÁUSULA LEONINA.

PACTO PENAL.
penalty clause, penal provision, clause which sets forth the penalties for breach of contract.

PACTO PROHIBIDO.
illegal agreement ‖ illegal clause.

PACTO REAL.
See CONTRATO REAL.

PACTO RESERVADO.
secret agreement (between private parties, which is legal but which has no legal effect upon the rights of third parties) ‖ secret agreement or clause (between nations).

PACTO SOCIAL.
agreement of a political or economic nature between the government and trade unions and business groups. Also see CONTRATO SOCIAL.

PACTO SUCESORIO.
See PACTO DE SUCESIÓN FUTURA.

PACTOS PREEXISTENTES.
interstate or interprovince agreements, generally occurring prior to the formation of a constitution.

"PACTUM ADJECTUM".
See PACTO ADICIONAL.

"PACTUM DE NON PETENDO".
agreement of obligee not to make a demand for payment or fulfillment of an obligation by the obligor.

"PACTUM DISPLICENTIAE".
See PACTO DE ARREPENTIMIENTO.

"PACTUM RESERVATI DOMINII".
See PACTO DE RESERVA DE DOMINIO.

"PACTUM RESERVATI HYPOTHECAE".
See PACTO DE RESERVA DE HIPOTECA.

PADRASTRO.
m, stepfather.

PADRE.
m, father (in all senses) ‖ head of family ‖ male, man ‖ protector ‖ author or inventor of something ‖ precursor ‖ cause.

PADRE ADOPTIVO.
adoptive father, man who adopts someone ‖ man who cares for and maintains someone.

PADRE ADULTERINO.
father of a child born of an adulterous relationship.

PADRE DE FAMILIA.
paterfamilias, father of the family ‖ head of the family ‖ head of household.

PADRE DE LA PATRIA.
statesman ‖ founding father ‖ meritorious citizen who has been of unusual service to his country ‖ liberator (of a people).

PADRE DE PILA.
baptismal godfather.

PADRE DESCONOCIDO.
unknown father.

PADRE ILEGÍTIMO.
natural father, father of an illegitimate child, father of a child born to a woman to whom father could have legally been married.

PADRE INCESTUOSO.
father by incest, father of a child born of an incestuous relationship.

PADRE INDIGNO.
father excluded from the legal right to inherit from his child or children.
See INDIGNIDAD PARA SUCEDER.

PADRE LEGÍTIMO.
legitimate father, father of child born to woman to whom he is married or from whom he has been divorced 300 days or less ‖ father of child born to woman after the first 180 days of their marriage.

PADRE NATURAL.
natural father, father of an illegitimate child ‖ father of a child born to a woman to whom father could have legally been married.

PADRE POLÍTICO.
father-in-law ‖ stepfather.

PADRE PUTATIVO.
putative father ‖ person who appears to be a father without being the natural father.

PADRE SUPUESTO.
See PADRE PUTATIVO.

PADRE VIUDO.
widowed father, widower who is a father (as long as he doesn't remarry).

PADRES.
m, parents ‖ fathers.

PADRINA.
See MADRINA.

PADRINAZGO.
m, godfathership ‖ (public) sponsorship ‖ protection.

PADRINO.
m, godfather (for purposes of a child's baptism, confirmation, marriage, and entering a religious order, if any of these events occurs) ‖ protector ‖ defender ‖ second (in a duel).

PADRINO DE DUELO.
second (in a duel).

PADRÓN.
m, census list, relationship or list of inhabitants (of a town) ‖ list of voters ‖ model, example, pattern ‖ doting father.

PAGA.
f, payment, act of paying ‖ payment, amount of payment ‖ pay, fee, wages, compensation, remuneration ‖ satisfaction, compensation (of injury) ‖ payment, punishment or fine or penalty for injury.

PAGA ADELANTADA,
PAGA VICIOSA.
payments made in advance are improper.

PAGA DE SUPERVIVENCIA.
widow's or orphan's payment (made by employer of diseased employee who did not reach the age at which he would have received a pension).

PAGA DE TOCAS.
See PAGA DE SUPERVIVENCIA.

PAGA INDEBIDA.
See PAGO DE LO INDEBIDO . Also see PAGA VICIOSA.

PAGA VICIOSA.
type of improper payment, payment which has no legal effect by reason of its being made by or to an improper party or at an improper time.

PAGABLE.
adj, payable, able to be paid ‖ due, owing ‖ easily paid.

PAGADERO.
adj, owing ‖ debit ‖ debt ‖ obligation ‖ easily payable. Used to indicate the time and place of payment.

PAGADERO A LA DEMANDA.
payable on demand.

PAGADERO A LA VISTA.
payable on sight.

PAGADO.
m, payment stamp, "PAID" stamp ‖ adj, paid.

PAGADOR.
m, payor ‖ paymaster ‖ accounts payable clerk ‖ obligor who fulfills his or her obligation ‖ debtor.

PAGADURÍA.
f, accounts payable office ‖ paymaster's general office, paymaster's office.

PAGÁNICO.
See TESTAMENTO PAGÁNICO.

PAGANISMO.
m, paganism.

PAGAR.
v, to pay ‖ to fulfill or satisfy (an obligation) ‖ to pay (a debt or salary) ‖ to pay, suffer a punishment ‖ to return (a favor or emotions).

PAGAR DE CONTADO.
to pay immediately.

PAGAR LAS VERDES Y LAS MADURAS.
to receive fitting punishment.

PAGARÉ.
m, promissory note, writing evidencing a payment for a sum and date certain in favor of a specified person, to the order of a specified person or to the bearer ‖ I.O.U.

PAGARÉ A LA ORDEN.
order note, promissory note written to the order of a specified person.

PAGARÉ AL PORTADOR.
bearer note, promissory note in favor of bearer.

PAGARÉ NOMINATIVO.
nominative note, promissory note written in favor of a specified person.

PAGARLA.
v, to receive fitting punishment ‖ to take revenge upon.

PAGARLA DOBLE.
to impose double punishment.

PAGARSE POR SU MANO.
to pay an expense directly of the corresponding account.

PÁGINA.
f, page

PAGINACIÓN.
f, pagination.

PAGINAR.
v, to paginate.

PAGO.
m, payment ‖ repayment of a debt) ‖ payment (of a salary) ‖ satisfaction (of an injury or obligation) ‖ delivery of money owed ‖ pay

ment (of punishment) ‖ remuneration, fee, salary, compensation ‖ county, district, region. See PAGADO.

PAGO A CUENTA.
down payment (on a purchase) ‖ partial payment (of a debt) ‖ payment on account.

PAGO A MEJOR FORTUNA.
See BENEFICIO DE COMPETENCIA.

PAGO A PLAZOS.
time payment, payment on time, payment in installments, installment payment.

PAGO ABREVIADO.
payment made offsetting debits against credits between parties who are at the same time debtors and creditors of each other.

PAGO AL CONTADO.
payment upon delivery (of service or goods).

PAGO ANTICIPADO.
pre-payment, payment made prior to due date.

PAGO CON BENEFICIO DE COMPETENCIA.
See BENEFICIO DE COMPETENCIA.

PAGO CON CHEQUE SIN PROVISIÓN DE FONDOS.
payment with a check against non-sufficient funds.

PAGO CON GIRO SIN PROVISIÓN DE FONDOS.
payment with a bill of exchange against non-sufficient funds.

PAGO CON SUBROGACIÓN.
subrogation payment, payment made pursuant to subrogation of creditor's rights to third party making the payment. May be either CONVENCIONAL (conventional) or LEGAL (legal).

PAGO CUANDO EL DEUDOR QUIERA.
See CLÁUSULA DE PAGO CUANDO EL DEUDOR QUIEBRA.

PAGO DE ACREEDORES DE LA HERENCIA.
payment of the creditors of a decedent's estate. Such payments may include taxes, costs incurred in administering the estate, outstanding debts against the estate, and legal heirs.

PAGO DE CONTRIBUCIONES.
payment of taxes ‖ payment of rent pursuant to USUFRUCTO, USO Y HABITACIÓN, CENSO, or ARRENDAMIENTO.

PAGO DE DEUDAS AJENAS.
payment of third party obligations by parties who are not directly liable (e.g. parents for the liabilities incurred by their children ‖ payment of accessory obligation (e.g. payment by guarantor)).

PAGO DE DEUDAS DE DINERO.
payment of monetary obligations.

PAGO DE DEUDAS HEREDITARIAS.
payment of debts by heirs.

PAGO DE LA LETRA DE CAMBIO.
payment of a negotiable instrument. See LETRA DE CAMBIO.

PAGO DE LEGADOS.
payment of legacies or bequests. See LEGADO.

PAGO DE LO INDEBIDO.
wrongful payment, payment resulting in unjust enrichment, payment of monies not owed ‖ payment of monies by person who is not the true debtor. Payment may be made pursuant to a mistake in either law of fact.

PAGO DE LO QUE NO SE DEBE.
See PAGO DE LO INDEBIDO.

PAGO DE OBLIGACIONES.
satisfaction or payment of obligations.

PAGO DE PENSIONES CENSUALES.
payment of rents pursuant to CENSO. See CENSO.

PAGO DE SALARIOS.
payment of salaries (to employees).

PAGO DE SERVICIOS.
fees, payment of services (to independent contractors) ‖ see PAGO DE SALARIOS.

PAGO DE VACACIONES.
vacation pay, payment for time spent on vacation or which should have been spent on vacation, but which was worked instead.

PAGO DEL INSOLVENTE.
preferential payment, payment made by insolvent person.

PAGO DIFERIDO.
deferred payment, delayed payment (upon agreement of creditor and debtor) ‖ late or delinquent payment, payment in arrears ‖ payment made after a moratorium.

PAGO EN CUOTAS.
payment made in installments.

PAGO EN EL ARRENDAMIENTO.
rent, rent payment

PAGO EN EL USUFRUCTO.
rent paid pursuant to USUFRUCTO.

PAGO EN MONEDA EXTRANJERA.
payment made in foreign currency.

PAGO EN ORO.
payment made in gold.

PAGO FICTICIO.
fictitious payment, payment made pursuant to a sham transaction ‖ fictitious payment, apparent (but not real) payment ‖ secret payment.

PAGO FORZOSO.
forced payment, payment made against the will of the debtor.

PAGO IMPOSIBLE.
payment which, due to force majeure, other physical factors, insolvency of payor, immorality or illegality thereof, is made impossible.

PAGO IMPUTADO.
See IMPUTACIÓN DE PAGOS.

PAGO INDEBIDO.
See PAGO DE LO INDEBIDO.

PAGO LIBERATORIO.
payment which extinguishes the obligation.

PAGO PARCIAL.
partial payment, part payment ‖ installment, installment payment.

PAGO POR CAUSA TORPE.
type of improper payment, payment made for an immoral or illegal purpose.

PAGO POR CESIÓN DE BIENES.
payment of debts by transfer of goods (by an insolvent debtor to creditors).

PAGO POR CONSIGNACIÓN.
payment into court.

PAGO POR CUENTA AJENA.
payment on behalf of third party (with or without consent or power of attorney of debtor.

PAGO POR ENTREGA DE BIENES.
payment in kind, payment in lieu of money ‖ payment in kind agreed to by creditor.

PAGO POR ERROR.
See PAGO DE LO INDEBIDO.

PAGO POR OTRO.
See PAGO DE DEUDAS AJENAS.

PAGO SIN CAUSA.
payment made against no valid obligation.

PAÍS.
m, land, territory ‖ country, nation, state ‖ place of a person's origin.

PAÍS DE DERECHO CONSUETUDINARIO.
nation ruled by customary law.

PAÍS DE DERECHO ESCRITO.
nation ruled by written law.

PAÍS DE DESTINO.
country of destination.

PAÍS DE ELECCIÓN.
country of election.

PAÍS DE ORIGEN.
country of birth ‖ country of family ancestors ‖ country of origin (e.g. of an emigrant or merchandise).

PAÍS ENEMIGO.
enemy nation or state ‖ belligerent nation ‖ unfriendly nation.

PAÍS IMPORTADOR.
importing nation.

PAÍS LEGAL.
legally recognized country, nation which has been recognized diplomatically.

PAÍS NO ALINEADO.
non-aligned nation or state.

PAISANA.
f, female civilian ‖ female compatriot, fellow countrywoman, female from the same country ‖ female peasant.

PAISANAJE.
m, civilians, body of civilians ‖ civilian population ‖ character of being compatriots or fellow countrymen ‖ ties between compatriots or fellow countrymen ‖ armed civilians (as opposed to militia).

PAISANO.
m, civilian ‖ compatriot, fellow countryman, person from the same country ‖ peasant.

PAJAREAR.
v, to roam, ramble ‖ to loaf about, live without working.

PÁJARO DE CUENTA.
m, habitual or dangerous criminal.

PALABRA.
f, word, term ‖ word, promise ‖ offer ‖ floor, right to speak (at a meeting) ‖ text, passage (of a writing) ‖ speech.

¡PALABRA!
On my word!

PALABRA DE HONOR.
word of honor.

PALABRA DE MATRIMONIO.
promise to marry.

PALABRA PESADA.
offensive or insulting words.

PALABRA PICANTE.
biting words.

PALABRA-PREGUNTA.
question (to a person taking a lie-detector test).

PALABRA-RESPUESTA.
answer (of a person taking a lie-detector test).

PALABRAS.
f, words ‖ passage, fragment (of a word).

PALABRAS COMPROMETEDORAS.
words of promise or of agreement ‖ words which are used by an interrogator to pin down facts about a crime.

PALABRAS DE DUELO.
fighting words, dueling words.

PALABRAS DUDOSAS.
ambiguous words.

PALABRAS GRUESAS.
strong words ‖ dirty words.

PALABRAS LIBRES.
obscenities, obscene and untrue words, defamatory words.

PALABRAS MAYORES.
(verbal) offenses, insults.

PALABRAS SOLEMNES.
words said emphatically ‖ words used to solemnize a contract or other obligation.

PALABROTA.
f, swear-word.

PALACIO.
m, palace ‖ building (of the Supreme Court of Justice).

**PALACIO
DE JUSTICIA.**
Palace of Justice, building of Supreme Court of Justice.

PALADINAMENTE.
adv, publicly, clearly.

PALADINO.
adj, public, patent, clear, unequivocal.

PALIAR.
v, to palliate.

PALINODIA.
f, public retraction, recantation.

PALINODISTA.
m, person who recants or retracts something.

PALIZA.
f, flogging, beating, thrashing ‖ complete rout or defeat.

PALMAS.
f, applause.

PALMO A PALMO.
little by little, slowly and steadily.

PALO.
m, stick, flog, switch.

PALO DE CIEGO.
unconsidered injury or offense ‖ aimless action.

PALOTEAR.
v, to thrash, hit by blows.

PALPABLE.
adj, palpable, tangible ‖ evident, manifest, clear.

PALPACIÓN.
f, palpation, touching, feeling, diddling.

PALPAR.
v, to diddle, feel up, touch.

PALPAR DE ARMAS.
pat down, body search (for arms).

PAN.
m, bread ‖ daily bread, living.

PAN DE LA BODA.
wedding gifts.

PAN DE PERRO.
injury to or punishment imposed on a person.

PAN PERDIDO.
lost cause, goner.

PAN Y AGUA.
bread and water (for prisoners).

PANACEA.
f, panacea.

PANAFRICANISMO.
m, Pan-Africanism.

PANAMERICANISMO.
m, Pan-Americanism.

PANDECTAS.
f, Pandects, recompilation of legal works and texts of Justinian.

"PANE LUCRANDO".
for the purpose of earning one's daily bread.

PANESLAVISMO.
m, Pan-Slavism.

PANEUROPA.
f, Pan-Europe.

PANGERMANISMO.
m, Pan-Germanism.

PANHELENISMO.
m, Pan-Hellenism.

PÁNICO.
m, panic, fear, terror.

PÁNICO COLECTIVO.
mass panic, collective panic.

PANISLAMISMO.
m, Pan-Islamism, movement to unite Islamic countries.

PANTEÍSMO.
m, pantheism.
PANTEÓN.
m, pantheon.
PAPA.
m, Pope.
PAPÁ.
m, papa, daddy, dad, father.
PAPEL.
m, paper ‖ sheet of paper ‖ paper, writing, document ‖ role, function, character ‖ bank-note ‖ commercial instrument, commercial paper market security ‖ paper money
PAPEL AL PORTADOR.
bearer paper.
PAPEL BLANCO.
blank sheet of paper.
PAPEL COMÚN.
ordinary paper ‖ ordinary sheet of paper.
PAPEL DE COMERCIO.
commercial paper.
PAPEL DE CRÉDITO.
credit instruments.
PAPEL DE OFICIO.
legal size paper, paper which fulfills the size, margin and line requirements of the law.
PAPEL DE PAGOS.
special invoice slip (to be used when billing a government entity).
PAPEL DEL ESTADO.
public debt ‖ public debt instrument.
PAPEL EN DERECHO.
pleading.
PAPEL MOJADO.
unimportant role ‖ writing which proves nothing ‖ worthless document or instrument ‖ unimportant or useless thing.
PAPEL MONEDA.
bill, paper money, paper currency.
PAPEL SELLADO.
official paper which is stamped and used for official purposes.
PAPEL TIMBRADO.
See PAPEL SELLADO.
PAPEL TIMBRADO COMÚN.
official paper used in Spain which bears special markings.
PAPEL TIMBRADO JUDICIAL.
legal paper used in Spain which bears special markings and is to be used in court proceedings. No longer in use.

PAPELEAR.
v, to look or rummage through papers.
PAPELEO.
m, bureaucratic paperwork, red tape ‖ action of looking or rummaging through papers.
PAPELES DE COMERCIO.
commercial paper, negotiable instruments, commercial documents.
PAPELES DEL BUQUE.
ship's papers.
PAPELES DEL FALLIDO.
business papers of a bankrupt.
PAPELES PRIVADOS.
private papers of essentially any type but which are normally handwritten.
PAPELETA.
f, slip of paper or form on which something is written or is to be written ‖ summons for certain legal purposes ‖ pawn slip or ticket ‖ complaint in an oral trial.
PAPELETA DE EMPEÑO.
pawn slip or ticket.
PAPELUCHO.
m, worthless writing ‖ writing which contains injurious statements or anonymous or blackmail threats.
PAPISMO.
m, papism, papistry.
PAPISTA.
m, papist.
PAQUETE.
m, package ‖ packet of papers kept in a file or envelope.
PAQUETE POSTAL.
postal package, package used for mailing things through the postal service.
PAR.
m, par ‖ even ‖ equal, analogous ‖ similar ‖ pair ‖ even number.
PARA MEJOR PROVEER.
See DILIGENCIAS PARA MEJOR PROVEER.
PARADERO.
m, resting or stopping place ‖ purpose, end ‖ home, actual abode.
PARADIGMA.
m, paradigm.
PARADO.
m, unemployed person (who is both able and willing to work) ‖ striker, employee who participates in a PARO FORZOSO. See PARO FORZOSO ‖ adj, stopped, blocked ‖ standing.

PARADOXIA SEXUAL.
f, homosexuality.
PARAFERNALES.
See BIEN PARAFERNAL.
PARAFISCAL.
See IMPUESTO PARAFISCAL.
PARAFRASEADOR.
m, person who paraphrases ‖ commentator ‖ annotator ‖ interpreter.
PARAFRASEAR.
v, to paraphrase, explain, comment, interpret (a legal text).
PARÁFRASIS.
f, explanation, clarification, interpretation (of a legal text) ‖ commentary, annotation, footnote ‖ malicious commentary.
PARÁLISIS.
f, paralysis.
PARÁLISIS INFANTIL.
infantile paralysis.
PARALÍTICO.
m, paralyzed person ‖ adj, paralytic, paralyzed.
PARALIZACIÓN.
f, paralyzation ‖ stoppage, blockage ‖ stagnation.
**PARALIZACIÓN
DEL PROCESO.**
paralyzation of a legal proceeding. May be due to the law, judicial determination, or actions taken by the parties.
PARALOGISMO.
m, false reasoning, faulty argumentation.
PARALOGIZAR.
v, to try to convince by false reasoning.
PARANOIA.
f, paranoia.
PARANOICO.
m, paranoid person ‖ adj, paranoid.
PARASITISMO.
m, parasitism, habit or custom of living off another.
PARÁSITO.
m, parasite ‖ adj, parasitic.
PARÁSITO SOCIAL.
social parasite, person who fails in his duties to society and lives off of others without doing anything useful.
PARATITLA.
f, summary or synthesis of legal treatise or writing ‖ jurisprudential summary.

PARCELA.
f, lot or parcel of land, plot.
PARCELACIÓN.
f, dividing or subdividing into parcels or lots of land.
PARCELAR.
v, to divide or subdivide into parcels or lots of land.
PARCELARIO.
adj, pertaining to parcels of land or parceling.
PARCIAL.
m, mid-term examination ‖ adj, partial ‖ incomplete, lacking ‖ partisan ‖ part (of a total) ‖ partial, biased, prejudiced.
PARCIALIDAD.
f, sector, faction ‖ partiality, prejudice, bias ‖ friendship.
PARCIALIZARSE.
v, to become a member or affiliate of a party or union.
PARCIALMENTE.
adv, partially, partly ‖ incompletely, insufficiently ‖ unjustly, unequally ‖ with prejudice or bias or partiality.
PARECER.
m, opinion, judgment, decision, belief ‖ v, to appear, be found ‖ to believe, opine ‖ to appear, seem.
PARECER BIEN.
to approve or accept.
**PARECER
EN JUICIO.**
to make an appearance (in court).
PARECER MAL.
to disapprove or reject.
PARED.
f, wall.
PARED AJENA.
neighboring wall, wall constructed entirely on the property of another.
PARED COMÚN.
adjoining wall which may be owned in different proportions by the different owners.
PARED DIVISORIA.
dividing wall. May be a PARED COMÚN, PARED PROPIA or PARED MEDIANERA.
PARED MAESTRA.
main wall.
PARED MEDIANERA.
adjoining wall which is owned in co-tenancy by neighboring property owners.

PARED POR MEDIO.
neighboring, continuity ‖ nearness ‖ separated by a wall.

PARED PROPIA.
dividing wall which is entirely located on one's own property.

PARED RUINOSA.
wall in threatening or dangerous condition.

PAREJA.
f, couple ‖ adj, pair ‖ equal, even.

PAREJA CRIMINAL.
See PAREJA DELINCUENTE.

PAREJA DELINCUENTE.
criminal association of two persons.

PAREJURA.
f, evenness, equality ‖ similarity.

"PARENS".
parent ‖ grandfather or grandmother ‖ founder ‖ author ‖ inventor.

"PARENS BINUBUS".
parent married for the second time.

"PARENS MANUMISSOR".
parent who emancipates his child.

PARENTESCO.
m, parentage, kinship, relationship.

PARENTESCO CARNAL.
blood relationship, kinship by blood.

PARENTESCO CIVIL.
relationship which occurs by law (e.g. adoption).

PARENTESCO COLATERAL.
indirect blood relationship.

PARENTESCO CONSANGUÍNEO.
See PARENTESCO POR CONSANGUINIDAD.

PARENTESCO DE AFINIDAD.
See PARENTESCO POR AFINIDAD.

PARENTESCO DE DOBLE VÍNCULO.
blood relationship, relationship through both the mother and the father (i.e. sibling relationship).

PARENTESCO DE SIMPLE VÍNCULO.
half-blood relationship, relationship through either the mother or the father (i.e. relationship between half siblings).

PARENTESCO DIRECTO.
direct relationship.

PARENTESCO DOBLE.
relationship between persons through two different ties.

PARENTESCO ESPIRITUAL.
spiritual relationship (e.g. that of godfather to godchild).

PARENTESCO ILEGÍTIMO.
illegitimate relationship.

PARENTESCO LEGAL.
legal relationship.

PARENTESCO LEGÍTIMO.
legitimate relationship.

PARENTESCO MATERNO.
maternal relationship.

PARENTESCO NATURAL.
blood relationship, relationship through blood lines.

PARENTESCO OBLICUO.
See PARENTESCO COLATERAL.

PARENTESCO PATERNO.
paternal relationship.

PARENTESCO POLÍTICO.
See PARENTESCO POR AFINIDAD.

PARENTESCO POR AFINIDAD.
relationship which arises between person due to their legal ties (e.g. that of mothers-in-law and sons-in law, etc.).

PARENTESCO POR CONSANGUINIDAD.
blood relationship, relationship by blood.

PARENTESCO SIMPLE.
relationship through parents.

PARIA.
f, m, pariah.

PARIDAD.
f, comparison ‖ equality, similarity, parity ‖ parity of par and true value of stock ‖ foreign currency rate of exchange.

PARIDAD DE CASOS.
similarity of cases.

PARIDAD DE EFECTOS PÚBLICOS.
parity of the quoted and nominal values of securities.

PARIDAD DE MONEDA.
parity of the metal and legal value of money.

PARIDAD POLÍTICA.
parity of the exchange rates imposed by government intervention.

PARIDAD REAL.
commercial parity of goods in markets of different countries.

PARIENTA.
f, female relative ‖ wife (in relation to her husband).

PARIENTE.
m, relative, relation ‖ male relative ‖ husband (in relation to his wife) ‖ adj, equal ‖ similar, like.
PARIENTE MÁS PRÓXIMO.
nearest of kin, closest relative.
PARIENTE MAYOR.
member of a family with priority as to an estate belonging to that family.
PARIENTES DEL TESTADOR.
relatives of the testator. Usually the next of kin.
PARIFICACIÓN.
f, proof by comparison ‖ exemplification, illustration.
PARIFICAR.
v, to prove by comparison or example ‖ to illustrate, exemplify.
PARIGUAL.
adj, identical, same ‖ very similar.
PARIR.
v, to give birth, bear.
PARITARIO.
adj, equal or similar in composition. Used to refer to groups organized to resolve labor disputes in which labor and management are equally represented.
PARITARISMO.
m, state support of equal treatment of all religions.
PARLAMENTAR.
v, to speak, talk, converse (between persons) ‖ to deal or negotiate with ‖ to deal with or negotiate in a military situation ‖ to negotiate with the enemy ‖ to negotiate a contract.
PARLAMENTARIO.
m, parliamentarian, member of parliament, congressman, legislator (in the United States) (including senator, deputy, representative) ‖ representative (of others) ‖ representative of nation at war used to negotiate truce ‖ adj, parliamentary.
PARLAMENTARISMO.
m, parliamentarianism ‖ government by or selected by parliament ‖ degeneration of parliament.
PARLAMENTARISTA.
f, m, defender of the parliamentary system.
PARLAMENTO.
m, parliament, legislative power, legislature, congress ‖ parliament building ‖ speech, address (to a meeting, congress, etc.) ‖ confe-

rence, meeting (to deal with a particular matter) ‖ negotiation, meeting.
PARO.
m, strike ‖ end of workday ‖ state of unemployment ‖ work stoppage ‖ stop ‖ see PARO FORZOSO ‖ lockout (by employers).
PARO DE BRAZOS CAÍDOS.
work stoppage, refusal to work ‖ passive strike.
PARO ESTRUCTURAL.
structural unemployment, unemployment caused by a surplus of employees in relation to the economy.
PARO FORZOSO.
unemployment due to involuntary causes (of salaried worker who is otherwise willing and able to work) ‖ layoff.
PARO OBRERO.
See PARO FORZOSO.
PARO PATRONAL.
lockout ‖ shutdown (of a business in order to improve the economic situation of the company).
PÁRRAFO.
m, paragraph.
PARRICIDA.
f, m, parricide, person who kills his or her mother or father ‖ adj, parricidal.
PARRICIDIO.
m, parricide, act of killing one's mother or father.
PARTE.
f, m, part, portion ‖ fragment, fraction, piece ‖ quota, share, interest ‖ period of time, lapse ‖ site, place, location ‖ section, subdivision ‖ communication, notice ‖ military communique ‖ routine informational report ‖ share of co-tenancy upon partition ‖ party, group, faction (of diverse interests) ‖ party (to a lawsuit), litigant (whether plaintiff, defendant, third party plaintiff, or third party defendant) ‖ party (to a contract), contracting party (usually referred to as offeror and offeree) ‖ notification of marriage, marriage announcement.
PARTE ACTORA.
plaintiff, complainant.
PARTE ALÍCUOTA.
proportionate share (e.g. one-half, one-third).
PARTE BELIGERANTE.
belligerent party, warring faction, rebel faction (whether national or international).

PARTE CAPAZ.
able individual ‖ legally competent party.
PARTE CIVIL.
plaintiff (in a civil action).
PARTE COMPARECIENTE.
party who makes an appearance in court.
PARTE CONTRARIA.
opposing party.
PARTE CONTRATANTE.
party (to a contract), contracting party (usually referred to as offeror and offeree).
PARTE DE GUERRA.
military communique, dispatch sent during wartime.
PARTE DE LIBRE DISPOSICIÓN.
portion of an inheritance which may be distributed at the will of the testator. Opposed to PARTE HEREDITARIA.
PARTE DE NOVEDADES.
military communique or report.
PARTE DEL LEÓN.
lion's share, greatest share.
PARTE DEL MUNDO.
area or part of the world.
PARTE DEMANDADA.
defendant.
PARTE DEMANDANTE.
plaintiff.
PARTE DISPOSITIVA.
dispositive part of a law, statute, etc. Opposed to the preamble or explanation of purposes of the law.
PARTE ESENCIAL.
requirement, part of a contract or legal act which is essential to its validity or characterization ‖ necessary party.
PARTE HEREDITARIA.
legal share of an inheritance, share which by law must be distributed to certain person ‖ share given by legacy, bequest, or devise.
PARTE IDEAL.
general portion, equally proportionate share of property. In wills, refers to general legacy or devise. Opposed to PARTE REAL.
PARTE ILEGÍTIMA.
party who lacks legal standing in a lawsuit ‖ party who has no legal interest in a matter.
PARTE INTEGRANTE.
integral part ‖ part of a whole ‖ principal part.
PARTE INTERESADA.
interested or participating party ‖ party who

has a legal interest in a matter ‖ party with standing.
PARTE INTERVINIENTE.
intervener (in a lawsuit).
PARTE LEGÍTIMA.
party to a lawsuit who has standing.
PARTE OFICIAL.
official communication (from government). See PARTE DE GUERRA.
PARTE PRINCIPAL.
main part ‖ essential part or thing ‖ principal party (to a lawsuit) ‖ principal body of a pleading.
PARTE PROCESAL.
litigant (whether plaintiff, defendant, prosecutor, or accused ‖ government representative or attorney (in a lawsuit), attorney general ‖ intervener (in a lawsuit).
PARTE PÚBLICA.
prosecutor, public prosecutor, attorney general (to criminal actions).
PARTE REAL.
specific portion, share of property not determined by equal proportionate shares. In wills, refers to specific legacy or devise. Opposed to PARTE IDEAL.
PARTE REBELDE.
party in default, party who fails to make an appearance in court ‖ party who makes an appearance in court but fails to defend or appear thereafter.
PARTE VIRIL.
proportionate share of a whole which is divided into equal parts.
PARTEAR.
v, to help as a midwife, assist at a birth.
PARTES.
f, m, plural of PARTE ‖ parties, factions, bands ‖ parties (to a lawsuit) which includes the defendant and plaintiff.
PARTES DESIGUALES.
unequal shares or portions.
PARTICIÓN.
f, partition, division, (into equal parts) ‖ distribution ‖ division ‖ separation.
PARTICIÓN AMISTOSA.
amicable distribution of decedent's estate.
PARTICIÓN ANTICIPADA.
advancement, gift causa mortis, anticipatory distribution of an estate prior to death (which distribution must not injure the rights of legal

heirs) ‖ distribution by will of an estate to legatees and devisees (which distribution must not
injure the rights of legal heirs).

PARTICIÓN DE ASCENDIENTE.
type of PARTICIÓN ANTICIPADA given to children and grand-children.

PARTICIÓN DE BIENES SOCIALES.
distribution of property upon dissolution of a
business organization.

PARTICIÓN DE LA HERENCIA.
distribution of the assets of a decedent's estate
‖ right of the heirs, estate creditors, and creditors of the heirs to demand the distribution
of the assets of a decedent's estate.

**PARTICIÓN DE LA HERENCIA
POR EL JUEZ.**
distribution of the assets of a decedent's estate
by court order.

**PARTICIÓN DE LA HERENCIA
POR EL TESTADOR.**
advancement, distribution of an estate causa
mortis by person prior to his death.

**PARTICIÓN DE LA HERENCIA
POR LOS HEREDEROS.**
distribution of an estate by the heirs.

PARTICIÓN ENTRE SOCIOS.
distribution of property upon dissolution of a
business organization.

PARTICIÓN JUDICIAL.
judicial distribution of property (in any situation).

PARTICIÓN POR COMISARIO.
distribution of decedent's estate carried out by
executor or executrix.

PARTICIÓN POR DONACIÓN.
inter-vivos distribution of assets carried out by
parent(s) or grandparent(s) to children or grand-
children.

PARTICIÓN POR JUEZ.
See PARTICIÓN JUDICIAL.

PARTICIÓN POR EL TESTADOR.
See PARTICIÓN POR TESTAMENTO ‖ also see
PARTICIÓN DE LA HERENCIA POR EL TES-
TADOR.

PARTICIÓN POR TESTAMENTO.
distribution of estate by will.

PARTICIÓN PROVISIONAL.
temporary distribution of assets of a decedent's estate ‖ division of assets of a decedent's estate which is to happen upon the occurrence of an event.

PARTICIPACIÓN.
f, participation, share ‖ part, fraction ‖ intervention ‖ communication, notice, information.

PARTICIPACIÓN CRIMINAL.
criminal participation, participation in a crime.
May be as a principal, instigator, accomplice,
conspirator, aider and abetter, etc.

**PARTICIPACIÓN EN LA GESTIÓN
DE LAS EMPRESAS.**
participation of employees in the management
of a company.

**PARTICIPACIÓN EN
LAS ADQUISICIONES.**
See PARTICIPACIÓN EN LOS GANANCIALES.

PARTICIPACIÓN EN LAS GANANCIAS.
See PARTICIPACIÓN EN LOS BENEFICIOS.

PARTICIPACIÓN EN LAS UTILIDADES.
See PARTICIPACIÓN EN LOS BENEFICIOS.

PARTICIPACIÓN EN LOS BENEFICIOS.
profit sharing by workers, annual sharing in
the profits.

PARTICIPACIÓN EN LOS GANANCIALES.
sharing of spouses in the property acquired by
them during the marriage.

PARTICIPACIÓN LABORAL.
worker participation (whether in the profits or
in the management of a business).

PARTICIPANTE.
m, participant, participator ‖ sharer, recipient
‖ adj, participating, sharing.

PARTICIPAR.
v, to participate ‖ to tell, communicate, inform
‖ to share or participate in.

PARTÍCIPE.
m, sharer, recipient ‖ participant, participator
‖ partner in crime ‖ partner ‖ co-owner ‖ adj,
participating, sharing.

PARTÍCIPE DE BUQUE.
co-owner or a ship or vessel.

PARTICULAR.
m, citizen ‖ civilian ‖ matter, subject, topic,
theme ‖ adj, particular, special ‖ private, intimate, one's own ‖ individual, singular ‖ extraordinary.

PARTICULARIDAD.
f, particularity ‖ singularity, individuality.

PARTICULARIZAR.
v, to go into detail, describe in detail ‖ to particularize, go into the particulars ‖ to make
concrete ‖ to prefer, pay special attention (to
a certain person).

PARTIDA.
f, departure ‖ march ‖ death ‖ site, place ‖ behavior, comportment ‖ amount ‖ lot, shipment, portion of merchandise ‖ registration of births, deaths, marriages, etc. by a civil registry ‖ certified record or certificate or copy of aforementioned registration ‖ guerilla group, band ‖ gang ‖ farm, estate ‖ item, entry (in accounting) ‖ financial allotment.

PARTIDA DE MATRIMONIO.
marriage certificate.

PARTIDA DE NACIMIENTO.
birth certificate.

PARTIDA DOBLE.
double entry (in accounting).
Opposed to PARTIDA SIMPLE.

PARTIDA EN SUSPENSO.
entry which cannot yet be entered on the account books.

PARTIDA SIMPLE.
simple entry (in accounting).
Opposed to PARTIDA DOBLE.

PARTIDAMENTE.
adv, separately.

PARTIDARIO.
m, party or group member or affiliate ‖ follower, supporter, partisan (of cause) ‖ guerilla member.

PARTIDARIO SUELTO.
irregular, irregular fighter.

PARTIDISMO.
m, partisanship.

PARTIDISTA.
adj, partisan ‖ fanatic.

PARTIDO.
m, benefit, advantage ‖ favor, help ‖ agreement, treaty, pact, contract ‖ district ‖ party, faction ‖ political party ‖ ready match, person who is ready to marry ‖ (sports) team ‖ game (of sports) ‖ partiality ‖ adj, divided ‖ distributed .

PARTIDO JUDICIAL.
jurisdiction of a trial or district court (in either civil or criminal matters).
See JUEZ DE PRIMERA INSTANCIA.

PARTIDO POLÍTICO.
political party.

PARTIDOR.
m, distributor ‖ executor (if male), executrix (if female).

PARTIJA.
f, lot or share of an inheritance ‖ division o partition of an inheritance ‖ distribution, divi sion.

PARTIMIENTO.
m, partition, division.

PARTIR.
v, to separate or divide into two ‖ to distribut ‖ to divide among common owners ‖ to ope ‖ to leave, depart, take off ‖ to attack ‖ to be gin an era or other time period ‖ to base, bac oneself.

PARTO.
m, delivery, childbirth ‖ birth ‖ newly borr newly born child.

PARTO DOBLE.
multiple delivery ‖ birth of two or more chi dren (in the same delivery).

PARTO MÚLTIPLE.
See PARTO DOBLE.

PARTURIENTA.
f, woman in labor or childbirth ‖ new mothe

PARTURIENTE.
adj, condition of a woman in labor or chil birth, or of a new mother.

PARVIFUNDIO.
See MINIFUNDIO.

PASAJE.
m, passage ‖ passageway, pass ‖ channe straight ‖ passage of a book or other writing entry fee ‖ passage, fare (paid on a boat o other transportation) ‖ (total group of) pa sengers ‖ ticket or other proof of payment passage.

PASAJERO.
m, traveler (by public transportation) ‖ hot guest ‖ adj, passing, temporary ‖ inconsisten unstable.

PASAMENTO.
m, transit, passage ‖ lack of heirs.

PASAMIENTO.
See PASAMENTO.

PASANTE.
m, law clerk (who is still a student) ‖ professo who teaches students prior to examination.

PASANTÍA.
f, law clerking ‖ law clerkship ‖ duration of la clerkship ‖ apprenticeship, training.

PASAPORTE.
m, passport ‖ license, permit, freedom.

PASAPORTE COMÚN.
common passport.
PASAPORTE DEL BUQUE.
ship's papers, sea letter (to show nationality of ship).
PASAPORTE DIPLOMÁTICO.
diplomatic passport.
PASAR POR ALTO.
to forget or omit (inadvertently).
PASAR POR ENCIMA.
to overcome (problems) ‖ to skip the chain of command, go over someone's head ‖ to lack due respect for the law or authority.
PASE.
m, pass, entry ‖ free ticket ‖ pass, document which authorizes entry to a specified site ‖ authorization, permission, license ‖ written approval of a court to use a license or privilege ‖ authorization to transport goods from one site to another for resale ‖ passport ‖ pass (provided by bus or other form of transportation).
PASE DE LIBRE CIRCULACIÓN.
document which authorizes free use of transportation.
PASE LIBRE.
free ticket, pass.
See PASE DE LIBRE CIRCULA-CIÓN.
PASIBLE.
m, person who may be penalized if he or she acts or fails to act ‖ adj, liable or subject to a certain consequence.
PASIÓN.
f, passion, strong desire ‖ omission, abstention ‖ suffering ‖ passivity, passiveness ‖ vehemence ‖ (in criminal law) heat, passion, violent emotion ‖ love.
PASIVO.
m, passive party, abstainer ‖ debt ‖ liability ‖ adj, lazy ‖ inactive ‖ passive.
PASIVO EXIGIBLE.
enforceable liability
PASIVO FICTICIO.
fictitious liability.
Opposed to PASIVO REAL.
PASIVO FUTURO.
liability enforceable at a future point in time.
PASIVO NO EXIGIBLE.
unenforceable liability
PASIVO PREVISIONAL.
liability toward social security agencies.

PASIVO REAL.
real liability. Opposed to PASIVO FICTICIO.
PASO.
m, passage. See SERVIDUMBRE DE PASO.
PASO A NIVEL.
train crossing, level crossing, grade crossing.
PASO AL ENEMIGO.
defection or crossing over to the enemy forces.
PASO ATRÁS.
step backwards ‖ retraction ‖ loss of power, force, benefit, organization, fortune, or discipline.
PASO EN FALSO.
false step ‖ error ‖ imprudence, unwise move.
PASO SUBTERRÁNEO.
underground passageway or passage.
PASQUÍN.
m, low quality newspaper ‖ anonymous poster or notice which satirizes the government.
PASTAR.
v, to pasture, take to pasture.
PASTEAR.
v, to pasture, take to pasture.
PASTOREO.
m, act of pasturing livestock.
PASTOREO ABUSIVO.
type of trespass consisting of pasturing livestock on another's property without permission.
PASTOS.
m, pasture land ‖ pasture.
PASTOS COMUNES.
commons, common pasture land.
PATAS ARRIBA.
f, disorder ‖ tremendous confusion.
PATEAR.
v, to kick (with one's feet) ‖ to treat rudely ‖ to carry out complicated business ‖ to hurry around trying to obtain something ‖ to show disapproval by stamping on the floor.
PATENTADO.
m, patent holder, patentee ‖ adj, patented.
PATENTAR.
v, to patent ‖ to request or obtain a patent.
PATENTE.
f, license to practice a profession ‖ business license or permit (for special types of businesses) ‖ patent, invention patent, letters patent, patent certificate ‖ registration papers ‖ membership card or carnet ‖ adj, patent, clear, obvious.

PATENTE DE CORSO.
authorization granted by the government to private vessels in order to allow them to make war on the ships of an enemy country.
PATENTE DE EMIGRACIÓN.
government permission granted to transport emigrants.
PATENTE DE INTRODUCCIÓN.
importation patent.
PATENTE DE INVENCIÓN.
patent, invention patent, letters patent, patent certificate.
PATENTE DE NAVEGACIÓN.
ship's registration papers, ship's papers.
PATENTE DE SANIDAD.
health certificate.
PATENTE INDUSTRIAL.
industrial or professional permit, permit which permits one to carry out certain industrial or professional activities.
PATENTE PRECAUCIONAL.
provisional patent.
"PATER FAMILIAS".
pater familias, father of the family.
PATERNIDAD.
f, fatherhood, paternity ‖ authorship.
PATERNIDAD CIVIL.
See ADOPCIÓN.
PATERNIDAD ILEGÍTIMA.
See HIJO ILEGÍTIMO and PADRE ILEGÍTIMO.
PATERNIDAD LEGÍTIMA.
See HIJO LEGÍTIMO and PADRE LEGÍTIMO.
PATERNIDAD NATURAL.
See HIJO NATURAL and PADRE NATURAL.
PATERNO.
adj, paternal.
PATIBULARIO.
adj, pertaining to hangman's scaffold ‖ horrifying, disgusting, repulsive.
PATÍBULO.
m, hangman's scaffold, gallows.
PATOTA.
f, gang, street gang, gang of delinquents.
PATRIA.
f, place, city, or nation of birth ‖ homeland, fatherland, motherland ‖ nation.
PATRIA POTESTAD.
parental rights and duties (which lie in the father or, if dead, in the mother) ‖ power to determine the family home and rule the family as well as duty to maintain and protect the family property and name.
"PATRIA POTESTAS".
See PATRIA POTESTAD.
PATRIARCA.
m, patriarch.
PATRIARCADO.
m, patriarchy, patriarchal society.
PATRIMONIO.
m, patrimony, totality of assets and liabilities capable of being evaluated ‖ net worth ‖ net assets, totality of assets less liabilities (whether tangible or intangible) ‖ capital, patrimony ‖ estate ‖ inheritance ‖ proprietorship.
PATRIMONIO ARTÍSTICO.
artistic patrimony or assets (of a nation), governmentally owned works of art.
PATRIMONIO BRUTO.
totality of assets, gross assets.
PATRIMONIO DEL ESTADO.
government property, State assets or patrimony.
PATRIMONIO FAMILIAR.
family property, family assets.
PATRIMONIO MARÍTIMO.
See FORTUNA DE MAR.
PATRIMONIO NACIONAL.
national patrimony, national wealth.
PATRIMONIO PRIVADO.
privately-held assets or capital or estate ‖ private property.
PATRIMONIO PÚBLICO.
publicly-held assets or capital or estate ‖ public property, government property.
PATRIMONIO REAL.
State patrimony or wealth.
PATRIMONIO SEPARADO.
separate property or estate (from another estate). May be separate from that of husband or father, or from the bankrupt's estate, etc.
PATRIMONIO SINDICAL.
union assets or capital, totality of economic rights and obligations of a union.
PATRIMONIO SOCIAL.
corporate assets (of civil or commercial corporations). See PATRIMONIO SINDICAL.
PATRIOTA.
m, patriot ‖ compatriot.
PATRIOTERÍA.
See PATRIOTERISMO.

PATRIOTERISMO.
m, superficial and excessive patriotism, jingoism.

PATRIÓTICO.
adj, patriotic, nationalistic.

PATRIOTISMO.
m, patriotism, nationalism.

PATROCINADOR.
m, sponsor, backer, supporter ‖ defender ‖ protector.

PATROCINAR.
v, to sponsor, back, support ‖ to defend ‖ to protect.

PATROCINIO.
m, sponsorship ‖ backing ‖ support ‖ defense ‖ protection ‖ advice ‖ help.

PATROCINIO LETRADO.
legal advice or representation.

PATRÓN.
m, norm, guideline ‖ criteria, measure ‖ defender, protector ‖ patron, boss, employer ‖ master, slave-owner ‖ inn or hotel keeper ‖ businessman, entrepreneur ‖ landlord ‖ skipper, captain ‖ standard (for metals, e.g. gold standard)

PATRÓN DE BOTE.
warship captain.

PATRÓN DE BUQUE.
ship captain.

PATRÓN DE LANCHA.
See PATRÓN DE BOTE.

PATRÓN MONETARIO.
monetary standard.

PATRÓN ORO.
gold standard.

PATRONA.
f, woman of the house ‖ female who is defender, protector, patron, boss, employer, master, slave-owner, innkeeper, hotelier, businessman, entrepreneur, skipper, or ship captain ‖ landlady.

PATRONAL.
adj, employment, pertaining to employment ‖ pertaining to PATRONATO; pertaining to PATRONO.

PATRONATO.
m, right or authority or power of employer ‖ employers' association ‖ patronage ‖ trust, foundation, non-profit association ‖ trusteeship ‖ board of trustees ‖ right to propose the appointment of bishops and other clerics.

PATRONATO DE LIBERADOS.
See LIBERTAD CONDICIONAL.

PATRONATO DE MENORES.
non-profit association for the protection and aid of minors and orphans.

PATRONO.
m, defender, protector ‖ holder of a right of PATRONATO ‖ master, slave-owner ‖ innkeeper, hotelier ‖ employer ‖ boss.

PATRULLA.
f, (army or police) patrol, squad ‖ policemen on the beat ‖ tax or customs inspection officers ‖ band, group.

PAULIANA.
See ACCIÓN PAULIANA.

PAULINO.
See PRIVILEGIO PAULINO.

PAUPERISMO.
m, poverty, pauperism.

PAUTA.
f, norm, guideline ‖ model, example, guide.

PAUTAR.
v, to set forth or draw up guidelines or norms.

PAZ.
f, peace, tranquility ‖ armistice.

PEAJE.
m, toll, highway toll.

PEATÓN.
m, pedestrian.

PECADO.
m, sin, holy sin ‖ transgression ‖ excess, abuse ‖ defect, fault.

PECADOR.
m, sinner.

PECOREA.
f, looting or pillage carried out by disbanded soldiers.

PECOREAR.
v, to rustle or steal cattle ‖ to loot, pillage.

PECULADO.
m, embezzlement (of public funds), peculation.

PECULIAR.
adj, peculiar, characteristic (of someone or something).

PECULIARIDAD.
f, essence, peculiarity, singularity, characteristic (as noun).

PECULIARISMO.
m, peculiarity, oddness, strangeness ‖ individuality.

PECULIO.

m, one's own money, private money ‖ separate property ‖ prisoner's pay (see PECULIO DEL CONDENADO) ‖ son's separate property.

PECULIO ADVENTICIO.

son's private property (resulting from his own labor, luck, gift, or inheritance from persons other than his father).

PECULIO CASTRENSE.

son's private property (resulting from military service or campaigns).

PECULIO CUASICASTRENSE.

son's private property (resulting from professional, public, or religious work).

PECULIO DEL CONDENADO.

prisoner's pay received for labor performed.

PECULIO PROFECTICIO.

property the administration of which a father transfers to his son, but title to which remains in the father.

PECUNIARIO.

adj, pecuniary.

PECHAR.

v, to pay a tax ‖ to pay a fine ‖ to hit up for a loan with no intention of returning it ‖ to assume (a responsibility).

PECHO.

m, tax ‖ fine.

PEDAGOGÍA.

f, pedagogy ‖ teachings, doctrine.

PEDAGOGO.

m, pedagogue ‖ teacher ‖ tutor.

PEDÁNEO.

m, mayor or judge of a village or hamlet.

PEDERASTA.

m, pederast, person who has sexual relations with children of same sex as the actor ‖ sodomite.

PEDERASTÍA.

f, pederasty ‖ sodomy.

PEDIDO.

m, request, petition ‖ order, purchase order.

PEDIMENTO.

m, petition, bill, complaint ‖ motion, written request presented to a judge ‖ claim, specific request set forth in the aforementioned documents.

PEDIR CUENTA.

to ask for an explanation ‖ to accuse.

PEDIR LA PALABRA.

v, to call for or request the floor (at a meeting).

PEGADO A LA PARED.

adj, nonplussed, confused, embarrassed.

PEGAR CUATRO TIROS.

to shoot dead, murder ‖ to execute by shooting ‖ to impose one's views violently.

PEGUJAL.

m, small plot of land given to certain farm employees as part of their pay. See PECULIO

PEGUJAR.

See PEGUJAL.

PELAR.

v, to shave or cut hair (as punishment) ‖ to skin alive, win all the money of another ‖ to take the shirt off one's back, fleece (by trickery or violence).

PELEA.

f, fight, combat, battle ‖ struggle.

PELEAR.

v, to fight, battle ‖ to struggle, resist ‖ to oppose.

PELEARSE.

v, to fight one another ‖ to have a tiff ‖ to make an enemy of another.

PELIGRAR.

v, to be in danger.

PELIGRO.

m, danger, peril, hazard ‖ risk ‖ threat of danger.

PELIGRO COMÚN.

ordinary danger or risk ‖ danger which affects a number of persons equally.

PELIGRO CONCRETO.

known danger ‖ in criminal law, danger intended to harm identified person(s) or property (as opposed to unidentified person(s) or property) ‖ danger in a particular situation (as distinguished from the danger which generally arises from certain types of conduct).

PELIGRO DE GUERRA.

state of war.

PELIGRO
DE MUERTE.

mortal danger, danger of death, peril of loss of life.

PELIGRO GRAVE.

serious risk or danger. In re persons, involves danger to life, body, honor, fundamental rights, and important interests ‖ in re things, entails their destruction, loss, or theft ‖ in re nations, involves the possible loss of indepen-dence or part of national territory.

PELIGRO INMINENTE.
imminent or impending danger, danger which is proximate in time and avoidable only with difficulty.

PELIGRO INTENCIONAL.
intentionally caused danger.

PELIGRO PERSONAL.
personal danger or peril.

PELIGRO ROJO.
red peril, i.e. Communism.

PELIGROSAMENTE.
adv, dangerously, hazardously, with peril.

PELIGROSIDAD.
f, dangerousness.

PELIGROSIDAD SOCIAL.
dangerousness to society.

PELIGROSO.
adj, dangerous, hazardous ‖ risky ‖ bad or threatening (person).

PENA.
f, punishment, sanction ‖ legal punishment ‖ penalty, fine ‖ physical pain ‖ trouble, difficulty ‖ embarrassment ‖ work ‖ fatigue ‖ grief, sorrow.

PENA ACCESORIA.
accessory or additional punishment, punishment which is imposed as a consequence of another principal punishment.

PENA ADMINISTRATIVA.
administrative penalty, fine, or punishment, one imposed by the executive branch.

PENA AFLICTIVA.
serious punishment ‖ corporal punishment.

PENA ALTERNATIVA.
alternative punishment.

PENA ARBITRARIA.
arbitrary punishment, discretionary punishment, punishment which is imposed at the discretion of the judge ‖ arbitrary and unjustly imposed punishment.

PENA CAPITAL.
capital punishment, death penalty.

PENA CIVIL.
civil penalty. Opposed to PENA CRIMINAL.

PENA COMPLEMENTARIA.
additional penalty or punishment (imposed to make another punishment more effective).

PENA COMPROMISORIA.
punishment imposed by an arbitrator for failure to comply with an arbitration decision or award.

PENA COMÚN.
ordinary criminal penalty or punishment.

PENA CONJUNTA.
cumulative punishment.

PENA CONMINATORIA.
non-criminal penalty or punishment which is imposed to make citizens comply with their civic duties.

PENA CONTRACTUAL.
contractual penalty.

PENA CONVENCIONAL.
contractual penalty.

PENA CORPORAL.
corporal penalty or punishment ‖ punishment which restricts the (limited) freedoms of a prisoner.

PENA CORRECCIONAL.
corrective punishment, punishment which is less severe than PENA AFLICTIVA ‖ punishment by incarceration.

PENA CRIMINAL.
criminal punishment or penalty.

PENA DE CASTIGO.
punishment, penalty imposed as a punishment.

PENA DE DERECHO COMÚN.
punishment or penalty which is set forth in the criminal code (as opposed to a special statute).

PENA DE LA VIDA.
See PENA DE MUERTE.

PENA DE MUERTE.
capital punishment, death penalty.

PENA DE NULIDAD.
sanction of nullifying the legal effects of a contract or other legal act.

PENA DE ORDEN MORAL.
punishment which affects the reputation of the convicted person.

PENA DE PECHO.
penalty which is determined by multiplying the harm suffered by the victim.

PENA DE POLICÍA.
administrative fine or penalty.

PENA DISCIPLINARIA.
disciplinary punishment ‖ punishment which is a warning, censure, or other preventative punishment.

PENA DISCIPLINARIA A PRISIONEROS.
prisoner punishment imposed for disciplinary violations.

PENA DIVISIBLE.
graduated punishment (which requires the adjudicator to impose the punishment to the extent he feels appropriate).

PENA GRAVE.
serious punishment.

PENA INDIVISIBLE.
indivisible punishment (which may or may not be applied, but which by its nature does not allow discretionary flexibility, e.g. death penalty).

PENA INFAMANTE.
punishment which affects one's public honor.

PENA JUDICIAL.
contractual penalty ‖ judicially imposed punishment.
Opposed to PENA ADMINISTRATIVA.

PENA LEGAL.
mandatory punishment (which permits no discretion on the part of the adjudicator).

PENA LEVE.
light punishment.

PENA MILITAR.
military punishment.

PENA PATRIMONIAL.
penalty imposed against the property of the defendant.

PENA PECUNIARIA.
fine, monetary penalty or punishment.

PENA POLÍTICA.
penalty imposed for breach of the peace or public order; punishment imposed for political crimes.

PENA PRINCIPAL.
main or principal punishment. Opposed to PENA ACCESORIA.

PENA PRIVADA.
punishment imposed for a DELITO PRIVADO ‖ penalty which is imposed for the benefit of an individual.

PENA PRIVATIVA DE DERECHOS.
punishment which deprives a person of rights (other than that of freedom).

PENA PRIVATIVA DE LIBERTAD.
punishment which deprives a person of freedom.

PENA PÚBLICA.
punishment imposed for a DELITO PÚBLICO penalty which is imposed for the benefit of society as a whole.

PENA RESTRICTIVA DE LIBERTAD.
punishment which restricts a person's freedom. Includes imprisonment, exclusion from an area or place, or deportation from a country.

PENA TEMPORAL.
punishment which is imposed for a period of time.

PENABLE.
adj, punishable.

PENADO.
m, convict, convicted person ‖ adj, worried ‖ difficult.

PENAL.
m, prison, penitentiary ‖ adj, criminal, penal.

PENALIDAD.
f, affliction, bother, hardship, discomfort ‖ quality of punishable ‖ penalty, sanction set forth by law.

PENALIDAD CIVIL.
civil sanction ‖ sanction imposed by civil law regarding void or illegal contracts or other legal acts.

PENALISTA.
f, m, criminal lawyer, lawyer specializing in criminal law.

PENALMENTE.
adv, criminally, pertaining to criminal law ‖ pertaining to penalties or sanctions ‖ repressively.

PENAR.
v, to penalize, punish, fine ‖ to fulfill a prison term ‖ to suffer (emotionally or physically).

PENAS PARALELAS.
parallel punishments.

PENAS PRIVATIVAS DE DERECHOS.
punishments involving deprivation of rights (e.g. voting, holding of public office, etc.).

PENAS PRIVATIVAS DE LIBERTAD.
punishments involving deprivation of freedom or liberty.

PENAS RESTRICTIVAS DE LA LIBERTAD.
punishments involving restrictions on freedom of movement.

PENDENCIA.
f, quarrel, dispute ‖ fight ‖ pendency of litigation, lite pendente ‖ quality of being pending or lacking resolution.

PENDENCIAR.
v, to quarrel, fight ‖ to have a dispute.

PENDENCIERO.
m, fighter, troublemaker.

"PENDENTE CONDITIONE".
condition pending.

"PENDENTE LITE".
pending litigation, pendente lite.

PENDIENTE.
adj, pending.

PENETRACIÓN.
f, penetration.

PENETRACIÓN ECONÓMICA.
economic penetration (of one country in the economy of another).

PENETRACIÓN PACÍFICA.
peaceful influence (of one country over the political or economic affairs of another country).

PENITENCIARÍA.
f, jail, prison, penitentiary, penal institution.

PENITENCIARIO.
adj, penitentiary, jail, pertaining to prisons or jails.

"PENITUS EXTRANEI".
uneffected by or beyond the penalty. Refers to those who are third parties to a contract and thus remain unaffected by contractual penalties.

PENOLOGÍA.
f, penology.

PENSAMIENTO CRIMINAL.
criminal mens rea.

PENSIÓN.
f, pension ‖ allowance, support, maintenance ‖ rent paid on a piece of rural property (either permanent or temporary) ‖ government pension ‖ annuity ‖ scholarship, grant, fellowship (for studying) ‖ hostelry, boarding house ‖ board, cost of lodging, board and rent.

PENSIÓN A LA VEJEZ.
pension for old age (usually granted by employer to employee.)

PENSIÓN ALIMENTARIA.
See PENSIÓN ALIMENTICIA.

PENSIÓN ALIMENTICIA.
allowance for food and other necessities ‖ in divorce law referred to as support or maintenance.

PENSIÓN DE VIUDEDAD.
widow or widower's pension.

PENSIÓN DE VIUDEZ.
See PENSIÓN DE VIUDEDAD.

PENSIÓN FAMILIAR.
family pension, pension granted to orphans, widows or widowers, or parents of certain state employees.

PENSIÓN GRACIABLE.
pension granted by government or governmental entity to certain persons based on merit or extraordinary service.

PENSIÓN LABORAL.
employment pension granted to employee or certain family members upon death or disability of employee. Includes disability pension or widow or widower or orphan's pension.

PENSIÓN MILITAR.
military pension. Includes retirement pension granted for extraordinary service, and widow or widower or orphan's pension.

PENSIÓN NO CONTRIBUTIVA.
pension (granted to certain persons) which is not based on prior contribution of pensioner to the pension fund.

PENSIÓN PERPETUA.
permanent pension.

PENSIÓN REMUNERATORIA.
See PENSIÓN GRACIABLE.

PENSIÓN VITALICIA.
annuity, life pension.

PENSIONADO.
m, pensioner ‖ adj, pensioned.

PENSIONAR.
v, to grant a pension ‖ to charge rent.

PENSIONARIO.
m, party who pays a tax or pension ‖ attorney, lawyer (within a republic) ‖ adj, pertaining to party who pays a tax or pension or an attorney or lawyer.

PENSIONISTA.
f, m, pensioner ‖ boarder, lodger ‖ boarding school boarder.

PENTÁGONO.
m, (United States) Pentagon ‖ pentagon.

PENTARQUÍA.
f, pentarchy, government formed of five persons.

PEÑO.
m, pledge.

PEÓN.
m, peon ‖ manual laborer ‖ day laborer ‖ pedestrian.

PEÓN CAMINERO.
road worker, person whose job is to maintain and repair public roads.

PEONADA.
f, day's work of a laborer ‖ totality of workers on a job, work gang or team or group.

PEONAJE.
m, totality of workers on a job, work gang or team or group.

PEQUEÑA EMPRESA.
small business, small business enterprise.

PEQUEÑA PROPIEDAD.
property of medium size (between LATIFUNDIO and MINIFUNDIO.)

PEQUEÑO DERECHO.
authorship rights of poets or composers (which gives them right to receive fees each time their work is played to a playing public.)

"PER ACCIDENS".
by accident.

PER CÁPITA.
per capita, per person, individually.

"PER SE".
for oneself, for one's own benefit and in one's own name.

PERCANCE.
m, accident ‖ mishap, misfortune ‖ perquisite, benefit received over and above salary.

PERCATAR.
v, to warn, consider ‖ to care for.

PERCATARSE.
v, to discover, notice, become aware of ‖ to hear of something.

PERCEPCIÓN.
f, perception, comprehension, understanding ‖ receipt (of something) ‖ charge, receipt, collection.

PERCEPCIÓN DE LOS FRUTOS.
receipt of benefits (of something.), e.g. fruits of a farm, factory, rental property, etc.

PERCEPCIÓN DEL SALARIO.
receipt of salary.

PERCEPTIBLE.
adj, understandable, comprehensible ‖ chargeable, collectable.

PERCEPTOR.
m, receiver (of something) ‖ collector.

PERCIBO.
m, receipt, act of receiving or hearing of (something).

PERCUSIÓN.
f, percussion ‖ blow, knock, hit ‖ wound, injury.

PERCUSOR.
m, person who hits or knocks.

PERCUTIR.
v, to hit, knock, give a blow to ‖ to injure, wound.

PERDEDOR.
m, loser (of a battle or lawsuit).

PERDER.
v, to lose, mislay ‖ to forfeit ‖ not to find ‖ to miss ‖ to lose a battle, etc. ‖ to be beaten ‖ to err ‖ to suffer emotional damage ‖ not to be worthy of a name or a reputation ‖ to go downhill, go to rack and ruin ‖ to corrupt, pervert.

PERDER DE SU DERECHO.
to settle, to give in.

PERDER EL TIEMPO.
to lose or waste time ‖ to work uselessly ‖ to lose an opportunity.

PERDER LA VIDA.
to lose one's life.

PERDERSE.
v, to be disoriented ‖ to sink, go down (re a ship) ‖ to risk one's life ‖ to be lost, fail to find a solution to a problem ‖ not to use to take advantage of something ‖ to become corrupt or perverted.

PERDICIÓN.
f, ruin ‖ eternal damnation, perdition ‖ act of PERDER or PERDERSE | unbridled or uncontrolled passion ‖ person who causes injury or damage.

PERDIDA.
f, loose woman ‖ lost thing ‖ adj, lost, mislaid ‖ wasted.

PÉRDIDA.
f, deficit ‖ loss ‖ negative balance ‖ deprivation of property or right ‖ loss of something, including shortage and shrinkage and leakage ‖ damage, injury ‖ waste, amount lost ‖ ship sinking ‖ loss of territory ‖ war dead and wounded.

PÉRDIDA DE AERONAVE.
loss of an airplane.

PÉRDIDA DE ARMAS.
loss of firearms.

PÉRDIDA DE BUQUE.
loss of a vessel.

ÉRDIDA DE EMPLEO.
loss of employment.

ÉRDIDA DE LA CIUDADANÍA.
loss of nationality ‖ rights pertaining to a citizen (other than nationality), e.g. political rights.

ÉRDIDA DE LA COSA DEBIDA.
loss of property owed to another party, e.g. property which already has been sold that is subsequently lost.

ÉRDIDA DE LA NACIONALIDAD.
loss of nationality.

ÉRDIDA DE LA PATRIA POTESTAD.
loss of parental rights (and obligations).

ÉRDIDA DE LA POSESIÓN.
loss of possession (of property). May occur due to the property no longer existing, physical impossibility of possession, transfer of the property, voluntary abandonment, a third party taking possession, loss of the property, etc.

ÉRDIDA DE PLAZA.
loss of military position during a war or in other circumstances.

ÉRDIDA DEL CAPITAL DE LA SOCIEDAD.
loss of corporate capital.

ÉRDIDA DEL EJERCICIO DE LA PATRIA POTESTAD.
loss of exercising parental rights. Differs from PÉRDIDA DE LA PATRIA POTESTAD in the facts or acts which cause this to occur.

ÉRDIDA DEL TIEMPO DE SERVICIO.
loss of time worked, loss of time employed.

ÉRDIDA EN LA COMPRAVENTA.
loss or destruction or diminution in value of the object of a sales contract.

ÉRDIDAS E INTERESES.
damages plus interest ‖ losses and damages, including interest.

ÉRDIDAS Y GANANCIAS.
profits and losses ‖ profit and loss.

ERDIDO.
m, stray or lost person ‖ adj, lost ‖ perverted, corrupted ‖ ruined ‖ without possibility of salvation.

ERDIDOR.
m, loser ‖ adj, easily lost.

ERDIGÓN.
m, young squanderer or prodigal ‖ one who loses heavily at gambling.

PERDIMIENTO.
See PERDICIÓN.

PERDÓN.
m, pardon ‖ forgiveness (of a debt or other obligation) ‖ indulgence, clemency ‖ amnesty ‖ reprieve ‖ exemption.

PERDÓN DE LA DEUDA.
forgiveness of the debt.

PERDÓN DEL OFENDIDO.
victim's pardon or forgiveness of the crime or tort.

PERDÓN JUDICIAL.
judicial pardon or clemency.

PERDONABLE.
adj, pardonable ‖ forgivable ‖ susceptible to clemency or amnesty or reprieve.

PERDONADOR.
m, forgiver ‖ party who grants a pardon or clemency or amnesty or reprieve.

PERDONAR.
v, to pardon, excuse ‖ to forgive ‖ to grant clemency ‖ to grant amnesty ‖ to grant a reprieve ‖ to exempt.

PERDURABLE.
adj, durable ‖ perpetual.

PERDURAR.
v, to endure, last (a long time) ‖ to persist ‖ to remain.

PERECEDERO.
m, place of loss ‖ dangerous place ‖ adj, perishable ‖ fleeting ‖ needy, lacking in basic necessities ‖ mortal.

PERECER.
v, to end, perish ‖ to die ‖ to suffer damage ‖ to endure emotional ruin ‖ to deserve eternal damnation ‖ to lack the life-sustaining necessities.

PERECIMIENTO.
m, act of perishing or dying or suffering damage or ruination.

PERENCIÓN.
See PERENCIÓN DE LA INSTANCIA.

PERENCIÓN DE LA INSTANCIA.
lapsing of a lawsuit due to inactivity.

PERENE.
See PERENNE.

PERENNE.
adj, perennial, perpetual, continual ‖ lasting ‖ permanent.

PERENNIDAD.
f, perpetuity ‖ permanence.

PERENTORIAMENTE.
adv, urgently, without delay ‖ peremptorily ‖ pursuant to a peremptory period of time.

PERENTORIO.
adj, peremptory ‖ conclusive, decisive ‖ urgent ‖ final.

PEREZA.
f, laziness ‖ negligence, carelessness.

PERFECCIÓN.
f, perfection ‖ perfect accord with the law ‖ perfection (of legal instrument or act to coincide with legal requisites), fulfillment of all legal requirements for an act to be legally valid.

PERFECCIÓN DEL CONTRATO.
perfection of a contract, fulfillment of all legal requirements for a contract to be legally valid.

PERFECCIONAR.
v, to perfect ‖ to improve, better ‖ to correct ‖ to perfect, fulfill all legal requirements needed for any act to be valid.

PERFECTO.
adj, perfect ‖ complete ‖ perfected, fully effective, in full legal effect.

PERICIA.
f, expertness, expert knowledge or qualification (in an art or science) ‖ skill ‖ know-how ‖ testimony of or report prepared by an expert witness.

PERICIAL.
adj, expert, pertaining to an expert ‖ with the assistance or opinion of an expert.

PERICIALMENTE.
adv, expertly ‖ with the assistance or opinion of an expert.

PERIÓDICAMENTE.
adv, periodically.

PERIODICIDAD.
f, periodicity ‖ totality of periods of time in a given period of time.

PERIÓDICO.
m, newspaper ‖ adj, periodical, cyclical.

PERÍODO.
m, period, term, period or space or lapse of time.

PERÍODO COMPLEMENTARIO.
executory period, term which is set for executing a judgment.

PERÍODO CONSTITUTIVO.
period which is set to establish a corporation and fulfill all legal requirements pertaining thereto.

PERÍODO DE ALERTA.
state of alert (after an enemy attack).

PERÍODO DE PRUEBA.
trial or test period (of an employee prior to offering employment).

PERÍODO DE SEGURIDAD.
safe period, period of time during female menstrual cycle during which she is infertile.

PERÍODO DE SILENCIO INTERNACIONAL.
period of international silence.

PERÍODO DE SOSPECHA.
See PERÍODO SOSPECHOSO.

PERÍODO ELECTORAL.
election period, period of time after election have been called for and prior to elections.

PERÍODO SOSPECHOSO.
period of time between the date of suspensión of payments and the final judgment thereof o immediately prior to the declaration of bankruptcy ‖ period of time before and after the commission of a crime for which a person doe not have an alibi.

PERISTA.
m, fence, person who purchases stolen goods

PERITACIÓN.
f, expert's research or investigation ‖ expert' report.

PERITAJE.
m, expert's report.

PERITO.
m, expert, specialist.

PERITO EN AVERÍAS.
expert in (maritime) average.

PERITO JUDICIAL.
legal expert who provides special legal information or advice to a judge in a law suit.

PERITO TERCERO.
disinterested expert assigned by a judge when the testimony of the experts of both partie may or does conflict.

PERITO TESTIGO.
expert witness.

PERJUDICADO.
m, injured or prejudiced party ‖ accident victim ‖ adj, prejudiced, injured, hurt, damaged

PERJUDICAR.
v, to injure, prejudice, hurt, harm, damage.

PERJUDICIAL.
adj, prejudicial, harmful, injurious, damaging

PERJUICIO.
m, prejudice ‖ emotional damage ‖ harm, injury ‖ damages, loss.
PERJUICIO CORPORAL.
bodily injury.
PERJUICIO ESTÉTICO.
damage to aesthetic appearance, especially of a person.
PERJUICIO EVENTUAL.
See DAÑO EVENTUAL.
PERJUICIO INDIRECTO.
consequential damages, losses which result from other damages.
PERJUICIO MATERIAL.
See DAÑO MATERIAL.
PERJUICIO MORAL.
See DAÑO MORAL.
PERJUICIOS E INTERESES.
See PÉRDIDAS E INTERESES.
PERJUICIOS RECÍPROCOS.
See DAÑOS RECÍPROCOS.
PERJURADOR.
See PERJURO.
PERJURAR.
v, to perjure, give false testimony, commit perjury.
PERJURARSE.
v, to commit perjury, perjure oneself.
PERJURIO.
m, perjury, false testimony.
PERJURO.
m, perjurer.
PERMANECER.
v, to remain, stay.
PERMANENCIA.
f, stay, duration of stay ‖ permanence ‖ residence ‖ permanency.
PERMANENTE.
adj, permanent, continuous, enduring, lasting.
PERMISIVAMENTE.
adv, with permission, permissively, with implied consent, without express approval or authorization.
PERMISIVO.
adj, permissive, that which authorizes or permits but which neither prohibits not obliges.
PERMISO.
m, permission, license, authorization, consent ‖ furlough, approved leave from military service ‖ leave, vacation, time-off.

PERMISO DE ARMAS.
gun license, license to bear arms.
PERMISO DE CONDUCIR.
driver's license.
PERMISO EXTRAORDINARIO.
authorized leave without pay.
PERMITIDO.
adj, authorized, permitted ‖ not prohibited.
PERMITIDOR.
m, permitter, authorizer, person who authorizes or permits ‖ grantor (of a license, authorization, or permit).
PERMITIR.
v, to permit, authorize, license, consent to ‖ to grant (a license, or authorization) ‖ to tolerate, put up with, stand.
PERMUTA.
f, permutation, exchange (of one thing for another) ‖ barter ‖ barter agreement ‖ change of destiny or profession.
PERMUTA AMIGABLE.
See PERMUTA VOLUNTARIA.
PERMUTA FORZOSA.
type of forced land exchange by which small land parcels are exchanged such that land is owned in larger portions.
PERMUTA MERCANTIL.
barter contract.
PERMUTA OBLIGATORIA.
See PERMUTA FORZOSA.
PERMUTA VOLUNTARIA.
consensual barter or exchange of property.
PERMUTABLE.
adj, exchangeable, subject to barter.
PERMUTACIÓN.
f, bartering ‖ barter, exchange.
PERMUTANTE.
m, barterer, party who participates in an exchange of property.
PERMUTAR.
v, to exchange property ‖ to interchange ‖ to barter (one thing for another).
PERMUTATIVO.
See ACTO PERMUTATIVO.
PERNICIOSAMENTE.
adv, perniciously.
PERNICIOSO.
adj, pernicious, highly damaging or harmful.
PEROGRULLADA.
f, truism, platitude, obvious truth.

PERORACIÓN.
f, final argument ‖ peroration, conclusion of speech.

PERORAR.
v, to give final argument ‖ to insist ‖ to make a speech.

PERORATA.
f, lengthy discourse ‖ insistence.

PERPETRACIÓN.
f, perpetration, commission ‖ provocation, perpetration (e.g. of a crime).

PERPETRADOR.
m, perpetrator, author of a crime.

PERPETRAR.
v, to perpetrate, commit (a crime).

PERPETUACIÓN.
f, perpetuation ‖ prolongation.

PERPETUAR.
v, to perpetuate ‖ to last, endure ‖ to cause to last or endure.

PERPETUARSE.
v, to perpetuate ‖ to remain in an office (at any price) ‖ to perpetuate oneself, have children.

PERPETUIDAD.
f, perpetuity, eternity ‖ prolonged duration.

PERPETUO.
adj, in perpetuity ‖ perpetual, eternal ‖ long lasting ‖ for life.

PERPETUO SILENCIO.
judicial order to remain silent regarding certain unfounded claims.

PERSECUCIÓN.
f, persecution ‖ pursuit ‖ right of replevin, right to recover goods in the possession of others.

PERSECUTORIO.
adj, pursuing ‖ persecuting.

PERSEGUIDO.
m, thing or person which is being pursued or persecuted ‖ defendant ‖ adj, pursued ‖ persecuted.

PERSEGUIDOR.
m, pursuer ‖ persecutor ‖ person who exercises his right of replevin.

PERSEGUIMIENTO.
See PERSECUCIÓN.

PERSEGUIR.
v, to pursue ‖ to persecute ‖ to bother, pester ‖ to file a criminal complaint ‖ to file a replevin action.

PERSONA.
f, individual, person, human being ‖ important person, personage, personality.

PERSONA A CARGO.
dependent (of a person involved in an on-the-job accident) ‖ dependent (of the taxpayer).

PERSONA ABSTRACTA.
See PERSONA ARTIFICIAL.

PERSONA ARTIFICIAL.
legal person or entity, artificial person.

PERSONA AUSENTE CON PRESUNCIÓN DE FALLECIMIENTO.
missing person presumed dead.

PERSONA CAPAZ.
capable person ‖ person who is legally competent ‖ qualified person.

PERSONA CIVIL.
person as defined by the civil law or for civil law purposes.

PERSONA COLECTIVA.
collective person. See PERSONA ARTIFICIAL.

PERSONA CORPORAL.
natural person.

PERSONA DE DERECHO PRIVADO.
artificial person organized for private purposes.

PERSONA DE DERECHO PUBLICO.
public corporation, artificial person which is organized for public purposes (e.g. municipalities, states, provinces, etc.).

PERSONA DE EXISTENCIA IDEAL.
See PERSONA ABSTRACTA.

PERSONA DE EXISTENCIA REAL.
See PERSONA NATURAL.

PERSONA DE EXISTENCIA VISIBLE.
See PERSONA NATURAL.

PERSONA FICTICIA.
See PERSONA ABSTRACTA.

PERSONA FÍSICA.
See PERSONA NATURAL.

PERSONA FUTURA.
future life, future being, person not yet born or created.

PERSONA GRATA.
diplomatic representative who is proposed and accepted by a foreign nation.

PERSONA INCAPAZ.
incompetent person ‖ person who is legally incompetent ‖ unqualified person.

PERSONA INCIERTA.
person whose existence or identity is uncertain.

PERSONA INCORPORAL.
See PERSONA ABSTRACTA.

PERSONA INDETERMINADA.
See PERSONA INCIERTA.

PERSONA INDIVIDUAL.
See PERSONA NATURAL.

PERSONA INHÁBIL.
incompetent person ‖ person who is legally incompetent ‖ unqualified person.

PERSONA INTERESADA.
interested party, person who has an interest in a matter.

PERSONA INTERNACIONAL.
nation recognized as independent pursuant to public international law ‖ person as recognized by public international law.

PERSONA INTERPUESTA.
straw party, straw man.

PERSONA INTERPÓSITA.
See PERSONA INTERPUESTA.

PERSONA JURÍDICA.
artificial person.

PERSONA LEGAL.
See PERSONA JURÍDICA.

PERSONA MORAL.
See PERSONA JURÍDICA.

PERSONA NATURAL.
natural person, person.

PERSONA NO FÍSICA.
artificial person.

PERSONA NON GRATA.
persona non grata.

PERSONA NOTORIAMENTE INSOLVENTE.
person who is well-known to be insolvent.

PERSONA POR NACER.
person yet to be born.

PERSONA PÚBLICA.
public entity, artificial person of the government.

PERSONA SOCIAL.
See PERSONA ABSTRACTA and PERSONA COLECTIVA.

PERSONA TORPE.
clumsy person ‖ immoral or indecent person.

PERSONA VISIBLE.
See PERSONA NATURAL.

PERSONAL.
m, personnel ‖ members of a class or entity ‖ adj, personal ‖ individual, private, intimate ‖ characteristic ‖ non-delegable ‖ face-to-face, personal, direct.

PERSONAL AERONÁUTICO.
aeronautic personnel in the Air Force.

PERSONAL CONSULAR.
consular personnel.

PERSONAL DE SERVICIO.
domestic, domestic help or personnel or staff.

PERSONAL NAVEGANTE.
flight personnel ‖ ship's crew.

PERSONAL NO NAVEGANTE.
ground personnel (re aviation).

PERSONAL SANITARIO.
garbage men ‖ sanitary engineers ‖ health personnel.

PERSONALIDAD.
f, personality ‖ character, legal capacity ‖ well-defined character ‖ personality, well-known personage ‖ legal standing, legal capacity to litigate.

PERSONALIDAD DE LA PENA.
individualization of punishment, making the punishment fit the circumstances.

PERSONALIDAD GREMIAL.
See PERSONERÍA GREMIAL.

PERSONALÍSIMO.
adj, strictly personal or individual.

PERSONALIZACIÓN DEL PODER.
f, personalization of power.

PERSONARSE.
v, to appear (in court) ‖ to present oneself ‖ to attend an administrative meeting ‖ to have an interview

PERSONAS.
f, persons, individuals. Used to refer to a classification or branch of civil law.

PERSONERÍA.
f, function and position of agent ‖ also see PERSONALIDAD.

PERSONERÍA GREMIAL.
legal status of a legally recognized union.

PERSONERO.
m, agent ‖ representative ‖ union representative ‖ solicitor.

PERSONIFICACIÓN.
f, personification.

PERSONIFICAR.
v, to personify.

PERSUADIR.
v, to persuade, convince, induce ‖ to seduce.

PERTENENCIA.

f, mining concession claim ‖ ownership ‖ legal right to something ‖ accessory, additional thing ‖ incumbency, duty.

PERTINENTE.

pertaining to ‖ related to ‖ concerning ‖ leading to litigation ‖ adj, admissible (evidence) ‖ germane ‖ pertinent.

PERTRECHAR.

v, to procure arms and munitions ‖ to prepare (precisely what is needed) ‖ to supply or equip.

PERTRECHOS.

m, military supplies ‖ arms, munitions and other items of defense for war ‖ ship's tools or instruments.

PERTURBACIÓN.

f, disturbance ‖ perturbation ‖ disorder, confusion ‖ mental imbalance ‖ lack of recognition or acknowledgement of a legal right.

PERTURBACIÓN DE DERECHO.

lack of recognition or acknowledgement of a legal right.

PERTURBACIÓN DE HECHO.

physical action in violation of a legal right ‖ breach of the peace, disturbance of public order.

PERTURBACIÓN DE LA POSESIÓN.

interruption of possession (whether it is the possession of the owner, the legitimate possessor or a person in adverse possession).

PERTURBACIÓN MENTAL.

mental imbalance ‖ insanity.

PERTURBADOR.

m, disturber, interrupter.

PERTURBAR.

v, to disturb ‖ to interrupt (possession or another's quiet enjoyment) ‖ to cause disorder or confusion ‖ to breach the peace or public order ‖ to bother ‖ to become mentally unbalanced.

PERVERSIDAD.

f, perversity ‖ evil ‖ extreme corruption ‖ sexual deviation or perversion.

PERVERSIÓN.

f, sexual perversion ‖ corruption, perversion, teaching of perversity ‖ depravity ‖ cruelty committed by a criminal.

PERVERSO.

m, war criminal ‖ vicious criminal ‖ adj, perverse, depraved ‖ evil, wicked.

PERVERTIDOR.

m, perverter, corruptor ‖ sexual seducer.

PERVERTIR.

v, to breach public order ‖ to corrupt morally deprave, pervert ‖ to induce criminal behavio ‖ to seduce.

PESADUMBRE.

f, harm, injury ‖ offense ‖ fatigue ‖ work bother, affliction ‖ regret ‖ unpleasantness weight, heaviness.

PESAS Y MEDIDAS.

weights and measures.

PESCA.

f, fishing ‖ fishing industry ‖ occupation of fisherman ‖ art of fishing ‖ catch, haul (c fish).

PESCA MARÍTIMA.

maritime or sea or salt water fishing.

PESCADOR.

m, fisherman.

PESCAR.

v, to fish ‖ to catch in a lie or contradiction ‖ t obtain ‖ to catch.

PESO.

m, weight ‖ power, influence ‖ monetary un in many Latin American countries ‖ weight scales, balances ‖ bothersome task.

PESO BRUTO.

gross weight.

PESO EN CARGA.

weight of loaded vehicle.

PESO MÁXIMO.

maximum weight.

PESO NETO.

net weight.

PESQUISA.

f, undercover policeman ‖ detective ‖ inve: tigation or inquiry or interrogation to dete: mine the facts of a crime or act.

PESQUISA EN LUGAR CERRADO.

search of an enclosed place to determine fac or obtain evidence of a crime.

PESQUISADOR.

m, person who carries out an inquiry, inte. rogation, investigation or search ‖ investigatc ‖ interrogator ‖ inquirer ‖ searcher.

PESQUISAR.

v, to search ‖ to investigate, carry out an i quiry, interrogate.

See PESQUISA.

PESTE.
f, pestilence, plague ‖ epidemic ‖ evil ‖ corruption, depravity, perversion ‖ scandal.
PETICIÓN.
f, complaint, legal complaint, demand ‖ request ‖ vote ‖ prayer, supplication ‖ request for a woman's hand in marriage ‖ pleading ‖ petition (e.g. to a government).
PETICIÓN COLECTIVA.
public petition or complaint (e.g. made by a group of people).
PETICIÓN DE HERENCIA.
demand or request for probate of a decedent's estate ‖ legal claim to receive part of an estate.
PETICIÓN DE MANO.
request for a woman's hand in marriage.
PETICIÓN IRRESPETUOSA.
disrespectful request.
PETICIONARIO.
m, petitioner ‖ complainant, plaintiff.
PETITORIO.
m, list of labor demands ‖ the part of a complaint or answer which sets forth the legal claims and the procedural action requested of the court ‖ adj, concerning a petition ‖ pertaining to the ownership of something (in contrast to its possession).
"PETITUM".
petition, request, supplication ‖ part of a complaint or answer which sets forth the legal claims or defenses.
PETRÓLEO.
m, petroleum ‖ gasoline, gas, petrol.
PETROLERO.
m, petrol or oil tanker ‖ adj, petroleum, petrol, oil.
PICAPLEITOS.
m, troublemaker ‖ ambulance chaser (attorney) ‖ pettifogger, attorney who engages in dilatory tactics.
PICARDÍA.
f, mischievous or improper act or comment ‖ lie, falsehood, dishonesty ‖ ability to get the better of another ‖ trickery, trick ‖ vileness, baseness ‖ mischievousness.
PIE.
m, foot ‖ foot, bottom, end (e.g. of a document) ‖ guideline, rule, norm ‖ motive ‖ occasion ‖ partial payment or down payment (to confirm a contract).

PIE DE ESCRITO.
foot or end of the document (left for signatures).
PIE DE IMPRENTA.
statement in a book or other work of its publisher, address, and date of its first printing.
PIEDAD.
f, piety.
PIEDRA DE ESCÁNDALO.
f, cause of a scandal.
PIEZA.
f, part, piece ‖ room ‖ bedroom ‖ coin ‖ animal which is hunted ‖ piece, short theatrical work ‖ each part or section of a court file or case ‖ plot of land ‖ component.
PIEZA DE CONVICCIÓN.
prosecutorial evidence ‖ piece of evidence which proves a crime ‖ material proof of a fact.
PIEZA DE PRUEBA.
piece of evidence.
PIEZA SEPARADA.
each of the special parts in which a complex case is divided.
PIGNORACIÓN.
f, act of pledging or hocking or pawning.
PIGNORACIÓN INMOBILIARIA.
See ANTICRESIS.
PIGNORACIÓN MOBILIARIA.
pledge; see PRENDA.
PIGNORAR.
v, to pledge (if personal property) ‖ to mortgage (if real property).
PIGNORATICIO.
adj, mortgage, pledge, related to pledge or mortgage.
PILOTAJE.
m, piloting, science and art of piloting ‖ pilotage, fee paid for being given assistance in landing a ship or plane by an expert pilot.
PILOTAJE AÉREO.
air piloting.
PILOTAR.
v, to pilot ‖ to manage or direct a matter ‖ to give advice.
PILOTEAR.
See PILOTAR.
PILOTÍN.
m, pilot trainee or assistant.
PILOTO.
m, pilot, captain ‖ driver (of an automobile) ‖ director (of a business) ‖ head thief.

PILOTO AVIADOR.
airline pilot.
PILOTO DE AERONAVE.
See PILOTO AVIADOR.
PILOTO DE BUQUE.
ship's pilot.
PILOTO DE PRUEBAS.
test pilot or driver.
PILOTO
DE PUERTO.
harbor pilot.
PILLAJE.
m, theft, robbery ‖ sacking, pillaging.
PILLAR.
v, to pillage, sack ‖ to steal, rob ‖ to discover a trick of a crime.
PILLEAR.
v, to be a habitual rogue.
PILLERÍA.
f, group of rogues ‖ roguishness.
PILLO.
m, rogue ‖ vagrant ‖ crafty person.
PINTURA.
f, painting.
PÍO.
adj, pious ‖ devoted.
PIQUETE.
m, jab, poke ‖ prick, injury from a pointed instrument ‖ picket, union picket ‖ small contingent of troops.
PIRÁMIDE DE POBLACIÓN.
f, population pyramid.
PIRÁMIDE JURÍDICA.
f, legal pyramid ‖ hierarchy of positive law (e.g. constitution over statutory law over administrative rules, etc.)
PIRATA.
m, pirate ‖ thief.
PIRATEAR.
v, to be a pirate or thief ‖ to pirate or copy or steal something that is copyrighted.
PIRATERÍA.
f, piracy ‖ theft, robbery.
PIRATERÍA AÉREA.
air piracy ‖ high-jacking.
PIROMANÍA.
f, pyromania.
PIRÓMANO.
m, pyromaniac.
PIROTECNIA.
f, fireworks.

PIRQUÍN.
m, type of mining concession by which the user pays the owner a stipulated fee for unrestricted mining rights.
PIRQUINEAR.
v, to work a mining concession.
See PIRQUÍN.
PIRQUINERO.
m, miner who works a mining concession per fee. See PIRQUÍN.
PISA.
f, whorehouse ‖ kicking.
PISAR.
v, to step ‖ to infringe or impinge upon ‖ to mistreat ‖ to humiliate.
PISO.
m, step ‖ floor, story (in a building) ‖ apartment ‖ ground ‖ rock bottom, minimum level.
PISTA.
f, trail of paw prints or footprints or fingerprints ‖ runway (of an airport, etc.) ‖ telltale sign, clue.
PISTOLA.
f, pistol.
PISTOLERO.
m, gunman, person who uses a pistol for unlawful purposes.
"PLACET".
placet.
PLAGA.
f, plague, pestilence, epidemic.
PLAGIAR.
v, to plagiarize.
PLAGIARIO.
m, plagiarist.
PLAGIO.
m, plagiarism.
PLAN.
m, plan, structure ‖ government program ‖ purpose, intent ‖ project.
PLAN DE VUELO.
flight plan.
PLAN QUINQUENAL.
five-year (economic) plan.
PLANETA.
m, planet.
PLANIFICACIÓN.
f, planning
PLANO.
m, chart, map, diagram ‖ plane ‖ adj, even, flat.

PLANTACIÓN.

f, planting, seeding ‖ plantation.

PLANTACIÓN EN SUELO AJENO.

planting on property of another.

PLANTADOR.

m, planter, person who plants, cultivator ‖ grave digger.

PLANTAR.

v, to plant, sow, cultivate ‖ to establish, found ‖ to hit, beat ‖ to make fun of (another) ‖ to bury ‖ to expel ‖ to throw (out or in) ‖ to stand (someone) up, fail to do as agreed, leave in a lurch.

PLANTARSE.

v, to take a firm stand on something ‖ to stand one's ground, resist pressure.

PLANTE.

m, rebellion, revolt (usually in prison) ‖ military rebellion or revolt, sedition.

PLANTEAR.

v, to outline, set forth ‖ to pose, raise (the problems or difficulties of a matter) ‖ to establish, found, start up (a system or institution).

PLANTEO.

m, layout ‖ arrangement ‖ also see PLANTE.

PLANTIFICAR.

v, to set up, establish, found, begin ‖ to hit, give a blow to ‖ to set forth (one's ideas about another).

PLATA.

f, silver ‖ money ‖ coin, change ‖ valuable item.

PLATAFORMA.

f, platform, stage ‖ shelf ‖ pretext, appearance ‖ (political) platform, program ‖ propaganda ‖ base, foundation.

PLATAFORMA CONTINENTAL.

continental shelf.

PLATAFORMA ELECTORAL.

political platform.

PLATAFORMA ESPACIAL.

space platform.

PLATAFORMA SUBMARINA.

seabed

PLATÓNICO.

adj, platonic.

PLAYA.

f, beach, shore ‖ seashore ‖ parking lot, car park.

PLAYA DE ESTACIONAMIENTO.

parking lot, car park.

PLAZA.

f, plaza, square ‖ space ‖ walled city ‖ protected or walled place ‖ office, ministry, department ‖ important commercial center ‖ merchants located at an important commercial center ‖ business carried out at an important commercial center ‖ market ‖ central market ‖ place, location, site ‖ vacancy.

PLAZO.

m, term, fixed time period ‖ expiration, termination (of term or time period) ‖ installment, partial payment ‖ period during which a party must appear in court, or answer or prove or allege or consent to or deny something.

PLAZO CIERTO.

fixed time period ‖ fixed time limit.

PLAZO CITATORIO.

period during which a party must appear in court.

PLAZO CONMINATORIO.

term fixed by express date the failure to comply with which will be penalized.

PLAZO CONTINUO.

continuous time period, period which counts all days or hours, etc.

PLAZO CONTRACTUAL.

contractual time period, contract term.

PLAZO CONVENCIONAL.

See PLAZO CONTRACTUAL.

PLAZO DE FAVOR.

grace period.

PLAZO DE GRACIA.

See PLAZO DE FAVOR.

PLAZO DE LAS OBLIGACIONES.

term or time period for payment of obligations.

PLAZO DE PREAVISO.

time period which must elapse after giving an employee notice of dismissal, before dismissal may be effective ‖ time period which must elapse between a notice and some legal action or resultant effect.

PLAZO DE VIUDEZ.

period during which a widow may not remarry.

PLAZO DELIBERATORIO.

period of deliberation or consideration.

PLAZO DETERMINADO.

time period set by reference to a express date.

PLAZO DILATORIO.

time period for the exercise of a right the expiration of which does not extinguish such right.

PLAZO EXTINTIVO.
time limit (after which certain rights are lost or extinguished).

PLAZO FATAL.
deadline, final time limit ‖ time period which may not be extended.

PLAZO FINAL.
time limit.

PLAZO IMPRORROGABLE.
See PLAZO FATAL.

PLAZO INCIDENTAL.
period during which a party must appear in court, or answer or prove or allege or consent to or deny something in a matter which is secondary to the principal case.

PLAZO INCIERTO.
time period set by reference to a future event of uncertain date.

PLAZO INDEFINIDO.
See PLAZO INCIERTO.

PLAZO INDETERMINADO.
See PLAZO INCIERTO.

PLAZO JUDICIAL.
judicially prescribed term or time period or time limit.

PLAZO LEGAL.
legal term, legal time period or legal time limit (i.e. set by law).

PLAZO PERENTORIO.
See TÉRMINO PERENTORIO.

PLAZO PRECLUSIVO.
time limit (after which certain actions are precluded).

PLAZO PRESCRIPTIVO.
See PRESCRIPCIÓN ADQUISITIVA Y EXTINTIVA.

PLAZO PROBATORIO.
period of discovery and during which proof is placed before the court, together.

PLAZO PRORROGABLE.
See TÉRMINO PRORROGABLE.

PLAZO RESOLUTORIO.
time period which extinguishes a right or legal relationship when it expires.

PLAZO SUSPENSIVO.
time period which suspends or stays the effects of a right or legal relationship until such period expires.

PLAZO ÚTIL.
term which counts only working days or hours.

PLEBISCITARIO.
adj, pertaining to a plebiscite.

PLEBISCITO.
m, plebiscite.

PLEBISCITO INTERNACIONAL.
international plebiscite, vote of the inhabitants of a territory that they oppose or support the annexation of their territory to another nation.

PLEITEADOR.
m, lawyer who files spurious actions ‖ lawyer who uses dilatory tactics ‖ adj, litigious, litigating.

PLEITEAR.
v, to litigate, sue ‖ to bring an action ‖ to bring actions on spurious bases.

PLEITISTA.
See PLEITEADOR.

PLEITO.
m, sentence, decision ‖ litigation, court action, judicial action ‖ cause of action, action, suit, case, lawsuit ‖ dispute, quarrel, argument.

PLEITO CIVIL.
civil action or suit. Involves any dispute regarding property, contracts, torts, family matters, marital status, wills, trust and estates, etc.

PLEITO CRIMINAL.
criminal action or suit.

PLEITO ORDINARIO.
See JUICIO ORDINARIO.

PLENAMENTE.
adv, fully, totally, wholly, entirely ‖ unconditionally.

PLENARIAMENTE.
adv, pertaining to JUICIO PLENARIO.
See PLENAMENTE.

PLENARIO.
adj, descriptive of second phase of a lawsuit beginning with an exposition of the facts and ending with a decision (may refer to the oral argument phase of a trial) ‖ descriptive of decision reached by several courts of appeals, acting together as a single court, regarding a legal issue upon which they had previously held conflicting positions ‖ full, total, whole, entire, complete ‖ fulfilled, complied with.

PLENIPOTENCIA.
m, unrestricted or full power of attorney ‖ power granted by a government to diplomats or other agents to act on its behalf, especially vis à vis treaties and other agreements.

PLENIPOTENCIARIO.

m, person in whom power of a government has been vested to act, especially vis à vis treaties and other agreements.

PLENO.

adj, full, complete ‖ in full attendance.

PLENO DOMINIO.

fee simple absolute, fee simple.

PLENO EMPLEO.

full employment.

PLENOS PODERES.

full powers ‖ exercise of legislative powers by the executive branch, either by legislative delegation or by usurpation.

PLICA.

f, sealed will or other document to be opened at an established point in date, under specified conditions, and in the presence of specified persons.

PLIEGO.

m, quadrangular piece of paper which is folded in the middle ‖ piece of paper ‖ section of book (usually of sixteen pages which used to be printed at one time) ‖ lease or rental contract, annotation of lease or rental ‖ sealed document or letter or communication.

PLIEGO DE CARGOS.

list of charges, list of infractions (in administrative hearings).

PLIEGO DE CONDICIONES.

bid specifications or specs, list of conditions relative to a government bid.

PLIEGO DE POSICIONES.

interrogatories (in a civil, labor, or administrative matter which must be answered by the parties).

PLURALIDAD.

f, plurality ‖ majority.

PLURALIDAD SINDICAL.

plurality of unions, allowance of representation of workers by various unions simultaneously.

PLURALISMO.

m, pluralism.

PLURALISMO JURÍDICO.

legal pluralism, existence of multiple and opposing legal organisms within one legal system.

PLURILATERAL.

adj, plurilateral, multisided.

PLUS.

m, bonus given to military troops at war ‖

bonus, perquisite, perk, fringe benefit.

PLUS PETICIÓN.

excessive demand, claim for more than is due ‖ decision which awards more than was claimed by petitioner.

"PLUS PETITIO".

See PLUS PETICIÓN.

PLUSEMPLEO.

m, moonlighting, overtime.

PLUSPETICIÓN.

See PLUS PETICIÓN.

PLUSVALÍA.

f, appreciation, increase in value ‖ population increase ‖ increase in wealth ‖ surplus value of product (over the cost of labor and material).

PLUTOCRACIA.

f, plutocracy, government by the wealthy ‖ predominance of wealthy in a country.

PLUTÓCRATA.

m, plutocrat. See PLUTOCRACIA.

PLUTOCRÁTICO.

adj, plutocratic. See PLUTOCRACIA.

P.O.

adj, per request. Abbreviation used to indicate that a document is signed by someone else pursuant to authorization.

POBLACIÓN.

f, population ‖ act of populating or settling a country ‖ city, town, village, urbanized area.

POBLACIÓN ACTIVA.

working population

POBLACIÓN CIVIL.

civilian population.

POBLACIÓN DE DERECHO.

legal population, population registered as born and still living with the Civil Registry. As opposed to POBLACIÓN DE HECHO.

POBLACIÓN DE HECHO.

actual population. As opposed to POBLACIÓN DE DERECHO.

POBLACIÓN PASIVA.

population which does not work (inclusive of those who are underage, unemployed, retirees, etc.).

POBLACIÓN RURAL.

rural population.

POBLACIÓN TRABAJADORA.

working population, population which is employed.

POBLACIÓN URBANA.

urban population, city dwellers, townsmen.

POBLADOR.
m, city founder, settler ‖ inhabitant.
POBLAR.
v, to settle, found ‖ to inhabit ‖ to populate,
people ‖ to colonize ‖ to father a large family.
POBRE.
m, pauper, poor person ‖ person of the lower
economic class ‖ legally indigent person (for
purposes of obtaining the benefits of free legal
representation) ‖ beggar, pauper ‖ adj, poor,
indigent ‖ modest ‖ unfortunate.
POBRE VOLUNTARIO.
person who is poor due to having taken a vow
of poverty.
POBRES.
m, the poor.
POBREZA.
f, poverty, indigence ‖ scarcity, lack of ‖ legal
indigence.
POBREZA LEGAL.
legal indigence (for purposes of obtaining the
benefits of free legal representation).
PODER.
m, power, faculty, right ‖ power, mandate ‖
jurisdiction ‖ power, force, strength ‖ attributions ‖ ability, capacity ‖ possibility ‖ power of
attorney, proxy, legal power ‖ power or letter
of attorney, document in which a power of attorney is granted ‖ possession of a power of attorney ‖ authority ‖ government ‖ military
force or might ‖ superiority ‖ v, to be able to
(either physically or in terms of authority or
power, i.e. can or may).
PODER ABSOLUTO.
absolute power (e.g. of a monarch).
PODER ADMINISTRATIVO.
administrative branch (of a government).
PODER ARMÓNICO.
combination of executive, judicial, and legislative functions and power in a single monarch.
PODER CONSTITUIDO.
constitutional power (of a government) ‖ each
one of the constitutional branches of government ‖ constitutionally ruling government.
PODER CONSTITUYENTE.
constitutional power (of a government).
PODER DE POLICÍA.
police power, power of the public administration to assure public order.
PODER DISCIPLINARIO.
disciplinary power.

**PODER DISCIPLINARIO
DEL EMPLEADOR.**
employer's disciplinary power.
PODER DISCRECIONAL.
discretionary power.
PODER EJECUTIVO.
the executive, executive branch (of a government) ‖ see PODER CONSTITUIDO ‖ government, administration ‖ head of state and his
ministers.
PODER EN DERECHO CIVIL.
See MANDATO.
PODER EN DERECHO POLÍTICO.
political power ‖ dominion, rule, faculty, and
jurisdiction to govern and carry out ‖ supreme
power of a state to govern.
PODER EN DERECHO PROCESAL.
power of representation, power of attorney
PODER ESPECIAL.
special power of attorney, special power.
PODER GENERAL.
general power of attorney, general power.
PODER GENERAL PARA PLEITOS.
general power of attorney to litigate.
PODER IMPLÍCITO.
implied power.
PODER JERÁRQUICO.
hierarchical power.
PODER JUDICIAL.
the judiciary, judicial branch (of a government) ‖ judiciary.
PODER LEGAL.
constitutional or legitimate or legal power (of
a government branch) ‖ legal capacity (of
person) ‖ legal power (to carry out certain
acts) ‖ special power of attorney which is legally solemnized.
PODER LEGISLATIVO.
the legislature, Congress, Parliament, legislative branch (of a government).
PODER MODERADOR.
head of state (in a constitutional monarchy or
parliamentary republic).
PODER PARA JUZGAR.
jurisdiction to adjudge.
PODER PARA TESTAR.
capacity to testify.
PODER PÚBLICO.
police power (in terms of U.S. law), power of
the state to regulate and rule the inhabitants
therein.

PODER REAL.
de facto government ‖ political power and rights of a monarchy or a de facto government ‖ real control.

PODER REGLAMENTARIO.
regulatory power (of the executive). This may be either pursuant or not to a legislative statute.

PODER REVOLUCIONARIO.
revolutionary power, power resulting from a successful revolution.

PODER TEMPORAL.
temporal power (of secular authorities). Opposed to spiritual power.

PODERDANTE.
m, principal ‖ constituent, person who grants a power.

PODERES CONCURRENTES.
concurrent powers, overlapping powers.

PODERES DEL ESTADO.
powers of the state, governmental powers.

PODERES DEL JUEZ.
judicial powers, powers of the judge.

PODERES DELEGADOS.
delegated powers (within the government) ‖ powers of attorney or agency or representative ‖ powers of trustee.

PODERES EXTRAORDINARIOS.
extraordinary powers (usually of executive granted by the legislative branch).

PODERES RESERVADOS.
reserved powers, powers which are not delegated ‖ powers reserved by the state or province (i.e. not granted to the federal government).

PODERES SINDICALES.
powers or rights of labor unions. Usually includes right to represent its members legally, to make regulations, to exact dues or fees, to discipline, and to administrate.

PODERHABIENTE.
m, attorney, agent, appointee ‖ proxy, proxyholder.

POGROM".
m, pogrom.

POLÉMICA.
f, controversy, dispute, argument.

POLEMIZAR.
v, to discuss, dispute, argue.

POLIANDRÍA.
f, polyandry, condition of one woman having two or more husbands.

POLIARQUÍA.
f, polyarchy, government ruled by many. Opposed to monarchy.

POLIÁRQUICO.
adj, polyarchic.

POLICÍA.
f, police, police force ‖ policeman ‖ peace, order ‖ cleanliness ‖ courtesy, urbanity ‖ undercover police or agent.

POLICÍA ADMINISTRATIVA.
police force acting within the administrative branch of government ‖ power to enforce the rules of administrative authorities.

POLICÍA ADUANERA.
customs inspection force ‖ customs inspector, customs inspection officer.

POLICÍA AÉREA.
maintenance of order and lawfulness in the air ‖ air patrol.

POLICÍA CIENTÍFICA.
investigative police force with scientific knowledge or research.

POLICÍA CRIMINAL.
police force in charge of criminal investigations.

POLICÍA DE COSTUMBRES.
maintenance of morality. See PODER DE POLICÍA.

POLICÍA DE ESTRADOS.
maintenance of order in the courtroom.

POLICÍA DE NAVEGACIÓN.
maintenance of order and lawfulness at sea and in inland waterways ‖ naval police, sea patrol.

POLICÍA DE SEGURIDAD.
police (either federal or state) which are to ensure the safety of the citizenry.

POLICÍA DEL TRABAJO.
employee safety inspectors ‖ inspectors in charge of controlling compliance with labor laws.

POLICÍA FEDERAL.
federal police.

POLICÍA FEMENINA.
policewoman ‖ female police force.

POLICÍA FISCAL.
tax inspector, tax man.

POLICÍA GUBERNATIVA.
See POLICÍA DE SEGURIDAD.

POLICÍA INTERNACIONAL.
international police force (e.g. INTERPOL or the United Nations Security Forces).
POLICÍA JUDICIAL.
police investigator ‖ investigative police force, police who are responsible for investigating crimes and arresting suspects. They form part of the judiciary and carry out judicial functions.
POLICÍA MARÍTIMA.
maritime police.
POLICÍA MILITAR.
military police (which performs civilian police functions) ‖ regulations pertaining to military orderliness.
POLICÍA MUNICIPAL.
city or municipal police force ‖ city or municipal policeman or woman.
POLICÍA PREVENTIVA.
preventive peacekeeping.
POLICÍA REPRESIVA.
police force in charge of repression.
POLICÍA SANITARIA.
sanitation inspectors (at borders who assure that persons with illnesses or contagious diseases do not enter the country).
POLICÍA SECRETA.
secret police.
POLICÍACO.
adj, police, pertaining to police.
POLICIAL.
adj, police, pertaining to police.
POLICIANO.
m, local police force.
POLICITACIÓN.
m, offer (not yet accepted).
POLIGAMIA.
f, polygamy ‖ see POLIANDRIA.
POLÍGAMO.
adj, polygamous.
POLIGINIA.
f, polygamy.
POLIGRAFÍA.
f, polygraphy, art of writing in code or decoding ‖ art of writing about diverse topics.
POLÍGRAFO.
m, polygraph, lie detector ‖ specialist in POLIGRAFÍA ‖ writer on widely diverse topics.
POLÍTICA.
f, policy, doctrine ‖ politics ‖ steps ‖ politeness, tact.

POLÍTICA CAMBIARIA.
foreign exchange policy.
POLÍTICA COMERCIAL.
trade policy.
POLÍTICA CONTRIBUTIVA.
tax policy.
POLÍTICA CRIMINAL.
study of the causes and punishment of criminal behavior and adoption of policies on that basis.
POLÍTICA DE LA GUERRA.
plan of war ‖ policy regarding war.
POLÍTICA ECONÓMICA.
economic policy.
POLÍTICA FISCAL.
fiscal policy.
POLÍTICA INDUSTRIAL.
industrial policy.
POLÍTICA INTERNA.
national policy ‖ national politics.
POLÍTICA INTERNACIONAL.
international politics ‖ international policy (of a nation).
POLÍTICA LABORAL.
labor policy.
POLÍTICA MILITAR.
military policy, governmental policy with regard to armed forces.
POLÍTICA MONETARIA.
monetary policy.
POLÍTICA SOCIAL.
social policy.
POLÍTICAMENTE.
adv, politically ‖ politely, urbanely.
POLÍTICO.
m, politician ‖ adj, political, pertaining to politics ‖ urbane, polite ‖ in-law, related.
POLÍTICOLABORAL.
adj, pertaining to labor policy.
POLIVIRIA.
See POLIANDRIA.
PÓLIZA.
f, policy, principal contract, document which establishes the conditions which regulate a specific contract ‖ promise ‖ order to pay draft, money order ‖ tax stamp ‖ customs clearance certificate.
PÓLIZA DE FLETAMIENTO.
freight policy, freight contract.
PÓLIZA DE SEGURO.
insurance policy, insurance contract.

PÓLIZA DE TURISMO.
tourist tax (on hotels, restaurants, etc.).

PÓLIZA FLOTANTE.
floating policy.

POLIZÓN.
m, vagabond, bum, tramp, hobo ‖ stowaway (in a plane or ship).

POLIZONAJE.
m, type of crime committed by being a stowaway.

PÓLVORA.
f, powder ‖ ill-tempered person.

PONDERACIÓN.
f, deliberation, care, thoughtfulness ‖ good judgment.

PONDERAR.
v, to ponder, think over, deliberate.

PONENCIA.
f, position, office, and functions of a PONENTE ‖ proposed decision or report offered by a PONENTE.

PONENTE.
m, justice or tribunal-member who is in charge of examining the documents, directing the discovery, and submitting a proposed decision to other members of the court for their approval ‖ reporter in a parliamentary commission, scientific congress, etc.

PONER A UNO EN EL PALO.
v, to strangle ‖ to execute, kill.

PONER ANTE.
v, to place before, put to (an authority).

PONER COBRO EN ALGO.
to attempt to collect ‖ to be cautious, proceed with caution.

PONER CONTRA LA PARED.
to place against the wall (either for purposes of punishment or of killing by firing squad) ‖ to be placed in a difficult position, be placed between a rock and a hard spot.

PONER DE PATAS.
to kick or throw out ‖ to say good-bye ‖ to break up (a love affair).

PONER DELANTE DE LOS OJOS UNA COSA.
to open another's eyes to the fallacy of his or her argument or position.

PONER EN CONDICIONES.
to prepare properly.

PONER EN CUENTA.
to put money to an account.

PONER EN LIBERTAD DE UNA OBLIGACIÓN.
to free from obligation.

PONER EN ORDEN.
to order, put in order ‖ to reestablish order ‖ to adjust to size or needs.

PONER EN PRECIO.
to set or designate a price ‖ to adjust the price.

PONER LA FIRMA.
to be sure about something, back something with certainty ‖ to sign, execute.

PONER LA MANO EN UNA COSA.
to see for oneself ‖ to intervene in a case.

PONER LOS OJOS EN ALGUIEN.
to choose or select someone.

PONER PLEITO.
to sue ‖ to bring an action, file a complaint.

PONER SITIO.
to lay siege to ‖ to pursue ‖ to seduce, woo.

PONER TÉRMINO.
to put an end to ‖ to conclude.

PONERSE DE PARTE DE UNO.
to take sides, side with.

POPULAR.
adj, popular ‖ of the people, plebeian, democratic ‖ well-known ‖ v, to populate.

POR ANTE.
before (me or them). Used in documents to indicate that the person swears to the contents thereof.

POR AVALÚO.
ad valorem.

POR CUENTA DE ALGUIEN.
in someone's name, at someone's expense.

POR CUENTA Y RIESGO DE.
for account and risk of.

POR CUERDA SEPARADA.
(filed) apart from main trial ‖ incidental to and apart from the main action. Court files may be physically tied together by a cord to show their separate but related nature.

POR EL TANTO.
for the same amount.

POR FAS O POR NEFÁS.
with or without justice, justly or unjustly.

POR FÓRMULA.
pro forma.

POR GRACIA.
gratuitously, by favor.

POR LA TREMENDA.
violently ‖ to extremes.

POR LO CLARO.
clearly, manifestly.
POR MAYOR.
wholesale.
POR MENOR.
retail.
POR MENUDO.
retail.
**POR MINISTERIO
DE LA LEY.**
by operation of law.
POR OÍDAS.
hearsay.
POR PROMEDIO.
on the average.
POR SÍ O POR NO.
guilty or not guilty. Used to describe the choice of a jury.
POR SU MANO.
on your own, on his own authority.
POR SU ORDEN.
by order, successively ‖ by preference ‖ in the order required by rules or procedure ‖ (legal costs) that are to be borne by the party which originally incurred the expense.
PORCENTAJE.
m, percentage.
PORCIENTO.
m, percent.
PORCIÓN.
f, portion, part ‖ quota, lot, share ‖ large number (of persons or things).
PORCIÓN ACRECIDA.
portion of lapsed inheritance which is distributed to the remaining heirs.
PORCIÓN DISPONIBLE.
disposable portion of an inheritance, part of an inheritance which may be disposed of freely. See PORCIÓN LEGÍTIMA.
PORCIÓN LEGÍTIMA.
portion of an inheritance which must be given to legal heirs. See LEGÍTIMA.
PORCIONERO.
m, participant ‖ adj, party.
PORCIONISTA.
m, shareholder, person who has a portion or share of something.
PORDIOSERO.
m, beggar.
PORMENOR.
See POR MENOR.

PORNOGRAFÍA.
f, pornography.
PORNOGRÁFICO.
adj, pornographic ‖ obscene.
PORNÓGRAFO.
m, pornographer, author of pornography.
PORTADOR.
m, bearer, holder ‖ transporter, carrier ‖ titleholder.
PORTADOR DE LETRA DE CAMBIO.
holder or bearer of a draft.
PORTALERA.
f, prostitute.
PORTAR.
v, to bear, hold ‖ to transport, carry ‖ to bring.
PORTAVOZ.
f, m, spokesperson, spokesman, spokeswoman.
PORTAZGAR.
v, to charge a toll or tax (for entering a place or using a road).
PORTAZGO.
m, tax or toll (for entering a place or using a road) ‖ tollhouse.
PORTAZGUERO.
m, toll collector.
PORTE.
m, transportation, carrying, transporting ‖ transportation fee, carrying charge ‖ conduct, comportment, bearing ‖ capacity, size ‖ tonnage (of ship) ‖ postage charge.
PORTE BRUTO.
tonnage, dead-weight (of ship to flotation line).
PORTE DEBIDO.
freight payable on delivery, freight owing.
PORTE PAGADO.
freight prepaid.
PORTE TOTAL.
See PORTE BRUTO.
PORTEADOR.
m, carrier, transporter, freight company ‖ porter ‖ stevedore, longshoreman.
PORTEAR.
v, to carry, transport, transfer (for a price).
PORTEO.
m, carrying, portage, transfer of a thing from one place to another.
PORTERÍA.
f, position of doorkeeper or janitor or concierge ‖ housing of such person ‖ gatekeeper's or concierge's or porter's lodge. See PORTERO

PORTERO.
m, doorkeeper, janitor, concierge, porter, gatekeeper.

PORTERO DE ESTRADOS.
court employee who secures order in the court.

PORTUARIO.
m, dock worker, laborer who loads and unloads ships ‖ adj, port, related to seaports.

PORVENIR.
m, future, the yet to come ‖ desired social position.

POSDATA.
See POSTDATA.

POSDATA.
f, post script, p.s. ‖ See POSFECHAR.

POSEEDOR.
m, possessor, holder

POSEEDOR DE BUENA FE.
holder in good faith, person who in good faith obtains title to property ‖ person who in good faith believes that he holds legal title to the thing possessed.

POSEEDOR DE MALA FE.
holder in bad faith, person who possesses property knowing that he does not hold any legal right to the thing possessed.

POSEER.
v, to possess, hold, have, be possessor (of something) ‖ to own, be owner (of something) ‖ to possess (sexually) ‖ to know (a subject or topic) well.

POSEERSE.
v, to be in possession, control oneself.

POSESIÓN.
f, act of possession, holding, detention (of something) ‖ use or enjoyment (of something) ‖ possession, holding, property (held) ‖ simple possession ‖ ownership (in a non-technical sense) ‖ tenancy (in a non-technical sense).

POSESIÓN ACTUAL.
actual possession.

POSESIÓN ANUAL.
possession from year to year, possession for periods of at least a year and a day.

POSESIÓN ARTIFICIAL.
constructive possession.

POSESIÓN CARNAL.
carnal knowledge.

POSESIÓN CIVIL.
legal possession (which usually requires actual use or enjoyment of something and the intent to possess).

POSESIÓN CIVILÍSIMA.
type of constructive possession over inherited property which is transferred automatically upon death, unless repudiated.

POSESIÓN CLANDESTINA.
possession obtained clandestinely or secretly.

POSESIÓN CONTINUA.
continuous possession ‖ constructive continuous possession.

POSESIÓN CORPORAL.
physical possession ‖ corpus, physical property ‖ See POSESIÓN CARNAL.

POSESIÓN DE BUENA FE.
property held in good faith. See POSEEDOR DE BUENA FE.

POSESIÓN DE COSAS MUEBLES.
possession of personal property.

POSESIÓN DE DERECHO.
legal possession.

POSESIÓN DE ESTADO.
holding or enjoyment of a legal status of some kind (e.g. marital, voting, nationality, etc.)

POSESIÓN DE HECHO.
actual possession. See POSESIÓN NATURAL.

POSESIÓN DE LA HERENCIA.
(automatic) possession of the inheritance.

POSESIÓN DE MALA FE.
property held in bad faith, knowing that one has no legal right to it. See POSEEDOR DE MALA FE.

POSESIÓN DIRECTA.
direct ownership or possession (i.e. not owned or possessed in the name of a third party).

POSESIÓN EN COMÚN.
joint tenancy or possession ‖ possession o tenancy in common. In both cases several persons possess property on the basis of a common right.

POSESIÓN EQUÍVOCA.
doubtful possession (as regards to whether i is possessed for oneself or on behalf of a thir party).

POSESIÓN FINGIDA.
See POSESIÓN ARTIFICIAL.

POSESIÓN ILEGÍTIMA.
wrongful or unlawful possession.

POSESIÓN IMAGINARIA.
See POSESIÓN ARTIFICIAL.

POSESIÓN IMPERFECTA.
simple possession, holding, detention.
See POSESION ILEGÍTIMA.

POSESIÓN INDIRECTA.
indirect possession or ownership (i.e. owned or possessed in the name of a third party).

POSESIÓN INMEMORIAL.
possession for time immemorial.

POSESIÓN JUDICIAL.
possession (obtained or retained) by court order.

POSESIÓN JURÍDICA.
See POSESIÓN DE DERECHO.

POSESIÓN JUSTA.
rightful possession, possession which is not obtained wrongfully, clandestinely, or by violence.

POSESIÓN LEGÍTIMA.
legal or lawful possession, rightful possession.

POSESIÓN NATURAL.
physical possession ‖ use or enjoyment of property.

POSESIÓN NO EQUÍVOCA.
possession as regards to which there is no doubt as to whether it is possessed for oneself or on behalf of a third party.

POSESIÓN NO INTERRUMPIDA.
uninterrupted possession.

POSESIÓN PACÍFICA.
quiet enjoyment ‖ possession obtained and held peacefully ‖ non-bothersome possession.

POSESIÓN POR ABUSO DE CONFIANZA.
possession by holding over.

POSESIÓN POR TOLERANCIA.
possession at sufferance.

POSESIÓN PRECARIA.
possession at will.

POSESIÓN PRETORIA.
type of possession with right to use, obtained by court order to pay a debt.

POSESIÓN PRO INDIVISO.
tenancy or possession such that several persons possess the whole of a given property, even though they may have only partial or shared rights to it.

POSESIÓN PROMISCUA.
actual tenancy or possession of property by several persons even though they may have no legal right to such joint possession.

POSESIÓN PÚBLICA.
open and notorious possession.

POSESIÓN SIMBÓLICA.
constructive possession.

POSESIÓN TURBATIVA.
possession obtained through non-peaceful means.

POSESIÓN VICIOSA.
defective possession, possession which in some way is unlawful. May be POSESIÓN CLANDESTINA, DE MALA FE, EQUÍVOCA, PRECARIA, PROMISCUA, or VIOLENTA.

POSESIÓN VIOLENTA.
possession obtained or retained by force or threats.

POSESIONAL.
adj, possessory, related to possession.

POSESIONAR.
v, to give possession of, place in possession (of a right, position, or property) ‖ to install (in a post).

POSESIONES.
f, possessions, territories, colonies (of a nation) ‖ real estate ‖ rural property.

POSESIVO.
adj, possessive.

POSESO.
m, possessed person, person controlled spiritually by another ‖ adj, possessed.

POSESOR.
See POSEEDOR.

POSESORIO.
adj, possessory.

POSFECHA.
f, postdate, date which is subsequent to the true date.

POSFECHAR.
v, to post-date, postdate.

POSGUERRA.
f, post-war period.

POSIBILIDAD.
f, possibility, potentiality ‖ power, force ‖ ability to work ‖ means, resources ‖ permission, authorization.

POSIBILITAR.
v, to make possible ‖ to ease ‖ to procure, provide.

POSIBLE.
adj, possible.

POSIBLES.
m, goods, property ‖ income ‖ means, resources.

POSICIÓN.

f, position || posture || disposition || social or economic status || supposition || interrogatory posed by a plaintiff to a defendant or vice versa, each question asked of the opposition to be answered in the affirmative or negative.

POSICIÓN SOCIAL.

social status or class or position.

POSICIONES.

f, interrogatories (which must be answered in writing or orally by the plaintiff or defendant)

POSITIVAMENTE.

adv, positively, affirmatively, surely, truly, certainly || undoubtedly || beneficially, usefully || absolutely || productively.

POSITIVISMO.

m, positivism || materialism.

POSITIVISTA.

f, m, positivist || materialist || adj, positivist || materialist.

POSITIVO.

adj, positive, affirmative || sure, true, certain || indisputable || absolute || productive || effective.

PÓSITO.

m, granary or silo (usually public or communal) || professional mutual benefit association.

POSLIMINIO.

See POSTLIMINIO.

POSMERIDIANO.

See POSTMERIDIANO.

POSPONER.

v, to postpone, delay, defer || to disparage, depreciate.

POSPOSICIÓN.

f, postponement, deferral || disparagement, depreciation.

POSPOSICIÓN DE LA HIPOTECA.

change of the order of mortgage interests (such that a more recently perfected mortgage prevails over an earlier one).

"POSSESSIO JURIS".

possession of a right.

"POSSESSIO REI".

See POSESIÓN NATURAL.

"POSSESSOR JURIS".

possessor of a right.

"POSSESSOR PRO EMPTORE".

possessor by purchase.

"POSSESSOR PRO HAEREDE".

See "POSSESSOR PRO HEREDE".

"POSSESSOR PRO HEREDE".

possessor by inheritance.

"POSSIDETIS".

See "UTI POSSIDETIS".

POST DATA.

See POSDATA.

POST MERIDIEM.

post meridian, p.m.

POSTDATA.

See POSDATA.

POSTERGACIÓN.

f, postponement, delay || administrative sanction which is imposed by placing a person ahead of another who has greater seniority || prejudice which is suffered when such a sanction is imposed.

POSTERGADO.

adj, postponed, delayed, put off.

POSTERGAR.

v, to postpone, delay (whether in time or order) || to impose an administrative sanction against an employee.

See POSTERGACIÓN.

POSTERIDAD.

f, posterity.

POSTERIOR.

adj, posterior (in order or time), later, subsequent || behind, rear, back.

POSTERIORI.

See A POSTERIORI.

POSTERIORIDAD.

f, posteriority.

POSTERIORMENTE.

adv, later, subsequently.

POSTEROS.

m, descendants, future generations.

POSTLIMINIO.

m, action by which property and persons taken in war by the enemy are returned to their prior status as soon as they are turned over to the country from which they come.

POSTOR.

m, bidder.

POSTRACIÓN.

f, prostration.

POSTRAR.

v, to prostrate || to humiliate || to give up, surrender || to destroy || to overthrow || to weaken, debilitate.

POSTRARSE.

v, to prostrate oneself.

POSTREMO.
m, see POSTRERO ‖ descendant.

POSTRERO.
adj, last, final (in order and time).

PÓSTULA.
See POSTULACIÓN.

POSTULACIÓN.
f, postulation ‖ petition, request, demand ‖ application ‖ request for donation.

POSTULANTE.
m, petitioner ‖ person who requests donations ‖ applicant.

POSTULAR.
v, to petition, request, demand ‖ to apply.

"POSTULATIO".
m, petition, request, demand ‖ allegation.

PÓSTUMO.
adj, posthumous, after death.

POSTURA.
f, posture ‖ position, situation, attitude, way ‖ price of food set by courts ‖ bid price, auction price ‖ settlement ‖ (amount of a) bet.

POTENCIA.
f, power, dominion, strength ‖ power, nation, sovereign state ‖ potency (in reference to procreation).

POTENCIA MARÍTIMA.
naval force or strength.

POTENCIA MILITAR.
military strength or force.

POTENCIA MUNDIAL.
world power.

POTENCIAL.
adj, potential, possible ‖ related to strength or power.

POTENCIAL BÉLICO.
military capability or strength.

POTENCIAL NACIONAL.
capability (of a nation) for militaristic or other purposes.

POTENCIALIDAD.
f, potentiality, possibility.

POTENTE.
adj, capable, able ‖ powerful, potent ‖ (sexually) potent.

POTESTAD.
f, power, authority ‖ dominion ‖ ability, attribution ‖ jurisdiction.

POTESTAD CIVIL.
authority granted under the civil code. Includes POTESTAD MARITAL and PATRIA POTESTAD.

POTESTAD DISCIPLINARIA.
See DERECHO DISCIPLINARIO.

POTESTAD MARITAL.
authority of husband over his wife and her property.

POTESTAD PATERNA.
See PATRIA POTESTAD.

POTESTAD PÚBLICA.
public authority or power, power or authority which may be exercised by a group or government over another or others.

POTESTATIVO.
adj, optional, that which one may chose to do or not to do.

PRÁCTICA.
f, practice, exercise ‖ method, means, procedure ‖ custom, usage, practice ‖ training, study, apprenticeship ‖ experience, ability, skill.

PRÁCTICA CONTRA LA LEY.
unlawful practice or custom.

PRÁCTICA DESLEAL.
disloyal practice (of an employee against his employer) ‖ unfair competition.

PRÁCTICA FORENSE.
practice of law ‖ study of law ‖ practical legal training or apprenticeship (after the study of law).

PRACTICABLE.
adj, practicable, possible, feasible ‖ passable, fit for traffic.

PRACTICAJE.
m, pilotage.

PRÁCTICAMENTE.
adv, customarily, as in practice ‖ with experience ‖ practically, virtually, for all intents and purposes.

PRACTICANTE.
m, trainee, apprentice ‖ (surgery) intern ‖ doctor's assistant ‖ pharmacist's assistant ‖ adj ‖ practicing.

PRACTICAR.
v, to practice (in all senses) ‖ to perform, carry out, exercise ‖ to apprentice, train.

PRÁCTICO.
m, pilot ‖ adj, practical ‖ practiced, experienced ‖ expert, skilled ‖ beneficial, useful.

PRÁCTICO DE COSTA.
pilot who navigates by or near the coast.

PRÁCTICO DE PUERTO.
harbor pilot, docking pilot.

PRÁCTICO DE RÍO.
river pilot.
PRÁCTICO MAYOR.
port master, harbor master.
"PRAEFECTUS".
See PREFECTO.
"PRAEJUDICIUM".
adj, pre-judgment.
"PRAESCRIPTIO".
See PRESCRIPCIÓN.
PRAGMÁTICA.
f, law, act, type of royal decree ‖ adj, pragmatic, practical.
PRAGMÁTICO.
m, commentator or interpreter of national laws ‖ adj, pragmatic, practical.
PRAGMATISMO.
m, pragmatism.
PRAGMATISMO JURÍDICO.
legal pragmatism.
PRAGMATISTA.
m, pragmatist.
PREÁMBULO.
m, preamble ‖ digression ‖ pretext, excuse ‖ constitutional preamble.
PREÁMBULO DE
LA CONSTITUCIÓN.
constitutional preamble.
PREAVISAR.
v, to give notice (of either dismissal or resignation from employment) ‖ to give advance notice.
PREAVISO.
m, notice (of either employment dismissal or resignation) ‖ pink slip ‖ forewarning ‖ advance notice.
PREBENDA.
f, sinecure, comfortable position.
PRECARIAMENTE.
adv, precariously ‖ without legal right (to receive or keep something) ‖ without legal right to continue exercising legal power or control.
PRECARIEDAD.
f, precariousness. See PRECARIAMENTE.
PRECARIO.
m, revocable bailment, possession and use subject to revocation at the will of the owner ‖ adj, precarious, unstable ‖ uncertain, unsure ‖ revocable.
PRECARISTA.
m, holder of a PRECARIO.

PRECAUCIÓN.
f, precaution, warning ‖ care ‖ circumspection.
PRECAUCIONARSE.
v, to take precautions, take precautionary measures or steps ‖ to be careful.
PRECAUTELAR.
See PRECAUCIONARSE.
PRECAUTORIO.
adj, precautionary, preventative, preventive.
PRECAVER.
v, to take precautions, take precautionary measures or steps.
PRECEDENCIA.
f, precedence, priority (in order) ‖ priority, previousness (in time) ‖ pre-eminence ‖ preference ‖ primacy, superiority.
PRECEDENTE.
f, (legal) precedent, case precedent ‖ example ‖ practice, usage ‖ adj, prior, precedent (in time and order) ‖ first ‖ antecedent.
PRECEDER.
v, to precede, be prior to ‖ to be preferred.
PRECEPTISTA.
m, one who formulates precepts.
PRECEPTIVO.
adj, obligatory, mandatory.
PRECEPTO.
m, precept, rule, norm ‖ mandate, order ‖ teaching, instruction ‖ commandment ‖ article, clause (of a law or regulation).
PRECEPTO LEGAL.
law, statute, regulation ‖ each article or clause of a law, statute, regulation, etc.
PRECEPTOR.
m, preceptor, teacher, professor, tutor ‖ advisor, adviser.
PRECEPTOS
DEL DERECHO.
legal precepts or rules or norms.
PRECEPTUAR.
v, to issue precepts or rules or norms ‖ to order, command, obligate.
PRECIADO.
adj, precious, valued, esteemed ‖ valuable ‖ boastful.
PRECIADOR.
See APRECIADOR.
PRECIAR.
v, to price, value, appraise, place a price on ‖ to boast.

PRECINTA.
f, customs seal or stamp placed on inspected goods.

PRECINTAR.
v, to bind with metal strapping ‖ to place a seal or binding strap on goods inspected by customs.

PRECINTO.
m, binding strap ‖ binding strap used by customs on inspected goods ‖ police station.

PRECIO.
m, price, value ‖ monetary value ‖ (contractual) consideration ‖ prize (given in jousts) ‖ importance ‖ estimation ‖ credit ‖ effort, sacrifice ‖ type of aggravating circumstance which consists of receiving pay for committing a crime.

PRECIO ABUSIVO.
abusive price, price which exceeds cost plus legal mark-up.

PRECIO AFECTIVO.
personal value, value placed on something due to the memories or associations which it bears or to the extraordinary feeling which one has toward it.

PRECIO AJUSTADO.
agreed-upon price, contract price ‖ moderate price ‖ adjusted price.

PRECIO AL CONTADO.
cash price.

PRECIO ALZADO.
fixed price (determined for a work without relation to the quantity, quality, time, or cost of materials).

PRECIO APLAZADO.
payment on credit, postponed payment.

PRECIO CALLEJERO.
street price.

PRECIO CIERTO.
sum certain, fixed price ‖ price paid for an identified good.

PRECIO CORRIENTE.
current or market or going price,

PRECIO DE ADJUDICACIÓN.
price upon partition of jointly-owned property ‖ auction price.

PRECIO DE ADQUISICIÓN.
purchase price ‖ price paid.

PRECIO DE AFECCIÓN.
See PRECIO AFECTIVO.

PRECIO DE APERTURA.
opening price.

PRECIO DE CIERRE.
closing price.

PRECIO DE COSTO.
cost price or value. Includes the cost of raw materials, labor, and capital earnings.

PRECIO DE FÁBRICA.
cost of raw material and manufacturing costs ‖ price less costs of middlemen and transportation ‖ see PRECIO DE COSTO ‖ ex-factory price.

PRECIO DE FACTURA.
invoice price, billing price, invoiced price.

PRECIO DE LA NOVIA.
price of the bride.

PRECIO DE PLAZA.
local price, market price.

PRECIO DE PRODUCCIÓN.
See PRECIO DE FÁBRICA ‖ production price (including cost of labor and materials).

PRECIO DE REPOSICIÓN.
replacement price.

PRECIO DE REVENTA.
resale price

PRECIO DE VENTA.
selling or sales price.

PRECIO DEL MERCADO.
market price, local price.

PRECIO FICTICIO.
fictitious or shadow price.

PRECIO FIJO.
fixed or set price, price which is not subject to bargaining.

PRECIO FINGIDO.
See PRECIO FICTICIO.

PRECIO FRAUDULENTO.
fraudulent price, stated price which differs from the real price (usually for purposes of tax evasion).

PRECIO FUERA DE LA BOLSA.
street price.

PRECIO INCIERTO.
indeterminate price, price which is not fixed.

PRECIO JUSTO.
fair price.

PRECIO LEGAL.
legal price, price which is set by law, regulation etc.

PRECIO LÍQUIDO.
net price (less transportation or other additional costs) ‖ discounted price ‖ cash price.

PRECIO MÁXIMO.
maximum or ceiling price.
PRECIO MEDIO.
average price ‖ mean price ‖ median price.
PRECIO MÍNIMO.
minimum or base price.
PRECIO NETO.
net price ‖ bottom price.
PRECIO NOMINAL.
nominal price ‖ par value.
PRECIO OFICIAL.
official price, government-set price.
PRECIO ORDINARIO.
market price, local price ‖ average price ‖
fixed price.
PRECIO PAGADO.
purchase price ‖ price paid.
PRECIO POLÍTICO.
government-set price ‖ artificial price.
**PRECIO
POR UNIDAD.**
unit price.
PRECIO REAL.
actual price paid (opposed to official price) ‖
actual price (opposed to nominal price).
PRECIO RECIBIDO.
price received.
PRECIO TECHO.
ceiling price.
PRECIO TOPE.
ceiling price.
PRECIO ÚNICO.
bulk price, price paid for a group of things ‖
identical price charged for a variety of items.
PRECIO UNITARIO.
unit price.
PRECIO VIL.
price below cost ‖ dumping price.
PRECISAMENTE.
adv, precisely, exactly ‖ justly, fairly ‖ as determined ‖ obligatorily, necessarily, as required ‖
inevitably.
PRECISAR.
v, to indicate, specify, determine ‖ to need, be
in need of ‖ to oblige, obligate,
PRECISIÓN.
f, precision, exactness ‖ necessity, obligation ‖
need.
PRECISO.
adj, precise, exact ‖ correct, accurate ‖ necessary,
indispensable ‖ punctual ‖ unique, only, sole.

PRECLARAMENTE.
adv, illustriously ‖ lucidly, with intellectual in-
sight.
PRECLARO.
adj, illustrious, admirable ‖ lucid, intellectually
penetrating.
PRECLUSIÓN.
f, preclusion, termination, extinction, limitation ‖ limitation or extinction of a procedural
right at law ‖ principle in procedural law whereby the start of one stage in a lawsuit termi-
nates the prior stage and precludes its being
raised again.
PRECLUSIVO.
adj, preventative, preclusive.
PRECOCIDAD.
f, precocity, precociousness.
PRECONCEBIR.
v, to preconceive.
PRECONTRATO.
m, letter of intent, pre-contract, contract by
which the execution of a future agreement is
agreed to.
PRECOZ.
adj, precocious.
PRECURSOR.
m, precursor, forerunner.
PREDATARIO.
m, predatory.
PREDIAL.
adj, concerning real property.
PREDILECTO.
adj, preferred.
PREDIO.
m, land, real estate, real property, estate ‖ lot.
PREDIO AJENO.
real property belonging to another.
PREDIO ALODIAL.
unencumbered estate, real property free of
encumbrances.
PREDIO DOMINANTE.
dominant estate or tenement (re easements).
PREDIO ENCLAVADO.
land-locked estate, real estate without access
to a public road.
PREDIO INFERIOR.
real estate or property through which waters
from a dominant estate flow.
PREDIO INTERMEDIO.
real estate or property between a dominant
and servient estate.

PREDIO RURAL.
See PREDIO RÚSTICO.
PREDIO RÚSTICO.
rural property.
PREDIO SIRVIENTE.
servient estate or tenement.
PREDIO SUBURBANO.
suburban property, real estate located in the outskirts of a city.
PREDIO SUPERIOR.
dominant estate ‖ property through which water runs before it arrives at other properties.
PREDIO URBANO.
urban real estate, city property.
PREDISPONER.
v, to predispose ‖ to prejudice, influence.
PREDISPOSICIÓN.
f, predisposition ‖ tendency, inclination ‖ prejudice.
PREDOMINACIÓN.
See PREDOMINIO.
PREDOMINANCIA.
See PREDOMINIO.
PREDOMINANTE.
adj, predominant.
PREDOMINAR.
v, to predominate, prevail ‖ to predominate or prevail over ‖ to abound.
PREDOMINIO.
m, predominance, superiority, power.
PREELECCIÓN.
f, pre-election ‖ predestination.
PREELEGIR.
v, to pre-elect, elect beforehand ‖ to predestine.
PREEMINENCIA.
f, preeminence, superiority ‖ privilege ‖ prerogative.
PREEMINENTE.
adj, preeminent, superior ‖ privileged ‖ honorific.
PREESTABLECIDO.
adj, pre-established.
PREEXISTENCIA.
f, pre-existence.
PREEXISTENTE.
adj, pre-existing.
PREFABRICADO.
adj, prefabricated.
PREFECTO.
m, prefect, chief administrative officer (who is

responsible for others carrying out their work)
PREFERENCIA.
f, preference, advantage ‖ predilection ‖ choce, selection ‖ inclination, propensity, tender cy.
PREFERENCIA DE CRÉDITOS.
priority or preference of secured loan.
PREFERENCIA EN EL PASO.
right of way.
PREFERENCIAL.
adj, preferential.
PREFERENTE.
adj, preferred, preferable ‖ the best ‖ prefe rential, having priority.
PREFERENTEMENTE.
adv, preferably, preferentially.
PREFERIBLEMENTE.
adv, preferably
PREFERIR.
v, to prefer ‖ to choose, select.
PREFIJAR.
v, to prearrange, pre-fix, pre-set ‖ to predete mine.
PREFIJO.
adj, prearranged, pre-set ‖ predetermined.
PREGÓN.
m, public announcement, announcement of town crier, proclamation ‖ street vendor's cr
PREGONADO.
m, person with a price on his head.
PREGONAR.
v, to announce or proclaim or cry out public ‖ to hawk, cry out prices of merchandise ‖ proscribe.
PREGONERO.
m, town crier ‖ public announcer ‖ street ver dor ‖ gossip.
PREGUERRA.
f, pre-war.
PREGUNTA.
f, interrogation, questioning ‖ question, inte rogatory.
PREGUNTAR.
v, to question, ask ‖ to interrogate.
PREGUNTAS A LITIGANTES.
interrogatories or written questions to parti to the case. These are usually posed by submi ting them in a sealed file to the judge who w not open them until the ABSOLUCIÓN DE POS CIONES occurs.

PREGUNTAS A TESTIGOS.
interrogatories or written questions to witnesses.
PREGUNTAS CAPCIOSAS.
tricky or captious questions.
PREGUNTAS GENERALES DE LA LEY.
standard legal questions or interrogatories (regarding name, age, marital status, etc.). Usually formulated by the court.
PREGUNTAS IMPERTINENTES.
irrelevant questions or interrogatories.
PREGUNTAS OFICIOSAS.
questions or interrogatories posed by persons who have no legal right to ask them.
PREGUNTAS SUGESTIVAS.
leading questions or interrogatories.
PREHUELGA.
adj, pre-strike.
PREINDUSTRIAL .
adj, pre-industrial.
PREINDUSTRIALISMO.
m, pre-industrialism.
PREJUDICIAL.
adj, prejudgmental, prejudicial ‖ requiring a decision prior to the final decision ‖ pretrial.
PREJUICIO.
m, prejudice, partiality, bias ‖ prejudgment.
PREJUICIO ANTIEMPRESARIAL.
anti-business prejudice.
PREJUICIO CLASISTA.
classism.
PREJUICIO DE CLASE.
See PREJUICIO CLASISTA.
PREJUICIO RACIAL.
racial prejudice, racism.
PREJUICIO RELIGIOSO.
religious prejudice.
PREJUICIO SOCIAL.
social prejudice.
PREJUZGAMIENTO.
m, prejudgment ‖ prejudice.
PREJUZGAR.
v, to prejudge.
PRELACIÓN.
f, priority (in time or rank that must be granted something) ‖ preference.
PRELACIÓN CONSENSUAL.
consensually agreed to order of preference of creditors' interests in a bankruptcy or insolvency proceeding (usually established by unanimous consent of creditors).

PRELACIÓN DE CRÉDITOS.
order of preference of creditors' claims in the case of an insolvent or debtor in default (as a result or agreement or law).
PRELACIÓN JUDICIAL.
judicially determined order of preference of creditors' interests in a bankruptcy or insolvency proceeding (usually established when the creditors are unable to agree).
PRELEGADO.
m, bequest in favor of an heir.
PRELIMINAR.
adj, preliminary, previous, antecedent ‖ introductory.
PRELIMINARES DE LA PAZ.
preliminary stipulations to a peace treaty ‖ initial contacts between warring factions or nations to initiate peace talks.
PRELIMINARMENTE.
adv, preliminarily, previously.
PRELUSIÓN.
f, prologue, preface.
PREMARITAL.
adj, pre-marital, anti-nuptial, pre-nuptial.
PREMATURA.
f, female who is under the age to have sexual relations ‖ adj, premature.
PREMATURAMENTE.
adv, prematurely.
PREMATURO.
adj, premature
PREMEDITACIÓN.
f, premeditation, malice aforethought.
PREMEDITADAMENTE.
adv, premeditatedly, with premeditation or malice aforethought.
PREMEDITAR.
v, to premeditate.
PREMIAR.
v, to award ‖ to reward.
PREMILITAR.
adj, before military service.
PREMIO.
m, recompense, remuneration ‖ award, prize ‖ premium, interest, return (on money) ‖ premium, extra money, bonus (given as a stimulus) ‖ premium, increase in the nominal value of money when it is exchanged ‖ (employee) bonus.
PREMIO DEL REASEGURO.
reinsurance premium.

PREMIO DEL SEGURO.
See PRIMA DEL SEGURO.

**PREMIO NOBEL
DE LA PAZ.**
Nobel Peace Prize.

PREMIO POR NATALIDAD.
bonus or extra pay given upon the birth of an employee's child.

PREMIO POR NUPCIALIDAD.
wedding bonus, bonus upon marriage of employee.

PREMISA.
f, premise ‖ indication, sign.

PREMISO.
adj, precedent, antecedent, preceding.

PREMORIENCIA.
f, antecedent death, death of one before another.

PREMORIENTE.
adj, pre-decedent, person who dies before another or others.

PREMORIR.
v, to predecease, die before another or others.

PREMOSTRAR.
v, to preview, show previously.

PREMUERTO.
See PREMORIENTE.

PRENATAL.
adj, prenatal, prior to birth.

PRENDA.
f, pledge, lien, security, security interest, chattel mortgage ‖ pledge agreement (whereby personal property is given as a guaranty of an obligation and is delivered to the pledgee) ‖ pledge, pledged property ‖ guaranty ‖ garment, piece of clothing ‖ jewelry or furniture or domestic wares (when put up for sale) ‖ loved one, dearheart ‖ token.

PRENDA AGRARIA.
pledge of agricultural property.

PRENDA AGRÍCOLA.
See PRENDA AGRARIA.

PRENDA AMORTIZADA.
See PRENDA VIVA.

PRENDA COMERCIAL.
commercial pledge or security agreement, contract by which a pledge or security interest is given in something to guaranty a commercial transaction.

PRENDA CON REGISTRO.
security interest which is registered with a go-

vernmental agency over property which remains in the pledgor's possession.

PRENDA DE CRÉDITOS.
security interest in a loan to a third party held by a debtor.

PRENDA FIJA.
security interest in identified chattel goods ‖ pledge.

PRENDA FLOTANTE.
floating security interest over chattels.

PRENDA IRREGULAR.
pledge or security interest in money of other fungible goods.

PRENDA JUDICIAL.
court-ordered lien, judicial lien, judgment lien.

PRENDA PRETORIA.
See PRENDA JUDICIAL.

PRENDA SIN DESPLAZAMIENTO.
See PRENDA CON REGISTRO.

PRENDA SOBRE DERECHOS.
pledge or security interest in a debtor's legal interests or rights.

PRENDA SOBRE VALORES.
pledge of securities.

PRENDA USUFRUCTUARIA.
pledge of goods which allows the pledgee to use the goods and their fruits.
See USUFRUCTO.

PRENDADO.
adj, pledged, hocked, pawned.

PRENDADOR.
m, pledger.

PRENDAMIENTO.
m, act of pledging or taking a pledge ‖ detention, arrest, capture.

PRENDAR.
v, to give as a pledge, give as security, grant a security interest in (something), place a lien on ‖ to hock, pawn ‖ to charm (someone).

PRENDARIO.
adj, related to a pledge or lien or security interest.

PRENDER.
v, to detain, grab, hold ‖ to arrest ‖ to deprive of liberty or freedom ‖ to subject (someone) to ‖ to turn on (e.g. lights).

PRENSA.
f, the press, newspapers (as a group) ‖ printing press ‖ journalism.

PRENSA AMARILLA.
yellow press.

PRENUPCIAL.
adj, prenuptial, antenuptial, pre-marital.
PREÑADA.
f, pregnant woman or animal ‖ adj, pregnant.
PREÑADO.
m, pregnancy ‖ duration of pregnancy ‖ fetus.
PREÑAR.
v, to impregnate, inseminate.
PREÑEZ.
f, pregnancy ‖ pending matter ‖ difficulty, confusion.
PREOCUPACIÓN.
f, preoccupation, worry, concern.
PRERROGATIVA.
f, prerogative, privilege ‖ exclusive or superior right.
PRESA.
f, capture, seizure, apprehension ‖ detention, prison ‖ irrigation ditch, channel, sluice ‖ dam, dike ‖ war booty, spoils ‖ plunder, pillage.
PRESA LEGÍTIMA.
booty which is legally taken at time of war.
PRESA MARÍTIMA.
prize, vessel and cargo which during time of war is taken as property of the capturing nation.
PRESAGIAR.
v, to presage.
PRESAGIO.
m, presage, omen, sign ‖ ability to tell the future.
PRESAR.
See APRESAR.
PRESCINDENCIA.
f, omission, deletion ‖ act of omission, deletion ‖ formal declaration of government impartiality in elections.
PRESCINDIBILIDAD.
f, expendability of employees.
PRESCINDIBLE.
adj, dispensable, expendable ‖ unnecessary, superfluous.
PRESCINDIR.
v, to omit, delete ‖ to dispense with, eliminate ‖ to abstain, deprive oneself.
PRESCRIBIR.
v, to prescribe, order, command ‖ to acquire (property) by adverse possession or prescription ‖ to lapse, become legally unenforceable due to the passage of time (re statutes of limitations regarding civil rights and obligations) ‖

to have run (re statute of limitations regarding criminal liability)
PRESCRIPCIÓN.
m, appearance or extinguishment of a legal right due to the passage of time ‖ prescription (if personal property) ‖ adverse possession (if real property) ‖ limitation or lapsing of a legal right ‖ limitation of criminal liability due to the passage of time, running of the statute of limitations regarding criminal liability ‖ command, order, prescript.
PRESCRIPCIÓN ABREVIADA.
shortened or short prescription or adverse possession or lapsing of a legal right.
PRESCRIPCIÓN ADQUISITIVA.
prescription (if personal property) ‖ adverse possession (if real property).
PRESCRIPCIÓN CIVIL.
civil prescription or adverse possession or lapsing. Opposed to criminal lapsing.
PRESCRIPCIÓN CRIMINAL.
limitation of criminal liability (due to passage of time), running of statute of limitations regarding criminal liability. Includes PRESCRIPCIÓN DE LA PENA and DEL DELITO.
PRESCRIPCIÓN DE ACCIONES.
limitation of action, running of statute of limitations.
PRESCRIPCIÓN DE LA PENA.
running of the statute of limitations regarding criminal liability after the criminal has been sentenced.
PRESCRIPCIÓN DEL DELITO.
limitation of criminal liability (due to passage of time), running of statute of limitations regarding criminal liability.
PRESCRIPCIÓN DEL DOMINIO.
adverse possession or prescription.
PRESCRIPCIÓN EN LAS OBLIGACIONES.
limitation or lapse of a legal right or obligation.
PRESCRIPCIÓN ENTRE MARIDO Y MUJER.
prescription or adverse possession or lapse of rights as between a husband and wife due to running of a statute of limitations.
PRESCRIPCIÓN EXTINTIVA.
See PRESCRIPCIÓN LIBERATORIA.
PRESCRIPCIÓN EXTRAORDINARIA.
lengthened or extraordinarily long prescription or adverse possession obtained despite lack of good faith or title.

PRESCRIPCIÓN LIBERATORIA.
extinction of an obligation due to the running of a statute of limitations.
PRESCRIPCIÓN MERCANTIL.
prescription or lapsing related to commercial or corporate matters.
PRESCRIPCIÓN ORDINARIA.
See PRESCRIPCIÓN ADQUISITIVA.
PRESCRIPCIÓN PENAL.
See PRESCRIPCIÓN CRIMINAL.
PRESCRIPCIÓN PERENTORIA.
prescription or adverse possession which arises instantaneously by reason of possession, not by reason of the passage of time.
PRESCRIPCIÓN TREINTAÑAL.
thirty year prescription or adverse possession (which requires no showing of good faith or title).
PRESCRIPCIÓN VEINTEAÑAL.
twenty year prescription or adverse possession (which requires no showing of good faith or title).
PRESCRIPTIBILIDAD.
f, ability to own by adverse possession or prescription or to extinguish an obligation or right, by lapsing.
PRESCRIPTIBLE.
adj, able to be owned by adverse possession or prescription or to be extinguished by lapsing (re an obligation or right).
PRESCRIPTIVO.
adj, prescriptive ‖ pertaining to prescription or adverse possession or lapsing.
PRESCRIPTO.
See PRESCRITO.
PRESCRITO.
adj, prescribed, taken or lost by adverse possession, adversely possessed ‖ lapsed ‖ ordered, commanded, prescribed ‖ barred by a statute of limitations.
PRESENCIA.
f, presence (in all senses) ‖ attendance, appearance ‖ appearance in court.
PRESENCIAL.
adj, pertaining to presence.
PRESENCIAR.
v, to be present, appear ‖ to appear in court ‖ to witness, be witness (of something).
PRESENTACIÓN.
f, presentation, introduction ‖ showing, exhibition, display ‖ recommendation of a person for

a position or honor ‖ appearance, attendance ‖ demand, complaint, petition ‖ presentation (of a draft) ‖ first registration in some Real Estate Registries.
PRESENTACIÓN DE CREDENCIALES.
presentation of credentials (of a diplomat to a foreign nation).
PRESENTACIÓN DE LA LETRA DE CAMBIO.
presentation of a draft (to a bank).
PRESENTACIÓN DE LA MEJOR PRUEBA.
exhibition or showing of the best evidence.
PRESENTACIÓN DE PRISIONERO.
presentation of a prisoner of war (to the military if he is in the armed forces).
PRESENTACIÓN DEL AUSENTE.
reappearance of a missing person who is presumed dead ‖ appearance of a person who has failed to properly appear in court.
PRESENTACIÓN ESPONTÁNEA DEL DELINCUENTE.
the act of a criminal turning himself in (to the police).
PRESENTADO.
m, manager who has been introduced to his subordinates ‖ armed forces personnel who has presented himself before the requisite authorities ‖ adj, presented.
PRESENTADOR.
m, presenter ‖ introducer.
PRESENTAR.
v, to present, introduce ‖ to show, display, exhibit ‖ to present, give ‖ to recommend (a person for a position).
PRESENTE.
m, attendant, witness ‖ present time ‖ gift, present ‖ person who is present ‖ real estate owner who lives in the province in which such property is located (re adverse possession) ‖ adj, present, in attendance ‖ present, current ‖ delivered by hand.
¡PRESENTE!
Here!. Present!
PRESERVACIÓN.
f, preservation ‖ protection ‖ support, backing ‖ custodianship, custody ‖ conservation.
PRESERVAR.
v, to preserve, keep, conserve ‖ to protect, defend ‖ to support, back.
PRESIDENCIA.
f, presidency ‖ office and functions of presi-

dent ‖ presidential term of office ‖ president's or manager's office ‖ right to preside over ‖ act of presiding over ‖ Presidency (of a nation).

PRESIDENCIAL.
adj, presidential.

PRESIDENCIALISMO.
m, presidentialism, governmental system in which the president is the head of state.

PRESIDENCIALISTA.
adj, pertaining to PRESIDENCIALISMO ‖ supporter of PRESIDENCIALISMO.

PRESIDENTA.
f, (female) president, chairwoman, female chairman ‖ first lady, president's wife ‖ female President (of a nation).

PRESIDENTE.
m, (male) president, chairman, chairperson, head (of a meeting or corporation, etc.) ‖ Speaker of the Senate or House (of Representatives) ‖ Lord Chancellor ‖ Speaker of Parliament ‖ President (of a nation) ‖ Chief Justice, Chief Supreme Court Justice ‖ Lord Chief Justice.

PRESIDENTE DE FACTO.
de facto president or head of state.

PRESIDENTE DE LA NACIÓN.
President of the Nation, national president.

PRESIDENTE DE LA REPÚBLICA.
President of the Republic, national president, President of the Nation.

PRESIDENTE DE MESA.
chairman of the meeting ‖ electoral president, person who presides over elections.

PRESIDENTE DE SALA.
lead judge (of a court of appeals or of a tribunal made up of judges from various courts).

PRESIDENTE DEL CONSEJO.
President ‖ Prime Minister ‖ president of the board of directors.

PRESIDENTE DEL CONSEJO SUPREMO.
chief justice of military court.

PRESIDENTE DEL TRIBUNAL SUPREMO.
Chief Justice, Chief Supreme Court Justice, Lord Chief Justice.

PRESIDENTE NATO.
leader or president who assumes such position by reason of his legal title or status, not election (e.g. Speaker of the Senate assumed by vice-president of executive branch).

PRESIDIABLE.
adj, imprisonable, meriting imprisonment.

PRESIDIARIO.
m, convict (who fulfills a prison sentence).

PRESIDIO.
m, presidio, military prison ‖ prison, penitentiary ‖ help, aid, assistance ‖ imprisonment, prison sentence ‖ convicts (as a whole) ‖ hard labor.

PRESIDIO CORRECCIONAL.
type of imprisonment (of limited duration).

PRESIDIO MAYOR.
long-term imprisonment.

PRESIDIO MENOR.
short-term imprisonment.

PRESIDIR.
v, to preside, govern or rule over (as president) ‖ to carry out the functions of president ‖ to dominate, influence.

PRESIÓN.
f, pressure (in all meanings) ‖ pressuring, act of pressuring; compression ‖ abuse of power or influence or authority.

PRESIÓN SOCIAL.
social pressure.

PRESIONAR.
v, to pressure, exercise power or influence or authority over.

PRESO.
m, person under arrest ‖ prisoner ‖ convict, con.

PRESO DE CONFIANZA.
prisoner who, for good behavior, is given special jobs requiring trust.

PRESTACIÓN.
f, loan ‖ lending, loaning, act of lending, loaning ‖ rendering (of work) ‖ work (done for the collective good) ‖ rent payment, charge, payment due the owner of a thing.

PRESTACIÓN ACCESORIA.
See OBLIGACIÓN ACCESORIA.

PRESTACIÓN ANUAL.
annuity, yearly payment ‖ yearly obligation (e.g. military service).

PRESTACIÓN DE ALIMENTOS.
support payment (provided by parent(s) of children), provision of food, clothing and housing (for children).

PRESTACIÓN DE SERVICIOS.
rendering of services.

PRESTACIÓN DE TRANSPORTES.
rendering of transportation services.
PRESTACIÓN NEGATIVA.
See OBLIGACIÓN DE NO HACER.
PRESTACIÓN PERSONAL.
obligatory community work.
PRESTACIÓN SOCIAL.
social service ‖ social services benefit or right.
PRESTADO.
m, loan, that which has been lent ‖ adj, loaned, lent.
PRESTADOR.
m, lender, loaner ‖ creditor ‖ renderer.
PRESTADOR DE TRABAJO.
renderer of services, worker.
PRESTAMENTE.
adv, promptly ‖ diligently.
PRESTAMISTA.
f, m, lender, loaner ‖ moneylender ‖ loan shark.
PRÉSTAMO.
m, loan ‖ loan contract.
PRÉSTAMO A LA GRUESA.
bottomry.
PRÉSTAMO A LA DEMANDA.
See PRÉSTAMO A LA VISTA.
PRÉSTAMO A LA VISTA.
demand loan, call loan
PRÉSTAMO A PLAZO FIJO.
fixed-term loan, time loan.
PRÉSTAMO A RIESGO MARÍTIMO.
See PRÉSTAMO A LA GRUESA.
PRÉSTAMO CON GARANTÍA.
guaranteed loan.
PRÉSTAMO CON GARANTÍA DE EFECTOS O DE VALORES PÚBLICOS.
collateral loan, loan secured by property or securities.
PRÉSTAMO CON GARANTÍA DE OBLIGACIONES AL PORTADOR.
loan secured by bearer instruments.
PRÉSTAMO CON INTERÉS.
interest-bearing loan, loan with interest.
PRÉSTAMO DE CONSUMO.
loan for consumption, loan of fungibles (e.g. money, food, etc.).
PRÉSTAMO DE DINERO.
loan of money, monetary loan.
PRÉSTAMO DE USO.
loan for use, loan of goods for use but not consumption.

PRÉSTAMO MERCANTIL.
commercial loan, loan in which one of the parties is a merchant or of which the purpose is commercial.
PRÉSTAMO SIMPLE.
See MUTUO ‖ loan of money or other fungible to be returned in kind. Interest-bearing only if expressly agreed to.
PRÉSTAMO USURARIO.
usurious loan.
PRESTANOMBRE.
See TESTAFERRO.
PRESTAR.
v, to loan, lend ‖ to borrow ‖ to give ‖ to contribute, collaborate ‖ to render (services) ‖ to pay (attention) ‖ to keep (silent) ‖ to swear to, state under oath ‖ to make (a statement).
PRESTAR FE.
to confirm testimony or a statement.
PRESTATARIO.
m, borrower.
PRESTIGIO.
m, fame, good reputation, prestige ‖ magic, trick ‖ influence, authority, power.
PRESTIGIOSO.
adj, prestigious, famous ‖ deceptive, illusory.
PRESUMIBLE.
adj, presumable, assumable.
PRESUMIR.
v, to suppose, guess, conjecture ‖ to suspect ‖ to assume, presume ‖ to deduce, infer ‖ to be vain.
PRESUNCIÓN.
f, supposition, guess, conjecture ‖ suspicion ‖ sign, indication ‖ presumption ‖ (legal) presumption ‖ (legal) inference ‖ vanity ‖ boastfulness.
PRESUNCIÓN ABSOLUTA.
total presumption, legal presumption which is applied equally against all persons or circumstances.
PRESUNCIÓN CONVENCIONAL.
contractual presumption, presumption which is agreed to by written contract.
PRESUNCIÓN DE AUSENCIA.
presumption of disappearance or absence (of a person).
PRESUNCIÓN DE COMMORIENCIA.
See COMMORIENCIA.
PRESUNCIÓN DE COSA JUZGADA.
presumption of res judicata.

PRESUNCIÓN DE FALLECIMIENTO.
presumption of death.
PRESUNCIÓN DE HECHO.
factual presumption.
**PRESUNCIÓN DE HECHO
Y DE DERECHO.**
irrebuttable presumption.
PRESUNCIÓN DE HOMBRE.
See PRESUNCIÓN "JURIS TANTUM".
PRESUNCIÓN DE INOCENCIA.
presumption of innocence.
PRESUNCIÓN DE JUEZ.
See PRESUNCIÓN "JURIS TANTUM".
PRESUNCIÓN DE LEY.
legal presumption.
PRESUNCIÓN DE MUERTE.
See PRESUNCIÓN DE FALLECIMIENTO.
PRESUNCIÓN DE SOLO DERECHO.
See PRESUNCIÓN DE LEY.
PRESUNCIÓN DE SUPERVIVENCIA.
presumption of survivorship.
PRESUNCIÓN DE VERACIDAD.
presumption of credibility, presumption that a
fact is true until proven otherwise.
PRESUNCIÓN DE VIDA.
presumption in favor of life (in case of doubt).
PRESUNCIÓN ESPECÍFICA.
presumption applicable under specific circumstances.
PRESUNCIÓN GENÉRICA.
presumption applicable under all circumstances.
PRESUNCIÓN JUDICIAL.
judicial presumption (accorded the facts).
PRESUNCIÓN "JURIS ET DE JURE".
irrebuttable presumption.
PRESUNCIÓN "JURIS TANTUM".
rebuttable presumption.
PRESUNCIÓN LEGAL.
statutory or code presumption ‖ legal presumption
PRESUNCIÓN NATURAL.
presumption about known facts or general
culture, presumption of which judicial notice
can be taken.
PRESUNCIÓN RELATIVA.
limited presumption, presumption which is
not applied to all persons or circumstances
equally.
PRESUNCIÓN VEHEMENTE.
conclusive presumption.

PRESUNCIÓN VIOLENTA.
See PRESUNCIÓN VEHEMENTE.
**PRESUNCIONES EN
EL ARRENDAMIENTO.**
presumptions regarding the rental (that the
leasehold is in good condition, etc.).
PRESUNCIONES EN EL CONDOMINIO.
presumptions regarding the joint ownership
(that the owners own equal shares, etc.).
PRESUNCIONES EN EL DEPÓSITO.
presumptions regarding the bailment (that the
thing bailed is not to be used, etc.).
PRESUNCIONES EN EL SEGURO.
presumptions regarding insurance (that it is
not contracted on behalf of a third party, etc.).
PRESUNCIONES EN EL TRANSPORTE.
presumptions regarding transportation (that
the goods are not defective, etc.).
PRESUNCIONES EN LA DONACIÓN.
presumptions regarding donations or gifts.
PRESUNCIONES EN LA FILIACIÓN.
presumptions of legitimacy.
PRESUNCIONES EN LA SOCIEDAD.
corporate presumptions (that corporate officers acted on behalf of the corporation, etc.).
PRESUNCIONES EN LAS SUCESIONES.
presumptions regarding succession (e.g. presumption of death, etc.).
PRESUNCIONES EN LO PENAL.
criminal presumptions, presumptions regarding crimes and accused persons (e.g. presumption of innocence, etc.).
**PRESUNCIONES EN LOS
CONTRATOS.**
presumptions regarding contracts (e.g. presumption of legality, etc.).
**PRESUNCIONES EN
LOS TESTAMENTOS.**
presumptions regarding wills (e.g. presumption of testator's sanity at writing of will, etc.).
PRESUNTAMENTE.
adv, presumably, assumably ‖ supposedly.
PRESUNTIVAMENTE.
adv, pursuant to conjecture or an assumption
‖ supposed.
PRESUNTIVO.
adj, presumed, supposed, based on a presumption ‖ able to be presumed or assumed.
PRESUPONER.
v, to presuppose, presume ‖ to budget, estimate (expenses).

PRESUPOSICIÓN.
f, presupposition ‖ budget, estimate ‖ pretext, reason.

PRESUPUESTAR.
v, to budget, calculate (expenses).

PRESUPUESTO.
m, budget, estimate (of expenses) ‖ reason, motive, pretext ‖ supposition, guess.

PRESUPUESTOS PROCESALES.
procedural requirements or circumstances (which must exist).

PRETENDER.
v, to try, attempt ‖ to request ‖ to procure.

PRETENDIENTE.
f, m, person who tries or attempts ‖ solicitor, requester ‖ procurer ‖ (woman's) suitor ‖ pretender (to the throne) ‖ candidate (for office) ‖ claimant, plaintiff.

PRETENSIÓN.
f, claim ‖ pretension ‖ request, solicitation ‖ petition, complaint, demand ‖ desire, aspiration ‖ legal basis (whether or not wellfounded).

PRETENSIÓN JUDICIAL.
judicially filed claim.

PRETENSIÓN PROCESAL.
filed claim.

PRETERICIÓN.
f, pretermission, omission of legal heirs from a will.

**PRETERICIÓN EN
LA PARTICIÓN.**
pretermission in the distribution of decedent's assets.

PRETERIDO.
See HEREDERO PRETERIDO.

PRETERINTENCIÓN.
f, criminal intent to cause injury less serious than that which actually occurs.

PRETERINTENCIONAL.
adj, unintended.
See PRETERINTENCIONALIDAD.

PRETERINTENCIONALIDAD.
f, type of criminal conduct which causes an injury more serious than that intended or than could reasonably have been expected. Usually an extenuating circumstance which may diminish the sentence imposed.

PRETERIR.
v, to pretermit, leave legal heirs out of will ‖ to omit, pass over.

PRETÉRITO.
adj, pretermitted, omitted, passed over.
See PRETERIR.

PRETERMISIÓN.
f, pretermission (from will of legal heir) ‖ omission; abandonment.

PRETERMITIR.
v, to act with lack of care.

PRETEXTO.
m, pretext, excuse.

PRETORIANISMO.
m, praetorianism, undue military influence in politics or the government ‖ political militarism.

PREVALECER.
v, to prevail, triumph ‖ to be superior to.

PREVALECIMIENTO.
m, triumph, victory, success (over).

PREVALER.
See PREVALECER.

PREVALERSE.
v, to take advantage of (in all senses) ‖ to abuse (with impunity).

PREVARICACIÓN.
f, breach of public duties, breach of duty (which is either intentional or reckless) of a public official or employee ‖ negligent or intentional injustice carried out by a judge ‖ legal prevarication.

PREVARICADOR.
m, public official or employee who breaches his public duties (either intentionally or recklessly) ‖ judge or prosecuting attorney who negligently or intentionally carries out an injustice ‖ attorney who prejudices the interests of his client or assists the interests of the opposition.

PREVARICAR.
v, to breach public duties (by a public official or employee) ‖ to carry out an injustice (by a judge or attorney) ‖ to fail to live up to one's duties ‖ to cause another to breach his or her duties ‖ to prevaricate (legally) ‖ to subvert ‖ to pervert, corrupt.

PREVARICATO.
m, (legal) prevarication, breach of public duty.

PREVENCIÓN.
f, detention, police jail (for holding suspects), holding tank ‖ type or disciplinary measure ‖ prevention (of a crime). preparation ‖ foresight ‖ precaution ‖ precautions, precaution

ary steps ‖ warning, advice ‖ prior knowledge of injury or harm ‖ concern, worry ‖ relief or resolution (of a problem or difficulty) ‖ aversion, repugnance ‖ bias, prejudice ‖ first instance, condition of being the first court to hear a case ‖ preliminary hearing of a case, anticipated hearing of a case.

REVENCIÓN DE ACCIDENTES.
prevention of accidents.

REVENCIÓN DE CAUSAS.
prevention or preventative measures of military crimes ‖ preliminary military hearing to determine the facts of the case and the persons who are accused of the crime.

REVENCIÓN DEL ABINTESTATO.
preliminary steps taken by a judge with regard to a person who dies intestate and without close relatives.

REVENCIÓN POLICIAL.
crime prevention by police ‖ preliminary hearing or investigation of crime by police.

REVENIDAMENTE.
adv, with PREVENCIÓN ‖ anticipatorily, previously ‖ with preparation.

REVENIDO.
m, suspect, criminal detainee (from the time of arrest until formal accusation) ‖ adj, prepared, ready ‖ foreseen ‖ foreseeable ‖ warned, forewarned ‖ supplied, furnished ‖ foresighted, careful.

REVENIR.
v, to prepare, make ready ‖ to foresee ‖ to avoid ‖ to make difficult ‖ to warn, forewarn ‖ to advise ‖ to take precautionary measures ‖ to worry ‖ to carry out a preliminary investigation or preliminary hearing ‖ to prevent (crime, lack of discipline, etc.) ‖ to prejudice, bias, predispose.

REVENTIVA.
See PRISIÓN PREVENTIVA.

REVENTIVAMENTE.
adv, preventively ‖ with PREVENCIÓN ‖ in prevention or avoidance of.

REVENTIVO.
adj, preventive.

REVER.
v, to foresee ‖ to take precautionary steps ‖ to conjecture.

REVIA CENSURA.
f, prior censorship, prior restraint on publication.

PREVIA INSCRIPCIÓN.
f, prior registration ‖ legal principle which establishes the necessity to register ownership and mortgage interests in a real estate registry (in order for them to be effective against third parties).

PREVIO.
adj, prior, previous ‖ preliminary.

PREVISIBILIDAD.
f, foreseeability.

PREVISIBLE.
adj, foreseeable.

PREVISIÓN.
f, foresight, prior knowledge ‖ conjecture ‖ prevision, precautionary measure ‖ adoption of precautionary measures.

PREVISIÓN OBRERA.
workers' pension plan, employees' retirement plan.

PREVISIÓN SOCIAL.
social welfare or security system. This term includes all governmental measures taken to assure the social welfare of citizens in case of unemployment, pregnancy, illness, invalidity, or old age.

PREVISIONAL.
adj, related to social security ‖ also see CLÁUSULA PREVISIONAL.

PREVISOR.
adj, foresighted, cautious.

PREVISTO.
adj, foreseen.

PRIMA.
f, (commercial) margin, mark-up ‖ insurance premium ‖ (employee) bonus, extra ‖ premium which a purchaser of stock pays over the nominal value of the stock ‖ export subsidy or grant (paid by government to encourage exports) ‖ female cousin.

**PRIMA A
LA PRODUCCIÓN.**
(employees') productivity bonus.

PRIMA DE EMISIÓN.
premium over par (value of stocks), mark-up margin over par.

**PRIMA
DEL SEGURO.**
insurance premium.

"PRIMA FACIE".
prima facie, at first sight. Used to indicate that the basis of a decision is not irrevocable.

PRIMACÍA.
f, preference, preferential right ‖ primacy, superiority ‖ excellency; priority.

"PRIMAE NOCTIS".
wedding night.

PRIMARIO.
adj, first, primary ‖ principal ‖ elemental ‖ initial.

PRIMAZGO.
m, relationship by cousins.

PRIMER.
See PRIMERO.

PRIMER MAGISTRADO.
m, president (of the nation), head of state (whether or not constitutional) ‖ commander in chief.

PRIMER MANDATARIO.
See PRIMER MAGISTRADO.

PRIMER MINISTRO.
prime minister.

PRIMERA COPIA.
first authorized copy of a document which has been witnessed by a special notary public.
See ESCRITURA MATRIZ.

PRIMERA GUERRA MUNDIAL.
First World War, World War I.

PRIMERA INSTANCIA.
first instance, inferior or lower or district or superior or circuit or county (court), common pleas.

PRIMERA INTENCIÓN.
See INTENCIÓN.

PRIMERA INTERNACIONAL.
First International (Socialist Association).

PRIMERA MATERIA.
raw material.

PRIMERA NECESIDAD.
See ARTÍCULO DE PRIMERA NECESIDAD.

PRIMERAMENTE.
adv, firstly, first of all ‖ with preference or priority ‖ previously.

PRIMERO.
adj, first (in all senses) ‖ excellent ‖ prior ‖ first (in hierarchy).

PRIMERO DE MAYO.
First of May, May Day ‖ Labor Day (in many but not all countries).

PRIMERO LA OBLIGACIÓN QUE LA DEVOCIÓN.
duty before devotion.

PRIMICIA.
f, first fruit (of something) ‖ fresh news.

PRIMO.
m, cousin, male cousin ‖ simpleton, fool ‖ adj, first, principal ‖ excellent.

PRIMO CARNAL.
See PRIMO HERMANO.

PRIMO HERMANO.
first cousin.

PRIMO SEGUNDO.
second cousin.

PRIMOGÉNITO.
m, first born, eldest child ‖ first born male child, eldest son ‖ eldest living child or son.

PRIMOGENITURA.
f, primogeniture.

PRIMORDIAL.
adj, primordial, primeval, primitive ‖ fundamental ‖ preferred.

PRINCESA.
f, princess ‖ wife of a prince.

PRINCIPADO.
m, honor and title of a prince ‖ princedom ‖ principality ‖ superiority, primacy.

PRINCIPAL.
m, (debt) principal ‖ manager of a commercial or industrial business ‖ principal (re agency law) ‖ basis of a matter or litigation ‖ principal claim or request or demand ‖ essential prayer or plea, e.g. damages, injunction, etc. ‖ adj principal, main, primary ‖ superior ‖ preferred ‖ primordial ‖ highly important ‖ essential fundamental (i.e. not accessory) ‖ independent.

PRINCIPALIDAD.
f, superiority ‖ primacy, state of being principal.

PRINCIPALMENTE.
adv, principally, primarily, essentially ‖ preferentially ‖ in the first place ‖ predominantly

PRÍNCIPE.
m, first born son of a monarch ‖ any son of a royal family ‖ prince.

PRÍNCIPE HEREDERO.
crown prince.

PRINCIPIO.
m, start, beginning, commencement ‖ principle, fundamental ‖ maxim, aphorism.

PRINCIPIO DE LA LEGALIDAD.
principle of no crime or punishment without prior law.

PRINCIPIO DE LA SEPARACIÓN DE PODERES.

principle of the separation of powers (i.e. separation of the executive, judiciary, and legislative branches of government).

PRINCIPIO DE PRUEBA POR ESCRITO.

existence of certain minimum written evidence, especially regarding a contract, regardless of whether or not additional parol evi-dence is necessary to prove the facts to which the written evidence refers.

PRINCIPIOS GENERALES DEL DERECHO.

general principles of law (which are to be applied when there is no applicable law and the case cannot be resolved by analogy).

PRINCIPIOS HIPOTECARIOS.

general principles regarding land ownership and mortgages.

PRINCIPIOS LABORALES.

general principles regarding labor law.

"PRIOR TEMPORE, POTIOR JURE".

The first in time is superior at law.

PRIORIDAD.

f, priority ‖ precedence ‖ privilege, preference;

PRIORIDAD DE PASO.

right of way at a traffic crossing.

PRIORIDAD EN EL NACIMIENTO.

priority at birth (regarding a multiple birth).

PRISIÓN.

f, prison (in all senses) ‖ jail, penitentiary ‖ imprisonment ‖ arrest ‖ capture, seizure. Seriousness varies from country to country. See RECLUSIÓN.

PRISIÓN ADMINISTRATIVA.

administrative hold or detention or arrest.

PRISIÓN ATENUADA.

detention pending judgment in which the prisoner is given special, better treatment (usually due to the position of the prisoner or the nature of the crime).

PRISIÓN CELULAR.

solitary isolation.

PRISIÓN CORRECCIONAL.

correctional institutionalization, punishment of imprisonment of a light nature.

PRISIÓN DE ESTADO.

state prison or penitentiary.

PRISIÓN ESTATAL.

See PRISIÓN DE ESTADO.

PRISIÓN MAYOR.

long-term imprisonment of a serious nature.

PRISIÓN MENOR.

short-term imprisonment of a less serious nature.

PRISIÓN MILITAR.

military imprisonment ‖ brig, stockade, military prison.

PRISIÓN PERPETUA.

life imprisonment, life.

PRISIÓN POR DEUDAS.

debtors' prison.

PRISIÓN PREVENTIVA.

temporary detention pending trial.

PRISIÓN PROVISIONAL.

See PRISIÓN PREVENTIVA.

PRISIÓN SUBSIDIARIA.

jail imposed for failure or inability to pay a fine.

PRISIÓN TEMPORAL.

imprisonment for a fixed term.

PRISIONERO.

m, prisoner, convict ‖ captive ‖ prisoner of war.

PRISIONERO DE GUERRA.

prisoner of war (whether military or civilian) ‖ damaged or sinking ship captured by the enemy.

PRISIONES.

f, means of imprisonment (e.g. bars, chains, etc.).

PRIVACIÓN.

f, deprivation, privation ‖ want, lack of ‖ disenfranchisement ‖ confiscation, seizure, impoundment ‖ divestment ‖ dispossession, eviction ‖ repossession, foreclosure.

PRIVACIÓN DE DERECHOS.

deprivation of civil rights and privileges and liberties (e.g. voting).

PRIVACIÓN DE EMPLEO.

See PÉRDIDA DE EMPLEO.

PRIVACIÓN DE LA PAZ.

exile, exclusion (from a tribal group).

PRIVACIÓN DE LIBERTAD.

imprisonment, deprivation of freedom (of movement).

PRIVADAMENTE.

adv, privately (in all senses) ‖ intimately ‖ separately.

PRIVADO.

adj, private (i.e. not public) ‖ individual, pertaining to persons ‖ personal ‖ intimate ‖ reserved, not freely available ‖ domestic, family.

PRIVAR.
v, to deprive, take away ‖ to disenfranchise ‖ to impound, seize, confiscate ‖ to divest ‖ to dispossess, evict ‖ to repossess, foreclose ‖ to prohibit, impede, block (entry) ‖ to spread a doctrine or theory.

PRIVARSE.
v, to deprive oneself, abstain.

PRIVATISTA.
m, lawyer who specializes in law pertaining to private matters (as opposed to public law) ‖ person who favors privatizing public enterprises.

PRIVATIVO.
m, cause of PRIVACIÓN ‖ exclusive ‖ personal, one's own ‖ excluding ‖ characteristic.

PRIVILEGIADO.
m, privileged person ‖ adj, privileged ‖ first, principal ‖ preferred ‖ favorite ‖ extraordinary.

PRIVILEGIAR.
v, to grant or recognize a privilege or preference ‖ to prefer ‖ to relieve of obligations or duties ‖ to create a lien ‖ to make payments to some but not all of one's creditors.

PRIVILEGIO.
m, privilege, preference ‖ security interest ‖ priority ‖ exemption ‖ license ‖ right ‖ instrument containing such privilege or preference or exemption.

PRIVILEGIO AFIRMATIVO.
grant of a privilege to act.

PRIVILEGIO CIVIL.
creditor's preference or privilege over the payment of other creditors (arising purely from the provisions of civil law).

PRIVILEGIO CONVENCIONAL.
contractual privilege or priority or preference or exemption.

PRIVILEGIO DE ACREEDORES.
creditors' preference (in bankruptcy or liquidation).

PRIVILEGIO DE AVOCACIÓN.
privilege to hear a case pending in another jurisdiction ‖ right of removal of a superior court, right of a superior court to remove a case from the jurisdiction of an inferior court to its jurisdiction.

PRIVILEGIO DE EMISIÓN.
privilege to issue bank notes (granted at times

to banking, industrial, or commercial institutions).

PRIVILEGIO DE INDUSTRIA.
See PATENTE INDUSTRIAL.

PRIVILEGIO DE INTRODUCCIÓN.
See PATENTE DE INTRODUCCIÓN.

PRIVILEGIO DE INVENCIÓN.
patent ‖ patent rights ‖ also see PATENTE DE INVENCIÓN.

PRIVILEGIO ESPECIAL.
priority of a creditor's interest in a special type of property held by a debtor in bankruptcy or liquidation.

PRIVILEGIO GENERAL.
priority of creditor's interest in all the property of a debtor in bankruptcy or liquidation.

PRIVILEGIO GRACIOSO.
privilege or priority or exemption or preference granted without regard to the merits of the recipient.

PRIVILEGIO GRATUITO.
gratuitous privilege or priority or preference or exemption.

PRIVILEGIO INTERNACIONAL.
international privilege(s) granted to diplomats of a foreign nation.

PRIVILEGIO NEGATIVO.
exemption from an obligation.

PRIVILEGIO ODIOSO.
privilege or priority or preference or exemption which is immoral or arbitrary or prejudices the rights of third party.

PRIVILEGIO ONEROSO.
privilege or priority or preference or exemption for value.

PRIVILEGIO PERSONAL.
personal privilege or priority or preference or exemption, one that is granted exclusively to a person without right of assignment.

PRIVILEGIO REMUNERATORIO.
privilege or priority or preference or exemption granted for extraordinary services.

PRIVILEGIOS EN LA QUIEBRA.
bankruptcy preferences, preferences granted to creditors within certain classes according to the type of priority interest held.

PRIVILEGIOS MARÍTIMOS.
priorities of creditors' interests resulting from shipping or navigation loans.

PRIVILEGIOS PARLAMENTARIOS.
See PRIVILEGIOS POLÍTICOS.

PRIVILEGIOS POLÍTICOS.
parliamentary or congressional privileges, e.g.
congressional immunity, etc.
PRIVILEGIO REAL.
real license, license or privilege or exemption
which runs with the land.
**PRIVILEGIOS SOBRE BIENES
INMUEBLES.**
creditors' preferences or security interests regarding real property, including those regarding mortgages.
**PRIVILEGIOS SOBRE
BIENES MUEBLES.**
creditors' preferences or security interests in
personal property.
**PRIVILEGIOS Y PRELACIÓN
DE CRÉDITOS.**
See ACREEDOR PRIVILEGIADO.
PRO.
m, advantage, benefit ‖ adj, pro ‖ positive.
"PRO DOMO SUA".
to the benefit of one's own house (to the ex-
clusion of others' interests).
PRO FORMA.
pro forma.
PRO FÓRMULA.
See PRO FORMA.
PRO INDIVISO.
pro indiviso, undivided, joint, in common
(regarding property ownership).
PRO OPERARIO.
in favor of the worker. Rule of statutory or
contractual interpretation, requiring a deci-
sion favorable to the worker, in case of doubt.
PRO RATA.
See PRORRATA.
PRO REO.
Doubtful cases must be resolved in favor of
the accused.
PRO TRIBUNAL.
before the court, in court.
PROBABLE.
adj, probable ‖ provable, demonstrable.
PROBANZA.
f, discovery ‖ proof, evidence.
PROBAR.
v, to prove, show, demonstrate ‖ to test (a person or thing) ‖ to taste ‖ to try (something) out
‖ to try.
PROBAR UNA COARTADA.
to establish an alibi (either by positive proof of

where one was, or negative proof of not having
been seen).
PROBATORIA.
f, discovery period, period during which evidence may be produced and submitted to the
court.
PROBATORIO.
m, discovery period, period during which evidence may be produced and submitted to the
court ‖ adj, evidentiary, discovery ‖ probative,
effective to prove the truth of a matter.
PROBIDAD.
f, rectitude, probity, honor ‖ moral integrity.
PROBLEMA.
m, problem, issue ‖ question ‖ conflict, matter
in dispute.
PROBLEMA SOCIAL.
social problem or question. Includes in particular problems and solutions arising out of
the class struggle.
PROBLEMÁTICA.
f, body or set of problems and issues related to
a given matter ‖ diplomatic inquiry or investigation into the nature and interests involved
in a problem and its solutions.
PROBLEMÁTICO.
adj, problematic ‖ doubtful, uncertain ‖ possible.
PROBO.
adj, honorable, fair, just ‖ impartial ‖ honest.
PROCACIDAD.
f, insolence ‖ obscenity ‖ shamelessness ‖ im-
pudence.
PROCAZ.
adj, insolent ‖ obscene ‖ shameless ‖ impu-
dent
PROCEDENCIA.
f, origin, source ‖ point or port or station or
airport of departure ‖ legal basis of a complaint or claim ‖ conformity with that which is
moral or reasonable or legal.
PROCEDENTE.
adj, proceeding, deriving, originating ‖ legal,
lawful, in agreement with the law ‖ according
to law ‖ according to reason or order or practice or usage.
PROCEDER.
m, comportment, conduct ‖ bearing ‖ action ‖
v, to proceed, originate, derive (from) ‖ to
conduct oneself ‖ to file or initiate a lawsuit ‖
to be legal or in accordance with the law.

PROCEDER CONTRA UNO.
to make or file a criminal complaint against someone ‖ to proceed against someone.

PROCEDIMENTAL.
adj, procedural.

PROCEDIMIENTO.
m, procedure, system, method ‖ regulatory rules by which certain governmental entities act ‖ act of proceeding ‖ (legal) proceeding or proceedings ‖ legal process or procedure.

PROCEDIMIENTO ACUSATORIO.
type of indictment or arraignment or information hearing, criminal procedure regarding an accusation against a defendant and his or her defense against such accusation, proceeding in which accusation against an accused is formally made. Distinguished from PROCEDIMIENTO INQUISITIVO.

PROCEDIMIENTO ADMINISTRATIVO.
administrative proceeding .
See PROCEDIMIENTO CONTENCIOSOADMINISTRATIVO.

PROCEDIMIENTO ARBITRAL DEL TRABAJO.
Arbitration proceeding in labour matters. See ARBITRAJE LABORAL and LAUDO ARBITRAL.

PROCEDIMIENTO CIVIL.
See PROCEDIMIENTO JUDICIAL.

PROCEDIMIENTO CONTENCIOSOADMINISTRATIVO.
judicial proceeding regarding administrative matters.

PROCEDIMIENTO CONTRADICTORIO.
adversary proceeding, one in which the parties hold contradictory positions.

PROCEDIMIENTO DE APREMIO.
See APREMIO.

PROCEDIMIENTO DE GUERRA.
military proceedings (at time of war or hostilities) ‖ war tactics.

PROCEDIMIENTO DE OFICIO.
judicially-initiated proceedings, those initiated sua sponte by the court.

PROCEDIMIENTO EJECUTIVO.
See JUICIO EJECUTIVO.

PROCEDIMIENTO EN REBELDÍA.
proceedings which must be followed when a defendant has failed to appear (e.g. giving notice by publication, registering the fact that the defendant has failed to appear, etc.).

PROCEDIMIENTO ESCRITO.
written proceeding, legal proceeding which is carried out entirely by submission of written documents.

PROCEDIMIENTO ESPECIAL DE MARINA.
special naval hearing (to deal with certain limited matters).

PROCEDIMIENTO EXTRAORDINARIO.
extraordinary proceeding subject to special rules (as distinguished from an ordinary proceeding).

PROCEDIMIENTO GUBERNATIVO.
See PROCEDIMIENTO ADMINISTRATIVO.

PROCEDIMIENTO INQUISITIVO.
inquisition, proceeding in which the judge inquires and accuses without requiring an accusation to be made by a private party or the state's attorney. Distinguished from PROCEDIMIENTO ACUSATORIO.

PROCEDIMIENTO INTERNACIONAL.
proceedings before the International Court of Justice ‖ proceedings before an international court or arbitrator of disputes between nations.

PROCEDIMIENTO JUDICIAL.
judicial proceeding or proceedings, entirety of legal steps and forms which regulate judicial dispute resolution.

PROCEDIMIENTO LABORAL.
employee grievance hearing, hearing which involves labor dispute (in such courts as have jurisdiction over such matters).

PROCEDIMIENTO LEGISLATIVO.
See PROCEDIMIENTO PARLAMENTARIO.

PROCEDIMIENTO MILITAR.
military hearing or proceedings.

PROCEDIMIENTO MONITORIO.
See PROCESO MONITORIO.

PROCEDIMIENTO ORAL.
oral proceeding, legal proceeding which is carried out by oral argumentation.

PROCEDIMIENTO ORDINARIO.
See JUICIO ORDINARIO.

PROCEDIMIENTO PARLAMENTARIO.
legislative or congressional or parliamentary law- making rules, all steps necessary to pass bill into law.

PROCEDIMIENTO PENAL.
criminal proceedings, entirety of steps involved in the investigation, indictment, trial, and sentencing of a criminally accused.

PROCEDIMIENTO POR FALTAS.
disciplinary hearing or proceeding.
PROCEDIMIENTO SUMARÍSIMO.
See JUICIO SUMARÍSIMO.
PROCEDIMIENTO SUMARIO.
See JUICIO SUMARIO.
PROCER.
m, founding father ‖ national hero.
PROCESADO.
m, accused, defendant ‖ indicted or arraigned defendant ‖ adj, indicted, arraigned.
PROCESAL.
adj, procedural (including trial), pertaining to legal proceedings.
PROCESALISTA.
f, m, lawyer specializing in procedural law.
PROCESAMIENTO.
m, processing, act of processing ‖ indictment, information, statement of the existence of prima facie evidence of guilt.
PROCESAR.
v, to prosecute, try ‖ to file a lawsuit ‖ to sue ‖ to indict.
PROCESIÓN.
f, procession ‖ action of proceeding.
PROCESO.
m, progress, advance ‖ passage or lapse of time ‖ phases, stages ‖ (legal) proceedings or proceeding or process, entirety of acts in a lawsuit ‖ litigation, legal proceeding, lawsuit, suit, case, (legal) action ‖ criminal or penal action ‖ trial.
PROCESO ACCESORIO.
collateral action (whether before, during, or after the principal action).
PROCESO ACUMULATIVO.
joint action, lawsuit in which a number of related actions are joined.
PROCESO ADMINISTRATIVO.
administrative action.
PROCESO ANORMAL.
legal process which is abused, use of proceeding for ends other than those for which it was intended ‖ irregular proceeding, lawsuit in which the procedural rules are not observed.
PROCESO CAUTELAR.
proceeding to obtain a preliminary order to protect a right which would otherwise be irreparably damaged.
PROCESO CIVIL.
civil action or proceeding, action deriving from a private right.

PROCESO COMERCIAL.
commercial action or proceeding (in courts of general jurisdiction or those which maintain separate jurisdictions for commercial matters).
PROCESO CONSTITUTIVO.
legal proceeding to establish, modify, or extinguish a legal right.
PROCESO CONTENCIOSO.
contentious or disputed litigation ‖ adversary proceeding.
PROCESO CRIMINAL.
See PROCESO PENAL.
PROCESO DE COGNICIÓN.
proceeding to decide a legal issue (as opposed to that to enforce such a decision).
PROCESO DE EJECUCIÓN.
executory proceeding, proceeding to enforce a judicial decision or a legal right.
PROCESO DE NUREMBERG.
Nuremberg trials.
PROCESO DECLARATIVO.
declaratory judgment action.
PROCESO DISPOSITIVO.
decision in a governing or leading or controlling or authoritative case which creates a legal principle or rule where there is no governing law.
PROCESO EJECUTIVO.
See PROCESO DE EJECUCIÓN.
PROCESO ESPECIAL.
extraordinary proceeding, any action which is not subject to ordinary legal procedure or trial. Opposed to PROCESO ORDINARIO.
PROCESO INCIDENTAL.
type of collateral proceeding which arises as a result of and during another.
PROCESO JURISDICCIONAL.
judicial proceeding.
PROCESO LABORAL COLECTIVO.
litigation pertaining to union or collective labor disputes.
PROCESO MONITORIO.
civil proceeding to obtain an injunction or court order ‖ also see PROCESO DE COGNICIÓN.
PROCESO ORDINARIO.
regular or ordinary proceeding. Opposed to PROCESO ESPECIAL.
PROCESO PENAL.
criminal proceeding.

PROCESO PREPARATORIO.
type or collateral action which is resolved prior to the principal action.

PROCESO PRINCIPAL.
principal action.

PROCESO SIMULADO.
type of collusive action to obtain judicial sanction of an illegal activity or action.

PROCESO SOCIAL.
social process.

PROCESOS CONTRA ANIMALES.
procedures or techniques which harm animals.

PROCLAMA.
f, proclamation, public notice ‖ (government) proclamation or announcement (whether written or oral) ‖ marriage banns.

PROCLAMACIÓN.
f, proclamation, declaration, publication of a law, decree, etc. ‖ inauguration of a new head of state ‖ public acclaim.

PROCLAMACIÓN DE CANDIDATOS.
issuance or publication of a slate of candidates

PROCLAMAR.
v, to proclaim, declare ‖ to publish legal notice ‖ to announce, designate (a person for a position) ‖ to declare (a candidate to be the winner of an election), announce (final election results) ‖ to inaugurate (a new head of state).

PROCLAMARSE.
v, to proclaim oneself (e.g. to be head of state).

PROCLAMAS DE MATRIMONIO.
marriage banns.

PROCLAMAS MATRIMONIALES.
See PROCLAMAS DE MATRIMONIO.

PROCLIVIDAD.
f, proclivity, inclination, propensity, tendency.

PROCREACIÓN.
f, procreation ‖ conception.

PROCREADOR.
m, procreator ‖ conceiver.

PROCREAR.
v, to procreate ‖ to conceive.

PROCURACIÓN.
f, careful or diligent treatment or management ‖ power of attorney, legal power or authorization, proxy ‖ procurer ‖ attorney's or lawyer's or barrister's office ‖ post of procurer ‖ post of attorney, lawyer, barrister.

PROCURACIÓN APUD ACTA.
power of attorney which results from the court file related to a given proceeding.

PROCURACIÓN ESPECIAL.
See PODER ESPECIAL.

PROCURACIÓN EXTRAJUDICIAL.
See MANDATO.

PROCURACIÓN GENERAL.
See MANDATO GENERAL.

PROCURACIÓN JUDICIAL.
See MANDATO JUDICIAL.

PROCURADOR.
m, prosecuting attorney, state's attorney ‖ attorney general; attorney, lawyer (in U.S.), barrister (in G.B.), person who is licensed to represent clients in court and has the corresponding power of attorney ‖ proxy, agent, representative, attorney ‖ town clerk or treasurer ‖ village or town representative.

PROCURADOR DE TRIBUNALES.
See PROCURADOR JUDICIAL.

PROCURADOR GENERAL DE LA NACIÓN.
Attorney General.

PROCURADOR JUDICIAL.
legal representative, attorney, lawyer (in U.S.), barrister (in G.B.), person who is licensed to represent clients in court and has the corresponding power of attorney

PROCURADOR VOLUNTARIO.
type of agent of absentee without his authorization (for reasons of friendship or family relations).

PROCURADORA.
f, female prosecuting attorney or state's attorney ‖ female attorney general ‖ female attorney or lawyer (in U.S.), female barrister (in G.B.), woman who is licensed to represent clients in court and has the corresponding power of attorney ‖ female proxy or agent or representative or attorney ‖ female town clerk or treasurer ‖ female village or town representative ‖ madame (of a bordello) ‖ female go-between or bawd.

PROCURADURÍA.
f, office of PROCURADOR or PROCURADORA ‖ position and functions of PROCURADOR or PROCURADORA.

PROCURAR.
v, to procure, obtain ‖ to try, endeavor, attempt ‖ to produce ‖ to act as agent or attor-

ney or proxy or representative ‖ to manage or take care of something for a specific purpose.

PROCURAR POR.
to act as agent or attorney or proxy or representative for.

"PROCURATOR".
See PROCURADOR.

PRODICIÓN.
See ALEVOSÍA.

PRODIGALIDAD.
f, prodigality, wastefulness, waste, extravagance ‖ abundance.

PRÓDIGAMENTE.
adv, prodigally, wastefully, extravagantly ‖ abundantly, excessively.

PRODIGAR.
v, to waste, squander ‖ to give abundantly ‖ to praise lavishly ‖ to lavish favors on.

PRODIGIADOR.
m, fortune teller.

PRODIGIO.
m, wonder, miracle ‖ prodigy, precocious person.

PRODIGIOSO.
adj, prodigious, extraordinary ‖ excellent.

PRÓDIGO.
m, prodigal, prodigal person, wastrel, squanderer ‖ generous person ‖ adj, generous, lavish ‖ wasteful, extravagant, prodigal.

PRODUCCIÓN.
f, production (in all senses) ‖ product ‖ products, produce, yield.

PRODUCIDOR.
m, producer ‖ adj, producing.

PRODUCIR.
v, to produce ‖ to create, found ‖ to manufacture, construct, fabricate ‖ to yield, bear (e.g. interest, fruits) ‖ to make ‖ to produce or present (proof or explanations to support a complaint or right).

PRODUCTIVIDAD.
f, productivity ‖ rate of production.

PRODUCTIVO.
adj, productive.

PRODUCTO.
m, product ‖ benefit ‖ return, yield, profit ‖ income ‖ production ‖ produce. PRODUCTO implies either a transformation of raw materials or production at irregular intervals.

PRODUCTO BRUTO.
gross product ‖ gross production.

PRODUCTO BRUTO INTERNO.
gross domestic product.

PRODUCTO BRUTO NACIONAL.
gross national product.

PRODUCTO NACIONAL NETO.
net national product.

PRODUCTO NETO.
net product ‖ net production.

PRODUCTO NETO INTERNO.
net domestic product.

PRODUCTOR.
m, producer ‖ farmer or industrialist.

PROFANACIÓN.
f, profanation ‖ desecration, irreverence ‖ abuse, lack of respect ‖ dishonor ‖ prostitution.

PROFANACIÓN DE CADÁVERES.
desecration of corpses. Usually considered to be a crime.

PROFANACIÓN DE LAS SAGRADAS FORMAS.
desecration of sacred forms of the Eucharist. Usually considered to be a crime.

PROFANACIÓN DE OBJETOS SAGRADOS.
desecration of sacred or religious objects. Usually considered to be a crime.

PROFANADOR.
m, profaner, defiler, desecrator.

PROFANAR.
v, to profane ‖ to desecrate, defile ‖ to abuse ‖ to dishonor, prostitute.

PROFANIDAD.
f, profanity.

PROFANO.
adj, profane, irreverent, disrespectful ‖ secular ‖ lacking in knowledge of a specific subject ‖ licentious, libertine.

PROFECTICIO.
adj, received from a father (in terms of property).

PROFESAR.
v, to exercise a profession, art or science ‖ to teach an art or science ‖ to profess ‖ to confess, admit (an opinion or doctrine) ‖ to feel affection.

PROFESIÓN.
f, profession (in all senses) ‖ occupation.

PROFESIÓN LIBERAL.
liberal arts profession, profession in which there is no regular employment relationship

between professional and client and regarding which the fees are determined by the professional.

PROFESIONAL.
f, m, professional ‖ prostitute ‖ liberal arts professional ‖ adj, professional.

PROFESIONALIDAD.
f, exercise of a profession ‖ professionalism

PROFESIONALIDAD DELICTIVA.
illegal exercise of a profession ‖ professional criminality, exercise of crime as a profession ‖ criminal career, crime exercised as a career.

PROFESIONALIDAD DELICTUAL.
See PROFESIONALIDAD DELICTIVA.

PROFESIONALISMO.
m, professionalism.

PROFESIONALIZAR.
v, to become a profession ‖ to become a professional.

PROFESOR.
m, professor, teacher ‖ person who practices an art or science.

PROFESORADO.
m, professorship ‖ professoriate, faculty, teaching staff ‖ body of professors or teachers in a certain field or physical area.

PROFESORAL.
adj, professorial, pertaining to a professor ‖ characteristic of a professorship.

PROFILÁCTICO.
m, prophylactic, condom, sheath ‖ adj, prophylactic, protective, preservative.

PROFILAXIS SOCIAL.
f, means (used by government) to halt the spread of sexually-communicated diseases.

PRÓFUGO.
m, fugitive, fugitive from justice, person imputed in, or accused or convicted of a crime who fails to a appear for trial ‖ escapee (from prison) ‖ draft dodger.

PROFUNDIDAD.
f, depth, deepness, profundity, profoundness ‖ great depth.

PROFUNDIZAR.
v, to go into (something) in detail or depth ‖ to make deeper, deepen.

PROFUNDO.
adj, profound ‖ deep ‖ extensive ‖ intense ‖ obscure, difficult to understand.

PROGENIE.
f, progeny, issue, offspring.

PROGENITOR.
m, progenitor, mother or father ‖ ancestor.

PROGENITURA.
f, progeny ‖ See PRIMOGÉNITO ‖ primogeniture.

PROGRAMA.
m, program ‖ plan, schedule ‖ edict, government notice, bann ‖ platform, (political) plan of action ‖ topic of discussion (for a talk) ‖ (course) program ‖ list of conditions or prerequisites.

PROGRAMACIÓN.
f, programming, establishment of a program or schedule.

PROGRAMAR.
v, to program ‖ to plan, schedule.

PROGRESAR.
v, to progress, improve ‖ to advance (socially, politically, or economically).

PROGRESISMO.
m, progressivism.

PROGRESISTA.
f, m, progressive, follower of progressivism.

PROGRESIVO.
adj, progressive ‖ increasing ‖ advancing, improving ‖ progressive (tax or freedom).

PROGRESO.
m, progress ‖ increase ‖ advance, advancement ‖ improvement, betterment.

PROGRESO SOCIAL.
social progress.

PROHIBICIÓN.
f, prohibition, interdiction ‖ impediment, inhibition.

PROHIBICIÓN DE COMERCIAR.
prohibition against dealing or trading or trafficking or doing business with.

PROHIBICIÓN DE COMPRAR.
prohibition against the purchase of.

PROHIBICIÓN DE ENAJENAR.
prohibition against the transfer of (property).

PROHIBICIÓN DE TRABAJO.
prohibition against working or employment.

PROHIBICIONES MATRIMONIALES.
See IMPEDIMENTOS MATRIMONIALES.

PROHIBICIONISMO.
m, prohibitionism.

PROHIBICIONISTA.
f, prohibitionist.

PROHIBIDO.
adj, prohibited, denied, forbidden.

PROHIBIDO ENTRAR.
no admittance, keep out.
PROHIBIDO ESTACIONAR.
no parking, parking prohibited.
PROHIBIDO FUMAR.
smoking forbidden or prohibited.
PROHIBIR.
v, to prohibit, forbid, deny ‖ to ban ‖ to impede, inhibit ‖ to be opposed to.
PROHIBITIVO.
adj, prohibitive.
PROHIBITORIO.
adj, prohibitory.
PROHIJADOR.
m, adoptive parent, adopter.
PROHIJACIÓN.
See PROHIJAMIENTO.
PROHIJAMIENTO.
m, adoption (of a child).
PROHIJAR.
v, to adopt (a child in law or in fact) ‖ to adopt (ideas) ‖ to protect, support.
PROINDIVISIÓN.
f, indivision, state of (property) being undivided.
PRÓJIMA.
f, slut.
PRÓJIMO.
m, fellow man ‖ mankind.
PROLACIÓN.
f, pronouncement ‖ declaration, statement.
PROLE.
f, offspring, progeny, issue ‖ descendant(s).
PROLETARIADO.
m, proletariat.
PROLETARIO.
m, worker ‖ indigent ‖ pleb ‖ proletarian ‖ adj, proletarian ‖ common ‖ poor, plebeian.
PROLIFERACIÓN.
f, proliferation.
PROLÍFICO.
adj, prolific.
PRÓLOGO.
m, prologue.
PROLONGACIÓN.
f, prolongation ‖ extension.
PROLONGACIÓN DE ATRIBUCIONES.
(illegal) extension of military rule.
PROLONGACIÓN DE FUNCIONES PÚBLICAS.
(illegal) continuation in or prolongation of public office.

PROLONGAR.
v, to prolong, extend.
PROMEDIAR.
v, to average ‖ to divide equally ‖ to mediate ‖ to split the difference ‖ to get to the middle (of a time period), be half way through (something).
PROMEDIO.
m, average, mean ‖ adj, average, mean.
PROMEDIO DE EDAD.
average age.
PROMEDIO DE VIDA.
average life span or lifetime.
PROMESA.
f, promise, unilateral statement of obligation ‖ unilateral contract (without consideration). May be considered to be an enforceable, contractual obligation.
PROMESA A DÍA CIERTO.
promise to be fulfilled by a date certain.
PROMESA CONDICIONAL.
conditional promise.
PROMESA DE ACCIONES.
stock option.
PROMESA DE COMPRA.
enforceable promise to purchase, unilateral purchase agreement (without consideration) although this is usually considered to be an enforceable contract.
PROMESA DE COMPRA Y VENTA.
buy-sell agreement, purchase agreement, sales agreement ‖ agreement to agree to purchase or sell, preliminary contract to purchase or sell ‖ earnest money agreement.
PROMESA DE COMPRAVENTA.
See PROMESA DE COMPRA Y VENTA.
PROMESA DE CONTRATO.
preliminary contract in which the parties agree to formally execute a contract at a future point in time.
PROMESA DE MATRIMONIO.
agreement to marry.
PROMESA DE MEJORAR.
enforceable promise to improve the promisee's share of an inheritance or estate.
PROMESA DE PAGO.
promise to pay ‖ offer to pay.
PROMESA DE RECOMPENSA.
See PROMESA PÚBLICA DE RECOMPENSA.
PROMESA DE VENTA.
option, enforceable promise to sell, unilateral

sales agreement (with or without consideration although this is usually considered to be
an enforceable contract).

PROMESA MIXTA.
conditional promise to be fulfilled by a date
certain.

PROMESA PARA DELINQUIR.
monetary agreement to commit a crime for
pay.

PROMESA PÚBLICA.
See PROMESA PÚBLICA DE RECOMPENSA.

PROMESA PÚBLICA DE RECOMPENSA.
formal promise to pay a reward or prize (a
member(s) of the public at large for doing or
not doing something).

PROMESA PURA.
simple promise, promise which is subject to
neither a term nor a condition.

PROMESA SIMPLE.
See PROMESA PURA ‖ promise which is formalized in no way.

PROMETER.
v, to promise ‖ to unilaterally obligate oneself
‖ to assure upon oath to the truth of a matter
‖ to offer, make an offer or proposal.

PROMETERSE.
v, to mutually agree to marry.

PROMETIDA.
f, fiancee.

PROMETIDO.
m, promise ‖ contents of a promise ‖ fiance ‖
adj, promised.

PROMETIENTE.
m, promisor ‖ offeror ‖ contractor, contracting party.

PROMETIMIENTO.
m, promise ‖ offer.

PROMISCUIDAD.
f, promiscuity ‖ mixture, confusion ‖ cohabitation.

PROMISCUIDAD SEXUAL.
sexual promiscuity.

PROMISCUO.
adj, promiscuous ‖ joint, in common.

PROMOCIÓN.
f, promotion (in all senses) ‖ advancement ‖
initiative ‖ progress ‖ class, year, group of students who finish their studies at the same time
‖ group of persons who are named to a position, or are given a promotion at the same time
‖ publicity.

PROMOCIÓN FAMILIAR.
promotion of large families.

PROMOCIÓN INDUSTRIAL.
industrial promotion.

PROMOTOR.
m, promoter ‖ leader or instigator of a revolt
or riot.

PROMOTOR DE LA FE.
devil's advocate.

PROMOTOR DE SEDICIÓN.
instigator or leader of sedition.

PROMOTOR FISCAL.
See MINISTERIO FISCAL.

PROMOVEDOR.
See PROMOTOR.

PROMOVER.
v, to promote ‖ to initiate, start ‖ to advance
progress ‖ to protect, provide protection ‖ to
be promoted.

PROMULGACIÓN.
f, promulgation ‖ public notification or notice
‖ legal publication ‖ propagation ‖ promulga
tion (of a statute).

PROMULGADOR.
m, promulgator ‖ head of state.

PRONÓSTICO.
m, prognosis ‖ omen, sign ‖ prognostication
prediction, forecast.

PRONÓSTICO DEL TIEMPO.
weather forecast.

**PRONÓSTICO
RESERVADO.**
reserved or provisional prognosis.

PRONTUARIO.
m, note, memo, notation (to jog one's memo
ry) ‖ compendium or summary of the rule
pertaining to an art of science ‖ handbook
manual ‖ (police) dossier, blotter.

PRONUNCIAMIENTO.
m, pronouncement, announcement ‖ judicia
order or decision or judgment ‖ issuance o
pronouncement of a judicial decision ‖ deci
sion regarding each disputed claim ‖ phas
during which a judicial decision is issued
military uprising or revolt ‖ rebellion, seditior

PRONUNCIAR.
v, to pronounce ‖ to determine, resolve ‖ to
pronounce or issue and publish a judicial sen
tence or decision or order or judgment ‖ to re
bel, revolt ‖ to instigate a coup d'etat or mili
tary uprising.

PRONUNCIARSE.

v, to rebel, revolt ‖ to instigate a coup d'etat or military uprising ‖ to go on record (regarding one's opinion).

PROPAGANDA.

f, propaganda.

PROPAGANDA DE GUERRA.

war propaganda.

PROPAGAR.

v, to propagate, multiply ‖ to spread ‖ to advertise, spread publicity (about a product, etc.) ‖ to divulge ‖ to increase.

PROPASAR.

v, to exceed the limits.

PROPENDER.

v, to have a propensity toward.

PROPENSIÓN.

m, propensity, inclination, tendency.

PROPENSIÓN A LA DETENCIÓN.

tendency to be arrested.

PROPENSIÓN A LA IMPORTACIÓN.

tendency or propensity to import.

PROPENSIÓN A LA INVERSIÓN.

tendency or propensity to invest.

PROPENSIÓN AL AHORRO.

tendency or propensity to save.

PROPENSIÓN AL ARRESTO.

See PROPENSIÓN A LA DETENCIÓN.

PROPENSIÓN AL CONSUMO.

tendency or propensity to consume.

PROPENSIÓN AL DELITO.

criminal tendency or propensity.

PROPIA IMAGEN.

one's own image.

PROPIAMENTE.

adv, properly, correctly ‖ strictly, strictly speaking ‖ appropriately.

PROPICIAR.

v, to propitiate, appease (anger) ‖ to support, defend (a cause) ‖ to sponsor ‖ to propose.

PROPICIO.

adj, propitious, favorable.

PROPIEDAD.

f, property (in all senses) ‖ possession, holding, holdings, estate ‖ ownership, proprietorship ‖ attribute, essential quality ‖ assets.

PROPIEDAD APARENTE.

apparent holding or estate ‖ apparent ownership or proprietorship.

PROPIEDAD ARTÍSTICA.

artistic property.

See PROPIEDAD INTELLECTUAL.

PROPIEDAD COLECTIVA.

collectively-held property or proprietorship.

PROPIEDAD COMUNAL.

communal property ‖ jointly held property, property held in common (by group of neighbors) ‖ joint ownership, ownership in common (by group of neighbors).

PROPIEDAD CONDICIONAL.

contingent or conditional ownership ‖ contingent or conditional estate, such as is subject to a contingency or condition subsequent or precedent.

PROPIEDAD DE LA PRODUCCIÓN.

ownership of property resulting from manufacturing or other types of production.

PROPIEDAD DE LOS MEDIOS DE PRODUCCIÓN.

ownership of means of production.

PROPIEDAD ENEMIGA.

enemy holdings or property.

PROPIEDAD HORIZONTAL.

condominium property or holding ‖ ownership of condominium property.

PROPIEDAD IMPERFECTA.

limited ownership, ownership subject to limitations (e.g. easement rights, etc.).

PROPIEDAD INDUSTRIAL.

industrial property, such as is used for industrial purposes ‖ intellectual property, industrial property, property rights of an inventor ‖ ownership of industrial property (in either of the above senses).

PROPIEDAD INMATERIAL.

intangible property ‖ ownership of intangible property.

PROPIEDAD INMOBILIARIA.

real property, real estate ‖ ownership of real property or real estate.

PROPIEDAD INCORPORAL.

See PROPIEDAD INMATERIAL.

PROPIEDAD INTELECTUAL.

intellectual property ‖ ownership of intellectual property.

PROPIEDAD LITERARIA.

literary property ‖ proprietorship of literary property.

PROPIEDAD MINERA.
mining property ‖ mine ownership ‖ ownership of mining rights.

PROPIEDAD PRIVADA.
private property ‖ private ownership ‖ private holdings.

Opposed to PROPIEDAD COLECTIVA.

PROPIEDAD PRO INDIVISO.
See PROINDIVISIÓN and CONDOMINIO.

PROPIEDAD RURAL.
agricultural or forest property ‖ ownership of agricultural or forest property ‖ agricultural or forest holding ‖ rural property ‖ rural ownership.

PROPIEDAD RÚSTICA.
See PROPIEDAD RURAL.

PROPIEDAD URBANA.
urban real estate ‖ ownership of urban real estate ‖ urban property or holding.

PROPIEDAD VERTICAL.
above- and under-ground property ‖ ownership of above- and under-ground property.

PROPIEDADES ESPECIALES.
properties which are not classified within a civil code.

PROPIETARIO.
m, owner, proprietor, title holder ‖ adj, proprietary.

PROPIETARIOS DE BUQUES.
ship owners. When a ship is owned by more than one person law may assume that it is owned as a type of partnership.

PROPINA.
f, tip, gratuity (for services rendered or to be rendered).

PROPINAR.
v, to hit, give a blow to.

PROPIO.
m, messenger, courier ‖ government real property or establishments that are used to pay public debts ‖ adj, ones' own ‖ characteristic ‖ peculiar ‖ private ‖ appropriate ‖ own, natural (vs. artificial) ‖ self.

PROPIOS.
See BIENES COMUNALES.

PROPONEDOR.
m, proponent, proposer.

PROPONENTE.
m, proponent, proposer.

PROPONER.
v, to propose, make a proposal, suggest ‖ to offer ‖ to move, put forward ‖ to develop a proposal ‖ to nominate (a person for a position) ‖ to set forth the pros and cons of a matter ‖ to pose a matter of discussion ‖ to intend, propose to.

PROPORCIÓN.
f, proportion (in all senses) ‖ opportunity, occasion ‖ size, dimension ‖ scale, proportion.

PROPORCIONADO.
adj, appropriate, apt ‖ able, suitable, fit.

PROPORCIONAL.
adj, proportional.

PROPORCIONALMENTE.
adv, proportionally.

PROPORCIONAR.
v, to apportion ‖ to procure, furnish, supply, provide ‖ to make proportionate.

PROPOSICIÓN.
f, proposition, proposal ‖ act of proposing ‖ offer ‖ reasoning, argument, support ‖ improper insinuation, proposition ‖ motion ‖ resolution.

PROPOSICIÓN DE DELITO.
See PROPOSICIÓN DELICTIVA.

PROPOSICIÓN DE LEY.
(legislative or congressional) bill ‖ draft bill.

PROPOSICIÓN DELICTIVA.
criminal proposition, proposal to commit a crime.

PROPOSICIÓN DESHONESTA.
(sexual) proposition or overtures or advances. May or may not be a crime.

PROPÓSITO.
m, intention, goal, objective, aim ‖ will ‖ theme, matter, issue.

PROPÓSITOS DE LAS NACIONES UNIDAS.
objectives of the United Nations.

PROPTER NUPTIAS.
because of marriage.

PROPTER REM.
the condition of obligations which are transferred together with the thing they refer to, specially real estate.

PROPUESTA.
f, proposal, proposition ‖ offer ‖ invitation ‖ requirement of a decision or opinion ‖ nomination (for a position, etc.).

PROPUESTO.
adj, proposed, offered ‖ resolved (on one's own).

PROPUGNAR.
v, to actively defend ‖ to protect, support.
PROPULSA.
f, impulse, stimulus ‖ repulse, rejection.
PROPULSAR.
v, to repulse, reject, rebuff ‖ to impel, propel, drive (forward).
PROPULSIÓN.
f, propulsion ‖ energy, force, drive ‖ stimulus, impulse.
PROPULSOR.
m, propeller ‖ driving force, stimulator ‖ protector.
PRORRATA.
adj, pro rata, proportional.
PRORRATEAR.
v, to divide proportionally or pro rata.
PRORRATEO.
m, proportional or pro rata division.
PRÓRROGA.
f, prorogation ‖ extension (of a term) ‖ deferral ‖ postponement, continuance (of a matter or case to another time) ‖ expansion of jurisdiction to things or person not initially covered.
PRÓRROGA ARRENDATICIA.
extension of a real property lease or rental agreement.
PRÓRROGA DE INCORPORACIÓN A FILAS.
draft deferral, deferral of military service.
PRÓRROGA DE JURISDICCIÓN.
jurisdictional clause, covenant submitting any possible disputes to a given jurisdiction.
PRORROGABLE.
adj, extendable ‖ continuable ‖ expandable ‖ deferrable.
PRORROGACIÓN.
See PRÓRROGA.
PRORROGADO.
adj, deferred ‖ extended ‖ continued ‖ amplified (jurisdictionally).
PRORROGAR.
v, to continue ‖ to extend (a term) ‖ to defer ‖ to continue (a matter or case) ‖ to expand jurisdiction ‖ to postpone, put off, defer.
PROSAPIA.
f, ancestry, lineage.
PROSCRIBIR.
v, to proscribe ‖ to deport, expel (from a nation) ‖ to prohibit ‖ to annul, void ‖ to invalidate ‖ to abolish.

PROSCRIPCIÓN.
f, proscription ‖ deportation, expulsion ‖ prohibition ‖ annulment, voidance ‖ invalidation ‖ abolition.
PROSCRIPTOR.
m, proscriber ‖ expeller ‖ prohibitor ‖ annuller, voider ‖ invalidator ‖ abolisher.
PROSCRIPTO.
m, deportee ‖ adj, proscribed ‖ deported, expelled ‖ prohibited ‖ annulled, voided ‖ invalidated ‖ abolished.
PROSECRETARIO.
m, vice-secretary, alternate or substitute secretary.
PROSECUCIÓN.
f, continuation ‖ pursuit.
PROSEGUIR.
v, to continue, persist, go on with ‖ to persevere, insist.
PROSÉLITO.
m, proselyte ‖ follower, believer ‖ member.
PROSPECCIÓN.
f, prospecting ‖ mineral exploration.
PROSPECTO.
m, prospectus ‖ catalogue.
PROSPERIDAD.
f, prosperity ‖ well-being ‖ success ‖ good luck or fortune.
PROSPERIDAD ECONÓMICA.
economic prosperity or well-being.
PROSTÍBULO.
m, brothel, whore-house.
PROSTITUCIÓN.
f, (sexual) prostitution ‖ corruption of a female ‖ degradation, prostitution.
PROSTITUIR.
v, to prostitute a female ‖ to dishonor ‖ to prostitute oneself ‖ to degrade ‖ to profane.
PROSTITUTA.
f, prostitute.
PROTAGONISTA.
f, m, protagonist ‖ principal litigants or parties to an action
PROTECCIÓN.
f, protection, support ‖ favor ‖ favoritism ‖ defense ‖ (economic) protectionism ‖ protection payment ‖ benefit(s) paid a woman for sexual services.
PROTECCIÓN A LA INFANCIA.
protection of minors.

PROTECCIÓN A LA MATERNIDAD.
protection of women during period of maternity (i.e. for a term before, during, and after delivery).
**PROTECCIÓN DE
LAS MINORÍAS.**
protection of minors.
PROTECCIONISMO.
m, (political or economic) protectionism.
PROTECCIONISTA.
f, m, protectionist, person who favors political or economic protectionism ‖ adj, protectionist.
PROTECTOR.
m, protector ‖ defender ‖ supporter ‖ patron ‖ adj, protecting, defending, supporting, defensive, protective.
PROTECTOR DE CHEQUES.
check protector, instrument used to perforate checks to avoid falsification.
PROTECTORADO.
m, protectorate.
PROTECTORADO INTERNACIONAL.
international protectorate, i.e. a protectorate which exists by international agreement.
PROTECTORÍA.
f, protectorate ‖ protectorship, position and functions of a protector.
PROTECTORIO.
adj, pertaining or including protection or support or defense.
PROTEGER.
v, to protect ‖ to support ‖ to defend ‖ to develop, drive forward.
PROTEGIDA.
f, protegee (woman) ‖ adj, kept (woman) ‖ protected.
PROTEGIDO.
m, protegee ‖ adj, protected ‖ supported ‖ defended ‖ favored ‖ adopted ‖ subject of a protectorate.
PROTESTA.
f, sworn statement or attestation to do something ‖ protestation or declaration or affirmation of agreement to do something ‖ protest, objection; legal notice of protest ‖ claim ‖ public statement of belief ‖ protest (of negotiable instrument).
PROTESTA CERTIFICATORIA.
declaratory PROTESTA, one which states the existence or not of a fact.

PROTESTA CONTRA EL MAR.
See PROTESTA DE MAR.
PROTESTA DECLARATORIA.
voluntary PROTESTA.
PROTESTA DE INOCENCIA.
protestation or declaration or statement of innocence (by an accused).
PROTESTA DE MAR.
ship's or captain's protest.
PROTESTA DIPLOMÁTICA.
diplomatic protest.
PROTESTA INHIBITORIA.
See PROTESTA PROHIBITORIA.
PROTESTA INVITATORIA.
PROTESTA which invites action.
PROTESTA MONITORIA.
See PROTESTA INVITATORIA.
PROTESTA PROHIBITORIA.
PROTESTA which prohibits or inhibits action.
PROTESTADO.
m, thing or matter which is the subject of protest or a protestation ‖ adj, protested.
PROTESTANTE.
m, protestant (in all senses) ‖ adj, protestant ‖ protesting.
PROTESTAR.
v, to protest, object ‖ to declare, protest ‖ to state openly ‖ to complain ‖ to make a formal protestation ‖ to file a protest ‖ to profess.
PROTESTAR CONTRA.
to protest against ‖ object to.
PROTESTAR DE.
to declare, protest, affirm ‖ to profess.
PROTESTAR UNA LETRA.
to protest a bill of exchange or draft.
PROTESTATIVO.
adj, declaratory, affirming, affirmative.
PROTESTO.
m, protest (of a negotiable instrument) ‖ document which sets forth such a protest ‖ legal filing or placing on record of such a protest by a notary or special notary ‖ also see PROTESTA.
**PROTESTO
PARA GARANTÍA.**
protest of holder of negotiable instrument for the purposes of guarantying that the payor has deposited funds necessary to cover the instrument.
PROTESTO PARA MAYOR SEGURIDAD.
protest of holder or negotiable instrument to obtain greater guaranty of payment.

PROTESTO POR QUIEBRA DEL LIBRADO.
protest of a negotiable instrument due to bankruptcy of the maker.

PROTOCOLAR.
adj, pertaining to a PROTOCOLO.

PROTOCOLARIO.
adj, formal ‖ ceremonial, ritual.

PROTOCOLIZACIÓN.
f, type of formal registration (of a document in the registry of a notary or special notary public). See ESCRIBANO.

PROTOCOLIZACIÓN DE EXPEDIENTES JUDICIALES.
formal registration of court files or records. See PROTOCOLIZACIÓN.

PROTOCOLIZACIÓN DE TESTAMENTOS.
registration of a will in the files of a notary public.

PROTOCOLIZAR.
v, to register a document formally or officially (with a notary or special notary public) ‖ to formalize, make official.

PROTOCOLO.
m, formal registry of a notary public or special notary public ‖ record of activities held during an international conference or diplomatic meeting ‖ protocol.

PROTONOTARIO.
m, head notary public.

PROTUTELA.
f, guardianship of minors.

PROTUTOR.
m, guardian of a minor ‖ institution which supervises the activities of guardians of minors.

PROVECHO.
m, benefit, utility, usefulness, enjoyment ‖ advantage ‖ profit, margin between purchase and resale price.

PROVECHOS.
m, return on capital ‖ profit.

PROVEEDOR.
m, supplier, purveyor ‖ provider.

PROVEEDURÍA.
f, position or functions or office of a supplier or purveyor ‖ warehouse ‖ wholesale cooperative ‖ retail outlet.

PROVEER.
v, to provide, supply, equip ‖ to issue a judicial decision ‖ to resolve a matter or file ‖ to fill a position or vacancy.

PROVEÍDO.
m, interlocutory order or decision or writ ‖ adj, provided, decided.

PROVEIMIENTO.
m, provision, act of providing.

PROVENIENCIA.
f, origin, start.

PROVENIENTE.
adj, proceeding, originating, resulting ‖ see ACCIÓN CIVIL PROVENIENTE DE DELITO or ACCIÓN PROVENIENTE DE CENSO.

PROVENIR.
v, to originate, start, arise from.

PROVIDENCIA.
f, providence, foresight ‖ prevention ‖ means to repair damage ‖ interlocutory order ‖ decision or writ or order which determines procedural or ancillary matters.

PROVIDENCIA DE MERO TRÁMITE.
interlocutory order.

PROVIDENCIAR.
v, to issue an interlocutory order or an order or decision regarding a procedural or ancillary matter ‖ to take or adopt steps ‖ to order, decide ‖ to command.

PROVIDENCIAS PARA MEJOR PROVEER.
See DILIGENCIAS PARA MEJOR PROVEER.

PROVINCIA.
f, province, part of a nation.

PROVINCIAL.
adj, provincial, pertaining to a province.

PROVINCIALISMO.
m, provincialism.

PROVINCIALIZAR.
v, to change into a province.

PROVINCIANISMO.
m, provincialism.

PROVINCIANO.
m, person from a province (vs. the capital) ‖ country bumpkin, hayseed ‖ adj, provincial.

PROVINCIAS.
f, provinces (vs. the federal district).

PROVISIÓN.
f, provision ‖ measures of care, precautionary steps ‖ provision, food, supply, stock ‖ supplying, provision, purveying ‖ means (to achieve an end) ‖ warehouse, deposit.

PROVISIÓN DE FONDOS.
supply of funds.

PROVISIONAL.
adj, temporary, provisional, interim.

PROVISIONES DE A BORDO.
on board or flight provisions.

PROVISOR.
m, provider ‖ supplier, purveyor.

PROVISTO.
adj, equipped, supplied.

PROVOCACIÓN.
f, provocation, incitement, instigation ‖ irritation ‖ challenge (to action or non-action) ‖ abuse of propriety or courtesy.

PROVOCACIÓN A LA REBELIÓN.
incitement to rebel.

PROVOCACIÓN ADECUADA.
sufficient provocation. Usually constitutes a defense to accusation of crime.

PROVOCACIÓN AL DELITO.
instigation or incitement to commit a crime. If as a result a crime is perpetrated, the PROVOCACIÓN is punished as INDUCCIÓN.
See INDUCCIÓN.

PROVOCACIÓN AL DUELO.
provocation to duel or fight.

PROVOCACIÓN DE DECLARACIÓN DE GUERRA.
provocation to declare war.

PROVOCACIÓN DEL OFENDIDO.
victim's provocation, provocation of the victim which may constitute a justification or an extenuating circumstance.

PROVOCADO.
adj, provoked ‖ done on one's own initiative.

PROVOCADOR.
m, provoker, inciter, instigator ‖ challenger ‖ trouble-maker ‖ adj, irritating, annoying.

PROVOCAR.
v, to provoke, excite, incite, instigate ‖ to challenge ‖ to irritate, annoy, anger, exasperate ‖ to help, cooperate, assist ‖ to cause ‖ to induce ‖ to challenge ‖ to look for a fight ‖ to tempt.

PROVOCATIVO.
adj, provocative (either sexually or otherwise) ‖ see PROVOCADOR.

PROXENETA.
f, m. pimp, procurer, pander, panderer.

PROXENÉTICO.
adj, pertaining to a pimp or procurer or panderer.

PROXENETISMO.
m, pimping, procuring, pandering.

PRÓXIMAMENTE.
adv, soon, immediately.

PROXIMIDAD.
f, proximity (in time and order) ‖ immediacy ‖ nearness, closeness.

PRÓXIMO.
adj, proximate (e.g. cause) ‖ near, close ‖ soon, immediate ‖ alleged; next.

PROYECTAR.
v, to project, throw forward ‖ to plan, prepare, think out.

PROYECTIL.
m, projectile, missile.

PROYECTO.
m, project, plan, design, preparation ‖ project design or plan.

PROYECTO DE LEY.
(legislative) bill, draft of a bill, proposed law.

PRUDENCIA.
f, prudence ‖ moderation ‖ good judgment, wisdom ‖ discretion ‖ care, caution ‖ cowardliness, fear, fright.

PRUDENCIAL.
adj, pertaining to prudence or moderation or good judgment or wisdom or discretion or care or caution or cowardliness or fear or fright.

PRUDENTE.
adj, prudent ‖ moderate ‖ wise ‖ discreet ‖ careful ‖ cautious ‖ cowardly, fearful.

PRUDENTEMENTE.
adv, prudently ‖ moderately ‖ wisely, with good judgment ‖ discreetly ‖ carefully ‖ cautiously ‖ fearfully.

PRUEBA.
f, test ‖ proof, evidence ‖ testimony ‖ supporting argument ‖ sample (of a product). Usually includes, INDICIOS (circumstantial evidence), PRESUNCIONES (legal presumptions or inferences), CONFESIÓN EN JUICIO (in-court confessions), INFORMES (reports), documentary and testimonial evidence (whether given by expert or other witnesses).

PRUEBA ABSOLUTA.
irrefutable or incontrovertible proof or evidence.

PRUEBA ADMISIBLE.
legal evidence ‖ legally admissible evidence ‖ competent evidence, admissible proof ‖ proof which requires judicial authorization to submit ‖ clear and convincing proof.

PRUEBA AISLADA.
uncorroborated proof or evidence.

PRUEBA ANTICIPADA.
pre-litigation obtaining or production of proof or evidence.
PRUEBA CIRCUNSTANCIAL.
See PRUEBA INDICIARIA.
PRUEBA CIVIL.
extrajudicial evidence, type of evidence submitted without the involvement of a judge.
PRUEBA COMERCIAL.
evidence which is regulated by the commercial code.
PRUEBA COMPUESTA.
See PRUEBA INDICIARIA.
PRUEBA COMÚN.
ordinary proof. Usually includes testimonial and documentary proof.
PRUEBA CONCLUYENTE.
conclusive evidence.
PRUEBA CONCURRENTE.
corroborating proof or evidence, cumulative evidence.
PRUEBA CONJETURAL.
See PRUEBA INDICIARIA.
PRUEBA CONTRARIA.
conflicting evidence.
PRUEBA CONVENCIONAL.
evidence the admissibility of which is agreed to by the parties.
PRUEBA CUMPLIDA.
See PRUEBA PLENA.
PRUEBA DE CONFESIÓN.
in-court or judicial confession.
PRUEBA DE FUEGO.
test of battle ‖ real or true test.
PRUEBA DE INDICIOS.
See PRUEBA INDICIARIA.
PRUEBA DE INFORMES.
information related to a court proceeding (obtained by means of requests addressed to public entities or special notaries public with regard to information which they maintain about persons which are the subject of litigation).
PRUEBA DE LA CULPA.
proof of liability or breach of duty.
PRUEBA DE LAS OBLIGACIONES.
proof regarding obligations and their fulfillment (or not).
PRUEBA DE LA PATERNIDAD.
proof of paternity.

PRUEBA DE LOS CONTRATOS.
contractual proof, proof of the existence of a contract.
PRUEBA DE PERITOS.
See PRUEBA PERICIAL.
PRUEBA DE SANGRE.
blood test (to prove blood kinship).
PRUEBA DERIVADA.
type of secondary evidence, non-original documentary evidence.
PRUEBA DIRECTA.
directly material proof or evidence ‖ judicial evidence, evidence obtained directly by the judge.
PRUEBA DOCUMENTAL.
documentary evidence. See DOCUMENTOS PRIVADOS and DOCUMENTOS PÚBLICOS.
PRUEBA EN ASUNTOS MERCANTILES.
proof regarding commercial matters.
PRUEBA EN CONTRARIO.
conflicting evidence ‖ rebutting proof, proof which is admissible to rebut prior evidence.
PRUEBA ESCRITA.
written evidence or proof.
See PRUEBA DOCUMENTAL.
PRUEBA IMPERTINENTE.
irrelevant evidence ‖ immaterial evidence ‖ extraneous evidence.
PRUEBA IMPRACTICABLE.
inadmissible evidence.
PRUEBA INDICIARIA.
circumstantial evidence.
PRUEBA INDIRECTA.
indirect proof or evidence.
PRUEBA INEFICAZ.
inadmissible evidence ‖ evidence which does not prove what was expected.
PRUEBA INMEDIATA.
See PRUEBA DIRECTA.
PRUEBA INMORAL.
evidence inadmissible due to its immoral character ‖ evidence related to immoral conduct.
PRUEBA INNOMINADA.
unclassified proof, that which is not subject to a given legal classification.
PRUEBA INSTRUMENTAL.
See PRUEBA DOCUMENTAL.
PRUEBA INÚTIL.
See PRUEBA INEFICAZ.
PRUEBA JUDICIAL.
in-court testimony or proof or evidence.

PRUEBA LEGAL.
legal proof or evidence ‖ legally-sufficient evidence of proof.

PRUEBA LIBRE.
evidence which may be produced by any means ‖ evidence that a court may weigh according to its own criteria, i.e. not subject to legal guidelines.

PRUEBA LITERAL.
See PRUEBA DOCUMENTAL.

PRUEBA MEDIATA.
See PRUEBA INDIRECTA.

PRUEBA MORAL.
evidence admissible due to its moral character ‖ evidence related to moral conduct ‖ also see PRUEBA LIBRE.

PRUEBA NEGATIVA.
negative proof ‖ ineffective proof, evidence which is ineffective to prove a fact.

PRUEBA NOMINADA.
classified proof, that which is subject to a given legal classification.

PRUEBA NULA.
incompetent evidence.

PRUEBA ORIGINAL.
type of primary evidence, original documentary evidence.

PRUEBA PERICIAL.
proof or testimony of expert witness.

PRUEBA PERSONAL.
type of primary evidence, evidence which comes from one of the litigants, a confession, witnesses, or expert witness.

PRUEBA PERTINENTE.
material evidence or proof ‖ persuasive evidence.

PRUEBA PLENA.
conclusive evidence, incontrovertible proof.

PRUEBA POR ESCRITO.
See PRUEBA DOCUMENTAL.

PRUEBA POR FAMA PÚBLICA.
hearsay, hearsay evidence.

PRUEBA POR PERITOS.
See PRUEBA PERICIAL.

PRUEBA POR PRESUNCIONES.
inferences, presumptions.

PRUEBA POR TESTIGOS.
See PRUEBA TESTIMONIAL.

PRUEBA POSITIVA.
affirmative proof ‖ persuasive evidence.

PRUEBA PRECONSTITUIDA.
documentary evidence which was created prior to litigation to establish the existence of a contract or action.

PRUEBA PRESUNTA.
See PRESUNCIÓN.

PRUEBA PRIVILEGIADA.
privileged proof or evidence, that which is admissible in some crimes and not in others.

PRUEBA PSICOLÓGICA.
psychological evidence, expert's testimony or report regarding psychological testing.

PRUEBA REAL.
real evidence ‖ autoptic evidence.

PRUEBA RELATIVA.
ineffective evidence (i.e. relatively non-persuasive) ‖ preliminary or foundational evidence, evidence which requires further evidence to be effective.

PRUEBA SEMIPLENA.
prima facie conclusive evidence, evidence which alone is satisfactory or accurate but which must be completed with additional evidence in order to prove the fact in question.

PRUEBA SINGULAR.
sole evidence.

PRUEBA SUFICIENTE.
sufficient evidence.

PRUEBA TASADA.
legal proof ‖ legally sufficient proof ‖ proof the effects of which are determined by statute not by the judge.

PRUEBA TESTIFICAL.
See PRUEBA TESTIMONIAL.

PRUEBA TESTIMONIAL.
testimony, testimonial proof or evidence.

PRUEBA ÚTIL.
See PRUEBA POSITIVA.

PRUEBA VOCAL.
oral testimony.

PRUEBAS.
f, evidence ‖ judicial interrogation or investigation (of a matter) ‖ proof of nobility or royal lineage.

P.S.
See POSTDATA.

PSICOANÁLISIS.
m, psychoanalysis.

PSICOLOGÍA.
f, psychology.

PSICOLOGÍA CRIMINAL.
criminal psychology.

PSICÓPATA.
m, f, psychopath.

PSICOPATÍA.
f, psychopathy.

PSICOPÁTICO.
adj, psychopathic.

PSICOPATOLOGÍA.
f, psychopathology.

PSICOSIS.
f, psychosis.

PSICOSIS CARCELARIA.
prison psychosis, that which is produced by being incarcerated.

PSIQUIATRA.
f, m, psychiatrist.

PSIQUIATRÍA.
f, psychiatry.

PSIQUIATRÍA FORENSE.
forensic psychiatry.

PÚBER.
m, person who has reached puberty || adj, pubescent.

PUBERO.
See PÚBER.

PUBERTAD.
f, puberty.

PUBERTAD LEGAL.
legal puberty, statutory puberty.

PÚBLICA PROMESA.
f, public promise || also see PROMESA PÚBLICA DE RECOMPENSA.

PÚBLICA SUBASTA.
f, public bid || public auction.

PÚBLICA VOZ Y FAMA.
common knowledge.

PUBLICABLE.
adj, publishable.

PUBLICACIÓN.
f, publication || divulgence || promulgation || proclamation || written or literary work || public notice || notice || banns.

PUBLICACIÓN DE DOCUMENTOS OFICIALES.
unauthorized publication or divulgence of government documents.

PUBLICACIÓN DE LA SENTENCIA.
publication or public notice in a newspaper of the criminal sentence. Used as an additional punishment.

PUBLICACIÓN DE LAS LEYES.
governmental publication of statutes or regulations or other legal texts.
See DIARIO OFICIAL.

PUBLICACIÓN OFICIAL.
official publication (by government department, ministry or other public entity).

PUBLICACIONES OBSCENAS.
obscene publication || spreading of obscene materials.

PUBLICADOR.
m, publisher || advertiser.

PÚBLICAMENTE.
adv, publicly.

PUBLICAR.
v, to publish || to make known, reveal || to show, display || to publish marriage banns.

PUBLICIDAD.
f, publicity || promotion, advertising || advertisement || disclosure || openness, publicity, state of being public or known.

PUBLICIDAD DE LOS JUICIOS.
openness or publicity of trials

PUBLICIDAD PENAL.
criminal use of the media, use of the press, radio, television, or other media to carry out a crime.

PUBLICIDAD REGISTRAL.
publicity or open disclosure of official registries || public notice through registration in real estate registries.

PUBLICISTA.
m, writer or specialist on public law || writer, author, journalist || advertising agent, ad man.

PÚBLICO.
m, public, people || the people or masses || multitude || social group || the people || audience || adj, public || open, known || wellknown || common, every-day || general || public, state, governmental.

PUDICIA.
f, modesty, shyness.

PUDOR.
m, sexual morality || modesty || chastity.

PUDOR PÚBLICO.
public rectitude or morality (especially regarding sexuality).

PUEBLO.
m, town, city, village || people, workers, working class || the poor || public opinion || nation || inhabitants || citizenry, society.

PUERICIA.
f, childhood, period from infancy and adolescence (approximately seven to fourteen years of age).

PUERPERIO.
m, puerperium, postpartum period (immediately after birth).

PUERTA.
f, door, entry way ‖ entry ‖ entry fee or tax.

PUERTA ABIERTA.
open door, free entry to work (re unions) ‖ free port, duty free port ‖ open to the public, free entry, public.

PUERTA CERRADA.
closed door.

PUERTA FRANCA.
exemption from consumption tax.
See PUERTO FRANCO.

PUERTO.
port, harbor ‖ protection, backing ‖ asylum, refuge ‖ (mountain) pass.

PUERTO ABIERTO.
open port (to foreign commerce).

PUERTO ADUANERO.
authorized customs port or entry.

PUERTO AÉREO.
airport.

PUERTO DE AMARRE.
port of registration, port where ship is legally registered ‖ home port (of a ship).

PUERTO DE DESTINO.
port of destination.

PUERTO DE EMBARQUE.
port of origin or embarkation.

PUERTO DE ESTADÍA.
port of stay or demurrage.

PUERTO DE MATRÍCULA.
See PUERTO DE AMARRE.

PUERTO DE ORIGEN.
See PUERTO DE AMARRE ‖ port of origin or embarkation.

PUERTO DE REFUGIO.
port of refuge.

PUERTO FRANCO.
free port, port where no entry tax is required.

PUERTO LIBRE.
See PUERTO FRANCO.

PUERTO MARÍTIMO.
seaport.

PUERTO NEUTRAL.
neutral port.

PUERTO SECO.
mountain pass ‖ border customs office.

PUESTA.
f, bet ‖ higher bid or offer.

PUESTERO.
m, caretaker of livestock or of a small rural establishment.

PUESTO.
m, position, place, site, locale ‖ post, position, office ‖ stall, stand, booth, space ‖ situation ‖ (military) post or camp ‖ sentry ‖ small cattle ranch near a town ‖ adj, placed.

PUGNA.
f, battle, fight ‖ opposition, rivalry.

PUGNANTE.
adj, hostile, contrary, opposing, enemy.

PUGNAR.
v, to fight, battle ‖ to require pugnaciously ‖ to struggle ‖ to be opposed to.

PUGNAR POR.
to struggle to.

PUJA.
f, bid, offer (in auctions, etc.) ‖ bidding.

PUJADOR.
m, bidder ‖ offerer.

PUJAR.
v, to bid, offer ‖ to outbid, better, top (another bid) ‖ to take advantage of ‖ to rise, ascend ‖ to struggle, strain.

PUNGUISTA.
m, pickpocket.

PUNIBILIDAD.
f, punishability.

PUNIBLE.
adj, punishable.

PUNICIÓN.
f, punishment, penalty, castigation.

PUNIDOR.
m, punisher.

PUNIR.
v, to punish, penalize, castigate.

PUNITIVO.
adj, punitive

PUNTEAR.
v, to check or tick off (e.g. on a checklist).

PUNTO.
m, point, dot ‖ site, space ‖ moment, instant ‖ occasion ‖ matter, issue, question, topic ‖ specific proposition ‖ situation, stage, status ‖ end, purpose ‖ end (of course studies or work).

PUNTO DE DERECHO.
point of law, legal issue.
PUNTO DE HECHO.
factual issue.
PUNTUAL.
adj, punctual ‖ exact, precise ‖ careful.
PUNTUALIDAD.
f, punctuality ‖ exactitude, precision.
PUNTUALIZAR.
v, to point out ‖ to imprint (in one's memory) ‖ to detail, describe in detail ‖ to put the finishing touches to or on ‖ to determine what doubts, proposals, areas of disagreement, etc. exist.
PUNTUALMENTE.
adv, punctually ‖ precisely.
PUÑO.
m, fist ‖ knife handle.
PUPILA.
f, minor orphaned girl ‖ prostitute.
PUPILAJE.
m, pupilage ‖ fees for pupilage ‖ legal system for the protection of minor orphans.
PUPILAR.
adj, pertaining to a minor orphan.
PUPILO.
m, minor orphaned boy (re his guardian) ‖ boarder, paying house guest ‖ student at a boarding school;
PURAMENTE.
adv, purely ‖ strictly ‖ without condition or term or tax or lien, etc.

PUREZA.
f, purity, chastity ‖ innocence.
PURGA.
f, tax exemption, exemption from payment of a tax or fee.
PURGA DE LA MORA.
exemption from late penalties (for a debtor in default).
PURGACIÓN.
f, exoneration (from accusations) ‖ claim of innocence (when accused of crimes) ‖ serving, fulfilling (of a punishment).
PURGAR.
v, to purify, purge ‖ to serve or fulfill a punishment or sentence) ‖ to exonerate ‖ to exempt ‖ to regain one's good reputation.
PURO.
adj, pure ‖ perfect ‖ chaste, virginal ‖ not subject to condition or term or tax or liens, etc.
PUTA.
See PROSTITUTA.
PUTATIVO.
adj, putative, reputed, supposed, apparent.
PUTO.
m, male prostitute ‖ male homosexual (derogatory).
PUTREFACCIÓN.
f, corruption.
PUTREFACTO.
adj, putrid, rotten ‖ corrupt, corrupted.

"QUAESTIO".
question ‖ inquiry, investigation ‖ consultation of a legal expert.

QUEBRADIZO.
adj, breakable, fragile ‖ perishable ‖ weak.

QUEBRADO.
m, bankrupt ‖ adj, broken ‖ breached ‖ bankrupt ‖ insolvent ‖ weak, weakened.

QUEBRADO CASUAL.
See QUEBRADO FORTUITO.

QUEBRADO CULPABLE.
negligent bankrupt.

QUEBRADO FORTUITO.
unintentional and non-negligent bankrupt.

**QUEBRADO
FRAUDULENTO.**
fraudulent bankrupt.

QUEBRADOR.
m, breaker ‖ lawbreaker, violator of a law, regulation, etc.

QUEBRANTABLE.
adj, bribable, able to be suborned ‖ fragile ‖ conquerable ‖ breakable, violable.

QUEBRANTADO.
adj, broken, violated ‖ weakened ‖ suborned.

QUEBRANTADURA.
See QUEBRANTAMIENTO.

QUEBRANTAMIENTO.
m, illegal breaking (into) ‖ violation, infraction, transgression ‖ breach, non-compliance ‖ procedural violation ‖ violation of terms of criminal sentence.

**QUEBRANTAMIENTO DE
ARRESTO.**
evasion of arrest.

QUEBRANTAMIENTO DE CONDENA.
violation of terms of criminal sentence.

QUEBRANTAMIENTO DE FORMA.
violation of procedural rules (by a lower court).

**QUEBRANTAMIENTO DE PRISIÓN
PREVENTIVA.**
escape from prison pending trial.

QUEBRANTAR.
v, to break ‖ to violate, transgress ‖ to breach, fail to comply ‖ to swear, profane ‖ to break out of (e.g. prison, etc.) ‖ to persuade ‖ to overcome, break (another's will) ‖ to revoke (e.g. a will, etc.).

QUEBRANTO.
m, see QUEBRANTAMIENTO ‖ ruin ‖ affliction ‖ weakness ‖ loss.

**QUEBRANTO
DE MONEDA.**
fixed sum granted to tellers and other employees who handle money in order to compensate for possible losses caused by receipt of counterfeit money and by missing bills or coins.

QUEBRAR.
v, see QUEBRANTAR ‖ to go into bankruptcy, go bankrupt.

QUEDA.
f, curfew.

QUEDAR.
v, to stay, remain ‖ to be (somewhere) ‖ to agree, contract ‖ to award an auction (to a bidder).

QUEHACER.
m, work, labor, task ‖ occupation, profession ‖ business, matter.

QUEJA.
f, complaint, claim, protest ‖ discontent ‖ criminal accusation ‖ probate proceeding to contest a will ‖ appeal (of a lower court deci-

sion) ‖ appeal filed directly with the appellate court when the lower court has refused to grant a hearing regarding such appeal or to allow such appeal to be filed or heard.
See RECURSO DE QUEJA.

QUEJARSE.
v, to complain, protest ‖ to express discontent.

QUEJAS DE PRISIONEROS.
prisoners' complaints (regarding conditions of detention).

QUEMA.
f, fire, blaze.

QUEMADERO.
m, crematorium, crematory, cinerarium ‖ pyre ‖ adj, to be burned.

QUEMADOR.
m, cremator ‖ person who burns.

QUEMADURA.
f, burn (by fire), scald (by water or steam).

QUEMAR.
v, to burn, burn up, incinerate ‖ to burn (by fire) ‖ to scald (by water or steam) ‖ to sell at a loss, hold a fire or bargain sale.

QUEMARROPA.
adj, pointblank (shooting) ‖ adv, pointblank.

QUEMARSE.
v, to burn oneself ‖ to burn oneself up ‖ to become irritated or impatient ‖ to be just about to find or solve something ‖ to waste one's time ‖ to lose one's reputation or good will.

QUEMAZÓN.
f, burn, blaze ‖ hurtful or cutting remark ‖ fire sale, bargain sale.

QUERELLA.
f, criminal complaint or charge or accusation (brought by the injured party for purposes of obtaining a conviction as well as indemnification for the injuries suffered) ‖ discord, quarrel ‖ moan ‖ contest of an invalid will (by the legal heirs).

QUERELLA CALUMNIOSA.
malicious prosecution (as a criminal offense).
See QUERELLA.

QUERELLA DE INOFICIOSO TESTAMENTO.
contest of an invalid will (by the legal heirs).

QUERELLADO.
m, accused, criminal defendant.
See QUERELLA.

QUERELLADOR.
See QUERELLANTE.

QUERELLANTE.
m, f, accuser.
See QUERELLA.

QUERELLARSE.
v, to moan, complain ‖ to accuse, bring or press charges, lodge a criminal complaint.

QUERIDA.
f, term of endearment (e.g. dearheart, dearest, honey) ‖ lover, mistress ‖ adj, dear.

QUIEBRA.
f, bankruptcy (of a merchant) ‖ break, rupture ‖ ruin, ruination, complete loss ‖ insolvency.

QUIEBRA CASUAL.
See QUIEBRA FORTUITA.

QUIEBRA CULPABLE.
negligent bankruptcy.

QUIEBRA FORTUITA.
unintentional and non-negligent bankruptcy.

QUIEBRA FRAUDULENTA.
fraudulent bankruptcy.

QUIEBRA IMPROPIA.
improper bankruptcy. Includes QUIEBRA CULPABLE and QUIEBRA FRAUDULENTA.

QUIEBRA PUNIBLE.
criminal bankruptcy, punishable bankruptcy. Includes QUIEBRA CULPABLE and QUIEBRA FRAUDULENTA.

QUIEN NO APARECE, PERECE.
He who is not present to defend his rights against others, loses.

QUINCENA.
f, fifteen-day period ‖ payment received every fifteen days. Although QUINCENA is used to describe the fifteen-year period, the accurate term is QUINDENIO.

QUINCENARIO.
m, habitual criminal ‖ adj, held for fifteen days.

QUINDENIO.
m, fifteen-year period.

QUINQUENAL.
adj, five-year, pertaining to a five-year period.

QUINQUENIO.
m, five-year period.

QUINTA.
f, country house ‖ military service lottery ‖ annual replacement of military.

QUINTAR.
v, to choose one out of every five ‖ to choose one out of every five military conscripts by lottery ‖ to kill one out of every five persons.

QUINTO.
m, one-fifth ‖ military conscript chosen by lots out of five ‖ tax of twenty percent ‖ five-cent piece ‖ adj, fifth.

QUIROGRAFARIO.
m, general or non-preferential creditor or credit, creditor or credit without a preference ‖ adj, pertaining to handwritten document.

QUIRÓGRAFO.
m, see MANUSCRITO ‖ acknowledgement of debt, I.O.U., document in which debtor acknowledges debt ‖ document signed by both parties as proof of a legal act ‖ acknowledgement of payment (given by creditor to debtor).

QUITA.
f, release, discharge of debt (whether partial or total) ‖ debt reduction.

QUITA Y ESPERA.
composition (if acceptance of partial payment), extension (if acceptance of extension of payment period).

QUITAR.
v, to remove, take something (from one place to another) ‖ to rob, steal ‖ to bother ‖ to prohibit, disallow ‖ to abrogate, repeal, nullify (a law) ‖ to exempt from (e.g. a punishment, tax) ‖ to release, free from an obligation ‖ to pardon or reduce a debt ‖ to eliminate.

QUITAR EL TIMÓN.
to take away the rights to navigate.

QUITARSE.
v, to leave, absent oneself, take off ‖ to give up (a habit) ‖ to take (one's life) ‖ to remove (things).

QUITARSE DE ENCIMA.
v, to get rid of (something or someone bothersome).

QUITARSE LA VIDA.
to suicide, commit suicide, take one's life.

QUITAS ZONALES.
f, pay reductions by area or zone (agreed to in collective bargaining agreements pursuant to the lower cost of living in certain areas or zones).

QUITO.
adj, free, exempt, released, discharged.

QUO.
quo.

QUÓRUM.
m, quorum.

R

R.D.
See REAL DECRETO.

RABIA.
f, rabies ‖ anger, furor, fury, ire ‖ hatred ‖ bitterness.

RABIAR.
v, to be angry or furious ‖ to have rabies.

RABIOSO.
adj, rabid ‖ angry, furious.

RÁBULA.
f, m, shyster lawyer, pettifogger.

RACIAL.
adj, racial.

RACIOCINAR.
v, to reason ‖ to reflect, meditate ‖ to discuss, argue.

RACIOCINIO.
m, reasoning ‖ argument.

RACIÓN.
f, rations ‖ daily allowance ‖ portion, ration.

RACIONABILIDAD.
f, reasoning, judgment, ability to reason.

RACIONAL.
adj, rational ‖ true ‖ well-founded, well-based.

RACIONALIDAD.
f, rationality.

RACIONALISMO.
m, rationalism.

RACIONALISMO JURÍDICO.
legal rationalism.

RACIONALISTA.
f, m, rationalist ‖ adj, rationalist.

RACIONALIZACIÓN.
f, rationalization.

RACIONALIZACIÓN LABORAL.
industrial organization to minimize labor costs and maximize efficiency.

RACIONALIZAR.
v, to rationalize.

RACIONALMENTE.
adv, rationally.

RACIONAMIENTO.
m, rationing.

RACIONAR.
v, to ration.

RACIONARSE.
v, to take one's rations.

RACIONERO.
m, person who rations out provisions.

RACIONISTA.
m, f, person who lives off of rations or an allowance.

RACISMO.
m, racism.

RACISTA.
m, f, racist ‖ adj, racist.

RADIACIÓN.
f, radiation ‖ disposal of antiquated or useless material ‖ radio broadcasting.

RADIACIONES PELIGROSAS.
dangerous radiation.

RADIACTIVO.
adj, radioactive.

RADIAL.
adj, pertaining to radio or radio broadcasting or radium or radius.

RADIAR.
v, to broadcast, spread by radio waves ‖ to throw or dispose of antiquated or useless material ‖ to keep apart or outside.

RADICAL.
m, radical, extremist ‖ adj, radical, extremist ‖ basic, fundamental ‖ pertaining to roots or

foundations ‖ radical, name of political parties (which vary in ideology).

RADICALISMO.
m, radicalism, extremism.

RADICALMENTE.
adv, radically ‖ basically, fundamentally.

RADICAR.
v, to live in ‖ to be domiciled ‖ to settle, be established, take root ‖ to be located, to be situated ‖ to consist of.

RADIO.
f, radio ‖ radio broadcast ‖ radio broadcasting ‖ m, radius ‖ zone ‖ area, sphere ‖ radio message ‖ radium.

RADIO DE ACCIÓN.
sphere of activity or influence ‖ arms length ‖ operating range.

RADIO DE LA PLAZA.
effective battle zone, radius of effective defensive fighting.

RADIO DE LA POBLACIÓN.
radius of populated area (from city center) ‖ urban zone, city limits.

RADIODIFUSIÓN.
f, radio broadcasting ‖ radio broadcast.

RAÍCES.
f, roots ‖ background, ancestry ‖ adj, real (property). See BIENES RAÍCES.

RAÍZ.
f, root ‖ basis.

RAMA.
f, branch ‖ branch, sector, area (of government, education, law, etc.) ‖ secondary aspect ‖ family relationship or branch.

RAMAS DE PARENTESCO.
family branches or relations.

RAMAS DEL DERECHO.
branches or areas of the law.

RAMERA.
f, prostitute.

RAMERÍA.
f, house of prostitution.

RAMIFICACIÓN.
f, ramification, consequence ‖ branching (out) ‖ propagation.

RAMO.
m, branch, field (of government, science, business, etc.) ‖ sub-branch, branch of a branch ‖ government department, ministry.

RANDAR.
v, to write ‖ to rob, steal.

RANGO.
m, class, hierarchy, level, category.

RANGO HIPOTECARIO.
priority of mortgage interest.

RAPAR.
v, to rob, steal ‖ to shave, crop (hair).

RAPAZ.
m, thief, robber ‖ lad, kid, young boy (between about 9 and 15 years of age).

RAPAZA.
f, lass, young girl (between about 9 and 15 years of age).

RAPIDEZ.
f, speed, velocity ‖ promptness.

RAPIÑA.
f, violent robbery (of a person) ‖ violent burglary (of a building).
See also HURTO VIOLENTO and ROBO.

RAPIÑADOR.
m, violent robber or burglar.

RAPIÑAR.
v, to rob or burgle with violence.

RAPTADA.
f, kidnap victim ‖ victim of an abduction (usually a woman, by her boyfriend or lover) ‖ adj, kidnapped ‖ abducted.

RAPTAR.
v, to abduct, kidnap ‖ to take a hostage.

RAPTO.
m, rapture, ecstasy ‖ loss of memory ‖ robbery ‖ abduction of a person (usually by the lover for purposes of marriage or sexual intercourse) ‖ child kidnapping or abduction (usually of a female child under 12 years of age) ‖ kidnapping ‖ hostage taking.

RAPTO CONSENTIDO.
See RAPTO IMPROPIO.

RAPTO
DE NIÑOS.
kidnapping or abduction of a minor, child kidnapping or abduction.

RAPTO IMPROPIO.
statutory kidnapping or abduction, consensual abduction (usually of a female under 12 years of age, with or without consent).

RAPTO PROPIO.
kidnapping, abduction (without consent).

RAPTOR.
m, kidnapper, abductor ‖ hostage taker ‖ thief ‖ person who commits a type of false imprisonment, person who holds a kidnap victim

(although not the original kidnapper or abductor).

RASCUÑO.
See RASGUÑO.

RASGADURA.
f, ripping, tearing, act of ripping.

RASGAR.
v, to tear, rip ‖ to destroy ‖ to rape ‖ to breach or break a treaty or agreement.

RASGO.
m, feature, characteristic (of a person whether physical or otherwise).

RASGUÑAR.
v, to scratch, injure (the surface of someone or thing).

RASGUÑO.
m, scratch.

RASPADURA.
f, scraping, act of scraping ‖ erasure, act of erasing.

RASPAR.
v, to scrape ‖ to erase ‖ to correct ‖ to steal, nab.

RASPONAZO.
m, scratch, graze, surface wound.

RASTILLADO.
adj, stolen, ripped off.

RASTILLERO.
m, thief.

RASTRA.
f, vestige, leftover ‖ consequence, result (of a crime, or a breach of duty if repair must be made).

RASTRAR.
See RASTREAR.

RASTREAR.
v, to investigate, question ‖ to dredge, drag (ocean floor) ‖ to track, trail.

RASTRO.
m, vestige, remains ‖ trace, trail ‖ track ‖ sign ‖ slaughterhouse ‖ wholesale meat market ‖ flea market.

RATEAR.
v, to distribute pro rata ‖ to reduce proportionally ‖ to pilfer, pinch, steal (habitually).

RATERÍA.
f, pilfering, petty theft ‖ vileness, baseness ‖ dishonesty (in business).

RATERO.
m, petty thief, pilferer ‖ pickpocket ‖ adj, thieving ‖ creeping.

RATIFICACIÓN.
f, ratification, ex post facto approval of unauthorized actions carried out on one's behalf by another ‖ confirmation ‖ reiteration of consent.

RATIFICACIÓN DE CONTRATOS.
ratification of contracts (by a principal of unauthorized signature by an agent or third party).

RATIFICACIÓN DE GESTIÓN DE NEGOCIOS.
ratification (by principal) of legal action (taken by agent or third party).

RATIFICACIÓN DE TESTIGOS.
confirmation of prior testimony (by reading the prior testimony and asking whether they wish to confirm, amend, or add anything thereto).

RATIFICACIÓN DE TRATADOS.
ratification of (international) treaties.

RATIFICACIÓN DEL PROCESADO.
confirmation of prior testimony of a suspect (by reading the testimony taken during the DECLARACIÓN INDAGATORIA and asking whether he or she wishes to confirm, amend, or add anything thereto).

RATIFICAR.
v, to ratify ‖ to confirm ‖ to reiterate an order, request, demand.

RATIFICATORIO.
adj, ratifying.

RATIHABICIÓN.
f, ratification (of unauthorized acts of a third party).

"RATIO".
reason, justification, excuse ‖ commentary (on a legal text) ‖ cause, motive ‖ type, genre ‖ measure ‖ basis of a legal norm.

"RATIONES".
plural of "RATIO" ‖ personal business or matters.

"RATIO AGENDI".
cause of litigation, legal cause of action.

"RATIO DECIDENDI".
justification of a legal decision.

"RATIO JURIS".
legal reason ‖ reason or argument based on legal rules or principles.

"RATIO LEGIS".
purpose of a law or rule.

"RATIONE MATERIAE".
subject matter jurisdiction.
"RATIONE PERSONAE".
personal jurisdiction.
RATO.
m, moment, brief lapse of time || adj, uncon-
summated. See MATRIMONIO RATO.
RAZA.
f, race (of humans) || breed || lineage || class.
RAZA AMARILLA.
race of non-white and non-black Asians, so-
metimes referred to as Oriental race.
RAZA BLANCA.
White race.
RAZA HUMANA.
human race.
RAZA NEGRA.
Black or Negroid race.
RAZA ROJA.
American Indian race.
RAZÓN.
f, reason, reasoning || truth || argument || mo-
tive, basis || cause || allegation || proof, eviden-
ce || explanation || right to act || fairness, rea-
sonableness || justice || proportion || relationship
|| account || notice || favorable verdict.
RAZÓN DE ESTADO.
State reasons, reasons of a nation.
RAZÓN
DE JUSTICIA.
reasons of justice or equity.
RAZÓN DEL DICHO.
basis of testimony, reason or basis upon which
the witness comes to have the information set
forth in his or her testimony.
RAZÓN HISTÓRICA.
historical reason, reason as applied in a given
historical context.
RAZÓN JURÍDICA.
legal reason or truth or motive or cause, reason or truth or motive or cause which is based
in law.
RAZÓN SOCIAL.
corporate name || firm name || partnership na-
me.
RAZÓN SUFICIENTE.
legally sufficient basis or reason || sufficient
basis or reason.
RAZONABLE.
adj, reasonable || just, fair || equitable || mode-
rate || average || acceptable.

RAZONABLEMENTE.
adv, reasonably || fairly || acceptably || probably.
RAZONADAMENTE.
adv, in a reasoned way.
RAZONADO.
adj, reasoned, well-founded, well-based || jus-
tified or supported by documents.
RAZONADOR.
m, reasoner, explainer || adj, reasoning, ex-
plaining.
RAZONAMIENTO.
m, reasoning || argument, basis, support.
RAZONAR.
v, to reason || to give reasons or proof || to base
(an opinion) || to justify an account (e.g. with
bills) || to document.
RAZZIA.
f, raid (to pillage) || police raid.
RE.
See IN RE.
REA.
f, female accused or defendant || prostitute.
REABRIR.
v, to reopen.
REACCIÓN.
f, reaction || resistance, opposition || type of
political party (usually conservative or of ex-
treme right) || defense (against an attack).
REACCIONAR.
v, to react || to defend.
REACCIONARIO.
m, reactionary || traditionalist || conservative ||
adj, reactionary.
REACTIVACIÓN.
f, reactivation.
REACTOR.
m, reactor.
REACUÑACIÓN.
f, recoining, reminting.
REACUÑAR.
v, to recoin (money).
READAPTACIÓN.
f, readaptation.
READAPTACIÓN PROFESIONAL.
employment readaptation, readjustment of an
employee to work after a work-related accident or sickness.
READMISIÓN.
f, readmission || reincorporation.
READMITIR.
v, to readmit.

REAFIRMACIÓN.
f, reaffirmation.
REAFIRMAR.
v, to reaffirm.
REAGRAVAR.
v, to get worse, become more serious, take a turn for the worse.
REAJUSTAR.
v, to readjust ‖ to increase (e.g. taxes, tariffs, prices).
REAJUSTE.
m, readjustment.
REAL.
m, Spanish monetary unit (one quarter of a peseta) ‖ fairground ‖ army camp headquarters ‖ adj, real, true ‖ exact ‖ concrete, existing ‖ royal ‖ monarchic ‖ real (estate).
REAL DECRETO.
royal decree.
REAL ORDEN.
royal or ministerial order.
REALENGO.
m, royal patrimony or property ‖ adj, of the king, royal.
REALEZA.
f, royalty ‖ royal sovereignty.
REALIDAD.
f, reality, truth ‖ essence.
REALISMO.
m, monarchism, royalism ‖ realism ‖ materialism.
REALISTA.
f, monarchist, royalist ‖ realist ‖ materialist ‖ adj, realistic ‖ royalist.
REALIZABLE.
adj, possible, feasible ‖ transferable, salable ‖ marketable.
REALIZACIÓN.
f, realization, achievement ‖ process of achieving ‖ execution, carrying out, performance ‖ sale (of goods for money), liquidation ‖ sale of commercial goods.
REALIZADO.
See CAPITAL REALIZADO.
REALIZAR.
v, to verify, prove ‖ to achieve, obtain, realize (one's objective) ‖ to execute, perform, carry out ‖ to sell, to exchange for money.
REALMENTE.
adv, really, truly ‖ without doubt, undoubtedly.

REALQUILAR.
v, to rent or lease again ‖ to sublease, sublet.
REANUDAR.
v, to renew, begin again ‖ to resume, continue after a break.
REAPARECER.
v, to reappear.
REAPERTURA.
f, reopening.
REAPERTURA DE CAUSA.
reopening of the case.
REAPERTURA DEL PROCEDIMIENTO.
reopening of the proceeding.
REAPRECIAR.
v, to revalue ‖ to reprice, readjust (prices).
REARGÜIR.
v, to reargue.
REARMAR.
v, to rearm.
REARMARSE.
v, to rearm oneself.
REARME.
m, rearmament.
REASEGURAR.
v, to reinsure.
REASEGURO.
m, reinsurance.
REASUMIR.
v, to reassume ‖ to resume, continue.
REASUNCIÓN.
f, resumption, continuation ‖ reassumption.
REBAJA.
f, discount, rebate, reduction ‖ bonus ‖ lowering, diminution.
REBAJA DE CATEGORÍA.
reduction of employment level or category.
REBAJA DE SALARIO.
salary reduction, cut in salary.
REBAJADO.
adj, reduced, cut ‖ discounted ‖ lowered, diminished.
REBAJAMIENTO.
f, debasement ‖ servility, submission.
See REBAJA.
REBAJAR.
v, to reduce, cut ‖ to discount ‖ to lower, lessen, diminish ‖ to humiliate ‖ to debase.
REBAÑO.
m, flock ‖ herd ‖ compliant workers ‖ people submissive to a dictatorship.

REBATE.
m, fight ‖ argument, dispute.
REBATIBLE.
adj, refutable ‖ arguable, disputable.
REBATIMIENTO.
m, refutation ‖ contradiction ‖ rebuttal.
REBATIR.
v, to overcome (force or violence), destroy ‖ to repel ‖ to eliminate or reduce a debt ‖ to refute, rebut, contradict (decisively) ‖ to impugn ‖ to object to ‖ to prove one's innocence ‖ to resist a temptation ‖ to strengthen.
REBELACIÓN.
See REBELDÍA and REBELIÓN.
REBELARSE.
v, to rebel ‖ to disobey (e.g. an authority, order, law) ‖ to encourage or take part in a rebellion ‖ to resist ‖ to break a friendship.
REBELDE.
m, rebel, insurgent ‖ disobedient person ‖ revolutionary ‖ person who is not docile or submissive ‖ anti-social person ‖ unreasonable person ‖ defaulter, person who fails to appear in court when summoned ‖ person who is in contempt of court order or decision ‖ adj, rebellious, insurgent ‖ disobedient ‖ revolutionary ‖ anti-social ‖ defaulting ‖ in contempt.
REBELDÍA.
f, disobedience ‖ rebellion, insurgency ‖ opposition, resistance ‖ non- appearance (in court when summoned), default ‖ contempt of court ‖ adj, rebelliousness ‖ disobedience.
REBELDÍA CIVIL.
non-appearance (in court when summoned in a civil suit), default ‖ contempt of court (in a civil suit).
REBELDÍA
DEL EJECUTADO.
default of defendant subject to an order of execution ‖ non-appearance of defendant subject to an order of execution.
REBELDÍA
PENAL.
criminal default or failure to appear in a criminal trial.
REBELIÓN.
f, rebellion, insurrection, revolt ‖ lack of discipline ‖ revolution ‖ civil war ‖ sedition.
REBELIÓN MILITAR.
military insurrection or revolt.

RECABAR.
v, to request authorization or a power to act ‖ to plead ‖ to obtain (a request or supplication).
RECADERO.
m, messenger, errand boy or girl.
RECADISTA.
See RECADERO.
RECADO.
m, verbal message ‖ response (made by the same means through a third party) ‖ gift ‖ package ‖ precaution, care ‖ daily shopping ‖ errand ‖ explanation or proof of account.
RECAER.
v, to fall again ‖ to repeat (e.g. offenses) ‖ to relapse (into) ‖ to come into, transfer a right to (e.g. an inheritance) ‖ to admit (guilt).
RECAÍDA.
f, repetition (of an offense) ‖ relapse ‖ recidivism ‖ adj, elapsed, taken place, occurred.
RECALADA.
f, return to port or airport.
RECALAR.
v, to return to port or airport.
RECAMBIAR.
v, to exchange again ‖ to issue a redraft.
RECAMBIO.
m, second exchange ‖ exchange ‖ usury ‖ redraft (which grants the holder the right to indemnification if not paid).
RECAPITULACIÓN.
f, summary, recapitulation, recap ‖ conclusions ‖ consolidated statement.
RECAPITULAR.
v, to recapitulate, recap, summarize (e.g. information, allegations, discussion).
RECARGAR.
v, to accuse or charge anew ‖ to recharge ‖ to overload ‖ to increase (e.g. charges, taxes, accusations) ‖ to accuse (of new offenses) ‖ to impose (a penalty for late payment) ‖ to impose (an additional payment), charge extra ‖ to increase (a punishment by a new judge or in a new action).
RECARGO.
m, recharge ‖ surcharge ‖ extra charge or payment ‖ increased punishment ‖ markup, increased charge ‖ surtax, tax increase ‖ surtax.
RECARGO EN EL SERVICIO.
extra service charge, tip ‖ increased punishment for serviceman.

RECATAR.
v, to hide ‖ to cover up ‖ to omit ‖ to remain silent.
RECATARSE.
v, to lack decisiveness.
RECATO.
m, circumspection, reserve ‖ care, caution ‖ honesty ‖ modesty.
RECAUDACIÓN.
f, collection ‖ amount collected ‖ receipt of payment ‖ collector'soffice. These terms are most commonly used to refer to collection of taxes and other government charges.
RECAUDADOR.
m, collector ‖ tax collector.
RECAUDAMIENTO.
m, collection ‖ functions and office of a collector or tax collector ‖ jurisdiction of tax collector.
RECAUDAR.
v, to collect ‖ to collect taxes ‖ to receive monies ‖ to care for.
RECAUDATORIO.
adj, collection, pertaining to collections or collecting or receipts.
RECAUDO.
m, collection ‖ charge ‖ care, caution, precaution ‖ slips which justify a charge or a credit ‖ guaranty ‖ bond, bail ‖ custody.
RECELAMIENTO.
See RECELO.
RECELAR.
v, to suspect, doubt ‖ to mistrust, distrust ‖ to fear.
RECELO.
m, suspicion, doubt ‖ lack of confidence, mistrust, distrust ‖ fear.
RECELOSO.
m, suspicious or doubting or mistrusting or fearful person ‖ adj, suspicious, doubting, mistrusting, mistrustful, fearful.
RECEPCIÓN.
f, reception ‖ receipt ‖ admission ‖ examination of witnesses ‖ verification of construction work (upon completion).
RECEPTACIÓN.
f, concealment, cover up (of a crime) ‖ receipt of stolen goods or criminal instruments ‖ hiding of criminal fugitives.
RECEPTÁCULO.
m, asylum, refuge.

RECEPTADOR.
m, type of criminal accessory who covers up a crime ‖ receiver or purchaser of stolen goods (with knowledge) ‖ person who hides fugitives.
RECEPTIVIDAD.
f, receptiveness, receptivity.
RECEPTIVO.
adj, receptive.
RECEPTO.
m, safe place ‖ asylum, refuge.
RECEPTOR.
m, receiver ‖ charger, person who charges ‖ fine collector ‖ criminal accessory, person who covers up a crime ‖ radio receiver.
RECEPTORÍA.
f, receiver's or collector's office or post ‖ commission of amounts received by collector ‖ treasury ‖ public treasury ‖ reception, reception office, office where goods or notices are received.
RECESIÓN.
f, (economic) recession.
RECESO.
m, recess ‖ adjournment ‖ separation ‖ deviation ‖ legislative recess or adjournment ‖ shareholders' appraisal rights.
RECIBÍ.
(literally) I received, payment received ‖ m, receipt, receipt form.
RECIBIDO.
adj, received ‖ graduated.
RECIBIDOR.
m, receiver.
RECIBIMIENTO.
m, receipt, reception ‖ admission ‖ acceptance, approval ‖ receipt of diploma, graduation.
RECIBIMIENTO A PRUEBA.
receipt of evidence, discovery period (in civil actions) ‖ reception of good for purposes of testing.
RECIBIMIENTO TRIUNFAL.
triumphal homecoming, hero's welcome.
RECIBIR.
v, to receive ‖ to admit, allow to enter ‖ to accept, approve ‖ to receive, hear.
RECIBIRSE.
v, to graduate, receive educational certification to practice a profession.

RECIBO.
m, receipt, receipt form, payment acknowledgement ‖ reception.
RECIBO DE CAPITAL.
acceptance of principal (on a debt).
RECIBOS EN LA TUTELA.
guardianship receipts, receipts which justify
guardian's expenditures.
RECIÉN NACIDO.
m, newly born ‖ adj, newly born.
RECÍPROCAMENTE.
adv, reciprocally, mutually ‖ equally.
RECIPROCIDAD.
f, reciprocity, mutuality ‖ equality ‖ international or interstate reciprocity.
RECÍPROCO.
adj, mutual, reciprocal ‖ equal ‖ bilateral.
RECLAMACIÓN.
f, reclamation ‖ claim, protest, complaint ‖
remonstrance, petition (between nations to
complain of a wrong).
RECLAMACIÓN COLECTIVA.
collective petition, petition.
RECLAMACIÓN DE ALIMENTOS.
complaint for the payment of alimony.
RECLAMACION PREVIA.
See EXCEPCIÓN DE FALTA DE RECLAMACIÓN
PREVIA.
RECLAMAR.
v, to reclaim ‖ to claim, protest, complain ‖ to
ask for ‖ to oppose ‖ to require ‖ to summons
a fugitive or person who fails to appear in
court ‖ to request the admission as immigrants
of persons who are related (by admitted immigrant).
RECLAMO.
m, claim, complaint, protest ‖ attraction ‖
commercial or political propaganda, advertisement ‖ inexpensive good ‖ summons, judicial summons.
RECLUIR.
v, to confine, enclose ‖ to imprison, jail ‖ to
punish by confinement.
RECLUSIÓN.
f, reclusion, seclusion ‖ isolation ‖ commitment (to a mental hospital) ‖ imprisonment,
confinement, deprivation of freedom.
RECLUSIÓN AISLADA.
solitary confinement.
RECLUSIÓN MAYOR.
long-term imprisonment.

RECLUSIÓN MENOR.
medium-term imprisonment.
RECLUSIÓN MILITAR.
serious military incarceration.
RECLUSIÓN PERPETUA.
life imprisonment. In many countries, cannot
last longer than thirty years.
RECLUSO.
m, prisoner, inmate ‖ imprisoned or confined
person ‖ adj, confined, imprisoned.
RECLUSORIO.
m, prison, place of confinement or imprisonment.
RECLUTA.
m, recruit, enlistee, (armed services) volunteer ‖ conscript, inductee, draftee ‖ rookie.
RECLUTADOR.
m, recruiter.
RECLUTAMIENTO.
m, enlistment, recruitment ‖ conscription, induction, draft.
RECLUTAR.
v, to recruit, enlist (others) ‖ to induct, draft,
conscript.
RECOBRAR.
v, to repossess, reacquire, retrieve ‖ to recuperate ‖ to reconquer.
See INTERDICTO DE RECOBRAR.
RECOBRARSE.
v, to be indemnified or have repair made ‖ to
be made whole ‖ to recuperate, regain (one's
health, wits) ‖ to recover.
RECOBRO.
m, recovery, recuperation ‖ reconquest ‖ recovery (of property).
RECOGER.
v, to take ‖ to collect, bring together ‖ to save
‖ to give asylum ‖ to pick up, collect ‖ to suspend (the use of something) ‖ to reorganize.
RECOGIDA.
f, collection ‖ withdrawal ‖ adj, collected ‖
withdrawn.
RECOGIDA DE AUTOS.
collection of court files (from the possession of
one of the parties, for the judge to study).
RECOLECCIÓN.
f, summary ‖ compilation ‖ tax collection ‖
collection.
RECOLECTAR.
v, to take a collection ‖ to compile ‖ to summarize.

RECOMENDACIÓN.
f, recommendation ‖ request ‖ advice.
RECOMENDANTE.
m, f, recommender.
RECOMENDAR.
v, to recommend ‖ to charge ‖ to request, ask ‖ to praise ‖ to advise ‖ to warn, forewarn.
RECOMPENSA.
f, award ‖ compensation, pay, remuneration ‖ amount of money offered for services to be rendered ‖ compensation for commission of crime ‖ reward.
RECOMPENSA INDUSTRIAL.
reward for industrial performance or innovations.
RECOMPENSABLE.
adj, worthy of compensation or pay.
RECOMPENSACIÓN.
See RECOMPENSA.
RECOMPENSAS A LA TRIPULACIÓN.
ship or aircraft crew's pay.
RECOMPONER.
v, to repair (damage), make as if new.
RECONCILIABLE.
adj, reconcilable.
RECONCILIACIÓN.
f, reconciliation.
RECONCILIACIÓN MATRIMONIAL.
marital reconciliation.
RECONCILIAR.
v, to reconcile, reestablish good relations (between others).
RECONCILIARSE.
v, to be reconciled, reestablish good relations (between each other).
RECONDENAR.
v, to reconvict ‖ to resentence ‖ to resentence to a harsher punishment.
RECONDUCCIÓN.
See TÁCITA RECONDUCCIÓN.
RECONDUCIR.
v, to extend by implication the term of a contract (esp. a rental contract).
RECONOCEDOR.
m, scrutinizer ‖ registrar ‖ observer ‖ recognizer (of something) ‖ identifier ‖ admitter ‖ person who is grateful.
See RECONOCIMIENTO.
RECONOCER.
v, to recognize (one's actions or position, another nation, a political regime) ‖ to scrutinize,

examine carefully ‖ to register ‖ to consider ‖ to warn ‖ to confess, admit ‖ to make a custom's inspection ‖ to concede.
RECONOCERSE.
v, to admit one's wrongdoing or guilt ‖ to confirm one's qualities.
RECONOCIDO.
adj, admitted ‖ confessed ‖ identified ‖ grateful, thankful ‖ acknowledged, recognized.
RECONOCIMIENTO.
m, recognition ‖ registration ‖ observation ‖ confession, admission, acknowledgement ‖ acceptance of another nation or political regime ‖ identification (of something or one) ‖ admission (of authenticity of writing or signature) ‖ recognition (of an obligation or paternity) ‖ appreciation, thankfulness.
RECONOCIMIENTO ACUSATORIO.
identification of a suspect.
RECONOCIMIENTO AUTÉNTICO.
formal identification or admission, etc.
See RECONOCIMIENTO.
RECONOCIMIENTO DE BELIGERANCIA.
declaration of war.
RECONOCIMIENTO DE CRÉDITOS.
acknowledgement of a debt ‖ stage in a bankruptcy or insolvency proceeding during which the debts are verified.
RECONOCIMIENTO DE CUENTAS.
examination or audit of accounts ‖ auditor's report.
RECONOCIMIENTO DE DEUDA.
See RECONOCIMIENTO DE LAS OBLIGACIONES.
RECONOCIMIENTO DE DOCUMENTOS.
admission or acknowledgement of one's writing in papers or documents.
RECONOCIMIENTO DE FACTO.
recognition of a de facto government.
RECONOCIMIENTO DE FIRMA.
recognition of signature ‖ authentication of signature, admission of authenticity of signature.
RECONOCIMIENTO DE GOBIERNOS.
recognition of governments.
RECONOCIMIENTO DE HIJOS EXTRAMATRIMONIALES.
recognition or acknowledgement of children born out of wedlock or illegitimate children.
RECONOCIMIENTO DE JURE.
recognition of a government pursuant to

terms of treaties and agreements pertaining to recognition.

RECONOCIMIENTO DE LAS OBLIGACIONES.
acknowledgement of obligations.

RECONOCIMIENTO DE LETRA.
recognition of handwriting.

RECONOCIMIENTO JUDICIAL.
judicial examination, examination or scrutiny of evidence or proof directly by a judge.

RECONOCIMIENTO JUDICIAL DE LOS ACUSADOS.
judicial examination of suspects or the accused, examination or scrutiny of suspects or the accused directly by a judge.

RECONOCIMIENTO PÓSTUMO.
posthumous recognition (of paternity or maternity of child which may be born after death of the father or mother or child).

RECONOCIMIENTO SIMULTÁNEO.
simultaneous recognition of paternity and maternity.

RECONOCIMIENTO SUCESIVO.
consecutive recognition of paternity and maternity.

RECONQUISTA.
f, reconquest, retaking (of territory in a battle).

RECONQUISTAR.
v, to conquer again, retake, regain.

RECONSIDERACIÓN.
f, reconsideration.

RECONSIDERAR.
v, to reconsider.

RECONSTITUCIÓN.
f, reconstitution.

RECONSTITUIR.
v, to reconstitute.

RECONSTRUCCIÓN.
f, reconstruction, recomposition, rebuilding ‖ new construction ‖ building repair or modification ‖ reconstruction, reproduction (of an event) ‖ imitation ‖ post-war reconstruction.

RECONSTRUCCIÓN DE LOS HECHOS.
reconstruction of the facts.

RECONSTRUCCIÓN DEL DELITO.
reconstruction of the crime or the scene of the crime.

RECONSTRUIR.
v, to reconstruct, rebuild ‖ to imitate ‖ to reproduce ‖ to redo.

RECONTAR.
v, to re-count, count again ‖ to recount, retell, relate.

RECONVENCIÓN.
f, counterclaim (if related to the matter in the complaint) ‖ cross-claim or cross-complaint (if not related to the matter in the complaint) ‖ recrimination, reproach ‖ charge, accusation.

RECONVENCIONAL.
adj, pertaining to a counterclaim or cross-claim or recrimination or charge.
See RECONVENCIÓN.

RECONVENIR.
v, to reproach, rebuke, recriminate ‖ to counterclaim or cross-claim.
See RECONVENCIÓN.

RECOPILACIÓN.
f, summary, compendium ‖ collection ‖ (legal) digest, codification.

RECOPILADOR.
m, codifier ‖ author of a compendium or collection or digest.

RECORDACIÓN.
f, memory (of the past), recollection ‖ commemoration, memorialization.

RECORDAR.
v, to remember, recollect ‖ to commemorate, memorialize.

RECORDATORIO.
m, memento, memorabilia ‖ notice, reminder (to do something) ‖ official reminder (regarding judicial orders or requests between judges).

RECORDATORIO JUDICIAL.
official reminder (regarding judicial orders or requests between judges).

RECRIMINACIÓN.
f, recrimination, reproach ‖ counter accusation (against one's accuser).

RECRIMINADOR.
m, recriminator, reproacher.

RECRIMINAR.
v, to recriminate, reproach ‖ to rebuke ‖ to bring a counter accusation.

RECRIMINARSE.
v, to accuse each other, exchange reproaches or accusations.

RECTAMENTE.
adv, honorably, honestly, with rectitude.

RECTIFICABLE.
adj, rectifiable.

RECTIFICACIÓN.
f, rectification, correction ‖ modification, amendment ‖ counter-order ‖ rectification of misstatement of opposing counsel ‖ misprint correction.

RECTIFICACIÓN DE ASIENTOS DE LOS REGISTROS.
correction of filings or registrations in public registries (e.g. real estate registry, marriage registry).

RECTIFICACIÓN PERIODÍSTICA.
misprint or erratum correction (by the press).

RECTIFICADOR.
m, corrector, rectifier.

RECTIFICAR.
v, to rectify, correct ‖ to amend, modify ‖ to clarify or rectify a misstatement ‖ to issue a counter-order.

RECTIFICATIVO.
adj, rectifying.

RECTITUD.
f, rectitude, honesty ‖ honor ‖ fairness, justness ‖ integrity, morality.

RECTA.
f, right-hand page ‖ straight line.

RECTO.
adj, upright, upstanding ‖ honest, honorable ‖ fair, just ‖ of integrity, moral ‖ literal (meaning).

RECTOR.
m, director ‖ university dean ‖ rector ‖ adj, guiding, leading.

RECTORADO.
m, deanship, directorship ‖ rectorship.

RECTORAL.
adj, concerning a dean or director or rector.

RECTORÍA.
f, post, functions and office of dean or director or rector.

RECUENTO.
m, re-count, count ‖ inventory, inventory check.

RECUERDO.
m, memory ‖ fame, celebrity ‖ warning, reminder ‖ gift, token.

RECUPERABLE.
adv, recoverable.

RECUPERACIÓN.
f, recuperation ‖ recovery, regaining ‖ reconquering.

RECUPERADOR.
m, person who recuperates or recovers or reconquers.

RECUPERAR.
v, to recuperate ‖ to recoup, recover.

RECUPERATORIO.
See ACTO RECUPERATORIO.

RECURRENTE.
m, appellant ‖ adj, recurring, recurrent.

RECURRIBLE.
adj, appealable.

RECURRIDO.
m, appellee ‖ adj, appealed.

RECURRIR.
v, to appeal, bring an appeal ‖ to resort to ‖ to petition.

RECURSO.
m, means, recourse ‖ extraordinary proceeding ‖ request ‖ written petition or demand, complaint ‖ legal recourse ‖ resource ‖ economic resource ‖ appeal ‖ motion.

RECURSO ADMINISTRATIVO.
administrative recourse or petition or claim.

RECURSO CONCEDIDO EN RELACIÓN.
appeal petition which permits no additional proof or claims.

RECURSO CONCEDIDO LIBREMENTE.
appeal petition which permits additional proof and claims.

RECURSO CONTENCIOSO ADMINISTRATIVO.
judicial complaint against an administrative decision or action.

RECURSO CONTENCIOSO ADMINISTRATIVO.
See RECURSO CONTENCIOSO ADMINISTRATIVO.

RECURSO DE ACLARACIÓN.
motion for clarification (presented to the same judge who issued the original decision).

RECURSO DE ACLARATORIA DE SENTENCIA.
See RECURSO DE ACLARACIÓN.

RECURSO DE AGRAVIO.
appeal to the head of state by a military serviceman complaining of superior officer's inaction regarding a complaint.

RECURSO DE ALZADA.
appeal.

RECURSO DE AMPARO.
complaint based on violation of constitutional

rights when such rights cannot be adequately and promptly protected by other procedural means. See JUICIO DE AMPARO or AMPARO.

RECURSO DE ANULACIÓN.
See RECURSO DE NULIDAD.

RECURSO DE APELACIÓN.
appeal, motion for appeal.

RECURSO DE AUDIENCIA.
motion for retrial (submitted by a party who fails to appear, based on the virtual impossibility of appearance).

RECURSO DE CASACIÓN.
type of extraordinary appeal to a supreme court (court of cassation) to request the reversal of a final lower court decision which violates either substantive or procedural law. Depending upon the legal system the court hearing the appeal may issue a new decision directly or may send it back to the prior court or to a new court for their reconsideration in line with the cassation decision.

RECURSO DE CASACIÓN DOBLE.
type of extraordinary appeal to a supreme court or a court of cassation requesting the reversal of a final lower court decision which violates both substantive and procedural law. See RECURSO DE CASACIÓN.

RECURSO DE CASACIÓN EN INTERÉS DE LA LEY.
type of extraordinary appeal to a supreme court or a court of cassation in which the Attorney General may join in the interests of assuring that the decision does not conflict with accepted legal doctrine. See RECURSO DE CASACIÓN.

RECURSO DE CASACIÓN EN LAS CAUSAS DE MUERTE.
type of extraordinary appeal to a supreme court or a court of cassation to request reversal of a death sentence. See RECURSO DE CASACIÓN.

RECURSO DE CASACIÓN POR INFRACCIÓN DE LEY.
type of extraordinary appeal to a supreme court or court of cassation requesting the reversal of a final lower court decision which violates substantive law. See RECURSO DE CASACIÓN.

RECURSO DE CASACIÓN POR QUEBRANTAMIENTO DE FORMA.
type of extraordinary appeal to a supreme court or court of cassation requesting the reversal of a final lower court decision which violates procedural law. See RECURSO DE CASACIÓN.

RECURSO DE DOCTRINA LEGAL.
See RECURSO DE INAPLICABILIDAD DE LA LEY.

RECURSO DE FUERZA.
appeal to civil courts which requests the reversal of a decision of an ecclesiastical court.

RECURSO DE FUERZA EN CONOCER.
See RECURSO DE FUERZA.

RECURSO DE HÁBEAS CORPUS.
habeas corpus appeal.

RECURSO DE INAPLICABILIDAD DE LA LEY.
appeal which requests the reversal of a decision which (allegedly) contradicts doctrine established by one of the chambers of the same appellate court during the prior ten years.

RECURSO DE INCONSTITUCIONALIDAD.
appeal which requests the reversal of a decision which (allegedly) violates the constitution.

RECURSO DE NULIDAD.
appeal based on procedural violations of the lower court trial ‖ also see RECURSO DE CASACIÓN. Meaning and use varies substantially from jurisdiction to jurisdiction.

RECURSO DE QUEJA.
type of appeal filed when a lower court judge improperly refuses to permit or delays the filing of an appeal.

RECURSO DE RECONSIDERACIÓN.
See RECURSO DE REPOSICIÓN.

RECURSO DE REFORMA.
interlocutory appeal (in a civil case).

RECURSO DE REPOSICIÓN.
appeal to a court requesting the reversal of its own decisions.

RECURSO DE RESCISIÓN.
See RECURSO DE AUDIENCIA.

RECURSO DE REVISIÓN.
motion to reopen a case (based on evidence of the falseness of the facts upon which the prior decision was made).

RECURSO DE REVOCACIÓN.
See RECURSO DE REVOCATORIA.

RECURSO DE REVOCATORIA.
See RECURSO DE REPOSICIÓN.

RECURSO DE SÚPLICA.
See RECURSO DE REFORMA and RECURSO DE REPOSICIÓN.

RECURSO EXTRAORDINARIO.
extraordinary appeal, appeal available when all other recourses have been exhausted. Includes RECURSO DE CASACIÓN, RECURSO DE REVISIÓN and RECURSO DE INCONSTITUCIONALIDAD. Opposed to RECURSO ORDINARIO.

RECURSO EXTRAORDINARIO DE APELACIÓN.
extraordinary appeal to the Supreme Court, available when all other recourses have been exhausted ‖ also see RECURSO DE REVISIÓN.

RECURSO GUBERNATIVO.
appeal before a court of special jurisdiction to require the registration of property or to request the lifting of clouds on the title to property such that it can be properly registered.

RECURSO JERÁRQUICO.
appeal before a higher administrative authority.

RECURSO JUDICIAL.
appeal before a judicial court.

RECURSO ORDINARIO.
ordinary appeal (before an appellate court or the lower court hearing the case). Opposed to RECURSO EXTRAORDINARIO.

RECURSO POR INFRACCIÓN DE LEY.
type of appeal to a military court requesting the reversal of a final lower court decision which violates either substantive or procedural law.

RECURSOS.
m, resources ‖ goods ‖ means ‖ provisions ‖ possibilities ‖ subsidies ‖ money ‖ appeals ‖ judicial remedies.

RECURSOS NATURALES.
natural resources.

RECUSABLE.
adj, recusable.

RECUSACIÓN.
f, recusation (of a judge, advisor, expert witness, secretary, special public notary, or other public official) ‖ rejection, refusal.

RECUSADO.
m, recused person (see RECUSACIÓN) ‖ person against whom a request for recusation has been made ‖ adj, recused, rejected, excused ‖ objected to, challenged.

RECUSANTE.
m, person who challenges or requests for recusation.

RECUSAR.
v, to recuse ‖ to reject ‖ to object to, challenge

RECHAZAMIENTO.
m, rejection, negative ‖ resistance ‖ opposition ‖ denial.

RECHAZAR.
v, to reject ‖ to resist ‖ to oppose, contradict ‖ to deny.

RECHAZO.
See RECHAZAMIENTO.

RED.
f, web ‖ ring (e.g. of spies) ‖ chain (of commercial establishments, etc.).

REDACCIÓN.
f, writing, drafting ‖ editing ‖ editorial staff group of editors ‖ editorial office.

REDACTAR.
v, to write, draw up, draft ‖ to edit.

REDACTOR.
m, writer, drafter ‖ editor ‖ journalist ‖ main writer.

REDACTORA.
f, female writer or drafter or editor or journalist or main writer.

REDARGUCIÓN.
f, counter-argument, refutation ‖ contradiction, denial (of an argument) ‖ impugnment.

REDARGÜIR.
v, to counter-argue, refute ‖ to contradict, deny ‖ to impugn.

REDENCIÓN.
f, recourse, remedy ‖ redemption (of a mortgage, etc.) ‖ restitution, restoration, recovery (of something lost).

REDENCIÓN DE CENSOS.
redemption or lifting of a CENSO.

REDENCIÓN DE SERVIDUMBRES.
redemption or lifting of easements.

REDENTOR.
m, redeemer ‖ provider.

REDESCUENTO.
m, rediscount.

REDESPACHAR.
v, to resend, reconsign (without passing through customs).

REDHIBICIÓN.
f, redhibition ‖ rescission of sale (by buyer) upon rejection of goods for hidden defects

and return of money paid.
See VICIOS REDHIBITORIOS.

REDHIBIR.
v, to rescind a sale (by buyer upon rejection of goods for hidden defects).
See REDHIBICIÓN.

REDHIBITORIA.
See ACCIÓN REDHIBITORIA.

REDHIBITORIO.
adj, pertaining to REDHIBICIÓN.

REDIMIBLE.
adj, redeemable.

REDIMIR.
v, to redeem ‖ to rescue, free (from slavery) ‖ to repurchase ‖ to free (from liens) ‖ to extinguish or terminate an obligation ‖ to free from guilt ‖ to exempt from a sentence.

RÉDITO.
m, income ‖ benefit ‖ profit ‖ earning ‖ interest.

REDITUABLE.
adj, interest bearing ‖ beneficial ‖ profitable.

REDITUAL.
See REDITUABLE.

REDITUAR.
v, to produce profits or earnings or income or benefits.

REDUCCIÓN.
f, reduction, diminution, decrease ‖ discount ‖ conversion, transformation ‖ summary ‖ conversion or change of money (from larger to smaller bills or coins) ‖ change ‖ concentration ‖ surrender, rendition ‖ persuasion.

REDUCCIÓN DE CRÉDITOS.
diminution or reduction of a borrowing or loan (through forgiveness or payment) ‖ composition, partial release of debtor in bankruptcy; cram-down or forced reduction of a debt (in a bankruptcy) ‖ partial discharge of a debt.

REDUCCIÓN DE DEUDAS.
See REDUCCIÓN DE DEUDAS.

REDUCCIÓN DE DONACIONES.
diminution of bequests to heirs who are not legal heirs (in order to insure that the legal heirs receive their due share).

REDUCCIÓN DE LA HIPOTECA.
reduction of the mortgage (possible only on property which is severable).

REDUCCIÓN DE LA PENA.
reduction of the (criminal) sentence.

REDUCCIÓN DE LOS ALIMENTOS.
reduction of alimony payments.

REDUCCIÓN DE LOS LEGADOS.
diminution of legatees in an inheritance (in order to insure that the legal heirs receive their due share).

REDUCCIÓN DEL PRECIO.
price discount, reduction in price.

REDUCCIÓN EN LAS SUCESIONES.
diminution of bequests among legal heirs (such that legal heirs receive their due share).
See REDUCCIÓN DE DONACIONES.

REDUCIR.
v, to reduce, diminish, decrease ‖ to discount ‖ to move ‖ to make changes ‖ to summarize ‖ to convert ‖ to subject, subjugate ‖ to persuade, convince ‖ to buy or sell stolen goods.

REDUCIR A PRISIÓN.
to jail, imprison, lock up.

REEDICIÓN.
f, republication.

REEDIFICACIÓN.
f, rebuilding, reconstruction ‖ remodeling.

REEDITAR.
v, to republish.

REEDUCACIÓN.
f, re-education.

REEDUCACIÓN PROFESIONAL.
professional retraining (of an accident victim whose injuries require him or her to acquire a new profession).

REEDUCAR.
v, to re-educate ‖ to retrain.

REELECCIÓN.
f, re-election.

REELECTO.
adj, re-elected.

REELEGIR.
v, to re-elect.

REEMBARCAR.
v, to ship again ‖ to re-embark.

REEMBARGAR.
v, to re-impose or increase a (pre-existing) garnishment or attachment.

REEMBARQUE.
m, reshipment ‖ re-embarkation.

REEMBOLSABLE.
adj, reimbursable.

REEMBOLSAR.
v, to reimburse, pay back ‖ to indemnify.

REEMBOLSO.
m, reimbursement ‖ indemnification.
REEMBOLSO EN LA LETRA DE CAMBIO.
indemnification of a dishonored draft.
REEMPLAZABLE.
adj, replaceable.
REEMPLAZAR.
v, to replace, substitute.
REEMPLAZO.
m, replacement, substitution.
REENDOSAR.
v, to re-endorse.
REENDOSO.
m, re-endorsement.
REENGANCHAMIENTO.
See REENGANCHE.
REENGANCHAR.
v, to reenlist.
REENGANCHE.
m, reenlistment.
REENVIAR.
v, to forward or send on ‖ to return back, return ‖ to return a copy ‖ to ship again.
REENVÍO.
m, return ‖ reshipment ‖ renvoi (in conflict of laws) ‖ forwarding.
REEXAMINACIÓN.
f, reexamination.
REEXAMINAR.
v, to reexamine.
REEXPEDICIÓN.
f, return to sender ‖ forwarding.
REEXPEDIR.
v, to return to sender ‖ to forward.
REEXPORTACIÓN.
f, re-exportation.
REEXPORTAR.
v, to reexport (usually from a free port).
REEXTRADICIÓN.
f, re-extradition (to original country).
REFACCIÓN.
f, repair, renovation ‖ bonus, extra ‖ upkeep ‖ upkeep expenses.
REFACCIONARIO.
adj, pertaining to REFACCIÓN.
REFERENCIA.
f, account, narration ‖ information ‖ reference, citation, notation, note ‖ (personal) reference.
REFERÉNDUM.
m, referendum.

REFERENTE.
adj, concerning, referring or pertaining to.
REFERIDO.
adj, said, referred ‖ according to a reference.
REFERIMIENTO.
See REFERENCIA.
REFERIR.
v, to narrate, tell, relate ‖ to tie together ‖ to inform ‖ to indicate ‖ to refer to.
REFERIRSE.
v, to refer or allude to.
REFIRMAR.
v, to resign ‖ to ratify or confirm (in writing).
REFLOTAMIENTO.
m, reflotation or refloating (of a damaged or sunken ship).
REFLOTAR.
v, to refloat.
REFORMA.
f, reform, change, innovation ‖ modification, variation ‖ correction, amendment ‖ restoration ‖ diminution, decrease ‖ (legislative) reform ‖ termination of an administrative agency ‖ termination or decrease of employment.
REFORMA AGRARIA.
agrarian reform.
REFORMA CONSTITUCIONAL.
constitutional reform.
REFORMA SOCIAL.
social reform or change.
REFORMABLE.
m, juvenile delinquent who is reformable ‖ adj, reformable, alterable, changeable ‖ modifiable, variable.
REFORMACIÓN.
f, reformation, action of reformation ‖ change, innovation, modification.
REFORMADO.
adj, reformed ‖ changed, altered ‖ modified.
REFORMAR.
v, to reform, redo ‖ to modify, change ‖ to repair ‖ to reestablish ‖ to restore ‖ to amend, correct ‖ to deprive of employment or salary ‖ to terminate an administrative agency ‖ to reduce ‖ to vary.
REFORMATORIO.
f, reformatory (usually for juvenile delinquents) ‖ adj, reforming.
REFORMATORIO DE DELINCUENTES.
criminal reformatory.

REFORMATORIO DE MENORES.
juvenile delinquent reformatory.
REFORMISMO.
m, reformism.
REFORMISTA.
m, f, reformer ‖ innovator, changer ‖ follower
of reformism.
REFORZAR.
v, to reinforce.
REFRACTARIO.
adj, rebellious, disobedient ‖ unwilling ‖ breaching.
REFRENDACIÓN.
See REFRENDO.
REFRENDAR.
v, to authorize ‖ to review a passport and visa
‖ to repeat, reiterate ‖ to countersign, legalize,
authenticate.
REFRENDARIO.
m, public official who legalizes or authenticates a document ‖ countersigner.
REFRENDATA.
f, countersignature ‖ legalizing or authenticating signature.
REFRENDO.
m, act of countersigning ‖ legalization, authentication ‖ visa ‖ stamp.
REFRIEGA.
f, fight ‖ dispute ‖ encounter, skirmish.
REFUGIADO.
m, refugee ‖ asylee ‖ adj, in refuge or hiding.
REFUGIAR.
v, to protect, give refuge or asylum.
REFUGIARSE.
v, to take refuge.
REFUGIO.
m, refuge, asylum ‖ sanctuary, protection ‖
poorhouse ‖ war or bomb shelter ‖ retreat.
REFUGIO ANTIAÉREO.
air-raid shelter.
REFUTABLE.
adj, arguable, rebuttable, able to be refuted.
REFUTACIÓN.
f, refutation, rebuttal, counter-argument ‖
counter-proof, counter-evidence.
REFUTAR.
v, to refute, rebut, counter-argue ‖ to give
counter-evidence ‖ to impugn.
REFUTATORIO.
adj, for the purpose of rebuttal or refutation.

REGALADOR.
m, giver, donator ‖ adj, giving.
REGALAR.
v, to give, donate.
REGALÍA.
f, royalty, royalty payment (for a license) ‖ exemption ‖ privilege ‖ rights of royalty, royal
prerogative or privilege ‖ (employment) perquisite, bonus, perk ‖ gift, present.
REGALO.
m, gift, present ‖ pleasure ‖ donation ‖ token.
REGALOS ENTRE CÓNYUGES.
spousal gifts, gifts between spouses.
REGATEAR.
v, to barter, discuss a price, haggle, bargain ‖
to resell at retail.
REGATEO.
m, bargaining, bartering, haggling.
REGENCIA.
f, regency ‖ management, governance ‖ post
or functions or term of a regent or manager.
REGENTA.
f, wife of a regent or manager ‖ female professor or teacher ‖ female regent or manager.
REGENTAR.
v, to govern, administrate ‖ to direct, manage
‖ to act as REGENTE ‖ to hold (a position or
post).
REGENTE.
m, manager, foreman ‖ director, rector, regent ‖ administrator ‖ temporary ruler (in the
stead of a monarch who lacks capacity due to
age, incapacity, or absence) ‖ university regent
‖ factor, agent (in small businesses).
REGENTEAR.
See REGENTAR.
REGICIDA.
f, m, regicide, person who assassinates a king
or queen. adj, regicidal.
REGICIDIO.
m, regicide, assassination of a king or queen
(or other royal family member).
REGIDOR.
m, ruler, governor, administrator ‖ alderman,
councilman ‖ adj, ruling, governing.
RÉGIMEN.
m, method, system ‖ regime, government ‖
norms, practices ‖ regulations.
RÉGIMEN CARCELARIO.
See RÉGIMEN PENITENCIARIO.

RÉGIMEN CELULAR.
system of solitary confinement (in a prison).
RÉGIMEN CONTRACTUAL.
system of common control over community property of spouses ‖ contractual system or regime.
RÉGIMEN CONYUGAL DE BIENES.
community property system of marital property.
RÉGIMEN CORPORATIVO.
See CORPORATIVISMO.
RÉGIMEN DE ABSORCIÓN DE BIENES.
system whereby husband owns all property of marital community.
RÉGIMEN DE COMUNIDAD LIMITADA.
limited community property system. In contrast to RÉGIMEN DE COMUNIDAD UNIVERSAL.
RÉGIMEN DE COMUNIDAD UNIVERSAL.
total community property system (whereby all present and future property becomes part of marital community).
RÉGIMEN DE SEPARACIÓN DE BIENES.
separate property system of marital community
RÉGIMEN DOTAL.
dowry system whereby the husband may use and administer the dowry but the ownership remains in the wife.
RÉGIMEN FEDERAL.
federal system.
RÉGIMEN INTERIOR.
military regulations, rules, norms and practices.
RÉGIMEN LEGAL DE BIENES EN EL MATRIMONIO.
legal system which regulates the property of the marital property.
RÉGIMEN MONÁRQUICO.
monarchical system.
RÉGIMEN PARLAMENTARIO.
parliamentary system.
RÉGIMEN PENAL.
See RÉGIMEN PENITENCIARIO.
RÉGIMEN PENITENCIARIO.
penal or prison system.
RÉGIMEN PRESIDENCIALISTA.
See PRESIDENCIALISMO.
RÉGIMEN REPRESENTATIVO.
representative system of government.
RÉGIMEN REPUBLICANO.
republican system of government.

RÉGIMEN SIN COMUNIDAD.
separate property system of marital community.
RÉGIMEN SINDICAL.
union regulations, norms, rules and practices.
RÉGIMEN UNITARIO.
See ESTADO UNITARIO.
REGIMENTAR.
v, to regiment.
REGIMIENTO.
m, regiment ‖ act of ruling or governing ‖ city council ‖ position and functions of a city councilman or alderman ‖ mob.
REGIO.
adj, regal, royal ‖ wonderful ‖ sumptuous.
REGIÓN.
f, region, area, territory, zone, sector, division.
REGIONALISMO.
m, regionalism, provincialism.
REGIR.
v, to rule, govern ‖ to direct, manage ‖ to be in effect ‖ to guide ‖ to carry.
REGISTRADO.
adj, registered ‖ patented.
REGISTRADOR.
m, registrar ‖ recorder, recording device ‖ public registrar ‖ official registrar of real estate ‖ government inspector.
REGISTRADOR DE LA PROPIEDAD.
recorder or registrar of the real estate registry.
REGISTRAL.
adj, registry, pertaining to registry ‖ registration, pertaining to registration.
REGISTRAR.
v, to register ‖ to examine closely, search, perform a search ‖ to deliver goods, etc. for inspection ‖ to record, make a filing, enter in a registry ‖ to transcribe or copy passages exactly from a public registry.
REGISTRO.
m, inspection, close examination ‖ search ‖ register, record, registry or record book ‖ registrar's office, registry ‖ registration, filing, entry, entry notation ‖ registration certificate ‖ asterisk, notation marker ‖ ship's tonnage.
REGISTRO BRUTO.
gross tonnage (of a ship).
REGISTRO CENTRAL DE PENADOS Y REBELDES.
central registry of convicts and fugitives.

REGISTRO CIVIL.
civil registry, registry in which births, deaths, marriages, adoptions, divorces, legitimizations of children, naturalizations, etc. are registered.

REGISTRO CONSULAR.
consular registry, registry which serves the same purpose as that of REGISTRO CIVIL for nationals residing abroad.

REGISTRO DE ACTOS DE ÚLTIMA VOLUNTAD.
probate office, office where last wills and testaments are registered after a death.

REGISTRO DE ASOCIACIONES.
registry of corporations and other legal associations, office where after having been duly authorized all legal associations are registered.

REGISTRO DE BUQUES.
registry of ships (registered within a given nation) ‖ registration book (of ships in port) ‖ registry of ship ownership and related contracts.

REGISTRO DE DEFUNCIONES.
registry of deaths ‖ death certificate.

REGISTRO DE EMBARGOS.
registration of attachments pertaining to real estate.

REGISTRO DE ESCRIBANOS.
registry of special notary publics.
See ESCRIBANO.

REGISTRO DE HIPOTECAS.
type of real estate registry (for the registry of mortgages).

REGISTRO DE INHIBICIONES.
registry of judicial restraints on alienation.

REGISTRO DE LA CORRESPONDENCIA.
recording of correspondence and other communications (by corporations).

REGISTRO DE LA PROPIEDAD.
real estate registry, real estate recording office.

REGISTRO DE LA PROPIEDAD INDUSTRIAL.
registry of industrial property rights. Includes patent office, trademark (and trade name) registry office, etc.

REGISTRO DE LA PROPIEDAD INTELECTUAL.
registry of intellectual property rights. Includes copyright office, official translator registry office, etc.

REGISTRO DE MATRIMONIOS.
marriage registry, marriage license office.

REGISTRO DE MINAS.
mining claims office.

REGISTRO DE NACIMIENTOS.
birth registry ‖ birth registration.

REGISTRO DE PAPELES.
registration of documents ‖ search for documents.

REGISTRO DE PENADOS.
court registry of convicted persons.

REGISTRO DE SOCIEDADES ANÓNIMAS.
registry of commercial corporations.
See SOCIEDADES ANÓNIMAS.

REGISTRO DE TESTAMENTOS.
See REGISTRO DE ACTOS DE ÚLTIMA VOLUNTAD.

REGISTRO DE TUTELAS.
registry of guardianships, registry of wards of the court.

REGISTRO MERCANTIL.
commercial registry (of documents in order that they become enforceable against third parties).

REGISTRO MINERO.
See REGISTRO DE MINAS.

REGISTRO NACIONAL DE REINCIDENCIA.
national registry of recidivism.

REGISTRO PARROQUIAL.
ecclesiastical registry (of births, deaths, baptisms, confirmations and marriages of members).

REGISTRO PRIVADO.
private notation or note ‖ unsworn writing ‖ private registry or list (i.e. maintained by non governmental authority).

REGISTRO PÚBLICO.
public registry ‖ public record book, public registry book, public registry ‖ public filing or entry or registration.

REGISTRO PÚBLICO DE COMERCIO.
See REGISTRO MERCANTIL.

REGLA.
f, rule, norm, principle, precept ‖ statute ‖ constitution ‖ ruler, measuring stick ‖ criterion ‖ moderation ‖ order, harmony ‖ law ‖ limitation ‖ guideline.

REGLA GENERAL.
general rule ‖ general legal principle or norm.

REGLADAMENTE.
adv, moderately, temperately.

REGLADO.
adj, moderate, temperate ‖ ordered ‖ ruled ‖ measured ‖ pursuant to measurement ‖ according to an order or precept.

REGLAMENTACIÓN.
f, regimentation, order ‖ regulation, rule ‖ regulations, rules ‖ establishment of regulations or norms.

REGLAMENTACIONES DE TRABAJO.
work rules or guidelines, rules of employment.

REGLAMENTAR.
v, to regulate, rule ‖ to issue norms or guidelines.

REGLAMENTARIO.
adj, regulatory, ruling, pertaining to a rule or regulation ‖ detailed.

REGLAMENTO.
m, administrative regulation or rule (issued pursuant to law) ‖ by- laws, constitution, written rules which regulate a government or business enterprise ‖ executive order or decree or proclamation.

REGLAMENTO ADMINISTRATIVO.
administrative regulation.

REGLAMENTO CONCORDADO DE TRABAJO.
work rules or guidelines or rules of employment agreed to by collective bargaining agreement.

REGLAMENTO DE LA ADMINISTRACIÓN PÚBLICA.
administrative rule or regulation.

REGLAMENTO DE TALLER.
See REGLAMENTACIONES DE TRABAJO.

REGLAMENTO DE TRABAJO.
See REGLAMENTACIONES DE TRABAJO.

REGLAMENTO EJECUTIVO.
executive order or decree of proclamation ‖ also see REGLAMENTO DE LA ADMINISTRACIÓN PÚBLICA.

REGLAR.
adj, ruled, regulated ‖ v, to regulate, rule.

REGLAS DE LA SANA CRÍTICA.
See SANA CRÍTICA.

REGLAS DEL DERECHO.
legal axioms ‖ rules of law ‖ legal principles or norms or precepts (usually unwritten).

REGNÍCOLA.
m, subject of a monarchy ‖ writer on topics particular to his country.

REGRESIÓN.
f, regression.

REGRESIVO.
adj, regressive.

REGRESO.
m, return ‖ reappearance (of a missing person thought to be dead) ‖ redraft.

REGULACIÓN.
f, regulation ‖ system, regulations, rules, guidelines.

REGULACIÓN LABORAL.
employment regulations. May be INDIVIDUAL (imposed unilaterally by the employer); CONTRACTUAL (pursuant to an employment contract); COLECTIVA (pursuant to collective bargaining); PROFESSIONAL (imposed by professional rules and regulations); or LEGAL (imposed by law).

REGULADO.
adj, ordered ‖ regulated ‖ organized ‖ regular.

REGULADOR.
m, regulator, controller ‖ organizer ‖ adj, regulating.

REGULAR.
m, regular (in the military) ‖ adj, regular ‖ regulating ‖ normal ‖ fair, ordinary ‖ habitual ‖ v, to regulate, establish a rule or norm or guideline ‖ to adjust ‖ to set or establish fees ‖ to compute, calculate ‖ to put in order.

REGULARIDAD.
f, regularity ‖ normality ‖ strict observance of a rule.

REGULARIZAR.
v, to impose or establish order ‖ to organize ‖ to discipline ‖ to regularize.

REGULARMENTE.
adv, regularly, habitually, usually, normally ‖ generally.

REHABILITACIÓN.
f, rehabilitation ‖ discharge.

REHABILITACIÓN DEL FALLIDO.
discharge of a bankrupt ‖ rehabilitation of an insolvent debtor.

REHABILITACIÓN DEL PENADO.
rehabilitation of a criminal.

REHABILITACIÓN DEL QUEBRADO.
discharge of a bankrupt.

REHABILITAR.
v, to rehabilitate ‖ to reinstate (rights or privileges) ‖ to restore (the reputation of a person who is wrongly accused) ‖ to return, restore

(things to their owner) ‖ to discharge (a bankrupt) ‖ to absolve (a criminal who has served
his sentence and paid proper indemnification).

REHABILITARSE.
v, to rehabilitate oneself ‖ to recover or regain
one's reputation or credit.

REHACER.
v, to redo, remake ‖ to rebuild, reconstruct ‖
to repair, indemnify ‖ to reform, correct.

REHÉN.
m, hostage ‖ enemy prisoner.

REHUIDA.
f, flight, avoidance ‖ breach ‖ excuse ‖ denial.

REHUIR.
v, to flee, avoid ‖ to excuse ‖ to deny.

REHUSAR.
v, to oppose, reject (something) ‖ to refuse,
turn down.

REIMPORTACIÓN.
f, re-importation.

REIMPORTAR.
v, to re-import.

REIMPRESIÓN.
f, reprint, reprinting.

REIMPRIMIR.
v, to reprint.

REINA.
f, queen, female monarch ‖ wife or widow of
king.

REINADO.
m, reign (duration of rule).

REINANTE.
adj, ruling ‖ reigning.

REINAR.
v, to rule, govern ‖ to dominate.

REINCIDENCIA.
f, recidivism, repetition of the same or similar
crime.

REINCIDENCIA ESPECÍFICA.
recidivism or repetition of the same crime.

REINCIDENCIA GENÉRICA.
generic recidivism, relapse into criminal activity (not necessarily the same crime).

REINCIDENTE.
f, m, recidivist, repeat offender ‖ backslider ‖
adj, repeating, relapsing, backsliding.

REINCIDIR.
v, to be a recidivist ‖ to repeat a crime ‖ to
backslide ‖ to relapse into crime.

REINCORPORACIÓN.
f, reincorporation ‖ rejoining.

REINCORPORAR.
v, to reincorporate, reintegrate ‖ to rejoin.

REINCORPORARSE.
v, to reincorporate or reintegrate oneself ‖ to
rejoin (a military unit).

REINGRESAR.
v, to rejoin (prior employment) ‖ to re-enter.

REINGRESO.
m, rejoining (prior employment) ‖ reentering.

REINO.
m, kingdom, realm.

REINSTALACIÓN.
f, reinstallation ‖ move, transfer ‖ restoration
‖ reinstatement.

REINSTALAR.
v, to reinstall ‖ to move, transfer ‖ to restore ‖
to reinstate.

REINTEGRABLE.
adj, able to be returned or restored ‖ refun-
dable.

REINTEGRACIÓN.
f, restoration, return, restitution (of property).

REINTEGRAR.
v, to refund ‖ to repay, reimburse ‖ to restore,
return ‖ to repair, indemnify, pay restitution ‖
to replace ‖ to re-establish.

REINTEGRARSE.
v, to recover (lost or loaned or mislaid property) ‖ to make payment.

REINTEGRO.
m, reintegration ‖ restitution, restoration, return ‖ repayment, reimbursement ‖ recovery
(of property) ‖ payment.

REINTEGRO DE CAUDALES PÚBLICOS.
repayment or reimbursement of public funds
(which were lost or stolen).

REINVERSIÓN.
f, reinvestment (e.g. of profits).

REITERACIÓN.
f, reiteration, repetition ‖ insistence ‖ recidivism ‖ repetition (of an action).

REITERADAMENTE.
adv, repeatedly ‖ insistently.

REITERADO.
adj, repeated ‖ reiterated.

REITERAR.
v, to reiterate ‖ to repeat ‖ to renew ‖ to become a recidivist.

REITERATIVO.
adj, repeatable, able to be repeated ‖ able to
be reiterated.

REIVINDICABLE.
adj, able to be replevied or repossessed or evicted or ousted or ejected.
REIVINDICACIÓN.
f, replevin, repossession ‖ eviction, ouster, ejectment ‖ action or legal proceeding of replevin or repossession ‖ action or legal proceeding of eviction or ouster or ejectment.
REIVINDICANTE.
f, m, replevisor, plaintiff in a replevin or repossession or eviction or ouster or ejectment action.
REIVINDICAR.
v, to replevy, repossess ‖ to evict, oust, eject ‖ to recover (property) ‖ to reclaim.
REIVINDICATORIO.
adj, replevying, repossessing ‖ evicting, ousting, ejecting ‖ recovering.
REJA.
f, bar, grille, grating ‖ (prison) bars.
RELACIÓN.
f, relation ‖ relationship, tie ‖ connection (to) ‖ treatment ‖ communication ‖ similarity ‖ account, narration, report ‖ nomination ‖ reference; statement.
RELACIÓN CON
EL ENEMIGO.
communication with the enemy.
RELACIÓN DE TRABAJO.
work relationship.
RELACIÓN JURADA.
sworn statement ‖ testimony.
RELACIÓN JURÍDICA.
legal relationship.
RELACIÓN PROCESAL.
procedural relationship, relationship between litigants.
RELACIÓN SOCIAL.
social relationship ‖ social communication (generally).
RELACIONAR.
v, to relate, narrate, state, report ‖ to tie together, connect ‖ to compare.
RELACIONES.
f, relations ‖ relationships ‖ communication.
RELACIONES CONSULARES.
consular relations.
RELACIONES DIPLOMÁTICAS.
diplomatic relations.
RELACIONES HUMANAS.
human relations ‖ human relationships.

RELACIONES PROFESIONALES.
professional relationships (as between colleagues or a client and lawyer) ‖ employee-employer relationships.
RELACIONES PÚBLICAS.
public relations.
RELACIONES SEXUALES.
sexual relations or intercourse.
RELAJACIÓN.
f, mitigation, reduction, relaxation (of a sentence) ‖ dispensing with (a vote or oath) ‖ lightening of or release from a burden or duty ‖ corruption ‖ relaxation (e.g. of traditions).
RELAJAR.
v, to relax ‖ to loosen, lighten (e.g. laws, rules) ‖ to dispense with (a vote or oath) ‖ to release or exempt from a duty ‖ to mitigate, reduce, relax (a sentence).
RELAJARSE.
v, to relax, rest ‖ to corrupt ‖ to relax (discipline or customs).
RELAPSO.
m, relapse, backsliding ‖ recidivism.
RELATAR.
v, to relate, narrate, tell ‖ to defend a legal position (in court) ‖ to tie together, connect ‖ to report.
RELATIVAMENTE.
adv, relatively.
RELATIVIDAD.
f, relativity.
RELATIVISMO.
m, relativism.
RELATIVO.
adj, relative ‖ related ‖ pertaining to ‖ doubtful, questionable.
RELATO.
m, story, narrative ‖ account, report.
RELATOR.
m, storyteller ‖ narrator ‖ reporter ‖ type of court reporter who provides a report or account of a case to a judge.
RELATORIA.
f, office of court reporter.
See RELATOR.
RELEGACIÓN.
f, relegation ‖ banishment, exile, deportation ‖ confinement (to a limited area).
RELEGAR.
v, to banish, exile, deport ‖ to confine (to a limited area).

RELEVACIÓN.

f, relief ‖ exemption, release (from a duty) ‖ forgiveness or cancellation (of a debt) ‖ lightening (of a duty) ‖ lifting (of a lien) ‖ absolution, pardon ‖ lifting of or exemption from an evidentiary requirement.

RELEVANCIA.

f, relevance.

RELEVANTE.

adj, relevant.

RELEVAR.

v, to relieve ‖ to pardon, absolve ‖ to lift (a lien) ‖ to forgive or cancel (a debt) ‖ to exempt, release ‖ to excuse a proof requirement.

RELEVO.

m, relief, soldier on relief duty.

RELICTO.

adj, (property) left at death.

RELICTOS.

m, decedent's estate.

RELIGIÓN.

f, religion.

RELIGIOSO.

adj, religious.

RELUCIR.

v, to shed light on, discover what is hidden ‖ to shine.

REMANDAR.

v, to resend, retransmit.

REMANENTE.

m, remnant, remainder, residue.

REMANENTE DE LA HERENCIA.

remainder from the inheritance (after fulfilling the terms of a will and the law) ‖ decedent's estate which a testator does not expressly dispose of.

REMATADO.

adj, hopeless ‖ auctioned, sold at auction.

REMATADOR.

m, auctioneer.

REMATAR.

v, to auction ‖ to end, conclude, terminate (a job) ‖ to put an end to ‖ to give the fatal blow to, finish off.

REMATE.

m, auction ‖ end, termination, conclusion ‖ closing bid ‖ closing (of an account).

REMBOLSAR.

See REEMBOLSAR.

REMEDIABLE.

adj, remediable, repairable.

REMEDIAR.

v, to remedy ‖ to repair ‖ to help, save ‖ to amend ‖ to correct.

REMEDIO.

m, remedy, repair, redress, reparation ‖ correction ‖ help, aid ‖ support ‖ remedy (as a procedural recourse) ‖ medication ‖ appeal.

REMISIBLE.

adj, pardonable, remissible.

REMISIÓN.

f, remission ‖ remittance, shipment, sending ‖ reference, note ‖ absolution, pardon (of a crime) ‖ release from or forgiveness or cancellation of (a debt) ‖ amnesty.

REMISIÓN DE DEUDA.

release from or forgiveness or cancellation of a debt.

REMISIÓN DE PRENDA.

release or lifting of a pledge or chattel mortgage.

REMISIÓN LEGAL.

legal reference or note in a text (to the full text of the law) ‖ reference made by or to a different statute.

REMISIVO.

adj, reference, referring.

REMISO.

adj, remiss ‖ late.

REMISORIA.

f, remitting court ‖ remanding court ‖ adj, remitting ‖ remanding.

REMISORIO.

adj, forgiving, with power to forgive or pardon.

REMITENTE.

m, sender, shipper.

REMITIDO.

m, type of individual notice published in the newspaper (for legal or other reasons) ‖ adj, remitted, sent.

REMITIR.

v, to send, transmit, dispatch, forward ‖ to ship ‖ to forgive, cancel (a debt) ‖ to pardon (a crime), grant amnesty ‖ to send up, remit, forward (e.g. a case from one court to another) ‖ to remand (a case to a lower court) ‖ to leave, give (a case to another for their decision) ‖ to make reference, refer, footnote (in writings to information located elsewhere in the text).

REMITIRSE.

v, to yield, defer, submit (to) ‖ to refer ‖ to loosen, slacken, relax.

REMOCIÓN.
f, dismissal, firing, removal (from job) ‖ transfer ‖ body removal (after an accident).
REMOCIÓN DE ALBACEAS.
removal of executor or executrix.
REMOCIÓN DE TUTORES.
removal or dismissal of a guardian of a minor.
REMORDER.
v, to feel remorse ‖ to bite again ‖ to bother (one's conscience).
REMORDIMIENTO.
m, remorse.
REMOTO.
adj, remote, distant (in time and place) ‖ improbable.
REMOVER.
v, to remove ‖ to move, change locations ‖ to leave destitute, throw out ‖ to overcome (a difficulty) ‖ to impassion, stir up ‖ to dismiss.
REMUNERACIÓN.
f, remuneration, compensation, pay, salary.
REMUNERADO.
adj, paid, remunerated, compensated, salaried.
REMUNERADOR.
m, remunerator, pay master ‖ adj, remunerating.
REMUNERAR.
v, to pay (a salary), compensate.
REMUNERATIVO.
adj, remunerative ‖ beneficial.
REMUNERATORIO.
adj, remunerative, given as compensation or remuneration ‖ advantageous.
RENDICIÓN.
f, rendition, surrender ‖ act of surrendering ‖ submission ‖ defeat ‖ restitution of dispossessed property ‖ yield, fruit, profit ‖ exhaustion, fatigue (from physical effort) ‖ rendering (of accounts).
RENDICIÓN DE CUENTAS.
rendering of accounts.
RENDICIÓN INCONDICIONAL.
unconditional surrender.
RENDICIÓN MERCANTIL DE CUENTAS.
rendering of commercial accounts.
RENDICIÓN MILITAR.
military surrender or rendition.
RENDIDO.
adj, rendered, surrendered ‖ defeated ‖ tired, exhausted ‖ submissive, servile ‖ humble.

RENDIMIENTO.
m, fatigue, exhaustion (from physical effort) ‖ profit, yield, output ‖ revenue, earnings ‖ performance, efficiency ‖ subordination, submission.
RENDIR.
v, to surrender, give up ‖ to be defeated ‖ to defeat, conquer ‖ to submit, render, deliver ‖ to wear out, exhaust ‖ to return, give back (something taken) ‖ to yield, produce (e.g. profits, benefits).
RENDIR CUENTA.
to present and justify accounts.
RENDIRSE.
v, to surrender, give up ‖ to become exhausted, become worn out.
RENOVABLE.
adj, renewable.
RENOVACIÓN.
f, renewal ‖ restoration ‖ insistence ‖ extension (in paying a debt) ‖ ratification (of mandate) ‖ substitution, replacement ‖ exchange ‖ reiteration ‖ reform.
RENOVAR.
v, to renew ‖ to restore ‖ to reestablish ‖ to exchange ‖ to reform ‖ to replace, substitute ‖ to reiterate ‖ to insist, persist.
RENOVARSE.
v, to renew, change (oneself).
RENTA.
f, income, revenue ‖ revenues ‖ rent, rental payment ‖ public debt ‖ government bonds (or other securities which represent public debt) ‖ annuity ‖ interest (on money).
RENTA BRUTA.
gross revenue or income.
RENTA ESTANCADA.
income from government monopoly.
RENTA GENERAL.
tax revenue, income produced from ordinary taxes and revenues.
RENTA GRAVABLE.
taxable income.
RENTA IMPONIBLE.
See RENTA GRAVABLE.
RENTA LÍQUIDA.
net income ‖ disposable income.
RENTA NACIONAL.
national revenue ‖ national product.
RENTA VITALICIA.
life annuity ‖ life annuity contract, contract by

which one party delivers money or goods to another such that the second party pay monies to the first party or another for the life of the first or second party.

RENTABILIDAD.
f, rentability ‖ income-producing capacity, revenue-yield capacity.

RENTABLE.
adj, rentable, leasable ‖ income-producing, revenue-producing ‖ remunerative.

RENTADO.
adj, rented, leased ‖ with income or revenue.

RENTAR.
v, to rent, lease ‖ to yield, produce (income or interest).

RENTAS PÚBLICAS.
public revenues.

RENTERO.
m, lessee, tenant, renter ‖ lessor, landlord ‖ taxpayer.

RENTISTA.
f, m, person who lives off his investments ‖ person of independent means ‖ annuitant, annuity recipient ‖ public finance expert ‖ bondholder ‖ financier.

RENTÍSTICO.
adj, pertaining to public revenues.

RENUENCIA.
f, reluctance (to do something).

RENUENTE.
adj, reluctant, unwilling (to do something) ‖ disobedient ‖ remiss, late.

RENUNCIA.
f, renunciation ‖ resignation, quitting (of a job or public office) ‖ abandonment ‖ rejection (e.g. of an offer) ‖ letter of resignation, document in which resignation is given ‖ depreciation ‖ giving up (a hope or effort) ‖ abdication ‖ relinquishment, surrender, cession, disclaimer, waiver, release (of a right) ‖ repudiation.

RENUNCIA ABDICATIVA.
resignation or rejection in favor of a specified successor (e.g. a simple rejection of a bequest). See RENUNCIA. Opposed to RENUNCIA TRASLATIVA.

RENUNCIA EXPRESA.
express resignation or rejection or waiver or release. See RENUNCIA.

RENUNCIA PERSONAL.
resignation or rejection which benefits a par-

ticular person. See RENUNCIA. Opposed to RENUNCIA REAL.

RENUNCIA REAL.
resignation or rejection which does not benefit any particular person. See RENUNCIA. Opposed to RENUNCIA PERSONAL.

RENUNCIA TÁCITA.
implied resignation or rejection or waiver or release. See RENUNCIA.

RENUNCIA TRASLATIVA.
resignation or rejection in favor of a specified successor(s). See RENUNCIA. Opposed to RENUNCIA ABDICATIVA.

RENUNCIABLE.
adj, renounceable ‖ rejectable ‖ able to be resigned ‖ able to be relinquished ‖ waivable, releasable.

RENUNCIACIÓN.
f, renunciation ‖ rejection ‖ resignation ‖ relinquishment ‖ waiver, release, disclaimer ‖ abandonment.

RENUNCIANTE.
m, person who waives or rejects or resigns or relinquishes or renounces or releases or disclaims or abandons.

RENUNCIAR.
v, to renounce ‖ to reject (e.g. an offer) ‖ to resign, quit (e.g. a job or public office) ‖ to relinquish, surrender, cede, waive, release, disclaim ‖ to abandon ‖ to give up (e.g. a hope or effort) ‖ to abdicate ‖ to repudiate.

RENUNCIATARIO.
m, beneficiary of a resignation or rejection. See RENUNCIA.

REO.
m, prisoner ‖ accused ‖ (criminal or civil) defendant ‖ criminal, offender ‖ convict, convicted person ‖ adj, guilty ‖ accused.

REO AUSENTE.
fugitive (from justice), criminal defendant who is in default (i.e. failed to appear in court when summoned).

REO DEL ESTADO.
defendant who is accused of a crime involving state security (e.g. treason, rebellion, sedition).

REORGANIZACIÓN.
f, reorganization ‖ re-establishment of order.

REORGANIZAR.
v, to reorganize ‖ to re-establish order.

REPARABLE.
adj, repairable, remediable ‖ indemnifiable ‖ amendable.

REPARACIÓN.
f, reparation, repair ‖ redress, remedy ‖ indemnification ‖ cure.

REPARACIÓN DE AVERÍAS.
repair of ship's average ‖ indemnification for ship's average.

REPARACIÓN DE BIENES INMUEBLES.
repair of real property.

REPARACIÓN DE BIENES MUEBLES.
repair of personal property.

REPARACIÓN DEL BUQUE.
repair of the ship.

REPARACIÓN DEL DAÑO.
indemnification for damage caused ‖ repair of damage suffered.

REPARACIÓN DEL DAÑO DEL DELITO.
repair of damage caused by the crime.

REPARACIÓN DEL OBJETO DEL CONTRATO.
cure of breach of the contractual purpose.

REPARACIONES DE GUERRA.
indemnification for war damage.

REPARACIONES EXTRAORDINARIAS.
extraordinary or major repairs (of property).

REPARACIONES ORDINARIAS.
ordinary and necessary repairs, up-keep, maintenance.

REPARADO.
adj, repaired, fixed ‖ provided ‖ reinforced ‖ indemnified ‖ cured.

REPARADOR.
m, repairer ‖ indemnifier ‖ censor.

REPARAMIENTO.
See REPARACIÓN.

REPARAR.
v, to repair, make reparation ‖ to redress, remedy ‖ to indemnify ‖ to cure.

REPARATIVO.
adj, repairable ‖ indemnifiable ‖ curable ‖ remediable.

REPARO.
m, reparation, repair ‖ remedy ‖ observation ‖ warning ‖ objection ‖ difficulty, inconvenience ‖ temporary defense ‖ port of refuge.

REPARTICIÓN.
f, partition, division ‖ distribution ‖ government department or office which has a degree of autonomy and importance.

REPARTIDO.
adj, distributed ‖ divided, partitioned.

REPARTIDOR.
m, distributor ‖ divider, partitioner ‖ telegram or cablegram deliveryman or delivery woman ‖ court clerk who must distribute the cases to the various courts, judges and secretaries.

REPARTIMIENTO.
m, division, partition ‖ distribution ‖ document which sets forth the terms of a division or partition ‖ apportionment, allotment (of an amount owing) ‖ distribution of cases to the various courts, judges, or secretaries ‖ office of the court clerk who distributes the cases to the various courts, judges, or secretaries.

REPARTIR.
v, to divide, partition ‖ to apportion, divide into shares ‖ to distribute ‖ to distribute cases to the various courts, judges, or secretaries ‖ to allot, divide an amount owing into shares ‖ to partition (property) ‖ to hand out (jobs subject to rotation).

REPARTO.
m, partition ‖ allotment ‖ distribution ‖ delivery ‖ division.

REPARTO A DOMICILIO.
home delivery.

REPARTO SOCIAL.
social or communal distribution (of property).

REPASAR.
v, to pass again ‖ to re-examine ‖ to scan, glance over ‖ to edit, correct (a work or article to be published).

REPASO.
m, re-examination ‖ scan, glance, scanning ‖ editing, correction (of a work or article to be published).

REPATRIACIÓN.
f, repatriation. May be VOLUNTARIA (voluntary) or FORZOSA (forced, e.g. ordered by a court or executive branch).

REPATRIACIÓN DE PRISIONEROS.
repatriation or return of prisoners.

REPATRIAR.
v, to repatriate.

REPELER.
v, to repel, turn back, repulse ‖ to contradict, impugn ‖ to throw off violently.

REPENSAR.
v, to rethink.

REPERCUSIÓN.
f, repercussion, consequence, effect, result.
REPERCUTIR.
v, to have or produce a repercussion or consequence or effect or result.
REPERTORIO.
m, repertory, repertoire ‖ digest, book which contains extracts of full texts which deal with a certain subject.
REPERTORIO DE LEGISLACIÓN.
legislative digest, book which contains extracts of full texts of legislation.
REPETICIÓN.
f, repetition ‖ duplication ‖ reiteration ‖ recidivism ‖ reproduction ‖ right of action for unjust enrichment ‖ action for unjust enrichment ‖ recovery of monies paid upon error or fraud or for some other legal reason, from either the payee or third parties.
REPETICIÓN EN
LA FIANZA.
action of a guarantor against joint obligors when the guarantor pays more than his share of the guaranteed obligation.
REPETICIÓN EN LOS CONTRATOS
REALES.
type of action for unjust enrichment (based on the performance of a contract by only one of the parties). See CONTRATO REAL.
REPETIDO.
adj, repeated.
REPETIR.
v, to repeat ‖ to reiterate ‖ to bring an action against third parties for improper payment or unjust enrichment.
RÉPLICA.
f, reply, answer ‖ replication, answer to a counterclaim or cross claim ‖ refutation ‖ objection ‖ argument.
REPLICACIÓN.
f, (plaintiff's) replication (to defendant's counterclaim or cross claim ‖ reply, answer ‖ reiteration ‖ repetition ‖ insistence.
REPLICADOR.
m, argumentative person ‖ adj, argumentative ‖ biting ‖ objecting.
REPLICAR.
v, to argue ‖ to refute, answer back ‖ to object ‖ to reply, answer (a legal complaint) ‖ to answer insolently ‖ to file a replication, answer a counterclaim or cross claim.

"REPLICATIO".
See RÉPLICA.
REPOBLACIÓN.
f, repopulation.
REPOBLACIÓN FORESTAL.
reforestation.
REPONER.
v, to replace ‖ to give back (e.g. a job or position) ‖ to reinstate (a dismissed worker) ‖ to reincorporate ‖ to substitute (an employee who is not at work) ‖ to oppose, object ‖ to replace (what was temporarily converted) ‖ to revise a decision against which an interlocutory appeal has been filed ‖ to put (something) back into its original condition.
REPONERSE.
v, to recover (one's health or lost property) ‖ to reorganize ‖ to calm down, return to peace.
REPOSICIÓN.
f, replacement ‖ reposition ‖ reinstatement (of a dismissed employee) ‖ return (of stolen or lost goods) ‖ to annul a judgment (ordered by a judge in order to return a case to its original state) ‖ presentation or filing of stamped legal paper when one of the parties has failed to do so.
REPREGUNTA.
f, second question (of a witness to verify the truth of prior testimony) ‖ cross-examination (of a witness to verify the truth of prior testimony).
REPREGUNTAR.
v, to requestion (a witness to verify the truth of prior testimony) ‖ to cross-examine (a witness to verify the truth of prior testimony).
REPRENDER.
v, to reprehend, rebuke, reprimand, admonish ‖ to castigate, punish ‖ to warn, caution.
REPRENDIDO.
adj, rebuked, reprimanded, admonished, reprehended ‖ castigated, punished ‖ warned, cautioned.
REPRENDIMIENTO.
See REPRENSIÓN.
REPRENSIBLE.
adj, reprehensible, meriting admonishment or rebuke ‖ punishable ‖ censurable.
REPRENSIÓN.
f, reprehension ‖ rebuke, admonishment ‖ admonition, reprimand ‖ castigation, punishment, warning, caution.

REPRENSIÓN DISCIPLINARIA.
disciplinary admonishment or rebuke, disciplinary warning.
REPRENSIÓN PRIVADA.
private reprehension or admonishment (e.g. by a judge in chambers).
REPRENSIÓN PÚBLICA.
public reprehension or admonishment (e.g. by a judge in open court).
REPRENSOR.
m, person who reprehends or rebukes ‖ castigator, punisher.
REPRESA.
f, dam, dike ‖ containment ‖ ship recovery, recapture of a ship (captured by pirates or enemy forces).
REPRESALIA.
f, type of lien which attaches upon breach of duty ‖ reprisal, retaliation, revenge.
REPRESALIAS.
f, reprisals ‖ war reprisals.
REPRESAR.
v, to recover or recapture a ship (captured by pirates or enemy forces) ‖ to contain, repress ‖ to dominate ‖ to build a dam or dike.
REPRESENTACIÓN.
f, representation (may include agency, guardianship, or other legal representation) ‖ right of succession by being heirs of the body of heir (see DERECHO DE REPRESENTACIÓN) ‖ statement, declaration ‖ representation, symbol, image (of something or someone) ‖ substitution (of a person) ‖ delegation ‖ request or petition which contains the bases therefor ‖ authority ‖ public performance.
REPRESENTACIÓN APARENTE.
apparent agency.
REPRESENTACIÓN DE LAS PERSONAS ABSTRACTAS.
corporate agency, representation of artificial persons. This terms includes not only the means, but also the legal capacity and power of such representation.
REPRESENTACIÓN DE LAS PERSONAS FÍSICAS.
agency or power of attorney (regarding natural persons), representation of natural persons.
REPRESENTACIÓN HEREDITARIA.
right of succession by reason of being heirs of the body. See DERECHO DE REPRESENTACIÓN.

REPRESENTACIÓN JUDICIAL.
court-ordered representation, agency or guardianship or other legal representation or right of succession ordered by a judge.
See REPRESENTACIÓN.
REPRESENTACIÓN LEGAL.
legal representation, agency or guardianship or other legal representation or right of succession which arises by reason of law (statutory, code, regulation, etc.).
REPRESENTACIÓN PROCESAL.
representation in a legal proceeding.
REPRESENTACIÓN PROPORCIONAL.
proportional representation (in elections).
REPRESENTACIÓN VOLUNTARIA.
voluntary representation, agency or guardianship or other legal representation arising as a result of the will of a party represented and the party representing.
See REPRESENTACIÓN.
REPRESENTADO.
adj, represented ‖ reproduced ‖ symbolized.
REPRESENTADOR.
adj, representing.
REPRESENTANTE.
m, representative ‖ congressional representative ‖ agent ‖ exclusive representative or agent ‖ symbol ‖ artist, actor ‖ adj, representing.
REPRESENTANTE DE COMERCIO.
business representative, commercial agent, factor ‖ commissioned agent.
REPRESENTANTE LEGAL.
legal representative, agent or guardian or other legal representative or successor whose right of representation arises by reason of law (statutory, code, regulation, etc.).
REPRESENTANTE LEGÍTIMO.
See REPRESENTANTE LEGAL.
REPRESENTANTE PATRONAL.
representative of an owner of a business, person who in a large business or a corporation represents and manages the interests of the owner ‖ representative of an employers' association.
REPRESENTANTE SINDICAL.
union representative ‖ union manager.
REPRESENTAR.
v, to represent ‖ to narrate, tell ‖ to inform ‖ to evidence, declare ‖ to replace, substitute ‖ to symbolize ‖ to act as a representative o

agent or guardian or other legal representative ‖ to enact or put on a play.

REPRESENTATIVO.
adj, representative.

REPRESIÓN.
f, repression ‖ containment ‖ check, curb, restraint, control.

REPRIMIR.
v, to repress ‖ to contain, dominate ‖ to refrain ‖ to check, curb, restrain, control.

REPROBABLE.
adj, reprehensible, condemnable.

REPROBACIÓN.
f, reprobation, condemnation, reprehension ‖ refusal, negation ‖ disqualification of a witness.

REPROBAR.
v, to reprove, condemn ‖ to exclude (from a privilege) ‖ to refuse, negate ‖ to disqualify a witness.

REPROBATORIO.
adj, reproving, condemning ‖ refusing, negating ‖ disqualifying.

RÉPROBO.
m, reprobate.

REPROCHABILIDAD.
f, reproachability.

REPROCHABLE.
adj, reproachable ‖ imperfect ‖ immoral ‖ accusable.

REPROCHAR.
v, to reproach ‖ to censure ‖ to accuse.

REPRODUCCIÓN.
f, reproduction ‖ copy, imitation ‖ repetition ‖ recidivism ‖ evidence of facts alleged ‖ procreation.

REPRODUCIR.
v, to reproduce ‖ to produce again.

REPRODUCTIVO.
adj, reproductive ‖ highly beneficial or profitable.

REPRODUCTOR.
m, reproducer, copier, imitator ‖ planter.

REPÚBLICA.
f, republic ‖ duration of a republic ‖ municipality.

REPÚBLICA ARISTÓCRATA.
republic formed by the aristocracy.

REPÚBLICA BURGUESA.
republic formed by the bourgeoisie.

REPÚBLICA DEMOCRÁTICA.
democratic republic.

REPÚBLICA FEDERAL.
federal republic.
Opposed to REPÚBLICA UNITARIA.

REPÚBLICA PARLAMENTARIA.
parliamentary republic.

REPÚBLICA POPULAR.
popular or people's republic, republic formed by the masses.

REPÚBLICA PRESIDENCIALISTA.
presidential republic ‖ republic in which the executive is distinct from the legislature.

REPÚBLICA SOCIALISTA.
socialist republic.

REPÚBLICA UNITARIA.
unitary republic, republic that is not a federation of subordinate states.
Opposed to REPÚBLICA FEDERAL.

REPUBLICANISMO.
m, republicanism, political form of government of a republic.

REPUBLICANO.
m, republican, person who supports republicanism ‖ statesman or stateswoman ‖ citizen of a republic ‖ republican, person who is member of U.S. Republican Party ‖ adj, republican.

REPÚBLICO.
m, statesman ‖ patriot ‖ person who is suited for carrying out important public posts.

REPUDIACIÓN.
f, repudiation, refusal ‖ renunciation ‖ repulsion.

REPUDIACIÓN DE LA HERENCIA.
renunciation of an inheritance (by an heir).

REPUDIACIÓN DE LOS LEGADOS.
renunciation by legatees (of a legacy or bequest).

REPUDIAR.
v, to repudiate, refuse, renounce ‖ to dissent ‖ to repudiate or renounce (e.g. one's wife).

REPUDIO.
m, repudiation or renunciation (e.g. of one's wife).

REPUDIO DE DEUDAS.
repudiation of or refusal to pay one's debts.

REPUESTO.
m, reinstatement (to a position or job after an illness or accident) ‖ stock, supply ‖ spare part ‖ adj, replaced ‖ restored ‖ reinstated ‖ recovered, cured.

REPULSA.
f, negation ‖ refusal ‖ disapproval ‖ censure ‖ condemnation.
REPULSA SOCIAL.
popular revolt or rejection of something (especially of the government).
REPULSAR.
v, to repulse ‖ to refuse ‖ to oppose ‖ to disapprove.
REPULSIÓN.
See REPULSA ‖ repulsion, repugnance.
REPUTACIÓN.
f, reputation, repute ‖ fame, celebrity.
REPUTAR.
v, to estimate, judge, consider ‖ to appreciate, esteem.
REQUERIDOR.
See REQUIRENTE.
REQUERIMIENTO.
m, requirement ‖ judicial order ‖ injunction ‖ mandamus ‖ sworn notification or interrogatory asking for a response to a question or statement ‖ summons ‖ demand.
REQUERIMIENTO JUDICIAL.
mandatory injunction, judicial order to do or refrain from doing something.
REQUERIMIENTO NOTARIAL.
notification or interrogatory sworn before a special notary asking for a response to a question or statement.
REQUERIR.
v, to require, demand ‖ to induce, persuade (someone to take a certain position) ‖ to be necessary ‖ to need ‖ to examine, investigate (a situation) ‖ to observe ‖ to notify ‖ to summon, issue a summons ‖ to enjoin, issue a mandatory injunction.
REQUILORIO.
m, circumlocution ‖ superfluous and bothersome request.
REQUIRENTE.
m, person who requires (something) ‖ summons server ‖ complaint server ‖ person who requests the issuance of or serves a mandatory injunction or other form of REQUERIMIENTO ‖ type of notarial examiner who asks for the response to a REQUERIMIENTO NOTARIAL ‖ judge who issues a mandatory injunction.
REQUISA.
f, requisition (by armed forces) ‖ tour of in-

spection ‖ daily inspection (e.g. of prison) ‖ confiscation.
REQUISABLE.
adj, able to be requisitioned or confiscated.
REQUISAR.
v, to requisition ‖ to confiscate.
REQUISICIÓN.
war donation.
See REQUERIMIENTO and REQUISA.
REQUISICIÓN EN TIEMPO DE GUERRA.
war-time requisition.
REQUISICIÓN EN TIEMPO DE PAZ.
peace-time requisition.
REQUISITO.
m, requirement, requisite.
REQUISITORIA.
f, criminal summons, judicial summons of a criminal ‖ adj, requisitory, pertaining to a request.
REQUISITORIO.
m, mandatory injunction.
"RES".
f, res.
"RES CORPORALES".
res corporales, corporal things.
"RES FURTIVAE".
stolen things.
"RES HEREDITARIAE.
inherited things.
"RES INCORPORALES".
res incorporales, incorporal things.
"RES JUDICATA".
res judicata.
"RES PUBLICA".
public entity ‖ public things, public property.
"RES UNIVERSITATIS".
universitates rerum, aggregate of things.
"RES UXORIA".
things of a wife.
RESACA.
f, redraft against a drawer or endorser.
RESARCIBLE.
adj, repairable, compensable, indemnifiable.
RESARCIMIENTO.
m, compensation, indemnification, redress ‖ restitution, reparation ‖ satisfaction.
RESARCIR.
v, to compensate, indemnify, redress ‖ to repair ‖ to satisfy.
RESCATAR.
v, to rescue ‖ to ransom ‖ to free, obtain the

release, save (from enemy control) ‖ to re-coup, recuperate, recover (what is lost) ‖ to exchange precious metals for merchandise ‖ to discharge, release (from a duty) ‖ to lift a lien ‖ to acquire foreign debt ‖ to pay foreign debt ‖ to save a sinking ship.

RESCATE.
m, rescue ‖ release ‖ ransom ‖ recuperation, recoupment, recovery ‖ redemption of a lien ‖ discharge, release (from a duty) ‖ acquisition of foreign debt ‖ payment of foreign debt ‖ ransom money ‖ saving of a sinking ship.

RESCINDIBLE.
adj, rescindable.

RESCINDIR.
v, to rescind.

RESCISIÓN.
f, rescission.

RESCISIÓN DE LOS CONTRATOS.
rescission of contracts.

RESCISIÓN DE PARTICIONES.
rescission of distribution of decedent's estate.

RESCISORIO.
adj, rescissory, rescinding, having the effect of rescinding.

RESELLAR.
v, to restamp ‖ to remint, recoin ‖ to change the value of government stamps.

RESELLO.
m, restamping ‖ reminting, recoining ‖ changing the value of government stamps.

RESENTIMIENTO.
m, resentment.

RESEÑA.
f, military inspection, review of the troops ‖ brief description, outline, sketch (to identify a person or thing).

RESEÑAR.
v, to review (a book or troops) ‖ to outline, sketch or describe briefly (to identify a person or thing) ‖ to write a review.

RESERVA.
f, reserve ‖ stock ‖ restraint ‖ reservation ‖ custody ‖ savings ‖ exception, exemption ‖ moderation, circumspection ‖ military reserve ‖ see BIENES RESERVABLES ‖ judicial statement that a judicial decision does not preju-dice the rights of third parties ‖ reservation of legal rights (in a contract) ‖ legal obligation to heirs of the body, legal obligation of parents of deceased son or daughter to bequeath part of

their estate to the heirs of said son or daughter ‖ secret ‖ reservation of right or power ‖ adj, reserve.

RESERVA DE ACCIONES.
reservation of right, statement by a party that an action shall not prejudice other rights of that party.

RESERVA DE BIENES.
restraint on alienation (of property).

RESERVA DE DERECHOS.
reservation of legal rights or without prejudice to legal rights, contractual term which is used to indicate that the terms of the contract are not intended to limit in any way the rights or powers of the parties to the contract or third parties whether granted by law or by other contracts.

RESERVA DE DOMINIO.
reservation of title or legal ownership, reserva-tion of right of legal ownership.

RESERVA DEL DERECHO DE ADMISIÓN.
reservation of the right to refuse entrance or admission or membership (e.g. to a country, a locale, a club).

RESERVA ESTATUTARIA.
reserve fund provided by the bylaws.

RESERVA EXTRAORDINARIA.
extraordinary reserves.

RESERVA FACULTATIVA.
voluntary or optional reserve.

RESERVA FAMILIAR.
See RESERVA TRONCAL.

RESERVA LEGAL.
legal reserve.

RESERVA LINEAL.
See RESERVA TRONCAL.

RESERVA MERCANTIL.
reserve fund, undistributed profits of a busi-ness.

RESERVA NACIONAL.
national guard, military reserve.

RESERVA ORDINARIA.
ordinary reserves.

RESERVA ORGÁNICA.
See RESERVA NACIONAL.

RESERVA TRONCAL.
legal obligation to heirs of the body, legal obli-gation of parents of deceased son or daughter to bequeath part of their estate to the heirs of said son or daughter.

RESERVA VIUDAL.
legal obligation of widow or widower to children of marital community (upon remarriage or having a child out of wedlock).

RESERVABLE.
adj, subject to a RESERVA.

RESERVACIÓN.
See RESERVA.

RESERVADAMENTE.
adv, with reservation or caution ‖ secretly, clandestinely.

RESERVADO.
m, reserved compartment or car (of a train) ‖ adj, reserved ‖ discreet, circumspect ‖ private (e.g. mail, writing).

RESERVAR.
v, to reserve ‖ to save, put aside ‖ to set aside, separate ‖ to restrict the use of ‖ to exempt (from the law) ‖ to separate and retain ‖ to shut up, quiet, keep secret ‖ to cover up, hide, conceal ‖ to put off, postpone, defer.

RESERVARSE.
v, to save oneself ‖ to be cautious ‖ to mark time, bide one's time ‖ to distrust ‖ to reserve a right (in a contract, etc.).

RESERVAS BANCARIAS.
central bank reserves (in hard currency) ‖ bank reserves.

RESERVATARIO.
m, child of a deceased parent who has a right to inherit part of grandparents' estate.
See RESERVA TRONCAL.

RESERVATIVO.
adj, reserved, pertaining to a RESERVA.

RESERVISTA.
m, reservist, person who serves in the military reserves ‖ person who is limited by a restraint on alienation.

RESGUARDAR.
v, to defend, protect ‖ to guard against or cover risks.

RESGUARDARSE.
v, to be cautious ‖ to protect or defend oneself ‖ to look for shelter or protection.

RESGUARDO.
m, defense, protection, shelter ‖ prevention ‖ safeguard ‖ pass, safe conduct pass ‖ slip, certificate, voucher (of payment) ‖ written proof of a contract or debt ‖ reserve corps, national guard ‖ border guard (to prevent entry of illegal immigrants or contraband).

RESGUARDO DE DEPÓSITO.
deposit slip (for bailed property) ‖ certificate of deposit (at a warehouse), warehouse receipt.

RESIDENCIA.
f, legal domicile (of a corporation) ‖ residence (where one intends to remain) ‖ housing ‖ domicile, abode, home ‖ period of stay (in a place or country ‖ presence and stay of certain government functionaries in a place as part of their job ‖ process to determine the liability of a government officer for conduct during his term after such term ends.

RESIDENCIAL.
f, position and function of a government functionary who must stay in a place to know it better as part of a job ‖ adj, residential.

RESIDENCIAR.
v, to subject a government officer to a proceeding to determine his liability for conduct during his term after such term ends.

RESIDENTE.
m, resident, person who lives in a place with the intent to reside there permanently ‖ inhabitant ‖ government functionary who must stay in a place as part of his job ‖ adj, residing, resident, residential.

RESIDIR.
v, to reside ‖ to dwell ‖ to live ‖ to be domiciled ‖ to live in a place as part of one's job ‖ to consist of ‖ to rest in, lie ‖ to stay.

RESIGNACIÓN.
f, resignation (in all senses) ‖ relinquishment.

RESIGNACIÓN DE MANDO.
relinquishment of authority.

RESIGNAR.
v, to resign, renounce ‖ to relinquish, hand over (a position).

RESIGNARSE.
v, to resign oneself (to something).

RESIGNATARIO.
m, resignee, beneficiary of a resignation or relinquishment.

RESISTENCIA.
f, resistance ‖ opposition ‖ tolerance, suffering, patience, resignation ‖ capacity, stamina, endurance ‖ firmness, strength ‖ obstacle, obstruction ‖ repugnance, aversion ‖ military resistance.

RESISTENCIA A LA AUTORIDAD.
resisting authority, resisting an officer. May in-

clude resisting arrest or breach of the peace.
RESISTENCIA A LA OPRESIÓN.
resisting (government) oppression, resisting illegal or unconstitutional government action.
RESISTENCIA PASIVA.
passive resistance.
RESISTENTE.
adj, resisting ‖ resistant, resilient, tough.
RESISTIDOR.
adj, resistance, tolerant.
RESISTIR.
v, to resist ‖ to oppose, fight against ‖ to last, remain (against opposition) ‖ to contradict ‖ to disobey ‖ to refuse ‖ to put up with, tolerate, suffer.
RESISTIRSE.
v, to resist.
RESOBRINA.
f, grandniece.
RESOBRINO.
m, grandnephew.
RESOLUBLE.
adj, resoluble ‖ resolvable, solvable.
RESOLUCIÓN.
f, resolution, act of solving or resolving ‖ rescission, revocation ‖ verdict, decision, judgment, order (of the judicial branch) ‖ decree, order, decision (of the executive branch) ‖ nullifying act or statement ‖ destruction ‖ nullification, abrogation ‖ termination, end, finish ‖ solution ‖ position ‖ resoluteness ‖ strength, energy ‖ courage ‖ promptness ‖ means, measure, step.
RESOLUCIÓN DE LA COMPRAVENTA.
rescission of the buy-sell contract or purchase or sale.
RESOLUCIÓN DE LA LOCACIÓN.
rescission of the rental or lease agreement.
RESOLUCIÓN DE LAS OBLIGACIONES.
nullification, nullifying act or statement (which abolishes or invalidates a duty in tort or contract).
RESOLUCIÓN DE LOS CONTRATOS.
contractual rescission or revocation, rescission of contracts.
RESOLUCIÓN JUDICIAL.
judicial verdict or decision or judgment or order or writ.
RESOLUTIVO.
adj, analytical ‖ with the power to resolve, terminate or rescind.

RESOLUTO.
adj, resolved ‖ summarized, brief ‖ expert, skilled ‖ resolute.
RESOLUTORIAMENTE.
adv, resolutely, firmly ‖ with the effect of nullifying or ending or rescinding ‖ by setting forth a decision or judgment.
RESOLUTORIO.
adj, resolute ‖ resolving, deciding ‖ nullifying, voiding, abrogating.
RESOLVER.
v, to resolve ‖ to solve ‖ to decide ‖ to adopt an attitude or position ‖ to clarify a doubt ‖ to put an end to a conflict or problem ‖ to destroy ‖ to analyze ‖ to annul, nullify, void, abrogate ‖ to summarize ‖ to rescind.
RESOLVERSE.
v, to take a stance or position ‖ to void or annul (something).
RESPALDAR.
m, to back, support, indorse ‖ to indorse, endorse, write on the back of.
RESPALDO.
m, backing, support ‖ indorsement ‖ endorsement.
RESPECTIVAMENTE.
adv, respectively ‖ in relation to, with respect to.
RESPECTIVO.
adj, pertaining or concerning or related to.
RESPECTO.
m, respect, relation, pertinence.
RESPECTO A.
See CON RESPECTO A.
RESPETABILIDAD.
f, respectability.
RESPETABLE.
m, respectable ‖ spectators, public ‖ honorable ‖ considerable.
RESPETAR.
v, to respect.
RESPETO.
m, respect ‖ fear, awe.
RESPETO AL SUPERIOR.
respect for an officer or public official.
RESPETO
DE PERSONAS.
respect for others.
RESPETUOSAMENTE.
adv, respectfully ‖ with consideration or deliberation.

RESPETUOSO.
adj, respectful.
RESPONDER.
v, to respond ‖ to answer (e.g. a question, letter) ‖ to comply ‖ to answer (a complaint or counterclaim or cross claim) ‖ to correspond ‖ to guarantee, warranty ‖ to keep proportion ‖ to be civilly liable ‖ to compensate (damages and losses) ‖ to be punished ‖ to assure ‖ to produce ‖ to obey.
RESPONDER POR OTRO.
to guarantee (another's obligation) ‖ to answer for or indemnify the losses caused by another.
RESPONSABILIDAD.
f, responsibility ‖ liability (whether contractual or tortious or criminal) ‖ legal obligation to compensate losses ‖ debt ‖ moral obligation ‖ reliability.
RESPONSABILIDAD ADMINISTRATIVA.
administrative responsibility ‖ liability for administrative acts.
RESPONSABILIDAD AERONÁUTICA.
aeronautic liability, criminal or civil liability for aeronautic breaches or violations.
RESPONSABILIDAD CIVIL.
civil liability.
RESPONSABILIDAD CONTRACTUAL.
contractual liability.
RESPONSABILIDAD CRIMINAL.
criminal liability.
RESPONSABILIDAD CUASICONTRACTUAL.
quasi-contractual liability.
RESPONSABILIDAD CUASIDELICTUAL.
liability for unintentional torts.
RESPONSABILIDAD DELICTUAL.
liability for intentional torts.
RESPONSABILIDAD EXTRACONTRACTUAL.
tortious liability, non-contractual liability.
RESPONSABILIDAD FUNCIONAL.
See RESPONSABILIDAD ADMINISTRATIVA ‖ civil liability of civil servants.
RESPONSABILIDAD JUDICIAL.
judicial liability, liability of a judge for violation of judicial duties. May be either criminal or civil.
RESPONSABILIDAD LEGAL.
statutory liability ‖ legal liability, liability imposed by law (as opposed to contract).

RESPONSABILIDAD LIMITADA.
limited liability.
RESPONSABILIDAD MILITAR.
military liability, liability for violation of military code.
RESPONSABILIDAD MORAL.
moral responsibility ‖ liability for emotional damages.
RESPONSABILIDAD OBJETIVA.
strict liability.
RESPONSABILIDAD PATRONAL.
employer's liability or obligation to compensate losses.
RESPONSABILIDAD PECUNIARIA.
monetary liability or obligation or responsibility.
RESPONSABILIDAD PENAL.
criminal liability.
RESPONSABILIDAD POR HECHO AJENO.
liability for acts of others.
RESPONSABILIDAD PROFESIONAL.
professional responsibility ‖ liability of professionals.
RESPONSABILIDAD SIN CULPA.
strict liability.
RESPONSABILIDAD SOLIDARIA.
See OBLIGACIÓN SOLIDARIA.
RESPONSABILIDAD SUBJETIVA.
liability based on breach of a duty (whether contractual or criminal).
RESPONSABLE.
m, manager, boss ‖ guilty party, criminal (includes author or principal, accomplice and accessory) ‖ liable party ‖ adj, responsible (in all senses) ‖ obligated to respond ‖ liable ‖ answerable ‖ criminally liable ‖ civilly liable ‖ civilly obligated ‖ guilty ‖ serious ‖ wise.
RESPONSABLE CIVILMENTE.
civilly liable (regardless of criminal innocence).
RESPUESTA.
f, response, answer ‖ answer to a complaint, counterclaim ‖ objection ‖ refutation ‖ argument ‖ reply ‖ revenge ‖ testimony, answer (of a witness) ‖ compensation.
RESPUESTA EVASIVA.
evasive response.
RESTABLECER.
v, to re-establish, restore ‖ to compensate ‖ to reinstate.

RESTABLECERSE.
v, to recover (e.g. influence, power, reputation).

RESTAURACIÓN.
m, restoration, recuperation, recovery ‖ reparation, refurbishment (e.g. of a painting) ‖ restoration, reinstatement, re-establishment (e.g. of a political party).

RESTAURAR.
v, to restore, recoup, recuperate, recover ‖ to reinstate, restore, re-establish (e.g. a political regime) ‖ to repair, refurbish (e.g. a painting).

RESTITUCIÓN.
f, restitution, return, restoration ‖ re-establishment ‖ restitution, redelivery of territories (after war).

RESTITUCIÓN DE DEPÓSITO.
return of bailed goods.

RESTITUCIÓN DE LA DONACIÓN.
return of the gift.

RESTITUCIÓN DE LA DOTE.
return or restitution of dowry (upon divorce).

RESTITUCIÓN EN LOS ACTOS JURÍDICOS.
nullification of legal acts ‖ revocation of legal acts.
See ACTO JURÍDICO.

RESTITUCIÓN IN INTEGRUM.
restitution or compensation in full ‖ revocation in full.

RESTITUIBLE.
adv, returnable, able to be returned or restored.

RESTITUIDOR.
m, returner, restorer, person who returns or restores something taken ‖ adj, returning, restoring.

RESTITUIR.
v, to return, restore ‖ to re-establish ‖ to reinstate, reintegrate.

RESTO.
m, residue, leftover ‖ remainder.

RESTOS.
m, cadaver, dead body, body, corpse.

RESTOS MORTALES.
mortal remains, cadaver, body, corpse

RESTRICCIÓN.
f, restriction, limitation ‖ restraint ‖ scarcity ‖ war restrictions (on consumption).

RESTRICCIONES DE COMERCIO.
restraint on trade.

RESTRICCIONES DE ENAJENAR.
See PROHIBICIÓN DE ENAJENAR.

RESTRICCIONES Y LIMITACIONES DEL DOMINIO.
restraints on ownership rights.

RESUELTO.
adj, resolved, taken care of ‖ decided, determined ‖ solved ‖ resolute ‖ prompt ‖ fearless ‖ rescinded.

RESULTA.
f, result, consequence, effect ‖ resolution, final outcome or determination ‖ vacancy of a position or office.
See RESULTADO.

RESULTADO.
m, result, consequence, effect ‖ profit, benefit ‖ remainder ‖ outcome.

RESULTANCIA.
See RESULTA and RESULTADO.

RESULTANDO.
m, whereas clause, clause in a judicial decision which sets forth the facts of a case ‖ factual bases of a judicial decision ‖ conj, whereas.

RESULTANTE.
f, result ‖ adj, resulting.

RESULTAR.
v, to produce a result or consequence ‖ to appear, seem ‖ to redound, lead to.

RESUMEN.
m, summary ‖ abstract ‖ synthesis ‖ digest ‖ conclusions of an allegation ‖ recap.

RETARDACIÓN.
f, retardation, delay.

RETARDADO.
m, retardate, retarded person ‖ adj, retarded ‖ late.

RETARDANTE.
adj, retarding.

RETARDAR.
v, to delay, slow down ‖ to leave to the last minute ‖ to suspend ‖ to make late, delay.

RETARDO.
m, lateness, delay ‖ retardation.

RETASA.
f, revaluation, reappraisal ‖ reduction in price (in an auction).

RETASACIÓN.
See RETASA.

RETASAR.
v, to revalue, reappraise ‖ to reduce (in order to sell at auction).

RETAZO.

m, fragment (e.g. of an allegation).

RETENCIÓN.

m, retention ‖ detention ‖ conservation, keeping ‖ memory ‖ retention, reduction (in salary) ‖ withholding, amount withheld ‖ retention (of a prior job or position after receiving a new one) ‖ arrest, detention, hold, lock-up.

RETENEDOR.

m, retainer ‖ detainer ‖ withholder.

RETENER.

v, to retain ‖ to detain ‖ to arrest, imprison ‖ to withhold, retain (from a salary) ‖ to keep, retain (a prior job or position after receiving a new one) ‖ to remember, recall ‖ to retain (jurisdiction over a case by a court) ‖ to retain (possession of something as guarantee) ‖ to reserve (a right).

RETENIDO.

adj, subject of a RETENCIÓN.

RETICENCIA.

f, reticence ‖ withholding of information demanded by the opposing party.

RETIRACIÓN.

m, withdrawal, retreat ‖ refuge, shelter.

RETIRADAMENTE.

adv, secretly, in secret.

RETIRADO.

m, retiree ‖ retired military serviceman ‖ adj, retired ‖ departed, left ‖ remote, far, distant.

RETIRAMIENTO.

m, separation ‖ departure ‖ retirement ‖ withdrawal, retreat.

RETIRAR.

v, to retire ‖ to leave, depart ‖ to hide, secrete ‖ to reserve ‖ to withdraw (funds) ‖ to withdraw, drop (a complaint) ‖ to revoke (a right or permission).

RETIRARSE.

v, to withdraw ‖ to retire ‖ to leave, depart ‖ to quit, resign from (e.g. a job).

RETIRO.

m, retirement ‖ withdrawal ‖ estrangement ‖ departure ‖ retreat (in all senses) ‖ withdrawal (of funds) ‖ retirement (from employment or military service) ‖ retirement pension or pay (of a military serviceman) ‖ voluntary retirement, resignation.

RETIRO DE COLABORACIÓN.

failure to put forth an effort or to work hard (in a job).

RETIRO VOLUNTARIO.

voluntary retirement.

RETO.

m, challenge ‖ threat ‖ dare ‖ provocation.

RETORCER.

v, to twist, distort (e.g. an argument or statement).

RETÓRICA.

f, rhetoric.

RETÓRICAS.

f, sophistries, false argument ‖ subtleties.

RETORNAR.

v, to return ‖ to return to one's country ‖ to insist, continue to try ‖ to recover ‖ to give back.

RETORNO.

m, return (of something), restitution ‖ return (to a place) ‖ reward, compensation for a thing or services ‖ exchange ‖ revenge ‖ return trip ‖ homecoming.

RETORNO A CAUTIVERIO.

return to captivity ‖ recapture.

**RETORNO AL LUGAR
DE LOS HECHOS.**

return to the scene of the crime.

RETORSIÓN.

m, retaliation ‖ distortion (of a statement).

RETRACCIÓN.

f, retraction.

RETRACTABLE.

adj, retractable.

RETRACTACIÓN.

f, retractation ‖ confession, admission (of guilt) ‖ withdrawal (of consent) ‖ revocation (of something said) ‖ negation.

RETRACTACIÓN DE LA CONFESIÓN.

retractation or withdrawal of the confession.

**RETRACTACIÓN EN
LAS INJURIAS.**

retractation of insults or offenses.

RETRACTACIÓN TESTAMENTARIA.

revocation of a will.

RETRACTAR.

v, to retract ‖ to revoke ‖ to repudiate.

RETRACTARSE.

v, to revoke or repudiate or take back (what one has said) ‖ to retract (a prior confession).

RETRACTO.

m, retraction ‖ revocation ‖ right of revocation (of a sales contract after the sale has occurred).

RETRACTO ADMINISTRATIVO.
right of government to revoke sales contract in order to condemn property.

RETRACTO CONVENCIONAL.
revocation by agreement ‖ right of revocation granted by reason of a sales contract. Opposed to RETRACTO LEGAL.

RETRACTO DE ABOLENGO.
See RETRACTO GENTILICIO.

RETRACTO DE ALEDAÑOS.
See RETRACTO DE COLINDANTES.

RETRACTO DE ASURCANOS.
See RETRACTO DE COLINDANTES.

RETRACTO DE COHEREDEROS.
legal right granted to heir to revoke the transfer of future property rights by a co-heir prior to probate of the estate, such that he can purchase it.

RETRACTO DE COLINDANTES.
legal right granted to property owner to require the revocation of the sale of the neighboring property such that he can purchase it.

RETRACTO DE COMUNEROS.
legal right granted to a co-tenant to require the revocation of the sale of property rights of the other co-tenant such that the first can purchase it.

RETRACTO DE SANGRE.
See RETRACTO GENTILICIO.

RETRACTO GENTILICIO.
legal right to revoke the sale of certain property by persons related to the seller by blood.

RETRACTO LEGAL.
legal revocation, revocation by reason of law ‖ right of revocation granted by law. Opposed to RETRACTO CONVENCIONAL.

RETRAER.
v, to bring again ‖ to revoke, exercise one's right of revocation ‖ to dissuade ‖ to paint or draw a portrait.

RETRASADO.
adj, backward, slow, behind ‖ in arrears ‖ mentally deficient, retarded, slow ‖ uncultured, boorish.

RETRASAR.
v, to go backwards ‖ to defer (an action) ‖ to procrastinate.

RETRASARSE.
v, to be late or tardy or behind ‖ to put off, procrastinate ‖ to fall behind.

RETRASO.
m, delay ‖ lateness, tardiness ‖ lack of punctuality ‖ procrastination ‖ reversal.

RETRASO MALICIOSO EN LA ADMINISTRACIÓN DE JUSTICIA.
intentional delay of the administration of justice. See PREVARICACIÓN.

RETRAYENTE.
m, revoker, person who revokes (pursuant to a right of RETRACTO).

RETRIBUCIÓN.
f, salary, wages, pay, compensation, remuneration ‖ retribution ‖ thanks or gift (for a favor or service performed).

RETRIBUIDO.
See MANDATO RETRIBUIDO.

RETRIBUIR.
v, to pay, compensate, remunerate ‖ to pay back in kind, take revenge ‖ to pay back (a favor).

RETRIBUTIVO.
adj, compensated, remunerated, salaried, paid.

RETROACCIÓN.
f, regression ‖ retroactivity ‖ retroaction.

RETROACCIÓN DE LA QUIEBRA.
retroactivity of the filing of bankruptcy.

RETROACCIÓN DE LAS OBLIGACIONES.
retroactivity of contractual obligations.

RETROACTIVIDAD.
f, retroactivity.

RETROACTIVIDAD DE LA LEY.
retroactivity of the law.

RETROACTIVIDAD DE LAS SENTENCIAS.
retroactivity of judicial decisions (from the date of their issuance to that of the filing of the corresponding complaint or some other point in time).

RETROACTIVIDAD E IRRETROACTIVIDAD DE LAS NORMAS JURÍDICAS.
retroactivity and non-retroactivity of legal norms.

RETROACTIVO.
adj, retroactive.

RETROCESIÓN.
f, retrocession, transfer back to transferor.

RETRODONACIÓN.
f, return of a thing given or donated back to giver or donor.

RETROTRAER.
v, to have retroactive effect.

RETROVENDENDO.
See CONTRATO DE RETROVENDENDO.
RETROVENDER.
v, to sell back to original seller ‖ to resell.
RETROVENDICIÓN.
See RETROVENTA.
RETROVENTA.
f, resale to the original seller ‖ repurchase by the original seller.
REUNIDO.
adj, reunited, joined ‖ called together, assembled, gathered.
REUNIÓN.
f, meeting, assembly ‖ interview ‖ fusion, consolidation ‖ annexation ‖ (right of) assembly.
REUNIÓN DE GABINETE.
cabinet meeting.
REUNIÓN PRIVADA.
private meeting.
REUNIÓN PÚBLICA.
public meeting.
REUNIR.
v, to meet, assemble, get together, gather ‖ to join, consolidate ‖ to congregate ‖ to aggregate, collect.
REUNIRSE.
v, to hold a meeting.
REVÁLIDA.
f, final examination to obtain an undergraduate university degree ‖ revalidation ‖ receipt of educational certification (from a university) to practise a profession ‖ revalidation of a foreign degree.
REVALIDACIÓN.
f, revalidation ‖ ratification ‖ confirmation.
REVALIDACIÓN DEL MATRIMONIO.
retroactive validation of a marriage (which is invalid due to a technicality).
REVALIDAR.
v, to revalidate, validate retroactively ‖ to ratify ‖ to take a final examination to obtain an undergraduate university degree;
REVALIDARSE.
v, to receive an educational certification (from a university) in order to practice a profession ‖ to revalidate a foreign degree.
REVALORACIÓN.
f, revaluation, reassessment, reappraisal.
REVALORIZAR.
v, to revalue, reassess.

REVALUACIÓN.
f, revaluation, reassessment, reappraisal.
REVEEDOR.
m, revisor.
REVELABLE.
adj, revealable ‖ discoverable.
REVELACIÓN.
f, revelation ‖ divulgence or divulging or disclosure of or making public of a secret or private information.
REVELACIÓN DE SECRETOS.
divulgence or divulging secrets.
REVELACIÓN DE SECRETOS MILITARES.
divulgence or divulging military secrets.
REVELADOR.
m, revealer ‖ divulger ‖ adj, probative, pertaining to proof.
REVELAR.
v, to reveal ‖ to divulge, disclose, make public ‖ to discover (something private) ‖ to prove demonstrate.
REVENDEDOR.
m, reseller ‖ retailer ‖ scalper.
REVENDER.
v, to resell ‖ to retail ‖ to scalp, overcharge on the resale of goods or tickets.
REVENIR.
v, to come back ‖ to re-adopt a prior position
REVENTA.
f, resale ‖ retail (of goods within a short period of time at a considerably higher price) ‖ scalping, overcharge on the resale of goods or tickets.
REVER.
v, to review, re-examine ‖ to re-register (something) ‖ to decide a dispute anew (by a different court or authority).
REVERENCIA.
f, reverence ‖ respect, veneration.
REVERENCIAL .
adj, reverential.
REVERENCIAR.
v, to pay respect or reverence to.
REVERENTE.
adj, reverent, respectful, with reverence respect.
REVERSIBILIDAD.
f, reversibility.
REVERSIBLE.
adj, reversible ‖ reversionary.

REVERSIÓN.
f, reversion ‖ return (to a prior state or condition). See RETRACTO and RETRODONACIÓN.
REVERSIÓN DE CONCESIONES.
reversion of public licenses or franchises or concessions.
REVERSIÓN DE LAS DONACIONES.
reversion or reverter of gifts or donations.
REVERSIÓN SUCESORIA.
testamentary reversion or reverter.
REVERTIR.
v, to revert ‖ to return (property to a person or country which held it previously).
REVÉS.
m, reverse ‖ slap with the back of the hand ‖ back ‖ adversity, misfortune ‖ frustration.
REVISABLE.
adj, reviewable ‖ verifiable ‖ able to be reheard.
REVISAR.
v, to review, inspect ‖ to revise ‖ to verify, check, audit, check over (e.g. an account, tickets).
REVISIÓN.
f, review, revision ‖ inspection, audit, examination ‖ re-examination ‖ account audit or inspection ‖ annual inspection of military conscription ‖ reconsideration ‖ verification, checking ‖ review or rehearing of a reopened case (based on evidence of the falseness of the facts upon which the prior decision was made).
REVISIÓN GENERAL.
general inspection or check over.
REVISOR.
m, reviewer, revisor ‖ inspector, auditor, examiner.
REVISTA.
f, inspection, examination ‖ rehearing of a case by a different court in the same division or a new judge ‖ magazine, periodical.
REVOCABILIDAD.
f, revocability.
REVOCACIÓN.
f, revocation, nullification, annulment ‖ repeal, abrogation ‖ resummoning ‖ retraction ‖ counter-order ‖ reversal.
REVOCACIÓN DE CONTRATOS.
contractual revocation, revocation of acceptance of a contract.
REVOCACIÓN DE LA PROPIEDAD.
reversion of property to prior owner.

REVOCACIÓN DE LAS DONACIONES.
reversion of donations or gifts to donor.
REVOCACIÓN DE LOS ACTOS FRAUDULENTOS.
revocation or nullification of fraudulent acts.
REVOCACIÓN DE LOS LEGADOS.
revocation of a testamentary gift.
REVOCACIÓN DE LOS TESTAMENTOS.
revocation of a will or testament.
REVOCACIÓN DE UNA SENTENCIA.
reversal of a judicial decision.
REVOCACIÓN DEL DOMINIO.
reversion of ownership subject to a condition subsequent. See DOMINIO REVOCABLE.
REVOCACIÓN DEL MANDATO.
revocation of powers of representation or agency.
REVOCACIÓN EN EL MATRIMONIO.
(judicial) revocation of a marriage.
REVOCACIÓN EN LAS SUCESIONES.
revocation as regards to inheritance.
REVOCACIÓN POPULAR.
recall vote (of an elected official).
REVOCADOR.
m, revoker, annuller ‖ repealer, abrogator ‖ reverser ‖ adj, revoking, annulling ‖ repealing, abrogating ‖ reversing.
REVOCAR.
v, to revoke, annul, void, cancel ‖ to repeal, abrogate ‖ to dissuade ‖ to resummon ‖ to retract ‖ to issue a counter-order ‖ to reverse.
REVOCATORIO.
adj, revocatory, revoking, annulling ‖ repealing, abrogating, reversing.
REVOLUCIÓN.
f, revolution ‖ revolt ‖ major change ‖ complete or total change.
REVOLUCIÓN INDUSTRIAL.
Industrial Revolution.
REVOLUCIONAR.
v, to revolt, bring about a revolution ‖ to revolutionize, change completely.
REVOLUCIONARIO.
m, revolutionary, person who supports a revolution ‖ rebel ‖ adj, revolutionary.
REVOLVER.
v, to incite to rebel or revolt ‖ to change public order ‖ to stir up, disturb (e.g. trouble) ‖ to retrace (one's steps).
REVUELTA.
f, revolt, rebellion ‖ sedition ‖ revolution ‖

change, modification ‖ quarrel, fight, row ‖
disturbance ‖ bend, twist.

REY.
m, king, ruling monarch, sovereign.

REY CONSORTE.
queen's husband.

REYERTA.
f, quarrel, row, fight ‖ altercation.

REYERTAR.
v, to fight, quarrel, have a row.

REYEZUELO.
m, tyrant ‖ petty king.

RICO.
m, rich or wealthy person ‖ adj, rich, wealthy ‖
abundant, plentiful ‖ well-made, sumptuous ‖
tasty, delicious.

RIESGO.
m, risk ‖ danger ‖ contingency or possibility or
probability of danger.

RIESGO CREADO.
created liability, legal liability assumed by a
person for the damage caused to third parties
by things or animals which he or she has in his
or her care or by the use thereof. Type of strict
liability in the sense that proof of breach of
duty is not necessary.

RIESGO
PROFESIONAL.
occupational hazard, professional risk ‖ professional liability, liability for the damage resulting from carrying out one's occupation or
profession.

RIFA.
f, raffle. See also RIÑA.

RIGIDEZ.
f, rigidity, stiffness ‖ intolerance ‖ severity ‖
despotism.

RÍGIDO.
adj, inflexible, rigid, stiff ‖ intolerant ‖ severe.

RIGOR.
m, scrupulousness ‖ hardness ‖ rigor ‖ vehemence ‖ precision.

RIGOROSO.
See RIGUROSO.

RIGUROSO.
adj, cruel, harsh ‖ severe ‖ rigorous ‖ exacting,
strict.

RIÑA.
f, quarrel, fight, row, dispute.

RIÑA TUMULTUARIA.
brawl, commotion, melee, fracas (which ma-

kes the identification of the parties and the
liability of such difficult or impossible).

RÍO.
m, river.

RÍO INTERNACIONAL.
international river, river which serves as the
border between two nations.

RIQUEZA.
f, abundance ‖ wealth, riches ‖ richness.

RIQUEZA IMPONIBLE.
taxable wealth.

ROBA.
See ROBO.

ROBADO.
m, victim of a ROBO ‖ adj, robbed, stolen.

ROBAR.
v, to take another's property by use of violence
or force or intimidation (includes: to rob, to
steal and to burgle) ‖ to abduct, kidnap ‖ to
erode ‖ to seduce, steal one's heart ‖ to persuade.

ROBO.
m, taking of another's property by means of
violence or force or intimidation (includes:
theft, robbery and burglary) ‖ stolen property
‖ abduction, kidnapping ‖ highway robbery,
abusive price ‖ excessive tax ‖ also see HURTO.

ROBO AGRAVADO.
aggravated taking of property of another. See
ROBO. Usually aggravating circumstances include: the use of weapons; taking from an inhabited building; taking from a car, train, bus,
plane, boat, or other means of transportation;
taking from a bank or other commercial establishment where monies are held.

ROBO CON HOMICIDIO.
taking of another's property which results in
the killing of a person. See ROBO.

ROBO FAMÉLICO.
taking of another's property caused by hunger
or necessity.

ROBORAR.
v, to corroborate, confirm.

ROBRA.
f, drink offered to seal a business deal.

ROGACIÓN.
f, resolution, substantive or dispositive part o
a law or statute ‖ concrete administrative mea
sure taken by voting ‖ request, petition.

ROGATORIO.
adj, rogatory.

ROL.

m, list, roll ‖ role, part ‖ master list (of a ship's crew).

ROL DE
LA TRIPULACIÓN.

master list (of a ship's crew).

ROMANISTA.

f, m, specialist in Roman law.

ROMANO.

adj, Roman ‖ catholic.

ROMANO PONTÍFICE.

m, the Pope.

ROMPER.

v, to break (e.g. a contract, the law, one's word) ‖ to mangle, shred ‖ to ruin, destroy ‖ to injure (bodily) ‖ to penetrate ‖ to interrupt ‖ to disobey ‖ to initiate certain actions ‖ to violate a peace treaty ‖ to violate or break the law ‖ to breach an obligation.

ROMPER EL HIELO.

to break the ice.

ROMPERSE.

v, to break one's own (e.g. body, spirit) ‖ to break one's back or carry efforts to an extreme.

ROMPIMIENTO.

m, break, breaking ‖ enmity, discord ‖ quarrel ‖ declaration of war ‖ break in diplomatic relations ‖ breach ‖ violation.

RONDA.

f, night watch ‖ round, beat ‖ surrounding road or path (of a city) ‖ street serenade or singing (usually at night).

ROPA REGLAMENTARIA.

f, uniform.

ROTACIÓN.

f, rotation ‖ shift, turn (of work).

ROTACIÓN
DE CAPITAL.

movement of capital (within a company).

ROTO.

adj, broken ‖ mangled, shredded ‖ ruined, destroyed ‖ injured (bodily) ‖ penetrated ‖ interrupted ‖ disobeyed ‖ violated ‖ breached.

RÓTULO.

m, title, name, label, denomination ‖ sign, poster ‖ notice.

RÓTULO DE ESTABLECIMIENTO.

name or drawing or label or any other sign which distinguishes one business from another. Includes business sign or label, etc.

ROTURA.

f, fracture ‖ break ‖ breakage ‖ breaking ‖ tear, rip, rent ‖ broken bone.

RÚBRICA.

f, flourish (of a signature) ‖ rubric, title, heading.

RUDO.

adj, rude.

RUEDA.

f, wheel ‖ circle ‖ shift, turn, rota.

RUEDA DE PRESOS.

line-up (of suspects for purposes of identification).

RUEDA ELECTORAL.

group of individuals who go from polling place to polling place voting in names of others.

RUEGO.

m, petition ‖ referendum ‖ supplication, request, petition, plea.

RUEGOS
Y PREGUNTAS.

parliamentary or legislative question and answer period (in certain legislative bodies during which the representatives are permitted to direct questions to other members to obtain information or clarifications).

RUFIÁN.

m, ruffian ‖ pimp.

RUFIANEAR.

v, to pimp.

RUFIANERÍA.

f, pimping.

RUFIANESCA.

f, group of pimps ‖ gang of ruffians ‖ bad manners ‖ adj, related to pimping.

RUIDO.

m, noise, sound ‖ confusion, banging ‖ discord, rumpus ‖ lawsuit, litigation.

RUÍN.

adj, base ‖ traitorous, disloyal ‖ cheap, miserly ‖ vengeful ‖ ungrateful.

RUINA.

f, ruin, destruction, fall ‖ decay ‖ downfall (of a person) ‖ loss ‖ decadence, decline ‖ ruination.

RUINAS.

f, ruins, remains.

RUINDAD.

f, baseness ‖ meanness ‖ disloyalty.

RUINOSO.

adj, ruinous.

RULETA.
f, roulette.
RUMOR.
m, rumor ‖ sign, indication ‖ information without confirmation.
RUMOREARSE.
v, to spread a rumor.
RUMORES FALSOS.
false rumors.
RUPTURA.
f, breaking, break, rupture.
RUPTURA DE ARMISTICIO.
breaking of armistice.
RUPTURA DE HOSTILIDADES.
break out of war.
RUPTURA DE NEGOCIACIONES.
break in negotiations.

RUPTURA DE TREGUA.
breaking of truce.
RUPTURA EN RELACIONES DIPLOMÁTICAS.
break in diplomatic relations.
RURAL.
adj, rural ‖ agricultural or forest ‖ from the countryside ‖ uncultured, rough.
RÚSTICO.
adj, rustic ‖ rural ‖ from the countryside ‖ uncultured, rough.
RUTA.
f, route ‖ road ‖ highway ‖ itinerary.
RUTA AÉREA.
air way or route.
RUTINA.
f, routine, pattern ‖ custom, habit.
RUTINARIO.
adj, routine ‖ habitual, customary.

S.A.
initials for SOCIEDAD ANÓNIMA.

S.A. DE C.V.
initials for SOCIEDAD ANÓNIMA DE CAPITAL VARIABLE.

SÁBADO.
m, Saturday ‖ Sabbath.

SÁBADO INGLÉS.
week-end rest, Saturday and Sunday (as days of rest from work).

SABÁTICO.
adj, sabbatical ‖ pertaining to Saturday or Sabbath.

SABATIZAR.
v, to keep the Sabbath.

SABER.
m, knowledge, learning ‖ wisdom ‖ v, to know ‖ to have knowledge of ‖ to be an expert in something.

SABIO.
m, wise man or woman, sage ‖ scholar ‖ adj, wise, sage ‖ learned.

SABOTAJE.
m, sabotage.

SABOTAJE LABORAL.
industrial sabotage, intentional destruction of, damage to, failure to use, hiding of, or removing from the country employer's property during a labor dispute.

SABOTEADOR.
m, saboteur.

SABOTEAR.
v, to sabotage.

SABUESO.
m, investigator, snoop ‖ spy ‖ sleuth, undercover investigator.

SACA.
f, extraction ‖ removal, taking away or out ‖ certified or notarized copy of an officially recorded document (DOCUMENTO PROTOCOLIZADO) ‖ election ‖ draft or conscription lottery ‖ liberation, freeing ‖ postal or mail sack ‖ livestock tax ‖ see also DERECHO DE RETRACTO and DERECHO DE TANTEO.

SACA
DE AGUA.
extraction or removal of water.

SACAR.
v, to remove, extract, take away or out, withdraw ‖ to export ‖ to free, liberate ‖ to resolve or work out or do accounts ‖ to draw by lots, choose by lottery ‖ to win a lottery ‖ to exempt, except ‖ to copy a writing ‖ to cite, refer ‖ to invent ‖ to make public ‖ to put into circulation ‖ to quote or take notes from a text ‖ to nickname ‖ to remove bullets.

SACAR PRENDAS.
to pawn, hock.

SACOMANO.
m, sacking, pillage (by military troops).

"SACRAMENTUM".
(sworn) oath.

SACRIFICIO.
m, sacrifice ‖ work, labor ‖ danger ‖ suffering ‖ death (for one's country).

SACRILEGIO.
m, sacrilege.

SÁDICO.
m, sadist ‖ adj, sadistic.

SADISMO.
m, sadism.

SADOMASOQUISMO.
m, sadomasochism.

SAFISMO.
m, lesbianism.

SAGACIDAD.
f, sagacity.
SAGAZ.
adj, sagacious, wise.
SAGRADO.
m, asylum, sanctuary ‖ adj, sacred.
SALA.
f, room ‖ hall, salon ‖ living or drawing room ‖ courtroom ‖ division of judiciary, entirety of judges who make up each of the divisions or departments of a court system ‖ court, tribunal ‖ one of several courts of appeals dealing with particular types of cases.
SALA DE APELACIÓN.
appeals or appellate court, court of appeals.
SALA DE GOBIERNO.
tribunal of judicial discipline, court which monitors and hears cases of judicial irregularities or regarding internal procedures.
Opposed to SALA DE JUSTICIA.
SALA DE JUSTICIA.
court of justice.
Opposed to SALA DE GOBIERNO.
SALA DE JUSTICIA MILITAR.
court of military justice.
SALA DE VACACIONES.
pro tem court, court which hears cases during judicial holidays.
SALARIADO.
m, social security and employment system based on the payment of regular salary ‖ working class ‖ adj, salaried, waged, compensated by salary.
SALARIO.
m, salary, wage, wages, pay ‖ compensation (for services rendered).
SALARIO A DESTAJO.
pay by the piece, compensation by a piecework system.
SALARIO ACCESORIO.
bonus, bonus pay (for overtime or extra production).
SALARIO ANUAL.
annual wages, yearly salary.
SALARIO BÁSICO.
basic wages or salary ‖ minimum salary (as set in collective bargaining agreements).
SALARIO COMPLEMENTARIO.
additional wages, all compensation paid in excess of basic salary.

SALARIO CON PRIMAS.
salary with bonus for overtime or extra production.
SALARIO CONVENCIONAL.
salary or compensation pursuant to contract.
SALARIO DIARIO.
daily wages or salary.
SALARIO DIFERIDO.
deferred compensation.
SALARIO DIRECTO.
direct compensation, salary.
Opposed to SALARIO INDIRECTO.
SALARIO EFECTIVO.
wages paid in cash ‖ take-home pay, salary less deductions.
SALARIO EN DINERO.
salary paid in money.
Opposed to SALARIO EN ESPECIE.
SALARIO EN ESPECIE.
salary paid in kind.
Opposed to SALARIO EN DINERO.
SALARIO FAMILIAR.
bonus paid to an employee who is married or has children or other dependents.
SALARIO GARANTIZADO.
guaranteed wage, minimum wage which must be paid under a system which offers bonuses for extra production or overtime.
SALARIO INCENTIVADO.
wages paid pursuant to a production incentive plan.
SALARIO INDIRECTO.
indirect compensation, fringe benefits, perquisites, compensation added to basic wages.
Opposed to SALARIO DIRECTO.
SALARIO INDIVIDUAL.
individual pay or salary ‖ pay received independent of SALARIO FAMILIAR.
SALARIO ÍNFIMO.
compensation inadequate to pay for worker's necessities ‖ unjust wages.
SALARIO JUDICIAL.
judicially set compensation or salary.
SALARIO LEGAL.
legal wages or compensation, pay stipulated by law. Includes minimum wage.
SALARIO MÁXIMO.
maximum compensation (pursuant to law, agreement, or regulation).

SALARIO MÍNIMO.
minimum wage (pursuant to law, agreement, or regulation).

SALARIO MIXTO.
salary paid partly in money and partly in kind.

SALARIO MÓVIL.
adjustable or fluctuating salary, salary which is adjusted automatically pursuant to the fluctuations of predetermined criteria.

SALARIO NOMINAL.
nominal salary, salary before deductions ‖ nominal wages, salary paid without regard to its buying power.

SALARIO POR PIEZA.
piece rate, compensation based on pieces completed.

SALARIO POR TAREA.
pay for completion of a minimum level of production.

SALARIO POR TIEMPO.
salary based on time spent at work.

SALARIO PROGRESIVO.
salary with bonus which increases as a function of overtime or extra production.

SALARIO REAL.
true compensation, basic wages plus all additional compensation and fringe benefits ‖ salary in relation to its buying power.

SALARIO VITAL.
living wage ‖ minimum wage (as set by law).

SALARIO VITAL MÍNIMO MÓVIL.
adjustable minimum living wage,

SALDAR.
v, to sell at a low price, have a fire sale ‖ to liquidate or close out an account (by paying the difference owing or withdrawing the excess).

SALDISTA.
m, businessman who sells existing stock ‖ buyer or seller of remnants or goods at liquidation sale.

SALDO.
m, payment, settlement (of a debt of obligation) ‖ balance, remaining balance, difference between assets and liabilities of an estate or account ‖ remnants, leftovers, goods to be sold at a lower price ‖ remainder ‖ extra.

SALDO ACREEDOR.
credit or positive balance.

SALDO DEUDOR.
debit or negative balance, balance due (on an account).

SALDO DISPONIBLE.
disposable balance, balance on hand, balance which may be withdrawn from an account.

SALDO EXIGIBLE.
balance payable on demand.

SALIDA.
f, exit ‖ departure, leaving ‖ departure day or hour ‖ transportation abroad ‖ accounting entry ‖ expenditure, expense, outlay ‖ end, finish ‖ escape, way out ‖ way out of or solution to a difficult problem ‖ easy merchantability or salability ‖ freeing or liberation of a prisoner.

SALIR CON EL PLEITO.
v, to win a lawsuit.

SALOMÓNICO.
adj, Solomonic.

SALÓN.
m, salon, hall, auditorium, room where meetings are held.

SALÓN DE SESIONES.
board room ‖ (chamber or floor of) senate or house of representatives or other formal body.

SALTAR.
v, to jump ‖ to jump over, skip over ‖ to protest, object to ‖ to put an end to something oppressive ‖ to set off (explosives) ‖ to omit, skip over (parts of a text) ‖ to shorten, abbreviate (a text).

SALTEADOR.
m, highwayman, street thief, robber who steals in streets, roads, and other uninhabited sites.

SALTEADORA.
f, female highwayman, female street thief, female robber who steals in streets, roads, and other uninhabited sites ‖ wife or concubine of a SALTEADOR.

SALTEAMIENTO.
m, armed robbery which takes place on the highway, street, or other uninhabited site.

SALTEAR.
v, to rob on the highway, street or other uninhabited site ‖ to jump or skip over ‖ to surprise.

SALTO.
m, jump ‖ omission ‖ shortening, abbreviation ‖ progress.

SALUBRE.
adj, healthful, healthy, good for one's health.

SALUBRIDAD.
f, healthiness, health.

SALUD.
f, health ‖ welfare ‖ salvation.
SALUD PÚBLICA.
public health ‖ public welfare ‖ department of public health.
SALUDABLE.
adj, healthy, fit, wholesome.
SALUDAR.
v, to greet ‖ to welcome ‖ to salute.
SALUDO.
m, greeting, salutation ‖ welcome.
SALUDOS.
m, regards, compliments.
SALVA.
f, salutation, welcome ‖ oath, word of honor ‖ solemn promise ‖ sworn oath, swearing on the bible ‖ (e.g. 21) gun salute ‖ food testing for poison.
SALVABLE.
adj, able to be saved, rescuable.
SALVACIÓN.
f, salvation ‖ rescue ‖ exculpation, absolution (of fault) ‖ see also SALVA and SALVACIÓN.
SALVAGUARDA.
See SALVAGUARDIA.
SALVAGUARDIA.
f, custodian, guard (of something or someone) ‖ safe-conduct pass, pass, safe pass ‖ protection.
SALVAJADA.
f, savagery, brutality, cruelty.
SALVAJE.
m, savage ‖ adj, uncivilized ‖ untamed, undomesticated ‖ savage.
SALVAJISMO.
m, savagery ‖ cruelty, atrocity ‖ total lack of respect or consideration.
SALVAMENTE.
adv, without any risk ‖ safely, securely.
SALVAMENTO.
m, rescue ‖ saving ‖ safe harbor, place of safety.
SALVAMENTO MARÍTIMO.
maritime rescue.
SALVAMIENTO.
See SALVAMENTO.
SALVAR.
v, to save, rescue ‖ to place in safety ‖ to salvage ‖ to defend, protect ‖ to guard against or cover risks ‖ to obtain an acquittal, get an accused off ‖ to prove innocence ‖ to obtain a reprieve (for a person sentenced to death) ‖ to

overcome (difficulties) ‖ to avoid (something undesirable) ‖ to add at the end of a document a list of mistakes and omissions and deletions which the parties initial ‖ to take an oath ‖ to exempt, except ‖ to test foods for poison ‖ to free.
SALVARSE.
v, to save oneself, escape a risk ‖ to overcome (e.g. a disgrace, accident) ‖ to free oneself (e.g. of problems, charges).
SALVAVIDAS.
m, life preserver.
SALVEDAD.
f, excuse ‖ reservation ‖ clarification ‖ limitation ‖ exception ‖ note added at the end of a document to list the mistakes, omissions and deletions which the parties initial ‖ see also SALVOCONDUCTO and GARANTÍA.
SALVO.
adj, safe, saved ‖ free ‖ exempt ‖ excepted ‖ omitted ‖ adv, except, barring, save.
SALVO ERROR U OMISIÓN.
barring errors and omissions, error and omissions excepted.
SALVOCONDUCTO.
m, safe conduct pass, safe pass, pass (e.g. for use through enemy or unknown territory).
SANA CRÍTICA.
f, reasoned opinion or judgment, judgment which is both freely arrived at and based on admissible evidence.
SANABLE.
adj, curable, amendable ‖ healable.
SANATORIO.
m, sanatorium.
SANCIÓN.
f, sanction, punishment, penalty ‖ law, statute, regulation, rule ‖ signing of a statute into law by a head of state ‖ sanction, sanctioning, approval ‖ authorization ‖ legislation, lawmaking, legislative enactment of a statute or approval or passage of a bill.
SANCIÓN ADMINISTRATIVA.
administrative sanction or punishment. May include administrative fine.
SANCIÓN ARBITRARIA.
arbitrary punishment.
SANCIÓN DE LAS LEYES.
signing of a statute into law by a head of state ‖ legislation, lawmaking, legislative enactment of a statute or approval or passage of a bill.

SANCIÓN DISCIPLINARIA.
disciplinary sanction or punishment.
SANCIÓN PENAL.
criminal punishment or penalty or sanction.
SANCIÓN SOCIAL.
social disapproval whether it be punishment or
a more subtle form of coercion.
SANCIONABLE.
adj, punishable ‖ worthy of sanction or punishment.
SANCIONADOR.
m, punisher, sanctioner ‖ legislator, enactor.
SANCIONAR.
v, to sanction ‖ to punish, penalize ‖ to pass a
law, regulation, rule ‖ to sign a statute into law
by a head of state ‖ to approve ‖ to authorize,
sanction ‖ to legislate ‖ to enact a statute ‖ to
approve or pass a bill.
**SANCIONES CONTRA
PRISIONEROS.**
punishment of prisoners of war.
SANCIONES INTERNACIONALES.
(international) sanctions. Includes military,
legal, political, or economic sanctions.
**SANCIONES
PROCESALES.**
procedural sanctions, sanctions imposed
against litigants for failure to comply with procedural requirements.
SANEADO.
adj, unencumbered (e.g. by liens) ‖ without
deductions, not subject to deductions ‖ free
from defects ‖ cured.
SANEAMIENTO.
m, indemnification, reparation, redress, compensation ‖ curing hidden defect of the property sold ‖ warranty, guaranty against risk of
possible harm ‖ warranty against hidden defects ‖ duty of seller to guaranty buyer's quiet
enjoyment ‖ duty of seller to guaranty buyer
against hidden defects.
SANEAR.
v, to guaranty, warrant (against harm) ‖ to assure ‖ to fix ‖ to indemnify, repair, compensate
(for hidden defects) ‖ to cure ‖ to unencumber,
free from encumbrances, have encumbrances
lifted ‖ to put a corporation or government
budget on sound economic ground, have a
surplus in a budget ‖ to correct, clean up.
SANGRAR.
v, to bleed ‖ to steal, pilfer ‖ to drain.

SANGRE.
f, blood ‖ vitality, energy ‖ family, lineage
bloodline, ascendancy.
SANGRE AZUL.
blue or noble blood.
SANGRE CALIENTE.
heat of passion.
SANGRE FRÍA.
cold blood ‖ stoicism, calm (in the face of dar
ger or chaos).
SANGRIENTO.
adj, bloody.
SANGUINARIO.
adj, bloody, cruel, sanguinary.
SANGUÍNEO.
adj, blood, pertaining to blood.
SANGUINOLENTO.
adj, bloody, blood-stained.
SANIDAD.
f, health ‖ healthiness, health ‖ see also SAN
DAD PÚBLICA.
SANIDAD MILITAR.
health department of the armed forces.
**SANIDAD
PÚBLICA.**
public health ‖ health department, depar
ment or board of health.
SANITARIO.
m, member of the health department of th
armed forces ‖ adj, sanitary, hygienic.
SANO.
adj, healthy, in good health, sound ‖ of nob
spirit ‖ free of risk ‖ free of harm ‖ free of hi
den defects ‖ free of mistakes ‖ whole, u
damaged, unharmed, unbroken ‖ honest, wi
‖ sane.
SANO Y SALVO.
safe and sound.
SANTO Y SEÑA.
m, password, watchword, countersign.
SAÑA.
f, anger, cruelty, rancor ‖ unnecessary violen
or harm.
SAQUEADOR.
m, plunderer, looter, person who sacks.
SAQUEAR.
v, to sack, plunder, loot, pillage.
SAQUEO.
m, sacking, plundering, pillage, looting.
SATÉLITE.
m, satellite, dependant, follower.

ATÉLITE ARTIFICIAL.
man-made satellite.
ATÉLITE DE COMUNICACIONES.
communications satellite.
ATISDACIÓN.
See FIANZA.
ATISFACCIÓN.
f, satisfaction ‖ satisfaction, full payment of a debt ‖ pleasure ‖ explanation or clarification of or apology for (e.g. an offense, insult) ‖ confidence ‖ conceit.
ATISFACCIÓN AL OFENDIDO.
explanation or clarification or apology to the offended person for (e.g. an offense, insult).
ATISFACER.
v, to satisfy ‖ to repay, pay a debt in full ‖ to be worthy of a pardon ‖ to explain (e.g. an offense, insult) ‖ to please ‖ to resolve a problem or doubt ‖ to atone for, expiate ‖ to indemnify, compensate ‖ to reward ‖ to answer, reply ‖ to convince.
ATISFACERSE.
v, to satisfy oneself ‖ to avenge one's honor ‖ to take revenge on one's enemy, get satisfaction ‖ to obtain a clarification or explanation of a doubt or problem.
ATISFACTORIO.
adj, satisfactory ‖ able to pay in full.
ATURACIÓN.
f, saturation.
ATURACIÓN DE MERCADO.
market saturation, flooding of the market.
ECANO.
m, dry land. See ABOGADO DE SECANO.
ECCIÓN.
f, section, part ‖ administrative or military subdivision.
ECESIÓN.
f, secession.
ECESIONISMO.
m, secessionism.
ECESIONISTA.
f, m, secessionist, separatist.
ECRETA.
f, impeachment inquest ‖ secret inquest or investigation ‖ secret police ‖ adj, secret.
ECRETARIA.
f, female secretary or office worker ‖ female form of SECRETARIO.
ECRETARÍA.
f, position and office of a SECRETARIO ‖ (go-

vernmental) ministry, secretariat, department.
SECRETARIADO.
m, secretarial profession ‖ see also SECRETARÍA ‖ unit or corps of secretaries.
SECRETARIAL.
adj, secretarial.
SECRETARIO.
m, secretary ‖ (governmental) minister, secretary ‖ clerk ‖ typist ‖ department notary public ‖ person to whom one reveals a secret ‖ special judicial notary public ‖ head court clerk, highest court officer below a judge.
SECRETARIO DE ESTADO.
cabinet secretary or minister.
SECRETARIO DE JUSTICIA.
Attorney General, head of the Department of Justice.
SECRETARIO DE SALA.
court clerk, bailiff.
SECRETARIO JUDICIAL.
judge's clerk ‖ special judicial notary public ‖ court clerk, bailiff.
SECRETO.
m, secret ‖ strong box, safe ‖ secrecy, concealment ‖ reserve ‖ mystery ‖ adj, secret ‖ confidential, private ‖ hidden ‖ reserved.
SECRETO DE ESTADO.
state secret.
SECRETO DE FABRICACIÓN.
manufacturing secret ‖ secrecy of manufacturing process.
SECRETO MILITAR.
military secret.
SECRETO PROFESIONAL.
professional confidentiality or secrecy ‖ professional secret.
SECUENCIA.
f, sequence ‖ derivation.
SECUESTRACIÓN.
See SECUESTRO.
SECUESTRADOR.
m, person who deposits property in litigation with the court ‖ kidnapper, abductor.
SECUESTRAR.
v, to sequester, attach, seize ‖ to abduct, kidnap ‖ to deposit property in litigation with the court.
SECUESTRO.
m, deposit in court (of property in litigation) ‖ judicial attachment ‖ kidnapping, abduction ‖ sequestration.

SECUESTRO CONVENCIONAL.
deposit of property in litigation with a third party pursuant to contract.

SECUESTRO DE BIENES.
attachment of personal property ‖ levy or embargo of personal property ‖ sequestration of personal property ‖ confiscation, taking.

SECUESTRO DE PERSONAS.
kidnapping or abduction of persons.

SECUESTRO JUDICIAL.
deposit with the court of property in litigation.

SECUESTRO POLÍTICOSOCIAL.
socio-political kidnapping or abduction, which is done for revolutionary or subversive purposes.

SECULARIZACIÓN.
f, secularization ‖ change from religious life.

SECUNDAR.
v, to cooperate, help, assist.

SECUNDARIO.
adj, secondary, accessory, subordinate ‖ unimportant.

SEDE.
f, seat ‖ headquarters, main offices ‖ legal domicile of a corporation or partnership.

SEDE SOCIAL.
legal domicile of a corporation or partnership ‖ headquarters, main administrative offices.

SEDICIÓN.
f, sedition.

SEDIENTES.
See BIENES SEDIENTES.

SEDUCCIÓN.
f, seduction ‖ sexual seduction ‖ attraction ‖ influence, pressure ‖ bribe ‖ suggestive action.

SEDUCIR.
v, to seduce ‖ to attract, entice ‖ to pressure, influence ‖ to bribe ‖ to corrupt ‖ to cause to fall in love.

SEDUCTOR.
m, seducer ‖ person who attracts or seduces ‖ sexual seducer.

SEGREGACIÓN.
f, segregation ‖ separation ‖ solitary confinement.

SEGREGACIÓN RACIAL.
racial segregation.

SEGREGAR.
v, to segregate ‖ to separate.

SEGÚN.
prep, according to, pursuant to ‖ conj, as ‖ according to how ‖ adv, depending on circumstances.

SEGÚN DERECHO.
according to law, in accordance with the law.

SEGÚN Y CÓMO.
just as, exactly as, precisely as.

SEGÚN Y CONFORME.
See SEGÚN Y CÓMO.

SEGUNDA GUERRA MUNDIAL.
Second World War, World War Two, WWII.

SEGUNDA HIPOTECA.
second mortgage.

SEGUNDA INSTANCIA.
first appeal, appeal from an inferior or lower or superior or circuit or district or county court ‖ appellate procedure.

SEGUNDA INTENCIÓN.
See INTENCIÓN.

SEGUNDA VUELTA.
second vote or election ‖ general election (after primary election).

SEGUNDAS COPIAS.
copies (from an original filing or document) copy of a copy.

SEGUNDAS NUPCIAS.
second marriage, remarriage (after a divorce or death of a spouse).

SEGUNDO.
m, second in command ‖ adj, second ‖ secondary.

SEGUNDO GRADO.
second in degree (of kinship) ‖ second grade or degree or level.

SEGUNDOGÉNITO.
m, second born ‖ second-born son ‖ adj, second-born.

SEGURIDAD.
f, security, safety, safeness ‖ solidarity ‖ certainty ‖ firm conviction ‖ confidence ‖ guaranty, warranty, surety ‖ sureness ‖ security interest ‖ safety measures or steps ‖ police ‖ surety bond.

SEGURIDAD COLECTIVA.
international security ‖ international peace.

SEGURIDAD DE LOS MEDIOS DE TRANSPORTE Y DE COMUNICACIONES.
security of the transportation and communication systems.

SEGURIDAD DE PRISIONEROS.
safety of prisoners.

EGURIDAD E HIGIENE EN EL TRABAJO.
health and safety at work.
EGURIDAD INTERNACIONAL.
See SEGURIDAD COLECTIVA.
EGURIDAD JURÍDICA.
legal certainty ‖ enforcement of the law and stability of legal institutions.
EGURIDAD LABORAL.
employment security ‖ assurance of work.
EGURIDAD PERSONAL.
personal security or safety ‖ governmental guaranty of right to due process ‖ police, security forces.
EGURIDAD SOCIAL.
social security ‖ social security system ‖ societal safety or protection.
EGURO.
m, insurance ‖ insurance policy ‖ certainty ‖ license ‖ safe pass, pass ‖ permission ‖ safety, safety lock (on guns) ‖ adj, safe, secure ‖ certain, sure, firm ‖ safe, private.
EGURO ACUMULATIVO.
type of concurrent insurance which is cumulative.
EGURO AÉREO.
flight insurance ‖ insurance against air navigation risks.
EGURO AERONÁUTICO.
See SEGURO AÉREO.
EGURO AGRÍCOLA.
agricultural or farm insurance ‖ crop insurance.
EGURO CON FRANQUICIA.
insurance with a deductible clause.
EGURO CONTRA ACCIDENTES.
accident insurance.
EGURO CONTRA EL GRANIZO.
hailstorm insurance (usually part of agricultural insurance).
EGURO CONTRA EL PARO.
unemployment insurance.
EGURO CONTRA INCENDIOS.
fire insurance.
EGURO CONTRA ROBO.
insurance against robbery or theft or burglary or other similar taking.
EGURO CONTRA TODO RIESGO.
all risk or comprehensive insurance.
EGURO DE ACCIDENTES DEL TRABAJO.
insurance against employment-related accidents or illnesses.

SEGURO DE CRÉDITO.
credit insurance.
SEGURO DE ENFERMEDAD.
health insurance.
SEGURO DE FLETE.
freight insurance.
SEGURO DE INVALIDEZ.
disability insurance.
SEGURO DE MATERNIDAD.
maternity leave insurance.
SEGURO DE MUERTE.
life insurance (paid upon death of the insured).
SEGURO DE NATALIDAD.
insurance paid upon live birth of child.
SEGURO DE NUPCIALIDAD.
insurance paid upon the marriage of a woman.
SEGURO DE RESPONSABILIDAD CIVIL.
civil liability insurance (excludes intentional torts).
SEGURO DE TRANSPORTE DE PASAJEROS.
travel insurance for passengers.
SEGURO DE TRANSPORTE TERRESTRE.
ground freight insurance.
SEGURO DE VEJEZ.
old age insurance.
SEGURO DE VIDA.
See SEGURO SOBRE LA VIDA.
SEGURO FACULTATIVO.
optional insurance.
SEGURO LIMITADO.
limited insurance, insurance with some form of limitation or condition.
SEGURO MARÍTIMO.
marine insurance.
SEGURO MERCANTIL.
type of commercial insurance, insurance which is regulated by the Commercial Code, insurance which covers commercial enterprises.
SEGURO MUTUO.
mutual insurance.
SEGURO OBLIGATORIO.
obligatory or mandatory insurance (i.e. required by law).
SEGURO PRIVADO.
private insurance.
SEGURO PÚBLICO.
government insurance, governmentally administered insurance.

SEGURO SOBRE BUENAS NOTICIAS.
maritime insurance against receipt of (inaccurately transmitted) good news.

SEGURO SOBRE LA VIDA.
life insurance (if the condition of payment is the death of the insured), or a form of life annuity insurance (providing for the payment of monies upon the occurrence of an event or for a certain period of time).

SEGURO SOBRE
MALAS NOTICIAS.
maritime insurance against receipt of (inaccurately transmitted) bad news.

SEGURO SOCIAL.
social insurance.

SEGURO TERRESTRE.
ground travel insurance.

SELECCIÓN.
f, selection, choice ‖ preference ‖ best selection.

SELECCIÓN DE PERSONAL.
employee selection, selection of personnel.

SELLADO.
adj, stamped, sealed.

SELLADOR.
m, sealer, stamper ‖ person who stamps or seals.

SELLAR.
v, to stamp ‖ to place a postage stamp ‖ to mark with an imprint ‖ to seal ‖ to mark ‖ to impress ‖ to conclude, finish, put an end to ‖ to seal (an envelope), enclose.

SELLO.
m, stamp, seal, machine to stamp or seal ‖ stamp or seal (placed on object) ‖ postal stamp ‖ stamp office, office which stamps documents ‖ see also PAPEL SELLADO.

SELLO POSTAL.
stamp, postage or postal stamp.

SELLOS OFICIALES.
government or official stamp.

SEMANA.
f, week ‖ work week (e.g. Monday through Friday).

SEMANA DE 40 HORAS.
40 hour work week ‖ work week.

SEMANA INGLESA.
week which includes Saturday afternoon and Sunday as days of rest from work.

SEMANAL.
adj, weekly, week, pertaining to a week.

SEMANALMENTE.
adv, weekly.

SEMANARIO.
m, weekly, weekly publication.

SEMEJANTE.
m, likeness, resemblance ‖ fellow man ‖ imitation ‖ adj, similar, like ‖ same.

SEMEJANZA.
f, similarity, likeness, resemblance.

SEMESTRAL.
adj, semestral, six-month.

SEMESTRE.
m, semester, period of six months ‖ semester payment, payment (e.g. of salary or rents or pensions) received on a semester basis ‖ semester, period of a two term school year which usually lasts between three and four months.

SEMICONFESIÓN.
f, partial confession.

SEMIDIRECTO.
adj, partially or somewhat direct.

SEMIHUELGA.
f, partial strike (includes: slow down, strike in which only part of the workers participate, strike during certain hours only, etc.).

SEMINARIO.
m, seminary, school ‖ seminar, discussion group (in a classroom setting) ‖ conference, convention.

SEMIPERMANENTE.
adj, semi-permanent.

SEMIPLENA PRUEBA.
f, prima facie evidence ‖ evidence which creates a presumption but is not conclusive.

SEMIPLENAMENTE.
adv, almost totally ‖ almost satisfactorily.

SEMIPLENO.
adj, almost complete ‖ almost satisfactory.
See SEMIPLENA PRUEBA.

SEMOVIENTE.
m, animal ‖ livestock ‖ adj, self-moving, moving on its own.

SENADO.
m, senate, upper chamber of bicameral congress or legislature) ‖ senate, senate building.

SENADOR.
m, senator, member of a senate.

SENADOR ELECTIVO.
(popularly) elected senator.

SENADOR VITALICIO.
senator for life. Usually not elected, but na-

med by a higher authority to such position.

SENADURÍA.
f, senatorship, position and functions of senator.

SENARA.
f, patch of land given to servants for their own use as a perk or part of their wages ‖ harvest of such property ‖ seeded or sown land ‖ commons, village common.

SENATORIAL.
adj, senatorial.

SENATORIO.
See SENATORIAL.

SENDA.
f, path, walkway ‖ see also SERVIDUMBRE DE PASO.

SENECTUD.
f, old age.

SENIL.
adj, senile ‖ pertaining to old age or the aged.

SENILIDAD.
f, senility.

SENIOR.
m, mister, Mr. ‖ sir, master ‖ senator ‖ adj, senior, older.

SENO MATERNO.
m, mother's womb.

SENSATO.
adj, sensible, judicious ‖ prudent ‖ dispassionate.

SENSUAL.
adj, sensual ‖ sensory ‖ sensuous.

SENTENCIA.
f, (judicial) decision, opinion, adjudication, judgment ‖ verdict, determination, decree, order, ruling, pronouncement ‖ finding ‖ award ‖ (non- judicial) award, judgment, opinion ‖ maxim, aphorism, saying.

SENTENCIA ABSOLUTORIA.
In criminal law: acquittal, verdict of not guilty, verdict of acquittal, acquittance, quittance, exculpation. In civil law: verdict in favor of defending party (not necessarily defendant).

SENTENCIA ARBITRAL.
arbitrium, arbitrament, arbitration award or judgment or decision.

SENTENCIA CAUTELAR.
temporary order, mandatory injunction pendente lite.

SENTENCIA "CITRA PETITA".
judicial decision which fails to decide the principal issue(s) in dispute.

SENTENCIA COLECTIVA.
type of decision pertaining to a class of people who may or may not have participated directly in the suit as named plaintiffs or defendants (e.g. labor cases).

SENTENCIA COMPLEMENTARIA.
clarifying ruling or decision (by a higher court of a lower court decision).

SENTENCIA CONDENATORIA.
(in criminal law) guilty verdict, verdict of guilty, conviction, sentence ‖ (in civil law) verdict in favor of petitioner. Opposed to SENTENCIA ABSOLUTORIA.

SENTENCIA CONDICIONAL.
conditional decision or sentence, decision subject to reservation, judicial determination which contains a condition or reservation. May be either criminal or civil decision.

SENTENCIA CONFIRMATORIA.
affirming decision or sentence, decision of an appellate court which affirms a lower court judgment.

SENTENCIA CONGRUENTE.
judicial decision which resolves all the issues in dispute as set forth in the complaint and answer.

SENTENCIA CONSENTIDA.
final (unappealed) decision or sentence, judgment which although appealable is not appealed (by choice of the parties).

SENTENCIA CONSTITUTIVA.
judicial decision which establishes, modifies, or abolishes a legal right. Opposed to SENTENCIA DECLARATIVA.

SENTENCIA CONTENCIOSA.
judicial decision of a disputed issue.

SENTENCIA DE CONDENA.
See SENTENCIA CONDENATORIA.

SENTENCIA DE MUERTE.
death sentence.

SENTENCIA DE PRIMERA INSTANCIA.
lower court decision, decision of a lower court. See PRIMERA INSTANCIA.

SENTENCIA DE REMATE.
order of judicial sale, type of writ of execution which orders a judicial sale of the goods which have been seized.

SENTENCIA DE SEGUNDA INSTANCIA.
appellate court decision, decision of an appellate court. See SEGUNDA INSTANCIA.
SENTENCIA DE TRIBUNAL EXTRANJERO.
decision or sentence of a foreign court.
See TRIBUNAL EXTRANJERO.
SENTENCIA DECISORIA.
substantive decision or sentence, judgment which resolves substantive issues.
SENTENCIA DECLARATIVA.
declaratory judgment. Opposed to SENTENCIA CONSTITUTIVA.
SENTENCIA DEFINITIVA.
final decision or sentence or order or judgment.
SENTENCIA DESESTIMATORIA.
See SENTENCIA ABSOLUTORIA.
SENTENCIA DISPOSITIVA.
dispositive decision, judgment which determines a matter or decides an issue.
SENTENCIA EJECUTORIA.
See SENTENCIA FIRME.
SENTENCIA EJECUTORIADA.
executed judgment, judgment which has been fully carried out.
SENTENCIA ESTIMATORIA.
See SENTENCIA CONDENATORIA.
SENTENCIA "EXTRA PETITA".
judicial decision which grants more than that requested by the petitioner in the complaint.
SENTENCIA EXTRANJERA.
foreign judgment.
SENTENCIA FIRME.
final order or judgment or sentence or decision ‖ judgment which although appealable is not appealed or from which no appeal can be taken.
SENTENCIA INDETERMINADA.
indeterminate sentence, criminal sentence for a period of time which is fixed in light of the individual, the degree of his or her dangerousness or conduct, and the degree of reform.
SENTENCIA INTERLOCUTORIA.
interlocutory order or decision.
SENTENCIA NULA.
void sentence or decision or judgment (for being issued in violation of substantive or procedural law).
SENTENCIA PASADA EN AUTORIDAD DE COSA JUZGADA.
See SENTENCIA FIRME.

SENTENCIA PREPARATORIA.
interlocutory procedural orders.
SENTENCIA PROVISIONAL.
temporary order ‖ interlocutory order ‖ judgment or decision which is reviewable ‖ judgment or decision which does not have the effect of res judicata, non-final judgment or decision.
SENTENCIA RESOLUTIVA.
judgment or decision which has the effect of voiding or nullifying something.
SENTENCIA "ULTRA PETITA".
judicial decision which grants more than that requested by the petitioner.
SENTENCIADO.
adj, condemned, sentenced.
SENTENCIADOR.
m, judge, court, person or court which decides a matter ‖ adj, sentencing, deciding.
SENTENCIAR.
v, to adjudge, decide ‖ (in criminal law) to condemn, sentence, issue a sentence or verdict ‖ (in civil law) to issue a decision or opinion or judgment ‖ to pass judgment on ‖ to designate (something for a certain purpose).
SENTIDO.
m, sense ‖ understanding, significance, meaning ‖ intelligence ‖ explanation ‖ interpretation ‖ easily offended person ‖ common sense, judgment ‖ way, direction (e.g. of traffic) ‖ injured party ‖ adj, experienced ‖ sensitive ‖ offended.
SENTIDO COMÚN.
common sense, good judgment, discernment.
SENTIMIENTO.
m, sentiment, emotion ‖ opinion, judgment, decision ‖ complaint; pleasure ‖ pain ‖ sensation ‖ grief, sorrow.
SENTIMIENTO DE NACIONALIDAD.
national sentiment ‖ patriotism ‖ national consciousness.
SEÑA.
f, sign ‖ scar ‖ mark ‖ down payment ‖ earnest money ‖ indicia ‖ signal.
SEÑAL.
f, mark ‖ differentiating note or mark ‖ marking post ‖ sign, signal ‖ indicia ‖ vestige ‖ scar ‖ symbol, representation ‖ notification, summons ‖ down payment ‖ earnest money.
SEÑALADAMENTE.
adv, specially, especially ‖ determinedly.

SEÑALADO.
m, person with an identifying mark ‖ adj, distinguished, notable ‖ famous ‖ noted ‖ infamous ‖ identifiable, with an identifying mark ‖ appropriate.

SEÑALAMIENTO.
m, summons (to appear in court) ‖ designation or indication of the date and time (of an appointment) ‖ matter, issue (of discussion or meeting) ‖ appointment, date.

SEÑALAR.
v, to make a sign or identifying mark ‖ to designate or appoint a person ‖ to identify, point out a person within a group ‖ to summon, cite ‖ to scar, mark ‖ to notify, give notice ‖ to designate, set (e.g. a date, place, time).

SEÑALARSE.
v, to stand out, distinguish oneself, be famous for.

SEÑALES CARRETERAS.
traffic signs.

SEÑALES DE TRÁFICO.
See SEÑALES CARRETERAS.

SEÑALIZAR.
v, to place traffic signs.

SEÑAS.
f, home address ‖ gestures, signals.

SEÑAS MORTALES.
indications of concealment of a crime or other illegal conduct.

SEÑAS PERSONALES.
personal description, identifying characteristics.

SEÑOR.
m, mister, Mr. ‖ (male) owner, master, proprietor ‖ nobleman ‖ God ‖ sir, sire ‖ father-in-law ‖ gentleman.

SEÑORA.
f, mistress, Mrs., missus, madam, madame ‖ Ms. (in English "Ms." indicates either married or unmarried status) ‖ wife, married woman ‖ (female) owner, mistress, proprietress ‖ woman ‖ widow, widowed woman ‖ mother-in-law.

SEÑORADA.
f, gentlemanly thing to do.

SEÑORÍA.
f, lordship, ladyship ‖ ownership ‖ senate ‖ your honor. Used to address judges formally.

SEÑORÍO.
m, dominion ‖ control (of one's emotions) ‖ group of gentlemen ‖ majesty, nobility ‖ elegance ‖ gentry, nobility ‖ estate ‖ fiefdom.

SEÑORITA.
f, miss, Miss, Ms. (in English, "Ms." indicates either married or unmarried status) ‖ unmarried woman.

SEPARABLE.
adj, separable ‖ subject to being partitioned.

SEPARACIÓN.
f, separation ‖ parting ‖ division ‖ partition ‖ distance, loss of contact ‖ separation from or loss of employment or position ‖ retirement ‖ voluntary dismissal or abandonment or dropping of a complaint ‖ dissolution of a partnership or a corporation ‖ dismissal, firing, removal, discharge, severance (from job) ‖ resignation, quitting (of a job or public office) ‖ (legal) separation (of a married couple) ‖ (legal) separation of marital property ‖ separate property within the marital community.

SEPARACIÓN CONYUGAL.
marital separation, (legal) separation (of a married couple) ‖ separation of a married couple due to causes of travel, work, etc.

SEPARACIÓN DE BIENES.
See SEPARACIÓN DE BIENES ENTRE CÓNYUGES.

SEPARACIÓN DE BIENES ENTRE CÓNYUGES.
separation of marital property.

SEPARACIÓN DE CUERPOS.
legal separation (of a married couple).

SEPARACIÓN DE HECHO.
de facto (marital) separation.

SEPARACIÓN DE LA DOTE.
return of the dowry property to the wife (for mismanagement by husband).

SEPARACIÓN DE LA IGLESIA Y EL ESTADO.
separation of church and state.

SEPARACIÓN DE LA TUTELA.
removal of guardian of a minor.

SEPARACIÓN DE LOS FRUTOS.
See FRUTOS PERCIBIDOS.

SEPARACIÓN DE LOS PATRIMONIOS DEL DIFUNTO.
division of decedent's estate, probate of a decedent's estate in order that it be distributed.

SEPARACIÓN DE LOS PATRIMONIOS DEL HEREDERO.
division of the heir's estate.

SEPARACIÓN DE PODERES.
See SEPARACIÓN POLÍTICA.
SEPARACIÓN DE PUESTO.
resignation, quitting (of a job or public office).
SEPARACIÓN DEL SERVICIO.
dishonorable discharge from military service.
SEPARACIÓN POLÍTICA.
separation of powers (between judicial, legislative, and executive branches).
SEPARADO.
m, person who has undergone a marital separation ‖ adj, separated.
SEPARAR.
v, to separate ‖ to distance ‖ to divide ‖ to leave ‖ to discharge, dismiss, fire, remove (from job) ‖ to separate the goods of a marital estate ‖ to reserve, set aside (e.g. goods for a customer).
SEPARAR DEL SERVICIO.
to discharge dishonorably (from military service).
SEPARARSE.
v, to distance or separate oneself ‖ to distance oneself ‖ to divorce ‖ to voluntarily dismiss or abandon or drop a complaint ‖ to waive or abandon a right or a claim ‖ to dissolve a partnership or a corporation.
SEPARATISMO.
m, separatism, separatist movement.
SEPARATISTA.
f, m, separatist ‖ adj, separatist.
SEPARATIVO.
adj, separative ‖ separable.
SEPTUAGENARIO.
m, septuagenarian.
SEPULCRAL.
adj, sepulchral, pertaining to a tomb.
SEPULCRO.
m, tomb, grave ‖ grave site.
SEPULTAR.
v, to bury ‖ to place in a grave or tomb, entomb, inter ‖ to hide, conceal ‖ to be wrapped up in one's own problems.
SEPULTURA.
f, burial, interment ‖ tomb, grave, pit ‖ burial or grave site.
SEPULTURERO.
m, grave digger ‖ mortician, undertaker ‖ official grave digger or exhumer.
SEQUÍA.
f, drought, dry spell ‖ dry season.

SÉQUITO.
m, entourage, retinue, train ‖ following.
SÉQUITO SEPULCRAL.
burial or funeral train.
SER
m, being ‖ essence ‖ nature ‖ value or reason of things ‖ v, to be, exist ‖ to possess, have (a quality) ‖ to pertain to ‖ to serve as ‖ to find oneself (in a place) ‖ to belong to ‖ to have been born in a certain place ‖ to form part of.
SER DE OTRO.
v, to be unfaithful (as a wife) ‖ to belong to another party.
SER DE VIDA.
life in being ‖ live being.
SERIE.
f, series.
SERIEDAD.
f, seriousness ‖ honesty ‖ honor ‖ formality ‖ sincerity ‖ loyalty ‖ importance.
SERIO.
adj, serious ‖ honest ‖ honorable ‖ formal ‖ sincere ‖ loyal ‖ important.
SERVICIO.
m, service ‖ work ‖ activity ‖ benefit, use, profit ‖ method ‖ time in service ‖ assistance, help ‖ group of tools or means used to carry something out ‖ domestic service ‖ military service ‖ money or other item that is given by government to pay for public's needs.
SERVICIO ACTIVO.
active duty or service ‖ active duty or service in the military.
SERVICIO CIVIL.
civil service, (non-military) public service ‖ administrative service ‖ military service.
**SERVICIO CIVIL
DE DEFENSA.**
civil defense service.
SERVICIO DE EMPLEO.
unemployment service, administrative agency which is charged with finding jobs for persons
SERVICIO DE INTELIGENCIA.
See SERVICIO SECRETO.
**SERVICIO DE UTILIDAD
PÚBLICA.**
See SERVICIO PÚBLICO.
SERVICIO DOMÉSTICO.
domestic service.
SERVICIO EXTERIOR DE LA NACIÓN.
foreign service, diplomatic corps.

SERVICIO MILITAR.

military service, service in the military ‖ obligation to do military service.

SERVICIO OBLIGATORIO.

obligatory military service.

SERVICIO PÚBLICO.

public service.

SERVICIO SECRETO.

secret or intelligence service.

SERVICIO SOCIAL.

social service.

SERVICIOS.

m, services ‖ plural of SERVICIO.
See LOCACIÓN DE SERVICIOS.

SERVIDERO.

adj, serviceable, useful, utile.

SERVIDOR.

m, servant, maid ‖ help, assistant ‖ server, waiter ‖ used to refer to oneself, I. This is often used by the writer or speaker to refer to him or herself, e.g. "TU SERVIDOR".

SERVIDUMBRE.

f, easement, servitude, right of way (if it allows the owner of the dominant estate to benefit from use of the property of the servient estate) ‖ right of way ‖ covenant (if it requires the owner of the servient estate to do or not do something) ‖ equitable servitude (if it requires the owner of the servient estate to do or not do something but does not fulfill the legal requirements of a covenant) ‖ slavery, servitude ‖ totality of household help or servants ‖ subjection ‖ obligation ‖ restriction of freedom.

SERVIDUMBRE AÉREA.

air space easement, easement to use air space for air travel.

SERVIDUMBRE AFIRMATIVA.

See SERVIDUMBRE POSITIVA.

SERVIDUMBRE APARENTE.

apparent easement.

SERVIDUMBRE CONTINUA.

continuing or continuous easement, easement which occurs naturally and requires no act of man (e.g. aqueduct).

SERVIDUMBRE CONVENCIONAL.

express easement, easement which is agreed to by contract ‖ express covenant, covenant which is agreed to by contract.
See SERVIDUMBRE.

SERVIDUMBRE DE ABREVADERO.

easement to allow livestock to drink water running through another's estate (but not to draw water in any other fashion).

SERVIDUMBRE DE ACUEDUCTO.

easement to run an aqueduct through another's property.

SERVIDUMBRE DE AGUAS.

easement to run water onto the estate of another.

SERVIDUMBRE DE ALBAÑAL.

sewer drainage easement.

SERVIDUMBRE DE CAMINO DE SIRGA.

See CAMINO DE SIRGA.

SERVIDUMBRE DE CANALETA.

easement to run roof water onto the estate of another.

SERVIDUMBRE DE CANALÓN.

See SERVIDUMBRE DE CANALETA.

SERVIDUMBRE DE ESTRIBO DE PRESA.

See SERVIDUMBRE DE PARADA.

SERVIDUMBRE DE LUCES.

light and air easement.

SERVIDUMBRE DE MEDIANERÍA.

easement related to a dividing or adjoining wall.

SERVIDUMBRE DE "NON AEDIFICANDI".

covenant not to build.

SERVIDUMBRE DE "NON ALTIUS TOLLENDI".

covenant not to build over a certain height.

SERVIDUMBRE DE PARADA.

easement to construct into a river to draw off water or to raise the water level.

SERVIDUMBRE DE PASO.

right of way, easement of access.

SERVIDUMBRE DE PASTOS.

easement to pasture livestock on another's estate.

SERVIDUMBRE DE SACA DE AGUA.

easement to draw water from another's estate.

SERVIDUMBRE DE SALVAMENTO.

easement to land a vessel or boat on another's estate in case of necessity.

SERVIDUMBRE DE SIRGA.

See CAMINO DE SIRGA.

SERVIDUMBRE DE TRÁNSITO.

See SERVIDUMBRE DE PASO.

SERVIDUMBRE DE UTILIDAD PÚBLICA.

See SERVIDUMBRE LEGAL.

SERVIDUMBRE DE VISTAS.

negative covenant prohibiting the opening of holes or windows which would allow a view of

the estate of another ‖ type of affirmative covenant or easement to permit the continued view of another's estate.
See SERVIDUMBRE.

SERVIDUMBRE DISCONTINUA.
discontinuous or non-continuous or non-apparent easement, easement which does not occur naturally and requires some act of man (e.g. right to draw water).

SERVIDUMBRE LEGAL.
easement by eminent domain, easement prescribed by law.

SERVIDUMBRE NATURAL.
easement prescribed by law.

SERVIDUMBRE NEGATIVA.
negative easement ‖ negative or restrictive covenant. See SERVIDUMBRE.

SERVIDUMBRE NO APARENTE.
non-continuing or discontinuing or non-apparent easement ‖ non-apparent covenant, covenant which is not apparent from any external indication (e.g. the covenant not to build over a certain height).
See SERVIDUMBRE.

SERVIDUMBRE PERSONAL.
easement in gross ‖ covenant in gross.
See SERVIDUMBRE.

SERVIDUMBRE POSITIVA.
affirmative easement ‖ affirmative covenant.
See SERVIDUMBRE.

SERVIDUMBRE PREDIAL.
easement which runs with the land.
See SERVIDUMBRE REAL.

SERVIDUMBRE PÚBLICA.
public easement.

SERVIDUMBRE REAL.
appurtenant easement ‖ covenant appurtenant, covenant running with the land, real covenant. See SERVIDUMBRE.

SERVIDUMBRE RURAL.
See SERVIDUMBRE RÚSTICA.

SERVIDUMBRE RÚSTICA.
rural easement or covenant ‖ easement pertaining to rural property ‖ covenant pertaining to rural property.
See SERVIDUMBRE.

SERVIDUMBRE TÁCITA.
easement by implication (includes easement by necessity or right of way by necessity, and quasi-easement) ‖ implied covenant.
See SERVIDUMBRE.

SERVIDUMBRE URBANA.
urban easement or covenant ‖ easement pertaining to urban property. See SERVIDUMBRE.

SERVIDUMBRE VISIBLE.
See SERVIDUMBRE APARENTE.

SERVIDUMBRE VOLUNTARIA.
easement by agreement or express act of the parties ‖ covenant by agreement or express act of the parties. See SERVIDUMBRE.

SERVIL.
adj, servile ‖ servants', pertaining to servant(s) ‖ slaves', pertaining to slaves ‖ lowly, humble ‖ despicable, vile.

SERVIR.
v, to serve ‖ to wait on (e.g. tables) ‖ to be of service, be useful ‖ to carry out a job or position, work for ‖ to do a service ‖ to serve (in the military), do military service ‖ to replace or substitute for someone ‖ to give ‖ to court, woo a woman ‖ to do a favor ‖ to be suitable or apt or appropriate for.

"SERVITUS".
slavery ‖ see also SERVIDUMBRE.

SESIÓN.
f, session ‖ meeting, conference, convention, assembly ‖ discussion ‖ consultation ‖ congressional or parliamentary session or meeting.

SESIÓN PÚBLICA.
public trial or hearing ‖ public congressional or parliamentary session, congressional or parliamentary session or meeting which is open to the public.

SEUDO.
adj, pseudo-, false, pretended, supposed.

SEUDÓNIMO.
m, pseudonym, alias, assumed name ‖ pen name, nom de plume.

S.E.U.O.
See SALVO ERROR U OMISIÓN.

SEVERAMENTE.
adv, severely, harshly.

SEVERIDAD.
f, severity, harshness, sternness, strictness ‖ cruelty ‖ strict adherence to the law.

SEVICIA.
f, extreme or excessive cruelty ‖ cruel treatment, mistreatment, maltreatment.

SEXO.
m, sex, gender ‖ sex, sexual intercourse ‖ female or male sex organs.

SICARIO.
m, paid assassin, hired gun ‖ member of a repressive police or military unit.

SIERVO.
m, slave, serf ‖ servant.

SÍFILIS.
f, syphilis.

SIFILÍTICO.
m, syphilitic ‖ adj, syphilitic.

SIGILACIÓN.
f, concealment, hiding ‖ sealing, stamping ‖ stamp, seal.

SIGILAR.
v, to stamp ‖ to seal ‖ to silence, quiet ‖ to hide, conceal.

SIGILARIO.
adj, able to be stamped or sealed.

SIGILO.
m, stamp, seal, instrument for stamping or sealing ‖ secrecy.

SIGILO PROFESIONAL.
See SECRETO PROFESIONAL.

SIGILOSO.
adj, silent, quiet ‖ secretive, hidden ‖ reserved ‖ discreet.

SIGLA.
f, acronym.

SIGLO.
m, century, period of 100 years ‖ very long time ‖ era, age, epoch, period ‖ the mundane or worldly.

SIGNAR.
v, to make a mark or seal ‖ to sign, autograph.

SIGNATARIO.
m, signatory ‖ adj, signatory.

SIGNATURA.
f, sign, mark ‖ library classification number or mark ‖ filing mark.

SIGNIFICACIÓN.
f, meaning, significance ‖ importance ‖ representation ‖ expression ‖ statement.

SIGNIFICADO.
m, meaning, sense ‖ interpretation ‖ adj, important ‖ well-known ‖ prominent.

SIGNIFICAR.
v, to signify, mean, represent ‖ to indicate, show, point out ‖ to have importance, be important, be of interest.

SIGNIFICARSE.
v, to distinguish oneself.

SIGNIFICATIVO.
adj, significant ‖ important ‖ relevant, probative.

SIGNO.
m, sign ‖ representation ‖ symbol ‖ mark ‖ signal ‖ each letter or punctuation mark ‖ flourish or mark (added to a notary's signature) ‖ indicia, proof ‖ fate, destiny.

SIGNO NOTARIAL.
flourish or mark (added to a notary's signature).

SIGNOS DE VIDA.
signs of life.

SILENCIAR.
v, to silence, quiet, impose silence on ‖ to be silent (about something).

SILENCIARIO.
m, person who is charged with enforcing silence.

SILENCIERO.
See SILENCIARIO.

SILENCIO.
m, silence, quiet ‖ lack of response ‖ pause ‖ lack of determination.

SILENCIO DEL ACUSADO.
silence of the accused (when questioned).

SILENCIO, OBSCURIDAD O INSUFICIENCIA DE LAS LEYES.
silence, obscurity, or inadequacy of the law.

SILENCIOSO.
adj, in silence ‖ silent, reserved.

SILOGISMO.
m, syllogism.

SILLA.
f, chair, seat ‖ headquarters, main office ‖ chair, head (e.g. of a university department).

SILLA ELÉCTRICA.
f, electric chair.

SIMBÓLICO.
adj, symbolic, representative.

SIMBOLISMO JURÍDICO.
m, legal symbolism ‖ symbolism which has legal significance.

SIMBOLIZAR.
v, to symbolize ‖ to appear.

SÍMBOLO.
m, symbol, representation, image ‖ emblem.

SÍMBOLO NACIONAL.
m, national emblem or symbol ‖ person who is a source of national pride.

SIMIL.
m, simile ‖ similarity ‖ comparison ‖ adj, similar.

SIMILAR.
adj, similar, alike ‖ analogous.

SIMILITUD.
f, similarity, resemblance ‖ analogy.

SIMPLE.
m, simpleton, fool ‖ adj, simple ‖ mere ‖ pure ‖ unconditional ‖ unceremonious ‖ common ‖ in one unit, single ‖ not combined, not compounded, uncombined ‖ non-complex ‖ unqualified ‖ without aggravating circumstances ‖ stupid, slow, simple ‖ unsigned ‖ unauthenticated ‖ uncomplicated, easy.

SIMPLE PRÉSTAMO.
See PRÉSTAMO SIMPLE.

SIMPLE SOCIEDAD CIVIL.
type of partnership regulated by the civil code.

SIMPLE TENEDOR.
simple holder or possessor.

SIMPLE TENENCIA.
simple tenancy ‖ simple possession ‖ simple holding.

SIMPLEMENTE.
adv, simply ‖ without duplicity or trickery ‖ unconditionally ‖ unqualifiedly.

SIMPLIFICADO.
adj, simplified.

SIMPOSIO.
m, symposium, conference.

SIMULACIÓN.
f, simulation ‖ fraud ‖ pretense, guise ‖ sham ‖ imitation ‖ hypocrisy ‖ fakery ‖ subterfuge ‖ action which disguises the true nature of a transaction.

SIMULACIÓN ABSOLUTA.
absolute or pure pretense or simulation (without no real transaction underlying the simulated act).
Opposed to SIMULACIÓN RELATIVA.

SIMULACIÓN DE DENUNCIA.
See FALSA DENUNCIA.

SIMULACIÓN DELICTIVA.
criminal fraud or subterfuge, sham, criminal act which attempts to conceal the true purpose of a transaction or act (e.g. sham transaction or contract).

SIMULACIÓN EN EL MATRIMONIO.
fraud in the marriage.

SIMULACIÓN FRAUDULENTA.
SIMULACIÓN with fraudulent intent.

SIMULACIÓN INOCENTE.
SIMULACIÓN without harmful intent.

SIMULACIÓN RELATIVA.
relative or partial fraud (for the purpose of concealing the true purpose or nature, but relative to which there is a real transaction)
Opposed to SIMULACIÓN ABSOLUTA.

SIMULACRO.
m, simulacrum, false image ‖ pretense ‖ model, example ‖ work, rehearsal, mock presentation.

SIMULADO.
adj, simulated, faked, false ‖ apparent fraudulent ‖ sham ‖ hypocritical.

SIMULADOR.
m, hypocrite ‖ faker ‖ pretender, feigner, author of a sham or simulation or fraud or subterfuge.

SIMULAR.
v, to simulate ‖ to defraud ‖ to disguise ‖ put up a pretense or guise or subterfuge ‖ imitate ‖ to be hypocritical ‖ to fake.

SIMULTÁNEAMENTE.
adv, simultaneously.

SIMULTANEAR.
v, to do or try to do two things at the same time ‖ to study two or more subjects or courses the same time.

SIMULTANEIDAD.
f, simultaneousness, duality.

SIMULTÁNEO.
adj, simultaneous.

SIN.
prep, without ‖ besides, apart from.

SIN EMBARGO.
notwithstanding, however, nevertheless.

SIN NÚMERO.
innumerable, countless.

SIN PERJUICIO DE TERCERO.
without prejudice to third party rights or interests, without affecting the rights or interests third parties.

SINALAGMÁTICO.
adj, mutually obligatory ‖ obligatory upon parties.

SINDICABLE.
adj, able to be syndicated ‖ able to be unionized.

SINDICACIÓN.
f, union membership or affiliation ‖ unionization ‖ syndication ‖ accusation ‖ entering into a voting trust or shareholders' agreement.
SINDICACIÓN DE ACCIONES.
entering into a voting trust or shareholders' agreement.
SINDICACIÓN OBLIGATORIA.
membership under union shop conditions, obligatory union membership ‖ obligatory unionization.
SINDICADO.
m, syndicate ‖ member of a trade union ‖ adj, unionized ‖ accused.
SINDICAL.
adj, union, pertaining to unions or a particular union ‖ syndicalist, pertaining to syndicalism.
SINDICALISMO.
m, syndicalism, trade or labor unionism, unionism.
SINDICALISTA.
f, m, unionist, follower of syndicalism or unionism ‖ adj, unionist.
SINDICAR.
v, to unionize ‖ to syndicate ‖ to accuse, denounce ‖ to suspect ‖ to put into a trust.
SINDICARSE.
v, to join a labor or trade union ‖ to form a union, unionize.
SINDICATO.
m, union ‖ labor organization ‖ local ‖ labor union ‖ trade union ‖ syndicate.
SINDICATO ACCIONARIO.
voting trust ‖ shareholders' agreement.
SINDICATO AGRÍCOLA.
grange, farm owners' association ‖ farm workers' union.
SINDICATO DE EMPRESA.
independent union, union which only includes workers of a single company regardless of their profession or trade.
SINDICATO DE FUNCIONARIOS.
public employees' union.
SINDICATO DE INDUSTRIA.
See SINDICATO INDUSTRIAL.
SINDICATO DE OFICIO.
horizontal union ‖ craft union, trade union.
SINDICATO GREMIAL.
See SINDICATO DE OFICIO.
SINDICATO HORIZONTAL.
craft union.

SINDICATO INDUSTRIAL.
industrial union.
SINDICATO MÁS REPRESENTATIVO.
most representative union (in cases in which there are competing unions).
SINDICATO MIXTO.
labor organization which associates both workers and employers.
SINDICATO OBRERO.
employees' labor or trade union. Opposed to SINDICATO PATRONAL.
SINDICATO PATRONAL.
employers' association (which usually includes both individual and corporate members). Opposed to SINDICATO OBRERO.
SINDICATO ÚNICO.
exclusive union, union which is the sole and exclusive labor representative of workers in a given area.
SINDICATO VERTICAL.
union including all the workers in a certain company or activity (e.g. steel plant union which included members regardless of their trade or position).
SINDICATURA.
f, trusteeship ‖ receivership ‖ position and office of shareholders' representative or corporate comptroller. See SÍNDICO.
SÍNDICO.
m, trustee or receiver (in bankruptcy or other insolvency proceedings) ‖ corporate comptroller ‖ shareholders' representative, special type of auditor who is charged by law with the permanent review of corporate books, records, and activities in order to protect the interests of shareholders or partners from fraud, abuse, or mismanagement.
SÍNDICO EN EL CONCURSO DE ACREEDORES.
receiver or trustee in an insolvency proceeding or reorganization.
See CONCURSO DE ACREEDORES.
SÍNDICO EN LA QUIEBRA.
trustee or receiver in bankruptcy.
"SINE DIE".
sine die, with no appointed date.
SINE QUA NON.
indispensable or essential condition ‖ adj, sine qua non, indispensable, essential.
SINECURA.
f, sinecure.

SINGLADURA.
f, day's run, distance traveled by a ship in a day.

SINGRAFA.
f, contract, document which contains the rights and obligations between two parties.

SINGULAR.
m, neighbor ‖ individual, person ‖ adj, singular, single ‖ unique, extraordinary, special ‖ private ‖ between two people only ‖ one.

SINGULARIDAD.
f, singularity ‖ peculiarity ‖ particularity ‖ uniqueness.

SINGULARIZAR.
v, to particularize, distinguish, single out.

SINGULARMENTE.
adv, singularly, particularly ‖ separately ‖ specially, especially.

SINIESTRADO.
m, accident victim, victim of a serious accident or disaster.

SINIESTRO.
m, disaster ‖ major accident ‖ adj, sinister, evil, wicked, fiendish, with bad intentions ‖ ill-fated ‖ perverse.

SINIESTRO MAYOR.
total disaster, disaster which causes a total loss.

SINIESTRO MENOR.
partial disaster, disaster which causes only a partial loss.

SINJUSTICIA.
f, injustice.

SINNÚMERO.
m, incalculable or countless number or amount.

SINONIMIA.
f, synonymy.

SINÓNIMO.
m, synonym ‖ adj, synonymous.

SINOPSIS.
f, synopsis ‖ summary, compendium, synthesis.

SINÓPTICO.
adj, synoptic, pertaining to a synopsis.

SÍNTESIS.
f, synthesis ‖ summary, synopsis, compendium ‖ informational bulletin.

SINTÉTICO.
m, synthetic or artificial product ‖ adj, synthetical, pertaining to a synthesis ‖ summarized ‖ synthetic, artificial.

SÍNTOMA.
m, symptom.

SIRVIENTA.
f, (female) servant or domestic help, maid.

SIRVIENTE.
m, manservant, (male) domestic help ‖ adj, servient (e.g. estate).

SISA.
f, petty theft or filching of money by a woman or a servant from the daily shopping money.

SISAR.
v, to filch. See SISA.

SISTEMA.
m, system ‖ method ‖ procedure ‖ technique ‖ doctrine.

SISTEMA ACUSATORIO.
accusatory system, system of criminal procedure whereby the court must decide based on evidence presented by others in a public or private hearing.
Opposed to SISTEMA INQUISITIVO.

SISTEMA CORPORATIVO.
corporative system ‖ trade union system.

SISTEMA DE GABINETE.
cabinet system (of government), system of government whereby a cabinet chosen from members of parliament constitutes a part of the executive branch.

SISTEMA DE PRUEBA.
See CONDENA CONDICIONAL.

SISTEMA ECONÓMICO.
economic system.

SISTEMA INQUISITIVO.
system of criminal procedure whereby the court is the accuser, the inquirer and the sentencer.
Opposed to SISTEMA ACUSATORIO.

SISTEMA PARLAMENTARIO.
parliamentary system (of government).

SISTEMA PRESIDENCIALISTA.
presidential system, system based on the election of a president as executive power.

SISTEMA PROGRESIVO.
progressive system of criminal readjustment consisting of five stages: observation, treatment, testing the treatment, freedom under observation and conditional freedom.

SISTEMA REPRESENTATIVO.
representative system (of government).

SISTEMA TORRENS.
Torrens title system.

SISTEMAS ELECTORALES.
electoral systems.
SISTEMAS HIPOTECARIOS.
mortgage filing systems.
SISTEMAS INSTITUCIONALES.
institutional systems, systems by which institutions are formed in relation to their field or sphere of activity.
SISTEMAS PENITENCIARIOS.
prison system ‖ penal system.
SISTEMAS SINDICALES.
union systems, systems of labor organization.
SISTEMÁTICAMENTE.
adv, systematically.
SISTEMÁTICO.
adj, systematic ‖ invariable, constant.
SISTEMATIZACIÓN.
f, systematization.
SISTEMATIZAR.
v, to systematize.
SITIADO.
m, person or thing under siege ‖ adj, besieged, under siege.
SITIADOR.
m, person imposing a siege, besieger ‖ adj, besieging.
SITIAL.
m, seat of honor ‖ elevated position.
SITIAR.
v, to besiege, place under siege ‖ to hem in, harass (a person).
SITIO.
m, (military) siege ‖ place, spot ‖ site, locale ‖ location ‖ space ‖ recreational house, country house ‖ hunting lodge ‖ small farm.
SITIO DE PLAZA.
siege of a military position.
SITIOS.
m, plural of SITIO ‖ adj, real (estate or property).
SITO.
adj, situated ‖ real (estate or property).
SITUACIÓN.
f, situation, position ‖ site ‖ disposition ‖ state, constitution (e.g. of person's health) ‖ fixed income ‖ phase, stage, point ‖ posing (e.g. a problem) ‖ political, economic, or social state of affairs of a country.
SITUACIÓN DE EXCEDENCIA.
condition of being laid off temporarily from a job (due to an unnecessary number of employees).

SITUACIÓN "EN COMISIÓN".
condition of being temporarily transferred from a job.
SITUACIÓN JURÍDICA.
legal relationship ‖ legally protected interest.
SITUACIÓN PELIGROSA.
dangerous state or condition, state or condition of things that pose a personal or societal risk.
SITUADO.
m, fixed income or salary based on the income produced by certain assets ‖ adj, situated, located.
SITUAR.
v, to situate, place ‖ to locate ‖ to earmark funds, assign or put monies aside for certain expenses ‖ to locate something on a map.
SOBERANÍA.
f, sovereignty, supremacy ‖ rule, power, sway ‖ source of public authority ‖ national independence ‖ highest quality or excellence ‖ pride, arrogance ‖ governance of a nation over a non-contiguous territory.
SOBERANÍA AÉREA.
aerial sovereignty.
SOBERANÍA NACIONAL.
national sovereignty ‖ governmental power to rule.
SOBERANÍA POPULAR.
popular sovereignty.
SOBERANÍA TERRITORIAL.
territorial sovereignty.
SOBERANO.
m, sovereign, monarch ‖ adj, sovereign ‖ independent ‖ excellent, supreme ‖ superior.
SOBORDO.
m, verification that freight list and cargo coincide ‖ freight list or manifest ‖ bonus paid a ship's crew during time of war or other unusual danger.
SOBORNABLE.
adj, able to be suborned, bribable.
SOBORNACIÓN.
See SOBORNO.
SOBORNADO.
adj, suborned, bribed.
SOBORNADOR.
m, briber, suborner ‖ adj, bribing, suborning.
SOBORNAR.
v, to suborn, bribe.

SOBORNO.
m, bribery, subornation ‖ bribing, suborning ‖ bribe ‖ corruption ‖ paid seduction.
See COHECHO.
SOBRANTE.
m, surplus ‖ extra ‖ remainder, leftover ‖ adj, surplus, extra, excess ‖ leftover, remaining.
SOBRAR.
v, to remain, be leftover ‖ to exceed, surpass ‖ to be more than enough, exceed, be leftover or in excess.
SOBRE.
m, envelope ‖ address (of a letter or package) ‖ prep, over.
SOBRE EL TERRENO.
on the spot, on-site.
SOBRECARGA.
f, overload ‖ extra charge ‖ overcharge ‖ extra problem or burden ‖ surcharge on a stamp.
SOBRECARGAR.
v, to overload ‖ to overcharge ‖ to stamp a surcharge (on a stamp).
SOBRECARGO.
m, purser, ship's officer in charge of freight.
SOBRECARTA.
f, second issuance of a judicial order.
SOBREENTENDER.
See SOBRENTENDER.
SOBREESCRITO.
adj, written over.
SOBREESTADÍA.
See SOBRESTADÍAS.
SOBREGIRO.
m, overdraft.
SOBREHERIDO.
adj, superficially or lightly wounded.
SOBREJUEZ.
m, appellate court judge.
SOBRENOMBRE.
See APODO.
See also SEUDÓNIMO.
SOBRENTENDER.
v, to be understood implicitly, go without saying ‖ to understand (something implied).
SOBREPAGA.
f, salary increase ‖ bonus, extra pay.
SOBREPARTO.
m, postpartum period, time immediately following birth ‖ adj, postpartum.
SOBREPRECIO.
m, overcharge ‖ surcharge.

SOBREPRIMA.
f, extra premium due on an insurance policy to cover increased or new risks.
SOBREPRODUCCIÓN.
f, overproduction, excess production.
SOBREPUJAR.
v, to outbid, up or increase a bid (at auction).
SOBRESCRITO.
m, instructions or information written on the outside of an envelope ‖ superscribed, written over.
SOBRESEER.
v, to acquit ‖ to desist, stop ‖ to abandon (e.g. a plan) ‖ to stay an investigative proceeding ‖ to stay (legal) proceedings ‖ to discontinue (legal) proceedings ‖ to dismiss a case, order a judgment of nonsuit ‖ to yield.
SOBRESEGURO.
m, overinsurance, insurance in excess of the value of the insured item.
SOBRESEIMIENTO.
m, acquittal ‖ abandonment (e.g. of a plan) ‖ staying of an investigative proceeding ‖ stay of (legal) proceedings ‖ discontinuance; dismissal ‖ nonsuit.
SOBRESEIMIENTO DEFINITIVO.
See SOBRESEIMIENTO LIBRE.
SOBRESEIMIENTO LIBRE.
dismissal with prejudice (to reopen a criminal prosecution) ‖ quashing of the charge or indictment. Occurs during the trial due to lack of proof.
SOBRESEIMIENTO PARCIAL.
partial dismissal of a criminal prosecution (e.g. against certain defendants).
SOBRESEIMIENTO PROVISIONAL.
dismissal without prejudice (to reopen a criminal prosecution).
SOBRESEIMIENTO TOTAL.
dismissal of a criminal case in full ‖ total dismissal of criminal prosecution (e.g. against all defendants).
SOBRESELLO.
m, second stamp or seal.
SOBRESTADÍAS.
f, demurrage, overstay of a vessel in port ‖ charge for such overstay or demurrage.
SOBRESTANTE.
m, foreman, overseer, supervisor.
SOBRESTANTE DE OBRAS PÚBLICAS.
overseer of public works projects.

SOBRESUELDO.
m, bonus, extra wages or pay.
SOBREVENIDO.
See HECHO SOBREVENIDO.
SOBREVENIR.
v, to supervene.
SOBREVIVENCIA.
See SUPERVIVENCIA.
SOBREVIVIENTE.
m, survivor, person who survives another or others ‖ adj, surviving.
SOBREVIVIR.
v, to survive (e.g. another person or a period of time) ‖ to be saved.
SOBRINA.
f, niece.
SOBRINAZGO.
m, familial relationship between a nephew or niece and an uncle or aunt ‖ nepotism.
SOBRINO.
m, nephew.
SOBRINO CARNAL.
nephew related by blood (i.e. son of brother or sister).
SOBRINO POLÍTICO.
nephew by marriage, nephew of husband or wife.
SOBRINO SEGUNDO.
cousin once removed, cousin's son.
SOCIAL.
adj, social ‖ societal ‖ sociable ‖ partner, related to partners ‖ member, related to members ‖ corporate ‖ partnership, related to a partnership ‖ sociological ‖ labor, worker, pertaining to labor or workers ‖ collective.
SOCIALISMO.
m, socialism.
SOCIALISTA.
f, m, socialist, supporter of socialism ‖ member of socialist party ‖ adj, socialist.
SOCIALIZACIÓN.
f, socialization, introduction or adoption of socialism in a society ‖ expropriation ‖ nationalization.
SOCIALIZACIÓN DE LA PROPRIEDAD.
nationalization or expropriation of private property ‖ see also COLECTIVISMO.
SOCIEDAD.
f, society ‖ societal order ‖ social relationship between countries or peoples ‖ high society ‖ association ‖ union, labor organization ‖ commercial company ‖ company, corporation, firm, partnership, society ‖ tie, relationship ‖ contract between two or more people such that they jointly invest labor and capital and share the profits.
SOCIEDAD ACCIDENTAL.
unincorporated association resulting from an agreement between parties to invest capital and labor for a particular purpose. The managing investors are jointly liable for the association debts to the full extent of their personal assets, whereas the non-managing partners are liable only to the extent of their investment. Business is carried out in the name of the managing partners.
SOCIEDAD ANÓNIMA.
corporation, stock company, incorporated association of two or more persons whose liability for acts of the association is limited to their initial investment and whose participation is represented by shares.
SOCIEDAD ANÓNIMA CON PARTICIPACIÓN ESTATAL MAYORITARIA.
type of partially government-owned corporation, incorporated association of two or more investors in which the government owns 51% or more of the stock.
SOCIEDAD CAPITALISTA.
capitalist society ‖ stock company, corporation in which the shareholders invest capital.
SOCIEDAD CIVIL.
corporation or partnership regulated by the civil code.
SOCIEDAD CLASIFICADORA.
vessel inspection association which is charged with classifying, inspecting and granting legal status to vessels.
SOCIEDAD COLECTIVA.
type of partnership, registered association of two or more persons who are jointly and severally liable to the full extent of their personal assets, organized to do business under a commercial name.
SOCIEDAD COMANDITARIA.
See SOCIEDAD EN COMANDITA.
SOCIEDAD COMERCIAL.
See SOCIEDAD MERCANTIL.
SOCIEDAD CONTROLADA.
subsidiary corporation, subsidiary, corporation in which a controlling block of stock is owned by another (parent) corporation.

SOCIEDAD CONYUGAL.
community property.
SOCIEDAD COOPERATIVA.
See COOPERATIVA and COOPERATIVISMO.
SOCIEDAD DE CAPITAL E INDUSTRIA.
type of limited partnership, registered association of two or more partners in which at least one partner invests money, is personally liable for partnership debts and has management powers, and in which at least one partner invests his services and labor, is personally liable only to the extent of the undistributed profits of the company and also has management powers.
SOCIEDAD DE CAPITALIZACIÓN.
corporation which obligates the shareholder to invest money over a period of time. Opposed to those requiring a one-time investment.
SOCIEDAD DE COMERCIO.
See SOCIEDAD MERCANTIL.
SOCIEDAD DE CRÉDITO.
cooperative, mutual benefit association or corporation the purpose of which is to allow the capital invested to be used by its members.
SOCIEDAD DE CUENTAS EN PARTICIPACIÓN.
See SOCIEDAD ACCIDENTAL and CUENTAS EN PARTICIPACIÓN.
SOCIEDAD DE DERECHO.
corporation de jure, de jure corporation.
SOCIEDAD DE ECONOMÍA MIXTA.
partially government-owned corporation.
SOCIEDAD DE EMPRESAS.
joint venture corporation or business association.
SOCIEDAD DE GANANCIALES.
community which arises relative to community property.
SOCIEDAD DE HABILITACIÓN.
See SOCIEDAD DE CAPITAL E INDUSTRIA.
SOCIEDAD DE HECHO.
de facto business association.
SOCIEDAD DE INVERSIÓN.
investment company.
SOCIEDAD DE LAS NACIONES.
League of Nations.
SOCIEDAD DE NACIONES.
See SOCIEDAD DE LAS NACIONES.
SOCIEDAD DE RESISTENCIA.
labor or trade union, labor organization, union.

SOCIEDAD DE RESPONSABILIDAD LIMITADA.
limited liability company, type of registered close corporation in which the number of stockholders is limited, the investment is made in fixed payments, the liability for corporate debts is limited to an amount established in the articles of incorporation, and the capital is divided in parts or quotas (i.e. not by shares).
SOCIEDAD DE SOCORROS MUTUOS.
mutual benefit association, not-for-profit or non- profit corporation the purpose of which is to allow the capital invested to be used by its members.
SOCIEDAD DOMÉSTICA.
family community. Includes SOCIEDAD CONYUGAL, SOCIEDAD PATERNOFILIAL and SOCIEDAD HERIL.
SOCIEDAD EN COMANDITA.
limited partnership.
SOCIEDAD EN COMANDITA POR ACCIONES.
type of limited partnership in which the limited partners are issued stock and the general partners are not.
SOCIEDAD EN COMANDITA SIMPLE.
limited partnership.
SOCIEDAD EN FORMACIÓN.
corporation in the process of formation which has been legally established and whose by-laws have been created, but relative to which the incorporation process is not yet complete.
SOCIEDAD EN LIQUIDACIÓN.
corporation in liquidation, dissolved corporation.
SOCIEDAD EN PARTICIPACIÓN.
See SOCIEDAD ACCIDENTAL.
SOCIEDAD EXTRANJERA.
foreign corporation, association that is incorporated in a foreign country ‖ foreign-controlled corporation, corporation controlled by foreigners ‖ foreign-owned corporation, corporation owned by foreigners ‖ foreign corporation with a local branch, agency, or affiliate.
SOCIEDAD FIADORA.
See FIADORA, EMPRESA.
SOCIEDAD GREMIAL.
labor or trade union, labor organization, union.

SOCIEDAD HERIL.
community of economic relations between an employer and his or her domestic staff or servants.

SOCIEDAD ILÍCITA.
corporation organized for illegal purposes.

SOCIEDAD INDUSTRIAL.
industrialized society ‖ society after the industrial revolution ‖ corporation or business association with industrial purposes.

SOCIEDAD IRREGULAR.
business association which has not been formed pursuant to formal legal requirements (e.g. written contract, registration).

SOCIEDAD LEONINA.
See CLÁUSULA LEONINA.

SOCIEDAD MATRIARCAL.
matriarchal society.

SOCIEDAD MERCANTIL.
business association.

SOCIEDAD NACIONAL.
domestic corporation, association that is incorporated nationally ‖ domestic corporation, corporation controlled by nationals ‖ locally-owned corporation, corporation owned by nationals.

SOCIEDAD PATERNOFILIAL.
community of family and economic relations between parents and children.

SOCIEDAD PATRIARCAL.
patriarchal society.

SOCIEDAD POLÍTICA.
human society ‖ political party or association.

SOCIEDAD POR CUOTAS.
See SOCIEDAD DE RESPONSABILIDAD LIMITADA.

SOCIEDAD PREINDUSTRIAL.
pre-industrial society.

SOCIEDAD RELIGIOSA.
religious organization or association ‖ religious society.

SOCIEDAD SECRETA.
secret society or order.

SOCIEDAD SIN FINES DE LUCRO.
not-for-profit corporation, non-profit corporation.

SOCIEDAD SOLIDARIA.
See SOCIEDAD COLECTIVA.

SOCIEDAD UNIVERSAL.
community which includes the entirety of property of its members.

SOCIEDAD VINCULADA.
affiliate, affiliated corporation, corporation which owns more than a given percentage in another corporation.

SOCIEDADES PRIMITIVAS.
primitive or undeveloped societies.

SOCINIANA.
See CAUTELA SOCINIANA.

SOCIO.
m, member, fellow ‖ (corporate) shareholder, stockholder ‖ partner, associate ‖ affiliate, affiliated member or partner ‖ (joint venture or partnership) partner.

SOCIO ACCIONISTA.
shareholder, stockholder ‖ shareholder or stockholder in a type of limited partnership in which the limited partners are issued stock and the general partners are not. See SOCIEDAD EN COMANDITA POR ACCIONES.

SOCIO ADMINISTRADOR.
manager or administrator who holds shares in the corporation ‖ managing partner.

SOCIO APARENTE.
apparent partner or shareholder or associate (in a corporation or partnership or association).

SOCIO CAPITALISTA.
capital partner or shareholder or stockholder, partner or stockholder or shareholder who invests capital or goods, as opposed to services.

SOCIO COLECTIVO.
general or full partner, partner who is unlimitedly liable for the debts of the partnership. See SOCIEDAD EN COMANDITA and SOCIEDAD COLECTIVA.

SOCIO COMANDITARIO.
limited or special partner, partner who is liable only to the extent of his or her investment. See SOCIEDAD EN COMANDITA.

SOCIO DE INDUSTRIA.
See SOCIO INDUSTRIAL.

SOCIO EMPLEADO.
partner or shareholder or stockholder who is obligated to invest not only capital but also labor.

SOCIO GESTOR.
managing partner, general partner.

SOCIO INDUSTRIAL.
partner or stockholder or shareholder who invests labor or services, as opposed to capital or goods.

SOCIO LIQUIDADOR.
partner or shareholder who is charged with winding up or liquidating a company.
SOCIO NO GESTOR.
non-managing partner.
SOCIO NO OSTENSIBLE.
See SOCIO OCULTO.
SOCIO OCULTO.
dormant or silent or secret partner ‖ secret shareholder or stockholder.
SOCIO OSTENSIBLE.
ostensible partner ‖ ostensible shareholder or stockholder.
SOCIOLOGÍA.
f, sociology.
SOCIOLOGÍA CRIMINAL.
criminology, criminal sociology.
SOCIOLOGÍA INDUSTRIAL.
industrial sociology.
SOCIOLOGÍA JURÍDICA.
legal sociology.
SOCIOLÓGICO.
adj, sociological.
SOCIÓLOGO.
m, sociologist.
SOCOLOR.
m, excuse, pretext ‖ appearance.
SOCORREDOR.
m, savior ‖ aid, assistant ‖ helper ‖ adj, helping, aiding ‖ saving.
SOCORRER.
v, to help ‖ to aid, assist ‖ to save (from harm or evil) ‖ to pay part of a debt, make a partial payment.
SOCORRIDO.
m, person who is saved ‖ person who is helped or aided ‖ adj, saved ‖ helped, aided ‖ well-stocked ‖ profitable ‖ trite ‖ handy, convenient.
SOCORRISMO.
m, aid or assistance organization.
SOCORRISTA.
m, emergency specialist, specialist in helping emergency victims.
SOCORRO.
m, help ‖ aid, assistance ‖ monetary assistance, subsidy ‖ salvation, redemption ‖ theft, robbery ‖ prostitute's earnings given to her pimp.
SOCORROS MUTUOS.
mutual assistance or help. See SOCIEDAD DE SOCORROS MUTUOS.

SODOMÍA.
f, sodomy (between man and woman or between men or between women or between human and animal) ‖ sexual deviation (of any kind) ‖ bestiality.
SODOMITA.
f, m, sodomite.
SOEZ.
adj, crude, vulgar, base, vile, gross, against nature.
SOFISMA.
m, sophism, false argument.
SOFISTA.
m, sophist, quibbler.
SOFISTERÍA.
f, sophistry ‖ trickery ‖ lie, fallacy.
SOFOCACIÓN.
f, suffocation.
SOFOCAR.
v, to suffocate, choke, stifle, smother ‖ to repress ‖ to suffocate, extinguish, put out (e.g. a fire) ‖ to embarrass, make blush ‖ to bother.
SOGA.
f, rope.
SOJUZGADOR.
m, oppressor, subjugator ‖ repressor.
SOJUZGAR.
v, to subjugate, oppress ‖ to repress ‖ to subdue ‖ to tyrannize.
SOLAMENTE.
adv, only, sole ‖ provided.
SOLAMENTE QUE.
provided that.
SOLAPADAMENTE.
adv, underhandedly ‖ deceitfully ‖ sneakily.
SOLAPADO.
adj, underhanded ‖ deceitful ‖ insincere ‖ sly.
SOLAPAR.
v, to act underhandedly or deceitfully ‖ to sneak, act slyly ‖ to deceive ‖ to cover up.
SOLAR.
m, ancestral home ‖ noble ancestry or lineage ‖ undeveloped urban real estate ‖ tenement ‖ adj, solar, sun ‖ ancestral.
SOLARIEGO.
adj, ancestral, pertaining to an ancestral home ‖ manorial ‖ pertaining to a sole proprietor.
SOLDADA.
f, female soldier ‖ salary, wages, pay ‖ stipend ‖ soldier's duty.

SOLDADO.

n, soldier ‖ military academy graduate ‖ serviceman.

SOLEMNE.

adj, solemn, serious ‖ yearly, annual, once per year ‖ binding ‖ formal ‖ valid ‖ legally compliant ‖ authentic ‖ serious ‖ ceremonious ‖ ostentatious ‖ important, high, grand.

SOLEMNEMENTE.

adv, solemnly, seriously ‖ formally ‖ validly ‖ seriously ‖ complying legally ‖ authentically ‖ bindingly ‖ ceremoniously.

SOLEMNIDAD.

, solemnity ‖ seriousness ‖ formality ‖ legal requirement, requirement for an act to be legal, valid and binding ‖ ceremony.

SOLEMNIZAR.

v, to solemnize ‖ to authorize (e.g. an act or contract) ‖ to carry out pursuant to all legal formalities.

SOLICITADA.

, advertisement for employees, want-ad ‖ statement (e.g. of opinion) published in a newspaper by a person or a group of people.

SOLICITADOR.

n, solicitor, petitioner, requester ‖ applicant ‖ agent.

SOLICITANTE.

n, solicitor, petitioner, requester.

SOLICITAR.

v, to try ‖ to request, petition, solicit ‖ to solicit a woman).

SOLICITUD.

, written request or petition ‖ application ‖ solicitation ‖ care, earnestness ‖ diligence ‖ solicitude.

SOLIDAMENTE.

adv, solidly, firmly ‖ with strong, legal reasons.

SOLIDARIAMENTE.

adv, joint and severally ‖ descriptive of situation in which a party may be sued for the entirety of an obligation which was incurred with others to whom he or she may then look for subrogation.

SOLIDARIDAD.

, solidarity ‖ cooperation, help, assistance ‖ personal support or identification (with a position or group) ‖ joint liability pursuant to which a party may be sued for the entirety of an obligation incurred with others to whom he or she may then look for subrogation.

See SOLIDARIDAD ACTIVA and SOLIDARIDAD PASIVA.

SOLIDARIDAD ACTIVA.

joint obligation or liability owed to multiple creditors (by one or more debtors), which requires the payment of the debt in full to any one or all of the creditors without regard to its distribution between them.

SOLIDARIDAD PASIVA.

joint obligation or liability owed by multiple debtors (to one or more creditors), which requires the payment of the debt in full by any one or all of the debtors without regard to spreading of the debt between them.

SOLIDARIDAD PENAL.

joint liability for criminal act.

SOLIDARIDAD POR DELITO.

See SOLIDARIDAD PENAL.

SOLIDARIDAD SOCIAL.

societal solidarity ‖ social assistance or cooperation.

SOLIDARIO.

adj, joint ‖ joint and several ‖ joined ‖ associated, sympathizing.

SOLIDARISMO.

m, solidarity movement ‖ solidarity ‖ cooperativism.

SOLIDARIZAR.

to solidify ‖ to make jointly and severally responsible or liable, obligate jointly and severally.

SOLIDARIZARSE.

v, to join together ‖ to obligate oneself jointly such that one may be held liable for the entirety of a joint obligation with the right to be subrogated by co-obligors.

SOLTAR.

v, to let go ‖ to free, liberate ‖ to acquit (a defendant) ‖ to explain, solve (e.g. a problem) ‖ to pardon, excuse ‖ to remit, send ‖ to relieve, free (from an obligation) ‖ to drop ‖ to untie, loosen.

SOLTAR LA PALABRA.

to forgive an obligation or promise ‖ to offer or promise something.

SOLTARSE.

v, to untie or disentangle oneself ‖ to help to escape ‖ to become practiced or skilled (at a job or activity) ‖ to fall into bad habits or ways.

SOLTERA.

f, single woman.

SOLTERÍA.
f, bachelorhood, condition of being a bachelor || celibacy.
SOLTERO.
m, single man, bachelor || celibate man || adj, single, lone || celibate || free.
SOLTURA.
f, freeing or release of a prisoner or a detainee granted by a judge || release of a prisoner upon completion of sentence || agility, ability || solution of a dialectic problem || insolence, impudence.
SOLUBLE.
adj, solvable, resolvable || soluble.
SOLUCIÓN.
f, solution || resolution || payment || satisfaction or payment of a debt || fulfillment of an obligation || conclusion, termination.
SOLUCIÓN DE CONTINUIDAD.
lack of continuity, interruption.
SOLUCIONAR.
v, to solve, resolve || to provide a solution.
"SOLUTIO".
payment || fulfillment, satisfaction, compliance in full.
"SOLUTIO INDEBITI".
payment of that which is not owed.
"SOLVE ET REPETE".
A complaint may be filed only upon making the payment complained of.
SOLVENCIA.
f, solvency || rendition of accounts || payment of a debt.
SOLVENCIA EN LA CESIÓN.
solvency (of a debtor) in assigning a right to payment.
SOLVENCIA EN LA SUCESIÓN.
solvency (of the heirs) in a inheritance.
SOLVENTAR.
v, to pay what is owed || to comply with or fulfill or satisfy an obligation || to resolve or solve a problem.
SOLVENTE.
adj, solvent || free of debts, debt-free || sound, capable of paying one's debts || resolved, solved || dissolved || capable, able (to carry out a job or position) || reliable, dependable.
SOMERO.
adj, superficial || unmeditated, not thought out || without reflection.

SOMETER.
v, to submit, put forward (the resolution of a problem to others for their decision) || to subdue, quell, dominate (e.g. an enemy, rebels) || to humiliate || to conquer || to pacify || to subordinate || to carry out work or tests || to subject.
SOMETERSE.
v, to submit oneself || to subject oneself || to quell, put down, subdue (e.g. rebellion) || to conquer || to give up, yield, surrender.
SOMETIMIENTO.
m, submission || subjection || subjugation || conquering || rendition, surrender || pacification || humiliation || subordination.
SOMNÍFERO.
m, soporific substance || adj, soporific.
SONAMBULISMO.
m, somnambulism || sleepwalking or talking in one's sleep.
SONÁMBULO.
m, somnambulist || sleepwalker || adj, somnambulistic.
SONDA.
f, depth sounding, fathoming, measuring the depth (in bodies of water) || exploration || sound, passage (of water).
SONDAR.
See SONDEAR.
SONDEAR.
v, to fathom, sound (for depth) || to explore | to sound out (a person).
SONDEO.
m, sounding || exploring.
SOPLO.
m, breath (of air), gust || whisper, secret communication || informer, rat, stool pigeon || accusation, denunciation.
SOPLÓN.
m, informer, rat, stool pigeon || traitorous conspirator || confidant.
SOPLONEAR.
v, to accuse, denounce || to tell a secret, inform or rat on.
SOPLONERÍA.
f, informing, squealing, ratting on || accusing denouncing.
SOR.
f, sister || nun.
SORDERA.
f, deafness.

SORDEZ.
See SORDERA.

SÓRDIDO.
adj, sordid || dirty || scandalous || miserable || abhorrent.

SORDO.
m, deaf person || adj, deaf || insensitive, unresponsive || reserved || rebellious.

SORDOMUDEZ.
f, deaf-muteness.

SORDOMUDO.
m, deaf-mute || adj, deaf and dumb.

SORPRENDER.
v, to surprise, astonish, give a surprise to || to surprise someone in the act || to discover something hidden.

SORPRENDIDO.
m, victim of surprise || adj, surprised.

SORPRESA.
f, surprise, astonishment || casual discovery of something hidden.

SORTEADOR.
m, person who draws lots or straws or who carries out a lottery; person who evades or eludes.

SORTEAMIENTO.
See SORTEO.

SORTEO.
m, lottery, raffle, drawing (of lots or lottery) || decision made by lottery or raffle or drawing || dodging, evasion.

S.O.S.
S.O.S., request for help or assistance.

SOSLAYAR.
v, to evade, dodge, ignore (a problem) || to avoid a difficulty.

SOSPECHA.
f, suspicion || guess or belief about someone's guilt || doubt || lack of confidence || mistrust || unfavorable presumption.

SOSPECHABLE.
See SOSPECHOSO.

SOSPECHADO.
adj, suspect || foreseen, surmised.

SOSPECHAR.
v, to suspect, surmise || to guess, conjecture || to doubt || to mistrust, distrust.

SOSPECHOSO.
m, suspect, person with doubtful background || adj, suspect || presumed guilty || mistrustful, distrustful.

SOSTÉN.
m, support, base, foundation || sustenance || protector.

SOSTENER.
v, to sustain || to support || to protect || to maintain, hold (e.g. an opinion) || to maintain, keep, provide sustenance, provide the essentials (e.g. food, clothing) || to help, aid || to save || to tolerate, endure, bear, put up with || to suffer || to defend (a thesis) || to affirm zealously || to resist, sustain || to hold (e.g. a meeting).

SOSTENIMIENTO.
m, sustenance || support || protection || maintenance || aid, help, assistance || tolerance || defence || resistance || affirmance.
See SOSTENER.

SOVIET.
m, soviet || council || adj, Soviet.

"SPONSIO".
promise, obligation || bet || treaty between peoples || bond, bail.

"SPONSOR".
guarantor || surety || debtor whose debt is guaranteed || guarantor of an oral contract whose debt is not binding on his heirs.

STANDARD.
m, standard, norm || model, pattern || gold standard || adj, standard.

"STATUS"
m, status, state || legal status.

STATUS QUO.
m, status quo.

"STIPULATIO".
stipulation || contract || contractual clause || offer, proposal.

"STRICTO SENSU".
stricto sensu, strict sense or interpretation, literally.

SUB JÚDICE.
sub judice, in litigation || under (judicial) consideration.

SUBALTERNAR.
v, to subordinate, subject || to oppress.

SUBALTERNO.
m, inferior, subordinate || lieutenant || adj, inferior, subordinate || lower in rank or standing.

SUBARRENDADOR.
m, sublessor, lessee or renter who sublets or subleases real property he or she has rented from another.

SUBARRENDAMIENTO.
See SUBARRIENDO.
SUBARRENDAR.
v, to sublet, sublease.
SUBARRENDATARIO.
m, subtenant, sublessee ‖ renter or lessee who sublets or subleases real property from another lessee or renter.
SUBARRIENDO.
m, subleasing, subletting, sublease, underlease ‖ sublease or under-lease payment.
SUBASTA.
f, public sale or auction ‖ private auction ‖ public bid or licitation.
SUBASTA ADMINISTRATIVA.
public bid or licitation (for government contract).
SUBASTA EXTRAJUDICIAL.
extrajudicial auction.
SUBASTA JUDICIAL.
judicial or court-ordered auction.
SUBASTA PÚBLICA.
public auction or sale ‖ public bid.
SUBASTACIÓN.
See SUBASTA.
SUBASTADOR.
m, auctioneer ‖ public auctioneer.
SUBASTAR.
v, to sell or lease or contract at auction or public sale or public auction.
SUBCLASE.
f, subclass.
SUBCOMISARÍA.
f, position, office and location of a subcommissary or subcommissioner.
SUBCOMISARIO.
m, deputy commissary or commissioner, subcommissioner.
SUBCOMISIÓN.
f, subcommission.
SUBCONTRATAR.
v, to subcontract.
SUBCONTRATISTA.
m, subcontractor.
SUBCONTRATO.
m, subcontract.
SUBDELEGADO.
m, delegate's assistant or collaborator ‖ delegate's agent ‖ agent ‖ adj, subdelegated.
SUBDELEGAR.
v, to assist a delegate ‖ to assign to another

that which has been delegated or granted by agency agreement.
SUBDESARROLLO.
m, underdevelopment ‖ economic underdevelopment.
SUBDESARROLLO ECONÓMICO.
economic underdevelopment.
SUBDIRECCIÓN.
f, position and office of assistant manager or director.
SUBDIRECTOR.
m, assistant manager or director.
SÚBDITO.
m, citizen, national ‖ subject (of a country or authority) ‖ adj, subjected (to some authority).
SÚBDITO ENEMIGO.
citizen or subject or national of an enemy nation (found in enemy territory).
SUBDIVIDIR.
v, to subdivide.
SUBDIVISIÓN.
f, subdivision ‖ subclassification.
SUBEJECUTOR.
m, subagent ‖ assistant executor.
SUBEMPLEO.
m, underemployment.
SUBENFITEUSIS.
f, sub-emphyteusis. See ENFITEUSIS.
SUBENTENDER.
See SOBREENTENDER.
SUBESPECIE.
f, sub-species.
SUBESTIMAR.
v, to underestimate, undervalue.
SUBFIADOR.
m, sub-guarantor, guarantor of a guarantor ‖ sub-surety, guarantor of a surety.
See FIADOR.
SUBFIANZA.
f, subguarantee, subguaranty ‖ sub-surety.
SUBFLETAMENTO.
m, sub-charter.
SUBGÉNERO.
m, subgenus.
SUBGOBERNADOR.
m, lieutenant or deputy governor.
SUBHIPOTECA.
f, mortgage of a mortgage ‖ second mortgage
SUBIDA.
f, rise ‖ increase ‖ ascent ‖ climb.

SUBIDO.
adj, heightened, extraordinary, intense.
SUBINQUILINO.
m, subtenant.
SUBINSPECCIÓN.
f, assistant inspectorship ‖ office of assistant inspector.
See INSPECCIÓN.
SUBINTENDENCIA.
f, subdivision or department within a super-intendent's jurisdiction ‖ assistant superinten-dency ‖ office of assistant superintendent.
SUBINTENDENTE.
m, assistant superintendent.
SUBIR.
v, to rise ‖ to ascend ‖ to increase ‖ to climb ‖ to obtain a better position ‖ to gain political or social power or influence, rise in the world.
SÚBITO.
adj, sudden, hasty ‖ violent ‖ impetuous ‖ un-expected ‖ adv, suddenly, hastily ‖ impetuous-ly ‖ unexpectedly.
SUBJEFE.
m, assistant chief.
SUBJETIVAMENTE.
adv, subjectively ‖ because of the person or subject ‖ intimately ‖ personally.
SUBJETIVIDAD.
f, subjectivity.
SUBJETIVISMO.
m, subjectivism.
SUBJETIVISMO JURÍDICO.
legal subjectivism, legal philosophy which em-phasizes the subjective.
SUBJÚDICE.
See SUB JÚDICE.
SUBLEVACIÓN.
f, uprising, revolt, insurrection ‖ act of sedition ‖ rebellion ‖ open protest.
SUBLEVADO.
m, rebel, person who starts, wins, or loses an uprising or revolt or insurrection ‖ adj, rebel-lious ‖ revolting, protesting.
SUBLEVAR.
v, to rebel, rise up, revolt ‖ to protest openly ‖ to incite to rebellion ‖ to stir up.
SUBLEVARSE.
v, to revolt, rise up.
SUBLOCACIÓN.
f, sublease, subletting.

SUBMARINO.
m, submarine.
SUBORDINACIÓN.
f, subordination ‖ submission ‖ condition of being secondary or accessory.
SUBORDINACIÓN JERÁRQUICA.
hierarchical subordination.
SUBORDINACIÓN LABORAL.
employee subordination (to the employer).
SUBORDINADO.
adj, subordinated, subordinate ‖ secondary ‖ accessory ‖ lower, inferior (in position).
SUBORDINAR.
v, to subordinate ‖ to oppress, quell ‖ to ar-range hierarchically or preferentially.
SUBORDINARSE.
v, to subordinate oneself ‖ to stop being insub-ordinate ‖ to follow the straight and narrow.
SUBPREFECTO.
m, assistant prefect, subprefect.
See PREFECTO.
SUBPREFECTURA.
f, assistant prefecture, subprefecture.
SUBPRODUCTO.
m, by-product.
SUBREPCIÓN.
f, concealment, hiding ‖ fraud.
SUBREPTICIO.
adj, surreptitious ‖ hidden, clandestine.
SUBROGACIÓN.
f, subrogation ‖ substitution, replacement.
SUBROGACIÓN CONVENCIONAL.
contractual subrogation, subrogation which is contractually agreed upon.
Opposed to SUBROGACIÓN LEGAL.
SUBROGACIÓN EN LA FIANZA.
guarantee or surety subrogation, subrogation of the guarantor or surety.
SUBROGACIÓN EN LA RELACION FAMILIAR.
subrogation of family relations to the rights and obligations of children.
SUBROGACIÓN EN LOS PRIVILEGIOS.
subrogation of new creditors to the liens and preferences corresponding to the previous creditors.
SUBROGACIÓN LEGAL.
legal subrogation, subrogation set forth by law. Opposed to SUBROGACIÓN CONVENCIO-NAL.

SUBROGACIÓN PARCIAL.
partial subrogation.
SUBROGACIÓN PERSONAL.
subrogation of persons (due to a substitution).
SUBROGACIÓN REAL.
substitution of one thing for another ‖ placing one thing in the legal position of another thing.
SUBROGACIÓN TOTAL.
complete or total subrogation.
SUBROGADO.
adj, subrogated ‖ substituted, replaced.
SUBROGAR.
v, to subrogate ‖ to substitute, replace.
SUBROGATORIO.
adj, subrogation, pertaining to subrogation.
SUBSANABLE.
adj, correctable, rectifiable ‖ repairable ‖ amendable ‖ excusable.
SUBSANACIÓN.
f, correction, rectification ‖ amendment ‖ repair ‖ exculpation, excusing ‖ pardon.
SUBSANAR.
v, to correct ‖ to amend, rectify ‖ to repair ‖ to amend ‖ to excuse ‖ to pardon ‖ to satisfy.
SUBSCRIBIR.
v, to subscribe ‖ to sign, subscribe (a document or contract) ‖ to agree or side with, support (e.g. a position) ‖ to purchase stocks or bonds before the shares are sold on the stock market ‖ to grant a request.
SUBSCRIBIRSE.
v, to subscribe (to a periodic publication) ‖ to agree to pay a business.
SUBSCRIPCIÓN.
f, subscription (e.g. to a magazine or a legal document) ‖ payment for such subscription ‖ signing ‖ signature ‖ acceptance to a contract, treaty, or accord ‖ assent, granting (of a request) ‖ support, agreement (with a position).
SUBSCRIPTO.
See SUBSCRITO.
SUBSCRIPTOR.
m, signor, signatory ‖ subscriber ‖ adj, paid (to a publication) ‖ subscribing ‖ signing.
SUBSCRITO.
m, signor, signatory ‖ subscriber ‖ adj, signed ‖ subscribed ‖ paid.
SUBSECRETARÍA.
f, under-secretaryship ‖ assistant secretaryship ‖ position and office of under-secretary or assistant secretary.

SUBSECRETARIO.
m, under-secretary ‖ assistant secretary.
SUBSECUENTE.
adj, subsequent ‖ last, most recent, latter.
SUBSEGUIR.
v, to follow directly or immediately or next.
SUBSIDIADO.
adj, subsidized.
SUBSIDIARIA.
f, subsidiary, corporation owned in part or in whole by another corporation.
SUBSIDIARIAMENTE.
adv, subsidiarily ‖ additionally ‖ secondly ‖ on the other hand.
SUBSIDIARIDAD.
f, nature of that which is subsidiary.
SUBSIDIARIO.
m, subsidiary, corporation owned in part or in whole by another corporation ‖ adj, subsidiary, additional, secondary.
SUBSIDIO.
m, subsidy ‖ assistance ‖ strike subsidy (from a union) ‖ allowance.
SUBSIDIO FAMILIAR.
family allowance, extra payment made to a worker for his family ‖ family subsidy, family maintenance payment, government payment made to maintain a person's family.
SUBSIDIO POR PARO.
unemployment assistance or pay or allowance.
SUBSIGUIENTE.
adj, subsequent, following ‖ after the next, following the next.
SUBSISTENCIA.
f, subsistence ‖ permanence, continuity ‖ survival ‖ maintenance ‖ sustenance, food ‖ livelihood, means of support.
SUBSISTENCIA HUMANA.
human survival.
SUBSISTENCIAS.
f, material sustenance, food, provisions.
SUBSISTENTE.
adj, in effect, existing ‖ prevailing.
SUBSISTIR.
v, to subsist ‖ to remain, continue, last, endure ‖ to live, exist ‖ to remain in effect, continue to exist (over the passage of time).
SUBSTANCIA.
f, substance, material ‖ food, sustenance, nutrition ‖ essence ‖ characteristic, nature ‖ ba-

sis ‖ wealth, fortune ‖ estate ‖ esteem, respect, estimation ‖ judgment, sense.
SUBSTANCIACIÓN.
f, a proceeding in a case.
SUBSTANCIAL.
adj, substantial (in all senses) ‖ pertaining to SUBSTANCIA ‖ material ‖ basic, fundamental ‖ essential ‖ important, considerable.
SUBSTANCIALMENTE.
adv, substantially.
SUBSTANCIAR.
v, to extract, summarize, abridge ‖ to try a case, litigate.
SUBSTANCIAS ABORTIVAS.
abortive substances, materials which produce an abortion.
SUBSTANCIAS CORROSIVAS.
corrosive substances or materials.
SUBSTANCIAS EXPLOSIVAS E INFLAMABLES.
explosive and inflammable materials.
SUBSTANCIAS TÓXICAS.
toxic substances or materials.
SUBSTANTIVIDAD.
f, substantiality.
SUBSTANTIVO.
m, fact, thing which exists ‖ substantive, noun ‖ adj, substantive ‖ substantive, pertaining to law which permits, prohibits, or requires. Opposed to PROCEDIMENTAL or ADJETIVO.
SUBSTITUCIÓN.
f, substitution, replacement.
SUBSTITUCIÓN CUASIPUPILAR.
substitution of a mentally incompetent heir.
SUBSTITUCIÓN DE HEREDERO.
substitution of an heir ‖ designation of a remainderman.
SUBSTITUCIÓN DEL MANDATO.
substitution of an agent or attorney in fact.
SUBSTITUCIÓN DIRECTA.
designation of an heir whose interest vests immediately (without a trust or intervening interests). Opposed to SUBSTITUCIÓN INDIRECTA.
SUBSTITUCIÓN EJEMPLAR.
See SUBSTITUCIÓN CUASIPUPILAR.
SUBSTITUCIÓN EXPRESA.
express designation of an heir or substitution.
SUBSTITUCIÓN INDIRECTA.
designation of person who will receive via a future interest or a trust.
Opposed to SUBSTITUCIÓN DIRECTA.

SUBSTITUCIÓN PUPILAR.
designation of a trustee of a protective trust for the benefit of a minor.
SUBSTITUCIÓN RECÍPROCA.
designation of heirs by reason of reciprocal wills.
SUBSTITUCIÓN TÁCITA.
implied designation of an heir or substitution.
SUBSTITUCIÓN VULGAR.
designation of a remainderman whose estate vests if the prior holder cannot or does not wish to inherit.
SUBSTITUIBLE.
adj, replaceable.
SUBSTITUIDOR.
m, substitute, person or thing that substitutes.
SUBSTITUIR.
v, to substitute, replace ‖ to subrogate.
SUBSTITUTIVO.
m, second-best ‖ substitute ‖ adj, substitutive.
SUBSTITUTIVOS PENALES.
alternative criminal sanctions.
SUBSTITUTO.
m, substitute, sub, replacement ‖ representative, agent ‖ alternate ‖ paid substitute for a military conscript ‖ type of alternate heir which may be a remainderman or reversioner, person who inherits an estate due to the failure to vest in the (primary) heir.
SUBSTITUTO DEL MANDATARIO.
alternative or substitute agent or attorney in fact.
SUBSTITUTO PROCESAL.
type of litigant of third party interests, person who in his own name litigates on behalf of another, for that other party's benefit.
SUBSTRACCIÓN.
f, substraction ‖ extraction, removal ‖ theft ‖ robbery ‖ separation ‖ misappropriation, embezzlement ‖ diminution ‖ kidnapping.
SUBSTRACCIÓN DE CADÁVERES.
removal of cadavers ‖ secretion or destruction of a cadaver.
SUBSTRACCIÓN DE CAUDALES PÚBLICOS.
embezzlement or misappropriation or defalcation of public monies or funds.
SUBSTRACCIÓN DE DOCUMENTOS.
type of theft of public property which consists of theft or removal of documents by the public

official to whom they were entrusted. Usually a crime.

SUBSTRACCIÓN DE EFECTOS HEREDITARIOS.
type of theft which consists of removal or theft of a decedent's estate.

SUBSTRACCIÓN DE LA CORRESPONDENCIA.
postal or mail theft, theft of and/or reading and/or revelation of contents of another's mail.

SUBSTRACCIÓN DE MENORES.
kidnapping of a minor.

SUBSTRACCIÓN DE OBEDENCIA.
aiding and abetting desertion or insubordination (of soldier or troop).

SUBSTRAER.
v, to subtract ‖ to separate ‖ to remove, extract ‖ to steal, rob ‖ to misappropriate, embezzle ‖ to diminish ‖ to kidnap.

SUBSTRAERSE.
v, to avoid, get out of (an obligation).

SUBSTRATO.
m, substance, essence ‖ basis ‖ characteristic ‖ summary.

SUBSUELO.
m, underground ‖ subsoil ‖ basement.

SUBSUNCIÓN.
f, action of subsuming a particular situation within the terms of the law.

SUBTERFUGIO.
m, subterfuge ‖ artifice ‖ evasion ‖ excuse, pretext.

SUBTERRÁNEO.
adj, subterranean, underground ‖ insincere, traitorous.

SUBTITULAR.
v, to subtitle.

SUBTÍTULO.
m, subtitle.

SUBURBANO.
m, suburban transportation ‖ suburbanite, person who lives in the suburbs ‖ adj, suburban.

SUBURBIO.
m, suburb.

SUBVENCIÓN.
f, subvention ‖ help, assistance ‖ subsidy ‖ allowance, payment for necessities ‖ welfare payment, financial assistance.

SUBVENCIONAR.
v, to grant or give a subvention or financial assistance.

SUBVERSIÓN.
f, subversion ‖ revolution ‖ destruction of moral values.

SUBVERSIVO.
m, subversive ‖ adj, subversive.

SUBVERSOR.
m, subversive ‖ revolutionary ‖ agitator ‖ subverter.

SUBVERTIR.
v, to subvert ‖ destroy ‖ to foment revolution, agitate.

SUBYUGABLE.
adj, able to be subjugated.

SUBYUGACIÓN.
f, subjugation, subjection ‖ domination ‖ enslavement.

SUBYUGADOR.
m, subjugator ‖ adj, subjecting.

SUBYUGAR.
v, to subjugate, subject ‖ to dominate ‖ to enslave ‖ to influence strongly.

SUCEDÁNEO.
m, substitute, substitution.

SUCEDER.
v, to occur, happen ‖ to follow the entrance ‖ to replace, succeed ‖ to proceed ‖ to inherit, agree to inherit.

SUCEDER POR CABEZA.
to inherit (as direct heir, in contrast to inheriting as heir of another heir).

SUCEDIDO.
m, occurrence, event, happening.

SUCEDIENTE.
m, successor ‖ follower.

SUCESIBLE.
m, heir, person who holds a right to inherit ‖ adj, able to inherit ‖ able to be granted by will or inherited.

SUCESIÓN.
f, succession, following ‖ substitution, replacement ‖ succession, transfer of rights and obligations of a deceased, inheritance ‖ devise (pertaining to real estate) ‖ legacy, bequest (pertaining to personal property) ‖ descendant, offspring, issue ‖ continuity.

SUCESIÓN A LA CORONA.
succession to the throne or the crown.

SUCESIÓN A TÍTULO DEFINITIVO.
succession to the estate of a person presumed dead ‖ irrevocable succession.

SUCESIÓN A TÍTULO PROVISIONAL.
provisional or conditional inheritance.

SUCESIÓN A TÍTULO SINGULAR.
succession under specific title, succession to a specific legacy or bequest (if personal property) or devise (if real property).

SUCESIÓN A TÍTULO UNIVERSAL.
succession under general title, succession to a general legacy or bequest (if personal property) or devise (if real property).

SUCESIÓN AB INTESTATO.
See SUCESIÓN INTESTADA.

SUCESIÓN CONTRACTUAL.
succession by mutual wills, succession pursuant to a contract or agreement to make a will.

SUCESIÓN DE LOS ASCENDIENTES.
succession of ascendants.

SUCESIÓN DE LOS AUSENTES.
succession of the estate of persons presumed dead.

SUCESIÓN DE LOS BIENES RESERVADOS.
succession to property reserved to certain classes of persons.

SUCESIÓN DE LOS COLATERALES.
succession of the collateral relatives (i.e. brothers and sisters, aunts and uncles, nieces and nephews, cousins).

SUCESIÓN DE LOS DESCENDIENTES LEGÍTIMOS.
succession of legitimate descendants.

SUCESIÓN DE LOS HIJOS NATURALES.
succession of illegitimate or naturalchildren.

SUCESIÓN DE LOS PADRES NATURALES.
succession of the natural parents.

SUCESIÓN DE MANDO.
transfer of power or mandate.

SUCESIÓN DEL CÓNYUGE SUPÉRSTITE.
succession of the surviving spouse.

SUCESIÓN DEL ESTADO.
escheat, succession of the state ‖ nationalization, transfer of property to the state.

SUCESIÓN DEL FISCO.
escheat, succession of the state.

SUCESIÓN DIRECTA.
direct succession which immediately vests,

without a trust or intervening interest. Opposed to SUCESIÓN INDIRECTA.

SUCESIÓN FORZOSA.
legal succession, succession required by law. In many civil law countries, the law requires that certain classes of persons (e.g. spouses, children) receive a set portion of a decedent's estate.

SUCESIÓN FUTURA.
See HERENCIA FUTURA.

SUCESIÓN HEREDITARIA.
succession by inheritance, transfer causa mortis, testamentary transfer or succession.

SUCESIÓN INDIRECTA.
succession via a future interest or a trust. Opposed to SUCESIÓN DIRECTA.

SUCESIÓN INTER VIVOS.
inter vivos transfer or succession.

SUCESIÓN INTESTADA.
See SUCESIÓN AB INTESTATO.

SUCESIÓN LEGÍTIMA.
intestate succession.

SUCESIÓN LEGITIMARIA.
See SUCESIÓN FORZOSA.

SUCESIÓN MORTIS CAUSA.
transfer causa mortis, testamentary or hereditary transfer or succession.

SUCESIÓN NECESARIA.
See SUCESIÓN FORZOSA.

SUCESIÓN POR CABEZAS.
per capita succession. Opposed to SUCESIÓN POR ESTIRPES and POR LÍNEAS. .

SUCESIÓN POR ESTIRPES.
per stirpes succession. Opposed to SUCESIÓN POR CABEZA and POR LÍNEAS.

SUCESIÓN POR LÍNEAS.
succession to ascendants of the same relation to the deceased (divided in half between maternal and paternal ascendants, regardless of the number of ascendants on the respective sides).

SUCESIÓN POR TRONCOS.
See SUCESIÓN POR ESTIRPES.

SUCESIÓN PROVISIONAL.
See SUCESIÓN DE LOS AUSENTES.

SUCESIÓN RECÍPROCA.
succession by mutual or reciprocal or joint wills.

SUCESIÓN SINGULAR.
secession of a specific devise (pertaining to real estate) or a specific legacy or bequest (pertaining to personal property).

liv

SUCESIÓN TESTADA.
See SUCESIÓN TESTAMENTARIA.

SUCESIÓN TESTAMENTARIA.
testate succession.

SUCESIÓN TRONCAL.
See SUCESIÓN INTESTADA.

SUCESIÓN UNIVERSAL.
secession of a general devise (pertaining to real estate) or a general legacy or bequest (pertaining to personal property).

SUCESIÓN VACANTE.
See HERENCIA VACANTE.

SUCESIÓN VOLUNTARIA.
See SUCESIÓN TESTAMENTARIA.

SUCESIVAMENTE.
adv, successively, consecutively.

SUCESIVO.
adj, successive, continuing ‖ following ‖ consecutive.

SUCESO.
m, occurrence, event, happening ‖ important fact or event ‖ passage or lapse of time ‖ outcome, result.

SUCESOR.
m, successor, substitute, replacement ‖ continuation ‖ heir, inheritor ‖ legatee (if personal property) ‖ devisee (if real property) ‖ successor in interest (in a corporation).

SUCESOR PARTICULAR.
See SUCESOR SINGULAR.

SUCESOR SINGULAR.
specific legatee or devisee. See SUCESOR.

SUCESOR UNIVERSAL.
general legatee or devisee.
See SUCESOR.

SUCESORIO.
adj, pertaining to SUCESIÓN.

SUCINTAMENTE.
adv, succinctly, briefly, concisely.

SUCINTO.
adj, succinct, brief, concise.

SUCUMBIR.
v, to succumb, give in ‖ to give up ‖ to die ‖ to lose a case ‖ to be defeated.

SUCURSAL.
f, branch, branch office.

SUDAMERICANO.
m, South American, person from South America ‖ adj, South American.

SUEGRA.
f, mother-in-law.

SUEGRO.
m, father-in-law.

SUELDO.
m, salary, pay, wages, compensation, rem neration (for work).

SUELDO ANUAL COMPLEMENTARIO.
year-end or Christmas bonus (often statutoi mandated).

SUELO.
m, ground, earth ‖ earth, world ‖ territory c nation or state or province or municipality other like jurisdiction ‖ floor, ground ‖ s‹ bottom, base ‖ end, finish ‖ plot (of land).

SUELO NATAL.
native soil, homeland, fatherland, motherla

SUELTO.
m, loose change, spare change ‖ short ne‹ paper article ‖ adj, loose ‖ at large, at liberi agile ‖ competent, able ‖ freed, released (fr detention or incarceration) ‖ unattached, committed ‖ licentious, incontinent, loc wanton ‖ free, easy.

SUEÑO.
m, dream ‖ sleep ‖ sleepiness.

SUERTE.
f, luck, chance ‖ good luck or fortune ‖ f lot ‖ decision or selection by lottery ‖ selec service lottery ‖ condition, state ‖ class, s‹ cies, kind ‖ way, manner (of doing somethi ‖ quality ‖ lottery ticket or stub ‖ plot of l demarcated by posts for special use.

SUFICIENCIA.
f, sufficiency ‖ aptitude, fitness, ability, c‹ petence, capacity (to carry out a position oi tivity) ‖ arrogance, over-assuredness.

SUFICIENTE.
adj, sufficient, adequate, enough ‖ apt, able, competent (to carry out a position oi tivity) ‖ arrogant, over-assured ‖ pedantic

SUFRAGAR.
v, to pay, satisfy (a debt) ‖ to help ‖ to voi

SUFRAGIO.
m, aid, assistance ‖ vote, suffrage.

SUFRAGISMO.
m, female suffrage movement, movemen the women's vote.

SUFRIBLE.
adj, sufferable, tolerable, bearable.

SUFRIDO.
m, cuckold who accepts his wife's adult‹ adj, enduring, resigned, patient, long-suffer

UFRIMIENTO.
m, (physical or emotional) pain, suffering ‖ unhappiness, grief ‖ resignation, tolerance.

UFRIR.
v, to suffer (in all senses) ‖ to tolerate, put up with, bear ‖ to resist ‖ to permit ‖ to repay (a wrong).

UFRIR LAS CONSECUENCIAS.
to suffer the consequences.

UGESTIBILIDAD.
f, suggestibility.

UGESTIÓN.
f, suggestion ‖ insinuation ‖ inspiration ‖ hypnosis ‖ control of another's will ‖ proposal, offer ‖ trick, illusion.

UGESTIÓN HIPNÓTICA.
hypnotic suggestion.

UGESTIONABLE.
adj, easy to influence.

UGESTIONADOR.
adj, able to influence or control by suggestion.

UGESTIONAR.
v, to suggest, inspire ‖ to hypnotize ‖ to dominate, control.

UI GÉNERIS.
sui generis.

UICIDA.
f, m, suicide, suicide victim ‖ person who has attempted suicide ‖ person who is sclf-destructive ‖ adj, suicidal ‖ self-destructive.

UICIDARSE.
v, to commit suicide, suicide, take one's life.

UICIDIO.
m, suicide, taking of one's life ‖ self-destruction.

UJECIÓN.
f, subjection, submission ‖ rigorous domination or discipline or control ‖ loss or restriction of freedom.

UJETAR.
v, to subject ‖ to oppress ‖ to retain by force ‖ to have under one's control.

UJETARSE.
v, to subject oneself ‖ to accept the control of another ‖ to control one's desires and impulses ‖ to accept discipline or oppression.

UJETO.
n, subject (in all senses) ‖ person, individual ‖ holder of a right or obligation ‖ theme, subject, topic ‖ adj, subject, liable (to) ‖ dependant, contingent (upon).

SUJETO A.
subject to.

SUJETO ACTIVO DEL DELITO.
criminal, participant in the crime. May be an AUTOR, CÓMPLICE or ENCUBRIDOR.

SUJETO DEL DERECHO.
person who holds a right ‖ person (whether natural or artificial) capable of holding legal rights or obligations.

SUJETO DEL LITIGIO.
See PARTE PROCESAL.

SUJETO PASIVO DEL DELITO.
crime victim, victim of the crime.

SUMA.
f, sum (in all senses) ‖ entirety, whole, aggregate ‖ sum, sum total ‖ addition ‖ quantity, amount ‖ essence ‖ the most important ‖ summary, recompilation.

SUMAR.
v, to add, add up ‖ to aggregate, bring together ‖ to summarize ‖ to add up to, amount to.

SUMARIA.
f, written legal file or proceedings or trial ‖ preliminary investigation.

SUMARIAL.
adj, pertaining to a SUMARIA or a SUMARIO.

SUMARIAMENTE.
adv, summarily, briefly.

SUMARIAR.
v, to submit to a preliminary investigation ‖ to conduct an investigation relative to a military indictment.

SUMARIO.
m, summary proceeding or hearing or trial ‖ summary, abstract, compendium ‖ preliminary stage in a criminal trial, consisting of an indictment or prosecutorial information and a subsequent investigation to determine the active participants in the crime (sometimes equivalent to grand jury investigation or a preliminary hearing) ‖ adj, summarized, brief, summary.

SUMARIO ADMINISTRATIVO.
administrative inquest.

SUMARÍSIMO.
m, extraordinary summary proceeding, highly accelerated summary proceeding ‖ adj, highly summarized or brief.

SUMARSE.
v, to join or affiliate oneself with a party or doctrine or movement ‖ to support an opinion ‖ to submit to or accept an abusive decision.

SUMERGIR.
v, to submerge ‖ to sink.
SUMINISTRACIÓN.
See SUMINISTRO.
SUMINISTRADOR.
m, provider, supplier.
SUMINISTRAR.
v, to supply, provide, furnish.
SUMINISTRO.
m, provision, supply, furnishing.
SUMINISTRO DE ARMAS.
supply of arms, weapons supply.
SUMINISTRO DE INFORMES AL ENEMIGO.
furnishing information to the enemy.
SUMINISTRO IRREGULAR.
improper supply of goods.
SUMISIÓN.
m, submission, subordination ‖ obedience ‖ submission to the jurisdiction of a court (esp. of a foreign jurisdiction).
SUMISO.
adj, submissive ‖ obedient ‖ subordinate ‖ subjugated.
"SUMMUN JUS, SUMMA INJURIA".
Inflexible application of the law represents the greatest injustice.
SUNTUARIO.
adj, luxury.
SUNTUOSO.
adj, luxurious, sumptuous.
SUPEDITACIÓN.
f, subordination ‖ submission ‖ oppression ‖ enslavement.
SUPEDITAR.
v, to conquer ‖ to subjugate ‖ to oppress ‖ to subject ‖ to subordinate.
SUPERÁVIT.
m, superavit, surplus.
SUPEREMPLEO.
m, over-employment.
SUPERENTENDER.
v, to inspect, supervise ‖ to rule, govern.
SUPEREROGACIÓN.
f, supererogation, doing more than is required.
SUPEREROGATORIO.
adj, pertaining to supererogation.
SUPERESTRUCTURA.
f, superstructure.

SUPERFICIAL.
adj, superficial ‖ frivolous ‖ apparent ‖ pertaining to the surface.
SUPERFICIARIO.
m, holder of surface rights ‖ person who holds right to the fruits of another's property in exchange for an annual fee.
SUPERFICIE.
f, surface ‖ surface rights.
SUPERINTENDENCIA.
f, superintendency ‖ jurisdiction, position and office of a superintendent.
SUPERINTENDENTE.
m, superintendent ‖ supervisor ‖ overseer.
SUPERIOR.
m, superior ‖ adj, superior ‖ top, upper, higher ‖ better ‖ the best ‖ the most ‖ greater ‖ the greatest ‖ excellent ‖ superior, advanced, higher (relative to educational institutions, etc.).
SUPERIOR JERÁRQUICO.
hierarchical superior, superior in rank.
SUPERIORIDAD.
f, superiority ‖ excellence ‖ advantage ‖ dominance ‖ decisive power or authority.
SUPERPOBLACIÓN.
f, over-population.
SUPERPRODUCCIÓN.
f, over-production.
SUPÉRSTITE.
adj, surviving (over another).
SUPERVACÁNEO.
See SUPERFLUO.
SUPERVENCIÓN.
f, supervention ‖ act of supervening.
SUPERVENIENCIA.
f, supervention ‖ action of supervening.
SUPERVENIENTE.
adj, supervening.
SUPERVENIR.
v, to supervene.
SUPERVISAR.
v, to supervise, inspect.
SUPERVISIÓN.
f, supervision.
SUPERVISOR.
m, supervisor.
SUPERVIVENCIA.
f, survival.
SUPERVIVIENTE.
m, survivor.

SUPLANTABLE.
adj, supplantable ‖ falsifiable.

SUPLANTACIÓN.
f, supplantation ‖ forgery ‖ fraudulent alteration (e.g. of a negotiable instrument) ‖ temporary replacement (of an employee).

SUPLANTADOR.
m, person who illegally supplants or substitutes ‖ usurper.

SUPLANTAR.
v, to supplant ‖ to forge ‖ to falsify, alter fraudulently (e.g. a negotiable instrument) ‖ to temporarily replace (an employee) ‖ to alter a text ‖ to usurp (e.g. functions) ‖ to pass oneself off.

SUPLEMENTAL.
See SUPLEMENTARIO.

SUPLEMENTARIO.
adj, supplementary, complementary ‖ additional ‖ substitute.

SUPLEMENTO.
m, supplement ‖ substitution ‖ complement ‖ additional payment.

SUPLEMENTO DE LEGÍTIMA.
See COMPLEMENTO DE LEGÍTIMA.

SUPLENCIA.
f, substitution, replacement (of an employee).

SUPLENTE.
m, substitute, replacement (of an employee) ‖ adj, substitute, alternate, replacement ‖ acting, provisional, temporary.

SUPLETORIO.
adj, replacing, substituting ‖ complementary ‖ supplemental ‖ requesting.

SÚPLICA.
f, plea ‖ petition, supplication ‖ entreaty ‖ written request ‖ plea, prayer for relief (in a complaint).

SUPLICACIÓN.
f, plea ‖ petition, supplication ‖ entreaty ‖ petition for reconsideration (before the same court).

SUPLICAR.
v, to plead ‖ to petition, request ‖ to beg ‖ to petition a court to reconsider a case or overturn a decision of another court.

SUPLICATORIA.
f, communication sent from one judge to a higher judge. May include letters rogatory.

SUPLICATORIO.
m, pleading sent by a court or tribunal to parliament to request authorization to initiate legal proceedings against a member of parliament ‖ also see SUPLICATORIA ‖ adj, requesting, pleading, petitioning.

SUPLICIO.
m, capital punishment ‖ execution chamber ‖ corporal punishment ‖ cruelty ‖ torture ‖ physical pain.

SUPLIDO.
adj, advance payment made by an agent on behalf of another.

SUPLIR.
v, to substitute, replace ‖ to complete, finish ‖ to supply, furnish, provide (what is missing or needed) ‖ to overlook, excuse (someone's defects or shortcomings, etc.).

SUPONEDOR.
m, presumer, person who assumes something incorrectly.

SUPONER.
v, to suppose, assume, presume ‖ to guess, conjecture ‖ to pretend, fake ‖ to exercise influence ‖ to imply.

SUPORTAR.
See SOPORTAR.

SUPOSICIÓN.
f, supposition ‖ guess, conjecture ‖ belief ‖ (false) assumption, presumption, supposition ‖ authority ‖ falsehood.

SUPOSICIÓN DE ESTADO CIVIL.
See SUPRESIÓN DE ESTADO CIVIL.

SUPOSICIÓN DE NOMBRE.
See NOMBRE SUPUESTO.

SUPOSICIÓN DE PARTO.
(false) posing as the natural mother (by another woman).

SUPREMA CORTE DE JUSTICIA.
Supreme Court of Justice, Supreme Court.

SUPREMACÍA.
f, supremacy ‖ superiority ‖ dominance ‖ advantage (at war) ‖ hegemony, leadership.

SUPREMAMENTE.
adv, supremely ‖ until the end.

SUPREMO.
m, absolute chief or head ‖ highest authority ‖ adj, supreme ‖ superior ‖ last, final ‖ definitive, absolute ‖ highest.

SUPRESIÓN.
f, suppression ‖ cessation ‖ disappearance, elimination ‖ abolition, derogation ‖ omission ‖ violent death (to an enemy).

SUPRESIÓN DE ESTADO CIVIL.
assumption of a false marital or legal status.

SUPRIMIR.
v, to suppress ‖ to cease ‖ to omit, strike out ‖ to eliminate, delete, cause to disappear ‖ to abolish.

SUPUESTO.
m, hypothesis ‖ basis of a position or opinion ‖ see also SUPOSICIÓN ‖ adj, supposed, presumed ‖ false ‖ inexact ‖ apparent.

SUSCEPTIBLE.
adj, susceptible (to modification) ‖ irritable, touchy.

SUSCITAR.
v, to originate, start ‖ to promote ‖ to provoke.

SUSCRIBIR.
See SUBSCRIBIR.

SUSCRIBIRSE.
See SUBSCRIBIRSE.

SUSCRIPCIÓN.
f, subscription, written obligation which requires making regular payments in exchange for the receipt of goods or services.

SUSCRIPTOR.
See SUBSCRIPTOR.

SUSCRITO.
See SUBSCRITO.

SUSPENDER.
v, to suspend ‖ to hang ‖ to stay, postpone (a judicial proceeding, etc.) ‖ to discontinue, adjourn, interrupt (an action, etc.) ‖ to suspend payment ‖ to fail, flunk (an examinee) ‖ to impose the sentence of SUSPENSIÓN, suspend one's rights or privileges ‖ to amaze, astound.

SUSPENDERSE.
v, to hang oneself ‖ to elevate oneself ‖ to be suspended or adjourned, interrupted.

SUSPENDIDO.
m, thing or person which is suspended ‖ adj, suspended ‖ hung. See SUSPENSIÓN.

SUSPENSIÓN.
f, suspension, act of suspending ‖ anxiety, suspense ‖ hanging ‖ stay, postponement (of a judicial proceeding) ‖ adjournment, interruption, suspension (e.g. of a meeting) ‖ (sanction consisting of) suspension of pay ‖ (temporary) suspension from work (as a sanction or for lack of work) ‖ suspension of constitutional rights and privileges or guarantees.

SUSPENSIÓN DE ABOGACÍA.
(temporary) SUSPENSIÓN of an attorney (from the practice of law), temporary disbarment.

SUSPENSIÓN DE ARMAS.
suspension of hostilities, temporary cease-fire ‖ truce.

SUSPENSIÓN DE CARGO PÚBLICO.
suspension from public duties.

SUSPENSIÓN DE CONDENA.
See CONDENA CONDICIONAL.

SUSPENSIÓN DE EMPLEO.
(employer sanction consisting of) suspension of pay ‖ (temporary) suspension from work (as a sanction).

SUSPENSIÓN DE GARANTÍAS.
suspension of constitutional rights and privileges or guarantees.

SUSPENSIÓN DE HOSTILIDADES.
suspension of hostilities, temporary cease-fire ‖ truce.

SUSPENSIÓN DE LA EJECUCIÓN DE PENAS.
suspension of a (criminal) sentence.

SUSPENSIÓN DE LA PRESCRIPCIÓN.
tolling of the statute of limitations.

SUSPENSIÓN DE LOS JUICIOS CIVILES.
dismissal (with prejudice) of a civil action.

SUSPENSIÓN DE OFICIO.
See SUSPENSIÓN DEL CONTRATO DE TRABAJO and SUSPENSIÓN PENAL.

SUSPENSIÓN DE PAGOS.
suspension of payments ‖ insolvency proceeding, type of reorganization proceedings (short of declaring bankruptcy) which usually requires the appointment of a trustee.

SUSPENSIÓN DE PROFESIÓN.
See SUSPENSIÓN PENAL.

SUSPENSIÓN DEL CONTRATO DE TRABAJO.
temporary suspension or interruption of (the effect of) a labor contract (with or without cause).

SUSPENSIÓN DEL EJERCICIO DE LA PATRIA POTESTAD.
suspension of parental rights.

SUSPENSIÓN DEL JUICIO ORAL.
stay, adjournment, postponement (of an oral trial).

SUSPENSIÓN DEL PROCEDIMIENTO.
See SUSPENSIÓN PROCESAL.

SUSPENSIÓN EN EL TRABAJO.
suspension from work (whether for legal re

sons (e.g. illness) or due to a unilateral decision of the employer).

SUSPENSIÓN PENAL.
punitive suspension, suspension as a punishment. Usually includes professional suspension or suspension of rights and privileges, etc.

SUSPENSIÓN PROCESAL.
stay, adjournment, postponement (of a judicial proceeding).

SUSPENSIVO.
adj, suspensive, interrupting || staying, adjourning.

SUSPENSO.
m, suspension || see also SUSPENSIÓN DE PAGOS || adj, suspended.

SUSPICACIA.
f, distrust, suspiciousness.

SUSPICAZ.
adj, distrustful, distrusting, suspicious.

SUSTANCIA.
See SUBSTANCIA.

SUSTANCIACIÓN.
See SUBSTANCIACIÓN.

SUSTANCIAL.
See SUBSTANCIAL.

SUSTANCIAR.
See SUBSTANCIAR.

SUSTANTIVIDAD.
See SUBSTANTIVIDAD.

SUSTANTIVO.
See SUBSTANTIVO.

SUSTENTABLE.
adj, sustainable, defensible, arguable.

SUSTENTACIÓN.
f, action of sustaining || suspension (in the air) || sustenance, food, nourishment || mainte-

nance, conservation || defense of a proposition.

SUSTENTADOR.
m, sustainer, person who sustains || adj, sustaining.

SUSTENTAR.
v, to sustain || to support, maintain || to defend (e.g. a proposition) || to sustain, give nourishment to || to conserve.

SUSTENTO.
m, sustenance, nourishment, food || basis, backing, support || maintenance.

SUSTITUCIÓN.
See SUBSTITUCIÓN.

SUSTITUIBLE.
See SUBSTITUIBLE.

SUSTITUIDOR.
See SUBSTITUIDOR.

SUSTITUIR.
See SUBSTITUIR.

SUSTITUTIVO.
See SUBSTITUTIVO.

SUSTITUTO.
See SUBSTITUTO.

SUSTRACCIÓN.
See SUBSTRACCIÓN.

SUSTRAER.
See SUBSTRAER.

SUSTRAERSE.
See SUBSTRAERSE.

SUTILEZA.
f, subtlety || detail || cunning.

SUTILIZAR.
v, to discuss something subtly || to make subtle distinctions || to perfect, sharpen.

TABANCO.
m, food stall or stand.

TABERNA.
f, tavern, bar, barroom, saloon, drinking establishment.

TABERNERO.
m, tavern keeper, saloon-keeper, owner of a drinking establishment.

TABLA.
f, board, plank, slab ‖ width of board ‖ tablet ‖ public notice or announcement ‖ index, table of contents ‖ table, list (of statistics, etc.) ‖ piece of cultivated land between two rows of trees ‖ customs house, customs outpost (at land borders).

TABLA DE MATERIALES.
table of contents.

TABLADO.
m, scaffold.

TABLAS DE MORTALIDAD.
mortality tables, tables of statistics (regarding sex, age, residence, profession, etc.) of deceased.

TABLAS DE VIDA.
life expectancy tables.

TABLÓN DE ANUNCIOS.
announcement board (of schools, courts, businesses, etc.).

TABÚ.
m, tabu.

TÁCITA RECONDUCCIÓN.
tenancy at sufferance, holding over, holdover, implied continuation of a lease after the contractual term expires.

TÁCITA RECONDUCCIÓN LABORAL.
implied continuation of an employment contract after the contractual term expires.

TÁCITAMENTE.
adv, by implication, implicitly, tacitly.

TÁCITO.
adj, implied, tacit ‖ constructive ‖ understoo ‖ supposed.

TÁCTICA.
f, tactic ‖ art of organizing ‖ tactics ‖ plan.

TÁCTICAMENTE.
adv, tactically.

TÁCTICO.
m, tactician, tactical expert ‖ adj, tactical.

TACHA.
f, mark, defect, flaw ‖ unfavorable mark c note ‖ legal basis for disqualifying a witness c discrediting a witness's testimony ‖ impeach ment or disqualification of a witness ‖ cha lenge or impugnment of a witness ‖ crossin out.

TACHA DE TESTIGOS.
legal basis for disqualifying a witness, or in peaching or discrediting a witness's testimor ‖ disqualification of a witness ‖ challenge c impeachment of a witness.

TACHABLE.
adj, able or appropriate to be crossed out deserving of disqualification or censure.

TACHADOR.
m, censure ‖ person who crosses out ‖ cha lenger, disqualifier, person who disqualifies c challenges a witness.

TACHADURA.
f, crossing out, erasure (of words or letters a writing, etc.).

TACHAR.
v, to cross out ‖ to flaw or mark something to challenge or impeach a witness's testimor

|| to object to a witness || to disqualify a witness || to censure.

TACHÓN.
m, crossing out a word or letter with a line.

TAIFA.
f, band, party, faction.

TAJANTE.
adj, slicing, cutting || decisive || rigorous.

TAJAR.
v, to slice, cut.

TAJO.
m, cut, slice || knife wound || blade, knife blade || blow with a sword || work, task, job || beheading block || mine site of a working mine or quarry or field.

TALA.
f, topping or trimming of trees || felling of trees (for use or to damage or take revenge upon their owner) || destruction, sacking devastation (of another's property or enemy property).

TÁLAMO.
m, marriage bed, bed of newlyweds || conjugal bed || marriage.

TALAR.
v, to fell trees || to trim or top trees || to destroy, demolish, sack.

TALIÓN.
m, revenge, retaliation || principle of an eye for an eye, a tooth for a tooth.

TALIONAR.
v, to retaliate, take revenge || to apply the principle of an eye for an eye, a tooth for a tooth.

TALÓN.
m, slip, coupon, stub || sight draft or order of payment which is detached from a stub book || stub book of a negotiable instrument || freight voucher, letter given to freight carrier || check stub || deposit slip.

TALÓN DE AQUILES.
Achilles heel || vulnerable point.

TALÓN DE VENTA.
sales slip.

TALONARIO.
m, stub book || negotiable instrument which is separated from a stub book.

TALLA.
f, reward (for the capture of a criminal) || stature, (person's) height.

TALLER.
m, workshop, shop || school || studio.

TALLER FAMILIAR.
family workshop or shop.

TALLERISTA.
f, m, person who works at home with material provided by an employer || person who employs persons who work at home with material provided by the employer.

TANDA.
f, turn, rotation, shift (in employment) || task, job, work || (work) shift or gang or group || (work) shift or relief, group of persons who replace others on the job.

TANGENTE.
adj, tangent, touching.

TANQUE.
m, tank || tanker, tanker ship (for transport of liquids) || water tank, reservoir.

TANTEAR.
v, to feel out, size up (something to determine it's appropriateness) || to inspect, measure, examine, scrutinize, test, try out, study, (something to see that it matches the requirements or stated measurements) || to examine (persons or things) || to exercise a right of first refusal (upon sale of real estate or personal property) || to think about carefully, consider, deliberate.

TANTEARSE.
v, to agree to pay an amount equal to that paid at public auction.

TANTEO.
m, sizing up, feeling out || examination, scrutiny (e.g. of the pros and cons of a case or problem) || right of first refusal (upon sale of real estate of personal property) || agreement by which a person pays the amount equal to that paid at public auction.

TANTO.
m, set or fixed amount or quantity || copy or sample of an original || a bit, commission or interest or part paid for a service rendered.

TANTO DE CULPA.
copy of deposition or confession which is extracted for the purpose of proving criminal guilt.

TANTO MÁS CUANTO.
barter between buyer and seller.

TANTO POR CIENTO.
certain or given percentage || rate of interest ||

bank discount rate ‖ commission or participation in a business or banking transaction.

TANTO POR TANTO.
at the same price or value.

TARA.
f, tare, allowance for weight of the container ‖ physical or mental defect ‖ dead weight.

TARADO.
adj, physically or mentally defective ‖ given as an allowance for the weight of the container.

TARDANZA.
f, lateness, tardiness ‖ delay ‖ slowness.

TARDAR.
v, to be late or tardy ‖ to delay ‖ to be slow (intentionally or otherwise) ‖ to put in more time than is worth or calculated.

TARDE.
f, afternoon ‖ early evening ‖ late afternoon ‖ dusk ‖ adv, late.

TARDÍAMENTE.
adv, belatedly, too late, slowly, tardily.

TARDÍO.
adj, late, belated, tardy ‖ slow, delayed, overdue.

TAREA.
f, work ‖ labor, employment ‖ task, chore, job ‖ homework ‖ activity ‖ service ‖ work responsibilities or assignments.

TARIFA.
f, tariff, rate ‖ tax table ‖ price list ‖ list of fees ‖ toll, fare.

TARIFA ADUANERA.
customs tariff table or list.

TARIFA DE AVALUO.
See TARIFA ADUANERA.

TARIFAR.
v, to establish a tariff or table of TARIFA ‖ to impose a TARIFA ‖ to make an enemy.

TARJETA.
f, ticket ‖ numbered ticket ‖ card ‖ identification, identity card ‖ postcard ‖ heading or title of a map or writing ‖ index card.

TARJETA DE COMPRA.
See TARJETA DE CRÉDITO.

TARJETA DE CRÉDITO.
credit card.

TARJETA DE IDENTIDAD.
identification, identity card,

TARJETA POSTAL.
postcard.

TARTAMUDEAR.
v, to stutter, stammer.

TARTAMUDEO.
m, act of stuttering or stammering.

TARTAMUDEZ.
f, stuttering, stammering (as a defect).

TARTAMUDO.
m, stutterer, stammerer.

TASA.
f, rate ‖ valuation, appraisal, assessment (c things) ‖ (governmentally set) maximum pric ‖ tax, duty, charge ‖ norm, rule ‖ measure rule, standard.

TASA DE INTERÉS.
rate of interest, interest rate.

TASA FISCAL.
tax rate.

TASACIÓN.
f, valuation, appraisal, assessment (of things) price regulation or control.

TASACIÓN DE COSTAS.
assessment of litigation expenses and fees (a judge).

TASACIÓN DE LOS BIENES HEREDITARIOS.
valuation or appraisal of the decedent's estat

TASACIÓN EN CASO DE EXPROPIACIÓ
eminent domain assessment, condemnatic assessment.

TASADAMENTE.
adv, with moderation or limitation ‖ scarcel

TASADO.
adj, valued, appraised, assessed ‖ taxed, d tied ‖ measured ‖ fixed with a maximum pri ‖ subject to a norm or rule.

TASADOR.
m, appraiser, assessor, valuator ‖ adj, appra ing, assessing, valuating.

TASAR.
v, to price, value, assess, appraise ‖ to regula measure, establish norms ‖ to reduce, restrict, tion ‖ to tax.

TATARABUELO.
m, great-great-grandparent ‖ great-great-gran father.

TATARANIETO.
m, great-great-grandchild ‖ great-great-gran son.

TAXATIVO.
adj, strict, literal ‖ limiting, restrictive ‖ ri rous.

TÉCNICA.
f, technique ‖ techniques ‖ series of procedures or recourses ‖ skill, ability ‖ adj, technical.
TÉCNICA ADMINISTRATIVA.
administrative procedures or recourses.
TÉCNICA FORENSE.
procedural technique.
TÉCNICA LEGISLATIVA.
legislative process, law-making procedure ‖ legislation drafting technique.
TÉCNICA SOCIAL.
social process.
TÉCNICAMENTE.
adv, technically.
TECNICISMO.
m, technicality ‖ technical term or word.
TÉCNICO.
m, expert, specialist ‖ expert witness ‖ adj, technical.
TÉCNICOJURÍDICO.
adj, related to or based on considerations that are both technical and legal.
TECNOCRACIA.
f, technocracy.
TECNOLOGÍA.
f, technology.
TEJADO.
m, roof, roofing.
TELA.
f, controversy, dispute ‖ subject, topic, theme ‖ money ‖ material, cloth ‖ web, net, gossip ‖ lie, trick, plot.
TELECOMUNICACIÓN.
f, telecommunication ‖ telecommunications.
TELEDIRIGIR.
v, to guide by remote control.
TELEFONÍA.
f, telephony.
TELEFÓNICAMENTE.
adv, telephonically.
TELEFÓNICO.
adj, telephone, phone, telephonic.
TELÉFONO.
m, telephone, phone.
TELEGRAFÍA.
f, telegraphy.
TELEGRÁFICAMENTE.
adv, telegraphically.
TELEGRÁFICO.
adj, telegraphic, telegraph.

TELÉGRAFO.
m, telegraph.
TELEGRAMA.
m, telegram.
TELEGRAMA COLACIONADO.
telegram-back, telegram returned to the original sender to check for accuracy.
TELEOLOGÍA JURÍDICA.
legal teleology, method of explanation based on the purposes of the law rather than the causes.
TELEPATÍA.
f, telepathy.
TELEVISIÓN.
f, television.
TELÓN DE HIERRO.
iron curtain.
TELÚRICO.
adj, telluric, terrestrial, pertaining to the earth.
TEMA.
m, subject, matter, theme, topic ‖ debate topic.
TEMARIO.
m, matters for consideration, meeting agenda, series of questions to be discussed and approved ‖ topics of discussion ‖ agenda, program.
TEMBLAR.
v, to tremble ‖ to be afraid ‖ to mistrust greatly.
TEMBLOR.
m, tremble, shake, shudder, shiver.
TEMER.
v, to be afraid, fear ‖ to suspect.
TEMERARIO.
adj, temerarious, reckless ‖ imprudent.
TEMERIDAD.
f, temerity, boldness ‖ foolhardiness.
TEMIBILIDAD.
See PELIGROSIDAD.
TEMIBLE.
adj, frightening.
TEMOR.
m, fear ‖ suspicion, presumption.
TEMORIZAR.
v, to frighten ‖ to inspire fear, terrorize.
TEMPERAMENTO.
m, temperament ‖ compromise, decision made to resolve a matter.
TEMPESTAD.
f, tempest, storm.

TEMPESTIVAMENTE.
adv, opportunely ‖ seasonably.
TEMPESTIVIDAD.
f, opportuneness, timeliness.
TEMPESTIVO.
adj, opportune ‖ timely, seasonable.
TEMPESTUOSAMENTE.
adv, tempestuously, stormily ‖ violently ‖ scandalously.
TEMPLADO.
adj, moderate, temperate ‖ warm ‖ lukewarm ‖ mild ‖ tempered ‖ brave and serene.
TEMPLANZA.
f, moderation, temperance ‖ sobriety ‖ continence ‖ courage, bravery.
TEMPLAR.
v, to moderate, temper (natural forces) ‖ to refrain ‖ to restrain (impulses) ‖ to pacify ‖ to calm ‖ to appease.
TEMPLARSE.
v, to moderate or temper one's actions ‖ to get used to adversity.
TEMPORADA.
f, period or lapse or spell (of time) ‖ season.
TEMPORAL.
m, storm, tempest ‖ strong wind (i.e. over 66 km. per hour) ‖ seasonal or migrant worker ‖ period of rainy weather ‖ weather conditions ‖ adj, temporal ‖ transitory, provisional ‖ secular, profane ‖ civil (i.e. not religious).
TEMPORALMENTE.
adv, temporarily, provisionally ‖ momentarily ‖ temporally, secularly.
TEMPORÁNEO.
adj, temporal ‖ transitory, provisional ‖ momentary.
TEMPORERO.
m, migrant or seasonal worker.
TEMPORIZAR.
See CONTEMPORIZAR.
TEMPRANO.
adv, early, prior to time, ahead of time, beforehand.
TENDENCIA.
f, tendency, inclination, proclivity ‖ intention, aspiration ‖ desire, passion ‖ goal ‖ trend.
TENDENCIA SOCIAL.
social tendency.
TENDENCIOSO.
adj, tendentious ‖ with ulterior motives.

TENDER.
v, to be inclined, tend ‖ to intend, aspire ‖ desire, want ‖ to stretch out (e.g. one's han‖ ‖ to break or split up (e.g. forces) ‖ to instal
TENDERO.
m, shopkeeper ‖ retailer.
TENDERSE.
v, to lie down ‖ to throw oneself on the grou‖ ‖ to let slide, neglect, be neglectful (of a matt or business).
TENEDOR.
m, (mere) holder, possessor (physically b without legal title) ‖ tenant in possession, c cupant ‖ holder of a negotiable instrumen‖ fork.
TENEDOR DE ACCIONES.
stockholder.
TENEDOR DE LA PÓLIZA.
(insurance) policyholder.
TENEDOR DE LIBROS.
bookkeeper.
TENEDURÍA.
f, position and office of bookkeeper.
TENEDURÍA DE LIBROS.
bookkeeping, profession and knowledge bookkeeping.
TENENCIA.
f, (simple) tenancy, (bare) possession ‖ c cupancy ‖ office and position of lieutenant.
TENENCIA DE ALCALDÍA.
office of deputy mayor or mayor's second command.
TENENCIA DE ARMAS.
possession of weapons or arms ‖ illegal poss sion of arms or weapons.
TENENCIA DE EFECTOS MILITARES.
possession of military property ‖ illegal poss sion of military property.
TENENCIA DE GANZÚAS.
possession of burglar's tools. Usually a cri ‖ see GANZÚA.
TENENCIA DE INSTRUMENTOS DELICTIVOS.
possession of criminal tools. May be a crim
TENENCIA DE LOS HIJOS.
custody of the children (in a divorce) ‖ le custody of the children (in a divorce).
TENENCIA DE MONEDA FALSA.
possession of counterfeit money ‖ illegal p session of counterfeit money.

:NENCIA PRECARIA.
ee PRECARIO.

:NER.
, to have ‖ to hold, possess ‖ to own ‖ to main-
ain ‖ to defend, sustain ‖ to dominate ‖ to en-
ompass, contain ‖ to be opposed to ‖ to resist,
ppose ‖ to keep (one's word) ‖ to carry out,
old, celebrate, perform ‖ to estimate, judge,
onsider ‖ to be wealthy or rich ‖ to receive (a
erson) ‖ to spend (time) ‖ to be (X years old).

:NER ALGO QUE PERDER.
o have something to lose, have an interest in
omething.

:NER DERECHO DE PISO.
o have paid one's dues, have a moral right to.

.NER EN CONTRA.
o dislike, have something against (someone)
to have (something) going against one.

NER LA CULPA.
o be to blame, be liable for, be at fault.

:NER LA PALABRA.
o have the floor (at a meeting) ‖ to give some-
ne the floor (at a meeting) ‖ to have the last
ord on something.

NER LA SARTÉN POR EL MANGO.
o have control or power over something ‖ to
ave something under control.

NER LO QUE HAY QUE TENER.
o have what it takes ‖ to have the guts (to do
omething).

NER PARTE CON UNA MUJER.
o have sexual relations with a woman.

NER PARTE EN ALGO.
o participate or share in something.

NERSE.
to sustain, maintain, stand firm ‖ to resist ‖
o consider oneself ‖ to stop, halt, hold back.

NIENTE.
a, lieutenant ‖ deputy, second-in-command ‖
abstitute, alternate ‖ adj, possessing, holding
owning.

NIENTE DE ALCALDE.
eputy mayor or mayor's second in command.

NSIÓN.
tension.

NSO.
dj, tense.

NTACIÓN.
temptation ‖ excitement.

NTADO.
a, victim of temptation ‖ adj, tried, attemp-ted.

TENTAR.
v, to attempt, try ‖ to touch, feel ‖ to frisk ‖ to
examine, inspect ‖ to test, try out ‖ to instigate,
induce.

TENTATIVA.
f, attempt ‖ try ‖ trial, experiment ‖ examination, scrutiny (e.g. of the pros and cons of a
case or problem) ‖ final college or university
graduation examination ‖ endeavor.

TENTATIVA DE DELITO.
attempt to commit a crime, criminal attempt.

TENTATIVA DE FUGA.
attempt to escape, attempted escape.

**TENTATIVA PARA PASAR
A PAÍS ENEMIGO.**
attempt to go over to enemy forces.

TENTATIVO.
adj, tentative ‖ experimental, under testing.

TEOCRACIA.
f, theocracy.

TEOCRÁTICO.
adj, theocratic.

TEOLOGÍA.
f, theology.

TEORÍA.
f, theory, speculation, supposition ‖ theory,
principle, doctrine ‖ proposition.

TEORÍA DE ESCEPTICISMO JURÍDICO.
theory of legal skepticism.

TEORÍA DE LA ACCESORIEDAD.
theory based on the idea that an accessory has
the same legal status as the principal.

TEORÍA DE LA CAUSALIDAD.
theory of causation.

TEORÍA DE LA CORTESÍA.
principle of full faith and credit ‖ principle of
reciprocity ‖ comity.

TEORÍA DE LA CULPA.
theory of fault-based liability.

TEORÍA DE LA IMPREVISIÓN.
doctrine of unforeseeability (which permits
the modification of contracts based on the unforeseeability of events).

TEORÍA DE LA LESIÓN.
doctrine of indemnification (which requires a
contractual party to indemnify the injured
party) ‖ doctrine of unconscionability.

TEORÍA DE LA NECESIDAD.
theory of necessity (which permits an aggressor state to invade a neutral state in time of
war) ‖ see also ESTADO DE NECESIDAD.

TEORÍA DE LA POSESIÓN.
theory regarding the legal status of possession.
TEORÍA DE LA RECIPROCIDAD.
principle of reciprocity (between states or nations).
TEORÍA DE LA SOLIDARIDAD.
See OBLIGACIÓN SOLIDARIA.
TEORÍA DE LA UBICUIDAD.
territorial principle of jurisdiction over a crime ‖ principle that criminal impunity may be obtained through an alibi.
TEORÍA DE REENVÍO.
doctrine of renvoi.
TEORÍA DEL ESCEPTICISMO JURÍDICO.
theory that permits judge-made law on the basis that statutory regulation cannot cover all circumstances.
TEORÍA DEL PELIGRO.
theory that attempted criminal conduct should not be a crime unless it creates a danger to society or a person.
TEORÍA DEL PRECIO.
price theory.
TEORÍA DEL RIESGO.
risk theory, theory of liability that he who creates the risk is liable therefore.
TEORÍA DEL RIESGO PROFESIONAL.
theory pertaining to liability for work-related accidents based on the risk inherent in professional activities.
TEORÍA GENERAL DEL DERECHO.
general theory of law ‖ jurisprudence.
TEORÍA GENERAL DEL ESTADO.
general theory of the state.
TEORÍA PURA DEL DERECHO.
pure theory of law.
TEÓRICA.
f, theory, intellectual speculation.
TEÓRICAMENTE.
adv, theoretically.
TEÓRICO.
m, theoretician, theorist ‖ adj, theoretic, theoretical ‖ speculative ‖ nominal.
TEORIZANTE.
adj, theorizing.
TEORIZAR.
v, to theorize (on or about).
TERCENA.
f, government monopoly store, state outlet in which monopolized goods are sold.

TERCER MUNDO.
third world, (countries of the) undevelop and underdeveloped world.
TERCER OPOSITOR.
third party litigant (either as a third pa plaintiff or third party defendant) ‖ co-litiga (either as a co-defendant or co-plaintif joined after the suit has been instigated).
TERCER POSEEDOR.
third party who possesses property sold.
TERCER REICH.
Third Reich.
TERCERA INSTANCIA.
second appeal or appeals.
TERCERA PERSONA.
arbitrator, mediator ‖ see TERCERO.
TERCEREAR.
v, to mediate, arbitrate.
TERCERÍA.
f, position of mediator or arbitrator ‖ th party intervention or joinder or litigation a co-litigant joined after the litigation is in gated.
TERCERÍA DE DOMINIO.
third party intervention or joinder of a co gant after the litigation is instigated such t such third party or co-litigant claims to c the property in dispute in the original actio
TERCERÍA DE MEJOR DERECHO.
third party intervention or joinder of a co gant after the litigation is instigated such t such third party or co-litigant claims to have interest in property preferential to those of other party litigants.
TERCERISTA.
third party plaintiff ‖ intervener ‖ plaintiff TERCERÍA
TERCERO.
m, mediator, arbitrator, arbiter, referee ‖ pi panderer ‖ third party, disinterested pa party who is not directly involved ‖ adj, thi
TERCERO DESCONOCIDO.
unknown third party holder (to a negotia instrument).
TERCERO EN DISCORDIA.
mediator, arbitrator, arbiter, referee ‖ in ested third party to a matter in litigation.
TERCERO EN EL PAGO.
See PAGO POR CUENTA AJENA.

ERCERO EN LA COSA JUZGADA.
non-party or non-litigant relative to an action
which has been decided.

ERCERO EN LA SOCIEDAD.
hird parties relative to a corporation or partnership. Such usually includes not only non-shareholders and non-partners, but shareholders and partners when they act in a capacity other than shareholder or partner.

ERCERO EXCLUYENTE.
hird party plaintiff or third party defendant or co-plaintiff joined after the litigation is instigated so that such third party or co-plaintiff claims to own or have a preferential interest in the disputed property.

ERCERO INTERVINIENTE.
hird party intervener who intervenes to defend property or rights claimed by others.

ERCERO PERJUDICADO.
hird party damaged by a contract or other action or transaction.

ERCEROS EN EL PROCESO.
hird party interveners.

ERCIA.
, third part, third.

ERCIADOR.
n, mediator, arbitrator, arbiter, referee.

ERCIAR.
, to intervene, mediate, arbitrate, referee ‖ to distribute into thirds ‖ to get mixed up in a war between other states.

ERCIO.
n, third, third part ‖ seamen's union or fishermen's guild (for fishing in a harbor) ‖ adj, third.

ERCIO DE LEGÍTIMA.
See LEGÍTIMA ESTRICTA.

ERCIO DE MEJORA.
See MEJORA HEREDITARIA.

ERCIO LIBRE.
See PARTE DE LIBRE DISPOSICIÓN.

ERGIVERSACIÓN.
, distortion or twisting of words or facts or a position (to confuse or defraud).

ERGIVERSAR.
, to twist or distort words or facts or a position to persuade or confuse or defraud).

ERMINABLE.
adj, terminable, subject to an end.

ERMINACIÓN.
, end, ending, finish, termination, conclusion

‖ finish, final touch or work (on a product).

TERMINAL.
f, conclusion ‖ (bus, train, etc.) station, terminal ‖ adj, terminal ‖ last, final ‖ latter.

TERMINANTE.
adj, definitive, conclusive, clear ‖ categorical.

TERMINAR.
v, to end, finish, conclude, terminate ‖ to put an end to.

TERMINARSE.
v, to end, terminate ‖ to put an end to.

TÉRMINO.
m, limit ‖ term, word ‖ end, finish (of something existing) ‖ term, period (of time) ‖ boundary, dividing line ‖ landmark ‖ expiration or maturity date, deadline ‖ objective, goal, purpose ‖ day and time for compliance ‖ site or place of an act or action ‖ state, condition (of something) ‖ term of speech, expression ‖ district (within the jurisdiction of a township).

TÉRMINO CIERTO.
term certain, fixed term ‖ date certain.

TÉRMINO CONVENCIONAL.
contractual or stipulated term ‖ contractual or stipulated expiration date.

TÉRMINO DE GRACIA.
grace period.

TÉRMINO DE LA PATRIA
POTESTAD.
period during which parental rights have effect.

TÉRMINO DE PRUEBA.
See TÉRMINO PROBATORIO.

TÉRMINO DE RIGOR.
See TÉRMINO IMPRORROGABLE.

TÉRMINO DE UNA AUDIENCIA.
court recess.

TÉRMINO EXPRESO.
express term or period ‖ express expiration date.

TÉRMINO EXTINTIVO.
expiration or maturity date ‖ expiration of a statutory or proscriptive period.

TÉRMINO EXTRAORDINARIO.
extraordinary term ‖ type of extraordinary discovery period, extended discovery period to carry out discovery abroad or at a distance and to present it to the judge.
Opposed to TÉRMINO ORDINARIO.

TÉRMINO FATAL.
See TÉRMINO IMPRORROGABLE.

TÉRMINO HÁBIL.
unexpired term or period.

TÉRMINO IMPRORROGABLE.
unextendable expiration date ‖ final deadline ‖ expiration date of a statute of limitation ‖ see also PLAZO FATAL.

TÉRMINO INCIERTO.
contingent or conditional term or period, term fixed in relation to future condition or contingency ‖ conditional or contingent expiration date, expiration date fixed in relation to future condition or contingency.

TÉRMINO INHÁBIL.
expired term or period.

TÉRMINO INICIAL.
initial term or period ‖ starting date, beginning.

TÉRMINO JUDICIAL.
judicial term, term fixed by a judge or court ‖ procedural term or period, term for fulfilling procedural requirements.

TÉRMINO LEGAL.
legal period or term, term fixed by law ‖ statutory period, term fixed by statute.

TÉRMINO MEDIO.
middle ground, compromise ‖ medium term ‖ average.

TÉRMINO NECESARIO.
waiting period, term which must run in order for something to occur.

TÉRMINO NO PERENTORIO.
procedural term or period which continues until its expiration date is set by court order. Opposed to TÉRMINO PERENTORIO.

TÉRMINO ORDINARIO.
ordinary term ‖ type of ordinary discovery period, normal period during which discovery is carried out and presented before the court. Opposed to TÉRMINO EXTRAORDINARIO.

TÉRMINO PERENTORIO.
procedural term or period which expires automatically. Opposed to TÉRMINO NO PERENTORIO.

TÉRMINO POSESORIO.
term of possession ‖ term in office.

TÉRMINO PRECLUSIVO.
See TÉRMINO IMPRORROGABLE.

TÉRMINO PROBATORIO.
discovery period, term during which evidence may be discovered and presented to the court.

May be TÉRMINO EXTRAORDINARIO or TÉRMINO ORDINARIO.

TÉRMINO PROCESAL.
procedural period or term, term during which procedural requirements must be fulfilled (set by statute, court or by agreement of the parties).

TÉRMINO PRORROGABLE.
extendable period or term ‖ extendable expiration date or deadline.

TÉRMINO RESOLUTORIO.
See PLAZO RESOLUTORIO.

TÉRMINO SUSPENSIVO.
See PLAZO SUSPENSIVO.

TÉRMINO TÁCITO.
implied term or period ‖ implied expiration date.

TERMINOLOGÍA.
f, terminology.

TERNA.
f, group of three candidates from which one will be selected for a position.

TERRATENIENTE.
m, property or land owner or possessor or holder.

TERRAZGO.
m, arable or cultivatable property ‖ rent paid for farm property.

TERRAZGUERO.
m, farm tenant, tenant farmer.

TERREMOTO.
m, earthquake.

TERRENO.
m, terrain ‖ land, earth, ground ‖ plot, piece of land, lot ‖ farm ‖ sphere of activity ‖ attitude ‖ order of ideas ‖ adj, earthly, pertaining to the earth ‖ worldly.

TERRENO ABIERTO.
open ground ‖ unenclosed terrain.

TERRENO BALDÍO.
uncultivated property or terrain ‖ vacant lot.

TERRENO CERCADO.
fenced plot or lot or terrain.

TERRENO CERRADO.
enclosed plot or lot or terrain.

TERRENO DEL ESTADO.
government or state land or piece of land.

TERRENO DEL HONOR.
field of honor, dueling site.

TERRENO EDIFICADO.
developed land or plot of land.

TERRENO FORESTAL.
forested property.

TERRENO FRANCO.
unexploited property which may be leased for mining purposes.

TERRENO YERMO.
wasteland, barren land || uninhabited land.

TERRERO.
m, public square || adj, earthy, from the earth || earthly || humble, lowly.

TERRESTRE.
adj, terrestrial || earthly || ground, on the ground.

TERRIBILIDAD.
f, terribleness.

TERRIBLE.
adj, terrible || atrocious || extremely violent || frightening || gruff.

TERRÍCOLA.
m, earthling, inhabitant of Earth.

TERRITORIAL.
adj, territorial || national || applicable to all inhabitants || terrestrial.

TERRITORIALIDAD.
f, territoriality.

TERRITORIALIDAD DE LA LEY.
territoriality of law.

TERRITORIALIDAD DE LAS NORMAS JURÍDICAS.
territoriality of legal norms.

TERRITORIALIDAD PENAL.
territoriality of criminal law.

TERRITORIO.
m, territory, region || zone, district || jurisdiction || national territory.

TERRITORIO CONQUISTADO.
conquered territory.

TERRITORIO ENEMIGO.
enemy territory.

TERRITORIO ESTATAL.
state or government territory.

TERRITORIO EXTRANJERO.
foreign territory, territory of a foreign state or government.
Opposed to TERRITORIO NACIONAL.

TERRITORIO NACIONAL.
national territory. Opposed to TERRITORIO EXTRANJERO.

TERRITORIOS NACIONALES.
national territories, (non-provincial) territories of the national government. Opposed to

territory of provincial or state government.

TERRITORIOS POLARES.
territory near the North and South Poles || the Antarctic.

TERROR.
m, terror || fear || period of terror after the French revolution.

TERRORÍFICO.
adj, terrifying || horrifying.

TERRORISMO.
m, terrorism.

TERRORISTA.
m, terrorist || adj, terrorist.

TERRUÑO.
m, plot or piece of land || territory || birthplace || motherland, fatherland, homeland || place of origin (of a person).

TESIS.
f, thesis || conclusion, proposition || dissertation || doctoral thesis.

TESÓN.
m, tenacity, perseverance || firmness.

TESONERÍA.
f, obstinacy || stubbornness.

TESORERÍA.
f, treasury, office and position of treasurer.

TESORERO.
m, treasurer.

TESORIZAR.
See ATESORAR.

TESORO.
m, treasure || riches, richness || public treasury, exchequer || national or public funds || unclaimed property, treasure || thesaurus.

TESORO ARTÍSTICO Y CULTURAL.
artistic and cultural treasures (of a nation, etc.).

TESORO NACIONAL.
public treasury, exchequer || national or public funds.

TESTACIÓN.
f, crossing out, obliteration, erasure (of words or letters in a writing).

TESTADO.
adj, testate, with a will || crossed out, erased.

TESTADOR.
m, testator.

TESTADORA.
f, testatrix.

TESTADURA.
See TESTACIÓN.

TESTAFÉRREA.
See TESTAFERRO.
TESTAFERRO.
m, straw man or party.
TESTAMENTARÍA.
f, testamentary execution, execution or fulfillment of the terms of a will ‖ probate proceeding, testamentary proceeding ‖ testamentary documents and instruments ‖ testamentary succession ‖ meeting of executors or executrix or administrators ‖ executor (if male), executrix (if female).
TESTAMENTARIO.
m, executor ‖ adj, testamentary.
TESTAMENTO.
m, testament, will ‖ act of making a will ‖ series of actions which are taken for personal benefit by an authority prior leaving office ‖ lengthy or voluminous writing.
TESTAMENTO A FAVOR DEL ALMA.
See ALMA DEL TESTADOR.
TESTAMENTO "AB IRATO".
will made during a moment of great anger.
TESTAMENTO ABIERTO.
nuncupative will (taken down by a notary public).
TESTAMENTO AD CAUTELAM.
testament which could not be revoked unless a special pass word was used. No longer in use.
TESTAMENTO ANTE TESTIGOS.
will made in fear of imminent death and attested to by witnesses.
TESTAMENTO CERRADO.
sealed will which is written by the testator or another person on his behalf.
TESTAMENTO COMÚN.
ordinary testament or will.
TESTAMENTO CORRESPECTIVO.
type of joint and mutual will which neither testator may revoke separately.
TESTAMENTO DE HERMANDAD.
See TESTAMENTO MANCOMUNADO.
TESTAMENTO DE MANCOMÚN.
See TESTAMENTO MANCOMUNADO.
TESTAMENTO DE PRISIONERO.
prisoner's will or testament.
TESTAMENTO DEL ANALFABETO.
testament or will of an illiterate.
TESTAMENTO DEL CIEGO.
testament or will of a blind person.

TESTAMENTO DEL EXTRANJERO.
testament or will of a foreigner.
TESTAMENTO DEL LOCO.
will or testament of an insane person.
TESTAMENTO DEL MENOR.
will or testament of a minor.
TESTAMENTO DEL MUDO.
will or testament of a person who is mute.
TESTAMENTO DEL SORDOMUDO.
will or testament of a deaf mute.
TESTAMENTO EN CASO DE EPIDEMIA.
will or testament made during an epidemic.
TESTAMENTO EN EL EXTRANJERO.
foreign will or testament, will made outside national territory.
TESTAMENTO EN LENGUA EXTRANJERA.
will or testament in a foreign language.
TESTAMENTO EN MANCOMÚN.
See TESTAMENTO MANCOMUNADO.
TESTAMENTO EN PELIGRO DE MUERTE.
testament or will made in imminent fear of death.
TESTAMENTO ESCRITO.
written will ‖ see also TESTAMENTO CERRADO.
TESTAMENTO ESPECIAL.
type of will which must fulfill different requirements than the TESTAMENTO COMÚN in order to be valid. Includes a soldier's will, seaman's will, foreign will, etc.
TESTAMENTO EXTRAORDINARIO.
type of simplified will which must fulfill less stringent standards in order to be valid. Includes TESTAMENTO DEL LOCO, DEL SORDOMUDO, TESTAMENTO DEL MUDO, TESTAMENTO DEL CIEGO, TESTAMENTO EN LENGUA EXTRANJERA, etc.
TESTAMENTO INOFICIOSO.
invalid will or testament ‖ will which in form is valid, but which is invalid due to the exclusion of heirs required by law.
TESTAMENTO MANCOMUNADO.
joint will (which is executed by two persons together to dispose of their jointly-held property).
TESTAMENTO MARÍTIMO.
seaman's will, mariner's will.
TESTAMENTO MILITAR.
soldier's will.
TESTAMENTO MÍSTICO.
See TESTAMENTO CERRADO.

TESTAMENTO MUTUO.
mutual will ‖ reciprocal will.

TESTAMENTO NUNCUPATIVO.
oral will ‖ nuncupative will ‖ oral will attested to by seven witnesses ‖ see also TESTAMENTO ABIERTO.

TESTAMENTO OLÓGRAFO.
holographic or olographic will.

TESTAMENTO ORDINARIO.
ordinary will or testament.

TESTAMENTO PAGÁNICO.
civilian testament, non-military will.

TESTAMENTO POR ACTO PÚBLICO.
nuncupative will (attested to by a notary public).

TESTAMENTO POR COMISARIO.
will made by another pursuant to a special power of attorney.

TESTAMENTO POR MANDATARIO.
See TESTAMENTO POR COMISARIO.

TESTAMENTO PRIVILEGIADO.
See TESTAMENTO EXTRAORDINARIO.

TESTAMENTO RECÍPROCO.
reciprocal will (which either testator may revoke separately).

TESTAMENTO SACRAMENTAL.
unwritten will which is determined by the in-court testimony regarding such sworn to by witnesses.

TESTAMENTO SECRETO.
See TESTAMENTO CERRADO.

TESTAMENTO SOLEMNE.
solemn will, will which has been solemnized and fulfills all the legal requirements.

TESTANTE.
m, witnessing, attesting.

TESTAR.
v, to make a will or testament ‖ to obliterate, erase ‖ to place a judicial lien (on property) ‖ to request an embargo of something.

TESTIFICACIÓN.
f, act of giving testimony ‖ attestation.

TESTIFICAL.
adj, witness's, pertaining to a witness ‖ witnesses', pertaining to witnesses.

TESTIFICANTE.
adj, testifying, deposing ‖ attesting, witnessing.

TESTIFICAR.
v, to testify, depose, give testimony (in a legal proceeding) ‖ to witness ‖ to bear witness to, attest.

TESTIFICATIVO.
adj, attesting, witnessing.

TESTIGO.
m, witness ‖ attester ‖ evidence, proof ‖ testimony.

TESTIGO ABONADO.
competent witness.

TESTIGO AURICULAR.
See TESTIGO DE OÍDAS.

TESTIGO CONTESTE.
witness whose testimony agrees with that of others.

TESTIGO DE ACTUACIÓN.
subscribing or attesting witness.

TESTIGO DE APREMIO.
subpoenaed witness, witness subject to a subpoena.

TESTIGO DE CARGO.
prosecuting witness, witness for the prosecution.

TESTIGO DE CONOCIMIENTO.
witness with personal knowledge of the party in question.

TESTIGO DE DESCARGO.
defense witness, witness for the defense (in a criminal case).

TESTIGO DE LOS TESTAMENTOS.
testamentary witness ‖ witness of a will or testament.

TESTIGO DE OÍDAS.
hearsay witness, witness of hearsay testimony.

TESTIGO DE VISTA.
eyewitness ‖ witness with personal knowledge of the facts about which he is to give testimony ‖ person who watches or spies on another.

TESTIGO EN LOS INSTRUMENTOS PÚBLICOS.
witness subscribing to or attesting public documents.

TESTIGO FALSO.
perjurer, false witness.

TESTIGO HÁBIL.
competent witness.

TESTIGO IDÓNEO.
competent witness.

TESTIGO INHÁBIL.
incompetent witness.

TESTIGO INSTRUMENTAL.
documentary witness ‖ subscribing or attesting witness.

TESTIGO JUDICIAL.
trial witness, witness who attests to facts in litigation.

**TESTIGO MAYOR
DE TODA EXCEPCIÓN.**
fully competent witness.

TESTIGO NECESARIO.
necessary witness ‖ incompetent witness whose testimony is permitted notwithstanding.

TESTIGO OCULAR.
eye witness.

TESTIGO PRESENCIAL.
eyewitness ‖ witness with personal knowledge of the facts about which he gives testimony.

TESTIGO REBELDE.
witness subject to a subpoena who fails to appear.

TESTIGO SINGULAR.
witness who is alone in what he testifies to ‖ witness whose testimony contradicts that of others.

TESTIGO TESTAMENTARIO.
See TESTIGO DE LOS TESTAMENTOS.

TESTIGO ÚNICO.
See TESTIGO SINGULAR.

TESTIGOS DEL MATRIMONIO.
marriage witnesses, witnesses to a marriage.

TESTIGUAR.
v, to testify.

TESTIMONIAL.
adj, testimonial.

TESTIMONIALES.
m, (original) documentary proof or evidence.

TESTIMONIAR.
v, to testify or attest to, bear witness, depose.

TESTIMONIERO.
m, perjurer, false witness.

TESTIMONIO.
m, testimony ‖ evidence, proof ‖ affidavit ‖ notarized document ‖ in-court testimony or statement ‖ false testimony, perjury.

**TESTIMONIO
DE SENTENCIA.**
certification of judicial decision or sentence (by court clerk).

TESTIMONIO FALSO.
perjury, false testimony.

TEXTO.
m, text ‖ legal text (e.g. of a law, regulation, ordinance) ‖ substantive contents of a document (excluding formalities).

TEXTO LEGAL.
text of a law ‖ collection of statutes ‖ legal text book.

TEXTUAL.
adj, textual ‖ literal.

TEXTUALMENTE.
adv, textually ‖ literally.

TÍA.
f, aunt ‖ great-aunt ‖ mother-in-law ‖ street walker, prostitute ‖ course woman ‖ step mother.

TÍA ABUELA.
great-aunt.

TÍA CARNAL.
aunt by blood relation.

TÍA POLÍTICA.
aunt by marriage ‖ wife of a great-uncle.

TÍA SEGUNDA.
second-aunt, female cousin of parent.

TIEMPO.
m, time, period ‖ duration, lapse (of time) ‖ age, era ‖ season ‖ weather ‖ age (esp. of babies under one year).

TIEMPO CIVIL.
time computed as required by law.

TIEMPO CONTINUO.
continuous period.

TIEMPO DE EFECTIVIDAD.
effective period, time which is computed as effective ‖ time in office or at a position.

TIEMPO DE ENSAYO.
training period.

TIEMPO DE GUERRA.
time of war, war-time.

TIEMPO DE PAZ.
peace-time.

TIEMPO DE SERVICIO.
time spent in military service.

TIEMPO DEL PAGO.
payment period (including the due date).

TIEMPO HÁBIL.
non-holiday period, period made up exclusively of working days ‖ period prior to the expiration of a term or deadline.

TIEMPO INMEMORIAL.
period before the expiration of a term or deadline ‖ time immemorial.

TIEMPO SUFICIENTE.
sufficient or adequate time (to do something)

TIEMPO SUPLEMENTARIO DE TRABAJO
overtime, overtime period.

TIEMPO ÚTIL.
See TIEMPO HÁBIL.

TIEMPO Y ESPACIO.
time and space.

TIENDA.
f, store, shop || retail shop || clothing or material store.

TIERRA.
f, earth || ground || soil || world || cultivated land or terrain || rural property || homeland, motherland, fatherland || country, land, region || district || territory, jurisdiction || land, shore.

TIERRA A TIERRA.
shore navigation, navigation in sight of land.

TIERRA ARRASADA.
land laid waste, especially during a war.

TIERRA DE NADIE.
no man's land.

TIERRA FIRME.
terra firma, dry land.

TIERRAS DE SECANO.
non-irrigated land.

TIERRAS TRIBUTARIAS.
taxable lands or real estate.

TIMBRADO.
adj, stamped, sealed.

TIMBRADOR.
m, person or machine which stamps or seals.

TIMBRAR.
v, to stamp || to seal || to place a stamp on.

TIMBRE.
m, stamp || tax stamp || revenue from stamp tax || bell, buzzer || doorbell || meritorious act, honorable deed.

TIMBRE DEL ESTADO.
state tax stamp.

TIMO.
m, swindle.

TIMOCRACIA.
f, timocracy, government of the wealthy.

TIMÓN.
m, rudder || government, rule.

TIMORATO.
adj, timid.

TÍO.
m, uncle.

TÍO ABUELO.
great-uncle.

TÍO CARNAL.
uncle by blood relation.

TÍO POLÍTICO.
uncle by marriage || husband of a great-aunt.

TÍO SEGUNDO.
second-uncle, male cousin of parent.

TIPICIDAD.
f, legal description or typification of a crime || requirement that only legally typified conduct be punished || requirement that business associations be organized under one of the accepted legal structures (e.g. partnership, limited partnership) provided by law.

TÍPICO.
adj, typical || characteristic, peculiar || representative.

TIPO.
m, type || model, class, example || standard, representation || strange person, character, customer || (letter) type || rate || legal description of a crime or other legal classification.

TIPO DE CAMBIO.
rate of exchange (of foreign currencies).

TIPOGRAFÍA.
f, typography || typesetting.

TIRA Y AFLOJA.
alternation between iron fist rule and liberalism, from one extreme to the other.

TIRADA.
f, distance, length (between two points) || lapse, length of time (between two moments) || series of arguments grouped together in an oral allegation or congressional or parliamentary debate || number of copies in a printing (of a book or newspaper) || prostitute.

TIRADO.
adj, give-away, very cheap, dirt cheap || easy, easily obtained || ruined || depreciated.

TIRANAMENTE.
See TIRÁNICAMENTE.

TIRANÍA.
f, tyranny || abusive or excessive command or rule.

TIRANÍA SIDICAL.
abusive leadership of a union.

TIRÁNICAMENTE.
adv, tyrannically.

TIRANICIDA.
f, m, tyrannicide, person who kills a tyrant.

TIRANICIDIO.
m, tyrannicide, act of killing a tyrant.

TIRÁNICO.
adj, tyrannical, tyrannic || oppressive.

TIRANIZACIÓN.
f, (act of) tyrannizing.
TIRANIZADAMENTE.
adv, tyrannically, like a tyrant.
TIRANIZAR.
v, to tyrannize || to have a tyrant govern || to oppress.
TIRANO.
m, tyrant || adj, tyrannical.
TIRANTE.
adj, tense || strained (e.g. friendship or diplomatic relations) || taut.
TIRANTEZ.
f, tension.
TIRANTEZ DE RELACIONES.
strain or tension in relations.
TIRAR.
v, to throw, hurl || to drop, throw away || to grab || to cast || to shoot, fire (e.g. a gun) || to drop (bombs) || to waste, squander (money) || to attract || to overcome (a difficult situation) || to be inclined or likely (to) || to try, attempt || to last, continue, remain.
TIRAR A DAR.
to shoot to injure or kill.
TIRO.
m, shot, shooting, report || trajectory, range (e.g. of a bullet) || explosion, report (e.g. of a gun) || bullet, round, charge || shooting range || injury, damage, harm || joke || trick || theft || hint, allusion || flight of stairs || shaft or length of a well || mine shaft || traction, tension.
TIRO AL AIRE.
shot in the air, stray bullet || warning shot || undirected person.
TIRO DE GRACIA.
coup de grace, final bullet, shot to kill injured person or animal.
TIROCINIO.
See APRENDIZAJE.
TIROS.
m, see TIRO || skirmish, volley.
TIROTEARSE.
v, to exchange shots, shoot at each another.
TIROTEO.
m, skirmish, volley (of shots).
TÍTERE.
m, puppet || instrument of another.
TITULACIÓN.
f, title documents, series of documents which demonstrate ownership of property.

TITULADO.
m, nobility, titled person || holder of an acade mic degree || adj, entitled || so-called.
TITULAR.
m, title-holder, legal owner || possessor, owner || named person, person who holds a position or practices a profession in his own name and right || adj, titular, nominal, so-called || regula || named || v, to name, entitle, call || to be gran ted a title of nobility.
TITULARIDAD.
f, title ownership || legal entitlement.
TÍTULO.
m, title || origin, cause, reason || pretext, ex cuse || academic degree || certificate, diploma || license || section, division of laws (between books and chapters) || basis or foundation (o a right or obligation) || certificate of title, title document which demonstrates a legal right noble title || nobility, titled person || bond.
TÍTULO A LA ORDEN.
nominative bond.
TÍTULO ACADÉMICO.
academic title || academic degree or diploma
TÍTULO AL PORTADOR.
bearer instrument || bearer bond.
TÍTULO ATRIBUTIVO.
document which shows transference of a righ or obligation. Opposed to TÍTULO DECLARA TIVO and TÍTULO CONSTITUTIVO.
TÍTULO AUTÉNTICO.
authentic title (properley issued by a goverr ment authority).
TÍTULO CONSTITUTIVO.
document which creates a legal right or obliga tion. Opposed to TÍTULO ATRIBUTIVO an TÍTULO DECLARATIVO.
TÍTULO DE ADQUISICIÓN.
title of purchase.
TÍTULO DE CRÉDITO.
credit instrument, document which demon trates a right to receive money. May be eithe nominative or bearer.
TÍTULO DE DEUDA.
debt or credit instrument || evidence of indel tedness.
TÍTULO DE LA DEUDA.
See TÍTULO DE LA DEUDA PÚBLICA.
TÍTULO DE LA DEUDA PÚBLICA.
public bond.

TÍTULO DE NOBLEZA.
See TÍTULO NOBILIARIO.

TÍTULO DE PILOTO.
pilot's license.

TÍTULO DE PROPIEDAD.
title, property title, title to property ‖ deed, title deed (to real estate).

TÍTULO DECLARATIVO.
document which merely declares the existence of a right. Opposed to TÍTULO ATRIBUTIVO and TÍTULO CONSTITUTIVO.

TÍTULO DERIVATIVO.
title by descent ‖ title derived from another title.

TÍTULO EJECUTIVO.
execution paper, document which grants right to execute on property by means of a summary proceeding (to satisfy an obligation).

TÍTULO ENDOSABLE.
negotiable or transferable or endorsable in-strument.

TÍTULO FACULTATIVO.
university diploma or degree (usually in law, philosophy, medicine, pharmacy).

TÍTULO GRATUITO.
gratuitous title.

TÍTULO HÁBIL.
perfect title.

TÍTULO INSCRIBIBLE.
registerable title, title which is legally sufficient for purposes of registration in a real estate registry.

TÍTULO JUSTO.
See JUSTO TÍTULO.

TÍTULO LUCRATIVO.
lucrative title.

TÍTULO NO TRASLATIVO DEL DOMINIO.
defective title, title which may not be trans-ferred due to some defect ‖ imperfect title, title which is not legally sufficient to transfer title.

TÍTULO NOBILIARIO.
title of nobility.

TÍTULO NOMINATIVO.
nominative instrument.

TÍTULO NULO.
void title ‖ imperfect title.

TÍTULO OFICIAL.
official certificate or diploma or degree certifi-cate.

TÍTULO ONEROSO.
onerous title, title for consideration.

TÍTULO ORIGINARIO.
original title, title without prior transfer.

TÍTULO PARTICULAR.
See TÍTULO SINGULAR.

TÍTULO POSESORIO.
legal basis of possession ‖ possessory title.

TÍTULO PRECARIO.
See A TÍTULO PRECARIO.

TÍTULO PRIMORDIAL.
original title.

TÍTULO PRIVADO.
See DOCUMENTO PRIVADO.

TÍTULO PROFESIONAL.
professional license ‖ professional degree or certificate or diploma.

TÍTULO PÚBLICO.
See DOCUMENTO PÚBLICO.

TÍTULO PUTATIVO.
presumptive title ‖ paper title ‖ apparent title.

TÍTULO QUE TRAE APAREJADA EJECUCIÓN.
See TÍTULO EJECUTIVO.

TÍTULO SINGULAR.
specific title, title to a specific thing or right. See A TÍTULO SINGULAR.

TÍTULO TRASLATIVO DEL DOMINIO.
good title, title which contains no defects and thus may be transferred ‖ perfect title, title which is legally sufficient to transfer title.

TÍTULO UNIVERSAL.
general title, title to unspecified things or rights. See A TÍTULO UNIVERSAL.

TÍTULO UNIVERSITARIO.
university degree or diploma.

TÍTULO VALOR.
credit instrument.

TÍTULO VERDADERO.
true or real title.

TÍTULO VICIADO.
See TÍTULO VICIOSO.

TÍTULO VICIOSO.
imperfect title ‖ defective title ‖ title defective in form, bad title.

TOCADO.
m, insane person ‖ nut, crazy ‖ adj, touched.

TOCAMIENTO.
m, touching, act of touching.

TOCAR.
v, to touch, feel ‖ to arrive (re. the moment) ‖

to be one's responsibility (re. a task or job, etc.) ‖ to have a right (to a lottery prize) ‖ to hold by right or title ‖ to be related ‖ to touch, feel up, diddle (a female) ‖ to abuse a child sexually ‖ to reach shore ‖ to touch bottom ‖ to influence.

TOCAR DE CERCA.
to be closely related ‖ to know a subject well ‖ to influence something personally.

TOCAYO.
m, namesake.

TODO.
m, totality, entirety ‖ maximum ‖ adj, all, entire, total ‖ whole ‖ complete ‖ full.

TOGA.
f, toga ‖ judge's robes ‖ gown, robe (for special persons and circumstances).

TOGADO.
m, person who wears a toga, robe, or gown ‖ judge ‖ attorney, lawyer ‖ chief justice (of a tribunal).

TOLERABLE.
adj, tolerable ‖ sufferable ‖ permissible.

TOLERANCIA.
f, tolerance ‖ toleration ‖ authorization, permission ‖ allowance (in discrepancy of weights, etc.).

TOLERANTE.
adj, tolerant.

TOMA.
f, taking (e.g. of possession) ‖ occupation (e.g. of a city by enemy forces).

TOMA DE MANDO.
assumption or taking of office ‖ taking command.

TOMA DE POSESIÓN.
taking possession, act of transferring a right ‖ occupation ‖ inauguration (of a president) ‖ (formal) assumption of an office or post.

TOMA DE RAZÓN.
public documentation of will or intent.

TOMA DE RAZÓN HIPOTECARIA.
mortgage filing or registration.

TOMA Y DACA.
simultaneous exchange (of property or services) ‖ give and take, reciprocity.

TOMADOR.
m, taker ‖ payee (of a negotiable instrument).

TOMAR.
v, to take ‖ to conquer, seize ‖ to occupy ‖ to adopt (e.g. a position, resolution) ‖ to acquire

‖ to charge ‖ to grab, seize ‖ to take responsibility for ‖ to begin (e.g. a position or job) to take (e.g. medicine, food) ‖ to accept ‖ t receive ‖ to employ, contract for services ‖ t rent, lease ‖ to understand, interpret ‖ to stea rob ‖ to buy ‖ to select, opt, choose ‖ to arriv (at port) ‖ to catch (in the act) ‖ to use, borrov ‖ to have sexual intercourse ‖ to gain.

TOMAR ALGO POR DONDE QUEMA.
to take something in its worst meaning or ser se.

TOMAR ALGO SOBRE SÍ.
to take responsibility for ‖ to accept an oblig tion ‖ to assume responsibility on behalf c another.

TOMAR CUENTAS.
to examine carefully the conduct of another to check accounts.

TOMAR LA VOZ DE ALGUIEN.
to take up someone's cause, defend ‖ to spea or act on behalf of someone.

TOMAR MEDIDAS.
to take measures or step ‖ to measure.

TOMAR PARTE.
to take part or participate or get mixed up ir

TOMAR PARTIDO.
to take sides in a dispute or controversy ‖ ▪ sign up (with a paramilitary group of band) to form an opinion or judgment.

TOMAR POR SU CUENTA.
to assume a position or responsibility.

TOMAR TIERRA.
to land, reach port ‖ to disembark ‖ to lan reach ground (re. an airplane) ‖ to return Earth ‖ to get practice or practical experienc

TOMAR UN PARTIDO.
to decide, make a decision, make up one mind (under difficult circumstances).

TOMARSE.
v, to get drunk ‖ to adopt a right or privileg

TOMO.
m, tome, volume (of books) ‖ bulk, body (things) ‖ importance, significance, value.

TONELADA.
f, ton ‖ tonnage.

TONELADA DE ARQUEO.
register ton.

TONELADA DE DESPLAZAMIENTO.
ton for purposes of calculating a ship's tc nage.

NELADA DE PESO.
n of 2,000 pounds ‖ ton of effective weight.

NELADA MÉTRICA DE ARQUEO.
bic meter.

NELADA MÉTRICA DE PESO.
etric ton, ton of 1,000 kilograms.

NELAJE.
, tonnage ‖ tonnage duty.

NELAJE BRUTO.
oss tonnage.

NELAJE DE CARGA.
rgo tonnage.

NELAJE NETO.
t tonnage.

NTINA.
ontine, association in which members invest
order that annuities be paid to those mem-
rs surviving at a later point in time.

PAR.
to hit, bump into, run into.

PE.
, collision, bump, accident ‖ limit ‖ maxi-
um price ‖ impediment, difficulty, obstacle ‖
arrel.

PICO.
, topic, subject, theme ‖ public place, com-
onplace ‖ common or trite expression ‖ adj,
pical.

QUE.
, touch, act of touching ‖ assaying of gold ‖
st, examination ‖ warning, recommendation
difficulty ‖ essence, heart (of a matter) ‖ fini-
ing touch.

QUE DE QUEDA.
rfew.

RCER.
to twist ‖ to deviate ‖ to misinterpret ‖ to
rrupt, bribe (e.g. a judge).

RMENTAR.
e ATORMENTAR.

RMENTO.
, torture, torment ‖ anguish, affliction ‖ un-
arable pain ‖ tormentor.

RNO.
, passing of auctioned property to the se-
nd-highest bidder, due to the failure of the
ghest bidder to fulfill the requirements of
e bid (e.g. guaranties, payments) within a
pulated time.

RPEDEAR.
to torpedo.

TORPEDEO.
m, torpedoing.

TORPEDERO.
m, torpedo boat ‖ (air) bomber.

TORPEDO.
m, torpedo.

TORPEZA.
f, deprivation of freedom of movement ‖ slowness, sluggishness ‖ rudeness ‖ dullness, mental slowness ‖ ineptitude, awkwardness, clum-
siness ‖ indecency, lasciviousness ‖ dishonesty
‖ infamy ‖ disloyalty.

TORTUOSA.
adj, tortuous ‖ devious ‖ disloyal.

TORTURA.
f, torture, torment ‖ cruelty ‖ martyrdom,
great pain or suffering.

TORTURA PSÍQUICA.
psychological torture.

TORTURADOR.
m, torturer, tormentor ‖ instrument of torture `
or torment.

TORTURAR.
v, to torture, torment.

TOTALIDAD.
f, totality, entirety, whole ‖ congressional or
parliamentary debate on the substance of a
law.

TOTALITARIO.
m, supporter of totalitarianism ‖ adj, totalitarian.

TOTALITARISMO.
m, totalitarianism.

TOTALITARISTA.
f, supporter of totalitarianism.

TOXICIDAD.
f, toxicity.

TÓXICO.
adj, toxic, poisonous.

TRABA.
f, union, joining ‖ tie, relationship, bond ‖
problem, beginning of a dispute ‖ difficulty,
obstacle, hindrance ‖ obstacle to execution ‖
effectiveness of an attachment or seizure.

**TRABA DE
LA LITIS.**
case in controversy, procedural point in time
at which a legal controversy is said to arise, e.g.
when the complaint is answered.

TRABADO.
adj, tied, related to ‖ difficult, with obstacles or

hindrances ‖ attached (re. property in a legal proceeding) ‖ slowed down.

TRABAJADO.
adj, tired or worn out (by work) ‖ worked ‖ very busy.

TRABAJADOR.
m, worker, laborer ‖ manual laborer ‖ day laborer ‖ working man, workman ‖ employee ‖ adj, work, related to work ‖ laborious, hard working ‖ working.

TRABAJADOR A DOMICILIO.
laborer who works at home.

TRABAJADOR ACCIDENTAL.
See TRABAJADOR OCASIONAL.

TRABAJADOR AÉREO.
aviation or airline personnel.

TRABAJADOR AGRÍCOLA.
farm or agricultural worker.

TRABAJADOR ASALARIADO.
salaried employee.

TRABAJADOR BANCARIO.
bank employee.

TRABAJADOR DE CASA DE RENTA.
worker in an income-producing office or store.

TRABAJADOR DE COMPAÑÍAS DE SEGUROS.
insurance company employee.

TRABAJADOR DE LA CONSTRUCCIÓN.
construction worker.

TRABAJADOR DE LA INDUSTRIA.
industrial worker ‖ factory worker.

TRABAJADOR DEL COMERCIO.
business employee ‖ employee whose work is regulated by the commerce code ‖ employee of a retailer or other trading company.

TRABAJADOR DEL ESTADO.
government employee or worker.

TRABAJADOR DEPENDIENTE.
employee (of an employer).
Opposed to TRABAJADOR INDEPENDIENTE.

TRABAJADOR DOCENTE.
teacher, professor.

TRABAJADOR DOMÉSTICO.
domestic servant or help ‖ cleaning person.

TRABAJADOR EVENTUAL.
temporary (non-emergency) worker, temp.

TRABAJADOR EXTRANJERO.
foreign worker or employee.
Opposed to TRABAJADOR INDÍGENA.

TRABAJADOR FAMILIAR.
employee who is a member of the family.

TRABAJADOR GASTRONÓMICO.
food worker, restaurant employee.

TRABAJADOR INDEPENDIENTE.
independent contractor.
Opposed to TRABAJADOR DEPENDIENTE.

TRABAJADOR INDÍGENA.
local worker, worker who is a national. Opposed to TRABAJADOR EXTRANJERO.

TRABAJADOR MANUAL.
manual laborer or worker.

TRABAJADOR MARÍTIMO.
maritime worker ‖ seaman, sailor.

TRABAJADOR OCASIONAL.
temporary emergency worker (for the purpose of taking care of an emergency).

TRABAJADOR RURAL.
farm or rural worker ‖ field hand.

TRABAJANTE.
adj, working, laboring.

TRABAJAR.
v, to work, labor, toil ‖ to do a job or task ‖ to try, attempt ‖ to be employed ‖ to be at work or working ‖ to work toward an end ‖ to do as planned ‖ to serve or work for a cause ‖ to bother, harass ‖ to put out good work ‖ to rob, steal.

TRABAJO.
m, work, labor, toil ‖ human effort ‖ job, task ‖ position, office, post ‖ employment ‖ profession ‖ craft, trade ‖ occupation ‖ service ‖ proposal, proposition ‖ care, carefulness ‖ difficulty, obstacle, inconvenience ‖ bother, irritation ‖ penalty, punishment ‖ operation working (of a machine) ‖ prison, jail.

TRABAJO A BORDO.
on-board work.

TRABAJO A CÓDIGO.
form of work slowdown by court employees work to code or rule which requires exacting conformity with procedural code (which otherwise is not required).

TRABAJO A COMISIÓN.
worker or employee on commission, commission worker.

TRABAJO A DESGANO.
work done reluctantly.

TRABAJO A DESTAJO.
piecework, work paid by the piece.

TRABAJO A DOMICILIO.
work performed at home.

TRABAJO A REGLAMENTO.
orm of work slowdown, work to code or regulation which, accordingly, is slower.

TRABAJO ACCIDENTAL.
See TRABAJO OCASIONAL.

TRABAJO AGRÍCOLA.
agricultural or farm worker, farmhand.

TRABAJO AL DETALLE.
orm of work slowdown, work done on unnecessary details.

TRABAJO AUTÓNOMO.
personal services, work which cannot be assigned || work not done for an employer, self employment.

TRABAJO CARCELARIO.
prison work, hard labor (performed by anyone who is detained or imprisoned, before or after sentencing).

TRABAJO CONTINUO.
continuous work.

TRABAJO DE GABINETE.
research or investigative work.

TRABAJO DE LA GENTE DE MAR.
maritime work.

TRABAJO DE LAS MUJERES.
women's work, work performed by women.

TRABAJO DE LOS EXTRANJEROS.
work performed by foreigners.

TRABAJO DE LOS MENORES.
work performed by minors. See MENOR.

TRABAJO DE PRISIONEROS.
work performed by prisoners.

TRABAJO DE TEMPORADA.
seasonal or migrant workers.

TRABAJO DIURNO.
day labor.

TRABAJO DOMÉSTICO.
domestic work or service or help.

TRABAJO EFECTIVO.
actual work, work actually done.

TRABAJO EN CADENA.
assembly line work.

TRABAJO EVENTUAL.
temporary (non-emergency) work or services.

TRABAJO FAMILIAR.
familiar or known work || work performed by family members in a business, industry, etc.

TRABAJO FORZADO.
forced or hard labor. Failure to perform such work results in physical punishment.

TRABAJO ILÍCITO.
illegal or illicit work.

TRABAJO IMPUESTO.
forced labor.

TRABAJO INDOLENTE.
work performed lazily.

TRABAJO INDUSTRIAL.
industrial labor || factory work.

TRABAJO INFANTIL.
child labor.

TRABAJO INSALUBRE.
unhealthy work.

TRABAJO INTELECTUAL.
intellectual work || non-manual labor.

TRABAJO INTERMITENTE.
work which is performed during different separate periods of a day (rather than in one eight or nine hour period).

TRABAJO LÍCITO.
legal or licit labor or work.

TRABAJO MANUAL.
manual labor or work.

TRABAJO MARÍTIMO.
maritime work.

TRABAJO NEGRO.
illegal work, work which is against the law in some way (e.g. by not paying employee deductions, working illegal overtime).

TRABAJO NOCTURNO.
night work, work performed at night.

TRABAJO OBLIGATORIO.
obligatory work, work which is required in order to obtain something. Failure to perform such work results in the imposition of a penalty or loss of benefits.

TRABAJO OCASIONAL.
temporary emergency work (for the purpose of taking care of an emergency).

TRABAJO ORDINARIO.
normal work, work done during an ordinary working day.

TRABAJO PARA TODOS.
employment for all.

TRABAJO PELIGROSO.
dangerous work or employment.

TRABAJO PENITENCIARIO.
prison work, hard labor (performed by a convict after sentencing).

TRABAJO POR EQUIPOS.
group work or labor.

TRABAJO PREPARATORIO.
preparatory work ‖ work done prior to incorporation.
TRABAJO PROFESIONAL.
professional work or employment.
TRABAJO PROHIBIDO.
prohibited work, work which is prohibited by law.
TRABAJO RURAL.
See TRABAJO AGRÍCOLA.
TRABAJO SOCIAL.
social work, work in human services.
TRABAJO SUBORDINADO.
subordinate employment or work, work performed under the supervision of another.
TRABAJO TÉCNICO.
technical work.
TRABAJOS.
m, hardships, difficulties ‖ penalties ‖ plural of TRABAJO.
TRABAJOSO.
adj, requiring a lot of work or effort ‖ laborious ‖ weak ‖ needy ‖ unspontaneous.
TRABAR.
v, to unite, join ‖ to tie, bond together ‖ to grab, seize ‖ to attach, seize (property in litigation) ‖ to make difficult, place an obstacle, hinder ‖ to retain rights ‖ to begin or initiate a lawsuit or dispute or battle ‖ to oppose another's actions.
TRABARSE.
v, to begin or initiate a lawsuit or dispute or battle ‖ to jam, foul (a firearm).
TRABARSE
DE PALABRAS.
to exchange words, insult, hurt someone verbally.
TRABAZÓN.
f, union, joining ‖ tie, bond ‖ dependency ‖ relationship, relation.
TRABUCACIÓN.
f, mistake, error ‖ obfuscation ‖ mix-up, confusion ‖ disorder.
TRABUCANTE.
See MONEDA TRABUCANTE.
TRABUCAR.
v, to mix up, confuse ‖ to get out of order ‖ to obfuscate ‖ to mix up words, letters, syllables, data, information, etc.
TRACCIÓN.
f, traction, pulling ‖ transportation.

TRACTO.
m, space, separation (between two things) ‖ lapse, interval, space, stretch (of time).
TRACTO SUCESIVO.
successive chain of title (in a real estate registry).
TRACTO ÚNICO.
See OBLIGACIÓN DE TRACTO ÚNICO.
"TRADENS".
transferor ‖ transmitter ‖ seller, vendor.
TRADENTE.
See "TRADENS".
TRADICIÓN.
f, delivery, act pursuant to which a person places something in the physical possession of another ‖ (physical) transfer or transference transmission, communication (of ideas) tradition, custom, rite, practice.
TRADICIÓN "BREVI MANU".
constructive delivery by agreement. Opposed to actual delivery or physical transfer. This takes place when a thing is held by a person under right that doesn't grant title as to that thing (e.g. a lease, subsequent to which the title is transferred to the lessee by a different agreement such as a sale).
TRADICIÓN CORPORAL.
See TRADICIÓN REAL.
TRADICIÓN DE ACCIONES.
delivery or physical transfer of stock or shares.
TRADICIÓN DE DERECHOS.
transfer of rights.
TRADICIÓN DE INMUEBLES.
transfer of real estate.
TRADICIÓN DE INSTRUMENTOS DE CRÉDITO.
delivery or physical transfer of negotiable instruments.
TRADICIÓN DE LA DONACIÓN.
physical transfer of donated property to the donee.
TRADICIÓN DE LA POSESIÓN.
transfer of possession.
TRADICIÓN DE LA PROPIEDAD.
physical transfer or delivery of property.
TRADICIÓN DE LA SIMPLE TENENCIA.
physical transfer or delivery of simple tenancy or simple possession or simple holding.
TRADICIÓN DE MUEBLES.
physical transfer or delivery of personal property.

TRADICIÓN DE RENTAS PÚBLICAS.
transfer or delivery of public income (by approving a budget by congress or legislature or parliament).
TRADICIÓN EN EL CONTRATO.
transfer or delivery pursuant to a contract.
TRADICIÓN EN LA OBLIGACIÓN.
transfer pursuant to an obligation.
TRADICIÓN FICTICIA.
See TRADICIÓN FINGIDA.
TRADICIÓN FINGIDA.
constructive delivery or transfer ‖ illusory or fictitious transfer or delivery.
TRADICIÓN "LONGA MANU".
constructive delivery by showing, but not physically transferring, the property to the transferee (e.g. placing property in a safe). Opposed to actual delivery or physical transfer.
TRADICIÓN POR MINISTERIO DE LA LEY.
statutory delivery, type of constructive delivery pursuant to statute.
TRADICIÓN REAL.
actual delivery or physical transfer.
TRADICIÓN SIMBÓLICA.
symbolic delivery or physical transfer.
TRADICIONAL.
adj, traditional, customary, habitual ‖ pertaining to delivery or physical transfer.
TRADICIONALISMO.
m, traditionalism.
TRADICIONALISTA.
f, m, traditionalist ‖ (political) conservative.
TRADUCCIÓN.
f, translation ‖ act of translating ‖ work which has been translated ‖ interpretation ‖ explanation ‖ exchange, trade.
TRADUCIR.
v, to translate ‖ to interpret ‖ to explain ‖ to exchange, trade.
TRADUCTOR.
m, translator ‖ interpreter ‖ explainer ‖ exchanging party, person who exchanges or trades.
TRAER.
v, to bring ‖ to carry with ‖ to cause, produce (an effect) ‖ to take care of something ‖ to oblige, require (performance) ‖ to deal with ‖ to have a matter pending ‖ to manage ‖ to attract, pull ‖ to wear, use ‖ to advance, put forward (e.g. an argument) ‖ to persuade ‖ to have, carry (merchandise).

TRAER A COLACIÓN.
to bring into a matter or discussion.
TRAER A COLACIÓN Y PARTICIÓN.
to include a thing in hotchpot.
TRAER ENTRE MANOS.
to manage a business ‖ to take care of something.
TRAERSE.
v, to bring or carry with one.
TRAÉRSELAS.
m, to be more malicious or problematic than appears at first glance.
TRAFICANTE.
m, trafficker, peddler, dealer, seller (usually of illegal goods).
TRAFICAR.
v, to traffic in, peddle (usually illegal goods) ‖ to exchange, trade (goods or monies) ‖ to deal in, sell.
TRÁFICO.
m, traffic ‖ commerce, trade ‖ trade or exchange of goods or monies ‖ negotiation ‖ railroad transportation ‖ transit ‖ contraband trade, peddling.
TRÁFICO AÉREO.
air traffic ‖ air transportation.
TRÁFICO DE DROGAS.
drug traffic or trade or peddling.
TRÁFICO DE INFLUENCIA.
influence peddling, power dealing.
TRAGEDIA.
f, tragedy ‖ calamity, disaster, catastrophe ‖ cause of great unhappiness.
TRAGEDIA AÉREA.
airplane disaster or accident.
TRÁGICO.
adj, tragic ‖ terrible ‖ calamitous, catastrophic, disastrous ‖ violent.
TRAGO.
m, drink ‖ gulp ‖ adversity.
TRAICIÓN.
f, treason ‖ treachery, disloyalty, unfaithfulness ‖ breaking of one's word ‖ lack of good faith ‖ marital unfaithfulness.
TRAICIÓN MILITAR.
military treason, aiding the enemy.
TRAICIONAR.
v, to commit treason ‖ to betray ‖ to be disloyal or unfaithful ‖ to break one's word ‖ to lack good faith ‖ to be unfaithful (a wife to her husband).

TRAICIONERO.
m, traitor ‖ adj, traitorous, disloyal, unfaithful ‖ treacherous.

TRAIDOR.
m, traitor ‖ adj, traitorous, disloyal, unfaithful ‖ treacherous ‖ false, tricky.

TRAIDORAMENTE.
traitorously, disloyally, unfaithfully ‖ treacherously ‖ falsely, trickily.

TRAJÍN.
m, transportation, carrying (of merchandise) ‖ hustle and bustle ‖ hectic work or activity.

TRAMA.
f, plot, scheme, plan, stratagem ‖ conspiracy.

TRAMAR.
v, to plot, scheme, plan (something evil or bad) ‖ to conspire ‖ to strategize, plan out something complicated.

TRAMITACIÓN.
f, administrative or judicial formalities and procedures (which must be fulfilled relative to a certain matter) ‖ course of litigation ‖ red-tapery, red-tape, series of transmissions of pleadings or documents through the adminis-trative or judicial bureaucracy ‖ negotiation, transaction.

TRAMITADOR.
m, expediter, person who attends to or requests the expedition of a matter through bureaucratic steps or procedures.

TRAMITAR.
v, to attend to, handle ‖ to request expedition of a matter through the steps of judicial or administrative bureaucracy.

TRÁMITE.
m, (bureaucratic or administrative or judicial) step, procedure, formality ‖ negotiation.

TRÁMITE JUDICIAL.
judicial step or procedure or formality.

TRÁMITES DE ESTILO.
routine judicial procedures, judicial formalities.

TRAMPA.
f, trap ‖ cheating ‖ trick, fraud ‖ artifice ‖ slight of hand ‖ unpaid or bad debt.

TRAMPEAR.
v, to cheat ‖ to trick, defraud, swindle ‖ to sponge off someone, borrow money with no intention of repayment ‖ to wriggle out of a difficult situation ‖ to elude one's obligations ‖ to get along.

TRAMPOSO.
m, cheater, swindler, defrauder ‖ sponger, bum ‖ bad debtor ‖ person who pays his debts late or not at all ‖ adj, cheating, swindling, tricky ‖ sponging.

TRANCE.
m, critical or decisive moment ‖ trance ‖ judicial attachment, seizure, levy (of property).

TRANCE DE ARMAS.
combat, battle ‖ war ‖ challenge.

TRANQUILAMENTE.
adv, tranquilly, peacefully, calmly ‖ without thinking of others ‖ without responsibility.

TRANQUILIDAD.
f, peace, tranquility, calm ‖ peace of mind.

TRANQUILIZAR.
v, to tranquilize ‖ to calm down.

TRANSACCIÓN.
f, settlement (of a case prior to trial) ‖ compromise, agreement (on a middle ground) ‖ transaction, business, commercial operation.

TRANSACCIONAL.
adj, settlement ‖ compromise, agreed-upon ‖ business, pertaining to a transaction of commercial operation. See TRANSACCIÓN.

TRANSAR.
See TRANSIGIR.

TRANSATLÁNTICO.
m, transatlantic ship ‖ adj, transatlantic.

TRANSBISABUELO.
See TATARABUELO.

TRANSBISNIETO.
See TATARANIETO.

TRANSBORDAR.
v, to change, switch (e.g. trains or planes or vessels) ‖ to go from one side of the river to the other ‖ to transfer (from one method of transportation to another).

TRANSBORDO.
m, change or switch (from one method of transportation to another).

TRANSCENDENCIA.
See TRASCENDENCIA.

TRANSCENDER.
See TRASCENDER.

TRANSCONTINENTAL.
adj, transcontinental.

TRANSCRIBIR.
v, to transcribe, copy.

TRANSCRIPCIÓN.
f, transcription, copy, reproduction ‖ (act of

verbatim filing of a title deed in a real estate registry.

TRANSCRITO.
m, deed which has been filed verbatim in a real estate registry ‖ adj, transcribed, copied, reproduced.

TRANSCURRIR.
v, to pass, go by, elapse (in terms of time).

TRANSCURSO.
m, passage, course (of time).

TRANSEÚNTE.
m, pedestrian ‖ vagabond, transient ‖ adj, passing, transitory ‖ momentary ‖ wandering.

TRANSFERENCIA.
f, transference, transfer ‖ alienation (of property) ‖ delivery ‖ cession, ceding ‖ transmission ‖ delay, recess ‖ assignment of rental agreement from one tenant to another ‖ assignment.

TRANSFERENCIA BANCARIA.
banking transfer.

TRANSFERENCIA DE CRÉDITOS NO ENDOSABLES.
transfer of non-negotiable or non-endorsable instruments.

TRANSFERENCIA DE LOS ARRENDAMIENTOS URBANOS.
assignment of rental agreement for urban property from one tenant to another.

TRANSFERENCIA DEL DOMINIO.
transfer of ownership.

TRANSFERENCIA DEL FONDO DE COMERCIO.
transfer of a business (which includes transfer of the commercial installations, merchandise, trade-name, trade-marks, clientele, rights to physical location, invention patents, industrial drawings and models, and all other commercial rights).

TRANSFERENCIA EN LAS OBLIGACIONES.
assignment or transfer of obligations.

TRANSFERENCIA EN LOS CONTRATOS.
assignment or transfer of contracts.

TRANSFERENCIA PSÍQUICA.
psychological transference.

TRANSFERIBLE.
adj, transferable ‖ alienable ‖ assignable ‖ able to be transmitted.

TRANSFERIDOR.
m, transferor ‖ assigner ‖ remitter.

TRANSFERIR.
v, to transfer, cede ‖ to alienate (property) ‖ to assign ‖ to transmit ‖ to transport ‖ to delay, postpone.

TRANSFIGURAR.
v, to transfigure.

TRANSFORMACIÓN.
f, transformation, conversion, change.

TRANSFORMACIÓN SOCIAL.
social change or transformation.

TRANSFORMADO.
adj, transformed, changed, converted.

TRANSFORMADOR.
m, transformer, changer.

TRANSFORMAR.
v, to transform, change, convert.

TRANSFUGA.
m, f, fugitive ‖ deserter ‖ traitor.

TRANSFUNDIR.
v, to transmit, spread (notice to various persons successively).

TRANSFUSIÓN.
f, transmission.

TRANSGREDIR.
v, to transgress, violate, break (e.g. a law, rule).

TRANSGRESIÓN.
f, transgression, violation, infraction (e.g. of a law, rule).

TRANSGRESOR.
m, transgressor, violator, breaker (e.g. of a law, rule, etc.).

TRANSICIÓN.
f, transition ‖ evolution ‖ change.

TRANSIGENCIA.
f, tolerance ‖ passivity ‖ changeability ‖ malleability ‖ also see TRANSACCIÓN.

TRANSIGENTE.
f, m, person who is compromising or tolerant or passive or malleable ‖ adj, compromising ‖ tolerant ‖ passive ‖ malleable.

TRANSIGIR.
v, to settle (prior to trial) ‖ to compromise, agree on a middle ground, settle (a dispute or difference) ‖ to demonstrate tolerance or passivity or changeability or malleability.

TRANSIR.
v, to pass on, die ‖ to come to an end.

TRANSITAR.
v, to transit, cross, go from one place to another (by public means) ‖ to travel, journey.

TRANSITARIO.
adj, re-expediter ‖ forwarder.

TRÁNSITO.
m, transit, movement ‖ travel (via public means) ‖ (vehicle) traffic ‖ mutation, alteration, change ‖ death, passing on ‖ passage, way, road.

TRÁNSITO AÉREO.
air traffic ‖ air travel.

TRANSITORIAMENTE.
adv, temporarily, for the time being ‖ until further notice or order.

TRANSITORIEDAD.
f, temporariness.

TRANSITORIO.
adj, transitory ‖ temporary ‖ limited in time.

TRANSLACIÓN.
See TRASLACIÓN.

TRANSLATIVO.
See TRASLATIVO.

TRANSLIMITACIÓN.
f, physical, legal, or moral transgression ‖ trespass ‖ invasion (of enemy troops).

TRANSLIMITAR.
v, to transgress physically or legally or morally ‖ to trespass ‖ to invade.

TRANSLINEAR.
v, to pass on certain hereditary rights in property from one line of heirs to another.

TRANSMARINO.
adj, transoceanic, across the sea.

TRANSMEDITERRÁNEO.
adj, across the Mediterranean.

TRANSMIGRACIÓN.
f, transmigration ‖ emigration as a group.

TRANSMIGRAR.
v, to emigrate as a group or nation ‖ to transmigrate.

TRANSMISIBILIDAD.
f, transferability, alienability ‖ transmissibility ‖ contagiousness.

TRANSMISIBLE.
adj, transferable, alienable ‖ transmittable, transmissible ‖ contagious.

TRANSMISIÓN.
f, transmission ‖ communication, statement of something to another ‖ transfer, alienation, transference ‖ succession ‖ assignment (of property) ‖ renunciation, waiver (of a right) ‖ radio or television transmission or communication ‖ contagion ‖ propagation.

TRANSMISIÓN DE CRÉDITO.
novation of creditor (pursuant to a new co tract) ‖ subrogation of creditor (pursuant the same contract).

TRANSMISIÓN DE DEUDA.
novation of debtor (pursuant to a new co tract) ‖ subrogation of debtor (pursuant to t same contract).

TRANSMISIÓN DE DERECHOS.
See CESIÓN DE DERECHOS (if inter vinos tra fer) ‖ see SUCESIÓN (if causa mortis transfe

TRANSMISIÓN DE LA COSA AJENA.
transfer of property of another.

TRANSMISIÓN DE LA COSA GRAVADA.
transfer of encumbered property.

TRANSMISIÓN DE LAS ACCIONES.
stock transfer.

TRANSMISIÓN DE LAS OBLIGACIONE:
novation of obligations (by a new contract subrogation of obligations (pursuant to ' same contract). May be ACTIVA (subrogat of the creditor, assignment of creditor's rig or PASIVA (subrogation of the debtor, assi ment of debtor's rights).

TRANSMISIÓN DE LOS ALIMENTOS.
assignment of right to receive alimony or c support payments.

TRANSMISIÓN DEL MANDO.
inauguration of a president ‖ transfer of wer.

TRANSMISIÓN DEL PENSAMIENTO.
telepathy.

TRANSMISIÓN HEREDITARIA.
transfer by heredity ‖ inheritance.

TRANSMISIONES.
military communications corps, signal corp

TRANSMISOR.
m, transmitter ‖ dispatcher (of commun tions) ‖ transmitting machine, transmitte telephone.

TRANSMITENTE.
f, m, transferor, person who alienates or ce or disposes of property.

TRANSMITIR.
v, to transmit ‖ to communicate ‖ to disp (communications) ‖ to establish commun tion ‖ to spread contagion, contaminate teach ‖ to reveal ‖ to transfer power ‖ tc augurate (as president or other governm authority) ‖ to transfer, alienate, cede, disp (of property) ‖ to transmit by third party

grant by testament ‖ to renounce or waive a right ‖ to leave rights or obligations due to death.

TRANSMUDACIÓN.
f, transmutation.

TRANSMUDAMIENTO.
See TRANSMUDACIÓN.

TRANSMUDAR.
v, to transmute, change.

TRANSMUTACIÓN.
transmutation, change, conversion.

TRANSMUTAR.
v, to transmute, change, convert.

TRANSPACÍFICO.
adj, transpacific.

TRANSPARENCIA.
f, transparency.

TRANSPONER.
v, to transfer ‖ to distance a person.

TRANSPONERSE.
v, to get out of sight, hide ‖ to set (re. the sun), go below the horizon.

TRANSPORTABLE.
adj, transportable.

TRANSPORTACIÓN.
f, transportation ‖ transport.

TRANSPORTADO.
adj, transported.

TRANSPORTADOR.
m, transporter, carrier.

TRANSPORTAR.
v, to transport, carry.

TRANSPORTARSE.
v, to be transported (beyond one's reason) ‖ to travel.

TRANSPORTE.
m, transport ‖ transportation, carriage, conveyance ‖ cargo ship ‖ transporting ‖ transportation contract ‖ costs of transportation ‖ passenger ship ‖ ship of war ‖ supply ship ‖ national transportation network.

TRANSPORTE AÉREO.
air transportation or transport.
See TRANSPORTE.

TRANSPORTE BENÉVOLO.
gratuitous transportation.
See TRANSPORTE.

TRANSPORTE DE ABASTECIMIENTOS POR AIRE.
food airlift.

TRANSPORTE DE CAUDALES.
transportation of wealth ‖ transport of funds.
See TRANSPORTE.

TRANSPORTE DE COSAS.
carriage of personal property.
See TRANSPORTE.

TRANSPORTE DE EMIGRANTES.
transportation of emigrants.
See TRANSPORTE.

TRANSPORTE DE EQUIPAJES.
transportation of baggage.
See TRANSPORTE.

TRANSPORTE DE NOTICIAS.
transmission of news or information.
See TRANSPORTE.

TRANSPORTE DE PERSONAS.
transportation of people. See TRANSPORTE.

TRANSPORTE DE VIAJEROS.
transportation of travelers. See TRANSPORTE.

TRANSPORTE FERROVIARIO.
rail transportation or transport.
See TRANSPORTE.

TRANSPORTE FLUVIAL.
river transportation. See TRANSPORTE.

TRANSPORTE LACUSTRE.
lake transportation. See TRANSPORTE.

TRANSPORTE MARÍTIMO.
maritime or ocean transportation.
See TRANSPORTE.

TRANSPORTE MERCANTIL.
commercial transportation, transportation for consideration. See TRANSPORTE.

TRANSPORTE POR AGUA.
transportation by water. See TRANSPORTE.

TRANSPORTE SANITARIO.
emergency evacuation ‖ transport or transfer of the sick or injured. See TRANSPORTE.

TRANSPORTE TERRESTRE.
ground transportation. See TRANSPORTE.

TRANSPORTE URBANO.
urban transportation. See TRANSPORTE.

TRANSPORTES.
m, military personnel transportation corps ‖ means of transportation.

TRANSPORTISTA.
f, m, (commercial) transporter or carrier.

TRANSPOSICIÓN.
m, transposition ‖ transfer ‖ hiding.

TRANSUBSTANCIACIÓN.
f, transubstantiation, change from one substance to another.

TRANSVERSAL.
f, cross street ‖ collateral relative ‖ adj, transversal ‖ oblique, diagonal ‖ cross.
TRANSVESTIMIENTO.
m, transvestism ‖ homosexuality.
TRANSVESTIDO.
adj, transvestite.
TRANSVESTE.
m, transvestite.
TRANZA.
f, judicial attachment, seizure, levy (of property).
TRAPICHEAR.
v, to sell at retail ‖ to use one's wits, devise, scheme (to do something illegal).
TRAPICHEO.
m, retail marketing or selling ‖ scheming activity (to do something illegal).
TRASATLÁNTICO.
See TRANSATLÁNTICO.
TRASBISABUELO.
See TATARABUELO.
TRASBISNIETO.
See TRANSBISNIETO.
TRASBORDAR.
See TRANSBORDAR.
TRASBORDO.
See TRANSBORDO.
TRASCENDENCIA.
f, transcendency ‖ importance ‖ repercussion, consequence, result, effect ‖ penetration ‖ publicity ‖ trespass (of a limit).
TRASCENDENTAL.
adj, transcendent ‖ important ‖ fundamental ‖ serious ‖ far-reaching.
TRASCENDENTE.
See TRASCENDENTAL.
TRASCENDER.
v, to transcend ‖ to come out, be known ‖ to learn about or know (something secret) ‖ to reach, spread (in effect or result) ‖ to ask about (something secret).
TRASCENDIDO.
m, person who learns of some private information very promptly ‖ rumor ‖ unofficial information ‖ adj, keen, sharp, perspicacious.
TRASCRIBIR.
See TRANSCRIBIR.
TRASCRIPCIÓN.
See TRANSCRIPCIÓN.
TRASCRITO.
See TRANSCRITO.

TRASCUENTA.
See TRABACUENTA.
TRASCURRIR.
See TRANSCURRIR.
TRASCURSO.
See TRANSCURSO.
TRASERO.
m, back, rear ‖ latter ‖ adj, back, rear ‖ fin latter.
TRASEROS.
m, ancestors.
TRASFERENCIA.
See TRANSFERENCIA.
TRASFERIBLE.
See TRANSFERIBLE.
TRASFERIR.
See TRANSFERIR.
TRASFIGURAR.
See TRANSFIGURAR.
TRASFIJO.
See TRANSFIJO.
TRASFIXIÓN.
See TRANSFIXIÓN.
TRASFORMACIÓN.
See TRANSFORMACIÓN.
TRASFORMADOR.
See TRANSFORMADOR.
TRASFORMAR.
See TRANSFORMAR.
TRÁSFUGA.
See TRÁNSFUGA.
TRASFUNDIR.
See TRANSFUNDIR.
TRASFUSIÓN.
See TRANSFUSIÓN.
TRASGREDIR.
See TRANSGREDIR.
TRASGRESIÓN.
See TRANSGRESIÓN.
TRASGRESOR.
See TRANSGRESOR.
TRASLACIÓN.
f, move, transfer (of an employee) ‖ tran tation, transport ‖ translation (into an language) ‖ back dating or postdating (e a contract) ‖ copy, transcription.
TRASLADAR.
v, to transfer, move (an employee) ‖ to port ‖ to back date or postdate (e.g. a me a contract) ‖ to translate (into anothe guage) ‖ to copy, transcribe ‖ to transpc

RASLADO.
m, move, transfer (of an employee) ‖ copy of a document ‖ translation (of a text) ‖ transportation, moving, passage, sending ‖ transmission ‖ forwarding.
RASLADO DE AUTOS.
forwarding of pleadings from one party to another such that the recipient respond.
RASLADO DE POBLACIONES.
transfer or removal of peoples (e.g. during war time).
RASLADO DE PRISIONEROS.
prisoner transfer.
RASLADO DE TRABAJO.
employee transfer, transfer of an employee
RASLADO LABORAL
DIARIO.
daily work commute.
RASLATIVO.
adj, transferring, moving ‖ translating ‖ transporting ‖ transmitting.
RASLINEAR.
See TRANSLINEAR.
RASLUCIRSE.
r, to be inferred or deduced.
RASMARINO.
See TRANSMARINO.
RASMEDITERRÁNEO.
See TRANSMEDITERRÁNEO.
RASMIGRACIÓN.
See TRANSMIGRACIÓN.
RASMIGRAR.
See TRANSMIGRAR.
RASMISIBLE.
See TRANSMISIBLE.
RASMISIÓN.
See TRANSMISIÓN.
RASMISOR.
See TRANSMISOR.
RASMITIR.
See TRANSMITIR.
RASMUDACIÓN.
See TRANSMUDACIÓN.
RASMUDAMIENTO.
See TRANSMUDAMIENTO.
RASMUDAR.
See TRANSMUDAR.
RASMUTACIÓN.
See TRANSMUTACIÓN.
RASNIETO.
See TATARANIETO.

TRASNOMBRAR.
v, to change or confuse names.
TRASPAPELARSE.
v, to disappear or be lost or confused (re. paper, files, etc.).
TRASPARENCIA.
See TRANSPARENCIA.
TRASPASABLE.
adj, transportable ‖ delegable ‖ alienable. See TRASPASO.
TRASPASADOR.
See TRANSGRESOR.
TRASPASAR.
v, to move ‖ to move ahead or up ‖ to cross, go over ‖ to exceed ‖ to wound (by firearm) ‖ to infringe, transgress ‖ to alienate, transfer, cede ‖ to waive a right ‖ to assign a rental contract ‖ to sell a commercial establishment.
TRASPASO.
m, transportation, transport ‖ transfer, move ‖ cross over, trespass ‖ excess, transgression ‖ ruse, scheme, plot ‖ affliction, torment ‖ waiver, renunciation (of a right) ‖ transfe-rence ‖ alienation, cession (of property rights) ‖ sale of a commercial establishment ‖ inheritance of a commercial establishment ‖ assignment of a rental contract.
TRASPASO DE CUENTA CORRIENTE.
transfer of a current account.
TRASPASO DE EMPRESA.
sale of a business ‖ corporate buy-out (by another corporation).
TRASPIÉ.
m, error, mistake ‖ slip-up ‖ mess.
TRASPLANTAR.
v, to transplant ‖ to change location.
TRASPLANTARSE.
v, to move, emigrate.
TRASPLANTE.
m, transplant, transplantation.
TRASPLANTE
DE ÓRGANOS.
organ transplant.
TRASPONER.
See TRANSPONER.
TRASPONERSE.
See TRANSPONERSE.
TRASPORTABLE.
See TRANSPORTABLE.
TRASPORTACIÓN.
See TRANSPORTACIÓN.

TRASPORTADOR.
See TRANSPORTADOR.

TRASPORTAR.
See TRANSPORTAR.

TRASPORTARSE.
See TRANSPORTARSE.

TRASPORTE.
See TRANSPORTE.

TRASPOSICIÓN.
See TRANSPOSICIÓN.

TRASTOCAR.
v, to mix-up, confuse, disturb, upset.

TRASTOCARSE.
v, to go crazy, go out of one's mind.

TRASTORNADOR.
m, disturber, person who disturbs or upsets or confuses || corrupter || agitator.

TRANSTORNAR.
v, to turn (something) around, turn upside down || to alter, change (a given order) || to confuse || to agitate, incite (to rebel) || to make (someone) crazy or go insane || to seduce || to change one's opinion or mind, switch sides || to corrupt.

TRASTORNO.
m, complete change in position, upset || social or political agitation || perturbation, disturbance || chaos, confusion || harm, injury, damage || insanity, mental derangement.

TRASTORNO MENTAL.
insanity, mental derangement.

TRASTORNO MENTAL TRANSITORIO.
temporary insanity.

TRASTOS.
m, tools of the trade || worthless objects.

TRASTRABILLAR.
v, to vacillate || to stutter, stammer.

TRASTROCAMIENTO.
m, revolution || disorder || upset || mental disturbance || insanity.

TRASTROCAR.
v, to change.

TRASUNTAR.
v, to copy, transcribe (exactly) || to suggest, imply.

TRASUNTO.
m, exact copy or transcription || imitation, representation.

TRASVERSAL.
See TRANSVERSAL.

TRATA.
f, slave trade, trade in human beings.

TRATA DE BLANCAS.
White slave trade.

TRATA DE ESCLAVOS.
slave trade || Black slave trade.

TRATA DE NEGROS.
Black slave trade.

TRATABLE.
adj, sociable || reasonable || accessible.

TRATADISTA.
f, m, writer of a treatise or other lengthy work.

TRATADO.
m, (international) treaty || convention, proto col, covenant, compact, concordat || treatise lengthy intellectual work || agreement, con tract || book, volume, tome (of a legal text).

TRATADO-CONTRATO.
m, (international) treaty || (international) trea ty-contract.

TRATADO DE ALIANZA.
treaty of alliance.

TRATADO DE AMISTAD.
treaty of friendship, friendship treaty.

TRATADO DE ASISTENCIA MUTUA.
treaty of mutual assistance.

TRATADO DE ASISTENCIA RECÍPROCA.
treaty of mutual assistance.

TRATADO DE COMERCIO.
commercial treaty.

TRATADO DE EXTRADICIÓN.
extradition treaty.

TRATADO DE INDEMNIZACIÓN.
indemnification treaty.

TRATADO DE JURISDICCIÓN.
jurisdictional treaty or convention.

TRATADO DE NEUTRALIDAD.
neutrality pact or treaty.

TRATADO DE NEUTRALIZACIÓN.
convention of neutrality, agreement of vario nations to recognize the neutrality of anoth nation.

TRATADO DE PAZ.
peace treaty.

TRATADO ECONÓMICO.
economic treaty or convention.

TRATADO GENERAL.
general treaty.

TRATADO INTERNACIONAL.
international treaty.

RATADO-LEY.
m, (international) treaty-law.

RATADO POLÍTICO.
political treaty.

RATAMIENTO.
m, treatment ‖ style, honorific title ‖ medical treatment ‖ experimental procedure.

RATAMIENTO DE DETENIDOS Y PRESOS.
treatment of detainees and prisoners.

RATAMIENTOS.
See MALOS TRATOS.

RATANTE.
n, dealer, trader, person who buys for resale and usually does not have a fixed locale from which he works.

RATANTE DE BLANCAS.
White slave trader.

RATAR.
v, to treat ‖ to deal with ‖ to manage ‖ to intervene in, get involved in (a matter) ‖ to arrange for, take steps to carry out ‖ to address, call a person (by a title) ‖ to take care of something ‖ to attempt, try ‖ to deal in, do business in ‖ to maintain a relationship of love or friendship.

RATAR MAL DE PALABRA.
to insult, injure verbally.

RATO.
n, treatment ‖ dealing, dealings ‖ management (of a thing) ‖ use, service (of a thing) ‖ comportment, manner, way ‖ loving relationship ‖ style, (honorific) title ‖ traffic, commerce, business ‖ interest, relationship ‖ business of a dealer or trader ‖ treaty, compromise, agreement, pact.

RATO CARNAL.
exual relations.

RATO DE PRISIONEROS.
prisoner treatment.

RATO DESIGUAL.
nequal treatment, favoritism.

RATO DOBLE.
double-dealing.

RAUMA.
n, trauma.

RAUMA PSÍQUICO.
psychological trauma.

RAVESÍA.
side road ‖ cross street ‖ portion of highway which crosses through a city ‖ ocean trip or crossing or voyage ‖ special seaman's pay (from one port to another) ‖ amount won or lost at gambling ‖ distance from one point to another.

TRAVESURA.
f, (youthful) prank.

TRAVIESO.
m, rogue, ne'er do well, miscreant ‖ adj, naughty, undisciplined.

TRAYECTO.
m, space from one point to another ‖ run, stretch ‖ distance, piece of road ‖ each of the distances of a bus or train trip for which a different fare is charged.

TRAYECTORIA.
f, trajectory ‖ path, course ‖ employment background, personal work history.

TRAZA.
f, plan, design ‖ idea ‖ means (of carrying something out) ‖ appearance, looks (of a person) ‖ trace.

TRAZAR.
v, to plan, design ‖ to conceive of, come up with (e.g. an idea) ‖ to trace ‖ to set forth the character of a person or the nature of a matter involved in a case.

TRAZO.
m, line ‖ trace ‖ tracing, delineation ‖ outline.

TRECHO.
m, stretch, distance, period (in time or space).

TREGUA.
f, truce, cease-fire ‖ rest.

TREINTAÑAL.
adj, thirty-year ‖ prolonged.

TREMENDO.
adj, terrible ‖ tremendous ‖ large, big.

TREN.
m, train.

TREN HOSPITAL.
hospital train.

TREN SANITARIO.
hospital train, train used to take emergency medical treatment to disaster victims.

TREPADO.
m, dotted line, line of perforations (upon which to tear a paper).

TREPIDAR.
v, to tremble.

TRIBADISMO.
m, lesbianism.

TRIBU.
f, tribe.

TRIBULACIÓN.
f, tribulation ‖ misfortune, adversity.

TRIBUNA.
f, tribune ‖ rostrum, dais, podium, pulpit, public platform ‖ gallery, stand ‖ body of political speakers (of a nation).

TRIBUNAL.
m, tribunal, court of justice, judicature, judiciary ‖ tribunal, group of judges who together hear and decide a case ‖ courtroom ‖ courthouse ‖ body of judges (in a given jurisdiction) ‖ board of examiners (at a university).

TRIBUNAL A QUO.
lower court tribunal or court, court from which an appeal is taken.

TRIBUNAL AD QUEM.
appellate or appeals court, court of appeals.

TRIBUNAL ADMINISTRATIVO.
administrative appeals court or tribunal.

TRIBUNAL ARBITRAL.
board of arbitration, arbitration board or court or tribunal.

TRIBUNAL CIVIL.
civil court or tribunal, court which has jurisdiction over civil matters (exclusive of commercial matters).

TRIBUNAL COLEGIADO.
three-judge court ‖ court in which three or more judges decide a case.

TRIBUNAL CONSTITUCIONAL.
constitutional court, court which has jurisdiction to hear cases involving constitutional issues.

TRIBUNAL CRIMINAL.
criminal court or tribunal, court which has jurisdiction over criminal matters.

TRIBUNAL DE CASACIÓN.
court of cassation, court which has jurisdiction to hear a RECURSO DE CASACIÓN.

TRIBUNAL DE COMERCIO.
commercial court.

TRIBUNAL DE CUENTAS.
government accounting office, administrative court which reviews the legitimacy of government expenditures and determines whether they fall within the budget.

TRIBUNAL DE EXAMEN.
board of examiners, board of examinations (in educational institutions).

TRIBUNAL DE EXCEPCIÓN.
court which has jurisdiction over extraord nary matters (e.g. military court).

TRIBUNAL DE FALTAS.
police or misdemeanor court (if criminal a tion) or small claims court (if civil action). M include traffic court.

TRIBUNAL DE GARANTÍAS CONSTITUCIONALES.
court with jurisdiction to hear cases involvi constitutional issues.

TRIBUNAL DE HONOR.
non-judicial court which is organized to he challenges to conduct of members of a body profession.

TRIBUNAL DE INSTANCIA.
court which has jurisdiction to hear questio of both fact and law.

TRIBUNAL DE LA INQUISICIÓN.
court of inquisition.

TRIBUNAL DE MENORES.
juvenile court.

TRIBUNAL DE POLICÍA.
police or misdemeanor court.

TRIBUNAL DE SIMPLE POLICÍA.
See TRIBUNAL DE POLICÍA

TRIBUNAL EXTRANJERO.
foreign court or tribunal.
Opposed to TRIBUNAL NACIONAL.

TRIBUNAL FEDERAL.
federal court.

TRIBUNAL INTERNACIONAL.
international tribunal or court of justice (w jurisdiction to hear either criminal or civil m ters).

TRIBINAL MARÍTIMO.
maritime court or tribunal.

TRIBUNAL MILITAR.
military court or tribunal.

TRIBUNAL NACIONAL.
national court.
Opposed to TRIBUNAL EXTRANJERO.

TRIBUNAL PERMAMENTE DE JUSTICI INTERNATIONAL.
International Court of Justice.

TRIBUNAL SENTENCIADOR.
sentencing court or tribunal ‖ military cou

TRIBUNAL SUPREMO.
supreme court.

TRIBUNAL UNIPERSONAL.
one-judge court or tribunal.

TRIBUNALES
DE TRABAJO.
labor court, courts which have jurisdiction to
hear labor disputes.
TRIBUTABLE.
adj, taxable ‖ dutiable ‖ able or appropriate to
be paid tribute or respect to.
TRIBUTACIÓN.
paying of taxes or duties ‖ act of paying taxes
tax ‖ tax system ‖ paying of tribute of respect
see also ENFITEUSIS.
TRIBUTANTE.
m, taxpayer ‖ adj, taxable ‖ contributing ‖
tribute payer.
TRIBUTAR.
to pay (government) taxes or duties ‖ to
contribute goods or services to the state as
payment of taxes ‖ to mark boundaries ‖ to
pay tribute or respect to.
TRIBUTARIO.
, taxpayer ‖ tributary ‖ adj, contributing ‖
tax, duty, pertaining to taxes or duties ‖ taxing
subject to tax ‖ pertaining to tribute or respect ‖ tributary (of a river).
TRIBUTO.
, tribute, respect, homage ‖ tax, impost, duty
right of way, easement, servitude.
TRIGAMIA.
third marriage, marriage for a third time ‖
gamy, marriage to three women.
TRILEMA.
multiple choices or opportunities.
TRILINGÜE.
adj, trilingual.
TRILLADO.
adj, everyday, commonplace, trite.
TRIMESTRE.
, trimester ‖ quarterly payment or annuity,
payment or annuity paid quarterly ‖ salary
paid quarterly ‖ adj, quarterly, trimestral, tri-
mestrial.
TRINIDAD.
(Holy) Trinity ‖ trio who run a business.
TRIPARTICIÓN.
m, tri-partition, division into thirds.
TRIPARTIR.
to divide into thirds.
TRIPARTITO.
adj, tripartite, divided into three parts ‖ elected by a group of three parties ‖ carried out by
three persons.

TRIPLE.
adj, triple ‖ treble ‖ three times as much ‖ of
thirds, made up of thirds.
TRÍPLICA.
f, surrejoinder, pleading written in answer to
defendant's rejoinder.
TRIPLICACIÓN.
f, triplication ‖ trebling ‖ plaintiff's third
rejoinder, act of answering a DÚPLICA.
TRIPLICAR.
v, to triple ‖ to file a (plaintiff's) third rejoinder, answer a DÚPLICA.
TRIPULACIÓN.
f, ship's crew ‖ airplane crew ‖ crew.
TRIPULANTE.
m, crew member, member of a crew (e.g. of a
ship, airplane).
TRIPULAR.
v, to man (e.g. a vessel), be a crew member ‖
to fly (e.g. a plane) or captain (a vessel).
TRIQUIÑUELA.
f, trick, trickery, underhanded deal.
TRISEMANAL.
adj, triweekly, three times per week ‖ every
three weeks.
TRISTE.
adj, sad, unhappy ‖ lamentable, miserable,
sorry ‖ painful ‖ ridiculous ‖ insignificant, insufficient, meager.
TRISTEZA.
f, sadness, unhappiness ‖ affliction ‖ pain, suffering ‖ death penalty.
TRITURAR.
v, to mistreat ‖ to crush, reduce (something)
to ashes or dust ‖ to bother ‖ to refute, contradict.
TRIUNFADOR.
m, winner, victor ‖ adj, triumphant, victorious,
winning.
TRIUNFAL.
adj, triumphant, victorious, winning.
TRIUNFAR.
v, to triumph (over), be victorious, win ‖ to
beat ‖ to spend money ostentatiously ‖ to conquer.
TRIUNFO.
m, triumph, victory, win ‖ trophy, winnings ‖
success.
TRIUNVIRATO.
m, triumvirate or group of three persons who
lead a revolution of civil war.

TRIVIAL.
adj, trivial, insignificant ‖ trite, commonplace ‖ vulgar, ordinary.

TRIZAR.
v, to break into little bits or pieces ‖ to destroy.

TROCABLE.
adj, exchangeable, able to be exchanged or switched.

TROCADO.
See DINERO TROCADO.

TROCADOR.
m, exchanger, switcher, person who exchanges something.

TROCAMIENTO.
See PERMUTA.

TROCAR.
v, to exchange, switch ‖ to confuse, mix-up, muddle ‖ to change, alter.

TRONCAL.
adj, trunk, pertaining to a trunk ‖ main. See TRONCO.

TRONCALIDAD.
f, principle of intestacy by which property is passed to one's ascendants.

TRONCO.
m, trunk, base from which two branches of a family are joined ‖ trunk (e.g. of a tree, person) ‖ boor.

TRONGA.
f, concubine.

TRONO.
m, throne.

TRONQUERO.
m, person who has right to inherit pursuant to TRONCALIDAD.

TROPA.
f, troop, troops ‖ group, crowd ‖ herd (of cattle).

TROPA CÍVICA.
civil defense troops.

TROPA IRREGULAR.
troops which are not part of the regular armed forces.

TROPAS.
f, (armed forces) unit ‖ troops (in the armed forces) ‖ forces.

**TROPAS
DE POLICÍA.**
police force.

TROPAS MERCENARIAS.
mercenary forces or troops or unit.

TRUEQUE.
See PERMUTA.

TRUHÁN.
m, cheat ‖ liar ‖ boaster ‖ disloyal person ‖ ac cheating ‖ lying ‖ boasting ‖ disloyal.

TRUHANADA.
See TRUJANERÍA.

TRUHANEAR.
v, to trick, cheat.

TRUJANERÍA.
f, lie ‖ trick, swindle ‖ gang of cheats or liars ◄ scoundrels.

TRUNCADO.
adj, cut off, truncated, truncate.

TRUNCAR.
v, to truncate, cut off ‖ to reduce, cut short to chop of a head ‖ to mutilate ‖ to frustrat impede.

TUICIÓN.
f, legal protection or defense.

TUITIVO.
adj, protecting, protective ‖ defense, defen ing ‖ defensive (legally).

TULLIDO.
m, adj, paralytic ‖ invalid ‖ crippled, maime

TULLIMIENTO.
m, disablement, state of being crippled or m med or paralytic.

TULLIR.
v, to cripple, maim, paralyze, disable.

TUMBA.
f, tomb ‖ grave.

**TUMBA
DE COMBATIENTE.**
soldier's grave (in the field of war).

TUMOR.
m, tumor.

TUMULTO.
m, mob ‖ riot, revolt ‖ public disorder ‖ cc fusion, commotion.

TUMULTUACIÓN.
See TUMULTO.

TUMULTUANTE.
m, rioter, person who revolts ‖ part or part pant of a mob ‖ adj, agitating ‖ rioting.

TUMULTUAR.
v, to incite to riot or revolt ‖ to agitate.

TUMULTUARIO.
See TUMULTUOSO.

TUMULTUOSO.
adj, agitating ‖ rioting.

"TUNC".
See EX TUNC.
TUNDA.
f, thrashing || defeat, rout.
TUNDEAR.
v, to thrash, beat.
TÚNEL.
m, tunnel.
TÚNICA.
f, tunic, robe, robes, gown.
TURBA.
f, mob, disorderly crowd.
TURBACIÓN.
f, disturbance || perturbation || embarrassment || disorder.
TURBACIÓN DE LA POSESIÓN.
disturbance of possessory rights || disturbance of use and quiet enjoyment.
TURBANTE.
adj, disturbing, perturbing || embarrassing.
TURBAR.
v, to disturb, perturb || to change, alter (the course of something) || to disconcert || to interrupt violently || to incite a riot or revolt || to bother || to confuse || to embarrass.
TURBULENCIA.
f, turbulence, perturbation (e.g. of peace, order, a legal right) || confusion || political or social agitation.
TURBULENTO.
adj, turbulent || disquieting || violent || confused.
TURNAR.
v, to alternate, take turns || to send a communication, file, or pleading from one judge or tribunal or government official to another.
TURNO.
m, turn, shift, rotation.
TURNO JUDICIAL.
rotation of judicial duties among various courts or judges.
TUTELA.
f, guardianship, custodianship, custody || protection || guardianship of minors || guardianship of the legally incapacitated.
TUTELA ADMINISTRATIVA.
institutional guardianship by a public institution.
TUTELA DADA POR LOS PADRES.
See TUTELA TESTAMENTARIA.

TUTELA DATIVA.
court-appointed guardianship.
TUTELA DE HECHO.
de facto guardianship.
TUTELA DE LOS HIJOS NATURALES.
guardianship of natural children.
TUTELA DE LOS LOCOS.
guardianship of the insane.
TUTELA DE LOS MENORES.
guardianship of minors.
TUTELA DE LOS PRÓDIGOS.
guardianship of spend-thrifts.
TUTELA DE LOS SORDOMUDOS.
guardianship of deaf-mutes.
TUTELA DE LOS SUJETOS A INTERDICCIÓN.
representation of persons who have been stripped of rights to administer their property. See INTERDICCIÓN CIVIL.
TUTELA EJEMPLAR.
guardianship of the mentally disabled or ill.
TUTELA ESPECIAL.
special guardianship.
TUTELA LEGÍTIMA.
statutory guardianship, guardianship pursuant to statute (due to the lack or invalidity of the TUTELA TESTAMENTARIA).
TUTELA PENAL.
custody in a minimum security prison.
TUTELA PLENA.
full guardianship (involving a TUTOR, PRO-TUTOR and the CONSEJO DE FAMILIA).
TUTELA RESTRINGIDA.
restricted guardianship (involving only a TU-TOR).
TUTELA TESTAMENTARIA.
guardianship of minor children pursuant to will || trusteeship for the care and protection of minors (pursuant to a will).
TUTELADO.
adj, guardianship, subject to a guardianship || tutelary || incapacitated.
TUTELAR.
adj, protective, defense, defensive || guardian, directive, guiding || pertaining to a guardianship of minors or incapacitated persons || v, to protect || to guard || to guide.
TUTOR.
m, tutor || guardian || custodian || administrator, director, guide, adviser || defender, protector.

TUTOR AD HOC.

ad hoc guardian, guardian for certain specified actions.

TUTOR DATIVO.

court-appointed guardian.

TUTOR DE HECHO.

de facto guardian.

TUTOR LEGÍTIMO.

statutory guardian, guardian appointed pursuant to statute.

TUTOR

TESTAMENTARIO.

guardian of minor children pursuant to wil trustee of minors (pursuant to will).

TUTORA.

f, female guardian.

TUTORÍA.

f, position, functions, and term of a guardia see also TUTELA.

U

UBICACIÓN.
f, location, situation, position ‖ work, employment ‖ purpose, destination.

UBICAR.
v, to locate or situate or position oneself (in a place) ‖ to become or get situated ‖ to employ ‖ to assign work (in a business or office).

UBICUIDAD.
f, ubiquity ‖ omnipresence ‖ intense activity which involves frequent changes of location.

UBICUO.
m, person who is able to do more than one thing at the same time ‖ adj, ubiquitous.

UCASE.
m, tyrannical or capricious decree or order.

UJIER.
m, doorman ‖ judicial employee who keeps order in a courtroom (i.e. bailiff), serves notices and orders of the president of the Courts of Appeals (i.e. sheriff), and takes care of other sundry matters (court clerk).

ULTERIOR.
adj, ulterior ‖ beyond (in time and space) ‖ posterior, subsequent, following.

ÚLTIMA ENFERMEDAD.
f, final illness (before death).

ÚLTIMA PALABRA.
final decision or resolution ‖ final word, last say ‖ final offer.

ÚLTIMA PENA.
death sentence.

ÚLTIMA VOLUNTAD.
last will and testament.

ULTIMACIÓN.
f, conclusion, end, finish (to something long and drawn out).

ULTIMADOR.
m, concluder, finisher, person who end killer, murderer.

ÚLTIMAMENTE.
adv, lately, recently ‖ final, decisively.

ULTIMAR.
v, to conclude, end, terminate ‖ to put finishing touches on ‖ to kill, finish off.

ÚLTIMAS NOTICIAS.
last word or news (of someone or somethin

ÚLTIMAS PALABRAS.
last words, conclusion (of a speech) ‖ dy words, last words (before death).

ULTIMATO.
See ULTIMÁTUM.

ULTIMÁTUM.
m, ultimatum.

ULTIMIDAD.
f, ultimateness, finality, condition of being l

ÚLTIMO.
m, final recourse ‖ final offer ‖ the latest, last ‖ the best ‖ the worst ‖ the highest ‖ farthest ‖ adj, last, final ‖ latest (in time) ‖ ter ‖ best ‖ worst ‖ highest ‖ farthest (in spa ‖ superior.

ÚLTIMO DOMICILIO.
present domicile ‖ last known domicile.

ÚLTIMO DOMICILIO CONOCIDO.
last known domicile.

ÚLTIMO PAGO.
last payment ‖ final payment (in an installm contract).

ÚLTIMO PLAZO.
last term ‖ final term ‖ maturity or expira date ‖ final extension period ‖ final extens for making an already late payment.

TIMO SUPLICIO.
ath penalty.

TIMO VIAJE.
t journey (of a ship prior to being sold).

TRA PETITA".
e SENTENCIA "ULTRA PETITA".

TRA VIRES HAEREDITATIS".
yond the decedent's estate. Refers to the ligation of the heir who has accepted the inritance unconditionally to pay the debts of e estate out of the estate's and his or her own nds.

TRAJADOR.
, injurer ‖ insulter, offender ‖ humiliator ‖ ist.

TRAJAR.
to injure ‖ to outrage ‖ to insult, offend ‖ to miliate ‖ to rape.

TRAJE.
injury ‖ outrage ‖ offense, insult ‖ humiliasn ‖ rape.

TRAJE A LA NACIÓN.
ason against the nation.

TRAJE A LOS SÍMBOLOS CIONALES.
ult to national symbols (e.g. flag, hymn).

TRAJE AL PUDOR.
ral offense, sex or sexual offense (exclusive such acts which include sexual intercourse).

TRAJOSO.
i, offensive, insulting ‖ humiliating ‖ outra-bus ‖ injurious.

TRAMAR.
overseas country, country which is overseas dj, overseas.

NIME.
j, unanimous.

NIMIDAD.
unanimity ‖ total agreement ‖ law, agree-ent, or statement adopted unanimously.

CAMENTE.
v, only, solely.

CAMERAL.
j, unicameral, one-chamber.

CAMERALISMO.
unicameralism, existence of one chamber a parliament, congress, or legislature.

CIDAD.
niqueness ‖ exclusivity.

CIDAD SINDICAL.
or union exclusivity. Refers to right of a la-bor union to be the exclusive representative of employees in a certain area or activity.

UNIDAD.
f, unity, indivisibility ‖ oneness ‖ union ‖ harmony, coordination ‖ conformity ‖ measure of comparison ‖ unit ‖ military unit ‖ military troop ‖ each one, each.

UNIDAD ADMINISTRATIVA.
administrative agency or unit.

UNIDAD DE ACCIÓN.
unity of action in both a general and procedural sense ‖ coordination of activity (toward one goal).

UNIDAD DE DEFENSA.
unity of defense. Refers to the indivisibility of various defendant's interests represented by one attorney.

UNIDAD DE FUERO.
unity of jurisdiction. Refers to the submission of all parties to the jurisdiction of the same court in order to avoid multiplicity of lawsuits.

UNIDAD DE MANDO.
unity of command or authority (in one individual).

UNIDAD DE MEDIDA.
unit of measurement, unit of weights and measures.

UNIDAD DE PESO.
unit of weight.

UNIDAD DE TIEMPO.
unit of time.

UNIDAD DEL ACTO.
unity of all stages of a legal action or contract such that they constitute one act.

UNIDAD MONETARIA.
monetary unit.

UNIDAD NACIONAL.
national unity ‖ centralist (governmental) regime ‖ constitutional and legal system pursuant to which the same laws and principles govern an entire nation.

UNIDAD ORGÁNICA.
organic unit, administrative unit which exists independently.

UNIDAMENTE.
adv, unitedly, indivisibly ‖ harmoniously ‖ with coordination ‖ together ‖ in agreement.

UNIDO.
adj, united, indivisible ‖ harmonious, coordinated ‖ in a block ‖ tied together ‖ gathered together.

UNIFICACIÓN.
f, unification ‖ national unification (of various territories, etc.).
UNIFICAR.
v, to unify, bring together ‖ to impose the same laws and principles over an entire nation.
UNIFORMAR.
v, to make uniform (two or more things), standardize ‖ to unify, bring together ‖ to outfit with uniforms.
UNIFORME.
m, uniform, outfit ‖ military uniform ‖ adj, uniform, equal ‖ similar.
UNIFORME DE TRABAJO.
work uniform or outfit.
UNIFORMEMENTE.
adv, uniformly ‖ equally ‖ similarly.
UNIFORMIDAD.
f, uniformity ‖ equality ‖ similarity.
UNIGÉNITO.
m, only child ‖ adj, only-begotten.
UNILATERAL.
adj, unilateral ‖ partial, one-sided ‖ half, related by one parent alone.
UNIÓN.
f, union ‖ tie, connection, bond ‖ confusion (of goods), mixing ‖ mixture ‖ joining together ‖ bringing together ‖ federation, league, confederation, alliance ‖ harmony ‖ marriage ‖ unity, unification ‖ labor organization, guild ‖ organization ‖ agreement.
UNIÓN ADMINISTRATIVA.
international organization to coordinate services and technical matters.
UNIÓN ADUANERA.
customs union, international tariff agreement, international customs duties agreement (to eliminate export or import duties).
UNIÓN DE COSAS DE DISTINTOS DUEÑOS.
union of personal property of different owners such that they form a new thing, whether its parts are distinguishable or not.
UNIÓN DE ESTADOS.
unification of independent states.
UNIÓN DE INTERESES.
unity of interest ‖ joining commercial interests of various businesses together.
UNIÓN ECONÓMICA.
international economic community, union of nations for economic purposes (e.g. European Economic Community).

UNIÓN LIBRE.
common law marriage, union of a man ar woman as husband and wife without the be fit of a legal marriage.
UNIÓN MONETARIA.
international monetary agreement, inte‌ tional agreement regarding questions of ‌ ment and currency exchange.
UNIÓN PERSONAL.
partial federation, alliance of two nations led by the same sovereign, but with total ir pendence internally and internationally.
UNIÓN PROFESIONAL.
professional organization.
UNIÓN REAL.
true federation, alliance of two nations r‌ by the same sovereign and same governn‌ internationally, but with total independe internally.
UNIONISMO.
m, unionism ‖ movement or ideology favo unification (of parties, groups, nations, t‌ tories, etc.).
UNIONISTA.
f, union member ‖ member of a confedera or alliance or union or organization or gu‌
UNIPERSONAL.
adj, unipersonal ‖ individual, one-person ‖ taining to one person.
UNIR.
v, to unite ‖ to link, join ‖ to bring togeth to tie, connect, bond together ‖ to con (goods), mix up ‖ to unify ‖ to incorpo‌ annex ‖ to marry (others).
UNIRSE.
v, to confederate, ally, federate ‖ to asso‌ oneself ‖ to wed, marry, get married ‖ to together ‖ to consolidate, merge, collect t ther, amalgamate, combine.
UNISEXUAL.
adj, unisex, unisexual.
UNÍSONO.
adj, unison.
UNITARIO.
m, unitarian, follower of unity of organiza‌ ‖ centralist ‖ adj, unitarian ‖ unitary ‖ un‌ ‖ unit, per unit.
UNITARISMO.
m, doctrine or movement supportive of p‌ cal and administrative unity ‖ Unitarianis

UNIVERSAL.
adj, universal, global, world ‖ earthly ‖ international ‖ all-encompassing ‖ pertaining to a personal estate as a whole. Opposed to NACIONAL, ORDINARIO, PARTICULAR, SINGULAR.

UNIVERSALIDAD.
f, universality ‖ (total) estate, totality of property (inclusive of rights and obligations) ‖ group of property.

UNIVERSALIDAD DE DERECHO.
group of property created by law and only divisible as permitted legally.

UNIVERSALIDAD DE HECHO.
group of property formed by the will of the owner and divisible by such owner.

UNIVERSALIDAD JURÍDICA.
See UNIVERSALIDAD DE DERECHO.

UNIVERSALISMO.
m, universalism.

UNIVERSALIZAR.
v, to universalize ‖ to generalize.

UNIVERSALMENTE.
adv, universally ‖ unanimously.

UNIVERSIDAD.
f, university, college ‖ university campus or building ‖ university authorities ‖ university as a corporation ‖ universality ‖ entirety of corporate members.

UNIVERSITARIO.
adj, university.

"UNIVERSITAS".
See UNIVERSALIDAD ‖ group of persons.

UNÍVOCO.
adj, univocal, of one voice.

UNTAR LA MANO.
to suborn.

URANISMO.
m, male homosexuality.

URANISTA.
m, male homosexual.

URBANIDAD.
f, urbanity, civility ‖ politeness, courtesy.

URBANISMO.
m, city planning, creation and development and reform of cities.

URBANIZACIÓN.
f, urbanization, real estate development ‖ city planning.

URBANIZAR.
v, to urbanize ‖ to develop real estate ‖ to make into a city.

URBANO.
m, member of city police force ‖ adj, urban, city ‖ built-up, developed ‖ populated, peopled ‖ urbane, polite, courteous, civil.

URBE.
m, big city, metropolis ‖ state capital.

URDIMBRE.
m, plot, scheme ‖ conspiracy.

URDIR.
v, to plot, scheme ‖ to conspire.

URGENCIA.
f, urgency ‖ necessity ‖ immediate legal obligation.

URGENTE.
adj, urgent, pressing ‖ immediate, unpostponable ‖ expedited.

URGIR.
v, to urge, push ‖ to oblige.

URNA.
f, urn ‖ ballot box ‖ election.

URNA CINERARIA.
cremation urn.

U.R.S.S.
f, UNIÓN DE LAS REPÚBLICAS SOCIALISTAS SOVIÉTICAS, Unión of Socialist Soviet Republics, U.S.S.R.

USADO.
adj, used, second-hand ‖ employed, utilized, used ‖ worn-out ‖ used up, wasted, spent ‖ ruined ‖ usual, ritual, customary.

USADOR.
m, user ‖ utilizer.

USANZA.
f, usage, custom, practice ‖ habit ‖ legal use.

USAR.
v, to use ‖ to employ, utilize, use ‖ to practice, carry out (an activity) ‖ to exercise (a right) ‖ to accustom ‖ to enjoy (a thing).

USAR DE SU DERECHO.
to file an action, to bring a complaint ‖ to exercise a right or liberty.

USÍA.
Your Honor, Your Lordship.

USO.
m, use ‖ usage, practice, custom ‖ fashion ‖ way, manner ‖ exercise of a right ‖ right to use ‖ right to gratuitous enjoyment of the fruits of another's property for the one's basic needs. Also see DERECHO DE USO and DERECHO CONSUETUDINARIO.

USO DE NOMBRE SUPUESTO.
use of an assumed name or alias.

USO DE RAZÓN.
use of (ability to) reason, use of reasoning.

USO ESTATAL.
government use.

USO ILEGÍTIMO DEL AUTOMOTOR.
car theft, illegal use of an automobile, joyriding.

USO INDEBIDO DE ATRIBUCIONES.
improper use of authority or powers.

USO INDEBIDO DE INSIGNIAS.
improper use of military insignia.

**USO INDEBIDO
DE UNIFORME.**
improper use of uniform.

USO JUDICIAL.
judicial practice or custom or usage.

USO PÚBLICO.
use of public property ‖ custom or practice regarding public property.

USOS CONVENCIONALES.
customary practices or usage ‖ customs.

USOS DEL COMERCIO.
business practices.

USOS INNOCUOS.
harmless uses (e.g. of other's property).

USOS LOCALES.
local customs or usage or practices.

USOS SOCIALES.
social customs or usage or practices.

USOS TÉCNICOS.
technical uses or practices.

USUAL.
adj, usual ‖ common ‖ habitual ‖ accustomed ‖ customary.

USUARIO.
m, user ‖ titleholder to a right of use ‖ license holder to right to public waters ‖ adj, having limited use of a thing.

USUCAPIÓN.
m, adverse possession, right to ownership by means of prolonged possession as owner.

USUCAPIR.
v, to acquire by adverse possession.

USUFRUCTO.
m, usufruct, right of enjoyment of or right to use another's property and to take the fruits therefrom without altering its substance. Usually temporary and may be gratuitous or for consideration.

USUFRUCTO CONVENCIONAL.
contractual usufruct.
See USUFRUCTO.

USUFRUCTO DE ANIMALES.
usufruct for the use of animals.
See USUFRUCTO.

USUFRUCTO DE COSAS CONSUMIBLES.
quasi-usufruct, usufruct for the use of consumables.
See CUASIUSUFRUCTO and USUFRUCTO.

USUFRUCTO DE EDIFICIOS.
usufruct for the use of buildings.
See USUFRUCTO.

USUFRUCTO ESPECIAL.
atypical usufruct.

USUFRUCTO IMPERFECTO.
See CUASIUSUFRUCTO and USUFRUCTO.

USUFRUCTO IMPROPIO.
See CUASIUSUFRUCTO and USUFRUCTO.

USUFRUCTO JUDICIAL.
usufruct imposed by court order.

USUFRUCTO LEGAL.
statutory usufruct, usufruct imposed by law
See USUFRUCTO.

USUFRUCTO NORMAL.
ordinary usufruct, usufruct for the use of non consummables. See USUFRUCTO.

USUFRUCTO PARTICULAR.
usufruct for the use of identified things.
See USUFRUCTO.

USUFRUCTO PERFECTO.
true usufruct.

USUFRUCTO PLENO.
unlimited usufruct.

USUFRUCTO POR PRESCRIPCIÓN.
usufruct acquired by adverse possession.

USUFRUCTO REMUNERATORIO.
usufruct for consideration or remuneration.

USUFRUCTO RESTRINGIDO.
restricted or limited usufruct.

USUFRUCTO SIMULTÁNEO.
usufruct granting simultaneous use to two o more persons.

USUFRUCTO SUCESIVO.
usufruct transmitted to successive persons du ring the life of the same owner of the property

USUFRUCTO TEMPORAL.
temporary usufruct.
See USUFRUCTO.

USUFRUCTO TESTAMENTARIO.
usufruct granted by will. See USUFRUCTO.

USUFRUCTO UNIVERSAL.
usufruct for the use of all or a share of a totality of property.
see USUFRUCTO.

USUFRUCTO VITALICIO.
usufruct granted for life.

USUFRUCTO VOLUNTARIO.
usufruct granted at will.

USUFRUCTUANTE.
see USUFRUCTUARIO.

USUFRUCTUAR.
, to hold a right of usufruct, hold in usufruct ‖ to enjoy the right of usufruct ‖ to be of benefit or utility.

USUFRUCTUARIO.
n, usufructuary, holder of right of usufruct.

USUFRUTO.
see USUFRUCTO.

USUFRUTUAR.
see USUFRUCTUAR.

USUFRUTUARIO.
see USUFRUCTUARIO.

USURA.
, usury ‖ interest-bearing loan contract ‖ interest ‖ profit ‖ profiteering.

USURAR.
see USUREAR.

USURARIAMENTE.
adv, usuriously ‖ with interest ‖ profitably ‖ with excessive profit.

USURARIO.
n, see USURERO ‖ adj, usurious ‖ pertaining to interest or profiteering or usury.

USUREAR.
, to charge interest on a loan ‖ to practice usury, charge usuriously ‖ to take out a usurious loan ‖ to profit or benefit (especially if it is excessive) ‖ to profiteer.

USURERO.
n, usurer ‖ profiteer ‖ moneylender, pawnbroker.

USURPACIÓN.
, usurpation ‖ arrogation ‖ assumption ‖ appropriation, seizure ‖ property that is usurped ‖ illegal taking.

USURPACIÓN DE AUTORIDAD.
illegal assumption of authority.

USURPACIÓN DE HONORES.
illegal assumption of honors or attributions.

USURPACIÓN DE INMUEBLES.
appropriation or illegal use of real property.

USURPACIÓN DE TÍTULOS.
illegal assumption of an honorific or professional title.

USURPADOR.
m, usurper ‖ adj, usurping.

USURPAR.
v, to usurp ‖ to assume (e.g. power without right) ‖ to appropriate, seize ‖ to encroach upon.

UT RETRO.
previously.

"UT SINGULI".
individually, singularly ‖ separately.

UT SUPRA.
as above ‖ as before ‖ above.

"UT UNIVERSI".
together, as a totality or entirety.

UTENSILIO.
m, utensil, tool, implement ‖ equipment ‖ device ‖ food and lodging given to soldiers by civilians.

UTERINO.
adj, maternal, from the maternal side ‖ uterine.

"UTI POSSIDETIS".
as previously held. Refers to holding boundaries or territories as they were prior to a dispute.

ÚTIL.
m, utensil, tool, implement ‖ equipment ‖ device ‖ adj, useful ‖ beneficial ‖ helpful ‖ usable, serviceable ‖ fruitful, fruit-bearing ‖ interest-bearing ‖ fit for military service ‖ working (day) ‖ within the required term or time.

ÚTILES DELICTIVOS.
tools or instruments of a crime.

UTILIDAD.
f, utility ‖ benefit, usefulness ‖ advantage ‖ interest ‖ profit ‖ fruit ‖ convenience, ease.

UTILIDAD BRUTA.
gross profit.

UTILIDAD COMUNAL.
community benefit, benefit of the community ‖ communal benefit.

**UTILIDAD
DE EXPLOTACIÓN.**
operating profit.

UTILIDAD DECRECIENTE.
diminishing return.

UTILIDAD MARGINAL.
marginal utility ‖ marginal profit.

UTILIDAD NETA.
net profit.

UTILIDAD PARTICULAR.
individual benefit.

UTILIDAD PÚBLICA.
public benefit or good.

UTILIDADES.
f, earnings, profits, returns, gains.

UTILIDADES A DISTRIBUIR.
undistributed or undivided profits.

UTILIDADES ANTICIPADAS.
anticipated profits.

UTILIDADES DE CAPITAL.
capital gains.

UTILIDADES ESPERADAS.
See UTILIDADES ANTICIPADAS.

UTILIDADES IMPOSITIVAS.
taxable profits.

UTILIDADES INCORPORADAS.
retained earnings or profits.

UTILIDADES PREVISTAS.
See UTILIDADES ANTICIPADAS.

UTILIZABLE.
adv, usable, serviceable.

UTILIZACIÓN.
f, utilization, use.

UTILIZAR.
v, to utilize, employ, use, make use of.

UTILIZARSE.
v, to be used frequently ‖ to serve as, be used for (a specific end).

ÚTILMENTE.
adv, usefully ‖ beneficially ‖ profitably ‖ fruitfully.

UTOPÍA.
f, Utopia.

UTÓPICO.
adj, Utopian.

UTOPISMO.
m, Utopianism.

UTOPISTA.
f, m, Utopian, follower of Utopian theory ‖ adj, Utopian.

UXORICIDA.
m, uxoricide, husband who kills his wife ‖ adj, uxoricidal.

UXORICIDIO.
m, uxoricide, wife killing, murder of a wife by her husband.

UXORIO.
adj, uxorious.

V

VACACIÓN.
f, vacation, holiday ‖ time off ‖ occurrence of a vacancy.

VACACIONES.
f, vacations, holidays, vacation.

VACACIONES JUDICIALES.
type of extended legal holidays, court or judicial holidays, term during which the courts are closed for one or two months each year.

VACACIONES LABORALES.
See VACACIONES PAGADAS.

VACACIONES PAGADAS.
paid vacation, vacation with pay.

VACANCIA.
f, vacancy.

VACANTE.
f, vacancy ‖ vacation, vacations, holiday, holidays ‖ adj, temporarily vacant (for rest) ‖ vacant, unoccupied ‖ unfilled ‖ unoccupied ‖ without lawful heirs ‖ unowned, without owner.

VACIAR.
v, to empty, drain (e.g. liquids) ‖ to cast (e.g. a mold).

VACIARSE.
v, to empty ‖ to reveal, divulge, tell (a secret) ‖ to spill the beans, blab.

VACIEDAD.
f, stupidity, nonsense ‖ ill-founded argument.

VACILACIÓN.
f, vacillation, lack of resolution, hesitation ‖ doubt.

VACILAR.
v, to vacillate, hesitate ‖ to doubt.

VACÍO.
m, vacuum ‖ void ‖ empty space, gap ‖ vacancy ‖ lack of ‖ adj, empty ‖ unoccupied, unren-

ted, vacant ‖ frustrated ‖ fruitless ‖ unpo-
lated ‖ vacuous ‖ vain, presumptuous ‖ va
ty ‖ lazy .

VACUO.
m, vacancy ‖ adj, empty ‖ unoccupied, unren
vacant ‖ frustrated ‖ fruitless ‖ unpo-pulat‹
vacuous ‖ vain, presumptuous ‖ lazy.

"VADIMONIUM".
m, sworn promise to appear (in court).

VAGABUNDAJE.
m, vagabonding, roaming ‖ vagrancy.

VAGABUNDEAR.
v, to roam, rove, wander ‖ to be a vagabon‹
hobo or bum or vagrant.

VAGABUNDEO.
See VAGABUNDAJE.

VAGABUNDO.
m, vagabond, wanderer, roamer ‖ vagr
bum, tramp, hobo ‖ adj, vagabond, wan‹
ing, roaming, roving.

VAGANCIA.
f, vagrancy ‖ indolence, laziness ‖ idlene
unemployment.

VAGANTE.
adj, vagrant ‖ idle ‖ wandering.

VAGAR.
f, leisure, free time, time off ‖ slowness ‖
ness ‖ idleness ‖ v, to wander, roam, rove
be idle or lazy ‖ to be a vagrant ‖ to vacati‹
to be unemployed.

VAGO.
m, vagrant, tramp ‖ deserter, fugitive ‖
empty, void ‖ unemployed ‖ vacant ‖ fr‹
without fixed purpose ‖ vague, imprecise
decisive ‖ wandering, roaming, vagrant ‖

VAGÓN.
m, wagon, car, coach (of a train).

VAGOROSO.
adj, wandering, roaming, roving ‖ idle, lazy ‖ vagrant ‖ unemployed ‖ vacillating from side to side.

VAGUEAR.
See VAGAR.

VAGUEDAD.
f, stupidity, vacuous comment ‖ vagrancy ‖ vagueness.

VAHÍDO.
m, vertigo, dizziness ‖ fainting, loss of consciousness.

VAIVÉN.
m, comings and goings ‖ fluctuation ‖ oscillation ‖ risk of loss ‖ changeableness, inconstancy.

VAIVÉN LABORAL.
See TRASLADO LABORAL DIARIO.

VALE.
m, promissory note (if to the order of someone) ‖ written promise to pay a sum certain (directly to someone) ‖ voucher ‖ receipt, signed document which entitles the person to receipt or delivery of a good ‖ certificate of good behavior ‖ see also VALE REAL.

VALE REAL.
public or government bonds.

VALEDERO.
adj, enforceable, legal ‖ valid, binding.

VALENTÍA.
f, courage, valor ‖ effort, vigor, energy ‖ heroic act ‖ boasting about a heroic deed ‖ calm opposition (to a despot).

VALENTÓN.
m, braggart, boaster (about heroic deeds) ‖ adj, bragging, boastful.

VALENTONA.
f, brag, boast.

VALENTONADA.
See VALENTONA.

VALER.
m, value, price, worth ‖ v, to be worth, be valued at ‖ to cost ‖ to protect, defend, safeguard ‖ to have energy ‖ to carry out to an end ‖ to be in effect ‖ to be usable ‖ to be profitable, render a profit ‖ to produce, yield, bear fruit ‖ to reach (a certain sum of money) ‖ to have authority or influence or power ‖ to prevail (re. a right or license) ‖ to have effect, be effective ‖ to be valid or binding or enforceable ‖ to circulate or be in circulation ‖ to be important or useful.

VALEROSIDAD.
f, courage, valor, bravery.

VALÍA.
f, value, worth, price ‖ favor ‖ partiality, bias ‖ merit, quality ‖ party, faction.

VALIDACIÓN.
f, validation ‖ validity, enforceability, binding quality ‖ security, sureness.

VÁLIDAMENTE.
adv, validly, bindingly, enforceably, legally.

VALIDAR.
v, to make valid or binding or enforceable or legal.

VALIDEZ.
f, validity, enforceability, binding quality ‖ legality ‖ effectiveness; firmness.

VALIDEZ DE LAS ESTIPULACIONES SOCIALES.
validity of clauses of a contract creating a business association.

VALIDEZ DE LOS ACTOS JURÍDICOS.
validity of legal acts.

VALIDEZ DE LOS CONTRATOS.
contractual validity.

VALIDEZ DE LOS INSTRUMENTOS PÚBLICOS.
validity of public documents.

VALIDEZ DE LOS TESTAMENTOS.
validity of wills.

VALIDEZ INTERNACIONAL DE LOS DOCUMENTOS Y DE LAS ACTAS NOTARIALES.
international validity of documents and public notarizations.

VALIDO.
m, political favorite ‖ prime minister ‖ adj, esteemed, respected ‖ believed, admitted ‖ accepted.

VÁLIDO.
adj, valid, binding, effective, enforceable, legal ‖ firm, solid ‖ strong, robust.

VALIENTE.
m, braggart, boaster ‖ brave person ‖ adj, valiant, brave, courageous ‖ strong, robust ‖ excellent, fine, superb.

VALIENTEMENTE.
adv, valiantly, bravely, courageously ‖ excessively ‖ excellently, finely, superbly.

VALIJA.
f, bag, suitcase, luggage ‖ mailbag, mail pouch ‖ mail.

VALIJA DIPLOMÁTICA.
diplomatic pouch.
VALIJERO.
m, mailman, mail carrier.
VALIOSO.
adj, valuable ‖ costly, expensive ‖ rich, wealthy ‖ decisive.
VALOR.
m, value ‖ worth, cost, price ‖ utility ‖ aptitude or capability to secure necessities of life ‖ profit, yield, revenue ‖ fruit, product ‖ significance, import, meaning ‖ importance ‖ merit, worth ‖ force, strength ‖ effectiveness, efficacy ‖ audacity ‖ power ‖ leading or noble person.
VALOR ACREDITADO.
book value, value on the books ‖ proven worth or merit of a person ‖ value credited, credit in an account ‖ check or other instrument which has been credited to an account.
VALOR ACTIVO.
asset.
VALOR ACTUAL.
present value.
VALOR ADQUISITIVO.
purchasing power.
VALOR AJUSTADO.
adjusted value.
VALOR AL COBRO.
note or promissory note or other document the payment of which is pending.
VALOR APARENTE.
apparent value.
VALOR ARBITRADO.
arbitrated value.
VALOR CIERTO.
fixed price ‖ value certain.
VALOR CÍVICO.
civic-mindedness.
VALOR COMERCIAL.
commercial value.
VALOR CONTABLE.
book value, value on the books.
VALOR DE AFECCIÓN.
emotional value (above and beyond market value, due to personal appreciation).
VALOR DE LAS COSAS.
(actual) value of things.
VALOR DE REPOSICIÓN.
See PRECIO DE REPOSICIÓN.
VALOR DECLARADO.
stated value.

VALOR EFECTIVO.
cash value.
VALOR EN CAMBIO.
effective or real market value.
VALOR EN CUENTA.
credited amount.
VALOR EN PLAZA.
market value.
VALOR EN SÍ MISMO.
interest value.
VALOR EN USO.
useful value.
VALOR ENTENDIDO.
agreed value ‖ also see VALOR EN CUENTA.
VALOR ESTIMADO.
estimated value or worth.
VALOR ESTIMATIVO.
See PRECIO AFECTIVO.
VALOR EXTRÍNSECO.
extrinsic value ‖ circumstantial value, val under given circumstances ‖ contractual or a bitrated value.
VALOR FICTICIO.
fictitious value ‖ stated price.
VALOR IMPOSITIVO.
tax value, value for tax purposes.
VALOR INMOBILIARIO.
real estate or real property value.
VALOR INMOVILIZADO.
value of capital assets (of a business).
VALOR INTRÍNSECO.
intrinsic value.
VALOR LÍQUIDO.
monetary value, value in money.
VALOR LOCATIVO.
rental value of real estate.
VALOR NOMINAL.
face value ‖ nominal value ‖ supposed valu
VALOR OFICIAL.
official price.
VALOR ORO.
See CLÁUSULA ORO.
VALOR PASIVO.
liability.
VALOR PROBADO.
See VALOR ACREDITADO.
VALOR REAL.
See PRECIO REAL.
VALOR RECIBIDO.
value received.

VALOR SUPUESTO.
supposed worth or merit (e.g. of a person).
VALOR VENAL.
sales price ‖ value for tax purposes based on the supposed sale price.
VALORACIÓN.
f, valuation ‖ evaluation, appraisal, assessment, estimation ‖ just price ‖ increase in price.
VALORACIÓN AGRÍCOLA.
agricultural value, value of agricultural goods.
VALORACIÓN COMERCIAL.
commercial valuation or appraisal.
VALORACIÓN DE LAS PRUEBAS.
See ESTIMACIÓN JURÍDICA.
VALORACIÓN DE MUEBLES Y UTENSILIOS.
valuation of personal property and tools.
VALORACIÓN JURÍDICA.
See ESTIMATIVA JURÍDICA.
VALORAR.
v, to appraise, evaluate, valuate, assess, estimate ‖ to fix the value ‖ to increase the value (of something).
VALORATIVO.
adj, which makes valuable ‖ which increases the value of ‖ which carries out (e.g. a work or activity) ‖ appraised, assessed, estimated ‖ wich appraises, evaluates, estimates.
VALOREAR.
See VALORAR.
VALÓREM.
See AD VALÓREM.
VALORES.
m, securities (including stocks and bonds) ‖ values, morals, principles (e.g. of a community) ‖ valuable goods ‖ liquid assets ‖ plural of VALOR.
VALORES AJUSTABLES.
adjustable values ‖ government bonds adjusted for inflation.
VALORES COTIZABLES.
negotiable securities.
VALORES DECLARADOS.
declared value (of goods and monies sent through the mails).
VALORES FIDUCIARIOS.
securities backed by a trust-like guaranty.

VALORES METÁLICOS.
certified letters (in which money is enclosed).
VALORES PÚBLICOS.
government bonds.
VALORÍA.
f, valuation ‖ evaluation, appraisal, assessment, estimation.
VALORIZACIÓN.
f, valuation ‖ evaluation, appraisal, assessment, estimation ‖ increase in value, raise or mark-up in price ‖ trading of a good for cash.
VALORIZAR.
v, to value ‖ to evaluate, appraise, assess, estimate ‖ to increase the value, raise or mark up the price ‖ to cash in, convert into cash.
VALUACIÓN.
See VALORIZACIÓN.
VALUAR.
v, to value ‖ to evaluate, appraise, assess, estimate.
VÁLVULA DE ESCAPE.
escape valve.
VALLA.
f, fence, barricade ‖ hurdle ‖ obstacle ‖ impediment ‖ limit, prohibition.
VALLADAR.
f, fence, barricade ‖ hurdle ‖ obstacle ‖ impediment.
VALLADO.
See VALLADAR.
VALLAR.
f, see VALLADAR ‖ adj, pertaining to a fence or barricade ‖ v, to fence, fence in, barricade.
VANDÁLICO.
adj, pertaining to vandals or vandalism ‖ destructive ‖ devastating.
VANDALISMO.
m, vandalism.
VÁNDALO.
m, vandal.
VANGUARDIA.
f, vanguard.
VANIDAD DELICTIVA.
pride in criminal acts ‖ boasting of crimes.
VARA.
f, rod, cane (for thrashing or caning) ‖ wand, long thin stick ‖ influence, pull ‖ rod, gavel (as sign of authority) ‖ jurisdiction of person with a rod or gavel (as sign of authority) ‖ linear measure equivalent to 86 centimeters.

VARA DE LA JUSTICIA.
judicial branch ‖ judicial power ‖ judicial officer who uses a gavel or rod as a sign of authority.

VARADA.
f, grounding, running aground (of a vessel).

VARIABLE.
adj, variable, susceptible to change ‖ tending to change or move.

VARIACIÓN.
f, variation, change, alteration ‖ transformation ‖ innovation ‖ difference ‖ falsification ‖ distortion ‖ distinction.

VARIANTE.
f, variation, variant, difference ‖ witness who contradicts him or herself ‖ difference between a copy and the original of a document ‖ temporary detour ‖ adj, varying, changing ‖ contradicting.

VARIAR.
v, to vary, change, alter, modify ‖ to differ ‖ to give contradictory evidence or statements (as a witness) ‖ to make a detour.

VARIEDAD.
f, variety ‖ distinction ‖ change.

VARIO.
adj, various ‖ different, diverse, distinct ‖ twisted ‖ changeable ‖ indeterminate.

VARÓN.
m, male, man ‖ male child ‖ male adult ‖ respected man of authority.

VARONÍA.
f, male issue, male children.

VARONIL.
adj, masculine, male, pertaining to a man ‖ courageous.

VASALLAJE.
m, dependance (of one person on another) ‖ subjection ‖ vassalage.

VASALLO.
m, vassal ‖ dependant ‖ subject (of a sovereign).

VASTACIÓN.
f, devastation, destruction, ruin ‖ decimation.

VÁSTAGO.
m, offshoot ‖ offspring, issue, descent.

VASTAR.
v, to devastate, ruin, destroy ‖ decimate.

VASTEDAD.
f, vastness, immensity ‖ amplitude.

VATICANO.
m, Vatican.

VECINAL.
adj, neighborhood, vicinal, pertaining to neighborhood ‖ neighboring, vicinal, pertaining to a neighbor ‖ adjacent.

VECINAMENTE.
adv, contiguously, abutting ‖ nearby, in the proximity.

VECINDAD.
f, vicinity ‖ quality of being a neighbor or bordering ‖ neighborhood, neighbors, members of a neighborhood ‖ unrelated householders, community, neighborhood ‖ environs ‖ nearness, proximity.

VECINDAD CIVIL.
legal neighborhood, neighborhood made up of a legal territory.

VECINDARIO.
m, neighborhood, totality of neighbors in a city ‖ townspeople, city inhabitants ‖ neighborhood, neighborhood members ‖ list of neighbors ‖ quality of being a neighbor or bordering.

VECINO.
m, neighbor ‖ non-resident homeowner (in an area) ‖ bordering country ‖ borderer ‖ person who owns or lives next door ‖ adj, close, neighboring, proximate ‖ similar, analogous, like ‖ resident, inhabitant, domiciled (for purposes of municipal administration).

VEDA.
f, prohibition, ban, disallowance, proscription ‖ injunction ‖ interdiction ‖ taboo ‖ closed season (for hunting or fishing).

VEDADO.
m, enclosed park or farm ‖ adj: prohibited, forbidden.

VEDAMIENTO.
See VEDA.

VEDAR.
v, to prohibit, ban, disallow, proscribe ‖ to impose an injunction ‖ to make difficult, hinder ‖ to obstruct.

VEEDOR.
m, inspector.

VEEDURÍA.
f, inspectorship ‖ jurisdiction, position and office of inspector.

VEHEMENCIA.
f, vehemence.

VEHEMENTE.
adv, vehemently.

HÍCULO.
vehicle ‖ carrier, means of transportation.

NTENIO.
score, twenty-year period.

NTEÑAL.
j, twenty-year.

ACIÓN.
mistreatment ‖ insult, verbal offense ‖ un-
r treatment ‖ injury ‖ rape ‖ sexual offense.

ACIONES DE PRISIONEROS.
istreatment of prisoners ‖ mistreatment of
isoners of war.

ADOR.
abuser ‖ insulter, offender ‖ rapist ‖ sexual
fender ‖ adj, offending, insulting ‖ mistreat-
, abusive ‖ injuring.

AMEN.
e VEJACIÓN.

AR.
to offend, insult ‖ to mistreat, maltreat ‖ to
rsecute ‖ to injure, hurt ‖ to bother ‖ to pre-
dice ‖ to rape (either male or female).

ATORIO.
j, offending, insulting ‖ mistreating, abusive
aping ‖ persecuting ‖ injuring, hurting ‖ bo-
ering ‖ prejudicing.

EZ.
old age ‖ decadence.

A.
candle ‖ vigil, watch ‖ night work ‖ night
tch or sentry.

ACIÓN.
vigil, watch ‖ night work ‖ night nurse ‖ night
tch or sentry ‖ careful observation ‖ wake-
ness.

ADA.
evening reunion ‖ also see VELA ‖ adj, hid-
n, disguised, veiled.

AR.
to watch or watch out (for) ‖ to do guard or
ntry duty ‖ to observe attentively ‖ to stay
ake ‖ to tend, watch over a sick person at
ght ‖ to hold a wake for (a dead person) ‖ to
ork late, do night work, work at night ‖ to
il, cover with a veil.

ATORIO.
wake (prior to burial).

EIDAD.
whim, caprice ‖ inconstancy, fickleness.

EIDOSO.
j, inconstant, fickle.

VELO.
m, veil ‖ pretext ‖ cover-up.

VELOCIDAD.
f, velocity, speed.

VENABLE.
adj, venal.

VENAL.
adj, venal, corruptible, bribable ‖ immoral ‖
offered for sale ‖ salable, able to be sold.

VENALIDAD.
f, venality, bribery ‖ corruption ‖ lack of scru-
ples.

VENCEDOR.
m, winner ‖ victor, conqueror ‖ adj, winning ‖
victorious, conquering.

VENCER.
v, to conquer, beat, win, vanquish, defeat ‖ to
dominate ‖ to surmount, overcome ‖ to expire, mature, come due ‖ to expire, no longer be
valid.

VENCIBLE.
adj, conquerable, beatable ‖ surmountable,
able to be overcome.

VENCIDO.
m, loser, defeated ‖ losing party ‖ adj, conquered, beaten ‖ surmounted, overcome ‖
mature, due, payable ‖ invalid, expired.

VENCIMIENTO.
m, defeat ‖ victory, action of conquering ‖ domination ‖ surmounting, action of surmounting ‖ due date, maturity date ‖ expiration date
‖ expiration, maturity.

VENCIMIENTO ANTICIPADO.
anticipatory expiration of a term ‖ accelera-
tion.

VENDAJE.
m, commission (on the sale of merchandise) ‖
tip, gratuity.

VENDEDOR.
m, seller, vendor ‖ merchant, salesman ‖ trader.

VENDEDOR AMBULANTE.
traveling salesman.

VENDEDOR DE UNA HERENCIA.
seller of rights to an inheritance.

VENDEDORA.
f, female seller or merchant ‖ saleswoman,
salesgirl.

VENDEJA.
f, public sale (e.g. in a market or fair) ‖ merchandise.

VENDER.
v, to sell, vend ‖ to offer a good for sale ‖ to betray, sell out ‖ to trick, abuse confidence ‖ to discover a secret (to someone's prejudice).

VENDERSE.
v, to sell ‖ to betray, sell out ‖ to sell oneself ‖ to be or let oneself be bribed ‖ to offer to do something dangerous, expose oneself to danger (for another's benefit) ‖ to give oneself away, show something that prejudices oneself.

VENDÍ.
m, bill of sale, certificate of sale.

VENDICIÓN.
See VENTA.

VENDIDA.
See VENTA.

VENDIDO.
m, traitor ‖ person who sells himself for a price ‖ adj, sold ‖ betrayed.

"VENDITIO".
m, sale.

VENENO.
m, poison, venom ‖ evil ‖ anger, rancor, venom.

VENENOSIDAD.
f, poisonousness.

VENENOSO.
adj, poisonous, venomous ‖ evil ‖ perverted ‖ baneful, ruinous.

VENERABLE.
adj, venerable ‖ virtuous.

VENERACIÓN.
f, veneration, respect ‖ submission.

VENERAR.
v, to venerate, respect, revere ‖ to admire.

VENÉREO.
adj, sensual, lascivious, carnal ‖ venereal.

VENGA LO QUE VENGA.
come what may.

VENGA LO QUE VINIERE.
See VENGA LO QUE VENGA.

VENGABLE.
adj, able to be avenged ‖ susceptible to revenge.

VENGADOR.
m, avenger ‖ adj, avenging, revenging.

VENGAINJURIAS.
f, prosecuting attorney.

VENGANZA.
f, vengeance ‖ revenge ‖ punishment ‖ retaliation.

VENIA.
f, pardon ‖ forgiveness ‖ dismissal ‖ amnesty authorization or permission or license to c something not prohibited ‖ permission or a thorization granted to a minor to manage h or her own property ‖ salutation, nod of tl head (as greeting or recognition) ‖ milita salute.

VENIA JUDICIAL.
court permission or authorization granted tc minor to manage his or her own property.

VENIA LEGISLATIVA.
statutory permission or authorization grant to a minor to manage his or her own proper

VENIA MARITAL.
marital permission or authorization granted a minor to manage his or her own property

VENIAL.
adj, venial.

VENIALIDAD.
f, veniality.

VENIDERO.
adj, future, coming.

VENIDEROS.
m, future generation, posterity ‖ heirs ‖ d cendants ‖ (as yet) unborn.

VENIR.
v, to come ‖ to arrive ‖ to approach, come nc ‖ to appear ‖ to fit, adjust (oneself to the nec of another) ‖ to return (to the topic) ‖ to pi ceed ‖ to receive property (from another) ‖ near (the end) ‖ to occur, come to mind ‖ to solve, decide ‖ to come from.

VENIR
A LAS MANOS.
to come to blows ‖ to attack ‖ to stick togeth

VENIR A MENOS.
to lose status ‖ to fall ‖ to become impo rished ‖ to deteriorate.

VENIR UNO
CONTRA SU PALABRA.
to break one's promise, go against one's wc

VENTA.
f, sale ‖ sales contract ‖ offer for sale (of goo ‖ roadside stop or inn.

VENTA A CRÉDITO.
credit sale, sale on credit.

VENTA A ENSAYO.
See COMPRAVENTA A ENSAYO.

VENTA A LA VISTA.
See COMPRAVENTA A LA VISTA.

NTA A PLAZOS.
ne-sale, installment sale, sale on an install-
ent plan.

NTA A SATISFACCIÓN
:L COMPRADOR.
le to the satisfaction of the customer.

NTA "AD CORPUS".
le of a specific thing for a price, regardless of
e actual characteristics or condition of the
ing.

NTA "AD GUSTUM".
e COMPRAVENTA A ENSAYO.

NTA ADMINISTRATIVA.
vernment sale, sale of property by the ad-
inistrative branch of the government.

NTA AL CONTADO.
sh sale.

NTA AL POR MAYOR.
olesale ‖ wholesale sale.

NTA AL POR MENOR.
tail ‖ retail sale.

NTA ALEATORIA.
e VENTA DE ESPERANZA.

NTA "C.I.F.".
e CLÁUSULA C.I.F.

NTA CIVIL.
n-commercial or private sale.

NTA COMERCIAL.
mmercial sale.

NTA COMPULSIVA.
rced sale.

NTA CON GARANTÍA.
le with guaranty or warranty (of goods).

NTA CON PACTO DE RETROVENTA.
le with right of redemption.

NTA CON PRIMAS.
le including buyer's bonuses, stamps, gifts or
her similar promotional gifts.

NTA CON REBAJA.
count sale.

NTA CONDICIONAL.
nditional sale (on approval of buyer).

NTA CONTRA DOCUMENTOS.
cumentary sale, sale against documents or
cumentation.

NTA DE CASA DE COMERCIO.
e of a business establishment.

NTA DE ESPERANZA.
e of fraudulent sale of services, agreement
* a price to use influence to obtain a favora-
: decision from an official or other person

known to the seller, when in fact such influence does not exist or is not used.

VENTA DE HUMO.
See VENTA DE ESPERANZA.

VENTA DE LA HIPOTECA.
sale of encumbered or mortgaged real estate
‖ assignment of a loan secured by a real estate
mortgage . See also EJECUCIÓN HIPOTECARIA.

VENTA
DE LA PRENDA.
sale of pledged property ‖ assignment of a
loan secured by a pledge.

VENTA DIRECTA.
direct sale (without middlemen) ‖ sale of securities with actual delivery of such securities.

VENTA EN BLOQUE.
bulk sale.

VENTA EN CONSIGNACIÓN.
consignment sale. Opposed to VENTA FIRME.

VENTA, ENTREGA O DISTRIBUCIÓN DE
MEDICAMENTOS NOCIVOS.
sale, delivery, or distribution of poisonous medicine.

VENTA FACULTATIVA.
sale which permits the seller to replace the
thing sold with another item.

VENTA FIDUCIARIA.
See VENTA CON PACTO DE RETROVENTA.

VENTA FIRME.
executed sale (without possibility of later returning the good).
Opposed to VENTA EN CONSIGNACIÓN.

VENTA F.O.B..
See CLÁUSULA F.O.B.

VENTA FORZOSA.
forced sale.

VENTA JUDICIAL.
judicial sale, court-ordered sale, execution sale
‖ sale of good for which judicial authorization
is required.

VENTA LEGAL.
legal sale, sale which is licit ‖ forced sale.

VENTA-LOCACIÓN.
type of installment sale subject to the condition that if all installments are not paid the sale
is converted automatically into a simple rental
or lease and the installments are treated as
rental payments. The definition of this term
varies greatly from country to country.

VENTA PARCIAL.
partial sale, sale of part of a larger piece or

block of property. There may or may not be later sales of other parts.

VENTA PARTICULAR.
private sale ‖ sale of private goods (as opposed to government or public property) ‖ see also VENTA DIRECTA.

VENTA PROHIBIDA.
illegal sale.

VENTA PÚBLICA.
public auction ‖ public sale ‖ sale carried out by a public official.

VENTA PURA Y SIMPLE.
absolute or unconditional sale.

VENTA RESERVADA.
sale subject to a right of first refusal.

VENTA SOBRE DOCUMENTOS.
See VENTA CONTRA DOCUMENTOS.

VENTA SOBRE MUESTRAS.
See COMPRAVENTA MERCANTIL SOBRE MUESTRAS.

VENTA VOLUNTARIA.
voluntary sale ‖ see also VENTA PARTICULAR.

VENTAJA.
f, advantage ‖ superiority ‖ profit ‖ benefit ‖ extra salary (as compared to others in similar positions) ‖ handicap (in a game or sport).

VENTAJERO.
m, wily person (who takes advantage in business transactions).

VENTAJISTA.
f, m, advantage seeker ‖ profiteer.

VENTAJOSAMENTE.
adv, advantageously.

VENTAJOSO.
adj, advantageous ‖ beneficial ‖ profitable.

VENTILACIÓN.
f, ventilation ‖ airing or discussion of a matter.

VENTILAR.
v, to ventilate ‖ to air, discuss (a matter).

VER.
m, sight ‖ v, to see ‖ to look, observe ‖ to examine ‖ to visit ‖ to foresee ‖ to experience ‖ to reflect, consider, meditate ‖ to decide ‖ to try, hear (a case) ‖ to appear to give concluding oral argument in a case.

VER EL PLEITO.
to air all the facts in court.

VER LA PAGA AL OJO.
to be paid in cash, really be paid.

VER Y CREER.
(Literally: to see and to believe.) Seeing is believing.

VERACIDAD.
f, truthfulness ‖ veracity.

VERAMENTE.
adv, truthfully ‖ truly, verily ‖ sincerely.

VERAS.
f, reality ‖ truth (of a matter) ‖ earnestness fervor, zeal.

VERAZ.
adj, true, real, honest ‖ truthful.

VERBAL.
adj, verbal, of words ‖ oral, of spoken word

VERBALISMO.
m, verbalism, tendency to reason through t use of words over concepts.

VERBALMENTE.
adv, verbally ‖ orally.

VERDAD.
f, truth ‖ reality ‖ rational judgment ‖ sinc rity.

VERDADERAMENTE.
adv, truthfully ‖ really, truly ‖ sincerely ‖ h nestly.

VERDADERO.
adj, truthful ‖ real, true ‖ authentic ‖ since ‖ honest.

VERDUGO.
m, (judicial) hangman or executioner.

VEREDICTO.
m, verdict, jury verdict ‖ decision, judgmen (judicial) decision, judgment, sentence.

VEREDICTO DE INCULPABILIDAD.
verdict of not guilty or of acquittal, acquitta

VERGONZOSO.
m, shy person ‖ adj, embarrassing ‖ immo or dishonorable or illegal ‖ shameful, disgra ful ‖ shy, timid.

VERGÜENZA.
f, embarrassment ‖ shame, disgrace ‖ shyne timidity, bashfulness ‖ integrity, honor ‖ ge talia.

VERÍDICO.
adj, true, truthful, honest.

VERIFICACIÓN.
f, verification, checking ‖ proof, evidenc comparison (of things for verification) ‖ amination, inspection ‖ revision, review ‖ f fillment of something ‖ termination of a p ject.

VERIFICACIÓN DE CRÉDITOS.
verification and acceptance by a trustee or a court of creditors' claims (to a bankrupt estate).
VERIFICADO.
m, thing that has been verified or checked or proven or compared or examined or inspected or reviewed or fulfilled or ended ‖ adj, verified, checked ‖ proven ‖ compared ‖ examined, inspected ‖ reviewed ‖ fulfilled ‖ ended.
VERIFICADOR.
m, verifier ‖ examiner, inspector, checker ‖ reviewer ‖ adj, verifying ‖ examining, inspecting, checking ‖ reviewing.
VERIFICAR.
v, to verify, check ‖ to examine, inspect ‖ to prove, evidence ‖ to compare (things for verification) ‖ to review ‖ to fulfill, carry out, comply with something ‖ to end a project.
See VERIFICACIÓN DE CRÉDITOS.
VERIFICARSE.
v, to be or prove true ‖ to comply with something ‖ to occur, happen, take place.
VEROSÍMIL.
adj, probable, likely ‖ credible.
VEROSIMILITUD.
f, probability, likelihood ‖ credibility ‖ appearance of truth ‖ admissibility of a hypothetical doctrine.
VERSÁTIL.
adj, versatile ‖ changeable, inconstant.
VERSIÓN.
m, version, opinion, (personal) account ‖ translation.
VERTICAL.
adj, vertical ‖ perpendicular.
VERTICALIDAD.
f, verticality.
VERTIENTE DE TEJADOS.
See SERVIDUMBRE DE DESAGÜE.
VESTIGIO.
m, vestige ‖ remains ‖ trace, sign, indicia ‖ fingerprint or footprint.
VESTUARIO
DE PRISIONEROS.
prisoners clothing or uniform.
VETAR.
v, to veto.
VETERANO.
m, (military) veteran ‖ veteran, experienced person.

VETO.
m, veto ‖ right or power to veto or prohibit.
VETUSTEZ.
f, antiquity ‖ old age.
VETUSTO.
adj, ancient, very old ‖ antique.
VEZ.
f, alternative ‖ turn, shift, rotation ‖ occasion, opportunity, time.
VÍA.
f, road, street ‖ avenue ‖ route, way ‖ track, rail ‖ railroad line ‖ conduit ‖ direction, way ‖ recourse, procedural path or process or route ‖ jurisdiction ‖ judgment ‖ method or means (of enforcing a right) ‖ way, manner (of being) ‖ path, course ‖ agent, medium.
VÍA CONTENCIOSA.
judicial recourse (rather than those of the executive or legislative) ‖ litigation.
VÍA DE APREMIO.
See JUICIO DE APREMIO.
VÍA DISCIPLINARIA.
disciplinary recourse.
VÍA EJECUTIVA.
See JUICIO EJECUTIVO.
VÍA GUBERNATIVA.
administrative recourse.
VÍA JERÁRQUICA.
hierarchical order.
VÍA ORDINARIA.
ordinary judicial recourse ‖ standard (judicial) procedures or routine ‖ regular channels.
VÍA SUMARIA.
summary proceedings or procedures.
See JUICIO SUMARIO.
VIABILIDAD.
f, viability ‖ possibility.
VIABLE.
adj, viable ‖ possible ‖ probable ‖ doable, feasible ‖ transitable.
VIAJANTE.
m, traveler ‖ traveling salesman ‖ adj, traveling.
VIAJANTE DE COMERCIO.
traveling salesman.
VIAJAR.
v, to travel ‖ to go by, travel by.
VIAJE.
m, trip, journey, travel ‖ way, road ‖ load, cargo ‖ navigation ‖ crossing ‖ thrust, jab (with a knife, sword, etc.) ‖ attack, assault.

VIAJE REDONDO.
round trip.
VIAJERO.
m, traveler ‖ passenger ‖ adj, traveling.
VIAL.
f, tree-lined avenue or boulevard ‖ adj, related to a public road or street or avenue or boulevard or lane, etc.
VIALIDAD.
f, administrative services and offices related to public road or street or avenue or boulevard or lane, etc.
VIANDANTE.
m, traveler ‖ pedestrian ‖ hiker, walker ‖ vagabond, tramp.
VÍAS DE DERECHO.
legal recourses.
VÍAS DE HECHO.
vigilante justice, non-legal recourses (e.g. force, violence).
VÍAS PECUARIAS.
livestock paths or routes.
VÍAS PÚBLICAS.
public thoroughfare or road or street or avenue or boulevard or lane, etc.
VIÁTICO.
m, traveler's provisions or possessions ‖ payment made to defray travel or moving expenses of diplomats or employees living away from home.
VIBRACIÓN.
f, vibration.
VIBRAR.
v, to vibrate ‖ to oscillate ‖ to agitate, work up.
VICARÍA.
f, office and position and court and jurisdiction of a vicar.
VICARIATO.
See VICARÍA.
VICARIO.
m, substitute, replacement ‖ vicar ‖ adj, substitute, replacement.
VICECÓNSUL.
m, vice-consul.
VICECONSULADO.
m, vice-consulate.
VICEPRESIDENCIA.
f, vice-presidency.
VICEPRESIDENTE.
m, vice-president.

VICEPRESIDENTE DE LA NACIÓN.
national vice-president.
VICEVERSA.
adv, vice versa ‖ conversely.
VICIADO.
adj, defectively ‖ fouled, foul, polluted ‖ with a vice.
VICIAR.
v, to injure (physically) ‖ to vitiate, corrupt (morally) ‖ to contaminate, foul, pollute ‖ to adulterate ‖ to falsify, forge, counterfeit ‖ to illegally alter (a document) ‖ to void or nullify or invalidate (e.g. a contract) ‖ to pervert ‖ to twist or misconstrue (the meaning).
VICIARSE.
v, to become corrupted ‖ to become engulfed or wrapped up in ‖ to become deformed or defective ‖ to become perverted or warped.
VICIO.
m, vice ‖ bad habit ‖ defect, flaw, fault ‖ physical defect ‖ material injury or harm ‖ poor quality ‖ immorality ‖ dishonesty ‖ falsity ‖ error ‖ defect which voids or invalidates a contract or other legal act ‖ perversion, corruption ‖ addiction to ‖ overindulgence, excessive tolerance.
VICIO COMERCIALIZADO.
commercial vice, vice as a business.
VICIO DE CONSTRUCCIÓN.
construction defect, fault of construction.
VICIO DE FONDO.
substantive defect.
VICIO DE FORMA.
procedural defect, defect of form.
VICIO DE LA COSA.
defect in the good (inclusive of product defect).
VICIO INSUBSANABLE.
See DEFECTOS INSUBSANABLES.
VICIO JURÍDICO.
legal defect.
VICIOS DE LA SENTENCIA.
errors of the (lower court) decision.
VICIOS DEL CONSENTIMIENTO.
flaws or defects in consent (of the parties).
VICIOS OCULTOS DE LA COSA.
hidden or latent defects in the good.
VICIOS REDHIBITORIOS.
hidden defects in the goods (which existed at the time when the good was sold, which make it unsuitable for the purpose for which it wa

ntended and which make the good such that
he buyer would not have purchased it had he
een aware of such defect).

CIOSAMENTE.
dv, defectively ‖ ineffectively, invalidly.

CIOSO.
dj, defective, flawed, faulty ‖ given to vice or
ad habits ‖ sinful ‖ immoral ‖ dishonest ‖ fal-
e ‖ erroneous ‖ void, invalid, null ‖ perverted,
orrupt ‖ overindulged, pampered, spoiled.

CISITUD.
, vicissitude, change of circumstances.

CTIMA.
, victim.

CTIMA DE ABUSO.
ictim of abuse.

CTIMARIO.
n, murderer ‖ author of a crime which injures
person.

CTIMOLOGÍA.
, victimology, study of victims.

CTORIA.
, victory, conquest, triumph.

CTORIOSO.
dj, victorious, triumphant.

DA.
, life ‖ signs of life ‖ lifetime, life span ‖ means
f occupation, livelihood, living ‖ way of life ‖
aily necessities ‖ person, being ‖ life history,
iography ‖ liveliness, vitality, animation ‖ pros-
itution ‖ life, duration (of a thing) ‖ term of
ndearment (e.g. darling, sweetheart).

DA CIVIL.
gal existence.

DA
N COMÚN.
fe shared together by a man and a woman.

DA LICENCIOSA.
w life, licentious living.

DA
RIVADA.
rivate life ‖ areas of living which are regula-
ed by DERECHO PRIVADO ‖ family life ‖ in-
ividual way of life ‖ love affairs.

DA PÚBLICA.
ublic life, life related to public functions and
ork.

DA SOCIAL.
ocial life.

DA ÚTIL.
seful life (of a product or person).

VIDENTE.
m, seer, prophet, clairvoyant ‖ fortune-teller.

VIDUAL.
adj, concerning widowhood.

VIEJA.
f, old woman ‖ mother.

VIEJO.
m, old man ‖ father ‖ adj, old, ancient ‖ antique ‖ much or very or well used ‖ used up, spent
‖ tarnished, spoiled.

VIENTO.
m, wind, breeze ‖ bragging, boasting, puffing
‖ stool pigeon, rat ‖ conceit, vanity.

VIENTRE.
m, womb ‖ fetus, unborn child ‖ belly (of a ship
or plane).

VIENTRE LIBRE.
child to be born free from slavery.

VIGENCIA.
f, effect, force ‖ obligation ‖ operation, use ‖
duration, life ‖ legal effect (in terms of time).

VIGENTE.
adj, in force and effect ‖ obligatory ‖ in operation, in use.

VIGÉSIMO.
adj, twentieth.

VIGÍA.
f, m, lookout, person who watches or listens ‖
vigilance, care.

VIGIAR.
v, to watch, keep a lookout ‖ to spy.

VIGILADO.
m, person who is being watched or spied on ‖
adj, watched, spied on.

VIGILANCIA.
f, vigilance, watchfulness ‖ care, diligence ‖
guard service ‖ punishment of being under the
care of a parole officer or other official who
watches one's conduct.

VIGILANTE.
m, police agent, policeman ‖ guard, watchman, watch ‖ adj, watching, watch ‖ guard,
guarding ‖ vigilant, watchful.

VIGILAR.
v, to keep vigil over, care for ‖ to spy on ‖ to
watch, observe ‖ to follow.

VIGILIA.
f, vigil, watch ‖ wakefulness, state of being
awake ‖ watchfulness, state of watching ‖ (military) night guard duty or watch ‖ night work or
study ‖ eve, day before.

VIGOR.
m, vigor ‖ effect, force ‖ energy, force ‖ operation, use.

VIGORAR.
See VIGORIZAR.

VIGORIZAR.
v, to give energy or force to, invigorate.

VIGOROSO.
adj, vigorous, strong, energetic.

VIL.
adj, vile ‖ despicable, base ‖ low ‖ disloyal ‖ infamous ‖ unthankful.

VILEZA.
f, vility ‖ despicableness, baseness ‖ disloyalty ‖ infamy ‖ ungratefulness ‖ unconscionability (of a contract).

VILIPENDIADOR.
m, denigrator, insulter.

VILIPENDIAR.
v, to denigrate, insult.

VILIPENDIO.
m, denigration, insult, affront.

VILMENTE.
adv, vilely, basely ‖ cowardly ‖ traitorously, disloyally ‖ infamously ‖ ungratefully.

VILLA MISERIA.
f, slum, shanty town.

VINCULABLE.
adj, able to be related ‖ able to be subject to a restriction or limitation.
See VINCULACIÓN.

VINCULACIÓN.
f, entailment, limitation on property rights ‖ prohibition against alienation ‖ predetermined succession ‖ permanent condition placed on property such that it will be used only for certain purposes or by certain people ‖ condition placed on the activities of foundations ‖ perpetuity ‖ association, relationship, tie, link.

VÍNCULO.
m, nexus, association, relationship, tie, link ‖ entailment against transfer of property ‖ entailed property.

VÍNCULO DE PARENTESCO.
family relationship or tie.

VÍNCULO JURÍDICO.
legal relationship or nexus.

VÍNCULO MATRIMONIAL.
marital relationship.

VÍNCULO OBLIGACIONAL.
obligational relationship, relationship of duty.

VÍNCULO REAL.
See DERECHO REAL.

VINDICABLE.
adj, able to be vindicated.

VINDICACIÓN.
f, vindication ‖ revenge ‖ defense ‖ see REIVINDICACIÓN.

VINDICACIÓN DE OFENSA.
vindication of an offense or insult.

VINDICADOR.
m, vindicator, avenger ‖ adj, vindicating, dictive, avenging.

VINDICAR.
v, to vindicate ‖ to avenge, take revenge respond in writing to an insult ‖ to punish, tigate ‖ to rehabilitate ‖ see also REIVINDI

"VINDICATIO".
See VINDICACIÓN and REIVINDICACIÓN.

VINDICATIVO.
m, writing which responds to an insult o fense ‖ adj, vengeful, vindictive.

VINDICATORIO.
adj, vengeful, vindictive ‖ vindicatory.

VINDICTA.
f, revenge ‖ vindication.

VINDICTA PÚBLICA.
public vindication, punishment for a crim rely for reasons of social justice and to s example ‖ public punishment (to replace vate revenge).

VIOLABLE.
adj, violable.

VIOLACIÓN.
f, violation ‖ infraction, transgression law) ‖ desecration ‖ infringement ‖ blot, ing ‖ misdemeanor, crime ‖ rape, rape of man ‖ statutory rape.

VIOLACIÓN DE ARMISTICIO.
violation of armistice.

VIOLACIÓN DE CORRESPONDENCIA Y PAPELES PRIVADOS.
tampering with mail and private pape another.

VIOLACIÓN DE DEBERES DE FUNCIONARIOS PÚBLICOS.
violation of duties of public employees o cials.

VIOLACIÓN DE DOMICILIO.
unauthorized entering of the home of an ‖ unauthorized staying in the home of an after having entered with permission.

OLACIÓN DE FUEROS.
iolation of rights and privileges of legislators
r congressmen or members of parliament.
OLACIÓN DE LA LEY.
iolation of the law.
OLACIÓN DE MUJER.
ape, rape of a woman.
OLACIÓN DE PAÍSES NEUTRALES.
iolation of a country's neutral status.
OLACIÓN DE SECRETOS.
iolation or breaking of a secret.
OLACIÓN DE SELLOS
' DOCUMENTOS.
ampering with public seals and documents.
OLACIÓN DE SEPULTURAS.
esecration of graves.
OLACIÓN DE TREGUA.
ee VIOLACIÓN DE ARMISTICIO.
OLADA.
, rape victim, woman who has been raped ‖
dj, raped ‖ violated, infringed.
OLADOR.
, rapist.
OLAR.
, to violate ‖ to transgress ‖ to rape, commit
ape ‖ to rape a woman ‖ to commit statutory
ape, have sexual relations with a minor girl ‖
spoil, ruin.
OLAR LA ORDENANZA.
violate the letter of (e.g. military) law or re-
ulation.
OLENCIA.
violence, use of force against the consent of
nother ‖ oppression ‖ force ‖ aggression ‖
ercion, compulsion ‖ rape.
OLENCIA DESHONESTA.
first degree rape, non-consensual sexual re-
tions which are carried out by violence or
reats of force.
OLENCIA EN EL MATRIMONIO.
arital violence, wife or husband beating.
OLENCIA EN LA POSESIÓN.
ee POSESIÓN VIOLENTA.
OLENCIA EN LA PRESCRIPCIÓN.
use of) violence in adverse possession.
OLENCIA EN LAS PERSONAS.
use of) violence against individuals.
OLENCIA EN LAS SUCESIONES.
use of) violence in alienation of property.
OLENCIA EN LOS TESTAMENTOS.
use of) violence in (the writing of) wills.

VIOLENCIA FÍSICA.
physical violence.
VIOLENCIA FÍSICA
IRRESISTIBLE.
irresistible physical force imposed to obtain
consent to a legal act.
VIOLENCIA MORAL.
moral aggression ‖ coercion, compulsion.
VIOLENTAMENTE.
adv, violently ‖ with force ‖ against another's
will ‖ with arms.
VIOLENTAR.
v, to use violence or force ‖ to do violence to, apply violence to ‖ to force ‖ to obligate ‖ to in-
tepret something arbitrarily, do violence to
(the correct interpretation) ‖ to anger, infuriate ‖ to break and enter (a building), to enter
the dwelling of another without the inhabitant's consent ‖ see also VIOLAR.
VIOLENTO.
adj, violent ‖ forceful ‖ unnatural, abnormal ‖
against the will (of someone) ‖ destructive,
ruinous ‖ angry ‖ false, twisted ‖ unjust, unreasonable, unfair ‖ accidental ‖ without legal
right ‖ energetic.
VIRGEN.
f, m, virgin ‖ fallow land ‖ unadulterated or
unmanufactured product ‖ adj, virgin (woman
or man), new, unused.
VIRGINAL.
adj, virginal ‖ with defect ‖ without fault.
VIRGINIDAD.
f, virginity ‖ purity ‖ perfectness, state of being
perfect or without defect.
VIRIL.
adj, virile ‖ masculine, male ‖ condition of a
part that results from dividing a whole in as
many equal parts as there are persons who are
to share in the division.
VIRILIDAD.
f, virility ‖ manhood, age at which a man becomes virile.
VIRREY.
m, viceroy.
VIRTUAL.
adj, virtual ‖ implicit, implied ‖ tacit ‖ with
capacity or ability to produce an effect.
VIRTUALIDAD.
f, capability, ability ‖ tacitness.
VIRTUALMENTE.
adv, virtually ‖ implicitly, tacitly.

VIRTUD.
f, virtue ‖ morality ‖ chastity ‖ force, power ‖ quality ‖ legality, conformity with the law ‖ merit ‖ advantage ‖ goodwill ‖ strict complian-ce (with professional duties).

VIRTUOSAMENTE.
adv, virtuously.

VIRTUOSO.
m, virtuoso ‖ adj, virtuous.

VIRULENCIA.
f, virulence ‖ perversity ‖ spite, rancor ‖ evil.

VIRULENTO.
adj, virulent ‖ perverse ‖ spiteful, rancorous ‖ evil.

VIRUS.
m, virus.

VIS.
f, force ‖ violence.

VIS ABSOLUTA.
physical violence.

VIS COMPULSIVA.
immediate threat of violence.

VISA.
f, visa.

VISADO.
m, visa ‖ grant of a visa (by a consul or embas-sy) ‖ certification or legalization (of a docu-ment).

VISADO CONSULAR.
consular visa, visa for consular officers.

VISADO DIPLOMÁTICO.
diplomatic visa, visa for diplomats.

VISAR.
v, to examine or review a document ‖ to au-thorize or certify (for certain purposes) ‖ to approve or authorize ‖ to grant a visa, stamp with a visa.

VISIBLE.
adj, visible ‖ evident, manifest ‖ notable ‖ ob-vious ‖ physical.

VISIÓN.
f, vision, sight ‖ fantasy, imagination ‖ halluci-nation.

VISITA.
f, visit, call ‖ inspection ‖ group of judges who inspect jails and prisons ‖ home visit (of a doc-tor) ‖ health inspection ‖ visitor, caller ‖ right to inspect, right of inspection ‖ visitation.

VISITA A LOS HIJOS.
visitation, child visitation (of a non-custodial parent).

VISITA A LOS MENORES.
See VISITA A LOS HIJOS.

VISITA DE BUQUES DE GUERRA EXTRANJEROS.
inspection of foreign warships.

VISITA DE CÁRCEL.
prison or jail inspection (by judges or othe thorities).

VISITA DE SANIDAD.
health inspection.

VISITA DOMICILIARIA.
police of judicial search or inspection of me ‖ home visit (e.g. of a doctor, priest).

VISITADOR.
m, visitor, caller ‖ inspector ‖ official o vernment or judicial inspector ‖ door-to-salesman.

VISITAR.
v, to visit, call on ‖ to make a home visit review cases and judicial work of a lower (by a superior court) ‖ to inspect, review ke an official inspection (e.g. of prisons, c ports or exports, weights and measures, h of ships) ‖ to inform oneself.

VISITARSE.
v, to visit a detainee or prisoner (to form a complaint or habeas corpus pleading) visit each other.

VISITAS A LOS HIJOS.
child visitation.

VISITAS A LOS MENORES.
See VISITAS A LOS HIJOS.

VISLUMBRAR.
v, to make out, see vaguely (for lack of li to guess at, surmise, conjecture.

VISLUMBRE.
f, conjecture, suspicion ‖ signs, indicia pearance, slight similarity ‖ weak sight ‖ mer, glimpse.

VISORIO.
m, inspection or examination of an expe

VÍSPERA.
f, eve, day before.

VISTA.
f, vision ‖ sight ‖ observation, percep view ‖ public trial or hearing or procee appearance, aspect, look ‖ exact knowle purpose, end, goal ‖ customs inspectio ficer (for registering goods imported a ported) ‖ oral hearing or trial or proce (before a judge) ‖ proceeding by which the

rders a response from one of the parties about matter (e.g. a request made by the opposing arty).

STA ACTUARIO.
ustoms official, customs inspection officer.

STA
E LA CAUSA.
nal public proceeding in a trial.

STA DE OJOS.
n-sight or personal inspection by a jury or adge.

STA EN PRIMERA INSTANCIA.
ublic hearing at the trial court level.

STA EN SEGUNDA INSTANCIA.
ublic hearing at the appellate court level.

STAS.
meeting ‖ nuptial gifts between fiance and ancee ‖ door, window, or balcony, etc., which lows one to look in or out ‖ easement of light nd air ‖ right to open a wall in order to look utside.

STAZO.
a, superficial inspection ‖ glance, glimpse.

STO.
onsidering, in view of, taking into considera-on that ‖ whereas ‖ administrative termino-gy used to indicate that a decision will not be sued in a case ‖ judicial terminology used to dicate that all evidence has been heard and atements entered ‖ judicial terminology sed to accept an appeal on cassation (see ASACIÓN) ‖ judicial terminology used to indi-ate that the judge has finished reviewing a ase or matter or document or file ‖ term used written judgments to set forth the applicable recepts and facts upon which the decision will e based.

STO BUENO.
dicial or administrative terminology used to pprove a request or ratify a resolution or re-uest from a subordinate, or certify a docu-ent or swear to a fact or the legality of some-ing ‖ authorization, approval ‖ ratification.

SU.
ee DE VISU.

SURA.
personal inspection ‖ on-sight inspection. ee also VISORIO.

TAL.
dj, vital ‖ pertaining to life ‖ essential, absolu-ly necessary ‖ decisive.

VITALICIO.
m, holder of a life estate ‖ holder of a position for life ‖ life insurance policy ‖ life pension or life annuity ‖ type of tax ‖ adj, for life, life, last-ing for a lifetime.

VITALICISTA.
m, annuity holder ‖ life insurance policy hol-der.

VITALIDAD.
f, vitality.

VITUPERABLE.
adj, worthy of reprobation or censure.

VITUPERACIÓN.
f, vituperation, censure.

VITUPERADOR.
m, censurer, person who criticizes another.

VITUPERAR.
v, to censure ‖ to criticize ‖ to vituperate, revi-le.

VITUPERIO.
adj, vituperative ‖ insulting ‖ critical ‖ censo-rious ‖ reviling.

VIUDA.
f, widow ‖ gallows.

VIUDA ALEGRE.
widow who takes a lover quickly after the death of her husband.

VIUDA DESHONESTA.
See VIUDA ALEGRE.

VIUDA ENCINTA.
pregnant widow.

VIUDAL.
adj, pertaining to a widow or widower ‖ that which a widow or widower has by right.

VIUDEDAD.
f, widowhood ‖ widow's pension ‖ right of use and enjoyment of the surviving spouse in com-munity property.

VIUDEZ.
f, widowhood (of either a widow or widower).

VIVA VOZ.
verbal, oral.

VIUDO.
m, widower.

VIVAZ.
adj, vivacious ‖ effective ‖ long-lived ‖ sharp, quick.

VIVENCIA.
f, life or personal experience ‖ experience which consciously or unconsciously is incorpo-rated into one's personality.

VÍVERES.
m, food, provisions ‖ edible foodstuffs.

VIVEZA.
f, sharpness, quickness ‖ energy ‖ thoughtless action or remark ‖ crookedness, trick, ruse, slyness, cunning ‖ perspicacity.

VIVIDOR.
m, sponger, moocher ‖ hard worker, hard-working person ‖ adj, living, alive ‖ hard-working, diligent.

VIVIENDA.
f, dwelling, habitation ‖ house ‖ home ‖ habitable place ‖ way or manner of living ‖ domicile ‖ residence ‖ housing.

VIVIENTE.
adj, live, alive.

VIVIR.
m, means of living or sustenance ‖ conduct, manner ‖ v, to live, be alive ‖ to last ‖ to exist ‖ to live, dwell ‖ to be domiciled ‖ to reside ‖ to adapt to the circumstances ‖ to outlive, survive (a danger).

VIVO.
m, cunning or sly or tricky person ‖ adj, alive, live ‖ intense ‖ vigorous, strong ‖ clever ‖ lively ‖ bright ‖ ingenious, astute ‖ cunning, sly, tricky ‖ diligent, hard-working ‖ expressive ‖ under-water (re. ships).

VIZCONDE.
m, viscount.

VO.BO.
See VISTO BUENO.

VOCABLO.
m, word, term.

VOCABULARIO.
m, vocabulary ‖ dictionary.

VOCACIÓN.
f, vocation, calling ‖ summons ‖ inclination or tendency to a certain profession or work.

VOCACIÓN HEREDITARIA.
right to inherit.

VOCACIONAL.
adj, vocational.

VOCAL.
m, voting member of a meeting or council or board of directors or committee (exclusive of the president, secretary, treasurer, etc.) ‖ adj, vocal.

VOCAL SUPLENTE.
substitute or alternate voting member of a meeting or council or board of directors or committee (exclusive of the president, secretary, treasurer, etc.).

VOCEADOR.
m, crier ‖ street vendor.

VOCEAR.
v, to voice ‖ to call or cry out ‖ to publicize ‖ to acclaim out loud, give voice to ‖ to boast, brag.

VOCERÍA.
f, position and functions of a spokesperson or spokesman or spokeswoman or proxy or representative or attorney ‖ crying out, protest.

VOCERO.
m, spokesperson, spokesman, spokeswoman ‖ proxy, representative ‖ attorney.

VOLADOR.
m, flyer ‖ adj, flying ‖ fast, quick ‖ hanging.

VOLADURA.
f, blowing up, explosion which destroys or makes things fly.

VOLANTE.
m, note with a request or question ‖ flyer, advertisement thrown into the air ‖ steering wheel ‖ adj, flying ‖ mobile ‖ easily moved ‖ wandering, roving, roaming ‖ unsettled.

VOLAR.
v, to fly ‖ to disappear, split, take off ‖ to escape, flee, run away ‖ to fly (re. rumors) ‖ to be around (in the air).

VOLAR LA MINA.
to find something hidden, reveal a secret ‖ confess.

VOLICIÓN.
f, volition ‖ will ‖ desire, wish ‖ consent.

VOLITIVO.
adj, volitional.

VOLUBLE.
adj, versatile, volatile ‖ changeable, inconstant ‖ capricious ‖ opportunistic.

VOLUMEN.
m, volume ‖ bulk, body.

VOLUMINOSO.
adj, voluminous.

VOLUNTAD.
f, will, disposition ‖ acceptance, acquiescence ‖ refusal ‖ desire ‖ intention ‖ proposal ‖ termination ‖ free will ‖ free choice ‖ love ‖ affection ‖ benevolence ‖ order, mandate ‖ consent.

VOLUNTAD EXPRESA.
express intention or will or consent.

LUNTAD GENERAL.
ollective or group intention or will or consent.

LUNTAD PRESUNTA.
onstructive acceptance or acquiescence or onsent || constructive refusal. This usually occurs from silence in a situation which demands response.

LUNTAD TÁCITA.
mplied intention or will or consent.

LUNTAD UNILATERAL.
unilateral intention or will or consent.

LUNTARIADO.
m, voluntary enlistment, volunteering (for the military).

LUNTARIAMENTE.
dv, voluntarily || spontaneously || freely.

LUNTARIEDAD.
condition of that which is voluntary || spontaneous determination of will.

LUNTARIO.
, volunteer || military volunteer || adj, voluntary || spontaneous || free || without obligation without coercion.

LUNTARIO DEL EJÉRCITO.
rmy volunteer.

LUNTARIOSAMENTE.
dv, willfully.

LUNTARIOSO.
dj, willful || capricious.

LUNTARISMO.
, voluntarism.

LVER.
to turn || to turn around || to correspond || to ay || to repay || to give back, return (e.g. property or change from a bill) || to translate || to sist, reiterate || to come back of return (from aving been away) || to persuade || to return to vilian life.

LVER EN SÍ.
regain one's senses.

LVER LO
E ABAJO ARRIBA.
turn things upside down || to bring about a volution.

LVER POR SÍ.
defend oneself || to vindicate oneself || to gain one's status.

LVERSE.
to look backward || to turn || to turn around o change one's opinion || to rebel || to switch les.

VORAZ.
adj, voracious.

VOTACIÓN.
f, election, vote || voting, balloting, act of voting || vote, total vote.

VOTACIÓN DE SENTENCIAS.
judicial vote (in a multi-judge court in order to reach a decision).

VOTACIÓN MECÁNICA.
mechanical voting or vote, voting or vote by a mechanical process.

VOTACIÓN NOMINAL.
voting or vote by roll call.

VOTACIÓN ORDINARIA.
ordinary voting or balloting (by standing up or by a show of hands).

VOTACIÓN PARLAMENTARIA.
parliamentary or legislative or congressional voting or vote.

VOTACIÓN POR ACLAMACIÓN.
voting or vote by acclamation.

VOTACIÓN POR REPRESENTACIÓN.
voting or vote by proxy.

VOTACIÓN SECRETA.
secret ballot || secret balloting.

VOTADO.
m, see VOTACIÓN || adj, elected.

VOTADOR.
m, voter || elector || blasphemer, person who swears or curses.

VOTANTE.
m, voter || elector || person who exercises his right to vote.

VOTAR.
v, to vote, cast a ballot or vote || to elect || to swear, curse || to state one's opinion in voting by acclamation.

VOTO.
m, vote, ballot || voter || elector || decision || opinion || plea || swearing, cursing || desire, wish || vow.

VOTO ACTIVO.
right to vote, suffrage.

VOTO ACUMULADO.
cumulative vote.

VOTO CALIFICADO.
conditional right to vote, right to vote which is limited by some condition to certain persons.

VOTO CONSULTIVO.
advisory or preliminary vote (which does not count as the final vote).

VOTO DE CALIDAD.
casting or deciding vote.
VOTO DE CENSURA.
vote of censure.
VOTO DE CONFIANZA.
vote of confidence (of a government) ‖ ratification of government action.
VOTO DECISIVO.
See VOTO DE CALIDAD ‖ see also VOTO DELIBERATIVO.
VOTO DELIBERATIVO.
final vote, vote which will have force and effect.
VOTO DIRECTO.
direct vote.
VOTO EN BLANCO.
blank vote, ballot which is left blank.
VOTO FACULTATIVO.
voluntary vote, vote which may or not be exercised (without imposition of penalty).
Opposed to VOTO OBLIGATORIO.
VOTO INDIRECTO.
indirect voting, voting by means of an electoral college or similar institution.
VOTO INFORMATIVO.
See VOTO CONSULTATIVO.
VOTO LIMITADO.
See VOTO RESTRINGIDO.
VOTO MÚLTIPLE.
multiple vote, right to vote more than once in the same election.
VOTO OBLIGATORIO.
obligatory voting.
Opposed to VOTO FACULTATIVO.
VOTO PARTICULAR.
minority opinion or objection or vote ‖ dissent opinion.
VOTO PERPETUO.
perpetual vote, vote for life ‖ right to vote (which exists for the life of the voter).
Opposed to VOTO TEMPORAL.
VOTO PLURAL.
vote which counts for two or more persons ‖ multiple voting, voting more than once in the same election.
VOTO POLÍTICO.
political vote. May be either VOTO DE CONFIANZA or VOTO DE CENSURA.

VOTO POR CORREO.
vote by mail.
VOTO POR PODER.
vote by proxy.
VOTO PREFERENCIAL.
preferential vote, vote in which a voter m change the order of the slate of candidates.
VOTO PREPONDERANTE.
See VOTO DE CALIDAD.
VOTO PÚBLICO.
voice or public vote.
VOTO RESERVADO.
minority or dissenting vote or opinion (fr the majority vote or opinion in a multi-ju court).
VOTO RESTRINGIDO.
restricted vote, vote cast for a number of c didates less than that which will be elected.
VOTO SECRETO.
secret vote or ballot.
VOTO SIMPLE.
simple suffrage, one vote per person.
VOTO SOLEMNE.
solemn vow.
VOTO TEMPORAL.
temporary vote.
Opposed to VOTO PERPETUO.
VOZ.
f, voice ‖ noise ‖ cry ‖ word, term ‖ tense (verb) ‖ say, sayso, authority to a say or opin ‖ right or power or capacity or authority represent oneself or work on one's own be ‖ vote ‖ opinion ‖ rumor, story.
VOZ ACTIVA.
suffrage, right to vote or opine.
VOZ DE CONCIENCIA.
remorse ‖ voice of one's conscience.
VOZ DE MANDO.
word of a boss or superior.
VOZ PASIVA.
non-voting right to voice one's opinion (meeting, etc.).
VOZ PÚBLICA.
See FAMA PÚBLICA.
VUELO.
m, flight ‖ soaring.
VUELTA.
f, return ‖ repetition ‖ time ‖ turning ‖ rev tion, revolving ‖ change, evolution ‖ altera ‖ change, money left over from a bill ‖ rest

‖ walk, stroll ‖ reverse, back, other side ‖ ...npensation.

..LTO.

..change, money left over from a bill ‖ adj, ...rned.

..GAR.

, vulgar, coarse ‖ common ‖ ordinary, eve-...ay.

..GARIDAD.

...ulgarity ‖ insolence ‖ triteness.

..GARISMO.

..common term or expression.

..GARIZACIÓN.

...ılgarization.

..GARIZADOR.

...person who vulgarizes or explains or popu-...zes something.

VULGARIZAR.

v, to vulgarize ‖ to explain or translate into everyday language.

VULGARMENTE.

adv, vulgarly ‖ commonly, generally ‖ ordinarily.

VULGO.

m, the people ‖ common people ‖ uneducated people.

VULNERABILIDAD.

f, vulnerability.

VULNERABLE.

adj, vulnerable ‖ censurable.

VULNERAR.

v, to injure, damage, hurt, prejudice ‖ to break, transgress.

WARRANT.
 f, guaranty, warranty ‖ pledge paper, bearer instrument which shows the deposit of goods in pledge ‖ certificate of deposit.

WARRANT AGRÍCOLA.
 certificate of deposit regarding agricult products.

WARRANT INDUSTRIAL.
 certificate of deposit regarding industrial ducts.

XENELAXIA.
f, right to expel or deport, to keep under watch, or to keep in a secure place such natio-nals of an enemy nation as are found in one's territory.

XENÓFILA.
f, person who shows friendliness toward or likes foreigners or strangers.

XENOFILIA.
f, friendliness or affection toward foreigners or strangers.

XENOFOBIA.
f, xenophobia, hatred or hostility toward . eigners or strangers.

XENÓFOBO.
m, xenophobe, person who hates or is hos to foreigners or strangers.

XENOMANÍA.
f, xenophobia, manic hatred or hostility ward foreigners or strangers.

XENÓMANO.
m, person who has a manic hatred or hosti toward foreigners or strangers.

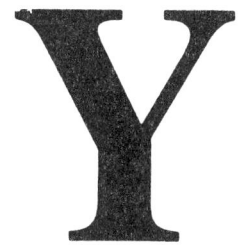

Y

Y ASÍ SUCESIVAMENTE.
and so on.
Y COMPAÑÍA.
and Company.
Y HNO(S).
and Brother(s).
Y/O.
conj, and/or.
YACENTE.
adj, prone lying down ‖ inheritance which has been neither accepted or refused ‖ inheritance which has not yet been divided among the heirs.
YACER.
v, to lie, lie down ‖ to lie with someone, have sexual intercourse ‖ to rest, be buried (somewhere).
YACIMIENTO MINERAL.
m, mineral bed or deposit.
YANACONA.
m, Indian serf to colonial Spaniards.
YANACONAZGO.
m, Indian serfdom to provide personal services to colonial Spaniards.
YANACONAJE.
See YANACONAZGO.
YANACONIZAR.
v, to distribute Indian serfs among colonial Spaniards.
YAPA.
f, extra something or little gift given to a purchaser as thanks.

YAPAR.
v, to give an extra something or little gift gi▮ to a purchaser as thanks.
YERMAR.
v, to depopulate ‖ to strip ‖ to let lie fallow, ve uncultivated.
YERMO.
m, fallow land ‖ wilderness ‖ wasteland or ▮ ren land ‖ adj, unpopulated ‖ uninhabi▮ deserted.
YERNO.
m, son-in-law.
YERRO.
m, crime or mistake committed witting or wittingly against morals or the law ‖ inad▮ tent mistake, blunder, slip-up ‖ error.
YERRO DE CUENTA.
accounting error or mistake.
YERTO.
m, person who is stiff with cold ‖ stiff ‖ adj gid, tense, stiff.
YUGO.
m, yoke ‖ oppression ‖ nuptial veil ‖ marri▮ ceremony ‖ burden ‖ bother ‖ encumbran▮ tyranny ‖ slavery.
YUGULAR.
v, to behead ‖ to murder ‖ to interrupt an▮ tivity abruptly.
YUNQUE.
m, anvil ‖ hard worker ‖ resistant person.
YUNTAMIENTO.
m, marriage ‖ union.

AS.
illegal, illicit.
TALINEAL.
parallel columns, in columns side-by-side.

YUXTAPONER.
v, to juxtapose.
YUXTAPOSICIÓN.
f, juxtaposition.

ZABARCERA.
f, retail vender of fruits, fruit vender ‖ green-grocer.

ZACAPELA.
f, scandalous quarrel, row.

ZAFARSE.
v, to escape ‖ to elude, avoid (danger) ‖ to slip away ‖ to hide ‖ to evade a problem of bother ‖ to give an excuse, excuse yourself.

ZANCADILLA.
f, trip, trip up ‖ trick, trap ‖ disloyalty ‖ treason.

ZANGUANGA.
f, pretending to be ill or injured to avoid work.

ZANJAR.
v, to resolve a conflict ‖ to overcome a dispute ‖ to settle a potential lawsuit.

ZAR.
m, tsar, czar, tzar.

ZARAGATA.
f, row, quarrel, brawl ‖ riot.

ZARISMO.
m, czarism, tsarism.

ZÓCALO.
m, public square, plaza.

ZÓCALO CONTINENTAL.
See PLATAFORMA SUBMARINA.

ZOCO.
m, public square.

ZONA.
f, zone, district ‖ area, region ‖ division.

ZONA AÉREA.
flight zone, area of sky in which planes are authorized to fly.

ZONA DE AÉREA PROHIBIDA.
See ZONA DE VUELO PROHIBIDO.

ZONA CÉNTRICA.
city center, center of the city or town.

ZONA COMERCIAL.
commercial center (of city or town).

ZONA CONTIGUA.
contiguous zone.

ZONA DE AISLAMIENTO.
blasting zone. ‖ isolation zone

ZONA DE COSTAS.
coastal area or zone.

ZONA DE ENSANCHE.
urban development zone (on the outsk a city).

ZONA DE FRONTERA.
border area or zone or strip.

ZONA DE GUERRA.
war zone.

ZONA DE INFLUENCIA.
zone or area of influence ‖ sphere of infl (of one power over other countries).

ZONA DE LIBRE CAMBIO.
duty-free area, area between various na in which customs barriers have been lift

ZONA DE OPERACIONES.
zone of operations.

ZONA DE RETAGUARDIA.
rear-guard zone (of a war).

ZONA DE SEGURIDAD.
safety zone.

ZONA DE TOLERANCIA.
red-light district, area of prostitutio other illegal vices which is tolerated by t lice.

ZONA DE VUELO PROHIBIDO.
prohibited air space.

ZONA DESMILITARIZADA.
demilitarized zone or area.

ONA FISCAL.
ax district.

ONA FORESTAL.
orestation or reforestation area, forest development area.

ONA FRANCA.
ee zone, duty-free zone ‖ tax-free area of a ountry.

ONA INDUSTRIAL.
industrial zone or area.

ONA MARÍTIMA.
maritime zone.

ONA MILITAR.
military zone.

ONA NEUTRALIZADA.
neutral zone or area (re. war).

ONA SANITARIA.
ospital area or zone ‖ military hospital zone ‖ zone demarcated for health reasons (e.g. quarantine zone).

ONA URBANA.
rban zone or area, urbanized area.

ONAL.
dj, zone, zonal, pertaining to a zone ‖ determined by a zone ‖ characteristic of a zone ‖ limited in space.

ONIFICACIÓN.
zoning.

ORRA.
prostitute ‖ astute woman ‖ drunkenness.

ORREAR.
, to work with care and astuteness ‖ to pimp ‖ to frequent prostitutes.

ORRERÍA.
care, caution ‖ astuteness ‖ cunning, foxiness.

ORRERO.
dj, cunning, foxy ‖ astute.

ORRO.
1, fox, wily person.

ORRÓN.
1, fox, wily person.

OZOBRA.
sinking, foundering ‖ swamping ‖ disquiet, worry, bother, affliction.

ZOZOBRAR.
v, to sink, founder (re. a vessel) ‖ to be in danger of sinking or being swamped ‖ to be in danger or jeopardy ‖ to worry.

ZURCIDOR DE VOLUNTADES.
m, pimp.

ZURCIR.
v, to weave ‖ to trump up, concoct (e.g. a story or lie).

ZURRA.
f, whipping ‖ thrashing ‖ beating ‖ dispute ‖ prolongation of time at work or study.

ZURRACO.
m, hidden money, treasure.

ZURRAPELO.
m, strong reprimand.

ZURRAR.
v, to reprimand ‖ to thrash, whip ‖ to beat, dominate ‖ to censure publicly.

ZURRIAGA.
See ZURRIAGO.

ZURRIAGADA.
f, confusion ‖ quarrel, dispute ‖ tumult, uproar.

ZURRIAGAR.
v, to whip, thrash ‖ to beat.

ZURRIAGAZO.
m, lash, whip ‖ unexpected disgrace or offense or rebuff ‖ unforeseen mistreatment.

ZURRIAGO.
m, whip, lash, horsewhip.

ZURRIBURI.
adj, miserable, vile ‖ plebeian ‖ disorder, uproar ‖ delinquency ‖ rabble ‖ ruffian.

ZURRIOTA.
m, prostitute.

ZURRONA.
f, prostitute ‖ female thief.

ZURUPETO.
m, unqualified stockbroker ‖ nosy notary public, notary public who intrudes into others' business.

ZUTANO.
m, Jo Blow ‖ Tom, Dick and Harry.